2nd Edition

Goldmine's
Price Guide to

Collectible Record Albums
1949-1989

By Neal Umphred

4

Published by

krause
publications

700 East State St.   Iola WI 54990
715-445-2214

Library of Congress Catalog Number: 89-83584
ISBN: 0-87341-175-7
Printed in the United States of America

Acknowledgements

This book would not be possible without the contributions of time and information from:

Steve Andrews
Kirkland, Wash.

Athanases
Redmond, Wash.

Christopher Chatman
Beyond Records
Los Angeles, Calif.

John Christensen
Renton, Wash.

Scott Davis
Rubato Records
Bellevue, Wash.

John DeBlaiso
Renton, Wash.

Charlie Essmeier
Retro Records
Salt Lake City, Utah

Joe Goldmark
San Francisco, Calif.

Thomas Grosh
Very English &
Rolling Stone
Lancaster, Pa.

Brian Guiberson
Seattle, Wash.

Rick Haney
Calendula Records
Seattle, Wash.

Alan Johnson
Rockaway Too
Mesa, Ariz.

Ashley Johnson
Corpus Christi, Texas

Gary Johnson
Rockaway Records
Los Angeles, Calif.

Kim Nott
San Francisco, Calif.

Bill Paquin
13th Floor Records
Stockton, N.J.

Alfred Pease
Edmonds, Wash.

Jeff Piehler
Los Angeles, Calif.

Rich Rockford
Vancouver, BC, Canada

Bill Shonk
Jazz Grooveyard
Seattle, Wash.

Neal Skok
Redmond, Wash.

Tom Ventris Jr.
Long Beach, Calif.

Barry Wickham
Terra Linda, Calif.

While I used many *Goldmine* discographies, special thanks are due to those contributors to the magazine who assisted me in my research for various articles and discographies over the past few years: Douglas Antreassian, Lees Brown Jr., John Cody, Travis Davidson, Bill DeYoung, Jack Haley, Ed Heath, John von Hoelle, John and Karen Lesniewski, Brian Nelson, Peter Reum, Ken Settle, and Joanna Zangrille.

Along with the mail I have received from *Goldmine* readers, during a spelunking adventure in the nether regions of my makeshift office, I uncovered a packet of letters addressed to me years ago during my tenure as editor for O'Sullivan Woodside. These letters contained various corrections and additions to my earlier work for that company. Thus, the following are due thanks: Frank Brockel, Jefferson City, Mo.; Ralph Bukofzer, Rockville Centre, N.Y.; Herbert Kamitz, Modling, Austria; Peter Kellner, Marinette, Wis.; Richard Kohler, Strabane, Pa.; Mad Louie, Buffalo, N.Y.; Kevin Rogers, London, Ontario; and Richard Balsam (Richard, wherever you are, please contact me via Goldmine!).

And a final thanks to those who, while not participating fully in this particular project, have provided me with data that eventually found its way into these pages and/or direction in where to take that info: Chuck DeMean, Norman Feinberg, Linda Jones, Lars Keilhau, John Kravett, Walter Piotrowski, Jeff Tamarkin, John Tefteller, and Todd "Scratch My K'nif" Van Sittert.

Goldmine's Price Guide
to Collectible Record Albums

An Introduction to the 2nd Edition

By Neal Umphred

The acknowledgements page that preceeds this introduction lists those collectors and dealers who were instrumental in the compilation and accuracy of this book; the contribution of each is valued, and necessary, if this guide is to be a growing concern. But there are several individuals who performed above and beyond the call of duty and they must be addressed separately. So, special thanks to John Christensen, Charlie Essmeier, Joe Goldmark, Ashley Johnson, Gary Johnson, Rich Rockford and Bill Shonk, without whom, I can assure you, this would be an immeasurably poorer book.

Now, I'd like to tell you what this book is not. This book is *not* the bible for record collectors; it is *not* the blue book of vinyl junkies. And it is certainly not the "official" price guide for anything. Nor does this book reflect my opinions of what your records are worth. The prices quoted here are an attempt to reflect the broad differences in markets from region to region, state to state and city to city. The prices here are an attempt to document what collectible records are worth on the open collectors market. While attention was given to the foreign market, this is an American price guide that will be purchased mostly by American collectors, therefore I did not allow the effects of the weakened American dollar to unduly affect the pricing.

Please note that the prices quoted reflect the market during the period in which this book was assembled; I cannot guarantee that they will remain the same for any length of time following the publication of this book. In fact, price guides tend to have a direct—and often immediate—effect on the very market they attempt to chronicle. That is, the release of the new information from such a book into the general market can influence what collectors collect and, consequently, what prices are paid. Thus prices listed here may be made obsolete by their very listing, especially when the listing offers new information or information that contradicts previously published (erroneous) information.

The market for truly rare and desirable albums continues at the same hectic pace it has for previous years; prices paid in the four-figure range are becoming a rather normal affair. In the past two years sealed copies of first-state, stereo "butcher covers" of the Beatles' *Yesterday And Today* sold for $12,000 and $15,000 (a mono, $5,000). The best copy yet offered of the *The Freewheelin' Bob Dylan* with the rare tracks ("Let Me Die In My Footsteps," "Talkin' John Birch Society Blues," etc.) was auctioned off for nearly $8,000 in less than very good condition! David Bowie's *Diamond Dogs* with the Bowiedog's genitals intact fetched $5,000; it, too, was less than nearly mint. (In an interesting move, the recent Ryko disc release of *Diamond Dog* restores the offending genitals.) A nearly mint copy of the Federal 10-inch *Billy Ward & The Dominoes* surfaced from a collection in the South and, after changing hands a couple of times, found its way into the hands of a collector who had sought it lustily for nearly two decades; the final price was $5,000.

Perhaps the most exciting—or portentous—news was the auctioning of a vinyl and CD version of Prince's notorious "Black Album," pulled from release by artist in 1988, although not until some copies were pressed and distributed among the company employees and Prince's party. Rockaway Records of Los Angeles acquired one of each and sold the LP for nearly $4,000 while the compact disc eventually reached $11,000 (not the $13,500 reported

by the media.) For those who think the price a fluke, there was contentious bidding by several parties during the final extended weeks of the auction.

Several labels have reached a point where virtually everything on them is collectible: rockabilly labels Sun and its subsidiary, Philips International; rhythm 'n' blues labels Aladdin, Score and King; original Atlantic and early Motown and anything related to Phil Spector's various entrepreneurial endeavors. Joe Goldmark's comments on country/western music makes note of the smaller country labels that are collectible.

As for the fluctuations in the market, well, for those readers who expect values to rise automatically, the collectibles market is not all that different from the commodities market or the stock market, and everyone knows the wild fluctuations that occur there. So, while most prices do remain stable, or rise gradually, some rise dramatically while others actually go down in value. Value is established almost solely by supply and demand: Prices go up when the current demand is greater than the available supply; prices go down when the available supply is greater than the current demand.

Any number of factors can cause prices to rise or decline, many of them tied in with an artist's status from year to year. The most dramatic leveller is probably the warehouse find, where boxes of a supposedly rare record turn up in sufficient quantities to meet the immediate demand, driving its value down for the near future. On the most mundane of levels, the value of a fairly common out-of-print album can decline when that album is released as a compact disc, although the drop is usually temporary, with the record slowly returning to its earlier value when the supply dropped on the market in the wake of its digitalized debut is exhausted.

What's Here and What's Not

Each book has boundaries (size, page, count, etc.) in which the author or editor must work. The more these boundaries can be defined, the more likely it is that the individual goals will be met. As most collectible records are the older ones, and, as that is where the main center of interest lies, I have centered the listings on those artists who started their careers in the 1950s and 1960s with select artists from the last 20 years. The expanded size of this edition has allowed greater leeway in choosing what to include. You will find thousands of new titles in all fields, especially folk, psych, country and audiophile pressings with hundreds of promotional albums included. The expanded page count also allowed the luxury of several related articles and the inclusion of twice as many photos as the first edition!

This book makes no attempt at completeness; rather, the reader will find approximately 25,000 listings that cover, more or less: 1) the most collectible records in the business; 2) those records that exchange hands the most often; an 3) those records most in need of attention at this point in time. While the discographies of many artists are complete, for others they are obviously incomplete. Let's use The Kinks as an example: their early Reprise album, from 1965 through 1968, were issued on that label's multi-colored (pink, gold and green) label with a large steamboat dominating the upper left "slice" of the label (approximately 9:00 through 12:00). Their next few LPs appeared on the company's modified label: brown with a green top with a considerably reduced steamboat and, more distinctly, the Warner-Seven Arts "W7" logo at midnight alongside the Reprise ":r" logo. This was followed by the brown label, on which several earlier titles were reissued.

With the group's move to RCA, they recorded a series of albums on that label's orange label, several of which were reissued later in the decade on a light brown label. The orange label originals are listed; the brown labels are not. The Kinks then signed with Arista, producing numerous albums which have no collectible value at this time excepting certain promotional items, which are listed. Thus for the rather popular Kinks, the reader will find a fairly complete discography of their Reprise albums, a reasonable look at their RCA origi-

nals, and some of the more recent half-speed and promos listed, with the regular, common pressings ignored. This approach was used on many artists and is not meant as an artistic judgment on my behalf but rather an economical one.

There are going to be instances where the information here is incomplete or wrong; it is almost unimaginable for any book listing 25,000 records not to make some errors. These may range in nature from common typographical errors, from pressing the wrong character on the keyboard to transferring erroneous data from an error-filled source, to incomplete research (missing catalog numbers, incorrect values assigned to records.)

Page Breakdown

The records are listed chronologically by label, interrupted by soundtrack appearances. I have used fairly standard alphabetization throughout; there should be no real surprises for anyone familiar with an encyclopedia. Necessary notes are usually listed in italics in parenthesis below the appropriate section or selections. Using Duane Eddy as an example:

Label/Catalogue #		Title	Year	VG+	NM
EDDY, DUANE					
Jamie JLP-3000	(M)	Have "Twangy" Guitar-Will Travel	1958	37.50	75.00
Jamie JLPS-3000	(S)	Have "Twangy" Guitar-Will Travel	1958	100.00	200.00
		(Yellow label. The title on the cover is in white print. Originally issued in true stereo.)			
Jamie JLPM-3000	(M)	Have "Twangy" Guitar-Will Travel	1959	16.00	40.00
Jamie JLPS-3000	(E)	Have "Twangy" Guitar-Will Travel	1959	12.00	30.00
		(Yellow label. The title on the cover is in red print. Reissued in electronically rechanneled stereo.)			
Jamie JLPM-3000	(M)	Have "Twangy" Guitar-Will Travel	196?	12.00	30.00
Jamie JLPS-3000	(E)	Have "Twangy" Guitar-Will Travel	196?	8.00	20.00
		(Gold & white label. The title on the cover is in red print.)			
Jamie JLPM-3006	(M)	(Especially) For You	1959	16.00	40.00
Jamie JLPS-3006	(E)	(Especially) For You	1959	10.00	25.00
Jamie JLPM-3009	(M)	The Twangs The Thang	1959	16.00	40.00
Jamie JLPS-3009	(E)	The Twangs The Thang	1959	10.00	25.00
Jamie JLPM-3011	(M)	Songs Of Our Heritage *(Gatefold cover)*	1960	14.00	35.00
Jamie JLPS-3011	(S)	Songs Of Our Heritage *(Gatefold cover)*	1960	20.00	50.00
Jamie JLPS-3011	(S)	Songs Of Our Heritage *(Blue vinyl)*	1960	100.00	200.00
Jamie JLPS-3011	(S)	Songs Of Our Heritage *(Red vinyl)*	1960	100.00	200.00
Jamie JLPM-3011	(M)	Songs Of Our Heritage *(Standard cover)*	1960	8.00	20.00
Jamie JLPS-3011	(S)	Songs Of Our Heritage *(Standard cover)*	1960	12.00	30.00
		—Original Jamie albums above have gold & white labels.—			

The first column indicates the label and catalog number. The second features a key notation for the record's sound: an "(M)" denotes a monaural recording, while an "(S)" means the entire record is in true stereo. An "(E)" indicates that the stereo effect of the album has been electronically created while a "(P)" indicates a partially true stereo record; i.e., while most of the tracks are true stereo, one or more are either mono or electronic stereo. "(Q)" indicates quadraphonic. Finally, "(DJ)" means that the record is a promotional disc, either uniquely promo or a promo label variation of the commercial title, which will be listed directly beneath it. Promos in the '50s and early '60s should be assumed to be mono; those from the late '60s on, stereo.

The record's title is the middle column; specific notes short enough to place on the same line follow. In this case, the existence of two different colored vinyl versions of Jamie 3011 are noted; all records are on black vinyl unless otherwise noted. This is followed by the year of release; dating the records was often problematic. The final two columns, the prices, are for two conditions, very-good-plus (VG+) and near-mint (NM) and are dealt with at length below.

For those artists who achieved a long lasting popularity that saw their recordings repeatedly reissued I have attempted to list brief notations about particular records. Notes indented beneath an album and enclosed in parentheses refer only to the title under which it is listed.

These may refer to that record's particular label or any other aspect that requires attention. In the example above, the note "(Yellow label. The title on the cover is in white print. Originally issued in true stereo.)" refers only to Jamie 3000, *Have "Twangy" Guitar-Will Travel*. In this particular note, there are two parts, the second referring specifically to the stereo release.

Notes that are centered and open (i.e., lacking parentheses) refer to two or more titles and are almost exclusively dealing with label specifications. These notes always include the qualifier "above" in their statements! As in the case of the above example which begins "—Original Jamie albums above," the note applies to all of the albums above it. For this work one book was invaluable: Joe Lindsay's *Record Label Guide For Domestic LPs*. Published by BioDisc, this is an absolute must for serious album collectors.

There are several other parenthetical notes that are used on the same line as the title (space allowing):"No cover" indicates a record issued in a plain, unmarked cardboard sleeve (usually privately printed albums). Most soundtracks albums are listed as "Soundtrack"; in some cases, the abbreviation "Sdtk" was used. Similarly, while it was necessary to denote titles by specialist labels (Mobile Fidelity, Nautilus, Direct Disk) as half-speed masters, major labels that dipped into the audiophile field with such products are noted as "Half-speed master" (or simply "Half-speed"). Other pecularities (color vinyl, white label promos, etc.) are also noted in parentheses with the title.

Regarding the artist listings: when a group's name is followed by another name in brackets, it means that the group has recorded under two names. If the two names are similar, the records are listed together under the first name. For instance, "CHICAGO (CHICAGO TRANSIT AUTHORITY)" tell the reader that albums listed under either of those two names can be found under that one listing.

For the sake of usefulness, certain artists who started out as members of a group and who then rose to dominate the group have all of the recordings listed under the individual artist's usually better-known name. For instance, while The Midnighters originally recorded under the group's name, the bulk of their material was recorded under the name Hank Ballard & The Midnighters, under which all of their recordings are grouped in this book. Similarly, the Crickets first album is listed under Buddy Holly; the Stone Poneys under Linda Ronstadt, etc.

References are kept to a bare minimum and refer the reader to another artist when the artist or group in question is named in the title of an album or is inseparably linked with the recording. Listing references for artists who appeared on other artist's recording is a book in itself. Should the reader desire one, Terry Hounsome and Tim Chambre's *Rock Record* is highly recommended, with thousands upon thousands of listings of who played on what, when and where!

Budget Labels

Many labels sprang up over the years that specialized in leasing masters of previously released material—usually of artists who were no longer hot—and all too often issuing albums in the cheapest possible manner: poor mastering, poor pressings on low grade vinyl, etc. These labels include Crown, Diplomat, Grand Prix, Guest Star, Spin-o-rama, Wyncote, and the undisputed kind of low budget labels in America, Pickwick. While some of these labels did collect important material—Crown especially began by issuing great r&b—most of them issued albums of less than collectible consequence. For that matter, most of them are not listed here unless they are of some real importance. Most of the albums have little value and can be nearly impossible to sell—even sealed—for more than a few bucks. Some minor titles listed in the previous edition have been deleted.

The premiere magazine for music collectors and fans

Goldmine
The collector's record & compact disc marketplace

Covering the music spectrum ...
- **Rock 'n Roll**
- **Blues**
- **Country**
- **Doo-Wop**
- **Pop**
- **Jazz**

Since 1974, GOLDMINE has been the number one source for the music fan and historian who's interested in collecting and preserving the music of our past and present.

Every two weeks, we deliver internationally renowned coverage of artists and groups from the '40s to the present, with complete discographies, in-depth interviews, reliable feature articles, and thousands of ads for buying, selling, and trading rare and collectible vinyl, CDs, and memorabilia.

1/2 year **13 issues $22.00**

1 year **26 issues $35.00**

To subscribe, send check or money order in U.S. funds to the address below, or call toll-free to charge subscription to MC or VISA.
--Or send for a free sample copy--
U.S. addresses only - write for foreign rates.

Write to Goldmine Magazine, Circulation Dept. BX4, 700 E. State Street, Iola, WI 54990-0001
OR CALL TOLL-FREE
(800) 258-0929, Goldmine Dept. BX4

Available nationwide at most used record & CD shops, Tower Records, and National Record Mart stores.

Elvis & The Beatles

The listings for Elvis Presley and The Beatles are the lengthiest yet only scratch the surface. There are thousands of label and cover variations, off label releases and many, many more that could not be squeezed in. While the listing here are more than adequate for most dealers and collectors to assess their acquisitions, they may be less than so for the completist. Recommended is the third column of *The Beatles Price Guide For American Records* by Perry Cox and Joe Lindsay. At 8½ x 11 inches and 240 pages, this is available for $23.95 (includes postage and handling) from: Perry Cox Ent., P.O. Box 82278, Phoenix, AZ 85071.

For the true Elvis collector, or the dealer who caters to such collectors' needs, I recommend my own *A Touch Of Gold: The American Record Collectors Price Guide To Elvis Presley Records & Memorabilia*. This book is 8½ x 11 inches with 350 pages containing nearly 5,000 listings covering singles, EPs, LPs, tapes, compact discs, sheet music and RCA released memorabilia. *A Touch Of Gold* is available for $23.95 (includes postage and handling) from: White Dragon Press, P.O. Box 800130, Santa Clarita, CA 91380.

There Are Producers...And Then There Are Producers

Unbeknownst to many a star-struck fan is the fact that many of the records that catch their attention and their disposable cash are far more the product of the technical people behind the scenes than the actual artists lip-syncing their way to fame and glory on MTV. Without a competent team of technicians, few records can make it through the rigors of selection that place records on top radio play-lists. While a good engineer is one of these people—a must, in fact—of more importance on the creative (sic) level is the role of producer who, more often than not, decides exactly how the final record will appear to the public, from the final sound to the actual selection of the tracks, including who writes what and who does or does not play on the record!

While the role of the producer and his efforts throughout the history of recorded music can fill an entire book with explanations and anecdotes, this brief chapter will merely point out that many of the classic records of rock 'n' roll era were created almost entirely by the production team. In fact, there are many "artists" who do not exist, but are merely a nom de plume—a front, if you will—for the otherwise nameless people who do this sort of thing for a living.

Some of these producers were also recording artists: Jan Berry of Jan & Dean; Steve Barri and Phil Sloan of The Fantastic Baggys; Ron Dante of The Trashmen; Brian Wilson of The Beach Boys; and Frank Zappa of The Mothers Of Invention, each of whom has references in their section for artists they produced. Most producers functioned solely at the board, from the well-known work of George Martin, who, aside from the Beatles, produced many of the best records of the Mersey Sound, to the lesser-known but equally impressive work of Jimmy Miller, responsible for The Rolling Stones' best albums *(Beggar's Banquet* through *Exile On Main Street)* and Traffic's first few albums. For this second edition, two producers have been selected and their work focused on: the late Gary Usher, responsible for some of the best records from the early '60s California sound, and the granddaddy of 'em of, Uncle Phil Spector.

Phil Spector is best known as the creator of the "wall of sound" production technique that led to such classic singles as "Da Do Ron Ron" and "Then He Kissed Me" for The Crystals; "Be My Baby" and "Walking In The Rain" for The Ronettes; "You've Lost That Loving Feeling" and "Just Once In My Life" for The Righteous Brothers; and Tina Turner's "River Deep-Mountain High." While Uncle Phil's forte was the two-minute-thirty single, he did produce a number of albums, several of which are gems, all of which are collectible. Aside from the various artists' compilations of his productions that are listed under his name, he is

represented in this book by albums by Bobb B. Soxx & The Blue Jeans, The Crystals, The Righteous Brothers, The Ronettes, The Teddy Bears and Ike & Tina Turner. Spector also co-produced The Beatles' *Let It Be;* George Harrison's *All Things Must Pass* and *Concert For Bangla Desh*; and John Lennon's *Plastic Ono Band, Imagine, Sometime In New York City, Roots* and *Rock 'N' Roll*.

Gary Usher's reputation is not quite so grandiose as Spector's (although Japanese collectors have long revered him alongside Brian Wilson). Gary's work as writer (he was involved on many of the early Beach Boys' car songs with Brian), arranger, producer, singer and instrumentalist has produced an enormous body of work, most of which currently languishes in the vaults of major record companies and the hoary recesses of too many collectors memories. Gary's work during this period includes albums by The Competitors, The Ghouls, The Hondells, Bruce Johnston, The Kickstands, The Knights, Mr. Gasser & The Weird-Ohs, The Revells, The Road Runners, The Silly Surfers, The Super Stocks, The Surfaris, and The Weird-Ohs, all of which are listed in these pages. (With Roger Christian, he also "produced" *The Beatles Story* for Capitol).

While Gary specialized in the single format, by the end of the '60s the demand for the type of record he loved (up-tempo and fun) was lost and he became a staff producer for Columbia Records, where he assisted The Byrds through their finest moments, *Younger Than Yesterday, The Notorious Byrd Brothers* and *Sweetheart Of The Rodeo*, and molded the sounds of Keith Allison, Chad & Jeremy, Millenium, The Peanut Butter Conspiracy and Sagittarius. His later work included projects with Curt Boetcher, Danny Cox, Andy Goldmark, Ship, The Spiral Starecase, and a pair of fascinating sets by philosopher Alan Watts.

Pricing the Records

If you will pardon my redundancy: This book is not the work of one person; it does not reflect my opinions of what your records are worth. Instead, I solicited the assistance of many collectors and dealers whom I had known for several years, both personally and professionally (the contributors list expanded somewhat, mainly through recommendations of other dealers and collectors from the previous book's contributors.) Each dealer and collector was requested to provide current values based on recent sales or purchases, not transactions from years ago. The records listed here are taken from a variety of printed sources plus the input of the contributors. This input and a constant scrutiny of the set-sale and auctions in the pages of *Goldmine* also played a part in the make-up of this book.

I strived for a sense of internal consistency with the pricing. That is, I did not attach East Coast prices to oldies, Northwest prices to garage, Midwest prices to Motown, L.A. prices to surf, etc., but rather sought a balance between them all so that the book as a whole works as a guideline for each region of the country to use as an outline for their own market. Every item in this book as been scrutinized by several contributors. The values that were decided upon represent a ballpark value that takes into account each of the prices submitted.

An example of the pricing technique used throughout is adequately summed up by the first few responses to my inquiries regarding *Them*, Van Morrison's original claim to fame. The first four prices below are those values submitted by four contributors who specialize in '60s rock. The fifth figure, "Avg.", is just that, the average of the four submitted values. The final figure is the value arrived at with the average rounded up or down (later submissions by other contributors fell in line with the above four.)

			#1	#2	#3	#4	Avg.	Value
Tower	ST-5104	Now And Them	50.00	40.00	50.00	60.00	48.00	50.00
Tower	ST-5116	Time Out! Time In For Them	60.00	60.00	50.00	75.00	57.00	60.00
Happy Tiger	1004	Them	35.00	40.00	50.00	40.00	41.00	40.00
Happy Tiger	1012	Them In Reality	40.00	40.00	75.00	75.00	55.00	60.00

While the early, Morrison-led albums receive the most critical attention, it is the later albums that are the hardest to find and, due to their punkish, pseudo-psychedelic sound, more in demand. The two Tower titles are the more desirable with *Time Out! Time In* the hottest. The two Happy Tiger titles are less desirable but *Them In Reality* is the rarest of the four. Also, while the mono versions of the two titles (same catalog number but with a plain "T" prefix) are more difficult to find, it is the stereo versions that the collectors want.

It should always be borne in mind that the price that anyone will buy (or sell) an item for is often linked closely with the geographic/economic environment he or she is living in. A collector in New York City should expect to pay more—sometimes considerably more—for a given item than a collector from Wilkes-Barre, Pa. After all, the Manhattan collector pays more for rent, for a restaurant dinner, for tickets to the Mets or Yankees, etc., because a New York City resident will be paid commensurately more for his job (i.e., a waiter in a moderately successful Manhattan restaurant would make more than double the tips than a waiter in many of northeastern Pennsylvania's finest restaurant would make). Similarly, just as a dealer takes for granted that he or she will pay less for records when stocking his or her shop in Seattle (a buyer's market), they should also expect to sell them for less in the same market.

My own opinion as both a participant and observer varies greatly with some of the values listed here, just as you, the reader, will—and should—disagree with some of the prices! Because of this, I have a bit of advice for any serious collector: "When you are offered a record for which you have been actively searching for over five years, do not argue with the price, pay it." The corollary to this little bit of wisdom would be: "If you don't, you may not see it again for another five years, and it will cost even more."

There are some cases where records are so rare in collectible condition that realistic values could not be assigned. In those cases no figure was assigned to the price column but an estimated range was noted parenthetically beneath the title. This is not to imply that the record is worth either the highest or the lowest of the estimated range but rather that this range is a reasonable assessment of the discrepancies in the submitted values. An example:

GRANDMA'S ROCKERS
Fredlo 6727   (M)   **Homemade Apple Pie**   1967   *See note below*
                                (Rare. Estimated near mint value $1,000-2,000.)

As noted in the price column, the reader's attention is referred to the note, which gives an estimated near mint value of $1,000 to $2,000. Essentially, what this means is that a seller with a near mint copy should expect to get at least $1,000 for this record in an open auction. While a buyer might win this record for as little as $1,000 (or conceivably less), he should not be surprised to find the bidding escalate to the $2,000 range. Similarly, records is lesser condition should cut the estimated range appropriately: a VG+ copy would have a range of approximately $500-1,000; a VG copy, $250-500.

If a price on a record with which you are familiar seems ludicrously wrong, don't feel obliged to accept it. If other dealers and collectors are puzzled by the same discrepancy, it may be just that, an error of mine. But, at the same time, the average dealer or collector is often years (at least months) behind the reality of the market when it comes to the specialized knowledge of truly rare records, mainly because they are so rare that few, if anyone, ever sees them for sale at any price. For example, the prices that are quoted for Marty Robbins may appear preposterous to a '60s rock specialist; but a Robbins collector knows that certain titles, even those from later in his career, are difficult to find at any price! And that exists for a good many artists. The more knowledgeable that you, the reader, are, the more useful and informative this book will be, if only that the informed reader will be better able to assimilate the information and make use of it on a day-to-day basis.

Many collectors have expressed concern over the effects the overseas buyer has had on American records; the continued slump in America's ability to cope with honest competition (versus the collusion of the domestic market in general) may have glutted the coffers of the multi-national corporations that bend our elected officials ears, but it has also led to a weakened dollar and, thus, the ability of the European and/or Japanese collector to outbid the American collector. To ignore these events would be both futile and counter-productive. Thus, an item that goes for a bigger dollar overseas but of which overseas collectors purchase only a fraction of the copies put up for sale/auction is not unduly affected in this book.

But a record that turns up infrequently (only a few times a year), and invariably leaves the country to an overseas collector who bids two or three times what American collectors believe the record is "really" worth, then those prices do determine the value of those records. I would, in effect, be doing you, the reader and user of this book, a disservice were I to choose any other option. The average American collector needs to know what he or she should expect to have to bid to win a truly rare and desirable record in an open auction on the open market.

So there are two prices listed for each record: The last and most important is the "Near Mint" price. I use a scale (see page 22) that evaluates the Very Good Plus, or Excellent, condition record as a sliding percentage of the NM value. For lesser condition records, VG price are, for easy reference, approximately one-half (50%) of the listed VG+ value. The normal rule of thumb for pricing is that the cover makes up 40-50% of the value and the record 50-60%, although there are many, many exceptions to this rule.

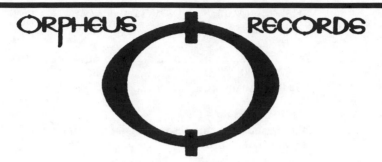

Near Mint Value	VG+ Value (%)
Less than $50	40%
$60-200	50%
$250-500	60%
$600-1,800	66%
$2,000 and up	70%

Always keep in mind that the accuracy of these prices are meaningless without a corresponding accuracy in the grading of records.

Grading the Records

Records are graded by visual standards, not aural; the reason being that when purchasing a record at a show or through the mail, the buyer does not get to listen to it. The biggest complaints against the visual method are 1) the subjectivity of the grader's eyes or viewpoint, and 2) the fact that records do not always play as well or as poorly as they look. Both of these are justifiable arguments and, of course, it is the first point that causes the need for articles such as this: records always look better when selling than when buying. The arguments against playgrading are similar. The subjectivity of the listener is also a factor, a factor that is multiplied by the type of equipment the grader is playing the record on to form his or her judgment. So, for the sake of convenience and necessity, visual grading is the standard by which almost all dealers and collectors work.

When grading a disc, grade the overall wear of the vinyl. A record advertised as "NM" or "VG" should tell the prospective buyer the shape of the playable vinyl (although common sense should be used: Un-played records that are warped cannot be Mint). Such defects as name stickers on the label, tape on the jacket, etc., should be addressed separately with abbreviated notations. A reliable set of these notations have been developed over the years, covering virtually every type of defect that can occur to a record or its cover; a list of most of the more common abbreviations and their meanings follow the grading definitions below. When defining the grades, it is difficult to describe several without discussing certain defects and/or the way the disc plays; these are included to help define the grade, not to cause confusion.

Visual grading is most important in mail-order transactions where a buyer doesn't see his purchase until his check has cleared the bank. Grading needs to be as strict and as accurate as possible. Put simply, the aim of grading is to make the buyer visualize the record he or she is purchasing through an advertisement and not be disappointed when that record arrives! A record that is accurately graded will play the same (or better) than the grading! In-person deals do not require a grade of any sort; if you are holding a record that has obviously been played a hundred times, you don't need a grade to determine whether or not you are going to purchase that disc.

Always grade records under a good steady light. A 100-watt lightbulb in a common desklamp will do an adequate job; most major defects will jump out at you and allow you to make an accurate assessment of the vinyl. Grading a record using light from the ceiling or from deflected sunlight entering the window will often "hide" paper scuffs, discoloration, groove wear and even some fingerprints. Everyone makes mistakes in grading. This is a problem all dealers and collectors are prone to make and must be aware of. Do not condemn a dealer for one mistake; but, when the mistake is the norm, find someone else from which to buy your records. Think of these definitions as guidelines around which your experience will build a better understanding of conditions.

Mint. A Mint ("M") record should appear to have just left the manufacturers without any handling; that is, it should appear perfect! No scuffs or scratches, blotches or stains, labels or writing, tears or splits; nothing. Perfect. And age has nothing to do with it; the same standard for Mint apply to a 10-inch soundtrack from 1954 as they do to a heavy metal album from 1989! There are no sliding values for Mint.

A Mint album cover should appear to have never have had a record in it; no ring-wear, dogeared corners, writing, seam-splits. I define ring-wear as any imprint on the cover from the record that it formerly held. Any imprint. To many dealers and collectors the ink has to be worn off for them to recognize ring-wear and grade a cover down. Uh-uh. Mint means perfect and nothing else.

Near Mint. A record that is otherwise Mint but has one or two tiny, inconsequential flaws that do not affect the play is Near Mint ("NM") and should command 85-95% of the Mint price. For many, Near Mint and Mint-Minus mean the same thing; for the sake of this article, they are interchangeable. When dealing with a seller that discriminates between the two grades, inquire as to what the dealer means when he calls one record M- and another NM. Many dealers and collectors take the position that any used (opened) record cannot be verified as Mint so they use M- to describe what appears to be a perfect record that has been opened. Covers should still be close to perfect with minor signs of wear or age just becoming evident: slight ring-wear, minor denting to a corner, or writing on the cover all be noted properly.

Many records are available in Near Mint/Mint condition, although these are generally more recent and the prices are nominal. That is, most dealers set a minimum price on the records they sell in their stores, usually dollars ($3.99-4.99), just for normal, everyday, all-too-readily-available records. Whether they are un-played or "merely" near mint the price will be the same: it wouldn't be worth the dealer's time to stock the single unless that minimum price was met.

Sometimes referred to as "Excellent," a Very Good Plus ("VG+") record has been handled and played either infrequently or very carefully. That is, an item obviously not perfect, but not too far from it. On a disc, this could mean that there are light paper scuffs from sliding in and out of a sleeve; the vinyl may have lost some—not all— of its original luster. A slight scratch that did not affect the play in an otherwise nearly Mint disc would be acceptable VG+ for most collectors; a scratch of any sort that audibly clicked throughout at a level greater than or equal to the music would not be acceptable. Always list the flaws in a VG+ record or cover.

As a rule of thumb, a VG+ item is worth 50%, or one-half, of the Near Mint value, although this ratio varies with the rarity of the item. That is, a record that is fairly common in NM/M condition has little real value in VG+ to most collectors; consequently 25-35% may be more appropriate. On the other hand, truly rare records will fetch 75% in VG+. (By rare, I am referring to items in which the supply is merely a fraction of the demand and the record sells for hundreds of dollars.) On covers, some wear from storage is acceptable, especially light wear that does not affect the beauty of the artwork. Again, listing the flaws when selling is safest.

Very Good ("VG") records will display visible signs of handling and playing, such as loss of vinyl luster, light surface scratches, groove wear, and spindle trails from countless spins on the turntable. A VG record looks as if it will have some audible surface noise when it is played, although any such noise should not overwhelm the music or ruin the listening experience. VG records should appear to have been well-played although well-loved by a responsible owner. Gouges, rips in the label, cracks, maple syrups in the grooves are all unacceptable.

As more and more collectors spend more and more money on their acquisitions, the lower limits of acceptability for an item to be admitted into their collection rises. That is, to many collectors, a record in VG condition is not acceptable unless the item is truly rare

and virtually unavailable in any other condition! And then, only if the price is scaled appropriately to match the condition. Used but not abused might sum up this grade. A VG record should command approximately 20-30% of the Near Mint price.

This is a difficult grade when discussing paper goods. Like a disc, usually a cover is VG when a variety of problems are evident: ring wear, seam splits, bent corners, loss of gloss on the photo, stains, etc. An aggravated combination of two of these problems—never all of them— would likely cause a sleeve to be graded VG.

Good ("G") in record collecting parlance all too often means a beat, trashed, take-it-to-the-flea-market frisbee. Good should mean that the record is well-played with any number of defects that collectors normally shy away from, such as an almost complete loss of surface sheen, aggravating surface noise, etc. Still, the purchaser, knowing full well that he or she is buying a Good record, should be able to take it home, slap it onto the turntable and have a good time listening to it. Records that do not provide this most fundamental requirement are just no good. A Good record should command 10-15% of the Near Mint price.

A Good cover has seen considerable handling over a course of years and displays the obvious physical signs: ring-wear on the front and back; some seam-splitting, particularly along the bottom, which would receive the brunt of the record's sliding in and out; corners may be dogeared to a light degree; an infatuated owner may have written his or her name somewhere; etc. If a record or cover is beneath your contempt, it is not in ("G") condition; look below for the appropriate grade.

Any record or cover that does not qualify for the above "Good" grading should be seen as Poor. A "P" record should command 0-5% of the Mint price. Make a friend and give any "P" record away as a freebee to anyone who expresses interest in it.

Finally, it should always be borne in mind that visual evidence can be deceiving: The quality of the vinyl and the plating make all the difference in the world. A record properly manufactured with a high quality plating may look VG+ and play Near Mint; this is particularly true of records from the '50s through the mid-'60s, when print runs were dramatically smaller, vinyl was fresher and more care was paid to the entire procedure. Records from this period are a better investment in VG+ condition than the more recent American product. In fact, many 45s from the '50s can be purchased in VG condition at reasonable prices and will play far better than the price paid would indicate. A record manufactured from recycled vinyl with poor plating (too many from the past 15 years) may look Mint and play VG. Still, most dealers do not have the time to listen to each item in their inventory, so visual standards remain.

Record Collecting Abbreviations

Listed here are several common abbreviations used when advertising to describe flaws and their location on a record or cover. Different collectors/dealers have different ways of using these abbreviations; some capitalize them ("DJ"), some use periods after each letter ("n.a.p.") and some use a slash ("c/o"). Those defects marked with an asterisk (*) should always be listed when advertising an item for sale or auction.

alt	alternate (take)
cc	cut corner*
co	cut out*
coh	cut-out hole*
c-33	compact-33⅓ rpm single or EP
cvr	cover

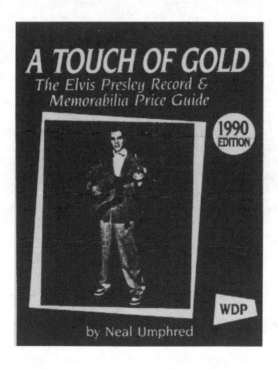

dj .... disc jockey or promotional copy
flexi .... flexible plastic disc
imp .... import
ips .... inches per second
lbl ....label
lp .... 12" 33⅓ rpm long playing album
mo .... mono, monaural
nap .... (does) not affect play
ol ....on label
org .... original
pln cvr .... plain paper jacket (no picture or titles)
promo .... promotional copy
quad .... quadraphonic
re .... reissue
reel .... reel to reel tape
repro .... reproduction, or counterfeit
sdtk ....soundtrack
se ....stereo effect electronically produced
2nd pr .... second pressing
slt wrp .... slight warp*
sm ....saw mark (a cut-out mark)*
sm splt ....seam split*
sol ....sticker on the label*
sr ....slight ring-wear on the front cover*
ss ....still sealed
st .... stereo
stkr ....sticker
10" .... 10" 33⅓ rpm album
t&ts ....(disc jockey) title & timing strip
toc .... tape on the cover*
tol .... tape on the label*
ts .... taped seams*
wlp ....white label promo
wol .... writing on the label*

Shrink-wrap, Stickers & Bonus Photos

Please note that the prices quoted are for opened copies in either VG+ or NM condition. In many cases collectors are willing to pay a premium for still-sealed copies. Depending on the age and desirability of the record, the premium may be a modest 10% above the NM price to 50%; in the case of certain items, the increase would be dramatically greater. Sealed copies of Beatles mono albums on Capitol are worth three to four times the NM price listed in these pages. Certain Elvis Presley albums with a "bonus" sticker on the sealed shrink-wrap would be worth two or more times the NM price. As in all cases, common sense should be used.

Two major points on purchasing still-sealed albums: First, shrink-wrapping of albums at the factory was not common practice until the early to mid-60s. A label as large as Capitol was using the fact that their albums were "poly-wrapped in the factory" as late as January 1964 as a selling point to the consumer. Thus, should you be offered an album from the '50s or early '60s still sealed in shrink-wrap, think twice. Generally, a dealer cannot be held responsible for what is inside a sealed jacket. For example, during

30

Elvis' career, RCA often printed far more covers than records on the initial run (it saved money) and subsequently used the covers until they ran out. Thus it is rather common to find second and third pressing records in original first pressing covers. Consequently, Elvis collectors are not as obsessed with sealed copies and would rather see an opened mint copy than take a chance on a sealed one.

There is also the practice of re-sealing albums. This was done over the years by the record companies and by firms specializing in remainders (I don't remember anyone calling them cut-outs in the '60s.) Prior to the sales boom of the mid-1970s, the industry had a very loose policy regarding returns; many of us over "thirtysomething" grew up able to test a purchase out on the store's turntable before taking it home (and were often able to return records that we just plain didn't like). Of course, those were pre-corporate days when retail operations were independently owned and operated and the proprietor knew most of his customers and catered to their needs.

When purchasing a valuable sealed collectible at a shop or show, pay for the record with the mutual understanding that you will open it immediately after purchase, in front of the dealer, and if the record inside is not what it should be, you may return it on the spot. Do not purchase a sealed record, leave the store or dealer's table, and return later claiming that you got the wrong record or a damaged copy. Naturally, very few dealers will offer a refund in such a case. On a less savory note, there are more than a few dealers and shops that do their own shrink-wrapping.

Promotional Records

The most common method of printing promotional records has been to press them on white labels with plain black print, hence the term "white label promo." As these white labels are obvious manifestations of the label's special attention, they are the most popular with collectors. Some labels used their regular label, or a slightly modified version, and had such mottos as "Audition Copy" and "Promotional Copy" incorporated into the label's typesetting; labels with such notices stamped on after the fact are not the same! Promotional records are usually pressed in small runs on quality vinyl—often at plants that specialize in small print runs—making it a better pressing than the stock copies; needless to say, they are quite collectible and generally command a premium above the normal value of the record, although the premium may be minimal.

The reader should assume that a promo for most records are worth more than the regular, listed version. In cases where the promo has an unusually high value, the promo is listed with its value. The following chart may be used to gauge the value of common promos; these figures are for estimates only and may vary. The column on the left is the listed value of the stock copy; the second column delineates the approximate increase in value that a promo normally commands.

Listed Value	Promo value
$8-45	add approximately 33%
$50-450	add approximately 40%
$500 and up	add approximately 50%

Certainly exceptions to this rule exist: White label promos of Phil Spector's Philles labels are very rare and sell for several times the stock copies listed value (one such promo recently sold for $1,500). Conversely, there are instances where the promo versions are more common than the stock; while this is probably more prevalent than we know, it was not dealt with in this edition. Should any reader be aware of cases that demand recognition in a price guide, please write.

MADE IN ENGLAND

NOT FOR SALE

Trademarks Reg. U.S. Pat. Off.

LONDON ffrr

FULL FREQUENCY RANGE RECORDING

SPEED 33-⅓   Side   (XARL.6291)

1   **LL.3375DJ**

1. NOT FADE AWAY (Petty, Hardin)
2. (GET YOUR KICKS ON) ROUTE 66 (Troup)
3. I JUST WANT TO MAKE LOVE TO YOU (Dixon)
4. HONEST I DO (Reed)
5. NOW I'VE GOT A WITNESS (Phelge)
(LIKE UNCLE PHIL AND UNCLE GENE)
6. LITTLE BY LITTLE (Phelge, Spector)

THE ROLLING STONES

ALL RIGHTS OF THE MANUFACTURER AND OF THE OWNER OF THE RECORDED WORK RESERVED · UNAUTHORISED PUBLIC PERFORMANCE BROADCASTING AND COPYING OF THIS RECORD PROHIBITED

COC 59100

THE ROLLING STONES
STICKY FINGERS

1. BROWN SUGAR (3:50)
Mick Jagger - Keith Richard

STEREO

SAMPLE COPY
NOT FOR SALE
SIDE ONE

TM

2. SWAY (3:45)
Mick Jagger - Keith Richard
3. WILD HORSES (5:41)
Mick Jagger - Keith Richard
4. CAN'T YOU HEAR ME KNOCKING (7:17)
Mick Jagger - Keith Richard
5. YOU GOTTA MOVE (2:32)
Fred McDowell

PRODUCED BY JIMMY MILLER

DIST. BY ATCO . DIV. OF ATLANTIC RECORDING CORP., 1841 B'WAY, N.Y., N.Y.

(ST-RS-712189 PR)

Caveat Emptor: Counterfeits

This then brings us to the subject of counterfeits. The reader will find notes that read "Counterfeits of this record exist!" throughout the book; these notes are applied to those albums where it is generally known that second, illegitimate pressings exist. This is to call the novice's attention to the fact that a record he/she finds at a shop or show for a steal may be a steal of a different nature. One concerned contributor wrote, "One thing I'd like to see emphasized is counterfeit identification. I've learned over the years that there is no polite way to tell someone that the record they have for sale is a fake. They always get defensive. Still, as many collectors don't know what to look for, it's only fair to try to warn them, so that they don't get taken in by a dealer who doesn't know better. Virtually every interesting album of the '70s has been counterfeited, and now we have to deal with these records being offered for sale as originals!"

A counterfeit is an exact copy (or an attempt at an exact copy) of a legitimate record. These are far more common than one might expect. Counterfeits range from the not-so-professional to the perfect. Examples include most if not all of the rare rhythm 'n' blues albums of the '50s and early '60s, especially King and Aladdin, and many rock 'n' rollers, including *Johnny Burnette & The Rock 'n' Roll Trio* and the first four volumes of Elvis' *Golden Records.* Such '60s stalwarts include the Epic Yardbirds stereo albums; the stereo Mothers Of Inventions On Verve; the stereo Left Banke on Smash; and The International Submarine Band's *Safe At Home.*

The Fab Four have probably received the most illicit attention: Most, if not all, of the Beatles Vee Jay catalogue (*Introducing The Beatles* may be the most over produced, with countless unreasonable facsimiles); *The Beatles Christmas Album* and *Let It Be* (which supposedly sold more copies than the legitimate pressing!) on Apple; John and Yoko's *Two Virgins*; and the Ed Rudy interview albums with The Beatles and The Stones. Virtually every garage/punk/psych album of the late '60s and early '70s on a small label has been reproduced, as have many collectible promos of the '70s and '80s, including the Warner Brothers Radio Show series of live albums by Van Morrison, The Pretenders, The Who and Talking Heads; Todd Rundgren's two Runt albums on Ampex; Elvis Costello *Live At The El Mocambo*; Nils Lofgren's *Authorized Bootleg* and Tom Petty's *Live 'leg*; David Bowie's *The Man Who Sold The World*; and such unexpected rarites (sic) as It's A Beautiful Day, The City, Saturday Night Fever; and the pre-Cheap Trick Fuse.

Many of these are fairly obvious, as the covers are blurred photocopies of the originals, the labels tend to be uneven and the sound quality is obviously "mastered" from another record. At the time of their "release" they were always sold on the collectors market as second pressings or bootlegs. Unfortunately, ten years after the fact, they are readily confused for the original by novice collectors. On the opposite end of the scale, many are of such professional duplication that it is nearly impossible to tell the real from the unreal without being made aware of the differences and having one of each in your hands to compare. There are even duplications of test pressing, acetates and Gold and Platinum Record Awards.

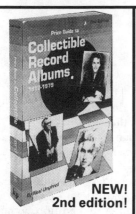

GOLDMINE publisher's foreword

By Greg Loescher

The advent of the compact disc initially sent shockwaves through the record collecting hobby. People wondered what would happen to the value of their vinyl.

Despite the CD's preponderance in the mainstream marketplace, collectible vinyl prices have been rising, as shown by the values in this reference. A collectible is a collectible, regardless of what is currently being purchased.

In this second edition of *Goldmine's Price Guide to Collectible Record Albums*, Neal Umphred has greatly expanded the number of records — and prices — listed for your usage. Neal had to cut quite a bit of his listings for our slimmer first edition, so both the author and the purchaser of this book have to be pleased with the more generous outcome of this second edition.

Neal has put a lot of work into this reference. Despite the tremendous amount of time spent calling aound the country to dealers and collectors for information and the many months spent poring over *Goldmine* ads and reference works, Neal's enthusiasm for this project has never faltered.

Such is the plight of us hard-core record collectors. I'm sure once you've broken the shrink wrap to this volume, you'll spend many long nights looking through your collection, watching the *Goldmine* ads for deals every two weeks and scouring flea markets, garage sales and used record shops for elusive records.

As with any price guide, you may find some pricing not to your liking. Sometimes regional variations or sudden surges in popularity of an artist cause prices to change more rapidly than we can keep up with.

We feel that Neal's pricing is as realistic, current and accurate as humanly possible, or else we wouldn't be stamping our *Goldmine* logo on the cover. This book is a great companion volume to *Goldmine's Rock 'n' Roll 45 RPM Record Price Guide*, also authored by Neal.

Regardless of the era, artists or musical style you collect, I think you'll find this guide to be of value. And if perchance you notice errors or have additions for the next edition, please let us know. The popularity of our first edition, and we hope this new edition, ensures continued updates in future years. And your input is welcome.

We are pleased with the outcome of this newly expanded edition and hope that you enjoy it also.

An Overview of Country & Western Record Collecting

By Joe Goldmark

What do you think of "Jimbo" Reeves on Abbott for $1,000, *Rock 'n Rollin' Robbins* for $750 or Waylon Jennings on Bat for $400? How about $350 for *Moon Over Mullican* or a Bob Wills 10-inch on Antones or *Rockin' With Wanda* for $300? Or George Jones' first Starday album for a mere $200? Do these prices for C&W records scare you or excite you? If they make you angry, you haven't been paying attention. Look at what baseball cards have done recently and you can't even listen to them!

What is your favorite aspect of record collecting? For me, it used to be just the music; I didn't care about the condition or value, since I was only listening for the great sounds and the hot licks. However, these days I think that it's the covers that turn me on more than anything, and condition is now an obsession. For example, I recently bought Sterling Blythe's *Night At The Showboat* on red vinyl (Sage C-14). I still haven't listened to this album, since I never really cared about ol' Sterling, but, geez, what a neat album to have! Or, get a copy of the Louvin Brothers *Satan Is Real* (Capitol T-1277), or *George Jones Salutes Hank Williams* (Mercury SR-60257), or, for that matter, any MGM yellow label Hank Williams album: The combination of the wonderful cover art, the classic sounds, and the appreciating monetary value combine to create the soul, or should we say the gestalt, of the record. This is what addicts collectors, and old C&W albums have this in spades. So, sneak out to your local used record palace and spend a few bucks on a Lefty Frizzell 10-inch album; you'll never regret it.

Country music collectors are a distinct minority in the record collecting hobby; I would guess that at a record swap only five out of 100 buyers are looking for C&W. It was not very long ago that a country collector could have carte blanche, that is, if anyone bothered to bring country records to sell. In fact, usually the response was, "Why should I lug 'em out when nobody buys 'em?" Nowadays, you will see a lot more C&W and, while the prices will be higher, they're still a much better deal than rare R&R records. In the long run, if you have patience and persevere, you have a good shot at actually getting most of the albums that you're looking for. So, let's talk records and prices.

Capitol, Columbia, Decca, RCA, Victor and, to a lesser extent, Mercury and MGM were the major country labels in the '50s and '60s. Most of the desirable artists' LPs of that era go for $15-$30 and the mid '50s stuff is currently up around $50. Ten-inch albums are quickly drawing serious bucks, generally in the $40-$100 range. And, we are talking clean near mint records throughout this article.

It seems that most collectors are completists. Country music feeds this obsession well, since successful artists traditionally have long careers. For example, on Capitol it's fun to get all the Hank Thompson, Wanda Jackson and Jean Shepard, not to mention Buck, Merle and Red's stuff. Then there's Decca, probably the largest and most predictable country label of that period, with Kitty Wells, Loretta Lynn, Webb Pierce, ET, Conway, etc. Some records were great, most just OK, but you should get at least the first dozen albums by each of these artists. OK, I'm a sick dog, but who can resist such neat records? I specialize in collecting guitar and steel guitar albums. Chet Atkins is by far the most collected instrumental artist in the country field and remains so today with his 10-inch albums and "off" label stuff the toughest to find. Believe it or not, there are over 500 steel guitar albums, with Jerry Byrd, Leon McAuliffe and Santo & Johnny the most collected.

Let's look at some interesting collectible labels: Starday started out with some new artists (George Jones and Buck Owens), some washed up artists (Red Sovine and Floyd Tillman), lots of middling bluegrass and gospel (Stringbean and Carl Story), compilation albums galore, and, lo and behold, instrumental albums (Pete Drake and Arthur Smith). When I first started collecting in the late '60s, these albums clogged the cut-out bins and were not taken seriously by collectors. However, as time goes on, Starday originals on the yellow label have become very collectible and now routinely go for $15-$30 a pop.

King Records out of Cincinnati, mainly thought of by collectors as a strong R&B label with James Brown, Little Willie John, Bill Doggett, etc., also had a lot of great bluegrass and country. The Stanley Brothers, Reno & Smiley, the Delmore Brothers, T. Tyler Texas and Moon Mullican all released very collectible albums on King. Slim Whitman, who sold a ton of records for Imperial, is an interesting artist who owned the country charts in the early '50s and then, for the next thirty-odd years, became an international pop star. (It makes you wonder how Imperial Records went under when they had the likes of Slim and Ricky and Fats selling platters galore.)

Sims, Cuca, Audio Lab, Shasta and Longhorn are some of the more collectible small labels; they all had rosters of decent regional artists but they suffered from a lack of national distribution and the resulting inability to break national hits. However, for us, the lack of commercial success means that fewer were pressed and that the records are more desirable now.

It's always been a country tradition for a singer to carry a hot band on the road; a lot of these bands recorded albums on their own. Ernest Tubb's Texas Troubadours, Buck Owen's Buckaroos and Merle Haggard's Strangers were the most successful and remain the most sought-after but there are many more that are fun to collect.

Finally, while I've mainly discussed older albums, I think that even recent records will become collectible now that CDs have taken over. You might want to get all the early albums by artists that you think will be consistent stars and records by the more obscure contemporary artists that you like. There are also many recent reissues on labels such as Stetson and See-For-Miles that are nice if you despair of ever finding the originals or don't want to wear out your original. Records are appreciating in value, especially with the preeminence of the CD. Soon we'll turn around and realize the good stuff is all gone, so now is the time to suck 'em up.

Joe Goldmark is a collector of country & western music and records with a special interest in the steel guitar. He is the author of the privately printed **International Steel Guitar Discography.**

Gold and Platinum Record Award Collecting: A Primer

By Christopher Chatman

The purpose of this article is to give the reader a general acquaintance with the terms and descriptions commonly used in the field of gold and platinum record award collecting. This is being done in order to give the reader added information about an aspect of record collecting of which little is commonly known. The easiest way to go about this is to take a listing of an item as an example, examine it section by section, define each term, and, by so doing, go through the basics of collecting these awards.

Example: 1) Beatles; 2) *Sgt. Pepper's Lonely Hearts Club Band;* 3) RIAA; 4) Gold; 5) White matte; 6) Awarded to Capitol Records; and 7) value unknown.

1) Artist. Obviously the artist whose records, cassettes or compact discs the award commemorates is of immense importance. An award for Elvis Presley or The Beatles (the most obvious examples) is generally worth more than one for Aerosmith (though probably not to any Aerosmith fan, for whom a Double-Platinum Award for their *Permanent Vacation* album may be the ultimate collectible). But generally, the same rules of collecting that help determine the values of records and related memorabilia hold for collecting awards.

2) Title. It is my opinion that the title of the record impacts greatly on the desirability of a given award. (This opinion is not held by *every* dealer or collector). I would rather have an award for Bob Dylan's *Bringing It All Back Home* than one for *Nashville Skyline*, all other factors being equal because to me, *Bringing It All Back Home* is more of a classic. Different people are going to have different opinions about what is classic or desirable. There are certain constants, such as an artist's first gold or platinum award; most collectors would place a premium on that. Again, personal preference and the generalization rule referred to above also apply here.

3) Organization Recognizing Sales Achievement. *This section deserves special notation because so many record award collectors place high emphasis on this.* Most collectors in the United States prefer to have RIAA certified awards. RIAA stands for Record Industry Association of America, the official organization in the United States which certifies the number of records, tapes and compact discs sold. The RIAA has many other functions but the main one which concerns us here is that it acts as an unbiased accounting firm to verify the actual number of units sold. It is for this reason that most award collectors give RIAA certification so much importance. However, it is important to note that record awards that are certified by the record company itself (commonly referred to as "in-house awards") are also desirable. Beside the beauty of some in-house awards, even after 1958 (the year the RIAA was formed), many record companies did not become members of the RIAA (Motown comes instantly to mind).

Another thing to keep in mind is that Platinum status (described below) was recognized by individual record companies years before the RIAA did in 1976. So a Platinum in-house award presented prior to 1976 can be just as valid as an RIAA gold award presented at the same time.

The official organization certifying sales achievement in the United Kingdom in the BPI, or British Phonographic Industry. Because of the blue, red and black cloth backgrounds of these awards, they can be especially nice to acquire.

4) RIAA Award Designation (Gold, Platinum or Multi-Platinum). Qualifiation for RIAA awards have varied over the years, as the following chart illustrates:

1958-1974	45 Gold Award	1,000,000	units in sales.
	LP Gold Award	1,000,000	dollars in sales.
1975-1988	45 Gold Award	1,000,000	units in sales.
	LP Gold Award	500,000	units in sales.
1976	45 Platinum Award	2,000,000	units in sales.
	LP Platinum Award	1,000,000	units in sales.
1984	LP Multi-Platinum Awards		
	LP Double-Platinum Awards	2,000,000	units in sales.
	LP Triple-Platinum Awards	3,000,000	units in sales.
1989	45 Gold Award *	500,000	units in sales.

* Single and album requirements are now the same.

5) RIAA Styles or Formats of Awards.

A. White Matte (1958-1975): The plaque background is an off-white linen material in an unpainted wood frame. Note that occasionally the linen material turns a reddish brown with age. New York Picture & Frame Company was the exclusive manufacturer of this style.

B. Floater (1975-1981): The plaque background is dark (usually black). The record, mini-cover (in the case of albums) and award plate appear to be floating between the background and the Plexiglas in a wood frame painted either gold or silver.

C. Strip Plate (1982-1984): The plaque background is dark. The engraving and RIAA logo (and mini-cover for album awards) are on the same strip of metal. These came with and without a cassette inside.

D. Hologram (1984-1989): The plaque background is dark. The engraving and mini-cover (for album awards) are on the same strip of metal with the RIAA logo designated in a hologram, rainbow-fashion, to avoid unauthorized duplication. All come with the cassette inside.

E. "R" Hologram (1989-present): The traditional RIAA seal was replaced with a symbol consisting of the letter "R" in a hologram pattern. All size and style restrictions were relaxed with the "R" hologram format.

Because of the increased popularity of collecting these awards in the last few years, many award recipients have taken to ordering extra awards to sell to the collectors market. Therefore, when buying a hologram (or any other style of award for that matter), try to make sure the award is in the *original format*. Original format means that the style of the award coincides with the time period in which the album or single was originally certified by the RIAA. The original format of any award will be the most desirable (most of the time).

Another thing to remember is that sometimes record companies have been known to reframe awards in a style other than the standard frame of a given style. This was done to replace damaged frames or because someone in the record company didn't like the standard frame. This practice was not met with favor by the RIAA and has been discontinued for the most part.

6) Recipient. In my opinion, the best way to get an award "presented to" is listed below in descending order.

A. The artist.

B. The record company.

C. Someone closely connected with the production of the record. Example: anyone listed in the album credits.

D. Production company.

E. Radio station.

F. A record company executive.

7) Price. Compare prices, which are going to vary, depending on how a dealer has invested in a given item and what the dealer thinks he can get out of that award. Consider all the preceding factors but be sure to consider a dealer's reputation. A good price is a *bad* price if you never receive the item or get a bogus one.

Gold and platinum awards are great investments if you invest in an artist who will maintain collector's interest over the years. As the interest in this field of collecting continues to grow, a wise purchase in the present has the potential to grow into a healthy investment for the future.

Christopher Chatman, owner of Beyond Records, is a collector/dealer who has specialized in rare records and memorabilia — including gold and platinum awards — for several years.

How to Realistically Sell Your Records

By Perry Cox

Collectors and dealers all over the world keep a watchful eye on current market trends to see how their investments are doing, as well as what they can expect to pay for items that remain on their want lists. The burning questions, then, are: "How does one realistically go about selling their records? Sure, the guide says it's worth X dollar amount, but how do I market my item(s) anywhere near its value estimate?" There are several answers, all of which depend on the seller's situation and needs.

Set Sale to Personal Contracts

This method is probably the only way to achieve near, at, or above market value in a relatively short period of time. At the point you wish to market your item(s), the sale may take no longer than a couple of phone calls to complete. Of course, this method involves plenty of prior invested time and interaction with others. As a collector among collectors, it is ideal to socialize, share one's finds, interact for feedback and advice, and keep on the lookout for other collectors' wants. By acquiring a current list of items your friends and colleagues are looking for, you will be better able to determine what you can sell and for how much. This is not only an ideal way to obtain maximum return from collectibles you have to sell, but this also allows you a keen advantage in terms of trading for items to fill your own collection. As well, many will appreciate your servicing their wants. The longer you are involved, the larger your customer/friendship base grows. That is, *if* you have kept the required high standards of dealing ethics which are absolutely essential in building a solid relationship with other collectors.

Ethics between buyer and sellers *must* be given preference over all other factors. Your records and money mean little if your code of conduct allows for dissatisfaction with the other party, especially if you do not promptly remedy the problem to their satisfaction. Universal dealing principles equate to honesty and fairly grading their items. Since most prospective buyers are unable to personally inspect the items prior to the sale, it is good policy to institute a full "money back, satisfaction guarantee" coupled with a reasonable limit for recourse (usually a couple of weeks is sufficient).

It is very important to formulate your selling prices *before* you contact prospective buyers. It is not wise to gauge your pricing on the customer's level of desire or by pitting one customer against another. These tactics spawn little more than frustration and discontent for everyone. If you agree to a set price, do not raise the price if you later realize another party expresses interest in it. (As well, if you agree to buy an item for a certain price, nitpicking at very minor, insignificant flaws in hopes of getting a discount is not wise.) In short, each must live by his own set of standards and always give great respect to another's valid concerns. Remember, if you get in the habit of making undesirable transactions, many will learn not to contact you the next time you have records to sell or trade.

Set Sale in Trade Publications

The term "set sale" means to list your items at fixed prices; i.e., the items are *not* being auctioned. The advantage with this method is that your market potential is far greater due to the mass attention your items receive. The *actual* level of exposure depends on what publications you choose. If you have several "high ticket" items or a large amount of quality merchandise to sell, ads in several publications at once is certainly a viable option. This method is a bit more time consuming: Ad preparation, distribution of the publication, and mail transactions involve time.

Preparing your ad needs special planning and considerations; you will need to figure the total number of lines each typewritten page gives you (normally between 50 and 60), the cost per ad, then the cost per line. Collectors tend to gravitate to the excellent condition items, so concentrate on listing in-demand items in quality shape. If you list thirty $10 items that take up half your full page ad space, you have only covered your ad cost, *if you sell them all.*

Keep in mind the costs of advertising with full page ads. Smaller space ads are considerably cheaper. The "Showcase" ad section in the back of *Goldmine* is very effective in presenting select items. The inexpensive rates include typesetting and placement among other eye-appealing ads. This is often the first section viewed by readers.

When preparing your ad, by all means grade your items very conservatively. Conservative, accurate grading provides a healthy, happy collecting environment for everyone. Also, you must be prepared to pack your items well with proper, snug packing and padding (2-3 inches of padding around the item is a good minimum). Always insure the items you are mailing; it is well worth the extra expense.

When dealing with mail-order, the buyers may notify you of their intent to reserve any particular item(s) they are interested in. Normally this is done by telephone (many buyers prefer to talk to the people they are dealing with, since it gives an added sense of security and provides an immediate response as to the availability of the item) or mail. The response you may receive from this type of advertising is an excellent way to broaden your list of other collectors.

Selling Via Auctions in Trade Publication

If one has the time, this method has the potential of being the most rewarding in terms of highest yield plus it is a good way to learn just how much customers are willing to spend at any given time on any given item. With the mail-order auction, the seller sets a bid deadline; normally an auction runs for one month from the beginning of the issue's publication date. At the deadline all bids are evaluated, and the highest bidders are then notified.

In some cases, auctions have yielded sales substantially over the going set value; in other cases the results can be most disappointing. The factors involved in determining the final results are far too numerous to detail, but the general spending mood of the public is probably the most important factor. When a given artist is focused on in the media, sales tend to surge accordingly. The death of a major star such as John Lennon is one example; the hoopla surrounding Madonna's or the Rolling Stones' latest tour is another.

Reputable auction establishments such as Sotheby's, Christie's and Phillips are alternative auction methods. They can, however, take the longest time in that they only hold their auctions a few times a year. Exposure to collectors is also limited, but the spending frenzy sometimes associated with these houses can often play a favorable role for the seller. One thing is certain: Auctions do take the longest period of time on average to sell your items. From start to completion, a mail-order auction consumes an average of two months. This is not the way to go if one wishes to liquidate in a hurry.

Selling Your Items to a Dealer

Probably the quickest manner to sell your items once you have exhausted retail sales to personal contacts is to sell them wholesale to a dealer. If you need cash and you need it right away, selling this way can be quite convenient. Your first responsibility is to contact a *reputable* dealer who is interested in mutual satisfaction between his interest and your own. One must keep in mind that a dealer is not in a position to pay top market dollar for your items. Like any commodity, the record dealer has to buy at a modest percentage of full value in order to make enough profit to stay in business.

As a rule, it is safe to say that the more significantly rare and valuable your item is, the more the dealer is probably willing to pay, especially if he has a ready buyer. Although the dealer takes into consideration many factors when evaluating, the bottom line is usually this: "How long will one have to keep his money tied up before one actually sells the goods and recovers his money?" Some very rare and valuable items have been known to fetch as much as 60-65% of market retail. A good average for slow movers is about 30-40% of the dealer's opinion of the market value. If the period is lengthy or if the dealer has several copies of the item you are trying to sell, he'll be less generous in his offer or may not express any interest at all!

If you intend to solicit offers from various dealers, please advise each dealer of this prior to negotiations to avoid hard feelings. This eliminates the impression the dealer may have in thinking he has an exclusive on your items. *(Editor's note: Similarly, never take the first offer without gettting offers from at least two other dealers!)*

The Consignment Method

Some dealers will agree to place items obtained from the owner on consignment. That is, he will not pay the owners until the item sells. Usually this method is not entertained unless the dealer feels the item is significant enough to yield a handsome return within a reasonable time. The retail value is mutually agreed upon, while the dealer assumes responsibility for the custody and sale of the item. The final say in retail value usually goes to the dealer who knows his area and market potential best. The average consignment fee is anywhere from 15% to 30% to the dealer, certainy better than the 40-50% usually obtained in a straight sale to the dealer.

Compared with some of the others, this selling method can be quite time consuming without guaranteed sales, a factor that must be considered before locking your item(s) in a consignment agreement (which is, in effect, a contract).

The Top 100 Most Valuable Albums

Those values preceeded by an asterisk indicate that the reocrd is listed in the book without a specific value but is represented by an estimated near mint range. Enough information is noted parenthetically to indicate exactly which pressing of a record holds the particular value; refer to the listings within the book for more information or other pressings. Please note that the mono (M) or stereo (S) assignation is important to identify which copy of a title holds the high(est) value.

1. **BOB DYLAN**
   Columbia CL-1986   (M)   The Freewheelin' Bob Dylan   1963   *10,000.00
   (Original pressings contain "Rocks And Gravel," "Let Me Die In My Footsteps," "John Birch Society Blues" and "Ramblin' Gamblin' Willie.")

2. **THE BEATLES**
   Vee Jay LPS-1085   (P)   The Beatles And Frank Ifield On Stage   1964   7,500.00
   (The cover has a full-color, painted portrait of the Beatles.)

   THE BEATLES
   Vee Jay PRO-202   (M)   Hear The Beatles Tell All *(White label)*   1964   *7,500.00

   THE BEATLES
   Capitol ST-2553   (P)   Yesterday And Today   1966   7,500.00
   ("First state butcher cover.")

5. **THE FIVE KEYS**
   Aladdin 806   (M)   The Best Of The Five Keys *(Blue label)*   1956   5,000.00

   BILLY WARD & HIS DOMINOES
   Federal 295-94   (M)   Billy Ward & His Dominoes *(10")*   1954   5,000.00

7. **DAVID BOWIE**
   RCA Victor APL1-0576   (S)   Diamond Dogs   1974   *4,500.00

   IKE & TINA TURNER
   Philles PHLP-4011   (M)   River Deep-Mountain High   1966   *4,500.00
   (No covers are to known to have been completed for Philles 4011.)

9. **THE BEATLES**
   Vee Jay SR-1062   (P)   Introducing The Beatles   1963   4,000.00
   (Includes "Love Me Do" and "P.S. I Love You." Black label with a rainbow border and oval logo. The back cover has ads for 25 other albums.)

   THE ROLLING STONES
   London LL-3402   (M)   12 X 5 *(Blue vinyl)*   1964   *4,000.00

11. **DAMON**
    Ankh 968   (M)   Song Of A Gypsy   1970   *3,500.00
    (Textured cover with the title an an ankh embossed. Copies in a plain jacket $1,500.)

    PRINCE
    Warner Bros. 25677   (S)   The Black Album   1987   *3,500.00

13. **BOB DYLAN**
    Columbia PC-33235   (S)   Blood On The Tracks *(Test pressing)*   1976   *2,500.00
    (Test pressing includes alternate takes of five songs.)

    THE BEATLES
    Capitol T-2553   (M)   Yesterday And Today   1966   2,500.00
    ("First state butcher cover.")

    PHAPHNER
    Dragon LP-101   (S)   Overdrive   197?   *2,500.00

16. **MARIANI**
    Sonobeat 1001   (M)   Perpetuum Mobile *(Issued without a cover)*   196?   *2,250.00

    THE MIDNIGHTERS
    Federal 295-90   (M)   Their Greatest Jukebox Hits   1955   *2,250.00

    THE BRIGADE
    Band'n Vocal BVRS-1066   (S)   Last Laugh   1970   *2,250.00

19. **THE BEATLES**
    Vee Jay LP-1062   (M)   Introducing The Beatles   1963   2,000.00
    (Includes "Love Me Do" and "P.S. I Love You." Black label with a rainbow border and oval logo. The back cover has ads for 25 other albums.)

THE BEATLES
Vee Jay SR-1062   (P)   Introducing The Beatles   1963   2,000.00
(Includes "Love Me Do" and "P.S. I Love You." Black label with a rainbow border. The back cover is blank.)

THE BEATLES
Vee Jay LP-1085   (M)   The Beatles And Frank Ifield On Stage   1964   2,000.00
(The cover has a full-color, painted portrait of the Beatles.)

BOYD BENNETT
King 594   (M)   Boyd Bennett   1956   2,000.00

THE FIVE SATINS
Ember ELP-100   (M)   The Five Satins Sing *(Blue label)*   1957   2,000.00

FRANK FROST & THE NIGHTHAWKS
Phillips International 1975   (M)   Hey! Boss Man   1961   *2,000.00

PAUL McCARTNEY
Apple MAS-3375   (M)   Ram *(Mono promo)*   1971   *2,000.00

AMOS MILBURN
Motown 608   (M)   The Blues Boss   1963   *2,000.00

27. THE BEATLES
United Artists UAL-3366   (M)   A Hard Day's Night *(White label promo)*   1964   1,800.00

28. THE BEATLES
Vee Jay DXS-30   (S)   The Beatles Vs. The Four Seasons *(2 LPs with poster)*   1964   1,700.00

29. THE PATRON SAINTS
No label   (M)   Fohhoh Bohob   1969   *1,600.00

30. BENT WIND
Trend T-1015   (S)   Sussex   196?   *1,500.00

CHARLES BROWN
Aladdin 702   (M)   Mood Music *(10" red vinyl)*   1952   1,500.00

FRANK BALLARD
Phillips International 1985   (M)   Rhythm-Blues Party   1962   1,500.00

JOHNNY BURNETTE & THE ROCK 'N' ROLL TRIO
Coral CRL-57080   (M)   Johnny Burnette & The Rock 'N' Roll Trio   1956   1,500.00

THE CRYSTALS
Philles DT-90722   (E)   Twist Uptown   1963   *1,500.00

BOB DYLAN
Columbia CL-1986   (M)   The Freewheelin' Bob Dylan *(White label promo)*   1963   *1,500.00
(The label lists the four deleted tracks but the album plays the four new tracks.)

THE EBON-KNIGHTS
Stepheny 4001   (M)   First Date With The Ebon-Knights   196?   *1,500.00

FRACTION
Angelus WR-5005   (S)   Moon Blood   197?   *1,500.00

GRANDMA'S ROCKERS
Fredlo 6727   (M)   Homemade Apple Pie   1967   *1,500.00

THE INDEX
D. C. *(No number)*   (M)   The Index (First Album)   1967   1,500.00
(Only a few copies were issued with an original cover and there are no documented sales from which to derive a value!)

THE JEFFERSON AIRPLANE
RCA Victor LPM-3584   (M)   The Jefferson Airplane Takes Off!   1966   *1,500.00
(Originally issued with "Runnin' Round The World.")

AMOS MILBURN
Aladdin 704   (M)   Rockin' The Boogie *(10" on red vinyl)*   1954   1,500.00

AMOS MILBURN / WYNONIE HARRIS / "CROWN PRINCE" WATERFORD
Aladdin 703   (M)   Party After Hours *(10" on red vinyl)*   1954   1,500.00

THE MUSIC EMPORIUM
Sentinal 69001   (S)   The Music Emporium   1969   *1,500.00

THE NEW TWEEDY BROTHERS
Ridon 234   (S)   The New Tweedy Brothers   196?   *1,500.00

ELVIS PRESLEY
RCA Victor VPSX-6089   *(Q)*   Aloha From Hawaii Via Satellite *(2 LPs)*   *1973*   1,500.00
                                              (With "Chicken Of The Sea Tuna" sticker.)

STACK
Charisma CRS-303   *(M)*   Above All   *1966*   *1,500.00

VARIOUS ARTISTS
No label   *(M)*   Rock, Rock, Rock *(Soundtrack)*   *1956*   1,500.00

48. **JIM REEVES**
Abbott LP-5001   *(M)*   Jim Reeves Sings   *1956*   *1,250.00

THE WEST COAST POP ART EXPERIMENTAL BAND
Fifo M-101   *(M)*   The West Coast Pop Art Experimental Band   *1966*   *1,250.00

50. **THE BEATLES**
Vee Jay VJS-1092   *(S)*   Songs, Pictures And Stories   *1964*   1,200.00

THE BEATLES
United Artists Help-Show   *(M)*   Help! *(One-sided open-end interview)*   *1965*   1,200.00

THE BEATLES
Capitol ST-2553   *(P)*   Yesterday And Today   *1966*   1,200.00
                         ("Second state butcher cover.")

THE BEATLES
Apple KAL-1004   *(M)*   Yellow Submarine Radio Spots   *1968*   1,200.00

THE FIVE ROYALES
Apollo LP-488   *(M)*   The Rockin' Five Royales *(Green or yellow label)*   *1956*   1,200.00

LITTLE ESTHER
King LP-622   *(M)*   Down Memory Lane With Little Esther   *1956*   1,200.00

ELVIS PRESLEY
RCA Victor *(No number)*   *(S)*   International Hotel Presents Elvis, 1970 *(Boxed set)*   *1970*   1,200.00

ELVIS PRESLEY
RCA Victor AFL1-2428   *(S)*   Moody Blue *("Splash" colored vinyl)*   *1977*   1,200.00

THE ROLLING STONES
London LL-3375   *(M)*   The Rolling Stones *(White label promo)*   *1964*   1,200.00

VARIOUS ARTISTS
No label   *(M)*   Go, Johnny, Go *(Soundtrack)*   *1956*   1,200.00

60. **ELVIS PRESLEY**
RCA Victor *No number*   *(S)*   International Hotel Presents Elvis, 1969 *(Boxed set)*   *1969*   1,100.00

61. **ARK**
Ark 810-71   *(S)*   Voyages   *1978*   1,000.00

THE BEATLES
Vee Jay LP-1062   *(M)*   Introducing The Beatles   *1963*   1,000.00
                         (Includes "Love Me Do" and "P.S. I Love You." Black label with a rainbow border. The back cover is blank.)

THE BEATLES
Vee Jay SR-1062   *(S)*   Introducing The Beatles   *1964*   1,000.00
                         (Includes "Please Please Me" and "Ask Me Why." Black label with a rainbow border and the "Vee Jay" logo in an oval. The back cover lists the song titles in two columns.)

THE BEATLES
Vee Jay SR-1062   *(S)*   Introducing The Beatles   *1964*   1,000.00
                         (Includes "Please Please Me" and "Ask Me Why." Solid black label with a plain "VJ" logo. The back cover lists the songs in two columns.)

THE CRICKETS
Brunswick BL-54038   *(M)*   The Chirping Crickets *(Yellow label promo)*   *1957*   1,000.0

THE FENDERMEN
Soma MG-1240   *(M)*   Mule Skinner Blues *(Opaque vinyl)*   *1960*   1,000.00

THE FIVE KEYS
Aladdin 806   *(M)*   The Best Of The Five Keys *(Maroon label)*   *1956*   1,000.00

BUDDY HOLLY
Decca DL-8707   *(M)*   That'll Be The Day *(Pink label promo)*   *1958*   1,000.00

	MARCUS NR 10788	(S)	From The House Of Trax	*1979*	1,000.00
	"BIG" JAY McNEELY Federal 295-96	(M)	Big Jay McNeely *(10")*	*1954*	1.000.00
	THE NIGHT SHADOWS Spectrum	(S)	The Square Root Of Two	*1968*	1,000.00
	ODYSSEY Organic ORG-1	(M)	Odyssey	*196?*	1,000.00
	THE PLATTERS Federal 395-549	(M)	The Platters	*1955*	1,000.00
	ELVIS PRESLEY RCA Victor LPM-1382	(M)	Elvis *(Contains an alternate take of "Old Shep.")*	*1956*	1,000.00
	ELVIS PRESLEY RCA Victor UNMR-5697	(M)	Special Christmas Programming	*1967*	1,000.00
	ELVIS PRESLEY RCA Victor AFL1-2428	(S)	Moody Blue *(Colored vinyl)*	*1977*	1,000.00
	THE ROLLING STONES Abkco MPD-1	(P)	Songs Of The Rolling Stones *(The cover features a photo taken from "Rock & Roll Circus.")*	*1975*	1,000.00
	TOUCH Mainline PS70-116-7	(S)	Street Suite	*197?*	1,000.00
	VARIOUS ARTISTS Warner Bros.	(M)	Jamboree *(Soundtrack)*	*1956*	1,000.00
	VARIOUS ARTISTS King 668	(M)	Battle Of The Blues, Volume 4	*1956*	1,000.00
	BILLY WARD & HIS DOMINOES Federal 395-559	(M)	Clyde McPhatter With Billy Ward & His Dominoes	*1956*	1,000.00
	BILLY WARD & HIS DOMINOES Federal 395-548	(M)	Billy Ward & His Dominoes	*1956*	1,000.00
	ZERFAS 700 West 730710	(S)	Zerfas	*197?*	1,000.00
84.	**HOOTCH** Pro-Gress PRS-4844	(S)	Hootch	*1974*	*950.00
85.	**THE BEATLES** Vee Jay SR-1062	(S)	Introducing The Beatles *(Includes "Please Please Me" and "Ask Me Why." Black label with a rainbow border and the "VJ" logo in brackets. The back cover lists the song titles in two columns.)*	*1964*	900.00
	THE BEATLES Atco 33-169	(M)	Ain't She Sweet *(White label promo)*	*1964*	900.00
	THE BEATLES United Artists SP-2362	(M)	A Hard Day's Night *(Radio Spots)*	*1964*	900.00
	THE BEATLES United Artists Help-INT	(M)	Help! *(Open-end Interview)*	*1965*	900.00
	FREDRIC Forte 301	(S)	Phases And Faces	*1968*	900.00
	THE ROLLING STONES London RSD-1	(M)	The Rolling Stones Promotional Album	*1969*	900.00
91.	**JACKSON BROWNE**	(S)	Jackson Browne's First Album	*1967*	*885.00
92.	**THE C.A. QUINTET** Candy Floss 7764	(M)	A Trip Through Hell	*1969*	800.00
93.	**JOHNNY ACE** Duke DLP-71	(M)	Memorial Album For Johnny Ace *(10")*	*1955*	750.00
	ANNETTE & HAYLEY MILLS Buena Vista BV-3508	(M)	Annette And Hayley *(Paper sleeve)*	*1964*	*750.00

THE BEATLES United Artists Help-A/B	(M)	Help! *(Radio spots)*	*1965*	750.00
THE BEATLES United Artists SP-2359	(M)	A Hard Day's Night *(Open-end interview)*	*1964*	750.00
CHARLES BROWN Aladdin 702	(M)	Mood Music *(10")*	*1952*	750.00
CHRISTOPHER Cris Tee	(S)	What'cha Gonna Do? *(Orange cover)*	*1969*	*750.00
THE CRYSTALS Philles PHLP-4000	(M)	Twist Uptown *(White label promo)*	*1962*	750.00
THE CRYSTALS Philles PHLP-4001	(M)	He's A Rebel *(White label promo)*	*1963*	750.00
THE FIVE KEYS Score LP-4003	(M)	The Five Keys On The Town	*1957*	750.00
THE FUGITIVES Hideout 1001	(M)	The Fugitives At Dave's Hideout	*1968*	750.00
JIMI HENDRIX Reprise 2R-6307	(M)	Electric Ladyland *(2 LPs)*	*1968*	750.00
THE INDEX D. C. *(No number)*	(M)	The Index (Second Album)	*1967*	*750.00
LAZY SMOKE Onyx 6903	(M)	Corridor Of Faces	*196?*	750.00
JOHN LENNON & YOKO ONO Apple SVBB-3392	(S)	Some Time In New York City *(2 LPs. Promo)*	*1972*	750.00
AMOS MILBURN Aladdin 704	(M)	Rockin' The Boogie *(10")*	*1954*	750.00
AMOS MILBURN / WYNONIE HARRIS / "CROWN PRINCE" WATERFORD Aladdin 703	(M)	Party After Hours *(10")*	*1954*	750.00
ELVIS PRESLEY RCA Victor LPM-3921	(M)	Elvis' Gold Records, Volume 4	*1968*	750.00
ELVIS PRESLEY RCA Victor LPM-3989	(M)	Speedway *(Soundtrack)*	*1968*	750.00
THE RISING STORM Remnant BBA-3571	(M)	Calm Before The Rising Storm	*1968*	750.00
MARTY ROBBINS Columbia CL-2601	(M)	Rock 'N Roll 'N Robbins *(10")*	*1956*	750.00
BRUCE SPRINGSTEEN Columbia PC-33795	(S)	Born To Run *(Advanced promo with the title on the cover in script. Includes promotional inserts.)*	*1975*	750.00
JACKIE WILSON Sesac	(M)	Jackie Wilson	*1958*	*750.00

Honorable Mention

JACK KEROUAC Dot DLP-3154	(M)	Poetry For The Beat Generation *(Pressed in minute quantities and then deleted, there are no known transactions from which to derive a value.)*	*1959*	—
VARIOUS ARTISTS *No label*	(M)	Carnival Rock *(Soundtrack)* *(So rare there is no estimated value)*	*1956*	—

Label & Catalog #		Title	Year	VG+	NM

A.F.O. EXECUTIVES, THE
| A.F.O. LP-0002 | (M) | **A Compendium** | 196? | **75.00** | **150.00** |

Abba, celebrated for their international success in the '70s, where they rivaled Elton John and The Bee Gees, have only a couple of collectibles from their U.S. catalog.

ABBA
| Atlantic PR-300 | (DJ) | **Abba** *(Sampler)* | 1978 | 10.00 | **25.00** |
| Nautilus NR-20 | (S) | **Arrival** | 198? | 6.00 | **15.00** |

ABICAIR, SHIRLEY
| Columbia CL-1531 | (M) | **With The Gentle Air** | 1960 | 6.00 | **15.00** |
| Columbia CS-8331 | (S) | **With The Gentle Air** | 1960 | 8.00 | **20.00** |

ACE, JOHNNY
Duke DLP-70 (10")	(M)	**Memorial Album For Johnny Ace**	1955	500.00	**750.00**
Duke DLP-71	(M)	**Memorial Album For Johnny Ace**	1956	150.00	**250.00**
		(Purple & yellow label. No card on the cover.)			
Duke DLP-71	(M)	**Memorial Album For Johnny Ace**	1961	75.00	**150.00**
		(Purple & yellow label. The cover has a playing card.)			

ACUFF, ROY
Columbia HL-9004 (10")	(M)	**Songs Of The Smokey Mountains**	1949	35.00	**70.00**
Columbia HL-9010 (10")	(M)	**Old Time Barn Music**	1949	35.00	**70.00**
Columbia HL-9013 (10")	(M)	**Songs Of The Saddle**	1949	35.00	**70.00**
Capitol T-617	(M)	**Songs Of The Smoky Mountains**	1955	20.00	**50.00**
Harmony HL-7082	(M)	**Great Speckled Bird**	1958	10.00	**25.00**
MGM E-3707	(M)	**Favorite Hymns**	1958	20.00	**50.00**

Label & Catalog #		Title	Year	VG+	NM
MGM E-4044	(M)	Hymn Time	1962	8.00	20.00
MGM SE-4044	(S)	Hymn Time	1962	10.00	25.00
Capitol T-1870	(M)	Songs Of The Smoky Mountains	1963	10.00	25.00
Capitol T-2103	(M)	The Great Roy Acuff	1964	8.00	20.00
Capitol ST-2103	(S)	The Great Roy Acuff	1964	10.00	25.00
Capitol T-2276	(M)	The Voice Of Country Music	1965	8.00	20.00
Capitol ST-2276	(S)	The Voice Of Country Music	1965	10.00	25.00
ADAMS, DON					
Signature SM-1010	(M)	Don Adams	1960	8.00	20.00
Crescendo GNP-91	(M)	Don Adams Meets The Roving Reporter	1963	5.00	12.00
Crescendo GNPS-91	(S)	Don Adams Meets The Roving Reporter	1963	6.00	15.00
Roulette R-25317	(M)	The Detective	1966	5.00	12.00
Roulette SR-25317	(S)	The Detective	1966	6.00	15.00
United Arts. UAL-3533	(M)	Get Smart (TV Soundtrack)	1966	8.00	20.00
United Arts. UAS-6533	(S)	Get Smart (TV Soundtrack)	1966	10.00	25.00
United Arts. UAL-3604	(M)	Don Adams Live	1967	5.00	12.00
United Arts. UAS-6604	(S)	Don Adams Live	1967	6.00	15.00
ADAMS, EDIE					
MGM E-3751	(M)	Music To Listen To Records To	1959	8.00	20.00
MGM SE-3751	(S)	Music To Listen To Records To	1959	12.00	30.00
ADAMS, FAYE					
Warwick 2031	(M)	Shake A Hand	1961	75.00	150.00
ADAMS, JERRI					
Columbia CL-916	(M)	It's Cool Inside	1956	16.00	40.00
Columbia CL-1259	(M)	Play For Keeps	1959	12.00	30.00
ADAMS, MIKE, & THE RED JACKETS					
Crown CLP-5312	(M)	Surfer's Beat	1963	4.00	10.00
Crown CST-312	(S)	Surfer's Beat	1963	5.00	12.00
Crown CST-312	(S)	Surfer's Beat (Colored vinyl)	1963	12.00	30.00
ADRIAN & THE SUNSETS					
Sunset 63-601	(M)	Breakthrough	1963	40.00	80.00
Sunset SE-63-601	(S)	Breakthrough	1963	60.00	120.00
Sunset 63-601	(M)	Breakthrough (Multi-colored vinyl)	1963	60.00	120.00
Sunset SE-63-601	(S)	Breakthrough (Multi-colored vinyl)	1963	80.00	160.00
ADVENTURERS, THE					
Columbia CL-2147	(M)	Can't Stop Twistin'	1961	16.00	40.00
Columbia CS-8547	(S)	Can't Stop Twistin'	1961	20.00	50.00
AEROSMITH					
Columbia KCQ-32847	(Q)	Get Your Wings	1974	10.00	25.00
Columbia JCQ-33479	(Q)	Toys In The Attic	1975	10.00	25.00
Columbia PCQ-34165	(Q)	Rocks	1976	10.00	25.00
Columbia A3S-187	(DJ)	Pure Gold (3 LPs)	1976	20.00	50.00
Columbia (No number)	(DJ)	The First Decade (8 LP box)	1980	50.00	100.00
AESOPS FABLE					
Cadet Concept LPS-323	(S)	In Due Time	1969	6.00	15.00
AFFECTION COLLECTION, THE					
Evolution 2007	(S)	The Affection Collection	196?	6.00	15.00
AFFINITY					
Paramount PAS-5027	(S)	Affinity	1970	6.00	15.00
AFTERGLOW					
M.T.A. 5010	(M)	Afterglow	1967	12.00	30.00
AGAPE					
Mark MRS-2170	(M)	Agape	196?	75.00	150.00
Renrut 101	(S)	Victims Of Tradition	197?	100.00	200.00

Label & Catalog #		Title	Year	VG+	NM
AGE OF REASON, THE					
Georgetown	(M)	The Age Of Reason	196?	75.00	150.00
AGGREGATION					
L.H.I. 12008	(S)	Mind Odyssey	1967	75.00	150.00
AIR SUPPLY					
Mobile Fidelity MFSL-113	(S)	The One That You Love	198?	6.00	15.00
Nautilus NR-31	(S)	Lost In Love	198?	4.00	10.00
AKENS, JEWEL					
Era EL-110	(M)	The Birds And The Bees	1965	12.00	30.00
Era ES-110	(S)	The Birds And The Bees	1965	16.00	40.00
ALABAMA					
Plantation PLP-44	(S)	Wild Country	1981	20.00	50.00
ALAIMO, STEVE					
Checker LP-2981	(M)	Twist With Steve Alaimo	1961	16.00	40.00
Checker LP-2983	(M)	Mashed Potatoes	1962	16.00	40.00
Checker LP-2986	(M)	Every Day I Have To Cry	1963	16.00	40.00
ABC-Paramount 501	(M)	Starring Steve Alaimo	1965	8.00	20.00
ABC-Paramount S-501	(S)	Starring Steve Alaimo	1965	10.00	25.00
ABC-Paramount 531	(M)	Where The Action Is	1965	8.00	20.00
ABC-Paramount S-531	(S)	Where The Action Is	1965	10.00	25.00
ABC-Paramount 551	(M)	Steve Alaimo Sings And Swings	1966	8.00	20.00
ABC-Paramount S-551	(S)	Steve Alaimo Sings And Swings	1966	10.00	25.00
ALBATROSS					
Anvil 8100	(S)	Albatross	197?	180.00	300.00
ALBERGHETTI, ANNA MARIA					
Mercury MG-20056	(M)	Songs By Anna Maria Alberghetti	1956	12.00	30.00
Capitol T-887	(M)	I Can't Resist You	1957	12.00	30.00
MGM E-4001	(M)	Love Makes The World Go 'Round	1962	6.00	15.00
MGM SE-4001	(S)	Love Makes The World Go 'Round	1962	8.00	20.00
ALBERGHETTI, ANNA MARIA, & KAYE BALLARD					
MGM E-3946	(M)	Carnival	1961	6.00	15.00
MGM SE-3946	(S)	Carnival	1961	8.00	20.00
ALBERT, EDDIE					
Kapp KP-1000	(M)	One God	1954	10.00	25.00
Kapp KP-1017	(M)	Eddie Albert And Margo	1956	10.00	25.00
Kapp KP-1083	(M)	September Song	1957	10.00	25.00
Dot DLP-3109	(M)	High Upon A Mountain	1960	8.00	20.00
Columbia CL-2599	(M)	The Eddie Albert Album	1966	6.00	15.00
Columbia CS-9399	(S)	The Eddie Albert Album	1966	8.00	20.00
ALBERTS, AL					
Alberts was formerly lead singer of The Four Aces.					
Coral CRL-57259	(M)	Man Has Got To Sing	1959	12.00	30.00
Coral CRL-757259	(S)	Man Has Got To Sing	1959	16.00	40.00
ALBRIGHT, LOLA					
Columbia CL-1327	(M)	Dreamsville	1959	8.00	20.00
Columbia CS-8133	(S)	Dreamsville	1959	12.00	30.00
ALDA, ROBERT					
Tops L-1589	(M)	Romance Of Rome	195?	10.00	25.00
Treasure TLP-804	(M)	For Continental Lovers	195?	10.00	25.00
ALEONG, ALI, & THE NOBLES					
Reprise R-6020	(M)	C'mon Baby, Let's Dance	1962	6.00	15.00
Reprise R9-6020	(S)	C'mon Baby, Let's Dance	1962	8.00	20.00
Reprise R-6011	(M)	Twistin' The Hits	1962	6.00	15.00
Reprise R9-6011	(S)	Twistin' The Hits	1962	8.00	20.00
Vee Jay LP-1060	(M)	Come Surf With Me	1963	8.00	20.00
Vee Jay SR-1060	(S)	Come Surf With Me	1963	12.00	30.00

Label & Catalog #		Title	Year	VG+	NM
ALEXANDER, ARTHUR					
Dot DLP-3434	(M)	You Better Move On	1962	40.00	80.00
Dot DLP-25434	(S)	You Better Move On	1962	75.00	150.00
Warner Bros. B-2592	(S)	Arthur Alexander	1972	8.00	20.00
ALEXANDER'S TIMELESS BLOOZBAND					
Smack 1001	(M)	Alexander's Timeless Bloozband	1967	50.00	100.00
Uni 73021	(S)	For Sale	1968	5.00	12.00
ALEXANDRIA, LOREZ					
King 542	(M)	This Is Lorez	1958	16.00	40.00
King 565	(M)	Lorez Sings Prez	1958	16.00	40.00
King 676	(M)	Songs Everybody Knows	1959	16.00	40.00
King 656	(M)	The Band Swings, Lorez Sings	1959	16.00	40.00
Argo LP-663	(M)	Early In The Morning	1960	8.00	20.00
Argo LPS-663	(S)	Early In The Morning	1960	10.00	25.00
Argo LP-682	(M)	Sing No Sad Songs For Me	1961	8.00	20.00
Argo LPS-682	(S)	Sing No Sad Songs For Me	1961	10.00	25.00
Argo LP-694	(M)	Deep Roots	1962	8.00	20.00
Argo LPS-694	(S)	Deep Roots	1962	10.00	25.00
Argo LP-720	(M)	For Swingers Only	1963	8.00	20.00
Argo LPS-720	(S)	For Swingers Only	1963	10.00	25.00
Impulse A-62	(M)	The Great Lorez Alexandria	1964	6.00	15.00
Impulse AS -62	(S)	The Great Lorez Alexandria	1964	8.00	20.00
Impulse A-76	(M)	More Of The Great Lorez Alexandria	1965	6.00	15.00
Impulse AS-76	(S)	More Of The Great Lorez Alexandria	1965	8.00	20.00
ALIOTTA-HAYNES [ALIOTTA-HAYNES-JEREMIAH]					
Ampex 10108	(S)	Aliotta-Haynes Music	1970	5.00	12.00
Ampex 10119	(S)	Aliotta-Haynes-Jeremiah	1970	5.00	12.00
Little Foot 711	(S)	Slippin' Away	1977	5.00	12.00
Big Foot 714	(S)	Lakeshore Drive	1978	10.00	20.00
ALIVE 'N KICKIN'					
Roulette SR-42052	(S)	Alive 'N Kickin'	1969	6.00	15.00
ALKIRE, EDDIE					
Full-Tone FM-647	(M)	Exciting New Colors	196?	12.00	30.00
Full-Tone FM-647	(M)	Exotic Steel Guitar	196?	12.00	30.00
Full-Tone FM-648	(M)	Steel Guitar Style	196?	12.00	30.00
Full-Tone FM-649	(M)	Jazz Steel Guitar	196?	12.00	30.00
ALL STARS, THE					
Gramophone 20192	(M)	Boogie Woogie	196?	20.00	50.00
ALLAN, CHAD, & THE EXPRESSIONS					
Chad Allan was an original member of The Guess Who.					
Scepter 533	(M)	Shakin' All Over	1966	12.00	30.00
Scepter SPS-533	(E)	Shakin' All Over	1966	8.00	20.00
ALLAN, DAVIE (& THE ARROWS)					
Tower T-5002	(M)	Apache '65	1965	16.00	40.00
Tower DT-5002	(E)	Apache '65	1965	12.00	30.00
Tower T-5043	(M)	The Wild Angels (Soundtrack)	1966	10.00	25.00
Tower DT-5043	(E)	The Wild Angels (Soundtrack)	1966	8.00	20.00
Tower T-5056	(M)	The Wild Angels, Volume 2 (Soundtrack)	1967	10.00	25.00
Tower DT-5056	(E)	The Wild Angels, Volume 2 (Soundtrack)	1967	8.00	20.00
Tower T-5074	(M)	Devil's Angels (Soundtrack)	1967	10.00	25.00
Tower DT-5074	(E)	Devil's Angels (Soundtrack)	1967	8.00	20.00
Tower T-5078	(M)	Blues Theme	1967	16.00	40.00
Tower DT-5078	(E)	Blues Theme	1967	12.00	30.00
Tower T-5083	(M)	Mondo Hollywood (Soundtrack)	1968	12.00	30.00
Tower DT-5083	(E)	Mondo Hollywood (Soundtrack)	1968	8.00	20.00
Tower DT-5094	(E)	Cycledelic Sounds	1968	12.00	30.00
Tower SKAO-5099	(E)	Wild In The Streets (Soundtrack)	1968	12.00	30.00
Tower ST-5124	(E)	The Hellcats (Soundtrack)	1968	10.00	25.00
Tower ST-5141	(S)	Killers Three (Soundtrack)	1968	10.00	25.00
Sidewalk T-5902	(M)	Thunder Alley (Soundtrack)	1967	8.00	20.00
Sidewalk ST-5902	(S)	Thunder Alley (Soundtrack)	1967	10.00	25.00

Label & Catalog #		Title	Year	VG+	NM

Davie Allan can be seen as the link between Dick Dale and Jeff Beck in the use of feedback and, as such, a progenitor of the punk/psychedelic guitar of the later '60s.

Sidewalk T-5903	(M)	**Teenage Rebellion** *(Soundtrack)*	1967	10.00	25.00
Sidewalk DT-5903	(E)	**Teenage Rebellion** *(Soundtrack)*	1967	8.00	20.00
Sidewalk T-5910	(M)	**Glory Stompers** *(Soundtrack)*	1967	12.00	30.00
Sidewalk DT-5910	(E)	**Glory Stompers** *(Soundtrack)*	1967	8.00	20.00
Sidewalk T-5911	(M)	**Mary Jane** *(Soundtrack)*	1968	8.00	20.00
Sidewalk DT-5911	(P)	**Mary Jane** *(Soundtrack)*	1968	8.00	20.00
Sidewalk T-5914	(M)	**Wild Racers** *(Soundtrack)*	1968	12.00	30.00
Sidewalk ST-5914	(S)	**Wild Racers** *(Soundtrack)*	1968	10.00	25.00

ALLEN, DAVE

International Art. 11	(S)	**Color Blind**	1969	20.00	50.00
International Art. 11	(S)	**Color Blind**	1979	6.00	15.00
		(Reissues have "Masterfonics" in the trail-off vinyl.)			

ALLEN, LEE

| Ember ELP-200 | (M) | **Walkin' With Mr. Lee** *(Red label)* | 1958 | 100.00 | 200.00 |
| Ember ELP-200 | (M) | **Walkin' With Mr. Lee** *(Black label)* | 196? | 40.00 | 80.00 |

ALLEN, REX

Decca DL-8402	(M)	**Under Western Skies**	1956	16.00	40.00
Decca DL-8776	(M)	**Mister Cowboy**	1959	10.00	25.00
Decca DL-78776	(S)	**Mister Cowboy**	1959	16.00	40.00
Hacienda LP-101	(M)	**Rex Allen Sings**	1960	12.00	30.00
Buena Vista BV-3307	(M)	**Rex Allen Sings 16 Favorites**	1961	12.00	30.00
Mercury MG-20719	(M)	**Faith Of A Man**	1962	8.00	20.00
Mercury SR-60719	(S)	**Faith Of A Man**	1962	12.00	30.00
Mercury MG-20752	(M)	**Rex Allen Sings And Tells Tales**	1962	8.00	20.00
Mercury SR-60752	(S)	**Rex Allen Sings And Tells Tales**	1962	12.00	30.00

ALLEN, RAY, & THE UPBEATS

| Blast BLP-6804 | (M) | **A Tribute To Six** | 196? | 20.00 | 50.00 |

ALLEN, RICHIE

| Imperial LP-9212 | (M) | **Stranger From Durango** | 1963 | 10.00 | 25.00 |

Label & Catalog #		Title	Year	VG+	NM
ALLEN, RICHIE					
Imperial LP-9212	(M)	**Stranger From Durango**	1963	10.00	25.00
Imperial LP-12212	(S)	**Stranger From Durango**	1963	16.00	40.00
Imperial LP-9229	(M)	**The Rising Surf**	1963	10.00	25.00
Imperial LP-12229	(S)	**The Rising Surf**	1963	16.00	40.00
Imperial LP-9243	(M)	**Surfer's Slide**	1963	10.00	25.00
Imperial LP-12243	(S)	**Surfer's Slide**	1963	16.00	40.00
ALLEN, ROSALIE					
Waldorf 150 (10")	(M)	**Rosalie Allen Sings Country & Western**	1954	20.00	50.00
Grand Award 330	(M)	**Songs Of The Golden West**	1957	10.00	25.00
ALLEN, TONY, & THE NIGHT OWLS					
Crown CLP-5231	(M)	**Rock & Roll With Tony Allen**	1960	20.00	50.00
ALLEN, WOODY					
Colpix CP-488	(M)	**Woody Allen**	1964	8.00	20.00
Colpix SCP-488	(S)	**Woody Allen**	1964	12.00	30.00
Colpix CP-518	(M)	**Woody Allen 2**	1965	6.00	15.00
Colpix SCP-518	(S)	**Woody Allen 2**	1965	10.00	25.00
Capitol T-2986	(M)	**The Third Woody Allen Album**	1968	8.00	20.00
Bell 6008	(S)	**Wonderful Wacky World Of Woody Allen**	1968	8.00	20.00
United Arts. UAS-9968	(S)	**The Night Club Years 1964-1968**	1972	6.00	15.00
Paramount PAS-1004	(S)	**Play It Again, Sam** (Soundtrack)	1972	8.00	20.00
ALLISON, GENE					
Vee Jay LP-1009	(M)	**Gene Allison** (Maroon label)	1959	50.00	100.00
Vee Jay LP-1009	(M)	**Gene Allison** (Black label)	196?	20.00	50.00
ALLISON, KEITH					
Produced by Gary Usher. Refer to The Falconaires; Paul Revere & The Raiders.					
Columbia CL-2641	(M)	**Keith Allison In Action**	1967	8.00	20.00
Columbia CS-9441	(S)	**Keith Allison In Action**	1967	12.00	30.00
ALLMAN, DUANE					
Capricorn PRO-545	(DJ)	**Dialogs**	1972	10.00	25.00
ALLMAN, DUANE & GREGG					
Bold 33-301	(S)	**Duane And Gregg Allman**	1972	8.00	20.00
Bold 33-302	(S)	**Duane And Gregg Allman**	1973	4.00	10.00
ALLMAN, SHELDON					
Hi Fi R-415	(M)	**Folk Songs For The 21st Century**	1960	10.00	25.00
Del Fi DFLP-1213	(M)	**Sing Along With Drac**	1961	8.00	20.00
Del Fi DFST-1213	(S)	**Sing Along With Drac**	1961	12.00	30.00
ALLMAN BROTHERS BAND, THE					
The Allman Brothers feature Duane and Gregg.					
Atco SD-33-308	(S)	**The Allman Brothers Band**	1969	6.00	15.00
Atco SD-33-342	(S)	**Idlewild South**	1970	6.00	15.00
Atco SD-33-805	(S)	**Beginnings**	1973	6.00	15.00
Capricorn SD2-802	(S)	**At Fillmore East** (2 LPs)	1971	8.00	20.00
Capricorn CX4-0102	(Q)	**Eat A Peach** (2 LPs)	1972	10.00	25.00
Capricorn CX4-0131	(Q)	**At Fillmore East** (2 LPs)	1974	10.00	25.00
Nautilus NR-30	(S)	**At Fillmore East** (2 LPs)	1980	30.00	60.00
Mobile Fidelity MFSL-157	(S)	**Eat A Peach** (2 LPs)	1984	30.00	60.00
ALLSUP, TOMMY					
Allsup was a member of The Crickets.					
Reprise R-6182	(M)	**The Buddy Holly Songbook**	1965	16.00	40.00
Reprise RS-6182	(S)	**The Buddy Holly Songbook**	1965	20.00	50.00
ALPAKA, ALFRED					
Decca DL-5423 (10")	(M)	**My Isle Of Golden Dreams**	195?	14.00	35.00
ALPHA CENTAURI					
Salt SAD-003	(S)	**Alpha Centauri**	1977	35.00	70.00

Label & Catalog #		Title	Year	VG+	NM

AMBOY DUKES, THE
The Amboy Dukes feature Ted Nugent.

Label & Catalog #		Title	Year	VG+	NM
Mainstream 56104	(M)	The Amboy Dukes	1968	16.00	40.00
Mainstream 6104	(S)	The Amboy Dukes	1968	12.00	30.00
Mainstream 6112	(S)	Journey To The Center Of The Mind	1968	12.00	30.00
Mainstream 6118	(S)	Migration	1968	12.00	30.00
Mainstream 6125	(S)	The Best Of The Original Amboy Dukes	1969	8.00	20.00
Mainstream 421	(S)	Ted Nugent & The Amboy Dukes	197?	8.00	20.00
Mainstream S-801	(S)	Journeys And Migrations (2 LPs)	1974	5.00	12.00
Polydor 24-4012	(S)	Marriage On The Rocks	1970	8.00	20.00
Polydor 24-4035	(S)	Survival Of The Fittest	1970	8.00	20.00
DiscReet 2181	(S)	Call Of The Wild	1974	5.00	12.00
DiscReet 2203	(S)	Tooth, Fang And Claw	1974	5.00	12.00

AMBROSE SLADE
Ambrose Slade later recorded as Slade.

Fontana SRF-67598	(DJ)	Ballzy (White label)	1969	12.00	30.00
Fontana SRF-67598	(S)	Ballzy	1969	20.00	50.00

AMBROSIA

Nautilus NR-23	(S)	Life Beyond L.A.	198?	6.00	15.00

AMERICA

Warner Bros. BS4-2808	(Q)	Holiday	1974	5.00	12.00
Warner Bros. BS4-2852	(Q)	Hearts	1975	5.00	12.00

AMERICAN BLUES, THE

Karma KLP-1001	(M)	The American Blues Is Here	1967	100.00	200.00
Uni 73044	(S)	The American Blues Do Their Thing	1969	16.00	40.00

AMERICAN BLUES EXCHANGE, THE

Tayl TLS-1	(M)	Blueprint	1969	50.00	100.00

AMERICAN BREED, THE

Acta 8003	(M)	The American Breed	1967	5.00	12.00
Acta 38003	(S)	The American Breed	1967	6.00	15.00
Acta 8003	(M)	Bend Me, Shape Me	1968	5.00	12.00
Acta 38003	(S)	Bend Me, Shape Me	1968	6.00	15.00
Dot DLP-25846	(S)	No Way To Treat A Lady (Soundtrack)	1968	8.00	20.00

AMERICAN DREAM, THE

Ampex 10101	(S)	The American Dream	1970	6.00	15.00

AMERICAN EAGLE

Decca DL-75258	(S)	American Eagle	1971	8.00	20.00

AMERICAN REVOULTION

Flick Disc FLS-54002	(S)	American Revolution	1968	10.00	25.00

AMES, NANCY

Libert LRP-3299	(M)	A Portrait Of Nancy	1963	5.00	12.00
Libert LST-7299	(S)	A Portrait Of Nancy	1963	6.00	15.00

AMES BROTHERS, THE

Coral CRL-56014 (10")	(M)	Sing A Song Of Christmas	1950	12.00	30.00
Coral CRL-56017 (10")	(M)	In The Evening By The Moonlight	1951	12.00	30.00
Coral CRL-56024 (10")	(M)	Sentimental Me	1951	12.00	30.00
Coral CRL-56025 (10")	(M)	Hoop-De-Hoo	1951	12.00	30.00
Coral CRL-56042 (10")	(M)	Sweet Leilani	1951	12.00	30.00
Coral CRL-56050 (10")	(M)	Favorite Spirituals	1952	12.00	30.00
Coral CRL-56079 (10")	(M)	Home On The Range	1952	12.00	30.00
Coral CRL-56080 (10")	(M)	Merry Christmas 1952	1952	12.00	30.00
Coral CRL-56097 (10")	(M)	Favorite Songs	1954	12.00	30.00
RCA Victor LPM-3186 (10")	(M)	It Must Be True	1954	12.00	30.00
Coral CRL-57031	(M)	Ames Brothers Concert	1956	10.00	25.00
Coral CRL-57054	(M)	Love's Old Sweet Song	1956	10.00	25.00
Coral CRL-57166	(M)	Sounds Of Christmas Harmony	1957	10.00	25.00
Coral CRL-57176	(M)	Love Serenade	1957	10.00	25.00
Coral CRL-57338	(M)	Our Golden Favorites	1960	10.00	25.00

Label & Catalog #		Title	Year	VG+	NM
RCA Victor LPM-1142	(M)	Exactly Like You	1956	10.00	25.00
RCA Victor LPM-1157	(M)	Four Brothers	1956	10.00	25.00
RCA Victor LPM-1228	(M)	The Ames Brothers With Hugo Winterhalter	1956	10.00	25.00
RCA Victor LPM-1487	(M)	Sweet Seventeen	1957	10.00	25.00
RCA Victor LPM-1541	(M)	There'll Always Be A Christmas	1957	10.00	25.00
RCA Victor LPM-1680	(M)	Destination Moon	1958	10.00	25.00
RCA Victor LPM-1855	(M)	Smoochin' Time	1958	10.00	25.00
RCA Victor LPM-1859	(M)	The Best Of The Ames Brothers	1958	8.00	20.00
RCA Victor LPM-1954	(M)	Famous Hits Of Famous Quartets	1959	8.00	20.00
RCA Victor LSP-1954	(S)	Famous Hits Of Famous Quartets	1959	10.00	25.00
RCA Victor LPM-1998	(M)	The Best In The Country	1959	8.00	20.00
RCA Victor LPM-1998	(S)	The Best In The Country	1959	10.00	25.00
RCA Victor LPM-2009	(M)	Words And Music	1959	8.00	20.00
RCA Victor LSP-2009	(S)	Words And Music	1959	10.00	25.00
RCA Victor LPM-2100	(M)	Hello, Amigos	1960	6.00	15.00
RCA Victor LSP-2100	(S)	Hello, Amigos	1960	8.00	20.00
RCA Victor LPM-2182	(M)	The Blend And The Beat	1960	6.00	15.00
RCA Victor LSP-2182	(S)	The Blend And The Beat	1960	6.00	20.00
RCA Victor LPM-2273	(M)	The Best Of The Bands	1960	6.00	15.00
RCA Victor LSP-2273	(S)	The Best Of The Bands	1960	6.00	20.00

— Original RCA mono albums above have "Long Play" on the bottom of the label;
stereo albums have "Living Stereo" on the bottom.—

Epic LN-24036	(M)	Hello Italy	1963	5.00	12.00
Epic BN-26036	(S)	Hello Italy	1963	6.00	15.00
Epic LN-24069	(M)	Knees Up, Mother Brown	1963	5.00	12.00
Epic BN-26069	(S)	Knees Up, Mother Brown	1963	6.00	15.00
RCA Victor LPM-2876	(M)	For Sentimental Reasons	1964	5.00	12.00
RCA Victor LSP-2876	(S)	For Sentimental Reasons	1964	6.00	15.00
RCA Victor LPM-2981	(M)	Down Memory Lane	1964	5.00	12.00
RCA Victor LSP-2981	(S)	Down Memory Lane	1964	6.00	15.00

— Original RCA albums above have black labels.—

AMON DUUL
Prophesy PRS-1003	(S)	Amon Duul	1970	10.00	25.00

AMULET
Shadow AC-00084	(S)	Amulet	1980	90.00	180.00

ANCIENT GREASE
Mercury SR-61305	(S)	Women And Children First	1970	8.00	20.00

ANDERS & PONCIA
Anders & Poncia also recorded as The Innocence; The Tradewinds.
Warner Bros. WS-1778	(S)	The Anders & Poncia Album	1969	8.00	20.00

ANDERSON, AL
Refer to NRBQ; Wildweeds.
Vanguard VSD-79324	(S)	Al Anderson	1972	6.00	15.00
Vanguard VSQ-79324	(Q)	Al Anderson	1972	8.00	20.00

ANDERSON, BILL
Decca DL-4192	(M)	Bill Anderson Sings Country Songs	1962	6.00	15.00
Decca DL-74192	(S)	Bill Anderson Sings Country Songs	1962	8.00	20.00
Decca DL-4427	(M)	Still	1963	6.00	15.00
Decca DL-74427	(S)	Still	1963	8.00	20.00
Decca DL-4499	(M)	Bill Anderson Sings	1964	6.00	15.00
Decca DL-74499	(S)	Bill Anderson Sings	1964	8.00	20.00
Decca DL-4600	(M)	Bill Anderson Showcase	1964	6.00	15.00
Decca DL-74600	(S)	Bill Anderson Showcase	1964	8.00	20.00
Decca DL-4646	(M)	From This Pen	1965	6.00	15.00
Decca DL-74646	(S)	From This Pen	1965	8.00	20.00
Decca DL-4686	(M)	Bright Lights And Country Music	1965	6.00	15.00
Decca DL-74686	(S)	Bright Lights And Country Music	1965	8.00	20.00

ANDERSON, CASEY
Elektra EKL-192	(M)	Goin' Places	1960	6.00	15.00
Elektra EKS-7192	(S)	Goin' Places	1960	8.00	20.00
Atco 33-149	(M)	The Bag I'm In	1962	6.00	15.00
Atco SD-33-149	(S)	The Bag I'm In	1962	8.00	20.00

Label & Catalog #		Title	Year	VG+	NM
Atco 33-166	(M)	More Pretty Girls Than One	1964	6.00	15.00
Atco SD-33-166	(S)	More Pretty Girls Than One	1964	8.00	20.00
Atco 33-172	(M)	Live At The Ice House	1965	6.00	15.00
Atco SD-33-172	(S)	Live At The Ice House	1965	8.00	20.00
Atco 33-176	(M)	Blues Is A Woman Gone	1965	6.00	15.00
Atco SD-33-176	(S)	Blues Is A Woman Gone	1965	8.00	20.00

ANDERSON, ERNESTINE

Label & Catalog #		Title	Year	VG+	NM
Mercury MG-20354	(M)	Hot Cargo	1958	12.00	30.00
Mercury MG-20400	(M)	Ernestine Anderson	1959	8.00	20.00
Mercury SR-60074	(S)	Ernestine Anderson	1959	12.00	30.00
Mercury MG-20492	(M)	Fascinating Ernestine	1959	8.00	20.00
Mercury SR-60171	(S)	Fascinating Ernestine	1959	12.00	30.00
Mercury MG-20496	(M)	My Kinda Swing	1959	8.00	20.00
Mercury SR-60175	(S)	My Kinda Swing	1959	12.00	30.00
Mercury MG-20582	(M)	Moanin,' Moanin,' Moanin'	1959	8.00	20.00
Mercury SR-60242	(S)	Moanin,' Moanin,' Moanin'	1959	12.00	30.00
Wing MG-12281	(M)	Ernestine Anderson	1964	5.00	12.00
Wing SR-16281	(S)	Ernestine Anderson	1964	6.00	15.00

ANDERSON, PINK

Label & Catalog #		Title	Year	VG+	NM
Bluesville BV-1038	(M)	Carolina Blues Man	1961	16.00	40.00
Bluesville BV-1051	(M)	Medicine Show Man	1962	16.00	40.00
Bluesville BV-1071	(M)	Ballad And Folksinger	1963	16.00	40.00

ANDREWS, JULIE

Label & Catalog #		Title	Year	VG+	NM
RCA Victor LOC-1018	(M)	The Boy Friend (Original Cast)	1954	16.00	40.00
Columbia OL-5090	(M)	My Fair Lady (Original Cast)	1956	12.00	30.00
Columbia OL-5190	(M)	Cinderella (Soundtrack)	1957	12.00	30.00
RCA Victor LPM-1403	(M)	The Lass With The Delicate Air	1957	10.00	25.00
RCA Victor LPM-1681	(M)	Julie Andrews Sings	1958	8.00	20.00
RCA Victor LSP-1681	(S)	Julie Andrews Sings	1958	10.00	25.00
RCA Victor LOP-1001	(M)	Rose Marie (Soundtrack)	1958	8.00	20.00
RCA Victor LSO-1001	(S)	Rose Marie (Soundtrack)	1958	12.00	30.00
Columbia OL-5615	(M)	My Fair Lady (Original Cast)	1959	8.00	20.00
Columbia OS-2015	(S)	My Fair Lady (Original Cast)	1959	10.00	25.00
Columbia OL-5620	(M)	Camelot (Original Cast)	1960	6.00	15.00
Columbia OS-2031	(S)	Camelot (Original Cast)	1960	8.00	20.00
Columbia OL-5840	(M)	Julie And Carol At Carnegie Hall	1962	6.00	15.00
Columbia OS-2240	(S)	Julie And Carol At Carnegie Hall	1962	8.00	20.00
Columbia CL-1712	(M)	Broadway's Fair Julie	1962	6.00	15.00
Columbia CS-8512	(S)	Broadway's Fair Julie	1962	8.00	20.00
Columbia CL-1886	(M)	Don't Go In The Lion's Cage Tonight	1962	6.00	15.00
Columbia CS-8686	(S)	Don't Go In The Lion's Cage Tonight	1962	8.00	20.00
Buena Vista BV-4026	(M)	Mary Poppins (Soundtrack)	1964	5.00	12.00
Buena Vista STER-4026	(S)	Mary Poppins (Soundtrack)	1964	6.00	15.00
RCA Victor LOCD-2005	(M)	The Sound Of Music (Soundtrack)	1965	4.00	10.00
RCA Victor LSOD-2005	(S)	The Sound Of Music (Soundtrack)	1965	5.00	12.00
Decca DL-1500	(M)	Thoroughly Modern Millie (Soundtrack)	1967	5.00	12.00
Decca DL-71500	(S)	Thoroughly Modern Millie (Soundtrack)	1967	6.00	15.00
RCA Victor LPM-3829	(M)	Christmas Treasure	1967	4.00	10.00
RCA Victor LSP-3829	(S)	Christmas Treasure	1967	5.00	12.00

— Original Columbia albums above have three white "eye" logos on each side of the spindle hole.—
— Original RCA albums above have black labels.—

ANDREWS SISTERS, THE
The Sisters recorded with Bing Crosby.

Label & Catalog #		Title	Year	VG+	NM
Decca DL-5019 (10")	(M)	Merry Christmas	1950	16.00	40.00
Decca DL-5020 (10")	(M)	Christmas Greetings	1950	16.00	40.00
Decca DL-5065 (10")	(M)	Tropical Songs	1950	16.00	40.00
Decca DL-5120 (10")	(M)	The Andrews Sisters	1950	16.00	40.00
Decca DL-5155 (10")	(M)	Club 15	1950	16.00	40.00
Decca DL-5264 (10")	(M)	Berlin Songs	1950	16.00	40.00
Decca DL-5282 (10")	(M)	Christmas Cheer	1950	16.00	40.00
Decca DL-5284 (10")	(M)	Mr. Music (Soundtrack)	1951	50.00	100.00
Decca DL-5306 (10")	(M)	I Love To Tell The Story	1951	16.00	40.00
Decca DL-5331 (10")	(M)	Country Style	1952	16.00	40.00
Decca DL-5423 (10")	(M)	My Isle Of Golden Dreams	1952	16.00	40.00
Decca DL-5438 (10")	(M)	Sing, Sing, Sing	1953	16.00	40.00

Label & Catalog #		Title	Year	VG+	NM
Decca DL-8354	(M)	Jingle Bells	1956	12.00	30.00
Decca DL-8360	(M)	By Popular Demand	1957	12.00	30.00
Capitol T-790	(M)	The Andrews Sisters In Hi-Fi	1957	12.00	30.00
Capitol T-860	(M)	Fresh And Fancy Free	1957	12.00	30.00
Capitol T-973	(M)	Dancing Twenties	1958	12.00	30.00
Dot DLP-3406	(M)	The Andrews Sisters' Greatest Hits	1961	6.00	15.00
Dot DLP-25406	(S)	The Andrews Sisters' Greatest Hits	1961	10.00	25.00
Dot DLP-3452	(M)	Great Golden Hits	1962	6.00	15.00
Dot DLP-25452	(S)	Great Golden Hits	1962	10.00	25.00
Dot DLP-3529	(M)	The Andrews Sisters Present	1963	6.00	15.00
Dot DLP-25529	(S)	The Andrews Sisters Present	1963	8.00	20.00
Dot DLP-3543	(M)	The Andrews Sisters' Greatest Hits	1963	6.00	15.00
Dot DLP-25543	(S)	The Andrews Sisters' Greatest Hits	1963	8.00	20.00
Capitol T-1924	(M)	The Hits Of The Andrews Sisters	1964	6.00	15.00
Capitol ST-1924	(S)	The Hits Of The Andrews Sisters	1964	8.00	20.00
Dot DLP-3567	(M)	Great Country Hits	1964	6.00	15.00
Dot DLP-25567	(S)	Great Country Hits	1964	8.00	20.00
Dot DLP-3632	(M)	The Andrews Sisters Go Hawaiian	1965	6.00	15.00
Dot DLP-25632	(S)	The Andrews Sisters Go Hawaiian	1965	8.00	20.00

ANGELO, MICHAEL

Guinn 1050	(S)	Michael Angelo	1976	180.00	300.00

One of the first successful white girl groups, The Angels had three albums released.
Their fourth on Ascot is a repackage of this, their first album on Caprice.

ANGELS, THE

Caprice LP-1001	(M)	And The Angels Sing	1962	30.00	60.00
Caprice SLP-1001	(S)	And The Angels Sing	1962	35.00	70.00
Smash MGS-27039	(M)	My Boyfriend's Back	1963	14.00	35.00
Smash SRS-67039	(P)	My Boyfriend's Back	1963	16.00	40.00
Smash MGS-27048	(M)	A Halo To You	1964	10.00	25.00
Smash SRS-67048	(S)	A Halo To You	1964	12.00	30.00
Ascot AM-13009	(M)	Twelve Of Their Greatest Hits	1964	10.00	25.00
Ascot ALS-6009	(S)	Twelve Of Their Greatest Hits	1964	12.00	30.00

(The Ascot album is a repackage of Caprice 1001.)

Label & Catalog #		Title	Year	VG+	NM

ANIMALS, THE
Eric Burdon, Chas Chandler, Alan Price, John Steel and Hilton Valentine. By 1966 Burdon was the sole surviving member, recording with a variety of different musicians as Eric Burdon & The Animals.

Label & Catalog #		Title	Year	VG+	NM
MGM E-4264	(M)	The Animals	1964	12.00	30.00
MGM SE-4264	(E)	The Animals	1964	8.00	20.00
MGM E-4281	(M)	The Animals On Tour	1965	12.00	30.00
MGM SE-4281	(E)	The Animals On Tour	1965	8.00	20.00
MGM E-4305	(M)	Animal Tracks	1965	16.00	40.00
MGM SE-4305	(E)	Animal Tracks	1965	12.00	30.00
MGM E-4324	(M)	The Best Of The Animals	1966	6.00	15.00
MGM SE-4324	(P)	The Best Of The Animals	1966	8.00	20.00
MGM E-4384	(M)	Animalization	1966	8.00	20.00
MGM SE-4384	(P)	Animalization	1966	8.00	20.00
MGM E-4414	(M)	Animalism	1966	8.00	20.00
MGM SE-4414	(E)	Animalism	1966	6.00	15.00

ANIMATED EGG

Label & Catalog #		Title	Year	VG+	NM
Alshire SF-5104	(S)	Animated Egg	196?	6.00	15.00

ANKA, PAUL

Label & Catalog #		Title	Year	VG+	NM
ABC-Paramount 240	(M)	Paul Anka	1958	18.00	45.00
ABC-Paramount S-240	(S)	Paul Anka	1958	30.00	60.00
ABC-Paramount 296	(M)	My Heart Sings	1959	14.00	35.00
ABC-Paramount S-296	(S)	My Heart Sings	1959	20.00	50.00
ABC-Paramount 323	(M)	Paul Anka Sings His Big 15	1960	14.00	35.00
ABC-Paramount S-323	(S)	Paul Anka Sings His Big 15	1960	20.00	50.00
ABC-Paramount 347	(M)	Paul Anka Swings For Young Lovers	1960	10.00	25.00
ABC-Paramount S-347	(S)	Paul Anka Swings For Young Lovers	1960	14.00	35.00
ABC-Paramount 353	(M)	Anka At The Copa	1960	10.00	25.00
ABC-Paramount S-353	(S)	Anka At The Copa	1960	14.00	35.00
ABC-Paramount 360	(M)	It's Christmas Everywhere	1960	10.00	25.00
ABC-Paramount S-360	(S)	It's Christmas Everywhere	1960	16.00	40.00
ABC-Paramount 371	(M)	Strictly Instrumental	1961	10.00	25.00
ABC-Paramount S-371	(S)	Strictly Instrumental	1961	16.00	40.00
ABC-Paramount 390	(M)	Paul Anka Sings His Big 15, Volume 2	1961	8.00	20.00
ABC-Paramount S-390	(S)	Paul Anka Sings His Big 15, Volume 2	1961	12.00	30.00
ABC-Paramount 409	(M)	Paul Anka Sings His Big 15, Volume 3	1962	8.00	20.00
ABC-Paramount S-409	(S)	Paul Anka Sings His Big 15, Volume 3	1962	12.00	30.00
ABC-Paramount 420	(M)	Diana	1962	8.00	20.00
ABC-Paramount S-420	(S)	Diana	1962	12.00	30.00
RCA Victor LPM-2502	(M)	Young, Alive And In Love!	1962	8.00	20.00
RCA Victor LSP-2502	(S)	Young, Alive And In Love!	1962	12.00	30.00
RCA Victor LPM-2575	(M)	Let's Sit This One Out!	1962	8.00	20.00
RCA Victor LSP-2575	(S)	Let's Sit This One Out!	1962	12.00	30.00
RCA Victor LPM-2614	(M)	Our Man Around The World	1963	8.00	20.00
RCA Victor LSP-2614	(S)	Our Man Around The World	1963	12.00	30.00
RCA Victor LPM-2691	(M)	Paul Anka's 21 Golden Hits	1963	8.00	20.00
RCA Victor LSP-2691	(S)	Paul Anka's 21 Golden Hits	1963	12.00	30.00

— Original RCA mono albums above have "Long Play" on the bottom of the label; stereo albums have "Living Stereo" on the bottom.—

Label & Catalog #		Title	Year	VG+	NM
RCA Victor LPM-2744	(M)	Songs I Wish I'd Written	1963	6.00	15.00
RCA Victor LSP-2744	(S)	Songs I Wish I'd Written	1963	8.00	20.00
RCA Victor LPM-2996	(M)	Excitement On Park Avenue	1964	6.00	15.00
RCA Victor LSP-2996	(S)	Excitement On Park Avenue	1964	8.00	20.00
RCA Victor LPM-3580	(M)	Strictly Nashville	1966	6.00	15.00
RCA Victor LSP-3580	(S)	Strictly Nashville	1966	8.00	20.00
RCA Victor LPM-3875	(M)	Paul Anka Alive	1967	6.00	15.00
RCA Victor LSP-3875	(S)	Paul Anka Alive	1967	8.00	20.00

— Original RCA albums above have black labels.—

ANN-MARGRET

Label & Catalog #		Title	Year	VG+	NM
RCA Victor LPM-2399	(M)	And Here She Is	1961	8.00	20.00
RCA Victor LSP-2399	(S)	And Here She Is	1961	12.00	30.00
RCA Victor LPM-2453	(M)	On The Way Up	1961	8.00	20.00
RCA Victor LSP-2453	(S)	On The Way Up	1961	12.00	30.00
Dot DLP-9011	(M)	State Fair *(Soundtrack)*	1962	12.00	30.00
Dot DLP-25011	(S)	State Fair *(Soundtrack)*	1962	16.00	40.00
RCA Victor LPM-2551	(M)	The Vivacious One	1962	8.00	20.00
RCA Victor LSP-2551	(S)	The Vivacious One	1962	12.00	30.00

Label & Catalog #		Title	Year	VG+	NM
RCA Victor LPM-2659	(M)	**Bachelor's Paradise**	1963	8.00	20.00
RCA Victor LSP-2659	(S)	**Bachelor's Paradise**	1963	12.00	30.00
RCA Victor LPM-2690	(M)	**Beauty And The Beard** (With Al Hirt)	1963	5.00	12.00
RCA Victor LSP-2690	(S)	**Beauty And The Beard** (With Al Hirt)	1963	6.00	15.00
RCA Victor LPM-2947	(M)	**Hits From Broadway Shows**	1964	5.00	12.00
RCA Victor LSP-2947	(S)	**Hits From Broadway Shows**	1964	6.00	15.00
		— Original RCA mono albums above have "Long Play" on the bottom of the label; stereo albums have "Living Stereo" on the bottom.—			
RCA Victor LOC-1081	(M)	**Bye Bye Birdie** (Soundtrack)	1963	8.00	20.00
RCA Victor LSO-1081	(S)	**Bye Bye Birdie** (Soundtrack)	1963	12.00	30.00
		(First pressings: Ann-Margret is not pictured on the cover.)			
RCA Victor LOC-1081	(M)	**Bye Bye Birdie** (Soundtrack)	1963	5.00	12.00
RCA Victor LSO-1081	(S)	**Bye Bye Birdie** (Soundtrack)	1963	6.00	15.00
		(Second pressings: Ann-Margret is pictured on the cover.)			
RCA Victor LOC-1101	(M)	**The Pleasure Seekers** (Soundtrack)	1965	16.00	40.00
RCA Victor LSO-1101	(S)	**The Pleasure Seekers** (Soundtrack)	1965	20.00	50.00
RCA Victor LPM-3710	(M)	**The Swinger** (Soundtrack)	1966	30.00	60.00
RCA Victor LSP-3710	(S)	**The Swinger** (Soundtrack)	1966	35.00	70.00
		—RCA albums above have black labels.—			

ANN-MARGRET, & LEE HAZLEWOOD

L.H.I. 12007	(S)	**The Cowboy And The Lady**	1969	6.00	15.00

ANN-MARGRET / KITTY KALLEN / DELLA REESE

RCA Victor LPM-2724	(M)	**Three Great Girls**	1963	5.00	12.00
RCA Victor LSP-2724	(S)	**Three Great Girls**	1963	6.00	15.00

Former Mousketeers turned teen queen, Annette Funicello enjoyed a string of successful films, a modest run on the singles charts, and a rather impressive catalog of albums.

ANNETTE (ANNETTE FUNICELLO)

Mickey Mouse MM-24	(M)	**Songs From Annette**	1959	40.00	80.00
Buena Vista BV-3301	(M)	**Annette**	1959	40.00	80.00
Buena Vista BV-3302	(M)	**Annette Sings Anka**	1960	40.00	80.00
Buena Vista BV-3303	(M)	**Hawaiiannette**	1960	30.00	60.00
Buena Vista BV-3304	(M)	**Italiannette**	1960	30.00	60.00

Label & Catalog #		Title	Year	VG+	NM
Buena Vista BV-3305	(M)	**Dance Annette**	1961	30.00	60.00
Buena Vista BV-4037	(M)	**Annette Funicello**	1962	20.00	50.00
Buena Vista BV-3312	(M)	**The Story Of My Teens**	1962	30.00	60.00
Buena Vista BV-3313	(M)	**Teen Street**	1962	20.00	50.00
Buena Vista BV-3314	(M)	**Muscle Beach Party** (Soundtrack)	1963	20.00	50.00
Buena Vista STER-3314	(S)	**Muscle Beach Party** (Soundtrack)	1963	50.00	100.00
Buena Vista BV-3316	(M)	**Annette's Beach Party** (Soundtrack)	1963	20.00	50.00
Buena Vista STER-3316	(S)	**Annette's Beach Party** (Soundtrack)	1963	50.00	100.00
Buena Vista BV-3320	(M)	**Annette On Campus**	1964	20.00	50.00
Buena Vista STER-3320	(S)	**Annette On Campus**	1964	50.00	100.00
Buena Vista BV-3324	(M)	**Annette At Bikini Beach**	1964	20.00	50.00
Buena Vista STER-3324	(S)	**Annette At Bikini Beach**	1964	50.00	100.00
Buena Vista BV-3325	(M)	**Annette's Pajama Party**	1964	16.00	40.00
Buena Vista STER-3325	(S)	**Annette's Pajama Party**	1964	50.00	100.00
Buena Vista BV-3327	(M)	**Golden Surfin' Hits**	1964	40.00	80.00
Buena Vista STER-3327	(S)	**Golden Surfin' Hits**	1964	75.00	150.00
Buena Vista BV-3328	(M)	**Something Borrowed, Something Blue**	1964	35.00	70.00
Wand WD-671	(M)	**How To Stuff A Wild Bikini** (Soundtrack)	1965	8.00	20.00
Wand WDS-671	(S)	**How To Stuff A Wild Bikini** (Soundtrack)	1965	12.00	30.00
Disneyland DQ-1245	(M)	**Walt Disney's Wonderful World Of Color**	1964	10.00	25.00
Disneyland DQS-1245	(S)	**Walt Disney's Wonderful World Of Color**	1964	16.00	40.00
Disneyland DQ-1267	(M)	**The Best Of Broadway**	1965	12.00	30.00
Disneyland DQ-1287	(M)	**Tubby The Tuba**	1966	10.00	25.00
Disneyland DQS-1287	(S)	**Tubby The Tuba**	1966	16.00	40.00
Disneyland DQ-1293	(M)	**State And College Songs**	1967	10.00	25.00
Disneyland DQS-1293	(S)	**State And College Songs**	1967	16.00	40.00
Disneyland DQS-1362	(S)	**Walt Disney's MM Club Mousekedances And Other Mousketeer Favorites**	1974	6.00	15.00
Sidewalk T-5902	(M)	**Thunder Alley** (Soundtrack)	1967	8.00	20.00
Sidewalk ST-5902	(S)	**Thunder Alley** (Soundtrack)	1967	10.00	25.00

ANNETTE & HAYLEY MILLS

Label & Catalog #		Title	Year	VG+	NM
Buena Vista BV-3508	(M)	**Annette And Hayley** (Paper sleeve)	1964	See note below	
		(Rare. Estimated near mint value $500-1,000.)			

ANNETTE & TOMMY SANDS

Label & Catalog #		Title	Year	VG+	NM
Buena Vista BV-3309	(M)	**The Parent Trap** (Soundtrack)	1961	16.00	40.00
Buena Vista STER-3309	(S)	**The Parent Trap** (Soundtrack)	1961	35.00	70.00
Buena Vista BV-4022	(M)	**Babes In Toyland** (Soundtrack)	1961	16.00	40.00
Buena Vista STER-4022	(S)	**Babes In Toyland** (Soundtrack)	1961	35.00	70.00

ANONYMOUS

Label & Catalog #		Title	Year	VG+	NM
A-Major AMLS-1002	(S)	**Inside The Shadow** (Blue on white cover)	1976	100.00	200.00
		(Issued with a booklet, priced separately below.)			
A-Major AMLS-1002		**Inside The Shadow Booklet**	1976	20.00	50.00
A-Major AMLS-1002	(S)	**Inside The Shadow** (Black on white cover)	1981	20.00	50.00

ANT TRIP CEREMONY

Label & Catalog #		Title	Year	VG+	NM
C.R.C. 2129	(M)	**Twenty-Four Hours**	1967	360.00	600.00

AORTA

Label & Catalog #		Title	Year	VG+	NM
Columbia CS-9785	(S)	**Aorta**	1968	8.00	20.00
Happy Tiger HT-1010	(S)	**Aorta 2**	1970	8.00	20.00

APHRODITE'S CHILD

Label & Catalog #		Title	Year	VG+	NM
Vertigo 2500	(S)	**666**	196?	8.00	20.00

APPEL, DAVE

Label & Catalog #		Title	Year	VG+	NM
Cameo C-1004	(M)	**Alone Together**	1959	12.00	30.00

APPLETREE THEATRE

Label & Catalog #		Title	Year	VG+	NM
Forecast FTS-302	(S)	**Playback**	1968	6.00	15.00

APOSTLES, THE

Label & Catalog #		Title	Year	VG+	NM
MG 79909	(M)	**On Crusade**	196?	180.00	300.00

APOSTLES, THE

Label & Catalog #		Title	Year	VG+	NM
Sound Recording CO-1245	(M)	**An Hour Of Prayer**	196?	50.00	100.00

Label & Catalog #		Title	Year	VG+	NM
AQUATONES, THE					
Fargo 3001	(M)	The Aquatones Sing	1964	300.00	500.00
ARCHIES, THE					
The sound of The Archies is a creation of Ron Dante.					
Calendar KES-101	(S)	The Archies	1968	8.00	20.00
Calendar KES-103	(S)	Everything's Archie	1969	6.00	15.00
Kirshner KES-103	(S)	Sugar Sugar	1969	6.00	15.00
		("Sugar Sugar" is a repackage of "Everything's Archie.")			
Calendar KES-105	(S)	Jingle Jangle	1969	5.00	12.00
Kirshner KES-107	(S)	Sunshine	1969	5.00	12.00
Kirshner KES-109	(S)	The Archies' Greatest Hits	1970	5.00	12.00
Kirshner KES-110	(S)	This Is Love	1971	8.00	20.00
Morgan MuscicA6-2345	(S)	Drive The Boulevard	1980	6.00	15.00
51 West Q-16002	(S)	The Archies	1979	5.00	12.00
ARCHITECT					
Architect AR-101	(S)	Architect	197?	50.00	100.00
ARDEN, TONI					
Decca DL-8651	(M)	Miss Toni Arden	1957	10.00	25.00
Decca DL-8875	(M)	Besame	1959	8.00	20.00
Decca DL-78875	(S)	Besame	1959	10.00	25.00
ARGENT					
Epic EQ-32195	(Q)	In Deep	1974	6.00	15.00
ARISTOCATS, THE					
High Fidelity R-610	(M)	Boogie And Blues	1959	12.00	30.00
High Fidelity SR-610	(S)	Boogie And Blues	1959	16.00	40.00
ARK					
Ark 810-71	(S)	Voyages	1978	660.00	1,000.00
ARKANGEL					
Joyeuse Garde JGR-001	(S)	Wind Face	1980	40.00	80.00
ARKANSAS BLUEGRASS BOYS, THE					
Smigar 6275	(M)	Bluegrass Special	1962	16.00	40.00
ARMAGEDDON					
Amos 73075	(S)	Armageddon	1969	8.00	20.00
ARMAGEDDON					
Armageddon features Keith Relf, formerly of The Yardbirds.					
A&M SP-4513	(S)	Armageddon	1975	8.00	20.00
ARNAZ, DESI					
RCA Victor LPM-3096 (10")	(M)	Babalu!	1954	50.00	100.00
ARNOLD, BILLY BOY					
Prestige PR-7389	(M)	Blues On The South Side	1965	6.00	15.00
Prestige PRST-7389	(S)	Blues On The South Side	1965	8.00	20.00
ARNOLD, EDDY					
RCA Victor LPM-3027 (10")	(M)	Anytime	1952	40.00	80.00
RCA Victor LPM-3031 (10")	(M)	All-Time Hits From The Hills	1952	30.00	60.00
RCA Victor LPM-3117 (10")	(M)	All-Time Favorites	1953	30.00	60.00
RCA Victor LPM-3219 (10")	(M)	The Chapel On The Hill	1954	30.00	60.00
RCA Victor LPM-3230 (10")	(M)	An American Institution (With booklet)	1954	40.00	80.00
RCA Victor LPM-3230 (10")	(M)	An American Institution (Without booklet)	1954	30.00	60.00
RCA Victor LPM-1111	(M)	Wanderin'	1955	16.00	40.00
RCA Victor LPM-1223	(M)	All-Time Favorites	1955	16.00	40.00
RCA Victor LPM-1224	(M)	Anytime	1955	16.00	40.00
RCA Victor LPM-1225	(M)	The Chapel On The Hill	1955	16.00	40.00
RCA Victor LPM-1293	(M)	A Dozen Hits	1956	16.00	40.00
RCA Victor LPM-1377	(M)	A Little On The Lonely Side	1956	16.00	40.00
RCA Victor LPM-1484	(M)	When They Were Young	1957	16.00	40.00
RCA Victor LPM-1575	(M)	My Darling, My Darling	1957	12.00	30.00

Label & Catalog #		Title	Year	VG+	NM
RCA Victor LPM-1733	(M)	Praise Him, Praise Him	1958	12.00	30.00
RCA Victor LPM-1928	(M)	Have Guitar, Will Travel	1959	8.00	20.00
RCA Victor LSP-1928	(S)	Have Guitar, Will Travel	1959	12.00	30.00
RCA Victor LPM-2036	(M)	Thereby Hangs A Tale	1959	8.00	20.00
RCA Victor LSP-2036	(S)	Thereby Hangs A Tale	1959	12.00	30.00
RCA Victor LPM-2185	(M)	Eddy Arnold Sings Them Again	1960	8.00	20.00
RCA Victor LSP-2185	(S)	Eddy Arnold Sings Them Again	1960	12.00	30.00
RCA Victor LPM-2268	(M)	You Gotta Have Love	1960	8.00	20.00
RCA Victor LSP-2268	(S)	You Gotta Have Love	1960	12.00	30.00
RCA Victor LPM-2337	(M)	Let's Make Memories Tonight	1961	8.00	20.00
RCA Victor LSP-2337	(S)	Let's Make Memories Tonight	1961	12.00	30.00
RCA Victor LPM-2471	(M)	One More Time	1961	8.00	20.00
RCA Victor LSP-2471	(S)	One More Time	1961	12.00	30.00
RCA Victor PRS-346	(DJ)	Christmas With Eddy Arnold	1961	20.00	50.00
RCA Victor LPM-2554	(M)	Christmas With Eddy Arnold	1961	8.00	20.00
RCA Victor LSP-2554	(S)	Christmas With Eddy Arnold	1961	12.00	30.00
RCA Victor LPM-2578	(M)	Cattle Call	1962	8.00	20.00
RCA Victor LSP-2578	(S)	Cattle Call	1962	12.00	30.00
RCA Victor LPM-2596	(M)	Our Man Down South	1962	8.00	20.00
RCA Victor LSP-2596	(S)	Our Man Down South	1962	12.00	30.00
RCA Victor LPM-2629	(M)	Faithfully Yours	1963	8.00	20.00
RCA Victor LSP-2629	(S)	Faithfully Yours	1963	12.00	30.00

— Original RCA mono albums above have "Long Play" on the bottom of the label;
stereo albums have "Living Stereo" on the bottom.—

RCA Victor LPM-2811	(M)	Folk Song Book	1964	6.00	15.00
RCA Victor LSP-2811	(S)	Folk Song Book	1964	8.00	20.00
RCA Victor LPM-2909	(M)	Sometimes I'm Happy, Sometimes I'm Blue	1964	5.00	12.00
RCA Victor LSP-2909	(S)	Sometimes I'm Happy, Sometimes I'm Blue	1964	6.00	15.00
RCA Victor LPM-2951	(M)	Pop Hits From The Country Side	1964	5.00	12.00
RCA Victor LSP-2951	(S)	Pop Hits From The Country Side	1964	6.00	15.00
RCA Victor LPM-3361	(M)	The Easy Way	1965	5.00	12.00
RCA Victor LSP-3361	(S)	The Easy Way	1965	6.00	15.00
RCA Victor LPM-3466	(M)	My World	1965	5.00	12.00
RCA Victor LSP-3466	(S)	My World	1965	6.00	15.00
RCA Victor LPM-3507	(M)	I Want To Go With You	1966	5.00	12.00
RCA Victor LSP-3507	(S)	I Want To Go With You	1966	6.00	15.00
RCA Victor LPM-3565	(M)	The Best Of Eddy Arnold	1966	5.00	12.00
RCA Victor LSP-3565	(S)	The Best Of Eddy Arnold	1966	6.00	15.00
RCA Victor LPM-3622	(M)	The Last Word In Lonesome	1966	5.00	12.00
RCA Victor LSP-3622	(S)	The Last Word In Lonesome	1966	6.00	15.00
RCA Victor LPM-3715	(M)	Somebody Like Me	1966	5.00	12.00
RCA Victor LSP-3715	(S)	Somebody Like Me	1966	6.00	15.00
RCA Victor LPM-3753	(M)	Lonely Again	1967	8.00	20.00
RCA Victor LSP-3753	(S)	Lonely Again	1967	6.00	15.00
RCA Victor LPM-3869	(M)	Turn The World Around	1967	8.00	20.00
RCA Victor LSP-3869	(S)	Turn The World Around	1967	6.00	15.00
RCA Victor LPM-3931	(M)	The Everlovin' World Of Eddy Arnold	1968	20.00	50.00
RCA Victor LSP-3931	(S)	The Everlovin' World Of Eddy Arnold	1968	6.00	15.00

— Original RCA albums above have black labels.—

ARNOLD, P.P.

Immediate Z1252016	(S)	Kafunta	197?	8.00	20.00

ARROWS, THE: *Refer to* DAVIE ALLAN

ARS NOVA

Elektra EKS-74020	(S)	Ars Nova	1968	5.00	12.00
Atlantic SD-8221	(S)	Sunshine And Shadows	1969	5.00	12.00

ARTHUR [ARTHUR LEE HARPER]

L.H.I. 12000	(S)	Dreams And Images	1967	10.00	25.00

ART OF LOVIN'

Mainstream S-6113	(S)	Art Of Lovin'	1968	5.00	12.00

ARTISTICS, THE

OKeh OKL-4119	(M)	Get My Hands On Some Lovin'	1967	6.00	15.00
OKeh OKS-14119	(S)	Get My Hands On Some Lovin'	1967	8.00	20.00

Label & Catalog #		Title	Year	VG+	NM
Brunswick BL-54123	(M)	I'm Gonna Miss You	1967	6.00	15.00
Brunswick BL-754123	(S)	I'm Gonna Miss You	1967	8.00	20.00
Brunswick BL-754139	(S)	The Articulate Artistics	1968	6.00	15.00
Brunswick BL-754153	(S)	What Happened	1969	6.00	15.00
ARZACHEL					
Roulette SR-42036	(S)	Arzachel	1969	40.00	80.00
ASGAERD					
Threshold 6	(S)	In The Realm Of Asgaerd	1972	6.00	15.00
ASHER, JANE					
London OSA-1206	(M)	Alice In Wonderland	1965	20.00	50.00
ASHER & LITTLE JIMMY					
Decca DL-4785	(M)	Mountain Ballads And Old Hymns	1966	8.00	20.00
Decca DL-74785	(S)	Mountain Ballads And Old Hymns	1966	12.00	30.00
ASHES					
Vault 125	(S)	Ashes	1968	10.00	25.00
ASHKAN					
Sire SES-97017	(S)	In From The Cold	1970	8.00	20.00
ASSOCIATION, THE					
Valiant VLM-5002	(M)	And Then Along Comes The Association	1966	6.00	15.00
Valiant VLS-25002	(S)	And Then Along Comes The Association	1966	8.00	20.00
Valiant VLM-5004	(M)	Renaissance	1966	6.00	15.00
Valiant VLS-25004	(S)	Renaissance	1966	8.00	20.00
		(First pressing covers do not mention "No Fair At All.")			
Valiant VLM-5004	(M)	Renaissance	1966	5.00	12.00
Valiant VLS-25004	(S)	Renaissance	1966	6.00	15.00
		(Second pressing covers have a blurb for "No Fair At All.")			
Warner Bros. W-1696	(M)	Insight Out	1967	6.00	15.00
Warner Bros. WS-1696	(S)	Insight Out	1967	8.00	20.00
Warner Bros. WS-1702	(S)	And Then Along Comes The Association	1968	5.00	12.00
Warner Bros. WS-1704	(S)	Renaissance	1968	5.00	12.00
		—Original Warner albums above have gold labels.—			
ASTAIRE, FRED					
Mercury MG-1001	(M)	The Fred Astaire Story, Volume 1	1952	20.00	50.00
Mercury MG-1002	(M)	The Fred Astaire Story, Volume 2	1952	20.00	50.00
Mercury MG-1003	(M)	The Fred Astaire Story, Volume 3	1952	20.00	50.00
Mercury MG-1004	(M)	The Fred Astaire Story, Volume 4	1952	20.00	50.00
"X" LVA-1001	(M)	Fred Astaire With Leo Reisman	1955	14.00	35.00
Coral CRL-57008	M)	Cavalcade Of Dance	1955	14.00	35.00
Epic LN-3103	(M)	Nothing Thrilled Us Half As Much	1955	14.00	35.00
Epic LN-3137	(M)	The Best Of Fred Astaire	1955	14.00	35.00
MGM E-3413	(M)	Shoes With Wings	1956	14.00	35.00
Verve V-2010	(M)	Mr. Top Hat	1956	14.00	35.00
Verve V-2114	(M)	Easy To Dance With	1958	14.00	35.00
Kapp KL-1165	(M)	Now	1959	10.00	25.00
Kapp KS-3165	(S)	Now	1959	14.00	35.00
ASTRONAUTS, THE					
RCA Victor LPM-2760	(M)	Surfin' With The Astronauts	1963	12.00	30.00
RCA Victor LSP-2760	(S)	Surfin' With The Astronauts	1963	16.00	40.00
RCA Victor LPM-2782	(M)	Everything Is A-OK	1964	10.00	25.00
RCA Victor LSP-2782	(S)	Everything Is A-OK	1964	12.00	30.00
RCA Victor LPM-2858	(M)	Competition Coupe	1964	16.00	40.00
RCA Victor LSP-2858	(S)	Competition Coupe	1964	20.00	50.00
RCA Victor LPM-2903	(M)	The Astronauts Orbit Campus	1964	10.00	25.00
RCA Victor LSP-2903	(S)	The Astronauts Orbit Campus	1964	12.00	30.00
RCA Victor PRM-183	(DJ)	Rockin' With The Astronauts	1964	8.00	20.00
RCA Victor LPM-3441	(M)	Wild On The Beach *(Soundtrack)*	1965	8.00	20.00
RCA Victor LSP-3441	(S)	Wild On The Beach *(Soundtrack)*	1965	12.00	30.00
RCA Victor LPM-3307	(M)	The Astronauts Go Go Go	1965	8.00	20.00
RCA Victor LSP-3307	(S)	The Astronauts Go Go Go	1965	10.00	25.00

Label & Catalog #		Title	Year	VG+	NM
RCA Victor LPM-3359	(M)	Favorites For You From Us	1965	8.00	20.00
RCA Victor LSP-3359	(S)	Favorites For You From Us	1965	10.00	25.00
RCA Victor LPM-3454	(M)	Down The Line	1965	8.00	20.00
RCA Victor LSP-3454	(S)	Down The Line	1965	10.00	25.00
RCA Victor LPM-3733	(M)	Travelin' Men	1967	6.00	15.00
RCA Victor LSP-3733	(S)	Travelin' Men	1967	8.00	20.00

ASTRONAUTS, THE / THE LIVERPOOL FIVE

RCA Victor PRS-251	(S)	Stereo Festival (Sampler)	1967	50.00	100.00

ATCHER, BOBBY, & THE COUNTRYMEN

Columbia HL-9006 (10")	(M)	Early American Folk Songs	1949	35.00	70.00
Columbia HL-9013 (10")	(M)	Songs Of The Saddle	1949	35.00	70.00
Columbia CL-2232	(M)	The Dean Of Cowboy Singers	1964	10.00	25.00
Columbia CS-9032	(E)	The Dean Of Cowboy Singers	1964	6.00	15.00

ATKINS, CHET

Refer to The Country All-Stars; The Nashville All-Stars.

RCA Victor LPM-3079 (10")	(M)	Chet Atkins' Gallopin' Guitar	1952	60.00	120.00
RCA Victor LPM-3169 (10")	(M)	Stringin' Along With Chet Atkins	1953	50.00	100.00
RCA Victor LPM-1090	(M)	A Session With Chet Atkins	1954	16.00	40.00
RCA Victor LPM-1197	(M)	Chet Atkins In Three Dimensions	1956	16.00	40.00
RCA Victor LPM-1236	(M)	Stringin' Along With Chet Atkins	1956	16.00	40.00
RCA Victor LPM-1383	(M)	Finger Style Guitar	1956	14.00	35.00
RCA Victor LPM-1544	(M)	Chet Atkins At Home	1957	12.00	30.00
RCA Victor LPM-1577	(M)	Hi Fi In Focus	1957	12.00	30.00
RCA Victor LPM-1993	(M)	Chet Atkins In Hollywood	1959	6.00	15.00
RCA Victor LSP-1993	(S)	Chet Atkins In Hollywood	1959	16.00	40.00
RCA Victor LPM-2025	(M)	Hum And Strung Along (With booklet)	1959	8.00	20.00
RCA Victor LSP-2025	(S)	Hum And Strung Along (With booklet)	1959	12.00	30.00
RCA Victor LPM-2025	(M)	Hum And Strung Along (Without booklet)	1959	6.00	15.00
RCA Victor LSP-2025	(S)	Hum And Strung Along (Without booklet)	1959	10.00	25.00
RCA Victor LPM-2103	(M)	Mister Guitar	1959	5.00	12.00
RCA Victor LSP-2103	(S)	Mister Guitar	1959	8.00	20.00
RCA Victor LPM-2161	(M)	Teensville	1960	5.00	12.00
RCA Victor LSP-2161	(S)	Teensville	1960	8.00	20.00
RCA Victor LPM-2175	(M)	The Other Chet Atkins	1960	5.00	12.00
RCA Victor LSP-2175	(S)	The Other Chet Atkins	1960	8.00	20.00
RCA Victor LPM-2232	(M)	Chet Atkins' Workshop	1961	4.00	10.00
RCA Victor LSP-2232	(S)	Chet Atkins' Workshop	1961	6.00	15.00
RCA Victor LPM-2346	(M)	The Most Popular Guitar	1961	4.00	10.00
RCA Victor LSP-2346	(S)	The Most Popular Guitar	1961	6.00	15.00
RCA Victor LPM-2424	(M)	Christmas With Chet Atkins	1961	5.00	12.00
RCA Victor LSP-2424	(S)	Christmas With Chet Atkins	1961	8.00	20.00
RCA Victor LPM-2450	(M)	Down Home	1962	4.00	10.00
RCA Victor LSP-2450	(S)	Down Home	1962	6.00	15.00
RCA Victor LPM-2549	(M)	Caribbean Guitar	1962	4.00	10.00
RCA Victor LSP-2549	(S)	Caribbean Guitar	1962	6.00	15.00
RCA Victor LPM-2601	(M)	Back Home Hymns	1962	5.00	12.00
RCA Victor LSP-2601	(S)	Back Home Hymns	1962	8.00	20.00
RCA Victor LPM-2616	(M)	Our Man In Nashville	1963	4.00	10.00
RCA Victor LSP-2616	(S)	Our Man In Nashville	1963	6.00	15.00
RCA Victor LPM-2678	(M)	Travelin'	1963	4.00	10.00
RCA Victor LSP-2678	(S)	Travelin'	1963	6.00	15.00
RCA Victor LPM-2719	(M)	Teen Scene	1963	4.00	10.00
RCA Victor LSP-2719	(S)	Teen Scene	1963	6.00	15.00

*— Original RCA mono albums above have "Long Play" on the bottom of the label;
stereo albums have "Living Stereo" on the bottom.—*

ATLANTA RHYTHM SECTION, THE

Mobile Fidelity MFSL-038	(S)	Champagne Jam	1980	6.00	15.00

ATLEE

Atlee features Atlee Yeager of Damon.

Dunhill DS-50084	(S)	Atlee	1969	6.00	15.00

ATOMIC ROOSTER

Elektra EKS-74094	(S)	Death Walks Behind You	1971	6.00	15.00
Elektra EKS-74109	(S)	In Hearing Of	1971	6.00	15.00

Label & Catalog #		Title	Year	VG+	NM
Elektra EKS-75039	(S)	**Made In England**	1972	5.00	12.00
Elektra EKS-75074	(S)	**Atomic Rooster IV**	1973	5.00	12.00

ATTILA
Attila features Billy Joel.

Epic E-30030	(S)	**Attila**	1970	10.00	25.00

AU-GO-GO SINGERS, THE
The Au-Go-Gos feature Steve Stills and Rich Furay, later of The Buffalo Springfield.

Roulette R-25280	(M)	**They Call Us The Au Go-Go Singers**	1964	16.00	40.00
Roulette SR-25280	(S)	**They Call Us The Au Go-Go Singers**	1964	20.00	50.00

AUM

Fillmore F-30002	(S)	**Resurrection**	1969	6.00	15.00
Sire SES-97007	(S)	**Bluesvibes**	1969	5.00	12.00

AUSTIN, CLAIRE

Good Time Jazz 24 (!)")	(M)	**Claire Austin Sings The Blues**	1954	35.00	70.00
Contemporary 5002	(M)	**When Your Lover Has Gone**	1956	14.00	35.00

AUSTIN, GENE

RCA Victor LPM-3200 (10")	(M)	**My Blue Heaven**	195?	20.00	50.00
"X" LVA-1007	(M)	**Gene Austin Sings All-Time Favorites**	195?	16.00	40.00
Decca DL-8433	(M)	**My Blue Heaven**	1957	16.00	40.00
Dot DLP-3300	(M)	**Great Hits**	1960	8.00	20.00
Dot DLP-25300	(S)	**Great Hits**	1960	12.00	30.00

AUTOSALVAGE

RCA Victor LSP-3940	(S)	**Autosalvage**	1968	8.00	20.00

AUTRY, GENE

Columbia JL-8001 (10")	(M)	**Gene Autry At The Rodeo**	1949	40.00	80.00
Columbia JL-8009 (10")	(M)	**Stampede**	1949	40.00	80.00
Columbia JL-8012 (10")	(M)	**Champion**	1950	40.00	80.00
Columbia HL-9001 (10")	(M)	**Western Classic, Volume 1**	1949	40.00	80.00
Columbia HL-9002 (10")	(M)	**Western Classic, Volume 2**	1949	40.00	80.00
Columbia CL-6020 (10")	(M)	**Easter Favorites**	1949	40.00	80.00
Columbia CL-6137 (10")	(M)	**Merry Christmas**	1950	40.00	80.00
Columbia MJV-82 (10")	(M)	**The Story Of The Nativity**	1955	35.00	70.00
Columbia MJV-83 (10")	(M)	**Little Johnny Pilgrim And Guffy**	1955	35.00	70.00
Columbia MJV-94 (10")	(M)	**Rusty, The Rocking Horse**	1955	35.00	70.00
Columbia CL-2547 (10")	(M)	**Merry Christmas**	1955	35.00	70.00
Columbia CL-2568 (10")	(M)	**Gene Autry Sings Peter Cottontail**	1955	35.00	70.00
Columbia CL-677	(M)	**Champion Western Adventures**	1955	35.00	70.00
Challenge CHL-600	(M)	**Christmas With Gene Autry**	1958	20.00	50.00
Columbia CL-1575	(M)	**Gene Autry's Greatest Hits**	1961	14.00	35.00
Harmony HL-9505	(M)	**Champion Western Advantures**	1959	16.00	40.00
Harmony HL-9550	(M)	**Christmas Favorites**	1960	12.00	30.00
Harmony HL-7332	(M)	**Gene Autry's Great Western Hits**	1965	10.00	25.00
RCA Victor LPM-2623	(M)	**Gene Autry's Golden Hits**	1962	10.00	25.00
RCA Victor LSP-2623	(S)	**Gene Autry's Golden Hits**	1962	10.00	25.00
Melody Ranch 101	(M)	**Melody Ranch**	1965	16.00	40.00
Republic 1970	(S)	**South Of The Border**	1970	12.00	30.00

AVALANCHES, THE

Warner Bros. W-1525	(M)	**Ski Surfin'**	1963	12.00	30.00
Warner Bros. WS-1525	(S)	**Ski Surfin'**	1963	16.00	40.00

AVALON, FRANKIE
Refer to Fabian / Frankie Avalon.

Chancellor CHL-5001	(M)	**Frankie Avalon** (Pink label)	1958	35.00	70.00
Chancellor CHL-5002	(M)	**The Young Frankie Avalon** (Pink label)	1959	35.00	70.00
Chancellor CHLX-5004	(M)	**Swingin' On A Rainbow**	1959	30.00	60.00
Chancellor CHL-69801	(M)	**Young And In Love**	1960	40.00	80.00
		(Boxed set with photos and a 3-D portrait.)			
Chancellor CHL-5011	(M)	**Summer Scene**	1960	16.00	40.00
Chancellor CHLS-5011	(S)	**Summer Scene**	1960	30.00	60.00
Chancellor CHL-5018	(M)	**A Whole Lot Of Frankie**	1961	16.00	40.00

Label & Catalog #		Title	Year	VG+	NM
Chancellor CHL-5022	(M)	**And Now About Mr. Avalon**	1961	16.00	40.00
Chancellor CHLS-5022	(S)	**And Now About Mr. Avalon**	1961	20.00	50.00
Chancellor CHL-5025	(M)	**Italiano**	1962	10.00	25.00
Chancellor CHLS-5025	(S)	**Italiano**	1962	16.00	40.00
Chancellor CHL-5027	(M)	**You Are Mine**	1962	10.00	25.00
Chancellor CHLS-5027	(S)	**You Are Mine**	1962	16.00	40.00
Chancellor CHL-5031	(M)	**Frankie Avalon's Christmas Album**	1962	10.00	25.00
Chancellor CHLS-5031	(S)	**Frankie Avalon's Christmas Album**	1962	16.00	40.00
Chancellor CHL-5032	(M)	**Cleopatra Plus 13 Other Great Hits**	1963	10.00	25.00
Chancellor CHLS-5032	(S)	**Cleopatra Plus 13 Other Great Hits**	1963	16.00	40.00
United Arts. UAL-3371	(M)	**Songs From Muscle Beach Party**	1964	8.00	20.00
United Arts. UAS-6371	(S)	**Songs From Muscle Beach Party**	1964	12.00	30.00
United Arts. UAL-3382	(M)	**Frankie Avalon's 15 Greatest Hits**	1964	8.00	20.00
United Arts. UAS-6382	(P)	**Frankie Avalon's 15 Greatest Hits**	1964	10.00	25.00
United Arts. UAL-4121	(M)	**I'll Take Sweden** (Soundtrack)	1965	8.00	20.00
United Arts. UAS-5121	(S)	**I'll Take Sweden** (Soundtrack)	1965	10.00	25.00
Metromedia 1034	(S)	**I Want You Near Me**	1970	6.00	15.00

AVENGERS VI, THE

Mark-56 Records	(M)	**Real Cool Hits**	1965	75.00	150.00

AVERAGE WHITE BAND, THE [AWB]

Atlantic QD-7308	(Q)	**AWB**	1975	5.00	12.00

AVONS, THE

Hull HLP-1000	(M)	**The Avons** (Red label)	1960	300.00	500.00

AYCOCK, EARL

Mercury MG-20282	(M)	**Earl Aycock**	1958	10.00	25.00

AZTECA

Columbia CQ-31776	(Q)	**Azteca**	1973	5.00	12.00

AZTECS, THE

World Artists WAM-2001	(M)	**Live At The Ad-Lib Club Of London**	1964	16.00	40.00

AZITIS

Elco SC-EC-5555	(S)	**Help!**	197?	300.00	500.00

B. F. TRIKE

Rockadellic	(S)	**B. F. Trike**	197?	20.00	50.00

BABY

Lone Starr 9782	(S)	**Baby**	1974	8.00	20.00

BABY HUEY

Curtom CRS-8007	(S)	**The Living Legend**	1970	16.00	40.00

BABY RAY

Imperial LP-9335	(M)	**Where Soul Lives**	1967	6.00	15.00
Imperial LP-12335	(S)	**Where Soul Lives**	1967	8.00	20.00

Label & Catalog #		Title	Year	VG+	NM
BABYSITTERS, THE					
Vanguard VRS-9042	(M)	The Babysitters	195?	8.00	20.00
BACK PORCH MAJORITY, THE					
The Back Porch Majority features Randy Sparks.					
Epic LN-24134	(M)	Live From Ledbetter's	1965	6.00	15.00
Epic BN-26134	(S)	Live From Ledbetter's	1965	8.00	20.00
Epic LN-24149	(M)	Riverboat Days	1965	5.00	12.00
Epic BN-26149	(S)	Riverboat Days	1965	6.00	15.00
Epic LN-24184	(M)	That's The Way It's Gonna Be	1966	5.00	12.00
Epic BN-26184	(S)	That's The Way It's Gonna Be	1966	6.00	15.00
Epic LN-24319	(M)	Willy Nilly Wonder Of Illusion	1967	5.00	12.00
Epic BN-26319	(S)	Willy Nilly Wonder Of Illusion	1967	6.00	15.00
BADFINGER					
Badfinger originally recorded as The Iveys.					
Commonwealth Un. 6004	(S)	The Magic Christian (Soundtrack)	1970	8.00	20.00
Apple ST-3364	(S)	Magic Christian Music	1970	10.00	25.00
Apple SKAO-3367	(S)	No Dice	1970	16.00	40.00
Apple SW-3387	(S)	Straight Up	1971	40.00	80.00
Apple SW-3411	(S)	Ass	1973	8.00	20.00
Warner Bros. BS-2762	(S)	Badfinger	1974	6.00	15.00
Warner Bros. BS-2827	(S)	Wish You Were Here	1974	8.00	20.00
Elektra 6E-175	(S)	Airwaves	1979	4.00	10.00
BADGE					
LPS-1	(S)	Badge & Co.	1977	180.00	300.00
BAEZ, JOAN					
Vanguard VRS-2077	(M)	Joan Baez	1960	10.00	25.00
Vanguard VRS-2097	(M)	Joan Baez, Volume 2	1961	8.00	20.00
Vanguard VRS-2122	(M)	Joan Baez In Concert, Volume 1	1962	8.00	20.00
Vanguard VRS-2123	(M)	Joan Baez In Concert, Volume 2	1963	8.00	20.00
Vanguard VRS-9160	(M)	Joan Baez/5	1964	8.00	20.00
Vanguard VRS-9200	(M)	Farewell Angelina	1965	6.00	15.00
Vanguard VSD-79200	(S)	Farewell Angelina	1965	8.00	20.00
Vanguard VRS-9230	(M)	Noel	1966	5.00	12.00
Vanguard VSD-79230	(S)	Noel	1966	6.00	15.00
Vanguard VRS-9240	(M)	Joan	1967	5.00	12.00
Vanguard VSD-79240	(S)	Joan	1967	6.00	15.00
Fantasy	(M)	Joan Baez In San Francisco	196?	12.00	30.00
Fantasy	(S)	Joan Baez In San Francisco	196?	16.00	40.00
Vanguard Q-40001	(Q)	Blessed Are (2 LPs)	1974	6.00	15.00
Vanguard Q-40332	(Q)	Hits/Greatest And Others	1974	4.00	10.00
A&M QU-54339	(Q)	Come From The Shadows	1974	4.00	10.00
A&M QU-54527	(Q)	Diamonds And Rust	1975	4.00	10.00
Portrait PRQ-34697	(Q)	Blowin' Away	1977	4.00	10.00
Nautilus NR-12	(S)	Diamonds And Rust	198?	12.00	30.00
BAG, THE					
Decca DL-75057	(S)	Real	1968	6.00	15.00
BAGDASARIAN, ROSS					
Bagdasarian as David Seville was the mastermind behind The Chipmunks.					
Liberty LRP-3451	(M)	The Crazy, Mixed-Up World Of Ross Bagdasarian	1966	12.00	30.00
Liberty LST-7451	(S)	The Crazy, Mixed-Up World Of Ross Bagdasarian	1966	16.00	40.00
BAILEY, MILDRED					
Columbia CL-6094 (10")	(M)	Mildred Bailey Serenade	1950	20.00	50.00
Allegro 3119 (10")	(M)	Mildred Bailey Sings	1951	20.00	50.00
Allegro 4007 (10")	(M)	Mildred Bailey Songs	1952	20.00	50.00
Allegro 4040 (10")	(M)	Mildred Bailey Songs	1952	20.00	50.00
Decca DL-5387 (10")	(M)	The Rockin' Chair Lady	1953	20.00	50.00
Regent 6032	(M)	Me And The Blues	1957	16.00	40.00
Columbia C3L-22	(M)	Greatest Performances (3 LPs with booklet)	1962	16.00	40.00
Savoy 12219	(M)	M.B.	1964	12.00	30.00

Label & Catalog #		Title	Year	VG+	NM

BAILEY, PEARL

Label & Catalog #		Title	Year	VG+	NM
Columbia CL-6099 (10")	(M)	Pearl Bailey Entertains	1950	20.00	50.00
Coral CRL-56068 (10")	(M)	Say Si Si	1953	20.00	50.00
Coral CRL-56078 (10")	(M)	I'm With You	1953	20.00	50.00
Columbia ML-4969	(M)	House Of Flowers (Soundtrack)	1954	20.00	50.00
Capitol L-355	(M)	St. Louis Woman (Soundtrack)	1955	50.00	100.00
Mercury MG-20187	(M)	The One And Only Pearl Bailey Sings	1956	16.00	40.00
Mercury MG-20277	(M)	The Intoxicating Pearl Bailey	1957	16.00	40.00
Coral CRL-57037	(M)	Birth Of The Blues	1956	16.00	40.00
Coral CRL-57162	(M)	Cultured Pearl	1957	16.00	40.00
Vocalion VL-3621	(M)	Gems By Pearl Bailey	1958	10.00	25.00
Columbia OL-5410	(M)	Porgy And Bess (Soundtrack)	1959	8.00	20.00
Columbia OS-2016	(S)	Porgy And Bess (Soundtrack)	1959	12.00	30.00
Roulette R-25012	(M)	Pearl Bailey A-Broad	1959	8.00	20.00
Roulette R-25016	(M)	Pearl Bailey Sings For Adults Only	1959	6.00	15.00
Roulette SR-25016	(S)	Pearl Bailey Sings For Adults Only	1959	8.00	20.00
Roulette R-25037	(M)	St. Louis Blues	1959	6.00	15.00
Roulette SR-25037	(S)	St. Louis Blues	1959	8.00	20.00
		— Original Roulette albums above have black labels.—			
Roulette R-25063	(M)	Porgy And Bess	1959	6.00	15.00
Roulette SR-25063	(S)	Porgy And Bess	1959	8.00	20.00
Roulette R-25101	(M)	More Songs For Adults Only	1960	6.00	15.00
Roulette SR-25101	(S)	More Songs For Adults Only	1960	8.00	20.00
Roulette R-25116	(M)	Songs Of The Bad Old Days	1960	6.00	15.00
Roulette SR-25116	(S)	Songs Of The Bad Old Days	1960	8.00	20.00
Roulette R-25125	(M)	Naughty But Nice	1960	6.00	15.00
Roulette SR-25125	(S)	Naughty But Nice	1960	8.00	20.00
Roulette R-25144	(M)	The Best Of Pearl Bailey	1961	5.00	12.00
Roulette SR-25144	(S)	The Best Of Pearl Bailey	1961	6.00	15.00
Roulette R-25155	(M)	Songs Of Harold Arlen	1961	5.00	12.00
Roulette SR-25155	(S)	Songs Of Harold Arlen	1961	6.00	15.00
Roulette R-25167	(M)	Happy Sounds	1962	5.00	12.00
Roulette SR-25167	(S)	Happy Sounds	1962	6.00	15.00
Roulette R-25181	(M)	Come On, Let's Play With Pearlie Mae	1962	5.00	12.00
Roulette SR-25181	(S)	Come On, Let's Play With Pearlie Mae	1962	6.00	15.00
		— Original Roulette albums above have white labels.—			
Roulette R-25195	(M)	All About Good Little Girls & Bad Little Boys	1963	5.00	12.00
Roulette SR-25195	(S)	All About Good Little Girls & Bad Little Boys	1963	6.00	15.00
Roulette R-25222	(M)	C'est La Vie	1963	5.00	12.00
Roulette SR-25222	(S)	C'est La Vie	1963	6.00	15.00
Roulette R-25259	(M)	The Risque World Of Pearl Bailey	1964	5.00	12.00
Roulette SR-25259	(S)	The Risque World Of Pearl Bailey	1964	6.00	15.00
RCA Victor LOC-1090	(M)	Les Poupees De Paris (Soundtrack)	1964	14.00	35.00
RCA Victor LSO-1090	(S)	Les Poupees De Paris (Soundtrack)	1964	20.00	50.00
RCA Victor LOC-1147	(M)	Hello, Dolly (Soundtrack)	1964	8.00	20.00
RCA Victor LSO-1147	(S)	Hello, Dolly (Soundtrack)	1964	10.00	25.00
Roulette R-25271	(M)	Songs By James Van Heusen	1964	5.00	12.00
Roulette SR-25271	(S)	Songs By James Van Heusen	1964	5.00	12.00
Roulette R-25300	(M)	For Women Only	1965	6.00	15.00
Roulette SR-25300	(S)	For Women Only	1965	5.00	12.00
Regent MG-6022	(M)	The Jazz Singer	1965	8.00	20.00
Regent MG-6032	(M)	Me And The Blues	1965	8.00	20.00

BAIN, BOB

Label & Catalog #		Title	Year	VG+	NM
Capitol T-965	(M)	Rockin,' Rollin'	1958	40.00	80.00

BAKER, JOSEPHINE

Label & Catalog #		Title	Year	VG+	NM
Columbia CL-9532 (10")	(M)	Josephine Baker	1951	30.00	60.00
Columbia CL-9533 (10")	(M)	Chansons Americaines	1951	30.00	60.00
Columbia ML-2608 (10")	(M)	Josephine Baker Sings	1952	20.00	50.00
Columbia ML-2609 (10")	(M)	Chansons Americaines	1952	30.00	60.00
Columbia ML-2613 (10")	(M)	Encores Americaines	1952	20.00	50.00
Jolly Roger 5015 (10")	(M)	Josephine Baker	1951	20.00	50.00
Mercury MG-25105 (10")	(M)	The Inimitable Josephine Baker	1952	20.00	50.00
Mercury MG-25151 (10")	(M)	Avec Josephine Baker	1952	20.00	50.00
RCA Victor LPM-2475	(M)	The Fabulous Josephine Baker	1962	12.00	30.00
RCA Victor LSP-2475	(S)	The Fabulous Josephine Baker	1962	16.00	40.00

Label & Catalog #		Title	Year	VG+	NM
BAKER, LAVERN					
Atlantic 8002	(M)	LaVern	1956	75.00	150.00
Atlantic 8007	(M)	LaVern Baker	1957	75.00	150.00
Atlantic 1281	(M)	LaVern Baker Sings Bessie Smith	1958	60.00	120.00
Atlantic 8030	(M)	Blues Ballads	1959	60.00	120.00
Atlantic 8036	(M)	Precious Memories	1959	50.00	100.00
		— Original Atlantic albums above have black labels.—			
Atlantic 8002	(M)	LaVern	1960	30.00	60.00
Atlantic 8030	(M)	Blues Ballads	1960	30.00	60.00
Atlantic 8050	(M)	Saved	1961	20.00	50.00
Atlantic SD-8050	(S)	Saved	1961	35.00	70.00
Atlantic 8071	(M)	See See Rider	1963	16.00	40.00
Atlantic SD-8071	(S)	See See Rider	1963	30.00	60.00
Atlantic 8078	(M)	The Best Of LaVern Baker	1963	18.00	45.00
Atlantic SD-8078	(S)	The Best Of LaVern Baker	1963	30.00	60.00
		—Mono Atlantic albums above have orange & purple labels with a white fan; stereo albums have green & blue labels with a white fan.—			
Brunswick BL-754160	(S)	Let Me Belong To You	1970	8.00	20.00
BAKER, MICKEY					
Formerly one half of Mickey & Sylvia. Refer to Champion Jack Dupree; Brother John Sellers.					
Atlantic 8035	(M)	Wildest Guitar (Black label)	1959	75.00	150.00
Atlantic SD-8035	(S)	Wildest Guitar (Green label)	1959	100.00	200.00
King K-839	(M)	But Wild	1963	35.00	70.00
King KS-839	(S)	But Wild	1963	45.00	90.00
BALDRY, LONG JOHN					
Ascot ALM-13022	(M)	Long John's Blues	1965	5.00	12.00
Ascot ALS-16022	(S)	Long John's Blues	1965	6.00	15.00
BALIN, MARTY					
Marty Balin was a founding member of The Jefferson Airplane.					
EMI SPRO-9673	(DJ)	Balin (Red vinyl)	1981	5.00	12.00
BALLADEERS, THE					
Del-Fi DFLP-1204	(M)	Alive-O	1959	16.00	40.00
BALLARD, FRANK					
Phillips Int. 1985	(M)	Rhythm-Blues Party	1962	1,000.00	1,500.00
BALLARD, HANK (& THE MIDNIGHTERS)					
Federal 295-90 (10")	(M)	Their Greatest Jukebox Hits	1955	*See note below*	
		(Rare. Estimated near mint value $1,500-3,000.)			
Federal 541	(M)	The Midnighters	1956	500.00	750.00
Federal 581	(M)	The Midnighters, Volume 2	1956	500.00	750.00
King 541	(M)	The Midnighters	1958	180.00	300.00
King 581	(M)	The Midnighters, Volume 2	1958	180.00	300.00
King 618	(M)	Singin And Swingin'	1959	75.00	150.00
King 674	(M)	The One And Only Hank Ballard	1960	75.00	150.00
King 700	(M)	Mr. Rhythm And Blues	1960	75.00	150.00
King 740	(M)	Spotlight On Hank Ballard	1961	75.00	150.00
King KS-740	(S)	Spotlight On Hank Ballard	1961	100.00	200.00
King 748	(M)	Let's Go Again	1961	50.00	100.00
King 759	(M)	Sing Along	1961	50.00	100.00
King 781	(M)	The Twistin' Fools	1962	50.00	100.00
King 793	(M)	Jumpin' Hank Ballard	1962	50.00	100.00
King 815	(M)	The 1963 Sound Of Hank Ballard	1963	50.00	100.00
King 867	(M)	Biggest Hits	1963	50.00	100.00
King 896	(M)	A Star In Your Eyes	1964	50.00	100.00
		— Original King albums above have crownless black labels.—			
King 913	(M)	Those Lazy, Lazy Days	1965	35.00	70.00
King 927	(M)	Glad Songs, Sad Songs	1966	35.00	70.00
King 950	(M)	24 Hit Tunes	1966	30.00	60.00
King 981	(M)	24 Great Songs	1968	16.00	40.00
King KSD-1052	(S)	You Keep A Good Man Down	1969	12.00	30.00
BALLARD, LIL' WILLIE					
King 737	(M)	Hit Makers And Record Breakers	1960	50.00	100.00

Label & Catalog #		Title	Year	VG+	NM
BALLARD, RUSS					
EMI SPRO-9404/5	(DJ)	**The Fire Still Burns** (2 LPs)	1985	8.00	20.00
BANANA SPLITS, THE					
Decca DL-75075	(S)	**We're The Banana Splits**	1969	50.00	100.00
Rhodes Prod.	(S)	**We're The Banana Splits** (Picture disc)	1985	50.00	100.00
BAND, THE					
The Band is Rick Danko, Levon Helm, Garth Hudson, Richard Manuel and Robbie Robertson. Refer to Bob Dylan; John Hammond; Ronnie Hawkins; Steve Miller.					
Capitol SKAO-2955	(S)	**Music From Big Pink** (Black label)	1968	8.00	20.00
Capitol ST-132	(S)	**The Band** (Black label)	1969	8.00	20.00
Capitol SKAO-2955	(S)	**Music From Big Pink** (Green label)	1970	5.00	12.00
Capitol ST-132	(S)	**The Band** (Green label)	1970	5.00	12.00
Capitol SW-425	(S)	**Stage Fright** (Green label)	1970	5.00	12.00
Capitol ST-651	(S)	**Cahoots** (Green label)	1971	5.00	12.00
Capitol SABB-11045	(S)	**Rock Of Ages** (2 LPs)	1972	8.00	20.00
		(Red label with a purple "C" logo on top.)			
Capitol SW-11214	(S)	**Moondog Matinee**	1973	8.00	20.00
		(Orange label. Originally issued with a fold-open "false" cover insert with a painting portraying the group in a bar scene.)			
Warner Bros. PRO-737	(DJ)	**The Last Waltz** (Sampler)	1978	6.00	15.00
Mobile Fidelity MFSL-039	(S)	**Music From Big Pink**	198?	10.00	25.00
BANDITS, THE					
The Bandits feature Glen Campbell.					
World Pacific T-1833	(M)	**The Electric 12 String**	1964	5.00	12.00
World Pacific ST-1833	(S)	**The Electric 12 String**	1964	6.00	15.00
BANGLES, THE					
Faulty 1302	(S)	**The Bangles** (5 tracks)	1982	8.00	20.00
Columbia CAS-2270	(DJ)	**Interchords** (Interview)	1986	10.00	25.00
BANGOR FLYING CIRCUS, THE					
Dunhill DS-50069	(S)	**The Bangor Flying Circus**	1969	6.00	15.00
BANKS, DARRELL					
Atco 33-216	(M)	**Darrell Banks Is Here**	1967	6.00	15.00
Atco SD-33-216	(P)	**Darrell Banks Is Here**	1967	8.00	20.00
Volt VOS-6002	(S)	**Here To Stay**	1969	6.00	15.00
BANTAMS, THE					
Warner Bros. W-1625	(M)	**Beware The Bantams**	1966	8.00	20.00
Warner Bros. WS-1625	(S)	**Beware The Bantams**	1966	10.00	25.00
BARBARIANS, THE					
Laurie LLP-2033	(M)	**Are You A Boy Or Are You A Girl?**	1966	20.00	50.00
Laurie SLP-2033	(S)	**Are You A Boy Or Are You A Girl?**	1966	35.00	70.00
BARDOT, BRIGITTE					
Poplar 33-1002	(M)	**The Girl In The Bikini** (Soundtrack)	1952	240.00	400.00
Decca DL-8685	(M)	**And God Created Woman** (Soundtrack)	1957	50.00	100.00
Warner Bros. W-1371	(M)	**Behind Brigitte Bardot**	1960	10.00	25.00
Warner Bros. WS-1371	(S)	**Behind Brigitte Bardot**	1960	14.00	35.00
Philips PC-204	(M)	**Brigitte Bardot Sings**	1963	10.00	25.00
Philips PCC-604	(S)	**Brigitte Bardot Sings**	1963	14.00	35.00
Burlington-Cameo 1000	(DJ)	**Special Bardot** (TV Soundtrack)	1968	50.00	100.00
BARDS, THE					
Piccadilly PIC-3419	(S)	**The Bards**	1980	8.00	20.00
BARE, BOBBY					
RCA Victor LPM-2776	(M)	**Detroit City And Other Hits**	1963	8.00	20.00
RCA Victor LSP-2776	(S)	**Detroit City And Other Hits**	1963	10.00	25.00
RCA Victor LPM-2835	(M)	**500 Miles Away From Home**	1963	8.00	20.00
RCA Victor LSP-2835	(S)	**500 Miles Away From Home**	1963	10.00	25.00
RCA Victor LPM-2955	(M)	**The Travelin' Bare**	1964	8.00	20.00
RCA Victor LSP-2955	(S)	**The Travelin' Bare**	1964	10.00	25.00

Label & Catalog #		Title	Year	VG+	NM
RCA Victor LPM-3336	(M)	Tunes For Two	1965	6.00	15.00
RCA Victor LSP-3336	(S)	Tunes For Two	1965	8.00	20.00
RCA Victor LPM-3395	(M)	Constant Sorrow	1965	6.00	15.00
RCA Victor LSP-3395	(S)	Constant Sorrow	1965	8.00	20.00
RCA Victor LPM-3515	(M)	Talk Me Some Sense	1966	5.00	12.00
RCA Victor LSP-3515	(S)	Talk Me Some Sense	1966	6.00	15.00
RCA Victor LPM-3618	(M)	The Streets Of Baltimore	1966	5.00	12.00
RCA Victor LSP-3618	(S)	The Streets Of Baltimore	1966	6.00	15.00
RCA Victor LPM-3688	(M)	This I Believe	1966	5.00	12.00
RCA Victor LSP-3688	(S)	This I Believe	1966	6.00	15.00
RCA Victor LPM-3764	(M)	The Game Of Triangles	1967	6.00	15.00
RCA Victor LSP-3764	(S)	The Game Of Triangles	1967	5.00	12.00
RCA Victor LPM-3831	(M)	A Bird Named Yesterday	1967	6.00	15.00
RCA Victor LSP-3831	(S)	A Bird Named Yesterday	1967	5.00	12.00
RCA Victor LPM-3896	(M)	The English Country Side	1967	6.00	15.00
RCA Victor LSP-3896	(S)	The English Country Side	1967	5.00	12.00

— *Original RCA albums above have black labels.*—

BARGE, GENE

Checker 2994	(M)	Dance With Daddy G	1965	12.00	30.00

BARKER, WARREN

Warner Bros. W-1289	(M)	77 Sunset Strip *(TV Soundtrack)*	1959	8.00	20.00
Warner Bros. WS-1289	(S)	77 Sunset Strip *(TV Soundtrack)*	1959	12.00	30.00
Warner Bros. W-1290	(M)	TV Guide/Top TV Themes	1959	8.00	20.00
Warner Bros. WS-1290	(S)	TV Guide/Top TV Themes	1959	12.00	30.00

BARNES, MAE

Atlantic ALS-404 (10")	(M)	Fun With Mae Barnes	1953	180.00	300.00

BARNETT, BOBBY

Sims 198	(M)	At The World Famous Crystal Palace	1964	12.00	30.00

BAROQUES, THE

Chess 1516	(M)	The Baroques	1967	10.00	25.00
Chess S-1516	(S)	The Baroques	1967	12.00	30.00

BARRACUDAS, THE

Justice 143	(M)	A Plane View	1968	180.00	300.00

BARRIER BROTHERS, THE

Philips PHM-200003	(M)	Golden Bluegrass Hits	1962	8.00	20.00
Philips PHS-600003	(S)	Golden Bluegrass Hits	1962	12.00	30.00
Philips PHM-200049	(M)	More Golden Bluegrass Hits	1962	8.00	20.00
Philips PHS-600049	(S)	More Golden Bluegrass Hits	1962	12.00	30.00
Philips PHM-200083	(M)	Gospel Songs, Bluegrass Style	1962	8.00	20.00
Philips PHS-600083	(S)	Gospel Songs, Bluegrass Style	1962	12.00	30.00

BARRY & THE TAMERLANES

A&M LP-406	(M)	I Wonder What She's Doing Tonight	1963	50.00	100.00

BARRY, GENE

RCA Victor LPM-2975	(M)	The Star Of "Burke's Law" Sings	1964	5.00	12.00
RCA Victor LSP-2975	(S)	The Star Of "Burke's Law" Sings	1964	6.00	15.00

BARRY, LEN

Len Barry was formerly a member of The Dovells.

Decca DL-4720	(M)	1-2-3	1965	8.00	20.00
Decca DL-74720	(P)	1-2-3	1965	10.00	25.00
RCA Victor LPM-3823	(M)	My Kind Of Soul	1967	5.00	12.00
RCA Victor LSP-3823	(S)	My Kind Of Soul	1967	6.00	15.00
Buddah BDS-5105	(S)	Ups & Downs	1972	4.00	10.00

BARTHOLOMEW, DAVE

Imperial LP-9162	(M)	Fats Domino Presents David Bartholomew	1961	30.00	60.00
Imperial LP-12076	(S)	Fats Domino Presents David Bartholomew	1961	40.00	80.00
Imperial LP-9217	(M)	New Orleans House Party	1963	20.00	50.00
Imperial LP-12217	(S)	New Orleans House Party	1963	35.00	70.00

Label & Catalog #		Title	Year	VG+	NM
BARTLEY, CHARLENE					
RCA Victor LPM-1478	(M)	**Weekend Of A Private Secretary**	1957	10.00	25.00
BASKERVILLE HOUNDS, THE					
Dot DLP-3823	(M)	**The Baskerville Hounds**	1967	10.00	25.00
Dot DLP-25823	(S)	**The Baskerville Hounds**	1967	12.00	30.00
BASS, FONTELLA					
Checker LP-2997	(M)	**The New Look**	1966	5.00	12.00
Checker LPS-2997	(S)	**The New Look**	1966	6.00	15.00
BATTERED ORNAMENTS					
Harvest SKAO-422	(S)	**Mantle-Piece**	1970	16.00	40.00
BAUGH, PHIL					
Longhorn LP-002	(M)	**Country Guitar**	1965	16.00	40.00
Toro T-502	(M)	**Country Guitar II**	1965	12.00	30.00
Era ES-801	(S)	**California Guitar**	196?	10.00	25.00
BAYSIDERS, THE					
Everest LPBR-5124	(M)	**Over The Rainbow**	1961	20.00	50.00
Everest BRST-5124	(S)	**Over The Rainbow**	1961	30.00	60.00
BE-BOP DELUXE					
Harvest SPRO-8531	(DJ)	**Be-Bop's Biggest**	1975	12.00	30.00
Harvest SKBB-11666	(DJ)	**Live! In The Air Age** (2 LPs)	1977	8.00	20.00
Harvest SW-11750	(DJ)	**Drastic Plastic** (White vinyl)	1978	8.00	20.00

BEACH BOYS, THE

The Beach Boys were Brian Wilson with brothers Carl and Dennis; Al Jardine, Mike Love and Bruce Johnston. Other members include David Marks (1963-64) and Rickie Fataar and Blondie Chaplin of The Flame (1971-1973). Refer to The Sunrays; Murry Wilson.

Capitol T-1808	(M)	**Surfin' Safari**	1962	14.00	35.00
Capitol DT-1808	(E)	**Surfin' Safari**	1962	30.00	60.00
		(Originally issued in a "Full Dimensional Stereo" cover.)			
Capitol DT-1808	(E)	**Surfin' Safari**	1963	12.00	30.00
		(Second pressings have the correct "Duophonic Stereo" cover.)			
Capitol T-1890	(M)	**Surfin' U.S.A.**	1963	12.00	30.00
Capitol ST-1890	(S)	**Surfin' U.S.A.**	1963	16.00	40.00
Capitol T-1981	(M)	**Shut Down**	1963	8.00	20.00
Capitol ST-1981	(S)	**Shut Down**	1963	8.00	20.00
		(Various artists compilation based around the group's singles. The Beach Boys appeared on other compilations; most are listed— though not identified— in the "Various Artists" section.)			
Capitol T-1981	(M)	**Surfer Girl**	1963	12.00	30.00
Capitol ST-1981	(S)	**Surfer Girl**	1963	14.00	35.00
		(Original covers mention the influence of The Four Freshmen style on "Your Summer Dreams" in the liner notes on the back.)			
Capitol T-1981	(M)	**Surfer Girl**	1963	14.00	35.00
Capitol ST-1981	(S)	**Surfer Girl**	1963	16.00	40.00
		(Later pressings make mention of "Their other new single-record hit Little Deuce Coupe" in the liner notes on the back.)			
Capitol T-1998	(M)	**Little Deuce Coupe**	1963	12.00	30.00
Capitol ST-1998	(S)	**Little Deuce Coupe**	1963	16.00	40.00
Capitol T-2027	(M)	**Shut Down, Volume 2**	1964	12.00	30.00
Capitol ST-2027	(P)	**Shut Down, Volume 2**	1964	14.00	35.00
Capitol T-2110	(M)	**All Summer Long**	1964	14.00	35.00
Capitol ST-2110	(S)	**All Summer Long**	1964	20.00	50.00
		(The front cover erroneously lists the last song on the album as "Don't Break Down.")			
Capitol T-2110	(M)	**All Summer Long**	1964	12.00	30.00
Capitol ST-2110	(P)	**All Summer Long**	1964	14.00	35.00
		(The front cover correctly lists the last song on the album as "Don't Back Down.")			
Capitol T-2164	(M)	**The Beach Boys' Christmas Album**	1964	10.00	25.00
Capitol ST-2164	(S)	**The Beach Boys' Christmas Album**	1964	14.00	35.00
Capitol PRO-2744	(DJ)	**Programming Aids From Capitol**	1964	100.00	200.00
		(Various artists compilation contains "Auld Lang Syne" without "The Christmas Album's" voice-over.)			

Label & Catalog #		Title	Year	VG+	NM
Capitol PRO-3123	(DJ)	**Silver Platter Service From Hollywood**	1964	100.00	200.00
		(Various artists compilation features Brian introducing selections			
		from The Hollyridge Strings' "Beach Boys Songbook.")			
Capitol PRO-3133	(DJ)	**The Beach Boys Christmas Special**	1964	210.00	350.00
Capitol TAO-2198	(M)	**Beach Boys Concert**	1964	8.00	20.00
Capitol STAO-2198	(S)	**Beach Boys Concert**	1964	10.00	25.00
Capitol T-2269	(M)	**The Beach Boys Today!**	1965	14.00	35.00
Capitol DT-2269	(E)	**The Beach Boys Today!**	1965	10.00	25.00
Capitol T-2354	(M)	**Summer Days (And Summer Nights!!)**	1965	14.00	35.00
Capitol DT-2354	(E)	**Summer Days (And Summer Nights!!)**	1965	16.00	40.00
		(Originally issued in a "Full Dimensional Stereo" cover.)			
Capitol DT-2354	(E)	**Summer Days (And Summer Nights!!)**	1965	10.00	25.00
		(Second pressings have the correct "Duophonic Stereo" cover.)			
Capitol MAS-2398	(M)	**Beach Boys Party!** *(With wallet photos)*	1965	12.00	30.00
Capitol DMAS-2398	(E)	**Beach Boys Party!***(With wallet photos)*	1965	10.00	25.00
Capitol MAS-2398	(M)	**Beach Boys Party!** *(Without the photos)*	1965	10.00	25.00
Capitol DMAS-2398	(E)	**Beach Boys Party!***(Without the photos)*	1965	8.00	20.00
Capitol T-2458	(M)	**Pet Sounds**	1966	12.00	30.00
Capitol DT-2458	(E)	**Pet Sounds**	1966	6.00	15.00
Capitol T-2545	(M)	**Best Of The Beach Boys, Volume 1**	1966	8.00	20.00
Capitol DT-2545	(E)	**Best Of The Beach Boys, Volume 1**	1966	6.00	15.00
Capitol T-2545	(M)	**Best Of The Beach Boys, Volume 1**	1966	12.00	30.00
Capitol DT-2545	(E)	**Best Of The Beach Boys, Volume 1**	1966	8.00	20.00
		(Black Starline label.)			
Capitol T-2545	(M)	**Best Of The Beach Boys, Volume 1**	1967	14.00	35.00
Capitol DT-2545	(E)	**Best Of The Beach Boys, Volume 1**	1967	5.00	12.00
		(Red & white "bullseye" Starline label.)			
Capitol DT-2545	(E)	**Best Of The Beach Boys, Volume 1**	1969	10.00	25.00
		(Red & white "star" Starline label.)			
Capitol T-2706	(M)	**Best Of The Beach Boys, Volume 2**	1967	8.00	20.00
Capitol DT-2706	(E)	**Best Of The Beach Boys, Volume 2**	1967	6.00	15.00
		(Red & white "bullseye" Starline label.)			
Capitol DT-2706	(E)	**Best Of The Beach Boys, Volume 2**	1969	6.00	15.00
		(Red & white "star" Starline label.)			
Brother T-9001	(M)	**Smiley Smile**	1967	12.00	30.00
Brother ST-9001	(E)	**Smiley Smile**	1967	6.00	15.00
		(First pressing covers do not credit Barry Turnbull.)			
Brother T-9001	(M)	**Smiley Smile**	1967	10.00	25.00
Brother ST-9001	(E)	**Smiley Smile**	1967	5.00	12.00
		(Later pressing read "Title for this album by Barry Turnbull.")			
Capitol PRO-3265	(DJ)	**Silver Platter Service From Hollywood**	1967	150.00	250.00
		(Various artists compilation features Brian briefly discussing			
		the scrapping of the "Smile" album.)			
Capitol TCL-2813	(M)	**The Beach Boys Deluxe Set** *(3 LP box)*	1967	100.00	200.00
		(The mono box has a black border and contains standard copies			
		of the albums with a "T" prefix.)			
Capitol DTCL-2813	(E)	**The Beach Boys Deluxe Set** *(3 LP box)*	1967	30.00	60.00
		(The stereo box has a maroon border and contains custom copies			
		of the albums with a "DTCL" prefix.)			
Capitol DTCL-8-2813	(E)	**The Beach Boys Deluxe Set** *(Record Club)*	1967	150.00	250.00
		(The stereo box has a blue border and contains custom copies			
		of the albums with a "DTCL" prefix.)			
Capitol T-2859	(M)	**Wild Honey**	1967	12.00	30.00
Capitol ST-2859	(E)	**Wild Honey**	1967	6.00	15.00
Capitol ST8-2891	(E)	**Smiley Smile** *(Record Club)*	1968	50.00	100.00
Capitol DKAO-2893	(E)	**Stack O' Tracks** *(With booklet)*	1968	40.00	80.00
Capitol DKAO-2893	(E)	**Stack O' Tracks** *(Without booklet)*	1968	16.00	40.00
Capitol DKAO-8-2893	(E)	**Stack O' Tracks** *(Record Club with booklet)*	1968	75.00	150.00
Capitol ST-2895	(S)	**Friends**	1968	8.00	20.00
Capitol DKAO-2945	(P)	**Best Of The Beach Boys, Volume 3**	1969	6.00	15.00
Capitol DKAO-2945	(P)	**Best Of The Beach Boys, Volume 3**	1969	8.00	20.00
		(Red & white "star" Starline label.)			
Capitol SKAO-133	(P)	**20/20**	1969	8.00	20.00
Capitol SKAO-133	(P)	**20/20** *(Red & white "star" Starline label)*	1969	10.00	25.00
Capitol SKAO-8-0133	(P)	**20/20** *(Record Club)*	1969	12.00	30.00
Capitol SKAO-8-0133	(P)	**20/20** *(Record Club. Lime label)*	197?	16.00	40.00
Capitol SWBB-253	(E)	**Close-Up** *(2 LPs)*	1969	8.00	20.00
Capitol SWBB-253	(E)	**Close-Up** *(2 LPs. Lime label)*	197?	16.00	40.00

— *Unless noted otherwise, Capitol albums above have black rainbows labels..* —

Label & Catalog #		Title	Year	VG+	NM
Capitol ST-442	(P)	**Good Vibrations** (Lime label)	1970	5.00	12.00
Capitol DT-80442	(P)	**Good Vibrations** (Record Club)	1970	10.00	25.00
Capitol ST-442	(P)	**Good Vibrations** (Orange label)	1972	8.00	20.00
Capitol SF-501/DF-502	(E)	**All Summer Long / California Girls**	1970	8.00	20.00
		(Lime label. Two single albums, edited versions of 2110 and 2354, bound together with a Special Double Play sticker.)			
Capitol SF-501/DF-502	(E)	**All Summer Long / California Girls** (2 LPs)	1971	12.00	30.00
		(Orange label with a purple "C" on top. This is two single albums bound together with a Special Double Play sticker.)			
Capitol SF-702/DF-703	(P)	**Fun, Fun, Fun / Dance, Dance, Dance**	1970	8.00	20.00
		(Lime label. Two single albums, edited versions of 2027 and 2269, bound together with a Special Double Play sticker.)			
Capitol SF-702/DF-703	(P)	**Fun, Fun, Fun / Dance, Dance, Dance** (2 LPs)	1971	12.00	30.00
		(Orange label with a purple "C" on top. This is two single albums bound together with a Special Double Play sticker.)			
Capitol R-233593	(P)	**American Summer** (2 LPs. Record Club)	1975	4.00	10.00
Capitol SVBB-11307	(P)	**Endless Summer** (2 LPs)	1974	6.00	15.00
		(Orange label. Issued with a poster, included in the price.)			
Capitol SLB-6994	(P)	**Golden Years Of The Beach Boys** (2 LPs)	1975	6.00	15.00
Era HTE-805	(M)	**The Beach Boys' Biggest Beach Hits**	1969	8.00	20.00
Sears SPS-609	(E)	**Summertime Blues**	1970	30.00	60.00
Reprise RS-6382	(DJ)	**Sunflower** (White label)	1970	12.00	30.00
Reprise RS-6382	(S)	**Sunflower** (Orange label)	1970	See note below	
		(Rare. Estimated near mint value $50-100)			
Reprise RS-6382	(S)	**Sunflower** (Yellow label)	1970	6.00	15.00
Reprise SKAO-93352	(S)	**Sunflower** (Record Club)	1970	65.00	130.00
Reprise RS-6453	(DJ)	**Surf's Up** (White label with lyric sheet)	1971	16.00	40.00
Reprise RS-6453	(S)	**Surf's Up** (With lyric sheet)	1971	4.00	10.00
Reprise R-113793	(S)	**Surf's Up** (RCA Record Club)	1971	8.00	20.00
Asylum R-113793	(S)	**Surf's Up** (RCA Record Club)	1971	65.00	130.00
Reprise 2MS-2083	(DJ)	**Carl And The Passion-So Tough / Pet Sounds** (2 LPs. White label)	1972	12.00	30.00
Reprise 2MS-2083	(S)	**Carl And The Passion-So Tough / Pet Sounds** (2 LPs)	1972	8.00	20.00
Reprise MS-2118	(DJ)	**Holland** (Test pressing with "We Got Love")	1973	240.00	400.00
Reprise MS-2118	(DJ)	**Holland** (White label)	1973	16.00	40.00
		(Issued with a white label EP, "Mt. Vernon & Fairway," with a PS.)			
Reprise MS-2118	(S)	**Holland**	1973	8.00	20.00
		(Issued with an EP, "Mt. Vernon & Fairway," with a PS. Note: The EP was taped to the back cover; small tape tears in the EP sleeve are common)			
Reprise 2MS-6484	(DJ)	**Beach Boys In Concert** (2 LPs. White label)	1973	12.00	30.00
Reprise 2MS-2166	(DJ)	**Wild Honey / 20/20** (2 LPs)	1974	8.00	20.00
Reprise 2MS-2167	(DJ)	**Friends / Smiley Smile** (2 LPs)	1974	8.00	20.00
Reprise MS-2223	(DJ)	**Good Vibrations-Best Of The Beach Boys**	1975	6.00	15.00
Caribou JZ-35752	(DJ)	**L.A. (Light Album)** (White label)	1979	6.00	15.00
Caribou JZ-36293	(DJ)	**Keepin' The Summer Alive** (White label)	1980	6.00	15.00
Mobile Fidelity MFSL-116	(S)	**Surfer Girl**	198?	8.00	20.00

BEACON STREET UNION
The Beacon Street Union later recorded as Eagle.

MGM SE-4517	(S)	**The Eyes Of The Beacon Street Union**	1968	6.00	15.00
MGM SE-4568	(S)	**The Clown Died In Marvin Gardens**	1968	6.00	15.00

BEANS

Avalanche 9200	(S)	**Beans**	1971	8.00	20.00

BEAR, YOGI, & THE THREE STOOGES

HBR HLP-2050	(M)	**The Mad, Mad Dr. No No**	1962	20.00	50.00

BEAR, YOGI

Colpix CP-472	(M)	**Hey There, It's Yogi Bear** (TV Soundtrack)	1964	14.00	35.00
Colpix SCP-472	(S)	**Hey There, It's Yogi Bear** (TV Soundtrack)	1964	20.00	50.00

BEARCATS, THE

Somerset P-20800	(M)	**Beatlemania**	1964	12.00	30.00

BEASLEY, JIMMY

Modern LMP-1214	(M)	**The Fabulous Jimmy Beasley**	1956	100.00	200.00

Label & Catalog #		Title	Year	VG+	NM
Crown CLP-5014	(M)	**The Fabulous Jimmy Beasley**	1957	50.00	100.00
Crown CLP-5247	(M)	**Twist With Jimmy Beasley**	1961	20.00	50.00

BEAT OF THE EARTH

Ardish AS-001	(S)	**Beat Of The Earth**	196?	180.00	300.00

BEATLE BUDDIES, THE

Diplomat 2313	(M)	**The Beatle Buddies**	1964	10.00	25.00

BEATLES, THE

The Fab Four were John Lennon, Paul McCartney, George Harrison and Ringo Starr; the fifth Beatle was producer George Martin. Peter Best was an early member replaced by Ringo before the group recorded under their own name. Both Billy Preston and Yoko Ono appeared on the group's late '60s recordings.

The Beatles are the single most collectible group in the hobby; every variation in sound, label or cover is pursued, documented and valued among aficionados. The listing here is excessively complete for all but the hardcore; for more info on more Beatles, refer to the section "Elvis & The Beatles" in the introduction. Finally, as Vee Jay issued mono albums with stereo labels, check for an "S" suffix on the master number in the trail-off vinyl. Many, many counterfeits of the Vee Jay albums exist!

— Vee Jay Records, 1963-1964 —

Vee Jay LP-1062	(M)	**Introducing The Beatles**	1963	1,400.00	2,000.00
Vee Jay SR-1062	(P)	**Introducing The Beatles**	1963	2,800.00	4,000.00

(Includes "Love Me Do" and "P.S. I Love You." Black label with a rainbow border and oval logo. The cover has "Printed In U.S.A" in the lower left corner. The back cover has ads for 25 other albums.)

Vee Jay LP-1062	(M)	**Introducing The Beatles**	1963	660.00	1,000.00
Vee Jay SR-1062	(P)	**Introducing The Beatles**	1963	1,400.00	2,000.00

(Includes "Love Me Do" and "P.S. I Love You." Black label with a rainbow border. The back cover is blank.)

Vee Jay LP-1062	(M)	**Introducing The Beatles**	1963	210.00	350.00

(Includes "Love Me Do" and "P.S. I Love You." Black label with a rainbow border and oval logo. The back cover lists the song titles in two columns.)

Vcc Jay LP 1062	(M)	**Introducing The Beatles**	1963	240.00	400.00

(Includes "Love Me Do" and "P.S. I Love You." Black label with a rainbow border and brackets logo. The back cover lists the song titles in two columns.)

Vee Jay LP-1062	(M)	**Introducing The Beatles**	1964	150.00	250.00
Vee Jay SR-1062	(S)	**Introducing The Beatles**	1964	660.00	1,000.00

(Includes "Please Please Me" and "Ask Me Why." Black label with a rainbow border and the "Vee Jay" logo in an oval. The back cover lists the song titles in two columns.)

Vee Jay LP-1062	(M)	**Introducing The Beatles**	1964	100.00	200.00
Vee Jay SR-1062	(S)	**Introducing The Beatles**	1964	600.00	900.00

(Includes "Please Please Me" and "Ask Me Why." Black label with a rainbow border and the "VJ" logo in brackets. The back cover lists the song titles in two columns.)

Vee Jay LP-1062	(M)	**Introducing The Beatles**	1964	150.00	250.00
Vee Jay SR-1062	(S)	**Introducing The Beatles**	1964	660.00	1,000.00

(Includes "Please Please Me" and "Ask Me Why." Solid black label with plain "VJ" logo. The back cover lists the songs in two columns.)

Vee Jay LP-1062	(M)	**Introducing The Beatles**	1964	150.00	250.00

(Includes "Please Please Me" and "Ask Me Why." Solid black label with the "VJ" logo in an oval. The back cover lists the songs in two columns.)

Vee Jay LP-1062	(M)	**Introducing The Beatles**	1964	180.00	300.00

(Includes "Please Please Me" and "Ask Me Why." Solid black label with "VJ" logo in brackets. The back cover lists the song titles in two columns.)

Vee Jay LP-1085	(M)	**The Beatles And Frank Ifield On Stage**	1964	100.00	200.00
Vee Jay LPS-1085	(P)	**The Beatles And Frank Ifield On Stage**	1964	240.00	400.00

(The cover has a drawing of a Victorian gentleman with a Beatles haircut. Original covers have printing along the spine.)

Vee Jay LP-1085	(M)	**The Beatles And Frank Ifield On Stage**	1964	1,400.00	2,000.00
Vee Jay LPS-1085	(P)	**The Beatles And Frank Ifield On Stage**	1964	5,250.00	7,500.00

(The cover has a full-color, painted portrait of the Beatles. Legitimate copies have printing along the spine.)

Label & Catalog		Title	Year	VG+	NM
Vee Jay D'		~easons (2 LPs)	1964	300.00	500.00
Vee Jay		easons (2 LPs)	1964	1,000.00	1,500.00

Vee Jay 1065, "Golden Hits Of The Four
nd version of Vee Jay 1062, "Introducing
ith full-color poster, priced separately below.)

Vee		r Seasons Poster	1964	100.00	200.00
Vee		ories	1964	90.00	180.00
Vee		ories	1964	800.00	1,200.00

epackages the second version of Vee Jay
er is 8" across and folds open.)

Vee		All (White label)	1964	See note below	
Vee J		l All (Black rainbow label)	1964	75.00	150.00

ear mint value $5,000-10,000.)
s have black rainbow labels.)

s, 1964-1968—

INS Ra		(Open-end interview)	1964	240.00	400.00
Radio P		th Ed Rudy (Yellow label)	1964	30.00	60.00
Radio P		, Ed Rudy New U.S. Tour	1965	50.00	100.00
Lloyds F		ia Tour	1965	300.00	500.00
Sterling		h bonus photo)	1966	100.00	200.00
Sterling F		thout photo)	1966	75.00	150.00
Capitol T		es	1964	30.00	60.00
Capitol ST		les	1964	16.00	40.00
Capitol PR		leases From The			
		itol Of The World	1964	50.00	100.00

rtists. The Beatles appeared on various Capitol compi-
oth promotional and commercial; these are listed— though
ified— in the "Various Artists" section of the book.)

Capitol T-208		Second Album	1964	30.00	60.00
Capitol ST-208		Second Album	1964	16.00	40.00
United Artists		ay's Night (Open-end interview)	1964	500.00	750.00
United Artists S		ay's Night (Radio Spots)	1964	600.00	900.00
United Artists U		ay's Night (White label)	1964	1,200.00	1,800.00
United Artists UA		Day's Night	1964	40.00	80.00
United Artists UA		Day's Night	1964	50.00	100.00
Capitol T-2108		hing New	1964	30.00	60.00
Capitol ST-2108		hing New	1964	16.00	40.00
Capitol TBO-2222		eatles' Story (2 LPs)	1964	40.00	80.00
Capitol STBO-2222		eatles' Story (2 LPs)	1969	20.00	50.00
Capitol T-2228		es '65	1964	30.00	60.00
Capitol ST-2228		les '65	1964	16.00	40.00
Capitol T-2309		Early Beatles	1965	30.00	60.00
Capitol ST-2309		Early Beatles	1965	16.00	40.00
Capitol T-2358	(M)	Beatles VI	1965	30.00	60.00
Capitol ST-2358	(P)	Beatles VI	1965	16.00	40.00
United Artists Help-A/B	(DJ)	Help! (Radio spots)	1965	500.00	750.00
United Artists Help-INT	(DJ)	Help! (Open-end Interview)	1965	600.00	900.00
United Artists Help-Show	(DJ)	Help! (One-sided open-end interview)	1965	800.00	1,200.00
Capitol MAS-2386	(M)	Help!	1965	30.00	60.00
Capitol SMAS-2386	(P)	Help!	1965	16.00	40.00
Capitol T-2442	(M)	Rubber Soul	1965	30.00	60.00
Capitol ST-2442	(S)	Rubber Soul	1965	16.00	40.00
Capitol T-2553	(M)	Yesterday And Today	1966	1,750.00	2,500.00
Capitol ST-2553	(P)	Yesterday And Today	1966	5,250.00	7,500.00

("First state butcher cover." This is the original cover with the
Fab Four in doctor's smocks covered with pieces of raw meat and
baby doll parts. "First state" means that this cover has never been
pasted over with the common trunk cover.)

Capitol T-2553	(M)	Yesterday And Today	1966	300.00	500.00
Capitol ST-2553	(P)	Yesterday And Today	1966	800.00	1,200.00

("Second state butcher cover." That is, the replacement cover with
the group posed around a steamer trunk, is pasted over the original
"butcher" cover with no attempts at peeling. Many copies of this
album are sold in various states of removal, or peeling; the prices for
these vary dramatically according to the success of the peel job;
Some are professionally perfect and virtually indistinguishable
from true "first states," commanding equivalent sums.)

First pressings of *Yesterday And Today* were released with the above cover, depicting the Fab Four in doctor's smocks, slabs of raw meat, baby doll parts and cheeky grins. Apparently a reaction to the American record company's annoying habit of breaking up their fourteen track U.K. albums and issuing them as eleven track albums in the U.S. (in effect, butchering their work).

Copies of the "butcher cover" album in their original condition are referred to as "first state." When the album was recalled, employees were instructed to remove the original cover slick and paste the new cover on. Many workers took the short route and simply pasted the new cover over the old; these copies are referred to as "second state." (Second state covers that have had the new cover removed are called "peel jobs," which vary in quality from destroyed to almost perfect.)

While mono copies of the butcher cover are plentiful in one form or another (the liner notes for Capitol's *Rarities* album estimates that anywhere from 60,000 to 600,000 may have been pressed), stereo copies in anything resembling collectible condition are rare.

Label & Catalog #		Title	Year	VG+	NM
Capitol T-2553	(M)	**Yesterday And Today** *(Trunk cover)*	*1966*	**30.00**	**60.00**
Capitol ST-2553	(P)	**Yesterday And Today** *(Trunk cover)*	*1966*	**16.00**	**40.00**
Capitol T-2576	(M)	**Revolver**	*1966*	**30.00**	**60.00**
Capitol ST-2576	(S)	**Revolver**	*1964*	**16.00**	**40.00**
Capitol MAS-2653	(M)	**Sgt. Pepper's Lonely Heart's Club Band**	*1967*	**60.00**	**120.00**
Capitol SMAS-2653	(S)	**Sgt. Pepper's Lonely Heart's Club Band**	*1967*	**16.00**	**40.00**
		(Issued with a sheet of cutouts and a red psychedelic inner sleeve.)			
Capitol MAL-2835	(M)	**Magical Mystery Tour**	*1967*	**65.00**	**130.00**
Capitol SMAL-2835	(P)	**Magical Mystery Tour**	*1967*	**16.00**	**40.00**
		— Original Capitol albums above have black labels with the logo on top.—			
Capitol ST-2047	(P)	**Meet The Beatles**	*1969*	**12.00**	**30.00**
Capitol ST-2080	(P)	**The Beatles Second Album**	*1969*	**12.00**	**30.00**
Capitol ST-2108	(S)	**Something New**	*1969*	**12.00**	**30.00**
Capitol ST-2228	(P)	**Beatles '65**	*1969*	**12.00**	**30.00**
Capitol ST-2309	(P)	**The Early Beatles**	*1969*	**12.00**	**30.00**
Capitol ST-2358	(P)	**Beatles VI**	*1969*	**12.00**	**30.00**
Capitol SMAS-2386	(P)	**Help!**	*1969*	**12.00**	**30.00**
Capitol ST-2442	(S)	**Rubber Soul**	*1969*	**12.00**	**30.00**
Capitol ST-2553	(P)	**Yesterday And Today**	*1969*	**12.00**	**30.00**
Capitol ST-2576	(S)	**Revolver**	*1969*	**12.00**	**30.00**
Capitol ST-2576	(S)	**Revolver** *(Red label)*	*197?*	**45.00**	**90.00**
Capitol SMAS-2653	(S)	**Sgt. Pepper's Lonely Heart's Club Band**	*1969*	**12.00**	**30.00**
Capitol SMAL-2835	(P)	**Magical Mystery Tour**	*1969*	**12.00**	**30.00**
		— Capitol reissues above have green labels.—			
		— Capitol Record Club, 1964-1969—			
Capitol ST-8-2047	(P)	**Meet The Beatles** *(Black label)*	*1964*	**65.00**	**130.00**
Capitol ST-8-2047	(P)	**Meet The Beatles** *(Green label)*	*1964*	**20.00**	**50.00**
Capitol ST-8-2080	(P)	**The Beatles Second Album** *(Black label)*	*1964*	**65.00**	**130.00**
Capitol ST-8-2080	(P)	**The Beatles Second Album** *(Green label)*	*1969*	**20.00**	**50.00**
United Artists T-90828	(M)	**A Hard Day's Night** *(Black label)*	*1964*	**240.00**	**400.00**
United Artists ST-90828	(P)	**A Hard Day's Night** *(Black label)*	*1964*	**180.00**	**300.00**
Capitol ST-8-2108	(S)	**Something New** *(Black label)*	*1964*	**65.00**	**130.00**
Capitol ST-8-2108	(S)	**Something New** *(Green label)*	*1969*	**20.00**	**50.00**
Capitol ST-8-2358	(P)	**Beatles VI** *(Black label)*	*1965*	**65.00**	**130.00**
Capitol ST-8-2358	(P)	**Beatles VI** *(Green label)*	*1969*	**20.00**	**50.00**
Capitol SMAS-8-2386	(P)	**Help!** *(Black label)*	*1965*	**65.00**	**130.00**
Capitol SMAS-8-2386	(P)	**Help!** *(Green label)*	*1969*	**30.00**	**60.00**
Capitol ST-8-2442	(S)	**Rubber Soul** *(Black label)*	*1965*	**65.00**	**130.00**
Capitol ST-8-2442	(S)	**Rubber Soul** *(Green label)*	*1969*	**20.00**	**50.00**
Capitol ST-8-2553	(P)	**Yesterday And Today** *(Black label)*	*1966*	**65.00**	**130.00**
Capitol ST-8-2553	(P)	**Yesterday And Today** *(Green label)*	*1969*	**20.00**	**50.00**
Capitol ST-8-2576	(S)	**Revolver** *(Black label)*	*1966*	**65.00**	**130.00**
Capitol ST-8-2576	(S)	**Revolver** *(Green label)*	*1969*	**20.00**	**50.00**
Capitol ST-8-2576	(S)	**Revolver** *(Orange label)*	*1969*	**30.00**	**60.00**
		— Apple Records, 1968-1974—			
Apple SWBO-101	(S)	**The Beatles (The White Album)** *(2 LPs)*	*1968*	**40.00**	**80.00**
		(First pressings have an Apple label with the Capitol logo on the bottom. The front cover has "The Beatles" in raised white letters and is sequentially numbered 1-3,000,000 in black. Copies with numbers under #10,000 affect the value— substantially. Issued with a fold-open poster/lyric sheet and four glossy, full-color portraits of the group, included in the price.)			
Apple SWBO-101	(S)	**The Beatles (The White Album)** *(2 LPs)*	*1968*	**20.00**	**50.00**
		(First pressing without the poster and photos.)			
Apple SWBO-101	(S)	**The Beatles (The White Album)** *(2 LPs)*	*1969*	**16.00**	**40.00**
		(Second pressing are the same as the first except there is no number on the cover; issued with the poster and photos.)			
Apple SWBO-101	(S)	**The Beatles (The White Album)** *(2 LPs)*	*1969*	**8.00**	**20.00**
		(Second pressing without the poster and photos.)			
Apple KAL-1004	(DJ)	**The Yellow Submarine** *(Radio spots)*	*1968*	**800.00**	**1,200.00**
Apple SW-153	(P)	**The Yellow Submarine**	*1969*	**10.00**	**25.00**
		(Apple label with Capitol logo.)			
Apple SW-153	(P)	**The Yellow Submarine**	*1971*	**6.00**	**15.00**
Apple SO-383	(S)	**Abbey Road** *(Apple label with Capitol logo)*	*1969*	**12.00**	**30.00**
Apple SO-383	(S)	**Abbey Road**	*1969*	**10.00**	**25.00**
Apple SO-385	(S)	**Hey Jude/The Beatles Again**	*1970*	**10.00**	**25.00**
Apple SW-385	(S)	**Hey Jude/The Beatles Again**	*1970*	**12.00**	**30.00**

Label & Catalog #		Title	Year	VG+	NM
Apple SW-385	(S)	**Hey Jude** (Apple label with Capitol logo)	1970	**20.00**	**50.00**
Apple SW-385	(S)	**Hey Jude**	1971	**6.00**	**15.00**
Apple AR-34001	(S)	**Let It Be**	1970	**8.00**	**20.00**
		(Red Apple label with "Bell Sound" stamped in the trail-off vinyl.)			

This album, issued to their fan club in 1970, has been heavily counterfeited. On originals, the words "Theatre Royal" can be read in the second photo from the left on the bottom of the cover.

Label & Catalog #		Title	Year	VG+	NM
Apple SBC-100	(DJ)	**The Beatles Christmas Album**	1970	**75.00**	**150.00**
Apple SKBO-3403	(P)	**The Beatles 1962-1966** (2 LPs)	1973	**10.00**	**25.00**
Apple SKBO-3404	(P)	**The Beatles 1967-1970** (2 LPs)	1973	**10.00**	**25.00**
Apple	(P)	**The Beatles Special Limited Edition**	1974	**660.00**	**1,000.00**
		(Boxed set of nine Apple label albums.)			
		—Apple/Capitol reissues, 1968-1974—			
Apple ST-2047	(P)	**Meet The Beatles**	1968	**16.00**	**40.00**
Apple ST-2080	(P)	**The Beatles Second Album**	1968	**16.00**	**40.00**
Apple ST-2108	(S)	**Something New**	1968	**16.00**	**40.00**
Apple ST-2222	(P)	**The Beatles' Story** (2 LPs)	1968	**20.00**	**50.00**
Apple ST-2228	(P)	**Beatles '65**	1968	**16.00**	**40.00**
Apple ST-2309	(P)	**The Early Beatles**	1968	**16.00**	**40.00**
Apple ST-2358	(P)	**Beatles VI**	1968	**16.00**	**40.00**
Apple ST-2386	(P)	**Help!**	1968	**16.00**	**40.00**
Apple ST-2442	(S)	**Rubber Soul**	1968	**16.00**	**40.00**
Apple ST-2553	(P)	**Yesterday And Today**	1968	**16.00**	**40.00**
Apple ST-2576	(S)	**Revolver**	1968	**16.00**	**40.00**
Apple SMAS-2653	(S)	**Sgt. Pepper's Lonely Heart's Club Band**	1968	**16.00**	**40.00**
Apple SMAL-2835	(P)	**Magical Mystery Tour**	1968	**16.00**	**40.00**
		— Original pressings of the Apple reissues above have "A subsidiary of Capitol" on the label.—			
Apple ST-2047	(P)	**Meet The Beatles**	1970	**8.00**	**20.00**
Apple ST-2080	(P)	**The Beatles Second Album**	1970	**8.00**	**20.00**
Apple ST-2108	(S)	**Something New**	1970	**8.00**	**20.00**
Apple ST-2222	(P)	**The Beatles' Story** (2 LPs)	1970	**12.00**	**30.00**
Apple ST-2228	(P)	**Beatles '65**	1970	**8.00**	**20.00**
Apple ST-2309	(P)	**The Early Beatles**	1970	**8.00**	**20.00**
Apple ST-2358	(P)	**Beatles VI**	1970	**8.00**	**20.00**
Apple ST-2386	(P)	**Help!**	1970	**8.00**	**20.00**
Apple ST-2442	(S)	**Rubber Soul**	1970	**8.00**	**20.00**

Label & Catalog #		Title	Year	VG+	NM
Apple ST-2553	(P)	**Yesterday And Today**	1970	**8.00**	**20.00**
Apple ST-2576	(S)	**Revolver**	1970	**8.00**	**20.00**
Apple SMAS-2653	(S)	**Sgt. Pepper's Lonely Heart's Club Band**	1970	**8.00**	**20.00**
Apple SMAL-2835	(P)	**Magical Mystery Tour**	1970	**8.00**	**20.00**

— Second pressings of the Apple reissues above have "Mfd. by Apple Records" on the label. —

Apple ST-2047	(P)	**Meet The Beatles**	1974	**5.00**	**12.00**
Apple ST-2080	(P)	**The Beatles Second Album**	1974	**5.00**	**12.00**
Apple ST-2108	(S)	**Something New**	1974	**5.00**	**12.00**
Apple ST-2222	(P)	**The Beatles' Story** (2 LPs)	1974	**8.00**	**20.00**
Apple ST-2228	(P)	**Beatles '65**	1974	**5.00**	**12.00**
Apple ST-2309	(P)	**The Early Beatles**	1974	**5.00**	**12.00**
Apple ST-2358	(P)	**Beatles VI**	1974	**5.00**	**12.00**
Apple ST-2386	(P)	**Help!**	1974	**5.00**	**12.00**
Apple ST-2442	(S)	**Rubber Soul**	1974	**5.00**	**12.00**
Apple ST-2553	(P)	**Yesterday And Today**	1974	**5.00**	**12.00**
Apple ST-2576	(S)	**Revolver**	1974	**5.00**	**12.00**
Apple SMAS-2653	(S)	**Sgt. Pepper's Lonely Heart's Club Band**	1974	**5.00**	**12.00**
Apple SMAL-2835	(P)	**Magical Mystery Tour**	1974	**5.00**	**12.00**

— Later pressings of the Apple reissues above have an "All rights reserved" disclaimer on the label. —

— Capitol Records, 1974-1987 —

Capitol (No number)	(DJ)	**The Beatles 10th Anniversary Box Set**	1974	**1,200.00**	**1,800.00**
		(Boxed set of seventeen Apple label albums.)			
Lingasong LS-2-7001	(DJ)	**Live At The Star Club** (2 LPs. Blue vinyl)	1977	**180.00**	**300.00**
Lingasong LS-2-7001	(DJ)	**Live At The Star Club** (2 LPs. Red vinyl)	1977	**65.00**	**130.00**
Lingasong LS-2-7001	(DJ)	**Live At The Star Club** (2 LPs. Black vinyl)	1977	**12.00**	**30.00**
Lingasong LS-2-7001	(E)	**Live At The Star Club** (2 LPs)	1977	**5.00**	**12.00**
Capitol SKBO-11537	(P)	**Rock 'N' Roll Music** (2 LPs)	1977	**8.00**	**20.00**
Capitol SMAS-11638	(DJ)	**The Beatles At The Hollywood Bowl**	1977	**150.00**	**250.00**
		(Tan label issued in a plain white jacket.)			
Capitol SMAS-11638	(S)	**The Beatles At The Hollywood Bowl**	1977	**6.00**	**15.00**
		(Both the title and the graphics on the front cover are raised.)			
Capitol SKBL-11711	(P)	**Love Songs** (2 LPs with embossed cover)	1977	**6.00**	**15.00**
Capitol SEAX-11840	(S)	**Sgt. Pepper's Lonely Heart's Club Band**	1978	**6.00**	**15.00**
		(Picture disc in die cut cover.)			
Capitol SEBX-11841	(S)	**The Beatles** (2 LPs. White vinyl)	1978	**12.00**	**30.00**
Capitol SEBX-11842	(P)	**The Beatles 1962-1966** (2 LPs. Red vinyl)	1978	**12.00**	**30.00**
Capitol SEBX-11843	(P)	**The Beatles 1967-1970** (2 LPs. Blue vinyl)	1978	**12.00**	**30.00**
Capitol SEAX-11900	(S)	**Abbey Road** (Picture disc)	1978	**16.00**	**40.00**
Capitol SN-12009	(P)	**The Beatles Rarities** (Green label)	1978	**75.00**	**150.00**
		(Capitol 12009 issued without a cover.)			
Capitol/EMI BC-13	(P)	**The Beatles Collection** (14 LP box)	1978	**100.00**	**200.00**
Capitol SPRO-8969	(DJ)	**Rarities**	1980	**16.00**	**40.00**
Capitol SHAL-12080	(P)	**Rarities**	1980	**6.00**	**15.00**
		(Original covers do not credit George Martin as producer.)			
Capitol SV-12199	(DJ)	**Reel Music** (Gold vinyl)	1982	**14.00**	**35.00**
		(Back cover stamped with a "Limited Edition" number.)			
Capitol SV-12199	(S)	**Reel Music** (Gold vinyl)	1982	**12.00**	**30.00**
		(Without the "Limited Edition" number.)			
Capitol	(DJ)	**The Platinum Collection** (18 LP box)	1984	**500.00**	**750.00**
		(Note: 2/3 of the price— $500— is for the box alone.)			

— Essential Various Artists Compilations —

MGM E-4215	(M)	**The Beatles With Tony Sheridan & Guests**	1964	**75.00**	**150.00**
MGM SE-4215	(P)	**The Beatles With Tony Sheridan & Guests**	1964	**240.00**	**400.00**
Atco 33-169	(DJ)	**Ain't She Sweet**	1964	**600.00**	**900.00**
Atco 33-169	(M)	**Ain't She Sweet**	1964	**75.00**	**150.00**
Atco SD-33-169	(P)	**Ain't She Sweet** (Banded label)	1964	**150.00**	**250.00**
Atco SD-33-169	(P)	**Ain't She Sweet** (Yellow label)	196?	**75.00**	**150.00**
Savage BM-69	(M)	**The Savage Young Beatles** (Yellow cover)	1964	**35.00**	**70.00**
Savage BM-69	(M)	**The Savage Young Beatles** (Orange cover)	1964	**300.00**	**500.00**
Clarion 601	(M)	**The Amazing Beatles**	1966	**40.00**	**80.00**
Clarion SD-601	(P)	**The Amazing Beatles**	1966	**100.00**	**200.00**
Polydor 24-4504	(P)	**In The Beginning/Circa 1960** (Red label)	1970	**8.00**	**20.00**

— Original Master Recordings, 1979-1987 —

Mobile Fidelity MFSL-023	(S)	**Abbey Road**	1979	**20.00**	**50.00**
Mobile Fidelity MFSL-047	(P)	**Magical Mystery Tour**	1980	**30.00**	**60.00**
Mobile Fidelity MFSL-072	(S)	**The Beatles (The White Album)** (2 LPs)	1982	**16.00**	**40.00**

Label & Catalog #		Title	Year	VG+	NM
Mobile Fidelity MFSL-100	(S)	**Sgt. Pepper's Lonely Heart's Club Band**	1982	**8.00**	**20.00**
Mobile Fidelity MFQR-100	(S)	**Sgt. Pepper's Lonely Heart's Club Band**	1982	**100.00**	**200.00**
		(UHQR issued in a box.)			
Mobile Fidelity MFSL-101	(S)	**Please Please Me**	1986	**8.00**	**20.00**

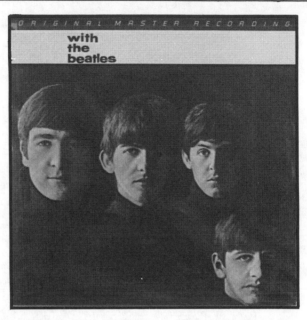

When the pressing plates for this album broke, an instant rarity was born. Thus, while all of the Mobile Fidelity albums have become collectible, this one will escalate the most in value over time.

Mobile Fidelity MFSL-102	(S)	**With The Beatles**	1986	**35.00**	**70.00**
Mobile Fidelity MFSL-103	(S)	**A Hard Day's Night**	1986	**8.00**	**20.00**
Mobile Fidelity MFSL-104	(S)	**Beatles For Sale**	1986	**8.00**	**20.00**
Mobile Fidelity MFSL-105	(S)	**Help!**	1986	**8.00**	**20.00**
Mobile Fidelity MFSL-106	(S)	**Rubber Soul**	1986	**8.00**	**20.00**
Mobile Fidelity MFSL-107	(S)	**Revolver**	1987	**8.00**	**20.00**
Mobile Fidelity MFSL-108	(P)	**Yellow Submarine**	1987	**8.00**	**20.00**
Mobile Fidelity MFSL-109	(S)	**Let It Be**	1987	**8.00**	**20.00**
Mobile Fidelity	(P)	**The Beatles: The Collection** *(14 LPs)*	1982	**240.00**	**400.00**

BEATLES, THE

Tower KAO-5000	(M)	**Sing A Song With The Beatles**	1965	**35.00**	**70.00**
Tower DKAO-5000	(E)	**Sing A Song With The Beatles**	1965	**35.00**	**70.00**
		(Instrumental versions of Beatle hits. While the Fab Four are on the cover, the playing is by unidentified studio musicians.)			

BEATS, THE [THE LIVERPOOL BEATS]

Rondo 2026	(M)	**The New Merseyside Sound**	1964	**12.00**	**30.00**
		(Released credited to either The Beats or The Liverpool Beats.)			

BEAU BRUMMELS, THE
Originally Ron Elliot, Declan Mulligan, Ron Meagher, John Petersen and Sal Valentino, by 1967 The Beau Brummels were a duo, Valentino and Elliot.

Autumn LP-103	(M)	**Introducing The Beau Brummels**	1965	**12.00**	**30.00**
Autumn SLP-103	(S)	**Introducing The Beau Brummels**	1965	**16.00**	**40.00**
Autumn LP-104	(M)	**The Beau Brummels, Volume 2**	1965	**12.00**	**30.00**
Autumn SLP-104	(S)	**The Beau Brummels, Volume 2**	1965	**16.00**	**40.00**
Warner Bros. WS-1644	(M)	**Beau Brummels '66**	1966	**8.00**	**20.00**
Warner Bros. WS-1644	(S)	**Beau Brummels '66**	1966	**12.00**	**30.00**

Label & Catalog #		Title	Year	VG+	NM
Warner Bros. W-1692	(M)	**Triangle**	1967	6.00	15.00
Warner Bros. WS-1692	(S)	**Triangle**	1967	8.00	20.00
Warner Bros. WS-1760	(S)	**Bradley's Barn**	1968	8.00	20.00
Vault LP-114	(M)	**The Best Of The Beau Brummels**	1967	6.00	15.00
Vault SLP-114	(S)	**The Best Of The Beau Brummels**	1967	8.00	20.00
Vault SLP-121	(E)	**The Beau Brummels, Volume 44**	1968	6.00	15.00
Post 6000	(P)	**The Beau Brummels**	196?	5.00	12.00
JAS 5000	(S)	**Original Hits Of The Beau Brummels**	1976	6.00	15.00

BEAUREGARDE
F-Empire	(S)	**Beauregarde**	196?	30.00	60.00

BEAVER, PAUL
Rapture 11111	(S)	**Perchance To Dream**	196?	12.00	30.00

BEAVER & KRAUSE
Paul Beaver and Bernie Krause.
Limelight 86069	(S)	**Ragnarok**	1969	12.00	30.00
Warner Bros. WS-1850	(S)	**In A Wild Sanctuary**	1969	6.00	15.00
Warner Bros. WS-1909	(S)	**Gandharva**	1971	5.00	12.00
Warner Bros. BS-2624	(S)	**All Good Men**	1972	5.00	12.00

BECK, BOGERT & APPICE
Jeff Beck, Tim Bogert, Carmine Appice
Epic EQ-32140	(Q)	**Beck, Bogert, & Appice**	1973	5.00	12.00

BECK, JEFF [JEFF BECK GROUP]
Beck was formerly a member of The Yardbirds. Epic 26413-26478 feature Rod Stewart and Ron Wood.
Epic BN-26413	(S)	**Truth** *(Yellow label)*	1968	6.00	15.00
Epic BN-26478	(S)	**Beck-Ola** *(Yellow label)*	1969	6.00	15.00
Epic EQ-30973	(Q)	**Rough And Ready**	1972	6.00	15.00
Epic EQ-31331	(Q)	**The Jeff Beck Group**	1972	6.00	15.00
Epic PEQ-33409	(Q)	**Blow By Blow**	1975	6.00	15.00
Epic PEQ-33849	(Q)	**Wired**	1976	6.00	15.00
Epic PEQ-34433	(Q)	**Live**	1977	6.00	15.00
Epic AS-151	(DJ)	**Everything You Always Wanted To Hear**	1977	8.00	20.00
Epic AS-796	(DJ)	**Musical Montage**	1979	8.00	20.00
Epic HE-43409	(S)	**Blow By Blow** *(Half-speed master)*	1982	12.00	30.00
Epic HE-43849	(S)	**Wired** *(Half-speed master)*	1982	12.00	30.00

BECK, PIA
Epic LN-3269	(M)	**Dutch Treat**	1957	16.00	40.00

BEDIENT, JACK, & THE CHESSMEN
Executive Prods.	(M)	**Jack Bedient**	196?	16.00	40.00
Trophy 101	(M)	**Two Sides Of Jack Bedient**	1964	16.00	40.00
Fantasy 3365	(M)	**Live At Harvey's**	1965	16.00	40.00
Satori LP-1001	(M)	**Where Did She Go?**	1966	30.00	60.00

BEE GEES, THE
The Bee Gees are the brothers Gibb: Barry, Maurice and Robin.
Atco 33-223	(M)	**The Bee Gees First**	1967	8.00	20.00
Atco SD-33-223	(S)	**The Bee Gees First**	1967	6.00	15.00
Atco 33-233	(M)	**Horizontal**	1968	10.00	25.00
Atco SD-33-233	(S)	**Horizontal**	1968	6.00	15.00
Atco SD-33-253	(S)	**Idea**	1968	5.00	12.00
Atco SD-33-264	(E)	**Rare, Precious And Beautiful**	1968	5.00	12.00
— Original Atco stereo albums above have brown & purple labels.—					
Atco SD-33-292	(S)	**The Best Of The Bee Gees**	1969	5.00	12.00
Atco ST-142	(DJ)	**Odessa** *(In-store sampler)*	1969	30.00	60.00
Atco SD-2-702	(S)	**Odessa** *(Red felt cover)*	1969	10.00	25.00
Atco SD-2-702	(S)	**Odessa** *(Record Club. Plain red cover)*	1969	16.00	40.00
Atco SD-33-321	(E)	**Rare, Precious And Beautiful, Volume 2**	1970	4.00	10.00
Atco SD-33-327	(S)	**Cucumber Castle**	1970	5.00	12.00
Atco SD-33-353	(S)	**Two Years On**	1971	5.00	12.00
Atco SD-33-363	(S)	**Melody** *(Soundtrack)*	1971	6.00	15.00
Atco SD-7003	(S)	**Trafalgar**	1971	5.00	12.00
Atco SD-7012	(S)	**To Whom It May Concern**	1972	5.00	12.00
— Original Atco albums above have yellow labels with an 1841 Broadway address on the bottom.—					

Label & Catalog #		Title	Year	VG+	NM
RSO SMP-1	(DJ)	The Words And Music Of Maurice, Barry And Robin Gibb (Sampler)	197?	12.00	30.00
RSO 3042	(S)	Spirits Having Flown (Picture disc)	1979	4.00	10.00
Nautilus NR-17	(S)	Spirits Having Flown	1981	6.00	15.00

Ms. Molly Bee, like many a pop singer, lent her pipes to a collection of country tunes in 1967 and graced the cover with this leather-clad shot.

BEE, MOLLY

Capitol T-1097	(M)	Young Romance	1958	16.00	40.00
MGM E-4303	(M)	It's Great, It's Molly Bee	1965	6.00	15.00
MGM SE-4303	(S)	It's Great, It's Molly Bee	1965	8.00	20.00
MGM E-4423	(M)	Swingin' Country	1967	6.00	15.00
MGM SE-4423	(S)	Swingin' Country	1967	8.00	20.00

BEEFHEART, CAPTAIN: *Refer to* **CAPTAIN BEEFHEART & THE MAGIC BAND**

BEETHOVEN SOUL, THE

Dot DLP-3821	(M)	The Beethoven Soul	1967	6.00	15.00
Dot DLP-25821	(S)	The Beethoven Soul	1967	8.00	20.00

BEHRKE TRIO, RICHARD

Atco 33-141	(M)	The Richard Behrke Trio	1962	6.00	15.00
Atco SD-33-141	(S)	The Richard Behrke Trio	1962	8.00	20.00

BELAFONTE, HARRY

RCA Victor LPM-1022	(M)	Mark Twain And Other Folk Favorites	1954	16.00	40.00
RCA Victor LPM-1150	(M)	Three For Tonight (Soundtrack)	1955	50.00	100.00
RCA Victor LPM-1248	(M)	Calypso	1956	12.00	30.00
RCA Victor LPM-1402	(M)	An Evening With Belafonte	1957	12.00	30.00
RCA Victor LPM-1505	(M)	Belafonte Sings Of The Caribbean	1957	12.00	30.00
RCA Victor LOP-1006	(M)	Belafonte Sings The Blues	1958	8.00	20.00
RCA Victor LPM-1887	(M)	To Wish You A Merry Christmas	1958	8.00	20.00
RCA Victor LPM-1927	(M)	Love Is A Gentle Thing	1959	6.00	15.00
RCA Victor LSP-1927	(S)	Love Is A Gentle Thing	1959	8.00	20.00
RCA Victor LOC-1507	(M)	Porgy And Bess	1959	6.00	15.00
RCA Victor LSO-1507	(S)	Porgy And Bess	1959	8.00	20.00

Label & Catalog #		Title	Year	VG+	NM
RCA Victor LOC-6006	(M)	Belafonte At Carnegie Hall	1959	6.00	15.00
RCA Victor LSO-6006	(S)	Belafonte At Carnegie Hall	1959	8.00	20.00
RCA Victor LPM-2022	(M)	My Lord What A Mornin'	1960	4.00	10.00
RCA Victor LSP-2022	(S)	My Lord What A Mornin'	1960	6.00	15.00
RCA Victor LOC-6007	(M)	Belafonte Returns To Carnegie Hall	1960	4.00	10.00
RCA Victor LSO-6007	(S)	Belafonte Returns To Carnegie Hall	1960	6.00	15.00
RCA Victor LPM-2194	(M)	Swing Dat Hammer	1960	4.00	10.00
RCA Victor LSP-2194	(S)	Swing Dat Hammer	1960	6.00	15.00
RCA Victor LPM-2388	(M)	Jump Up Calypso	1961	4.00	10.00
RCA Victor LSP-2388	(S)	Jump Up Calypso	1961	6.00	15.00
RCA Victor LPM-2499	(M)	The Midnight Special	1962	8.00	20.00
RCA Victor LSP-2499	(S)	The Midnight Special	1962	10.00	25.00
		(RCA 2499 features Bob Dylan's first appearance on record, playing harmonica on one track.)			
RCA Victor LPM-2574	(M)	The Many Moods Of Belafonte	1962	4.00	10.00
RCA Victor LSP-2574	(S)	The Many Moods Of Belafonte	1962	6.00	15.00
RCA Victor LPM-2626	(M)	To Wish You A Merry Christmas	1962	4.00	10.00
RCA Victor LSP-2626	(S)	To Wish You A Merry Christmas	1962	6.00	15.00
RCA Victor LPM-2695	(M)	Streets I Have Walked	1963	4.00	10.00
RCA Victor LSP-2695	(S)	Streets I Have Walked	1963	6.00	15.00

— Original RCA mono albums above have "Long Play" on the bottom of the label; stereo albums have "Living Stereo" on the bottom.—

BELEW, CARL

Decca DL-4074	(M)	Carl Belew	1960	12.00	30.00
Decca DL-74074	(S)	Carl Belew	1960	16.00	40.00
RCA Victor LPM-2848	(M)	Hello Out There	1964	5.00	12.00
RCA Victor LSP-2848	(S)	Hello Out There	1964	6.00	15.00
RCA Victor LPM 3381	(M)	Am I That Easy To Forget?	1965	5.00	12.00
RCA Victor LSP-3381	(S)	Am I That Easy To Forget?	1965	6.00	15.00
RCA Victor LPM-3919	(M)	Twelve Shades Of Belew	1968	12.00	30.00
RCA Victor LSP-3919	(S)	Twelve Shades Of Belew	1968	6.00	15.00

BELL, ARCHIE, & THE DRELLS

Atlantic 8181	(M)	Tighten Up	1968	10.00	25.00
Atlantic SD-8181	(S)	Tighten Up	1968	10.00	25.00
Atlantic SD-8204	(S)	I Can't Stop Dancing	1968	8.00	20.00
Atlantic SD-8226	(S)	There's Gonna Be A Showdown	1969	6.00	15.00

BELL, FREDDIE, & THE BELL BOYS

Mercury MG-20289	(M)	Rock And Roll—All Flavors	1958	100.00	200.00
20th Century TF-4146	(M)	Bells Are Swinging	1964	8.00	20.00
20th Century TFS-4146	(S)	Bells Are Swinging	1964	10.00	25.00

BELLINE, DENNY, & THE RICH KIDS

RCA Victor LPM-3655	(M)	Denny Belline And The Rich Kids	1966	6.00	15.00
RCA Victor LSP-3655	(S)	Denny Belline And The Rich Kids	1966	8.00	20.00

BELLUS, TONY

N.R.C. LPA-8	(M)	Robbin' The Cradle	1960	50.00	100.00

BELMONTS, THE
Refer to Dion & The Belmonts.

Sabina SALP-5001	(M)	The Belmonts' Carnival Of Hits	1962	50.00	100.00
Dot DLP-25949	(S)	Summer Love	1969	12.00	30.00
Buddah BDS-5123	(S)	Cigars, Acappella, Candy	1972	16.00	40.00
Strawberry 6001	(S)	Cheek To Cheek	1978	6.00	15.00

BELVIN, JESSE

RCA LPM-2089	(M)	Just Jesse Belvin	1959	14.00	35.00
RCA LSP-2089	(S)	Just Jesse Belvin	1959	20.00	50.00
RCA LPM-2105	(M)	Mr. Easy	1960	12.00	30.00
RCA LSP-2105	(S)	Mr. Easy	1960	16.00	40.00
Camden CAL-960	(M)	Jesse Belvin's Best	1966	5.00	12.00
Camden CAS-960	(S)	Jesse Belvin's Best	1966	6.00	15.00

BENATAR, PAT
Pat was formerly a member of Coxan's Army.

Mobile Fidelity MFSL-057	(S)	In The Heat Of The Night	197?	6.00	15.00

Label & Catalog #		Title	Year	VG+	NM
BENDIX, WILLIAM					
Cricket CR-30	(M)	**Famous Pirate Stories**	1959	12.00	30.00

Vicki Benet, a French torch singer, has yet to receive any real attention from collectors, unless one happens to collect attractive female cover photos.

BENET, VICKI					
Decca DL-8233	(M)	**Vicki Benet**	1956	10.00	25.00
Decca DL-8381	(M)	**The French Touch**	1956	10.00	25.00
Liberty LRP-3103	(M)	**Sing To Me Of Love**	1960	8.00	20.00
Liberty LST-7103	(S)	**Sing To Me Of Love**	1960	10.00	25.00
BENNETT, BETTY					
Trend TL-1006 (10")	(M)	**Betty Bennett Sings Previn Arrangements**	1954	30.00	60.00
Atlantic 1226	(M)	**Nobody Else But Me**	1956	16.00	40.00
Kapp LP-1052	(M)	**Blue Sunday**	1957	16.00	40.00
United Arts. UAL-3070	(M)	**I Love To Sing**	1959	10.00	25.00
United Arts. UAS-6070	(S)	**I Love To Sing**	1959	14.00	35.00
BENNETT, BOYD					
King 594	(M)	**Boyd Bennett**	1956	1,400.00	2,000.00
BENNETT, TONY					
Columbia CL-6221 (10")	(M)	**Because Of You**	1952	30.00	60.00
Columbia CL-2507 (10")	(M)	**Alone At Last With Tony Bennett**	1955	20.00	50.00
Columbia CL-2550 (10")	(M)	**Because Of You**	1956	20.00	50.00
Columbia CL-613	(M)	**Treasure Chest Of Song Hits**	1955	16.00	40.00
Columbia CL-621	(M)	**Cloud Seven**	1955	16.00	40.00
— Original Columbia albums above have "Long Playing" on the bottom.—					
Columbia CL-938	(M)	**Tony**	1957	12.00	30.00
Columbia CL-1079	(M)	**The Beat Of My Heart**	1957	12.00	30.00
Columbia CL-1186	(M)	**Long Ago And Far Away**	1958	12.00	30.00
Columbia CL-1229	(M)	**Tony's Greatest Hits**	1958	12.00	30.00
Columbia CL-1292	(M)	**Blue Velvet**	1959	12.00	30.00
Columbia CL-2343	(M)	**If I Ruled The World**	1959	12.00	30.00
Columbia CL-1294	(M)	**Tony Bennett In Person**	1959	6.00	15.00
Columbia CS-8104	(S)	**Tony Bennett In Person**	1959	8.00	20.00

Label & Catalog #		Title	Year	VG+	NM
Columbia CL-1301	(M)	Hometown, My Hometown	1959	6.00	15.00
Columbia CS-8107	(S)	Hometown, My Hometown	1959	8.00	20.00
Columbia CL-1429	(M)	To My Wonderful One	1960	6.00	15.00
Columbia CS-8226	(S)	To My Wonderful One	1960	8.00	20.00
Columbia CL-1446	(M)	Tony Sings For Two	1960	6.00	15.00
Columbia CS-8242	(S)	Tony Sings For Two	1960	8.00	20.00
Columbia CL-1471	(M)	Alone Together	1960	6.00	15.00
Columbia CS-8262	(S)	Alone Together	1960	8.00	20.00
Columbia CL-1535	(M)	More Tony's Greatest Hits	1960	6.00	15.00
Columbia CS-8335	(S)	More Tony's Greatest Hits	1960	8.00	20.00
Columbia CL-1559	(M)	A String Of Harold Arlen	1960	6.00	15.00
Columbia CS-8359	(S)	A String Of Harold Arlen	1960	8.00	20.00
Roulette R-25072	(M)	Count Basie Swings/Tony Sings	1961	6.00	15.00
Roulette SR-25072	(S)	Count Basie Swings/Tony Sings	1961	8.00	20.00
Roulette R-25231	(M)	Bennett And Basie Strike Up The Band	1961	6.00	15.00
Roulette SR-25231	(S)	Bennett And Basie Strike Up The Band	1961	8.00	20.00
Columbia CL-1658	(M)	My Heart Sings	1961	6.00	15.00
Columbia CS-8458	(S)	My Heart Sings	1961	8.00	20.00
Columbia CL-1763	(M)	Mr. Broadway	1962	6.00	15.00
Columbia CS-8563	(S)	Mr. Broadway	1962	8.00	20.00
Columbia CL-1852	(M)	Tony's Greatest Hits	1962	8.00	20.00
Columbia CS-8652	(E)	Tony's Greatest Hits	1962	5.00	12.00
Columbia CL-1869	(M)	I Left My Heart In San Francisco	1962	6.00	15.00
Columbia CS-8669	(S)	I Left My Heart In San Francisco	1962	8.00	20.00
Columbia C2L-23	(M)	Tony Bennett At Carnegie Hall	1962	6.00	15.00
Columbia C2S-23	(S)	Tony Bennett At Carnegie Hall	1962	8.00	20.00
— Original Columbia albums above have three white "eye" logos on each side of the spindle hole.—					
Columbia CL-2000	(M)	I Wanna Be Around	1963	5.00	12.00
Columbia CS 8800	(S)	I Wanna Be Around	1963	6.00	15.00
Columbia CL-2056	(M)	This Is All I Ask	1963	5.00	12.00
Columbia CS-8856	(S)	This Is All I Ask	1963	6.00	15.00
Columbia CL-2141	(M)	The Many Moods Of Tony	1964	5.00	12.00
Columbia CS-8941	(S)	The Many Moods Of Tony	1964	6.00	15.00
Columbia CL-2175	(M)	When Lights Are Low	1964	5.00	12.00
Columbia CS-8975	(S)	When Lights Are Low	1964	6.00	15.00
Columbia CL-2285	(M)	Who Can I Turn To?	1964	5.00	12.00
Columbia CS-9085	(S)	Who Can I Turn To?	1964	6.00	15.00
Columbia CL-2343	(M)	Songs For The Jet Set	1965	5.00	12.00
Columbia CS-9143	(S)	Songs For The Jet Set	1965	6.00	15.00
Columbia CL-2373	(M)	Tony's Greatest Hits, Volume 3	1965	5.00	12.00
Columbia CS-9173	(S)	Tony's Greatest Hits, Volume 3	1965	6.00	15.00
Columbia CL-2472	(M)	The Movie Song Album	1966	5.00	12.00
Columbia CS-9272	(S)	The Movie Song Album	1966	6.00	15.00
Columbia CL-2560	(M)	A Time For Love	1966	5.00	12.00
Columbia CS-9360	(S)	A Time For Love	1966	6.00	15.00
Columbia OL-6550	(M)	The Oscar (Soundtrack)	1966	14.00	35.00
Columbia OS-2950	(S)	The Oscar (Soundtrack)	1966	20.00	50.00
Columbia CSL-552	(M)	Singer Presents Tony Bennett	1966	6.00	15.00
Columbia CSS-552	(S)	Singer Presents Tony Bennett	1966	8.00	20.00
Columbia CL-2653	(M)	Tony Makes It Happen!	1967	4.00	10.00
Columbia CS-9453	(S)	Tony Makes It Happen!	1967	5.00	12.00
Columbia CS-9573	(S)	For Once In My Life	1968	5.00	12.00
Columbia CS-9814	(S)	Tony Bennett's Greatest Hits, Volume 4	1969	5.00	12.00
Columbia CS-9882	(S)	I've Gotta Be Me	1969	5.00	12.00
Columbia CS-9980	(S)	Tony Sings The Great Hits Of Today	1970	5.00	12.00
—Original Columbia albums above have "360 Sound" on the bottom of the label.—					
Mobile Fidelity MFSL-117	(S)	The Bennett/Evans Album	1981	8.00	20.00

BENT WIND

Trend T-1015	(S)	Sussex	196?	See note below	
		(Rare. Estimated near mint value $1,000-2,000.)			

BENTON, BROOK

Epic LG-3573	(M)	Brook Benton At His Best	195?	12.00	30.00
Mercury MG-20421	(M)	It's Just A Matter Of Time	1959	12.00	30.00
Mercury SR-60421	(M)	It's Just A Matter Of Time	1959	16.00	40.00
Mercury MG-20464	(M)	Brook Benton	1959	12.00	30.00
Mercury SR-60146	(S)	Brook Benton	1959	16.00	40.00

Label & Catalog #		Title	Year	VG+	NM
Mercury MG-20565	(M)	So Many Ways I Love You	1959	12.00	30.00
Mercury SR-60225	(S)	So Many Ways I Love You	1959	16.00	40.00
Mercury MG-20602	(M)	Songs I Love To Sing	1960	8.00	20.00
Mercury SR-60602	(S)	Songs I Love To Sing	1960	10.00	25.00
Mercury MG-20607	(M)	Brook Benton's Golden Hits	1961	8.00	20.00
Mercury SR-60607	(S)	Brook Benton's Golden Hits	1961	10.00	25.00
Mercury MG-20619	(M)	If You Believe	1961	6.00	15.00
Mercury SR-60619	(S)	If You Believe	1961	8.00	20.00
Mercury MG-20641	(M)	The Boll Weevil Song	1961	6.00	15.00
Mercury SR-60641	(S)	The Boll Weevil Song	1961	8.00	20.00
Mercury MG-20673	(M)	There Goes That Song Again	1962	6.00	15.00
Mercury SR-60673	(S)	There Goes That Song Again	1962	8.00	20.00
Mercury MG-20740	(M)	Singing The Blues	1962	6.00	15.00
Mercury SR-60740	(S)	Singing The Blues	1962	8.00	20.00
Mercury MG-20774	(M)	Brook Benton's Golden Hits, Volume 2	1963	6.00	15.00
Mercury SR-60774	(S)	Brook Benton's Golden Hits, Volume 2	1963	8.00	20.00
Mercury MG-20830	(M)	Best Ballads Of Broadway	1963	6.00	15.00
Mercury SR-60830	(S)	Best Ballads Of Broadway	1963	8.00	20.00
Mercury MG-20886	(M)	Born To Sing The Blues	1964	6.00	15.00
Mercury SR-60886	(S)	Born To Sing The Blues	1964	8.00	20.00
— Original Mercury albums above have black labels with silver print.—					
Mercury MG-20918	(M)	On The Country Side	1964	5.00	12.00
Mercury SR-60918	(S)	On The Country Side	1964	6.00	15.00
Mercury MG-20934	(M)	This Bitter Earth	1964	5.00	12.00
Mercury SR-60934	(S)	This Bitter Earth	1964	6.00	15.00
RCA Victor LPM-3514	(M)	That Old Feeling	1966	5.00	12.00
RCA Victor LSP-3514	(S)	That Old Feeling	1966	6.00	15.00
RCA Victor LPM-3526	(M)	Mother Nature, Father Time	1966	5.00	12.00
RCA Victor LSP-3526	(S)	Mother Nature, Father Time	1966	6.00	15.00
RCA Victor LPM-3590	(M)	My Country	1966	5.00	12.00
RCA Victor LSP-3590	(S)	My Country	1966	6.00	15.00
Reprise R-6268	(M)	Laura, What's He Got That I Ain't Got?	1967	5.00	12.00
Reprise RS-6268	(S)	Laura, What's He Got That I Ain't Got?	1967	6.00	15.00

BENTON, BROOK, & DINAH WASHINGTON

Mercury MG-20588	(M)	The Two Of Us	1960	8.00	20.00
Mercury SR-60244	(S)	The Two Of Us	1960	10.00	25.00

BERGEN, POLLY

Jubilee 14 (10")	(M)	Polly Bergen	1955	16.00	40.00
Columbia CL-994	(M)	Bergen Sings Morgan	1957	12.00	30.00
Columbia CL-1031	(M)	The Party's Over	1957	12.00	30.00
Columbia CL-1138	(M)	Polly And Her Pop	1958	10.00	25.00
Columbia OL-2014	(M)	First Impressions	1959	10.00	25.00
Columbia CL-1218	(M)	My Heart Sings	1959	8.00	20.00
Columbia CS-8018	(S)	My Heart Sings	1959	10.00	25.00
Columbia CL-1300	(M)	All Alone By The Telephone	1959	8.00	20.00
Columbia CS-8100	(S)	All Alone By The Telephone	1959	10.00	25.00
Columbia CL-1481	(M)	Four Seasons Of Love	1960	6.00	15.00
Columbia CS-8246	(S)	Four Seasons Of Love	1960	8.00	20.00
Columbia CL-1632	(M)	"Do Re Mi" And "Annie Get Your Gun"	1961	6.00	15.00
Columbia CS-8432	(S)	"Do Re Mi" And "Annie Get Your Gun"	1961	8.00	20.00
— Original Columbia albums above have three white "eye" logos on each side of the spindle hole.—					
Columbia CL-2171	(M)	My Heart Sings	1964	5.00	12.00
Columbia CS-8971	(S)	My Heart Sings	1964	6.00	15.00
Philips PHM-200084	(M)	Act One-Sing, Too	1963	5.00	12.00
Philips PHS-600084	(S)	Act One-Sing, Too	1963	6.00	15.00

BERGEN, FRANCES

Columbia CL-873	(M)	Beguiling Miss	1956	12.00	30.00

BERLE, MILTON

Forum F-9005	(M)	Songs My Mother Loved	195?	12.00	30.00

BERNARD, ROD

Jin LP-4007	(M)	Rod Bernard	196?	20.00	50.00

BERRY, BROOKS

Bluesville BV-1074	(M)	Brooks Berry	1963	10.00	25.00

Label & Catalog #		Title	Year	VG+	NM
BERRY, CHUCK					
Berry also recorded with Bo Diddley.					
Chess LP-1426	(DJ)	**After School Session**	1958	180.00	300.00
Chess LP-1426	(M)	**After School Session**	1958	50.00	100.00
Chess LP-1432	(DJ)	**One Dozen Berrys**	1958	180.00	300.00
Chess LP-1432	(M)	**One Dozen Berrys**	1958	50.00	100.00
Chess LP-1435	(DJ)	**Berry Is On Top**	1959	180.00	300.00
Chess LP-1435	(M)	**Berry Is On Top**	1959	50.00	100.00
Chess LP-1448	(DJ)	**Rockin' At The Hops**	1960	150.00	250.00
Chess LP-1448	(M)	**Rockin' At The Hops**	1960	40.00	80.00
Chess LP-1456	(DJ)	**New Juke Box Hits**	1961	150.00	250.00
Chess LP-1456	(M)	**New Juke Box Hits**	1961	40.00	80.00
Chess LP-1465	(DJ)	**Chuck Berry Twist**	1962	100.00	200.00
Chess LP-1465	(M)	**Chuck Berry Twist**	1962	30.00	60.00
Chess LP-1465	(DJ)	**More Chuck Berry**	1963	100.00	200.00
Chess LP-1465	(M)	**More Chuck Berry**	1963	30.00	60.00
Chess LP-1480	(DJ)	**Chuck Berry On Stage**	1963	100.00	200.00
Chess LP-1480	(M)	**Chuck Berry On Stage**	1963	20.00	50.00
Chess LP-1485	(DJ)	**Chuck Berry's Greatest Hits**	1964	75.00	150.00
Chess LP-1485	(M)	**Chuck Berry's Greatest Hits**	1964	16.00	40.00
Chess LP-1488	(DJ)	**St. Louis To Liverpool**	1964	75.00	150.00
Chess LP-1488	(M)	**St. Louis To Liverpool**	1964	20.00	50.00
Chess LPS-1488	(P)	**St. Louis To Liverpool**	1964	30.00	60.00
— Original Chess albums above have black & silver labels.—					
Chess LP-1495	(DJ)	**Chuck Berry In London** (White label)	1965	75.00	150.00
Chess LP-1495	(M)	**Chuck Berry In London**	1965	14.00	35.00
Chess LPS-1495	(S)	**Chuck Berry In London**	1965	16.00	40.00
Chess LP-1498	(DJ)	**Fresh Berry's** (White label)	1965	75.00	150.00
Chess LP-1498	(M)	**Fresh Berry's**	1965	14.00	35.00
Chess LPS-1498	(S)	**Fresh Berry's**	1965	16.00	40.00
— Original Chess albums above have blue labels with a silver knight logo on top.—					
Chess LPS-1426	(E)	**After School Session**	1966	8.00	20.00
Chess LPS-1432	(E)	**One Dozen Berrys**	1966	8.00	20.00
Chess LPS-1435	(E)	**Berry Is On Top**	1966	8.00	20.00
Chess LPS-1448	(E)	**Rockin' At The Hops**	1966	8.00	20.00
Chess LPS-1456	(E)	**New Juke Box Hits**	1966	8.00	20.00
Chess LPS-1465	(E)	**More Chuck Berry**	1966	8.00	20.00
Chess LPS-1480	(E)	**Chuck Berry On Stage**	1966	8.00	20.00
Chess LPS-1485	(E)	**Chuck Berry's Greatest Hits**	1966	8.00	20.00
Chess LPS-1488	(P)	**St. Louis To Liverpool**	1966	8.00	20.00
Chess LPS-1495	(S)	**Chuck Berry In London**	1966	8.00	20.00
Chess LPS-1498	(S)	**Fresh Berry's**	1966	8.00	20.00
Chess LP-1514	(M)	**Chuck Berry's Golden Decade**	1967	10.00	25.00
Chess LPS-1514	(E)	**Chuck Berry's Golden Decade**	1967	6.00	15.00
— Chess albums above have blue & white labels.—					
Mercury MG-21103	(M)	**Chuck Berry's Golden Hits**	1967	6.00	15.00
Mercury SR-61103	(S)	**Chuck Berry's Golden Hits**	1967	6.00	15.00
Mercury MG-21123	(M)	**Chuck Berry In Memphis**	1967	8.00	20.00
Mercury SR-61123	(S)	**Chuck Berry In Memphis**	1967	10.00	25.00
Mercury MG-21138	(M)	**Live At The Fillmore Auditorium**	1967	8.00	20.00
Mercury SR-61138	(S)	**Live At The Fillmore Auditorium**	1967	10.00	25.00
		(Berry is backed by The Steve Miller Blues Band.)			
Mercury SR-61176	(S)	**From St. Louis To Frisco**	1968	8.00	20.00
Mercury SR-61223	(S)	**Concerto In B. Goode**	1969	8.00	20.00
Mercury SRM-2-6501	(S)	**St. Louie To Frisco To Memphis** (2 LPs)	1972	6.00	15.00
		(Repackage of previous Mercury material.)			
Chess LPS-1550	(S)	**Back Home**	1970	8.00	20.00
Chess CH-50008	(S)	**San Francisco Dues**	1971	8.00	20.00
Chess CH-60020	(P)	**The London Sessions** (Gatefold cover)	1972	6.00	15.00
— Original Chess albums above have blue labels.—					
Chess 2CH-60023	(P)	**Golden Decade, Volume 2** (2 LPs)	1973	6.00	15.00
Chess CH-50043	(S)	**Bio** (Gatefold cover)	1973	5.00	12.00
Chess 2CH-60028	(P)	**Golden Decade, Volume 3** (2 LPs)	1974	6.00	15.00
BERRY, RICHARD (& THE SOUL SEARCHERS)					
Crown CLP-5371	(M)	**Richard Berry And The Dreamers**	1963	14.00	35.00
Crown CST-371	(E)	**Richard Berry And The Dreamers**	1963	10.00	25.00
Pam 1001	(M)	**Live At The Century Club**	196?	20.00	50.00
Pam 1002	(M)	**Wild Berry**	196?	20.00	50.00

Label & Catalog #		Title	Year	VG+	NM
BEST, PETE					
Best was a member of the Beatles before they recorded for EMI/Parlophone.					
Savage BM-71	(M)	**Best Of The Beatles**	1965	75.00	150.00
BETHLEHEM ASYLUM					
Ampex 10106	(S)	**Commit Yourself**	1970	6.00	15.00
Ampex 10124	(S)	**Bethlehem Asylum**	1971	6.00	15.00
BEVERLY HILL BILLIES, THE					
The Hill Billies are a studio concoction featuring Elton Britt.					
Rar-Arts 1000	(M)	**Those Fabulous Beverly Hill Billies**	196?	20.00	50.00
BEZALEL & THE SABRAS: *Refer to* **THE SABRAS**					
BIBB, LEON					
Vanguard VRS-2067	(M)	**Love Songs**	1960	10.00	25.00
Vanguard VRS-9041	(M)	**Folksongs**	1961	10.00	25.00
Vanguard VRS-9058	(M)	**Tol' My Captain**	1962	10.00	25.00
BIG BEATS, THE					
Liberty LRP-3407	(M)	**The Big Beats Live**	1965	8.00	20.00
Liberty LST-7407	(S)	**The Big Beats Live**	1965	10.00	25.00
BIG BOPPER, THE [J.P. RICHARDSON]					
Mercury MG-20402	(M)	**Chantilly Lace** *(Black label)*	1959	180.00	300.00
Mercury MG-20402	(M)	**Chantilly Lace**	1964	75.00	150.00
		(Red label with black & white logo on top.)			
Mercury MG-20402	(M)	**Chantilly Lace**	1971	6.00	15.00
		(Red label with twelve oval logos around the perimeter.)			
BIG BROTHER					
All American 5770	(M)	**Confusion**	1970	90.00	180.00
BIG BROTHER & THE HOLDING COMPANY					
Big Brother's first two albums feature Janis Joplin; the final two albums feature Nick Gravenites.					
Mainstream 56099	(M)	**Big Brother & The Holding Company**	1967	8.00	20.00
Mainstream S-6099	(S)	**Big Brother & The Holding Company**	1967	6.00	15.00
Columbia KCL-2900	(M)	**Cheap Thrills**	1968	16.00	40.00
Columbia KCS-9700	(S)	**Cheap Thrills** *("360 Sound" label)*	1968	8.00	20.00
Columbia C-30222	(S)	**Be A Brother**	1970	8.00	20.00
Columbia C-30738	(S)	**How Hard It Is**	1971	8.00	20.00
BIG DADDY					
Gee G-704	(M)	**Big Daddy's Blues** *(Red label)*	1960	20.00	50.00
Gee SG-704	(S)	**Big Daddy's Blues** *(Red label)*	1960	40.00	80.00
Regent 6106	(M)	**Twist Party**	1962	10.00	25.00
BIG FOOT					
Winro 1004	(S)	**Big Foot**	1968	8.00	20.00
BIG MAYBELLE					
Savoy MG-14005	(M)	**Big Maybelle Sings**	1957	40.00	80.00
Savoy MG-14011	(M)	**Blues, Candy And Big Maybelle**	1958	40.00	80.00
Brunswick BL-54107	(M)	**What More Can A Woman Do**	1962	10.00	25.00
Brunswick BL-754107	(S)	**What More Can A Woman Do**	1962	12.00	30.00
Scepter S-522	(M)	**The Soul Of Big Maybelle**	1964	5.00	12.00
Scepter SS-522	(S)	**The Soul Of Big Maybelle**	1964	6.00	15.00
Rajac R-522	(M)	**Got A Brand New Bag**	1967	5.00	12.00
Rajac RS-522	(S)	**Got A Brand New Bag**	1967	6.00	15.00
BIG MILLER					
United Arts. UAL-3047	(M)	**Did You Ever Hear The Blues?**	1959	12.00	30.00
United Arts. UAS-6047	(S)	**Did You Ever Hear The Blues?**	1959	16.00	40.00
BIG STAR					
Big Star features Alex Chilton, formerly of The Box Tops.					
Ardent ADS-2803	(S)	**#1 Record**	1972	10.00	25.00
Ardent ADS-1501	(S)	**Radio City**	1974	10.00	25.00
PVC 7903	(S)	**Big Star's Third**	1978	10.00	25.00

Label & Catalog #		Title	Year	VG+	NM

BIG THREE, THE
The Big Three are Cass Elliot, James Hendricks and Tim Rose.

Label & Catalog #		Title	Year	VG+	NM
FM 307	(M)	The Big Three	1963	12.00	30.00
FM FS-307	(S)	The Big Three	1963	14.00	35.00
FM 311	(M)	Live At The Recording Studio	1964	12.00	30.00
FM FS-311	(S)	Live At The Recording Studio	1964	14.00	35.00
Roulette R-42000	(M)	The Big Three Featuring Cass Elliot	1967	6.00	15.00
Roulette SR-42000	(S)	The Big Three Featuring Cass Elliot	1967	8.00	20.00

BIKEL, THEODORE

Elektra EKL-32	(M)	Songs Of Israel	195?	8.00	20.00
Elektra EKL-105	(M)	Actor's Holiday	195?	8.00	20.00
Elektra EKL-175	(M)	Bravo Bikel	195?	8.00	20.00

BIKEL, THEODORE, & GEULA GILL

Elektra EKL-150	(M)	Russian Gypsy	195?	8.00	20.00
Elektra EKL-161	(M)	Songs From Just About Everywhere	195?	8.00	20.00
Elektra EKL-185	(M)	Songs Old And New	195?	8.00	20.00

BIKEL, THEODORE, & CYNTHIA GOODING

Elektra EKL-109	(M)	A Young Man And A Maid	195?	8.00	20.00

BILLION DOLLAR BABIES, THE
The Babies were former members of Alice Cooper's band.

Polydor PRO-022	(DJ)	Battle Axe (Sampler)	1977	8.00	20.00
Polydor PD1-6100	(S)	Battle Axe	1977	5.00	12.00

BIRTH CONTROL

Prophesy PRS-1002	(S)	A New German Rock Group	1970	10.00	25.00

BISHOP, ELVIN [THE ELVIN BISHOP GROUP]

Fillmore F-30001	(S)	The Elvin Bishop Group	1969	6.00	15.00
Fillmore Z-30239	(S)	Feel It	1970	6.00	15.00

BISHOP, JOEY

ABC-Paramount 408	(M)	Joey Bishop Sings Country & Western	1962	6.00	15.00
ABC-Paramount S-408	(S)	Joey Bishop Sings Country & Western	1962	8.00	20.00

BITTER END SINGERS, THE

Mercury MG-20986	(M)	Discover The Bitter End Singers	1965	5.00	12.00
Mercury SR-60986	(S)	Discover The Bitter End Singers	1965	6.00	15.00
Mercury MG-21018	(M)	Through Our Eyes	1965	5.00	12.00
Mercury SR-61018	(S)	Through Our Eyes	1965	6.00	15.00

BLACK, CILLA

Capitol T-2308	(M)	Is It Love?	1965	8.00	20.00
Capitol ST-2308	(S)	Is It Love?	1965	10.00	25.00

BLACK, JEANNE

Capitol T-1513	(M)	A Little Bit Lonely	1961	6.00	15.00
Capitol ST-1513	(S)	A Little Bit Lonely	1961	8.00	20.00

BLACK COMBO, BILL
Bill Black was Elvis Presley's bass player from his first recordings for Sun in 1954 through his first golden era with RCA Victor, 1956-1959.

Hi 12001	(M)	Smokie	1960	12.00	40.00
Hi SHL-32001	(E)	Smokie	196?	8.00	20.00
Hi 12002	(M)	Saxy Jazz	1960	12.00	40.00
Hi SHL-32002	(E)	Saxy Jazz	196?	8.00	20.00
Hi 12003	(M)	Solid And Raunchy	1960	12.00	40.00
Hi SHL-32003	(E)	Solid And Raunchy	1960	8.00	20.00
Hi 12004	(M)	That Wonderful Feeling	1961	8.00	20.00
Hi SHL-32004	(S)	That Wonderful Feeling	1961	10.00	30.00
Hi 12005	(M)	Movin'	1961	8.00	20.00
Hi SHL-32005	(S)	Movin'	1961	10.00	30.00
Hi 12006	(M)	Bill Black's Record Hop	1961	8.00	20.00
Hi SHL-32006	(S)	Bill Black's Record Hop	1961	10.00	30.00

Label & Catalog #		Title	Year	VG+	NM
Hi 12006	(M)	Let's Twist Her	1962	6.00	15.00
Hi SHL-32006	(S)	Let's Twist Her	1962	8.00	20.00
Hi 12009	(M)	The Untouchable Sound	1963	6.00	15.00
Hi SHL-32009	(S)	The Untouchable Sound	1963	8.00	20.00
Hi SR-8689	(DJ)	Sears Silvertone Presents	1963	12.00	30.00
		(Stereo presentation album.)			
Hi 12012	(M)	Bill Black's Greatest Hits	1963	5.00	12.00
Hi SHL-32012	(S)	Bill Black's Greatest Hits	1963	6.00	15.00
Hi 12013	(M)	Bill Black's Combo Goes West	1963	5.00	12.00
Hi SHL-32013	(S)	Bill Black's Combo Goes West	1963	6.00	15.00
Hi 12015	(M)	Bill Black Plays The Blues	1964	6.00	15.00
Hi SHL-32015	(S)	Bill Black Plays The Blues	1964	8.00	20.00
Hi 12017	(M)	Bill Black Plays Tunes By Chuck Berry	1964	6.00	15.00
Hi SHL-32017	(S)	Bill Black Plays Tunes By Chuck Berry	1964	8.00	20.00
Hi 12020	(M)	Bill Black's Combo Goes Big Band	1964	5.00	12.00
Hi SHL-32020	(S)	Bill Black's Combo Goes Big Band	1964	6.00	15.00
Hi 12023	(M)	More Solid And Raunchy	1965	5.00	12.00
Hi SHL-32023	(S)	More Solid And Raunchy	1965	6.00	15.00
Hi 12027	(M)	Mr. Beat	1965	5.00	12.00
Hi SHL-32027	(S)	Mr. Beat	1965	6.00	15.00
Hi 12032	(M)	All Timers	1966	5.00	12.00
HI SHL-32032	(S)	All Timers	1966	6.00	15.00
Hi 12033	(M)	Black Lace	1967	5.00	12.00
Hi SHL-32033	(S)	Black Lace	1967	6.00	15.00
Hi 12041	(M)	Beat Goes On	1968	6.00	15.00
Hi SHL-32041	(S)	Beat Goes On	1968	6.00	15.00

— Original Hi albums above have greyish labels.—

BLACK DIAMONDS, THE

Alshire 5220	(S)	Tribute To Jimi Hendrix	1971	6.00	15.00

BLACK LIGHTNING

Tower ST-5129	(S)	Shades Of Black Lightning	1968	6.00	15.00

BLACK MERDA

Chess LP-1551	(S)	Black Merda	1970	12.00	30.00

BLACK OAK ARKANSAS

Atco QD-7019	(Q)	Raunch And Roll/Live	1973	6.00	15.00
Capricorn CEP-0005	(DJ)	I'd Rather Be Sailing	1978	6.00	15.00

BLACK ORCHIDS, THE

NR 4680	(S)	The Black Orchids (No cover)	1972	30.00	60.00

BLACK PEARL

Atlantic SD-8220	(S)	Black Pearl	1969	6.00	15.00
Prophesy PRS-1001	(S)	Black Pearl Live	1970	8.00	20.00

BLACK SABBATH

The original Sabbath featured Ozzie Osbourne, later replaced by Ronnie James Dio and Ian Gillan.

Warner Bros. WS-1871	(S)	Black Sabbath	1969	6.00	15.00
Warner Bros. WS-1887	(S)	Paranoid	1971	5.00	12.00
Warner Bros. WS4-1887	(Q)	Paranoid	1974	8.00	20.00

BLACKFOOT, J. D.

Mercury SRM-1-61288	(S)	The Ultimate Prophecy	1970	20.00	50.00

BLACKHORSE

DSDA 001	(S)	Blackhorse	197?	20.00	50.00

BLACKMAN, HONOR

London LL-3408	(M)	Everything I've Got	1964	8.00	20.00
London PS-408	(S)	Everything I've Got	1964	12.00	30.00

BLACKWELL, OTIS

Davis 109	(M)	Singin' The Blues	1956	75.00	150.00

BLACKWOOD APOLOGY

Fontana SRF-67591	(S)	House Of Leather	1969	6.00	15.00

Label & Catalog #		Title	Year	VG+	NM
BLAINE, HAL, & THE YOUNG COUGARS					
RCA Victor LPM-2834	(M)	Deuces, T's, Roadsters And Drums	1963	12.00	30.00
RCA Victor LSP-2834	(S)	Deuces, T's, Roadsters And Drums	1963	16.00	40.00
BLAINE, HAL					
Dunhill D-50019	(M)	Psychedelic Percussion	1967	5.00	12.00
Dunhill DS-50019	(S)	Psychedelic Percussion	1967	6.00	15.00
BLAINE, VIVIAN					
Mercury MG-20233	(M)	Songs From The Ziegfield Follies	1957	12.00	30.00
Mercury MG-20234	(M)	Songs From "The Great White Way"	1957	12.00	30.00
Mercury MG-20321	(M)	Pal Joey	1958	12.00	30.00
BLAIR, SALLIE					
Bethlehem BCP-6009	(M)	Squeeze Me	1957	16.00	40.00
MGM E-3723	(M)	Hello, Tiger!	1959	14.00	35.00
BLAKE, BETTY					
Bethlehem 6059	(M)	In A Tender Mood	1956	16.00	40.00
BLANC, MEL					
Capitol H-436 (10")	(M)	Party Panic	1953	35.00	70.00
Capitol JAO-3251	(M)	Woody Woodpecker And His Talent Show	1961	20.00	50.00
Capitol J-3257	(M)	Bugs Bunny And His Friends	1961	20.00	50.00
Capitol J-3261	(M)	Tweety Pie And Other Favorites	1962	20.00	50.00
Capitol J-3263	(M)	Woody Woodpecker's Picnic	1962	20.00	50.00
Capitol J-3266	(M)	Bugs Bunny In Storyland	1963	20.00	50.00
BLAND, BOBBY "BLUE"					
Duke DLP-74	(M)	Two Steps From The Blues	1961	50.00	100.00
		(Originally issued on a purple & yellow label.)			
Duke DLP-74	(M)	Two Steps From The Blues	1961	20.00	50.00
Duke DLP-75	(M)	Here's The Man	1962	20.00	50.00
Duke DLP-77	(M)	Call On Me	1963	20.00	50.00
Duke DLP-78	(M)	Ain't Nothing You Can Do	1964	20.00	50.00
Duke DLP-79	(M)	The Soul Of The Man	1966	12.00	30.00
Duke DLPS-79	(S)	The Soul Of The Man	1966	16.00	40.00
Duke DLP-84	(M)	The Best Of Bobby Bland	1967	6.00	20.00
Duke DLPS-84	(S)	The Best Of Bobby Bland	1967	6.00	25.00
Duke DLP-88	(M)	Touch Of The Blues	1967	8.00	20.00
Duke DLPS-88	(S)	Touch Of The Blues	1967	6.00	25.00
Duke DLP-86	(M)	The Best Of Bobby Bland, Volume 2	1968	6.00	15.00
Duke DLPS-86	(P)	The Best Of Bobby Bland, Volume 2	1968	8.00	20.00
Duke DLPS-89	(S)	Spotlighting The Man	1969	6.00	15.00
Duke X-90	(S)	If Loving You Is Wrong	1970	6.00	15.00
		— Original Duke albums above have orange labels.—			
BLASTERS, THE					
Rollin' Rock 021	(S)	American Music	1980	30.00	60.00
BLESSED END					
T.N.S.	(M)	Movin' On	1971	180.00	300.00
BLIND FAITH					
Blind Faith is Ginger Baker, Eric Clapton, Rick Grech and Steve Winwood.					
Atco SD-33-304A	(S)	Blind Faith (Naked girl on cover)	1969	10.00	25.00
Atco SD-33-304B	(S)	Blind Faith (Attired group on cover)	1969	6.00	15.00
Mobile Fidelity MFSL-186	(S)	Blind Faith	198?	8.00	20.00
BLOCKER, DAN					
Trey TLP-903	(M)	Tales For Young 'Uns	196?	20.00	50.00
RCA Victor LPM-2896	(M)	Our Land, Our Heritage	1964	8.00	20.00
RCA Victor LSP-2896	(S)	Our Land, Our Heritage	1964	10.00	25.00
BLODWYN PIG					
A&M SP-4210	(S)	Ahead Rings Out	1969	6.00	15.00
A&M SP-4243	(S)	Getting To This	1970	6.00	15.00

Label & Catalog #		Title	Year	VG+	NM
BLOND					
Fontana SRF-67607	(S)	**Blond**	1969	8.00	20.00
BLONDE ON BLONDE					
Janus JLS-3003	(S)	**Contrasts**	1969	10.00	25.00
BLONDIE					
Blondie features Debbie Harry, formerly of Wind In The Willows.					
Private Stock PS-2035	(S)	**Blondie**	1975	8.00	20.00
Chrysalis CHP-5001	(S)	**Parallel Lines** (Picture disc)	1978	8.00	20.00
Chrysalis CHS-24	(DJ)	**At Home With Debbie Harry & Chris Stein** (Open-end interview with script.)	1981	10.00	25.00
Mobile Fidelity MFSL-050	(S)	**Parallel Lines**	1981	10.00	25.00
BLOOD, SWEAT & TEARS					
Originally the brainchild of Blues Project members Al Kooper and Steve Katz, BS&T was later fronted by David Clayton-Thomas.					
Columbia CS-9616	(S)	**Child Is Father To The Man**	1968	6.00	15.00
Columbia CS-9720	(S)	**Blood, Sweat And Tears**	1969	5.00	12.00
— Original Columbia albums above have "360 Sound" on the bottom of the label.—					
Columbia CQ-30994	(Q)	**Blood, Sweat And Tears**	1973	8.00	20.00
Columbia CQ-31170	(Q)	**Blood, Sweat And Tears' Greatest Hits**	1973	6.00	15.00
Columbia PCQ-32929	(Q)	**Mirror Image**	1974	6.00	15.00
Columbia HC-49619	(S)	**Child Is Father To The Man** (Half-speed)	1981	14.00	35.00
LAX L33-1865	(DJ)	**Nuclear Blues** (Gold vinyl)	1980	6.00	15.00
Direct Disk SD-16605	(S)	**Blood, Sweat And Tears**	198?	14.00	35.00
BLOOMFIELD, MIKE; AL KOOPER & STEPHEN STILLS					
Columbia CS-9701	(S)	**Super Session** ("360 Sound" label)	1968	6.00	15.00
Columbia PCQ-9701	(Q)	**Super Session**	1974	6.00	15.00
Mobile Fidelity MFSL-178	(S)	**Super Session**	198?	8.00	20.00
BLOSSOM DEARIE					
Verve V-2037	(M)	**Blossom Dearie**	1956	20.00	50.00
Verve V-2081	(M)	**Give Him The Ooh-La-La**	1958	16.00	40.00
Verve V-2109	(M)	**Comden And Green**	1959	12.00	30.00
Verve VS-6050	(S)	**Comden And Green**	1959	16.00	40.00
Verve V-2111	(M)	**Once Upon A Summertime**	1959	12.00	30.00
Verve VS-6020	(S)	**Once Upon A Summertime**	1959	16.00	40.00
Verve V-2125	(M)	**My Gentleman Friend**	1959	12.00	30.00
Verve VS-6112	(S)	**My Gentleman Friend**	1959	16.00	40.00
Verve V-2133	(M)	**Broadway Hit Songs**	1960	10.00	25.00
Verve V6-2133	(S)	**Broadway Hit Songs**	1960	14.00	35.00
BLOSSOMS, THE					
Lion 1007	(S)	**Shockwave**	1972	6.00	15.00
BLUE BARONS, THE					
Philips PHM-200017	(M)	**Twist To The Great Blues Hits**	1962	8.00	20.00
Philips PHS-600017	(S)	**Twist To The Great Blues Hits**	1962	10.00	25.00
BLUE BEATS, THE					
A.A. 133	(M)	**The Beatle Beat**	1964	20.00	50.00
BLUE CHEER					
Philips PHM-200264	(M)	**Vincebus Eruptum**	1968	14.00	35.00
Philips PHS-600264	(S)	**Vincebus Eruptum**	1968	10.00	25.00
Philips PHS-600278	(S)	**Outsideinside**	1968	10.00	25.00
Philips PHS-600305	(S)	**New! Improved! Blue Cheer**	1969	10.00	25.00
Philips PHS-600333	(S)	**Blue Cheer**	1970	10.00	25.00
— Original Philips albums above have black labels with no print on the bottom perimeter.—					
Philips PHS-600264	(S)	**Vincebus Eruptum**	1970	6.00	15.00
Philips PHS-600278	(S)	**Outsideinside**	1970	6.00	15.00
Philips PHS-600305	(S)	**New! Improved! Blue Cheer**	1970	6.00	15.00
Philips PHS-600333	(S)	**Blue Cheer**	1970	6.00	15.00
Philips PHS-600347	(S)	**The Original Human Being**	1970	8.00	20.00
Philips PHS-600350	(S)	**Oh! Pleasant Hope**	1971	8.00	20.00
— Philips albums above have black labels with "Distributed by Mercury" on the bottom.—					

Label & Catalog #		Title	Year	VG+	NM
BLUE DIAMONDS, THE					
London LL-3235	(M)	**Ramona**	1963	10.00	25.00
BLUE EMOTIONS, THE					
Ambient Sound 38346	(S)	**Doo-Wop Doo-Wop**	1982	4.00	10.00
BLUE JAYS, THE					
Milestone 1001	(M)	**The Blue Jays Meet Little Caesar**	196?	20.00	50.00
BLUE MOUNTAIN EAGLE					
Atco SD-33-324	(S)	**Blue Mountain Eagle**	1970	8.00	20.00
Atco (No number)	(DJ)	**Blue Mountain Eagle Two**	1970	12.00	30.00
BLUE OYSTER CULT					
Columbia XSM-157265	(DJ)	**Live 'Leg** (No cover)	1972	35.00	70.00
Columbia PCQ-32017	(Q)	**Tyranny And Mutation**	1973	8.00	20.00
Columbia PCQ-32858	(Q)	**Secret Treaties**	1974	8.00	20.00
Columbia AS-986	(DJ)	**Blue Oyster Cult** (Sampler)	1981	8.00	20.00
Columbia AS-1441	(DJ)	**Blue Oyster Cult Live** (Sampler)	1982	8.00	20.00
BLUE RIDGE RANGERS , THE					
The Blue Ridge Rangers are John Fogerty of Creedence Clearwater.					
Fantasy F-9415	(S)	**The Blue Ridge Rangers**	1973	8.00	20.00
BLUE SKY BOYS, THE					
Starday SLP-205	(M)	**Rare Treasury Of Old Song Gems**	1963	12.00	30.00
Starday SLP-257	(M)	**Together Again**	1964	12.00	30.00
Starday SLP-269	(M)	**The Blue Sky Boys**	1964	12.00	30.00
Capitol T-2483	(M)	**Presenting The Blue Sky Boys**	1966	6.00	15.00
Capitol ST-2483	(S)	**Presenting The Blue Sky Boys**	1966	8.00	20.00
BLUE THINGS, THE					
RCA Victor LPM-3603	(M)	**The Blue Things**	1966	30.00	60.00
RCA Victor LSP-3603	(S)	**The Blue Things**	1966	40.00	80.00
BLUE VELVET BAND, THE					
Warner Bros. WS-1802	(S)	**Sweet Moments**	1969	12.00	30.00
BLUEBIRD					
Piccadilly PIC-	(S)	**Bluebird**	1980	16.00	40.00
BLUES MAGOOS, THE					
Mercury MG-21096	(M)	**Psychedelic Lollipop**	1966	10.00	25.00
Mercury SR-61096	(S)	**Psychedelic Lollipop**	1966	12.00	30.00
Mercury MG-21104	(M)	**Electric Comic Book** (With comic book)	1967	14.00	35.00
Mercury SR-61104	(S)	**Electric Comic Book** (With comic book)	1967	16.00	40.00
Mercury MG-21104	(M)	**Electric Comic Book** (Without comic book)	1967	10.00	25.00
Mercury SR-61104	(S)	**Electric Comic Book** (Without comic book)	1967	12.00	30.00
Mercury SR-61167	(M)	**Basic Blues Magoos**	1968	10.00	25.00
Mercury SR-61167	(S)	**Basic Blues Magoos**	1968	10.00	25.00
— Original Mercury albums above have red labels with a black & white logo on top.—					
ABC S-697	(S)	**Never Goin' Back To Georgia**	1969	6.00	15.00
ABC S-710	(S)	**Gulf Coast Bound**	1970	6.00	15.00
BLUES PROJECT, THE					
The Blues Project consisted of Roy Blumenfeld, Tommy Flanders, Danny Kalb, Steve Katz, Al Kooper and Andy Kulberg. Refer to Blood, Sweat & Tears; Seatrain.					
Forecast FT-3000	(M)	**Live At The Cafe Au-Go-Go**	1966	6.00	15.00
Forecast FTS-3000	(S)	**Live At The Cafe Au-Go-Go**	1966	8.00	20.00
Folkways FT-3008	(M)	**Projections**	1966	6.00	15.00
Folkways FTS-3008	(S)	**Projections**	1966	8.00	20.00
Forecast FT-3025	(M)	**Live At Town Hall**	1967	6.00	15.00
Forecast FTS-3025	(S)	**Live At Town Hall**	1967	8.00	20.00
Forecast FTS-3046	(S)	**Planned Obsolescence**	1968	5.00	12.00
Forecast FTS-3069	(S)	**Flanders/Kalb/Katz, Etc.**	1969	5.00	12.00
Forecast FTS-3077	(S)	**The Best Of The Blues Project**	1969	5.00	12.00
BLUES SPECTRUM, THE					
DB 8970	(S)	**We Were The Blues Spectrum**	1970	75.00	150.00

Label & Catalog #		Title	Year	VG+	NM
BLYTHE, STERLING					
Sage C-14	(M)	**Night At The Showboat** (Red vinyl)	1962	12.00	30.00
BOA					
Snakefield SN-001	(S)	**Wrong Road**	1969	50.00	100.00
BOB & EARL					
Bob Garrett and Earl Cosby.					
Tip TLP-1011	(M)	**Harlem Shuffle**	1964	10.00	25.00
Tip TLS-9011	(S)	**Harlem Shuffle**	1964	14.00	35.00
BOB & RAY					
Unicorn 1001 (10")	(M)	**Bob & Ray**	1954	20.00	50.00
RCA Victor LPM-2131	(M)	**On A Platter**	1960	5.00	12.00
RCA Victor LSP-2131	(S)	**On A Platter**	1960	8.00	20.00
BOBB B. SOXX & THE BLUE JEANS					
The Blue Jeans feature Darlene Love. Produced by Phil Spector.					
Philles PHLP-4002	(DJ)	**Zip-A-Dee-Doo-Dah** (White label)	1963	300.00	500.00
Philles PHLP-4002	(M)	**Zip-A-Dee-Doo-Dah**	1963	100.00	200.00
BOETCHER, CURT					
Produced by Gary Usher. Boetcher was formerly a member of Milennium.					
Elektra EKS-75037	(DJ)	**There's An Innocent Face**	1972	6.00	15.00
BOGARDE, DIRK					
London LL-3147	(M)	**Lyrics For Lovers**	1960	10.00	25.00
BOGGS, NOEL					
Repeat 100-10	(M)	**Anytime**	196?	16.00	40.00
Repeat 310-8	(M)	**Western Swing**	196?	16.00	40.00
Shasta 503	(M)	**Magic Steel Guitar** (Red cover)	196?	16.00	40.00
BOHEMIAN VENDETTA					
Mainstream 56106	(M)	**Bohemian Vendetta**	1968	14.00	35.00
Mainstream 6106	(S)	**Bohemian Vendetta**	1968	20.00	50.00
BOMBERS, THE					
West End 104	(S)	**The Bombers**	1979	6.00	15.00
West End 106	(S)	**The Bombers 2**	1979	6.00	15.00
BONADUCE, DANNY					
Lion LN-1015	(S)	**Danny Bonaduce**	1973	8.00	20.00
BOND, EDDIE					
Philips Int. 1980	(M)	**The Greatest Country Gospel Hits**	1961	150.00	250.00
BOND, JOHNNY					
Johnny also recorded with Merle Travis.					
Starday SLP-147	(M)	**That Wild, Wicked, But Wonderful West**	1961	12.00	30.00
Starday SLP-227	(M)	**Songs That Made Him Famous**	1963	12.00	30.00
Starday SLP-298	(M)	**Hot Rod Lincoln**	1964	16.00	40.00
Starday SLP-333	(M)	**Ten Little Bottles**	1965	12.00	30.00
Starday SLP-354	(M)	**Famous Hot Rodders I Have Known**	1965	16.00	40.00
Harmony HL-7308	(M)	**Johnny Bond's Best**	1964	8.00	20.00
Harmony HL-7353	(M)	**Bottled In Bond**	1965	8.00	20.00
BONDS, GARY "U.S."					
Legrand LLP-3001	(M)	**Dance 'Til Quarter To Three**	1961	50.00	100.00
Legrand LLP-3002	(M)	**Twist Up Calypso**	1962	40.00	80.00
Legrand LLP-3003	(M)	**Greatest Hits Of Gary U.S. Bonds**	1962	40.00	80.00
BONFIRE, MARS					
Uni 73027	(S)	**Mars Bonfire**	1968	6.00	15.00
Columbia CS-9834	(S)	**Faster Than The Speed Of Life**	1969	5.00	12.00
BONNEVILLES, THE					
Drum Boy DLM-1001	(M)	**Meet The Bonnevilles**	1963	35.00	70.00
Drum Boy DLS-1001	(S)	**Meet The Bonnevilles**	1963	45.00	90.00

Label & Catalog #		Title	Year	VG+	NM

BONNIE LOU

King 335	(M)	Bonnie Lou Sings	1958	20.00	50.00
King 389	(M)	Daddy-O	1958	20.00	50.00
King 595	(M)	Bonnie Lou Sings	1958	20.00	50.00

BONNIWELL, T.S.

Capitol ST-277	(S)	Close	1969	8.00	20.00

BONNIWELL'S MUSIC MACHINE
Sean Bonniwel was formerly a member of The Music Machine.

Warner Bros. W-1732	(M)	Bonniwell's Music Machine	1967	10.00	25.00
Warner Bros. WS-1732	(S)	Bonniwell's Music Machine	1967	16.00	40.00

BONZO DOG (DOO DAH) BAND, THE
Refer to Roger Ruskin-Spear; The Rutles.

Imperial LP-12370	(S)	Gorilla	1968	10.00	25.00
Imperial LP-12432	(S)	Urban Spaceman	1969	10.00	25.00
Imperial LP-12445	(S)	Tadpoles	1969	10.00	25.00
Imperial LP-12457	(S)	Keynsham	1970	10.00	25.00
United Arts. UAS-5517	(S)	Beast Of The Bonzos	1972	6.00	15.00
United Arts. UAS-5584	(S)	Let's Make Up And Be Friendly	1972	8.00	20.00
		(With postcard still attached to the cover.)			
United Arts. LA321H2	(S)	The History Of The Bonzos *(2 LPs)*	1974	8.00	20.00

BOOGIE KINGS, THE

Montel 104	(M)	The Boogie Kings	1966	8.00	20.00
Montel 109	(M)	Blue Eyed Soul	1967	8.00	20.00

BOOKER T. & THE M.G.'S

Stax 701	(M)	Green Onions	1962	16.00	40.00
Stax 705	(M)	Soul Dressing	1965	8.00	20.00
Stax STS-705	(S)	Soul Dressing	1965	10.00	25.00
Stax 711	(M)	And Now	1966	8.00	20.00
Stax STS-711	(S)	And Now	1966	10.00	25.00
Stax 713	(M)	In The Christmas Spirit	1966	8.00	20.00
Stax STS-713	(S)	In The Christmas Spirit	1966	10.00	25.00
Stax 717	(M)	Hip Hug-Her	1967	6.00	15.00
Stax STS-717	(S)	Hip Hug-Her	1967	8.00	20.00
Stax 724	(M)	Doin' Our Thing	1968	5.00	12.00
Stax STS-724	(S)	Doin' Our Thing	1968	6.00	15.00
Atlantic 8202	(S)	The Best Of Booker T. & The MG's	1968	6.00	15.00
Stax	(DJ)	Funktion *(In-store sampler)*	1972	8.00	20.00

BOOKER T. & THE M.G.'S & THE MAR-KEYS

Stax 720	(S)	Back To Back	1967	5.00	12.00
Stax STS-720	(S)	Back To Back	1967	6.00	15.00

BOONE, PAT

Dot DLP-3012	(M)	Pat Boone	1956	12.00	30.00
Dot DLP-3030	(M)	Howdy!	1956	12.00	30.00
		— Original Dot albums above have maroon labels.—			
Dot DLP-3012	(M)	Pat Boone	1957	6.00	15.00
Dot DLP-25012	(E)	Pat Boone	196?	4.00	10.00
Dot DLP-3030	(M)	Howdy!	1957	6.00	15.00
Dot DLP-25030	(E)	Howdy!	196?	4.00	10.00
Dot DLP-3050	(M)	Pat	1957	10.00	25.00
Dot DLP-25050	(E)	Pat	196?	4.00	10.00
Dot DLP-3068	(M)	Hymns We Love	1957	8.00	20.00
Dot DLP-25068	(S)	Hymns We Love	1957	12.00	30.00
Dot DLP-3071	(M)	Pat's Great Hits	1957	8.00	20.00
Dot DLP-25071	(S)	Pat's Great Hits	1957	12.00	30.00
Dot DLP-9000	(M)	April Love	1957	10.00	25.00
Dot DLP-3077	(M)	Pat Boone Sings Irving Berlin	1958	6.00	15.00
Dot DLP-25077	(S)	Pat Boone Sings Irving Berlin	1958	10.00	25.00
Dot DLP-3118	(M)	Star Dust	1958	6.00	15.00
Dot DLP-25118	(S)	Star Dust	1958	10.00	25.00
Dot DLP-3121	(M)	Yes Indeed!	1958	8.00	20.00
Dot DLP-3158	(M)	Pat Boone Sings	1959	6.00	15.00
Dot DLP-25158	(S)	Pat Boone Sings	1959	10.00	25.00

Label & Catalog #		Title	Year	VG+	NM
Dot DLP-3180	(M)	**Tenderly**	*1959*	**6.00**	**15.00**
Dot DLP-25180	(S)	**Tenderly**	*1959*	**10.00**	**25.00**
Dot DLP-3181	(M)	**Great Millions**	*1959*	**6.00**	**15.00**
Dot DLP-25181	(S)	**Great Millions**	*1959*	**10.00**	**25.00**
Dot DLP-3199	(M)	**Side By Side**	*1959*	**6.00**	**15.00**
Dot DLP-25199	(S)	**Side By Side**	*1959*	**8.00**	**20.00**
Dot DLP-3222	(M)	**White Christmas**	*1959*	**5.00**	**12.00**
Dot DLP-25222	(S)	**White Christmas**	*1959*	**8.00**	**20.00**
Dot DLP-3234	(M)	**He Leadeth Me**	*1960*	**5.00**	**12.00**
Dot DLP-25234	(S)	**He Leadeth Me**	*1960*	**8.00**	**20.00**
Dot DLP-3261	(M)	**Pat's Great Hits, Volume 2**	*1960*	**5.00**	**12.00**
Dot DLP-25261	(S)	**Pat's Great Hits, Volume 2**	*1960*	**8.00**	**20.00**
Dot DLP-3270	(M)	**Moonglow**	*1960*	**5.00**	**12.00**
Dot DLP-25270	(S)	**Moonglow**	*1960*	**8.00**	**20.00**
Dot DLP-25270	(S)	**Moonglow** *(Blue vinyl)*	*1960*	**20.00**	**50.00**
Dot DLP-3285	(M)	**This And That**	*1960*	**5.00**	**12.00**
Dot DLP-25285	(S)	**This And That**	*1960*	**8.00**	**20.00**
Dot DLP-3346	(M)	**Great! Great! Great!**	*1961*	**5.00**	**12.00**
Dot DLP-25346	(S)	**Great! Great! Great!**	*1961*	**6.00**	**15.00**

One of the most successful artists of the pre-Beatles era, Pat ranks with Frank Sinatra as the most successful white pop (i.e., non-rock'n roll) artist of the '50s. Pat placed nearly 60 sides on the charts over the course of his career, the bulk of them in an eight year span beginning in 1955. This success did not phase album buyers, where a mere dozen of his albums made the charts.

Dot DLP-3384	(M)	**Moody River**	*1961*	**5.00**	**12.00**
Dot DLP-25384	(S)	**Moody River**	*1961*	**6.00**	**15.00**
Dot DLP-3386	(M)	**My God And I**	*1961*	**4.00**	**10.00**
Dot DLP-25386	(S)	**My God And I**	*1961*	**5.00**	**12.00**
Dot DLP-3399	(M)	**I'll See You In My Dreams**	*1962*	**4.00**	**10.00**
Dot DLP-25399	(S)	**I'll See You In My Dreams**	*1962*	**5.00**	**12.00**
Dot DLP-3402	(M)	**Pat Boone Reads From The Holy Bible**	*1962*	**5.00**	**12.00**
Dot DLP-3455	(M)	**Pat Boone's Golden Hits**	*1962*	**4.00**	**10.00**
Dot DLP-25455	(S)	**Pat Boone's Golden Hits**	*1962*	**5.00**	**12.00**
Dot DLP-9011	(M)	**State Fair** *(Soundtrack)*	*1962*	**6.00**	**15.00**
Dot DLP-29011	(S)	**State Fair** *(Soundtrack)*	*1962*	**8.00**	**20.00**

Label & Catalog #		Title	Year	VG+	NM
Dot DLP-3475	(M)	**I Love You Truly**	1962	**4.00**	**10.00**
Dot DLP-25475	(S)	**I Love You Truly**	1962	**5.00**	**12.00**
Dot DLP-3501	(M)	**Pat Boone Sings Guess Who?**	1963	**16.00**	**40.00**
Dot DLP-25501	(S)	**Pat Boone Sings Guess Who?**	1963	**20.00**	**50.00**
		("White Bucks" Boone sings "Blue Suede" Presley.)			

BOONE, RANDY

Decca DL-4619	(M)	**The Singing Star Of The Virginian**	1965	**12.00**	**30.00**
Decca DL-74619	(S)	**The Singing Star Of The Virginian**	1965	**14.00**	**35.00**
Decca DL-4663	(M)	**Ramblin' Randy**	1965	**8.00**	**20.00**
Decca DL-74663	(S)	**Ramblin' Randy**	1965	**10.00**	**25.00**
Gre-Gar 22170006	(S)	**Randy Boone**	196?	**8.00**	**20.00**

BOOT

Agape 2601	(S)	**Boot**	197?	**10.00**	**25.00**
Guinness 36002	(S)	**Turn The Other Cheek**	197?	**6.00**	**15.00**

BORDERSONG
Ann and Nancy Wilson of Heart provide backing vocals on one track.

Real Good 1001	(S)	**Morning**	1975	**16.00**	**40.00**

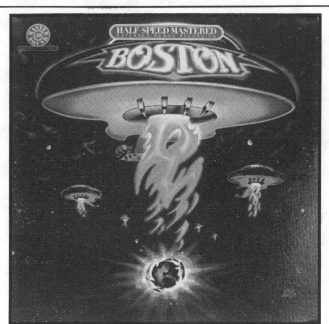

Issued as one of the first of CBS' ill-fated "Half-speed Master" series as HE-34188, Boston's eponymous first LP was quickly replaced with the HE-44188 designation.

BOSTON

Epic E99-44188	(S)	**Boston** *(Picture disc)*	1978	**6.00**	**15.00**
Epic HE-34188	(S)	**Boston** *(Half-speed master)*	1981	**16.00**	**40.00**
Epic HE-44188	(S)	**Boston** *(Half-speed master)*	1982	**12.00**	**30.00**
Epic E99-45050	(DJ)	**Don't Look Back** *(Picture disc)*	1982	**12.00**	**30.00**
Epic HE-45050	(S)	**Don't Look Back** *(Half-speed master)*	1982	**12.00**	**30.00**

BOSTON TEA PARTY, THE

Flick Disc 45000	(S)	**The Boston Tea Party**	1968	**6.00**	**15.00**
American Inter. ST-A-1033	(S)	**The Cycle Savages** *(Soundtrack)*	1970	**10.00**	**25.00**

Label & Catalog #		Title	Year	VG+	NM

BOSWELL, CONNEE
Ms. Boswell also recorded with Bing Crosby.

Decca DL-6013 (10")	(M)	The Star Maker	1951	20.00	50.00
Decca DL-5445 (10")	(M)	Singing The Blues	1953	16.00	40.00
RCA LPM-1426	(M)	Connee Boswell & The Original Memphis 5	1957	12.00	30.00
Decca DL-8356	(M)	Connee	1956	12.00	30.00
Design 68	(M)	Connee Boswell Sings Irving Berlin	195?	10.00	25.00
Design 101	(M)	The New Sound Of Connee Boswell	195?	10.00	25.00
Decca DL-4254	(M)	The Star Maker	1962	10.00	25.00

BOW STREET RUNNERS, THE

| B.T. Puppy BTPS-1026 | (S) | The Bow Street Runners | 1969 | 300.00 | 500.00 |

BOWAZ

| Blue Moon | (S) | Three Of A Kind | 1978 | 45.00 | 90.00 |

BOWEN, JIMMY
Jimmy also recorded with Buddy Knox.

Roulette R-25004	(M)	Jimmy Bowen	1957	50.00	100.00
Reprise R-6210	(M)	Sunday Morning With The Comics	1966	12.00	30.00
Reprise RS-6210	(S)	Sunday Morning With The Comics	1966	16.00	40.00

BOWIE, DAVID

Deram DE-16003	(M)	David Bowie	1967	50.00	100.00
Deram DES-18003	(S)	David Bowie	1967	75.00	150.00
Mercury SR-61246	(S)	Man Of Words, Man Of Music	1969	75.00	150.00
Mercury 61325	(S)	The Man Who Sold The World	1971	20.00	50.00
		(The matrix number is stamped in the trail-off vinyl of originals;			
		counterfeits have those numbers hand-etched.)			
RCA Victor LSP-4623	(S)	Hunky Dory	1972	6.00	15.00
RCA Victor LSP-4702	(S)	The Rise And Fall Of Ziggy Stardust	1972	6.00	15.00
RCA Victor LSP-4813	(S)	Space Oddity *(With poster)*	1972	10.00	25.00
RCA Victor LSP-4813	(S)	Space Oddity *(Without poster)*	1972	6.00	15.00
RCA Victor LSP-4816	(S)	Man Who Sold The World *(With poster)*	1972	10.00	25.00
RCA Victor LSP-4816	(S)	Man Who Sold The World *(Without poster)*	1972	6.00	15.00
RCA Victor LSP-4852	(S)	Aladdin Insane	1973	6.00	15.00
London 628/9	(P)	Images 1966-1967 *(2 LPs)*	1973	12.00	30.00
RCA Victor APL1-0291	(S)	Pin Ups	1974	6.00	15.00
RCA Victor APL1-0576	(S)	Diamond Dogs	1974		See note below
		(The Bowie/dog's genitals on the cover are clearly discernible.			
		Rare. Estimated near mint value $4,000-5,000.)			
RCA Victor APL1-0576	(S)	Diamond Dogs	1974	6.00	15.00
RCA Victor CPL2-0771	(S)	David Live *(2 LPs)*	1974	6.00	15.00
RCA Victor APL1-0998	(S)	Young Americans	1975	6.00	15.00
		— Original RCA albums above have orange labels. —			
RCA Victor APL1-1327	(S)	Station To Station *(Brown label)*	1975	4.00	10.00
RCA Victor APL1-1732	(S)	Changesonebowie	1976	50.00	100.00
		(Contains an alternate take of "John, I'm Only Dancing.")			
London 50007	(S)	Starting Point	1977	4.00	10.00
RCA Victor DJL1-2697	(DJ)	Bowie Now	1978	14.00	35.00
RCA Victor ARL1-2743	(S)	Peter And The Wolf *(Black vinyl)*	1978	6.00	15.00
RCA Victor ARL1-2743	(S)	Peter And The Wolf *(Green vinyl)*	1978	6.00	15.00
RCA Victor CPL2-2913	(S)	Stage *(2 LPs)*	1978	4.00	10.00
RCA Victor DJL1-3016	(DJ)	An Evening With David Bowie	1978	30.00	60.00
		(Originals have a black border along the bottom of the cover.)			
RCA Victor DJL1-3545	(DJ)	1980 All Clear	1979	10.00	25.00
RCA Victor DJL1-3829	(DJ)	Special Radio Series, Volume 1:			
		Scary Monsters Interview Album	1980	10.00	25.00
RCA Victor DJL1-3829	(DJ)	College Radio Series, Volume 1:			
		Scary Monsters Interview Album	1980	12.00	30.00
RCA Victor DJL1-3840	(DJ)	Scary Monsters Interview Album	1980	12.00	30.00
RCA Victor CPL2-4862	(DJ)	Ziggy Stardust, The Motion Picture *(2 LPs)*	1983	45.00	90.00
		Promo issued on clear vinyl.)			
EMI SPRO-9960/1	(DJ)	Let's Talk	1983	12.00	30.00
Mobile Fidelity MFSL-064	(S)	The Rise And Fall Of Ziggy Stardust	1983	16.00	40.00
Mobile Fidelity MFSL-083	(S)	Let's Dance	1983	8.00	20.00
EMI SPRO-79112/3	(DJ)	Never Let Me Down: The Interview	1987	35.00	70.00
Rykodisc LSD-4702	(DJ)	The Rise And Fall Of Ziggy Stardust	1990	50.00	100.00
		(Rykodisc 4702 contains an album and a CD.)			

Label & Catalog #		Title	Year	VG+	NM
BOX TOPS, THE					
The Box Tops feature Alex Chilton. Refer to Big Star.					
Bell 6011	(M)	**The Letter/Neon Rainbow**	*1967*	**6.00**	**15.00**
Bell S-6011	(S)	**The Letter/Neon Rainbow**	*1967*	**8.00**	**20.00**
Bell S-6017	(S)	**Cry Like A Baby**	*1968*	**8.00**	**20.00**
Bell S-6023	(S)	**Non-Stop**	*1968*	**6.00**	**15.00**
Bell S-6025	(S)	**Super Hits**	*1968*	**6.00**	**15.00**
Bell S-6032	(S)	**Dimensions**	*1969*	**6.00**	**15.00**
Cotillon SD-057	(S)	**A Lifetime Believing**	*1971*	**5.00**	**12.00**
BOYCE, TOMMY					
Camden CAL-2202	(M)	**A Twofold Talent**	*1967*	**6.00**	**15.00**
Camden CAS-2202	(S)	**A Twofold Talent**	*1967*	**8.00**	**20.00**
BOYCE, TOMMY, & BOBBY HART					
Refer to Dolenz, Jones, Boyce & Hart.					
A&M LP-126	(M)	**Test Patterns**	*1967*	**6.00**	**15.00**
A&M SP-4126	(S)	**Test Patterns**	*1967*	**8.00**	**20.00**
A&M LP-143	(M)	**I Wonder What She's Doing Tonight**	*1968*	**6.00**	**15.00**
A&M SP-4143	(S)	**I Wonder What She's Doing Tonight**	*1968*	**8.00**	**20.00**
A&M SP-4162	(S)	**It's All Happening On The Inside**	*1968*	**8.00**	**20.00**
BOYD, BILLY					
Crown CST-196	(S)	**Twangy Guitars** *(Red vinyl)*	*196?*	**12.00**	**30.00**
BOYD, EDDIE					
Epic BN-26409	(S)	**7936 South Rhodes**	*1968*	**16.00**	**40.00**
London PS-554	(S)	**I'll Dust My Broom**	*1969*	**16.00**	**40.00**
BRACKEN, EDDIE					
Sea Horse CSH-7002	(M)	**Bat Masterson**	*1960*	**20.00**	**50.00**
BRADBURY, RAY					
Tower ST-5172	(S)	**Dark Carnival**	*196?*	**10.00**	**25.00**
BRADLEY, OWEN					
Decca DL-8868	(M)	**Big Guitar**	*1958*	**12.00**	**30.00**
Decca DL-78868	(S)	**Big Guitar**	*1958*	**16.00**	**40.00**
BRADLEY, WILL					
Epic LG-1005 (10")	(M)	**Boogie Woogie**	*1954*	**50.00**	**100.00**
Epic LG-1127 (10")	(M)	**Will Bradley**	*1955*	**50.00**	**100.00**
Epic LN-3115	(M)	**Boogie Woogie**	*1955*	**16.00**	**40.00**
Epic LN-3119	(M)	**The House Of Bradley**	*1956*	**16.00**	**40.00**
BRADSHAW, TINY					
King 295-74 (10")	(M)	**Off And On**	*1955*	**100.00**	**200.00**
King 395-501	(M)	**Selections**	*1958*	**40.00**	**80.00**
King 653	(M)	**Great Composer**	*1959*	**20.00**	**50.00**
King 953	(M)	**24 Great Songs**	*1966*	**10.00**	**25.00**
BRADY BUNCH, THE					
Paramount 6032	(S)	**Meet The Brady Bunch**	*1972*	**8.00**	**20.00**
Paramount 6037	(S)	**The Kids From The Brady Bunch**	*1972*	**8.00**	**20.00**
Paramount 5026	(S)	**Merry Christmas From The Brady Bunch**	*1972*	**10.00**	**25.00**
Paramount 6058	(S)	**The Brady Bunch Phonograph Record**	*1973*	**12.00**	**30.00**
BRAINBOX					
Capitol ST-596	(S)	**Brainbox**	*1970*	**6.00**	**15.00**
BRAND X					
Mirror Image	(S)	**Brand X Squared**	*198?*	**8.00**	**20.00**
BRASSELLE, KEEFE					
Coral CRL-57295	(M)	**Minstrel Man**	*1959*	**8.00**	**20.00**
Coral CRL-757295	(S)	**Minstrel Man**	*1959*	**10.00**	**25.00**
BRAUTIGAN, RICHARD					
Harvest ST-424	(S)	**Listening To Richard Brautigan**	*1969*	**8.00**	**20.00**

Label & Catalog #		Title	Year	VG+	NM
BREAD					
Elektra BRD-1	(DJ)	**Bread** *(In-store sampler)*	1969	10.00	25.00
Elektra EQ-5015	(Q)	**Baby, I'm A-Want You**	1973	5.00	12.00
Elektra EQ-5056	(Q)	**The Best Of Bread**	1973	5.00	12.00
BRENDA & THE TABULATIONS					
Dionn LPM-2000	(M)	**Dry Your Eyes**	1967	12.00	30.00
Dionn LPS-2000	(P)	**Dry Your Eyes**	1967	16.00	40.00
BRENNAN, WALTER					
Dot DLP-3309	(M)	**Dutchman's Gold**	1960	6.00	15.00
Dot DLP-25309	(M)	**Dutchman's Gold**	1960	8.00	20.00
Everest DBR-5103	(M)	**World Of Miracles**	1960	6.00	15.00
Everest SDBR-1103	(S)	**World Of Miracles**	1960	8.00	20.00
Everest DBR-5123	(M)	**The President**	1960	6.00	15.00
Everest SDBR-1123	(S)	**The President**	1960	8.00	20.00
Liberty LRP-3233	(M)	**Old Rivers**	1962	6.00	15.00
Liberty LST-7233	(S)	**Old Rivers**	1962	8.00	20.00
Liberty LRP-3241	(M)	**The President**	1962	6.00	15.00
Liberty LST-7241	(S)	**The President**	1962	6.00	15.00
Liberty LRP-3244	(M)	**World Of Miracles**	1962	5.00	12.00
Liberty LST-7244	(S)	**World Of Miracles**	1962	6.00	15.00
Liberty LRP-3257	(M)	**'Twas The Night Before Christmas Back Home**	1962	5.00	12.00
Liberty LST-7257	(S)	**'Twas The Night Before Christmas Back Home**	1962	6.00	15.00
Liberty LRP-3266	(M)	**Mama Sang A Song**	1963	5.00	12.00
Liberty LST-7266	(S)	**Mama Sang A Song**	1963	6.00	15.00
Liberty LRP-3317	(M)	**Talkin' From The Heart**	1964	5.00	12.00
Liberty LST-7317	(S)	**Talkin' From The Heart**	1964	6.00	15.00
Liberty LRP-3372	(M)	**Gunfight At The O.K. Corral**	1964	5.00	12.00
Liberty LST-7372	(S)	**Gunfight At The O.K. Corral**	1964	6.00	15.00
BRETT, PAUL					
ABC 672	(S)	**Very Strange Brew**	1969	8.00	20.00
Janus 3026	(S)	**Paul Brett Sage**	1971	6.00	15.00
BREWER, TERESA					
London APB-1006 (10")	(M)	**Teresa Brewer**	1952	16.00	40.00
Coral CRL-56072 (10")	(M)	**A Bouquet Of Hits**	1952	12.00	30.00
Coral CRL-56093 (10")	(M)	**Till I Waltz Again With You**	1954	12.00	30.00
Coral CRL-57027	(M)	**Music, Music, Music**	1956	10.00	25.00
Coral CRL-57053	(M)	**Teresa**	1956	10.00	25.00
Coral CRL-57135	(M)	**For Teenagers In Love**	1957	10.00	25.00
Coral CRL-57144	(M)	**Teresa Brewer At Christmas Time**	1957	10.00	25.00
Coral CRL-57179	(M)	**Miss Music**	1958	10.00	25.00
Coral CRL-57232	(M)	**Time For Teresa**	1958	10.00	25.00
Coral CRL-57245	(M)	**Teresa Brewer And The Dixieland Band**	1959	8.00	20.00
Coral CRL-757245	(S)	**Teresa Brewer And The Dixieland Band**	1959	10.00	25.00
Coral CRL-57257	(M)	**When Your Love Has Gone**	1959	8.00	20.00
Coral CRL-757257	(S)	**When Your Love Has Gone**	1959	10.00	25.00
Coral CRL-57297	(M)	**Heavenly Lover**	1959	8.00	20.00
Coral CRL-757297	(S)	**Heavenly Lover**	1959	10.00	25.00
Coral CRL-57315	(M)	**Ridin' High**	1960	6.00	15.00
Coral CRL-757315	(S)	**Ridin' High**	1960	8.00	20.00
Coral CRL-57329	(M)	**Naughty, Naughty, Naughty**	1960	6.00	15.00
Coral CRL-757329	(S)	**Naughty, Naughty, Naughty**	1960	8.00	20.00
Coral CRL-57351	(M)	**My Golden Favorites**	1960	6.00	15.00
Coral CRL-757351	(S)	**My Golden Favorites**	1960	8.00	20.00
Coral CRL-57361	(M)	**Songs Everybody Knows**	1961	6.00	15.00
Coral CRL-757361	(S)	**Songs Everybody Knows**	1961	8.00	20.00
Coral CRL-57374	(M)	**Aloha From Teresa**	1961	6.00	15.00
Coral CRL-757374	(S)	**Aloha From Teresa**	1961	8.00	20.00
Coral CRL-57414	(M)	**Don't Mess With Tess**	1962	6.00	15.00
Coral CRL-757414	(S)	**Don't Mess With Tess**	1962	8.00	20.00
Philips PHM-200062	(M)	**Teresa Brewer's Greatest Hits**	1962	6.00	15.00
Philips PHS-600062	(S)	**Teresa Brewer's Greatest Hits**	1962	8.00	20.00
Philips PHM-200099	(M)	**Terrific Teresa**	1963	5.00	12.00
Philips PHS-600099	(S)	**Terrific Teresa**	1963	6.00	15.00

Label & Catalog #		Title	Year	VG+	NM
Philips PHM-200119	(M)	**Moments To Remember**	1964	5.00	12.00
Philips PHS-600119	(S)	**Moments To Remember**	1964	6.00	15.00
Philips PHM-200147	(M)	**Golden Hits Of 1964**	1964	5.00	12.00
Philips PHS-600147	(S)	**Golden Hits Of 1964**	1964	6.00	15.00
Philips PHM-200163	(M)	**Goldfinger/Other Great Movie Songs**	1965	5.00	12.00
Philips PHS-600163	(S)	**Goldfinger/Other Great Movie Songs**	1965	6.00	15.00
Philips PHM-200200	(M)	**Songs For Our Fighting Men**	1966	5.00	12.00
Philips PHS-600200	(S)	**Songs For Our Fighting Men**	1966	6.00	15.00
Philips PHM-200216	(M)	**Gold Country**	1966	5.00	12.00
Philips PHS-600216	(S)	**Gold Country**	1966	6.00	15.00
Philips PHM-200230	(M)	**Texas Leather And Mexican Lace**	1967	5.00	12.00
Philips PHS-600230	(S)	**Texas Leather And Mexican Lace**	1967	6.00	15.00

BRICE, FANNY, & HELEN MORGAN

Vik 997	(M)	**Torch Songs**	195?	20.00	50.00

BRIDGES, LLOYD

Carlton CHH-17	(M)	**Hear How To Skin Dive**	195?	10.00	25.00

BRIGADE

Band'n Vocal BVRS-1066	(S)	**Last Laugh**	1970	See note below	
		(Rare. Estimated near mint value $1,500-3,000.)			

BRIGG

Susquehanna LP-301	(S)	**Brigg**	1973	90.00	180.00

BRIGMAN, GEORGE

Solid SR-001	(S)	**Jungle Rot**	1975	75.00	150.00

BRILL, MARTY

Mercury MG-20178	(M)	**A Roving Balladeer**	1956	10.00	25.00

BRILLIANT, ASHLEIGH

Dorash 1001	(M)	**In The Haight-Ashbury** *(Documentary)*	1967	40.00	80.00

BRIMSTONE

"S" 30534	(M)	**Paper Winged Dreams**	1968	75.00	150.00

BRINSLEY SCHWARZ
Brinsley Schwarz features Nick Lowe.

Capitol ST-589	(S)	**Brinsley Schwarz**	1970	6.00	15.00
Capitol ST-744	(S)	**Despite It All**	1971	6.00	15.00
United Arts. UAS-5566	(S)	**Silver Pistol**	1972	6.00	15.00
United Arts. UAS-5647	(S)	**Nervous On The Road**	1972	6.00	15.00

BRITT, ELTON
Refer to The Beverly Hill Billies.

RCA Victor LPM-3222 (10")	(M)	**Yodel Songs**	1954	40.00	80.00
RCA Victor LPM-1288	(M)	**Yodel Songs**	1956	20.00	50.00
ABC-Paramount 293	(M)	**The Wandering Cowboy**	1959	14.00	35.00
ABC-Paramount S-293	(S)	**The Wandering Cowboy**	1959	20.00	50.00
ABC-Paramount 322	(M)	**Beyond The Sunset**	1960	10.00	25.00
ABC-Paramount S-322	(S)	**Beyond The Sunset**	1960	14.00	35.00
ABC-Paramount 331	(M)	**I Heard A Forest Praying**	1960	10.00	25.00
ABC-Paramount S-331	(S)	**I Heard A Forest Praying**	1960	14.00	35.00
ABC-Paramount 521	(M)	**The Singing Hills**	1965	8.00	20.00
ABC-Paramount S-521	(S)	**The Singing Hills**	1965	10.00	25.00
ABC-Paramount 566	(M)	**Somethin' For Everybody**	1966	8.00	20.00
ABC-Paramount S-566	(S)	**Somethin' For Everybody**	1966	10.00	25.00
RCA Victor LPM-2669	(M)	**The Best Of Elton Britt** *(Black label)*	1963	10.00	25.00
RCA Victor LSP-2669	(E)	**The Best Of Elton Britt** *(Black label)*	1963	6.00	15.00
RCA Victor LSP-4073	(S)	**When Evening Shadows Fall**	1968	6.00	15.00

BROOKS, DONNA

Dawn DLP-1105	(M)	**I'll Take Romance**	1956	16.00	40.00

BROOKS, DONNIE

Era EL-105	(M)	**The Happiest**	1961	20.00	50.00

Label & Catalog #		Title	Year	VG+	NM
BROOKS, HADDA					
Modern LMP-1210	(M)	**Femme Fatale**	1956	50.00	100.00
Crown CLP-5010	(M)	**Femme Fatale**	1957	20.00	50.00
Crown CLP-5374	(M)	**Hadda Brooks Sings And Swings**	1963	10.00	25.00
Crown CST-574	(E)	**Hadda Brooks Sings And Swings**	1963	6.00	15.00
BROOKS, HADDA / PETE JOHNSON					
Crown CLP-5058	(M)	**Boogie**	1958	20.00	50.00
BROOKS, TINA					
Blue Note 4041	(M)	**True Blue**	1960	10.00	25.00
BROONZY, BIG BILL					
Big Bill also recorded with Josh White.					
Dial 306 (10')	(M)	**Blues Concert**	1952	75.00	150.00
Period 1114 (10")	(M)	**Big Bill Broonzy Sings**	1955	150.00	250.00
EmArcy MG-20634 (10")	(M)	**Folk Blues**	1954	50.00	100.00
Folkways FA-2315	(M)	**Big Bill Broonzy**	1957	12.00	30.00
Folkways FA-2326	(M)	**Country Blues**	1957	12.00	30.00
Folkways FA-3586	(M)	**His Songs And Story**	1957	8.00	20.00
EmArcy MG-36137	(M)	**Blues By Broonzy**	1958	35.00	70.00
Columbia WL-111	(M)	**Big Bill's Blues**	1958	35.00	70.00
Verve V-3001	(M)	**Last Session, Part 1**	1959	10.00	25.00
Verve V-3002	(M)	**Last Session, Part 2**	1959	10.00	25.00
Verve V-3003	(M)	**Last Session, Part 3**	1959	10.00	25.00
Mercury MG-20822	(M)	**Memorial**	1963	8.00	20.00
Mercury SR-60822	(S)	**Memorial**	1963	10.00	25.00
Mercury MG-20905	(M)	**Remembering Big Bill Broonzy**	1964	8.00	20.00
Mercury SR-60905	(S)	**Remembering Big Bill Broonzy**	1964	10.00	25.00
Epic EE-22017	(M)	**Big Bill's Blues**	1969	12.00	30.00
BROONZY, BIG BILL; SONNY TERRY & BROWNIE McGHEE					
Folkways FA-3817	(M)	**Big Bill Broonzy, Sonny Terry**			
		And Brownie McGhee	1959	12.00	30.00
BROONZY, BIG BILL, & PETE SEEGER					
Folkways FVS-9008	(S)	**Big Bill Broonzy And Pete Seeger**	1965	10.00	25.00
BROONZY, BIG BILL, & WASHBOARD SAM					
Chess LP-1468	(M)	**Big Bill Broonzy And Washboard Sam**	1962	35.00	70.00
BROTHER FOX & TAR BABY					
Oracle 1001	(S)	**Brother Fox & Tar Baby**	1969	12.00	30.00
Capitol ST-544	(S)	**Brother Fox & Tar Baby**	1969	8.00	20.00
BROTHERHOOD					
Smitty, Drake and Fang of Paul Revere's Raiders, who also recorded as Friendsound.					
RCA Victor LSP-4092	(S)	**Brotherhood**	1968	6.00	15.00
RCA Victor LSP-4228	(S)	**Brotherhood, Brotherhood**	1969	6.00	15.00
BROTHERHOOD					
BH 501	(S)	**Stavia**	1972	80.00	160.00
BROTHERHOOD OF MAN, THE					
Deram DES-18046	(S)	**United We Stand**	1970	6.00	15.00
BROTHERS JOHNSON, THE					
A&M PR-4714	(DJ)	**Blam!** *(Picture disc)*	1978	8.00	20.00
A&M PR-4714	(S)	**Blam!** *(Picture disc)*	1978	4.00	10.00
BROWN, AL, & HIS TUNE TOPPERS					
Amy A-1	(M)	**The Madison Dance Party**	1960	14.00	35.00
Amy AS-1	(P)	**The Madison Dance Party**	1960	16.00	40.00
BROWN, ARTHUR					
Atlantic/Track SD-8198	(S)	**The Crazy World Of Arthur Brown**	1968	8.00	20.00

Label & Catalog #		Title	Year	VG+	NM
BROWN, BOBBY					
Destiny 4001	(S)	Bobby Brown Live	1972	6.00	15.00
Destiny 4002	(S)	The Enlightening Beam Of Axonda	1972	10.00	25.00
BROWN, BOOTS, & HIS BLOCKBUSTERS / DAN DREW & HIS DAREDEVILS					
RCA Victor LG-1000	(M)	Rock That Beat	1958	75.00	150.00
BROWN, BUSTER					
Fire FLP-102	(M)	The New King Of The Blues	1960	300.00	500.00
BROWN, CHARLES					
Aladdin 702 (10")	(M)	Mood Music	1952	500.00	750.00
Aladdin 702 (10")	(M)	Mood Music (Red vinyl)	1952	1,000.00	1,500.00
Aladdin 809	(M)	Mood Music	1956	300.00	500.00
Score SLP-4011	(M)	Driftin' Blues	1958	180.00	300.00
Imperial A-9178	(M)	Million Sellers	1961	50.00	100.00
King 775	(M)	Sings Christmas Songs	1961	50.00	100.00
King 878	(M)	Great Charles Brown	1963	50.00	100.00
Mainstream 56035	(M)	Ballads My Way	1965	8.00	20.00
Mainstream S-6035	(S)	Ballads My Way	1965	12.00	30.00
BluesWay BLS-6039	(S)	Legend	1970	6.00	15.00
BROWN, CHARLES / AMOS MILBURN					
Grand Prix K0421	(M)	Original Blues Sounds	196?	6.00	15.00
BROWN, GEORGIA					
London LL-3286	(M)	Georgia Brown	1962	8.00	20.00
London LL-3331	(M)	Georgia Brown Loves Gershwin	1963	6.00	15.00
London PS-331	(S)	Georgia Brown Loves Gershwin	1963	8.00	20.00
Coral CRL-57436	(M)	Georgia Brown	1964	6.00	15.00
Coral CRL-757436	(S)	Georgia Brown	1964	8.00	20.00
Capitol T-2329	(M)	The Many Shades Of Georgia Brown	1965	6.00	15.00
Capitol ST-2329	(S)	The Many Shades Of Georgia Brown	1965	8.00	20.00
BROWN, HYLO					
Capitol T-1168	(M)	Hylo Brown	1959	30.00	60.00
BROWN, JAMES (& HIS FAMOUS FLAMES)					
King 395-610	(M)	Please Please Please	1959	150.00	250.00
King 395-635	(M)	Try Me	1959	210.00	350.00
King LP-683	(M)	Think	1960	150.00	250.00
King LP-743	(M)	The Always Amazing James Brown	1961	50.00	100.00
King LP-771	(M)	Jump Around	1962	45.00	90.00
King KS-771	(S)	Jump Around	1962	65.00	130.00
King LP-780	(M)	The Exciting James Brown	1962	45.00	90.00
King LP-826	(M)	James Brown Live At The Apollo!	1963	45.00	90.00
King KS-826	(S)	James Brown Live At The Apollo!	1963	65.00	130.00
King LP-851	(M)	Prisoner Of Love	1963	45.00	90.00
King KS-851	(S)	Prisoner Of Love	1963	60.00	120.00
King LP-883	(M)	Pure Dynamite! Live At The Royal	1964	40.00	80.00
King KS-909	(E)	Please Please Please	1964	16.00	40.00
King LP-919	(M)	The Unbeatable 16 Hits	1964	20.00	50.00
King LP-938	(M)	Papa's Got A Brand New Bag	1965	20.00	50.00
King KSD-938	(E)	Papa's Got A Brand New Bag	1965	16.00	40.00
King LP-946	(M)	I Got You, I Feel Good	1966	16.00	40.00
King KSD-946	(S)	I Got You, I Feel Good	1966	20.00	50.00
King LP-961	(M)	Mighty Instrumentals	1966	16.00	40.00
King LP-985	(M)	It's A Man's Man's Man's World	1966	16.00	40.00
King KS-985	(S)	It's A Man's Man's Man's World	1966	20.00	50.00
King LP-1010	(M)	Christmas Songs	1966	20.00	50.00
		— Original King albums above have crownless black labels.—			
Smash MGS-27054	(M)	Showtime	1964	6.00	15.00
Smash SRS-67054	(S)	Showtime	1964	8.00	20.00
Smash MGS-27057	(M)	Grits And Soul	1965	6.00	15.00
Smash SRS-67057	(S)	Grits And Soul	1965	8.00	20.00
Smash MGS-27072	(M)	Today And Yesterday	1965	6.00	15.00
Smash SRS-67072	(S)	Today And Yesterday	1965	8.00	20.00
Smash MGS-27080	(M)	James Brown Plays New Breed	1966	6.00	15.00
Smash SRS-67080	(S)	James Brown Plays New Breed	1966	8.00	20.00

Label & Catalog #		Title	Year	VG+	NM
Smash MGS-27084	(M)	Handful Of Soul	1966	6.00	15.00
Smash SRS-67084	(S)	Handful Of Soul	1966	8.00	20.00
Smash MGS-27093	(M)	James Brown Plays The Real Thing	1967	6.00	15.00
Smash SRS-67093	(S)	James Brown Plays The Real Thing	1967	8.00	20.00
Smash SRS-67109	(S)	James Brown Sings Out Of Sight	1968	8.00	20.00
King LP-1016	(M)	Raw Soul	1967	16.00	40.00
King KS-1016	(E)	Raw Soul	1967	12.00	30.00
King LP-1018	(M)	Live At The Garden	1967	16.00	40.00
King KS-1018	(S)	Live At The Garden	1967	20.00	50.00
King K-1020	(M)	Cold Sweat	1967	12.00	30.00
King KS-1020	(M)	Cold Sweat	1967	16.00	40.00
King KS-1022	(S)	Live At The Apollo, Volume 2	1968	12.00	30.00
King KS-1024	(S)	His Show Of Tomorrow	1968	12.00	30.00
King KS-1030	(S)	I Can't Stand Myself When You Touch Me	1968	12.00	30.00
King KS-1031	(S)	I Got The Feelin'	1968	12.00	30.00
King KS-1038	(S)	Thinking About Little Willie John	1968	12.00	30.00
King KS-1040	(S)	A Soulful Christmas	1968	12.00	30.00
King KS-1047	(S)	Say It Loud—I'm Black And I'm Proud	1969	12.00	30.00
King KS-1051	(S)	Gettin' Down To It	1969	12.00	30.00
King KS-1054	(S)	Nothing But Soul	1968	12.00	30.00
King KSO-1055	(S)	The Popcorn	1969	12.00	30.00
King KS-1063	(S)	It's A Mother	1969	12.00	30.00
King KSD-1092	(S)	Ain't It Funky	1970	12.00	30.00
King KS-1095	(S)	It's A New Day So Let A Man Come In	1970	12.00	30.00
King KS-1100	(S)	Soul On Top	1970	12.00	30.00
King KSD-1110	(S)	Sho Is Funky Down Here	1970	12.00	30.00
King KSD-1115	(S)	Sex Machine	1970	12.00	30.00
King KSD-1124	(S)	Hey America!	1970	12.00	30.00
King KS-1127	(S)	Super Bad	1971	12.00	30.00

BROWN, MAXINE
Maxine Brown also recorded with Chuck Jackson.

Wand WD-656	(M)	The Fabulous Sound Of Maxine Brown	1963	10.00	25.00
Wand WD-663	(M)	Spotlight On Maxine Brown	1965	6.00	15.00
Wand WDS-663	(S)	Spotlight On Maxine Brown	1965	8.00	20.00
Wand WD-684	(M)	Maxine Brown's Greatest Hits	1967	6.00	15.00
Wand WDS-684	(P)	Maxine Brown's Greatest Hits	1967	8.00	20.00

BROWN, MILTON

Decca DL-5561 (10")	(M)	Dance-O-Rama #1	1955	90.00	180.00

BROWN, NAPPY

Savoy MG-14002	(M)	Nappy Brown Sings	1958	150.00	250.00
Savoy MG-14025	(M)	The Right Time	1960	85.00	170.00

BROWN, ROY

King 956	(M)	Roy Brown Sings 24 Hits	1966	20.00	50.00
King KS-956	(S)	Roy Brown Sings 24 Hits	1966	30.00	60.00
BluesWay BLS-6019	(S)	The Blues Are Brown	1968	6.00	15.00
BluesWay BLS-6056	(S)	Hard Times	197?	6.00	15.00
King KS-1130	(S)	Hard Luck Blues	1971	6.00	15.00
Epic BG-30473	(S)	Live At Monterey	1971	6.00	15.00

BROWN, ROY / WYNONIE HARRIS

King 607	(M)	Battle Of The Blues, Volume 1	1958	300.00	500.00
King 627	(M)	Battle Of The Blues, Volume 2	1959	300.00	500.00

BROWN, ROY / WYNONIE HARRIS / EDDIE VINSON

King 668	(M)	Battle Of The Blues, Volume 4	1960	500.00	750.00

BROWN, RUTH

Atlantic 115 (10")	(M)	Ruth Brown Sings Favorites	1956	See note below	
		(Atlantic 115 apparently does not exist.)			
Atlantic 8004	(M)	Ruth Brown (Black label)	1957	75.00	150.00
Atlantic 1308	(M)	Late Date With Ruth Brown (Black label)	1959	75.00	150.00
Atlantic SD-1308	(S)	Late Date With Ruth Brown (Green label)	1959	75.00	150.00
Atlantic 8026	(M)	Miss Rhythm (Black label)	1959	50.00	100.00
Atlantic 8026	(M)	Miss Rhythm (White label)	1959	75.00	150.00

Label & Catalog #		Title	Year	VG+	NM
Atlantic 8080	(M)	**The Best Of Ruth Brown**	1963	**16.00**	**40.00**
Atlantic SD-8080	(S)	**The Best Of Ruth Brown**	1963	**20.00**	**50.00**
Phillips PHM-200-028	(M)	**Along Comes Ruth**	1962	**16.00**	**40.00**
Phillips PHS-600-028	(S)	**Along Comes Ruth**	1962	**20.00**	**50.00**
Phillips PH-200-055	(M)	**Gospel Time**	1962	**12.00**	**30.00**
Phillips PHS-600-055	(S)	**Gospel Time**	1962	**16.00**	**40.00**
Mainstream 16044	(S)	**Ruth Brown '65**	1965	**10.00**	**25.00**
Mainstream S-6044	(S)	**Ruth Brown '65**	1965	**12.00**	**30.00**

BROWN'S FERRY FOUR, THE
Country supergroup features Granpa Jones, The Delmore Brothers and Merle Travis.

King 551	(M)	**Sacred Songs**	1957	**35.00**	**70.00**
King 590	(M)	**Sacred Songs**	1958	**35.00**	**70.00**
King 943	(M)	**Sacred Songs**	1964	**10.00**	**25.00**

BROWNE, JACKSON

(No label)	(DJ)	**Jackson Browne's First Album** (2 LPs)	1967	*See note below*	
		(Rare publisher's demo. Estimated near mint value $750-1,000.)			
Asylum SD-5051	(S)	**Jackson Browne** (With burlap cover)	1972	**12.00**	**30.00**
Asylum SD-5067	(S)	**For Everyman**	1973	**10.00**	**25.00**
		(Asylum 5051-5067 have white labels with a door-in-a-circle logo.)			
Reprise RS-	(S)	**Late For The Sky**	197?	**12.00**	**30.00**
		(RCA Record Club mis-pressing with a Reprise label.)			
Mobile Fidelity MFSL-055	(S)	**The Pretender**	1983	**12.00**	**30.00**

From 1955-67, siblings Bonnie, Maxine and Jim Ed scored on the country charts, the best of which is gathered here. While the cover states "Electronically Reprocessed," some of the hits are in true stereo.

BROWNS, THE

RCA Victor LPM-1438	(M)	**Jim Edward, Maxine And Bonnie Brown**	1957	**20.00**	**50.00**
RCA Victor LPM-2144	(M)	**Sweet Sounds By The Browns**	1959	**10.00**	**25.00**
RCA Victor LSP-2144	(S)	**Sweet Sounds By The Browns**	1959	**12.00**	**30.00**
RCA Victor LPM-2174	(M)	**Town And Country**	1960	**6.00**	**15.00**
RCA Victor LSP-2174	(S)	**Town And Country**	1960	**10.00**	**25.00**
RCA Victor LPM-2260	(M)	**The Browns Sing Their Hits**	1960	**6.00**	**15.00**
RCA Victor LSP-2260	(S)	**The Browns Sing Their Hits**	1960	**10.00**	**25.00**

Label & Catalog #		Title	Year	VG+	NM
RCA Victor LPM-2333	(M)	Our Favorite Folk Songs	1961	6.00	15.00
RCA Victor LSP-2333	(S)	Our Favorite Folk Songs	1961	10.00	25.00
RCA Victor LPM-2345	(M)	The Little Brown Church Hymnal	1961	6.00	15.00
RCA Victor LSP-2345	(S)	The Little Brown Church Hymnal	1961	10.00	25.00

— Original RCA mono albums above have "Long Play" on the bottom of the label;
stereo albums have "Living Stereo" on the bottom.—

RCA Victor LPM-2860	(M)	This Young Land	1964	5.00	12.00
RCA Victor LSP-2860	(S)	This Young Land	1964	6.00	15.00
RCA Victor LPM-2784	(M)	Grand Ole Opry Favorites	1965	5.00	12.00
RCA Victor LSP-2784	(S)	Grand Ole Opry Favorites	1965	6.00	15.00
RCA Victor LPM-2987	(M)	Three Shades Of Brown	1965	5.00	12.00
RCA Victor LSP-2987	(S)	Three Shades Of Brown	1965	6.00	15.00
RCA Victor LPM-3423	(M)	When Love Is Gone	1965	5.00	12.00
RCA Victor LSP-3423	(S)	When Love Is Gone	1965	6.00	15.00
RCA Victor LPM-3561	(M)	The Best Of The Browns	1966	5.00	12.00
RCA Victor LSP-3561	(P)	The Best Of The Browns	1966	6.00	15.00
RCA Victor LPM-3668	(M)	Our Kind Of Country	1966	5.00	12.00
RCA Victor LSP-3668	(S)	Our Kind Of Country	1966	6.00	15.00
RCA Victor LPM-3798	(M)	The Old Country Church	1967	6.00	15.00
RCA Victor LSP-3798	(S)	The Old Country Church	1967	6.00	15.00

— Original RCA abums above have black labels.—

BROWNSVILLE STATION [BROWNSVILLE]

Palladium P-1004	(S)	Brownsville Station	1970	12.00	30.00
Epic JE-35606	(DJ)	Air Special (Orange vinyl)	1979	6.00	15.00

BRUCE, CAROL

Tops L-1574	(M)	Carol Bruce Sings	195?	10.00	25.00

BRUCE, LENNY
Refer to Lawrence Schiller.

Fantasy 7001	(M)	Interviews Of Our Times (Thick red vinyl)	1959	16.00	40.00
Fantasy 7001	(M)	Interviews Of Our Times (Thin red vinyl)	196?	8.00	20.00
Fantasy 7001	(M)	Interviews Of Our Times	1959	8.00	20.00
Fantasy 7003	(M)	Sick Humor (Thick red vinyl)	1959	16.00	40.00
Fantasy 7003	(M)	Sick Humor (Thin red vinyl)	196?	8.00	20.00
Fantasy 7003	(M)	Sick Humor Of Lenny Bruce	1959	8.00	20.00
Fantasy 7007	(M)	I Am Not A Nut, Elect Me (Thick red vinyl)	1960	16.00	40.00
Fantasy 7007	(M)	I Am Not A Nut, Elect Me (Thin red vinyl)	196?	8.00	20.00
Fantasy 7007	(M)	I Am Not A Nut, Elect Me	1960	8.00	20.00
Fantasy 7011	(M)	Lenny Bruce, American (Thick red vinyl)	1962	16.00	40.00
Fantasy 7011	(M)	Lenny Bruce, American (Thin red vinyl)	196?	8.00	20.00
Fantasy 7011	(M)	Lenny Bruce, American	1962	8.00	20.00

— Fantasy 7001-7011 were originally pressed on thick, non-flexible red vinyl.
Later pressings were on a thinner, more flexible red and black vinyl.—

Fantasy 7012	(M)	The Best Of Lenny Bruce	1962	8.00	20.00
Philles PHLP-4010	(M)	Lenny Bruce Is Out Again	1966	10.00	25.00
United Arts. UAL-3580	(M)	Lenny Bruce	1967	6.00	15.00
Douglas SD-788	(M)	The Essential Lenny Bruce	1968	6.00	15.00
Bizarre 6329	(M)	The Berkeley Concert	1969	10.00	25.00
Fantasy 7017	(M)	Thank You, Masked Man	1972	6.00	15.00
Fantasy 34201	(M)	Live At The Curran Theater	1972	6.00	15.00
United Arts. UAS-6794	(M)	The Midnight Concert	197?	6.00	15.00
United Arts. UAS-9800	(M)	Carnegie Hall (3 LPs)	1975	6.00	15.00
Fantasy 79003	(M)	The Real Lenny Bruce (2 LPs)	1975	6.00	15.00
Warner Bros. SP-9101	(M)	The Law, The Language And Lenny Bruce	1975	4.00	10.00
Fantasy FP-1	(DJ)	Lenny Bruce Promo Album	197?	8.00	20.00
Douglas 2	(M)	To Is A Preposition, Come Is A Verb	197?	8.00	20.00
Douglas 30872	(M)	What I Was Arrested For	197?	6.00	15.00

BRYAN, JOY

Mode 108	(M)	Joy Bryan Sings	1957	30.00	60.00
Contemporary C3604	(M)	Make The Man Love Me	1961	10.00	25.00
Contemporary S7604	(S)	Make The Man Love Me	1961	14.00	35.00

BRYANT, JIMMY
Bryant also recorded with Speedy West.

Capitol T-1314	(M)	Country Cabin Jazz	1960	40.00	80.00
Capitol ST-1314	(S)	Country Cabin Jazz	1960	50.00	100.00

Label & Catalog #		Title	Year	VG+	NM
Dolton BLP-16505	(M)	**Play Country Guitar With Jimmy Bryant**	*1965*	**6.00**	**15.00**
Dolton BST-17505	(S)	**Play Country Guitar With Jimmy Bryant**	*1965*	**8.00**	**20.00**
Imperial LP-9310	(M)	**Bryant's Back In Town**	*1966*	**6.00**	**15.00**
Imperial LP-12310	(S)	**Bryant's Back In Town**	*1966*	**8.00**	**20.00**
Imperial LP-9315	(M)	**Laughing Guitar, Crying Guitar**	*1966*	**6.00**	**15.00**
Imperial LP-12315	(S)	**Laughing Guitar, Crying Guitar**	*1966*	**8.00**	**20.00**
Imperial LP-9338	(M)	**We Are Young**	*1966*	**6.00**	**15.00**
Imperial LP-12338	(S)	**We Are Young**	*1966*	**8.00**	**20.00**
Imperial LP-9349	(M)	**Wingin' It With Norval & Ivy**	*1967*	**6.00**	**15.00**
Imperial LP-12349	(S)	**Wingin' It With Norval & Ivy**	*1967*	**8.00**	**20.00**
Imperial LP-9360	(M)	**The Fastest Guitar In The Country**	*1967*	**6.00**	**15.00**
Imperial LP-12360	(S)	**The Fastest Guitar In The Country**	*1967*	**8.00**	**20.00**

BRYANT (COMBO), RAY

Label & Catalog #		Title	Year	VG+	NM
Columbia CL-1449	(M)	**Little Susie**	*1960*	**6.00**	**15.00**
Columbia CS-8244	(S)	**Little Susie**	*1960*	**8.00**	**20.00**
Columbia CL-1467	(M)	**Madison Time**	*1960*	**6.00**	**15.00**
Columbia CS-8267	(S)	**Madison Time**	*1960*	**8.00**	**20.00**
Columbia CL-1746	(M)	**Dancing The Big Twist**	*1962*	**6.00**	**15.00**
Columbia CS-8546	(S)	**Dancing The Big Twist**	*1962*	**8.00**	**20.00**

— Original Columbia albums above have three white "eye" logos on each side of the spindle hole.—

Sue 1016	(M)	**Groove House**	*1964*	**14.00**	**35.00**

BUBBLE GUM MACHINE, THE

Label & Catalog #		Title	Year	VG+	NM
Senate 1002	(M)	**The Bubble Gum Machine**	*1967*	**6.00**	**15.00**
Senate 21002	(S)	**The Bubble Gum Machine**	*1967*	**8.00**	**20.00**

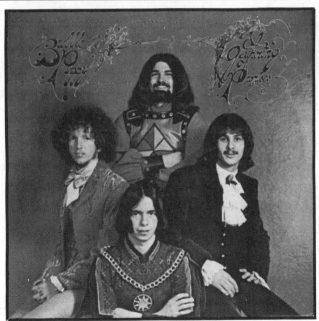

*After hitting with their sole chart entry, the psychedelicized confection "Hot Smoke And Sasafrass,"
Bubble Puppy opted for a harder rock and recorded as Demian.*

BUBBLE PUPPY
Bubble Puppy later recorded as Demian.

International Arts. 10	(S)	**A Gathering Of Promises**	*1969*	**30.00**	**60.00**
International Arts. 10	(S)	**A Gathering Of Promises**	*1979*	**8.00**	**20.00**

(Reissues have "Masterfonics" stamped in the trail-off vinyl.)

Label & Catalog #		Title	Year	VG+	NM
BUCCANEER					
Blunderbuss	(S)	**Buccaneer**	*1980*	**35.00**	**70.00**
		(The title on the cover is gold; issued with two singles.)			
Blunderbuss	(S)	**Buccaneer**	*198?*	**18.00**	**45.00**
		(Second pressings: the title on the cover is red.)			
BUCHANAN & GOODMAN					
Rori 3301	(M)	**The Many Heads Of Buchana & Goodman**	*195?*	**40.00**	**80.00**
BUCHANAN BROTHERS, THE					
The Buchanan Brothers are Terry Cashman, Gene Pistilli and Tommy West.					
Event 101	(S)	**Medicine Man**	*1969*	**10.00**	**25.00**
BUCKAROOS, THE [BUCK OWENS' BUCKAROOS]					
Capitol T-2436	(M)	**The Buck Owens' Songbook**	*1965*	**8.00**	**20.00**
Capitol ST-2436	(S)	**The Buck Owens' Songbook**	*1965*	**12.00**	**30.00**
Capitol T-2722	(M)	**America's Most Wanted Band**	*1967*	**8.00**	**20.00**
Capitol ST-2722	(S)	**America's Most Wanted Band**	*1967*	**10.00**	**25.00**
Capitol T-2828	(M)	**Again**	*1967*	**8.00**	**20.00**
Capitol ST-2828	(S)	**Again**	*1967*	**8.00**	**20.00**
Capitol ST-2902	(S)	**A Night On The Town**	*1968*	**8.00**	**20.00**
Capitol ST-2973	(S)	**Meanwhile, Back At The Ranch**	*1968*	**8.00**	**20.00**
Capitol ST-194	(S)	**Anywhere, U.S.A.**	*1969*	**6.00**	**15.00**
Capitol ST-322	(S)	**Roll Your Own With Buck Owens' Buckaroos**	*1969*	**6.00**	**15.00**
Capitol ST-440	(S)	**Rompin' And Stompin'**	*1970*	**6.00**	**15.00**
Capitol ST-550	(S)	**Boot Hill**	*1970*	**6.00**	**15.00**
Capitol ST-767	(S)	**The Buckaroos Play The Hits**	*1971*	**6.00**	**15.00**
BUCKINGHAM/NICKS					
Lindsay Buckingham and Stevie Nicks. Refer to Fleetwood Mac.					
Polydor PD-5058	(S)	**Buckingham/Nicks** *(Gatefold cover)*	*1973*	**16.00**	**40.00**
Polydor PD-5058	(S)	**Buckingham/Nicks** *(Standard cover)*	*1973*	**6.00**	**15.00**
BUCKINGHAMS, THE					
U.S.A. 107	(M)	**Kind Of A Drag** *(With "I'm A Man")*	*1967*	**180.00**	**300.00**
U.S.A. 107	(M)	**Kind Of A Drag**	*1967*	**8.00**	**20.00**
U.S.A. 107	(S)	**Kind Of A Drag**	*1967*	**10.00**	**25.00**
Columbia CL-2669	(M)	**Time And Charges**	*1967*	**5.00**	**12.00**
Columbia CS-9469	(S)	**Time And Charges**	*1967*	**6.00**	**15.00**
Columbia CL-2798	(M)	**Portraits**	*1968*	**5.00**	**12.00**
Columbia CS-9598	(S)	**Portraits**	*1968*	**6.00**	**15.00**
Columbia CS-9703	(S)	**In One Ear And Gone Tomorrow**	*1968*	**5.00**	**12.00**
Columbia CS-9812	(S)	**The Buckinghams' Greatest Hits**	*1969*	**5.00**	**12.00**
		— Original Columbia albums above have "360 Sound " on the bottom of the label.—			
BUCKLEY, LORD					
RCA Victor LPM-3246 (10")	(M)	**Hipsters, Flipsters And Finger**			
		Poppin' Daddies, Knock Me Your Lobes	*1955*	**75.00**	**150.00**
Vaya 101 (10")	(M)	**Euphoria**	*1955*	**75.00**	**150.00**
Vaya 107/8	(M)	**Euphoria, Volume 2**	*1957*	**20.00**	**50.00**
World Pacific WP-1279	(M)	**The Way Out Humor Of Lord Buckley**	*1959*	**20.00**	**50.00**
Crestview CRV-801	(M)	**The Best Of Lord Buckley**	*1963*	**14.00**	**35.00**
Crestview CRV7-801	(S)	**The Best Of Lord Buckley**	*1963*	**14.00**	**35.00**
World Pacific WP-1815	(M)	**Lord Buckley In Concert**	*1964*	**14.00**	**35.00**
World Pacific WP-1849	(M)	**Blowing His Mind And Yours, Too**	*1966*	**14.00**	**35.00**
World Pacific WPS-21879	(S)	**Buckley's Best**	*1968*	**14.00**	**35.00**
World Pacific WPS-21889	(S)	**Bad Rapping The Marquis De Sade**	*1969*	**14.00**	**35.00**
Elektra EKS-74047	(S)	**The Best Of Lord Buckley**	*1969*	**10.00**	**25.00**
Straight STS-1054	(S)	**A Most Immaculately Hip Autocrat**	*1970*	**14.00**	**35.00**
Bizarre RS-6389	(S)	**Lord Buckley**	*1970*	**10.00**	**25.00**
BUCKLEY, TIM					
Elektra EKL	(M)	**Tim Buckley**	*1966*	**6.00**	**15.00**
Elektra EKS-	(S)	**Tim Buckley**	*1966*	**8.00**	**20.00**
Elektra EKL-4028	(M)	**Goodbye And Hello**	*1967*	**6.00**	**15.00**
Elektra EKS-74028	(S)	**Goodbye And Hello**	*1967*	**8.00**	**20.00**
Elektra EKS-74045	(S)	**Happy Sad**	*1969*	**6.00**	**15.00**
Elektra EKS-74074	(S)	**Lorca**	*1970*	**6.00**	**15.00**
Straight STS-1060	(S)	**Blue Afternoon**	*1969*	**10.00**	**25.00**

Label & Catalog #		Title	Year	VG+	NM
Warner Bros. WS-1842	(S)	**Blue Afternoon**	1970	6.00	15.00
Warner Bros. WS-1881	(S)	**Starsailor**	1970	6.00	15.00
Warner Bros. B-2631	(S)	**Greetings From L.A.**	1972	8.00	20.00
		(Fold-open cover with postcard.)			
DiscReet 2157	(S)	**Sefronia**	1973	8.00	20.00
DiscReet 2201	(S)	**Look At The Fool**	1974	5.00	12.00

BUD & TRAVIS
Bud Dashiell and Travis Edmonson.

Liberty LRP-3125	(M)	**Bud & Travis**	1959	8.00	20.00
Liberty LST-7125	(S)	**Bud & Travis**	1959	10.00	25.00
Liberty LDR-8001	(M)	**Bud & Travis In Concert**	1960	6.00	15.00
Liberty LDS-12001	(S)	**Bud & Travis In Concert**	1960	8.00	20.00
Liberty LRP-3138	(M)	**Spotlight On Bud & Travis**	1961	6.00	15.00
Liberty LST-7138	(S)	**Spotlight On Bud & Travis**	1961	8.00	20.00
Liberty LRP-3222	(M)	**Bud & Travis In Concert, Volume 2**	1962	6.00	15.00
Liberty LST-7222	(S)	**Bud & Travis In Concert, Volume 2**	1962	8.00	20.00
Liberty LRP-3295	(M)	**Naturally**	1963	6.00	15.00
Liberty LST-7295	(S)	**Naturally**	1963	8.00	20.00
Liberty LRP-3341	(M)	**Perspective On Bud & Travis**	1964	6.00	15.00
Liberty LST-7341	(S)	**Perspective On Bud & Travis**	1964	8.00	20.00
Liberty LRP-3386	(M)	**Bud & Travis In Person**	1964	6.00	15.00
Liberty LST-7386	(S)	**Bud & Travis In Person**	1964	8.00	20.00
Liberty LRP-3398	(M)	**Bud & Travis' Latin Album**	1965	6.00	15.00
Liberty LST-7398	(S)	**Bud & Travis' Latin Album**	1965	8.00	20.00

BUDDIES, THE

Wing MGW-12293	(M)	**The Buddies And The Compacts**	1965	10.00	25.00
Wing SRW-16293	(S)	**The Buddies And The Compacts**	1965	12.00	30.00
Wing MGW-12306	(M)	**Go Go With The Buddies**	1965	8.00	20.00
Wing SRW-16306	(S)	**Go Go With The Buddies**	1965	10.00	25.00

BUDGIE

Kapp KS-3656	(S)	**Budgie**	1971	12.00	30.00
Kapp KS-3669	(S)	**Squawk**	1972	10.00	25.00
MCA 429	(S)	**In For The Kill**	1973	8.00	20.00

BUFFALO NICKEL JUGBAND, THE

Happy Tiger 1018	(S)	**The Buffalo Nickel Jugband**	1971	10.00	25.00

BUFFALO SPRINGFIELD, THE
The Springfield consisted of Neil Young, Steve Stills, Richie Furay, Dewey Martin and Bruce Palmer, replaced by Jim Messina in 1968.

Atco 33-200	(M)	**Buffalo Springfield**	1966	See note below	
Atco SD-33-200	(S)	**Buffalo Springfield**	1966	See note below	
		(First pressings contain the track "Baby Don't Scold Me," This was replaced in 1967 with the hit "For What It's Worth." Rare. Estimated near mint value for the mono $75-150; estimated near mint value for the stereo $100-200.)			
Atco 33-200A	(M)	**Buffalo Springfield**	1967	10.00	25.00
Atco SD-33-200A	(S)	**Buffalo Springfield**	1967	6.00	15.00
		(With "For What It's Worth.")			
Atco 33-226	(M)	**Buffalo Springfield Again**	1967	10.00	25.00
Atco SD-33-226	(S)	**Buffalo Springfield Again**	1967	6.00	15.00
Atco SD-33-256	(S)	**Last Time Around**	1968	6.00	15.00
		— Original Atco stereo albums above purple & brown labels.—			

BUFFETT, JIMMY

ABC SPDJ-43	(DJ)	**Special Jimmy Buffett Sampler**	1978	6.00	15.00

BUGALOOS, THE

Capitol SW-621	(S)	**Bugaloos**	1970	6.00	15.00

BUMP

Pioneer	(S)	**Bump**	1970	180.00	300.00

BUNNY, BUGS: *Refer to* MEL BLANC

Label & Catalog #		Title	Year	VG+	NM

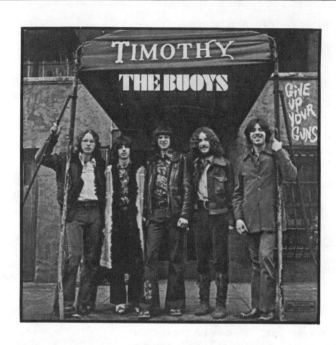

*Honeycombed with abandoned coal mines, their home town, Wilkes-Barre, PA, provided The Buoys'
with a perfect setting for their hit, "Timothy," a cheeky tale of cannibalism.*

BUOYS, THE

Scepter SPS-593	(S)	**Timothy**	*1971*	**6.00**	**15.00**

BURDON, ERIC, & THE ANIMALS
This is a completely different group than the one who recorded as The Animals.

MGM E-4433	(M)	**Eric Is Here**	*1967*	**4.00**	**10.00**
MGM SE-4433	(S)	**Eric Is Here**	*1967*	**5.00**	**12.00**
MGM E-4454	(M)	**Best Of Eric Burdon & The Animals, Vol. 2**	*1967*	**5.00**	**12.00**
MGM SE-4454	(P)	**Best Of Eric Burdon & The Animals, Vol. 2**	*1967*	**6.00**	**15.00**
MGM E-4484	(M)	**Winds Of Change**	*1967*	**5.00**	**12.00**
MGM SE-4484	(S)	**Winds Of Change**	*1967*	**6.00**	**15.00**
MGM E-4537	(M)	**The Twain Shall Meet**	*1968*	**12.00**	**30.00**
MGM SE-4537	(S)	**The Twain Shall Meet**	*1968*	**6.00**	**15.00**
MGM E-4553	(M)	**Every One Of Us**	*1968*	**12.00**	**30.00**
MGM SE-4553	(S)	**Every One Of Us**	*1968*	**5.00**	**12.00**
MGM SE-4591	(S)	**Love Is** *(2 LPs)*	*1969*	**20.00**	**50.00**
MGM SE-4602	(S)	**Greatest Hits Of Eric Burdon & The Animals**	*1969*	**4.00**	**10.00**

BURDON, ERIC, & WAR

MGM SAMP-4710	(DJ)	**Black Man's Burdon** *(Radio sampler)*	*1970*	**10.00**	**25.00**

BURDON, ERIC [THE ERIC BURDON BAND]

Capitol ST-11359	(S)	**Sun Secrets**	*1974*	**6.00**	**15.00**
Capitol SMAS-11426	(S)	**Stop!**	*1975*	**6.00**	**15.00**

BURGHOFF, GARY

Shalom 651	(S)	**Just For Fun**	*197?*	**8.00**	**20.00**

BURKE, SOLOMON

Apollo ALP-498	(M)	**Solomon Burke**	*1962*	**100.00**	**200.00**
Atlantic 8067	(M)	**Solomon Burke's Greatest Hits**	*1962*	**16.00**	**40.00**
Atlantic SD-8067	(S)	**Solomon Burke's Greatest Hits**	*1962*	**20.00**	**50.00**

Label & Catalog #		Title	Year	VG+	NM
Atlantic 8085	(M)	**If You Need Me**	1963	16.00	40.00
Atlantic SD-8085	(S)	**If You Need Me**	1963	20.00	50.00
Atlantic 8096	(M)	**Rock 'N' Roll Soul**	1964	16.00	40.00
Atlantic SD-8096	(S)	**Rock 'N' Roll Soul**	1964	20.00	50.00
Atlantic 8109	(M)	**The Best Of Solomon Burke**	1965	12.00	30.00
Atlantic SD-8109	(S)	**The Best Of Solomon Burke**	1965	16.00	40.00
Atlantic SD-8185	(S)	**I Wish I Knew**	1968	10.00	25.00
Atlantic SD-8158	(S)	**King Solomon**	1968	10.00	25.00
Bell 6033	(S)	**Proud Mary**	1969	6.00	15.00
MGM SE-4767	(S)	**Electronic Magnetism**	1971	4.00	10.00
MGM SE-4830	(S)	**We're Almost Home**	1972	4.00	10.00

BURNETTE, DORSEY

Era EL-102	(M)	**Tall Oak Tree**	1960	75.00	150.00
Era ES-102	(S)	**Tall Oak Tree**	1960	180.00	300.00
Dot DLP-3456	(M)	**Dorsey Burnette Sings**	1963	16.00	40.00
Dot DLP-25456	(S)	**Dorsey Burnette Sings**	1963	20.00	50.00
Era ES-800	(S)	**Dorsey Burnette's Greatest Hits**	1969	10.00	25.00
Capitol ST-11094	(S)	**Here And Now**	1972	6.00	15.00
Capitol ST-11219	(S)	**Dorsey Burnette**	1973	6.00	15.00

BURNETTE, JOHNNY

Liberty LRP-3179	(M)	**Dreamin'**	1960	16.00	40.00
Liberty LST-7179	(S)	**Dreamin'**	1960	20.00	50.00
Liberty LRP-3183	(M)	**Johnny Burnette**	1961	16.00	40.00
Liberty LST-7183	(S)	**Johnny Burnette**	1961	20.00	50.00
Liberty LRP-3190	(M)	**Johnny Burnette Sings**	1961	16.00	40.00
Liberty LST-7190	(S)	**Johnny Burnette Sings**	1961	20.00	50.00
Liberty LRP-3206	(M)	**Hits And Other Favorites**	1962	16.00	40.00
Liberty LST-7206	(S)	**Hits And Other Favorites**	1962	20.00	50.00
Liberty LRP-3255	(M)	**Roses Are Red**	1962	16.00	40.00
Liberty LST-7255	(S)	**Roses Are Red**	1962	20.00	50.00
Liberty LRP-3389	(M)	**The Johnny Burnette Story**	1964	16.00	40.00
Liberty LST-7389	(S)	**The Johnny Burnette Story**	1964	20.00	50.00

BURNETTE, JOHNNY, & THE ROCK 'N' ROLL TRIO

Coral CRL-57080	(M)	**Johnny Burnette & The Rock 'N' Roll Trio** *(Convincing counterfeits exist.)*	1956	1,000.00	1,500.00

BURNETTE, T-BONE

Warner Bros. 23921	(DJ)	**Proof Through The Night** *(Quiex II vinyl)*	1983	6.00	15.00

BURNS, RANDY, & THE SKY DOG BAND

ESP 2007	(S)	**Song For An Uncertain Lady**	1971	6.00	15.00

BURNT SUITE

B.J.W. 9	(M)	**Burnt Suite**	1967	75.00	150.00

BURRITO BROTHERS: Refer to FLYING BURRITO BROTHERS

BURROUGHS, WILLIAM

ESP 1050	(M)	**Call Me Burroughs**	196?	20.00	50.00

BURROWS, ABE

Columbia CL-6128 (10")	(M)	**Abe Burrows Sings**	195?	16.00	40.00
Decca DL-5288 (10")	(M)	**The Girl With The Three Blue Eyes**	1950	16.00	40.00

BURTON, JAMES
Refer to Longbranch Pennywhistle; Ralph Mooney.

A&M SP-4293	(S)	**James Burton**	1971	10.00	25.00

BUSH, JOHNNY

Million 1001	(M)	**The Best Of Johnny Bush**	1972	16.00	40.00

BUSH, KATE

EMI ST-17171	(DJ)	**Hounds Of Love** *(Marble vinyl)*	1986	16.00	40.00
EMI ST-17171	(DJ)	**Hounds Of Love** *(Marble vinyl)*	1986	50.00	100.00
		(Promo package issued with poster, press kit and ribbon.)			

Label & Catalog #		Title	Year	VG+	NM

An institution in Great Britain, the idiosyncratic Ms. Bush remains a bit of a cult item in the U.S., although anything remotely collectible gets scarfed up by her rabid followers.

BUSHES, THE

Growth LPS-200-08	(S)	**Assorted Shrubbery**	*197?*	**50.00**	**100.00**

BUSKERS, THE

RCA Victor LPM-104	(M)	**Ave A Go With The Buskers**	*1961*	**6.00**	**15.00**
RCA Victor LSP-104	(S)	**Ave A Go With The Buskers**	*1961*	**8.00**	**20.00**

BUTCH

Sunndial	(S)	**The Bitch Of Rock & Roll**	*1977*	**80.00**	**160.00**

BUTERA, SAM, & THE WITNESSES

Dot DLP-3272	(M)	**The Wildest Clan**	*1960*	**8.00**	**20.00**
Dot DLP-25272	(S)	**The Wildest Clan**	*1960*	**10.00**	**25.00**

BUTLER, BILLY

OKeh OKM-12115	(M)	**Right Track**	*1966*	**6.00**	**15.00**
OKeh OKS-12115	(S)	**Right Track**	*1966*	**6.00**	**15.00**
Prestige PRST-7734	(S)	**Guitar Soul**	*1969*	**5.00**	**12.00**

BUTLER, CARL

Columbia CL-2002	(M)	**Don't Let Me Cross Over**	*1963*	**6.00**	**15.00**
Columbia CS-8802	(S)	**Don't Let Me Cross Over**	*1963*	**8.00**	**20.00**

BUTLER, CARL & PEARL

Columbia CL-2125	(M)	**Loving Arms**	*1964*	**5.00**	**12.00**
Columbia CS-8925	(S)	**Loving Arms**	*1964*	**6.00**	**15.00**
Columbia CL-2308	(M)	**The Old And The New**	*1965*	**5.00**	**12.00**
Columbia CS-9108	(S)	**The Old And The New**	*1965*	**6.00**	**15.00**
Columbia CL-2640	(M)	**Avenue Of Prayer**	*1967*	**5.00**	**12.00**
Columbia CS-9440	(S)	**Avenue Of Prayer**	*1967*	**6.00**	**15.00**

BUTLER, JERRY

Abner R-2001	(M)	**Jerry Butler Esquire**	*1959*	**75.00**	**150.00**

Label & Catalog #		Title	Year	VG+	NM
Vee Jay LP-1027	(M)	Jerry Butler Esquire	1961	20.00	50.00
Vee Jay LP-1029	(M)	He Will Break Your Heart	1960	20.00	50.00
Vee Jay LP-1034	(M)	Love Me	1961	14.00	35.00
Vee Jay LP-1038	(M)	Aware Of Love	1961	10.00	25.00
Vee Jay SR-1038	(S)	Aware Of Love	1961	12.00	30.00
Vee Jay LP-1046	(M)	Moon River	1962	10.00	25.00
Vee Jay SR-1046	(S)	Moon River	1962	12.00	30.00
Vee Jay LP-1048	(M)	The Best Of Jerry Butler	1962	8.00	20.00
Vee Jay SR-1048	(P)	The Best Of Jerry Butler	1962	10.00	25.00
Vee Jay LP-1057	(M)	Folk Songs	1963	8.00	20.00
Vee Jay SR-1057	(S)	Folk Songs	1963	10.00	25.00
Vee Jay LP-1075	(M)	For Your Precious Love	1963	8.00	20.00
Vee Jay VJS-1075	(S)	For Your Precious Love	1963	10.00	25.00
Vee Jay LP-1076	(M)	Giving Up On Love/Need To Belong	1963	8.00	20.00
Vee Jay VJS-1076	(S)	Giving Up On Love/Need To Belong	1963	10.00	25.00
Vee Jay LP-1119	(M)	More Of The Best Of Jerry Butler	1965	5.00	12.00
Vee Jay VJS-1119	(S)	More Of The Best Of Jerry Butler	1965	6.00	15.00
Vee Jay VJS-2-1003	(M)	Jerry Butler's Gold (2 LPs)	196?	6.00	15.00

BUTLER, JERRY, & BETTY EVERETT

Vee Jay LP-1099	(M)	Delicious Together	1964	6.00	15.00
Vee Jay VJS-1099	(S)	Delicious Together	1964	8.00	20.00

BUTTERFIELD, PAUL [THE BUTTERFIELD BLUES BAND]

Elektra EKL-294	(M)	Paul Butterfield Blues Band	1965	6.00	15.00
Elektra EKS-7294	(S)	Paul Butterfield Blues Band	1965	8.00	20.00
Elektra EKL-315	(M)	East-West	1966	6.00	15.00
Elektra EKS-7315	(S)	East-West	1966	8.00	20.00
Elektra EKL-4015	(M)	Resurrection Of Pigboy Crabshaw	1967	6.00	15.00
Elektra EKS-74015	(S)	Resurrection Of Pigboy Crabshaw	1967	8.00	20.00
Elektra EKS-74025	(S)	In My Own Dream	1968	6.00	15.00
Elektra EKS-75031	(S)	Sometimes I Just Feel Like Smilin'	1971	5.00	12.00
Elektra EKS-75053	(S)	Keep On Moving	1971	5.00	12.00
Elektra 7E-2001	(S)	Paul Butterfield Blues Band Live (2 LPs)	1971	6.00	15.00
Elektra 7E-2005	(S)	Golden Butter (2 LPs)	1972	5.00	12.00
Red Lightnin'	(M)	Offer You Can't Refuse	1972	12.00	30.00

BUTTERSWORTH, MARY

Custom Fidelity	(S)	Mary Buttersworth	1971	100.00	200.00

BYRD, BOBBY
Bobby Byrd originally recorded as Bobby Day.

King KS-1118	(S)	I Need Help	1970	12.00	30.00

BYRD, JERRY
Jerry also recorded as a member of The Country All-Stars.

Mercury MG-25077 (10")	(M)	Nani Hawaii	1954	20.00	50.00
Mercury MG-25134 (10")	(M)	Pagan Love Song	1954	20.00	50.00
Mercury MG-25169 (10")	(M)	Byrd's Expedition	1954	20.00	50.00
Mercury MG-20693	(M)	Hawaiian Golden Hits	1962	8.00	20.00
Mercury SR-60693	(S)	Hawaiian Golden Hits	1962	12.00	30.00
Mercury MG-20856	(M)	Blue Hawaiian Steel Guitar	1963	8.00	20.00
Mercury SR-60856	(S)	Blue Hawaiian Steel Guitar	1963	12.00	30.00
Mercury MG-20932	(M)	The Man Of Steel	1964	8.00	20.00
Mercury SR-60932	(S)	The Man Of Steel	1964	12.00	30.00
Decca DL-8643	(M)	Hi Fi Guitar	1958	16.00	40.00
Decca DL-4078	(M)	Paradise Island	1961	8.00	20.00
Decca DL-74078	(S)	Paradise Island	1961	12.00	30.00
Wing MGW-12315	(M)	Country Steel Guitar Favorites	196?	8.00	20.00
Wing SRW-16315	(S)	Country Steel Guitar Favorites	196?	12.00	30.00
Monument M-4003	(M)	Byrd Of Paradise	1961	6.00	15.00
Monument SM-14008	(S)	Memories Of Maria	1962	8.00	20.00
Monument LP-8018	(M)	Admirable Byrd	1963	6.00	15.00
Monument SLP-18018	(S)	Admirable Byrd	1963	8.00	20.00
Monument LP-8033	(M)	Satin Strings Of Steel	1965	6.00	15.00
Monument SLP-18033	(S)	Satin Strings Of Steel	1965	8.00	20.00
Monument LP-8040	(M)	Potpourri	1965	6.00	15.00
Monument SLP-18040	(S)	Potpourri	1965	8.00	20.00

Label & Catalog #		Title	Year	VG+	NM
Monument LP-8081	(M)	**Burning Sands/Pearly Shells**	*1966*	6.00	15.00
Monument SLP-18081	(S)	**Burning Sands/Pearly Shells**	*1966*	8.00	20.00
Monument LP-8107	(M)	**Polynesian Suite**	*1967*	6.00	15.00
Monument SLP-18107	(S)	**Polynesian Suite**	*1967*	8.00	20.00

BYRD, JERRY / SHOT JACKSON

Sesac PA-228	(M)	**Just A Minute**	*195?*	50.00	100.00

BYRDS, THE

Original members were Gene Clark, Michael Clarke, David Crosby, Chris Hillman and Jim/Roger McGuinn. Later members include Gram Parsons, Clarence White, John York, Gene Parsons and Skip Battin. Also refer to the Beefeaters.

Columbia CL-2372	(DJ)	**Mr. Tambourine Man** *(White label)*	*1965*	40.00	80.00
Columbia CL-2372	(M)	**Mr. Tambourine Man**	*1965*	16.00	40.00
		(Original mono pressing labels read "Guaranteed High Fidelity.")			
Columbia CL-2372	(M)	**Mr. Tambourine Man**	*1965*	8.00	20.00
Columbia CS-9172	(P)	**Mr. Tambourine Man**	*1965*	8.00	20.00
Columbia CL-2454	(DJ)	**Turn, Turn, Turn** *(White label)*	*1965*	30.00	60.00
Columbia CL-2454	(M)	**Turn, Turn, Turn**	*1965*	8.00	20.00
Columbia CS-9254	(P)	**Turn, Turn, Turn**	*1965*	8.00	20.00
Columbia ZLP-116003	(DJ)	**5D Open-End Interview**	*1966*	180.00	300.00
		(Issued in a special paper sleeve with inserts.)			
Columbia CL-2549	(DJ)	**5D (Fifth Dimension)** *(White label)*	*1966*	30.00	60.00
Columbia CL-2549	(M)	**5D (Fifth Dimension)**	*1966*	8.00	20.00
Columbia CS-9349	(S)	**5D (Fifth Dimension)**	*1966*	8.00	20.00
Columbia CL-2642	(DJ)	**Younger Than Yesterday** *(White label)*	*1967*	30.00	60.00
Columbia CL-2642	(M)	**Younger Than Yesterday**	*1967*	10.00	25.00
Columbia CS-9442	(S)	**Younger Than Yesterday**	*1967*	8.00	20.00
MGM E-4484	(M)	**Don't Make Waves** *(Soundtrack)*	*1967*	6.00	15.00
MGM SE-4484	(S)	**Don't Make Waves** *(Soundtrack)*	*1967*	8.00	20.00
Columbia CL-2716	(DJ)	**The Byrds' Greatest Hits** *(White label)*	*1967*	30.00	60.00
Columbia CL-2716	(M)	**The Byrds' Greatest Hits**	*1967*	10.00	25.00
Columbia CS-9516	(P)	**The Byrds' Greatest Hits**	*1967*	6.00	15.00
Columbia CL-2775	(DJ)	**The Notorious Byrd Brothers** *(White label)*	*1968*	30.00	60.00
Columbia CL-2775	(M)	**The Notorious Byrd Brothers**	*1968*	12.00	30.00
Columbia CS-9575	(S)	**The Notorious Byrd Brothers**	*1968*	6.00	15.00
Columbia CS-9670	(DJ)	**Sweetheart Of The Rodeo** *(White label)*	*1968*	12.00	30.00
Columbia CS-9670	(S)	**Sweetheart Of The Rodeo**	*1968*	6.00	15.00
ABC S-OC-9	(S)	**Candy** *(Soundtrack)*	*1968*	6.00	15.00
Columbia CS-9755	(DJ)	**Dr. Byrds And Mr. Hyde** *(White label)*	*1969*	12.00	30.00
Columbia CS-9755	(S)	**Dr. Byrds And Mr. Hyde**	*1969*	6.00	15.00
Columbia CS-9942	(DJ)	**The Ballad Of Easy Rider** *(White label)*	*1969*	10.00	25.00
Columbia CS-9942	(S)	**The Ballad Of Easy Rider**	*1969*	6.00	15.00
		—Original Columbia albums above have "360 Sound" on the bottom of the label.—			
Together ST-1-1001	(S)	**Preflyte**	*1969*	6.00	15.00

BYRNES, ED "KOOKIE"

Warner Bros. W-1309	(M)	**Kookie**	*1959*	10.00	25.00
Warner Bros. WS-1309	(S)	**Kookie**	*1959*	12.00	30.00

C.A. QUINTET, THE

Candy Floss 7764	(M)	**A Trip Through Hell**	*1969*	530.00	800.00

A quintessential black vocal group featuring Earl "Speedo" Carroll, who later quit to join The Coasters, the Cadillacs produced exciting music during doo wop's heyday and placed two songs high in the pop charts, "Speedo" and "Peek-A-Boo." While popular they were known for their uptempo numbers (both the aforementioned hits), although most vocal group collectors prefer their slow ones, such as the oft-covered "Gloria," written by their manager. They recorded well into the '60s for Smash, Capitol and Mercury, but none of these labels saw fit to release an album.

Label & Catalog #		Title	Year	VG+	NM
C.C.S.					
Rak KZ-30559	(S)	Whole Lotta Love	1971	10.00	25.00
Rak KZ-31569	(S)	C.C.S.	1972	10.00	25.00
CABOT, SEBASTIAN					
MGM E-4431	(M)	Sebastian Cabot, Actor/Bob Dylan, Poet	1967	6.00	15.00
MGM SE-4431	(S)	Sebastian Cabot, Actor/Bob Dylan, Poet	1967	8.00	20.00
CADETS, THE					
The Cadets also recorded as The Jacks.					
Crown CLP-5015	(M)	Rockin' 'N' Reelin	1957	75.00	150.00
Crown CLP-5370	(M)	The Cadets	1963	20.00	50.00
Crown CST-370	(E)	The Cadets	1963	20.00	50.00
CADILLACS, THE					
Jubilee JGM-1045	(M)	The Fabulous Cadillacs *(Blue label)*	1957	180.00	300.00
Jubilee JGM-1045	(M)	The Fabulous Cadillacs *(Flat black label)*	1959	100.00	200.00
Jubilee JGM-1045	(M)	The Fabulous Cadillacs *(Glossy black label)*	1960	35.00	70.00
Jubilee JGM-1089	(M)	The Crazy Cadillacs *(Flat black label)*	1959	100.00	200.00
Jubilee JGM-1089	(M)	The Crazy Cadillacs *(Glossy black label)*	1960	35.00	70.00
Jubilee JGM-5009	(M)	Twisting With The Cadillacs	1962	75.00	150.00
CADILLACS, THE / THE ORIOLES					
Jubilee JGM-1117	(M)	The Cadillacs Meet The Orioles	1961	75.00	150.00
CAIN					
A.S.I. 204	(S)	A Pound Of Flesh	1974	14.00	35.00
A.S.I. 214	(S)	Stinger	1975	8.00	20.00
CAIN, JACKIE, & ROY KRAL					
Storyville STLP-322 (10")	(M)	Jackie & Roy	1955	35.00	70.00
Storyville STLP-904	(M)	Storyville Presents Jackie And Roy	1956	20.00	50.00
Storyville STLP-915	(M)	Sing Baby, Sing!	1956	20.00	50.00
Brunswick BL-54026	(M)	Jackie Cain And Roy Kral	1956	16.00	40.00
Regent 6057	(M)	Jackie Cain And Roy Kral	1957	16.00	40.00
ABC-Paramount 120	(M)	The Glory Of Love	1956	16.00	40.00
ABC-Paramount 163	(M)	Bits And Pieces	1957	16.00	40.00
ABC-Paramount 207	(M)	Free And Easy	1958	16.00	40.00
ABC-Paramount 267	(M)	In The Spotlight	1959	12.00	30.00
ABC-Paramount S-267	(S)	In The Spotlight	1959	16.00	40.00
Columbia CL-1469	(M)	Sweet And Low Down	1960	8.00	20.00
Columbia CS-8260	(S)	Sweet And Low Down	1960	12.00	30.00
Columbia CL-1704	(M)	Double Take	1961	6.00	15.00
Columbia CS-8504	(S)	Double Take	1961	8.00	20.00
Columbia CL-1934	(M)	Like Sing	1962	6.00	15.00
Columbia CS-8734	(S)	Like Sing	1962	8.00	20.00
Roulette R-25278	(M)	By Jupiter/Girl Crazy	1964	6.00	15.00
Roulette R-25278	(S)	By Jupiter/Girl Crazy	1964	8.00	20.00
CAKE, THE					
Decca DL-4927	(M)	The Cake	1967	6.00	15.00
Decca DL-74927	(S)	The Cake	1967	8.00	20.00
Decca DL-75039	(S)	A Slice Of The Cake	1968	8.00	20.00
CALE, JOHN					
Cale was formerly a member of the Velvet Underground.					
Columbia CS-1037	(S)	Vintage Violence *("360 Sound" label)*	1970	6.00	15.00
Reprise MS-2079	(S)	The Academy In Peril	1972	5.00	12.00
Reprise MS-2131	(S)	Paris, 1919	1973	4.00	10.00
CALE, JOHN, & TERRY RILEY					
Columbia CS-30131	(S)	Church Of Anthrax	1971	6.00	15.00
CALIFORNIA, RANDY					
California was formerly a member of Spirit.					
Epic KE-31755	(S)	Kapt. Kopter & The Fabulous Twirly Birds *(Yellow label)*	1972	6.00	15.00

Label & Catalog #		Title	Year	VG+	NM
CALIFORNIA POPPY PICKERS, THE					
Alshire 5152	(S)	**Sounds Of '69**	1969	10.00	25.00
Alshire 5153	(S)	**Let The Sunshine In**	1969	10.00	25.00
Alshire 5163	(S)	**Today's Chart Busters**	1969	10.00	25.00
CALLIOPE					
Calliope features Danny O'Keefe.					
Buddah BDS-5023	(S)	**Steamed**	1968	8.00	20.00
CALLOWAY, CAB					
Epic LN-3265	(M)	**Cab Calloway**	195?	16.00	40.00
RCA Victor LPM-2021	(M)	**Hi De Hi, Hi De Ho**	1959	12.00	30.00
RCA Victor LSP-2021	(S)	**Hi De Hi, Hi De Ho**	1959	16.00	40.00
Coral CRL-57408	(M)	**Blues Make Me Happy**	1962	6.00	15.00
Coral CRL-757408	(S)	**Blues Make Me Happy**	1962	8.00	20.00
CAMPBELL, CECIL					
Starday SLP-254	(M)	**Steel Guitar Jamboree**	1963	12.00	30.00
Winston 1001	(M)	**Greatest Hawaiian Instrumentals**	196?	8.00	20.00
CAMPBELL, CHOKER					
Motown 620	(M)	**Hits Of The Sixties**	1965	8.00	20.00
Motown MS-620	(S)	**Hits Of The Sixties**	1965	12.00	30.00
CAMPBELL, DICK					
Mercury MG-21060	(M)	**Dick Campbell Sings Where It's At**	1966	8.00	20.00
Mercury SR-61060	(S)	**Dick Campbell Sings Where It's At**	1966	10.00	25.00
CAMPBELL, GLEN					
Campbell was formerly a member of The Bandits; The Folkswingers; The Green River Boys.					
Capitol T-1810	(M)	**Big Bluegrass Special**	1962	16.00	40.00
Capitol T-1810	(S)	**Big Bluegrass Special**	1962	20.00	50.00
Capitol T-1881	(M)	**Too Late To Worry, Too Blue To Cry**	1963	6.00	15.00
Capitol ST-1881	(S)	**Too Late To Worry, Too Blue To Cry**	1963	8.00	20.00
Capitol T-2023	(M)	**Astounding 12-String Guitar**	1964	4.00	10.00
Capitol ST-2023	(S)	**Astounding 12-String Guitar**	1964	5.00	12.00
Capitol T-2392	(M)	**The Big Bad Rock Guitar Of Glen Campbell**	1965	5.00	12.00
Capitol ST-2392	(S)	**The Big Bad Rock Guitar Of Glen Campbell**	1965	6.00	15.00
Capitol SW-11722	(DJ)	**Basic** *(Picture disc)*	1978	20.00	50.00
CAMPBELL, IAN					
Elektra EKL-268	(M)	**The Ian Campbell Folk Group**	1964	5.00	12.00
Elektra EKS-7268	(S)	**The Ian Campbell Folk Group**	1964	6.00	15.00
Elektra EKL-309	(M)	**Rights Of Man**	1966	5.00	12.00
Elektra EKS-7309	(S)	**Rights Of Man**	1966	6.00	15.00
CAMPBELL, JO ANN					
End LP-306	(M)	**I'm Nobody's Baby**	1959	20.00	50.00
ABC-Paramount 393	(M)	**Twistin' And Listenin'**	1962	35.00	70.00
ABC-Paramount S-393	(S)	**Twistin' And Listenin'**	1962	50.00	100.00
Cameo C-1026	(M)	**All The Hits Of Jo Ann Campbell**	1962	12.00	30.00
Cameo SC-1026	(S)	**All The Hits Of Jo Ann Campbell**	1962	16.00	40.00
Roulette R-25168	(M)	**Hey, Let's Twist** *(Soundtrack)*	1962	12.00	30.00
Roulette SR-25168	(S)	**Hey, Let's Twist** *(Soundtrack)*	1962	16.00	40.00
Coronet CX-199	(M)	**Starring Jo Ann Campbell**	196?	6.00	15.00
Coronet CXS-199	(S)	**Starring Jo Ann Campbell**	196?	6.00	15.00
CAMPUS SINGERS, THE					
Argo 4023	(M)	**The Campus Singers At The Fickle Pickle**	1963	10.00	25.00
CANADIAN BEADLES, THE					
Tide 2005	(M)	**Three Faces North**	1964	20.00	50.00
CANADIAN SWEETHEARTS, THE					
A&M LP-106	(M)	**Introducing The Canadian Sweethearts**	1964	8.00	20.00
A&M SP-106	(S)	**Introducing The Canadian Sweethearts**	1964	12.00	30.00
CANARIES, THE					
B.T. Puppy BTS-1007	(S)	**Flying High With The Canaries**	1970	16.00	40.00

Label & Catalog #		Title	Year	VG+	NM
CANDYMEN, THE					
ABC 616	(M)	The Candymen	1967	5.00	12.00
ABC S-616	(S)	The Candymen	1967	6.00	15.00
ABC S-633	(S)	The Candymen Bring You Candypower	1968	6.00	15.00
CANDY STORE, THE					
Decca DL-75147	(S)	Turned On Christmas	1969	10.00	25.00
CANNED HEAT					
Canned Heat also recorded with John Lee Hooker.					
Liberty LRP-3526	(M)	Canned Heat	1967	8.00	20.00
Liberty LST-7526	(S)	Canned Heat	1967	6.00	15.00
Liberty LST-7541	(S)	Boogie With Canned Heat	1968	6.00	15.00
Liberty LST-7618	(S)	Hallelujah	1968	6.00	15.00
Liberty LST-27200	(S)	Living The Blues	1968	6.00	15.00
Liberty LST-11000	(S)	Canned Heat Cookbook	1969	4.00	10.00
Liberty LST-11002	(P)	Future Blues	1970	4.00	10.00
Wand WDS-693	(S)	Live At Topanga Canyon	1970	8.00	20.00
Liberty LST-35002	(S)	Hooker 'N' Heat	1971	6.00	15.00
United Arts. UAS-9955	(S)	Living The Blues	1971	4.00	10.00
United Arts. UAS-5509	(S)	Live In Europe	1971	4.00	10.00
United Arts. LA049	(S)	New Age	1973	4.00	10.00
Atlantic SD-7239	(S)	One More River To Cross	1973	4.00	10.00
CANNED HEAT & LITTLE RICHARD					
United Arts. UAS-5557	(S)	Historical Figures *(With comic book)*	1972	4.00	10.00
CANNIBAL & THE HEADHUNTERS					
Rampart RM-3302	(M)	Land Of 1,000 Dances	1966	16.00	40.00
Rampart RS-3302	(S)	Land Of 1,000 Dances	1966	20.00	50.00
Date TEM-3001	(M)	Land Of 1,000 Dances	1966	12.00	30.00
Date TES-3001	(S)	Land Of 1,000 Dances	1966	16.00	40.00
CANNON, FREDDY					
Swan LP-502	(M)	The Explosive! Freddie Cannon	1960	50.00	100.00
Swan LPS-502	(P)	The Explosive! Freddie Cannon	1960	75.00	150.00
Swan LP-504	(M)	Happy Shades Of Blue	1960	50.00	100.00
Swan LP-505	(M)	Solid Gold Hits	1961	50.00	100.00
Swan 506	(M)	Twistin' All Night Long	1961	50.00	100.00
		(Freddy is backed by Danny & The Juniors.)			
Swan LP-507	(M)	Freddie Cannon At Palisades Park	1962	50.00	100.00
Swan LP-511	(M)	Freddie Cannon Steps Out	1963	50.00	100.00
Warner Bros. W-1544	(M)	Freddie Cannon	1964	8.00	20.00
Warner Bros. WS-1544	(S)	Freddie Cannon	1964	10.00	25.00
Warner Bros. W-1612	(M)	Action!	1965	8.00	20.00
Warner Bros. WS-1612	(S)	Action!	1965	10.00	25.00
Warner Bros. W-1628	(M)	Freddie Cannon's Greatest Hits	1966	8.00	20.00
Warner Bros. WS-1628	(S)	Freddie Cannon's Greatest Hits	1966	10.00	25.00
CANNON, GUS					
Stax 702	(M)	Walk Right In	1962	16.00	40.00
CANTELON, WILLARD					
Supreme M-113	(M)	L.S.D. Battle For The Mind	1966	6.00	15.00
Supreme S-113	(S)	L.S.D. Battle For The Mind	1966	8.00	20.00
CAPES & MASKS, THE					
Mainstream 16069	(M)	Comic Book Heroes	1966	5.00	12.00
Mainstream 6069	(S)	Comic Book Heroes	1966	6.00	15.00
CAPITAL CITY ROCKETS, THE					
Elektra EKS-75059	(S)	Capital City Rockets	1973	6.00	15.00
CAPITOLS, THE					
Atco 33-190	(M)	Dance The Cool Jerk	1966	12.00	30.00
Atco SD-33-190	(S)	Dance The Cool Jerk	1966	16.00	40.00
Atco 33-201	(M)	We Got A Thing That's In The Groove	1966	12.00	30.00
Atco SD-33-201	(S)	We Got A Thing That's In The Groove	1966	14.00	40.00

Label & Catalog #		Title	Year	VG+	NM
CAPOTE, TRUMAN					
United Arts. UAS-6621	(S)	**Christmas Memory**	1968	6.00	15.00
United Arts. UAS-6682	(S)	**Thanksgiving Visitor**	1968	6.00	15.00
CAPRIS, THE					
Ambient Sound 37714	(S)	**There's A Moon Out Tonight**	1982	4.00	10.00
CAPTAIN & TENNILLE, THE					
Daryl Dragon and Toni Tenille.					
A&M QU-54552	(Q)	**Love Will Keep Us Together**	1975	5.00	12.00
CAPTAIN BEEFHEART & THE MAGIC BAND					
The Captain also recorded with Frank Zappa.					
Buddah BDM-1001	(M)	**Safe As Milk**	1967	16.00	40.00
Buddah BDS-5001	(E)	**Safe As Milk** *(Red label)*	1967	12.00	30.00
		(With custom inner sleeve and bumper sticker.)			
Buddah BDS-5001	(E)	**Safe As Milk** *(Multi-color label)*	1969	6.00	15.00
Blue Thumb BTS-1	(S)	**Strictly Personal**	1968	8.00	20.00
Straight STS-1053	(S)	**Trout Mask Replica** *(2 LPs.)*	1969	16.00	40.00
		(Produced by Frank Zappa.)			
Reprise RS-6420	(S)	**Lick My Decals Off, Baby**	1970	10.00	25.00
		(Orange label with the lyric sheet.)			
Reprise RS-6420	(S)	**Lick My Decals Off, Baby**	197?	6.00	15.00
		(Brown label with the lyric sheet.)			
Buddah BDS-5077	(S)	**Mirror Man** *(Fold open, die-cut cover)*	1971	10.00	25.00
Reprise M2S-2027	(S)	**Trout Mask Replica** *(2 LPs)*	1972	6.00	15.00
Reprise MS-2050	(S)	**Spotlight Kid** *(Orange label)*	1972	8.00	20.00
Reprise MS-2050	(S)	**Spotlight Kid** *(Brown label)*	197?	5.00	12.00
Reprise MS 2115	(S)	**Clear Spot** *(Clear jacket)*	1972	10.00	25.00
Mercury SRM-1-709	(S)	**Unconditionally Guaranteed**	1974	4.00	10.00
Mercury SRM-1-1018	(S)	**Bluejeans And Moonbeams**	1974	6.00	15.00
Warner Bros. BSK-3256	(S)	**Shiny Beast (Bat Chain Puller)**	1978	4.00	10.00
CAPTAIN BEEFHEART / RY COODER					
Reprise PRO-447	(DJ)	**Capt. Beefheart / Ry Cooder Interview**	1972	150.00	250.00
CAPTAIN BEYOND					
Capricorn CP-0105	(S)	**Captain Beyond** *(3-D cover)*	1972	8.00	20.00
CARAVAN, JIMMY					
Tower ST-5103	(S)	**Look Into the Flower**	1968	8.00	20.00
Vault 9007	(S)	**Hey Jude**	1969	6.00	15.00
CARAVELLES, THE					
Smash MGS-27044	(M)	**You Don't Have To Be A Baby To Cry**	1963	20.00	50.00
Smash SRS-67044	(E)	**You Don't Have To Be A Baby To Cry**	1963	16.00	40.00
CARAWAN, GUY					
Folkways FA-3544	(M)	**Guy Carawan**	195?	8.00	20.00
CAREFREES, THE					
London LL-3379	(M)	**We Love You All**	1964	16.00	40.00
London PS-379	(S)	**We Love You All**	1964	20.00	50.00
CARLISLE, BILL					
Hickory HL-129	(M)	**The Best Of Bill Carlisle**	1966	6.00	15.00
Hickory HLS-129	(S)	**The Best Of Bill Carlisle**	1966	8.00	20.00
CARLISLE BROTHERS, THE					
Mercury MG-20359	(M)	**On Stage With The Carlisles**	1958	20.00	50.00
King 643	(M)	**Fresh From The Country**	1959	20.00	50.00
CARMEN, ERIC					
Carmen was formerly a member of The Raspberries.					
Arista AL-4057	(S)	**Eric Carmen** *(Gold foil cover)*	1975	4.00	10.00
Arista AQ-4057	(Q)	**Eric Carmen**	1975	5.00	12.00
CARMEN, JENKS "TEX"					
Modern 7037	(M)	**Country Caravan**	1959	12.00	30.00

Label & Catalog #		Title	Year	VG+	NM
Sage 9	(M)	Jenks "Tex" Carmen	1962	12.00	30.00
Sage 26	(M)	The Ole Indian (Red vinyl)	1962	16.00	40.00
Sage 40	(M)	Tex Carmen Plays And Sings	1962	12.00	30.00
CARMICHAEL, HOAGY					
Kapp KL-1086	(M)	Old Buttermilk Sky	195?	16.00	40.00
Decca DL-8588	(M)	The Stardust Road	1958	16.00	40.00
Capitol T-1819	(M)	I Can Dream, Can't I?	1962	8.00	20.00
Capitol ST-1819	(S)	I Can Dream, Can't I?	1962	12.00	30.00
CARNES, KIM					
Refer to The Sugar Bears.					
Amos 7016	(S)	Rest On Me	1971	5.00	12.00
EMI SPRO-9626/7	(DJ)	Kim Carnes & The Hate Boys (Sampler)	1981	6.00	15.00
Mobile Fidelity MFSL-073	(S)	Mistaken Identity	1982	6.00	15.00
CARNEY, ART					
Columbia CL-2595 (10")	(M)	Doodle-Li-Boops And Rhinocelopes	195?	16.00	40.00
CAROLINA SLIM					
Sharp 2002	(M)	Blues From The Cotton Fields	195?	100.00	200.00
CARPENTER, IKE					
Discovery DL-3003 (10")	(M)	Dancers In Love	1949	150.00	250.00
Intro 950 (10")	(M)	Lights Out	1952	150.00	250.00
Aladdin LP-811	(M)	Lights Out	1956	150.00	250.00
Score SLP-4010	(M)	Lights Out	1957	75.00	150.00
CARPENTERS, THE					
The Carpenters are siblings Karen and Richard.					
A&M SP-4205	(S)	Offering	1969	16.00	40.00
A&M SP-4205	(S)	Ticket To Ride	1970	6.00	15.00
A&M SP-4271	(S)	Close To You	1970	5.00	12.00
A&M QU-54271	(Q)	Close To You	1970	6.00	15.00
A&M SP-4322	(S)	Bless The Beasts And The Children	1971	4.00	10.00
A&M SP-3502	(S)	Carpenters	1971	5.00	12.00
A&M QU-53502	(Q)	Carpenters	1971	6.00	15.00
A&M SP-3511	(S)	A Song For You	1972	5.00	12.00
A&M QU-53511	(Q)	A Song For You	1972	6.00	15.00
A&M SP-3519	(S)	Now & Then	1973	5.00	12.00
A&M QU-53519	(Q)	Now & Then	1973	6.00	15.00
A&M QU-53601	(Q)	The Singles 1969-1973	1973	6.00	15.00
A&M QU-54530	(Q)	Horizon	1975	6.00	15.00
		— Original A&M albums above have brown labels.—			
CARR, CATHY					
Fraternity 1005	(M)	Ivory Tower	1957	20.00	50.00
Dot DLP-3674	(M)	Ivory Tower	1964	8.00	20.00
Dot DLP-25674	(S)	Ivory Tower	1964	12.00	30.00
CARR, GEORGIA					
Tops 1617	(M)	Songs By A Moody Miss	1958	14.00	35.00
Roulette R-25077	(M)	Shy	1959	8.00	20.00
Roulette SR-25077	(S)	Shy	1959	10.00	25.00
Vee Jay LP-1105	(M)	Rocks In My Bed	1964	6.00	15.00
Vee Jay VJS-1105	(S)	Rocks In My Bed	1964	8.00	20.00
CARR, HELEN					
Bethlehem 1027 (10")	(M)	Down In The Depths On The 90th Floor	1954	35.00	70.00
Bethlehem 45	(M)	Why Do I Love You	1956	20.00	50.00
CARR, LEROY					
Columbia CL-1911	(M)	Blues Before Sunrise	1962	8.00	20.00
Columbia CS-8511	(S)	Blues Before Sunrise	1962	12.00	30.00
CARROLL, DIAHANN					
RCA Vicor LPM-1467	(M)	Diahann Carroll Sings Harold Arlen	1957	14.00	35.00
United Arts. UAL-4021	(M)	Porgy And Bess	1960	6.00	15.00
United Arts. UAS-5021	(S)	Porgy And Bess	1960	8.00	20.00

Label & Catalog #		Title	Year	VG+	NM
United Arts. UAL-3069	(M)	**Diahann Carroll And Andre Previn**	1960	6.00	15.00
United Arts. UAS-6069	(S)	**Diahann Carroll And Andre Previn**	1960	8.00	20.00
United Arts. UAL-3080	(M)	**Diahann Carroll At The Persian Room**	1960	6.00	15.00
United Arts. UAS-6080	(S)	**Diahann Carroll At The Persian Room**	1960	8.00	20.00
Atlantic 8048	(M)	**Fun Life**	1961	6.00	15.00
Atlantic SD-8048	(S)	**Fun Life**	1961	10.00	25.00
United Arts. UAL-4091	(M)	**Goodbye Again** *(Soundtrack)*	1961	14.00	35.00
United Arts. UAS-5091	(S)	**Goodbye Again** *(Soundtrack)*	1961	20.00	50.00
United Arts. UAL-3229	(M)	**The Fabulous Diahann Carroll**	1962	5.00	12.00
United Arts. UAS-6229	(S)	**The Fabulous Diahann Carroll**	1962	6.00	15.00
Columbia CL-2571	(M)	**Nobody Sees Me Cry**	1967	4.00	10.00
Columbia CS-9371	(S)	**Nobody Sees Me Cry**	1967	5.00	12.00

CARROLL BROTHERS

Cameo C-1015	(M)	**College Twist Party**	1962	8.00	20.00
Cameo CS-1015	(S)	**College Twist Party**	1962	12.00	30.00

CARS, THE

Elektra 5E-567	(DJ)	**Shake It Up** *(Picture disc)*	1981	20.00	50.00
Nautilus NR-14	(S)	**The Cars**	198?	8.00	20.00
Nautilus NR-49	(S)	**Candy-O**	198?	8.00	20.00

CARSON, MARTHA (LOU)

RCA Victor LPM-1145	(M)	**Journey To The Sky**	1955	14.00	35.00
RCA Victor LPM-1490	(M)	**Rock-A My Soul**	1957	14.00	35.00
Sims LP-100	(M)	**Martha Carson**	195?	12.00	30.00
Sims LP-109	(M)	**Martha Carson**	195?	10.00	25.00
Capitol T-1507	(M)	**Satisfied**	1960	8.00	20.00
Capitol T-1607	(M)	**A Talk With The Lord**	1962	6.00	15.00
Capitol ST-1607	(S)	**A Talk With The Lord**	1962	8.00	20.00

CARTER, ANITA

Mercury MG-20770	(M)	**Folk Songs Old And New**	1963	8.00	20.00
Mercury SR-60770	(S)	**Folk Songs Old And New**	1963	10.00	25.00

CARTER, BETTY
Ms. Carter also recorded with Ray Charles.

Epic LN-3202	(M)	**Meet Betty Carter**	1956	30.00	60.00
ABC-Paramount 363	(M)	**The Modern Sound Of Betty Carter**	1960	12.00	30.00
ABC-Paramount S-363	(S)	**The Modern Sound Of Betty Carter**	1960	16.00	40.00
Atco 33-152	(M)	**'Round Midnight**	1963	8.00	20.00
Atco SD-33-152	(S)	**'Round Midnight**	1963	12.00	30.00
United Arts. UAL-3379	(M)	**Inside Betty Carter**	1963	8.00	20.00
United Arts. UAS-6379	(S)	**Inside Betty Carter**	1963	12.00	30.00

CARTER, CALVIN

Vee Jay LP-1041	(M)	**Twist Along With Calvin Carter**	1962	10.00	25.00
Vee Jay SR-1041	(S)	**Twist Along With Calvin Carter**	1962	16.00	40.00

CARTER, CLARENCE

Atlantic SD-8192	(S)	**This Clarence Carter**	1968	10.00	25.00
Atlantic SD-8199	(S)	**The Dynamic Clarence Carter**	1969	8.00	20.00
Atlantic SD-8238	(S)	**Testifyin'**	1969	8.00	20.00
Atlantic SD-8267	(S)	**Patches**	1970	8.00	20.00
Atlantic SD-8282	(S)	**The Best Of Clarence Carter**	1971	6.00	15.00

CARTER, LYNDA

Epic JE-35308	(S)	**Portrait** *(Picture disc)*	1978	12.00	30.00

CARTER, "MOTHER" MAYBELLE
Refer to The Carter Family.

Ambassador 98069	(M)	**Mother Maybelle Carter**	195?	75.00	150.00
Kapp KL-1413	(M)	**Queen Of The Autoharp**	1964	6.00	15.00
Kapp KS-3413	(S)	**Queen Of The Autoharp**	1964	8.00	20.00
Columbia CL-2475	(M)	**A Living Legend**	1965	6.00	15.00
Columbia CS-9275	(S)	**A Living Legend**	1965	8.00	20.00

CARTER, MEL

Derby LPM-702	(M)	**When A Boy Falls In Love**	1963	75.00	150.00

Label & Catalog #		Title	Year	VG+	NM
Imperial LP-9289	(M)	Hold Me, Thrill Me, Kiss Me	1965	6.00	15.00
Imperial LP-12289	(S)	Hold Me, Thrill Me, Kiss Me	1965	8.00	20.00
Imperial LP-9300	(M)	My Heart Sings	1965	5.00	12.00
Imperial LP-12300	(S)	My Heart Sings	1965	6.00	15.00
Imperial LP-9319	(M)	Easy Listening	1966	5.00	12.00
Imperial LP-12319	(S)	Easy Listening	1966	6.00	15.00
Liberty LRP-3530	(M)	Be My Love	1967	5.00	12.00
Liberty LSP-7530	(S)	Be My Love	1967	6.00	15.00

CARTER FAMILY, THE
The Carters feature Mother Maybelle.

Acme LP-1	(M)	All Time Favorites	195?	75.00	150.00
Acme LP-2	(M)	In Memory Of A.P. Carter	195?	100.00	200.00
Camden CAL-586	(M)	The Original And Great Carter Family	195?	6.00	15.00
Decca DL-4404	(M)	The Carter Family	1960	16.00	40.00
Decca DL-4404	(M)	A Collection Of Favorites	1963	12.00	30.00
Decca DL-4557	(M)	More Favorites By The Carter Family	1964	16.00	40.00
Columbia CL-2152	(M)	Keep On The Sunny Side	1964	6.00	15.00
Columbia CS-8952	(S)	Keep On The Sunny Side	1964	8.00	20.00
Columbia CL-2617	(M)	The Country Album	1966	6.00	15.00
Columbia CS-9417	(S)	The Country Album	1966	8.00	20.00

CARTOONE

Atlantic SD-8219	(S)	Cartoone (With Jimmy Page)	1969	8.00	20.00

CARTWRIGHT, ANGELA

Star-Bright HLP-102	(M)	Angela Cartwright Sings	195?	16.00	40.00

CASCADES

Valiant W-405	(M)	Rhythm Of The Rain	1963	20.00	50.00
Valiant WS-405	(P)	Rhythm Of The Rain	1963	35.00	70.00
Cascade 681001	(S)	What Goes On	1968	20.00	50.00
Uni 73069	(S)	Maybe The Rain Will Fall	1969	8.00	20.00

CASE, ALAN

Columbia CL-1402	(M)	The "Deputy" Sings	1960	8.00	20.00
Columbia CS-8202	(S)	The "Deputy" Sings	1960	12.00	30.00

CASEY, AL

Prestige W-2007	(M)	Buck Jumpin'	1960	20.00	50.00
Prestige MV-12	(M)	The Al Casey Quartet	1961	16.00	40.00
Stacy STM-100	(M)	Surfin' Hootenanny (Surf-colored vinyl)	1963	20.00	50.00
Stacy STMS-100	(S)	Surfin' Hootenanny (Surf-colored vinyl)	1963	30.00	60.00

CASH, JOHNNY

Sun 1220	(M)	Johnny Cash With His Hot & Blue Guitar	1956	20.00	50.00
Sun 1235	(M)	The Songs That Made Him Famous	1958	16.00	40.00
Sun 1240	(M)	Johnny Cash's Greatest!	1959	16.00	40.00
Sun 1245	(M)	Johnny Cash Sings Hank Williams	1960	16.00	40.00
Sun 1255	(M)	Now Here's Johnny Cash	1961	12.00	30.00
Sun 1270	(M)	All Aboard The Blue Train	1963	10.00	25.00
Sun 1275	(M)	The Original Sun Sound Of Johnny Cash	1965	10.00	25.00
Columbia CL-1253	(M)	The Fabulous Johnny Cash	1958	10.00	25.00
Columbia CS-8122	(S)	The Fabulous Johnny Cash	1958	14.00	35.00
Columbia CL-1284	(M)	Hymns By Johnny Cash	1959	8.00	20.00
Columbia CS-8125	(S)	Hymns By Johnny Cash	1959	12.00	30.00
Columbia CL-1339	(M)	Songs Of Our Soil	1959	8.00	20.00
Columbia CS-8148	(S)	Songs Of Our Soil	1959	12.00	30.00
Columbia CL-1463	(M)	Now, There Was A Song!	1960	8.00	20.00
Columbia CS-8254	(S)	Now, There Was A Song!	1960	12.00	30.00
Columbia CL-1464	(M)	Ride This Train	1960	8.00	20.00
Columbia CS-8255	(S)	Ride This Train	1960	12.00	30.00
Columbia CL-1622	(M)	The Lure Of The Grand Canyon	1961	12.00	30.00
Columbia CS-8422	(S)	The Lure Of The Grand Canyon	1961	16.00	40.00
Columbia CL-1722	(M)	Hymns From The Heart	1962	6.00	15.00
Columbia CS-8522	(S)	Hymns From The Heart	1962	8.00	20.00
Columbia CL-1802	(M)	The Sound Of Johnny Cash	1962	6.00	15.00
Columbia CS-8602	(S)	The Sound Of Johnny Cash	1962	8.00	20.00

— *Original Columbia albums above have three white "eye" logos on each side of the spindle hole.* —

Label & Catalog #		Title	Year	VG+	NM
Columbia CL-1930	(M)	Blood, Sweat And Tears	1963	5.00	12.00
Columbia CS-8730	(S)	Blood, Sweat And Tears	1963	6.00	15.00
Columbia CL-2053	(M)	Ring Of Fire/The Best Of Johnny Cash	1963	5.00	12.00
Columbia CS-8853	(S)	Ring Of Fire/The Best Of Johnny Cash	1963	6.00	15.00
Columbia CL-2117	(M)	Christmas Spirit	1963	5.00	12.00
Columbia CS-8917	(S)	Christmas Spirit	1963	6.00	15.00
Columbia CL-2190	(M)	I Walk The Line	1964	5.00	12.00
Columbia CS-8990	(S)	I Walk The Line	1964	6.00	15.00
Columbia CL-2248	(M)	Bitter Tears	1964	6.00	15.00
Columbia CS-9048	(S)	Bitter Tears	1964	8.00	20.00
Columbia CL-2309	(M)	Orange Blossom Special	1965	5.00	12.00
Columbia CS-9109	(S)	Orange Blossom Special	1965	6.00	15.00
Columbia CL-2446	(M)	Mean As Hell	1965	5.00	12.00
Columbia CS-9246	(S)	Mean As Hell	1965	6.00	15.00
Columbia OL-6420	(M)	The Sons Of Katie Elder (Soundtrack)	1965	75.00	150.00
Columbia OS-2820	(S)	The Sons Of Katie Elder (Soundtrack)	1965	100.00	200.00
Columbia C2L-838	(M)	Ballads Of The True West (2 LPs)	1965	6.00	15.00
Columbia C2S-838	(S)	Ballads Of The True West (2 LPs)	1965	8.00	20.00
Columbia CL-2492	(M)	Everybody Loves A Nut	1966	3.50	8.00
Columbia CS-9292	(S)	Everybody Loves A Nut	1966	4.00	10.00
Columbia CL-2537	(M)	Happiness Is You	1966	3.50	8.00
Columbia CS-9337	(S)	Happiness Is You	1966	4.00	10.00
Columbia CL-2537	(M)	That's What You Get For Loving Me	1966	3.50	8.00
Columbia CS-9337	(S)	That's What You Get For Loving Me	1966	4.00	10.00
Columbia CL-2647	(M)	From Sea To Shining Sea	1967	3.50	8.00
Columbia CS-9447	(S)	From Sea To Shining Sea	1967	4.00	10.00
Columbia CL-2678	(M)	Johnny Cash's Greatest Hits, Volume 1	1967	3.50	8.00
Columbia CS-9478	(S)	Johnny Cash's Greatest Hits, Volume 1	1967	4.00	10.00
Columbia CL-2728	(M)	Carryin' On	1967	3.50	8.00
Columbia CS-9528	(S)	Carryin' On	1967	4.00	10.00
Columbia CS-9639	(S)	Johnny Cash At Folsom Prison	1968	3.50	8.00
Columbia CS-9726	(S)	The Holy Land (3D cover)	1969	4.00	10.00
Columbia CS-9726	(S)	The Holy Land (2D cover)	1969	3.50	8.00
Columbia CS-9827	(S)	Johnny Cash At San Quentin	1969	3.50	8.00
Columbia CS-9943	(S)	Hello, I'm Johnny Cash	1970	3.50	8.00
— Original Columbia albums above have "360 Sound" labels.—					
Columbia 7425	(S)	Grand Canyon Suite	1969	8.00	20.00
(Grey label with white "Masterworks" logo)					
Columbia 32253	(S)	The Gospel Road	1973	8.00	20.00

CASHMAN & WEST
Terry Cashman and Tommy West. Refer to The Chevrons.

Dunhill SPDJ-17	(DJ)	Tale Of Two Cities (American City Suite)	1972	6.00	15.00

CASINOS, THE

Fraternity 1019	(M)	Then You Can Tell Me Goodbye	1967	12.00	30.00
Fraternity LPS-1019	(S)	Then You Can Tell Me Goodbye	1967	16.00	40.00

CASSIDY, DAVID
David was formerly a member of The Partridge Family.

Bell 6070	(S)	Cherish	1972	6.00	15.00
Bell 1109	(S)	Rock Me, Baby	1972	6.00	15.00
Bell 1132	(S)	Dreams Are Nuthin' More Than Wishes	1973	6.00	15.00
Bell 1321	(S)	David Cassidy's Greatest Hits	1974	6.00	15.00
Bell 1312	(S)	Cassidy Live	1974	8.00	20.00
RCA Victor APL1-1066	(DJ)	The Higher They Climb... (Blue vinyl)	1975	20.00	50.00

CASTELLS, THE

Era EL-109	(M)	So This Is Love	1962	35.00	70.00
Era ES-109	(S)	So This Is Love	1962	50.00	100.00

CASTLE, PAULA

Bethlehem BCP-1036 (10")	(M)	Lost Love	1955	35.00	70.00

CASTOR BUNCH, JIMMY

Smash MGS-27091	(M)	Hey Leroy!	1967	8.00	20.00
Smash SRW-67091	(S)	Hey Leroy!	1967	10.00	25.00

Chad Stuart and Jeremy Clyde are more than likely remembered as "soft rock" artists, although they began their career recording folk material, all of which is found on *Chad & Jeremy Sing For You* and *Yesterday's Gone* (both readily available in most used record stores). With six of the tracks from this pair of long players making American charts, they were signed by Columbia. Meanwhile, Capitol acquired their World Artists catalog and quickly repackaged them. With Columbia they produced several excellent albums, including some pleasing excursions into folk-rock, ending their career with two albums of psychedelicized pop!

Label & Catalog #		Title	Year	VG+	NM

CATALINAS, THE
The Catalinas feature Bruce Johnston and Terry Melcher.

Ric M-1006	(M)	**Fun, Fun, Fun**	1964	30.00	60.00
Ric S-1006	(S)	**Fun, Fun, Fun**	1964	40.00	80.00

CATHEDRAL

Delta DRC-1002	(S)	**Stained Glass Stories**	197?	210.00	300.00
Symphonic	(S)	**Stained Glass Stories**	198?	8.00	20.00

CATHY JEAN & THE ROOMATES

Valmor 789	(M)	**At The Hop!** *(Original cover)*	1961	300.00	500.00
Valmor 789	(M)	**At The Hop!** *(Group photo cover)*	1961	75.00	150.00

CATANOOGA CATS, THE

Forward ST-F-1018	(S)	**The Catanooga Cats**	1969	12.00	30.00

CAVALIERE, FELIX
Felix was formerly a member of The Young Rascals/Rascals.

Epic AS-705	(DJ)	**Castles In The Air Sampler/Interview**	197?	8.00	20.00

CENTRAL NERVOUS SYSTEM

Music Factory MFS-12003	(S)	**I Could Have Danced All Night**	1968	5.00	12.00

CENTURIONS, THE

Del-Fi DFLP-1228	(M)	**Surfer's Pajama Party**	1963	12.00	30.00
Del-Fi DFST-1228	(S)	**Surfer's Pajama Party**	1963	16.00	40.00

*(This album has the same title, catalog number and cover photo as
The Bruce Johnston Surfing Band, but it plays The Centurions.)*

CESANA

Modern M-100	(M)	**Tender Emotions**	1964	8.00	20.00

CEYLIB PEOPLE, THE

Vault LP-117	(S)	**Tanyet**	1968	16.00	40.00

CHAD & JEREMY
Chad Stuart and Jeremy Clyde.

World Artists WAM-2002	(M)	**Yesterday's Gone**	1964	4.00	10.00
World Artists WAS-3002	(P)	**Yesterday's Gone**	1964	5.00	12.00
World Artists WAM-2005	(M)	**Chad & Jeremy Sing For You**	1965	4.00	10.00
World Artists WAS-3005	(P)	**Chad & Jeremy Sing For You**	1965	5.00	12.00
Fidu FM-101	(M)	**5 + 10 = 15 Fabulous Hits**	1965	4.00	10.00
Fidu FS-101	(P)	**5 + 10 = 15 Fabulous Hits**	1965	5.00	12.00
Capitol T-2470	(M)	**The Best Of Chad & Jeremy**	1966	4.00	10.00
Capitol ST-2470	(P)	**The Best Of Chad & Jeremy**	1966	5.00	12.00
Capitol TT-2546	(M)	**More Chad & Jeremy**	1966	4.00	10.00
Capitol ST-2546	(P)	**More Chad & Jeremy**	1966	5.00	12.00
Columbia CL-2374	(M)	**Before And After**	1965	6.00	15.00
Columbia CS-9174	(S)	**Before And After**	1965	8.00	20.00
Columbia CL-2398	(M)	**I Don't Want To Lose You Baby**	1965	6.00	15.00
Columbia CS-9198	(S)	**I Don't Want To Lose You Baby**	1965	8.00	20.00
Columbia CL-2564	(M)	**Distant Shores**	1966	6.00	15.00
Columbia CS-9364	(P)	**Distant Shores**	1966	8.00	20.00
Columbia CL-2657	(M)	**Of Cabbages And Kings**	1967	6.00	15.00
Columbia CS-9457	(S)	**Of Cabbages And Kings**	1967	8.00	20.00
Columbia CL-2899	(M)	**The Ark**	1968	8.00	20.00
Columbia CS-9699	(S)	**The Ark**	1968	8.00	20.00

(Columbia 9457 and 9699 produced by Gary Usher.)

Sidewalk ST-5918	(S)	**Three In The Attic** *(Soundtrack)*	1969	8.00	20.00

CHAIRMEN OF THE BOARD

Invictus SKAO-7300	(S)	**Chairmen Of The Board**	1970	6.00	15.00
Invictus SKAO-7304	(S)	**In Session**	1971	6.00	15.00
Invictus ST-9801	(S)	**Bittersweet**	1972	6.00	15.00
Invictus KZ-32526	(S)	**The Skin I'm In**	1974	6.00	15.00

CHALKER, CURLY

Columbia CL-2496	(M)	**Big Hits On Big Steel**	1965	6.00	15.00
Columbia CS-9296	(S)	**Big Hits On Big Steel**	1965	8.00	20.00

Label & Catalog #		Title	Year	VG+	NM

CHALLENGERS, THE
The Challengers also recorded as The Good Guys.

Vault LP-100	(M)	Surfbeat	1963	16.00	40.00
Vault VS-100	(S)	Surfbeat	1963	20.00	50.00
Vault VS-100	(S)	Surfbeat *(Orange vinyl)*	1963	50.00	100.00
Vault VS-100	(S)	Surfbeat *(Red vinyl)*	1963	50.00	100.00
Vault VS-100	(S)	Surfbeat *(Yellow vinyl)*	1963	50.00	100.00
Vault LP-101	(M)	Surfing	1963	16.00	40.00
Vault VS-101	(S)	Surfing	1963	20.00	50.00
Vault VS-101	(S)	Surfing *(Orange vinyl)*	1963	50.00	100.00
Vault VS-101	(S)	Surfing *(Red vinyl)*	1963	50.00	100.00
Vault VS-101	(S)	Surfing *(Yellow vinyl)*	1963	50.00	100.00
Vault VS-101	(S)	Surfing *(Blue vinyl)*	1963	50.00	100.00
Vault LP-102	(M)	The Challengers On The Move	1963	12.00	30.00
Vault VS-102	(S)	The Challengers On The Move	1963	14.00	35.00
Vault LP-107	(M)	K-39	1964	20.00	50.00
Vault LP-109	(M)	The Surf's Up	1965	12.00	30.00
Vault VS-109	(S)	The Surf's Up	1965	14.00	35.00
Vault LP-110	(M)	The Challengers Au Go Go	1966	12.00	30.00
Vault VS-110	(S)	The Challengers Au Go Go	1966	14.00	35.00
Vault LP-111	(M)	The Challengers' Greatest Hits	1967	10.00	25.00
Vault VS-111	(S)	The Challengers' Greatest Hits	1967	8.00	20.00
Triumph 100	(M)	Sidewalk Surfing	1965	8.00	20.00
Triumph TR-100	(S)	Sidewalk Surfing	1965	10.00	25.00
Crescendo GNP-2010	(M)	The Challengers At The Teenage Fair	1965	6.00	15.00
Crescendo GNPS-2010	(S)	The Challengers At The Teenage Fair	1965	5.00	12.00
Crescendo GNP-2018	(M)	The Man From U.N.C.L.E.	1965	6.00	15.00
Crescendo GNPS-2018	(M)	The Man From U.N.C.L.E.	1965	5.00	12.00
Crescendo GNP-2025	(M)	California Kicks	1966	6.00	15.00
Crescendo GNPS-2025	(S)	California Kicks	1966	5.00	12.00
Crescendo GNP-2030	(M)	Billy Strange And The Challengers	1967	6.00	15.00
Crescendo GNPS-2030	(S)	Billy Strange And The Challengers	1967	5.00	12.00
Crescendo GNP-2031	(M)	Wipe Out	1966	6.00	15.00
Crescendo GNPS-2031	(S)	Wipe Out	1966	5.00	12.00
Crescendo GNP-609	(M)	25 Great Instrumental Hits	1967	6.00	15.00
Crescendo GNPS-609	(S)	25 Great Instrumental Hits	1967	5.00	12.00
Crescendo GNPS-2045	(S)	Light My Fire With Classical Gas	1968	4.00	10.00
Crescendo GNPS-2056	(S)	Vanilla Funk	1970	4.00	10.00

— Original GNP Crescendo albums above have red labels.—

CHAMBERLAIN, RICHARD

MGM E-4088	(M)	Richard Chamberlain Sings	1963	6.00	15.00
MGM SE-4088	(S)	Richard Chamberlain Sings	1963	8.00	20.00
MGM E-4185	(M)	Twilight Of Honor *(Soundtrack)*	1963	6.00	15.00
MGM SE-4185	(S)	Twilight Of Honor *(Soundtrack)*	1963	8.00	20.00
MGM E-4287	(M)	Joy In The Morning	1964	5.00	12.00
MGM SE-4287	(S)	Joy In The Morning	1964	6.00	15.00
Metro M-564	(M)	Theme From "Dr. Kildare"	1966	6.00	15.00
Metro MS-564	(S)	Theme From "Dr. Kildare"	1966	8.00	20.00

CHAMBERS BROTHERS, THE

Vault 9003	(M)	People Get Ready	1966	5.00	12.00
Vault 9003	(S)	People Get Ready	1966	6.00	15.00
Vault 115	(M)	The Chambers Brothers Now	1967	5.00	12.00
Vault 115	(S)	The Chambers Brothers Now	1967	6.00	15.00
Vault 120	(S)	The Chambers Brothers Shout	1968	6.00	15.00
Vault 128	(S)	Feelin' The Blues	1969	6.00	15.00
Vault 135	(S)	Chambers Brothers' Greatest Hits *(2 LPs)*	1970	6.00	15.00
Columbia CL-2722	(M)	The Time Has Come	1967	6.00	15.00
Columbia CS-9522	(S)	The Time Has Come	1967	6.00	15.00
Columbia CS-9671	(S)	A New Time/A New Day	1968	5.00	12.00
Columbia KGP-20	(S)	Love, Peace & Happiness *(2 LPs)*	1969	6.00	15.00

— Original Columbia albums above have "360 Sound " on the bottom of the label—

CHAMPS, THE

Challenge CHL-601	(M)	Go Champs Go	1958	75.00	150.00
Challenge CHL-601	(M)	Go Champs Go *(Blue vinyl)*	1958	360.00	600.00
Challenge CHL-605	(M)	Everybody's Rockin' With The Champs	1959	50.00	100.00
Challenge CHS-605	(S)	Everybody's Rockin' With The Champs	1959	75.00	150.00

Label & Catalog #		Title	Year	VG+	NM
Challenge CHL-613	(M)	**Great Dance Hits**	1962	20.00	50.00
Challenge CHS-613	(S)	**Great Dance Hits**	1962	30.00	60.00
Challenge CHL-614	(M)	**All American Music From The Champs**	1962	20.00	50.00
Challenge CHS-614	(S)	**All American Music From The Champs**	1962	30.00	60.00
CHANDLER, GENE					
Vee Jay MR-1040	(M)	**The Duke Of Earl**	1962	40.00	80.00
Vee Jay SR-1040	(S)	**The Duke Of Earl**	1962	150.00	250.00
		(Original stereo albums have a "Stereophonic" banner across the top of the back cover; those with the banner on the front are reproductions with mono albums inside.)			
Constellation LP-1421	(M)	**Greatest Hits By Gene Chandler**	1964	10.00	25.00
Constellation LP-1423	(M)	**Just Be True**	1964	10.00	25.00
Constellation LP-1425	(M)	**Gene Chandler/Live On Stage In '65**	1965	10.00	25.00
Checker LP-3003	(M)	**The Duke Of Soul**	1967	8.00	20.00
Checker LPS-3003	(E)	**The Duke Of Soul**	1967	5.00	12.00
CHANDLER, JEFF					
Liberty LRP-3067	(M)	**Jeff Chandler Sings To You**	1957	12.00	30.00
Liberty LRP-3074	(M)	**Warm And Easy**	1957	12.00	30.00
Sunset SUM-1127	(M)	**Sincerely Yours**	196?	6.00	15.00
Sunset SUS-5127	(E)	**Sincerely Yours**	196?	5.00	12.00

The harmonica intro to the #1 smash, "Hey! Baby," remains one of the most familiar refrains in all of pop music. Unfortunately, the album containing the hit was issued in rechanneled stereo.

CHANNEL, BRUCE					
Smash MGS-27008	(M)	**Hey! Baby**	1962	30.00	60.00
Smash SRS-67008	(E)	**Hey! Baby**	1962	20.00	50.00
CHANTAYS, THE					
Downey DLP-1002	(M)	**Pipeline**	1963	60.00	120.00
Downey DLPS-1002	(S)	**Pipeline**	1963	75.00	150.00
Dot DLP-3516	(M)	**Pipeline**	1963	16.00	40.00
Dot DLP-25516	(S)	**Pipeline**	1963	20.00	50.00
Dot DLP-3771	(M)	**Two Sides Of The Chantays**	1966	10.00	25.00
Dot DLP-25771	(S)	**Two Sides Of The Chantays**	1966	12.00	30.00

Label & Catalog #		Title	Year	VG+	NM

CHANTELS, THE

End LP-301	(M)	**We're The Chantels** (Grey label)	1958	360.00	600.00
		(Grey label. The cover has a photo of the group on the front.)			
End LP-301	(M)	**We're The Chantels**	1959	100.00	200.00
		(Grey label. The cover has a photo of a jukebox on the front.)			
End LP-301	(M)	**We're The Chantels**	1962	20.00	50.00
		(Grey label with 1962 in the trail-off vinyl. Jukebox cover.)			
End LP-301	(M)	**We're The Chantels**	1965	12.00	30.00
		(Color label with 1965 in the trail-off vinyl. Jukebox cover.)			
Carlton LP-144	(M)	**The Chantels On Tour**	1961	50.00	100.00
Carlton STLP-144	(P)	**The Chantels On Tour**	1961	100.00	200.00
End LP-312	(M)	**There's Our Song Again**	1962	35.00	70.00
Forum 9104	(M)	**The Chantels Sing Their Favorites**	196?	10.00	25.00

CHAPIN BROTHERS, THE [HARRY & TOM CHAPIN]

Rockland 66	(M)	**Chapin Music**	1966	8.00	20.00

CHARIOTEERS, THE

Columbia CL-6014 (10")	(M)	**Sweet And Low**	1950	100.00	200.00

CHARITY

Uni 73061	(S)	**Charity Now**	1969	8.00	20.00

CHARLATANS, THE

Phillips PHS-600309	(S)	**The Charlatans**	1969	20.00	50.00

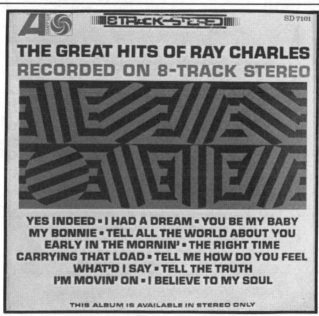

Working from the original session multi-tracks, Atlantic's engineers mixed up a batch of
the best of Ray and issued this unique, stereo-only album in 1964.

CHARLES, RAY

Atlantic 8006	(M)	**Ray Charles/Rock And Roll**	1957	20.00	50.00
Atlantic 1259	(M)	**The Great Ray Charles**	1957	20.00	50.00
Atlantic 1279	(M)	**Soul Brothers**	1958	20.00	50.00
Atlantic 1289	(M)	**Ray Charles At Newport**	1958	20.00	50.00
Atlantic 8025	(M)	**Yes, Indeed!**	1959	16.00	40.00
Atlantic 8029	(M)	**What'd I Say**	1959	16.00	40.00
Atlantic 8039	(M)	**Ray Charles In Person**	1960	16.00	40.00

— Original Atlantic albums above have black labels.—

Label & Catalog #		Title	Year	VG+	NM
Atlantic 1312	(M)	The Genius Of Ray Charles	1960	10.00	25.00
Atlantic SD-1312	(S)	The Genius Of Ray Charles	1960	14.00	35.00
Atlantic 8052	(M)	The Genius Sings The Blues	1961	10.00	25.00
Atlantic SD-8052	(S)	The Genius Sings The Blues	1961	14.00	35.00
Atlantic 8054	(M)	Do The Twist With Ray Charles!	1961	10.00	25.00
Atlantic 1360	(M)	Soul Meeting	1961	10.00	25.00
Atlantic SD-1360	(S)	Soul Meeting	1961	14.00	35.00

—Atlantic mono albums above have orange and purple labels with a white fan; stereo albums have green and blue labels with a white fan.—

Atlantic 1369	(M)	The Genius After Hours	1961	10.00	25.00
Atlantic SD-1369	(S)	The Genius After Hours	1961	14.00	35.00
Atlantic 8063	(M)	The Ray Charles Story, Volume 1	1962	8.00	20.00
Atlantic SD-8063	(P)	The Ray Charles Story, Volume 1	1962	10.00	25.00
Atlantic 8064	(M)	The Ray Charles Story, Volume 2	1962	8.00	20.00
Atlantic SD-8064	(P)	The Ray Charles Story, Volume 2	1962	10.00	25.00
Atlantic 8083	(M)	The Ray Charles Story, Volume 3	1963	8.00	20.00
Atlantic SD-8083	(P)	The Ray Charles Story, Volume 3	1963	10.00	25.00
Atlantic 8094	(M)	The Ray Charles Story, Volume 4	1964	8.00	20.00
Atlantic SD-8094	(P)	The Ray Charles Story, Volume 4	1964	10.00	25.00
Atlantic SD-7101	(S)	Great Hits Recorded On 8-Track Stereo	1964	10.00	25.00
Hollywood 504	(M)	Ray Charles	1959	35.00	70.00
Hollywood 505	(M)	The Fabulous Ray Charles	1959	35.00	70.00
ABC-Paramount 335	(M)	The Genius Hits The Road	1960	8.00	20.00
ABC-Paramount S-335	(S)	The Genius Hits The Road	1960	12.00	30.00
ABC-Paramount 355	(M)	Dedicated To You	1961	8.00	20.00
ABC-Paramount S-355	(S)	Dedicated To You	1961	12.00	30.00

— Original ABC albums above have black labels with "ABC-PARAMOUNT" on the top and "Am-Par Record Corp." on the bottom.—

Impulse A-2	(M)	Genius + Soul = Jazz	1961	12.00	30.00
Impulse AS-2	(S)	Genius + Soul = Jazz	1961	16.00	40.00
ABC-Paramount 410	(M)	Modern Sounds In Country And Western	1962	8.00	20.00
ABC-Paramount S-410	(S)	Modern Sounds In Country And Western	1962	10.00	25.00

(Original pressing covers do not have the RIAA Gold Record logo.)

ABC-Paramount 415	(M)	Ray Charles' Greatest Hits	1962	6.00	15.00
ABC-Paramount S-415	(S)	Ray Charles' Greatest Hits	1962	8.00	20.00
ABC-Paramount 435	(M)	Modern Sounds In Country & Western, Volume 2	1962	6.00	15.00
ABC-Paramount S-435	(S)	Modern Sounds In Country & Western, Volume 2	1962	8.00	20.00
ABC-Paramount 465	(M)	Ingredients In A Recipe For Soul	1963	6.00	15.00
ABC-Paramount S-465	(S)	Ingredients In A Recipe For Soul	1963	8.00	20.00
ABC-Paramount 480	(M)	Sweet And Sour Tears	1964	6.00	15.00
ABC-Paramount S-480	(S)	Sweet And Sour Tears	1964	8.00	20.00
ABC-Paramount 495	(M)	Have A Smile With Me	1964	6.00	15.00
ABC-Paramount S-495	(S)	Have A Smile With Me	1964	8.00	20.00
MGM E-4313	(M)	The Cincinnati Kid (Soundtrack)	1965	6.00	15.00
MGM SE-4313	(S)	The Cincinnati Kid (Soundtrack)	1965	8.00	20.00
ABC-Paramount 500	(M)	Live In Concert	1965	4.00	10.00
ABC-Paramount S-500	(S)	Live In Concert	1965	5.00	12.00
ABC-Paramount 520	(M)	Country & Western Meets Rhythm & Blues	1965	6.00	15.00
ABC-Paramount S-520	(S)	Country & Western Meets Rhythm & Blues	1965	8.00	20.00
ABC-Paramount 520	(M)	Together Again	1966	5.00	12.00
ABC-Paramount S-520	(S)	Together Again	1966	6.00	15.00
ABC-Paramount 544	(M)	Crying Time	1966	5.00	12.00
ABC-Paramount S-544	(S)	Crying Time	1966	6.00	15.00

— Original ABC albums above have black labels with "ABC-PARAMOUNT" on top.—

ABC 2-590	(M)	A Man And His Soul (2 LPs)	1967	8.00	20.00
ABC Y-2-590	(S)	A Man And His Soul (2 LPs)	1967	10.00	25.00
United Artists UAL-4160	(M)	In The Heat Of The Night (Soundtrack)	1967	6.00	15.00
United Artists UAS-5160	(S)	In The Heat Of The Night (Soundtrack)	1967	8.00	20.00

CHARLES, RAY, & BETTY CARTER

ABC-Paramount 385	(M)	Ray Charles And Betty Carter	1961	30.00	60.00
ABC-Paramount S-385	(S)	Ray Charles And Betty Carter	1961	40.00	80.00

CHARLIE

Janus/GRT JXS-7036	(DJ)	Lines (Picture disc)	1978	20.00	50.00

Label & Catalog #		Title	Year	VG+	NM
CHARMERS, THE					
Illusion CM-1070	(S)	**Your Presence Requested**	1976	40.00	80.00
Illusion CM-1071	(S)	**Do It To It**	1976	40.00	80.00
CHASE					
Epic EQ-30472	(Q)	**Chase**	1974	6.00	15.00
Epic EQ-32572	(Q)	**Pure Music**	1974	6.00	15.00
CHASE, LINCOLN					
Liberty LRP-3076	(M)	**The Explosive Lincoln Chase**	1958	16.00	40.00
CHEAP TRICK					
Epic 35773	(DJ)	**Dream Police** (Picture disc)	1980	12.00	30.00
CHECKER, CHUBBY					
Chubby Checker is a pseudonym for Ernest Evans. Refer to Bobby Rydell; Dee Dee Sharp.					
Parkway 5001	(M)	**Chubby Checker**	1960	20.00	50.00
Parkway P-7001	(M)	**Twist With Chubby Checker**	1960	14.00	35.00
Parkway P-7002	(M)	**For Twisters Only**	1960	14.00	35.00
Parkway P-7003	(M)	**It's Pony Time**	1961	14.00	35.00
Parkway P-7004	(M)	**Let's Twist Again**	1961	14.00	35.00
Parkway P-7007	(M)	**Your Twist Party**	1961	14.00	35.00
Parkway P-7008	(M)	**Twistin' Round The World**	1962	14.00	35.00
Parkway P-7009	(M)	**For Teen Twisters Only**	1962	14.00	35.00
Parkway SP-7009	(S)	**For Teen Twisters Only**	1962	20.00	50.00
Parkway P-7011	(M)	**Don't Knock The Twist** (Soundtrack)	1962	20.00	50.00
Parkway P-7014	(M)	**All The Hits For Your Dancin' Party**	1962	14.00	35.00
Parkway P-7020	(M)	**Limbo Party**	1962	10.00	25.00
Parkway SP-7020	(S)	**Limbo Party**	1962	16.00	40.00
Parkway P-7022	(M)	**Chubby Checker's Biggest Hits**	1962	14.00	35.00
Parkway SP-7022	(E)	**Chubby Checker's Biggest Hits**	1962	14.00	35.00
Parkway P-7026	(M)	**Chubby Checker In Person**	1963	10.00	25.00
Parkway SP-7026	(S)	**Chubby Checker In Person**	1963	16.00	40.00
Parkway P-7027	(M)	**Let's Limbo Some More**	1963	10.00	25.00
Parkway SP-7027	(S)	**Let's Limbo Some More**	1963	20.00	50.00
Parkway P-7030	(M)	**Beach Party**	1963	10.00	25.00
Parkway SP-7030	(S)	**Beach Party**	1963	20.00	50.00
Parkway P-7040	(M)	**Folk Album**	1963	10.00	25.00
Parkway SP-7040	(S)	**Folk Album**	1963	20.00	50.00
Parkway P-7045	(M)	**Discotheque**	1965	10.00	25.00
Parkway SP-7045	(S)	**Discotheque**	1965	20.00	50.00
Parkway P-7048	(M)	**Eighteen Golden Hits**	1966	10.00	25.00
Parkway SP-7048	(P)	**Eighteen Golden Hits**	1966	14.00	35.00
CHECKMATES, LTD., THE					
A&M SP-4183	(S)	**Checkmates, Ltd.**	1969	6.00	15.00
CHER					
Refer to Sonny & Cher.					
Imperial LP-9292	(M)	**All I Really Want To Do**	1965	6.00	15.00
Imperial LP-12292	(S)	**All I Really Want To Do**	1965	8.00	20.00
Imperial LP-9301	(M)	**The Sonny Side Of Cher**	1966	5.00	12.00
Imperial LP-12301	(S)	**The Sonny Side Of Cher**	1966	6.00	15.00
Imperial LP-9320	(M)	**Cher**	1966	5.00	12.00
Imperial LP-12320	(S)	**Cher**	1966	6.00	15.00
Imperial LP-9358	(M)	**With Love**	1967	5.00	12.00
Imperial LP-12358	(S)	**With Love**	1967	6.00	15.00
Imperial LP-12373	(S)	**Backstage**	1968	5.00	12.00
Imperial LP-12406	(S)	**Cher's Golden Greats**	1968	5.00	12.00
Casablanca NBPIX-7133	(S)	**Take Me Home** (Picture disc)	1979	5.00	12.00
CHEROKEE					
ABC S-719	(S)	**Cherokee**	1970	6.00	15.00
CHESTER, GARY					
DCP DCL-3803	(M)	**Yeah, Yeah, Yeah**	1964	6.00	15.00
DCP DCS-6803	(S)	**Yeah, Yeah, Yeah**	1964	8.00	20.00

Label & Catalog #		Title	Year	VG+	NM
CHEVRONS, THE					
The Chevrons feature Terry Cashman.					
Time 10008	(M)	**Sing A Long Rock & Roll**	1961	35.00	70.00
CHICAGO [CHICAGO TRANSIT AUTHORITY]					
Columbia GP-8	(S)	**Chicago Transit Authority** *(2 LPs)*	1969	12.00	30.00
Columbia KGP-24	(S)	**Chicago** *(2 LPs)*	1970	12.00	30.00
— Original Columbia albums above have "360 Sound " on the bottom of the label.—					
Columbia C2Q-30110	(Q)	**Chicago III** *(2 LPs)*	1974	10.00	25.00
Columbia CQ-30865	(Q)	**Chicago IV (Carnegie Hall)** *(4 LP box)*	1974	12.00	30.00
Columbia CQ-31102	(Q)	**Chicago V**	1974	8.00	20.00
Columbia CQ-32400	(Q)	**Chicago VI**	1974	8.00	20.00
Columbia C2Q-32810	(Q)	**Chicago VII** *(2 LPs)*	1974	10.00	25.00
Columbia PCQ-33100	(Q)	**Chicago VIII**	1975	8.00	20.00
Columbia GQ-33255	(Q)	**Chicago Transit Authority**	1975	8.00	20.00
Columbia GQ-33258	(Q)	**Chicago II**	1975	8.00	20.00
Columbia PCQ-33900	(Q)	**Chicago IX/Greatest Hits**	1975	8.00	20.00
Columbia PCQ-34200	(Q)	**Chicago X**	1976	8.00	20.00
Columbia *(No number)*	(DJ)	**Chicago** *(17 LP box)*	1976	100.00	200.00
Columbia HC-43900	(S)	**Greatest Hits** *(Half-speed master)*	1982	12.00	30.00
Columbia HC-44200	(S)	**Chicago X** *(Half-speed master)*	1982	8.00	20.00
Mobile Fidelity MFSL-128	(S)	**Chicago Transit Authority** *(2 LPs)*	1983	12.00	30.00
Full Moon 25060	(DJ)	**Chicago 17** *(Quiex II vinyl)*	1984	6.00	15.00
CHICKEN SHACK					
Epic BN-26414	(S)	**Forty Blue Fingers, Freshly Packed And Ready To Serve**	1968	8.00	20.00
Blue Horizon BH-7705	(S)	**O.K. Ken?**	1969	10.00	25.00
Blue Horizon BH-7706	(S)	**100 Ton Chicken**	1969	8.00	20.00
Blue Horizon BH-4809	(S)	**Accept Chicken Shack**	1970	8.00	20.00
Deram DES-18063	(S)	**Imagination Lady**	1972	8.00	20.00
CHIFFONS, THE					
Laurie LLP-2018	(M)	**He's So Fine**	1963	20.00	50.00
Laurie LLP-2020	(M)	**One Fine Day**	1963	20.00	50.00
Laurie LLP-2036	(M)	**Sweet Talkin' Guy**	1966	16.00	40.00
Laurie SLP-2036	(S)	**Sweet Talkin' Guy**	1966	20.00	50.00
B.T. Puppy S-1011	(S)	**My Secret Love**	1970	20.00	50.00
CHILD'S ART					
Gold 3000	(S)	**Uncut**	1982	40.00	80.00
CHILDREN, THE					
Cinema CLP-1	(S)	**Rebirth**	1968	35.00	70.00
Atco SD-33-271	(S)	**Rebirth**	1968	6.00	15.00
CHIPMUNKS, THE					
The Chipmunks are the creation of Ross Bagdasarian, a.k.a. David Seville.					
Liberty LRP-3132	(M)	**Sing With The Chipmunks** *(Red vinyl)*	1959	20.00	50.00
Liberty LST-7132	(S)	**Sing With The Chipmunks** *(Red vinyl)*	1959	30.00	60.00
Liberty LRP-3132	(M)	**Sing With The Chipmunks**	1959	10.00	25.00
Liberty LST-7132	(S)	**Sing With The Chipmunks**	1959	14.00	35.00
Liberty LRP-3159	(M)	**Sing Again With The Chipmunks**	1960	10.00	25.00
Liberty LST-7159	(S)	**Sing Again With The Chipmunks**	1960	14.00	35.00
Liberty LRP-3170	(M)	**Around The World With The Chipmunks**	1960	10.00	25.00
Liberty LST-7170	(S)	**Around The World With The Chipmunks**	1960	14.00	35.00
— Original pressings above have "realistic" drawings of the Chipmunks on the covers.—					
Liberty LRP-3132	(M)	**Sing With The Chipmunks**	1961	8.00	20.00
Liberty LST-7132	(S)	**Sing With The Chipmunks**	1961	10.00	25.00
Liberty LRP-3159	(M)	**Sing Again With The Chipmunks**	1961	8.00	20.00
Liberty LST-7159	(S)	**Sing Again With The Chipmunks**	1961	10.00	25.00
Liberty LRP-3170	(M)	**Around The World With The Chipmunks**	1961	8.00	20.00
Liberty LST-7170	(S)	**Around The World With The Chipmunks**	1961	10.00	25.00
— Later pressings have drawings of the Chipmunks on the covers as the familar cartoons.—					
Liberty LRP-3209	(M)	**The Alvin Show**	1961	8.00	20.00
Liberty LST-7209	(S)	**The Alvin Show**	1961	10.00	25.00
Liberty LRP-3229	(M)	**The Chipmunks Songbook**	1962	8.00	20.00
Liberty LST-7229	(S)	**The Chipmunks Songbook**	1962	10.00	25.00

Label & Catalog #		Title	Year	VG+	NM
Liberty LRP-3256	(M)	**Christmas With The Chipmunks**	*1962*	8.00	20.00
Liberty LST-7256	(S)	**Christmas With The Chipmunks**	*1962*	10.00	25.00
Liberty LRP-3334	(M)	**Christmas With The Chipmunks, Volume 2**	*1963*	8.00	20.00
Liberty LST-7334	(S)	**Christmas With The Chipmunks, Volume 2**	*1963*	10.00	25.00
Liberty LRP-3388	(M)	**The Chipmunks Sing The Beatles Hits**	*1964*	10.00	25.00
Liberty LST-7388	(S)	**The Chipmunks Sing The Beatles Hits**	*1964*	12.00	30.00
Liberty LRP-3424	(M)	**The Chipmunks A Go-Go**	*1965*	6.00	15.00
Liberty LST-7424	(S)	**The Chipmunks A Go-Go**	*1965*	8.00	20.00
Liberty LRP-3405	(M)	**The Chipmunks Sing With Children**	*1965*	6.00	15.00
Liberty LST-7405	(S)	**The Chipmunks Sing With Children**	*1965*	8.00	20.00

CHOATES, HARRY

"D" 7000	(M)	**Jole Blon**	*195?*	20.00	50.00

CHOCOLATE WATCH BAND, THE

Tower T-5096	(M)	**No Way Out**	*1967*	75.00	150.00
Tower ST-5096	(S)	**No Way Out**	*1967*	75.00	150.00
Tower ST-5016	(S)	**The Inner Mystique**	*1968*	75.00	150.00
Tower ST-5153	(S)	**One Step Beyond**	*1969*	50.00	100.00

(Original copies have the front cover slick trimmed and pasted on; counterfeits have the slick wrapped around the three sides.)

CHORDETTES, THE

Columbia CL-6111 (10")	(M)	**Harmony Time**	*1950*	16.00	40.00
Columbia CL-6170 (10")	(M)	**Harmony Time, Volume 2**	*1951*	16.00	40.00
Columbia CL-6218 (10")	(M)	**Harmony Encores**	*1952*	16.00	40.00
Columbia CL-6285 (10")	(M)	**Your Requests**	*1953*	16.00	40.00
Columbia CL-2519 (10")	(M)	**The Chordettes**	*1955*	16.00	40.00
Columbia CL-956	(M)	**Listen**	*1957*	12.00	30.00
Cadence CLP-1002 (10")	(M)	**Close Harmony**	*1955*	16.00	40.00
Cadence LP-3001	(M)	**The Chordettes**	*1957*	12.00	30.00
Cadence CLP-3002	(M)	**Close Harmony**	*1957*	12.00	30.00
Cadence CLP-3062	(M)	**Never On Sunday**	*1962*	8.00	20.00
Cadence CLP-25062	(S)	**Never On Sunday**	*1962*	12.00	30.00

CHOSEN FEW, THE

RCA Victor LSP-4242	(S)	**The Chosen Few**	*1969*	8.00	20.00

CHRISTIE, LOU

Lou Christie is a pseudonym for Lugee Sacco.

Roulette R-25208	(M)	**Lou Christie**	*1963*	12.00	30.00
Roulette SR-25208	(P)	**Lou Christie**	*1963*	16.00	40.00
MGM E-4360	(M)	**Lou Christie Strikes**	*1966*	6.00	15.00
MGM SE-4360	(S)	**Lou Christie Strikes**	*1966*	8.00	20.00
Co&Ce LP-1231	(M)	**Lou Christie Strikes Back**	*1966*	16.00	40.00
Colpix CP-4001	(M)	**Lou Christie Strikes Again**	*1966*	8.00	20.00
Colpix SCP-4001	(S)	**Lou Christie Strikes Again**	*1966*	12.00	30.00
Roulette R-25332	(M)	**Lou Christie Strikes Again**	*1966*	6.00	15.00
Roulette SR-25332	(P)	**Lou Christie Strikes Again**	*1966*	8.00	20.00
MGM E-4394	(M)	**Painter Of Hits**	*1966*	6.00	15.00
MGM SE-4394	(P)	**Painter Of Hits**	*1966*	8.00	20.00

CHRISTOPHER

Chris Tee	(S)	**What'cha Gonna Do?** *(Orange cover)*	*1969*	*See note below*	

(Rare. Estimated near mint value $500-1,000.)

CHRISTOPHER

Metromedia 1024	(DJ)	**Christopher**	*197?*	100.00	200.00

CHRISTY, JUNE

Capitol H-516 (10")	(M)	**Something Cool**	*1954*	20.00	50.00
Capitol T-516	(M)	**Something Cool**	*1955*	12.00	30.00
Capitol T-656	(M)	**Duet**	*1955*	12.00	30.00
Capitol T-725	(M)	**The Misty Miss Christy**	*1955*	12.00	30.00
Capitol T-833	(M)	**June Fair And Warmer**	*1957*	12.00	30.00
Capitol T-902	(M)	**Gone For The Day**	*1957*	12.00	30.00
Capitol T-1006	(M)	**This Is June Christy!**	*1958*	12.00	30.00

— Original Capitol albums above hace turquoise labels. —

Capitol T-1076	(M)	**June's Got Rhythm**	*1958*	10.00	25.00

Label & Catalog #		Title	Year	VG+	NM
Capitol T-1114	(M)	The Song Is June!	1959	10.00	25.00
Capitol T-1202	(M)	June Christy Recalls Those Kenton Days	1959	10.00	25.00
Capitol T-1308	(M)	Ballads For Night People	1959	10.00	25.00
Capitol T-1398	(M)	The Cool School	1960	10.00	25.00
Capitol T-1498	(M)	Off Beat	1961	10.00	25.00
Capitol T-1586	(M)	Do Re Mi	1961	6.00	15.00
Capitol ST-1586	(S)	Do Re Mi	1961	10.00	25.00
Capitol T-1605	(M)	That Time Of Year	1961	6.00	15.00
Capitol ST-1605	(S)	That Time Of Year	1961	10.00	25.00

— Original Capitol albums above have black labels with the Capitol logo on the left side.—

Capitol T-1693	(M)	The Best Of June Christy	1962	6.00	15.00
Capitol ST-1693	(S)	The Best Of June Christy	1962	8.00	20.00
Capitol T-1845	(M)	Big Band Specials	1962	6.00	15.00
Capitol ST-1845	(S)	Big Band Specials	1962	8.00	20.00
Capitol T-1953	(M)	The Intimate June Christy	1962	6.00	15.00
Capitol ST-1953	(S)	The Intimate June Christy	1962	8.00	20.00
Capitol T-2410	(M)	Something Broadway, Something Latin	1965	6.00	15.00
Capitol ST-2410	(S)	Something Broadway, Something Latin	1965	8.00	20.00

— Original Capitol albums above have black label with the Capitol logo on the top.—

CIRCUIT RIDERS, THE

C.R. 666	(S)	The Circuit Riders	1980	35.00	70.00

CIRCUS

Metromedia LPS-7401	(S)	Circus	197?	10.00	25.00

CIRCUS MAXIMUS

Circus Maximus features Jerry Jeff Walker.

Vanguard VRS-9260	(M)	Circus Maximus	1967	6.00	15.00
Vanguard VSD-79260	(S)	Circus Maximus	1967	8.00	20.00
Vanguard VSD-79274	(S)	Never Land Revisited	1968	8.00	20.00

CITY

City features Carole King.

Ode Z-1244012	(S)	Now That Everything's Been Said	1969	16.00	40.00
		(Originals have color covers, counterfeits have black & white covers.)			

CITY FOLK

20th Century TF-4153	(M)	Here Come The City Folk	1964	5.00	12.00
20th Century TFS-4153	(S)	Here Come The City Folk	1964	6.00	15.00

CLANTON, JIMMY

Ace 1001	(M)	Just A Dream	1959	20.00	50.00
Ace 1007	(M)	Jimmy's Happy	1960	20.00	50.00
Ace 1007	(M)	Jimmy's Happy (Red vinyl)	1960	35.00	70.00
Ace 1008	(M)	Jimmy's Blue	1960	20.00	50.00
Ace 1008	(M)	Jimmy's Blue (Blue vinyl)	1960	35.00	70.00
		(The records for "Jimmy's Happy" and "Jimmy's Blue" on red and blue vinyl have both the single album catalog numbers, 1007-8 and the double album catalog number, 100, on their labels.)			
Ace DLP-100	(M)	Jimmy's Happy/Blue (2 LPs. Colored vinyl)	1960	100.00	200.00
		(Issued with a poster, priced separately below.)			
Ace DLP-100		Jimmy's Happy/Jimmy's Blue Poster	1960	20.00	50.00
Ace 1011	(M)	My Best To You	1961	30.00	60.00
Ace 1014	(M)	Teenage Millionaire	1961	30.00	60.00
Ace 1026	(M)	Venus In Bluejeans	1962	35.00	70.00
Phillips PHM-200154	(M)	The Best Of Jimmy Clanton	1964	8.00	20.00
Phillips PHS-600154	(S)	The Best Of Jimmy Clanton	1964	10.00	25.00

CLAP

Nova Sol 1001	(S)	Have You Reached Yet?	197?	240.00	400.00

CLAPTON, ERIC

Refer to Blind Faith; Cream; Derek & The Dominos; John Mayall's Bluesbreakers; The Yardbirds.

Atco SD-33-329	(S)	Eric Clapton	1970	4.00	10.00
Atco SD-2-803	(S)	The History Of Eric Clapton (2 LPs)	1972	5.00	12.00
Polydor PD-3503	(S)	Clapton At His Best (2 LPs)	1972	6.00	15.00
RSO QD-4801	(Q)	461 Ocean Boulevard	1974	10.00	25.00
RSO QD-4806	(Q)	There's One In Every Crowd	1975	8.00	20.00

Label & Catalog #		Title	Year	VG+	NM
RSO 035	(DJ)	**Slowhand** (White vinyl)	1978	12.00	30.00
RSO 1009	(DJ)	**Backless** (White vinyl)	1978	10.00	25.00
RSO PRO-22-015	(DJ)	**Classic Cuts** (2 LPs)	1980	12.00	30.00
Mobile Fidelity MFSL-030	(S)	**Slowhand**	1980	20.00	50.00
Nautilus NR-32	(S)	**Just One Night**	198?	16.00	40.00

CLARK, CHRIS

Motown 664	(M)	**Soul Sounds**	1967	12.00	30.00
Motown 664	(S)	**Soul Sounds**	1967	16.00	40.00

CLARK, CLAUDINE

Chancellor CHL-5029	(M)	**Party Lights**	1962	35.00	70.00

CLARK, DAVE [THE DAVE CLARK FIVE]

Crown CLP-5400	(M)	**The Dave Clark Five With The Playbacks**	1964	6.00	15.00
Crown CST-400	(E)	**The Dave Clark Five With The Playbacks**	1964	5.00	12.00
Crown CLP-5473	(M)	**Chaquita In Your Heart**	1964	6.00	15.00
Crown CST-473	(E)	**Chaquita In Your Heart**	1964	5.00	12.00
Cortleigh 1073	(M)	**The Dave Clark Five With Ricky Astor**	1964	8.00	20.00
Epic LN-24093	(M)	**Glad All Over**	1964	20.00	50.00
Epic BN-26093	(E)	**Glad All Over**	1964	16.00	40.00
		(The band has no instruments on the cover.)			
Epic LN-24093	(M)	**Glad All Over**	1964	12.00	30.00
Epic BN-26093	(E)	**Glad All Over**	1964	8.00	20.00
		(The band has their instruments on the cover.)			
Epic LN-24104	(M)	**The Dave Clark Five Return**	1964	12.00	30.00
Epic BN-26104	(E)	**The Dave Clark Five Return**	1964	8.00	20.00
Epic LN-24117	(M)	**American Tour, Volume 1**	1964	12.00	30.00
Epic BN-26117	(E)	**American Tour, Volume 1**	1964	8.00	20.00
Epic XEM-77238	(DJ)	**The Dave Clark 5** (Interview)	1964	150.00	250.00
Radio Pulsebeat	(M)	**The Ed Rudy Interview**	1964	50.00	100.00
Epic LN-24128	(M)	**Coast To Coast**	1965	12.00	30.00
Epic BN-26128	(E)	**Coast To Coast**	1965	8.00	20.00
Epic LN-24139	(M)	**Weekend In London**	1965	12.00	30.00
Epic BN-26139	(E)	**Weekend In London**	1965	8.00	20.00
Warner Bros. 3248	(DJ)	**Having A Wild Weekend** (Radio spots)	1965	100.00	200.00
Warner Bros. 3296	(DJ)	**Having A Wild Weekend** (Interview)	1965	180.00	300.00
Epic LN-24162	(M)	**Having A Wild Weekend** (Soundtrack)	1965	12.00	30.00
Epic BN-26162	(E)	**Having A Wild Weekend** (Soundtrack)	1965	8.00	20.00
Epic LN-24178	(M)	**I Like It Like That**	1965	12.00	30.00
Epic BN-26178	(E)	**I Like It Like That**	1965	8.00	20.00
Epic LN-24185	(M)	**Greatest Hits**	1966	10.00	25.00
Epic BN-26185	(E)	**Greatest Hits**	1966	6.00	15.00
Epic BN-26185	(E)	**Greatest Hits** (Orange label)	1973	14.00	35.00
Epic LN-24198	(M)	**Try Too Hard**	1966	10.00	25.00
Epic BN-26198	(E)	**Try Too Hard**	1966	6.00	15.00
Epic LN-24212	(M)	**Satisfied With You**	1966	10.00	25.00
Epic BN-26212	(E)	**Satisfied With You**	1966	6.00	15.00
Epic LN-24221	(M)	**More Greatest Hits**	1966	10.00	25.00
Epic BN-26221	(E)	**More Greatest Hits**	1966	6.00	15.00
Epic LN-24236	(M)	**Five By Five**	1967	8.00	20.00
Epic BN-26236	(S)	**Five By Five**	1967	10.00	25.00
Epic LN-24312	(M)	**You Got What It Takes**	1967	8.00	20.00
Epic BN-26312	(S)	**You Got What It Takes**	1967	10.00	25.00
Epic LN-24354	(M)	**Everybody Knows**	1968	8.00	20.00
Epic BN-26354	(S)	**Everybody Knows**	1968	10.00	25.00
		—Original Epic albums above have yellow labels with a oval logo on top.—			
Epic EG-30434	(P)	**The Dave Clark Five** (2 LPs)	1971	35.00	70.00
Epic KEG-33459	(M)	**Glad All Over Again**	1975	14.00	35.00

CLARK, DEE

Abner LP-2000	(M)	**Dee Clark**	1959	18.00	45.00
Abner SR-2000	(S)	**Dee Clark**	1959	30.00	60.00
Abner LP-2002	(M)	**How About That**	1960	18.00	45.00
Abner SR-2002	(S)	**How About That**	1960	30.00	60.00
Vee Jay LP-1019	(M)	**You're Looking Good**	1960	14.00	35.00
Vee Jay LP-1028	(M)	**Dee Clark**	1961	14.00	35.00
Vee Jay LP-1037	(M)	**Hold On, It's Dee Clark**	1961	14.00	35.00
Vee Jay SR-1037	(S)	**Hold On, It's Dee Clark**	1961	20.00	50.00

Label & Catalog #		Title	Year	VG+	NM
Vee Jay LP-1047	(M)	The Best Of Dee Clark	1964	10.00	25.00
Vee Jay SR-1047	(P)	The Best Of Dee Clark	1964	14.00	35.00

CLARK, DOTTIE
| Mainstream 56006 | (M) | I'm Lost | 1966 | 6.00 | 15.00 |
| Mainstream S-6006 | (S) | I'm Lost | 1966 | 8.00 | 20.00 |

CLARK, GENE
Clark was formerly a member of The Byrds. Refer to Dillard & Clark; McGuinn, Clark & Hillman
Columbia CL-2618	(M)	Gene Clark With The Gosdin Brothers	1967	12.00	30.00
Columbia CS-9418	(S)	Gene Clark With The Gosdin Brothers	1967	20.00	50.00
A&M SD-4292	(S)	White Light	1971	6.00	15.00
MediaArts 41-12	(S)	American Flyer (Soundtrack)	1971	6.00	15.00
Columbia KC-31123	(S)	Early L.A. Sessions	1972	5.00	12.00
Asylum 7E-1016	(S)	No Other (With bonus photo)	1974	5.00	12.00
RSO RS-1-3011	(S)	Two Sides To Every Story	1976	6.00	15.00

CLARK, PETULA
Imperial LP-9079	(M)	Pet Clark	1959	12.00	30.00
Imperial LP-12027	(S)	Pet Clark	1959	16.00	40.00
Imperial LP-9281	(M)	Uptown With Petula Clark	1965	5.00	12.00
Imperial LP-12281	(S)	Uptown With Petula Clark	1965	6.00	15.00
Laurie LLP-2032	(M)	In Love	1966	5.00	12.00
Laurie LLPS-2032	(S)	In Love	1966	6.00	15.00
Laurie LLP-2043	(M)	Petula Clark Sings For Everybody	1967	5.00	12.00
Laurie LLPS-2043	(S)	Petula Clark Sings For Everybody	1967	6.00	15.00
Warner Bros. W-1590	(M)	Downtown	1964	5.00	12.00
Warner Bros. WS-1590	(S)	Downtown	1964	6.00	15.00
Warner Bros. W-1598	(M)	I Know A Place	1965	5.00	12.00
Warner Bros. WS-1598	(S)	I Know A Place	1965	6.00	15.00
Warner Bros. W-1608	(M)	The World's Greatest International Hits	1965	5.00	12.00
Warner Bros. WS-1608	(S)	The World's Greatest International Hits	1965	6.00	15.00
		— Original Warner albums above have grey labels.—			
Warner Bros. W-1630	(M)	My Love	1966	4.00	10.00
Warner Bros. WS-1630	(S)	My Love	1966	5.00	12.00
Warner Bros. W-1645	(M)	I Couldn't Live Without Your Love	1966	4.00	10.00
Warner Bros. WS-1645	(S)	I Couldn't Live Without Your Love	1966	5.00	12.00
Warner Bros. W-1673	(M)	Color My World/Who Am I	1967	4.00	10.00
Warner Bros. WS-1673	(S)	Color My World/Who Am I	1967	5.00	12.00
Warner Bros. W-1698	(M)	These Are My Songs	1967	4.00	10.00
Warner Bros. WS-1698	(S)	These Are My Songs	1967	5.00	12.00
Warner Bros. W-1719	(M)	The Other Man's Grass Is Always Greener	1968	5.00	12.00
Warner Bros. WS-1719	(S)	The Other Man's Grass Is Always Greener	1968	5.00	12.00
Warner Bros. W-1743	(M)	Petula	1968	5.00	12.00
Warner Bros. WS-1743	(S)	Petula	1968	5.00	12.00
		— Original Warner albums above have gold labels.—			
Warner Bros. 93215	(S)	Hits My Way (2 LPs. Capitol Record Club)	196?	8.00	20.00

CLARK, TODD
Todd originally recorded with Eyes.
| No label | (S) | We're Not Safe | 197? | 150.00 | 250.00 |
| T.M.I. 020 | (S) | Into Vision | 198? | 8.00 | 20.00 |

CLARK, "YODELING SLIM"
Playhouse 2017 (10")	(M)	Western Songs Anmd Dances	1954	20.00	50.00
Continental 1505	(M)	Cowboy And Yodel Songs	1962	10.00	25.00
Masterseal 57	(M)	Cowboy Songs	1963	8.00	20.00
Masterseal 135	(M)	Cowboy Songs (Volume 2)	1964	8.00	20.00
Palomino 300	(M)	Yodeling Slim Clark Sings Jimmie Rodgers	1966	30.00	60.00
Palomino 301	(M)	Favorite Montana Slim Songs	1966	16.00	40.00
Palomino 303	(M)	Favorite Montana Slim Songs	1966	16.00	40.00
Palomino 306	(M)	I Feel A Trip Coming On	1966	12.00	30.00
Palomino 307	(M)	Old Chestnuts	1967	12.00	30.00
Palomino 314	(M)	50th Anniversary Album	1968	12.00	30.00

CLARK-HUTCHINSON
| Sire SES-97027 | (S) | A=MH2 | 1969 | 6.00 | 15.00 |

While the career of Gram Parsons as the progenitor of modern country-rock is well documented, little attention is paid to the early work of former Byrd Gene Clark. His solo album for Columbia, *Gene Clark With The Gosdin Brothers*, featured future country superstars Vern and Rex Gosdin and a host of L.A.'s finest, including former Dillard Doug and soon-to-be Byrd Clarence White. The sound was far too country for 1967 and the album died unceremoniously. Teaming with Dillard in 1969, Gene released what may be the finest of all country rock albums, *The Fantastic Expedition Of Dillard & Clark*. (Gene Clark died on June 7, 1991.)

Label & Catalog #		Title	Year	VG+	NM
CLARY, ROBERT					
Epic LN-3171	(M)	**Meet Robert Clary**	195?	10.00	25.00
Epic LN-3281	(M)	**Hooray For Love**	195?	10.00	25.00
Mercury MG-20367	(M)	**Gigi**	1958	8.00	20.00
CLASH, THE					
Epic JE-35543	(S)	**Give 'Em Enough Rope** (Orange label)	1979	5.00	12.00
Epic 4E-36846 (10")	(S)	**Black Market Clash**	1980	6.00	15.00
Epic AS-952	(DJ)	**Interchords**	1981	12.00	30.00
Epic AS-1594	(DJ)	**The World According To The Clash**	1982	12.00	30.00
Epic AS-	(DJ)	**Sandinista Now!** (Sampler)	1981	10.00	25.00
Epic AS-99-1595	(DJ)	**Combat Rock** (Picture disc)	1983	6.00	30.00
CLASS-AIRES, THE					
Honey Bee	(M)	**Tears Start To Fall**	195?	180.00	300.00
CLAY, CASSIUS					
Cassius Clay later performed as Muhammed Ali.					
Columbia CL-2093	(M)	**I Am The Greatest!**	1963	14.00	35.00
Columbia CS-8893	(S)	**I Am The Greatest!**	1963	16.00	40.00
CLAY, JUDY, & BILLY VERA					
Atlantic 8174	(M)	**Storybook Children**	1967	6.00	15.00
Atlantic 8174	(S)	**Storybook Children**	1967	8.00	20.00
CLAYTON, PAUL					
Folkways FA-2007	(M)	**Cumberland Mountain Folksongs**	195?	8.00	20.00
Folkways FA-2106	(M)	**Bay State Ballads**	195?	8.00	20.00
Folkways FA-2110	(M)	**Folksongs And Ballads Of Virginia**	195?	8.00	20.00
Folkways FA 2378	(M)	**American Broadside**			
		Ballads In Popular Tradition	195?	8.00	20.00
Folkways FA-2382	(M)	**Dulcimer Songs And Solos**	195?	8.00	20.00
Folkways FA-2429	(M)	**Foc'sle Songs And Shanties**	195?	8.00	20.00
Folkways FA-8708	(M)	**British Broadside Ballads**	195?	8.00	20.00
Riverside RLP-12-615	(M)	**Bloody Ballads**	195?	8.00	20.00
Riverside RLP-12-640	(M)	**Wanted For Murder:**			
		Songs Of Outlaws And Desperados	195?	8.00	20.00
Riverside RLP-12-648	(M)	**Timber-r-r! Songs Of The Lumberjacks**	195?	8.00	20.00
Elektra EKL-147	(M)	**Unholy Matrimony**	195?	8.00	20.00
Elektra EKL-155	(M)	**Bobby Burns' Merry Muses Of Caledonia**	195?	8.00	20.00
Tradition 1005	(M)	**Whaling And Sailing Songs**			
		From The Days Of Moby Dick	196?	6.00	15.00
Stinson 69	(M)	**Whaling Songs And Ballads**	196?	6.00	15.00
Monument MLP-8017	(M)	**Folk Singer**	1965	6.00	15.00
Monument SLP-18017	(S)	**Folk Singer**	1965	8.00	20.00
CLAYTON-THOMAS, DAVID					
Refer to Blood, Sweat & Tears.					
Decca DL-75146	(S)	**David Clayton-Thomas**	1969	6.00	15.00
RCA Victor APD1-0173	(Q)	**David Clayton-Thomas**	1974	6.00	15.00
CLEANLINESS & GODLINESS SKIFFLE BAND, THE					
Vanguard VSD-79285	(S)	**Greatest Hits**	1968	10.00	25.00
CLEAR LIGHT					
Elektra EKL-4011	(M)	**Clear Light**	1967	6.00	15.00
Elektra EKS-74011	(S)	**Clear Light**	1967	8.00	20.00
CLEARY, DON					
Palomino 302	(M)	**Traditional Cowboy Songs**	1966	12.00	30.00
CLEFTONES, THE					
Gee GLP-705	(M)	**Heart And Soul**	1961	75.00	150.00
Gee SGLP-705	(S)	**Heart And Soul**	1961	180.00	300.00
Gee GLP-707	(M)	**For Sentimental Reasons**	1962	75.00	150.00
Gee SGLP-707	(S)	**For Sentimental Reasons**	1962	180.00	300.00

— Original Gee albums above have grey labels.—

Label & Catalog #		Title	Year	VG+	NM
CLIFFORD, BUZZ					
Columbia CL-1616	(M)	**Baby Sittin' With Buzz**	1961	20.00	50.00
Columbia CS-8416	(S)	**Baby Sittin' With Buzz**	1961	35.00	70.00
Dot DLP-25965	(S)	**See Your Way Clear**	1969	6.00	15.00
CLIFFORD, MIKE					
United Arts. UAL-6409	(M)	**For The Love Of Mike**	1965	8.00	20.00
United Arts. UAS-6409	(P)	**For The Love Of Mike**	1965	10.00	25.00
CLINE, PATSY					
Decca DL-8611	(M)	**Patsy Cline** (Black & silver label)	1957	35.00	70.00
Decca DL-8611	(M)	**Patsy Cline**	1957	20.00	50.00
Decca DL-4202	(M)	**Patsy Cline Showcase**	1961	16.00	40.00
Decca DL-74202	(S)	**Patsy Cline Showcase**	1961	20.00	50.00
Decca DL-4282	(M)	**Sentimentally Yours**	1962	10.00	25.00
Decca DL-74282	(S)	**Sentimentally Yours**	1962	14.00	35.00
Decca DXB-176	(M)	**The Patsy Cline Story** (With booklet)	1963	12.00	30.00
Decca DSXB-176	(S)	**The Patsy Cline Story** (With booklet)	1963	16.00	40.00
Decca DL-4508	(M)	**A Portrait Of Patsy Cline**	1964	10.00	25.00
Decca DL-74508	(S)	**A Portrait Of Patsy Cline**	1964	14.00	35.00
Decca DL-4586	(M)	**That's How A Heartache Begins**	1964	10.00	25.00
Decca DL-74586	(S)	**That's How A Heartache Begins**	1964	14.00	35.00
— Decca albums above have black labels with "Mfrd. by Decca" beneath the rainbow.—					
Decca DL-4854	(M)	**Patsy Cline's Greatest Hits**	1967	8.00	20.00
Decca DL-74854	(S)	**Patsy Cline's Greatest Hits**	1967	10.00	25.00
Everest D-5200	(M)	**Patsy Cline's Golden Hits**	1962	8.00	20.00
Everest SD-1200	(S)	**Patsy Cline's Golden Hits**	1962	10.00	25.00
Everest D-5204	(M)	**Encores**	1963	6.00	15.00
Everest SD-1204	(S)	**Encores**	1963	8.00	20.00
Everest D-5217	(M)	**In Memoriam**	1963	6.00	15.00
Everest SD-1217	(S)	**In Memoriam**	1963	8.00	20.00
Everest D-5223	(M)	**Patsy Cline-A Legend**	1963	6.00	15.00
Everest SD-1223	(S)	**Patsy Cline-A Legend**	1963	8.00	20.00
Everest D-5229	(M)	**Reflections**	1964	6.00	15.00
Everest SD-1229	(S)	**Reflections**	1964	8.00	20.00
Vocalion VL-3753	(M)	**Here's Patsy Cline**	1965	6.00	15.00
Vocalion VL-73753	(S)	**Here's Patsy Cline**	1965	8.00	20.00
Columbia CSP-5280	(S)	**A Portrait Of Patsy** (Record Club)	1969	8.00	20.00
CLIQUE, THE					
White Whale WWS-7126	(S)	**The Clique**	1969	6.00	15.00
CLOCKWORK					
Green Bottle 1013	(S)	**Clockwork**	1973	6.00	15.00
CLOONEY, ROSEMARY					
Refer to The Clooney Sisters; Bing Crosby; The Ferrers; The Hi-Lo's; The Reprise Repertory Theatre.					
Columbia CL-6224 (10")	(M)	**Hollywood's Best**	1952	20.00	50.00
Columbia CL-6297 (10")	(M)	**Rosemary Clooney**	1954	20.00	50.00
Columbia CL-6338 (10")	(M)	**White Christmas**	1954	20.00	50.00
Columbia CL-6282 (10")	(M)	**Red Garters** (Soundtrack)	1954	50.00	100.00
Columbia CL-2525 (10")	(M)	**Tenderly**	1955	20.00	50.00
Columbia CL-2569 (10")	(M)	**Children's Favorites**	1956	16.00	40.00
Columbia CL-2572 (10")	(M)	**A Date With The King**	1956	16.00	40.00
Columbia CL-2597 (10")	(M)	**My Fair Lady**	1956	16.00	40.00
MGM E-3153	(M)	**Deep In My Heart** (Soundtrack. Boxed set)	1954	50.00	100.00
MGM E-3153	(M)	**Deep In My Heart** (Soundtrack)	1955	20.00	50.00
Columbia CL-585	(M)	**Hollywood's Best**	1955	12.00	30.00
Columbia CL-872	(M)	**Blue Rose**	1956	12.00	30.00
Columbia CL-969	(M)	**Clooney Tunes**	1957	12.00	30.00
Columbia CL-1230	(M)	**Rosie's Greatest Hits**	1958	12.00	30.00
— Columbia albums above have three white "eye" logos on each side of the spindle hole.—					
Coral CRL-57266	(M)	**Swing Around Rosie**	1958	12.00	30.00
MGM E-3687	(M)	**Oh, Captain!**	1958	12.00	30.00
MGM E-3782	(M)	**Hymns From The Heart**	1959	8.00	20.00
MGM SE-3782	(S)	**Hymns From The Heart**	1959	12.00	30.00
MGM E-3834	(M)	**Rosemary Clooney Swings Softly**	1960	8.00	20.00
MGM SE-3834	(S)	**Rosemary Clooney Swings Softly**	1960	12.00	30.00

Label & Catalog #		Title	Year	VG+	NM
RCA Victor LPM-1854	(M)	**Fancy Meeting You Here**	1958	8.00	20.00
RCA Victor LSP-1854	(S)	**Fancy Meeting You Here**	1958	12.00	30.00
RCA Victor LPM-2133	(M)	**A Touch Of Tobasco**	1960	8.00	20.00
RCA Victor LSP-2133	(S)	**A Touch Of Tobasco**	1960	12.00	30.00
RCA Victor LPM-2212	(M)	**Clap Hands, Here Comes Rosie**	1960	8.00	20.00
RCA Victor LSP-2212	(S)	**Clap Hands, Here Comes Rosie**	1960	12.00	30.00
RCA Victor LPM-2265	(M)	**Rosie Solves The Swingin' Riddle**	1961	8.00	20.00
RCA Victor LSP-2265	(S)	**Rosie Solves The Swingin' Riddle**	1961	12.00	30.00
RCA Victor LPM-2565	(M)	**Country Hits From The Heart**	1963	8.00	20.00
RCA Victor LSP-2565	(S)	**Country Hits From The Heart**	1963	12.00	30.00
		—Mono RCA albums above have "Long Play" on the bottom of the label;			
		stereo albums have "Living Stereo" on the bottom.—			
Reprise R-6088	(M)	**Love**	1963	5.00	12.00
Reprise R9-6088	(S)	**Love**	1963	6.00	15.00
Reprise R-6108	(M)	**Thanks For Nothing**	1964	5.00	12.00
Reprise R9-6108	(S)	**Thanks For Nothing**	1964	6.00	15.00

CLOONEY SISTERS, THE
The Sisters feature Rosemary Clooney.

Epic LN-3160	(M)	**The Clooney Sisters With Tony Pastor**	1955	12.00	30.00

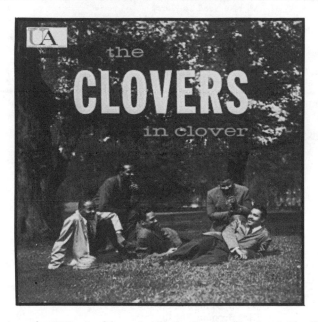

One of the most popular R&B acts of the early '50s, by the end of the decade The Clovers were recording pop for United Artists, where they hit with "Love Potion No. 9" in 1959.

CLOVERS, THE

Atlantic LP-1248	(M)	**The Clovers**	1956	180.00	300.00
Atlantic LP-8009	(M)	**The Clovers** *(Reissue of 1248)*	1957	100.00	200.00
Atlantic LP-8034	(M)	**Dance Party**	1959	100.00	200.00
		—Original Atlantic albums above have black labels.—			
Atlantic LP-8009	(M)	**The Clovers** *(Orange & purple label)*	195?	50.00	100.00
Atlantic LP-8034	(M)	**Dance Party** *(Orange & purple label)*	196?	50.00	100.00
Poplar 1001	(M)	**In Clover**	1958	75.00	150.00
United Arts. UAL-3033	(M)	**In Clover**	1959	50.00	100.00
United Arts. UAS-6033	(E)	**In Clover**	1959	75.00	150.00
United Arts. UAL-3099	(M)	**Love Potion Number Nine**	1959	50.00	100.00
United Arts. UAS-6099	(S)	**Love Potion Number Nine**	1959	100.00	200.00

Label & Catalog #		Title	Year	VG+	NM
COASTERS, THE					
Atco 33-101	(M)	**The Coasters** (Yellow harp label)	1958	180.00	300.00
Atco 33-111	(M)	**The Coasters' Greatest Hits**	1959	50.00	100.00
Atco 33-123	(M)	**One By One**	1960	30.00	60.00
Atco SD-33-123	(S)	**One By One**	1960	50.00	100.00
Atco 33-135	(M)	**Coast Along With The Coasters**	1962	16.00	40.00
Atco SD-33-135	(P)	**Coast Along With The Coasters**	1962	30.00	60.00
Clarion 605	(M)	**That's Rock And Roll**	1964	8.00	20.00
Clarion 605	(P)	**That's Rock And Roll**	1964	10.00	25.00
COCHRAN, EDDIE					
Liberty LRP-3061	(M)	**Singin' To My Baby** (Green label)	1957	180.00	300.00
Liberty LRP-3061	(M)	**Singin' To My Baby** (Black label)	1960	30.00	60.00
Liberty LRP-3172	(M)	**Eddie Cochran (Memorial Album)**	1960	40.00	80.00
Liberty LRP-3220	(DJ)	**Never To Be Forgotten** (Yellow label)	1962	75.00	150.00
Liberty LRP-3220	(M)	**Never To Be Forgotten**	1962	30.00	60.00
Sunset SUM-1123	(M)	**Summertime Blues**	1966	10.00	25.00
Sunset SUS-5123	(E)	**Summertime Blues**	1966	6.00	15.00
United Arts. UAS-9959	(M)	**Legendary Master** (2 LPs)	1971	10.00	25.00
COCHRAN, STEVIE					
No label	(DJ)	**No Need To Worry**	1984	100.00	200.00
COCHRAN, WAYNE (& THE C.C. RIDERS)					
Chess LP-1519	(M)	**Wayne Cochran**	1967	6.00	15.00
Chess LPS-1519	(S)	**Wayne Cochran**	1967	8.00	20.00
King KS-1116	(S)	**Livin' In A Bitch Of A World**	1970	6.00	15.00
Bethlehem 10002	(S)	**High And Ridin'**	1970	6.00	15.00
Epic KE-30989	(S)	**Cochran**	1972	5.00	12.00
COCKBURN, BRUCE					
True North APHT-5008	(S)	**Dancing In The Dragon's Jaw** (Half-speed master)	1982	6.00	15.00
True North APHT-5009	(S)	**Humans** (Half-speed master)	1982	6.00	15.00
COCKER, JOE					
A&M QU-54182	(Q)	**With A Little Help From My Friends**	1974	6.00	15.00
A&M QU-54224	(Q)	**Joe Cocker!**	1974	6.00	15.00
Asylum 6E-145	(DJ)	**Luxury You Can Afford** (Picture disc)	1978	4.00	10.00
COE, DAVID ALLAN					
SSS Inter. 9	(S)	**Penitentiary Blues**	196?	14.00	35.00
COLD BLOOD					
San Francisco 200	(S)	**Cold Blood**	1969	6.00	15.00
San Francisco 205	(S)	**Sisyphus**	1970	6.00	15.00
COLDER, BEN					
Ben Colder is a pseudonym for Sheb Wooley.					
MGM E-4117	(M)	**Spoofing The Big Ones**	1961	8.00	20.00
MGM SE-4117	(S)	**Spoofing The Big Ones**	1961	10.00	25.00
MGM E-4173	(M)	**Ben Colder**	1963	8.00	20.00
MGM SE-4173	(S)	**Ben Colder**	1963	10.00	25.00
MGM E-4421	(M)	**Big Ben Strikes Again**	1966	6.00	15.00
MGM SE-4421	(S)	**Big Ben Strikes Again**	1966	8.00	20.00
MGM E-4482	(M)	**Wine, Women And Song**	1967	5.00	12.00
MGM SE-4482	(S)	**Wine, Women And Song**	1967	6.00	15.00
COLE, JERRY, & HIS SPACEMEN					
Mr. Cole also recorded as Jerry Kole.					
Capitol T-2044	(M)	**Outer Limits**	1963	10.00	25.00
Capitol ST-2044	(S)	**Outer Limits**	1963	14.00	35.00
Capitol T-2061	(M)	**Hot Rod Dance Party**	1964	10.00	25.00
Capitol ST-2601	(S)	**Hot Rod Dance Party**	1964	14.00	35.00
Capitol T-2112	(M)	**Surf Age**	1964	16.00	40.00
Capitol ST-2112	(S)	**Surf Age**	1964	20.00	50.00
		(With bonus single, "Thunder Wave," by Dick Dale.)			
Capitol T-2112	(M)	**Surf Age** (Without the single)	1964	10.00	25.00
Capitol ST-2112	(S)	**Surf Age** (Without the single)	1964	14.00	35.00

Label & Catalog #		Title	Year	VG+	NM
COLE, MARIA					
Kapp 102 (10")	(M)	**Maria Cole**	1954	20.00	50.00
Capitol T-2612	(M)	**Love Is A Special Feeling**	1966	5.00	12.00
Capitol ST-2612	(S)	**Love Is A Special Feeling**	1966	6.00	15.00
COLE, NAT "KING"					
Capitol H-8 (10")	(M)	**The King Cole Trio**	1950	16.00	40.00
Capitol H-29 (10")	(M)	**The King Cole Trio, Volume 2**	1950	16.00	40.00
Capitol H-59 (10")	(M)	**The King Cole Trio, Volume 3**	1950	16.00	40.00
Capitol H-156 (10")	(M)	**Nat King Cole At The Piano**	1950	16.00	40.00
Capitol H-177 (10")	(M)	**The King Cole Trio, Volume 4**	1950	16.00	40.00
Capitol H-213 (10")	(M)	**Harvest Of Hits**	1950	16.00	40.00
Capitol H-220 (10")	(M)	**The Nat King Cole Trio, Volume 1**	1950	16.00	40.00
Capitol H-332 (10")	(M)	**Penthouse Serenade**	1952	16.00	40.00
Capitol H-357 (10")	(M)	**Unforgettable**	1952	16.00	40.00
Capitol H-420 (10")	(M)	**Two In Love**	1954	16.00	40.00
Capitol H-514 (10")	(M)	**Tenth Anniversary Album**	1954	16.00	40.00
Capitol T-332	(M)	**Penthouse Serenade**	1954	10.00	25.00
Capitol T-357	(M)	**Unforgettable**	1954	10.00	25.00
Capitol T-420	(M)	**Two In Love**	1954	10.00	25.00
Capitol W-514	(M)	**Tenth Anniversary Album**	1954	10.00	25.00
Capitol T-591	(M)	**Vocal Classics**	1955	10.00	25.00
Capitol T-592	(M)	**Instrumental Classics**	1955	10.00	25.00
Capitol T-680	(M)	**Ballads Of The Day**	1956	10.00	25.00
Capitol W-689	(M)	**The Piano Style Of Nat King Cole**	1956	10.00	25.00
Capitol W-782	(M)	**After Midnight**	1956	10.00	25.00

— Original Capitol albums above have turquoise or grey labels with "Long Playing" on the bottom.—

Label & Catalog #		Title	Year	VG+	NM
Decca DL-8260	(M)	**In The Beginning**	1956	16.00	40.00
Score SLP-4019	(M)	**The King Cole Trio And Lester Young**	1957	35.00	70.00
Capitol W 824	(M)	**Love Is The Thing**	1957	6.00	15.00
Capitol SW-824	(S)	**Love Is The Thing**	1957	10.00	25.00
Capitol T-870	(M)	**This Is Nat King Cole**	1957	10.00	25.00
Capitol W-903	(M)	**Just One Of Those Things**	1958	6.00	15.00
Capitol SW-903	(S)	**Just One Of Those Things**	1958	10.00	25.00
Capitol W-993	(M)	**Saint Louis Blues** *(Soundtrack)*	1958	16.00	40.00

— Original Capitol albums above have turquoise or grey labels with "Long Playing High Fidelity."—

Label & Catalog #		Title	Year	VG+	NM
Capitol W-1031	(M)	**Cole Espanol**	1958	6.00	15.00
Capitol DW-1031	(E)	**Cole Espanol**	196?	4.00	10.00
Capitol W-1084	(M)	**The Very Thought Of You**	1958	5.00	12.00
Capitol SW-1084	(S)	**The Very Thought Of You**	1958	6.00	15.00
Capitol W-1120	(M)	**Welcome To The Club**	1959	5.00	12.00
Capitol SW-1120	(S)	**Welcome To The Club**	1959	6.00	15.00
Capitol W-1190	(M)	**To Whom It May Concern**	1959	5.00	12.00
Capitol SW-1190	(S)	**To Whom It May Concern**	1959	6.00	15.00
Capitol W-1220	(M)	**A Mis Amigos**	1959	5.00	12.00
Capitol SW-1220	(S)	**A Mis Amigos**	1959	6.00	15.00
Capitol T-1249	(M)	**Every Time I Feel The Spirit**	1960	5.00	12.00
Capitol ST-1249	(S)	**Every Time I Feel The Spirit**	1960	6.00	15.00
Capitol W-1331	(M)	**Tell Me All About Yourself**	1960	5.00	12.00
Capitol SW-1331	(S)	**Tell Me All About Yourself**	1960	6.00	15.00
Capitol WAK-1392	(M)	**Wild Is Love**	1960	5.00	12.00
Capitol SWAK-1392	(S)	**Wild Is Love**	1960	6.00	15.00
Capitol W-1444	(M)	**The Magic Of Christmas**	1960	5.00	12.00
Capitol SW-1444	(S)	**The Magic Of Christmas**	1960	6.00	15.00
Capitol W-1574	(M)	**The Touch Of Your Lips**	1961	5.00	12.00
Capitol ST-1574	(S)	**The Touch Of Your Lips**	1961	6.00	15.00
Capitol WCL-1613	(M)	**The Nat King Cole Story** *(3 LPs)*	1961	10.00	25.00
Capitol SWCL-1613	(P)	**The Nat King Cole Story** *(3 LPs)*	1961	12.00	30.00
Capitol W-1675	(M)	**Nat King Cole Sings/George Shearing Plays**	1962	8.00	20.00
Capitol ST-1675	(S)	**Nat King Cole Sings/George Shearing Plays**	1962	10.00	25.00
		(Issued with a bonus album, PRO-2003.)			
Capitol W-1675	(M)	**Nat King Cole Sings/George Shearing Plays**	1962	5.00	12.00
Capitol ST-1675	(S)	**Nat King Cole Sings/George Shearing Plays**	1962	6.00	15.00
		(Without the bonus album.)			
Capitol W-1713	(M)	**Nat King Cole Sings The Blues**	1962	4.00	10.00
Capitol SW-1713	(S)	**Nat King Cole Sings The Blues**	1962	5.00	12.00

— Original Capitol albums above have black labels with the Capitol logo on the left side.—

Label & Catalog #		Title	Year	VG+	NM
Capitol W-1929	(M)	**Nat King Cole Sings The Blues, Volume 2**	1963	4.00	10.00
Capitol SW-1929	(S)	**Nat King Cole Sings The Blues, Volume 2**	1963	5.00	12.00

Label & Catalog #		Title	Year	VG+	NM
Capitol T-2311	(M)	The Nat King Cole Trio	1965	6.00	15.00
Capitol T-2340	(M)	"Cat Ballou" And Other Motion Pictures	1965	5.00	12.00
Capitol ST-2340	(S)	"Cat Ballou" And Other Motion Pictures	1965	6.00	15.00
Capitol T-2529	(M)	The Vintage Years	1966	6.00	15.00
Capitol TCL-2873	(M)	Deluxe Set (3 LP box)	1967	6.00	15.00
Capitol STCL-2873	(P)	Deluxe Set (3 LP box)	1967	8.00	20.00

— *Original Capitol albums above have black labels with the Capitol logo on top.* —

COLE, NATALIE

Mobile Fidelity MFSL-032	(S)	Thankful	197?	6.00	15.00
Mobile Fidelity MFSL-081	(S)	Natalie Cole Sings/George Shearing Plays	198?	5.00	12.00

COLEMAN, EARL

Prestige 7045	(M)	Earl Coleman Returns	1956	20.00	50.00

COLLAGE

Smash SRS-67101	(S)	The Collage	1968	6.00	15.00
Cream 9008	(S)	Collage	1971	6.00	15.00

COLLECTORS, THE

Warner Bros. WS-1746	(S)	The Collectors	1968	6.00	15.00
Warner Bros. WS-1774	(S)	Grass And Wild Strawberries	1969	5.00	12.00

COLLEGIANS, THE

Winley LP-6004	(M)	Sing Along With The Collegians	195?	240.00	400.00

COLLINS, ALBERT

T.C.F. Hall 8002	(M)	The Cool Sound Of Albert Collins	1965	12.00	30.00
Imperial LP-12428	(S)	Love Can Be Found Anywhere	1968	6.00	15.00
Imperial LP-12438	(S)	Trash Talkin'	1969	6.00	15.00
Imperial LP-12449	(S)	The Complete Albert Collins	1969	6.00	15.00
Blue Thumb BTS-8	(S)	Truckin' With Albert Collins	1969	6.00	15.00

COLLINS, DOROTHY

Coral CRL-57105	(M)	At Home	1957	10.00	25.00
Coral CRL-57106	(M)	Songs By Dorothy Collins	1957	10.00	25.00

COLLINS, JUDY

Elektra EQ-5030	(Q)	Colors Of The Day/Best Of Judy Collins	1972	4.00	10.00
Direct Disk SD-16607	(S)	Judith	197?	8.00	20.00

COLLINS, TOMMY

Capitol T-776	(M)	Words And Music Country Style	1957	40.00	80.00
Capitol T-1125	(M)	Light Of The Lord	1959	45.00	90.00
Capitol T-1196	(M)	This Is Tommy Collins	1959	37.50	75.00
Capitol T-1436	(M)	Songs I Love To Sing	1961	20.00	50.00
Capitol ST-1436	(S)	Songs I Love To Sing	1961	30.00	60.00
Tower T-5021	(M)	Let's Live A Little	1966	16.00	40.00
Tower DT-5021	(E)	Let's Live A Little	1966	10.00	25.00
Tower T-5107	(M)	Shindig	1968	10.00	25.00
Tower DT-5107	(E)	Shindig	1968	6.00	15.00
Columbia CL-2510	(M)	The Dynamic Tommy Collins	1966	14.00	35.00
Columbia CS-9310	(S)	The Dynamic Tommy Collins	1966	20.00	50.00
Columbia CL-2778	(M)	Tommy Collins On Tour	1968	20.00	50.00
Columbia CS-9578	(S)	Tommy Collins On Tour	1968	14.00	35.00
Starday SLP-474	(M)	Callin'	196?	10.00	25.00

COLOURS

Dot DLP-25854	(S)	Colours	1968	6.00	15.00
Dot DLP-25935	(S)	Atmosphere	1969	6.00	15.00

COLWELL-WINFIELD BLUES BAND, THE

Forecast FVS-3056	(S)	Cold Wind Blues	1968	6.00	15.00
ZaZoo 1	(S)	Live Bust	1971	12.00	30.00

COMFORTABLE CHAIR, THE

Ode Z12-44005	(S)	The Comfortable Chair	1968	5.00	12.00

Label & Catalog #		Title	Year	VG+	NM
COMMON PEOPLE, THE					
Capitol ST-266	(S)	**Of The People, By The People**	1969	30.00	60.00
COMO, PERRY					
RCA Victor LPM-51 (10")	(M)	**Merry Christmas**	1951	12.00	30.00
RCA Victor LPM-3013 (10")	(M)	**TV Favorites**	1952	12.00	30.00
RCA Victor LPM-3035 (10")	(M)	**Sentimental Date**	1952	12.00	30.00
RCA Victor LPM-3044 (10")	(M)	**Supper Club Favorites**	1952	12.00	30.00
RCA Victor LPM-3124 (10")	(M)	**Hits From Broadway Shows**	1953	12.00	30.00
RCA Victor LPM-3133 (10")	(M)	**Around The Christmas Tree**	1953	12.00	30.00
RCA Victor LPM-3188 (10")	(M)	**I Believe**	1954	12.00	30.00
RCA Victor LPM-3224 (10")	(M)	**Como's Golden Records**	1954	12.00	30.00
RCA Victor LPM-1085	(M)	**So Smooth**	1955	10.00	25.00
RCA Victor LPM-1172	(M)	**I Believe**	1955	10.00	25.00
RCA Victor LPM-1176	(M)	**Relaxing With Perry Como**	1955	10.00	25.00
RCA Victor LPC-1177	(M)	**A Sentimental Date With Perry Como**	1955	10.00	25.00
RCA Victor LPM-1191	(M)	**Hits From Broadway Shows**	1956	10.00	25.00
RCA Victor LPM-1243	(M)	**Merry Christmas Music**	1956	10.00	25.00
RCA Victor LPM-1463	(M)	**We Get Letters**	1957	10.00	25.00
RCA Victor LOP-1004	(M)	**Saturday Night With Mr. C**	1958	10.00	25.00
RCA Victor LOP-1007	(M)	**Como's Golden Records**	1958	10.00	25.00
RCA Victor LPM-1885	(M)	**When You Come To The End Of The Day**	1959	6.00	15.00
RCA Victor LPM-2010	(M)	**Como Swings**	1959	6.00	15.00
RCA Victor LSP-2010	(S)	**Como Swings**	1959	8.00	20.00
RCA Victor LPM-2066	(M)	**Season's Greetings**	1959	6.00	15.00
RCA Victor LSP-2066	(S)	**Season's Greetings**	1959	8.00	20.00
RCA Victor LPM-2343	(M)	**For The Young At Heart**	1961	5.00	12.00
RCA Victor LSP-2343	(S)	**For The Young At Heart**	1961	6.00	15.00
RCA Victor LPM-2390	(M)	**Sing To Me, Mr. C**	1961	5.00	12.00
RCA Victor LSP-2390	(S)	**Sing To Me, Mr. C**	1961	6.00	15.00
RCA Victor LPM-2567	(M)	**By Request**	1962	5.00	12.00
RCA Victor LSP-2567	(S)	**By Request**	1962	6.00	15.00
RCA Victor LPM-2630	(M)	**Irving Berlin's Songs For "Mr. President"**	1962	5.00	12.00
RCA Victor LSP-2630	(S)	**Irving Berlin's Songs For "Mr. President"**	1962	6.00	15.00

*— Original RCA mono albums above have "Long Play" on the bottom of the label;
stereo albums have "Living Stereo" on the bottom.—*

COMPETITORS, THE					
The Competitors are a creation of Gary Usher & Co.					
Dot DLP-3542	(M)	**Hits Of The Street And Strip**	1963	75.00	150.00
Dot DLP-25542	(S)	**Hits Of The Street And Strip**	1963	100.00	200.00
COMSTOCK, BOBBY, & THE COUNTS					
Ascot ALM-13026	(M)	**Out Of Sight**	1966	8.00	20.00
Ascot ALS-16026	(S)	**Out Of Sight**	1966	10.00	25.00
CONDELLO					
Condello is Michael Condello.					
Scepter SP-542	(M)	**Phase 1**	1968	8.00	20.00
Scepter SPS-542	(S)	**Phase 1**	1968	10.00	25.00
CONLEY, ARTHUR					
Atco 33-215	(M)	**Sweet Soul Music**	1967	10.00	25.00
Atco SD-33-215	(S)	**Sweet Soul Music**	1967	12.00	30.00
Atco 33-220	(M)	**Shake, Rattle And Roll**	1967	8.00	20.00
Atco SD-33-220	(S)	**Shake, Rattle And Roll**	1967	10.00	25.00
Atco SD-33-243	(S)	**Soul Directions**	1968	8.00	20.00
Atco SD-33-276	(S)	**More Sweet Soul**	1969	8.00	20.00
CONNELLY, CHRIS					
Phillips PHM-200173	(M)	**The Boy From Peyton Place**	1965	6.00	15.00
Phillips PHS-600173	(S)	**The Boy From Peyton Place**	1965	8.00	20.00
CONNELLY, PEGGY					
Bethlehem BCP-53	(M)	**Peggy Connelly**	1956	16.00	40.00
CONNOR, CHRIS					
Bethlehem 1001 (10")	(M)	**Lullabys Of Birdland**	1954	35.00	70.00
Bethlehem 1002 (10")	(M)	**Lullabys For Lovers**	1954	35.00	70.00

Label & Catalog #		Title	Year	VG+	NM
Bethlehem BCP-20	(M)	**This Is Chris**	1955	20.00	50.00
Bethlehem BCP-56	(M)	**Chris**	1956	20.00	50.00
Bethlehem BCP-6004	(M)	**Lullabys Of Birdland**	1957	20.00	50.00
Bethlehem BCP-6005	(M)	**Lullabys For Lovers**	1957	20.00	50.00
Bethlehem BCP-6006	(M)	**Bethlehem Girls**	1957	20.00	50.00
— Original Bethlehem albums above have maroon labels.—					
Atlantic 1228	(M)	**Chris Connor**	1956	20.00	50.00
Atlantic 1240	(M)	**He Loves Me, He Loves Me Not**	1956	20.00	50.00
Atlantic 8014	(M)	**I Miss You So**	1956	20.00	50.00
Atlantic 1286	(M)	**A Jazz Date With Chris Connor**	1957	20.00	50.00
Atlantic 2-601	(M)	**The George Gershwin Almanac Of Songs**	1957	20.00	50.00
Atlantic 1290	(M)	**Chris Craft**	1958	20.00	50.00
— Original Atlantic albums above have black labels.—					
Atlantic 1307	(M)	**Ballads Of The Sad Cafe**	1959	10.00	25.00
Atlantic SD-1307	(S)	**Ballads Of The Sad Cafe**	1959	16.00	40.00
Atlantic 8032	(M)	**Witchcraft**	1959	10.00	25.00
Atlantic SD-8032	(S)	**Witchcraft**	1959	16.00	40.00
Atlantic 8040	(M)	**Chris In Person**	1959	10.00	25.00
Atlantic SD-8040	(S)	**Chris In Person**	1959	16.00	40.00
Atlantic 8046	(M)	**A Portrait Of Chris**	1960	10.00	25.00
Atlantic SD-8046	(S)	**A Portrait Of Chris**	1960	14.00	35.00
Atlantic 8049	(M)	**Double Exposure**	1961	10.00	25.00
Atlantic SD-8049	(S)	**Double Exposure**	1961	14.00	35.00
Atlantic 8061	(M)	**Free Spirits**	1962	8.00	20.00
Atlantic SD-8061	(S)	**Free Spirits**	1962	12.00	30.00
—Mono Atlantic albums above have orange and purple labels with a white fan;					
stereo albums have green and blue labels with a white fan.—					
Roulette R-52068	(M)	**Two's Company**	1960	10.00	25.00
Roulette SR-52068	(S)	**Two's Company**	1960	16.00	40.00
FM 300	(M)	**Chris Connor At The Village Gate**	1963	8.00	20.00
FM S-300	(S)	**Chris Connor At The Village Gate**	1963	12.00	30.00
FM 312	(M)	**A Weekend In Paris**	1964	8.00	20.00
FM S-312	(S)	**A Weekend In Paris**	1964	12.00	30.00
ABC-Paramount 529	(M)	**Gentle Bossa Nova**	1965	8.00	20.00
ABC-Paramount S-529	(S)	**Gentle Bossa Nova**	1965	10.00	25.00
ABC-Paramount 585	(M)	**Now**	1966	8.00	20.00
ABC-Paramount S-585	(S)	**Now**	1966	10.00	25.00
CONRIED, HANS					
RCA Victor LPM-1923	(M)	**Monster Rally**	1959	8.00	20.00
RCA Victor LSP-1923	(S)	**Monster Rally**	1959	12.00	30.00
CONTOURS, THE					
Gordy 901	(M)	**Do You Love Me**	1962	100.00	200.00
CONWAY, TIM					
Liberty LRP-3512	(M)	**Are We On?**	1967	5.00	12.00
Liberty LST-7512	(S)	**Are We On?**	1967	6.00	15.00
Liberty LST-7552	(S)	**Bull!**	1968	6.00	15.00
COODER, RY					
Refer to Capt. Beefheart / Ry Cooder; Longbranch Pennywhistle					
Reprise RS-6402	(S)	**Ry Cooder**	1970	6.00	15.00
Reprise MS-2117	(S)	**Boomer's Story**	1972	5.00	12.00
Reprise MS-2052	(S)	**Into The Purple Valley**	1972	5.00	12.00
Mobile Fidelity MFSL-085	(S)	**Jazz**	1984	16.00	40.00
COOKE, SAM					
Sam Cooke originally recorded with The Soul Stirrers.					
Keen A-2001	(M)	**Sam Cooke**	1958	20.00	50.00
Keen 2003	(M)	**Encore**	1958	16.00	40.00
Keen 2004	(M)	**Tribute To The Lady—Billie Holiday**	1959	16.00	40.00
Keen 86101	(M)	**Hit Kit**	1959	16.00	40.00
Keen 86103	(M)	**I Thank God**	1960	14.00	35.00
Keen 86106	(M)	**The Wonderful World Of Sam Cooke**	1960	14.00	35.00
RCA Victor LPM-2221	(M)	**Cooke's Tour**	1960	12.00	30.00
RCA Victor LSP-2221	(S)	**Cooke's Tour**	1960	16.00	40.00
RCA Victor LPM-2236	(M)	**Hits Of The 50's**	1960	12.00	30.00
RCA Victor LSP-2236	(S)	**Hits Of The 50's**	1960	16.00	40.00

Label & Catalog #		Title	Year	VG+	NM
RCA Victor LPM-2293	(M)	**Swing Low**	1960	12.00	30.00
RCA Victor LSP-2293	(S)	**Swing Low**	1960	16.00	40.00
RCA Victor LPM-2392	(M)	**My Kind Of Blues**	1961	12.00	30.00
RCA Victor LPM-2392	(S)	**My Kind Of Blues**	1961	16.00	40.00
RCA Victor LPM-2555	(M)	**Twistin' The Night Away**	1962	12.00	30.00
RCA Victor LSP-2555	(S)	**Twistin' The Night Away**	1962	16.00	40.00
RCA Victor LPM-2625	(M)	**The Best Of Sam Cooke**	1962	10.00	25.00
RCA Victor LSP-2625	(E)	**The Best Of Sam Cooke**	1962	8.00	20.00
RCA Victor AYL1-3863	(P)	**The Best Of Sam Cooke**	197?	6.00	15.00
RCA Victor LPM-2673	(M)	**Mr. Soul**	1963	8.00	20.00
RCA Victor LSP-2673	(S)	**Mr. Soul**	1963	12.00	30.00
RCA Victor LPM-2709	(M)	**Night Beat**	1963	8.00	20.00
RCA Victor LSP-2709	(S)	**Night Beat**	1963	12.00	30.00

— Original RCA mono albums above have "Long Play" on the bottom of the label;
stereo albums have "Living Stereo" on the bottom.—

RCA Victor LPM-2899	(M)	**Ain't That Good News**	1964	6.00	15.00
RCA Victor LSP-2899	(S)	**Ain't That Good News**	1964	8.00	20.00
RCA Victor LPM-2970	(M)	**Sam Cooke At The Copa**	1964	6.00	15.00
RCA Victor LSP-2970	(S)	**Sam Cooke At The Copa**	1964	8.00	20.00
RCA Victor LPM-3367	(M)	**Shake**	1965	6.00	15.00
RCA Victor LSP-3367	(S)	**Shake**	1965	8.00	20.00
RCA Victor LPM-3373	(M)	**The Best Of Sam Cooke, Volume 2**	1965	6.00	15.00
RCA Victor LSP-3373	(P)	**The Best Of Sam Cooke, Volume 2**	1965	8.00	20.00
RCA Victor LPM-3435	(M)	**Try A Little Love**	1965	6.00	15.00
RCA Victor LSP-3435	(S)	**Try A Little Love**	1965	8.00	20.00
RCA Victor LPM-3517	(M)	**The Unforgettable Sam Cooke**	1966	6.00	15.00
RCA Victor LSP-3517	(S)	**The Unforgettable Sam Cooke**	1966	8.00	20.00
RCA Victor LSP-3991	(S)	**The Man Who Invented Soul**	1968	6.00	15.00

— Original RCA albums above have black labels.—

COOL, CALVIN, & THE SURF KNOBS

Charter CLP-103	(M)	**The Surfer's Beat**	1963	12.00	30.00
Charter CLS-103	(S)	**The Surfer's Beat**	1963	16.00	40.00

COOLEY, SPADE

Columbia IIL-9007 (10")	(M)	**Sagebrush Swing**	1949	50.00	100.00
Decca DL-5563 (10")	(M)	**Dance-O-Rama #3**	1955	90.00	180.00
Raynote R-5007	(M)	**Fidoolin'**	1959	16.00	40.00
Raynote RS-5007	(S)	**Fidoolin'**	1959	20.00	50.00
Roulette R-25145	(M)	**Fidoolin'**	1961	8.00	20.00
Roulette SR-25145	(M)	**Fidoolin'**	1961	12.00	30.00

COOLIDGE, RITA

Nautilus NR-16	(S)	**Anytime... Anywhere**	198?	6.00	15.00

COOPER, ALICE

Originally the name of the group, Alice Cooper has become pseudonymous with leader Vince Furnier.

Straight STS-1051	(S)	**Pretties For You**	1969	20.00	50.00
Straight WS-1845	(S)	**Easy Action**	1970	20.00	50.00
		("Alice Cooper" is in black letters on the cover)			
Straight WS-1845	(S)	**Easy Action**	1970	12.00	30.00
		("Alice Cooper" is in white letters on the cover)			
Straight WS-1883	(S)	**Love It to Death**	1971	20.00	50.00
Warner Bros. WS-1883	(S)	**Love It to Death**	1971	12.00	30.00
		(Cooper is gripping his cape in such a manner			
		that his right thumb has a phallic appearance.)			
Warner Bros. WS-1883	(S)	**Love It to Death**	1971	8.00	20.00
		(The thumb remains and a white box that reads			
		"Including Their Hit I'm Eighteen" in the corner.)			
Warner Bros. WS-1883	(S)	**Love It to Death**	197?	8.00	20.00
		(The cover has a broad white border at the top and bottom.)			
Warner Bros. WS-1883	(S)	**Love It to Death**	197?	5.00	12.00
		(Restored cover with the offending phalange airbrushed off.)			
Warner Bros. BS-2567	(S)	**Killer** *(With calendar and poster)*	1971	12.00	30.00
Warner Bros. BS-2623	(S)	**School's Out** *(With panties)*	1972	12.00	30.00
Warner Bros. BS4-2685	(Q)	**Billion Dollar Babies**	1974	8.00	20.00
Warner Bros. BS4-2748	(Q)	**Muscle Of Love**	1973	8.00	20.00
Mobile Fidelity MFSL-063	(S)	**Welcome To My Nightmare**	1980	12.00	30.00

Label & Catalog #		Title	Year	VG+	NM
COOPER, JACKIE					
Dot DLP-3146	(M)	**The Movies Swing!**	1958	12.00	30.00
Signature SM-1049	(M)	**Hennesey** (Soundtrack)	195?	35.00	70.00
COOPER, LES, & THE SOUL ROCKERS					
Everlast ELP-202	(M)	**Wiggle Wobble**	1963	16.00	40.00
COPAS, COWBOY					
King 553	(M)	**His All-Time Hits**	1957	30.00	60.00
King 556	(M)	**Favorite Scared Songs**	1957	20.00	50.00
King 619	(M)	**Sacred Songs**	1969	20.00	50.00
King 714	(M)	**Tragic Tales Of Love And Life**	1960	20.00	50.00
King 720	(M)	**Broken Hearted Melodies**	1960	20.00	50.00
King 817	(M)	**Country Gentleman Of Song**	1963	16.00	40.00
King 824	(M)	**As You Remember Cowboy Copas**	1963	16.00	40.00
Starday SLP-118	(M)	**All Time Country Music Great**	1960	16.00	40.00
Starday SLP-133	(M)	**Inspirational Songs**	1961	14.00	35.00
Starday SLP-144	(M)	**Cowboy Copas**	1961	14.00	35.00
Starday SLP-175	(M)	**Mr. Country Music**	1962	14.00	35.00
Starday SLP-184	(M)	**Songs That Made Him Famous**	1962	14.00	35.00
Starday SLP-208	(M)	**Country Music Entertainer #1**	1963	14.00	35.00
Starday SLP-212	(M)	**Beyond The Sunset**	1963	14.00	35.00
Starday SLP-234	(M)	**The Unforgettable Cowboy Copas**	1963	14.00	35.00
Starday SLP-247	(M)	**Star Of The Grand Ole Opry**	1963	12.00	30.00
Starday SLP-268	(M)	**Cowboy Copas And His Friends**	1964	12.00	30.00
Starday SLP-347	(M)	**The Cowboy Copas Story**	1965	12.00	30.00
COPAS, COWBOY / HAWKSHAW HAWKINS					
King 835	(M)	**In Memory**	1963	12.00	30.00
King 850	(M)	**Legend Of Cowboy Copas And Hawksahw Hawkins**	1964	12.00	30.00
CORBIN, HAROLD					
Roulette R-25079	(M)	**Soul Brother**	1961	8.00	20.00
Roulette SR-25079	(S)	**Soul Brother**	1961	10.00	25.00
CORNELLS, THE					
Garex LPGA-100	(M)	**Beach Bound**	1963	180.00	300.00
CORPORATION, THE					
Age of Aquarius 4150	(S)	**Get On Our Swing**	1969	10.00	25.00
Age of Aquarius 4250	(S)	**Hassels In My Mind**	1969	10.00	25.00
Capitol ST-175	(S)	**The Corporation**	1969	16.00	40.00
CORPUS					
Acorn 1001	(S)	**Creation A Child**	1972	210.00	350.00
CORTEZ, DAVE "BABY"					
RCA Victor LPM-2099	(M)	**Dave "Baby" Cortez And His Happy Organ**	1959	14.00	35.00
RCA Victor LSP-2099	(P)	**Dave "Baby" Cortez And His Happy Organ**	1959	20.00	50.00
Clock C-331	(M)	**Dave "Baby" Cortez**	1960	12.00	30.00
Chess LP-1473	(M)	**Rinky Dink**	1962	10.00	25.00
Roulette R-25298	(M)	**Organ Shindig**	1965	5.00	12.00
Roulette SR-25298	(S)	**Organ Shindig**	1965	6.00	15.00
Roulette R-25315	(M)	**Tweety Pie**	1966	5.00	12.00
Roulette SR-25315	(S)	**Tweety Pie**	1966	6.00	15.00
Roulette R-25328	(M)	**In Orbit With Dave "Baby" Cortez**	1966	5.00	12.00
Roulette SR-25328	(S)	**In Orbit With Dave "Baby" Cortez**	1966	6.00	15.00
Metro M-550	(M)	**The Fabulous Organ Of Dave "Baby" Cortez**	1965	5.00	12.00
Metro MS-550	(S)	**The Fabulous Organ Of Dave "Baby" Cortez**	1965	6.00	15.00
COSTELLO, ELVIS (& THE ATTRACTIONS)					
Columbia JC-35037	(S)	**My Aim Is True** (Yellow back cover)	1977	6.00	15.00
Columbia JC-35331	(S)	**This Year's Model** ("Costello" label) (Red label with "Costello" around the perimeter.)	1978	8.00	20.00
CBS CDN-10	(DJ)	**Live At The El Mocambo** (Canadian) (Counterfeits have excessive tape hiss.)	1978	150.00	250.00
Columbia (No number)	(DJ)	**My Aim Is True** (Picture disc)	1979	50.00	100.00

While other artists have amassed more critical and popular acclaim in the past two decades, it is Elvis Costello, that has written and recorded the most impressive body of contemporary rock'n roll. Released in Canada, *Live At The El Mocambo* (only 500 promo copies were supposedly pressed) reached many American stations and was eventually heavily counterfeited and sold on the U.S. collector's market. These fakes were "mastered" off of a copy of the album and have a hissy background; the sound on the original is clean and clear throughout. After several albums that failed to set rock's pundits on fire, 1982's *Imperial Bedroom* was greeted by many as album of the year...

Label & Catalog #		Title	Year	VG+	NM
Columbia JC-35709	(S)	**Armed Forces**	1979	6.00	15.00
		(Issued with a 7" EP, "Live At Hollywood High.")			
Costello AS-847	(DJ)	**Taking Liberties** *(Radio sampler)*	1980	16.00	40.00
Columbia AS-958	(DJ)	**The Tom Snyder Interview**	1981	12.00	30.00
Columbia AS-1318	(DJ)	**Almost Blue** *(Radio sampler)*	1981	16.00	40.00
Columbia HC-48157	(S)	**Imperial Bedroom** *(Half-speed master)*	1982	12.00	30.00

COSTELLO, ELVIS / NICK LOWE / MINK DeVILLE

Label & Catalog #		Title	Year	VG+	NM
Columbia/Capitol AS-443	(DJ)	**Radio Radio** *(Orange vinyl)*	1979	10.00	25.00

COTTON, JAMES [THE JAMES COTTON BLUES BAND]

Label & Catalog #		Title	Year	VG+	NM
Folkways FT-3023	(M)	**The James Cotton Blues Band**	1967	5.00	12.00
Folkways FTS-3023	(S)	**The James Cotton Blues Band**	1967	6.00	15.00
Folkways FTS-3038	(S)	**Pure Cotton**	1968	6.00	15.00
Vanguard VSD-79283	(S)	**Cut You Loose**	1968	6.00	15.00
Forecast FTS-3060	(S)	**Cotton In Your Ears**	1969	6.00	15.00
Capitol ST-814	(S)	**Taking Care Of Business**	1971	4.00	10.00

COUGAR, JOHN: Refer to JOHN COUGAR MELLANCAMP

COUNT FIVE, THE

Label & Catalog #		Title	Year	VG+	NM
Double Shot DSM-1001	(M)	**Psychotic Reaction**	1966	12.00	30.00
Double Shot DSS-5001	(E)	**Psychotic Reaction**	1966	8.00	20.00
		(Reproductions of DSS-5001 exist.)			

COUNTRY ALL-STARS, THE
The All-Stars feature Chet Atkins, Jerry Byrd and Henry "Homer" Haynes.

Label & Catalog #		Title	Year	VG+	NM
RCA Victor LPM-3167 (10")	(M)	**String Dustin'**	1953	60.00	120.00

COUNTRY GENTLEMEN, THE

Label & Catalog #		Title	Year	VG+	NM
Folkways FA-2409	(M)	**The Country Gentlemen**	195?	10.00	25.00
Starday SLP-109	(M)	**Traveling Dobro Blues**	1959	16.00	40.00
Cimarron 2001	(M)	**Songs Of The Pioneers**	1962	12.00	30.00

COUNTRY JOE & THE FISH
Country Joe MacDonald with Fish Barry Melton, Chicken Hirsch, Bruce Barthol and David Cohen.

Label & Catalog #		Title	Year	VG+	NM
Vanguard VRS-9244	(M)	**Electric Music For The Mind And Body**	1967	8.00	20.00
Vanguard VSD-79244	(S)	**Electric Music For The Mind And Body**	1967	6.00	15.00
Vanguard VRS-9266	(M)	**I-Feel-Like-I'm-Fixin'-To-Die**	1967	8.00	20.00
Vanguard VSD-79266	(S)	**I-Feel-Like-I'm-Fixin'-To-Die**	1967	6.00	15.00
		(Originally issued with a fold-open, "Fish game" poster, priced separately below.)			
Vanguard		**I-Feel-Like-I'm-Fixin'-To-Die Poster**	1967	6.00	15.00
Vanguard VSD-79277	(S)	**Together**	1968	5.00	12.00
Vanguard VSD-6545	(S)	**Country Joe & The Fish's Greatest Hits**	1969	5.00	12.00
Vanguard VSD-79299	(S)	**Here We Are Again**	1969	5.00	12.00
Vanguard VSD-6555	(S)	**C.J. Fish**	1970	4.00	10.00

COUSINS, THE

Label & Catalog #		Title	Year	VG+	NM
Parkway P-7005	(M)	**Music Of The Strip**	1961	6.00	15.00
Parkway SP-7005	(S)	**Music Of The Strip**	1961	8.00	20.00

COVAY, DON

Label & Catalog #		Title	Year	VG+	NM
Atlantic 8104	(M)	**Mercy**	1965	16.00	40.00
Atlantic SD-8104	(S)	**Mercy**	1965	20.00	50.00
Atlantic 8120	(M)	**See Saw**	1966	16.00	40.00
Atlantic SD-8120	(S)	**See Saw**	1966	20.00	50.00
Atlantic SD-8237	(S)	**The House Of Blue Lights**	1969	10.00	25.00

COWSILL, BILL

Label & Catalog #		Title	Year	VG+	NM
MGM SE-4706	(S)	**Nervous Breakthrough**	1971	6.00	15.00

COWSILLS, THE

Label & Catalog #		Title	Year	VG+	NM
MGM E-4498	(M)	**The Cowsills**	1967	5.00	12.00
MGM SE-4498	(S)	**The Cowsills**	1967	6.00	15.00
MGM SE-4534	(S)	**We Can Fly**	1968	4.00	10.00
MGM SE-4554	(S)	**Captain Sad And His Ship Of Fools**	1968	5.00	12.00
MGM SE-4597	(S)	**The Best Of The Cowsills**	1969	5.00	12.00
MGM SE-4619	(S)	**The Cowsills In Concert**	1969	5.00	12.00

Label & Catalog #		Title	Year	VG+	NM
MGM SE-4639	(S)	II By II	1970	6.00	15.00
London 587	(S)	On My Side	1971	8.00	20.00

COWSILLS, THE / THE LINCOLN PARK ZOO

Wing SRW-16354	(S)	The Cowsills Plus The Lincoln Park Zoo	1968	4.00	10.00

COX, DANNY
Produced by Gary Usher.

Together ZR-1011	(S)	Birth Announcement (2 LPs)	1970	12.00	30.00

COXAN'S ARMY
Coxan's Army features Pat Benatar.

Label unknown	(S)	Coxan's Army	1972	180.00	300.00

CRADDOCK, BILLY "CRASH"

King 912	(M)	I'm Tore Up	1964	20.00	50.00

CRAIN, JIMMY

Ray-O LP-2005	(M)	Miles To Go	196?	50.00	100.00

CRANE, BOB

Epic LN-246224	(M)	The Funny Side Of TV	1967	6.00	15.00
Epic BN-26224	(S)	The Funny Side Of TV	1967	8.00	20.00

CRAWFORD, DON

Folkways FV-3002	(M)	Don Crawford	1966	5.00	12.00
Folkways FVS-3002	(S)	Don Crawford	1966	6.00	15.00

CRAWFORD, JIMMY

Cumberland MGC-29531	(M)	We're Moving On	195?	10.00	25.00

CRAWFORD, JOAN

Universal Int. DCLA-1086	(DJ)	Personal Interview With Joan Crawford	195?	50.00	100.00
		(One sided promo for "Female On The Beach" on red vinyl.)			

CRAWFORD, JOHNNY

Del-Fi DFLP-1220	(M)	The Captivating Johnny Crawford	1962	16.00	40.00
Del-Fi DFLP-1223	(M)	A Young Man's Fancy	1963	12.00	30.00
Del-Fi DFST-1223	(S)	A Young Man's Fancy	1963	16.00	40.00
Del-Fi DFLP-1224	(M)	Rumors	1963	12.00	30.00
Del-Fi DFST-1224	(S)	Rumors	1963	16.00	40.00
Del-Fi DFLP-1229	(M)	His Greatest Hits	1963	12.00	30.00
Del-Fi DFST-1229	(S)	His Greatest Hits	1963	16.00	40.00
Del-Fi DFLP-1248	(M)	Greatest Hits, Volume 2	1964	8.00	20.00
Del-Fi DFST-1248	(S)	Greatest Hits, Volume 2	1964	12.00	30.00
Supreme S-210	(S)	Songs From "The Restless Ones"	196?	12.00	30.00

CRAYTON, PEE WEE

Crown CLP-5175	(M)	Pee Wee Crayton	1959	20.00	50.00
Vanguard VSD-6566	(S)	The Things I Used To Do	1971	6.00	15.00

CRAZY ELEPHANT

Bell 6034	(S)	Crazy Elephant	1969	6.00	15.00

CRAZY HORSE
Original members include Danny Whitten, Billy Talbot and Ralph Molina, who originally recorded as The Rockets. The first album includes Nils Lofgren and Jack Nitzsche. Refer to Neil Young.

Reprise RS-6438	(S)	Crazy Horse	1971	6.00	15.00

CREAM
Cream was Ginger Baker, Jack Bruce, and Eric Clapton with Felix Pappalardi.

Atco 33-206	(M)	Fresh Cream	1967	14.00	35.00
Atco SD-33-206	(S)	Fresh Cream	1967	10.00	25.00
Atco 33-232	(M)	Disraeli Gears	1967	20.00	50.00
Atco SD-33-232	(S)	Disraeli Gears	1967	6.00	15.00
Atco SD-33-245	(S)	The Savage Seven (Soundtrack)	1968	6.00	15.00
Atco PR-119/20	(DJ)	Wheels Of Fire (Radio sampler)	1968	35.00	70.00
Atco SD-2-700	(S)	Wheels Of Fire (2 LPs)	1968	10.00	25.00
		— Original Atco stereo albums above have purple & brown labels.—			

Label & Catalog #		Title	Year	VG+	NM
Atco SD-7001	(S)	**Goodbye** *(Yellow label)*	1969	6.00	15.00
Atco SD-33-328	(S)	**Live Cream** *(Yellow label)*	1970	5.00	12.00
Atco SD-7005	(S)	**Live Cream (Volume 2)** *(Yellow label)*	1972	5.00	12.00
Mobile Fidelity MFSL-066	(S)	**Wheels Of Fire** *(2 LPs)*	1980	16.00	40.00

CREAM / THE VANILLA FUDGE

Atco TL-ST-141	(DJ)	**Goodbye / Rock'n Roll**	1969	20.00	50.00
		(Radio sampler with one side by each artist.)			

CREATION OF SUNLIGHT

Windi 1001	(S)	**Creation Of Sunlight**	196?	240.00	400.00

CREATURES, THE

RCA Victor LPM-1923	(M)	**Monster Rally**	1959	12.00	30.00
RCA Victor LSP-1923	(S)	**Monster Rally**	1959	16.00	40.00

CREEDENCE CLEARWATER REVIVAL

CCR was John Fogerty, Tom Fogerty, Stu Cook and Doug Clifford, who originally recorded as The Golliwogs.

Fantasy F-8382	(S)	**Creedence Clearwater Revival**	1968	8.00	20.00
		(Without the blurb for "Suzie Q" on the cover.)			
Fantasy F-8382	(S)	**Creedence Clearwater Revival**	1968	6.00	15.00
		(With a blurb for "Suzie Q" on the cover.)			
Fantasy F-8387	(P)	**Bayou Country**	1969	6.00	15.00
Fantasy F-8393	(S)	**Green River**	1969	6.00	15.00
Fantasy F-8397	(S)	**Willy And The Poor Boys**	1969	6.00	15.00
Fantasy F-8402	(S)	**Cosmo's Factory**	1970	5.00	12.00
Fantasy F-8410	(S)	**Pendulum**	1970	5.00	12.00
Fantasy F-9404	(S)	**Mardi Gras**	1972	5.00	12.00
		— Original copies of Fantasy albums above have blue labels.—			
Liberty	(S)	**Green River**	197?	35.00	70.00
		(Creedence albums on Liberty— other titles may exist— were manufactured for either record club or foreign distribution.)			
Mobile Fidelity MFSL-037	(S)	**Cosmo's Factory**	1979	16.00	40.00
Sweet Thunder	(S)	**Green River**	198?	12.00	30.00

CREME SODA

Trinity CST-11	(S)	**Tricky Zingers** *(Group photo cover)*	1975	40.00	80.00
Trinity CST-11	(S)	**Tricky Zingers** *(Plain white cover)*	1976	16.00	40.00

CRESCENDOS, THE

Guest Star G-1453	(M)	**Oh Julie**	196?	16.00	40.00

CRESTS, THE

The Crests feature Johnny Maestro. Refer to The Brooklyn Bridge.

Coed LPC-901	(M)	**The Crests Sing All The Biggies**	1960	180.00	300.00
Coed LPC-904	(M)	**The Best Of The Crests**	1961	150.00	250.00
Coed LPS-904	(S)	**The Best Of The Crests**	1961	*See note below*	
		(While a stereo cover of Coed 904 has been found, it contained a mono album. Thus, no stereo records are known to exist.)			
Post 3000	(E)	**The Crests Sing**		12.00	30.00

CREW CUTS, THE

Mercury MG-25200 (10")	(M)	**The Crew Cuts Go Longhair**	1956	30.00	60.00
Mercury MG-20140	(M)	**The Crew Cuts On The Campus**	1957	20.00	50.00
Mercury MG-20140	(M)	**The Crew Cuts On The Campus**	1957	20.00	50.00
Mercury MG-20143	(M)	**Crew Cut Capers**	1957	20.00	50.00
Mercury MG-20144	(M)	**Rock And Roll Bash**	1957	30.00	60.00
Mercury MG-20199	(M)	**Music Ala Carte**	1957	20.00	50.00
RCA Victor LPM-1933	(M)	**Surprise Package**	1958	10.00	25.00
RCA Victor LSP-1933	(S)	**Surprise Package**	1958	16.00	40.00
RCA Victor LPM-2037	(M)	**The Crew Cuts Sing**	1959	10.00	25.00
RCA Victor LSP-2037	(S)	**The Crew Cuts Sing**	1959	16.00	40.00
RCA Victor LPM-2067	(M)	**You Must Have Been A Beautiful Baby**	1960	10.00	25.00
RCA Victor LSP-2067	(S)	**You Must Have Been A Beautiful Baby**	1960	16.00	40.00
Wing MGW-12177	(M)	**The Crew Cuts**	1962	8.00	20.00
Wing MGW-12180	(M)	**High School Favorites**	1962	8.00	20.00
Camay CA-1002	(M)	**The Crew Cuts Sing Folk**	196?	8.00	20.00
Camay CA-3002	(S)	**The Crew Cuts Sing Folk**	196?	10.00	25.00

Label & Catalog #		Title	Year	VG+	NM

CREWE, BOB [BOB CREWE GENERATION]

Warwick W-2009	(M)	**Kicks**	1966	5.00	12.00
Warwick WST-2009	(S)	**Kicks**	1966	6.00	15.00
Warwick W-2034	(M)	**Crazy In The Heart**	1967	5.00	12.00
Warwick WST-2034	(M)	**Crazy In The Heart**	1967	6.00	15.00

CRICKETS, THE

The Crickets featured Buddy Holly; refer to Holly for more listings. Original members were Jerry Allison, Don Guess and Sonny Curtis; later members included Tommy Allsup, Glen Hardin, and Niki Sullivan. Refer to Bobby Vee; The Ventures.

Coral CRL-57320	(DJ)	**In Style With The Crickets** (Blue label)	1960	180.00	300.00
Coral CRL-57320	(M)	**In Style With The Crickets**	1960	75.00	150.00
Liberty LRP-3272	(M)	**Something Old, Something New**	1962	30.00	60.00
Liberty LST-7272	(S)	**Something Old, Something New**	1962	35.00	70.00
Liberty LRP-7351	(M)	**California Sun**	1964	16.00	40.00
Liberty LST-7351	(S)	**California Sun**	1964	20.00	50.00
Barnaby Z-30268	(S)	**Rockin' 50's Rock 'N' Roll**	1970	8.00	20.00
Vertigo VEL-1020	(S)	**Remnants**	1973	8.00	20.00

CRISS, PETER

Criss is a member of Kiss.

Casablanca NBLP-7240	(S)	**Out Of Control**	1980	4.00	10.00

CRITTERS, THE

Kapp KL-1485	(M)	**Younger Girl**	1966	8.00	20.00
Kapp KS-3485	(S)	**Younger Girl**	1966	10.00	25.00
Project-3 PR-4001	(S)	**Touch'n Go With The Critters**	1968	5.00	12.00
Project-3 PR-4002	(S)	**The Critters**	1968	5.00	12.00

CROCE, JIM

Croce (No number)	(S)	**Faucets**	1966	180.00	300.00
Capitol ST-315	(S)	**Croce**	1969	8.00	20.00
Command QD-40006	(Q)	**You Don't Mess Around With Jim**	1974	6.00	15.00
Command QD-40007	(Q)	**Life And Times**	1974	6.00	15.00
Command QD-40008	(Q)	**I Got A Name**	1974	6.00	15.00
Command QD-40020	(Q)	**Photographs And Memories**	1974	6.00	15.00
Mobile Fidelity MFSL-079	(S)	**You Don't Mess Around With Jim**	1980	12.00	30.00

CROME SYRCUS, THE

Command 925	(S)	**Love Cycle**	1968	8.00	20.00

CROSBY, BING

Due to Der Bingle's prolific career, his albums are listed chronologically by label with no interruptions. Refer to The Reprise Repertory Theatre.

Decca DL-5000 (10")	(M)	**Hits From Musical Comedies**	1949	20.00	50.00
Decca DL-5001 (10")	(M)	**Jerome Kern Songs**	1949	20.00	50.00
Decca DL-5010 (10")	(M)	**Stephen Foster Songs**	1949	20.00	50.00
Decca DL-5011 (10")	(M)	**El Bingo**	1949	14.00	35.00
Decca DL-5020 (10")	(M)	**Christmas Greetings**	1949	14.00	35.00
Decca DL-5028 (10")	(M)	**Auld Lang Syne**	1950	14.00	35.00
Decca DL-5037 (10")	(M)	**St. Patrick's Day**	1950	14.00	35.00
Decca DL-5039 (10")	(M)	**St. Valentine's Day**	1950	14.00	35.00
Decca DL-5042 (10")	(M)	**Blue Skies**	1950	14.00	35.00
Decca DL-5052 (10")	(M)	**Going My Way**	1950	14.00	35.00
Decca DL-5052 (10")	(M)	**The Bells Of St. Mary's** (Soundtrack)	1950	50.00	100.00
Decca DL-5060 (10")	(M)	**Showboat Selections** (Soundtrack)	1950	35.00	70.00
Decca DL-5063 (10")	(M)	**Don't Fence Me In**	1950	14.00	35.00
Decca DL-5064 (10")	(M)	**Cole Porter Songs**	1950	14.00	35.00
Decca DL-5081 (10")	(M)	**Songs By Gershwin**	1950	14.00	35.00
Decca DL-5092 (10")	(M)	**Holiday Inn** (Soundtrack)	1950	35.00	70.00
Decca DL-5102 (10")	(M)	**Blue Of The Night**	1950	14.00	35.00
Decca DL-5105 (10")	(M)	**Blue Of The Night**	1950	14.00	35.00
Decca DL-5107 (10")	(M)	**Cowboy Songs**	1950	14.00	35.00
Decca DL-5119 (10")	(M)	**Drifting And Dreaming**	1950	14.00	35.00
Decca DL-5122 (10")	(M)	**Hawaiian Songs**	1950	14.00	35.00
Decca DL-5126 (10")	(M)	**Stardust**	1950	14.00	35.00
Decca DL-5129 (10")	(M)	**Cowboy Songs, Volume 2**	1950	14.00	35.00
Decca DL-5207 (10")	(M)	**South Pacific**	1950	14.00	35.00
Decca DL-5220 (10")	(M)	**Bing Sings Hits**	1950	14.00	35.00

Label & Catalog #		Title	Year	VG+	NM
Decca DL-5272 (10")	(M)	Top O' The Morning	1950	14.00	35.00
Decca DL-5284 (10")	(M)	Mr. Music	1950	14.00	35.00
Decca DL-5298 (10")	(M)	Hits From Broadway Shows	1951	14.00	35.00
Decca DL-5299 (10")	(M)	Favorite Hawaiian Songs	1951	14.00	35.00
Decca DL-5302 (10")	(M)	Go West, Young Man	1951	14.00	35.00
Decca DL-5310 (10")	(M)	Way Back Home	1951	14.00	35.00
Decca DL-5316 (10")	(M)	Bing Crosby	1951	14.00	35.00
Decca DL-5323 (10")	(M)	Bing And The Dixieland Bands	1951	14.00	35.00
Decca DL-5326 (10")	(M)	Yours Is My Heart Alone	1951	14.00	35.00
Decca DL-5331 (10")	(M)	Country Style	1951	14.00	35.00
Decca DL-5340 (10")	(M)	Down Memory Lane	1951	14.00	35.00
Decca DL-5343 (10")	(M)	Down Memory Lane, Volume 2	1951	14.00	35.00
Decca DL-5351 (10")	(M)	Beloved Hymns	1951	14.00	35.00
Decca DL-5355 (10")	(M)	Bing Sings Victor Herbert	1951	14.00	35.00
Decca DL-5403 (10")	(M)	When Irish Eyes Are Smiling	1952	14.00	35.00
Decca DL-5417 (10")	(M)	Just For You	1952	14.00	35.00
Decca DL-5444 (10")	(M)	The Road To Bali (Soundtrack)	1952	35.00	70.00
Decca DL-5499 (10")	(M)	Song Hits Of Paris/Le Bing	1953	14.00	35.00
Decca DL-5508 (10")	(M)	Some Fine Old Chestnuts	1954	14.00	35.00
Decca DL-5520 (10")	(M)	Bing Sings The Hits	1954	14.00	35.00
Decca DL-5556 (10")	(M)	Country Girl	1953	14.00	35.00
Decca DL-6000 (10")	(M)	The Small One / The Happy Prince (Sdtk)	1950	35.00	70.00
Decca DL-6001 (10")	(M)	Ichabod Crane	1951	14.00	35.00
Decca DL-6008 (10")	(M)	Collector's Classics	1951	14.00	35.00
Decca DL-6009 (10")	(M)	Two For Tonight	1951	14.00	35.00
Decca DL-6010 (10")	(M)	Rhythm On The Range (Soundtrack)	1951	50.00	100.00
Decca DL-6011 (10")	(M)	Waikiki Wedding (Soundtrack)	1951	35.00	70.00
Decca DL-6012 (10")	(M)	Collector's Classics	1951	14.00	35.00
Decca DL-6013 (10")	(M)	The Star Maker (Soundtrack)	1951	35.00	70.00
Decca DL-6014 (10")	(M)	Collector's Classics	1951	14.00	35.00
Decca DL-6015 (10")	(M)	The Road To Singapore (Soundtrack)	1951	35.00	70.00

— Decca 6008-6015 are a series of "Collector's Classics" from Bing's '30s recordings; soundtrack titles are listed where known.—

Decca DX-151	(M)	A Musical Autobiography (5 LP box)	1954	75.00	150.00

(The five abums were released separately as Decca 8702-8706.)

Decca DX-152	(M)	Old Masters (3 LPs)	1954	75.00	150.00
Decca DL-8020	(M)	A Man Without A Country	1954	10.00	25.00
Decca DL-8083	(M)	White Christmas (Soundtrack)	1954	20.00	50.00
Decca DL-8110	(M)	Lullabye Time	1955	10.00	25.00
Decca DL-8128	(M)	Merry Christmas	1955	10.00	25.00
Decca DL-8207	(M)	Shillelaghs And Shamrocks	1956	10.00	25.00
Decca DL-8210	(M)	Home On The Range	1956	10.00	25.00
Decca DL-8262	(M)	When Irish Eyes Are Smiling	1956	10.00	25.00
Decca DL-8268	(M)	Drifting And Dreaming	1956	10.00	25.00
Decca DL-8269	(M)	Blue Hawaii	1956	10.00	25.00
Decca DL-8272	(M)	High Tor (Soundtrack)	1956	240.00	400.00
Decca DL-8318	(M)	Anything Goes (Soundtrack)	1956	10.00	25.00
Decca DL-8352	(M)	Songs I Wish I Had Sung	1956	10.00	25.00
Decca DL-8365	(M)	Twilight On The Trail	1956	10.00	25.00
Decca DL-8374	(M)	Some Fine Old Chestnuts	1957	10.00	25.00
Decca DL-8419	(M)	A Christmas Sing Around The World	1957	10.00	25.00
Decca DL-8493	(M)	Bing And The Dixieland Bands	1957	10.00	25.00
Decca DL-8575	(M)	New Tricks	1957	10.00	25.00
Decca DL-8687	(M)	Around The World	1958	10.00	25.00
Decca DL-8702	(M)	A Musical Autobiography 1927-1934	1958	10.00	25.00
Decca DL-8703	(M)	A Musical Autobiography 1934-1941	1958	10.00	25.00
Decca DL-8704	(M)	A Musical Autobiography 1941-1944	1958	10.00	25.00
Decca DL-8705	(M)	A Musical Autobiography 1944-1947	1958	10.00	25.00
Decca DL-8706	(M)	A Musical Autobiography 1947-1953	1958	10.00	25.00
Decca DL-8780	(M)	Bing In Paris	1958	10.00	25.00
Decca DL-8781	(M)	That Christmas Feeling	1958	10.00	25.00

—Original Decca albums above have black labels with silver print.—

Decca DL-8846	(M)	In A Little Spanish Town	1959	10.00	25.00
Decca DL-9106	(M)	Ichabod	1959	10.00	25.00
Decca DL-4086	(M)	My Golden Favorites	1961	8.00	20.00
Decca DL-4250	(M)	Easy To Remember	1962	8.00	20.00
Decca DL-4251	(M)	Pennies From Heaven	1962	8.00	20.00
Decca DL-4252	(M)	Pocketful Of Dreams	1962	8.00	20.00
Decca DL-4253	(M)	East Side Of Heaven	1962	8.00	20.00

Label & Catalog #		Title	Year	VG+	NM
Decca DL-4254	(M)	The Road Begins	1962	8.00	20.00
Decca DL-4255	(M)	Only Forever	1962	8.00	20.00
Decca DL-4256	(M)	Holiday Inn	1962	8.00	20.00
Decca DL-4257	(M)	Swinging On A Star	1962	8.00	20.00
Decca DL-4258	(M)	Accentuate The Positive	1962	8.00	20.00
Decca DL-4259	(M)	Blue Skies	1962	8.00	20.00
Decca DL-4260	(M)	But Beautiful	1962	8.00	20.00
Decca DL-4261	(M)	Sunshine Cake	1962	8.00	20.00
Decca DL-4262	(M)	Cool Of The Evening	1962	8.00	20.00
Decca DL-4263	(M)	Zing A Little Zong	1962	8.00	20.00
Decca DL-4264	(M)	Anything Goes	1962	8.00	20.00
— Decca 4250-4264 above are known as "Bing's Hollywood Series" and collect a variety of his earlier soundtrack recordings onto LP.—					
Decca DL-4281	(M)	Holiday In Europe	1962	6.00	15.00
Decca DL-74281	(S)	Holiday In Europe	1962	8.00	20.00
Decca DL-4283	(M)	The Small One	1962	6.00	15.00
Decca DL-74283	(S)	The Small One	1962	8.00	20.00
Decca DL-4415	(M)	Songs Everybody Knows	1964	6.00	15.00
Decca DL-74415	(S)	Songs Everybody Knows	1964	8.00	20.00
Decca DX-184	(M)	The Best Of Bing Crosby	1965	6.00	15.00
Decca DXS-184	(S)	The Best Of Bing Crosby	1965	6.00	15.00
— Original Decca albums above have black labels with "Mfrd By Decca" beneath the rainbow.—					
Columbia CL-6027 (10")	(M)	Crosby Classics, Volume 1	1949	20.00	50.00
Columbia CL-6105 (10")	(M)	Crosby Classics, Volume 2	1950	20.00	50.00
Columbia CL-2502 (10")	(M)	Der Bingle	1955	16.00	40.00
Brunswick BL-58000 (10")	(M)	Bing Crosby, Volume 1	1950	20.00	50.00
Brunswick BL-58001(10")	(M)	Bing Crosby, Volume 2	1950	20.00	50.00
Brunswick BL-54005	(M)	The Voice Of Bing In The 30s	1955	10.00	25.00
"X" XLVA-4250	(M)	Young Bing Crosby	1955	20.00	50.00
Verve V-2020	(M)	Bing Sings Whilst Bregman Swings	1956	10.00	25.00
Capitol W-750	(M)	High Society (Soundtrack)	1956	16.00	40.00
United Arts. UAL-4001	(M)	Paris Holiday (Soundtrack)	1958	14.00	35.00
Grand Award 298:20	(M)	Ali Baba And The Forty Thieves	1957	8.00	20.00
Grand Award 298:21	(M)	Christmas Story	1957	8.00	20.00
RCA Victor LPM-1473	(M)	Bing With A Beat	1957	10.00	25.00
RCA Victor LPM-1854	(M)	Fancy Meeting You Here	1958	8.00	20.00
RCA Victor LSP-1854	(S)	Fancy Meeting You Here	1958	12.00	30.00
RCA Victor LPM-2071	(M)	Young Bing Crosby	1959	10.00	25.00
RCA Victor LPM-2314	(M)	High Time (Soundtrack)	1960	16.00	40.00
RCA Victor LSP-2314	(S)	High Time (Soundtrack)	1960	30.00	60.00
Warner Bros. W-1363	(M)	Join With Bing And Sing Along	1960	6.00	15.00
Warner Bros. WS-1363	(S)	Join With Bing And Sing Along	1960	8.00	20.00
Warner Bros. 2W-1401	(M)	101 Gang Songs	1961	6.00	15.00
Warner Bros. 2WS-1401	(S)	101 Gang Songs	1961	8.00	20.00
Warner Bros. W-1422	(M)	Join Bing In A Gang Sing Along	1961	6.00	15.00
Warner Bros. WS-1422	(S)	Join Bing In A Gang Sing Along	1961	8.00	20.00
Warner Bros. W-1435	(M)	Join Bing And Sing Along	1962	6.00	15.00
Warner Bros. WS-1435	(S)	Join Bing And Sing Along	1962	8.00	20.00
Warner Bros. W-1482	(M)	On The Happy Side	1962	6.00	15.00
Warner Bros. WS-1482	(S)	On The Happy Side	1962	8.00	20.00
Warner Bros. W-1484	(M)	I Wish You A Merry Christmas	1962	6.00	15.00
Warner Bros. WS-1484	(S)	I Wish You A Merry Christmas	1962	8.00	20.00
— Original Warner albums above have grey labels.—					
MGM E-3890	(M)	Senor Bing	1961	6.00	15.00
MGM SE-3890	(S)	Senor Bing	1961	8.00	20.00
Liberty LOM-16002	(M)	The Road To Hong Kong (Soundtrack)	1962	14.00	35.00
Liberty LOS-17002	(S)	The Road To Hong Kong (Soundtrack)	1962	20.00	50.00
MGM E-4129	(M)	The Great Standards	1963	6.00	15.00
MGM SE-4129	(S)	The Great Standards	1963	8.00	20.00
MGM E-4203	(M)	The Very Best Of Bing Crosby	1964	6.00	15.00
MGM SE-4203	(S)	The Very Best Of Bing Crosby	1964	8.00	20.00
Reprise R-6106	(M)	Return To Paradise Islands	1964	6.00	15.00
Reprise R9-6106	(S)	Return To Paradise Islands	1964	8.00	20.00
Metro M-523	(M)	Bing Crosby	1965	4.00	10.00
Metro MS-523	(S)	Bing Crosby	1965	5.00	12.00
Capitol T-2300	(M)	That Travelin' Two-Beat	1965	6.00	15.00
Capitol ST-2300	(S)	That Travelin' Two-Beat	1965	8.00	20.00
Capitol T-2346	(M)	Great Country Hits	1965	6.00	15.00
Capitol ST-2346	(S)	Great Country Hits	1965	8.00	20.00

Label & Catalog #		Title	Year	VG+	NM

CROSBY, BING, & THE ANDREWS SITERS

| Decca DL-5019 (10") | (M) | Merry Christmas | 1949 | 14.00 | 35.00 |

CROSBY, BING, & CONNEE BOSWELL

| Decca DL-5390 (10") | (M) | Bing And Connee | 1951 | 20.00 | 50.00 |

CROSBY, BING, & LOUIS ARMSTRONG

| MGM E-3882 | (M) | Bing And Satchmo | 1960 | 6.00 | 15.00 |
| MGM SE-3882 | (S) | Bing And Satchmo | 1960 | 8.00 | 20.00 |

CROSBY, CHRIS

| MGM E-4226 | (M) | Meet Chris Crosby | 1964 | 6.00 | 15.00 |
| MGM SE-4226 | (S) | Meet Chris Crosby | 1964 | 8.00 | 20.00 |

CROSBY, STILLS & NASH [CROSBY, STILLS, NASH & YOUNG]
David Crosby, Stephen Stlls, Graham Nash and Neil Young.

Atlantic PR-165	(DJ)	Celebration *(Radio sampler)*	197?	20.00	50.00
Atlantic 18102	(DJ)	A Rap With CSN&Y *(Interview)*	197?	20.00	50.00
Nautilus NR-48	(S)	Crosby, Stills & Nash	1982	10.00	25.00
Mobile Fidelity MFSL-088	(S)	Deja Vu	1983	30.00	60.00

CROSSFIRES, THE

| Strand SL-1083 | (M) | Limbo Rock | 1963 | 6.00 | 15.00 |
| Strand SLS-1083 | (S) | Limbo Rock | 1963 | 8.00 | 20.00 |

CROSSROADS

| Strawberry Jamm 801 | (S) | Crossroads | 1980 | 75.00 | 150.00 |

CROTHERS, SCATMAN

Tops 1511	(M)	Rock 'N Roll With Scatman	1956	35.00	70.00
Craftsman 8036	(M)	Gone With Scatman	1960	16.00	40.00
Motown M-777L	(S)	Big Ben Sings	1973	6.00	15.00

CROWS, THE / THE HARPTONES

| Roulette RE-114 | (M) | The Crows & The Harptones *(2 LPs)* | 1972 | 8.00 | 20.00 |

CRUDUP, ARTHUR "BIG BOY"

Fire 103	(M)	Mean Ol' Frisco	1960	300.00	500.00
Delmark DS-614	(S)	Look On Yonders Wall	1969	10.00	25.00
Delmark DS-621	(S)	Crudup's Mood	1969	10.00	25.00
RCA Victor LVP-573	(M)	Father Of Rock And Roll	1971	8.00	20.00

CRUM, SIMON
Simon Crum is a pseudonym for Ferlin Husky.

| Capitol T-1880 | (M) | The Unpredictable Simon Crum | 1963 | 20.00 | 50.00 |
| Capitol ST-1880 | (S) | The Unpredictable Simon Crum | 1963 | 35.00 | 70.00 |

CRYAN' SHAMES, THE
The Cryan' Shames feature Isaac Guillory.

Columbia CL-2589	(M)	Sugar And Spice	1966	6.00	15.00
Columbia CS-9389	(P)	Sugar And Spice *("360 Sound" label)*	1966	8.00	20.00
Columbia CL-9586	(M)	A Scratch In The Sky	1967	6.00	15.00
Columbia CS-9586	(S)	A Scratch In The Sky *("360 Sound" label)*	1967	8.00	20.00
Columbia CS-9719	(S)	Synthesis	1969	5.00	12.00

CRYSTAL HASE

| No label | (S) | Crystal Hase | 1977 | 50.00 | 100.00 |

CRYSTALS, THE
The Crystals were produced by Phil Spector.

Philles PHLP-4000	(DJ)	Twist Uptown *(White label)*	1962	500.00	750.00
Philles PHLP-4000	(M)	Twist Uptown *(Blue label)*	1962	150.00	250.00
Philles DT-90722	(E)	Twist Uptown *(Capitol Record Club)*	1963	See note below	
		(Although rechanneled, this is among the rarest "stereo" albums.			
		Estimated near mint value $1,000-2,000.)			
Philles PHLP-4001	(DJ)	He's A Rebel *(White label)*	1963	500.00	750.00
Philles PHLP-4001	(M)	He's A Rebel *(Blue label)*	1963	100.00	200.00
Philles PHLP-4003	(DJ)	The Greatest Hits *(White label)*	1963	300.00	500.00
Philles PHLP-4003	(M)	The Greatest Hits *(Blue label)*	1963	80.00	160.00

Label & Catalog #		Title	Year	VG+	NM
CUBY & THE BLIZZARDS					
Phillips PHS-600307	(S)	Cuby And The Blizzards/Live	1969	6.00	15.00
Phillips PHS-600331	(S)	King Of The World	1970	6.00	15.00
CUMBERLAND THREE, THE					
The Cumberland Three features John Stewart.					
Roulette R-25121	(M)	Folk Scene, U.S.A.	1960	8.00	20.00
Roulette SR-25121	(S)	Folk Scene, U.S.A.	1960	12.00	30.00
Roulette R-25132	(M)	Civil War Almanac/The Yankees	1960	6.00	15.00
Roulette SR-25132	(S)	Civil War Almanac/The Yankees	1960	10.00	25.00
Roulette R-25133	(M)	Civil War Almanac/The Rebels	1960	6.00	15.00
Roulette SR-25133	(S)	Civil War Almanac/The Rebels	1960	10.00	25.00
CUMMINGS, BOB					
Renner RC-100	(M)	Sounds Of Aviation	195?	10.00	25.00
CUMMINGS, BURTON					
Cummings was formerly a member of The Guess Who.					
Portrait PRQ-34261	(Q)	Burton Cummings	1976	5.00	12.00
CURLESS, DICK					
Tiffany 1016	(M)	Songs Of The Open Country	1958	20.00	50.00
Tiffany 1028	(M)	Singing Just For Fun	1959	16.00	40.00
Tiffany 1033	(M)	I Love To Tell A Story	1960	16.00	40.00
CURTIS, KEN					
Capitol T-2418	(M)	Gunsmoke's Festus	1965	8.00	20.00
Capitol ST-2418	(S)	Gunsmoke's Festus	1965	10.00	25.00
Dot DLP-3859	(M)	Gunsmoke's Festus Calls Out Ken Curtis	1967	8.00	20.00
Dot DLP-25859	(S)	Gunsmoke's Festus Calls Out Ken Curtis	1967	10.00	25.00
CURTIS, SONNY					
Curtis was formerly a member of The Crickets.					
Imperial LP-9276	(M)	Beatle Hits Flamenco Guitar Style	1964	12.00	30.00
Imperial LP-12276	(S)	Beatle Hits Flamenco Guitar Style	1964	16.00	40.00
Viva V-36012	(S)	The First Of Sonny Curtis	1968	8.00	20.00
Viva V-36021	(S)	The Sonny Curtis Style	1969	8.00	20.00
CYKLE, THE					
Label 9-261	(S)	The Cykle	1969	240.00	400.00
CYMBAL, JOHNNY					
Kapp KL-1324	(M)	Mr. Bass Man	1963	10.00	25.00
Kapp KS-3324	(S)	Mr. Bass Man	1963	14.00	35.00
CYRKLE, THE					
Columbia CL-2544	(M)	Red Rubber Ball	1966	10.00	25.00
Columbia CS-9344	(S)	Red Rubber Ball	1966	16.00	40.00
Columbia CL-2632	(M)	Neon	1967	3.50	8.00
Columbia CS-9432	(S)	Neon	1967	8.00	20.00
Amsterdam AMS-12007	(S)	The Minx *(Soundtrack)*	1970	8.00	20.00

Records With Estimated Values

Records with "See note below" in the price column have fluctuating values in the current market, illustrated by the estimated prices. A seller with a near mint copy should expect to get the minimum listed in the price spread in an open auction. While a buyer might win this record for the minimum, he should not be surprised to find the bidding escalate to the maximum listed value.

Label & Catalog #		Title	Year	VG+	NM

DALE & GRACE
Dale Houston and Grace Broussard.

Montel LP-100	(M)	**I'm Leaving It Up To You**	1964	35.00	70.00

DALE, DICK (& HIS DEL-TONES)
Refer to Jerry Cole.

Deltone LPM-1001	(M)	**Surfer's Choice**	1962	75.00	150.00
Deltone T-1886	(M)	**Surfer's Choice**	1962	12.00	30.00
Deltone DT-1886	(E)	**Surfer's Choice**	1962	10.00	25.00
Capitol T-1930	(M)	**King Of The Surf Guitar**	1963	16.00	40.00
Capitol ST-1930	(S)	**King Of The Surf Guitar**	1963	20.00	50.00
Capitol T-2002	(M)	**Checkered Flag**	1963	14.00	35.00
Capitol ST-2002	(S)	**Checkered Flag**	1963	18.00	45.00
Capitol T-2053	(M)	**Mr. Eliminator**	1964	14.00	35.00
Capitol ST-2053	(S)	**Mr. Eliminator**	1964	18.00	45.00
Capitol T-2111	(M)	**Summer Surf**	1964	20.00	50.00
Capitol ST-2111	(S)	**Summer Surf**	1964	30.00	60.00
		(Issued with a bonus single, "Racing Waves" by Jerry Cole,			
		in a special pocket on the front cover.)			
Capitol T-2111	(M)	**Summer Surf** *(Without the single)*	1964	14.00	35.00
Capitol ST-2111	(S)	**Summer Surf** *(Without the single)*	1964	18.00	45.00
Capitol T-2293	(M)	**Rock Out/Live At Ciro's**	1965	14.00	35.00
Capitol ST-2293	(S)	**Rock Out/Live At Ciro's**	1965	18.00	45.00

DALE, DICK / THE HOLLYWOOD SURFERS

Dub Tone LP-1246	(M)	**The Surf Family**	1964	14.00	35.00

DALE, DICK / THE STOMPERS

Cloister CLP-6301	(M)	**Silver Sounds Of The Surf** *(Felt cover)*	1963	75.00	150.00

DALEY, JIMMY

Decca DL-8429	(M)	**Rock Pretty Baby** *(Soundtrack)*	1958	35.00	70.00

DALLAS

No label 9715	(S)	**Casualty Of Love**	1979	12.00	30.00

DALLAS, DEAN
Dean Dallas is a pseudonym for Pete Drake.

Cumberland MGC-29516	(M)	**Golden Country Hits**	195?	8.00	20.00

DAMIN EIH [DAMIN EIH & BROTHER CLARK]

Demelot 7310	(S)	**Never Mind**	1974	90.00	180.00

DAMITA JO
Damita Jo was formerly a member of Steve Gibson's Red Caps.

ABC 378	(M)	**The Big Fifteen**	1961	12.00	30.00
Mercury MG-20642	(M)	**I'll Save The Last Dance For You**	1961	8.00	20.00
Mercury SR-60642	(S)	**I'll Save The Last Dance For You**	1961	12.00	30.00
Mercury MG-20734	(M)	**Sing A Country Song**	1962	8.00	20.00
Mercury SR-60734	(S)	**Sing A Country Song**	1962	12.00	30.00
Mercury MG-20703	(M)	**Damita Jo At The Diplomat**	1962	8.00	20.00
Mercury SR-60703	(S)	**Damita Jo At The Diplomat**	1962	12.00	30.00
Vee Jay LP-1137	(M)	**Damita Jo Sings**	1965	6.00	15.00
Vee Jay SR-1137	(S)	**Damita Jo Sings**	1965	10.00	25.00
Epic LN-24131	(M)	**If You Go Away**	1965	6.00	15.00
Epic BN-26131	(S)	**If You Go Away**	1965	8.00	20.00
Epic LN-24244	(M)	**This Is Damita Jo**	1967	6.00	15.00
Epic BN-26244	(S)	**This Is Damita Jo**	1967	8.00	20.00
Ranwood 8037	(S)	**Miss Damita Jo**	1968	6.00	15.00

Label & Catalog #		Title	Year	VG+	NM
DAMNATION					
United Arts. UAS-6738	(S)	**The Damnation Of Adam Blessing**	1969	6.00	15.00
United Arts. UAS-6773	(S)	**The Second Damnation**	1970	5.00	12.00
United Arts. UAS-5533	(S)	**Which Is The Justice, Which Is The Thief**	1971	5.00	12.00
DAMON					
Damon features Atlee Yeager.					
Ankh 968	(M)	**Song Of A Gypsy**	1970	*See note below*	
		(Issued in a textured cover with an embossed title and ankh.			
		Rare. Estimated near mint value $3,000-4,000.)			
Ankh 968	(M)	**Song Of A Gypsy**	1970	1,000.00	1,500.00
		(Issued in a regular single pocket cover.)			
DAMONE, VIC					
Mercury MG-25028 (10")	(M)	**Vic Damone**	1950	16.00	40.00
Mercury MG-25029 (10")	(M)	**Vic Damone**	1950	16.00	40.00
Mercury MG-25045 (10")	(M)	**Vic Damone**	1950	16.00	40.00
Mercury MG-25054 (10")	(M)	**Song Hits**	1950	16.00	40.00
Mercury MG-25092 (10")	(M)	**Christmas Favorites**	1951	16.00	40.00
Mercury MG-25100 (10")	(M)	**Vic Damone And Others**	1952	16.00	40.00
Mercury MG-25131 (10")	(M)	**The Night Has A Thousand Eyes**	1952	16.00	40.00
Mercury MG-25132 (10")	(M)	**Vocals By Vic**	1952	16.00	40.00
Mercury MG-25133 (10")	(M)	**April In paris**	1952	16.00	40.00
Mercury MG-25156 (10")	(M)	**Vic Damone**	1952	16.00	40.00
Mercury MG-25202 (10")	(M)	**Athena** *(Soundtrack)*	1954	100.00	200.00
MGM E-86 (10")	(M)	**Rich, Young And Pretty** *(Soundtrack)*	1951	50.00	100.00
MGM E-3153	(M)	**Deep In My Heart** *(Soundtrack. Boxed set)*	1954	50.00	100.00
MGM E-3153	(M)	**Deep In My Heart** *(Soundtrack)*	1955	20.00	50.00
MGM E-3236	(M)	**Rich, Young And Pretty** *(Soundtrack)*	1955	20.00	50.00
Mercury MG-20163	(M)	**Yours For A Song**	1957	10.00	25.00
Mercury MG-20193	(M)	**The Voice Of Vic Damone**	1957	10.00	25.00
Mercury MG-25-0194	(M)	**My Favorites**	1957	10.00	25.00
Columbia CL-900	(M)	**That Towering Feeling!**	1956	10.00	25.00
Columbia CL-950	(M)	**The Stingiest Man In Town** *(Soundtrack)*	1956	20.00	50.00
Columbia CL-1113	(M)	**The Gift Of Love** *(Soundtrack)*	1958	50.00	100.00
Columbia CL-1219	(M)	**Closer Than A Kiss**	1959	6.00	15.00
Columbia CS-8019	(S)	**Closer Than A Kiss**	1959	8.00	20.00
Columbia CL-1246	(M)	**Angela Mia**	1959	6.00	15.00
Columbia CS-8046	(S)	**Angela Mia**	1959	8.00	20.00
Columbia CL-1369	(M)	**This Game Of Love**	1959	6.00	15.00
Columbia CS-8169	(S)	**This Game Of Love**	1959	8.00	20.00
Columbia CL-1573	(M)	**On The Swingin' Side**	1961	6.00	15.00
Columbia CS-8373	(S)	**On The Swingin' Side**	1961	8.00	20.00
— *Original Columbia albums above have three white "eye" logos on each side of the spindle hole.*—					
Capitol T-1646	(M)	**Linger Awhile With Vic Damone**	1962	5.00	12.00
Capitol ST-1646	(S)	**Linger Awhile With Vic Damone**	1962	6.00	15.00
Capitol T-1691	(M)	**Strange Enchantment**	1962	5.00	12.00
Capitol ST-1691	(S)	**Strange Enchantment**	1962	6.00	15.00
Capitol T-1748	(M)	**The Lively Ones**	1962	5.00	12.00
Capitol ST-1748	(S)	**The Lively Ones**	1962	6.00	15.00
Capitol T-1811	(M)	**My Baby Loves To Swing**	1963	5.00	12.00
Capitol ST-1811	(S)	**My Baby Loves To Swing**	1963	6.00	15.00
Capitol T-1944	(M)	**The Liveliest**	1963	5.00	12.00
Capitol ST-1944	(S)	**The Liveliest**	1963	6.00	15.00
Capitol T-2123	(M)	**On The Street Where You Live**	1964	5.00	12.00
Capitol ST-2123	(S)	**On The Street Where You Live**	1964	6.00	15.00
RCA Victor LOC-1132	(M)	**Arrivederci Baby** *(Soundtrack)*	1966	8.00	20.00
RCA Victor LSO-1132	(S)	**Arrivederci Baby** *(Soundtrack)*	1966	10.00	25.00
RCA Victor LPM-3671	(M)	**Stay With Me**	1966	5.00	12.00
RCA Victor LSP-3671	(S)	**Stay With Me**	1966	6.00	15.00
RCA Victor LPM-3765	(M)	**On The South Side Of Chicago**	1967	6.00	15.00
RCA Victor LSP-3765	(S)	**On The South Side Of Chicago**	1967	6.00	15.00
RCA Victor LPM-3916	(M)	**The Damone Type Of Thing**	1968	6.00	15.00
RCA Victor LSP-3916	(S)	**The Damone Type Of Thing**	1968	6.00	15.00
RCA Victor LSP-3984	(S)	**Why Can't I Walk Away**	1968	6.00	15.00
DAN & DALE					
Tifton M-8002	(M)	**Batman And Robin**	1966	12.00	30.00
Tifton S-78002	(S)	**Batman And Robin**	1966	16.00	40.00

Label & Catalog #		Title	Year	VG+	NM

DANE, BARBARA

San Francisco 33014	(M)	Good Morning Blues	1957	16.00	40.00
Dot DLP-3177	(M)	Livin' With The Blues	1959	12.00	30.00
Dot DLP-25177	(S)	Livin' With The Blues	1959	16.00	40.00
Capitol T-1758	(M)	On My Way	1962	8.00	20.00
Capitol ST-1758	(S)	On My Way	1962	10.00	25.00

DANIELS, CHARLIE

Epic HE-44365	(S)	Fire On The Mountain (Half-speed master)	1982	8.00	20.00
Epic HE-45751	(S)	Million Mile Reflections (Half-speed master)	1982	6.00	15.00
Mobile Fidelity MFSL-176	(S)	Million Mile Reflections	1982	6.00	15.00

DANTE, RON

Dante was the mastermind behind The Detergents; The Archies; Mercy.

Kirshner KES-106	(S)	Ron Dante Brings You Up	1970	6.00	15.00

DANTE & THE EVERGREENS

Madison MA-1002	(M)	Dante & The Evergreens	1961	180.00	300.00

DARIN, BOBBY

Atco 22-102	(M)	Bobby Darin	1958	30.00	60.00
Atco 33-104	(M)	That's All	1959	12.00	30.00
Atco SD-33-104	(S)	That's All	1959	20.00	50.00
Atco 33-115	(M)	This Is Darin	1960	12.00	30.00
Atco SD-33-115	(S)	This Is Darin	1960	20.00	50.00
Atco 33-122	(M)	Darin At The Copa	1960	12.00	30.00
Atco SD-33-122	(S)	Darin At The Copa	1961	20.00	50.00
Atco SP-1001	(M)	For Teenagers Only (Paper cover)	1960	50.00	100.00
Atco 33-125	(M)	The 25th Of December	1960	12.00	30.00
Atco SD-33-125	(S)	The 25th Of December	1960	20.00	50.00
Colpix CP-507	(M)	Pepe (Soundtrack)	1960	8.00	20.00
Colpix SCP-507	(S)	Pepe (Soundtrack)	1960	12.00	30.00
Atco 33-126	(M)	Two Of A Kind	1961	12.00	30.00
Atco SD-33-126	(S)	Two Of A Kind	1961	20.00	50.00
Atco 33-131	(M)	The Bobby Darin Story	1961	12.00	30.00
Atco SD-33-131	(P)	The Bobby Darin Story	1961	16.00	40.00
Atco 33-134	(M)	Love Swings	1961	12.00	30.00
Atco SD-33-134	(S)	Love Swings	1961	16.00	40.00

— Original Atco albums above have yellow labels with a harp on top.—

Atco 22-102	(M)	Bobby Darin	196?	12.00	30.00
Atco 33-104	(M)	That's All	196?	6.00	15.00
Atco SD-33-104	(S)	That's All	196?	8.00	20.00
Atco 33-115	(M)	This Is Darin	196?	6.00	15.00
Atco SD-33-115	(S)	This Is Darin	196?	8.00	20.00
Atco 33-122	(M)	Darin At The Copa	196?	6.00	15.00
Atco 33-122	(S)	Darin At The Copa	196?	8.00	20.00
Atco 33-125	(M)	The 25th Of December	196?	6.00	15.00
Atco SD-33-125	(S)	The 25th Of December	196?	8.00	20.00
Atco 33-126	(M)	Two Of A Kind	196?	6.00	15.00
Atco SD-33-126	(S)	Two Of A Kind	196?	8.00	20.00
Atco 33-131	(M)	The Bobby Darin Story	196?	6.00	15.00
Atco SD-33-131	(S)	The Bobby Darin Story	196?	8.00	20.00
Atco 33-134	(M)	Love Swings	196?	6.00	15.00
Atco SD-33-134	(S)	Love Swings	196?	8.00	20.00

— Reissues of the early Atco mono albums above have gold, grey & white labels;
stereo albums have brown, purple & white labels.—

Atco 33-138	(M)	Twist With Bobby Darin	1961	8.00	20.00
Atco SD-33-138	(S)	Twist With Bobby Darin	1961	10.00	25.00
Atco 33-140	(M)	Bobby Darin Sings Ray Charles	1962	8.00	20.00
Atco SD-33-140	(S)	Bobby Darin Sings Ray Charles	1962	10.00	25.00
Atco 33-146	(M)	Things And Other Things	1962	8.00	20.00
Atco SD-33-146	(S)	Things And Other Things	1962	10.00	25.00
Atco 33-124	(M)	It's You Or No One	1963	8.00	20.00
Atco SD-33-124	(S)	It's You Or No One	1963	10.00	25.00
Atco 33-167	(M)	Winners	1964	6.00	15.00
Atco SD-33-167	(S)	Winners	1964	8.00	20.00
Dot DLP-9011	(M)	State Fair (Soundtrack)	1962	12.00	30.00
Dot DLP-25011	(S)	State Fair (Soundtrack)	1962	16.00	40.00

Label & Catalog #		Title	Year	VG+	NM
Capitol T-1791	(M)	Oh! Look At Me Now	1962	6.00	15.00
Capitol ST-1791	(S)	Oh! Look At Me Now	1962	8.00	20.00
Capitol T-1826	(M)	Earthy	1963	6.00	15.00
Capitol ST-1826	(S)	Earthy	1963	8.00	20.00
Capitol T-1866	(M)	You're The Reason I'm Living	1963	6.00	15.00
Capitol ST-1866	(S)	You're The Reason I'm Living	1963	8.00	20.00
Capitol T-1942	(M)	18 Yellow Roses	1963	6.00	15.00
Capitol ST-1942	(S)	18 Yellow Roses	1963	8.00	20.00
Capitol T-2007	(M)	Golden Folk Hits	1963	6.00	15.00
Capitol ST-2007	(S)	Golden Folk Hits	1963	8.00	20.00
Capitol T-2194	(M)	From "Hello Dolly" To "Goodbye Charlie"	1964	6.00	15.00
Capitol ST-2194	(S)	From "Hello Dolly" To "Goodbye Charlie"	1964	8.00	20.00
Decca DL-9119	(M)	The Lively Set (Soundtrack)	1964	14.00	35.00
Decca DL7-9119	(S)	The Lively Set (Soundtrack)	1964	20.00	50.00
Capitol T-2322	(M)	Venice Blue	1965	6.00	15.00
Capitol ST-2322	(S)	Venice Blue	1965	8.00	20.00
Capitol T-2571	(M)	The Best Of Bobby Darin	1966	6.00	15.00
Capitol ST-2571	(S)	The Best Of Bobby Darin	1966	8.00	20.00
Clarion 603	(M)	Clementine	1964	6.00	15.00
Clarion 603	(S)	Clementine	1964	8.00	20.00
Atlantic 8121	(M)	The Shadow Of Your Smile	1966	6.00	15.00
Atlantic SD-8121	(S)	The Shadow Of Your Smile	1966	8.00	20.00
Atlantic 8126	(M)	In A Broadway Bag	1966	6.00	15.00
Atlantic SD-8126	(S)	In A Broadway Bag	1966	8.00	20.00
Atlantic 8135	(M)	If I Were A Carpenter	1966	6.00	15.00
Atlantic SD-8135	(S)	If I Were A Carpenter	1966	16.00	40.00
Atlantic 8142	(M)	Inside Out	1967	6.00	15.00
Atlantic SD-8142	(S)	Inside Out	1967	8.00	20.00
Atlantic 8154	(M)	Bobby Darin Sings Doctor Doolittle	1967	6.00	15.00
Atlantic SD-8154	(S)	Bobby Darin Sings Doctor Doolittle	1967	8.00	20.00
Direction 1936	(S)	Born Walden Robert Cassotto	1968	8.00	20.00
Direction 1937	(S)	Commitment	1969	8.00	20.00
Motown M-753L	(S)	Bobby Darin	1972	5.00	12.00

DARIUS

Chartmaker 1102	(S)	Darius	1969	100.00	200.00

DARLING, DENVER

Audio Lab AL-107	(M)	Denver Darling	195?	20.00	50.00

DARLING, ERIC
Darling was a member of The Tarriers; The Rooftop Singers.

Vanguard VRS-9099	(M)	True Religion	1961	8.00	20.00
Vanguard VRS-9131	(M)	Train Time	1962	8.00	20.00
Elektra EKL-154	(M)	Folksongs	196?	8.00	20.00

DARREN, JAMES

Colpix CLP-406	(M)	James Darren	1960	16.00	40.00
Colpix CLP-406	(M)	James Darren (Green vinyl)	1960	50.00	100.00
Colpix CLP-418	(M)	Gidget Goes Hawaiian	1961	10.00	25.00
Colpix SCP-418	(S)	Gidget Goes Hawaiian	1961	16.00	40.00
Colpix CLP-424	(M)	James Darren Sings For All Sizes	1962	10.00	25.00
Colpix SCP-424	(S)	James Darren Sings For All Sizes	1962	16.00	40.00
Colpix CLP-428	(M)	Love Among The Young	1962	10.00	25.00
Colpix SCP-428	(S)	Love Among The Young	1962	16.00	40.00
Colpix CLP-454	(M)	Bye Bye Birdie	1963	10.00	25.00
Colpix SCP-454	(S)	Bye Bye Birdie	1963	16.00	40.00
Decca DL-9119	(M)	The Lively Set (Soundtrack)	1964	14.00	35.00
Decca DL7-9119	(S)	The Lively Set (Soundtrack)	1964	20.00	50.00
Warner Bros. W-1688	(M)	All	1964	5.00	12.00
Warner Bros. WS-1688	(S)	All	1964	6.00	15.00
Kirshner KES-115	(S)	Mammy Blue	1971	6.00	15.00
Kirshner KES-116	(S)	Love Songs From The Movies	1972	6.00	15.00

DARTELLS, THE

Dot DLP-3522	(M)	Hot Pastrami	1963	10.00	25.00
Dot DLP-25522	(S)	Hot Pastrami	1963	14.00	35.00

Label & Catalog #		Title	Year	VG+	NM
DARTS, THE					
Del-Fi DF-1244	(M)	**Hollywood Drag**	1963	8.00	20.00
Del-Fi DFST-1244	(S)	**Hollywood Drag**	1963	12.00	30.00
DASHIEL, BUD (& THE KINSMEN)					
Refer to Bud & Travis.					
Warner Bros. W-1429	(M)	**Bud Dashiell With The Kinsmen**	1961	6.00	15.00
Warner Bros. WS-1429	(S)	**Bud Dashiell With The Kinsmen**	1961	8.00	20.00
Warner Bros. W-1432	(M)	**Live Concert Extraordinaire**	1962	6.00	15.00
Warner Bros. WS-1432	(S)	**Live Concert Extraordinaire**	1962	8.00	20.00
Warner Bros. WS-1731	(S)	**I Think It's Gonna Rain Today**	1968	6.00	15.00
DAUGHTERS OF ALBION, THE					
Fontana SRF-68586	(S)	**The Daughters Of Albion** *(With inserts)*	1968	6.00	15.00
DAVE DEE, DOZY, BEAKY, MICK & TICH					
Fontana MGF-27567	(M)	**Greatest Hits**	1967	10.00	25.00
Fontana SRF-67567	(P)	**Greatest Hits**	1967	12.00	30.00
Imperial LP-12402	(P)	**Time To Take Off**	1968	10.00	25.00
DAVEY & THE BADMEN					
Gothic WA-63054	(M)	**Wanted**	1963	150.00	250.00
DAVID, THE					
V.M.C. 124	(S)	**Another Day, Another Lifetime**	1968	30.00	60.00
DAVID & JONATHAN					
David & Jonathan were Rogers Cook and Greenaway.					
Capitol T-2473	(M)	**Michelle**	1966	5.00	12.00
Capitol ST-2473	(S)	**Michelle**	1966	6.00	15.00
20th Century-Fox 3182	(M)	**Modesty Blaise** *(Soundtrack)*	1966	6.00	15.00
20th Century-Fox S-4182	(S)	**Modesty Blaise** *(Soundtrack)*	1966	8.00	20.00
DAVIS, BETTE					
Citadel CT-7030	(M)	**Miss Bette Davis Sings!**	196?	12.00	30.00
DAVIS, JIMMIE					
Decca DL-5500 (10")	(M)	**Jimmie Davis**	1954	20.00	50.00
Decca DL-8174	(M)	**Jimmie Davis**	1955	12.00	30.00
Decca DL-8572	(M)	**Hymn Time With The Anita Kerr Singers**	1957	12.00	30.00
Decca DL-8896	(M)	**You Are My Sunshine**	1959	12.00	30.00
Decca DL-8953	(M)	**Suppertime**	1960	12.00	30.00
DAVIS, JOHNNY					
King 626	(M)	**Johnny "Scat" Davis**	1959	12.00	30.00
DAVIS, LINK					
Mercury SR-61243	(S)	**Cajun Crawdaddy**	1969	10.00	25.00
DAVIS, JR., SAMMY					
Refer to The Reprise Repertory Theatre.					
Decca DL-8118	(M)	**Starring Sammy Davis, Jr.**	1955	12.00	30.00
Decca DL-8170	(M)	**Just For Lovers**	1955	12.00	30.00
Decca DL-9032	(M)	**Mr. Wonderful** *(Soundtrack)*	1956	16.00	40.00
Decca DL-8351	(M)	**Here's Looking At You**	1956	10.00	25.00
Decca DL-8486	(M)	**Sammy Swings**	1957	10.00	25.00
Decca DL-8641	(M)	**It's All Over But The Swingin'**	1957	10.00	25.00
Decca DL-8676	(M)	**Mood To Be Wooed**	1958	10.00	25.00
Decca DL-8779	(M)	**All The Way And Then Some**	1958	10.00	25.00
Decca DL-8841	(M)	**Sammy Davis, Jr. At Town Hall**	1959	8.00	20.00
Decca DL-78841	(S)	**Sammy Davis, Jr. At Town Hall**	1959	12.00	30.00
Decca DL-8854	(M)	**Porgy And Bess**	1959	8.00	20.00
Decca DL-78854	(S)	**Porgy And Bess**	1959	12.00	30.00
Decca DL-8921	(M)	**Sammy Awards**	1960	8.00	20.00
Decca DL-78921	(S)	**Sammy Awards**	1960	12.00	30.00
Decca DL-8981	(M)	**I Got A Right To Swing**	1960	8.00	20.00
Decca DL-78981	(S)	**I Got A Right To Swing**	1960	12.00	30.00

— Original Decca albums above have black & silver labels.—

Label & Catalog #		Title	Year	VG+	NM
Decca DL-4153	(M)	Mr. Entertainment	1961	6.00	15.00
Decca DL-74153	(S)	Mr. Entertainment	1961	8.00	20.00
Decca DL-4381	(M)	Forget-Me-Nots For First Nighters	1963	5.00	12.00
Decca DL-74381	(S)	Forget-Me-Nots For First Nighters	1963	6.00	15.00
Decca DL-4582	(M)	Try A Little Tenderness	1965	5.00	12.00
Decca DL-74582	(S)	Try A Little Tenderness	1965	6.00	15.00
Decca DXB-192	(M)	The Best Of Sammy Davis, Jr. (2 LPs)	1966	5.00	12.00
Decca DXSB-192	(S)	The Best Of Sammy Davis, Jr. (2 LPs)	1966	6.00	15.00
Decca DL-71502	(S)	Sweet Charity (Soundtrack)	1969	6.00	15.00
Reprise R-2003	(M)	The Wham Of Sam	1961	5.00	12.00
Reprise RS-2003	(S)	The Wham Of Sam	1961	6.00	15.00
Reprise R-2010	(M)	Belts The Best Of Broadway	1962	5.00	12.00
Reprise RS-2010	(S)	Belts The Best Of Broadway	1962	6.00	15.00
Reprise R-6033	(M)	All Star Spectacular	1962	5.00	12.00
Reprise R9-6033	(S)	All Star Spectacular	1962	6.00	15.00
Reprise R-6051	(M)	What Kind Of Fool Am I?	1962	5.00	12.00
Reprise R9-6051	(S)	What Kind Of Fool Am I?	1962	6.00	15.00
Reprise R-6063	(M)	At The Coconut Grove (2 LPs)	1963	6.00	15.00
Reprise R9-6063	(S)	At The Coconut Grove (2 LPs)	1963	8.00	20.00
Reprise R-6082	(M)	As Long As She Needs Me	1963	5.00	12.00
Reprise R9-6082	(S)	As Long As She Needs Me	1963	6.00	15.00
United Arts. UAL-4111	(M)	Johnny Cool (Soundtrack)	1963	10.00	25.00
United Arts. UAS-5111	(S)	Johnny Cool (Soundtrack)	1963	12.00	30.00
Capitol VAS-2124	(M)	Golden Boy (Soundtrack)	1964	10.00	25.00
Capitol SVAS-2124	(S)	Golden Boy (Soundtrack)	1964	12.00	30.00
Reprise R-6095	(M)	Salutes The Stars Of The London Palladium	1964	4.00	10.00
Reprise R9-6095	(S)	Salutes The Stars Of The London Palladium	1964	5.00	12.00
Reprise R-6096	(M)	A Treasury Of Golden Hits	1963	4.00	10.00
Reprise R9-6096	(S)	A Treasury Of Golden Hits	1963	5.00	12.00
Reprise R-6114	(M)	The Shelter Of Your Arms	1964	4.00	10.00
Reprise RS-6114	(S)	The Shelter Of Your Arms	1964	5.00	12.00
Reprise R-6126	(M)	California Suite	1964	4.00	10.00
Reprise RS-6126	(S)	California Suite	1964	5.00	12.00
Reprise R-6131	(M)	The Big Ones For Young Lovers	1964	4.00	10.00
Reprise RS-6131	(S)	The Big Ones For Young Lovers	1964	5.00	12.00
Reprise R-6144	(M)	When The Feeling Hits You	1965	4.00	10.00
Reprise RS-6144	(S)	When The Feeling Hits You	1965	5.00	12.00
Reprise R-6159	(M)	If I Ruled The World	1965	4.00	10.00
Reprise RS-6159	(S)	If I Ruled The World	1965	5.00	12.00
Reprise R-6164	(M)	The Nat King Cole Songbook	1965	4.00	10.00
Reprise RS-6164	(S)	The Nat King Cole Songbook	1965	5.00	12.00
Reprise R-6169	(M)	Sammy's Back On Broadway	1965	4.00	10.00
Reprise RS-6169	(S)	Sammy's Back On Broadway	1965	5.00	12.00
Reprise R-6180	(M)	A Man Called Adam (Soundtrack)	1966	10.00	25.00
Reprise RS-6180	(S)	A Man Called Adam (Soundtrack)	1966	12.00	30.00

— Original Reprise albums above have pink, gold & green labels.—

DAVIS, JR., SAMMY, & CARMEN McRAE

Decca DL-8490	(M)	Boy Meets Girl	1957	12.00	30.00

DAVIS, SKEETER

Ms. Davis also recorded with Porter Wagoner.

RCA Victor LPM-2197	(M)	I'll Sing You A Song And Harmonize, Too	1960	8.00	20.00
RCA Victor LSP-2197	(S)	I'll Sing You A Song And Harmonize, Too	1960	12.00	30.00
RCA Victor LPM-2327	(M)	Here's The Answer	1961	8.00	20.00
RCA Victor LSP-2327	(S)	Here's The Answer	1961	12.00	30.00
RCA Victor LPM-2699	(M)	The End Of The World	1962	8.00	20.00
RCA Victor LSP-2699	(S)	The End Of The World	1962	12.00	30.00
RCA Victor LPM-2736	(M)	Cloudy, With Occasional Tears	1963	8.00	20.00
RCA Victor LSP-2736	(S)	Cloudy, With Occasional Tears	1963	12.00	30.00

— Original RCA mono albums above have "Long Play" on the bottom of the label;
stereo albums have "Living Stereo" on the bottom.—

RCA Victor LPM-2980	(M)	Let Me Get Close To You	1964	6.00	15.00
RCA Victor LSP-2980	(S)	Let Me Get Close To You	1964	8.00	20.00
RCA Victor LPM-3374	(M)	The Best Of Skeeter Davis	1965	6.00	15.00
RCA Victor LSP-3374	(P)	The Best Of Skeeter Davis	1965	8.00	20.00
RCA Victor LPM-3382	(M)	Written By The Stars	1965	6.00	15.00
RCA Victor LSP-3382	(S)	Written By The Stars	1965	8.00	20.00

Label & Catalog #		Title	Year	VG+	NM
RCA Victor LPM-3463	(M)	**Skeeter Sings Standards**	1965	6.00	15.00
RCA Victor LSP-3463	(S)	**Skeeter Sings Standards**	1965	8.00	20.00
RCA Victor LPM-3567	(M)	**Singin' In The Summer Sun**	1966	6.00	15.00
RCA Victor LSP-3567	(S)	**Singin' In The Summer Sun**	1966	8.00	20.00
RCA Victor LPM-3667	(M)	**My Heart's In The Country**	1966	6.00	15.00
RCA Victor LSP-3667	(S)	**My Heart's In The Country**	1966	8.00	20.00
RCA Victor LPM-3763	(M)	**Hand In Hand With Jesus**	1967	6.00	15.00
RCA Victor LSP-3763	(S)	**Hand In Hand With Jesus**	1967	8.00	20.00
RCA Victor LPM-3790	(M)	**Skeeter Davis Sings Buddy Holly**	1967	12.00	30.00
RCA Victor LSP-3790	(S)	**Skeeter Davis Sings Buddy Holly**	1967	16.00	40.00
RCA Victor LPM-3876	(M)	**What Does It Take**	1967	6.00	15.00
RCA Victor LSP-3876	(S)	**What Does It Take**	1967	6.00	15.00
RCA Victor LPM-3960	(M)	**Why So Lonely?**	1968	12.00	30.00
RCA Victor LSP-3960	(S)	**Why So Lonely?**	1968	6.00	15.00

— Original RCA albums above have black labels.—

DAVIS, SPENCER [SPENCER DAVIS GROUP]
Steve Winwood is featured on each album except 6652.

United Arts. UAL-3578	(M)	**Gimme Some Lovin'**	1967	16.00	40.00
United Arts. UAS-6578	(E)	**Gimme Some Lovin'**	1967	12.00	30.00
United Arts. UAL-3589	(M)	**I'm A Man**	1967	14.00	35.00
United Arts. UAS-6589	(P)	**I'm A Man**	1967	16.00	40.00
United Arts. UAS-6641	(P)	**Spencer Davis' Greatest Hits**	1968	8.00	20.00
United Arts. UAS-6652	(S)	**With Their New Face On**	1968	5.00	12.00
United Arts. UAS-6691	(S)	**Heavies**	1969	5.00	12.00

DAVIS, TYRONE

Daker DK-9005	(S)	**Can I Change My Mind**	1969	6.00	15.00
Daker DK-9027	(S)	**Turn Back The Hands Of Time**	1970	5.00	12.00
Daker DK-76901	(S)	**I Had It All The Time**	1972	5.00	12.00

DAWE, TIM
Dawe was formerly a member of Iron Butterfly.

Straight STS-1058	(S)	**Penrod**	1969	10.00	25.00
Warner Bros. WS-1841	(S)	**Penrod**	1970	5.00	12.00

DAY, BOBBY
Bobby Day is a pseudonym for Bobby Byrd.

Class LP-5002	(M)	**Rockin' With Robin**	1959	100.00	200.00

DAY, DORIS
Ms. Day also recorded with Frank Sinatra.

Columbia CL-6071 (10")	(M)	**You're My Thrill**	1949	20.00	50.00
Columbia CL-6106 (10")	(M)	**Young Man With A Horn** (Soundtrack)	1950	50.00	100.00
Columbia CL-6149 (10")	(M)	**Tea For Two** (Soundtrack)	1950	50.00	100.00
Columbia CL-6168 (10")	(M)	**Lullaby Of Broadway** (Soundtrack)	1951	50.00	100.00
Columbia CL-6186 (10")	(M)	**On Moonlight Bay** (Soundtrack)	1951	50.00	100.00
Columbia CL-6198 (10")	(M)	**I'll See You In My Dreams** (Soundtrack)	1951	50.00	100.00
Columbia CL-6248 (10")	(M)	**By The Light Of The Silvery Moon** (Sdtk)	1953	50.00	100.00
Columbia CL-6273 (10")	(M)	**Calamity Jane** (Soundtrack)	1953	50.00	100.00
Columbia CL-2518 (10")	(M)	**Lights, Cameras, Action**	195?	12.00	30.00
Columbia CL-2530 (10")	(M)	**Boys And Girls Together**	195?	12.00	30.00
Columbia CL-2534 (10")	(M)	**Hot Canaries** (With Peggy Lee)	195?	12.00	30.00
Columbia CL-582	(M)	**Young Man With A Horn**	1954	10.00	25.00
Columbia CL-624	(M)	**Day Dreams**	1955	10.00	25.00
Columbia CL-710	(M)	**Love Me Or Leave Me** (Soundtrack)	1955	16.00	40.00
Columbia CL-749	(M)	**Day In Hollywood**	1955	10.00	25.00

— Original Columbia albums above have "Long Playing" on the bottom of the label —

Columbia CL-942	(M)	**Day By Day**	1957	10.00	25.00
Columbia OL-5210	(M)	**The Pajama Game** (Soundtrack)	1957	10.00	25.00
Columbia CL-1210	(M)	**Doris Day's Greatest Hits**	1958	10.00	25.00
Columbia C2L-5	(M)	**Hooray For Hollywood**	1959	10.00	25.00
Columbia C2S-5	(S)	**Hooray For Hollywood**	1959	12.00	30.00
Columbia CL-1266	(M)	**Hooray For Hollywood, Volume 1**	1959	5.00	12.00
Columbia CS-8066	(S)	**Hooray For Hollywood, Volume 1**	1959	6.00	15.00
Columbia CL-1267	(M)	**Hooray For Hollywood, Volume 2**	1959	5.00	12.00
Columbia CS-8067	(S)	**Hooray For Hollywood, Volume 2**	1959	6.00	15.00
Columbia CL-1278	(M)	**Cuttin' Capers**	1959	6.00	15.00
Columbia CS-8078	(S)	**Cuttin' Capers**	1959	8.00	20.00

Label & Catalog #		Title	Year	VG+	NM
Columbia CL-1289	(M)	**Day By Night**	1959	6.00	15.00
Columbia CS-8089	(S)	**Day By Night**	1959	8.00	20.00
Columbia DD-1	(M)	**Listen To Day**	1960	6.00	15.00
Columbia DDS-1	(S)	**Listen To Day**	1960	8.00	20.00
Columbia CL-1434	(M)	**What Every Girl Should Know**	1960	6.00	15.00
Columbia CS-8234	(S)	**What Every Girl Should Know**	1960	8.00	20.00
Columbia CL-1461	(M)	**Show Time**	1960	6.00	15.00
Columbia CS-8261	(S)	**Show Time**	1960	8.00	20.00
Columbia CL-1660	(M)	**I Have Dreamed**	1961	6.00	15.00
Columbia CS-8460	(S)	**I Have Dreamed**	1961	8.00	20.00
Columbia OL-5860	(M)	**Jumbo** (Soundtrack)	1962	6.00	15.00
Columbia OS-2260	(S)	**Jumbo** (Soundtrack)	1962	8.00	20.00
Columbia CL-1752	(M)	**Duet** (With Andre Previn)	1962	6.00	15.00
Columbia CS-8552	(S)	**Duet** (With Andre Previn)	1962	8.00	20.00

— Original Columbia albums above have three white "eye" logos on each side of the spindle hole.—

Columbia CL-1904	(M)	**You'll Never Walk Alone**	1962	5.00	12.00
Columbia CS-8704	(S)	**You'll Never Walk Alone**	1962	6.00	15.00
Columbia OL-5960	(M)	**Annie Get Your Gun** (Soundtrack)	1963	6.00	15.00
Columbia OS-2360	(S)	**Annie Get Your Gun** (Soundtrack)	1963	8.00	20.00
Columbia CL-1973	(M)	**Love Me Or Leave Me** (Soundtrack)	1963	6.00	15.00
Columbia CS-8773	(E)	**Love Me Or Leave Me** (Soundtrack)	1963	8.00	20.00
Columbia CL-2131	(M)	**Love Him!**	1964	5.00	12.00
Columbia CS-8931	(S)	**Love Him!**	1964	6.00	15.00
Columbia CL-2226	(M)	**Christmas Album**	1964	5.00	12.00
Columbia CS-9026	(S)	**Christmas Album**	1964	6.00	15.00
Columbia CL-2266	(M)	**With A Smile And A Song**	1964	5.00	12.00
Columbia CS-9066	(S)	**With A Smile And A Song**	1964	6.00	15.00
Columbia CL-2310	(M)	**Latin For Lovers**	1965	5.00	12.00
Columbia CS-9110	(S)	**Latin For Lovers**	1965	6.00	15.00

— Columbia albums above have "360 Sound Mono/Stereo" on the bottom of the label.—

DAY, DORIS; FRANKIE LAINE & JO STAFFORD

Columbia CL-2598 (10")	(M)	**Most Happy Fella**	1956	20.00	50.00

DAY, DORIS, & ROCK HUDSON

U.I. DCLA-1316	(DJ)	**Selections From "Pillow Talk"** (One sided)	195?	20.00	50.00

DAY, JIMMY

Phillips PHM-200016	(M)	**Golden Steel Guitar Hits**	196?	8.00	20.00
Phillips PHS-600016	(S)	**Golden Steel Guitar Hits**	196?	12.00	30.00
Phillips PHM-200075	(M)	**Steel And Strings**	196?	8.00	20.00
Phillips PHS-600075	(S)	**Steel And Strings**	196?	12.00	30.00

DAY BLINDNESS
Day Blindness features Sammy Hagar.

Studio 10 DBX-101	(S)	**Day Blindness**	1969	16.00	40.00

DE-FENDERS, THE
The De-Fenders feature Bruce Johnston.

World Pacific WP-1810	(M)	**The Big Ones**	1963	12.00	30.00
World Pacific ST-1810	(S)	**The Big Ones**	1963	16.00	40.00
World Pacific ST-1810	(S)	**The Big Ones** (Green vinyl)	1963	50.00	100.00
World Pacific ST-1810	(S)	**The Big Ones** (Red vinyl)	1963	50.00	100.00
Del-Fi DFLP-1242	(M)	**Drag Beat**	1963	14.00	35.00
Del-Fi DFSP-1242	(S)	**Drag Beat**	1963	20.00	50.00

DEAD BOYS, THE

Sire SR-6038	(S)	**Young, Loud And Snotty**	1977	10.00	25.00
Sire SRK-6054	(S)	**We Have Come For Your Children**	1978	10.00	25.00

DEAD KENNEDYS, THE

Alt. Tentacles	(S)	**Fresh Fruit For Rotting Vegetables**	1981	6.00	15.00

(Orange cover with a photo of an old band on the back.)

DEADLY ONES, THE

Vee Jay LP-1090	(M)	**It's Monster Surfing Time**	1964	12.00	30.00
Vee Jay VS-1090	(S)	**It's Monster Surfing Time**	1964	20.00	50.00

Label & Catalog #		Title	Year	VG+	NM
DEAL, BILL, & THE RHONDELS					
Heritage HTS-35006	(P)	The Best Of Bill Deal & The Rhondels	1969	6.00	15.00
Heritage HTS-35003	(P)	Vintage Rock	1969	6.00	15.00
DEAN, AL					
Warrior 506	(M)	Fragile Heart	195?	50.00	100.00
DEAN, EDDIE					
Sage & Sand C- 1	(M)	Greatest Westerns	1956	20.00	50.00
Sage & Sand C- 5	(M)	Hi-Country	1957	16.00	40.00
Sage & Sand C- 16	(M)	Hillbilly Heaven	1961	12.00	30.00
Sound 603	(M)	Greatest Westerns	1957	12.00	30.00
DEAN, JIMMY					
Mercury MG-20319	(M)	His Television Favorites	1957	16.00	40.00
Columbia CL-1025	(M)	Hour Of Prayer	1957	14.00	35.00
King 686	(M)	Favorites Of Jimmy Dean	1961	20.00	50.00
Starday SLP-325	(M)	Bummin' Around	1965	12.00	30.00
DEBRIS					
Static Disposal	(S)	Debris	196?	14.00	35.00
DeCARLO, YVONNE					
Masterseal (No number)	(M)	Yvonne DeCarlo Sings	1957	20.00	50.00
DeCASTRO SISTERS, THE					
Abbott 5002	(M)	The DeCastro Sisters	195?	20.00	50.00
Capitol T-1402	(M)	The DeCastros Sing	1960	8.00	20.00
Capitol ST-1402	(S)	The DeCastros Sing	1960	10.00	25.00
Capitol T-1501	(M)	The Rockin' Beat	1961	8.00	20.00
Capitol ST-1501	(S)	The Rockin' Beat	1961	10.00	25.00
DEE, JOEY (& THE STARLIGHTERS)					
Roulette R-25166	(M)	Doin' The Twist	1961	10.00	25.00
Roulette SR-25166	(S)	Doin' The Twist	1961	14.00	35.00
Roulette R-25168	(M)	Hey, Let's Twist (Soundtrack)	1962	12.00	30.00
Roulette SR-25168	(S)	Hey, Let's Twist (Soundtrack)	1962	16.00	40.00
Roulette R-25171	(M)	All The World Is Twistin'	1962	8.00	20.00
Roulette SR-25171	(S)	All The World Is Twistin'	1962	12.00	30.00
Roulette R-25173	(M)	Back To The Peppermint Lounge Twistin'	1962	8.00	20.00
Roulette SR-25173	(S)	Back To The Peppermint Lounge Twistin'	1962	12.00	30.00
Roulette R-25182	(M)	Two Tickets To Paris (Soundtrack)	1962	8.00	20.00
Roulette SR-25182	(S)	Two Tickets To Paris (Soundtrack)	1962	12.00	30.00
Roulette R-25197	(M)	Joey Dee	1963	6.00	15.00
Roulette SR-25197	(S)	Joey Dee	1963	8.00	20.00
Roulette R-25221	(M)	Dance, Dance, Dance	1963	6.00	15.00
Roulette SR-25221	(S)	Dance, Dance, Dance	1963	8.00	20.00
DEEP, THE					
Parkway P-7051	(M)	Psychedelic Moods	1966	50.00	100.00
Parkway SP-7051	(S)	Psychedelic Moods	1966	75.00	150.00
DEEP PURPLE					
Deep Purple features Ritchie Blackmore, Ian Paice and Jon Lord.					
Tetragrammaton T-102	(S)	Shades Of Deep Purple	1968	8.00	20.00
Tetragrammaton T-107	(S)	Book Of Taliesyn	1969	8.00	20.00
Tetragrammaton T-119	(S)	Deep Purple	1969	8.00	20.00
Tetragrammaton T-131	(S)	Deep Purple & The Royal Philharmonic	1969	75.00	150.00
		(Withdrawn from circulation immediately after release.)			
Warner Bros. BS4-2607	(Q)	Machine Head	1973	8.00	20.00
Warner Bros. PR4-2832	(Q)	Stormbringer	1974	8.00	20.00
DEEP RIVER BOYS, THE					
Waldorf 108 (10")	(M)	Spirituals And Jubilees	1956	50.00	100.00
Waldorf 120 (10")	(M)	Spirituals	1956	50.00	100.00
Vik LXA-1019	(M)	The Deep River Boys	1956	50.00	100.00
Camden CAL-303	(M)	Presenting The Deep River Boys	1956	35.00	70.00
Que FLS-104	(M)	Midnight Magic	1957	35.00	70.00

Label & Catalog #		Title	Year	VG+	NM
DEEP SIX, THE					
Liberty LRP-3475	(M)	The Deep Six	1966	5.00	12.00
Liberty LST-7475	(S)	The Deep Six	1966	6.00	15.00
DEERFIELD					
Flat Rock FRS-1	(S)	Nil Desperandum	196?	50.00	100.00

One of the first— and only— real examples of Jamaican ska/rock steady to make a dent on the constricted American play-lists (at least since Millie Small's "My Boy Lollipop" in 1964), this style of music eventually evolved into reggae.

Label & Catalog #		Title	Year	VG+	NM
DEKKER, DESMOND (& THE ACES)					
Uni 73059	(P)	Israelites	1969	12.00	30.00
DEL SATINS, THE					
B.T. Puppy 1019	(S)	Out To Lunch	1972	50.00	100.00
DEL VIKINGS, THE [THE DELL VIKINGS]					
Luniverse LP-1000	(M)	Come Go With The Del Vikings	1957	240.00	400.00
Mercury MG-20314	(M)	They Sing-They Swing	1957	180.00	300.00
Mercury MG-20353	(M)	A Swinging, Singing Record Session	1958	180.00	300.00
Dot DLP-3695	(M)	Come Go With Me	1966	100.00	200.00
Dot DLP-25695	(S)	Come Go With Me	1966	180.00	300.00
DEL VIKINGS, THE / THE SONNETS					
Crown CLP-5368	(M)	The Del Vikings & The Sonnets	1963	16.00	40.00
DELFONICS, THE					
Philly Groove 1150	(S)	La La Means I Love You	1968	12.00	30.00
Philly Groove 1151	(S)	The Sexy Sound Of Soul	1969	8.00	20.00
Philly Groove 1152	(S)	The Super Hits	1969	8.00	20.00
Philly Groove 1153	(S)	The Delfonics	1970	8.00	20.00
Philly Groove 1154	(S)	Tell Me This Is A Dream	1972	8.00	20.00
Philly Groove 1501	(S)	Alive & Kicking	1974	8.00	20.00

Label & Catalog #		Title	Year	VG+	NM
DELLS, THE					
Vee Jay VJLP-1010	(M)	**Oh What A Nite** (Maroon label)	1959	180.00	300.00
Vee Jay VJLP-1010	(M)	**Oh What A Nite** (Black label)	196?	75.00	150.00
Vee Jay LP-1141	(M)	**It's Not Unusual**	1965	10.00	25.00
Vee Jay LPS-1141	(S)	**It's Not Unusual**	1965	12.00	30.00
Cadet LPS-804	(S)	**There Is**	1968	5.00	12.00
Cadet LPS-822	(S)	**Musical Menu/Always Together**	1969	5.00	12.00
Cadet LPS-829	(S)	**Love Is Blue**	1969	5.00	12.00
Cadet LPS-837	(S)	**Like It Is, Like It Was**	1970	5.00	12.00
Upfront UPF-103	(S)	**Stay In My Corner**	1968	5.00	12.00
Buddah BDS-5053	(S)	**The Dells**	1969	5.00	12.00
DELLWOODS, THE					
Big Top 1306	(M)	**Fink Along With Mad**	1963	14.00	35.00
DELMORE BROTHERS, THE					
The Delmores also recorded as members of The Brown's Ferry Four.					
King 589	(M)	**Songs By The Delmore Brothers**	1958	35.00	70.00
King 785	(M)	**30th Anniversary Album**	1962	20.00	50.00
King 910	(M)	**In Memory**	1964	14.00	35.00
King 920	(M)	**In Memory, Volume 2**	1964	14.00	35.00
King 983	(M)	**24 Great Country Songs**	1966	12.00	30.00
King S-983	(E)	**24 Great Country Songs**	1966	12.00	30.00
		— *Original King albums above have crownless black labels.*—			
DELTA RHYTHM BOYS, THE					
Mercury MG-25153 (10")	(M)	**The Delta Rhythm Boys**	1952	75.00	150.00
RCA Victor LPM-3085 (10")	(M)	**Dry Bones**	1953	50.00	100.00
Camden CAL-313	(M)	**The Delta Rhythm Boys**	1956	35.00	70.00
Elektra EKL-138	(M)	**The Delta Rhythm Boys**	1957	35.00	70.00
Jubilee LP-1022	(M)	**In Sweden**	1957	50.00	100.00
Jubilee LP-1022	(M)	**In Sweden** (Red vinyl)	1957	75.00	150.00
Coral CRL-57358	(M)	**Swingin' Spirituals**	1961	20.00	50.00
DEMENSIONS, THE					
Coral CRL-57430	(M)	**My Foolish Heart**	1963	75.00	150.00
DEMIAN					
Demian originally recorded as Bubble Puppy.					
ABC S-718	(S)	**Demian**	1970	12.00	30.00
DEREK & THE DOMINOS					
Derek is Eric Clapton; The Dominos feature Duane Allman.					
Atco SD-2-704	(S)	**Layla** (2 LPs)	1970	10.00	25.00
RSO 2-8800	(S)	**Derek & The Dominos In Concert** (2 LPs)	1973	6.00	15.00
Direct Disk SD-16629	(S)	**Layla** (2 LPs)	198?	20.00	50.00
DERRINGER, RICK					
Blue Sky PRO-265	(DJ)	**Live In Cleveland**	1977	8.00	20.00
DESANTO, SUGAR PIE					
Checker LP-2979	(M)	**Sugar Pie**	1961	20.00	50.00
DeSHANNON, JACKIE					
Liberty LRP-3320	(M)	**Jackie DeShannon**	1963	12.00	30.00
Liberty LST-7320	(S)	**Jackie DeShannon**	1963	16.00	40.00
Liberty LRP-3390	(M)	**Breakin' It Up On The Beatles Tour**	1964	20.00	50.00
Liberty LST-7390	(S)	**Breakin' It Up On The Beatles Tour**	1964	30.00	60.00
Imperial LP-9286	(M)	**This Is Jackie DeShannon**	1965	6.00	15.00
Imperial LP-12286	(S)	**This Is Jackie DeShannon**	1965	8.00	20.00
Imperial LP-9294	(M)	**You Won't Forget Me**	1965	6.00	15.00
Imperial LP-12294	(S)	**You Won't Forget Me**	1965	8.00	20.00
Imperial LP-9296	(M)	**In The Wind**	1965	6.00	15.00
Imperial LP-12296	(S)	**In The Wind**	1965	8.00	20.00
		— *Original Imperial albums above have black & pink labels.*—			
Imperial LP-9328	(M)	**Are You Ready For This?**	1966	5.00	12.00
Imperial LP-12328	(S)	**Are You Ready For This?**	1966	6.00	15.00
Imperial LP-9344	(M)	**New Image**	1967	5.00	12.00
Imperial LP-12344	(S)	**New Image**	1967	6.00	15.00

Label & Catalog #		Title	Year	VG+	NM
Imperial LP-9352	(M)	**For You**	1967	5.00	12.00
Imperial LP-12352	(S)	**For You**	1967	6.00	15.00
Imperial LP-9404	(M)	**What The World Needs Now Is Love**	1967	5.00	12.00
Imperial LP-12404	(P)	**What The World Needs Now Is Love**	1967	6.00	15.00
Imperial LP-12415	(M)	**Laurel Canyon**	1968	5.00	12.00
Imperial LP-12386	(S)	**Me About You**	1968	5.00	12.00
Imperial LP-12442	(S)	**Put A Little Love In Your Heart**	1969	5.00	12.00
Imperial LP-12453	(S)	**To Be Free**	1970	5.00	12.00

DETERGENTS, THE
The Detergents feature Ron Dante.

Roulette R-25308	(M)	**The Many Faces Of The Detergents**	1965	20.00	50.00
Roulette SR-25308	(E)	**The Many Faces Of The Detergents**	1965	16.00	40.00

DEUCE COUPES, THE

Del-Fi DFLP-1243	(M)	**Hotrodders' Choice**	1963	12.00	30.00
Del-Fi DFS-1243	(S)	**Hotrodders' Choice**	1963	16.00	40.00

DEUCE COUPES, THE

Crown CLP-5393	(M)	**The Shut Downs**	1964	5.00	12.00
Crown CST-393	(S)	**The Shut Downs**	1964	6.00	15.00

DEVIANTS, THE

Sire SES-97001	(S)	**Poof**	1969	30.00	60.00
Sire SES-97005	(S)	**Disposable**	1969	30.00	60.00
Sire SES-97016	(S)	**The Deviants, No. 3**	1969	30.00	60.00

DEVILED HAM

Super-K SKS-6003	(S)	**I Had Too Much To Dream Last Night**	1968	8.00	20.00

DEVIL'S ANVIL, THE

Columbia CL-2664	(M)	**Hard Rock From The Middle East**	1967	8.00	20.00
Columbia CS-9464	(S)	**Hard Rock From The Middle East**	1967	12.00	30.00

DEVROE, BILLY, &THE DEVILAIRES

Tampa 31	(M)	**Billy Devroe & The Devilaires, Volume 1**	196?	10.00	25.00
Tampa 39	(M)	**Billy Devroe & The Devilaires, Volume 2**	196?	10.00	25.00

DEXTER, AL

Columbia HL-9005 (10")	(M)	**Songs Of The Southwest**	1954	16.00	40.00
Harmony HL-7293	(M)	**Pistol Packin' Mama**	1961	8.00	20.00
Capitol T-1701	(M)	**His Greatest Hits**	1962	8.00	20.00
Capitol ST-1701	(S)	**His Greatest Hits**	1962	12.00	30.00

DIALOGUE

No label	(M)	**Dialogue** *(White cover with insert)*	196?	75.00	150.00
Cold Studio	(M)	**Dialogue** *(Orange cover with insert)*	196?	20.00	50.00

DIALS, THE

Time 2100	(M)	**It's Monkey Time**	1964	6.00	15.00
Time S-2100	(S)	**It's Monkey Time**	1964	8.00	20.00

DIAMOND, NEIL
Refer to Diana Ross / Neil Diamond.

Bang BLP-214	(M)	**The Feel Of Neil Diamond**	1966	16.00	40.00
Bang BLPS-214	(S)	**The Feel Of Neil Diamond**	1966	35.00	70.00
Bang BLP-217	(M)	**Just For You**	1967	8.00	20.00
Bang BLPS-217	(S)	**Just For You**	1967	12.00	30.00
Bang BLPS-219	(P)	**Neil Diamond's Greatest Hits**	1968	12.00	30.00
		(First pressings were issued with the original single versio of "Solitary Man" in rechanneled stereo.)			
Bang BLPS-219	(S)	**Neil Diamond's Greatest Hits**	1968	6.00	15.00
		(Later pressings were issued with a rerecorded "Solitary Man" in stereo, the version that is now played endlessly on the radio.)			
Bang BLPS-221	(S)	**Shilo**	1970	12.00	30.00
Bang BLPS-224	(P)	**Do It!**	1970	10.00	25.00
Bang BLPS-227	(P)	**Double Gold** *(2 LPs)*	1970	10.00	25.00

— Original Bang albums above have red & white labels.—

Label & Catalog #		Title	Year	VG+	NM

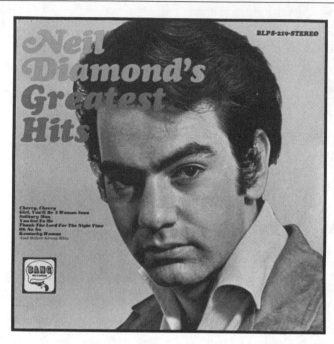

First pressings of "Neil Diamond's Greatest Hits" contain the original single "Solitary Man"
in rechanneled stereo; later pressings contain a re-recorded version in true stereo.
Unfortunately, the second version has little of the charm or impact of the original!

Label & Catalog #		Title	Year	VG+	NM
Uni ST-73030	(S)	Velvet Gloves And Spit	1968	8.00	20.00
Uni ST-73047	(S)	Brother Love's Traveling Salvation Show	1969	8.00	20.00
Uni ST-73071	(S)	Touching You, Touching Me	1969	8.00	20.00
Uni ND-11	(DJ)	Neil Diamond *(Radio sampler)*	1970	75.00	150.00
Uni ST-73084	(S)	Neil Diamond Gold	1970	8.00	20.00
Uni ST-73092	(S)	Tap Root Manuscript	1970	8.00	20.00
Uni ST-1913	(DJ)	Neil Diamond Open-End Interview	1971	100.00	200.00
Frog King AAR-1	(S)	Early Classics *(With songbook)*	1972	20.00	50.00
Frog King AAR-1	(S)	Early Classics *(Without book)*	1972	12.00	30.00
Columbia PCQ-32919	(Q)	Serenade	1974	10.00	25.00
Columbia HC-42550	(S)	Jonathan Livingston Seagull *(Half-speed)*	1982	10.00	25.00
Columbia HC-45625	(S)	You Don't Bring Me Flowers *(Half-speed)*	1982	10.00	25.00
Columbia HC-47628	(S)	On The Way To The Sky *(Half-speed)*	1982	10.00	25.00
Columbia HC-48068	(S)	12 Greatest Hits, Volume 2 *(Half-speed)*	1982	10.00	25.00
Columbia HC-48359	(S)	Heartlight *(Half-speed master)*	1982	10.00	25.00
Columbia 9C9-39915	(S)	Primitive *(Picture disc)*	1983	6.00	15.00
Harmony HS-30023	(S)	Chartbusters	197?	6.00	15.00
		(Various artist compilation contains both sides of Neil's first single, "Clown Town" and "I've Never Been The Same.")			
Mobile Fidelity MFSL-024	(S)	Hot August Night *(2 LPs)*	1979	16.00	40.00
Mobile Fidelity MFSL-071	(S)	Jazz Singer	1980	8.00	20.00
Direct Disk SD-16612	(S)	His 12 Greatest Hits	1982	8.00	20.00

DIAMONDS, THE

Label & Catalog #		Title	Year	VG+	NM
Mercury MG-20213	(M)	Collection Of Golden Hits	1956	50.00	100.00
Mercury MG-20309	(M)	The Diamonds	1957	50.00	100.00
Mercury MG-20368	(M)	The Diamonds Meet Pete Rugolo	1958	20.00	50.00
Mercury SR-60076	(S)	The Diamonds Meet Pete Rugolo	1958	35.00	70.00
Wing MGW-12114	(M)	The Diamonds	1962	12.00	30.00
Wing MGW-12178	(M)	Pop Hits By The Diamonds	1962	12.00	30.00
Sound Recorders SRS-4644	(S)	The Diamonds' '70s	1971	8.00	20.00

Label & Catalog #		Title	Year	VG+	NM

DICK & DEE DEE
Dick St. John and Dee Dee Sperling.

Liberty LRP-3236	(M)	Tell Me/The Mountain's High	1962	14.00	35.00
Liberty LST-7236	(E)	Tell Me/The Mountain's High	1962	12.00	30.00
Warner Bros. W-1500	(M)	Young & In Love	1963	6.00	15.00
Warner Bros. WS-1500	(S)	Young & In Love	1963	8.00	20.00
Warner Bros. W-1538	(M)	Turn Around	1964	6.00	15.00
Warner Bros. WS-1538	(S)	Turn Around	1964	8.00	20.00
Warner Bros. W-1586	(M)	Thou Shalt Not Steal	1965	6.00	15.00
Warner Bros. WS-1586	(S)	Thou Shalt Not Steal	1965	8.00	20.00
Warner Bros. W-1623	(M)	Songs We've Sung On Shindig	1965	6.00	15.00
Warner Bros. WS-1623	(S)	Songs We've Sung On Shindig	1965	8.00	20.00

DICKENS, LITTLE JIMMY

Columbia CL-9053 (10")	(M)	Old Country Church	1954	20.00	50.00
Columbia CL-1047	(M)	Raisin' The Dickens	1957	30.00	60.00
Columbia CL-1545	(M)	Big Songs	1960	8.00	20.00
Columbia CS-8345	(S)	Big Songs	1960	12.00	30.00
Columbia CL-1887	(M)	Out Behind The Barn	1962	8.00	20.00
Columbia CS-8687	(S)	Out Behind The Barn	1962	12.00	30.00

— *Original Columbia albums above have three white "eye" logos on each side of the spindle hole.*—

| Harmony HL-7311 | (M) | Little Jimmy Dickens' Best | 1964 | 10.00 | 25.00 |

DICKEY DOO & THE DONT'S

United Arts. UAL-3094	(M)	Madison	1960	16.00	40.00
United Arts. UAS-6094	(S)	Madison	1960	20.00	50.00
United Arts. UAL-3097	(M)	Teen Scene	1960	16.00	40.00
United Arts. UAS-6097	(S)	Teen Scene	1960	20.00	50.00

DICTATORS, THE

Epic KE-33348	(S)	The Dictators Go Girl Crazy	1975	5.00	12.00
Asylum 7E-1109	(S)	Manifest Destiny	1977	4.00	10.00
Asylum 6E-147	(S)	Bloodbrothers	1978	4.00	10.00

DIDDLEY, BO
Bo Diddley is a pseudonym for Ellas McDaniel.

Chess LP-1431	(M)	Bo Diddley	1958	40.00	80.00
Chess LP-1436	(M)	Go Bo Diddley	1959	35.00	70.00
Checker LP-2974	(M)	Have Guitar, Will Travel	1960	35.00	70.00
Checker LP-2976	(M)	Bo Diddley In The Spotlight	1960	35.00	70.00
Checker LP-2977	(M)	Bo Diddley Is A Gunslinger	1960	40.00	80.00
Checker LP-2980	(M)	Bo Diddley Is A Lover	1961	40.00	80.00
Checker LP-2982	(M)	Bo Diddley's A Twister	1962	35.00	70.00
Checker LP-2984	(M)	Bo Diddley	1962	35.00	70.00
Checker LP-2985	(M)	Bo Diddley And Company	1963	40.00	80.00
Checker LP-2987	(M)	Surfin' With Bo Diddley	1963	20.00	50.00
Checker LPS-2987	(E)	Surfin' With Bo Diddley	1963	12.00	30.00
Checker LP-2988	(M)	Bo Diddley's Beach Party	1963	30.00	60.00
Checker LPS-2988	(E)	Bo Diddley's Beach Party	1963	20.00	50.00
Checker LP-2989	(M)	16 All Time Greatest Hits	1964	16.00	40.00
Checker LPS-2989	(E)	16 All Time Greatest Hits	1964	12.00	30.00
Checker LP-2992	(M)	Hey! Good Lookin'	1965	12.00	30.00
Checker LPS-2992	(E)	Hey! Good Lookin'	1965	10.00	25.00
Checker LP-2996	(M)	500% More Man	1965	14.00	35.00
Checker LPS-2996	(E)	500% More Man	1965	12.00	30.00

— *Original Chess 1 albums above have black labels with silver logo on the left.*
The back covers read "Chess Producing Corporation."—

Checker LP-3001	(M)	The Originator	1966	10.00	25.00
Checker LPS-3001	(S)	The Originator	1966	12.00	30.00
Checker LP-2982	(M)	Road Runner	1967	30.00	60.00
Checker LPS-2982	(E)	Road Runner	1967	20.00	50.00

("Road Runner is a reissue of "Bo Diddley's A Twister.")

Checker LP-3006	(M)	Go Bo Diddley (Reissue of Chess 1436)	1967	16.00	40.00
Checker LPS-3006	(E)	Go Bo Diddley (Reissue of Chess 1436)	1967	14.00	35.00
Checker LP-3007	(M)	Boss Man (Reissue of Chess 1431)	1967	35.00	70.00
Checker LPS-3007	(E)	Boss Man (Reissue of Chess 1431)	1967	30.00	60.00

— *Original Chess albums above have blue & white labels with red, white & blue logo on top.*—

| Checker LP-3013 | (M) | The Black Gladiator | 1970 | 12.00 | 30.00 |
| Checker LPS-3013 | (S) | The Black Gladiator | 1970 | 14.00 | 35.00 |

Label & Catalog #		Title	Year	VG+	NM
Chess CH-50001	(S)	Another Dimension	1971	16.00	40.00
Chess 2CH-60005	(E)	Got My Own Bag Of Tricks (2 LPs)	1972	10.00	25.00
Chess CH-50016	(S)	Where It All Began	1972	16.00	40.00
Chess CH-50029	(S)	The London Bo Diddley Sessions	1973	10.00	25.00
Chess CH-50047	(S)	Big Bad Bo	1974	10.00	25.00
RCA Victor APL1-1229	(S)	The 20th Anniversary Of Rock N' Roll	1976	8.00	20.00
MF 2002	(S)	I'm A Man (2 Lps)	1977	50.00	100.00
Accord SN-7812	(S)	Toronto Rock And Roll Revival, Volume 5	1982	8.00	20.00
Check Mate 1960	(S)	Give Me A Break	1988	6.00	15.00

DIDDLEY, BO, & CHUCK BERRY

Checker LP-2991	(M)	Two Great Guitars	1964	20.00	50.00
Checker LPS-2991	(E)	Two Great Guitars	1964	16.00	40.00

DIDDLEY, BO; MUDDY WATERS & HOWLIN' WOLF

Checker LP-3010	(M)	Super, Super Blues Band	1968	16.00	40.00
Checker LPS-3010	(S)	Super, Super Blues Band	1968	20.00	50.00

(Blue/white label with red, white & blue logo on top.)

DIDDLEY, BO; MUDDY WATERS & LITTLE WALTER

Checker LP-3008	(M)	Super Blues	1968	16.00	40.00
Checker LPS-3008	(S)	Super Blues	1968	20.00	50.00

The inimitable Ms. Dietrich's "style" of singing and performing was mocked with loving perfection by Madeline Kahn's hilarious Lili von Stupf in Mel Brooks' "Blazing Saddles."

DIETRICH, MARLENE

Decca DL-5100 (10")	(M)	Souvenir Album	1950	20.00	50.00
Polydor PL-3040 (10")	(M)	Marlene Dietrich Sings	1950	20.00	50.00
Vox PL-3040 (10")	(M)	Marlene Dietrich Sings	1951	16.00	40.00
Columbia GL-105 (10")	(M)	American Songs In German For The OSS	1952	20.00	50.00
Columbia GL-164 (10")	(M)	Marlene Dietrich In Rio	1953	20.00	50.00
Columbia ML-4975	(M)	Cafe De Paris	1955	16.00	40.00
Decca DL-8465	(M)	Marlene	1957	16.00	40.00
Columbia CL-1275	(M)	Lile Marlene	1959	12.00	30.00
Capitol T-10397	(M)	Marlene	1965	8.00	20.00
Capitol ST-10397	(S)	Marlene	1965	10.00	25.00
Capitol OTCR-300	(M)	The Magic Of Marlene	1969	10.00	25.00

Label & Catalog #		Title	Year	VG+	NM

DIGA RHYTHM BAND, THE
The Digas are Mickey Hart and Bill Kreutzmann of The Grateful Dead.

Round RX-110	(S)	**The Diga Rhythm Band**	1976	10.00	25.00

DILLARD, DOUG
Refer to Dillard & Clark; The Dillards; Dillard & Boyce.

Together STT-1003	(S)	**Banjo Album**	1970	30.00	60.00

DILLARD & CLARK [THE DILLARD & CLARK EXPEDITION]
Doug Dillard and Gene Clark.

A&M SD-4158	(S)	**The Fantastic Expedition** *(Brown label)*	1969	8.00	20.00
A&M SD-4203	(S)	**Through The Morning, Through The Night**	1970	6.00	15.00

DILLARDS, THE
Features Doug Dillard.

Elektra EKL-232	(M)	**Back Porch Bluegrass**	1963	10.00	25.00
Elektra EKS-7232	(S)	**Back Porch Bluegrass**	1963	14.00	35.00
Elektra EKL-265	(M)	**The Dillards Live! Almost!**	1964	8.00	20.00
Elektra EKS-7265	(S)	**The Dillards Live! Almost!**	1964	10.00	25.00
Elektra EKL-285	(M)	**Pickin' And Fiddlin' With Byron Berline**	1965	8.00	20.00
Elektra EKS-7285	(S)	**Pickin' And Fiddlin' With Byron Berline**	1965	10.00	25.00
Elektra EKS-74035	(S)	**Wheatstraw Suite**	1969	6.00	15.00
Elektra EKS-74054	(S)	**The Dillards-Copperfields**	1969	6.00	15.00
Crystal Clear CCS-5007	(S)	**Mountain Rock**	1979	8.00	20.00

DIMENSIONS, THE

No label	(M)	**From All Dimensions**	1966	300.00	500.00

DING DONGS, THE

Motown 716	(S)	**Gimme Dat Ding**	1970	6.00	15.00

DINNING, MARK

MGM E-3828	(M)	**Teen Angel**	1960	35.00	70.00
MGM SE-3828	(S)	**Teen Angel**	1960	50.00	100.00
MGM E-3855	(M)	**Wanderin'**	1960	20.00	50.00
MGM SE-3855	(S)	**Wanderin'**	1960	35.00	70.00

DINO, DESI & BILLY
Dino Martin, Desi Arnez, Jr. and Billy Hinsche.

Reprise R-6176	(M)	**I'm A Fool**	1965	6.00	15.00
Reprise RS-6176	(S)	**I'm A Fool**	1965	8.00	20.00
Reprise R-6194	(M)	**Our Times Coming**	1966	5.00	12.00
Reprise RS-6194	(S)	**Our Times Coming**	1966	6.00	15.00
Reprise R-6198	(M)	**Memories Are Made Of This**	1966	5.00	12.00
Reprise RS-6198	(S)	**Memories Are Made Of This**	1966	6.00	15.00
Reprise R-6224	(M)	**Souvenir**	1966	5.00	12.00
Reprise RS-6224	(S)	**Souvenir**	1966	6.00	15.00
Uni 73056	(S)	**Follow Me** *(Soundtrack)*	1969	8.00	20.00

DION

Laurie LLP-2004	(M)	**Alone With Dion**	1960	35.00	70.00
Laurie LLP-2009	(M)	**Runaround Sue**	1961	35.00	70.00
Laurie LLP-2009	(M)	**Runaround Sue** *(Blue/green vinyl)*	1961	75.00	150.00
Capitol DT-91027	(E)	**Runaround Sue** *(Capitol Record Club)*	1962	50.00	100.00
Laurie LLP-2012	(M)	**Lovers Who Wander**	1962	35.00	70.00
Laurie LLP-2015	(M)	**Love Came To Me**	1963	35.00	70.00
Laurie LLP-2017	(M)	**Dion Sings To Sandy & All Other Girls**	1963	20.00	50.00
Laurie LLP-2019	(M)	**Dion Sings The 15 Million Sellers**	1963	20.00	50.00
Laurie LLP-2022	(M)	**More Of Dion's Greatest Hits**	1963	20.00	50.00
		— Original Laurie albums above have black & gold labels;			
		the five points of the background star have large ben-day dots.—			
Columbia CL-2010	(M)	**Ruby Baby**	1963	8.00	20.00
Columbia CS-8810	(S)	**Ruby Baby**	1963	12.00	30.00
Columbia CL-2107	(M)	**Donna The Prima Donna**	1963	8.00	20.00
Columbia CS-8907	(S)	**Donna The Prima Donna**	1963	12.00	30.00
Columbia CS-9773	(S)	**Wonder Where I'm Bound**	1969	6.00	15.00
		— Original Columbia albums above have "360 Sound" on the bottom of the label.—			
Laurie SLP-2047	(S)	**Dion**	1968	8.00	20.00
Warner Bros. WS-1826	(S)	**Sit Down Old Friend**	1969	6.00	15.00

Label & Catalog #		Title	Year	VG+	NM
Warner Bros. WS-1872	(S)	**You're Not Alone**	1971	6.00	15.00
Warner Bros. WS-1945	(S)	**Sanctuary**	1971	6.00	15.00
Warner Bros. BS-2642	(S)	**Suite For Late Summer**	1972	4.00	10.00
Warner Bros. BS-2954	(S)	**Streetheart**	1976	4.00	10.00

DION & THE BELMONTS
Features Dion DiMucci.

Laurie LLP-2002	(M)	**Presenting Dion & The Belmonts**	1959	75.00	150.00
Laurie LLP-2006	(M)	**Wish Upon A Star**	1960	35.00	70.00
Laurie LLP-2013	(M)	**Dion Sings His Greatest Hits**	1962	35.00	70.00
Laurie LLPS-2013	(S)	**Dion Sings His Greatest Hits**	1962	75.00	150.00
Laurie LLP-2016	(M)	**By Special Request**	1963	20.00	50.00

— Original Laurie albums above have black & gold labels;
the five points of the background star have large, coarse ben-day dots.—

ABC 599	(M)	**Together Again**	1967	10.00	25.00
ABC S-599	(S)	**Together Again**	1967	12.00	30.00
Warner Bros. BS-2664	(S)	**Dion & The Belmonts Live 1972**	1973	8.00	20.00
Laurie SLP-6000	(P)	**60 Greatest** *(3 LPs in a box)*	197?	8.00	20.00
Laurie SLP-6000	(P)	**60 Greatest** *(3 LPs in a sleeve)*	197?	4.00	10.00
Laurie LES-4002	(S)	**Everything You Always Wanted To Hear**	197?	4.00	10.00

DIRE STRAITS

Warner Bros. 23738	(DJ)	**Love Over Gold** *(Quiex II vinyl)*	1982	6.00	15.00
Warner Bros. 25264	(DJ)	**Brothers In Arms** *(Quiex II vinyl)*	1983	6.00	15.00
Warner Bros. 27085	(DJ)	**Alchemy** *(2 LPs. Quiex II vinyl)*	1984	8.00	20.00

DIRTY BLUES BAND, THE

BluesWay BLS-6010	(S)	**Dirty Blues Band**	1968	6.00	15.00
BluesWay BLS-6020	(S)	**Stone Dirt**	1968	6.00	15.00

*One of the classic girl group numbers of the early '60s, "Chapel Of Love" was originally intended
for The Ronettes! This album was repackaged as "Iko Iko" when that song became a hit.*

DIXIE CUPS, THE

Red Bird RB-20-100	(M)	**Chapel Of Love**	1964	14.00	35.00
Red Bird RBS-20-100	(S)	**Chapel Of Love**	1964	20.00	50.00

Label & Catalog #		Title	Year	VG+	NM
Red Bird RB-20-103	(M)	Iko Iko	1965	14.00	35.00
Red Bird RBS-20-103	(S)	Iko Iko	1965	20.00	50.00
ABC-Paramount 525	(M)	Riding High	1965	10.00	25.00
ABC-Paramount S-525	(S)	Riding High	1965	14.00	35.00
DIXIE DREGS, THE					
No label	(S)	The Great Spectacular	1975	100.00	200.00
Direct Disk SD-16620	(S)	Dregs Of The Earth	198?	12.00	30.00
DIXIEBELLES, THE					
Sound Stage-7 SSM-5000	(M)	Down At Poppa Joe's	1963	12.00	30.00
Sound Stage-7 SM-1500	(E)	Down At Poppa Joe's	1963	10.00	25.00
DIXON, WILLIE					
Columbia CS-9987	(S)	I Am The Blues ("360 Sound" label)	1970	6.00	15.00
DIXON, WILLIE, & MEMPHIS SLIM					
Bluesville BV-1003	(M)	Willie's Blues	1960	12.00	30.00
Verve V-3007	(M)	Blues Every Which Way	1961	8.00	20.00
Verve V6-3007	(S)	Blues Every Which Way	1961	10.00	25.00
Battle BV-6122	(M)	In Paris	1963	8.00	20.00
Battle BVS-6122	(S)	In Paris	1963	10.00	25.00

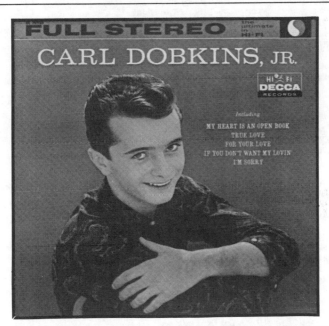

Carl's big hit, 1959's "My Heart Is An Open Book," and the minor follow-up, "If You Don't Want My Lovin,'" appear on his eponymous first album in stereo.

DOBKINS, JR., CARL					
Decca DL-8938	(M)	Carl Dobkins, Jr.	1959	18.00	45.00
Decca DL-78938	(S)	Carl Dobkins, Jr.	1959	30.00	60.00
DR. FEELGOOD & THE INTERNS					
OKeh OKM-12101	(M)	Doctor Feelgood & The Interns	1962	14.00	35.00
OKeh OKS-14101	(S)	Doctor Feelgood & The Interns	1962	20.00	50.00
DR. JOHN (THE NIGHT TRIPPER)					
Dr. John is a pseudonym for Mac Rebennack.					
Atco SD-33-234	(S)	Gris-Gris	1968	6.00	15.00

Label & Catalog #		Title	Year	VG+	NM
Atco SD-33-270	(S)	Babylon	1969	6.00	15.00
Atco SD-33-316	(S)	Remedies	1970	6.00	15.00
Atco SD-33-362	(S)	The Sun, Moon And Herbs	1971	6.00	15.00

DR. ROSS

Testament 2206	(M)	Doctor Ross	196?	8.00	20.00
Fortune FS-3011	(S)	Doctor Ross, The Harmonica Boss	196?	8.00	20.00

DR. WEST'S MEDICINE SHOW & JUG BAND
Dr. West's Band features Norman Greenbaum.

Go Go 22-17-002	(M)	The Eggplant That Ate Chicago	1967	8.00	20.00
Go Go 22-17-002	(E)	The Eggplant That Ate Chicago	1967	6.00	15.00

DODD, DICK
Dodd was formerly a member of The Standells.

Tower ST-5142	(S)	First Evolution Of Dick Dodd	1968	20.00	50.00

DODD, JIMMIE

Imperial LP-9121	(M)	Swing-A-Spell	1960	12.00	30.00
Disneyland DQ-1235	(M)	Sing Along With Jimmie Dodd	1962	10.00	25.00
Disneyland WDL-3014	(M)	His Favorite Hymns	1963	6.00	15.00

DODSON, MARGE

Columbia CL-1309	(M)	In The Still Of The Night	1959	10.00	25.00
Columbia CS-8134	(S)	In The Still Of The Night	1959	14.00	35.00
Columbia CL-1458	(M)	New Voice In Town	1960	10.00	25.00

DOHERTY, DENNY
Mr. Doherty was formerly a member of The Mugwumps; The Mamas & The Papas.

Dunhill DS-50096	(S)	Watcha' Gonna Do?	1970	6.00	15.00
Ember EMS-1036	(S)	Waiting For A Song	1975	4.00	10.00

DOJO

Eclipse ES-7309	(S)	Down For The Last Time	1971	10.00	25.00

DOLENZ, JONES, BOYCE & HART
Mickey Dolenz, Davey Jones, Tommy Boyce and Bobby Hart. Refer to The Monkees.

Capitol ST-11513	(S)	Dolenz, Jones, Boyce And Hart	1976	10.00	25.00

DOMINO, FATS

Imperial LP-9004	(M)	Rock And Rollin' With Fats Domino	1956	65.00	130.00
Imperial LP-9009	(M)	Rock And Rollin'	1956	65.00	130.00
Imperial LP-9028	(M)	This Is Fats Domino!	1957	65.00	130.00
Imperial LP-9038	(M)	Here Stands Fats Domino	1957	65.00	130.00
Imperial LP-9040	(M)	This Is Fats	1957	65.00	130.00
— *Original Imperial albums above have maroon labels.*—					
Imperial LP-9004	(M)	Rock And Rollin' With Fats Domino	1958	20.00	50.00
Imperial LP-9009	(M)	Rock And Rollin'	1958	20.00	50.00
Imperial LP-9028	(M)	This Is Fats Domino!	1958	20.00	50.00
Imperial LP-9038	(M)	Here Stands Fats Domino	1958	20.00	50.00
Imperial LP-9055	(M)	The Fabulous Mr. D	1958	20.00	50.00
Imperial LP-9062	(M)	Fats Domino Swings	1959	20.00	50.00
Imperial LP-9103	(M)	Million Record Hits	1960	20.00	50.00
Imperial LP-9127	(M)	A Lot Of Dominos	1961	16.00	40.00
Imperial LP-12066	(S)	A Lot Of Dominos	1961	50.00	100.00
Imperial LP-9138	(M)	I Miss You So	1961	16.00	40.00
Imperial LP-12398	(E)	I Miss You So	1961	16.00	40.00
Imperial LP-9153	(M)	Let The Four Winds Blow	1961	16.00	40.00
Imperial LP-12073	(S)	Let The Four Winds Blow	1961	50.00	100.00
Imperial LP-9164	(M)	What A Party	1962	16.00	40.00
Imperial LP-9170	(M)	Twistin' The Stomp	1962	16.00	40.00
Imperial LP-9195	(M)	Million Sellers By Fats	1962	12.00	30.00
Imperial LP-9208	(M)	Just Domino	1962	16.00	40.00
Imperial LP-9227	(M)	Walking To New Orleans	1963	12.00	30.00
Imperial LP-9239	(M)	Let's Dance With Domino	1963	12.00	30.00
Imperial LP-9248	(M)	Here He Comes Again	1963	12.00	30.00

— *Imperial mono albums above have black labels with colored stars on top; stereo album have black labels with silver print.*—

Label & Catalog #		Title	Year	VG+	NM
Imperial LP-9004	(M)	Rock And Rollin' With Fats Domino	1964	10.00	25.00
Imperial LP-12387	(E)	Rock And Rollin' With Fats Domino	1964	8.00	20.00
Imperial LP-9009	(M)	Rock And Rollin'	1964	10.00	25.00
Imperial LP-12388	(E)	Rock And Rollin'	1964	8.00	20.00
Imperial LP-9028	(M)	This Is Fats Domino!	1964	10.00	25.00
Imperial LP-12389	(E)	This Is Fats Domino!	1964	8.00	20.00
Imperial LP-9038	(M)	Here Stands Fats Domino	1964	10.00	25.00
Imperial LP-12390	(E)	Here Stands Fats Domino	1964	8.00	20.00
Imperial LP-9040	(M)	This Is Fats	1964	10.00	25.00
Imperial LP-12391	(E)	This Is Fats	1964	8.00	20.00
Imperial LP-9055	(M)	The Fabulous Mr. D	1964	10.00	25.00
Imperial LP-12394	(E)	The Fabulous Mr. D	1964	8.00	20.00
Imperial LP-9062	(M)	Fats Domino Swings	1964	10.00	25.00
Imperial LP-12091	(E)	Fats Domino Swings	1964	8.00	20.00
Imperial LP-9065	(M)	Let's Play Fats Domino	1964	10.00	25.00
Imperial LP-12395	(E)	Let's Play Fats Domino	1964	8.00	20.00
Imperial LP-9103	(M)	Million Record Hits	1964	10.00	25.00
Imperial LP-12103	(E)	Million Record Hits	1964	8.00	20.00
Imperial LP-9127	(M)	A Lot Of Dominos	1964	10.00	25.00
Imperial LP-12066	(S)	A Lot Of Dominos	1964	14.00	35.00
Imperial LP-9138	(M)	I Miss You So	1964	10.00	25.00
Imperial LP-12398	(E)	I Miss You So	1964	8.00	20.00
Imperial LP-9153	(M)	Let The Four Winds Blow	1964	10.00	25.00
Imperial LP-12073	(S)	Let The Four Winds Blow	1964	14.00	35.00
Imperial LP-9195	(M)	Million Sellers By Fats	1964	10.00	25.00
Imperial LP-12195	(S)	Million Sellers By Fats	1964	12.00	30.00
Imperial LP-9227	(M)	Walking To New Orleans	1964	10.00	25.00
Imperial LP-12227	(E)	Walking To New Orleans	1964	8.00	20.00
Imperial LP-9239	(M)	Let's Dance With Domino	1964	10.00	25.00
Imperial LP-12239	(E)	Let's Dance With Domino	1964	8.00	20.00
Imperial LP-9248	(M)	Here He Comes Again	1964	10.00	25.00
Imperial LP-12248	(E)	Here He Comes Again	1964	8.00	20.00
		— Imperial albums above have black & pink labels.—			
ABC Paramount 455	(M)	Here Comes Fats Domino	1963	8.00	20.00
ABC Paramount S-455	(S)	Here Comes Fats Domino	1963	10.00	25.00
ABC Paramount 479	(M)	Fats On Fire	1964	8.00	20.00
ABC Paramount S-479	(S)	Fats On Fire	1964	10.00	25.00
ABC Paramount 510	(M)	Getaway With Fats Domino	1965	8.00	20.00
ABC Paramount S-510	(S)	Getaway With Fats Domino	1965	10.00	25.00
Grand Award G-267	(M)	Fats Domino	196?	6.00	15.00
Grand Award GS-267	(E)	Fats Domino	196?	5.00	12.00
Mercury MG-21029	(M)	Fats Domino '65	1965	16.00	40.00
Mercury MG-21029	(M)	Fats Domino '65	1965	10.00	25.00
Mercury SR-61029	(S)	Fats Domino '65	1965	12.00	30.00
Mercury MG-21065	(M)	Southland U.S.A.	1966	See note below	
Mercury SR-61065	(S)	Southland U.S.A.	1966	See note below	
		(Mercury 21/61065 was withdrawn before commercial distribution. Should copies, exist they are rare.)			
Sunset SUM-1103	(M)	Fats Domino	1966	5.00	12.00
Sunset SUS-5103	(S)	Fats Domino	1966	8.00	20.00
Sunset SUM-1158	(M)	Stompin' Fats Domino	1967	5.00	12.00
Sunset SUS-5158	(S)	Stompin' Fats Domino	1967	8.00	20.00
Sunset SUS-5200	(S)	Trouble In Mind	1968	8.00	20.00
Sunset SUS-5299	(S)	Ain't That A Shame	1970	8.00	20.00
Reprise RS-6304	(S)	Fats Is Back	1968	8.00	20.00
Reprise RS-6439	(S)	Fats	1971	See note below	
		(Reprise 6439 was withdrawn before commercial distribution. Should copies, exist they are rare!.			
Reprise RS-6439	(S)	Fats (Test pressing)	1971	See note below	
		(Rare. Estimated near mint value $300-500.)			
United Arts. UAS-9958	(M)	Legendary Masters (2 LPs)	1971	6.00	15.00
United Artists LA122	(M)	Cookin' With Fats (2 LPs)	1974	8.00	20.00

DON & DEWEY
Don "Sugarcane" Harris and Dewey Terry.

Specialty SPS-2131	(E)	They're Rockin' Til Midnight, Rollin' Til Dawn	1970	8.00	20.00

Label & Catalog #		Title	Year	VG+	NM

DON & THE GOOD TIMES
Refer to Jim Valley.

Label & Catalog #		Title	Year	VG+	NM
Burdette 300	(M)	Don & The Goodtimes' Greatest Hits	1966	20.00	50.00
Epic LN-24311	(M)	So Good	1967	5.00	12.00
Epic BN-26311	(S)	So Good	1967	6.00	15.00
Wand WDS-679	(S)	Where The Action Is	1969	12.00	30.00

DON, DICK & JIMMY

Modern LMP-1205	(M)	Spring Fever	195?	16.00	40.00
Verve MGV-2084	(M)	Medium Rare	195?	6.00	15.00
Verve MGV-2107	(M)	Songs For The Hearth	195?	6.00	15.00

DONEGAN, LONNIE

Mercury MG-20229	(M)	An Englishman Sings American Folk Songs	1957	12.00	30.00
Dot DLP-3159	(M)	Lonnie Donegan	1959	10.00	25.00
Dot DLP-3394	(M)	Lonnie Donegan	1961	8.00	20.00
Atlantic 8038	(M)	Skiffle Folk Music	1960	8.00	20.00
Atlantic SD-8038	(S)	Skiffle Folk Music	1960	10.00	25.00
ABC-Paramount 433	(M)	Sing Hallelujah	1963	5.00	12.00
ABC-Paramount S-433	(S)	Sing Hallelujah	1963	6.00	15.00

DONNER, RAL

Gone LP-5012	(M)	Takin' Care Of Business	1961	100.00	200.00

DONNER, RAL / RAY SMITH / BOBBY DALE

Crown CLP-5335	(M)	Ral Donner, Ray Smith And Bobby Dale	1963	8.00	20.00
Crown CST-335	(E)	Ral Donner, Ray Smith And Bobby Dale	1963	6.00	15.00

DONOVAN (DONOVAN LEITCH)

Hickory LPM-123	(M)	Catch The Wind	1965	8.00	20.00
Hickory LPS-123	(E)	Catch The Wind	1965	6.00	15.00
Hickory LPM-127	(M)	Fairy Tale	1965	8.00	20.00
Hickory LPS-127	(E)	Fairy Tale	1965	6.00	15.00
Hickory LPM-135	(M)	The Real Donovan	1966	8.00	20.00
Hickory LPS-135	(E)	The Real Donovan	1966	6.00	15.00
Hickory LPS-143	(E)	Like It Is, Was And Evermore Shall Be	1968	8.00	20.00
Hickory LPS-149	(E)	The Best Of Donovan	1969	6.00	15.00
Epic LN-24217	(M)	Sunshine Superman	1966	8.00	20.00
Epic BN-26217	(E)	Sunshine Superman	1966	5.00	12.00
Epic LN-24239	(M)	Mellow Yellow	1967	8.00	20.00
Epic BN-26239	(E)	Mellow Yellow	1967	5.00	12.00
Epic LN-24349	(M)	Wear Your Love Like Heaven	1967	6.00	15.00
Epic BN-26349	(S)	Wear Your Love Like Heaven	1967	5.00	12.00
Epic LN-24350	(M)	For Little Ones	1967	6.00	15.00
Epic BN-26350	(S)	For Little Ones	1967	5.00	12.00
Epic L2N-171	(M)	A Gift From A Flower To A Garden	1968	16.00	40.00
Epic B2N-171	(S)	A Gift From A Flower To A Garden	1968	10.00	25.00

(Boxed set of the two previous albums, "Wear Your Love Like Heaven" and "For Little Ones." Issued with a portfolio of lyrics, drawings, and poetry, which are included in the price.)

Epic BN-26386	(S)	Donovan In Concert	1968	5.00	12.00
Epic BXN-26439	(P)	Donovan's Greatest Hits	1969	5.00	12.00
Epic BN-26481	(S)	Barabajagal	1969	5.00	12.00
Epic E-30125	(S)	Open Road	1970	5.00	12.00

— Original Epic albums above have yellow labels.—

DOOBIE BROTHERS, THE

Warner Bros. BS4-2634	(Q)	Toulouse Street	1974	6.00	15.00
Warner Bros. BS4-2694	(Q)	The Captain And Me	1974	6.00	15.00
Warner Bros. WS4-2750	(Q)	What Were Once Vices Are Now Habits	1974	6.00	15.00
Warner Bros. BS4-2835	(Q)	Stampede	1975	6.00	15.00
Nautilus NR-5	(S)	The Captain And Me	1980	10.00	25.00
Nautilus NR-18	(S)	Minute By Minute	1981	6.00	15.00
Mobile Fidelity MFSL-122	(S)	Takin' It To The Streets	198?	6.00	15.00

DOONICAN, VAL

Decca DL-4962	(M)	If The Whole World Stopped Lovin'	1966	5.00	12.00
Decca DL-74962	(S)	If The Whole World Stopped Lovin'	1966	6.00	15.00

Since breaking through in 1967 with one of the most impressive first albums of the decade, The Doors have watched their reputation as a band eclipsed by the excesses of their self-destructive lead singer. Mono copies of this album are in demand due to the different mix, particularly on the final track, "The End," where a certain expletive can be heard that was mixed out in stereo. Regardless of the claims for the remastered sterility of the CD, the Mobile Fidelity pressing is the best sounding version, being a truer representation of the original sound the group sought.

Label & Catalog #		Title	Year	VG+	NM
London PL-3515	(M)	The Many Shades Of Val Doonican	1967	5.00	12.00
London PS-515	(S)	The Many Shades Of Val Doonican	1967	6.00	15.00

DOORS, THE
The Doors are John Densmore, Robbie Krieger, Ray Manzarek and Jim Morrison.

Elektra EKL-4007	(M)	The Doors	1967	20.00	50.00
Elektra EKS-74007	(S)	The Doors	1967	8.00	20.00
Elektra EKL-4014	(M)	Strange Days	1967	20.00	50.00
Elektra EKS-74014	(S)	Strange Days	1967	8.00	20.00
Elektra EKL-4024	(M)	Waiting For The Sun	1968	50.00	100.00
Elektra EKS-74024	(S)	Waiting For The Sun	1968	8.00	20.00
		— Original Elektra albums above have brown labels.—			
Elektra EKS-75005	(S)	The Soft Parade (Red label)	1969	6.00	15.00
Elektra EKS-75007	(S)	Morrison Hotel/Hard Rock Cafe (Red label)	1970	6.00	15.00
Elektra EKS-2-9002	(S)	Absolutely Live (2 LPs)	1970	8.00	20.00
Elektra EKS-74079	(S)	The Doors 13	1970	4.00	10.00
Elektra EKS-75011	(S)	L.A. Woman (Die-cut window cover)	1971	10.00	25.00
Elektra EKS-75017	(S)	Other Voices	1971	4.00	10.00
Elektra EKS-2-6001	(S)	Weird Scenes Inside The Gold Mine (2 LPs)	1972	5.00	12.00
Elektra EKS-75038	(S)	Full Circle	1972	4.00	10.00
Elektra EQ-5035	(Q)	Best Of The Doors	1973	10.00	25.00
		— Original Elektra albums above have "butterfly" labels.—			
Mobile Fidelity MSFL-051	(S)	The Doors	1980	16.00	40.00

DORS, DIANA

Columbia CL-1436	(M)	Swinging Dors	1960	14.00	35.00
Columbia CS-8236	(S)	Swinging Dors	1960	20.00	50.00

DORSEY, LEE

Fury 1002	(M)	Ya Ya	1962	30.00	60.00
Sphere Sound SR-7003	(M)	Ya Ya	1963	16.00	40.00
Sphere Sound SSR-7003	(E)	Ya Ya	1963	12.00	30.00
Amy 8010	(M)	Ride Your Pony	1966	8.00	20.00
Amy S-8010	(S)	Ride your Pony	1966	10.00	25.00
Amy 8011	(M)	The New Lee Dorsey	1966	8.00	20.00
Amy 8011	(S)	The New Lee Dorsey	1966	10.00	25.00

DOUGLAS, GLEN

Decca DL-8748	(M)	Heartbreak Alley	1958	16.00	40.00

DOUGLAS, K.C.

Cook LP-5002	(M)	Road Recordings	1954	100.00	200.00
Bluesville BV-1023	(M)	K.C. Douglas	1961	12.00	30.00
Bluesville BV-1050	(M)	K.C. Douglas	1962	12.00	30.00

DOVELLS, THE
The Dovells feature Len Barry. Refer to the Orlons.

Parkway P-7006	(M)	The Bristol Stomp	1961	30.00	60.00
Parkway P-7010	(M)	All The Hits Of The Teen Groups	1962	20.00	50.00
Parkway P-7011	(M)	Don't Knock The Twist (Soundtrack)	1962	20.00	50.00
Parkway P-7021	(M)	For Your Hully Gully Party	1963	20.00	50.00
Parkway P-7025	(M)	You Can't Sit Down	1963	20.00	50.00

DOWELL, JOE

Smash MGS-27000	(M)	Wooden Heart	1961	12.00	30.00
Smash SRS-67000	(S)	Wooden Heart	1961	16.00	40.00
Smash MGS-27011	(M)	German American Hits	1962	8.00	20.00
Smash SRS-67011	(S)	German American Hits	1962	10.00	25.00

DOWN FROM NOTHING

No label	(S)	Down From Nothing	197?	100.00	200.00

DOWNS, HUGH

Epic LN-3597	(M)	An Evening With Hugh Downs	195?	10.00	25.00

DOYLE, MIKE

Fleetwood FLP-3018	(M)	The Secrets Of Surfing	1963	8.00	20.00

Label & Catalog #		Title	Year	VG+	NM
DRAGONFLY					
Megaphone MS-1202	(S)	**Dragonfly**	1968	35.00	70.00
DRAGONWYCK					
No label	(S)	**Dragonwyck**	197?	360.00	600.00
DRAGSTERS, THE					
Wing MGW-12269	(M)	**Drag City**	1964	8.00	20.00
Wing SRW-16269	(S)	**Drag City**	1964	10.00	25.00
DRAKE, NICK					
Island SMAS-9307	(S)	**Nick Drake**	1971	10.00	25.00
Island SMAS-9318	(S)	**Pink Moon**	1972	6.00	15.00
DRAKE, PETE					
Drake also recorded as Dean Dallas.					
Starday SLP-180	(M)	**The Fabulous Steel Guitar Of Pete Drake**	195?	16.00	40.00
Starday SLP-319	(M)	**The Amazing And Incredible Pete Drake**	196?	12.00	30.00
Smash MGS-27053	(M)	**Forever**	1964	5.00	12.00
Smash SRS-67053	(S)	**Forever**	1964	6.00	15.00
Smash MGS-27060	(M)	**Talking Steel Guitar**	1965	5.00	12.00
Smash SRS-67060	(S)	**Talking Steel Guitar**	1965	6.00	15.00
Smash MGS-27064	(M)	**Talking Steel And Singing Strings**	1965	5.00	12.00
Smash SRS-67064	(S)	**Talking Steel And Singing Strings**	1965	6.00	15.00
Cumberland MGC-29053	(M)	**Country Steel Guitar**	196?	6.00	15.00
Canaan LP-4640	(M)	**Steel Away**	196?	5.00	12.00
Canaan LP-9640	(S)	**Steel Away**	196?	6.00	15.00
DRAPER, RUSTY					
Mercury MG-20068	(M)	**Music For A Rainy Night**	1956	12.00	30.00
Mercury MG-20117	(M)	**Encores**	1957	12.00	30.00
Mercury MG-20118	(M)	**Rusty Draper Sings**	1957	12.00	30.00
Mercury MG-20173	(M)	**Rusty Meets Hoagy**	1957	12.00	30.00
DREAMLOVERS, THE					
Columbia CL-2020	(M)	**The Bird/Other Golden Dancing Grooves**	1963	8.00	20.00
Columbia CS-8820	(S)	**The Bird/Other Golden Dancing Grooves**	1963	10.00	25.00
DREW, DORIS					
Mode MOD-126	(M)	**Delightful Doris Drew**	1957	30.00	60.00
DREW, PATTI					
Capitol T-2804	(M)	**Tell Him**	1967	6.00	15.00
Capitol ST-2804	(S)	**Tell Him**	1967	8.00	20.00
Capitol ST-156	(S)	**I've Been Here All The Time**	1969	4.00	10.00
Capitol ST-408	(S)	**Wild Is Love**	1970	4.00	10.00
Capitol ST-408	(DJ)	**Wild Is Love** (Picture disc)	1979	16.00	40.00
DRIFTERS, THE					
Originally formed by Clyde McPhatter, lead singers over the years included Johnny Moore, Bobby Hendricks and Ben E. King.					
Atlantic 8003	(M)	**Clyde McPhatter & The Drifters**	1956	150.00	250.00
Atlantic 8022	(M)	**Rockin' And Driftin'**	1958	150.00	250.00
		— Original Atlantic albums above have black albums.—			
Atlantic 8003	(M)	**Clyde McPhatter & The Drifters**	1960	50.00	100.00
Atlantic 8022	(M)	**Rockin' And Driftin'**	1960	50.00	100.00
Atlantic 8041	(M)	**The Drifters' Greatest Hits**	1960	35.00	70.00
Atlantic 8059	(M)	**Save The Last Dance For Me**	1962	35.00	70.00
Atlantic SD-8059	(S)	**Save The Last Dance For Me**	1962	50.00	100.00
Atlantic 8073	(M)	**Up On The Roof**	1963	20.00	50.00
Atlantic SD-8073	(S)	**Up On The Roof**	1963	35.00	70.00
Atlantic 8093	(M)	**Our Biggest Hits**	1964	16.00	40.00
Atlantic SD-8093	(S)	**Our Biggest Hits**	1964	30.00	60.00
Atlantic 8099	(M)	**Under The Boardwalk**	1964	20.00	50.00
Atlantic SD-8099	(S)	**Under The Boardwalk**	1964	35.00	70.00
Clarion 608	(M)	**The Drifters**	1964	8.00	20.00
Clarion SD-608	(P)	**The Drifters**	1964	12.00	30.00
Atlantic 8103	(M)	**The Good Life With The Drifters**	1965	12.00	30.00
Atlantic SD-8103	(S)	**The Good Life With The Drifters**	1965	20.00	50.00

Label & Catalog #		Title	Year	VG+	NM
Atlantic 8113	(M)	I'll Take You Where The Music's Playing	1965	12.00	30.00
Atlantic SD-8113	(S)	I'll Take You Where The Music's Playing	1965	20.00	50.00
Atlantic 8153	(M)	The Drifters' Golden Hits	1968	8.00	20.00
Atlantic SD-8153	(M)	The Drifters' Golden Hits	1968	8.00	20.00

—Mono Atlantic albums above have orange & purple labels;
stereo albums have green & blue labels.—

DRIFTIN' SLIM
Driftin' Slim is a pseudonym for Elmon Mickle.

Milestone 93004	(M)	Driftin' Slim And His Blues Band	1968	8.00	20.00

DRIFTWOOD, JIMMY

RCA Victor LPM-1635	(M)	Newly Discovered Early American Folk Songs	1958	16.00	40.00
RCA Victor LPM-1994	(M)	Wilderness Road	1959	12.00	30.00
RCA Victor LSP-1994	(S)	Wilderness Road	1959	16.00	40.00
RCA Victor LPM-2171	(M)	The Westward Movement	1959	12.00	30.00
RCA Victor LSP-2171	(S)	The Westward Movement	1959	16.00	40.00
RCA Victor LPM-2228	(M)	Tall Tales In Song	1960	8.00	20.00
RCA Victor LSP-2228	(S)	Tall Tales In Song	1960	12.00	30.00
RCA Victor LPM-2316	(M)	Songs Of Billy Yank And Johnny Reb	1961	8.00	20.00
RCA Victor LSP-2316	(S)	Songs Of Billy Yank And Johnny Reb	1961	12.00	30.00
RCA Victor LPM-2443	(M)	Driftwood At Sea	1962	8.00	20.00
RCA Victor LSP-2443	(S)	Driftwood At Sea	1962	12.00	30.00
Monument MLP-8006	(M)	Voice Of The People	1963	6.00	15.00
Monument SLP-18006	(S)	Voice Of The People	1963	8.00	20.00
Monument MLP-8019	(M)	Down In The Arkansas	1965	6.00	15.00
Monument SLP-18019	(S)	Down In The Arkansas	1965	8.00	20.00
Monument MLP-8043	(M)	The Best Of Johnny Driftwood	1966	5.00	12.00
Monument SLP-18043	(S)	The Best Of Johnny Driftwood	1966	6.00	15.00

DRUIDS OF STONEHENGE, THE

Uni 3004	(M)	Creation	1967	12.00	30.00
Uni 73004	(S)	Creation	1967	16.00	40.00

DRUSKY, ROY

Decca DL-4160	(M)	Anymore With Roy Drusky	1961	8.00	20.00
Decca DL-74160	(S)	Anymore With Roy Drusky	1961	12.00	30.00
Decca DL-4340	(M)	It's My Way	1962	8.00	20.00
Decca DL-74340	(S)	It's My Way	1962	12.00	30.00

DRYEWATER

J.T.B. NRS-122	(S)	Dryewater	1974	50.00	100.00

DU DROPPERS, THE

Groove	(M)	Du Droppin'	1955	180.00	300.00

DU SHON, JEAN

Argo 4039	(M)	Make Way For Jean Du Shon	1964	8.00	20.00
Argo LPS-750	(M)	You Better Believe It	1965	10.00	25.00

DUALS, THE

Sue LP-2002	(M)	Stick Shift *(Cartoon cover)*	1961	65.00	130.00
Sue LP-2002	(M)	Stick Shift *(Photo cover)*	1964	45.00	90.00

DUBS, THE

Josie JM-4001	(M)	The Dubs Meet The Shells	196?	30.00	60.00
Josie JSS-4001	(P)	The Dubs Meet The Shells	196?	40.00	80.00

DUDLEY, DAVE

Golden Ring 110	(M)	Six Days On The Road	1963	50.00	100.00

DUKE, PATTY, & NORMAN VINCENT PEALE

Guideposts GP-101	(M)	Guideposts For Christmas	1963	16.00	40.00

DUKE, PATTY

United Arts. UAL-4131	(M)	Billie *(Soundtrack)*	1965	8.00	20.00
United Arts. UAS-5131	(S)	Billie *(Soundtrack)*	1965	10.00	25.00
United Arts. UAL-3452	(M)	Don't Just Stand There	1965	5.00	12.00
United Arts. UAS-6452	(S)	Don't Just Stand There	1965	6.00	15.00

Label & Catalog #		Title	Year	VG+	NM
United Arts. UAL-3492	(M)	Patty	1966	4.00	10.00
United Arts. UAS-6492	(S)	Patty	1966	5.00	12.00
United Arts. UAL-3535	(M)	Patty Duke's Greatest Hits	1966	4.00	10.00
United Arts. UAS-6535	(S)	Patty Duke's Greatest Hits	1966	5.00	12.00
Unart 20005	(M)	TV's Teen Star	1967	4.00	10.00
Unart 520005	(S)	TV's Teen Star	1967	5.00	12.00
United Arts. UAS-6632	(S)	Songs From The Valley Of The Dolls	1968	8.00	20.00

DUPREE, "CHAMPION" JACK

Label & Catalog #		Title	Year	VG+	NM
Atlantic 8019	(M)	Blues From The Gutter	1959	50.00	100.00
Atlantic SD-8019	(S)	Blues From The Gutter	1959	75.00	150.00
		(Original mono pressings have black labels; stereos, green labels.)			
Atlantic SD-8019	(S)	Blues From The Gutter	1959	35.00	70.00
Atlantic 8045	(S)	Natural And Soulful Blues	1961	20.00	50.00
Atlantic SD-8045	(S)	Natural And Soulful Blues	1961	35.00	70.00
Atlantic 8056	(M)	Champion Of The Blues	1961	16.00	40.00
Atlantic SD-8056	(S)	Champion Of The Blues	1961	20.00	50.00

—Atlantic mono albums above have orange & purple labels with a white fan; stereo albums have green & blue labels with a white fan.—

Label & Catalog #		Title	Year	VG+	NM
King LP-735	(M)	Sings The Blues	1961	40.00	80.00
Folkways FS-3825	(M)	Women Blues Of Champion Jack Dupree	1961	10.00	25.00
OKeh OKM-12103	(M)	Cabbage Greens	1963	12.00	30.00
Blue Horizon 7702	(S)	When You Feel The Feeling	1969	10.00	25.00
London PS-553	(S)	From New Orleans To Chicago	1969	8.00	20.00
Atlantic SD-8255	(S)	Blues From The Gutter	1970	6.00	15.00
King KS-1084	(S)	Walking The Blues	1970	6.00	15.00

DUPREE, "CHAMPION" JACK, & MICKEY BAKER

Label & Catalog #		Title	Year	VG+	NM
Sire 97010	(S)	In Heavy Blues	1969	10.00	25.00

DUPREE, SIMON, & THE BIG SOUND

Label & Catalog #		Title	Year	VG+	NM
Tower ST-5097	(S)	Without Reservations	1968	8.00	20.00

DUPREES, THE

Label & Catalog #		Title	Year	VG+	NM
Coed LPC-905	(M)	You Belong To Me	1962	50.00	100.00
Coed LPC-906	(M)	Have You Heard	1963	35.00	70.00
Heritage 35002	(S)	Total Recall	1968	8.00	20.00
Post 1000	(E)	The Duprees Sing	196?	6.00	15.00

DURAN DURAN

Label & Catalog #		Title	Year	VG+	NM
Mobile Fidelity MFSL-182	(S)	Seven And The Ragged Tiger	198?	6.00	15.00

DURANTE, JIMMY

Label & Catalog #		Title	Year	VG+	NM
Decca DL-9040	(M)	Club Durante	1959	14.00	35.00
Roulette R-25123	(M)	Jimmy Durante At The Copacabana	1961	8.00	20.00
Roulette SR-25123	(S)	Jimmy Durante At The Copacabana	1961	10.00	25.00
Warner Bros. W-1506	(M)	September Song	1963	6.00	15.00
Warner Bros. WS-1506	(S)	September Song	1963	8.00	20.00
Warner Bros. W-1531	(M)	Hello Young Lovers	1964	6.00	15.00
Warner Bros. WS-1531	(S)	Hello Young Lovers	1964	8.00	20.00
MGM E-4207	(M)	The Very Best Of Jimmy Durante	1964	5.00	12.00
MGM SE-4207	(S)	The Very Best Of Jimmy Durante	1964	6.00	15.00
Warner Bros. W-1577	(M)	A Way Of Life	1965	6.00	15.00
Warner Bros. WS-1577	(S)	A Way Of Life	1965	8.00	20.00
Warner Bros. W-1655	(M)	One Of Those Songs	1966	6.00	15.00
Warner Bros. WS-1655	(S)	One Of Those Songs	1966	8.00	20.00
Warner Bros. W-1713	(M)	Songs For Sunday	1967	6.00	15.00
Warner Bros. WS-1713	(S)	Songs For Sunday	1967	8.00	20.00
Decca DL-78884	(S)	In Person At The Piano	1970	6.00	15.00

DURBIN, DEANNA

Label & Catalog #		Title	Year	VG+	NM
Decca DL-8785	(M)	Deanna Durbin	1958	10.00	25.00

DUROCS, THE

Label & Catalog #		Title	Year	VG+	NM
Capitol ST-11981	(S)	The Durocs	1979	6.00	15.00

DWARR

Label & Catalog #		Title	Year	VG+	NM
Brand-X	(S)	Starting Over	1985	14.00	35.00
Brand-X	(S)	Animals	1986	14.00	35.00

Label & Catalog #		Title	Year	VG+	NM

DYER-BENNET, RICHARD

Label & Catalog #		Title	Year	VG+	NM
Decca DLP-5046	(M)	Folksongs	195?	8.00	20.00
Stinson 2	(M)	20th Century Minstrel	195?	8.00	20.00
Stinson 60	(M)	More Songs By The 20th Century Minstrel	195?	8.00	20.00
Dyer-Bennet 1	(M)	Richard Dyer-Bennet Songs, Volume 1	195?	8.00	20.00
Dyer-Bennet 2	(M)	Richard Dyer-Bennet Songs, Volume 2	195?	8.00	20.00
Dyer-Bennet 3	(M)	Richard Dyer-Bennet Songs, Volume 3	195?	8.00	20.00
Dyer-Bennet 4	(M)	Richard Dyer-Bennet Songs, Volume 4	195?	8.00	20.00
Dyer-Bennet 5	(M)	Richard Dyer-Bennet Songs, Volume 5	195?	8.00	20.00
Dyer-Bennet 6000	(M)	Songs With Young People In Mind	195?	8.00	20.00

DYKE & THE BLAZERS

Label & Catalog #		Title	Year	VG+	NM
Original Sound LP-8876	(M)	The Funky Broadway	1967	10.00	25.00
Original Sound LPS-8876	(S)	The Funky Broadway	1967	12.00	30.00
Original Sound LPS-8877	(S)	Dyke's Greatest Hits	1968	10.00	25.00

DYNAMICS, THE

Label & Catalog #		Title	Year	VG+	NM
Bolo BLP-8001	(M)	The Dynamics With Jimmy Hanna	1963	20.00	50.00

DYNATONES, THE

Label & Catalog #		Title	Year	VG+	NM
HBR HLP-8509	(M)	The Fife Piper	1966	6.00	15.00
HBR HST-9509	(S)	The Fife Piper	1966	8.00	20.00

DYLAN, BOB

Refer to Harry Belafonte; George Harrison; Doug Sahm.

Label & Catalog #		Title	Year	VG+	NM
Columbia CL-1779	(DJ)	Bob Dylan *(Red promo label)*	1962	150.00	250.00
Columbia CL-1779	(M)	Bob Dylan	1962	100.00	200.00
Columbia CS-8579	(S)	Bob Dylan	1962	180.00	300.00
		(Original copies of "Bob Dylan" have three white "eye" logo on each side of the spindle hole.)			
Columbia CL-1986	(M)	The Freewheelin' Bob Dylan	1963	*See note below*	
		(Original pressings contain "Rocks And Gravel," "Let Me Die In My Footsteps," "John Birch Society Blues" and "Ramblin' Gamblin' Willie." These four tracks were deleted and replaced by "Masters Of War," "Talkin' World War III Blues," "Girl From North Country" and "Bob Dylan's Dream" on all subsequent pressings. All known copies are mono with covers and labels that list the replacement tracks; must be played to identify. Estimated near mint value $8,000-12,000.)			
Columbia CL-1986	(DJ)	The Freewheelin' Bob Dylan *(White label)*	1963	*See note below*	
		(The label lists the four deleted tracks but the album plays the four new tracks. Estimated near mint value $1,000-2,000.)			
Columbia CL-1986	(DJ)	The Freewheelin' Bob Dylan *(White label)*	1963	300.00	500.00
		(The DJ title & timing strip on the cover lists the four deleted tracks but the label lists, and the album plays, the four new tracks.)			
Columbia CL-1986	(M)	The Freewheelin' Bob Dylan	1963	12.00	30.00
		(Original labels read "Guaranteed High Fidelity" on the bottom.)			
Columbia CS-8786	(S)	The Freewheelin' Bob Dylan	1963	12.00	30.00
		(Original labels read "360 Sound Stereo" in black on the bottom.)			
Columbia CL-2105	(DJ)	The Times They Are A-Changin' *(White label)*	1964	150.00	250.00
Columbia CL-2105	(M)	The Times They Are A-Changin'	1964	12.00	30.00
		(Original labels read "Guaranteed High Fidelity" on the bottom. Issued with a sheet continuing "11 Outlined Epitaphs.")			
Columbia CS-8905	(S)	The Times They Are A-Changin'	1964	12.00	30.00
		(Original labels read "360 Sound Stereo" in black on the bottom. Issued with a sheet continuing "11 Outlined Epitaphs.")			
Columbia CL-2193	(DJ)	Another Side Of Bob Dylan *(White label)*	1964	150.00	250.00
Columbia CL-2193	(M)	Another Side Of Bob Dylan	1964	12.00	30.00
		(Original labels read "Guaranteed High Fidelity" on the bottom.)			
Columbia CS-8993	(S)	Another Side Of Bob Dylan	1964	12.00	30.00
		(Original labels read "360 Sound Stereo" in black on the bottom.)			
Columbia CL-2328	(DJ)	Bringing It All Back Home *(White label)*	1965	150.00	250.00
Columbia CL-2328	(M)	Bringing It All Back Home	1965	12.00	30.00
		(Original labels read "Guaranteed High Fidelity" on the bottom.)			
Columbia CS-9128	(S)	Bringing It All Back Home	1965	12.00	30.00
		(Original labels read "360 Sound Stereo" in black on the bottom.)			
Columbia CL-2389	(DJ)	Highway 61 Revisited *(White label)*	1965	150.00	250.00
Columbia CL-2389	(M)	Highway 61 Revisited	1965	12.00	30.00
Columbia CS-9189	(S)	Highway 61 Revisited	1965	8.00	20.00

Psychedelic music for the end of a long, arduous trip, *Blonde On Blonde* remains, twenty-five years after the fact, an enormous accomplishment, personal, impressionistic, *filled with tender images, flashes* of insight and wit. Originally pressed with what has become known as the "female photos" inner sleeve, the two photos of the unidentified beauties (Claudia Cardinale is the one on the right) were deleted and replaced in all subsequent pressings. PS: If you have any doubts as to the real meaning of "Visions Of Johanna," substitute the word "nirvana" for "Johanna" and listen to the lyrics in your mind...

Label & Catalog #		Title	Year	VG+	NM
Columbia CS-9189	(S)	**Highway 61 Revisited**	1965	100.00	200.00
		(Some copies of the first pressing were issued with			
		an alternate take of "From A Buick 6.")			
Columbia DS-155	(S)	**Disco Teen '66**	1966	16.00	40.00
		(Various artists compilation contains an alternate stereo mix			
		of "Positively 4th Street." Dylan appears on many compilations,			
		both promotional and commercial; these are listed— though not			
		identified— in the "Various Artists" section of the book.)			
Columbia C2L-41	(DJ)	**Blonde On Blonde** (2 LPs. White label)	1966	300.00	500.00
Columbia C2L-41	(M)	**Blonde On Blonde** (2 LPs)	1966	30.00	60.00
Columbia C2S-41	(S)	**Blonde On Blonde** (2 LPs)	1966	12.00	30.00
		(Known as the "female photos" cover, the inside cover			
		has nine photos, including one of Claudia Cardinale.)			
Columbia C2S-41	(S)	**Blonde On Blonde**	1966	10.00	25.00
		(The inside cover has seven photos, omitting Claudia Cardinale.)			
Columbia KCL-2663	(DJ)	**Bob Dylan's Greatest Hits** (White label)	1967	35.00	70.00
Columbia KCL-2663	(M)	**Bob Dylan's Greatest Hits**	1967	10.00	25.00
Columbia KCS-9463	(S)	**Bob Dylan's Greatest Hits**	1967	8.00	20.00
		(Available for years with a poster by Milton Glaser, worth $5-10.)			
Columbia CL-2804	(DJ)	**John Wesley Harding** (White label)	1968	50.00	100.00
Columbia CL-2804	(M)	**John Wesley Harding**	1968	35.00	70.00
Columbia CS-9604	(S)	**John Wesley Harding**	1968	6.00	15.00
Columbia KCS-9825	(S)	**Nashville Skyline**	1969	6.00	15.00
Columbia CQ-32825	(Q)	**Nashville Skyline**	1973	12.00	30.00
Columbia HE-49825	(S)	**Nashville Skyline** (Half-speed master)	1975	16.00	40.00
Folkways FB-5322	(M)	**Bob Dylan Versus A.J. Weberman**	197?	150.00	250.00
Columbia C2X-30050	(S)	**Self Portrait** (2 LPs)	1970	35.00	70.00
		— Columbia albums above read "360 Sound" on the bottom of the label.—			
Columbia C2X-30050	(S)	**Self Portrait** (2 LPs)	1970	6.00	15.00
Columbia KC-30290	(S)	**New Morning**	1970	4.00	10.00
Columbia KG-31120	(S)	**Bob Dylan's Greatest Hits, Volume 2** (2 LPs)	1971	4.00	10.00
Columbia KC-32460	(S)	**Pat Garrett And Billy The Kid** (Soundtrack)	1973	6.00	15.00
		(The title on the front cover is in raised black letters.)			
Columbia KC-32747	(S)	**Dylan**	1973	4.00	10.00
Asylum 7E-1003	(DJ)	**Planet Waves** (White label)	1974	6.00	15.00
Asylum 7E-1003	(S)	**Planet Waves**	1974	8.00	20.00
		(Recorded with The Band. Issued with a wraparound second cover.)			
Asylum EQ-1003	(Q)	**Planet Waves**	1974	20.00	50.00
Island AB-201	(S)	**Before The Flood** (2 LPs with The Band)	1974	16.00	40.00
Asylum AB-201	(S)	**Before The Flood** (2 LPs with The Band)	1974	10.00	25.00
Columbia PC-33235	(DJ)	**Blood On The Tracks** (Test pressing)	1976	See note below	
		(Test pressing includes alternate takes of "Idiot Wind,"			
		"Lily, Rosemary And The Jack Of Hearts," "Tangled Up In Blue"			
		"If You See Her Say Hello" and "You're A Big Girl Now."			
		Estimated near mint value $2,000-3,000.)			
Columbia PC-33235	(DJ)	**Blood On The Tracks** (White label)	1975	6.00	15.00
Columbia PC-33235	(S)	**Blood On The Tracks**	1975	4.00	10.00
		(First pressing: The liner notes on the back are in black print.)			
Columbia PC-33235	(S)	**Blood On The Tracks**	1976	8.00	20.00
		(The back cover features a full-cover drawing.)			
Columbia HC-43235	(S)	**Blood On The Tracks** (Half-speed master)	1975	16.00	40.00
Columbia CS2-33682	(DJ)	**The Basement Tapes** (2 LPs. White label)	1975	6.00	15.00
Columbia PC-33893	(DJ)	**Desire** (White label)	1976	6.00	15.00
Columbia PCQ-33893	(Q)	**Desire**	1976	14.00	35.00
Columbia PC-34349	(DJ)	**Hard Rain** (White label)	1976	5.00	12.00
Columbia AS-422	(DJ)	**Renaldo And Clara**	1976	14.00	35.00
		(Originals have a title sticker on the cover.)			
Columbia JC-35453	(DJ)	**Street Legal** (White label)	1978	6.00	15.00
Columbia PC2-36067	(DJ)	**Bob Dylan At Budokan** (2 LPs. White label)	1979	5.00	12.00
Columbia FC-36120	(DJ)	**Slow Train Coming** (White label)	1979	5.00	12.00
Columbia AS-798	(DJ)	**Saved** (White label)	1980	8.00	20.00
Columbia TC-37496	(DJ)	**Shot Of Love**	1981	4.00	10.00
Columbia AS-1259	(DJ)	**The Dylan London Interview, July 1981**	1981	6.00	15.00
Columbia AS-1471	(DJ)	**Electric Lunch**	1983	6.00	15.00
Columbia C5S-38830	(S)	**Biograph** (5 LPs)	1985	8.00	20.00
Columbia CAS-2222	(DJ)	**Time Passes Slowly: Biograph Sampler**	1985	8.00	20.00
Mobile Fidelity MFSL-114	(S)	**The Times They Are A-Changin'**	1988	8.00	20.00

Label & Catalog #		Title	Year	VG+	NM

EAGLE
Eagle originally recorded as The Beacon Street Union.

Janus JLS-3011	(S)	**Come Under Nancy's Tent**	1970	6.00	15.00

EAGLES, THE

Asylum SD-5054	(S)	**The Eagles** (Gatefold cover)	1972	5.00	12.00
Asylum EQ-1004	(Q)	**The Long Run**	1979	6.00	15.00
Mobile Fidelity MFSL-126	(S)	**Hotel California**	1981	16.00	40.00

EAGLIN, "BLIND" SNOOKS

Folkways FA-2476	(M)	**New Orleans Street Singer**	1959	12.00	30.00
Bluesville BV-1046	(M)	**That's All Right**	1962	12.00	30.00

EARLS, THE

Old Town LP-104	(M)	**Remember Me Baby**	1963	100.00	200.00

EARTH OPERA

Elektra EKS-74016	(S)	**Earth Opera**	1968	6.00	15.00
Elektra EKS-74038	(S)	**The Great American Eagle Tragedy**	1969	6.00	15.00

EARTH QUAKE

A&M SP-4308	(S)	**Earth Quake**	1971	6.00	15.00
A&M SP-4337	(S)	**Why Don't You Try Me?**	1972	6.00	15.00

EARTH, WIND & FIRE

Columbia CQ-32194	(Q)	**Head To The Sky**	1974	6.00	15.00
Columbia CQ-32712	(Q)	**Open Our Eyes**	1974	6.00	15.00
Columbia FC-035647	(DJ)	**Best Of Earth, Wind & Fire** (Picture disc)	1979	6.00	15.00
Columbia HC-45647	(S)	**Best Of Earth, Wind & Fire** (Half-speed)	1981	8.00	20.00
Columbia HC-45730	(S)	**I Am** (Half-speed master)	1981	8.00	20.00
Columbia HC-47548	(S)	**Raise** (Half-speed master)	1982	8.00	20.00
Columbia HC-48490	(S)	**Secret Messages** (Half-speed master)	1982	8.00	20.00
Mobile Fidelity MFSL-159	(S)	**That's The Way Of The World**	198?	6.00	15.00

EARTHERN VESSEL

NRS 2587	(S)	**Hard Rock (Life Everlasting)**	1971	150.00	250.00

EAST SIDE KIDS, THE

Uni 73032	(S)	**Tiger And The Lamb**	1968	8.00	20.00

EASTFIELD MEADOWS

V.M.C. 133	(S)	**Eastfield Meadows**	1969	8.00	20.00

EASTWOOD, CLINT

Cameo C-1056	(M)	**Cowboy Favorites**	1963	40.00	80.00
Cameo CS-1056	(S)	**Cowboy Favorites**	1963	50.00	100.00

EASY CHAIR, THE
The Easy Chair features Jeff Simmons.

Vanco 1004	(M)	**The Easy Chair** (One sided)	1968	210.00	350.00

EASY RIDERS, THE

Columbia CL-990	(M)	**Marianne And Other Songs**	1957	14.00	35.00
Columbia CL-1302	(M)	**Wanderin' Folk Songs**	1959	12.00	30.00
Epic LN-24033	(M)	**Easy Riders**	1962	8.00	20.00
Epic BN-26033	(S)	**Easy Riders**	1962	12.00	30.00

EASYBEATS, THE

United Arts. UAL-3588	(M)	**Friday On My Mind**	1967	16.00	40.00
United Arts. UAS-6588	(P)	**Friday On My Mind**	1967	20.00	50.00

Label & Catalog #		Title	Year	VG+	NM
United Arts. UAS-6667	(S)	**Falling Off The Edge Of The World**	1968	16.00	40.00
Rare Earth 517	(S)	**Easy Ridin'**	1970	6.00	15.00
EBON-KNIGHTS, THE					
Stepheny 4001	(M)	**First Date With The Ebon-Knights**	196?	*See note below*	
		(Rare. Estimated near mint value $1,000-2,000.)			
EBSEN, BUDDY					
Reprise R-6174	(M)	**Buddy Ebsen Says Howdy**	1965	8.00	20.00
Reprise R9-6174	(S)	**Buddy Ebsen Says Howdy**	1965	10.00	25.00
Columbia CL-2402	(M)	**The Beverly Hillbillies** *(TV Soundtrack)*	1965	16.00	40.00
Columbia CS-9202	(S)	**The Beverly Hillbillies** *(TV Soundtrack)*	1965	20.00	50.00
ECKSTINE, BILLY					
Mr. B also recorded with Sarah Vaughan.					
National 2001 (10")	(M)	**Billy Eckstine Sings**	1950	20.00	50.00
MGM E-153 (10")	(M)	**Rodgers & Hemmerstein**	1952	20.00	50.00
MGM E-219 (10")	(M)	**Tenderly**	1953	20.00	50.00
MGM E-257 (10")	(M)	**I Let A Song Go Out Of My Heart**	1954	20.00	50.00
MGM E-523 (10")	(M)	**Songs By Billy Eckstine**	1951	20.00	50.00
MGM E-548 (10")	(M)	**Favorites**	1951	20.00	50.00
King 265-12 (10")	(M)	**The Great Mr. B**	1953	50.00	100.00
EmArcy 26025 (10")	(M)	**Blues For Sale**	1954	20.00	50.00
EmArcy 26027 (10")	(M)	**Love Songs Of Mr. B**	1954	20.00	50.00
MGM E-3176	(M)	**Mister B With A Beat**	1955	16.00	40.00
MGM E-3209	(M)	**Rendezvous**	1955	16.00	40.00
MGM E-3275	(M)	**That Old Feeling**	1955	16.00	40.00
EmArcy MG-36010	(M)	**I Surrender, Dear**	1955	16.00	40.00
EmArcy MG-36029	(M)	**Blues For Sale**	1955	16.00	40.00
EmArcy MG-36030	(M)	**Love Songs Of Mr. B**	1955	16.00	40.00
EmArcy MG-36129	(M)	**Imagination**	1958	16.00	40.00
Regent 6052	(M)	**Prisoner Of Love**	1957	12.00	30.00
Regent 6053	(M)	**The Duke, The Blues And Me**	1957	12.00	30.00
Regent 6054	(M)	**My Deep Blue Dream**	1957	12.00	30.00
Regent 6058	(M)	**You Call It Madness**	1957	12.00	30.00
Audio Lab AL-1549	(M)	**Mr. B**	1960	20.00	50.00
Roulette R-25052	(M)	**No Cover, No Minimum**	1960	8.00	20.00
Roulette SR-25052	(S)	**No Cover, No Minimum**	1960	12.00	30.00
Roulette R-25104	(M)	**Once More With Feeling**	1960	8.00	20.00
Roulette SR-25104	(S)	**Once More With Feeling**	1960	12.00	30.00
Mercury MG-20333	(M)	**Billy's Best**	1960	8.00	20.00
Mercury SR-60333	(S)	**Billy's Best**	1960	12.00	30.00
Mercury MG-20637	(M)	**Broadway, Bongos And Mr. B**	1961	8.00	20.00
Mercury SR-60637	(S)	**Broadway, Bongos And Mr. B**	1961	12.00	30.00
Mercury MG-20674	(M)	**Basin St. East**	1962	8.00	20.00
Mercury SR-60674	(S)	**Basin St. East**	1962	12.00	30.00
Mercury MG-20736	(M)	**Don't Worry 'Bout Me**	1962	8.00	20.00
Mercury SR-60736	(S)	**Don't Worry 'Bout Me**	1962	12.00	30.00
Mercury MG-20796	(M)	**The Golden Hits Of Billy Eckstine**	1963	8.00	20.00
Mercury SR-60796	(S)	**The Golden Hits Of Billy Eckstine**	1963	10.00	25.00
— Original Mercury albums above have black labels with silver print.—					
Metro M-537	(S)	**Everything I Have Is Yours**	1965	6.00	15.00
Metro MS-537	(E)	**Everything I Have Is Yours**	1965	4.00	10.00
Motown 632	(M)	**Prime Of My Life**	1965	8.00	20.00
Motown S-632	(S)	**Prime Of My Life**	1965	12.00	30.00
Motown 646	(M)	**My Way**	1966	8.00	20.00
Motown S-646	(S)	**My Way**	1966	12.00	30.00
Motown 677	(S)	**For Love Of Ivy**	1969	10.00	25.00
EDDY, DUANE					
Jamie JLP-3000	(M)	**Have "Twangy" Guitar-Will Travel**	1958	30.00	60.00
Jamie JLPS-3000	(S)	**Have "Twangy" Guitar-Will Travel**	1958	100.00	200.00
		(Yellow label. The title on the cover is in white print. Originally issued in true stereo.)			
Jamie JLPM-3000	(M)	**Have "Twangy" Guitar-Will Travel**	1959	16.00	40.00
Jamie JLPS-3000	(E)	**Have "Twangy" Guitar-Will Travel**	1959	12.00	30.00
		(Yellow label. The title on the cover is in red print. Reissued in electronically rechanneled stereo.)			

Label & Catalog #		Title	Year	VG+	NM
Jamie JLPM-3000	(M)	Have "Twangy" Guitar-Will Travel	196?	8.00	20.00
Jamie JLPM-3000	(E)	Have "Twangy" Guitar-Will Travel	196?	6.00	15.00
Jamie JLPM-3006	(M)	(Especially) For You	1959	16.00	40.00
Jamie JLPS-3006	(E)	(Especially) For You	1959	10.00	25.00
Jamie JLPM-3009	(M)	The Twangs The Thang	1959	16.00	40.00
Jamie JLPS-3009	(E)	The Twangs The Thang	1959	10.00	25.00
Jamie JLPM-3011	(M)	Songs Of Our Heritage (Gatefold cover)	1960	14.00	35.00
Jamie JLPS-3011	(S)	Songs Of Our Heritage (Gatefold cover)	1960	20.00	50.00
Jamie JLPS-3011	(S)	Songs Of Our Heritage (Blue vinyl)	1960	100.00	200.00
Jamie JLPS-3011	(S)	Songs Of Our Heritage (Red vinyl)	1960	100.00	200.00
Jamie JLPM-3011	(M)	Songs Of Our Heritage (Standard cover)	1960	8.00	20.00
Jamie JLPS-3011	(S)	Songs Of Our Heritage (Standard cover)	1960	12.00	30.00
Jamie JLPM-3014	(M)	$1,000,000 Worth Of Twang	1960	12.00	30.00
Jamie JLPS-3014	(E)	$1,000,000 Worth Of Twang	1960	8.00	20.00
Jamie JLPM-3019	(M)	Girls! Girls! Girls!	1961	8.00	20.00
Jamie JLPS-3019	(S)	Girls! Girls! Girls!	1961	12.00	30.00
Jamie JLPM-3021	(M)	$1,000,000 Worth Of Twang, Volume 2	1962	8.00	20.00
Jamie JLPS-3021	(P)	$1,000,000 Worth Of Twang, Volume 2	1962	12.00	30.00
Jamie JLPM-3022	(M)	Twisting With Duane Eddy	1962	8.00	20.00
Jamie JLPS-3022	(S)	Twisting With Duane Eddy	1962	12.00	30.00
Jamie JLPM-3024	(M)	Surfin' With Duane Eddy	1963	8.00	20.00
Jamie JLPS-3024	(S)	Surfin' With Duane Eddy	1963	12.00	30.00
Jamie JLPM-3025	(M)	Duane Eddy In Person	1963	8.00	20.00
Jamie JLPS-3025	(S)	Duane Eddy In Person	1963	12.00	30.00
Jamie JLPM-3026	(M)	16 Greatest Hits	1964	10.00	25.00
Jamie JLPS-3026	(E)	16 Greatest Hits	1964	6.00	15.00
— Original Jamie albums above have gold & white labels.—					
RCA Victor LPM-2525	(M)	Twistin' And Twangin'	1962	8.00	20.00
RCA Victor LSP-2525	(S)	Twistin' And Twangin'	1962	10.00	25.00
RCA Victor LPM-2576	(M)	Twangy Guitar, Silky Strings	1962	8.00	20.00
RCA Victor LSP-2576	(S)	Twangy Guitar, Silky Strings	1962	10.00	25.00
RCA Victor LPM-2648	(M)	Dance With The Guitar Man	1962	8.00	20.00
RCA Victor LSP-2648	(S)	Dance With The Guitar Man	1962	10.00	25.00
RCA Victor LPM-2681	(M)	Twang A Country Song	1963	8.00	20.00
RCA Victor LSP-2681	(S)	Twang A Country Song	1963	10.00	25.00
RCA Victor LPM-2700	(M)	Twangin' Up A Storm	1963	8.00	20.00
RCA Victor LSP-2700	(S)	Twangin' Up A Storm	1963	10.00	25.00
— Original RCA mono albums above have "Long Play" on the bottom of the label;					
stereo albums have "Living Stereo" on the bottom.—					
RCA Victor LPM-2798	(M)	Lonely Guitar	1964	8.00	20.00
RCA Victor LSP-2798	(S)	Lonely Guitar	1964	12.00	30.00
RCA Victor LPM-2918	(M)	Water Skiing	1964	8.00	20.00
RCA Victor LSP-2918	(S)	Water Skiing	1964	12.00	30.00
RCA Victor LPM-2993	(M)	Twangin' The Golden Hits	1965	8.00	20.00
RCA Victor LSP-2993	(S)	Twangin' The Golden Hits	1965	12.00	30.00
RCA Victor LPM-3432	(M)	Twangsville	1965	8.00	20.00
RCA Victor LSP-3432	(S)	Twangsville	1965	12.00	30.00
RCA Victor LPM-3477	(M)	The Best Of Duane Eddy	1966	6.00	15.00
RCA Victor LSP-3477	(P)	The Best Of Duane Eddy	1966	8.00	20.00
— Original RCA albums above have black labels.—					
Colpix CP-490	(M)	Duane A-Go-Go	1965	10.00	25.00
Colpix CPS-490	(S)	Duane A-Go-Go	1965	14.00	35.00
Colpix CP-494	(M)	Duane Eddy Does Bob Dylan	1965	14.00	35.00
Colpix CPS-494	(S)	Duane Eddy Does Bob Dylan	1965	20.00	50.00
Reprise R-6218	(M)	The Biggest Twang Of Them All	1966	8.00	20.00
Reprise RS-6218	(S)	The Biggest Twang Of Them All	1966	10.00	25.00
Reprise R-6240	(M)	The Roaring Twangies	1967	8.00	20.00
Reprise RS-6240	(S)	The Roaring Twangies	1967	10.00	25.00
Sire SASH-3707	(P)	Vintage Years (2 LPs)	1975	10.00	25.00
EDEN, BARBARA					
Dot DLP-3795	(M)	Miss Barbara Eden	1967	10.00	25.00
Dot DLP-25795	(S)	Miss Barbara Eden	1967	12.00	30.00
EDEN'S CHILDREN					
ABC S-624	(S)	Eden's Children	1968	6.00	15.00
ABC S-652	(S)	Sure Looks Real	1968	6.00	15.00

Label & Catalog #		Title	Year	VG+	NM

EDGE, THE
| Nose NRS-48003 | (S) | The Edge | 1970 | 16.00 | 40.00 |

EDMONSON, TRAVIS
Refer to Bud & Travis; The Gateway Singers.
Reprise R-6035	(M)	Travis On His Own	1962	6.00	15.00
Reprise R9-6035	(S)	Travis On His Own	1962	8.00	20.00
Horizon T-1606	(M)	Travis On Cue	1962	6.00	15.00
Horizon ST-1606	(S)	Travis On Cue	1962	8.00	20.00

EDMUNDS, DAVE
Edmunds was formerly a member of Love Sculpture.
MAM 3	(S)	Rockpile	1972	8.00	20.00
Atlantic PR-320	(DJ)	College Network Interview	1978	12.00	30.00
		(Copies with white labels are counterfeits.)			

EDWARDS, JONATHAN & DARLENE
Westminster WGAP-68104	(M)	American Popular Songs	195?	10.00	25.00
Columbia CL-1513	(M)	In Paris	1960	8.00	20.00
Columbia CS-8313	(S)	In Paris	1960	10.00	25.00
RCA Victor LPM-2495	(M)	Sing Along With Jonathan And Darlene	1962	6.00	15.00
RCA Victor LSP-2495	(S)	Sing Along With Jonathan And Darlene	1962	8.00	20.00
Dot DLP-3792	(M)	Songs For Sheiks And Flappers	1967	5.00	12.00
Dot DLP-25792	(S)	Songs For Sheiks And Flappers	1967	6.00	15.00

EDWARDS, TOMMY
Regent MG-6096	(M)	Tommy Edwards Sings	195?	20.00	50.00
Lion 70120	(M)	Tommy Edwards	195?	20.00	50.00
MGM E-3732	(M)	It's All In The Game	1959	10.00	25.00
MGM SE-3732	(S)	It's All In The Game	1959	14.00	35.00
MGM E-3760	(M)	For Young Lovers	1959	8.00	20.00
MGM SE-3760	(S)	For Young Lovers	1959	12.00	30.00
		— Original MGM albums above have yellow labels.—			
MGM E-3805	(M)	You Started Me Dreaming	1960	6.00	15.00
MGM SE-3805	(S)	You Started Me Dreaming	1960	8.00	20.00
MGM E-3822	(M)	Step Out Singing	1960	6.00	15.00
MGM SE-3822	(S)	Step Out Singing	1960	8.00	20.00
MGM E-3838	(M)	Tommy Edwards In Hawaii	1960	6.00	15.00
MGM SE-3838	(S)	Tommy Edwards In Hawaii	1960	8.00	20.00
MGM E-3884	(M)	Tommy Edwards' Greatest Hits	1961	6.00	15.00
MGM SE-3884	(S)	Tommy Edwards' Greatest Hits	1961	8.00	20.00
MGM E-3959	(M)	Golden Country Hits	1961	6.00	15.00
MGM SE-3959	(S)	Golden Country Hits	1961	8.00	20.00
MGM E-4020	(M)	Stardust	1962	6.00	15.00
MGM SE-4020	(S)	Stardust	1962	8.00	20.00
MGM E-4060	(M)	Soft Strings And Two Guitars	1962	6.00	15.00
MGM SE-4060	(S)	Soft Strings And Two Guitars	1962	8.00	20.00
MGM E-4141	(M)	The Very Best Of Tommy Edwards	1963	5.00	12.00
MGM SE-4141	(S)	The Very Best Of Tommy Edwards	1963	6.00	15.00
		— Original MGM albums above have black labels.—			

EIRE APPARENT
| Buddah BDS-5031 | (S) | Sunrise | 1969 | 8.00 | 20.00 |

EL DORADOS, THE
| Vee Jay VJLP-1001 | (M) | Crazy Little Mama *(Maroon label)* | 1959 | 180.00 | 300.00 |
| Vee Jay VJLP-1001 | (M) | Crazy Little Mama *(Black label)* | 1959 | 100.00 | 200.00 |

ELBERT, DONNIE
| King 629 | (M) | The Sensational Donnie Elbert Sings | 1959 | 75.00 | 150.00 |

ELECTRIC FLAG, THE
The Original Flag includes Mike Bloomfield, Barry Goldberg and Nick Gravenites.
Sidewalk T-5908	(M)	The Trip *(Soundtrack)*	1967	12.00	30.00
Sidewalk ST-5908	(S)	The Trip *(Soundtrack)*	1967	16.00	40.00
Columbia CS-9597	(S)	A Long Time Comin'	1968	6.00	15.00
Columbia CS-9714	(S)	An American Music Band	1968	6.00	15.00
		— Original Columbia albums above have "360 Sound" on the bottom of the label.—			

Label & Catalog #		Title	Year	VG+	NM
ELECTRIC INDIAN, THE					
United Arts. UAS-6728	(S)	**Keem 'O Sabe**	1969	4.00	10.00
ELECTRIC JUNKYARD					
RCA Victor LSP-4158	(S)	**The Electric Junkyard**	1969	6.00	15.00
ELECTRIC LIGHT ORCHESTRA, THE (E.L.O.)					
E.L.O. features Roy Wood and Jeff Lynne. Refer to The Idle Race; The Move.					
Jet/United Arts. LA546	(DJ)	**Face The Music** *(Banded for air-play)*	1975	8.00	20.00
Jet/United Arts. LA823	(DJ)	**Out Of The Blue** *(2 LPs. Blue vinyl)*	1977	10.00	25.00
Jet SP-123	(DJ)	**Ole ELO** *(Gold vinyl)*	1978	8.00	20.00
Jet SP-123	(DJ)	**Ole ELO** *(Blue vinyl)*	1978	40.00	80.00
Jet SP-123	(DJ)	**Ole ELO** *(Red vinyl)*	1978	40.00	80.00
Jet SP-123	(DJ)	**Ole ELO** *(White vinyl)*	1978	40.00	80.00
Jet HZ-45769	(S)	**Discovery** *(Half-speed master)*	1981	10.00	25.00
Jet HZ-46310	(S)	**ELO's Greatest Hits** *(Half-speed master)*	1981	12.00	30.00
Jet HZ-47371	(S)	**Time** *(Half-speed master)*	1981	10.00	25.00
Jet HZ-48490	(S)	**Secret Messages** *(Half-speed master)*	1983	12.00	30.00
ELECTRIC PRUNES, THE					
Reprise R-6248	(M)	**I Had Too Much To Dream**	1967	12.00	30.00
Reprise RS-6248	(S)	**I Had Too Much To Dream**	1967	16.00	40.00
Reprise R-6262	(M)	**Underground**	1967	14.00	35.00
Reprise RS-6262	(S)	**Underground**	1967	10.00	25.00
Reprise R-6275	(M)	**Mass In F Minor**	1967	14.00	35.00
Reprise RS-6275	(S)	**Mass In F Minor**	1967	8.00	20.00
Reprise R-6316	(M)	**Release Of An Oath**	1968	10.00	25.00
Reprise RS-6316	(S)	**Release Of An Oath**	1968	6.00	15.00
		— Original Reprise albums above have pink, gold & green labels.—			
Reprise RS-6342	(S)	**Just Good Rock N' Roll**	1969	6.00	15.00
ELECTRIC TOILET					
Nasco 9004	(S)	**In The Hands Of Karma**	1970	75.00	150.00
ELECTROMAGNETS, THE					
E.C.M. 1001	(S)	**The Electromagnets** *(Green cover)*	197?	100.00	200.00
E.C.M. 1001	(S)	**The Electromagnets** *(Red/orange cover)*	197?	90.00	180.00
ELEPHANT'S MEMORY					
Buddah BDS-5033	(S)	**Elephant's Memory**	1969	5.00	12.00
Buddah BDS-5038	(S)	**Songs From "Midnight Cowboy"**	1969	5.00	12.00
Metromedia MD-1035	(S)	**Take It To The Streets**	1970	6.00	15.00
Apple SMAS-3389	(S)	**Elephants Memory**	1972	8.00	20.00
		(Apple 3389 produced by John & Yoko)			
ELF					
Epic KE-31789	(S)	**Elf**	1972	8.00	20.00
MGM M3G-4974	(S)	**L.A. 59**	1974	6.00	15.00
MGM M3G-4994	(S)	**Trying To Burn The Sun**	1975	6.00	15.00
ELGINS, THE					
V.I.P. 400	(M)	**Darling Baby**	1966	12.00	30.00
V.I.P. S-400	(S)	**Darling Baby**	1966	16.00	40.00
ELIMINATORS, THE					
Liberty LRP-3365	(M)	**Liverpool, Dragsters, Cycles & Surfing**	1964	12.00	30.00
Liberty LST-7365	(S)	**Liverpool, Dragsters, Cycles & Surfing**	1964	16.00	40.00
ELLINGTON, HARVEY					
Stepheny MF-4010	(M)	**I Can't Hide The Blues**	1959	40.00	80.00
ELLIOT, "MAMA" CASS					
Refer to The Mugwumps; The Mamas & The Papas; Dave Mason.					
Dunhill DS-50040	(S)	**Dream A Little Dream**	1968	6.00	15.00
Dunhill DS-50055	(S)	**Bubble Gum, Lemonade**			
		& Something For Mama	1969	5.00	12.00
Dunhill DS-50071	(S)	**Make Your Own Kind Of Music**	1970	5.00	12.00
Dunhill DS-50093	(S)	**Mama's Big Ones**	1970	5.00	12.00
RCA Victor LSP-4619	(S)	**Cass Elliot**	1971	4.00	10.00

Label & Catalog #		Title	Year	VG+	NM
RCA Victor LSP-4753	(S)	The Road Is No Place For A Lady	1972	4.00	10.00
RCA Victor APL1-0303	(S)	Don't Call Me Mama No More	1973	4.00	10.00
ELLIOT, RAMBLIN' JACK					
Prestige INT-13016	(M)	Songs Of Woody Guthrie	1961	8.00	20.00
Prestige INT-13045	(M)	Country Style	1962	8.00	20.00
Prestige INT-13065	(M)	At The Second Fret	1962	8.00	20.00
Prestige INT-13083	(M)	Ramblin' Jack Elliott	1963	8.00	20.00
Prestige F-14019	(M)	Hootenanny With Jack Elliott	1964	8.00	20.00
Prestige F-14029	(M)	Country Style	1964	8.00	20.00
Monitor MF-379	(M)	Ramblin' Cowboy	1962	8.00	20.00
Monitor MF-380	(M)	Sings Woody Guthrie And Jimmie Rodgers	1962	8.00	20.00
Monitor MS-380	(S)	Sings Woody Guthrie And Jimmie Rodgers	1962	8.00	20.00
Vanguard VRS-9151	(M)	Jack Elliott	1964	6.00	15.00
Vanguard VSD-79151	(S)	Jack Elliott	1964	6.00	15.00
Delmark D-801	(M)	Talking Woody Guthrie	1968	4.00	10.00
Prestige 7221	(S)	Ramblin'	1968	4.00	10.00
Prestige 7453	(S)	Songs Of Woody Guthrie	1968	4.00	10.00
Reprise RS-6284	(S)	Young Brigham	1968	4.00	10.00
Reprise RS-6387	(S)	Bull Durham Sacks And Railroad Tracks	1970	4.00	10.00
Vanguard VSD-89	(M)	The Essential Ramblin' Jack Elliott	1970	4.00	10.00
ELLIOT, RON					
Ron Elliott was formerly a member of the Beau Brummels.					
Warner Bros. WS-1833	(S)	Candlestickmaker *(With booklet)*	1969	8.00	20.00
ELLIS, ANITA					
Epic LN-3280	(M)	I Wonder What Became Of Me	1956	20.00	50.00
Epic LN-3419	(M)	Him	1958	16.00	40.00
Elektra EKL-179	(M)	The World In My Arms	1960	12.00	30.00
Elektra EKS-7179	(S)	The World In My Arms	1960	16.00	40.00
ELLIS, DOLAN					
Reprise R-6038	(M)	Almost Authentic Folk Songs	1962	6.00	15.00
Reprise R9-6038	(S)	Almost Authentic Folk Songs	1962	8.00	20.00
ELLIS, JIMMY					
Jimmy Ellis also recorded as Orion.					
Boblo 78-829	(S)	Ellis Sings Elvis By Request	1978	20.00	50.00
ELLIS, SHIRLEY					
Congress CGL-3002	(M)	Shirley Ellis In Action	1964	6.00	15.00
Congress CGS-3002	(S)	Shirley Ellis In Action	1964	8.00	20.00
Congress CGL-3003	(M)	The Name Game	1965	6.00	15.00
Congress CGS-3003	(S)	The Name Game	1965	8.00	20.00
Columbia CL-2679	(M)	Sugar, Let's Shing A Ling	1967	5.00	12.00
Columbia CS-9479	(S)	Sugar, Let's Shing A Ling	1967	6.00	15.00
ELLIS, STEVE, & THE STARFIRES					
I.G.L. 105	(M)	The Steve Ellis Songbook	1967	300.00	500.00
ELMER CITY RAMBLING DOGS, THE					
Dog Dirt DD-1	(S)	Jam It	1975	10.00	25.00
ELMER GANTRY'S VELVET OPERA					
Epic BN-26415	(S)	Elmer Gantry's Velvet Opera	1968	16.00	40.00
EMBERS, THE					
J.C.P. Recording 2006	(M)	Rock And Roll Eleven	196?	75.00	150.00
EMBERS, THE					
E.E.E. 1069	(S)	The Embers Burn You A New One	197?	12.00	30.00
EMERALD CHOIR, THE					
Boat 1017	(S)	Timber Timbre Burn	198?	5.00	12.00
EMERSON, LAKE & PALMER					
Atlantic PR-277	(DJ)	Works, Volume 1 *(Sampler)*	197?	6.00	15.00
Mobile Fidelity MFSL-031	(S)	Pictures At An Exhibition	1980	12.00	30.00

Label & Catalog #		Title	Year	VG+	NM
EMERY, TIM					
Ros-Sound 130	(S)	**Alias Red Garrett**	*1978*	**50.00**	**100.00**
EMMONS, BUDDY					
Refer to Longbranch Pennywhistle.					
Mercury MG-20843	(M)	**Steel Guitar Jazz**	*1963*	**20.00**	**50.00**
Mercury SR-60843	(S)	**Steel Guitar Jazz**	*1963*	**35.00**	**70.00**
Emmons ELP-1001	(M)	**Buddy Emmons (The Black Album)**	*196?*	**8.00**	**20.00**
Cumberland MGC-29507	(M)	**Best Of Western Swing**	*196?*	**8.00**	**20.00**
EMMONS, BUDDY, & SHOT JACKSON					
Starday SLP-230	(M)	**Singing Strings Of Steel And Dobro**	*196?*	**20.00**	**50.00**
K-Ark 6028	(M)	**Two Aces**	*196?*	**8.00**	**20.00**
EMPEROR HUDSON					
Hook 100	(M)	**The Adventures Of Emperor Hudson**	*196?*	**10.00**	**25.00**
END, THE					
London PS-560	(S)	**Introspection** *(Produced by Bill Wyman)*	*1969*	**16.00**	**40.00**
ENDLE ST. CLOUD					
International Arts. 12	(S)	**Thank You All Very Much**	*1968*	**10.00**	**25.00**
ENGEL, SCOTT, & JOHN STEWART					
Scott and John were members of The Walker Brothers.					
Tower T-5026	(M)	**I Only Came To Dance With You**	*1966*	**5.00**	**12.00**
Tower ST-5026	(S)	**I Only Came To Dance With You**	*1966*	**6.00**	**15.00**
ENNIS, ETHEL					
Jubilee 1021	(M)	**Lullabies For Losers**	*1956*	**16.00**	**40.00**
Capitol T-941	(M)	**Changes Of Scenery**	*1957*	**12.00**	**30.00**
Capitol T-1078	(M)	**Have You Forgotten?**	*1958*	**12.00**	**30.00**
Jubilee 5024	(M)	**Ethel Ennis Sings**	*1963*	**8.00**	**20.00**
RCA Victor LPM-2984	(M)	**Eyes For You**	*1964*	**6.00**	**15.00**
RCA Victor LSP-2984	(S)	**Eyes For You**	*1964*	**8.00**	**20.00**
ENO, BRIAN					
Formerly a member of Roxy Music. Eno also recorded with Robert Fripp.					
Antilles AN-7018	(S)	**Evening Star**	*1973*	**4.00**	**10.00**
Antilles AN-7030	(S)	**Discreet Music**	*1973*	**4.00**	**10.00**
Island ILPS-9268	(S)	**Here Come The Warm Jets**	*1973*	**6.00**	**15.00**
Island ILPS-9309	(S)	**Taking Tiger Mountain By Strategy**	*1974*	**6.00**	**15.00**
Island ILPS-9351	(S)	**Another Green World**	*1975*	**5.00**	**12.00**
Island ILPS-9478	(S)	**Before And After Science**	*1978*	**4.00**	**10.00**
ENTWHISTLE, JOHN					
Mr. Entwhistle is a member of The Who.					
Decca DL-79183	(S)	**Smash Your Head Against The Wall**	*1971*	**6.00**	**15.00**
Decca DL-79190	(S)	**Whistle Rhymes**	*1972*	**6.00**	**15.00**
EPPS, PRESTON					
Original Sound 8851	(M)	**Bongo, Bongo, Bongo**	*1960*	**8.00**	**20.00**
Original Sound S-8851	(S)	**Bongo, Bongo, Bongo**	*1960*	**12.00**	**30.00**
EPPS, PRESTON / THE BONGO TEENS					
Original Sound OS-8872	(M)	**Surfin' Bongos**	*1963*	**8.00**	**20.00**
Original Sound OSS-8872	(S)	**Surfin' Bongos**	*1963*	**12.00**	**30.00**
EQUALS, THE					
Laurie LP-2045	(M)	**Unequalled**	*1967*	**8.00**	**20.00**
Laurie SLP-2045	(S)	**Unequalled**	*1967*	**10.00**	**25.00**
RCA Victor LSP-4078	(S)	**Baby Come Back**	*1968*	**8.00**	**20.00**
President PTL-1015	(S)	**Equal Sensation**	*1968*	**6.00**	**15.00**
President PTL-1020	(S)	**The Sensational Equals**	*1968*	**6.00**	**15.00**
President PTL-1025	(S)	**Equal Sensation**	*1968*	**6.00**	**15.00**
President PTL-1030	(S)	**Strikeback**	*1969*	**6.00**	**15.00**
ERIK & THE VIKINGS					
Karate 1401	(M)	**Sing Along Rock 'N Roll**	*1965*	**8.00**	**20.00**

Label & Catalog #		Title	Year	VG+	NM
ESQUERITA					
Capitol T-1186	(M)	**Esquerita**	1959	300.00	500.00
ESQUIRES, THE					
Bunky 300	(S)	**Get On Up And Get Away**	1968	10.00	25.00
ESSEX, THE					
Roulette R-25234	(M)	**Easier Said Than Done**	1963	14.00	35.00
Roulette SR-25234	(S)	**Easier Said Than Done**	1963	18.00	45.00
Roulette R-25235	(M)	**A Walkin' Miracle**	1963	10.00	25.00
Roulette SR-25235	(S)	**A Walkin' Miracle**	1963	14.00	35.00
Roulette R-25246	(M)	**Young And Lively**	1964	10.00	25.00
Roulette SR-25246	(S)	**Young And Lively**	1964	14.00	35.00
ESSEX, DAVID					
Columbia CQ-32560	(Q)	**Rock On**	1974	6.00	15.00
ESTES, "SLEEPY" JOHN					
Delmark 608	(M)	**Broke And Hungry**	1966	8.00	20.00
Delmark 613	(M)	**Sleepy John Estes**	1969	8.00	20.00
Delmark 619	(M)	**Electric Sheep**	1969	8.00	20.00
ETC.					
Windi WLPS-1011	(S)	**Etc. Is The Name Of The Band!**	1976	20.00	50.00
ETERNITY'S CHILDREN					
Tower ST-5123	(S)	**Eternity's Children**	1968	8.00	20.00
Tower ST-5144	(S)	**Timeless** (Canadian)	1968	8.00	20.00
EUCLID					
Amsterdam AMS-12005	(S)	**Heavy Equipment**	197?	8.00	20.00
EUPHORIA					
Heritage HTS-35,005	(S)	**Euphoria**	1969	6.00	15.00
EUPHORIA					
Capitol SKAO-363	(S)	**A Gift From Euphoria**	1969	40.00	80.00
EUPHORIA					
Rainbow 1003	(S)	**Lost In Trance**	197?	150.00	250.00
EVANS, DALE					
Ms. Evans also recorded with her hubby, Roy Rogers.					
Capitol T-2772	(M)	**It's Real**	1967	8.00	20.00
Capitol ST-2772	(S)	**It's Real**	1967	10.00	25.00
EVANS, PAUL					
Guaranteed GUL-1000	(M)	**Fabulous Teens**	1960	20.00	50.00
Guaranteed GUS-1000	(S)	**Fabulous Teens**	1960	35.00	70.00
Carlton TLP-129	(M)	**Hear Paul Evans In Your Home Tonight**	1961	14.00	35.00
Carlton STLP-129	(P)	**Hear Paul Evans In Your Home Tonight**	1961	20.00	50.00
Carlton TLP-130	(M)	**Folk Songs Of Many Lands**	1961	14.00	35.00
Carlton STLP-130	(S)	**Folk Songs Of Many Lands**	1961	20.00	50.00
Kapp KL-1346	(M)	**21 Years In A Tennessee Jail**	1964	8.00	20.00
Kapp KS-3346	(S)	**21 Years In A Tennessee Jail**	1964	10.00	25.00
Kapp KL-1475	(M)	**Another Town, Another Jail**	1966	8.00	20.00
Kapp KS-3475	(S)	**Another Town, Another Jail**	1966	10.00	25.00
EVEN DOZEN JUG BAND, THE					
Elektra EKL-246	(M)	**The Even Dozen Jug Band**	196?	8.00	20.00
EVERETT, BETTY					
Ms. Everett also recorded with Jerry Butler.					
Vee Jay LP-1077	(M)	**It's In His Kiss**	1964	14.00	35.00
Vee Jay VJS-1077	(S)	**It's In His Kiss**	1964	20.00	50.00
Vee Jay LP-1122	(M)	**The Very Best Of Betty Everett**	1965	8.00	20.00
Vee Jay VJS-1122	(S)	**The Very Best Of Betty Everett**	1965	12.00	30.00

Label & Catalog #		Title	Year	VG+	NM
EVERLY BROTHERS, THE					
The Everlys are Don and Phil.					
Cadence CLP-3003	(M)	**The Everly Brothers**	*1958*	**30.00**	**60.00**
Cadence CLP-3106	(M)	**Songs Our Daddy Taught Us**	*1958*	**30.00**	**60.00**
Cadence CLP-3025	(M)	**The Everly Brothers' Best**	*1959*	**30.00**	**60.00**
Cadence CLP-3040	(M)	**The Fabulous Style Of The Everly Brothers**	*1960*	**30.00**	**60.00**
Cadence CLP-25040	(P)	**The Fabulous Style Of The Everly Brothers**	*1960*	**35.00**	**70.00**
Cadence CLP-3059	(M)	**Folk Songs Of The Everly Brothers**	*1962*	**30.00**	**60.00**
Cadence CLP-25059	(E)	**Folk Songs Of The Everly Brothers**	*1962*	**20.00**	**50.00**
Cadence CLP-3062	(M)	**15 Everly Hits 15**	*1963*	**20.00**	**50.00**
Cadence CLP-25062	(P)	**15 Everly Hits 15**	*1963*	**30.00**	**60.00**
Warner Bros. W-1381	(M)	**It's Everly Time**	*1960*	**12.00**	**30.00**
Warner Bros. WS-1381	(S)	**It's Everly Time**	*1960*	**16.00**	**40.00**
Warner Bros. W-1395	(M)	**A Date With The Everly Brothers**	*1960*	**16.00**	**40.00**
Warner Bros. WS-1395	(S)	**A Date With The Everly Brothers**	*1960*	**20.00**	**50.00**
		(Fold-open cover with a sheet of photos.)			
Warner Bros. PRO-135	(DJ)	**Souvenir Sampler**	*1961*	**50.00**	**100.00**
Warner Bros. W-1418	(M)	**Both Sides Of An Evening**	*1961*	**12.00**	**30.00**
Warner Bros. WS-1418	(S)	**Both Sides Of An Evening**	*1961*	**16.00**	**40.00**
Warner Bros. W-1430	(M)	**Instant Party**	*1962*	**12.00**	**30.00**
Warner Bros. WS-1430	(S)	**Instant Party**	*1962*	**16.00**	**40.00**
Warner Bros. W-1471	(M)	**The Everly Brothers' Golden Hits**	*1962*	**10.00**	**25.00**
Warner Bros. WS-1471	(S)	**The Everly Brothers' Golden Hits**	*1962*	**14.00**	**35.00**
		— Original Warner albums above have grey labels with a black & yellow logo.—			
Warner Bros. W-1483	(M)	**Christmas With The Everly Brothers**	*1962*	**12.00**	**30.00**
Warner Bros. WS-1483	(S)	**Christmas With The Everly Brothers**	*1962*	**16.00**	**40.00**
Warner Bros. W-1513	(M)	**Great Country Hits**	*1963*	**12.00**	**30.00**
Warner Bros. WS-1513	(S)	**Great Country Hits**	*1963*	**16.00**	**40.00**
Warner Bros. W-1554	(M)	**Very Best Of The Everly Brothers**	*1964*	**8.00**	**20.00**
Warner Bros. WS-1554	(S)	**Very Best Of The Everly Brothers**	*1964*	**12.00**	**30.00**
		(Originally issued with a yellow cover.)			
Warner Bros. W-1578	(M)	**Rock N' Soul**	*1965*	**12.00**	**30.00**
Warner Bros. WS-1578	(S)	**Rock N' Soul**	*1965*	**16.00**	**40.00**
Warner Bros. W-1585	(M)	**Gone, Gone, Gone**	*1965*	**12.00**	**30.00**
Warner Bros. WS-1585	(S)	**Gone, Gone, Gone**	*1965*	**16.00**	**40.00**
Warner Bros. W-1605	(M)	**Beat N' Soul**	*1965*	**12.00**	**30.00**
Warner Bros. WS-1605	(S)	**Beat N' Soul**	*1965*	**16.00**	**40.00**
Warner Bros. W-1620	(M)	**In Our Image**	*1966*	**12.00**	**30.00**
Warner Bros. WS-1620	(S)	**In Our Image**	*1966*	**16.00**	**40.00**
		— Original Warner albums above have grey labels with a black & white logo.—			
Warner Bros. W-1646	(M)	**Two Yanks In London**	*1966*	**16.00**	**40.00**
Warner Bros. WS-1646	(S)	**Two Yanks In London**	*1966*	**20.00**	**50.00**
		(Although uncredited, the Hollies back up the Everlys throughout this album.)			
Warner Bros. W-1676	(M)	**The Hit Sound Of The Everly Brothers**	*1967*	**16.00**	**40.00**
Warner Bros. WS-1676	(S)	**The Hit Sound Of The Everly Brothers**	*1967*	**20.00**	**50.00**
Warner Bros. W-1708	(M)	**The Everly Brothers Sing**	*1967*	**16.00**	**40.00**
Warner Bros. WS-1708	(S)	**The Everly Brothers Sing**	*1967*	**20.00**	**50.00**
		— Original Warner albums above have gold labels.—			
Warner Bros. WS-1752	(S)	**Roots**	*1968*	**16.00**	**40.00**
Warner Bros. WS-1858	(S)	**The Everly Brothers' Show**	*1970*	**8.00**	**20.00**
Harmony HS-11304	(S)	**The Everly Brothers**	*1968*	**6.00**	**15.00**
Harmony HS-11350	(S)	**Christmas With The Everly Brothers**	*1969*	**6.00**	**15.00**
Harmony HS-11388	(S)	**Chained To A Memory**	*1970*	**4.00**	**10.00**
RCA Victor LSP-4781	(S)	**Pass The Chicken And Listen**	*1972*	**6.00**	**15.00**
RCA Victor LSP-4620	(S)	**Stories We Could Tell**	*1972*	**6.00**	**15.00**
Passport 4006DJ	(DJ)	**Reunion Concert**	*1983*	**20.00**	**50.00**
EVERLY, DON					
Ode 77005	(S)	**Don Everly**	*1970*	**6.00**	**15.00**
Ode 77023	(S)	**Sunset Towers**	*1974*	**5.00**	**12.00**
Hickory AH-44003	(S)	**Brother Jukebox**	*1976*	**4.00**	**10.00**
EVERLY, PHIL					
RCA Victor APL1-0092	(S)	**Star Spangled Banner**	*1973*	**6.00**	**15.00**
Pye 12104	(S)	**Phil's Diner**	*1975*	**6.00**	**15.00**
Pye 12121	(S)	**Mystic Line**	*1976*	**5.00**	**12.00**

Label & Catalog #		Title	Year	VG+	NM
EVERY MOTHER'S SON					
MGM E-3471	(M)	**Every Mother's Son**	1967	5.00	12.00
MGM SE-4471	(S)	**Every Mother's Son**	1967	6.00	15.00
MGM E-4504	(M)	**Every Mother's Son's Back**	1967	4.00	10.00
MGM SE-4504	(S)	**Every Mother's Son's Back**	1967	5.00	12.00
EVERPRESENT FULLNESS					
White Whale 7132	(S)	**Everpresent Fullness**	1970	12.00	30.00
EVERYTHING IS EVERYTHING					
Vanguard VSD-6512	(S)	**Everything Is Everything**	1969	10.00	25.00
EVESLAGE, ROBERT					
Mark 5208	(M)	**Reflecting/Portraits Of Loneliness**	196?	20.00	50.00
EXCEPTIONS, THE					
Flair 6444	(S)	**Rock 'N' Roll Mass**	1968	6.00	15.00
EXCITERS, THE					
United Arts. UAL-3264	(M)	**Tell Him**	1963	14.00	35.00
United Arts. UAS-6264	(S)	**Tell Him**	1963	18.00	45.00
Roulette R-25326	(M)	**The Exciters**	1966	8.00	20.00
Roulette RS-25326	(S)	**The Exciters**	1966	12.00	30.00
RCA Victor LSP-4211	(S)	**Caviar And Chitlin's**	1969	4.00	10.00
EXCURSIONS					
No label	(S)	**Excursions**	197?	60.00	120.00
EYES, THE					
World Theatre	(S)	**New Gods (Aardvark Thru Zymurgy)**	1977	300.00	500.00
EYES OF BLUE, THE					
Mercury SR-61184	(S)	**Crossroads Of Time**	1968	6.00	15.00
Mercury SR-61220	(S)	**In Fields Of Ardath**	1969	6.00	15.00

Label & Catalog #		Title	Year	VG+	NM
FABARES, SHELLY					
Colpix CLP-426	(M)	**Shelly**	1962	35.00	70.00
Colpix CST-426	(S)	**Shelly**	1962	100.00	200.00
Colpix CLP-431	(M)	**The Things We Did Last Summer**	1962	20.00	50.00
Colpix CST-431	(S)	**The Things We Did Last Summer**	1962	75.00	150.00
MGM SE-4540	(S)	**A Time To Sing** *(Soundtrack)*	1968	8.00	20.00
FABIAN (FABIAN FORTE)					
Chancellor CHL-5003	(M)	**Hold That Tiger**	1959	20.00	50.00
Chancellor CHLS-5003	(S)	**Hold That Tiger**	1959	35.00	70.00
Chancellor CHL-5005	(M)	**The Fabulous Fabian**	1959	20.00	50.00
Chancellor CHLX-5005	(S)	**The Fabulous Fabian**	1959	35.00	70.00
Chancellor CHL-5012	(M)	**The Good Old Summertime**	1960	12.00	30.00
Chancellor CHLS-5012	(S)	**The Good Old Summertime**	1960	16.00	40.00
Chancellor CHL-5019	(M)	**Rockin' Hot**	1961	20.00	50.00
Chancellor CHL-5024	(M)	**Fabian's 16 Fabulous Hits**	1962	16.00	40.00

Label & Catalog #		Title	Year	VG+	NM

FABIAN / FRANKIE AVALON

Chancellor CHL-5009	(M)	The Hit Makers	1960	20.00	50.00

FACES, THE: *Refer to* THE SMALL FACES

FAGEN, DONALD

Warner Bros. 23696	(DJ)	The Nightfly *(Quiex II vinyl)*	1982	6.00	15.00
Mobile Fidelity MFSL-120	(S)	The Nightfly	1984	8.00	20.00

FAIER, BILLY

Riverside RLP-12-427	(M)	Travelin' Man	195?	10.00	25.00
Riverside RLP-12-	(M)	The Art Of The Five String Banjo	195?	10.00	25.00

FAINE JADE

R.S.V.P. 8002	(S)	Introspection: A Faine Jade Recital	1968	100.00	200.00

FAIRPORT CONVENTION

A&M SP-4185	(S)	Fairport Convention	1969	6.00	15.00
A&M SP-4206	(S)	Unhalfbricking	1969	6.00	15.00

FAITH

Brown Bag LA085	(S)	Faith	1973	6.00	15.00
		(Originally issued as "Limousine" by Limousine.)			

FAITH, ADAM

MGM E-3591	(M)	England's Top Singer	1961	12.00	30.00
MGM SE-3591	(S)	England's Top Singer	1961	16.00	40.00
Amy 8005	(M)	Adam Faith	1965	6.00	15.00
Amy S-8005	(S)	Adam Faith	1965	8.00	20.00

FAITHFULL, MARIANNE

London LL-3423	(M)	Marianne Faithfull	1965	8.00	20.00
London PS-423	(E)	Marianne Faithfull	1965	5.00	12.00
London LL-3452	(M)	Go Away From My World	1965	5.00	12.00
London PS-452	(P)	Go Away From My World	1965	6.00	15.00
London LL-3482	(M)	Faithfull Forever	1966	5.00	12.00
London PS-482	(S)	Faithfulol Forever	1966	6.00	15.00
London PS-547	(P)	Marianne Faithfull's Greatest Hits	1969	5.00	12.00
Island 90066	(DJ)	A Child's Adventure *(Quiex II vinyl)*	1983	5.00	12.00

FALCONAIRES, THE
The Falconaires feature Steve Alaimo, Keith Allison and Mark Lindsay of Paul Revere's Raiders.

USAF 70-3/4	(S)	Something From The Falconaires	1970	16.00	40.00

FALLEN ANGELS, THE

Roulette SR-25358	(S)	The Fallen Angels	1968	8.00	20.00
Roulette SR-42011	(S)	It's A Long Way Down	1968	100.00	200.00

FAME, GEORGIE

Imperial LP-9282	(M)	Yeh, Yeh	1965	8.00	20.00
Imperial LP-12282	(E)	Yeh, Yeh	1965	6.00	15.00
Imperial LP-9331	(M)	Get Away	1966	8.00	20.00
Imperial LP-12331	(E)	Get Away	1966	6.00	15.00
Epic BN-26368	(S)	The Ballad Of Bonnie And Clyde	1968	10.00	25.00

FAMILY

Reprise RS-6312	(S)	Music In A Doll's House	1968	8.00	20.00
Reprise RS-6340	(S)	Family Entertainment	1969	6.00	15.00
Reprise RS-6384	(S)	A Song For Me	1970	6.00	15.00

FANKHAUSER, MERRELL (& HIS H.M.S. BOUNTY)
Refer to Fapardockly; The Impacts.

Shamley SS-701	(S)	Things	197?	10.00	25.00
Maui 101	(S)	Merrell Fankhauser	1976	30.00	60.00

FANTASTIC BAGGYS, THE
The Baggys are the creation of Steve Barri and Phil Sloan.

Imperial LP-9270	(M)	Tell 'Em I'm Surfin'	1964	50.00	100.00
Imperial LP-12270	(S)	Tell 'Em I'm Surfin'	1964	80.00	160.00

Label & Catalog #		Title	Year	VG+	NM
FANTASTIC DEE JAY'S, THE					
Stone SLP-4003	(S)	The Fantastic Dee Jay's	196?	360.00	600.00
FANTASTIC FOUR, THE					
Soul 717	(S)	Best Of The Fantastic Four	1969	6.00	15.00
FANTASTIC JOHNNY C, THE					
Phil-L.A. 4000	(S)	Boogaloo Down Broadway	1968	16.00	40.00
FAPARDOKLY					
Fapardockly is Merrell Fankhauser.					
V.I.P. 250	(S)	Fapardokly	1966	300.00	500.00
FAR EAST FAMILY BAND					
Muland 7002	(S)	The Cave Down To The Earth	197?	6.00	15.00
Muland 7139	(S)	Parallel World	197?	6.00	15.00
FARINA, RICHARD & MIMI					
Vanguard VRS-9174	(M)	Celebrations For A Gray Day	1965	5.00	12.00
Vanguard VSD-79174	(S)	Celebrations For A Gray Day	1965	6.00	15.00
Vanguard VRS-9204	(M)	Reflections In A Crystal Mind	1966	5.00	12.00
Vanguard VSD-79204	(S)	Reflections In A Crystal Mind	1966	6.00	15.00
Vanguard VSD-79263	(S)	Memories	1968	6.00	15.00
FARLOWE, CHRIS (& THE THUNDERBIRDS)					
Columbia CL-2593	(M)	The Fabulous Chris Farlowe	1967	6.00	15.00
Columbia CS-9393	(S)	The Fabulous Chris Farlowe	1967	8.00	20.00
Immediate Z12-52010	(S)	Paint It Farlowe	1968	6.00	15.00
FARM					
Series-2 F2001	(S)	The Inner Most Limits Of Pure Fun	197?	50.00	100.00
		(Issued with an insert cover.)			
FARM BAND, THE					
Mantra 777	(S)	The Farm Band *(2 LPs with poster)*	197?	14.00	35.00
Farm 1001	(S)	On The Rim Of The Nashville Basin	197?	6.00	15.00
Farm 1013	(S)	Communion	197?	6.00	15.00
Farm 1776	(S)	Up In Your Thing	197?	6.00	15.00
FARRELL, EILEEN					
Columbia CL-1465	(M)	I've Got A Right To Sing The Blues	1960	8.00	20.00
Columbia CS-8256	(S)	I've Got A Right To Sing The Blues	1960	12.00	30.00
FAT					
Dream Merchant OU812	(S)	Footloose	1976	10.00	25.00
FATHER YOD					
Higher Key 3301	(S)	Kohoutek	1973	75.00	150.00
Higher Key 3302	(S)	To Our Children	1973	100.00	200.00
Higher Key 3304	(S)	All Or Nothing At All	1974	75.00	150.00
Higher Key 3307	(S)	An Aquarian Symphony/Penetration	1974	75.00	150.00
FAUN					
Gregar 7000	(S)	Faun	1969	12.00	30.00
FAYE, ALICE					
Columbia CL-3068	(M)	Alice Faye In Hollywood 1934-1937	196?	8.00	20.00
Reprise R-6029	(M)	Alice Faye Sings Her Famous Movie Hits	1962	6.00	15.00
Reprise R9-6029	(S)	Alice Faye Sings Her Famous Movie Hits	1962	8.00	20.00
FAYE, FRANCES					
Capitol H-512 (10")	(M)	No Reservations	1954	30.00	60.00
Capitol T-512	(M)	No Reservations	1955	16.00	40.00
Bethlehem 23	(M)	I Am Wild Again	1955	16.00	40.00
Bethlehem 62	(M)	Relaxin' With Frances Faye	1956	16.00	40.00
Bethlehem EXLP-1	(M)	Porgy & Bess *(3 LPs)*	1956	30.00	60.00
Bethlehem 6017	(M)	Frances Faye Sings Folk Songs	1957	16.00	40.00
Gene Norman GNP-41	(M)	Caught In The Act	1958	12.00	30.00
Gene Norman GNP-41ST	(S)	Caught In The Act	1958	16.00	40.00

Label & Catalog #		Title	Year	VG+	NM
Imperial LP-9059	(M)	**Frances Faye Swings Fats Domino**	1959	8.00	20.00
Imperial LP-12059	(S)	**Frances Faye Swings Fats Domino**	1959	12.00	30.00
Imperial LP-9158	(M)	**Frances Faye Sings The Blues**	1961	8.00	20.00
Imperial LP-12158	(S)	**Frances Faye Sings The Blues**	1961	12.00	30.00
Verve V-2147	(M)	**In Frenzy**	1961	6.00	15.00
Verve V6-2147	(S)	**In Frenzy**	1961	8.00	20.00
Verve V-8434	(M)	**Swinging All The Way**	1962	6.00	15.00
Verve V6-8434	(S)	**Swinging All The Way**	1962	8.00	20.00
Crescendo GNP-92	(M)	**Caught In The Act, Volume 2**	1963	5.00	12.00
Crescendo GNPS-92	(S)	**Caught In The Act, Volume 2**	1963	6.00	15.00
Regina 315	(M)	**You Gotta Go! Go! Go!**	1964	6.00	15.00

FEAR ITSELF

Dot DLP-25942	(S)	**Fear Itself**	1969	8.00	20.00

FEATHER

Magic	(S)	**Feather**	1978	16.00	40.00

FELT

Nasco 9006	(S)	**Felt**	1971	60.00	120.00

FENDERMEN, THE

Soma MG-1240	(M)	**Mule Skinner Blues** (Opaque vinyl)	1960	660.00	1,000.00
Soma MG-1240	(M)	**Mule Skinner Blues** (Non-opaque vinyl)	1960		See note below

(The "non-opaque vinyl" listing refers to the highly sought-after colored vinyl copies of Soma 1240. There are no colored vinyls: there are non-opaque black vinyl copies that, when held up to a light, the light will shine through the vinyl with a brown, red or blue tint. Estimated near mint value $1,000-2,000.)

FERGUSON, JAY

Jay was formerly a member of Spirit.

Asylum AS-11394	(DJ)	**Jay Ferguson Live**	1978	8.00	20.00

FERLINGHETTI, LAWRENCE

Fantasy 7002	(M)	**Poetry Readings In The Cellar** (Red vinyl)	1957	30.00	60.00
Fantasy 7004	(M)	**Impeachment Of Eisenhower** (Red vinyl)	1958	30.00	60.00

FERRERS, THE

Mr. and Mrs. Jose Ferrer. Mrs. Ferrer also recorded under her maiden name, Rosemary Clooney.

MGM E-3709	(M)	**The Ferrers At Home**	1958	12.00	30.00

FEVER TREE

Uni 73024	(S)	**The Fever Tree**	1968	8.00	20.00
Uni 73040	(S)	**Another Time, Another Place**	1968	6.00	15.00
Uni 73067	(S)	**Creation**	1970	6.00	15.00
Uni 73091	(S)	**Angels Die Hard** (Soundtrack)	1970	8.00	20.00
Ampex A-10113	(S)	**For Sale**	1970	6.00	15.00

FIELD, SALLY

Colgems COL-106	(M)	**Star Of "The Flying Nun"**	1967	8.00	20.00
Colgems COS-106	(S)	**Star Of "The Flying Nun"**	1967	10.00	25.00

FIELDING, JANE

Jazz=West JWLP-3	(M)	**Jazz Trio**	1955	35.00	70.00
Jazz=West JWLP-5	(M)	**Embers Glow**	1955	35.00	70.00

FIFTH ESTATE, THE

Jubilee JGM-8005	(M)	**Ding Dong The Witch Is Dead**	1967	6.00	15.00
Jubilee JGS-8005	(S)	**Ding Dong The Witch Is Dead**	1967	8.00	20.00

FIFTY FOOT HOSE

Limelight 86062	(S)	**Cauldron**	1969	20.00	50.00

FILET OF SOUL

Mongoloid	(M)	**Freedom**	196?	60.00	120.00

FINCHLEY BOYS, THE

Golden Throat 200-19	(S)	**Everlasting Tribute**	1971	75.00	150.00

Label & Catalog #		Title	Year	VG+	NM
FIRE ESCAPE, THE					
Crescendo GNP-2034	(M)	**Psychotic Reaction** (Red label)	1967	10.00	25.00
Crescendo GNPS-2034	(S)	**Psychotic Reaction** (Red label)	1967	6.00	15.00
FIRE TOWN					
Boat 1013	(S)	**In The Heart Of The Heart Country**	1987	5.00	12.00
FIREBALLS, THE: *Refer to* **JIMMY GILMER & THE FIREBALLS**					
FIREBIRDS, THE					
Crown CST-589	(S)	**Light My Fire**	1968	16.00	40.00
FIREFLIES, THE					
Taurus 1002	(M)	**You Were Mine**	1961	50.00	100.00
Taurus S-1002	(S)	**You Were Mine**	1961	100.00	200.00
FIRESIGN THEATRE					
Philip Austin, Peter Bergman, David Ossman And Philip Proctor.					
Columbia CL-2719	(M)	**Waiting For The Electrician**	1968	10.00	25.00
Columbia CS-9519	(S)	**Waiting For The Electrician**	1968	6.00	15.00
Columbia CS-9884	(S)	**How Can You Be In Two Places At Once When You're Not Anywhere At All**	1969	6.00	15.00
— Original Columbia albums above have "360 Sound" on the bottom of the label.—					
Columbia C-30102	(S)	**Don't Crush That Dwarf, Hand Me The Pliers** (With poster)	1970	6.00	15.00
Columbia CQ-30737	(Q)	**I Think We're All Bozos On This Bus**	1971	8.00	20.00
Columbia CQ-33141	(Q)	**Everything You Know Is Wrong**	1974	8.00	20.00
FIRST CHIPS, THE					
Clay Pigeon CPP-SFCV1	(S)	**First Chips, Volume 1**	1972	75.00	150.00
FIRST EDITION, THE					
The First Edition features Kenny Rogers.					
Reprise R-6276	(M)	**The First Edition**	1967	8.00	20.00
Reprise RS-6276	(S)	**The First Edition**	1967	6.00	15.00
Reprise RS-6328	(S)	**The First Edition '69**	1969	4.00	10.00
FIRST FRIDAY					
Webster's Last Word 2895	(S)	**First Friday**	197?	50.00	100.00
FISCHER & EPSTEIN					
Swan 514	(M)	**It's A Beatle (Coo Coo) World**	1964	10.00	25.00
FISCHER, WILD MAN					
"Produced" by Frank Zappa.					
Bizarre 2XS-6332	(S)	**An Evening With Wild Man Fischer** (2 LPs)	1969	12.00	30.00
FISHER, CHIP					
RCA Victor LPM-1797	(M)	**Chipper At The Sugar Bowl**	1958	20.00	50.00
RCA Victor LSP-1797	(S)	**Chipper At The Sugar Bowl**	1958	35.00	70.00
FISHER, EDDIE					
RCA Victor LPM-3025 (10")	(M)	**Fisher Sings**	1952	16.00	40.00
RCA Victor LPM-3058 (10")	(M)	**I'm In The Mood For Love**	1952	16.00	40.00
RCA Victor LPM-3065 (10")	(M)	**Christmas With Fisher**	1952	16.00	40.00
RCA Victor LPM-3122 (10")	(M)	**Irving Berlin Favorites**	1954	16.00	40.00
RCA Victor LPM-3185 (10")	(M)	**May I Sing To You?**	1954	16.00	40.00
RCA Victor LPM-3375 (10")	(M)	**The Best Of Eddie Fisher**	1954	16.00	40.00
RCA Victor LOC-1024	(M)	**Academy Award Winners**	1955	12.00	30.00
RCA Victor LPM-1097	(M)	**I Love You**	1955	12.00	30.00
RCA Victor LPM-1180	(M)	**I'm In The Mood For Love**	1955	12.00	30.00
RCA Victor LPM-1181	(M)	**May I Sing To You?**	1955	12.00	30.00
RCA Victor LPM-1399	(M)	**Bundle Of Joy** (Soundtrack)	1956	12.00	30.00
RCA Victor LPM-1548	(M)	**Thinking Of You**	1957	12.00	30.00
RCA Victor LPM-1647	(M)	**As Long As There's Music**	1958	12.00	30.00
RCA Victor LSP-1647	(S)	**As Long As There's Music**	1958	16.00	40.00
Ramrod T-6001	(M)	**Scent Of Mystery** (Soundtrack)	1960	180.00	300.00
Ramrod ST-6001	(S)	**Scent Of Mystery** (Soundtrack)	1960	240.00	400.00

Label & Catalog #		Title	Year	VG+	NM
RCA Victor LPM-2504	(M)	Eddie Fisher's Greatest Hits	1962	6.00	15.00
RCA Victor LSP-2504	(S)	Eddie Fisher's Greatest Hits	1962	8.00	20.00
		— Original RCA mono albums above have "Long Play" on the bottom of the label; stereo albums have "Living Stereo" on the bottom.—			
Ramrod RR-1	(M)	Eddie Fisher At The Winter Garden	1963	6.00	15.00
Ramrod RRS-1	(S)	Eddie Fisher At The Winter Garden	1963	8.00	20.00
Dot DLP-3631	(M)	Eddie Fisher Today!	1965	5.00	12.00
Dot DLP-25631	(S)	Eddie Fisher Today!	1965	6.00	15.00
Dot DLP-3648	(M)	When I Was Young	1965	5.00	12.00
Dot DLP-25648	(S)	When I Was Young	1965	6.00	15.00
Dot DLP-3785	(M)	His Greatest Hits	1966	5.00	12.00
Dot DLP-25785	(S)	His Greatest Hits	1966	6.00	15.00
RCA Victor LPM-3726	(M)	Games That Lovers Play	1966	5.00	12.00
RCA Victor LSP-3726	(S)	Games That Lovers Play	1966	6.00	15.00
RCA Victor LPM-3820	(M)	People Like You	1967	6.00	15.00
RCA Victor LSP-3820	(S)	People Like You	1967	6.00	15.00
		— Original RCA albums above have black labels.—			

FISHER, KEVIN

P. Pan P-101	(S)	The First Of Fisher	1977	60.00	120.00

FISHER, MISS TONI

Signet WP-509	(P)	The Big Hurt	1960	20.00	50.00

FITZGERALD, ELLA

Decca DL-5084 (10")	(M)	Souvenir Album	1950	50.00	100.00
Decca DL-5300 (10")	(M)	Gershwin Songs	1951	50.00	100.00
Decca DL-8068	(M)	Songs In A Mellow Mood	1955	20.00	50.00
Decca DL-8155	(M)	Sweet And Hot	1955	20.00	50.00
Decca DL-8149	(M)	Lullabies Of Birdland	1955	20.00	50.00
Decca DL-8166	(M)	Pete Kelly's Blues (Soundtrack)	1955	30.00	60.00
Decca DL-8378	(M)	Gershwin Songs	1957	16.00	40.00
Decca DL-8477	(M)	Ella And Her Fellas	1957	16.00	40.00
Decca DL-8695	(M)	First Lady Of Song	1958	16.00	40.00
Decca DL-8696	(M)	Listen And Relax	1958	16.00	40.00
Decca DL-8832	(M)	For Sentimental Reasons	1958	16.00	40.00
Decca DX-156	(M)	The Best Of Ella	1958	16.00	40.00
		— Original Decca albums above have black & silver labels.—			
Decca DL-4129	(M)	Golden Favorites	1961	8.00	20.00
Decca DL-4447	(M)	Early Ella	1964	8.00	20.00
Decca DL-74447	(E)	Early Ella	1964	6.00	15.00
Decca DL-4446	(M)	Stairway To The Stars	1964	8.00	20.00
Decca DL-74446	(E)	Stairway To The Stars	1964	6.00	15.00
Decca DL-4451	(M)	Gershwin Songs	1964	8.00	20.00
Decca DL-74451	(E)	Gershwin Songs	1964	6.00	15.00
Verve V-4001-2	(M)	The Cole Porter Songbook (2 LPs)	1956	20.00	50.00
Verve V-4002-2	(M)	The Rodgers And Hart Songbook (2 LPs)	1956	20.00	50.00
Verve V-4004	(M)	Like Someone In Love	1957	16.00	40.00
Verve V-6000	(S)	Like Someone In Love	1957	30.00	60.00
Verve V-4008-2	(M)	Duke Ellington Songbook, Volume 1 (2 LPs)	1957	20.00	50.00
Verve V-4009-2	(M)	Duke Ellington Songbook, Volume 2 (2 LPs)	1957	20.00	50.00
Verve V-4010	(M)	Duke Ellington Songbook (4 LP box)	1957	50.00	100.00
Verve V-4011-2	(M)	Porgy And Bess (2 LPs)	1957	20.00	50.00
Verve V-6040-2	(S)	Porgy And Bess (2 LPs)	1957	35.00	70.00
Verve V-8264	(M)	Ella Fitzgerald At The Opera House	1958	14.00	35.00
Verve V-6026	(S)	Ella Fitzgerald At The Opera House	1958	20.00	50.00
Verve V-4019-2	(M)	The Irving Berlin Songbook (2 LPs)	1958	20.00	50.00
Verve V-6005-2	(S)	The Irving Berlin Songbook (2 LPs)	1958	35.00	70.00
Verve V-8288	(M)	One O' Clock Jump	1959	14.00	35.00
Verve V-4021	(M)	Ella Swings Lightly	1959	14.00	35.00
Verve V-6019	(S)	Ella Swings Lightly	1959	20.00	50.00
Verve (No number)	(M)	George & Ira Gershwin Songbook (5 LP box)	1959	300.00	500.00
		(The albums are in a leather pockets in a walnut box.)			
Verve V-4029-5	(M)	George & Ira Gershwin Songbook (5 LP box)	1959	75.00	150.00
Verve V-4032	(M)	Sweet Songs For Swingers	1959	14.00	35.00
Verve V-6072	(S)	Sweet Songs For Swingers	1959	20.00	50.00
Verve V-4034	(M)	Hello, Love	1959	14.00	35.00
Verve V-6100	(S)	Hello, Love	1959	20.00	50.00

Label & Catalog #		Title	Year	VG+	NM
Verve V-4036	(M)	Get Happy	1959	14.00	35.00
Verve V6-4036	(S)	Get Happy	1959	20.00	50.00
Verve V-4041	(M)	Mack The Knife/Ella In Berlin	1960	14.00	35.00
Verve V-4042	(M)	Wishes You A Merry Christmas	1960	14.00	35.00
Verve V6-4042	(S)	Wishes You A Merry Christmas	1960	20.00	50.00
Verve V-4043	(M)	Let No Man Write My Epitaph (Soundtrack)	1960	20.00	50.00
Verve V6-4043	(S)	Let No Man Write My Epitaph (Soundtrack)	1960	35.00	70.00
Verve V-4046	(M)	The Harold Glen Songbook	1961	14.00	35.00
Verve V6-4046	(S)	The Harold Glen Songbook	1961	20.00	50.00
Verve V-4049	(M)	Ella Fitzgerald Sings Cole Porter	1961	14.00	35.00
Verve V-4050	(M)	Ella Fitzgerald Sings More Cole Porter	1961	12.00	30.00
Verve V-4052	(M)	Ella Fitzgerald In Hollywood	1961	14.00	35.00
Verve V6-4052	(S)	Ella Fitzgerald In Hollywood	1961	20.00	50.00
Verve V-4053	(M)	Clap Hands, Here Comes Charlie	1962	14.00	35.00
Verve V6-4053	(S)	Clap Hands, Here Comes Charlie	1962	50.00	100.00
Verve V-4054	(M)	Ella Fitzgerald Swings Brightly	1962	14.00	35.00
Verve V6-4054	(S)	Ella Fitzgerald Swings Brightly	1962	20.00	50.00
Verve V-4055	(M)	Ella Fitzgerald Swings Gently	1962	14.00	35.00
Verve V6-4055	(S)	Ella Fitzgerald Swings Gently	1962	20.00	50.00
Verve V-4056	(M)	Rhythm Is My Business	1962	14.00	35.00
Verve V6-4056	(S)	Rhythm Is My Business	1962	20.00	50.00
Verve V-4057	(M)	The Harold Arlen Songbook	1962	14.00	35.00
Verve V6-4057	(S)	The Harold Arlen Songbook	1962	20.00	50.00
— Original Verve albums above have black & silver label with "Verve Records Inc" on the bottom.—					
Verve V-4059	(M)	Ella Sings Broadway	1963	8.00	20.00
Verve V6-4059	(S)	Ella Sings Broadway	1963	12.00	30.00
Verve V-4060	(M)	The Jerome Kern Songbook	1963	8.00	20.00
Verve V6-4060	(S)	The Jerome Kern Songbook	1963	12.00	30.00
Verve V-4061	(M)	Ella And Basie	1963	8.00	20.00
Verve V6-4061	(S)	Ella And Basie	1963	12.00	30.00
Verve V-4062	(M)	These Are The Blues	1963	8.00	20.00
Verve V6-4062	(S)	These Are The Blues	1963	12.00	30.00
Verve V-4063	(M)	The Best Of Ella Fitzgerald	1964	8.00	20.00
Verve V6-4063	(S)	The Best Of Ella Fitzgerald	1964	10.00	25.00
Verve V-4064	(M)	Hello Dolly	1964	8.00	20.00
Verve V6-4064	(S)	Hello Dolly	1964	10.00	25.00
Verve V-4066	(M)	A Tribute To Cole Porter	1964	10.00	25.00
Verve V-4067	(M)	The Johnny Mercer Songbook	1965	8.00	20.00
Verve V6-4067	(S)	The Johnny Mercer Songbook	1965	10.00	25.00
Verve V-8720	(M)	The Best Of Ella Fitzgerald	1967	6.00	15.00
Verve V6-8720	(S)	The Best Of Ella Fitzgerald	1967	8.00	20.00
— Original Verve albums above have black & silver label with "Metro Goldwyn Mayer" on the bottom.—					
Capitol T-2685	(M)	Brighten The Corner	1967	6.00	15.00
Capitol ST-2685	(S)	Brighten The Corner	1967	6.00	15.00
Capitol ST-2888	(S)	Misty Blue	1968	6.00	15.00
Reprise RS-6354	(S)	Ella	1969	6.00	15.00

FITZGERALD, ELLA, & LOUIS ARMSTRONG

Verve V-4003	(M)	Ella And Louis	1956	16.00	40.00
Verve V-4006-2	(M)	Ella And Louis Again (2 LPs)	1956	20.00	50.00
Verve V-4017	(M)	Ella And Louis Again, Volume 1	1958	8.00	20.00
Verve V-4018	(M)	Ella And Louis Again, Volume 2	1958	8.00	20.00

FITZGERALD, ELLA, & BILLIE HOLIDAY

A.R.S. G-433	(M)	Ella And Billie At Newport	1958	30.00	60.00
		(Issued in a plastic sleeve with four page insert.)			
Verve V-8234	(M)	Ella And Billie At Newport	1958	16.00	40.00

FITZGERALD, ELLA / LENA HORNE / BILLIE HOLIDAY

Columbia CL-2531 (10")	(M)	Ella, Lena And Billie	1955	35.00	70.00

FIVE AMERICANS, THE

HBR HLP-8503	(M)	I See The Light	1966	6.00	15.00
HBR HST-9503	(S)	I See The Light	1966	8.00	20.00
Abnak AB-2067	(M)	Western Union/Sound Of Love	1967	6.00	15.00
Abnak ABST-2067	(S)	Western Union/Sound Of Love	1967	8.00	20.00
Abnak AB-2069	(M)	Progressions	1967	5.00	12.00
Abnak ABST-2069	(P)	Progressions	1967	6.00	15.00
Abnak ABST-2071	(P)	Now And Then (2 LPs)	1968	6.00	15.00

Label & Catalog #		Title	Year	VG+	NM

FIVE EMPREES, THE

Freeport FR-3001	(M)	The Five Emprees	1965	35.00	70.00
Freeport FRS-4001	(S)	The Five Emprees	1965	45.00	90.00
Freeport FR-3001	(M)	Little Miss Sad	1966	12.00	30.00
Freepot FRS-4001	(S)	Little Miss Sad	1966	20.00	50.00

FIVE KEYS, THE

Aladdin 806	(M)	The Best Of The Five Keys (Blue label)	1956	3,500.00	5,000.00
Aladdin 806	(M)	The Best Of The Five Keys (Maroon label)	1956	660.00	1,000.00
Score LP-4003	(M)	The Five Keys On The Town	1957	500.00	750.00
Capitol T-828	(M)	The Five Keys On Stage	1957	75.00	150.00
		(The cover photo has the first member's hand against his body so that his thumb has a phallic appearance.)			
Capitol T-828	(M)	The Five Keys On Stage	1957	100.00	200.00
		(The cover has the thumb airbrushed out.)			
King 688	(M)	The Five Keys	1960	180.00	300.00
King 692	(M)	Rhythm & Blues Hits Past And Present	1960	180.00	300.00
		— Original King albums above have crownless black labels.—			
Capitol T-1769	(M)	The Fantastic Five Keys	1962	100.00	200.00

FIVE MAN ELECTRICAL BAND, THE

Capitol ST-165	(S)	The Five Man Electrical Band	1969	8.00	20.00

FIVE ROYALES, THE

Apollo LP-488	(M)	The Rockin 5 Royales (Green label)	1956	800.00	1,200.00
Apollo LP-488	(M)	The Rockin 5 Royales (Yellow label)	1956	660.00	1,000.00
King 580	(M)	Dedicated To You	1957	210.00	350.00
King 616	(M)	The 5 Royales Sing For You	1959	100.00	200.00
King 678	(M)	The Five Royales	1960	100.00	200.00
King 955	(M)	24 All Time Hits	1966	40.00	80.00
		— Original King albums above have crownless black labels.—			

FIVE SATINS, THE

Refer to Fred Parris & The Satins.

Ember ELP-100	(M)	The Five Satins Sing (Red label)	1957	180.00	300.00
Ember ELP-100	(M)	The Five Satins Sing (Blue vinyl)	1957	1,400.00	2,000.00
Ember ELP-100	(M)	The Five Satins Sing (Logs label)	1959	50.00	100.00
Ember ELP-100	(M)	The Five Satins Sing (Black label)	1961	20.00	50.00
Ember ELP-401	(M)	Encore, Volume 2 (Logs label)	1960	50.00	100.00
Ember ELP-401	(M)	Encore, Volume 2 (Black label)	1961	20.00	50.00
Mt. Vernon 108	(M)	The Five Satins Sing	196?	12.00	30.00
Celebrity Show. JB-7671	(M)	The Best Of The Five Satins	1970	10.00	25.00

FLAIRS, THE

Crown CLP-5356	(M)	The Flairs	1963	20.00	50.00
Crown CST-356	(E)	The Flairs	1963	14.00	35.00

FLAME, THE

Features Blondie Chaplin And Rickie Fataar. Also refer to the Beach Boys.

Brother BR-2500	(S)	Flame (With poster)	1970	10.00	25.00

FLAMIN' GROOVIES, THE

Snazz (10")	(S)	Sneekers	1969	30.00	60.00
Epic BN-26487	(S)	Supersnazz	1969	16.00	40.00
Kama Sutra KSBS-2021	(S)	Flamingo (Pink label)	1970	10.00	25.00
Kama Sutra KSBS-2021	(S)	Flamingo (Blue label)	1972	6.00	15.00
Kama Sutra KSBS-2031	(S)	Teenage Head (Pink label)	1971	10.00	25.00
Kama Sutra KSBS-2031	(S)	Teenage Head (Blue label)	1972	6.00	15.00
Sire D-7521	(S)	Shake Some Action	1976	6.00	15.00
Buddah BDS-5683	(S)	Still Shakin'	1977	6.00	15.00
Sire SRK-6059	(S)	The Flamin' Groovies Now (12 tracks)	1978	6.00	15.00
Sire SRK-6059	(S)	The Flamin' Groovies Now (14 tracks)	1978	5.00	12.00
Sire SRK-6067	(S)	Jumpin' In The Night	1979	5.00	12.00

FLAMING EMBER

Hot Wax HA-702	(S)	Westbound #9	1970	5.00	12.00
Hot Wax HA-705	(S)	Sunshine	1970	4.00	10.00

Starting with the now legendary Chance label, The Flamingos had a lengthy career spanning the '50s and '60s, which saw an array of personnel changes and label moves. While they are best remembered for their 1959 hit, "I Only Have Eyes For You," a pop standard since its first appearance, the group had a successful series of R&B hits, many of which enjoyed modest success as cross-over pop hits. As was common then, their albums sold in minute quantities and are highly sought after today.

Label & Catalog #		Title	Year	VG+	NM

FLAMING YOUTH
Flaming Youth features Phil Collins, later of of Genesis.

Label & Catalog #		Title	Year	VG+	NM
Uni 73075	(S)	**Ark 2**	1969	12.00	30.00

FLAMINGOS, THE

Checker LP-1433	(M)	**The Flamingos** (Black label)	1959	100.00	200.00
Checker LP-1433	(M)	**The Flamingos** (Blue label)	1965	20.00	50.00
Checker LPS-3005	(E)	**The Flamingos** (Blue label)	1965	10.00	25.00
End LP-304	(M)	**Flamingo Serenade**	1959	75.00	150.00
End LPS-304	(S)	**Flamingo Serenade**	1959	100.00	200.00
		(Original covers correctly list the record as "Stereo.")			
End STLP-304	(S)	**Flamingo Serenade**	196?	75.00	150.00
		(Later covers incorrectly read "Rechanneled Stereo.")			
End LP-307	(M)	**Flamingo Favorites**	1960	35.00	70.00
End LPS-307	(E)	**Flamingo Favorites**	1960	20.00	50.00
End LP-308	(M)	**Requestfully Yours**	1960	35.00	70.00
End LPS-308	(E)	**Requestfully Yours**	1960	20.00	50.00
End LP-316	(M)	**The Sound Of The Flamingos**	1962	20.00	50.00
End LPS-316	(S)	**The Sound Of The Flamingos**	1962	35.00	70.00
Constallation CS-3	(M)	**Collectors Showcase: The Flamingos**	1964	10.00	25.00
Phillips PHM-200206	(M)	**Their Hits-Then And Now**	1966	10.00	25.00
Phillips PHS-600206	(S)	**Their Hits-Then And Now**	1966	14.00	35.00

FLAMINGOS, THE / THE MOONGLOWS

Vee Jay LP-1052	(M)	**The Flamingos Meet The Moonglows**	1962	40.00	80.00

FLARES, THE

Press PR-73001	(M)	**Encore Of Foot Stompin' Hits**	1961	8.00	20.00
Press PRS-83001	(S)	**Encore Of Foot Stompin' Hits**	1961	16.00	40.00

FLAT EARTH SOCIETY

Fleetwood 3027	(S)	**Waleeco**	1968	100.00	200.00

FLATT, LESTER, & EARL SCRUGGS

Columbia CL-1019	(M)	**Foggy Mountain Jamboree**	1957	20.00	50.00
Mercury MG-20358	(M)	**Country Music**	1958	16.00	40.00
Mercury MG-20542	(M)	**Lester Flatt And Earl Scruggs**	1959	20.00	50.00
Mercury MG-20773	(M)	**The Original Sound Of Flatt And Scruggs**	1963	10.00	25.00
Mercury SR-60773	(E)	**The Original Sound Of Flatt And Scruggs**	1963	6.00	15.00
Columbia CL-1421	(M)	**Songs Of Glory**	1960	8.00	20.00
Columbia CS-8221	(S)	**Songs Of Glory**	1960	10.00	25.00
Columbia CL-1564	(M)	**Foggy Mountain Banjo**	1961	8.00	20.00
Columbia CS-8364	(S)	**Foggy Mountain Banjo**	1961	10.00	25.00
Columbia CL-1664	(M)	**Songs Of The Famous Carter Family**	1961	8.00	20.00
Columbia CS-8464	(S)	**Songs Of The Famous Carter Family**	1961	10.00	25.00
Columbia CL-1830	(M)	**Folk Songs Of Our Land**	1962	8.00	20.00
Columbia CS-8630	(S)	**Folk Songs Of Our Land**	1962	10.00	25.00
		— Original Columbia albums above have three white "eye" logos on each side of the spindle hole.—			
Columbia CL-2045	(M)	**Flatt And Scruggs At Carnegie Hall**	1963	6.00	15.00
Columbia CS-8845	(S)	**Flatt And Scruggs At Carnegie Hall**	1963	8.00	20.00
Columbia CL-2134	(M)	**Live At Vanderbilt University**	1964	6.00	15.00
Columbia CS-8934	(S)	**Live At Vanderbilt University**	1964	8.00	20.00
Columbia CL-2255	(M)	**The Fabulous Sound Of Flatt And Scruggs**	1964	6.00	15.00
Columbia CS-9055	(S)	**The Fabulous Sound Of Flatt And Scruggs**	1964	8.00	20.00
Columbia CL-2354	(M)	**The Versatile**	1965	6.00	15.00
Columbia CS-9154	(S)	**The Versatile**	1965	8.00	20.00
		— Original Columbia albums above have "360 Sound" on the bottom of the label.—			
Starday SLP-365	(M)	**Stars Of The Grand Ole Opry**	1966	8.00	20.00

FLEETWOOD MAC
Over the years members have included Mick Fleetwood, John McVie, Peter Green, Jeremy Spencer, Christine McVie, Bob Welch, Lindsay Buckingham and Stevie Nicks. Refer to Otis Spann.

Epic BN-26402	(S)	**Fleetwood Mac**	1968	6.00	15.00
Epic BN-26446	(S)	**English Rose**	1969	6.00	15.00
Epic KE-30632	(S)	**Black Magic Woman** (2 LPs)	1971	6.00	15.00
Reprise RS-6368	(S)	**Then Play On** (With "When You Say")	1969	8.00	20.00
Reprise RS-6408	(S)	**Kiln House**	1970	6.00	15.00
Reprise RS-6465	(S)	**Future Games** (Yellow cover)	1971	6.00	15.00
Reprise MS-2080	(S)	**Bare Trees** (With lyric sheet)	1972	6.00	15.00

Label & Catalog #		Title	Year	VG+	NM
Reprise MS-2138	(S)	Penguin	1973	5.00	12.00
Reprise MS-2158	(S)	Mystery To Me (With lyric sheet)	1973	6.00	15.00
		(With "Good Things Come To Those Who Wait.")			
Reprise MS-2196	(S)	Heroes Are Hard To Find	1974	5.00	12.00
Reprise MS-2225	(S)	Fleetwood Mac	1975	5.00	12.00
Sire SASH-3706	(S)	Vintage Years (2 LPs)	1975	6.00	15.00
Sire 2XS-6006	(S)	Vintage Years (2 LPs)	1977	5.00	12.00
Warner Bros. PRO-652	(DJ)	Rumours (Embossed promo cover)	1976	30.00	60.00
Warner Bros. PRO-866	(DJ)	Tusk Remix	1979	6.00	15.00
Warner Bros. PRO	(DJ)	The Fleetwood Mac Story (2 LPs)	1979	20.00	50.00
Warner Bros. 23607	(DJ)	Mirage (Quiex II vinyl)	1982	6.00	15.00
Mobile Fidelity MFSL-012	(S)	Fleetwood Mac	1980	16.00	40.00
Mobile Fidelity MFSL-119	(S)	Mirage	198?	10.00	25.00
Nautilus NR-8	(S)	Rumours	1980	10.00	25.00

FLEETWOODS, THE

Dolton BLP-2001	(M)	Mr. Blue	1959	16.00	40.00
Dolton BST-8001	(P)	Mr. Blue	1959	20.00	50.00
Dolton BLP-2002	(M)	The Fleetwoods	1960	12.00	30.00
Dolton BST-8002	(S)	The Fleetwoods	1960	16.00	40.00
Dolton BLP-2005	(M)	Softly	1961	12.00	30.00
Dolton BST-8005	(S)	Softly	1961	16.00	40.00
Dolton BLP-2007	(M)	Deep In A Dream	1961	12.00	30.00
Dolton BST-8007	(S)	Deep In A Dream	1961	16.00	40.00
Dolton BLP-2011	(M)	The Best Of The Oldies	1962	12.00	30.00
Dolton BST-8011	(S)	The Best Of The Oldies	1962	16.00	40.00

— *Original Dolton albums above have light blue labels with the fish logo above the spindle hole.*—

Dolton BLP-2018	(M)	The Fleetwoods' Greatest Hits	1962	8.00	20.00
Dolton BST-8018	(P)	The Fleetwoods' Greatest Hits	1962	12.00	30.00
Dolton BLP-2025	(M)	Goodnight My Love	1963	8.00	20.00
Dolton BST-8025	(S)	Goodnight My Love	1963	12.00	30.00
Dolton BLP-2020	(M)	The Fleetwoods Sing For Lovers By Night	1963	8.00	20.00
Dolton BST-8020	(S)	The Fleetwoods Sing For Lovers By Night	1963	12.00	30.00
Dolton BLP-2030	(M)	Before And After	1965	8.00	20.00
Dolton BST-8030	(S)	Before And After	1965	12.00	30.00
Dolton BLP-2039	(M)	Folk Rock	1965	8.00	20.00
Dolton BST-8039	(S)	Folk Rock	1965	12.00	30.00

— *Dolton albums above have dark blue labels with a color logo on the left side.*—

FLEMING, RHONDA

Columbia CL-1080	(M)	Rhonda	1958	16.00	40.00

FLEMONS, WADE

Vee Jay LP-1011	(M)	Wade Flemons (Maroon label)	1959	40.00	80.00
Vee Jay LP-1011	(M)	Wade Flemons (Black label)	196?	16.00	40.00

FLINT, SHELBY

Valiant LP-401	(M)	Shelby Flint (The Quiet Girl)	1961	12.00	30.00
Valiant LPS-401	(S)	Shelby Flint (The Quiet Girl)	1961	16.00	40.00
Valiant LP-403	(M)	Shelby Flint Sings Folk	1962	8.00	20.00
Valiant LPS-403	(S)	Shelby Flint Sings Folk	1962	12.00	30.00
Valiant VL-25003	(M)	Cast Your Fate To The Wind	1966	6.00	15.00
Valiant VLS-25003	(S)	Cast Your Fate To The Wind	1966	8.00	20.00

FLINTSTONES, THE

Colpix CLP-302	(M)	The Flintstones (TV Soundtrack)	1963	35.00	70.00
HBR HLP-2055	(M)	A Man Called Flintstone (TV Soundtrack)	1966	16.00	40.00

FLIRTATIONS, THE

Deram DES-18028	(S)	Nothing But A Heartache	1969	8.00	20.00

FLO & EDDIE

Mark Volman And Howard Kaylan, formerly members of the Turtles and the Mothers Of Invention.

Reprise MS-2099	(S)	The Phlorescent Leech And Eddie	1972	6.00	15.00
Reprise MS-2141	(S)	Flo And Eddie	1973	6.00	15.00
Columbia PC-33554	(S)	Illegal, Immoral And Fattening	1975	5.00	12.00
Columbia PC-34262	(S)	Moving Targets	1976	5.00	12.00

Label & Catalog #		Title	Year	VG+	NM
FLOCK, THE					
Columbia CS-9911	(S)	The Flock ("360 Sound" label)	1969	6.00	15.00
Columbia C-30007	(S)	Dinosaur Swamps	1970	5.00	12.00
Mercury SRM-1-1035	(S)	Inside Out	1975	4.00	10.00
FLOWERS, PHIL					
Guest Star G-1456	(M)	I Am The Greatest	196?	8.00	20.00
Guest Star G-1457	(M)	Phil Flowers Sings A Tribute	196?	8.00	20.00
Mt. Vernon 154	(M)	Rhythm 'N' Blues	196?	10.00	25.00
Dot DLP-25849	(S)	Our Man In Washington	1968	6.00	15.00
FLOYD, EDDIE					
Stax 714	(M)	Knock On Wood	1967	10.00	25.00
Stax S-714	(S)	Knock On Wood	1967	12.00	30.00
Stax STS-2002	(S)	I've Never Found A Girl	1968	8.00	20.00
Stax STS-2011	(S)	Rare Stamps	1969	6.00	15.00
Stax STS-2017	(S)	You've Got To Have Eddie	1969	6.00	15.00
Stax STS-2029	(S)	California Girl	1970	6.00	15.00
Stax STS-2041	(S)	Down To Earth	1971	6.00	15.00
Stax STS-3016	(S)	Baby Lay Your Head Down	1973	5.00	12.00
Stax STS-5512	(S)	Soul Street	1974	5.00	12.00
FLYING BURRITO BROTHERS, THE [THE BURRITO BROTHERS]					
Features Chris Hillman and Gram Parsons amongst a cast of thousands.					
A&M SD-4175	(S)	The Gilded Palace Of Sin	1969	6.00	15.00
A&M SD-4258	(S)	Burrito Deluxe	1970	5.00	12.00
A&M SD-4295	(S)	Flying Burrito Brothers	1971	5.00	12.00
A&M SD-4343	(S)	The Last Of The Red Hot Burritos	1972	5.00	12.00
		—Original A&M albums above have brown labels.—			
A&M SP-8070	(DJ)	Hot Burrito	1975	8.00	20.00
FLYING MACHINE, THE					
Janus JLS-3007	(P)	The Flying Machine	1969	5.00	12.00
FLYNN, ERROL / BASIL RATHBONE					
Columbia CL-4162 (10")	(M)	The Three Musketeers/Oliver Twist	195?	10.00	25.00
Columbia CL-674	(M)	The Three Musketeers/Oliver Twist	1955	8.00	20.00
		("Musketeers" is narrated by Flynn, "Twist" by Rathbone.)			
FOGELBERG, DAN					
Full Moon PEQ-33499	(Q)	Captured Angel *(2 LPs)*	1975	6.00	15.00
Full Moon A2S-1335	(DJ)	Interchords *(2 LPs)*	1982	10.00	25.00
Full Moon HE-45634	(S)	Phoenix *(Half-speed master)*	1982	6.00	15.00
Full Moon HE-48308	(S)	Greatest Hits *(Half-speed master)*	1982	6.00	15.00
FOGELBERG, DAN, & TIM WEISBURG					
Full Moon HE-45339	(S)	Twin Sons Of Different Mothers *(Half-speed)*	1982	6.00	15.00
FOGERTY, JOHN					
Refer to The Blue Ridge Rangers; Creedence Clearwater Revival; The Golliwogs.					
Asylum 7E-1046	(S)	John Fogerty	1975	5.00	12.00
Warner Bros. 25203	(DJ)	Centerfield *(Quiex II vinyl)*	1985	6.00	15.00
Warner Bros. 25203	(S)	Centerfield *(With "Zantz Kant Danz.")*	1985	4.00	10.00
FOGERTY, TOM					
Refer to Creedence Clearwater Revival; The Golliwogs.					
Fantasy F-9407	(S)	Tom Fogerty	1972	6.00	15.00
Fantasy F-9413	(S)	Excalibur	1972	6.00	15.00
Fantasy F-9448	(S)	Zephyr National	1974	5.00	12.00
Fantasy F-9469	(S)	Myopia	1974	5.00	12.00
Fantasy F-9611	(S)	Deal It Out	1981	4.00	10.00
FOLEY, RED					
Decca DL-5303 (10")	(M)	Souvenir Album	1951	35.00	70.00
Decca DL-5338 (10")	(M)	Lift Up Your Voice	1951	35.00	70.00
Decca DL-8294	(M)	Souvenir Album	1956	20.00	50.00
Decca DL-8296	(M)	Red Foley Beyond The Sunset	1956	16.00	40.00
Decca DL-8767	(M)	He Walks With Thee	1958	12.00	30.00

Label & Catalog #		Title	Year	VG+	NM
Decca DL-8806	(M)	My Keepsake Album	1958	12.00	30.00
Decca DL-8847	(M)	Let's All Sing With Red Foley	1959	12.00	30.00
Decca DL-8903	(M)	Let's All Sing To Him	1959	12.00	30.00
— Original Decca albums above have black & silver labels.—					
Decca DL-4107	(M)	Red Foley's Golden Favorites	1961	10.00	25.00
Decca DL-74107	(S)	Red Foley's Golden Favorites	1961	10.00	25.00
Decca DL-4140	(M)	Company's Comin'	1961	10.00	25.00
Decca DL-74140	(S)	Company's Comin'	1961	12.00	30.00
Decca DL-4198	(M)	Songs Of Devotion	1961	8.00	20.00
Decca DL-74198	(S)	Songs Of Devotion	1961	12.00	30.00
Decca DL-4290	(M)	Dear Hearts And Gentle People	1962	8.00	20.00
Decca DL-74290	(S)	Dear Hearts And Gentle People	1962	12.00	30.00
Decca DL-4341	(M)	The Red Foley Show	1963	6.00	15.00
Decca DL-74341	(S)	The Red Foley Show	1963	8.00	20.00
Decca DXB-177	(M)	The Red Foley Story (2 LPs)	1964	6.00	15.00
Decca DXSB-177	(S)	The Red Foley Story (2 LPs)	1964	8.00	20.00
Decca DL-4603	(M)	Songs Everybody Knows	1965	5.00	12.00
Decca DL-74603	(S)	Songs Everybody Knows	1965	6.00	15.00
— Original Decca albums above have black labels with "Mfrd by Decca" beneath the rainbow.—					

FOLEY, RED, & ERNEST TUBB

Decca DL-8298	(M)	Red And Ernie	1956	20.00	50.00

FOLKSINGERS, THE

Elektra EKL-157	(M)	Run Come Here	195?	10.00	25.00

FOLKSTERS, THE

Mercury MG-20749	(M)	New In Folk	1962	5.00	12.00
Mercury SR-60749	(S)	New In Folk	1962	6.00	15.00

FOLKSWINGERS, THE
The Folkswingers feature Glen Campbell.

World Pacific WP-1812	(M)	12 String Guitar	1963	6.00	15.00
World Pacific ST-1812	(S)	12 String Guitar	1963	8.00	20.00
World Pacific ST-1812	(S)	12 String Guitar (Red vinyl)	1963	20.00	50.00
World Pacific WP-1814	(M)	12 String Guitar, Volume 2	1963	5.00	12.00
World Pacific ST-1814	(S)	12 String Guitar, Volume 2	1963	6.00	15.00
World Pacific WP-1846	(M)	Raga Rock	1966	6.00	15.00
World Pacific ST-1846	(S)	Raga Rock	1966	8.00	20.00

FONDA, HENRY

Coral CRL-57308	(M)	Voices Of The 20th Century	1959	16.00	40.00

FONTANA, WAYNE, & THE MINDBENDERS
Refer to The Mindbenders.

Fontana MGF-27542	(M)	The Game Of Love	1965	10.00	25.00
Fontana SRF-67542	(E)	The Game Of Love	1965	8.00	20.00

FONTANA, WAYNE

MGM E-4459	(M)	Wayne Fontana	1967	6.00	15.00
MGM SE-4459	(S)	Wayne Fontana	1967	8.00	20.00

FONTANE SISTERS, THE

Dot DLP-3004	(M)	The Fontane Sisters	1956	12.00	30.00
Dot DLP-3042	(M)	The Fontanes Sing	1957	12.00	30.00
Dot DLP-3531	(M)	Tips Of My Fingers	1963	6.00	15.00
Dot DLP-25531	(S)	Tips Of My Fingers	1963	8.00	20.00

FOOL, THE

Mercury SR-61178	(S)	The Fool	1968	5.00	12.00

FORD, FRANKIE

Ace LP-1005	(M)	Let's Take A Sea Cruise	1959	100.00	200.00

FORD, NEAL, & THE FANATICS

Hickory LPS-141	(S)	Neal Ford & The Fanatics	1968	6.00	15.00

FORD, ROCKY BILL

Audio Lab AL-1561	(M)	A New Singing Star	1960	35.00	70.00

Label & Catalog #		Title	Year	VG+	NM

FORD, TENNESSE ERNIE
Ernie Ford's considerable catalog is primarily gospel, which is not covered in this edition.

Label & Catalog #		Title	Year	VG+	NM
Capitol T-888	(M)	**Ol' Rockin' Ern'** *(Turquoise label)*	1957	**20.00**	**50.00**

FOREIGNER

Mobile Fidelity MFSL-052	(S)	**Double Vision**	1979	**8.00**	**20.00**

FORREST, HELEN

Capitol T-704	(M)	**The Voice Of The Name Bands**	1956	**20.00**	**50.00**

FORTUNE, JOHNNY

Park Avenue 401	(M)	**Soul Surfer**	1963	**20.00**	**50.00**
Park Avenue 1301	(S)	**Soul Surfer**	1963	**50.00**	**100.00**

FORTUNE-TELLER

R.M.T. 4956	(S)	**Inner-City Scream**	1978	**75.00**	**150.00**

FORTUNES, THE

Press PR7-3002	(M)	**The Fortunes**	1965	**10.00**	**25.00**
Press PRS-83002	(S)	**The Fortunes**	1965	**12.00**	**30.00**
World Pacific WPS-21904	(S)	**That Same Old Feeling**	1970	**5.00**	**12.00**
Capitol ST-647	(S)	**Freedom**	1971	**5.00**	**12.00**
Capitol ST-809	(S)	**Here Comes That Rainy Day Feeling Again**	1971	**6.00**	**15.00**

FORUM, THE

Mira MLP-301	(M)	**The River Is Wide**	1967	**5.00**	**12.00**
Mira MLPS-301	(P)	**The River Is Wide**	1967	**6.00**	**15.00**

FOUL DOGS, THE

Rhythm Sound GA-481	(M)	**No. 1**	1966	**150.00**	**250.00**

FOUNDATIONS, THE

Uni 73016	(P)	**Baby, Now That I've Found You**	1968	**6.00**	**15.00**
Uni 73043	(P)	**Build Me Up Buttercup**	1969	**6.00**	**15.00**
Uni 73058	(S)	**Digging The Foundations**	1969	**5.00**	**12.00**

FOUR ACES, THE
The lead Ace was Al Alberts.

Decca DL-5429 (10")	(M)	**The Four Aces**	1952	**30.00**	**60.00**
Decca DL-8122	(M)	**The Mood For Love**	1955	**20.00**	**50.00**
Decca DL-8191	(M)	**Merry Christmas**	1956	**20.00**	**50.00**
Decca DL-8227	(M)	**Sentimental Souvenirs**	1956	**20.00**	**50.00**
Decca DL-8228	(M)	**Heart And Soul**	1956	**20.00**	**50.00**
Decca DL-8312	(M)	**She Sees All The Hollywood Hits**	1957	**20.00**	**50.00**
Decca DL-8424	(M)	**Written On The Wind** *(Soundtrack)*	1957	**50.00**	**100.00**
Decca DL-8567	(M)	**Shuffling Along**	1957	**20.00**	**50.00**
Decca DL-8693	(M)	**Hits From Hollywood**	1958	**20.00**	**50.00**
Decca DL-8766	(M)	**The Swingin' Aces**	1958	**14.00**	**35.00**
Decca DL-78766	(S)	**The Swingin' Aces**	1958	**20.00**	**50.00**
Decca DL-8855	(M)	**Hits From Broadway**	1959	**14.00**	**35.00**
Decca DL-78855	(S)	**Hits From Broadway**	1959	**20.00**	**50.00**
Decca DL-8944	(M)	**Beyond The Blue Horizon**	1959	**14.00**	**35.00**
Decca DL-78944	(S)	**Beyond The Blue Horizon**	1959	**20.00**	**50.00**
		—Original Decca albums above have black & silver labels.—			
Decca DL-4013	(M)	**The Golden Hits Of The Four Aces**	1960	**8.00**	**20.00**
Decca DL-74013	(S)	**The Golden Hits Of The Four Aces**	1960	**8.00**	**20.00**
United Arts. UAL-3337	(M)	**Record Oldies**	1963	**6.00**	**15.00**
United Arts. UAS-6337	(S)	**Record Oldies**	1963	**8.00**	**20.00**

FOUR FRESHMEN, THE

Capitol H-522 (10")	(M)	**Voices In Modern**	1955	**20.00**	**50.00**
Capitol T-522	(M)	**Voices In Modern**	1955	**14.00**	**35.00**
Capitol T-683	(M)	**Four Freshmen And Five Trombones**	1956	**14.00**	**35.00**
Capitol T-743	(M)	**Freshmen Favorites**	1956	**14.00**	**35.00**
Capitol T-763	(M)	**Four Freshmen And Five Trumpets**	1957	**14.00**	**35.00**
Capitol T-844	(M)	**Four Freshmen And Five Saxes**	1957	**14.00**	**35.00**

Label & Catalog #		Title	Year	VG+	NM
Capitol T-992	(M)	Voices In Latin	1958	10.00	25.00
Capitol T-1008	(M)	The Four Freshmen In Person	1958	10.00	25.00
Capitol ST-1008	(S)	The Four Freshmen In Person	1958	14.00	35.00
— Original Capitol albums above have turquoise labels.—					
Capitol T-1074	(M)	Voices In Love	1958	8.00	20.00
Capitol ST-1074	(S)	Voices In Love	1958	12.00	30.00
Capitol T-1103	(M)	Freshmen Favorites, Volume 2	1959	8.00	20.00
Capitol ST-1103	(S)	Freshmen Favorites, Volume 2	1959	12.00	30.00
Capitol T-1189	(M)	Love Lost	1959	8.00	20.00
Capitol ST-1189	(S)	Love Lost	1959	12.00	30.00
Capitol T-1255	(M)	The Four Freshmen And Five Guitars	1960	8.00	20.00
Capitol ST-1255	(S)	The Four Freshmen And Five Guitars	1960	10.00	25.00
Capitol T-1295	(M)	Voices And Brass	1960	8.00	20.00
Capitol ST-1295	(S)	Voices And Brass	1960	10.00	25.00
Capitol T-1378	(M)	First Affair	1960	8.00	20.00
Capitol ST-1378	(S)	First Affair	1960	10.00	25.00
Capitol T-1485	(M)	Freshmen Year	1961	8.00	20.00
Capitol ST-1485	(S)	Freshmen Year	1961	10.00	25.00
Capitol T-1543	(M)	Voices In Fun	1961	8.00	20.00
Capitol ST-1543	(S)	Voices In Fun	1961	10.00	25.00
Capitol T-1640	(M)	The Best Of The Four Freshmen	1962	8.00	20.00
Capitol ST-1640	(S)	The Best Of The Four Freshmen	1962	10.00	25.00
Capitol T-1682	(M)	Stars In Our Eyes	1962	8.00	20.00
Capitol ST-1682	(S)	Stars In Our Eyes	1962	10.00	25.00
— Original Capitol albums above have black labels with the Capitol logo on the left side.—					
Capitol T-1753	(M)	Swingers	1962	6.00	15.00
Capitol ST-1753	(S)	Swingers	1962	8.00	20.00
Capitol T-1860	(M)	The Four Freshmen In Person, Volume 2	1963	6.00	15.00
Capitol ST-1860	(S)	The Four Freshmen In Person, Volume 2	1963	8.00	20.00
Capitol T-1950	(M)	Got That Feelin'	1963	6.00	15.00
Capitol ST-1950	(S)	Got That Feelin'	1963	8.00	20.00
Capitol T-2067	(M)	Funny How Time Slips Away	1964	6.00	15.00
Capitol ST-2067	(S)	Funny How Time Slips Away	1964	8.00	20.00
Capitol T-2168	(M)	More Four Freshmen And Five Trombones	1964	6.00	15.00
Capitol ST-2168	(S)	More Four Freshmen And Five Trombones	1964	8.00	20.00
— Original Capitol albums above have black labels with the Capitol logo on top.—					
Liberty LST-7563	(S)	Today Is Tomorrow	1968	6.00	15.00
Liberty LST-7590	(S)	In A Class By Themselves	1969	6.00	15.00

FOUR KNIGHTS, THE

Label & Catalog #		Title	Year	VG+	NM
Capitol H-345 (10")	(M)	Spotlight Songs	1953	100.00	200.00
Capitol T-345	(M)	Spotlight Songs	1956	50.00	100.00
Coral CRL-57221	(M)	The Four Knights	1959	50.00	100.00
Coral CRL-57309	(M)	Million Dollar Baby	1960	20.00	50.00
Coral CRL-757309	(S)	Million Dollar Baby	1960	35.00	70.00

FOUR LADS, THE

Label & Catalog #		Title	Year	VG+	NM
Columbia CL-6329 (10")	(M)	Stage Show	1954	20.00	50.00
Columbia CL-2545 (10")	(M)	The Four Lads Sing Frank Loesser	1956	16.00	40.00
Columbia CL- 2577 (10")	(M)	Stage Show	1956	16.00	40.00
Columbia CL-861	(M)	The Four Lads With Frankie Laine	1956	16.00	40.00
Columbia CL-912	(M)	On The Sunny Side	1956	16.00	40.00
Columbia CL-950	(M)	The Stingiest Man In Town (Soundtrack)	1956	20.00	50.00
Columbia CL-1045	(M)	The Four Lads Sing Frank Loesser	1957	20.00	50.00
Columbia CL-1235	(M)	The Four Lads' Greatest Hits	1958	12.00	30.00
Columbia CL-1???	(M)	Breezin' Along	1959	10.00	25.00
Columbia CS-8035	(S)	Breezin' Along	1959	12.00	30.00
Columbia CL-1111	(M)	Four On The Aisle	1959	10.00	25.00
Columbia CS-8047	(S)	Four On The Aisle	1959	12.00	30.00
Columbia CL-1299	(M)	The Four Lads Swing Along	1959	10.00	25.00
Columbia CS-8106	(S)	The Four Lads Swing Along	1959	12.00	30.00
Columbia CL-1407	(M)	High Spirits!	1959	10.00	25.00
Columbia CS-8203	(S)	High Spirits!	1959	12.00	30.00
Columbia CL-1502	(M)	Love Affair	1960	6.00	15.00
Columbia CS-8293	(S)	Love Affair	1960	8.00	20.00
Columbia CL-1550	(M)	Everything Goes	1960	6.00	15.00
Columbia CS-8350	(S)	Everything Goes	1960	8.00	20.00
— Original Columbia albums above have three white "eye" logos on each side of the spindle hole.—					

Label & Catalog #		Title	Year	VG+	NM
Kapp KL-1224	(M)	**Twelve Hits**	*1961*	**6.00**	**15.00**
Kapp KS-3224	(S)	**Twelve Hits**	*1961*	**8.00**	**20.00**
Kapp KL-1254	(M)	**Dixieland Doin's**	*1961*	**6.00**	**15.00**
Kapp KS-3254	(S)	**Dixieland Doin's**	*1961*	**8.00**	**20.00**
Dot DLP-3438	(M)	**Hits Of The 60's**	*1962*	**6.00**	**15.00**
Dot DLP-25438	(S)	**Hits Of The 60's**	*1962*	**8.00**	**20.00**
Dot DLP-3533	(M)	**Oh, Happy Day**	*1963*	**6.00**	**15.00**
Dot DLP-25533	(S)	**Oh, Happy Day**	*1963*	**8.00**	**20.00**
United Arts. UAL-3356	(M)	**This Year's Top Movie Hits**	*1964*	**6.00**	**15.00**
United Arts. UAS-6356	(S)	**This Year's Top Movie Hits**	*1964*	**8.00**	**20.00**
United Arts. UAL-3399	(M)	**Songs Of World War I**	*1964*	**6.00**	**15.00**
United Arts. UAS-6399	(S)	**Songs Of World War I**	*1964*	**8.00**	**20.00**

FOUR LOVERS, THE
Members Frankie Valli, Nick DeVito and Hank Majewski formed the Four Seasons.

RCA Victor LPM-1317	(M)	**Joyride**	*1956*	**360.00**	**600.00**

FOUR MOST, THE

Dawn DLP-1112	(M)	**The Four Most Sing**	*1956*	**20.00**	**50.00**

FOUR PREPS, THE

Capitol T-994	(M)	**The Four Preps** *(Turquoise label)*	*1958*	**12.00**	**30.00**
Capitol T-1090	(M)	**The Things We Did Last Summer**	*1958*	**10.00**	**25.00**
Capitol T-1216	(M)	**Dancing And Dreaming**	*1959*	**8.00**	**20.00**
Capitol ST-1216	(S)	**Dancing And Dreaming**	*1959*	**12.00**	**30.00**
Capitol T-1291	(M)	**Early In The Morning**	*1960*	**10.00**	**25.00**
Capitol DT-1291	(E)	**Early In The Morning**	*1960*	**6.00**	**15.00**
Capitol T-1566	(M)	**Four Preps On Campus**	*1961*	**8.00**	**20.00**
Capitol ST-1566	(S)	**Four Preps On Campus**	*1961*	**10.00**	**25.00**
Capitol T-1647	(M)	**Campus Encore**	*1962*	**8.00**	**20.00**
Capitol ST-1647	(S)	**Campus Encore**	*1962*	**10.00**	**25.00**

— Original Capitol albums above have black labels with the Capitol logo on the left side.—

Capitol T-1814	(M)	**Campus Confidential**	*1963*	**5.00**	**12.00**
Capitol ST-1814	(S)	**Campus Confidential**	*1963*	**6.00**	**15.00**
Capitol T-1976	(S)	**Songs For A Campus Party**	*1963*	**5.00**	**12.00**
Capitol ST-1976	(S)	**Songs For A Campus Party**	*1963*	**6.00**	**15.00**
Capitol T-2169	(S)	**How To Succeed In Love**	*1964*	**5.00**	**12.00**
Capitol ST-2169	(S)	**How To Succeed In Love**	*1964*	**6.00**	**15.00**
Capitol T-2708	(S)	**The Best Of The Four Preps**	*1967*	**5.00**	**12.00**
Capitol ST-2708	(S)	**The Best Of The Four Preps**	*1967*	**6.00**	**15.00**

— Original Capitol albums above have black labels with the Capitol logo on top.—

FOUR SEASONS, THE [FRANKIE VALLI & THE FOUR SEASONS]
Refer to The Beatles; Four Lovers; Franki Valli.

Vee Jay LP-1053	(M)	**Sherry And 11 Others**	*1962*	**12.00**	**30.00**
Vee Jay SR-1053	(P)	**Sherry And 11 Others**	*1962*	**16.00**	**40.00**
Vee Jay LP-1055	(M)	**Four Seasons' Greetings**	*1963*	**12.00**	**30.00**
Vee Jay SR-1055	(S)	**Four Seasons' Greetings**	*1963*	**16.00**	**40.00**
Vee Jay LP-1056	(M)	**Big Girls Don't Cry**	*1963*	**12.00**	**30.00**
Vee Jay SR-1056	(P)	**Big Girls Don't Cry**	*1963*	**16.00**	**40.00**
Vee Jay LP-1059	(M)	**Ain't That A Shame**	*1963*	**8.00**	**20.00**
Vee Jay SR-1059	(P)	**Ain't That A Shame**	*1963*	**12.00**	**30.00**
Vee Jay LP-1065	(M)	**Golden Hits Of The Four Seasons**	*1963*	**8.00**	**20.00**
Vee Jay SR-1065	(P)	**Golden Hits Of The Four Seasons**	*1963*	**12.00**	**30.00**
Vee Jay LP-1082	(M)	**Folk-Nanny**	*1963*	**8.00**	**20.00**
Vee Jay SR-1082	(P)	**Folk-Nanny**	*1963*	**12.00**	**30.00**
Vee Jay LP-1082	(M)	**Stay** *(Repackage of "Folk-Nanny")*	*1964*	**6.00**	**15.00**
Vee Jay SR-1082	(P)	**Stay** *(Repackage of "Folk-Nanny")*	*1964*	**8.00**	**20.00**
Vee Jay LP-1088	(M)	**More Golden Hits**	*1964*	**8.00**	**20.00**
Vee Jay SR-1088	(P)	**More Golden Hits**	*1964*	**12.00**	**30.00**
		(First pressings includes "Long Lonely Nights.")			
Vee Jay LP-1088	(M)	**More Golden Hits**	*1965*	**6.00**	**15.00**
Vee Jay SR-1088	(P)	**More Golden Hits**	*1965*	**8.00**	**20.00**
		(Later pressings replace "Nights" with "Apple Of My Eye.")			
Vee Jay LP-1121	(M)	**We Love Girls**	*1965*	**8.00**	**20.00**
Vee Jay SR-1121	(S)	**We Love Girls**	*1965*	**12.00**	**30.00**
Vee Jay LP-1154	(M)	**Recorded Live On Stage**	*1965*	**8.00**	**20.00**
Vee Jay SR-1154	(S)	**Recorded Live On Stage**	*1965*	**12.00**	**30.00**

— Original Vee Jay albums above have black labels with a rainbow border.—

Label & Catalog #		Title	Year	VG+	NM

Original pressings of this double-album, containing many early hits in stereo, featured the "4" on the cover in unadorned red print; on later pressings it is either red print with black trim or solid white.

Label & Catalog #		Title	Year	VG+	NM
Philips PHM-200124	(M)	**Dawn (Go Away) & 11 Other Great Songs**	1964	6.00	15.00
Philips PHS-600124	(S)	**Dawn (Go Away) & 11 Other Great Songs**	1964	8.00	20.00
Philips PHM-200129	(M)	**Born To Wander**	1964	6.00	15.00
Philips PHS-600129	(S)	**Born To Wander**	1964	8.00	20.00
Philips PHM-200146	(M)	**Rag Doll**	1964	6.00	15.00
Philips PHS-600146	(P)	**Rag Doll**	1964	8.00	20.00
Philips PHM-200150	(M)	**All The Song Hits Of The Four Seasons**	1964	6.00	15.00
Philips PHS-600150	(S)	**All The Song Hits Of The Four Seasons**	1964	8.00	20.00
Philips PHM-200164	(M)	**The Four Seasons Entertain You**	1965	6.00	15.00
Philips PHS-600164	(S)	**The Four Seasons Entertain You**	1965	8.00	20.00
Philips PHM-200193	(M)	**Big Hits By Bacharach, David & Dylan**	1965	8.00	20.00
Philips PHS-600193	(S)	**Big Hits By Bacharach, David & Dylan**	1965	10.00	25.00
		(The cover has a medieval motif.)			
Philips PHM-200193	(M)	**Big Hits By Bacharach, David & Dylan**	1965	12.00	30.00
Philips PHS-600193	(S)	**Big Hits By Bacharach, David & Dylan**	1965	16.00	40.00
		(The cover features photos of the group.)			
Philips PHM-200196	(M)	**Gold Vault Of Hits**	1965	6.00	15.00
Philips PHS-600196	(S)	**Gold Vault Of Hits**	1965	8.00	20.00
		(Original pressings: the title on the cover is in unadorned red print.)			
Philips PHM-200196	(M)	**Gold Vault Of Hits**	196?	5.00	12.00
Philips PHS-600196	(S)	**Gold Vault Of Hits**	196?	6.00	15.00
		(Later pressings the title is red with black trim or solid black.)			
Philips PHM-200201	(M)	**Working My Way Back To You**	1966	6.00	15.00
Philips PHS-600201	(S)	**Working My Way Back To You**	1966	8.00	20.00
Philips PHM-200221	(M)	**2nd Gold Vault Of Hits**	1966	5.00	12.00
Philips PHS-600221	(S)	**2nd Gold Vault Of Hits**	1966	6.00	15.00
Philips PHM-200222	(M)	**Lookin' Back**	1966	6.00	15.00
Philips PHS-600222	(S)	**Lookin' Back**	1966	8.00	20.00
Philips PHM-200223	(M)	**The Four Seasons' Christmas Album**	1966	8.00	20.00
Philips PHS-600223	(S)	**The Four Seasons' Christmas Album**	1966	10.00	25.00
Philips PHM-200243	(M)	**New Gold Hits**	1967	6.00	15.00
Philips PHS-600243	(S)	**New Gold Hits**	1967	8.00	20.00

Label & Catalog #		Title	Year	VG+	NM
Philips PHS-2-6501	(S)	**Edizone D'Oro** (2 LPs)	1969	12.00	30.00
		(The "4" on the cover is in unadorned red print.)			
Philips PHS-2-6501	(S)	**Edizone D'Oro** (2 LPs)	1969	16.00	40.00
		(The "4" on the cover is in white print or red with black trim.)			
Philips PHS-600290	(S)	**Genuine Imitation Life Gazette**	1969	10.00	25.00
		(Original covers are yellow newspaper.)			
Philips PHS-600290	(S)	**Genuine Imitation Life Gazette**	1969	5.00	12.00
		(Later covers are white newspaper.)			
Philips PHS-600341	(S)	**Half And Half**	1970	6.00	15.00
Sears 609	(S)	**Brotherhood Of Man**	1970	8.00	20.00

FOUR TOPS, THE

Workshop 217	(M)	**Jazz Impressions**	1962	See note below	
		(Workshop was a subsidiary of the Motown family; 217 was advertised but never released.)			
Motown 622	(M)	**The Four Tops**	1964	6.00	15.00
Motown MS-622	(S)	**The Four Tops**	1964	8.00	20.00
Motown 634	(M)	**The Four Tops, No. 2**	1964	6.00	15.00
Motown MS-634	(S)	**The Four Tops, No. 2**	1965	8.00	20.00
Motown 647	(M)	**The Four Tops On Top**	1966	6.00	15.00
Motown MS-647	(S)	**The Four Tops On Top**	1966	8.00	20.00
Motown 654	(M)	**The Four Tops Live**	1966	6.00	15.00
Motown MS-654	(S)	**The Four Tops Live**	1966	8.00	20.00
Motown 657	(M)	**The Four Tops On Broadway**	1967	5.00	12.00
Motown MS-657	(S)	**The Four Tops On Broadway**	1967	6.00	15.00
Motown 660	(M)	**Reach Out**	1967	5.00	12.00
Motown MS-660	(S)	**Reach Out**	1967	6.00	15.00
Motown 662	(M)	**The Four Tops' Greatest Hits**	1967	5.00	12.00
Motown MS-662	(S)	**The Four Tops' Greatest Hits**	1967	6.00	15.00
Motown MS-669	(S)	**Yesterday Dreams**	1968	4.00	10.00
Motown MS-675	(S)	**The Four Tops Now**	1969	4.00	10.00
Motown MS-695	(S)	**Soul Spin**	1969	4.00	10.00
Motown MS-704	(S)	**Still Waters Run Deep**	1970	4.00	10.00
Motown MS-721	(S)	**Changing Times**	1970	4.00	10.00
Motown MS-740	(S)	**The Four Tops' Greatest Hits, Volume 2**	1971	4.00	10.00
Motown MS-748	(S)	**Nature Planned It**	1972	4.00	10.00
Command QD-40011	(Q)	**Keeper Of The Castle**	1974	5.00	12.00
Command QD-40012	(Q)	**Mainstreet People**	1974	5.00	12.00

FOUR TUNES, THE

Jubilee LP-1039	(M)	**12 X 4**	1957	35.00	70.00

FOURTH WAY, THE

Capitol ST-317	(S)	**The Fourth Way**	1969	6.00	15.00
Harvest SKAO-423	(S)	**Sun And Moon Have Come Together**	1970	5.00	12.00
Harvest ST-666	(S)	**Werewolf**	1971	5.00	12.00

FOWLEY, KIM

Tower T-5080	(M)	**Love Is Alive And Well**	1967	8.00	20.00
Tower ST-5080	(S)	**Love Is Alive And Well**	1967	10.00	25.00
Imperial LP-12413	(S)	**Born To Be Wild**	1968	12.00	30.00
Imperial LP-12423	(S)	**Outrageous**	1969	12.00	30.00
Imperial LP-12443	(S)	**Good Clean Fun**	1969	12.00	30.00

FOWLER, WALLY, & THE OAK RIDGE QUARTET

King 702	(M)	**Gospel Song Festival**	1960	16.00	40.00
Starday SLP-112	(M)	**All Night Songing Gospel Concert**	1960	12.00	30.00

FOX, CURLY, & TEXAS RUBY

Starday SLP-235	(M)	**Curly Fox And Texas Ruby**	196?	16.00	40.00
Harmony HL-7302	(M)	**Travelling Blues**	196?	10.00	25.00

FOXX, INEZ & CHARLIE

Symbol SYM-4400	(M)	**Mockingbird**	1963	30.00	60.00
Sue LP-1037	(M)	**Inez And Charlie Foxx**	1965	12.00	30.00
Sue LP-1037	(S)	**Inez And Charlie Foxx**	1965	16.00	40.00
Dynamo D-7000	(M)	**Come By Here**	1967	6.00	15.00
Dynamo DS-8000	(S)	**Come By Here**	1967	8.00	20.00

Label & Catalog #		Title	Year	VG+	NM
Dynamo D-7002	(M)	**Inez And Charlie Foxx's Greatest Hits**	1967	6.00	15.00
Dynamo DS-8002	(S)	**Inez And Charlie Foxx's Greatest Hits**	1967	8.00	20.00

FRACTION

Angelus WR-5005	(S)	**Moon Blood**	197?		*See note below*
		(Die-cut, red window in cover allows the moon on the inner sleeeve to show. Estimated near mint value $1,000-2,000.)			

FRAMPTON, PETER

A&M PR-3703	(S)	**Frampton Comes Alive** *(Picture disc)*	1978	4.00	10.00
A&M SP-4704	(DJ)	**I'm In You** *(Picture disc)*	1978	6.00	15.00
A&M SP-27200	(DJ)	**The Peter Frampton Radio Special**	197?	10.00	25.00
Sweet Thunder	(S)	**Frampton Comes Alive** *(2 LPs. Half-speed)*	198?	10.00	25.00

FRANCIS, CONNIE

MGM E-3686	(M)	**Who's Sorry Now?**	1958	20.00	50.00
MGM E-3761	(M)	**The Exciting Connie Francis**	1959	12.00	30.00
MGM SE-3761	(S)	**The Exciting Connie Francis**	1959	16.00	40.00
		—Original MGM albums above have yellow labels.—			
MGM E-3686	(M)	**Who's Sorry Now?**	196?	10.00	25.00
MGM SE-3686	(E)	**Who's Sorry Now?**	196?	8.00	20.00
MGM E-3761	(M)	**The Exciting Connie Francis**	196?	8.00	20.00
MGM SE-3761	(S)	**The Exciting Connie Francis**	196?	10.00	25.00
MGM E-3776	(M)	**My Thanks To You**	1959	10.00	25.00
MGM SE-3776	(S)	**My Thanks To You**	1959	12.00	30.00
MGM E-3791	(M)	**Italian Favorites**	1959	8.00	20.00
MGM SE-3791	(S)	**Italian Favorites**	1959	10.00	25.00
MGM E-3792	(M)	**Christmas In My Heart**	1959	10.00	25.00
MGM SE-3792	(S)	**Christmas In My Heart**	1959	12.00	30.00
MGM E-3793	(M)	**Connie's Greatest Hits**	1960	10.00	25.00
MGM SE-3793	(E)	**Connie's Greatest Hits**	1960	8.00	20.00
MGM E-3794	(M)	**Rock 'N' Roll Million Sellers**	1960	10.00	25.00
MGM SE-3794	(S)	**Rock 'N' Roll Million Sellers**	1960	12.00	30.00
MGM E-3795	(M)	**Country And Western Golden Hits**	1960	8.00	20.00
MGM SE-3795	(S)	**Country And Western Golden Hits**	1960	10.00	25.00
MGM E-3853	(M)	**Spanish And Latin American Favorites**	1960	6.00	15.00
MGM SE-3853	(S)	**Spanish And Latin American Favorites**	1960	8.00	20.00
MGM E-3869	(M)	**Jewish Favorites**	1961	6.00	15.00
MGM SE-3869	(S)	**Jewish Favorites**	1961	8.00	20.00
MGM E-3871	(M)	**More Italian Favorites**	1961	6.00	15.00
MGM SE-3871	(S)	**More Italian Favorites**	1961	8.00	20.00
MGM E-3893	(M)	**Songs To A Swinging Band**	1961	8.00	20.00
MGM SE-3893	(S)	**Songs To A Swinging Band**	1961	10.00	25.00
MGM E-3913	(M)	**Connie At The Copa**	1961	8.00	20.00
MGM SE-3913	(S)	**Connie At The Copa**	1961	10.00	25.00
MGM E-3942	(M)	**More Greatest Hits**	1961	8.00	20.00
MGM SE-3942	(S)	**More Greatest Hits**	1961	10.00	25.00
MGM E-3965	(M)	**Never On Sunday**	1961	8.00	20.00
MGM SE-3965	(S)	**Never On Sunday**	1961	10.00	25.00
MGM E-3969	(M)	**Folk Song Favorites**	1961	8.00	20.00
MGM SE-3969	(S)	**Folk Song Favorites**	1961	10.00	25.00
MGM E-4013	(M)	**Irish Favorites**	1962	8.00	20.00
MGM SE-4013	(S)	**Irish Favorites**	1962	10.00	25.00
MGM E-4022	(M)	**Do The Twist With Connie Francis**	1962	8.00	20.00
MGM SE-4022	(S)	**Do The Twist With Connie Francis**	1962	10.00	25.00
MGM E-4022	(M)	**Dance Party** *(Repackage of "Do The Twist")*	196?	8.00	20.00
MGM SE-4022	(S)	**Dance Party** *(Repackage of "Do The Twist")*	196?	10.00	25.00
MGM L-70126	(M)	**Fun Songs For Children**	196?	30.00	60.00
MGM E-4023	(M)	**Fun Songs For Children**	1962	12.00	30.00
MGM E-4048	(M)	**Award Winning Motion Picture Hits**	1962	8.00	20.00
MGMS E-4048	(S)	**Award Winning Motion Picture Hits**	1962	10.00	25.00
MGM E-4049	(M)	**Second Hand Love And Other Hits**	1962	8.00	20.00
MGM SE-4049	(S)	**Second Hand Love And Other Hits**	1962	10.00	25.00
MGM E-4079	(M)	**Country Music, Connie Style**	1962	8.00	20.00
MGM SE-4079	(S)	**Country Music, Connie Style**	1962	10.00	25.00
MGM E-4102	(M)	**Modern Italian Hits**	1963	8.00	20.00
MGM SE-4102	(S)	**Modern Italian Hits**	1963	10.00	25.00
MGM E-4123	(M)	**Follow The Boys** *(Soundtrack)*	1963	8.00	20.00
MGM SE-4123	(S)	**Follow The Boys** *(Soundtrack)*	1963	10.00	25.00

Label & Catalog #		Title	Year	VG+	NM
MGM E-4124	(M)	German Favorites	1963	8.00	20.00
MGM SE-4124	(S)	German Favorites	1963	10.00	25.00
MGM E-4145	(M)	Greatest American Waltzes	1963	8.00	20.00
MGM SE-4145	(S)	Greatest American Waltzes	1963	10.00	25.00
MGM E-4161	(M)	Mala Femmina And Big Hits From Italy	1963	8.00	20.00
MGM SE-4161	(S)	Mala Femmina And Big Hits From Italy	1963	10.00	25.00
MGM E-4167	(M)	The Very Best Of Connie Francis	1963	8.00	20.00
MGM SE-4167	(S)	The Very Best Of Connie Francis	1963	10.00	25.00
MGM E-4210	(M)	In The Summer Of His Years	1964	8.00	20.00
MGM SE-4210	(S)	In The Summer Of His Years	1964	10.00	25.00
MGM E-4229	(M)	Looking For Love (Soundtrack)	1964	8.00	20.00
MGM SE-4229	(S)	Looking For Love (Soundtrack)	1964	10.00	25.00
MGM E-4253	(M)	A New Kind Of Connie	1964	8.00	20.00
MGM SE-4253	(S)	A New Kind Of Connie	1964	10.00	25.00
MGM E-4294	(M)	For Mama	1965	8.00	20.00
MGM SE-4294	(S)	For Mama	1965	10.00	25.00
MGM E-4298	(M)	All Time International Hits	1965	8.00	20.00
MGM SE-4298	(S)	All Time International Hits	1965	10.00	25.00
MGM E-4334	(M)	When The Boys Meet The Girls (Sdtk)	1965	3.50	8.00
MGM SE-4334	(S)	When The Boys Meet The Girls (Sdtk)	1965	4.00	10.00
MGM E-4355	(M)	Jealous Heart	1965	8.00	20.00
MGM SE-4355	(S)	Jealous Heart	1965	10.00	25.00
MGM E-4382	(M)	Movie Greats Of The 60's	1966	8.00	20.00
MGM SE-4382	(S)	Movie Greats Of The 60's	1966	10.00	25.00
MGM E-4399	(M)	Connie's Christmas (Repackage of 3792)	1966	8.00	20.00
MGM SE-4399	(S)	Connie's Christmas (Repackage of 3792)	1966	10.00	25.00
MGM E-4411	(M)	Live At The Sahara In Las Vegas	1966	8.00	20.00
MGM SE-4411	(S)	Live At The Sahara In Las Vegas	1966	10.00	25.00
MGM E-4448	(M)	Love, Italian Style	1967	8.00	20.00
MGM SE-4448	(S)	Love, Italian Style	1967	10.00	25.00
MGM E-4472	(M)	Connie Francis On Broadway Today	1967	8.00	20.00
MGM SE-4472	(S)	Connie Francis On Broadway Today	1967	10.00	25.00
MGM E-4474	(M)	Grandes Exitos del Cine de los Anos 60	1967	8.00	20.00
MGM SE-4474	(S)	Grandes Exitos del Cine de los Anos 60	1967	10.00	25.00
MGM E-4487	(M)	My Heart Cries For You	1967	8.00	20.00
MGM SE-4487	(S)	My Heart Cries For You	1967	10.00	25.00
		— Original MGM albums above have black labels.—			
MGM E-4522	(M)	Hawaii: Connie	1968	10.00	25.00
MGM SE-4522	(S)	Hawaii: Connie	1968	6.00	15.00
MGM SE-4573	(S)	Connie & Clyde	1968	6.00	15.00
MGM SE-4585	(S)	Connie Francis Sings Bacharach & David	1968	6.00	15.00
MGM SE-4637	(S)	The Wedding Cake	1969	6.00	15.00
MGM SE-4655	(S)	The Songs Of Les Reed	1969	6.00	15.00
MGM GAS-109	(S)	Greatest Golden Groovy Goodies	1970	8.00	20.00
MGM LES-903	(S)	Connie Francis And The Kids Next Door	197?	6.00	15.00
MGM 91145	(S)	My Best To You (Capitol Record Club)	196?	6.00	15.00
MGM E6PS-2	(S)	A Connie Francis Spectacular (5 LP box)	197?	12.00	30.00
Mati-Mor 8002	(M)	Brylcreem Presents "Sing Along With Connie Francis"	195?	6.00	15.00

FRANCIS, CONNIE, & HANK WILLIAMS, JR.

MGM E-4251	(M)	Great Country Favorites	1964	6.00	15.00
MGM SE-4251	(S)	Great Country Favorites	1964	8.00	20.00

FRANKLIN, ALAN [THE ALAN FRANKLIN EXPLOSION]

Horne JC-888	(S)	The Blues Climax	1969	50.00	100.00
Aladdin 104049	(S)	Come Home, Baby	1979	18.00	45.00

FRANKLIN, ARETHA

Columbia CL-1612	(M)	Aretha	1961	10.00	25.00
Columbia CS-8412	(S)	Aretha	1961	12.00	30.00
Columbia CL-1761	(M)	The Electrifying Aretha Franklin	1962	10.00	25.00
Columbia CS-8561	(S)	The Electrifying Aretha Franklin	1962	12.00	30.00
Columbia CL-1876	(M)	The Tender... Swinging Aretha Franklin	1962	10.00	25.00
Columbia CS-8676	(S)	The Tender... Swinging Aretha Franklin	1962	12.00	30.00
		— Original Columbia albums above have three white "eye" logos on each side of the spindle hole.—			
Columbia CL-2079	(M)	Laughing On The Outside	1963	8.00	20.00
Columbia CS-8879	(S)	Laughing On The Outside	1963	10.00	25.00

Label & Catalog #		Title	Year	VG+	NM
Columbia CL-2163	(M)	Unforgettable	1964	8.00	20.00
Columbia CS-8963	(S)	Unforgettable	1964	10.00	25.00
Columbia CL-2281	(M)	Runnin' Out Of Fools	1964	8.00	20.00
Columbia CS-9081	(S)	Runnin' Out Of Fools	1964	10.00	25.00
Columbia CL-2351	(M)	Yeah!!!	1965	8.00	20.00
Columbia CS-9151	(S)	Yeah!!!	1965	10.00	25.00
Columbia CL-2521	(M)	Soul Sister	1966	8.00	20.00
Columbia CS-9321	(S)	Soul Sister	1966	10.00	25.00
Columbia CL-2629	(M)	Take It Like You Give It	1967	6.00	15.00
Columbia CS-9429	(S)	Take It Like You Give It	1967	8.00	20.00
Columbia CL-2673	(M)	Aretha Franklin's Greatest Hits	1967	6.00	15.00
Columbia CS-9473	(S)	Aretha Franklin's Greatest Hits	1967	8.00	20.00
Columbia CL-2754	(M)	Take A Look	1967	6.00	15.00
Columbia CS-9554	(S)	Take A Look	1967	8.00	20.00
Columbia CS-9601	(S)	Aretha Franklin's Greatest Hits, Volume 2	1968	6.00	15.00
Columbia CS-9776	(S)	Soft And Beautiful	1969	6.00	15.00
		— Columbia albums above have "360 Sound" on the bottom of the label.—			
Atlantic 8139	(M)	I Never Loved A Man (The Way I Love You)	1967	8.00	20.00
Atlantic SD-8139	(S)	I Never Loved A Man (The Way I Love You)	1967	6.00	15.00
Atlantic 8150	(M)	Aretha Arrives	1967	8.00	20.00
Atlantic SD-8150	(S)	Aretha Arrives	1967	6.00	15.00
Atlantic SD-8176	(S)	Lady Soul	1968	6.00	15.00
Atlantic SD-8186	(S)	Aretha Now	1968	6.00	15.00
		— Original Stereo Atlantic albums above have green & blue labels.—			
Atlantic SD-8207	(S)	Aretha In Paris	1968	5.00	12.00
Atlantic SD-8212	(S)	Soul '69	1969	5.00	12.00
Atlantic QD-7205	(Q)	Live At The Fillmore West	1971	6.00	15.00
Atlantic QD	(Q)	The Best Of Aretha Franklin	1971	10.00	25.00
FRANKLIN, CAROLYN					
RCA Victor LSP-4160	(S)	Baby Dynamite	1969	4.00	10.00
RCA Victor LSP-4317	(S)	Chain Reaction	1969	4.00	10.00
RCA Victor LSP-4411	(S)	I'd Rather Be Lonely	1969	4.00	10.00
FRANKLIN, ERMA					
Epic LN-3824	(S)	Her Name Is Erma	1962	5.00	12.00
Epic BN-619	(S)	Her Name Is Erma	1962	6.00	15.00
Brunswick BL-754147	(S)	Soul Sister	1969	4.00	10.00
FRANKS, MICHAEL					
Direct Disk SD-16611	(S)	Tiger In The Rain	197?	6.00	15.00
FRANTIC					
Lizard 20103	(S)	Conception	197?	6.00	15.00
FRATERNITY OF MAN, THE					
ABC S-647	(S)	The Fraternity Of Man	1968	8.00	20.00
Dot DLP-25955	(S)	Get It On	1969	8.00	20.00
FRAWLEY, WILLIAM					
Dot DLP-3061	(M)	The Old Ones	1957	12.00	30.00
FRAZIER, DALLAS					
Capitol T-2552	(M)	Elvira	1966	6.00	15.00
Capitol ST-2552	(S)	Elvira	1966	8.00	20.00
Capitol T-2764	(M)	Tell It Like It Is	1967	8.00	20.00
Capitol ST-2764	(S)	Tell It Like It Is	1967	10.00	25.00
FREAK SCENE, THE					
Columbia CL-2656	(M)	Psychedelic Psoul	1967	10.00	25.00
Columbia CS-9456	(S)	Psychedelic Psoul	1967	20.00	50.00
FREBERG, STAN					
Capitol T-732	(M)	Comedy Caravan	1956	20.00	50.00
Capitol T-777	(M)	A Child's Garden Of Freberg	1957	20.00	50.00
		— Original Capitol albums above have turquoise labels.—			
Capitol WBO-1035	(M)	The Best Of The Stan Freberg Show	1958	20.00	50.00
Capitol T-1242	(M)	Stan Freberg With The Original Cast	1959	12.00	30.00

Label & Catalog #		Title	Year	VG+	NM
Capitol W-1573	(M)	The United States Of America	1961	8.00	20.00
Capitol SW-1573	(S)	The United States Of America	1961	12.00	30.00
Capitol T-1694	(M)	Face The Funnies	1962	8.00	20.00
Capitol ST-1694	(S)	Face The Funnies	1962	12.00	30.00

— Original Capitol albums above have black labels with the Capitol logo on the left side.—

Capitol T-1816	(M)	Madison Avenue Werewolf	1962	8.00	20.00
Capitol J-3264	(M)	Mickey Mouse's Birthday Party	1963	10.00	25.00
Capitol T-2020	(M)	The Best Of Stan Freberg	1964	8.00	20.00
Capitol T-2551	(M)	Underground Show #1	1966	6.00	15.00
Capitol ST-2551	(S)	Underground Show #1	1966	8.00	20.00

— Original Capitol albums above have black labels with the Capitol logo on top.—

FRED, JOHN, & HIS PLAYBOY BAND

Paula LP-2191	(M)	John Fred And His Playboys	1966	5.00	12.00
Paula LPS-2191	(S)	John Fred And His Playboys	1966	6.00	15.00
Paula LP-2193	(M)	34:40 Of John Fred And His Playboys	1967	5.00	12.00
Paula LPS-2193	(S)	34:40 Of John Fred And His Playboys	1967	6.00	15.00
Paula LP-2197	(M)	Agnes English	1967	5.00	12.00
Paula LPS-2197	(S)	Agnes English	1967	6.00	15.00
Paula LPS-2197	(S)	Judy In Disguise With Glasses	1968	6.00	15.00
		("Judy" is a repackage of "Agnes.")			
Paula LPS-2201	(S)	Permanently Stated	1968	5.00	12.00
Uni 73077	(S)	Love In My Soul	1970	4.00	10.00

FREDDIE & THE DREAMERS

Tower T-5003	(M)	I'm Telling You Now	1965	8.00	20.00
Tower DT-5003	(E)	I'm Telling You Now	1965	6.00	15.00
Mercury MG-21017	(M)	Freddie & The Dreamers	1965	8.00	20.00
Mercury SR-61017	(E)	Freddie & The Dreamers	1965	6.00	15.00
Mercury MG-21026	(M)	Do The Freddie	1965	6.00	15.00
Mercury SR-61026	(S)	Do The Freddie	1965	8.00	20.00
Mercury MG-21031	(M)	Seaside Swingers (Soundtrack)	1965	6.00	15.00
Mercury SR-61031	(S)	Seaside Swingers (Soundtrack)	1965	8.00	20.00
Mercury MG-21053	(M)	Frantic Freddie	1965	6.00	15.00
Mercury SR-61053	(S)	Frantic Freddie	1965	8.00	20.00
Mercury MG-21061	(M)	Fun Lovin' Freddie	1966	6.00	15.00
Mercury SR-61061	(S)	Fun Lovin' Freddie	1966	8.00	20.00

FREDRIC

Forte 301	(S)	Phases And Faces	1968	600.00	900.00

FREE BAND, THE

Vanguard VSD-6507	(S)	The Free Band	1969	5.00	12.00

FREE SPIRITS, THE
Free Spirits features Larry Coryell.

ABC 593	(M)	Out Of Sight And Sound	1967	6.00	15.00
ABC S-593	(S)	Out Of Sight And Sound	1967	8.00	20.00

FREEBORNE

Monitor MPS-607	(S)	Peak Impressions	1967	35.00	70.00

FREED, ALAN

MGM E-293 (10")	(M)	The Big Beat	195?	75.00	150.00
Coral CRL-57063	(M)	Rock 'N' Roll Dance Party, Volume 1	1956	40.00	80.00
Coral CRL-57115	(M)	Rock 'N' Roll Dance Party, Volume 2	1957	40.00	80.00
Coral CRL-57177	(M)	TV Record Hop	1957	35.00	70.00
Coral CRL-57213	(M)	Rock Around The Block	1958	35.00	70.00
Brunswick BL-54043	(M)	The Alan Freed Rock & Roll Show	1959	50.00	100.00

FREEMAN, BOBBY

Jubilee JLP-1086	(M)	Do You Wanna Dance?	1959	35.00	70.00
Jubilee JLPS-1086	(S)	Do You Wanna Dance?	1959	50.00	100.00
Jubilee JGM-5010	(M)	Twist With Bobby Freeman	1962	12.00	30.00
Autumn LP-102	(M)	C'Mon And S-W-I-M	1964	12.00	30.00
King 930	(M)	The Lovable Style Of Bobby Freeman	1965	16.00	40.00
Josie JM-4007	(M)	Get In The Swim With Bobby Freeman	1965	10.00	25.00
Josie JGS-4007	(E)	Get In The Swim With Bobby Freeman	1965	8.00	20.00

Label & Catalog #		Title	Year	VG+	NM

FREHELY, ACE: *Refer to* KISS

FREIGHT TRAIN

Fly-by-Nite LPFBN-1001	(S)	**Just The Beginning**	1971	20.00	50.00

FREY, GLENN
Frey was formerly a member of The Eagles.

MCA 5501	(DJ)	**The Allnighter** *(Quiex II vinyl)*	1984	6.00	15.00

FRIAR TUCK

Mercury MG-21111	(M)	**Friar Tuck & His Psychedelic Guitar**	1967	8.00	20.00
Mercury SR-61111	(S)	**Friar Tuck & His Psychedelic Guitar**	1967	10.00	25.00

FRIEND & LOVER

Forecast FTS-3055	(S)	**Reach Out In Darkness**	1968	5.00	12.00

FRIENDS OF DISTINCTION, THE

RCA Victor APD1-0276	(Q)	**Friends Of Distinction's Greatest Hits**	1973	6.00	15.00

FRIENDSOUND
Features Phil Volk, Drake Levin and Mike Smith, of Paul Revere's Raiders. Also refer to Brotherhood.

RCA Victor LSP-4114	(S)	**Joyride**	1969	6.00	15.00

FRIJID PINK

Parrot PAS-71033	(S)	**Frijid Pink**	1970	8.00	20.00
Parrot PAS-71041	(S)	**Frijid Pink Defrosted**	1970	8.00	20.00
Lion LN-1004	(S)	**Earth Omen**	1972	8.00	20.00
Fantasy F-9464	(S)	**All Pink Inside**	1974	6.00	15.00

FRIPP & ENO
Robert Fripp of King Crimson and Brian Eno of Roxy Music.

Antilles ANM-7001	(S)	**No Pussy Footing**	1973	6.00	15.00

FRIZZELL, LEFTY
Refer to Carl Smith / Lefty Frizzel / Marty Robbins.

Columbia HL-9019 (10")	(M)	**The Songs Of Jimmie Rodgers**	1951	75.00	150.00
Columbia HL-9021 (10")	(M)	**Listen To Lefty**	1952	75.00	150.00
Columbia CL-1342	(M)	**The One And Only Lefty Frizzell**	1959	20.00	50.00
		— Original Columbia albums above have three white "eye" logos on each side of the spindle hole.—			
Columbia CL-2169	(M)	**Saginaw, Michigan**	1964	14.00	35.00
Columbia CS-8969	(S)	**Saginaw, Michigan**	1964	16.00	40.00
Columbia CL-2386	(M)	**The Sad Side Of Love**	1965	14.00	35.00
Columbia CS-9186	(S)	**The Sad Side Of Love**	1965	16.00	40.00
Columbia CL-2488	(M)	**Lefty Frizzell's Greatest Hits**	1966	14.00	35.00
Columbia CS-9288	(S)	**Lefty Frizzell's Greatest Hits**	1966	16.00	40.00
Columbia CL-2772	(M)	**Puttin' On**	1967	14.00	35.00
Columbia CS-9572	(S)	**Puttin' On**	1967	16.00	40.00
		—Columbia albums above have "360 Sound Mono/Stereo" on the bottom of the label.—			

FROGGIE BEAVER

Froggie Beaver 7301	(S)	**From The Pond**	1973	12.00	30.00

FROLK HAVEN

LRS RF-6023	(S)	**At The Apex Of High**	196?	75.00	150.00

FROM BRITAIN WITH BEAT

Modern Sound 544	(M)	**From Britain With Beat**	196?	40.00	80.00

FROMAN, JANE

RCA Victor LPT-3055 (10")	(M)	**Gems From Gershwin**	1952	20.00	50.00
Capitol H-309 (10")	(M)	**With A Song In My Heart** *(Soundtrack)*	1952	50.00	100.00
Capitol H-310 (10")	(M)	**Pal Joey**	1952	50.00	100.00
Capitol H-354 (10")	(M)	**Yours Alone**	1952	20.00	50.00
Capitol T-309	(M)	**With A Song In My Heart** *(Soundtrack)*	1955	16.00	40.00
Capitol T-310	(M)	**Pal Joey**	1952	50.00	100.00
Capitol T-726	(M)	**Faith**	1956	12.00	30.00
Capitol T-889	(M)	**Songs At Sunset**	1957	12.00	30.00

Label & Catalog #		Title	Year	VG+	NM
FROST, THE					
Vanguard VSD-6520	(S)	**Frost Music**	1969	6.00	15.00
Vanguard VSD-6541	(S)	**Rock And Roll Music**	1969	6.00	15.00
Vanguard VSD-6556	(S)	**Through The Eyes Of Music**	1970	6.00	15.00
FROST, FRANK, & THE NIGHTHAWKS					
Phillips Int. 1975	(M)	**Hey Boss Man!**	1961	See note below	
		(Rare. Estimated near mint value $1,500-2,500.)			
FROST, MAX, & THE TROOPERS					
Tower ST-5147	(S)	**Shape Of Things To Come**	1968	16.00	40.00
FRUMMOX					
Probe 4511	(S)	**From Here To There**	1969	6.00	15.00
FRUT					
Trash 1001	(S)	**Keep On Truckin'**	1971	8.00	20.00
FUGITIVES, THE					
Hideout 1001	(M)	**The Fugitives At Dave's Hideout**	1968	500.00	750.00

Greenwich Village Beat poets cum sexual/social satirists Ed Sanders and Tuli Kupferberg picked their name from Norman Mailer's first novel, "Armies Of The Night," where the author substituted "fug" for a more widely known four-letter expletive.

FUGS, THE [THE VILLAGE FUGS]
The Fugs are Tuli Kupferburg, Ed Sanders and Ken Weaver.

Broadside 304	(M)	**Ballads Of Contemporary Protest**	1966	50.00	100.00
		(Credited to The Village Fugs with backing by Peter Stampfel and Steve Weber, later The Holy Modal Rounders.)			
ESP 1018	(M)	**The Fugs First Album**	1966	8.00	20.00
ESP 1028	(S)	**The Fugs**	1966	8.00	20.00
ESP 1038	(S)	**Virgin Fugs: For Adults Minds Only**	1967	8.00	20.00
ESP 2018	(S)	**Fugs Four, Rounders Score**	1967	8.00	20.00

Label & Catalog #		Title	Year	VG+	NM
Reprise R-6280	(M)	**Tenderness Junction**	1967	8.00	20.00
Reprise RS-6280	(S)	**Tenderness Junction**	1967	10.00	25.00
Reprise RS-6305	(S)	**It Crawled Into My Hand, Honest**	1968	10.00	25.00
Reprise RS-6359	(S)	**Belle Of Avenue A**	1969	10.00	25.00
Reprise RS-6396	(S)	**Golden Filth**	1970	10.00	25.00

FULLER, BOBBY [THE BOBBY FULLER FOUR]

Label & Catalog #		Title	Year	VG+	NM
Mustang M-900	(M)	**KRLA King Of The Wheels**	1965	30.00	60.00
Mustang MS-900	(S)	**KRLA King Of The Wheels**	1965	50.00	100.00
Mustang M-901	(M)	**I Fought The Law**	1966	20.00	50.00
Mustang MS-901	(S)	**I Fought The Law**	1966	35.00	70.00

(The mono and stereo versions of "I Fouht The Law" contain different takes of several songs. Both Mustang 900 and 901 have been convincingly counterfeited.)

FULLER, JERRY

Label & Catalog #		Title	Year	VG+	NM
Lin LP-100	(M)	**Teenage Love**	1960	20.00	50.00

FULLER, JESSE

Label & Catalog #		Title	Year	VG+	NM
Cavalier 5006 (10")	(M)	**Frisco Bound**	195?	75.00	150.00
Cavalier 6009	(M)	**Frisco Bound**	195?	40.00	80.00

FULSON, LOWELL [LOWELL FOLSOM]

Label & Catalog #		Title	Year	VG+	NM
Kent KLP-5016	(M)	**Lowell Fulson**	1965	8.00	20.00
Kent KLP-5020	(M)	**Lowell Fulson**	1965	8.00	20.00
Kent KLP-520	(M)	**The Tramp**	1967	5.00	12.00
Kent KST-520	(S)	**The Tramp**	1967	6.00	15.00
Kent KST-531	(S)	**Lowell Fulson Now**	1969	5.00	12.00

FUN & GAMES, THE

Label & Catalog #		Title	Year	VG+	NM
Uni 73042	(S)	**Elephant Candy**	1968	8.00	20.00

FUNKADELIC

Funkadelic, who also recorded as Parliament, is the brainchild of George Clinton.

Label & Catalog #		Title	Year	VG+	NM
Invictus 7302	(S)	**Osmium**	1970	40.00	80.00
Westbound 2000	(S)	**Funkadelic**	1970	8.00	20.00
Westbound 2001	(S)	**Free Your Mind And Your Ass Will Follow**	1970	8.00	20.00
Westbound 2007	(S)	**Maggot Brain**	1971	8.00	20.00
Westbound 2020	(S)	**America Eats Its Young**	1972	8.00	20.00
Westbound 2022	(S)	**Cosmic Slop**	1973	8.00	20.00
Westbound 1001	(S)	**Standing On The Verge Of Getting It On**	1974	8.00	20.00
Westbound 215	(S)	**Let's Take It To The Stage**	1975	8.00	20.00
Westbound 227	(S)	**Tales Of Kidd Funkadelic**	1976	8.00	20.00

FUSE

Fuse features Rick Nielson And Tom Peterson of Cheap Trick.

Label & Catalog #		Title	Year	VG+	NM
Epic BN-26502	(S)	**Fuse** *(Counterfeits exist)*	1970	16.00	40.00

FUTURE

Label & Catalog #		Title	Year	VG+	NM
Shamley 703	(S)	**Down The Country Road**	1969	8.00	20.00

Do You Want To Assist With The Next Volume Of This Book?

We need all the help we can get! If you know of mistakes that we have made
— labels, catalog numbers, titles, dates and especially the prices—
don't grouch, get involved! Send corrections and additions to:

Neal Umphred/LP Guide
Goldmine Magazine, 700 East State Street, Iola, WI 54990

Label & Catalog #		Title	Year	VG+	NM

G.T.O.'S, THE
Girls Together Outrageously were produced by Frank Zappa.

Straight STS-1059	(S)	**Permanent Damage** *(With booklet)*	*1969*	**50.00**	**100.00**
Reprise RS-6390	(S)	**Permanent Damage** *(With booklet)*	*1970*	**16.00**	**40.00**

GABRIEL, PETER
Gabriel was formerly the leader of Genesis.

Direct Disk SD-16615	(S)	**Peter Gabriel**	*198?*	**30.00**	**60.00**
Geffen GHS-2011	(DJ)	**Peter Gabriel** *(Quiex II vinyl)*	*1982*	**6.00**	**15.00**

GALAHADS, THE

Liberty LRP-3371	(M)	**The Galahads**	*1964*	**8.00**	**20.00**
Liberty LST-7371	(S)	**The Galahads**	*1964*	**10.00**	**25.00**

GALE, SUNNY

RCA LPM-1277	(M)	**Sunny And Blue**	*1956*	**10.00**	**25.00**

GALS & PALS

Fontana MGF-27538	(M)	**Gals And Pals**	*1965*	**6.00**	**15.00**
Fontana SRS-67538	(S)	**Gals And Pals**	*1965*	**8.00**	**20.00**

GAME

Faithful Virtue 2003	(S)	**Game**	*1969*	**8.00**	**20.00**
Evolution 2021	(S)	**Game**	*1970*	**5.00**	**12.00**
Evolution 3008	(S)	**Long Hot Summer**	*1970*	**5.00**	**12.00**

GANDALF

Capitol ST-121	(S)	**Gandalf**	*1969*	**60.00**	**120.00**

GANDALF THE GREY

G.W.R. 7	(S)	**The Grey Wizard Am I**	*196?*	**180.00**	**300.00**

GANT, CECIL

King 671	(M)	**Cecil Gant**	*1958*	**50.00**	**100.00**
Sound 601	(M)	**The Incomparable Cecil Gant**	*1958*	**50.00**	**100.00**

GANTS, THE

Liberty LRP-3432	(M)	**Road Runner**	*1965*	**8.00**	**20.00**
Liberty LST-7432	(P)	**Road Runner**	*1965*	**12.00**	**30.00**
Liberty LRP-3455	(M)	**The Gants Galore**	*1966*	**6.00**	**15.00**
Liberty LST-7455	(S)	**The Gants Galore**	*1966*	**10.00**	**25.00**
Liberty LRP-3473	(M)	**The Gants Again**	*1966*	**6.00**	**15.00**
Liberty LST-7473	(S)	**The Gants Again**	*1966*	**10.00**	**25.00**

GARAGIOLA, JOE
Joe was formerly a member of The Pittsburgh Pirates.

United Arts. UAS-6032	(S)	**That Holler Guy**	*1973*	**6.00**	**15.00**

GARBO, GRETA

MGM E-4201	(M)	**Garbo**	*1964*	**12.00**	**30.00**
MGM SE-4201	(E)	**Garbo**	*1964*	**12.00**	**30.00**

GARCIA, JERRY
Refer to The Grateful Dead; Old & In The Way; Merl Saunders; Howard Wales.

Warner Bros. BS-2582	(S)	**Garcia**	*1972*	**10.00**	**25.00**
Round RX-102	(S)	**Garcia**	*1974*	**10.00**	**25.00**
Round RX-107	(S)	**Reflections**	*1975*	**10.00**	**25.00**
United Arts. LA565	(S)	**Reflections**	*1976*	**8.00**	**20.00**

Label & Catalog #		Title	Year	VG+	NM

Popular figurehead and nominal leader of The Grateful Dead, Jerry Garcia's solo albums are fairly accurate duplications of the band's sound at the time of recording.

GARDNER, DON, & DEE DEE FORD

Fire LP-105	(M)	**Need Your Lovin'**	*1962*	**75.00**	**150.00**
Sue LP-1044	(M)	**In Sweden**	*1965*	**14.00**	**35.00**

GARFUNKEL, ART
Refer to Simon & Garfunkel.

Columbia CQ-31474	(Q)	**Angel Clare**	*1974*	**6.00**	**15.00**
Columbia CQ-33700	(Q)	**Breakaway**	*1975*	**6.00**	**15.00**
Columbia HE-47392	(S)	**Scissors Cut** *(Half-speed master)*	*1982*	**6.00**	**15.00**

GARLAND, HANK
Hank also recorded as a member of The Nashville All-Stars.

Columbia CL-1572	(M)	**Jazz Winds From A New Direction**	*1961*	**8.00**	**20.00**
Columbia CS-8372	(S)	**Jazz Winds From A New Direction**	*1961*	**12.00**	**30.00**
Columbia CL-1913	(M)	**The Unforgettable Guitar Of Hank Garland**	*1962*	**8.00**	**20.00**
Columbia CS-8713	(S)	**The Unforgettable Guitar Of Hank Garland**	*1962*	**8.00**	**20.00**
H.G. 1001 LPS	(S)	**Jazz In New York**	*197?*	**20.00**	**50.00**

GARLAND, JUDY

MGM E-501 (10")	(M)	**Tills The Clouds Roll By** *(Soundtrack)*	*1950*	**50.00**	**100.00**
MGM E-502 (10")	(M)	**Easter Parade** *(Soundtrack)*	*1950*	**50.00**	**100.00**
MGM E-505 (10")	(M)	**Words And Music** *(Soundtrack)*	*1950*	**50.00**	**100.00**
MGM E-519 (10")	(M)	**Summer Stock** *(Soundtrack)*	*1950*	**50.00**	**100.00**
MGM E-21 (10")	(M)	**The Pirate / Summer Stock** *(Soundtracks)*	*1951*	**50.00**	**100.00**
MGM E-82 (10")	(M)	**Judy Garland Sings**	*1951*	**30.00**	**60.00**
MGM E-3149	(M)	**If You Feel Like Singing, Sing**	*1955*	**30.00**	**60.00**
MGM E-3227	(M)	**Easter Parade** *(Soundtrack)*	*1955*	**30.00**	**60.00**
MGM E-3231	(M)	**Tills The Clouds Roll By** *(Soundtrack)*	*1955*	**30.00**	**60.00**
MGM E-3232	(M)	**In The Good Old Summertime** *(Soundtrack)*	*1955*	**30.00**	**60.00**
MGM E-3233	(M)	**Words And Music** *(Soundtrack)*	*1955*	**30.00**	**60.00**
MGM E-3234	(M)	**Summer Stock / The Pirate** *(Soundtracks)*	*1955*	**30.00**	**60.00**
MGM E-3249	(M)	**Judy Garland With The MGM Orchestra**	*1956*	**16.00**	**40.00**
MGM E-3464	(M)	**The Wizard Of Oz** *(Soundtrack)*	*1956*	**50.00**	**100.00**
MGM E-3770	(M)	**Tills The Clouds Roll By** *(Soundtrack)*	*1959*	**20.00**	**50.00**
MGM E-3771	(M)	**Words & Music / Good News** *(Soundtracks)*	*1959*	**20.00**	**50.00**

— Original MGM albums above have yellow labels.—

Label & Catalog #		Title	Year	VG+	NM
MGM E-3989	(M)	The Star Years	1962	12.00	30.00
MGM E-3996	(M)	The Wizard Of Oz	1962	12.00	30.00
MGM SE-3996	(E)	The Wizard Of Oz	1962	10.00	25.00
MGM E-4005	(M)	The Hollywood Years	1962	12.00	30.00
MGM E-4204	(M)	The Very Best Of Judy Garland	1962	12.00	30.00
— Original MGM albums above have black labels.—					
Metro M-505	(M)	Judy Garland	1965	6.00	15.00
Metro MS-505	(E)	Judy Garland	1965	4.00	10.00
MGM SDP-1	(P)	Golden Years At M-G-M	1969	6.00	15.00
MGM GAS-113	(P)	Judy Garland	1970	6.00	15.00
Capitol T-676	(M)	Miss Show Business	1955	16.00	40.00
Capitol T-734	(M)	Judy	1956	16.00	40.00
Capitol T-835	(M)	Alone	1957	14.00	35.00
— Original Capitol albums above have turquoise labels.—					
Capitol T-1036	(M)	In Love	1958	14.00	35.00
Capitol ST-1036	(S)	In Love	1958	20.00	50.00
Capitol T-1118	(M)	Garland At The Grove	1959	14.00	35.00
Capitol ST-1118	(S)	Garland At The Grove	1959	20.00	50.00
Capitol T-1188	(M)	The Letter (With letter attached to cover)	1959	16.00	40.00
Capitol ST-1188	(S)	The Letter (With letter attached to cover)	1959	30.00	60.00
Capitol T-1188	(M)	The Letter (Without the letter)	1959	12.00	30.00
Capitol ST-1188	(S)	The Letter (Without the letter)	1959	16.00	40.00
Capitol T-1467	(M)	That's Entertainment	1960	10.00	25.00
Capitol ST-1467	(S)	That's Entertainment	1960	14.00	35.00
Capitol WBO-1569	(M)	Judy At Carnegie Hall	1961	10.00	25.00
Capitol SWBO-1569	(S)	Judy At Carnegie Hall	1961	14.00	35.00
— Original Capitol albums above have black labels with the Capitol logo on the left side.—					
Capitol W-1710	(M)	The Garland Touch	1962	10.00	25.00
Capitol SW-1710	(S)	The Garland Touch	1962	12.00	30.00
Capitol W-1861	(M)	I Could Go On Singing (Soundtrack)	1963	20.00	50.00
Capitol SW-1861	(S)	I Could Go On Singing (Soundtrack)	1963	35.00	70.00
Capitol T-1941	(M)	Our Love Letter	1963	10.00	25.00
Capitol ST-1941	(S)	Our Love Letter	1963	12.00	30.00
Capitol T-1999	(M)	The Hits Of Judy Garland	1963	8.00	20.00
Capitol ST-1999	(S)	The Hits Of Judy Garland	1963	10.00	25.00
Capitol W-2062	(M)	Just For Openers	1964	8.00	20.00
Capitol DW-2062	(S)	Just For Openers	1964	10.00	25.00
Capitol TAO-2295	(M)	Live At The London Palladium	1965	6.00	15.00
Capitol STAO-2295	(S)	Live At The London Palladium	1965	8.00	20.00
Capitol STCL-2988	(S)	Deluxe Set	1967	16.00	40.00
— Original Capitol albums above have black labels with the Capitol logo on top.—					
Decca DL-6020 (10")	(M)	Judy At The Palace	1952	30.00	60.00
Decca DL-5152 (10")	(M)	The Wizard Of Oz	1951	50.00	100.00
Decca DL-5412 (10")	(M)	Girl Crazy (Soundtrack)	1953	50.00	100.00
Decca DL-8190	(M)	Judy Garland's Greatest Performances	1955	16.00	40.00
Decca DL-8387	(M)	The Wizard Of Oz	1957	16.00	40.00
Decca DL-8498	(M)	Meet Me In St. Louis / The Harvey Girls (Soundtracks)	1957	75.00	150.00
Decca DL-4199	(M)	The Magic Of Judy Garland	1961	12.00	30.00
Decca DXB-172	(M)	The Best Of Judy Garland	1964	6.00	15.00
Decca DXSB-172	(S)	The Best Of Judy Garland	1964	8.00	20.00
Decca DL-75150	(S)	Judy Garland's Greatest Hits	1970	6.00	15.00
Decca DL-5	(E)	Collectors Items 1936-1945	1970	6.00	15.00
Columbia CL-1101	(M)	A Star Is Born (Soundtrack; boxed set)	1958	50.00	100.00
Columbia CL-1101	(M)	A Star Is Born (Soundtrack)	1958	20.00	50.00
Columbia CL-1940	(M)	A Star Is Born (Soundtrack)	1963	10.00	25.00
Columbia CS-8740	(E)	A Star Is Born (Soundtrack)	1963	6.00	15.00
Colpix CP-507	(M)	Pepe (Soundtrack)	1961	30.00	60.00
Colpix SCP-507	(S)	Pepe (Soundtrack)	1961	50.00	100.00
Warner Bros. B-1479	(M)	Gay Purr-ee (Soundtrack)	1962	20.00	50.00
Warner Bros. BS-1479	(S)	Gay Purr-ee (Soundtrack)	1962	30.00	60.00
ABC 620	(M)	At Home At The Palace	1967	8.00	20.00
ABC S-620	(S)	At Home At The Palace	1967	8.00	20.00
Mark-56	(S)	Live In San Francisco (Picture disc)	1978	20.00	50.00

GARLAND, JUDY, & LIZA MINELLI

Label & Catalog #		Title	Year	VG+	NM
Mobile Fidelity MFSL-048	(S)	Live At The London Palladium	1979	6.00	15.00

Label & Catalog #		Title	Year	VG+	NM

GARNETT, GALE

Label & Catalog #		Title	Year	VG+	NM
RCA Victor LPM-2833	(M)	My Kind Of Folk Songs	1964	5.00	12.00
RCA Victor LSP-2833	(S)	My Kind Of Folk Songs	1964	6.00	15.00
RCA Victor LSP-3305	(M)	Lovin' Place	1965	5.00	12.00
RCA Victor LSP-3305	(S)	Lovin' Place	1965	6.00	15.00
RCA Victor LPM-3325	(M)	The Many Faces Of Gale Garnett	1965	5.00	12.00
RCA Victor LSP-3325	(S)	The Many Faces Of Gale Garnett	1965	6.00	15.00
RCA Victor LPM-3498	(M)	Variety Is The Spice Of Gale Garnett	1966	5.00	12.00
RCA Victor LSP-3498	(S)	Variety Is The Spice Of Gale Garnett	1966	6.00	15.00
RCA Victor LPM-3586	(M)	New Adventures	1966	5.00	12.00
RCA Victor LSP-3586	(S)	New Adventures	1966	6.00	15.00
RCA Victor LPM-3747	(M)	Flying And Rainbows And Love	1967	5.00	12.00
RCA Victor LSP-3747	(S)	Flying And Rainbows And Love	1967	6.00	15.00
Columbia CS-9625	(S)	An Audience With The King Of Wands	1968	6.00	15.00
Columbia CS-9760	(S)	Sausalito Heliport	1969	5.00	12.00

GAS MASK

Label & Catalog #		Title	Year	VG+	NM
Tonsil 4001	(S)	Gas Mask	1970	8.00	20.00

GASLIGHT SINGERS, THE

Label & Catalog #		Title	Year	VG+	NM
Mercury MG-20848	(M)	The Gaslight Singers	1963	5.00	12.00
Mercury SR-60848	(S)	The Gaslight Singers	1963	6.00	15.00
Mercury MG-20923	(M)	Turning It On	1964	5.00	12.00
Mercury SR-60923	(S)	Turning It On	1964	6.00	15.00

GATES, DAVID

Gates was formerly a member of Bread.

Label & Catalog #		Title	Year	VG+	NM
Elektra EQ-5066	(Q)	David Gates' First	1973	6.00	15.00

GATES, HEN, & HIS GATERS

Label & Catalog #		Title	Year	VG+	NM
Masterseal M-700	(M)	Let's Go Dancing To Rock And Roll	195?	12.00	30.00

GATEWAY SINGERS, THE

The Gateways feature Travis Edmonson.

Label & Catalog #		Title	Year	VG+	NM
Decca DL-8413	(M)	Puttin' On The Style	1958	12.00	30.00
Decca DL-8671	(M)	The Gateway Singers At The Hungry i	1958	12.00	30.00
Decca DL-8742	(M)	The Gateway Singers In Hi Fi	1958	12.00	30.00
Warner Bros. W-1295	(M)	The Gateway Singers On The Lot	1959	8.00	20.00
Warner Bros. WS-1295	(S)	The Gateway Singers On The Lot	1959	10.00	25.00
Warner Bros. W-1334	(M)	Wagons West	1960	8.00	20.00
Warner Bros. WS-1334	(S)	Wagons West	1960	10.00	25.00
MGM E-3905	(M)	Down In The Valley	1961	6.00	15.00
MGM SE-3905	(S)	Down In The Valley	1961	8.00	20.00
MGM E-4154	(M)	Hootenanny	1963	6.00	15.00
MGM SE-4154	(S)	Hootenanny	1963	8.00	20.00

GATEWAY TRIO, THE

Label & Catalog #		Title	Year	VG+	NM
Capitol T-1868	(M)	The Mad, Mad, Mad, Mad Gateway Trio	1963	6.00	15.00
Capitol ST-1868	(S)	The Mad, Mad, Mad, Mad Gateway Trio	1963	8.00	20.00
Capitol T-2184	(M)	The Gateway Trio	1964	5.00	12.00
Capitol ST-2184	(S)	The Gateway Trio	1964	6.00	15.00

GAUCHOS, THE

Label & Catalog #		Title	Year	VG+	NM
ABC-Paramount 506	(M)	The Gauchos Featuring Jim Doval	1965	10.00	25.00
ABC-Paramount S-506	(S)	The Gauchos Featuring Jim Doval	1965	12.00	30.00

GAVIN, KEVIN

Label & Catalog #		Title	Year	VG+	NM
Charlie Parker 810	(M)	Hey! This Is Kevin Gavin	1962	8.00	20.00

GAYE, MARVIN

Marvin also recorded with Diana Ross; Mary Wells.

Label & Catalog #		Title	Year	VG+	NM
Tamla 221	(M)	Soulful Moods Of Marvin Gaye	1961	180.00	300.00
		(Label has a disc over-lapping a glope at the top.)			
Tamla 239	(M)	That Stubborn Kind Of Fella	1963	100.00	200.00
Tamla 242	(M)	On Stage Recorded Live	1963	35.00	70.00
Tamla 251	(M)	When I'm Alone I Cry	1964	35.00	70.00
Tamla 258	(M)	How Sweet It Is To Be Loved By You	1965	12.00	30.00
Tamla TS-258	(S)	How Sweet It Is To Be Loved By You	1965	16.00	40.00

abel & Catalog #		Title	Year	VG+	NM
amla 259	(M)	Hello Broadway, This Is Marvin	1965	10.00	25.00
amla TS-259	(S)	Hello Broadway, This Is Marvin	1965	12.00	30.00
amla 261	(M)	Tribute To The Great Nat King Cole	1965	10.00	25.00
amla TS-261	(S)	Tribute To The Great Nat King Cole	1965	12.00	30.00
amla 266	(M)	Moods Of Marvin Gaye	1966	8.00	20.00
amla TS-266	(S)	Moods Of Marvin Gaye	1966	10.00	25.00
amla 270	(M)	Marvin Gaye And Kim Weston	1966	8.00	20.00
amla TS-270	(S)	Marvin Gaye And Kim Weston	1966	8.00	20.00
amla 278	(M)	Marvin Gaye's Greatest Hits, Volume 2	1967	6.00	15.00
amla TS-278	(S)	Marvin Gaye's Greatest Hits, Volume 2	1967	8.00	20.00
		—Tamla albums above have two side-by-side circles at the top of the label.—			
amla TS-285	(S)	In The Groove	1968	8.00	20.00
amla TS-285	(S)	I Heard It Through The Grapevine	1968	6.00	15.00
amla TS-292	(S)	M.P.G.	1969	6.00	15.00
amla TS-293	(S)	Marvin Gaye And His Girls	1969	5.00	12.00
amla TS-299	(S)	That's The Way Love Is	1970	6.00	15.00
amla TS-300	(S)	Marvin Gaye's Super Hits	1970	6.00	15.00
Iotown M9-791A3	(S)	Anthology (3 LPs)	1974	6.00	15.00 —
Columbia HC-48197	(S)	Midnight Love (Half-speed master)	198?	12.00	30.00

AYE, MARVIN, & TAMI TERRELL

amla 277	(M)	United	1967	5.00	12.00
amla TS-277	(S)	United	1967	6.00	15.00
amla TS-284	(S)	You're All I Need	1968	6.00	15.00
amla TS-294	(S)	Easy	1969	6.00	15.00
amla TS-302	(S)	Greatest Hits	1970	5.00	12.00

AYLE, CRYSTAL

Jnited Artists LA-856	(DJ)	Somebody Loves You (Picture disc)	1978	20.00	50.00
Iobile Fidelity MFSL-043	(S)	We Must Believe In Magic	197?	6.00	15.00
Jautilus NR-36	(S)	When I Dream	198?	6.00	15.00

AYLORDS, THE

Iercury MG-25198 (10")	(M)	By Request	1955	16.00	40.00
Iercury MG-20075	(M)	Let's Have A Pizza Party	1956	10.00	25.00
Iercury MG-20186	(M)	Italia	1957	10.00	25.00
Ving MGW-12139	(M)	Italiano Favorites	1959	6.00	15.00
Iercury MG-20620	(M)	American Hits In Italian	1961	5.00	12.00
Iercury SR-60620	(S)	American Hits In Italian	1961	6.00	15.00
Iercury MG-20695	(M)	The Gaylords At The Shamrock	1962	5.00	12.00
Iercury SR-60695	(S)	The Gaylords At The Shamrock	1962	6.00	15.00
Iercury MG-20742	(M)	Party Style	1963	5.00	12.00
Iercury SR-60742	(S)	Party Style	1963	6.00	15.00

AYNOR, MITZI

erve MGV-2115	(M)	The Lyrics Of Ira Gershwin	195?	16.00	40.00
erve MGVS-6014	(S)	Mitzi	195?	16.00	40.00
rmstrong ICPR 3-77	(DJ)	Mitzi Zings Into Spring (One sided)	1977	10.00	25.00

EILS BAND, J.

tlantic QD-7260	(Q)	Bloodshot	1973	6.00	15.00
tlantic QD-7286	(Q)	Ladies Invited	1973	6.00	15.00
tlantic QD-18107	(Q)	Nightmares	1974	6.00	15.00
tlantic SD-7260	(S)	Bloodshot (Red vinyl)	1973	6.00	15.00
Jautilus NR-25	(S)	Love Stinks	198?	6.00	15.00

ENE & DEBBIE

.R.X. LPS-1001	(S)	Hear And Now	1968	10.00	25.00

ENE & EUNICE

core 4018	(M)	Rock 'N Roll Sock Hop	1957	100.00	200.00

ENESIS

Iercury SR-61175	(S)	In The Beginning (Red label)	1968	6.00	15.00

ENESIS

Genesis features Peter Gabriel And Phil Collins.

npulse AS-9025	(S)	Trespass	1970	10.00	25.00
amous Charisma 1052	(S)	Nursery Cryme (Pink label)	1972	5.00	12.00

Label & Catalog #		Title	Year	VG+	NM
Famous Charisma 1058	(S)	**Foxtrot** *(Pink label)*	1972	5.00	12.00
London PS-643	(S)	**From Genesis To Revelation**	1974	12.00	30.00
Buddah BDS-5659	(S)	**The Best Of Genesis**	1976	6.00	15.00
Mobile Fidelity MFSL-062	(S)	**A Trick Of The Tail**	1981	16.00	40.00

GENTLE GIANT

Vertigo VE-1005	(S)	**Acquiring The Taste**	1971	6.00	15.00

GENTLE SOUL

Epic BN-26374	(S)	**Gentle Soul**	1968	10.00	25.00

GENTRYS, THE

MGM E-4336	(M)	**Keep On Dancing**	1965	8.00	20.00
MGM SE-4336	(S)	**Keep On Dancing**	1965	10.00	25.00
MGM E-4346	(M)	**Time**	1966	6.00	15.00
MGM SE-4346	(S)	**Time**	1966	8.00	20.00
MGM GAS-127	(S)	**The Gentrys**	1966	8.00	20.00
Sun 117	(S)	**The Gentrys**	1970	12.00	30.00

GEORDIE

MGM SE-4903	(S)	**Hope You Like It**	1973	12.00	30.00

GEORGE, BARBARA

A.F.O. 5001	(M)	**I Know (You Don't Love Me Anymore)**	1962	75.00	150.00

GEORGE, LOWELL
Lowell was the founder of Little Feat.

Warner Bros. 3194	(S)	**Thanks, I'll Eat It Here**	1979	4.00	10.00

GERONIMO BLACK

Uni 73132	(S)	**Geronimo Black**	1972	10.00	25.00
Helios 4405	(S)	**Welcome Back**	1980	5.00	12.00

GERRY & THE PACEMAKERS

Laurie LLP-2024	(M)	**Don't Let The Sun Catch You Crying**	1964	14.00	35.00
Laurie SLP-2024	(E)	**Don't Let The Sun Catch You Crying**	1964	10.00	25.00
Laurie LLP-2027	(M)	**Second Album**	1964	14.00	35.00
Laurie SLLP-2027	(E)	**Second Album**	1964	10.00	25.00
Laurie LLP-2030	(M)	**I'll Be There**	1964	14.00	35.00
Laurie SLLP-2030	(E)	**I'll Be There**	1964	10.00	25.00
United Arts. UAL-3387	(M)	**Ferry Across The Mersey** *(Soundtrack)*	1965	14.00	35.00
United Arts. UAS-6387	(S)	**Ferry Across The Mersey** *(Soundtrack)*	1965	20.00	50.00
Laurie LLP-2031	(M)	**Gerry & The Pacemakers' Greatest Hits**	1965	10.00	25.00
Laurie SLLP-2031	(E)	**Gerry & The Pacemakers' Greatest Hits**	1965	8.00	20.00
Laurie LLP-2037	(M)	**Girl On A Swing**	1966	14.00	35.00
Laurie SLP-2037	(E)	**Girl On A Swing**	1966	10.00	25.00

GHOULS, THE
The Ghouls are a creation of Gary Usher & Co.

Capitol T-2215	(M)	**Dracula's Deuce**	1965	75.00	150.00
Capitol ST-2215	(S)	**Dracula's Deuce**	1965	100.00	200.00

GIANT CRAB

Uni 73037	(S)	**A Giant Crab Comes Forth**	1968	6.00	15.00
Uni 73057	(S)	**Cool It, Helios**	1969	6.00	15.00

GIBB, ROBIN
Robin Gibb is a member of The Bee Gees.

Atco SD-33-323	(S)	**Robin's Reign**	1970	8.00	20.00

GIBBS, GEORGIA

Coral CRL-56037 (10")	(M)	**Ballin' The Jack**	1951	10.00	25.00
Mercury MG-25175 (10")	(M)	**Georgia Gibbs Sings Oldies**	1953	20.00	50.00
Mercury MG-25199 (10")	(M)	**The Man That Got Away**	1954	20.00	50.00
Mercury MG-20071	(M)	**Music And Memories**	1956	12.00	30.00
Mercury MG-20114	(M)	**Song Favorites**	1956	12.00	30.00
Mercury MG-20170	(M)	**Swingin' With Her Nibs**	1956	12.00	30.00
Coral CRL-57183	(M)	**Her Nibs**	1957	10.00	25.00

Label & Catalog #		Title	Year	VG+	NM
Epic LN-24059	(M)	Georgia Gibbs' Greatest Hits	1963	6.00	15.00
Epic BN-26059	(S)	Georgia Gibbs' Greatest Hits	1963	8.00	20.00
Imperial LP-9264	(M)	Something's Gotta Give	1964	6.00	15.00
Imperial LP-12264	(S)	Something's Gotta Give	1964	8.00	20.00
Bell 6000	(M)	Call Me	1966	6.00	15.00
Bell 6000	(S)	Call Me	1966	8.00	20.00

GIBSON, BOB

Riverside RLP-12-802	(M)	Offbeat Folk Songs	1957	12.00	30.00
Riverside RLP-12-806	(M)	I Come For To Sing	1957	12.00	30.00
Riverside RLP-12-816	(M)	Carnegie Concert	1958	12.00	30.00
Riverside RLP-12-830	(M)	There's A Meetin' Here Tonight	1958	12.00	30.00
Elektra EKL-177	(M)	Ski Songs	1959	6.00	15.00
Elektra EKS-7177	(S)	Ski Songs	1959	8.00	20.00
Elektra EKL-197	(M)	Yes I See	1961	6.00	15.00
Elektra EKS-7197	(S)	Yes I See	1961	8.00	20.00
Elektra EKL-239	(M)	Where I'm Bound	1963	6.00	15.00
Elektra EKS-7239	(S)	Where I'm Bound	1963	8.00	20.00
Stinson 76	(M)	Folksongs Of Ohio	196?	8.00	20.00

GIBSON, BOB, & BOB CAMP

Elektra EKL-207	(M)	At The Gate Of Horn	1961	6.00	15.00
Elektra EKS-7207	(S)	At The Gate Of Horn	1961	8.00	20.00

GIBSON, DON

Lion 70069	(M)	Songs By Don Gibson	1958	30.00	60.00
RCA Victor LPM-1743	(M)	Oh Lonesome Me	1958	16.00	40.00
RCA Victor LPM-1918	(M)	No One Stands Alone	1959	12.00	30.00
RCA Victor LSP-1918	(S)	No One Stands Alone	1959	16.00	40.00
RCA Victor LPM-2038	(M)	That Gibson Boy	1959	12.00	30.00
RCA Victor LSP-2038	(S)	That Gibson Boy	1959	16.00	40.00
RCA Victor LPM-2184	(M)	Look Who's Blue	1960	12.00	30.00
RCA Victor LSP-2184	(S)	Look Who's Blue	1960	16.00	40.00
RCA Victor LPM-2269	(M)	Sweet Dreams	1960	12.00	30.00
RCA Victor LSP-2269	(S)	Sweet Dreams	1960	16.00	40.00
RCA Victor LPM-2361	(M)	Girls, Guitars And Gibson	1961	8.00	20.00
RCA Victor LSP-2361	(S)	Girls, Guitars And Gibson	1961	12.00	30.00
RCA Victor LPM-2448	(M)	Some Favorites Of Mine	1962	8.00	20.00
RCA Victor LSP-2448	(S)	Some Favorites Of Mine	1962	12.00	30.00
RCA Victor LPM-2702	(M)	I Wrote A Song	1963	8.00	20.00
RCA Victor LSP-2702	(S)	I Wrote A Song	1963	12.00	30.00

— Original RCA mono albums above have "Long Play" on the bottom of the label;
stereo albums have "Living Stereo" on the bottom.—

RCA Victor LPM-2878	(M)	God Walks These Hills	1964	6.00	15.00
RCA Victor LSP-2878	(S)	God Walks These Hills	1964	8.00	20.00
RCA Victor LPM-3376	(M)	The Best Of Don Gibson	1965	6.00	15.00
RCA Victor LSP-3376	(S)	The Best Of Don Gibson	1965	8.00	20.00
RCA Victor LPM-3470	(M)	Too Much Hurt	1965	6.00	15.00
RCA Victor LSP-3470	(S)	Too Much Hurt	1965	8.00	20.00
RCA Victor LPM-3594	(M)	Don Gibson With Spanish Guitar	1966	6.00	15.00
RCA Victor LSP-3594	(S)	Don Gibson With Spanish Guitar	1966	8.00	20.00
RCA Victor LPM-3680	(M)	Great Country Songs	1966	6.00	15.00
RCA Victor LSP-3680	(S)	Great Country Songs	1966	8.00	20.00
RCA Victor LPM-3843	(M)	All My Love	1967	6.00	15.00
RCA Victor LSP-3843	(S)	All My Love	1967	8.00	20.00
RCA Victor LSP-3974	(S)	The King Of Country Soul	1968	6.00	15.00
RCA Victor LSP-4053	(S)	More Country Soul	1968	6.00	15.00

— Original RCA albums above have black labels.—

GIBSON, HARRY

Sutton SSU-313	(M)	Rockin' Rhythm	196?	6.00	15.00

GIBSON, STEVE, & THE RED CAPS

Mercury MG-25115 (10")	(M)	Steve Gibson & The Red Caps	1954	150.00	250.00
Mercury MG-25116 (10")	(M)	Steve Gibson & The Red Caps	1954	150.00	250.00

GILBERT, ANN

Groove LG-1004	(M)	The Many Moods Of Ann Gilbert	1956	12.00	30.00
Vik LX-1090	(M)	In A Swingin' Mood	1957	12.00	30.00

Label & Catalog #		Title	Year	VG+	NM
GILBERT, JOHN					
No label	(S)	**Mead River**	1971	30.00	60.00
GILES, GILES & FRIPP					
Deram DES-18019	(S)	**Cheerful Insanity**	1968	16.00	40.00
GILKYSON, TERRY					
Decca DL-5263 (10")	(M)	**Folksongs**	1950	20.00	50.00
Decca DL-5457 (10")	(M)	**Golden Minutes Of Folk Music**	1952	20.00	50.00
Kapp KL-1196	(M)	**Rollin'**	1960	6.00	15.00
Kapp KS-3196	(S)	**Rollin'**	1960	8.00	20.00
Kapp KL-1327	(M)	**Cry Of The Wild Goose**	1963	5.00	12.00
Kapp KS-3327	(S)	**Cry Of The Wild Goose**	1963	6.00	15.00
GILLESPIE, DARLENE					
Disneyland WDL-3010	(M)	**Darlene Of The Teens**	195?	20.00	50.00
GILLEY, MICKEY					
Astro 101	(M)	**Lonely Wine**	1964	180.00	300.00
Paula LP-2195	(M)	**Down The Line**	1967	16.00	40.00
Paula LPS-2195	(S)	**Down The Line**	1967	20.00	50.00
GILMER, JIMMY, & THE FIREBALLS [THE FIREBALLS]					
Top Rank RM-324	(M)	**The Fireballs**	1960	35.00	70.00
Top Rank RM-343	(M)	**Vaquero**	1960	35.00	70.00
Top Rank RS-643	(S)	**Vaquero**	1960	50.00	100.00
Warwick W-2042	(M)	**Here Are The Fireballs**	1961	35.00	70.00
Dot DLP-3512	(M)	**Torquay**	1963	14.00	35.00
Dot DLP-25512	(S)	**Torquay**	1963	20.00	50.00
Dot DLP-3545	(M)	**Sugar Shack**	1963	10.00	25.00
Dot DLP-25545	(S)	**Sugar Shack**	1963	14.00	35.00
Dot DLP-3577	(M)	**Buddy's Buddy**	1964	20.00	50.00
Dot DLP-25577	(S)	**Buddy's Buddy**	1964	35.00	70.00
Dot DLP-3643	(M)	**Lucky 'Leven**	1965	8.00	20.00
Dot DLP-25643	(S)	**Lucky 'Leven**	1965	10.00	25.00
Dot DLP-3668	(M)	**Folkbeat**	1965	8.00	20.00
Dot DLP-25668	(S)	**Folkbeat**	1965	10.00	25.00
Dot DLP-3709	(M)	**Campusology**	1966	8.00	20.00
Dot DLP-25709	(S)	**Campusology**	1966	10.00	25.00
Dot DLP-25856	(P)	**Firewater**	1968	8.00	20.00
Atco SD-33-239	(S)	**Bottle Of Wine**	1968	6.00	15.00
Atco SD-33-275	(S)	**Come On, React!**	1969	6.00	15.00
GINNY & GALLIONS					
Downey DS-1003	(S)	**Two Sides Of Ginny And Gallions**	1964	14.00	35.00
GINSBERG, ALLEN					
Fantasy 7006	(M)	**Howl And Other Poems** (Red vinyl)	1959	20.00	50.00
Atlantic 4001	(M)	**Allen Ginsberg Reads Kaddish**	1966	8.00	20.00
Forecast FVS-3083	(M)	**Songs Of Innocence And Experience**	1969	8.00	20.00
GIRARD, CHUCK					
Chuck was formerly the lead singer for The Hondells. Refer to Lovesong.					
Good News GNR-001	(DJ)	**The Chuck Girard Radio Special**	1979	6.00	15.00
GLACIERS, THE					
Mercury MG-20895	(M)	**From Sea To Ski**	1964	8.00	20.00
Mercury SR-60895	(S)	**From Sea To Ski**	1964	10.00	25.00
GLASER, TOMPALL (& THE GLASER BROTHERS)					
Decca DL-4041	(M)	**This Land-Folk Songs**	1960	12.00	30.00
Decca DL-74041	(S)	**This Land-Folk Songs**	1960	16.00	40.00
United Arts. UAL-3540	(M)	**The Ballad Of Namu The Killer Whale**	1966	6.00	15.00
United Arts. UAS-6540	(S)	**The Ballad Of Namu The Killer Whale**	1966	8.00	20.00
GLASS HARP, THE					
Decca DL-75261	(S)	**Glass Harp**	1971	6.00	15.00
Decca DL-75306	(S)	**Synergy**	1971	6.00	15.00
Decca DL-75358	(S)	**It Makes Me Glad**	1972	8.00	20.00

Label & Catalog #		Title	Year	VG+	NM
GLAZER, TOM, & THE DO-RE-MI CHILDREN'S CHORUS					
Washington 301	(M)	Tom Glazer Concert	1959	8.00	20.00
Wonderland 1492	(M)	Songs Children Sing In Latin America	1963	5.00	12.00
Kapp KL-1331	(M)	On Top Of Spaghetti	1963	5.00	12.00
Kapp KS-3331	(S)	On Top Of Spaghetti	1963	6.00	15.00
GLENN, DARRELL					
NRC LPA-5	(M)	Crying In The Chapel	1959	6.00	15.00
NRC SLPA-5	(S)	Crying In The Chapel	1959	8.00	20.00
GLENN, LLOYD					
Alladin 808	(M)	Chica Boo	1956	100.00	200.00
Alladin 808	(M)	Chica Boo (Red vinyl)	1956	240.00	400.00
GLORY					
Texas Revolution CFS-2531	(S)	A Meat Music Sampler	197?	30.00	60.00
GLORY					
Avalanche LA148	(S)	Glory	1973	8.00	20.00
GNARLY, PHIL & THE TOUGH GUYS					
Flaming Pie 319	(S)	Philville	1987	5.00	12.00
GO-GO'S, THE					
RCA Victor LPM-2930	(M)	Swim With The Go-Go's	1964	5.00	12.00
RCA Victor LSP-2930	(S)	Swim With The Go-Go's	1964	6.00	15.00
GO ZOO BAND					
Go Go 22170004	(S)	Sounds That Are Happening	196?	6.00	15.00
GOBEL, GEORGE					
Decca DL-4163	(M)	Lonesome George	1962	5.00	12.00
Decca DL-74163	(S)	Lonesome George	1962	6.00	15.00
GODCHAUX, KEITH & DONNA					
Refer to The Grateful Dead; The Heart Of Gold Band.					
Round RX-104	(S)	Keith And Donna	1975	12.00	30.00
GODFREY, ARTHUR					
Columbia CL-1580	(M)	Arthur Godfrey's Greatest Hits	1960	8.00	20.00
Columbia CS-8380	(S)	Arthur Godfrey's Greatest Hits	1960	10.00	25.00
GODZ, THE					
ESP 1037	(S)	Contact High With The Godz	1967	12.00	30.00
ESP 1047	(S)	Godz 2	1968	12.00	30.00
ESP 1077	(S)	Third Testament	1969	12.00	30.00
ESP 2017	(S)	Godzundheit	1970	12.00	30.00
GOGGLES, THE					
Audio Fidelity AFS-6244	(S)	The Goggles	1971	6.00	15.00
GOLDBERG, BARRY					
Refer to The Electric Flag.					
Epic LN-24199	(M)	Blowing My Mind	1966	6.00	15.00
Epic BN-26199	(S)	Blowing My Mind	1966	8.00	20.00
Buddah BDS-5012	(S)	The Barry Goldberg Reunion	1968	5.00	12.00
Buddah BDS-5051	(S)	Street Man	1969	5.00	12.00
Buddah BDS-5081	(S)	Blast From My Past	1971	4.00	10.00
Record Man 5015	(S)	Barry Goldberg And Friends	1972	4.00	10.00
Atco SD-36-740	(S)	Barry Goldberg	1974	5.00	12.00
GOLDEBRIARS, THE					
Epic LN-24087	(M)	The Goldebriars	1964	5.00	12.00
Epic BN-26087	(S)	The Goldebriars	1964	6.00	15.00
Epic LN-24114	(M)	Straight Ahead	1964	5.00	12.00
Epic BN-26114	(S)	Straight Ahead	1964	6.00	15.00

Label & Catalog #		Title	Year	VG+	NM
GOLDEN DAWN					
International Art. 4	(S)	**Power Plant**	*1968*	**16.00**	**40.00**
International Art. 4	(S)	**Power Plant**	*1979*	**6.00**	**15.00**
		(Reissues have "Masterfonics" stamped in the trail-off vinyl.)			

Hailing from the Netherlands, the Earring had been an international fixture for a decade before scoring with "Radar Love" in America. The album containing that hit was released with a portrait of a nude dancer, which has modestly enhanced its desirability.

GOLDEN EARRING					
Capitol T-2823	(M)	**Winter Harvest**	*1967*	**12.00**	**30.00**
Capitol ST-2823	(S)	**Winter Harvest**	*1967*	**14.00**	**35.00**
Capitol ST-164	(S)	**Miracle Mirror**	*1969*	**12.00**	**30.00**
Atlantic SD-8244	(S)	**Eight Miles High**	*1969*	**8.00**	**20.00**
Track 396	(S)	**Moontan** *(Nude dancer cover)*	*1973*	**8.00**	**20.00**
Capitol ST-11315	(S)	**Golden Earring**	*1974*	**5.00**	**12.00**
GOLDEN GATE QUARTET, THE					
Mercury MG-25063 (10")	(M)	**Spirituals**	*1950*	**100.00**	**200.00**
Columbia CL-6102 (10")	(M)	**The Golden Gate Spirituals**	*1953*	**100.00**	**200.00**
Camden CAL-308	(M)	**The Golden Gate Quartet** *(Purple label)*	*1956*	**50.00**	**100.00**
Harmony HL-7018	(M)	**That Golden Chariot** *(Maroon label)*	*1957*	**50.00**	**100.00**
GOLDENROD					
Chartmaker CSG-1101	(S)	**Goldenrod**	*1968*	**65.00**	**130.00**
GOLDMARK, ANDY					
Andy was produced by Gary Usher.					
Warner Bros. BS-2703	(S)	**Andy Goldmark**	*1973*	**5.00**	**12.00**
GOLDSBORO, BOBBY					
United Arts. UAL-3358	(M)	**The Bobby Goldsboro Album**	*1964*	**5.00**	**12.00**
United Arts. UAS-6358	(S)	**The Bobby Goldsboro Album**	*1964*	**6.00**	**15.00**
United Arts. UAL-3381	(M)	**I Can't Stop Loving You**	*1964*	**5.00**	**12.00**
United Arts. UAS-6381	(S)	**I Can't Stop Loving You**	*1964*	**6.00**	**15.00**

Label & Catalog #		Title	Year	VG+	NM
United Arts. UAL-3425	(M)	**Little Things**	1965	5.00	12.00
United Arts. UAS-6425	(S)	**Little Things**	1965	6.00	15.00
United Arts. UAL-3471	(M)	**Broomstick Cowboy**	1966	4.00	10.00
United Arts. UAS-6471	(S)	**Broomstick Cowboy**	1966	5.00	12.00
United Arts. UAL-3486	(M)	**It's Too Late**	1966	4.00	10.00
United Arts. UAS-6486	(S)	**It's Too Late**	1966	5.00	12.00
United Arts. UAL-3552	(M)	**Blue Autumn**	1966	4.00	10.00
United Arts. UAS-6552	(S)	**Blue Autumn**	1966	5.00	12.00
United Arts. UAL-3561	(M)	**Solid Goldsboro/Greatest Hits**	1967	4.00	10.00
United Arts. UAS-6561	(S)	**Solid Goldsboro/Greatest Hits**	1967	5.00	12.00
United Arts. UAL-3599	(M)	**Romantic, Soulful, Wacky**	1967	4.00	10.00
United Arts. UAS-6599	(S)	**Romantic, Soulful, Wacky**	1967	5.00	12.00

GOLDTONES, THE

LaBrea L-8011	(M)	**The Goldtones Featuring Randy Seol**	196?	30.00	60.00

GOLLIWOGS, THE

The Golliwogs was an early incarnation of Creedence Clearwater Revival.

Fantasy F-9474	(S)	**Pre-Creedence**	1975	8.00	20.00

GOOD & PLENTY

Senate 21001	(S)	**The World Of Good & Plenty**	196?	8.00	20.00

GOOD GUYS, THE

The Good Guys is a pseudonym for The Challengers.

Crescendo GNP-2001	(M)	**Sidewalk Surfing** (Red label)	1964	6.00	15.00
Crescendo GNPS-2001	(S)	**Sidewalk Surfing** (Red label)	1964	8.00	20.00

GOOD GUYS, THE

United Arts. UAL-3370	(M)	**The Good Guys Sing**	1964	5.00	12.00
United Arts. UAS-6370	(S)	**The Good Guys Sing**	1964	6.00	15.00

GOOD OLD BOYS, THE

Round 576	(S)	**Pistol Packin' Mama**	1976	6.00	15.00

GOOD RATS, THE

Kapp KS-3580	(S)	**The Good Rats**	1969	8.00	20.00
Passport SP-20	(DJ)	**Rats The Way You Like It-Live**	1978	30.00	60.00

GOOD TIMES, THE

Kama Sutra KLP-8052	(M)	**The Good Times**	1966	5.00	12.00
Kama Sutra KLPS-8052	(S)	**The Good Times**	1966	6.00	15.00

GOODIES, THE

Hip HIS-7002	(S)	**Candy Coated Goodies**	1969	10.00	25.00

GOODING, CYNTHIA

Ms. Gooding also recorded with Theodore Bikel.

Elektra EKL-8	(M)	**Mexican Folk Songs**	195?	8.00	20.00
Elektra EKL-17	(M)	**Italian Folk Songs**	195?	8.00	20.00
Elektra EKL-107	(M)	**Faithful Lovers And Other Phenomena**	195?	8.00	20.00
Elektra EKL-131	(M)	**Queen Of Hearts**	195?	8.00	20.00
Riverside RLP-12-830	(M)	**Languages Of Love**	195?	8.00	20.00

GOODMAN, DICKIE

Refer to Buchanan & Goodman.

Rori 3301	(M)	**The Many Heads Of Dickie Goodman**	1962	20.00	50.00
Cash 451	(M)	**Mr. Jaws**	1974	10.00	25.00
Comet 69	(M)	**My Son, The Joke**	197?	6.00	15.00

GOODMAN, DODY

Coral CRL-57196	(M)	**Dody Goodman Sings**	1957	10.00	25.00

GORDON, HONI

Prestige PRLP-7230	(M)	**Honi Gordon Sings**	1962	16.00	40.00

GORDON, ROBERT

Private Stock PS-2030	(S)	**Robert Gordon With Link Wray**	1977	4.00	10.00
Private Stock PS-7008	(S)	**Fresh Fish Special**	1978	4.00	10.00

Label & Catalog #		Title	Year	VG+	NM
RCA Victor AFL1-3294	(DJ)	**Rock Billy Boogie** (White vinyl)	1979	6.00	15.00
RCA Victor DJL1-3411	(DJ)	**The Essential Robert Gordon**	1979	6.00	15.00
GORE, CHARIE					
Audio Lab AL-1526	(M)	**The Country Gentleman**	1959	35.00	70.00
GORE, LESLEY					
Mercury MG-20805	(M)	**I'll Cry If I Want To**	1963	8.00	20.00
Mercury SR-60805	(S)	**I'll Cry If I Want To**	1963	12.00	30.00
Mercury MG-20849	(M)	**Lesley Gore Sings Of Mixed Up Hearts**	1963	8.00	20.00
Mercury SR-60849	(S)	**Lesley Gore Sings Of Mixed Up Hearts**	1963	12.00	30.00
Mercury MG-20901	(M)	**Boys, Boys, Boys**	1964	8.00	20.00
Mercury SR-60901	(S)	**Boys, Boys, Boys**	1964	12.00	30.00
Mercury MG-20943	(M)	**Girl Talk**	1964	8.00	20.00
Mercury SR-60943	(S)	**Girl Talk**	1964	12.00	30.00
Mercury MG-21024	(M)	**The Golden Hits Of Lesley Gore**	1965	6.00	15.00
Mercury SR-61024	(S)	**The Golden Hits Of Lesley Gore** (12 tracks)	1965	8.00	20.00
Mercury SR-61024	(S)	**The Golden Hits Of Lesley Gore** (10 tracks)	196?	5.00	12.00
Mercury MG-21042	(M)	**My Town, My Guy And Me**	1965	8.00	20.00
Mercury SR-61042	(S)	**My Town, My Guy And Me**	1965	12.00	30.00
Mercury MG-21066	(M)	**All About Love**	1966	8.00	20.00
Mercury SR-61066	(S)	**All About Love**	1966	12.00	30.00
Mercury MG-21120	(M)	**California Nights**	1967	8.00	20.00
Mercury SR-61120	(S)	**California Nights**	1967	12.00	30.00
Mercury SR-61185	(S)	**The Golden Hits Of Lesley Gore, Volume 2**	1968	8.00	20.00
Wing SRW-16350	(S)	**Girl Talk** (Repackage of Mercury 60943)	1968	5.00	12.00
Wing SRW-16382	(S)	**Love, Love, Love**	1968	5.00	12.00
		(Repackage of Mercury 61066.)			
Wing PKW-2-119	(S)	**The Sound Of Young Love** (2 LPs)	1969	12.00	30.00
Mowest MW-117L	(S)	**Someplace Else Now**	1972	6.00	15.00
A&M SP-4564	(S)	**Love Me By Name**	1975	4.00	10.00
GORME, EYDIE					
Ms. Gorme also recorded with Steve Lawrence.					
Coral CRL-57109	(M)	**Delight**	1957	12.00	30.00
ABC-Paramount 150	(M)	**Eydie Gorme**	1957	10.00	25.00
ABC-Paramount 192	(M)	**Eydie Swings The Blues**	1957	10.00	25.00
ABC-Paramount 218	(M)	**Eydie Gorme Vamps The Roaring '20s**	1958	10.00	25.00
ABC-Paramount 246	(M)	**Eydie In Love**	1958	10.00	25.00
ABC-Paramount 254	(M)	**Showstoppers**	1958	8.00	20.00
ABC-Paramount S-254	(S)	**Showstoppers**	1958	10.00	25.00
ABC-Paramount 273	(M)	**Love Is A Season**	1958	8.00	20.00
ABC-Paramount S-273	(S)	**Love Is A Season**	1958	10.00	25.00
ABC-Paramount 307	(M)	**Eydie Gorme On Stage**	1959	8.00	20.00
ABC-Paramount S-307	(S)	**Eydie Gorme On Stage**	1959	10.00	25.00
United Arts. UAL-3143	(M)	**Come Sing With Me**	1961	5.00	12.00
United Arts. UAS-6143	(S)	**Come Sing With Me**	1961	6.00	15.00
United Arts. UAL-3189	(M)	**The Very Best Of Eydie Gorme**	1962	5.00	12.00
United Arts. UAS-6189	(S)	**The Very Best Of Eydie Gorme**	1962	6.00	15.00
Columbia CL-2012	(M)	**Blame It On The Bossa Nova**	1963	6.00	15.00
Columbia CS-8812	(S)	**Blame It On The Bossa Nova**	1963	8.00	20.00
Columbia CL-2065	(M)	**Let The Good Times Roll**	1963	4.00	10.00
Columbia CS-8865	(S)	**Let The Good Times Roll**	1963	5.00	12.00
Columbia CL-2120	(M)	**Gorme Country Style**	1964	4.00	10.00
Columbia CS-8920	(S)	**Gorme Country Style**	1964	5.00	12.00
Columbia CL-2203	(M)	**Amor**	1964	4.00	10.00
Columbia CS-9003	(S)	**Amor**	1964	5.00	12.00
Columbia CL-2300	(M)	**The Sound Of Music**	1965	4.00	10.00
Columbia CLS-9100	(S)	**The Sound Of Music**	1965	5.00	12.00
Columbia CL-2376	(M)	**More Amor**	1965	4.00	10.00
Columbia CS-9176	(S)	**More Amor**	1965	5.00	12.00
Columbia CL-2476	(M)	**Don't Go To Strangers**	1966	4.00	10.00
Columbia CS-9276	(S)	**Don't Go To Strangers**	1966	5.00	12.00
Columbia CL-2594	(M)	**Softly, As I Leave You**	1967	4.00	10.00
Columbia CS-9394	(S)	**Softly, As I Leave You**	1967	5.00	12.00
Columbia CL-2764	(M)	**Eydie Gorme's Greatest Hits**	1967	4.00	10.00
Columbia CS-9564	(S)	**Eydie Gorme's Greatest Hits**	1967	5.00	12.00

— Original Columbia albums above have "360 Sound" labels. —

A true teen phenom, Lesley Gore hit #1 with "It's My Party" before renewing her first driver's license. From 1963 through 1967 she placed nearly two dozen singles on the charts, although her albums never really set the retail racks afire. While it is common for albums in 1967 to be more difficult to find in mono than stereo, such is not the case with *California Nights*, a much sought after stereo release. The double album, *The Sound Of Young Love*, was a chance for Mercury to recycle her two previous Wing albums. It is also difficult to find *and*, often contains two albums with two different labels from different periods!

Label & Catalog #		Title	Year	VG+	NM

GOSDIN BROTHERS, THE
Vern and Rex Gosdin. Refer to Gene Clark; The Hillmen.

Capitol ST-2852	(S)	**Sounds Of Goodbye**	1968	8.00	20.00

GOULDMAN, GRAHAM

RCA Victor LPM-3954	(M)	**Graham Gouldman Thing**	1968	30.00	60.00
RCA Victor LSP-3954	(S)	**Graham Gouldman Thing**	1968	20.00	50.00

GRACEFUL HEAD

Excelsior	(S)	**Graceful Head**	1976	180.00	300.00

GRACIOUS
Gracious features Paul Davis.

Capitol ST-602	(S)	**Gracious**	1970	16.00	40.00

GRACEN, THELMA

EmArcy MG-36096	(M)	**Thelma Gracen**	1956	20.00	50.00
Wing MGW-60005	(M)	**Thelma Gracen**	1956	14.00	35.00

GRAHAM CENTRAL STATION

Warner Bros. BS4-2763	(Q)	**Graham Central Station**	1975	6.00	15.00
Warner Bros. BS4-2876	(Q)	**Ain't No 'Bout-A-Doubt It**	1975	6.00	15.00

GRAMMER, BILLY

Monument MLP-4000	(M)	**Travelin' On**	1961	10.00	25.00
Monument SLP-14000	(S)	**Travelin' On**	1961	16.00	40.00

GRAND FUNK RAILROAD
Mark Farner, Don Brewer, Mel Schacher and Craig Frost. Refer to Terry Knight.

Capitol ST-307	(S)	**On Time**	1969	6.00	15.00
Capitol SKAO-406	(S)	**Grand Funk**	1969	6.00	15.00
Capitol SKAO-471	(S)	**Closer To Home**	1970	6.00	15.00
Capitol SWBB-633	(S)	**Grand Funk/Live Album**	1970	5.00	12.00
Capitol SW-764	(S)	**Survival**	1971	5.00	12.00
Capitol SW-853	(S)	**E Pluribus Funk**	1971	5.00	12.00
— Original Capitol albums above have green labels.—					
Capitol SMAS-11207	(DJ)	**We're An American Band** *(Gold vinyl)*	1973	10.00	25.00

GRAND THEFT

No label	(S)	**Grand Theft** *(No cover)*	197?	150.00	250.00

GRANDMA'S ROCKERS

Fredlo 6727	(M)	**Homemade Apple Pie**	1967	*See note below*	
		(Rare. Estimated near mint value $1,000-2,000.)			

GRANMAX

Panam 1002	(S)	**A Ninth Alive** *(White vinyl)*	1977	6.00	15.00
Panam 1023	(S)	**Kiss Heaven Goodbye**	1978	30.00	60.00

GRANT, GOGI

Era 20001	(M)	**Suddenly There's Gogi Grant** *(Red vinyl)*	1956	40.00	80.00
Era 20001	(M)	**Suddenly There's Gogi Grant**	1957	16.00	40.00
RCA Victor LOC-1030	(M)	**The Helen Morgan Story** *(Soundtrack)*	1957	20.00	50.00
RCA Victor LPM-1716	(M)	**Gigi** *(Studio Cast)*	1958	10.00	25.00
RCA Victor LPM-1717	(M)	**Welcome To My Heart**	1958	14.00	35.00
RCA Victor LPM-1940	(M)	**Torch Time**	1959	10.00	25.00
RCA Victor LSP-1940	(S)	**Torch Time**	1959	14.00	35.00
RCA Victor LPM-1984	(M)	**Kiss Me, Kate**	1959	10.00	25.00
RCA Victor LSP-1984	(S)	**Kiss Me, Kate**	1959	14.00	35.00
Liberty LRP-3144	(M)	**If You Want To Get To Heaven, Shout**	1959	8.00	20.00
Liberty LST-7144	(S)	**If You Want To Get To Heaven, Shout**	1959	10.00	25.00
Era EL-106	(M)	**The Wayward Wind**	1960	16.00	40.00
Charter C-107	(S)	**City Girl In The Country**	1964	6.00	15.00
Charter CS-107	(M)	**City Girl In The Country**	1964	8.00	20.00

GRAPEFRUIT

Dunhill DS-50050	(S)	**Around Grapefruit**	1968	8.00	20.00
RCA Victor LSP-4215	(S)	**Deep water**	1969	5.00	12.00

Label & Catalog #		Title	Year	VG+	NM

GRASS ROOTS, THE
Originally a studio concoction of Steve Barri and Phil Sloan (Dunhill 50011), their initial success lead to the formation of a "real" group based around vocalist Rob Grill.

Label & Catalog #		Title	Year	VG+	NM
Dunhill D-50011	(M)	**Where Were You When I Needed You?**	1966	16.00	40.00
Dunhill D-50011	(S)	**Where Were You When I Needed You?**	1966	20.00	50.00
Dunhill D-50020	(M)	**Let's Live For Today**	1967	8.00	20.00
Dunhill DS-50020	(S)	**Let's Live For Today**	1967	10.00	25.00
Dunhill D-50027	(M)	**Feelings**	1968	8.00	20.00
Dunhill DS-50027	(S)	**Feelings**	1968	6.00	15.00
Dunhill DS-50047	(S)	**Golden Grass**	1968	6.00	15.00
Dunhill DS-50052	(S)	**Lovin' Things**	1969	4.00	10.00
Dunhill DS-50067	(S)	**Leavin' It All Behind**	1969	4.00	10.00
Dunhill DS-50087	(S)	**More Golden Grass**	1970	4.00	10.00
Command QD-40013	(Q)	**Their 16 Greatest Hits**	1974	6.00	15.00

GRATEFUL DEAD, THE
Original members were Jerry Garcia, Bill Kreutzmann, Phil Lesh, Ron "Pig Pen" McKernan (died 1973), Bob Weir and lyricist Robert Hunter. Mickey Hart joined in 1967, left 1970 and rejoined 1974. Tom Constanten was a member 1968-70; Keith and Donna Godchaux, 1971-1978; Brent Mydland, 1979 trhough his death in 1990. Refer to Bob Dylan; Ken Kesey; The Rhythm Devils; Touchstone.

Label & Catalog #		Title	Year	VG+	NM
Warner Bros. W-1689	(M)	**The Grateful Dead** (Gold label)	1967	20.00	50.00
Warner Bros. WS-1689	(S)	**The Grateful Dead** (Gold label)	1967	16.00	40.00
Warner Bros. WS-1689	(S)	**The Grateful Dead** (Green "W7" label)	1968	8.00	20.00
Warner Bros. WS-1749	(S)	**Anthem Of The Sun** (Purple cover)	1968	8.00	20.00
Warner Bros. WS-1790	(S)	**Auxamoxa**	1969	8.00	20.00
Warner Bros. 2WS-1830	(S)	**Live/Dead** (2 LPs with booklet)	1970	8.00	20.00
Warner Bros. WS-1869	(S)	**Workingman's Dead**	1970	8.00	20.00
Warner Bros. WS-1893	(S)	**American Beauty**	1970	8.00	20.00
		— Original Warner albums above have green labels with the "W7" logo on top.—			
Warner Bros. WS-1749	(S)	**Anthem Of The Sun** (White cover)	197?	16.00	40.00
		(Green label with "WB" logo. Contains a remix by Lesh; apparently only copies with the white bordered cover contain this remix.)			
Warner Bros. 2WS-1935	(S)	**The Grateful Dead** (2 LPs)	1971	10.00	25.00
		(First pressing with a "Skull & Roses" sticker on the front.)			
Warner Bros. 2WS-1935	(S)	**The Grateful Dead** (2 LPs)	1972	6.00	15.00
		(Without the "Skull & Roses" sticker.)			
Warner Bros. 3WX-2668	(S)	**Europe '72** (3 LPs)	1972	8.00	20.00
Warner Bros. BS-2721	(S)	**The History Of The Grateful Dead, Vol. 1**	1973	4.00	10.00
Warner Bros. B-2764	(S)	**Skeletons From The Closet**	1974	4.00	10.00
		— Original Warner albums above have green labels with the "WB" logo on top.—			
Sunflower SUN-5001	(S)	**Vintage Dead**	1972	8.00	20.00
		(Counterfeits are 1/4" shorter than normal album covers.)			
Sunflower SNF-5004	(S)	**Historic Dead**	1972	8.00	20.00
Pride PRD-0016	(S)	**History Of The Grateful Dead**	1972	10.00	25.00
Grateful Dead GD-01	(S)	**Wake Of The Flood** (Green vinyl)	1973	150.00	250.00
Grateful Dead GD-01	(S)	**Wake Of The Flood**	1973	6.00	15.00
		(First pressings do not have contributing artists on the back.)			
Grateful Dead GD-01	(S)	**Wake Of The Flood**	1975	4.00	10.00
		(Second pressings have contributing artists listed on the back.)			
Grateful Dead GD-102	(S)	**From The Mars Hotel**	1974	8.00	20.00
Grateful Dead LA-494	(S)	**Blues For Allah**	1975	6.00	15.00
Grateful Dead LA-620	(S)	**Steal Your Face** (2 LPs)	1976	6.00	15.00
United Arts. SP-114	(DJ)	**For Dead Heads**	1975	12.00	30.00
Arista SP-35	(DJ)	**Grateful Dead Sampler**	1977	10.00	25.00
Arista AL-7001	(DJ)	**Terrapin Station** (Banded for air-play)	1977	10.00	25.00
Mobile Fidelity MFSL-014	(S)	**American Beauty**	1978	20.00	50.00
Mobile Fidelity MFSL-172	(S)	**From The Mars Hotel**	1980	10.00	25.00
Direct Disk SD-16619	(S)	**Terrapin Station**	1980	50.00	100.00

GRAVES, TERESA

Label & Catalog #		Title	Year	VG+	NM
Kirshner KES-104	(S)	**Teresa Graves**	1970	8.00	20.00

GRAY, BILLY

Label & Catalog #		Title	Year	VG+	NM
Decca DL-5567	(M)	**Dance-O-Rama #7**	1955	90.00	180.00

GRAY, DOBIE

Label & Catalog #		Title	Year	VG+	NM
Charger CHR-M-2002	(M)	**Dobie Gray Sings For In Crowders**	1965	10.00	25.00
Charger CHR-S-2002	(S)	**Dobie Gray Sings For In Crowders**	1965	16.00	40.00
Decca DL-75397	(S)	**Drift Away**	1973	5.00	12.00

Label & Catalog #		Title	Year	VG+	NM

Dobie Gray's first album is tough to find in stereo and often overlooked by collectors: the only way to note the stereo on the cover is the "S" in the catalog number in the upper right corner.

GRAY, DOLORES

Capitol T-897	(M)	**Warm Brandy**	*1957*	**12.00**	**30.00**

GRAYCO, HELEN

Vik LX-1066	(M)	**After Midnight**	*1957*	**10.00**	**25.00**

GRAYSON, KATHRYN

MGM E-551 (10")	(M)	**Kathryn Grayson**	*1952*	**20.00**	**50.00**
MGM E-3077 (10")	(M)	**Kiss Me Kate** (Soundtrack)	*1953*	**50.00**	**100.00**
RCA Victor LOC-3000 (10")	(M)	**So This Is Love** (Soundtrack)	*1953*	**50.00**	**100.00**
RCA Victor LPM-3105 (10")	(M)	**The Desert Song** (Soundtrack)	*1953*	**50.00**	**100.00**
MGM E-3257	(M)	**Kathryn Grayson Sings**	*1956*	**14.00**	**30.00**

GREAT SOCIETY, THE
The Great Society features Grace Slick, later of The Jefferson Airplane.

Columbia CS-9624	(S)	**Conspicuous Only In It's Absence**	*1968*	**6.00**	**15.00**
Columbia CS-9702	(S)	**How It Was**	*1968*	**6.00**	**15.00**

— Original Columbia albums above have "360 Sound" on the bottom of the label.—

GREAVES, R.B.

Atco SD-33-311	(S)	**R.B. Greaves**	*1969*	**6.00**	**15.00**

GRECO, JULIETTE

Columbia CL-569	(M)	**Juliette Greco**	*1954*	**10.00**	**25.00**
Columbia CL-992	(M)	**Greco**	*1957*	**10.00**	**25.00**

GREEK FOUNTAIN RIVER FRONT BAND, THE

Montel LLP-110	(M)	**Takes Requests**	*1965*	**50.00**	**100.00**

GREEN, AL

Hot Line 1500	(M)	**Back Up Train**	*1967*	**10.00**	**25.00**
Hot Line 1500	(S)	**Back Up Train**	*1967*	**12.00**	**30.00**
Bell 6076	(S)	**Al Green**	*1971*	**5.00**	**12.00**
Hi SHL-32055	(S)	**Green Is Blues**	*1969*	**5.00**	**12.00**
Hi SHL-32062	(S)	**Al Green Gets Next To You**	*1971*	**4.00**	**10.00**
Hi SHL-32070	(S)	**Let's Stay Together**	*1972*	**4.00**	**10.00**

Label & Catalog #		Title	Year	VG+	NM
Hi SHL-32074	(S)	I'm Still In Love With You	1972	4.00	10.00
Hi SHL-32077	(S)	Call Me	1973	4.00	10.00
Hi SHL-32082	(S)	Livin' For You	1973	4.00	10.00
Hi SHL-32087	(S)	Al Green Explores Your Mind	1974	4.00	10.00
Hi SHL-32089	(S)	Al Green's Greatest Hits	1975	4.00	10.00
Hi SHL-32092	(S)	Al Green Is Love	1975	4.00	10.00

— Original Hi albums above have grey labels.—

GREEN, PETER
Green was formerly a member of Fleetwood Mac.

Reprise RS-6436	(S)	The End Of The Game	1971	8.00	20.00

GREEN BULLFROG
Green Bullfrog features Richie Blackmore and Jon Lord of Deep Purple.

Decca DL-75269	(S)	Green Bullfrog	1971	10.00	25.00

GREEN RIVER BOYS (FEATURING GLEN CAMPBELL), THE

Capitol T-1810	(M)	Big Bluegrass Special	1962	30.00	60.00
Capitol ST-1810	(S)	Big Bluegrass Special	1962	40.00	80.00

GREENBRIAR BOYS, THE
The Greenbriar Boys also recorded with Dian James.

Vanguard VR-9104	(M)	The Greenbriar Boys	1962	6.00	15.00
Vanguard VRS-9104	(S)	The Greenbriar Boys	1962	8.00	20.00
Vanguard VSD-9159	(M)	Ragged But Right!	1964	5.00	12.00
Vanguard VSD-79159	(S)	Ragged But Right!	1964	6.00	15.00
Vanguard VSD-9233	(M)	Better Late Than Never	1966	5.00	12.00
Vanguard VSD-79233	(S)	Better Late Than Never	1966	6.00	15.00

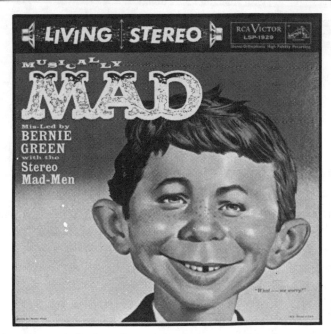

This album owes the enormous bulk of its collectibility to the presence of popular "Mad" magazine cover boy Alfred E. Newman, rendered by his official portraitist, Norman Mingo.

GREENE, BERNIE, & HIS STEREO MAD-MEN

RCA Victor LPM-1929	(M)	Musically Mad	1958	14.00	35.00
RCA Victor LSP-1929	(S)	Musically Mad	1958	20.00	50.00

Label & Catalog #		Title	Year	VG+	NM
GREENE, DODO					
Blue Note 9001	(M)	**My Hour Of Need**	1962	16.00	40.00
Blue Note 89001	(S)	**My Hour Of Need**	1962	20.00	50.00
		(Original label with "New York" on top.)			
Blue Note 9001	(M)	**My Hour Of Need**	1965	8.00	20.00
Blue Note 89001	(S)	**My Hour Of Need**	1965	10.00	25.00
		(Later pressings have "A division of Liberty" on the label.)			
GREENE, LORNE					
RCA Victor LPM-2661	(M)	**Young At Last**	1963	6.00	15.00
RCA Victor LSP-2661	(S)	**Young At Last**	1963	8.00	20.00
RCA Victor LPM-2843	(M)	**Welcome To The Ponderosa**	1964	6.00	15.00
RCA Victor LSP-2843	(S)	**Welcome To The Ponderosa**	1964	8.00	20.00
RCA Victor LPM-3302	(M)	**The Man**	1965	5.00	12.00
RCA Victor LSP-3302	(S)	**The Man**	1965	6.00	15.00
RCA Victor LPM-3409	(M)	**Lorne Greene's American West**	1965	5.00	12.00
RCA Victor LSP-3409	(S)	**Lorne Greene's American West**	1965	6.00	15.00
RCA Victor LPM-3410	(M)	**Have A Happy Holiday**	1965	5.00	12.00
RCA Victor LSP-3410	(S)	**Have A Happy Holiday**	1965	6.00	15.00
RCA Victor LPM-3678	(M)	**Portrait Of The West**	1966	5.00	12.00
RCA Victor LSP-3678	(S)	**Portrait Of The West**	1966	6.00	15.00
GREENHILL SINGERS					
United Arts. UAL-3347	(M)	**50 Fabulous Folk Favorites**	1964	5.00	12.00
United Arts. UAS-6347	(S)	**50 Fabulous Folk Favorites**	1964	6.00	15.00
GREENSLEEVES, EDDIE					
Cameo C-1031	(M)	**Humorous Folk Songs**	1963	5.00	12.00
Cameo SC-1031	(S)	**Humorous Folk Songs**	1963	6.00	15.00
GREENWICH, ELLIE					
Ms. Greenwich was formerly a member of The Raindrops.					
United Arts. UAS-6648	(S)	**Composes, Produces And Sings**	1968	8.00	20.00
Verve V6-5091	(S)	**Let It Be Written, Let It Be Sung**	1973	5.00	12.00
GREENWOODS, THE					
Decca DL-4496	(M)	**Folk Instrumentals**	1964	5.00	12.00
Decca DL-74496	(S)	**Folk Instrumentals**	1964	6.00	15.00
GREER					
Sugarbush SBS-109	(S)	**Between Two Worlds**	197?	75.00	150.00
GREGG, BOBBY, & HIS FRIENDS					
Epic LN-24051	(M)	**Let's Stomp And Wild Weekend**	1963	8.00	20.00
Epic BN-26051	(S)	**Let's Stomp And Wild Weekend**	1963	12.00	30.00
GRIFFIN, JAMES					
Refer to Bread.					
Reprise R-6091	(M)	**Summer Holiday**	1963	12.00	30.00
Reprise R9-6091	(S)	**Summer Holiday**	1963	16.00	40.00
GRIFFITH, ANDY					
Capitol T-962	(M)	**Just For Laughs**	1958	12.00	30.00
Capitol T-1105	(M)	**Shouts The Blues And Old Time Songs**	1959	12.00	30.00
Capitol T-1215	(M)	**This Here Andy Griffith**	1959	10.00	25.00
Capitol T-1611	(M)	**The Andy Griffith Show**	1961	8.00	20.00
Capitol ST-1611	(S)	**The Andy Griffith Show**	1961	12.00	30.00
Capitol T-2066	(M)	**Andy And Cleopatra**	1964	6.00	15.00
Capitol ST-2066	(S)	**Andy And Cleopatra**	1964	8.00	20.00
GRISSOM, JIMMY					
Argo 729	(M)	**World Of Trouble**	1963	8.00	20.00
GRODECK WHIPPERJENNY					
People 3000	(S)	**Grodeck Whipperjenny**	196?	45.00	90.00
GROOM, DEWEY, & THE TEXAS LONGHORNS					
Longhorn LP-004	(M)	**Last Of The Big Bands**	196?	20.00	50.00

Label & Catalog #		Title	Year	VG+	NM
GROOV-U					
Gateway GLP-3010	(M)	**Groov-U On Campus**	196?	12.00	30.00
GROOVIE GOOLIES, THE					
RCA Victor LSP-4420	(S)	**The Groovie Goolies**	1970	8.00	20.00
GROUNDHOGS, THE					
Cleve CH-82871	(S)	**The Groundhogs With John Lee Hooker**			
		And John Mayall	1968	35.00	70.00
World Pacific WPS-21892	(S)	**Scratching The Surface**	1968	16.00	40.00
Imperial LP-12452	(S)	**Blues Obituary**	1969	16.00	40.00
Liberty LST-7644	(S)	**Thank Christ For The Bomb**	1970	14.00	35.00
United Arts. UAS-5513	(S)	**The Groundhogs Split**	1971	10.00	25.00
United Arts. UAS-5570	(S)	**Who Will Save The World**	1972	10.00	25.00
United Arts. LA008	(S)	**Hogwash**	1973	6.00	15.00
United Arts. LA603	(S)	**Crosscut Saw**	1976	6.00	15.00
United Arts. LA680	(S)	**Black Diamond**	1976	6.00	15.00
GROUNDSTAR					
Stellar SR-2549	(S)	**Forced Landing**	1980	16.00	40.00
GROUP, THE					
Bell 6038	(S)	**The Group**	1970	8.00	20.00
GROUP, THE					
RCA Victor LPM-2663	(M)	**The Group**	1963	8.00	20.00
RCA Victor LSP-2663	(S)	**The Group**	1963	10.00	25.00
GROUP IMAGE, THE					
Community A-101	(S)	**A Mouth In The Clouds**	1968	6.00	15.00
GROUP ONE					
RCA Victor LPM-3524	(M)	**Brothers Go To Mothers And Others**	1966	6.00	15.00
RCA Victor LST-3524	(S)	**Brothers Go To Mothers And Others**	1966	8.00	20.00
GROUP THERAPY					
RCA Victor LSP-3976	(S)	**People Get Ready For Group Therapy**	1968	6.00	15.00
Philips PHS-600303	(S)	**37 Minutes Of Group Therapy**	1969	5.00	12.00
GROVE, BOBBY					
King 831	(M)	**It Was For You**	1963	14.00	35.00
GROWING CONCERN, THE					
Mainstream S-6108	(S)	**Growing Concern**	1968	16.00	40.00
GRYPHON					
No label 80-1230	(S)	**Gryphon**	197?	20.00	50.00
GUARD, DAVE, & THE WHISKEYHILL SINGERS					
The Whiskeyhill Singers feature Dave Guard of The Kingston Trio.					
Capitol T-1728	(M)	**Dave Guard & The Whiskeyhill Singers**	1962	10.00	25.00
Capitol ST-1728	(S)	**Dave Guard & The Whiskeyhill Singers**	1962	14.00	35.00
MGM 1E-5	(M)	**How The West Was Won** *(Soundtrack)*	1963	14.00	35.00
MGM S1E-5	(S)	**How The West Was Won** *(Soundtrack)*	1963	16.00	45.00
GUESS WHO, THE					
Members include Chad Allan, Randy Bachman, and Burton Cummings.					
Wand WDS-691	(E)	**Born In Canada**	1969	8.00	20.00
MGM SE-4645	(S)	**The Guess Who**	1969	8.00	20.00
RCA Victor LSP-4141	(S)	**Wheatfield Soul**	1969	8.00	20.00
RCA Victor LSP-4157	(S)	**Canned Wheat**	1969	6.00	15.00
RCA Victor LSP-4779	(S)	**Live At The Paramount**	1972	12.00	30.00
RCA Victor LSP-4830	(S)	**Artificial Paradise** *(With paper bag)*	1972	6.00	15.00
RCA Victor APD1-0130	(Q)	**Guess Who No. 10**	1973	8.00	20.00
RCA Victor APD1-0269	(Q)	**The Best Of The Guess Who, Volume 2**	1974	8.00	20.00
RCA Victor APD1-0405	(Q)	**Road Food**	1974	8.00	20.00
		— Original RCA albums above have orange labels.—			
Hilltak PR-331	(DJ)	**Track And Dialogue**	1979	10.00	25.00

Label & Catalog #		Title	Year	VG+	NM

GUILD, THE
The Guild is a creation of Gary Usher & Co.
| Elektra EKS- | (S) | The Guild | 1972 | 10.00 | 25.00 |

GUITAR, BONNIE
Dot DLP-3069	(M)	Moonlight And Shadows	1957	14.00	35.00
Dot DLP-3151	(M)	Whispering Hope	1958	10.00	25.00
Dot DLP-25151	(S)	Whispering Hope	1958	14.00	35.00
Dot DLP-3335	(M)	Dark Moon	1961	8.00	20.00
Dot DLP-25335	(E)	Dark Moon	1961	5.00	12.00
Dot DLP-3696	(M)	Two Worlds	1966	5.00	12.00
Dot DLP-25696	(S)	Two Worlds	1966	6.00	15.00
Dot DLP-3737	(M)	Miss Bonnie Guitar	1966	5.00	12.00
Dot DLP-25737	(S)	Miss Bonnie Guitar	1966	6.00	15.00
Dot DLP-3746	(M)	Merry Christams From Bonnie Guitar	1966	5.00	12.00
Dot DLP-25746	(S)	Merry Christams From Bonnie Guitar	1966	6.00	15.00
Dot DLP-3793	(M)	Award Winner	1967	5.00	12.00
Dot DLP-25793	(S)	Award Winner	1967	6.00	15.00

GUITAR JR.
| Goldband 1085 | (M) | Pick Me Up On Your Way Down | 1960 | 10.00 | 25.00 |

GUITAR SLIM
Guitar Slim is a pseudonym for Lee Baker.
| Capitol ST-403 | (S) | Broke And Hungry | 1969 | 6.00 | 15.00 |
| Specialty 2120 | (S) | Things That I Used To Do | 1969 | 6.00 | 15.00 |

GUN
Gun features Adrian and Paul Gurvitz (aka Curtis). Refer to The Baker-Gurvitz Army.
| Epic BN-26468 | (S) | Gun | 1969 | 5.00 | 12.00 |
| Epic BN-26551 | (S) | Gunsight | 1970 | 6.00 | 15.00 |

GUNS & ROSES
| Uzi Suicde USR-001 | (S) | Live! Like A Suicide | 1986 | 50.00 | 100.00 |

GUNTER, ARTHUR
| Excello 8017 | (M) | Black And Blues | 1971 | 10.00 | 25.00 |

GUTHRIE, ARLO
Reprise R-6267	(M)	Alice's Restaurant	1967	8.00	20.00
Reprise RS-6267	(S)	Alice's Restaurant (Green, gold & pink label)	1967	6.00	15.00
United Arts. UAS-5196	(S)	Alice's Restaurant (Soundtrack)	1969	6.00	15.00
Reprise MS4-2142	(Q)	The Last Of The Brooklyn Cowboys	1973	6.00	15.00

GUTHRIE, JACK
| Capitol T-2456 | (M) | Jack Guthrie's Greatest Songs | 1966 | 8.00 | 20.00 |
| Capitol ST-2456 | (S) | Jack Guthrie's Greatest Songs | 1966 | 8.00 | 20.00 |

GUTHRIE, WOODY
| Folkways FA-2011 | (M) | Talking Dust Bowl | 195? | 12.00 | 30.00 |
| Folkways FC-7015 | (M) | Songs To Grow On | 195? | 12.00 | 30.00 |

GUTHRIE, WOODY, & CISCO HOUSTON
Stinson 32	(M)	Cowboy Songs	196?	8.00	20.00
Stinson 44	(M)	Folksongs	196?	8.00	20.00
Stinson 53	(M)	More Songs	196?	8.00	20.00

GUY, BUDDY
Vanguard VSD-79272	(S)	A Man And The Blues	1968	8.00	20.00
Vanguard VSD-79290	(S)	This Is Buddy Guy	1968	8.00	20.00
Chess LPS-1527	(S)	Left My Blues In San Francisco	1969	6.00	15.00
Blue Thumb 20	(S)	Buddy And The Juniors (Colored vinyl)	1970	12.00	30.00

Label & Catalog #		Title	Year	VG+	NM

H.P. LOVECRAFT [LOVECRAFT]

Label & Catalog #		Title	Year	VG+	NM
Phillips PHM-200252	(M)	H. P. Lovecraft	1967	8.00	20.00
Phillips PHS-600252	(S)	H. P. Lovecraft	1967	10.00	25.00
Phillips PHS-600279	(S)	Lovecraft II	1968	10.00	25.00
Reprise RS-6419	(S)	Valley Of The Moon	1970	6.00	15.00
Mercury SRM-1-1031	(S)	We Love You	1976	6.00	15.00

HAGAR, ERNIE

Sage C-42	(M)	Swinging Steel Guitar	195?	20.00	50.00

HAGGARD, MERLE, & THE STRANGERS

Capitol T-2373	(M)	Strangers	1965	8.00	20.00
Capitol ST-2373	(S)	Strangers	1965	10.00	25.00
Capitol T-2585	(M)	Swinging Doors	1966	8.00	20.00
Capitol ST-2585	(S)	Swinging Doors	1966	10.00	25.00
Capitol T-2702	(M)	I'm A Lonesome Fugitive	1967	8.00	20.00
Capitol ST-2702	(S)	I'm A Lonesome Fugitive	1967	10.00	25.00
Capitol T-2789	(M)	Branded Man/I Threw Away The Rose	1967	6.00	15.00
Capitol ST-2789	(S)	Branded Man/I Threw Away The Rose	1967	8.00	20.00
Capitol ST-2848	(S)	Sing Me Back Home	1968	8.00	20.00
Capitol ST 2912	(S)	Legend Of Bonnie & Clyde	1968	6.00	15.00
Capitol SKAO-2951	(S)	Best Of Merle Haggard	1968	6.00	15.00
Capitol ST-2972	(S)	Mama Tried	1969	6.00	15.00
Capitol SKAO-168	(S)	Pride In What I Am	1969	6.00	15.00
Capitol ST-223	(S)	Same Train, A Different Time (2 LPs)	1969	10.00	25.00
Capitol ST-319	(S)	Portrait Of Merle Haggard	1969	6.00	15.00
Capitol ST-384	(S)	Okie From Muskogee	1969	5.00	12.00
Capitol ST-451	(S)	The Fighting Side Of Me	1970	5.00	12.00
Capitol ST-638	(S)	Tribute To The Best Damn Fiddle Player	1970	8.00	20.00
Capitol ST-735	(S)	Hag	1971	6.00	15.00
Capitol ST-803	(S)	Land Of Many Churches (2 LPs)	1971	20.00	50.00
Capitol ST-823	(S)	Truly The Best Of Merle Haggard	1971	16.00	40.00
Capitol ST-835	(S)	Someday We'll Look Back	1972	6.00	15.00

HAGGARD, MERLE, & BONNIE OWENS

Capitol T-2453	(M)	Just Between The Two Of Us	1966	6.00	15.00
Capitol ST-2453	(S)	Just Between The Two Of Us	1966	8.00	20.00

HAGGARD'S STRANGERS, MERLE

Capitol ST-169	(S)	The Instrumental Sound Of The Strangers	1969	10.00	25.00
Capitol ST-445	(S)	Introducing My Friends, The Strangers	1970	6.00	15.00
Capitol ST-590	(S)	Gettin' To Know Merle Haggard's Strangers	1970	6.00	15.00
Capitol ST-796	(S)	Honky Tonkin'	1971	6.00	15.00

HAINES, CONNIE

Coral CRL-56055 (10")	(M)	Connie Haines Sings	1955	14.00	35.00
RCA Victor LPM-2264	(M)	Faith, Hope And Charity	1960	6.00	15.00
RCA Victor LSP-2264	(S)	Faith, Hope And Charity	1960	8.00	20.00

HALE, CORKY

Gene Norman GNP-17	(M)	Corky Hale	1957	10.00	25.00

HALEN, VAN

Warner Bros. 23985	(DJ)	1984 (Quiex II vinyl)	1984	6.00	15.00

HALEY, BILL, & HIS COMETS
Refer to Trini Lopez / Scott Gregory.

Essex LP-202	(M)	Rock With Bill Haley And The Comets	1954	180.00	300.00
Somerset P-4600	(M)	Rock With Bill Haley And The Comets	1954	75.00	150.00
Trans World 202	(M)	Rock With Bill Haley And The Comets	1956	100.00	200.00

Label & Catalog #		Title	Year	VG+	NM
Decca DL-5560 (10")	(M)	**Shake, Rattle And Roll**	1955	300.00	500.00
Decca DL-8225	(M)	**Rock Around The Clock**	1956	100.00	200.00
Decca DL-78225	(E)	**Rock Around The Clock**	1960	75.00	150.00
Decca DL-8315	(M)	**Music For The Boyfriend**	1956	75.00	150.00
Decca DL-8345	(DJ)	**Rock And Roll Stage Show** (Pink label)	1956	300.00	500.00
Decca DL-8345	(M)	**Rock And Roll Stage Show**	1956	75.00	150.00
Decca DL-8569	(DJ)	**Rockin' The Oldies** (Pink label)	1957	300.00	500.00
Decca DL-8569	(M)	**Rockin' The Oldies**	1957	50.00	100.00
Decca DL-8692	(DJ)	**Rockin' Around The World** (Pink label)	1958	240.00	400.00
Decca DL-8692	(M)	**Rockin' Around The World**	1958	50.00	100.00
Decca DL-8775	(DJ)	**Rockin' The Joint** (Pink label)	1958	240.00	400.00
Decca DL-8775	(M)	**Rockin' The Joint**	1958	50.00	100.00
Decca DL-8821	(DJ)	**Bill Haley's Chicks** (Pink label)	1959	240.00	400.00
Decca DL-8821	(M)	**Bill Haley's Chicks**	1959	20.00	50.00
Decca DL-78821	(S)	**Bill Haley's Chicks**	1959	50.00	100.00
Decca DL-8964	(DJ)	**Strictly Instrumental** (Pink label)	1960	240.00	400.00
Decca DL-8964	(M)	**Strictly Instrumental**	1960	20.00	50.00
Decca DL-78964	(S)	**Strictly Instrumental**	1960	50.00	100.00

— Original Decca mono albums above have black labels with "Long Play 33 1/3 RPM" on the bottom; stereo albums have black labels with "Decca Stereo" on top.—

Label & Catalog #		Title	Year	VG+	NM
Warner Bros. W-1378	(M)	**Bill Haley And His Comets** (Grey label)	1960	20.00	50.00
Warner Bros. WS-1378	(S)	**Bill Haley And His Comets** (Grey label)	1960	40.00	80.00
Warner Bros. WS-1378	(S)	**Bill Haley And His Comets** (Gold label)	196?	16.00	40.00
Warner Bros. W-1391	(DJ)	**Bill Haley's Jukebox** (White label)	1960	150.00	250.00
Warner Bros. W-1391	(M)	**Bill Haley's Jukebox** (Grey label)	1960	20.00	50.00
Warner Bros. WS-1391	(S)	**Bill Haley's Jukebox** (Grey label)	1960	40.00	80.00
Vocalion VL-3696	(M)	**Bill Haley And The Comets**	1963	10.00	25.00
Guest Star 1454	(M)	**Rock Around The Clock King**	1964	10.00	25.00
Guest Star S-1454	(S)	**Rock Around The Clock King**	1964	6.00	15.00
Decca DL-75027	(S)	**Bill Haley's Greatest Hits**	1969	8.00	20.00
Kama Sutra KLPS-2104	(S)	**Scrapbook/Live At The Bitter End**	1970	12.00	30.00
Janus 3035	(S)	**Travelin' Band**	1970	10.00	25.00
Janus JX25-7003	(S)	**Razzle Dazzle** (2 LPs)	1971	6.00	15.00
Ambassador 98089	(S)	**Bill Haley & His Comets**	1970	8.00	20.00
Warner Bros. WS-1831	(S)	**Rock 'N' Roll Revival**	1971	6.00	15.00
Decca DXSE-211	(P)	**Golden Hits** (2 LPs)	1972	6.00	15.00
Sun 143	(S)	**R-O-C-K**	1979	6.00	15.00

HALFNELSON
Halfnelson is Ron and Russell Mael, later of Sparks.

Bearsville BV-2048	(S)	**Halfnelson** (Reissued as "Sparks")	1971	6.00	15.00

HALL, CONNIE

Decca DL-4217	(M)	**Connie Hall**	1962	6.00	15.00
Decca DL-74217	(S)	**Connie Hall**	1962	8.00	20.00

HALL, DARYL, & JOHN OATES

RCA Victor AFL1-2804	(S)	**Along The Red Ledge** (Red vinyl)	1978	5.00	12.00
RCA Victor DJL1-3832	(DJ)	**RCA Special Radio Series** (Interview)	1980	4.00	10.00
Mobile Fidelity MFSL-069	(S)	**Abandoned Luncheonette**	1979	6.00	15.00

HALL, DICKSON [DIXON HALL]

MGM E-329 (10")	(M)	**Outlaws Of The Old West**	1954	16.00	40.00
MGM E-3263	(M)	**Outlaws Of The Old West**	1956	10.00	25.00
Kapp KL-1067	(M)	**Fabulous Country Hits Way Out West**	1957	10.00	25.00
Kapp KL-1464	(M)	**24 Fabulous Country Hits**	1966	5.00	12.00
Kapp KS-3464	(S)	**24 Fabulous Country Hits**	1966	6.00	15.00
Epic LN-3427	(M)	**25 All-Time Country And Western Hits**	1958	10.00	25.00

HALL, JUANITA

Counterpoint 556	(M)	**Jaunita Hall Sings The Blues**	195?	20.00	50.00

HALL, LARRY

Strand 1005	(M)	**Sandy**	1960	20.00	50.00
Strand S-1005	(E)	**Sandy**	1960	16.00	40.00

HALLYDAY, JOHNNY

Phillips PHM-200019	(M)	**America's Rockin' Hits**	1961	16.00	40.00
Phillips PHS-600019	(S)	**America's Rockin' Hits**	1961	20.00	50.00

Label & Catalog #		Title	Year	VG+	NM
HALOS, THE					
Warwick W-2046	(M)	**The Halos**	1962	75.00	150.00
HAMBLEN, STUART					
Refer to Webb Pierce / Marvin Rainwater / Stuart Hamblen.					
RCA Victor LPM-3265 (10")	(M)	**It Is No Secret**	1954	20.00	50.00
RCA Victor LPM-1253	(M)	**It Is No Secret**	1956	12.00	30.00
RCA Victor LPM-1436	(M)	**Grand Old Hymns**	1957	12.00	30.00
Coral CRL-57254	(M)	**Remember Me**	1960	10.00	25.00
Columbia CL-1588	(M)	**The Spell Of The Yukon**	1961	6.00	15.00
Columbia CS-8388	(S)	**The Spell Of The Yukon**	1961	8.00	20.00
Columbia CL-1769	(M)	**Of God I Sing**	1962	6.00	15.00
Columbia CS-8569	(S)	**Of God I Sing**	1962	8.00	20.00
— Original Columbia albums above have three white "eye" logos on each side of the spindle hole.—					
HAMILTON, FRANK					
Hamilton was formerly a member of The Weavers.					
Capitol T-2005	(M)	**Sing A Song With The Kingston Trio**	1964	6.00	15.00
Capitol ST-2005	(S)	**Sing A Song With The Kingston Trio**	1964	8.00	20.00
HAMILTON, GEORGE, IV					
ABC-Paramount 220	(M)	**George Hamilton IV On Campus**	1958	8.00	20.00
ABC-Paramount S-220	(S)	**George Hamilton IV On Campus**	1958	12.00	30.00
ABC-Paramount 251	(M)	**Sing Me A Sad Song**	1958	8.00	20.00
ABC-Paramount S-251	(S)	**Sing Me A Sad Song**	1958	12.00	30.00
ABC-Paramount 461	(M)	**Big Fifteen**	1963	8.00	20.00
ABC-Paramount S-461	(S)	**Big Fifteen**	1963	12.00	30.00
ABC-Paramount 535	(M)	**By George**	1966	6.00	15.00
ABC-Paramount S-535	(S)	**By George**	1966	8.00	20.00
HAMILTON, ROY					
Epic LN-1103 (10")	(M)	**The Voice Of Roy Hamilton**	195?	40.00	80.00
HAMILTON, RUSS					
Kapp KL-1076	(M)	**Rainbow**	1957	30.00	60.00
HAMILTON STREETCAR					
Dot DLP-25939	(S)	**Hamilton Streetcar**	1969	6.00	15.00
HAMMER					
San Francisco SD-203	(S)	**Hammer**	1970	8.00	20.00
HAMMOND, JOHN					
Vanguard VRS-9153	(M)	**Big City Blues**	1964	8.00	20.00
Vanguard VSD-79153	(S)	**Big City Blues**	1964	12.00	30.00
Vanguard VRS-9178	(M)	**So Many Roads**	1966	12.00	30.00
Vanguard VSD-79178	(S)	**So Many Roads**	1966	16.00	40.00
Vanguard VRS-9198	(M)	**Country Blues**	1966	8.00	20.00
Vanguard VSD-79198	(S)	**Country Blues**	1966	12.00	30.00
Vanguard VRS-9245	(M)	**Mirrors**	1967	12.00	30.00
Vanguard VSD-79245	(S)	**Mirrors**	1967	16.00	40.00
		(Vanguard 9178 and 9245 feature Levon Helm, Garth Hudson and Robbie Robertson of The Band.)			
Atlantic SD-8206	(S)	**Sooner Or Later**	1968	8.00	20.00
Atlantic 8152	(M)	**I Can Tell**	1967	16.00	40.00
Atlantic SD-8152	(S)	**I Can Tell**	1967	20.00	50.00
		(Atlantic 8152 features Robertson, Rick Danko and Bill Wyman.)			
Atlantic SD-8251	(S)	**Southern Fried**	1969	6.00	15.00
HANGMEN, THE					
Monument MLP-8077	(M)	**Bitter Sweet**	1967	6.00	15.00
Monument SLP-18077	(S)	**Bitter Sweet**	1967	8.00	20.00
HAPPENINGS, THE					
B.T. Puppy BT-1001	(M)	**The Happenings**	1966	8.00	20.00
B.T. Puppy BTS-1001	(S)	**The Happenings**	1966	10.00	25.00
B.T. Puppy BT-1003	(M)	**Psycle**	1967	8.00	20.00
B.T. Puppy BTS-1003	(S)	**Psycle**	1967	10.00	25.00
B.T. Puppy BTS-1004	(S)	**The Happenings' Golden Hits!**	1968	16.00	40.00

Label & Catalog #		Title	Year	VG+	NM
Jubilee JGS-8028	(S)	Piece Of Mind	1969	8.00	20.00
Jubilee JGS-8030	(S)	The Happenings' Greatest Hits!	1969	8.00	20.00
HAPPENINGS, THE / THE TOKENS					
B.T. Puppy BT-1002	(M)	Back To Back	1967	5.00	12.00
B.T. Puppy BTS-1002	(S)	Back To Back	1967	6.00	15.00
HAPPY DRAGON BAND, THE					
Fiddler's Music 1157	(S)	The Happy Dragon Band	1977	50.00	100.00
HAPSHASH & THE COLOURED COAT					
Imperial LP-12377	(S)	Hapshash & The Coloured Coat	1968	8.00	20.00
Imperial LP-12430	(S)	Western Flyer	1969	8.00	20.00
HARD WATER					
Capitol ST-2954	(S)	Hard Water	1968	8.00	20.00
HARDIN, TIM					
Atco 33-210	(M)	Tim Hardin	1967	5.00	12.00
Atco SD-33-210	(S)	Tim Hardin	1967	6.00	15.00
HARDTIMES, THE					
World Pacific WP-1867	(M)	Blew Mind	1968	6.00	15.00
World Pacific ST-1867	(S)	Blew Mind	1968	8.00	20.00
HARDY, FRANCOISE					
Four Corners FC-4231	(M)	Francoise	196?	8.00	20.00
Four Corners FCS-4231	(S)	Francoise	196?	12.00	30.00
Four Corners FC-4238	(M)	Je Vous Aime	196?	8.00	20.00
Four Corners FCS-4238	(S)	Je Vous Aime	196?	12.00	30.00
Reprise RS-6290	(S)	Francoise Hardy	1968	12.00	30.00
HARDY BOYS, THE					
RCA Victor LSP-4217	(S)	Here Come The Hardy Boys	1969	6.00	15.00
RCA Victor LSP-4315	(S)	Wheels	1970	5.00	12.00
HARPER, ARTHUR LEE					
Mr. Harper also recorded as Arthur.					
Nocturne NRS-905	(S)	Love Is The Revolution	1975	180.00	300.00
HARPER, ROY					
Sunset SLS-50373	(S)	Folkjokeopus	1969	10.00	25.00
Harvest SKAO-418	(S)	Flat, Baroque And Berserk	1970	5.00	12.00
World Pacific WPS-21888	(S)	Folkjokeopus	1972	5.00	12.00
Chrysalis PRO-620	(DJ)	Introduction To Roy Harper	1976	12.00	30.00
HARPER, TONI					
Verve V-2001	(M)	Toni	1956	12.00	30.00
RCA Victor LPM-2092	(M)	Lady Lonely	1960	6.00	15.00
RCA Victor LSP-2092	(S)	Lady Lonely	1960	10.00	25.00
RCA Victor LPM-2253	(M)	Night Mood	1960	6.00	15.00
RCA Victor LSP-2253	(S)	Night Mood	1960	10.00	25.00
HARPERS BIZARRE					
Warner Bros. W-1693	(M)	Feelin' Groovy (Gold label)	1967	5.00	12.00
Warner Bros. WS-1693	(S)	Feelin' Groovy (Gold label)	1967	6.00	15.00
Warner Bros. WS-1716	(S)	Anything Goes	1968	5.00	12.00
Warner Bros. WS-1739	(S)	Secret Life Of Harpers Bazaar	1968	5.00	12.00
Warner Bros. WS-1784	(S)	Harpers Bazaar	1969	5.00	12.00
Forest Bay BS-7545LP	(S)	As Time Goes By	1976	4.00	10.00
HARPO, SLIM					
Excello LP-8003	(M)	Raining In My Heart	1961	50.00	100.00
Excello LP-8005	(M)	Baby, Scratch My Back	1966	20.00	50.00
Excello LP-8008	(S)	Tip On In	1968	12.00	30.00
Excello LP-8010	(S)	The Best Of Slim Harpo	1969	12.00	30.00
Excello LP-8013	(M)	Slim Harpo Knew The Blues	1970	10.00	25.00

Label & Catalog #		Title	Year	VG+	NM
HARPTONES, THE					
Refer to The Crows; The Paragons.					
Ambient Sound 37718	(S)	**Love Needs**	1982	4.00	10.00
HARRIS, EMMYLOU					
Jubilee JGS-8031	(S)	**Gliding Bird** *(Full color cover)*	1969	50.00	100.00
Mobile Fidelity MFSL-015	(S)	**Quarter Moon In A Ten Cent Town**	1979	12.00	30.00
HARRIS, PEPPERMINT					
Time 5	(M)	**Peppermint Harris**	1962	16.00	40.00
HARRIS, ROLF					
Epic LN-24053	(M)	**The Original Sun Arise**	1963	8.00	20.00
Epic BN-26053	(S)	**The Original Sun Arise**	1963	12.00	30.00
Epic LN-24110	(M)	**The Court Of King Caractacus**	1964	8.00	20.00
Epic BN-26110	(S)	**The Court Of King Caractacus**	1964	12.00	30.00
HARRIS, SHAUN					
Harris was formerly a member of The West Coast Pop Art Experimental Band.					
Capitol ST-11168	(S)	**Shaun Harris**	1973	8.00	20.00
HARRIS, WYNONIE					
Refer to Roy Brown; Amos Milburn.					
King KS-1086	(E)	**Good Rockin' Blues**	1970	10.00	25.00
HARRISON, GEORGE					
Harrsion was formerly a member of The Beatles. Refer to The Radha Krsna Temple.					
Apple ST-3350	(S)	**Wonderwall Music**	1969	35.00	70.00
		(Apple label with Capitol logo)			
Apple ST-3350	(S)	**Wonderwall Music**	1969	8.00	20.00
		(Apple label with "Apple Inc.")			
Zapple ST-3358	(S)	**Electronic Sound**	1969	14.00	35.00
Apple STCH-639	(S)	**All Things Must Pass** *(3 LP box)*	1970	8.00	20.00
		(Produced by Phil Spector)			
Apple STCX-3385	(S)	**The Concert For Bangla Desh** *(3 LP box)*	1972	8.00	20.00
		(With performances by Harrison, Bob Dylan			
		and Ringo produced by Phil Spector.)			
Apple SMAS-3410	(S)	**Living In The Material World**	1973	4.00	10.00
Apple SMAS-3418	(S)	**Dark Horse**	1974	6.00	15.00
Apple SW-3420	(S)	**Extra Texture** *(Die-cut title cover)*	1975	5.00	12.00
Dark Horse *(No number)*	(DJ)	**Dark Horse Radio Special**	1975	100.00	200.00
Dark Horse PRO-649	(DJ)	**Personal Music Dialogue At 33 & 1/3**	1976	16.00	40.00
Dark Horse 23734	(DJ)	**Gone Troppo** *(Quiex II vinyl)*	1982	8.00	20.00
Capitol STCH-639	(S)	**All Things Must Pass** *(3 LP box)*	1970	6.00	15.00
Capitol ST-11578	(S)	**Best Of George Harrison** *(Photo label)*	1976	5.00	12.00
Capitol ST-11578	(S)	**Best Of George Harrison** *(Orange label)*	1976	18.00	45.00
Capitol SABB-12248	(S)	**The Concert For Bangla Desh** *(2 LPs)*	1982	210.00	350.00
Capitol SN-16216	(S)	**Living In The Material World**	198?	6.00	15.00
Capitol SN-16217	(S)	**Extra Texture**	198?	8.00	20.00
HARRISON, NOEL					
London LL-3459	(M)	**Noel Harrison**	1965	6.00	15.00
London PS-459	(P)	**Noel Harrison**	1965	10.00	25.00
Reprise R-6321	(M)	**Santa Monica Pier**	1967	5.00	12.00
Reprise RS-6321	(S)	**Santa Monica Pier**	1967	6.00	15.00
Reprise RS-6321	(S)	**The Great Electric Experiment Is Over**	1968	6.00	15.00
HARRISON, WILBERT					
Sphere Sound SR-7000	(M)	**Kansas City**	1965	50.00	100.00
Sphere Sound SSR-7000	(E)	**Kansas City**	1965	40.00	80.00
Sue SSLP-8801	(S)	**Let's Work Together**	1970	12.00	30.00
Juggernaut ST-8803	(S)	**Shoot You Full Of Love**	1971	6.00	15.00
Buddah BDS-5092	(S)	**Wilbert Harrison**	1971	6.00	15.00
HARROW, NANCY					
Candid 8008	(M)	**Wild Women Don't Have The Blues**	1962	6.00	15.00
Candid 9008	(S)	**Wild Women Don't Have The Blues**	1962	10.00	25.00
Atlantic 8075	(M)	**You Never Know**	1963	6.00	15.00
Atlantic SD-8075	(S)	**You Never Know**	1963	10.00	25.00

Label & Catalog #		Title	Year	VG+	NM
HART, MICKEY					
Refer to The Diga Rhythm Band; The Grateful Dead; The Heart Of Gold Band.					
Warner Bros. BS-2635	(S)	**Rolling Thunder** *(With insert)*	1972	16.00	40.00
HARTMAN, DAN					
Blue Sky ASZ-246	(DJ)	**Who Is Dan Hartman?**	1976	6.00	15.00
HARTMAN, JOHNNY					
Regent 6014	(M)	**Just You, Just Me**	1956	20.00	50.00
Bethlehem BCP-43	(M)	**Songs From The Heart**	1956	20.00	50.00
Bethlehem BCP-6014	(M)	**The Debonair Mr. Hartman**	1958	20.00	50.00
Impulse 40	(M)	**John Coltrane And Johnny Hartman**	1963	12.00	30.00
Impulse S-40	(S)	**John Coltrane And Johnny Hartman**	1963	16.00	40.00
Impulse 57	(M)	**Dropped By To Say Hello**	1964	8.00	20.00
Impulse S-57	(S)	**Dropped By To Say Hello**	1964	10.00	25.00
Impulse 74	(M)	**The Voice That Is**	1965	8.00	20.00
Impulse S-74	(S)	**The Voice That Is**	1965	10.00	25.00
HARUMI					
Forecast FTS-3030	(S)	**Harumi** *(2 LPs)*	1968	6.00	15.00
HARVEST FLIGHT					
Destiny D-3303	(S)	**One Way**	197?	50.00	100.00
HASKELL, JIMMIE					
Capitol T-1915	(M)	**Sunset Surf**	1963	6.00	15.00
Capitol ST-1915	(S)	**Sunset Surf**	1963	8.00	20.00
Capitol T-2151	(M)	**Teen Love Themes**	1964	5.00	12.00
Capitol ST-2151	(S)	**Teen Love Themes**	1964	6.00	15.00
HASSLES, THE					
The Hassles feature Billy Joel.					
United Arts. UAS-6631	(S)	**The Hassles**	1968	8.00	20.00
United Arts. UAS-6699	(S)	**The Hour Of The Wolf**	1969	8.00	20.00
HAWKINS, DALE					
Chess 1429	(M)	**Suzie-Q**	1958	300.00	500.00
Roulette R-25175	(M)	**Let's All Twist**	1962	50.00	100.00
Roulette SR-25175	(S)	**Let's All Twist**	1962	75.00	150.00
Bell 6036	(S)	**L.A., Memphis And Tyler, Texas**	1969	12.00	30.00
HAWKINS, HAWKSHAW					
Refer to Cowboy Copas / Hawkshaw Hawkins.					
Gladwynne 2006	(M)	**Country Western Cavalcade**	195?	50.00	100.00
LaBrea 8020	(M)	**Hawkshaw Hawkins**	195?	50.00	100.00
King 587	(M)	**Hawkshaw Hawkins**	1958	35.00	70.00
King 592	(M)	**Grand Ole Opry Favorites**	1958	35.00	70.00
King 599	(M)	**Hawkshaw Hawkins**	1959	35.00	70.00
King 808	(M)	**The All New Hawkshaw Hawkins**	1963	12.00	30.00
King 858	(M)	**Taken From Our Vaults, Volume 1**	1963	12.00	30.00
King 870	(M)	**Taken From Our Vaults, Volume 2**	1963	12.00	30.00
King 873	(M)	**Taken From Our Vaults, Volume 3**	1963	12.00	30.00
HAWKINS, JENNELL					
Amazon AM-1001	(M)	**The Many Moods Of Jenny**	1961	6.00	15.00
Amazon AS-1001	(S)	**The Many Moods Of Jenny**	1961	8.00	20.00
Amazon AM-1002	(M)	**Moments To Remember**	1962	6.00	15.00
Amazon AS-1002	(S)	**Moments To Remember**	1962	8.00	20.00
HAWKINS, RONNIE					
The Hawks, a.k.a. The Band, is Ronnie's group on many of the Roulette sides.					
Roulette R-25078	(M)	**Ronnie Hawkins**	1959	40.00	80.00
Roulette SR-25078	(S)	**Ronnie Hawkins**	1959	50.00	100.00
Roulette SR-25078	(S)	**Ronnie Hawkins** *(Red vinyl)*	1959	180.00	300.00
Roulette R-25102	(M)	**Mr. Dynamo**	1960	40.00	80.00
Roulette SR-25102	(S)	**Mr. Dynamo**	1960	50.00	100.00
Roulette SR-25102	(S)	**Mr. Dynamo** *(Red vinyl)*	1960	180.00	300.00
Roulette R-25120	(M)	**The Folk Ballads Of Ronnie Hawkins**	1960	20.00	50.00
Roulette SR-25120	(S)	**The Folk Ballads Of Ronnie Hawkins**	1960	35.00	70.00

Label & Catalog #		Title	Year	VG+	NM
Roulette R-25137	(M)	The Songs Of Hank Williams	1960	20.00	50.00
Roulette SR-25137	(S)	The Songs Of Hank Williams	1960	35.00	70.00
Roulette SR-42045	(S)	The Best Of Ronnie Hawkins & His Band	1970	10.00	25.00
HAWKINS, "SCREAMIN' JAY"					
Epic LN-3448	(M)	At Home With Screamin' Jay Hawkins	1958	300.00	500.00
Epic LN-3457	(M)	I Put A Spell On You	1959	100.00	200.00
Epic BN-26457	(E)	I Put A Spell On You	1969	20.00	50.00
Phillips PHS-600319	(S)	What That Is	1969	16.00	40.00
Phillips PHS-600336	(S)	Screamin' Jay Hawkins	1970	16.00	40.00
Sounds Of Hawaii 5015	(S)	A Night At Forbidden City	196?	20.00	50.00
HAWKWIND					
United Arts. UAS-5519	(S)	In Search Of Space	1971	5.00	12.00
United Arts. UAS-5567	(S)	Hawkwind	1971	4.00	10.00
United Arts. LA001	(S)	Doremi Fasol Latido	1973	4.00	10.00
United Arts. LA120	(S)	Space Ritual Alive	1973	5.00	12.00
United Arts. LA328	(S)	Hall Of The Mountain Grill	1974	4.00	10.00
HAYDEN, WILLIE					
Dooto DTL-293	(M)	Blame It On The Blues	1960	180.00	300.00
HAYES, CATHY					
HiFi R-416	(M)	It's All Right With Me	1959	10.00	25.00
HAYES, ISAAC					
Atlantic SD-1599	(S)	Presenting Isaac Hayes	1968	8.00	20.00
HAYES, MARTHA					
Jubilee 1023	(M)	A Hayes Named Martha	1956	12.00	30.00
HAYMARKET SQUARE					
Chaparral 201	(S)	Magic Lantern	1968	360.00	600.00
HAYMES, DICK					
Decca DL-5023 (10")	(M)	Dick Haymes Sings	1950	12.00	30.00
Decca DL-5038 (10")	(M)	Little Shamrocks	1950	12.00	30.00
Decca DL-8773	(M)	Little White Lies	1958	8.00	20.00
Hollywood 138	(M)	Look At Me Now	195?	8.00	20.00
Capitol T-713	(M)	Rain Or Shine	1956	8.00	20.00
Capitol T-787	(M)	Moondreams	1956	8.00	20.00
Hallmark 301	(M)	The Name's Haymes	195?	8.00	20.00
Warwick W-2023	(M)	Richard The Lion-Hearted	195?	8.00	20.00
HAYNES, WALTER					
Mercury MG-20715	(M)	Steel Guitar Sounds	1962	6.00	15.00
Mercury SR-60715	(S)	Steel Guitar Sounds	1962	8.00	20.00
HAYWARD, JUSTIN, & JOHN LODGE					
Hayward and Lodge are members of The Moody Blues.					
Threshold THSX-1	(DJ)	Blue Jays *(Open-end interview with script)*	1975	20.00	50.00
HEAD					
Buddah BDS-5062	(S)	Head *(With coloring book)*	1970	8.00	20.00
HEAD, JIM, & HIS DEL RAY'S					
HP 22893	(M)	Jim Head & His Del Ray's	1964	20.00	50.00
HEAD, ROY					
TNT 101	(M)	Roy Head And The Traits	1965	50.00	100.00
Scepter S-532	(M)	Treat Me Right	1965	10.00	25.00
Scepter SS-532	(S)	Treat Me Right	1965	12.00	30.00
Dunhill DS-50080	(S)	Some People	1970	4.00	10.00
HEAD SHOP, THE					
Epic BN-26476	(S)	The Head Shop	1969	20.00	50.00
HEADS, THE					
Liberty LST-7581	(S)	Heads Up	1968	8.00	20.00

Label & Catalog #		Title	Year	VG+	NM
HEADSTONE					
Starr 740539	(S)	**Still Looking**	1974	100.00	200.00
HEART					
Heart features Ann and Nancy Wilson. Refer to Bordersong.					
Mushroom MRS-5005	(S)	**Dreamboat Annie**	1976	6.00	15.00
Mushroom MRS-5008	(S)	**Magazine**	1977	8.00	20.00
		(Original pressings have a contractual dispute disclaimer printed on the back cover.)			
Mushroom MRS-5008	(DJ)	**Magazine** *(Picture disc)*	1978	12.00	30.00
Mushroom MRS-1-SP	(S)	**Magazine** *(Picture disc)*	1978	6.00	15.00
Mushroom MRS-2-SP	(S)	**Dreamboat Annie** *(Picture disc)*	1979	8.00	20.00
Columbia AS-884	(DJ)	**Heart** *(Sampler)*	197?	8.00	20.00
Portrait HR-44799	(S)	**Little Queen** *(Half-speed master)*	1981	12.00	30.00
Nautilus NR-3	(S)	**Dreamboat Annie**	1980	10.00	25.00
HEARTBEATS, THE					
Roulette R-25107	(M)	**A Thousand Miles Away**	1960	75.00	150.00
Roulette SR-25107	(E)	**A Thousand Miles Away**	1960	50.00	100.00
		(Original labels are white with four crossed color bars.)			
HEARTS & FLOWERS					
Heart & Flowers features Rick Cunha. Linda Ronstadt supplies backing vocals.					
Capitol T-2762	(M)	**Now Is The Time For Hearts And Flowers**	1967	10.00	25.00
Capitol ST-2762	(S)	**Now Is The Time For Hearts And Flowers**	1967	12.00	30.00
Capitol ST-2868	(S)	**Of Horses, Kids And Forgotten Women**	1968	12.00	30.00
HEATHER BLACK					
American Playboy 1001	(S)	**Heather Black** *(2 LPs)*	197?	50.00	100.00
American Playboy 1001	(S)	**Heather Black** *(Single LP)*	197?	20.00	50.00
Double Bayou 2000	(S)	**Heather Black**	197?	16.00	40.00
HEAVEN					
W.W. 8701	(S)	**Heaven**	197?	75.00	150.00
HEAVY BALLOON, THE					
Elephant EVS-104	(S)	**32,000 Lbs.**	196?	14.00	35.00
HEAVY CRUISER					
Family 2706	(S)	**Heavy Cruiser**	1972	6.00	15.00
Family 2712	(S)	**Lucky Dog**	1973	6.00	15.00
Tiger Lily 14034	(S)	**Heavy Cruiser II**	197?	4.00	10.00
HEBB, BOBBY					
Phillips PHM-200212	(M)	**Sunny**	1966	8.00	20.00
Phillips PHS-600212	(S)	**Sunny**	1966	10.00	25.00
HELL, RICHARD, & THE VOIDOIDS					
Sire SR-6037	(S)	**Blank Generation**	1977	10.00	25.00
HELM, LEVON					
Helm was formerly a member of The Band.					
ABC SPPD-4-5	(DJ)	**Levon Helm** *(Picture disc)*	1978	5.00	12.00
HELMS, BOBBY					
Decca DL-8638	(M)	**To My Special Angel**	1957	30.00	60.00
Columbia CL-2060	(M)	**The Best Of Bobby Helms**	1963	8.00	20.00
Columbia CS-8860	(S)	**The Best Of Bobby Helms**	1963	10.00	25.00
Kapp KL-13463	(M)	**I'm The Man**	1966	5.00	12.00
Kapp KS-3463	(M)	**I'm The Man**	1966	6.00	15.00
Kapp KL-1505	(S)	**Sorry My Name Isn't Fred**	1966	5.00	12.00
Kapp KS-3505	(S)	**Sorry My Name Isn't Fred**	1966	6.00	15.00
HELMS, DON					
Smash MGS-27001	(M)	**Steel Guitar Sounds Of Hank Williams**	1963	8.00	20.00
Smash SRS-67001	(S)	**Steel Guitar Sounds Of Hank Williams**	1963	12.00	30.00
Smash MGS-27019	(M)	**Don Helms' Steel Guitar**	1963	6.00	15.00
Smash SRS-67019	(S)	**Don Helms' Steel Guitar**	1963	8.00	20.00

Label & Catalog #		Title	Year	VG+	NM
HELP					
Decca DL-75257	(S)	**Help**	1971	10.00	25.00
Decca DL-75304	(S)	**Second Chance**	1971	10.00	25.00
HENDERSON, BILL					
Vee Jay LP-1015	(M)	**Bill Henderson Sings**	1960	10.00	25.00
Vee Jay LP-1031	(M)	**Bill Henderson**	1960	10.00	25.00
Vee Jay SR-1031	(S)	**Bill Henderson**	1960	14.00	35.00
MGM E-4128	(M)	**With The Oscar Peterson Trio**	1963	8.00	20.00
MGM SE-4128	(S)	**With The Oscar Peterson Trio**	1963	10.00	25.00
Verve V-8619	(M)	**When My Dreamboat Comes Home**	1965	6.00	15.00
Verve V6-8619	(S)	**When My Dreamboat Comes Home**	1965	8.00	20.00
HENDERSON, BUGS					
Armadillo LP-78-1	(S)	**The Bugs Henderson Group At Last**	195?	12.00	30.00
HENDERSON, JOE					
Todd MT-2701	(M)	**Snap Your Fingers**	1962	12.00	30.00
Todd ST-2701	(S)	**Snap Your Fingers**	1962	16.00	40.00
Capitol T-1765	(M)	**You'd Be So Nice To Come Home To**	1962	8.00	20.00
Capitol ST-1765	(S)	**You'd Be So Nice To Come Home To**	1962	10.00	25.00
Milestone 9040	(S)	**Black Is The Color**	1972	4.00	10.00
HENDRICKS, JON					
Refer to Lambert, Hendricks and Ross.					
World Pacific WP-1283	(M)	**A Good Git-Together**	1959	12.00	30.00
Columbia CL-1583	(M)	**Evolution Of The Blues**	1961	10.00	25.00
Columbia CS-8383	(S)	**Evolution Of The Blues**	1961	12.00	30.00
Columbia CL-1805	(M)	**Fast Livin' Blues**	1961	10.00	25.00
Columbia CS-8605	(S)	**Fast Livin' Blues**	1961	12.00	30.00
— *Original Columbia albums above have three white "eye" logos on each side of the spindle hole.*—					
Reprise R-20167	(M)	**Salud**	1963	6.00	15.00
Reprise RS-6089	(S)	**Salud**	1963	8.00	20.00
Smash MGS-27069	(M)	**Recorded In Person At The Trident**	1965	6.00	15.00
Smash SRS-67069	(S)	**Recorded In Person At The Trident**	1965	8.00	20.00
HENDRIX, JIMI					
Refer to The Isley Brothers; Curtis Knight.					
Reprise R-6261	(DJ)	**Are You Experienced?** *(White label)*	1967	100.00	200.00
Reprise R-6261	(M)	**Are You Experienced?**	1967	30.00	60.00
Reprise RS-6261	(P)	**Are You Experienced?**	1967	12.00	30.00
Reprise R-6281	(DJ)	**Axis: Bold As Love** *(White label)*	1968	150.00	250.00
Reprise R-6281	(M)	**Axis: Bold As Love**	1968	180.00	300.00
Reprise RS-6281	(S)	**Axis: Bold As Love**	1968	180.00	300.00
— *Original Reprise albums have pink, gold & green labels.*—					
Reprise 2R-6307	(DJ)	**Electric Ladyland** *(2 LPs. Mono)*	1968	240.00	400.00
Reprise 2RS-6307	(DJ)	**Electric Ladyland** *(2 LPs. Stereo)*	1968	50.00	100.00
Reprise 2R-6307	(M)	**Electric Ladyland** *(2 LPs)*	1968	500.00	750.00
Reprise 2RS-6307	(S)	**Electric Ladyland** *(2 LPs)*	1968	14.00	35.00
— *Original Reprise albums above have brown & orange labels.*—					
Reprise MS-2025	(P)	**Smash Hits**	1969	14.00	35.00
		(Original covers advertised a poster in the lower right corner.			
		Issued with a poster, priced separately below.			
Reprise MS-2025		**Smash Hits Poster**	1969	16.00	40.00
Reprise MS-2025	(P)	**Smash Hits**	1969	8.00	20.00
		(The cover makes no mention of the poster.)			
Capitol STAO-472	(S)	**Band Of Gypsies** *(Green label)*	1970	6.00	15.00
Capitol STAO-8-472	(S)	**Band Of Gypsies** *(Record Club)*	1970	10.00	25.00
Reprise MS-2034	(S)	**The Cry Of Love**	1971	6.00	15.00
Reprise MS-2040	(S)	**Rainbow Bridge**	1971	10.00	25.00
Reprise MS-2049	(S)	**Hendrix In The West**	1972	10.00	25.00
Reprise MS-2103	(S)	**War Heroes**	1972	8.00	20.00
Reprise MS-2204	(S)	**Crash Landing**	1975	6.00	15.00
Reprise MS-2229	(S)	**Midnight Lightning**	1975	8.00	20.00
Reprise PRO-A-840	(DJ)	**Jimi Hendrix Medley**	1979	40.00	80.00
Maple 6004	(S)	**Together With Lonnie Youngblood**	1971	10.00	25.00
Crawdaddy 5-1975	(DJ)	**The Jimi Hendrix Interview LP**	1975	100.00	200.00

Label & Catalog #		Title	Year	VG+	NM
HENDRIX, JIMI / OTIS REDDING					
Reprise MS-2029	(S)	**Historic Performances Recorded At The Monterey International Pop Festival**	1970	6.00	15.00
HENRI, ADRIAN, & ROGER McGOUGH					
Epic LN-26336	(M)	**The Incredible New Liverpool Scene**	1967	8.00	20.00
Epic BN-24336	(S)	**The Incredible New Liverpool Scene**	1967	10.00	25.00
HENRY, CLARENCE "FROGMAN"					
Argo LP-4009	(M)	**You Always Hurt The One You Love**	1961	50.00	100.00
Roulette SR-42039	(S)	**Alive And Well And Living In New Orleans**	1969	8.00	20.00
HENSKE & YESTER					
Judy Henske and Jerry Yester.					
Straight STS-1052	(S)	**Farewell Aldebaran**	1968	12.00	30.00
Reprise RS-6388	(S)	**Farewell Aldebaran**	1971	6.00	15.00
HENSON, COUSIN HERB, & THE TRADING POST GANG					
Tally	(M)	**Herb Henson & The Trading Post Gang**	195?	50.00	100.00
HERD, THE					
The Herd features Peter Frampton.					
Fontana SRF-67579	(S)	**Lookin' Thru You**	1968	10.00	25.00
HERE COMES EVERYBODY					
Cab 101	(S)	**Here Comes Everybody**	1971	16.00	40.00
HERMAN, PEE WEE					
Fatima	(S)	**The Pee Wee Herman Show** *(Picture disc)*	1981	20.00	50.00
HERMAN'S HERMITS					
MGM E-4282	(M)	**Introducing Herman's Hermits**	1965	12.00	30.00
MGM SE-4282	(E)	**Introducing Herman's Hermits**	1965	8.00	20.00
		(The front cover reads "Featuring I'm Into Something Good.")			
MGM E-4282	(M)	**Introducing Herman's Hermits**	1965	12.00	30.00
MGM SE-4282	(E)	**Introducing Herman's Hermits**	1965	8.00	20.00
		(The front cover reads "Featuring I'm Into Something Good" with a sticker on the cover that reads "Featuring Mrs. Brown You Have A Lovely Daughter.")			
MGM E-4282	(M)	**Introducing Herman's Hermits**	1965	6.00	15.00
MGM SE-4282	(E)	**Introducing Herman's Hermits**	1965	5.00	12.00
		(Cover reads "Featuring Mrs. Brown You've Got A Lovely Daughter.")			
MGM E-4295	(M)	**On Tour: Their Second Album**	1965	6.00	15.00
MGM SE-4295	(E)	**On Tour: Their Second Album**	1965	4.00	10.00
MGM E-4315	(M)	**The Best Of Herman's Hermits**	1965	5.00	12.00
MGM SE-4315	(E)	**The Best Of Herman's Hermits**	1965	3.50	8.00
MGM E-4342	(M)	**Hold On!** *(Soundtrack)*	1966	3.50	8.00
MGM SE-4342	(P)	**Hold On!** *(Soundtrack)*	1966	4.00	10.00
MGM E-4386	(M)	**Both Sides Of Herman's Hermits**	1966	4.00	10.00
MGM SE-4386	(E)	**Both Sides Of Herman's Hermits**	1966	3.50	8.00
MGM E-4416	(M)	**Best Of Herman's Hermits, Volume 2**	1966	4.00	10.00
MGM SE-4416	(P)	**Best Of Herman's Hermits, Volume 2**	1966	5.00	12.00
		(Issued with a bonus photo, priced separately below.)			
MGM 4416	(M)	**Best Of , Volume 2 Bonus Photo**	1966	4.00	10.00
MGM E-4438	(M)	**There's A Kind Of Hush**	1967	3.50	8.00
MGM SE-4438	(E)	**There's A Kind Of Hush**	1967	1.50	6.00
MGM E-4478	(M)	**Blaze**	1967	1.50	6.00
MGM SE-4478	(P)	**Blaze**	1967	3.50	8.00
MGM E-4505	(M)	**The Best Of Herman's Hermits, Volume 3**	1967	4.00	10.00
MGM SE-4505	(P)	**The Best Of Herman's Hermits, Volume 3**	1967	4.00	10.00
MGM E-4548	(M)	**Mrs. Brown You've Got A Lovely Daughter**	1968	4.00	10.00
MGM SE-4548	(P)	**Mrs. Brown You've Got A Lovely Daughter**	1968	4.00	10.00
HERMON KNIGHTS, THE					
C.O. 2323	(S)	**The Hermon Knights**	1968	20.00	50.00
HESITATIONS, THE					
Kapp KL-1525	(M)	**Soul Superman**	1967	5.00	12.00
Kapp KS-3525	(S)	**Soul Superman**	1967	6.00	15.00

Label & Catalog #		Title	Year	VG+	NM
Kapp KS-3548	(S)	The New Born Free	1968	6.00	15.00
Kapp KS-3561	(S)	Where We're At	1968	6.00	15.00
Kapp KS-3574	(S)	Solid Gold	1968	6.00	15.00
HESTER, BENNY					
V.M.I. 72001	(S)	Benny Hester	1972	35.00	70.00
HESTER, CARLOYN					
Columbia CL-1796	(M)	Carloyn Hester ("Eyes" logo label)	1962	6.00	15.00
Columbia CS-8596	(S)	Carloyn Hester ("Eyes" logo label)	1962	8.00	20.00
Columbia CL-2031	(M)	This Is My Living	1963	5.00	12.00
Columbia CS-8831	(S)	This Is My Living	1963	6.00	15.00
Dot DLP-3604	(M)	That's My Song	1964	5.00	12.00
Dot DLP-25604	(S)	That's My Song	1964	6.00	15.00
Dot DLP-3649	(M)	Carloyn Hester At The Town Hall	1965	5.00	12.00
Dot DLP-25649	(S)	Carloyn Hester At The Town Hall	1965	6.00	15.00
HI-LITES, THE					
Dandee DLP-206	(M)	For Your Precious Love	195?	12.00	30.00
HI-LO'S, THE					
Refer to The Reprise Repertory Theatre.					
Starlite 6004 (10")	(M)	The Hi-Lo's	1955	16.00	40.00
Starlite 6005 (10")	(M)	The Hi-Lo's, I Presume	1955	16.00	40.00
Starlite 7005	(M)	Under Glass	1956	12.00	30.00
Starlite 7006	(M)	Listen To The	1956	12.00	30.00
Starlite 7007	(M)	The Hi-Lo's, I Presume	1956	12.00	30.00
Starlite 7008	(M)	On Hand	1956	12.00	30.00
Kapp KL 1027	(M)	The Hi-Lo's	1956	8.00	20.00
Kapp KL-1184	(M)	Under Glass	1959	8.00	20.00
Kapp KL-1194	(M)	On Hand	1960	8.00	20.00
Columbia CL-952	(M)	Suddenly It's The Hi-Lo's	1957	12.00	30.00
Columbia CL-1023	(M)	Now Hear This	1957	10.00	25.00
Columbia CL-1259	(M)	All That Jazz	1959	8.00	20.00
Columbia CS-8077	(S)	All That Jazz	1959	10.00	25.00
Columbia CL-1416	(M)	Broadway Playbill	1959	8.00	20.00
Columbia CS-8213	(S)	Broadway Playbill	1959	10.00	25.00
Columbia CL-1509	(M)	All Over The Place	1960	8.00	20.00
Columbia CS-8300	(S)	All Over The Place	1960	10.00	25.00
Columbia CL-1723	(M)	This Time It's Love	1962	6.00	15.00
Columbia CS-8523	(S)	This Time It's Love	1962	8.00	20.00
— Original Columbia albums above have three white "eye" logos on each side of the spindle hole.—					
Reprise R-6066	(M)	The Hi-Lo's Happen To Bossa Nova	1963	5.00	12.00
Reprise RS-6066	(S)	The Hi-Lo's Happen To Bossa Nova	1963	6.00	15.00
Omega 11	(S)	The Hi-Lo's In Stereo	196?	8.00	20.00
HI-LO'S, THE, & ROSEMARY CLOONEY					
Columbia CL-1006	(M)	Ring Around Rosie	1957	12.00	30.00
HIBBLER, AL					
Refer to Billie Holiday.					
Norgran N-4 (10")	(M)	Favorites	1954	35.00	70.00
Norgran N-415(10")	(M)	Al Hibbler	1954	35.00	70.00
Columbia CL-2593 (10")	(M)	Al Hibbler With The Duke	1956	20.00	50.00
Verve V-4000	(M)	Al Hibbler Sings Love Songs	1956	20.00	50.00
Score 4013	(M)	I Surrender, Dear	195?	35.00	70.00
Decca DL-8328	(M)	Starring Al Hibbler	1956	20.00	50.00
Decca DL-8420	(M)	Here's Hibbler	1958	20.00	50.00
Decca DL-8697	(M)	Torchy And Blue	1958	20.00	50.00
Decca DL-8757	(M)	Hits By Hibbler	1958	20.00	50.00
Decca DL-8862	(M)	Remember The Big Songs Of The Big Bands	1959	20.00	50.00
Atlantic 1251	(M)	After The Lights Go Down	1957	35.00	70.00
Brunswick BL-54036	(M)	Al Hibbler With The Ellingtonians	1958	20.00	50.00
Marterry 601	(M)	Melodies By Al Hibbler	195?	20.00	50.00
Reprise R-2005	(M)	Monday Every Day	1961	12.00	30.00
Reprise R9-2005	(S)	Monday Every Day	1961	16.00	40.00
L.M.I. 10001	(M)	Al Hibbler With The Roland Hanna Trio	196?	12.00	30.00
Atlantic SD-1630	(S)	A Meeting Of The Times	1972	6.00	15.00

Label & Catalog #		Title	Year	VG+	NM

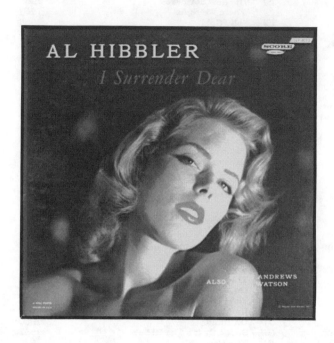

Al Hibbler made a name for himself as a big band crooner with the Ellington Orchestra in the '30s and then enjoyed renewed success as a pop balladeer in the '50s. This album, like virtually all albums on Score, is becoming increasingly more difficult to find in any condition.

HICKMAN, DWAYNE

Label & Catalog #		Title	Year	VG+	NM
Capitol T-1441	(M)	**Dobie!**	1960	8.00	20.00
Capitol ST-1441	(S)	**Dobie!**	1960	12.00	30.00

HIGGINS, CHUCK

Combo LP-300	(M)	**Pachuko Hop** *(Nude woman on cover)*	1960	180.00	300.00
Combo LP-300	(M)	**Pachuko Hop** *(Attired Higgins on cover)*	1961	85.00	170.00

HIGGINS, CHUCK / ROY MILTON

Dooto DL-223	(M)	**Rock 'N' Roll Versus Rhythm 'N' Blues**	1959	100.00	200.00

HIGH TIDE

Liberty LST-7638	(S)	**Sea Shanties**	1969	10.00	25.00

HIGH TREASON

Abbott ABS-1209	(S)	**High Treason**	197?	18.00	45.00

HIGHTOWER, DEAN

ABC-Paramount 312	(M)	**Guitar-Twangy With A Beat**	1959	8.00	20.00
ABC-Paramount S-312	(S)	**Guitar-Twangy With A Beat**	1959	12.00	30.00

HIGHTOWER, DONNA

Capitol T-1133	(M)	**Take One**	1959	10.00	25.00
Capitol T-1273	(M)	**Gee Baby, Ain't I Good To You?**	1959	10.00	25.00

HIGHWAY, THE

No label	(S)	**The Highway**	197?	75.00	150.00

Label & Catalog #		Title	Year	VG+	NM

HIGHWAYMEN, THE

Label & Catalog #		Title	Year	VG+	NM
United Arts. UAL-3125	(M)	The Highwaymen	1961	5.00	12.00
United Arts. UAS-6125	(S)	The Highwaymen	1961	6.00	15.00
United Arts. UAL-3168	(M)	Standing Room Only!	1962	5.00	12.00
United Arts. UAS-6168	(S)	Standing Room Only!	1962	6.00	15.00
United Arts. UAL-3225	(S)	Encore!	1962	5.00	12.00
United Arts. UAS-6225	(S)	Encore!	1962	6.00	15.00
United Arts. UAL-3245	(M)	March On, Brothers	1963	5.00	12.00
United Arts. UAS-6245	(M)	March On, Brothers	1963	6.00	15.00
United Arts. UAL-3294	(M)	Hootenanny With The Highwaymen	1963	5.00	12.00
United Arts. UAS-6294	(S)	Hootenanny With The Highwaymen	1963	6.00	15.00
United Arts. UAL-3323	(S)	One More Time	1964	5.00	12.00
United Arts. UAS-6323	(S)	One More Time	1964	6.00	15.00

HILL, GOLDIE

Decca DL-4034	(M)	Goldie Hill	1960	12.00	30.00
Decca DL-74034	(S)	Goldie Hill	1960	16.00	40.00
Decca DL-4148	(M)	Lonely Heartaches	1961	8.00	20.00
Decca DL7-4148	(S)	Lonely Heartaches	1961	12.00	30.00
Decca DL-4219	(M)	According To My Heart	1962	8.00	20.00
Decca DL7-4219	(S)	According To My Heart	1962	10.00	25.00
Decca DL-4492	(M)	Country Hit Parade	1964	6.00	15.00
Decca DL7-4492	(S)	Country Hit Parade	1964	8.00	20.00

HILLMEN, THE

Members include Chris Hillmen; Vern & Rex Gosdin. Refer to The Byrds; The Scottsville Squirrel Barkers.

Together STT-1012	(S)	The Hillmen	1970	20.00	50.00

HILLOW HAMMET

House Of Fox 2	(S)	Hammer	197?	20.00	50.00
L&BJ 14028	(S)	Hammer	197?	35.00	70.00

HINES, MIMI

Decca DL-8434	(M)	Mimi Hines Is A Happening	1958	8.00	20.00
Decca DL-78434	(S)	Mimi Hines Is A Happening	1958	10.00	25.00
Decca DL-4709	(M)	Mimi Hines Sings	1965	4.00	10.00
Decca DL-74709	(S)	Mimi Hines Sings	1965	5.00	12.00

HINSON, DON, & THE RIGORMORTICIANS

Capitol T-2219	(M)	Monster Dance Party	1964	6.00	15.00
Capitol ST-2219	(S)	Monster Dance Party	1964	8.00	20.00

HINTON, JOE

Backbeat B-60	(M)	Funny How Time Slips Away	1965	8.00	20.00
Backbeat B-60	(S)	Funny How Time Slips Away	1965	10.00	25.00

HINTON, SAM

Decca DL-8108	(M)	Singing Across The Land	1956	14.00	35.00

HITCHCOCK, ALFRED

Imperial LP-9052	(M)	Music To Be Murdered By	1958	16.00	40.00
Imperial LP-12052	(S)	Music To Be Murdered By	1958	20.00	50.00
Golden Record LP-89	(M)	Ghost Stories For Young People	1962	12.00	30.00

HOBBITS, THE

Decca DL-4290	(M)	Down To Middle Earth	1967	8.00	20.00
Decca DL-74290	(S)	Down To Middle Earth	1967	12.00	30.00
Decca DL-5009	(M)	Men And Doors	1968	5.00	12.00
Decca DL-75009	(S)	Men And Doors	1968	6.00	15.00
Perception	(S)	Return To Middle Earth	1971	12.00	30.00

HOFFMAN, ABBIE

Big Toe 1	(M)	Wake Up, America!	196?	12.00	30.00

HOFFMAN, JEANNIE

Capitol T-2021	(M)	Folk-Type Singer	1964	5.00	12.00
Capitol ST-2021	(S)	Folk-Type Singer	1964	6.00	15.00

Label & Catalog #		Title	Year	VG+	NM
HOBBITS, THE					
Decca DL-4290	(M)	**Down To Middle Earth**	1967	8.00	20.00
Decca DL-74290	(S)	**Down To Middle Earth**	1967	12.00	30.00
Decca DL-5009	(M)	**Men And Doors**	1968	5.00	12.00
Decca DL-75009	(S)	**Men And Doors**	1968	6.00	15.00
Perception	(S)	**Return To Middle Earth**	1971	12.00	30.00
HOFFMAN, ABBIE					
Big Toe 1	(M)	**Wake Up, America!**	196?	12.00	30.00
HOFFMAN, JEANNIE					
Capitol T-2021	(M)	**Folk-Type Singer**	1964	5.00	12.00
Capitol ST-2021	(S)	**Folk-Type Singer**	1964	6.00	15.00
HOFNER, ADOLPH					
Decca DL-5564 (10")	(M)	**Dance-O-Rama #4**	1955	90.00	180.00
HOGAN, CLAIRE					
MGM E-3349	(M)	**Just Imagine**	1956	10.00	25.00
HOGAN'S HEROES					
Sunset SUM-1137	(M)	**The Best Of World War II**	196?	6.00	15.00
Sunset SUS-5137	(S)	**The Best Of World War II**	196?	8.00	20.00
HOGG, ANDREW "SMOKEY"					
Time 6	(M)	**Smokey Hogg**	1962	35.00	70.00
Crown CLP-5226	(M)	**Smokey Hogg Sings The Blues**	1962	12.00	30.00
United 7745	(M)	**Smokey Hogg**	1970	4.00	10.00
HOLDEN, RANDY					
Holden was formerly a member of The Other Half; Blue Cheer.					
Hobbit 5002	(S)	**Population II**	1968	80.00	160.00
HOLDEN, RON					
Donna DLP-2111	(M)	**I Love You So**	1960	35.00	70.00
Donna DLPS-2111	(S)	**I Love You So**	1960	50.00	100.00
HOLIDAY, BILLIE					
Refer to Ella Fitzgerald					
Commodore 20005 (10")	(M)	**Billie Holiday, Volume 1**	1950	50.00	100.00
Commodore 20006 (10")	(M)	**Billie Holiday, Volume 2**	1950	50.00	100.00
Columbia CL-6040 (10")	(M)	**Teddy Wilson Featuring Billie Holiday**	1949	50.00	100.00
Columbia CL-6129 (10")	(M)	**Billie Holiday Sings**	1950	50.00	100.00
Columbia CL-6163 (10")	(M)	**Favorites**	1950	50.00	100.00
Jolly Roger 5020 (10")	(M)	**Billie Holiday, Volume 1**	1951	35.00	70.00
Jolly Roger 5021 (10")	(M)	**Billie Holiday, Volume 2**	1951	35.00	70.00
Jolly Roger 5022 (10")	(M)	**Billie Holiday, Volume 3**	1951	35.00	70.00
Dale 25 (10")	(M)	**Billie And Stan**	1951	50.00	100.00
Decca DL-5345 (10")	(M)	**Lover Man**	1951	50.00	100.00
Clef 144 (10")	(M)	**An Evening With Billie**	1953	50.00	100.00
Clef 118 (10")	(M)	**Favorites**	1953	50.00	100.00
Clef 161 (10")	(M)	**Favorites**	1954	50.00	100.00
Clef 169 (10")	(M)	**Jazz At The Philharmonic**	1954	50.00	100.00
Clef 669	(M)	**Music For Torching**	1955	30.00	60.00
Clef 686	(M)	**A Recital**	1955	30.00	60.00
Clef 690	(M)	**Solitude**	1956	30.00	60.00
Clef 713	(M)	**Velvet Moods**	1956	30.00	60.00
Clef 718	(M)	**Jazz Recital**	1956	30.00	60.00
Clef 721	(M)	**Lady Sings The Blues**	1956	30.00	60.00
A.R.S. G-409	(M)	**Billie Holiday Sings**	1956	30.00	60.00
A.R.S. G-431	(M)	**Lady Sings The Blues**	1956	30.00	60.00
		(Issued in a plastic sleeve with a four page insert.)			
Jazztone 1209	(M)	**Billie Holiday Sings**	1956	20.00	50.00
Columbia CL-637	(M)	**Lady Day** *(Red label with gold print)*	1954	20.00	50.00
Columbia CL-637	(M)	**Lady Day**	1966	16.00	40.00
Columbia CL-1157	(M)	**Lady In Satin**	1958	16.00	40.00
Columbia CS-8048	(S)	**Lady In Satin**	1959	16.00	40.00
Columbia C3L-21	(M)	**The Golden Years** *(3 LPs)*	1962	16.00	40.00

— Original Columbia albums above have three white "eye" logos on each side of the spindle hole.—

Label & Catalog #		Title	Year	VG+	NM
Columbia C3L-40	(M)	The Golden Years, Volume 2	1966	8.00	20.00
Columbia CL-2666	(M)	Billie Holiday's Greatest Hits	1967	6.00	15.00
Score LP-4014	(M)	Billie Holiday Sings The Blues	1957	50.00	100.00
Decca DL-8215	(M)	The Lady Sings	1956	16.00	40.00
Decca DL-8701	(M)	Blues Are Brewin'	1958	16.00	40.00
Decca DL-8702	(M)	Lover Man	1958	16.00	40.00
Decca DXB-161	(M)	The Billie Holiday Story (2 LPs)	196?	12.00	30.00
Decca DXSB-161	(E)	The Billie Holiday Story (2 LPs)	196?	8.00	20.00
Decca DL-75040	(S)	Billie Holiday's Greatest Hits	1968	6.00	15.00
Verve V-8026	(M)	Music For Torching	1957	20.00	50.00
Verve V-8027	(M)	A Recital	1957	20.00	50.00
Verve V-8074	(M)	Solitude	1957	20.00	50.00
Verve V-8096	(M)	Velvet Moods	1957	20.00	50.00
Verve V-8098	(M)	Jazz Recital	1957	20.00	50.00
Verve V-8099	(M)	Lady Sings The Blues	1957	20.00	50.00
Verve V-8197	(M)	Body And Soul	1957	20.00	50.00
Verve V-8257	(M)	Songs For Distingue' Lovers	1959	16.00	40.00
Verve VS-6021	(S)	Songs For Distingue' Lovers	1959	20.00	50.00
Verve V-8302	(M)	Stay With Me	1959	16.00	40.00
Verve V-8329	(M)	All Or Nothing At All	1959	16.00	40.00
Verve V-8338	(M)	The Unforgettable Lady Day	1960	16.00	40.00
— Original Verve albums above have black labels with "Verve Records, Inc." on the bottom.—					
MGM E-3764	(M)	Billie Holiday	1959	16.00	40.00
MGM SE-3764	(S)	Billie Holiday	1959	20.00	50.00
MGM E-3764	(M)	Billie Holiday	1959	16.00	40.00
Commodore 30008	(M)	Billie Holiday, Volume 2	1959	16.00	40.00
Commodore 30011	(M)	Billie Holiday, Volume 1	1959	16.00	40.00
Verve MGV-8410	(M)	The Essential Billie Holiday	1961	12.00	30.00
United Arts. UAL-14014	(M)	Lady Love	1962	10.00	25.00
United Arts. UAS-15014	(S)	Lady Love	1962	16.00	40.00
Ric 2001	(M)	Rare Live Recordings	1964	10.00	25.00
Mainstream 6000	(M)	The Commodore Recordings	1965	8.00	20.00
Mainstream 56000	(E)	The Commodore Recordings	1965	6.00	15.00
Mainstream 6022	(M)	Once Upon A Time	1965	8.00	20.00
Mainstream 56022	(E)	Once Upon A Time	1965	6.00	15.00

HOLIDAY, BILLIE / AL HIBBLER

Label & Catalog #		Title	Year	VG+	NM
Imperial LP-9185	(M)	Billie Holiday, Al Hibbler And The Blues	1962	20.00	50.00

HOLLAND, EDDIE

Label & Catalog #		Title	Year	VG+	NM
Motown 604	(M)	Eddie Holland	1963	50.00	100.00

HOLLIDAY, JUDY

Label & Catalog #		Title	Year	VG+	NM
Columbia OL-5170	(M)	Bells Are Ringing (Original Cast)	1956	12.00	30.00
Columbia CL-1153	(M)	Trouble Is A Man	1958	8.00	20.00
Columbia CS-8041	(S)	Trouble Is A Man	1958	12.00	30.00
Capitol W-1435	(M)	Bells Are Ringing (Soundtrack)	1960	8.00	20.00
Capitol SW-1435	(S)	Bells Are Ringing (Soundtrack)	1960	12.00	30.00

HOLLIES, THE

Original members include Allan Clarke, Graham Nash, Tony Hicks, Eric Haydock and Donald Rathbone. Rathbone was replaced by Bobby Elliott in 1963; Haydock by Bernie Calvert, 1966; and Nash by Terry Sylvester, 1968. Mikael Rikfors replaced Clarke on "Romany." Refer to The Everly Brothers; Peter Sellers.

Label & Catalog #		Title	Year	VG+	NM
Imperial LP-9265	(M)	Here I Go Again (Black label with stars)	1964	50.00	100.00
Imperial LP-12265	(E)	Here I Go Again (Black & silver label)	1964	35.00	70.00
Imperial LP-9265	(M)	Here I Go Again	1964	20.00	50.00
Imperial LP-12265	(E)	Here I Go Again	1964	14.00	35.00
Imperial LP-9299	(M)	Hear! Here!	1965	16.00	40.00
Imperial LP-12299	(E)	Hear! Here!	1965	12.00	30.00
Imperial LP-9312	(M)	The Hollies (Beat Group)	1966	12.00	30.00
Imperial LP-12312	(E)	The Hollies (Beat Group)	1966	8.00	20.00
Imperial LP-9330	(M)	Bus Stop	1966	12.00	30.00
Imperial LP-12330		Bus Stop	1966	8.00	20.00
— Imperial albums above have black, pink & white labels.—					
Imperial LP-9339	(M)	Stop! Stop! Stop!	1966	8.00	20.00
Imperial LP-12339	(S)	Stop! Stop! Stop!	1966	12.00	30.00
Imperial LP-9350	(M)	The Hollies' Greatest Hits	1967	8.00	20.00
Imperial LP-12350	(P)	The Hollies' Greatest Hits	1967	8.00	20.00
— Original Imperial albums above have black & green label that read "A Division Of Liberty Records."—					

Label & Catalog #		Title	Year	VG+	NM

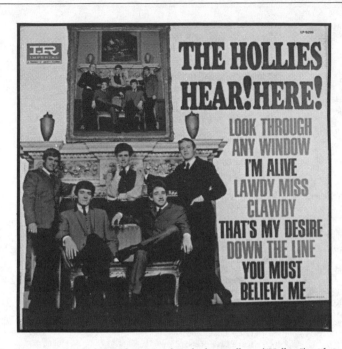

By replacing the two weakest tracks on the original Parlophone album ("Hollies") with two hit singles, "Look Through Any Window" and "I'm Alive," Imperial created "Hear! Here!," which was, along with the first two Beatles albums, the finest representation of British beat music.

Label & Catalog #		Title	Year	VG+	NM
Epic LN-24315	(M)	**Evolution**	1967	6.00	15.00
Epic BN-26315	(S)	**Evolution**	1967	8.00	20.00
Epic LN-24344	(M)	**Dear Eloise / King Midas In Reverse**	1967	6.00	15.00
Epic BN-26344	(S)	**Dear Eloise / King Midas In Reverse**	1967	8.00	20.00
Epic BN-26447	(S)	**Words And Music By Bob Dylan**	1969	5.00	12.00
Epic BN-26538	(S)	**He Ain't Heavy, He's My Brother**	1969	6.00	15.00
Epic KE-30255	(S)	**Moving Finger**	1970	6.00	15.00
		— Original Epic albums above have yellow labels.—			
Epic AS-138	(DJ)	**Everything You Always Wanted To Hear**	1977	6.00	15.00
HOLLIN'S FERRY					
Port City	(S)	**Hollin's Ferry**	197?	35.00	70.00
HOLLOWAY, BRENDA					
Tamla 257	(M)	**Every Little Bit Hurts**	1964	20.00	50.00
HOLLY, BUDDY (& THE CRICKETS)					
Refer to The Crickets; Norman Petty.					
Brunswick BL-54038	(DJ)	**The Chirping Crickets** *(Yellow label)*	1957	660.00	1,000.00
Brunswick BL-54038	(M)	**The Chirping Crickets**	1957	300.00	500.00
		(Reissued on Coral as "Buddy Holly & The Crickets.")			
Decca DL-8707	(DJ)	**That'll Be The Day** *(Pink label)*	1958	660.00	1,000.00
Decca DL-8707	(M)	**That'll Be The Day** *(Maroon label)*	1958	360.00	600.00
Decca DL-8707	(M)	**That'll Be The Day** *(Black label)*	196?	150.00	250.00
Coral CRL-57210	(DJ)	**Buddy Holly** *(Blue label)*	1958	300.00	500.00
Coral CRL-57210	(M)	**Buddy Holly**	1958	100.00	200.00
Coral CRL-57279	(DJ)	**The Buddy Holly Story** *(Blue label)*	1959	300.00	500.00
Coral CRL-57279	(M)	**The Buddy Holly Story**	1959	75.00	150.00
		(The print on the back cover is in red and black.)			
Coral CRL-57279	(M)	**The Buddy Holly Story**	1959	50.00	100.00
Coral CRL-757279	(E)	**The Buddy Holly Story**	1959	40.00	80.00
		(The print on the back cover is in black only.)			

Label & Catalog #		Title	Year	VG+	NM
Coral CRL-57326	(DJ)	The Buddy Holly Story, Vol. 2 (Blue label)	1959	300.00	500.00
Coral CRL-57326	(M)	The Buddy Holly Story, Vol. 2	1959	50.00	100.00
Coral CRL-57405	(DJ)	Buddy Holly & The Crickets (Blue label)	1962	300.00	500.00
Coral CRL-57405	(M)	Buddy Holly & The Crickets	1962	50.00	100.00
Coral CRL-757405	(E)	Buddy Holly & The Crickets	1962	35.00	70.00
Coral CRL-57426	(DJ)	Reminiscing (Blue label)	1963	180.00	300.00
Coral CRL-57426	(M)	Reminiscing	1963	40.00	80.00
Coral CRL-757426	(E)	Reminiscing	1963	30.00	60.00
		— Original Coral albums above have maroon labels.—			
Coral CRL-57210	(M)	Buddy Holly	1953	50.00	100.00
Coral CRL-57279	(M)	The Buddy Holly Story	1963	30.00	60.00
Coral CRL-757279	(E)	The Buddy Holly Story	1963	20.00	50.00
Coral CRL-57326	(M)	The Buddy Holly Story, Vol. 2	1963	30.00	60.00
Coral CRL-757326	(E)	The Buddy Holly Story, Vol. 2	1963	20.00	50.00
Coral CRL-57426	(DJ)	Reminiscing (Yellow label)	1963	180.00	300.00
Coral CRL-57426	(M)	Reminiscing	1964	40.00	80.00
Coral CRL-757426	(E)	Reminiscing	1964	30.00	60.00
Coral CRL-57450	(DJ)	Showcase (Yellow label)	1964	180.00	300.00
Coral CRL-57450	(M)	Showcase	1964	40.00	80.00
Coral CRL-757450	(E)	Showcase	1964	30.00	60.00
Coral CRL-57463	(DJ)	Holly In The Hills (Yellow label)	1965	180.00	300.00
Coral CRL-57463	(M)	Holly In The Hills	1965	40.00	80.00
Coral CRL-757463	(E)	Holly In The Hills	1965	30.00	60.00
Coral CXB-8	(DJ)	The Best Of Buddy Holly (Yellow label)	1966	100.00	200.00
Coral CXB-8	(M)	The Best Of Buddy Holly	1966	30.00	60.00
Coral CXSB-8	(E)	The Best Of Buddy Holly	1966	20.00	50.00
Coral CRL-57492	(M)	Buddy Holly's Greatest Hits	1967	30.00	60.00
Coral CRL-757492	(E)	Buddy Holly's Greatest Hits	1967	20.00	50.00
Coral CRL-757504	(E)	Giant	1969	16.00	40.00
		— Coral albums above have black labels. with "A subsidiary of Decca."—			
Vocalion VL-3811	(M)	The Great Buddy Holly	1967	35.00	70.00
Vocalion VL-73811	(E)	The Great Buddy Holly	1967	20.00	50.00
		(Vocalion 3811 is a repackage of "That'll Be The Day.")			
Vocalion VL-73923	(E)	Good Rockin'	1971	50.00	100.00
Decca DXSE-207	(F)	A Rock & Roll Collection	1972	8.00	20.00
Cricket C001000	(M)	Buddy Holly Live (Volume 1)	197?	6.00	15.00
Solid Smoke 8002	(M)	A Portrait In Music, Volume 1 (Picture disc)	1979	6.00	15.00
Solid Smoke 8003	(M)	A Portrait In Music, Volume 2 (Picture disc)	1979	6.00	15.00
MCA 6-8000	(M)	The Complete Buddy Holly (6 LP box)	1981	16.00	40.00

HOLLYWOOD ARGYLES, THE

Lute L-9001	(M)	Ally Oop	1960	240.00	400.00

HOLLYWOOD PERSUADERS, THE

Original Sound 8874	(M)	Drums A Go-Go	1965	14.00	35.00
Original Sound S-8874	(S)	Drums A Go-Go	1965	20.00	50.00

HOLT, WILL

Coral CRL-57114	(M)	The World Of Will Holt	1956	16.00	40.00
Stinson 64	(M)	Songs And Ballads	196?	6.00	15.00

HOLY MACKEREL

Reprise 6311	(S)	Holy Mackerel	1968	8.00	20.00

HOLY MODAL ROUNDERS, THE

The Rounders are Peter Stampfel and Steve Weber. Refer to The Fugs.

Prestige PR-7410	(M)	The Holy Modal Rounders	1965	8.00	20.00
Prestige PR-14031	(M)	The Holy Modal Rounders	1965	8.00	20.00
Prestige PRS-7451	(S)	The Holy Modal Rounders, Volume 2	1967	8.00	20.00
Elektra EKS-74026	(S)	The Moray Eels Eat The Holy Modal Rounders	1968	8.00	20.00
ESP 1068	(S)	Indian War Whoop	1969	8.00	20.00
Metromedia MD-1039	(S)	Good Taste Is Timeless	1971	8.00	20.00
Rounder 3004	(S)	Alleged In Their Own Time	1972	6.00	15.00
Fantasy F-24711	(S)	Stampfel And Weber	1972	6.00	15.00

HOMBRES, THE

Forecast FT-3036	(M)	Let It Out	1967	8.00	20.00
Forecast FTS-3036	(S)	Let It Out	1967	10.00	25.00

Label & Catalog #		Title	Year	VG+	NM

HOMER

| Universal Rec. Art. HS-101 | (S) | **Grown In U.S.A** | 197? | 150.00 | 250.0 |

HOMER & JETHRO

Homer & Jethro are Henry Haynes and Kenny Burns. Refer to The Country All-Stars.

RCA Victor LPM-3112 (10")	(M)	**Homer & Jethro Fracture Frank Loesser**	1953	50.00	100.0
Audio Lab AL-1513	(M)	**Musical Madness**	1958	20.00	50.0
King 639	(M)	**They Sure Are Corny**	1959	20.00	50.0
King 848	(M)	**Cornier Than Corn**	1963	12.00	30.
RCA Victor LPM-1412	(M)	**Barefoot Ballads**	1957	20.00	50.0
RCA Victor LPM-1560	(M)	**The Worst Of Homer & Jethro**	1957	20.00	50.0
RCA Victor LPM-1880	(M)	**Life Can Be Miserable**	1958	14.00	35.0
RCA Victor LSP-1880	(S)	**Life Can Be Miserable**	1958	20.00	50.0
RCA Victor LPM-2181	(M)	**At The Country Club**	1960	5.00	12.0
RCA Victor LSP-2181	(S)	**At The Country Club**	1960	12.00	30.0
RCA Victor LPM-2286	(M)	**Songs My Mother Never Sang**	1961	8.00	20.0
RCA Victor LSP-2286	(S)	**Songs My Mother Never Sang**	1961	12.00	30.0
RCA Victor LPM-2455	(M)	**Zany Songs Of The '30s**	1962	8.00	20.0
RCA Victor LSP-2455	(S)	**Zany Songs Of The '30s**	1962	12.00	30.0
RCA Victor LPM-2459	(M)	**Playing It Straight**	1962	12.00	30.0
RCA Victor LSP-2459	(S)	**Playing It Straight**	1962	16.00	40.0
RCA Victor LPM-2492	(M)	**At The Convention**	1962	8.00	20.0
RCA Victor LSP-2492	(S)	**At The Convention**	1962	12.00	30.0
RCA Victor LPM-2674	(M)	**Homer & Jethro Go West**	1963	8.00	20.0
RCA Victor LSP-2674	(S)	**Homer & Jethro Go West**	1963	12.00	30.0

— Original RCA mono albums above have "Long Play" on the bottom of the label; stereo albums have "Living Stereo" on the bottom.—

RCA Victor LPM-2743	(M)	**Ooh, That's Corny**	1963	6.00	15.0
RCA Victor LSP-2743	(S)	**Ooh, That's Corny**	1963	8.00	20.0
RCA Victor LPM-2928	(M)	**Cornfucius Say**	1964	6.00	15.0
RCA Victor LSP-2928	(S)	**Cornfucius Say**	1964	8.00	20.0
RCA Victor LPM-2954	(M)	**Fractured Folk Songs**	1964	6.00	15.0
RCA Victor LSP-2954	(S)	**Fractured Folk Songs**	1964	8.00	20.0
RCA Victor LPM-3357	(M)	**Homer And Jethro Sing Tenderly**	1965	6.00	15.0
RCA Victor LSP-3357	(S)	**Homer And Jethro Sing Tenderly**	1965	8.00	20.0
RCA Victor LPM-3462	(M)	**The Old Crusty Minstrels**	1965	5.00	12.0
RCA Victor LSP-3462	(S)	**The Old Crusty Minstrels**	1965	6.00	15.0
RCA Victor LPM-3474	(M)	**The Best Of Homer And Jethro**	1966	5.00	12.0
RCA Victor LSP-3474	(S)	**The Best Of Homer And Jethro**	1966	6.00	15.0
RCA Victor LPM-3538	(M)	**Any News From Nashville**	1966	5.00	12.0
RCA Victor LSP-3538	(S)	**Any News From Nashville**	1966	6.00	15.0
RCA Victor LPM-3673	(M)	**Wanted For Murder**	1966	5.00	12.0
RCA Victor LSP-3673	(S)	**Wanted For Murder**	1966	5.00	12.0
RCA Victor LPM-3701	(M)	**It Ain't Necessarily Square**	1967	8.00	20.0
RCA Victor LSP-3701	(S)	**It Ain't Necessarily Square**	1967	10.00	25.0
RCA Victor LPM-3822	(M)	**Nashville Cats**	1967	5.00	12.0
RCA Victor LSP-3822	(S)	**Nashville Cats**	1967	6.00	15.0
RCA Victor LPM-3877	(M)	**Somethin' Stupid**	1967	5.00	12.0
RCA Victor LSP-3877	(S)	**Somethin' Stupid**	1967	6.00	15.0
RCA Victor LSP-3973	(S)	**There's Nothing Like An Old Hippie**	1968	5.00	12.0
RCA Victor LSP-4001	(S)	**Cool Crazy Christmas**	1968	5.00	12.0
RCA Victor LSP-4024	(S)	**Live At Vanderbilt U**	1968	5.00	12.0

— Original RCA albums above have black labels.—

HONDELLS, THE

The Hondells are a creation of Gary Usher & Co. featuring Chuck Girard.

Mercury MG-20940	(M)	**Go Little Honda**	1964	12.00	30.0
Mercury SR-60940	(S)	**Go Little Honda**	1964	20.00	50.0
Mercury MG-20982	(M)	**The Hondells**	1965	20.00	50.0
Mercury SR-60982	(S)	**The Hondells**	1965	35.00	70.0

HONEYCOMBS, THE

Vee Jay IN-88001	(M)	**Here Are The Honeycombs**	1964	16.00	40.0
Vee Jay IN-88001	(E)	**Here Are The Honeycombs**	1964	14.00	35.0
Interphon IN-88001	(M)	**Here Are The Honeycombs**	1964	12.00	30.0
Interphon IN-88001	(E)	**Here Are The Honeycombs**	1964	10.00	25.0

HONEYDREAMERS, THE

| Fantasy 3-207 | (M) | **The Honeydreamers Sing Gershwin** | 1956 | 10.00 | 25.0 |

Label & Catalog #		Title	Year	VG+	NM
RKO ULP-134	(M)	An Evening With The Honeydreamers	1958	8.00	20.00
HOOKER, D.R.					
On XTL-1029	(S)	The Truth	1972	180.00	300.00
On 40725	(S)	Armaggedon	1979	20.00	50.00
HOOKER, JOHN LEE					
Refer to The Groundhogs; Big Maceo Merriweather..					
Vee Jay LP-1007	(M)	I'm John Lee Hooker (Maroon label)	1959	100.00	200.00
Vee Jay LP-1007	(M)	I'm John Lee Hooker (Black label)	1960	40.00	80.00
Vee Jay LP-1023	(M)	Travelin'	1960	30.00	60.00
Vee Jay LP-1033	(M)	The Folk Lore Of John Lee Hooker	1961	14.00	35.00
Vee Jay SR-1033	(S)	The Folk Lore Of John Lee Hooker	1961	20.00	50.00
Vee Jay LP-1043	(M)	Burnin'	1962	14.00	35.00
Vee Jay SR-1043	(S)	Burnin'	1962	20.00	50.00
Vee Jay LP-1049	(M)	The Best Of John Lee Hooker	1962	14.00	35.00
Vee Jay SR-1049	(S)	The Best Of John Lee Hooker	1962	20.00	50.00
Vee Jay LP-1066	(M)	John Lee Hooker On Campus	1963	14.00	35.00
Vee Jay SR-1066	(S)	John Lee Hooker On Campus	1963	20.00	50.00
Vee Jay LP-1078	(M)	John Lee Hooker At Newport	1964	14.00	35.00
Vee Jay SR-1078	(S)	John Lee Hooker At Newport	1964	20.00	50.00
— Original Vee Jay albums above have black rainbow labels.—					
King 727	(M)	John Lee Hooker Sings The Blues	1960	50.00	100.00
Chess LP-1438	(M)	House Of The Blues	1960	50.00	100.00
Chess LP-1454	(M)	Plays And Sings The Blues	1961	50.00	100.00
Chess LP-1508	(M)	Real Folk Blues	1966	14.00	35.00
Chess LPS-1508	(S)	Real Folk Blues	1966	20.00	50.00
Atco 33-151	(M)	Don't Turn Me From Your Door	1963	16.00	40.00
Atco SD-33-151	(S)	Don't Turn Me From Your Door	1963	20.00	50.00
Riverside RLP-12-838	(M)	Folk Blues	1962	14.00	35.00
Folkways FT-3003	(M)	Seven Nights	1965	10.00	25.00
Folkways FTS-3003	(S)	Seven Nights	1965	14.00	35.00
Impulse A-9103	(M)	It Serves Me Right To Suffer	1966	6.00	15.00
BluesWay BL-6002	(M)	Live At Cafe Au-Go-Go	1966	8.00	20.00
BluesWay BLS-6002	(S)	Live At Cafe Au-Go-Go	1966	10.00	25.00
BluesWay BLS-6012	(S)	Urban Blues	1968	8.00	20.00
BluesWay 6023	(S)	Simply The Truth	1969	8.00	20.00
BluesWay BLS-6038	(S)	If You Miss 'Im	1970	6.00	15.00
BluesWay BLS-6052	(S)	Live At Kabuki Wuki	1973	6.00	15.00
Stax STS-2013	(S)	That's Where It's At	1969	6.00	15.00
Buddah BDS-4002	(S)	The Very Best Of John Lee Hooker	1969	6.00	15.00
Buddah BDS-7506	(S)	Big Band Blues	1969	6.00	15.00
Wand WDS-689	(S)	John Lee Hooker On The Waterfront	1970	6.00	15.00
Specialty SPS-2125	(S)	Alone	1970	6.00	15.00
ABC S-720	(S)	Endless Boogie (2 LPs)	1970	8.00	20.00
King KS-1085	(S)	Moanin' And Stompin' Blues	1970	6.00	15.00
Jewel 5005	(S)	I Feel Good	1971	6.00	15.00
HOOKER, JOHN LEE, & CANNED HEAT					
Liberty LST-35003	(S)	Hooker 'N' Heat (2 LPs)	1971	6.00	15.00
HOOTCH					
Pro-gress PRS-4844	(S)	Hootch	1974	See note below	
		(Rare. Estimated near mint value $700-1,2000.)			
HOPE, BOB					
Decca DL-4396	(M)	Hope In Russia And Other Places	1963	6.00	15.00
Decca DL7-4396	(S)	Hope In Russia And Other Places	1963	8.00	20.00
HOPE, LYNN					
Aladdin 707 (10")	(M)	Lynn Hope And His Tenor Sax	1953	180.00	300.00
Aladdin 805	(M)	Lynn Hope And His Tenor Sax	1955	100.00	200.00
Aladdin 820	(M)	Lynn Hope	1957	100.00	200.00
Score LP-4015	(M)	Tenderly	1957	75.00	150.00
HOPKIN, MARY					
Apple SW-3351	(S)	Postcard	1969	6.00	15.00
Apple SW-53351	(S)	Postcard (Record club)	1969	12.00	30.00
Apple SMAS-3381	(S)	Earth Song/Ocean Song	1969	6.00	15.00

Label & Catalog #		Title	Year	VG+	NM

Welsh songstress Hopkin enjoyed international success with Paul McCartney's "Those Were The Days,"
which apppears here in mono, but was in stereo on the earlier "Postcard."

Label & Catalog #		Title	Year	VG+	NM
Apple SW-3395	(P)	Those Were The Days	1972	14.00	35.0
Paramount PAS-5005	(S)	Where's Jack (Soundtrack)	1969	16.00	40.0
American Int. STA-1042	(S)	Kidnapped (Soundtrack)	1972	10.00	25.0
HOPKINS, LIGHTNIN'					
Fire 104	(M)	Mojo Hand	1960	360.00	600.0
Herald 1012	(M)	Lightnin' And The Blues	1960	360.00	600.0
Score 4022	(M)	Lightnin' Hopkins Strums The Blues	1960	300.00	500.0
Tradition TLP-1035	(M)	Country Blues	1960	20.00	50.0
Tradition TLP-1040	(M)	Autobiography In Blues	1960	20.00	50.0
Time 70004	(M)	Last Of The Great Blues Singers	1960	20.00	50.0
Time 1	(M)	Blues/Folk	1962	20.00	50.0
Time 3	(M)	Blues/Folk, Volume 2	1962	20.00	50.0
Bluesville BV-1019	(M)	Lightnin'	1961	20.00	50.0
Bluesville BV-1029	(M)	Last Night Blues	1961	20.00	50.0
Bluesville BV-1045	(M)	Blues In My Bottle	1962	16.00	40.0
Bluesville BV-1057	(M)	Walkin' This Road By Myself	1962	16.00	40.0
Bluesville BV-1070	(M)	Smokes Like Lightnin'	1963	16.00	40.0
Bluesville BV-1073	(M)	Goin' Away	1964	16.00	40.0
Bluesville BV-1084	(M)	His Greatest Hits	1964	16.00	40.0
Bluesville BV-1986	(M)	Down Home Blues	1964	16.00	40.0
Vee Jay LP-1044	(M)	Lightnin' Hopkins	1962	20.00	50.0
Verve V-8453	(M)	Fast Life Woman	1962	20.00	50.0
Imperial LP-9180	(M)	Lightnin' Hopkins On Stage	1962	50.00	100.0
Imperial LP-9211	(M)	Lightnin' Hopkins And The Blues	1962	35.00	70.0
Imperial LP-12211	(S)	Lightnin' Hopkins And The Blues	1962	50.00	100.0
Mt. Vernon 104	(M)	Nothin' But The Blues	196?	8.00	20.0
World Pacific WP-1817	(M)	First Meetin'	1963	8.00	20.0
World Pacific ST-1817	(S)	First Meetin'	1963	10.00	25.0
World Pacific ST-1817	(S)	First Meetin' (Red vinyl)	1963	20.00	50.0
Folkways FV-9000	(M)	The Roots Of Lightnin' Hopkins	1965	8.00	20.0
Folkways FVS-9000	(S)	The Roots Of Lightnin' Hopkins	1965	10.00	25.0

Label & Catalog #		Title	Year	VG+	NM
Folkways FV-9022	(M)	**Lightnin' Strikes**	1965	8.00	20.00
Folkways FVS-9022	(S)	**Lightnin' Strikes**	1965	10.00	25.00
Folkways FV-3013	(M)	**Something Blue**	1967	8.00	20.00
Folkways FVS-3013	(S)	**Something Blue**	1967	10.00	25.00
Prestige PR-7370	(M)	**My Life In The Blues**	1965	10.00	25.00
Prestige PR-7377	(M)	**Soul Blues**	1966	8.00	20.00
Prestige PRS-7377	(S)	**Soul Blues**	1966	10.00	25.00
Prestige PRS-7592	(S)	**Lightnin' Hopkins' Greatest Hits**	1969	5.00	12.00
Prestige PRS-7714	(S)	**The Best Of Lightnin' Hopkins**	1969	6.00	15.00
Prestige PRS-7806	(S)	**Hootin' The Blues**	1970	6.00	15.00
Prestige PRS-7811	(S)	**The Blues Of Lightnin' Hopkins**	1970	6.00	15.00
International Art. 6	(S)	**Free Form Patterns**	1968	75.00	150.00
		(With a picture of Hopkins on the cover.)			
International Art. 6	(S)	**Free Form Patterns** *("Art" cover)*	1968	16.00	40.00
Vault 129	(S)	**California Mudslide**	1969	8.00	20.00
Poppy 60002	(S)	**Lightnin'**	1969	8.00	20.00

HOPNEY

Illusion CM-1032	(S)	**End And Means**	197?	50.00	100.00
Illusion CM-1033	(S)	**Perils Of Love**	197?	150.00	250.00
Illusion CM-1034	(S)	**Cosmic Rockout**	197?	240.00	400.00

HORN, SHIRLEY

Stereocraft 16	(M)	**Embers And Ashes**	1961	14.00	35.00
Mercury MG-20761	(M)	**Loads Of Love**	1963	6.00	15.00
Mercury SR-60761	(S)	**Loads Of Love**	1963	8.00	20.00
Mercury MG-20835	(M)	**Shirley Horn With Horns**	1964	6.00	15.00
Mercury SR-60835	(S)	**Shirley Horn With Horns**	1964	8.00	20.00
ABC-Paramount 538	(M)	**Travelin' Light**	1965	6.00	15.00
ABC-Paramount S-538	(S)	**Travelin' Light**	1965	8.00	20.00

HORNE, LENA
Refer to Ella Fitzgerald.

MGM E-545 (10")	(M)	**Lena Horne Sings**	1952	20.00	50.00
RCA Victor LPT-3061 (10")	(M)	**This Is Lena Horne**	1952	20.00	50.00
RCA Victor LPM-1148	(M)	**It's Love**	1955	20.00	50.00
RCA Victor LPM-1375	(M)	**Stormy Weather**	1956	20.00	50.00
RCA Victor LOC-1028	(M)	**Lena Horne At The Waldorf Astoria**	1957	14.00	35.00
RCA Victor LSO-1028	(S)	**Lena Horne At The Waldorf Astoria**	1957	20.00	50.00
RCA Victor LOC-1036	(M)	**Jamaica** *(Soundtrack)*	1957	14.00	35.00
RCA Victor LSO-1036	(S)	**Jamaica** *(Soundtrack)*	1957	20.00	50.00
Jazztone 1262	(M)	**Lena And Ivie**	1957	20.00	50.00
RCA Victor LPM-1879	(M)	**Give The Lady What She Wants**	1958	14.00	35.00
RCA Victor LSP-1879	(S)	**Give The Lady What She Wants**	1958	20.00	50.00
RCA Victor LPM-1895	(M)	**Songs Of Burke And Van Heusen**	1959	14.00	35.00
RCA Victor LSP-1895	(S)	**Songs Of Burke And Van Heusen**	1959	20.00	50.00
RCA Victor LOC-1507	(M)	**Porgy And Bess** *(Soundtrack)*	1959	10.00	25.00
RCA Victor LSO-1507	(S)	**Porgy And Bess** *(Soundtrack)*	1959	14.00	35.00
RCA Victor LPM-2364	(M)	**Lena Horne At The Sands**	1961	8.00	20.00
RCA Victor LSP-2364	(S)	**Lena Horne At The Sands**	1961	12.00	30.00
RCA Victor LPM-2465	(M)	**On The Blue Side**	1962	8.00	20.00
RCA Victor LSP-2465	(S)	**On The Blue Side**	1962	12.00	30.00

— Original RCA mono albums above have "Long Play" on the bottom of the label;
stereo albums have "Living Stereo" on the bottom.—

RCA Victor LPM-2587	(M)	**Lovely And Alive**	1963	6.00	15.00
RCA Victor LSP-2587	(S)	**Lovely And Alive**	1963	8.00	20.00
Charter CL-101	(M)	**Lena Horne Sings Your Requests**	1963	6.00	15.00
Charter CLS-101	(S)	**Lena Horne Sings Your Requests**	1963	8.00	20.00
Charter CL-106	(M)	**Like Latin**	1964	6.00	15.00
Charter CLS-106	(S)	**Like Latin**	1964	8.00	20.00
Movietone 71005	(M)	**Once In A Lifetime**	196?	6.00	15.00
Movietone 72005	(S)	**Once In A Lifetime**	196?	8.00	20.00
20th Century TF-4115	(M)	**Here's Lena Now**	1964	6.00	15.00
20th Century TFS-4115	(S)	**Here's Lena Now**	1964	8.00	20.00
RCA Victor LOC-1103	(M)	**Jamaica** *(Soundtrack)*	1965	6.00	15.00
RCA Victor LSO-1103	(S)	**Jamaica** *(Soundtrack)*	1965	8.00	20.00
United Arts. UAL-3433	(M)	**Feelin' Good**	1965	6.00	15.00
United Arts. UAS-6433	(S)	**Feelin' Good**	1965	8.00	20.00

Label & Catalog #		Title	Year	VG+	NM
United Arts. UAL-3470	(M)	**Lena In Hollywood**	*1966*	6.00	15.00
United Arts. UAS-6470	(S)	**Lena In Hollywood**	*1966*	8.00	20.00
United Arts. UAL-3496	(M)	**Soul**	*1966*	8.00	20.00
United Arts. UAS-6496	(S)	**Soul**	*1966*	8.00	20.00
Mobile Fidelity MFSL-094	(S)	**A Lady And Her Music**	*1980*	10.00	25.00
HORNETS, THE					
Liberty LRP-3348	(M)	**Motorcycles U.S.A.**	*1963*	8.00	20.00
Liberty LST-7348	(S)	**Motorcycles U.S.A.**	*1963*	12.00	30.00
Liberty LRP-3364	(M)	**Big Drag Boats U.S.A.**	*1964*	8.00	20.00
Liberty LST-7364	(S)	**Big Drag Boats U.S.A.**	*1964*	12.00	30.00
HORSES, THE					
White Whale 7121	(S)	**Horses**	*1970*	8.00	20.00
HORTON, JOHNNY					
Briar Int. 104	(M)	**Done Rovin'**	*195?*	50.00	100.00
Sesac 1201	(M)	**Free And Easy Songs**	*1959*	75.00	150.00
Mercury MG-20478	(M)	**The Fantastic Johnny Horton**	*1959*	20.00	50.00
Columbia CL-1362	(M)	**The Spectacular Johnny Horton**	*1960*	10.00	25.00
Columbia CS-8167	(S)	**The Spectacular Johnny Horton**	*1960*	14.00	35.00
Columbia CL-1478	(M)	**Johnny Horton Makes History**	*1960*	10.00	25.00
Columbia CS-8269	(S)	**Johnny Horton Makes History**	*1960*	14.00	35.00
Columbia CL-1596	(M)	**Greatest Hits** *(With bonus photo)*	*1961*	14.00	35.00
Columbia CS-8396	(S)	**Greatest Hits** *(With bonus photo)*	*1961*	16.00	40.00
Columbia CL-1596	(M)	**Greatest Hits** *(Without bonus photo)*	*1961*	10.00	25.00
Columbia CS-8396	(S)	**Greatest Hits** *(Without bonus photo)*	*1961*	12.00	30.00
Columbia CL-1721	(M)	**Honky-Tonk Man**	*1962*	12.00	30.00
Columbia CS-8779	(E)	**Honky-Tonk Man**	*1962*	6.00	15.00
— Original Columbia albums above have three white "eye" logos on each side of the spindle hole.—					
Dot DLP-3221	(M)	**Johnny Horton**	*1962*	12.00	30.00
Dot DLP-25221	(E)	**Johnny Horton**	*1962*	6.00	15.00
Columbia CL-2299	(M)	**I Can't Forget You**	*1965*	10.00	25.00
Columbia CS-9099	(E)	**I Can't Forget You**	*1965*	6.00	15.00
Columbia CL-2566	(S)	**Johnny Horton On The Louisiana Hayride**	*1966*	8.00	20.00
Columbia CS-9366	(S)	**Johnny Horton On The Louisiana Hayride**	*1966*	10.00	25.00
Columbia CS-9940	(S)	**Johnny Horton On The Road**	*1969*	6.00	15.00
—Columbia albums above have "360 Sound Mono/Stereo" on the bottom of the label.—					
HORTON, ROBERT					
Columbia CL-2202	(M)	**The Very Thought Of You**	*1964*	6.00	15.00
Columbia CS-9002	(S)	**The Very Thought Of You**	*1964*	8.00	20.00
Columbia CL-2408	(M)	**The Man Called Shenendoah**	*1965*	10.00	25.00
Columbia CS-9208	(S)	**The Man Called Shenendoah**	*1965*	12.00	30.00
HORTON, WALTER "SHAKEY"					
Argo 4037	(M)	**The Soul Of Blues Harmonica**	*195?*	40.00	80.00
HORWITZ, BILL					
ESP 3020	(S)	**Lies, Lies, Lies**	*1970*	6.00	15.00
HOT BUTTER					
Musicor MS-3242	(S)	**Popcorn** *(Die-cut shaped cover)*	*1972*	6.00	15.00
HOT DOGGERS, THE					
The Hot Doggers feature Bruce Johnston.					
Epic LN-24054	(M)	**Surfin' USA**	*1963*	50.00	100.00
Epic BN-26054	(S)	**Surfin' USA**	*1963*	75.00	150.00
HOT POOP					
Hot Poop 3072	(S)	**Hot Poop Does Their Own Stuff**	*1975*	35.00	70.00
HOT RODDERS, THE					
Crown CLP-5378	(M)	**Big Hot Rod**	*1963*	5.00	12.00
Crown CST-378	(S)	**Big Hot Rod**	*1963*	6.00	15.00
HOT TUNA					
Hot Tuna is Jorma Kaukonen and Jack Casady of The Jefferson Airplane.					
Grunt BFD1-0820	(Q)	**America's Choice**	*1975*	6.00	15.00

Label & Catalog #		Title	Year	VG+	NM
Grunt BFD1-1238	(Q)	**Yellow Fever**	1975	6.00	15.00
Grunt DJL1-2852	(DJ)	**The Last Interview** (With poster)	1978	8.00	20.00
		(Features a live track by Janis Joplin.)			
HOTLEGS					
Capitol ST-587	(S)	**Hotlegs Thinks: School Stinks**	1971	8.00	20.00
HOTZ, JIMMY					
Vision VR-777	(S)	**Beyond The Crystal Sea**	1980	90.00	180.00
HOUR GLASS, THE					
Hour Glass features Duane and Gregg Allman.					
Liberty LRP-3536	(M)	**The Hour Glass**	1967	6.00	15.00
Liberty LST-7536	(S)	**The Hour Glass**	1967	8.00	20.00
Liberty LST-7555	(S)	**The Power Of Love**	1968	8.00	20.00
HOUSE, SON					
Columbia CL-2417	(M)	**Father Of The Folk Blues**	1965	5.00	12.00
Columbia CS-9217	(S)	**Father Of The Folk Blues**	1965	6.00	15.00
		("360 Sound" label.)			
HOUSE, SON, & J.D. SHORT					
Folkways FT-9035	(M)	**Son House And J. D. Short**	1966	12.00	30.00
Folkways FTS-9035	(E)	**Son House And J. D. Short**	1966	8.00	20.00
HOUSE, WALLACE					
Folkways FA-2152	(M)	**Ballads Of The Revolution**	195?	8.00	20.00
HOUSTON, CISCO					
Houston also recorded with Woody Guthrie.					
Folkways FA-2013	(M)	**900 Miles And Other Railroad Ballads**	195?	10.00	25.00
Folkways FA-2022	(M)	**Cowboy Songs**	195?	10.00	25.00
Folkways FA-2042	(M)	**Hard Travellin'**	195?	10.00	25.00
Folkways FA-2346	(M)	**Folk Songs**	195?	10.00	25.00
Vanguard VRS-	(M)	**The Cisco Special!**	195?	10.00	25.00
Stinson 37	(M)	**Traditional Songs Of The Old West**	196?	8.00	20.00
HOUSTON, DOLLY					
RKO Unique 107	(M)	**Dolly's Lullabye**	1057	8.00	20.00
HOUSTON, JOE					
Combo LP-100	(M)	**Where Is Joe?**	1960	50.00	100.00
Combo LP-400	(M)	**Rockin' At The Drive In**	1960	50.00	100.00
Modern LMP-1206	(M)	**Joe Houston Blows All Night Long**	1960	20.00	50.00
Crown CLP-5006	(M)	**Joe Houston Rocks & Rolls All Nite Long**	1961	8.00	20.00
Crown CLP-5203	(M)	**Wild Man Of The Tenor Sax**	1962	8.00	20.00
Crown CLP-5313	(M)	**Surf Rockin'**	1963	8.00	20.00
Crown CLP-5319	(M)	**Limbo**	1963	6.00	15.00
Tops L-1518	(M)	**Rock And Roll**	1962	12.00	30.00
HOUSTON, THELMA, & PRESSURE COOKER					
Sheffield Lab 2	(S)	**I've Got The Music In Me**	1974	6.00	15.00
HOUSTON FEARLESS					
Imperial LP-12421	(S)	**Houston Fearless**	1969	8.00	20.00
HOWARD, DAVE					
Choreo 5	(M)	**I Love Everybody**	1961	10.00	25.00
HOWARD, HARLAN					
Capitol T-1631	(M)	**Harlan Howard Sings Harlan Howard**	1961	12.00	30.00
Capitol ST-1631	(S)	**Harlan Howard Sings Harlan Howard**	1961	16.00	40.00
Monument MLP-8038	(M)	**All-Time Favorite Country Songwriter**	1965	8.00	20.00
Monument SLP-18038	(S)	**All-Time Favorite Country Songwriter**	1965	12.00	30.00
RCA Victor LPM-3729	(M)	**Mr. Songwriter**	1967	6.00	15.00
RCA Victor LSP-3729	(S)	**Mr. Songwriter**	1967	8.00	20.00
RCA Victor LPM-3886	(M)	**Down To Earth**	1968	6.00	15.00
RCA Victor LSP-3886	(S)	**Down To Earth**	1968	8.00	20.00

Label & Catalog #		Title	Year	VG+	NM
HOWARD, JAN					
Wrangler 1005	(M)	**Jan Howard**	1962	12.00	30.00
Wrangler S-1005	(S)	**Jan Howard**	1962	16.00	40.00
Capitol T-1779	(M)	**Sweet And Sentimental**	1962	8.00	20.00
Capitol ST-1779	(S)	**Sweet And Sentimental**	1962	12.00	30.00
Forum 7G-505	(M)	**Jan Howard**	196?	12.00	30.00
Decca DL-4793	(M)	**Evil On Your Mind**	1966	6.00	15.00
Decca DL-74793	(S)	**Evil On Your Mind**	1966	8.00	20.00
Decca DL-4832	(M)	**Bad Seed**	1966	6.00	15.00
Decca DL-74832	(S)	**Bad Seed**	1966	8.00	20.00
Decca DL-4931	(M)	**This Is Jan Howard Country**	1967	6.00	15.00
Decca DL-74931	(S)	**This Is Jan Howard Country**	1967	8.00	20.00
HOWLIN' WOLF					
Howlin' Wolf is a pseudonym for Chester Burnett. Refer to Bo Diddley.					
Chess LP-1434	(M)	**Moanin' In The Moonlight**	1958	100.00	200.00
Chess LP-1469	(M)	**Howlin' Wolf**	1962	75.00	150.00
		— Chess albums above have black & silver labels.—			
Chess LP-1502	(M)	**The Real Folk Blues**	1966	20.00	50.00
Chess LP-1512	(M)	**More Real Folk Blues**	1967	20.00	50.00
		— Chess albums above have black labels with a color logo on top.—			
Crown CLP-5240	(M)	**Howlin' Wolf Sings The Blues**	1962	10.00	25.00
Custom CM-2055	(M)	**Big City Blues**	196?	14.00	35.00
Custom CS-2055	(S)	**Big City Blues**	196?	14.00	35.00
Kent KLP-526	(M)	**Original Folk Blues**	1967	6.00	15.00
Kent KST-526	(E)	**Original Folk Blues**	1967	5.00	12.00
Kent KST-527	(E)	**Howlin' Wolf's Twenty Greatest R&B Hits**	1967	6.00	15.00
Kent KST-535	(E)	**Underground Blues**	1967	6.00	15.00
United 7717	(E)	**Big City Blues**	1969	5.00	12.00
United 7747	(E)	**Original Folk Blues**	1969	5.00	12.00
Cadet 319	(S)	**This Is Howlin' Wolf's New Album**	1969	10.00	25.00
Chess LP-1540	(S)	**Evil**	1969	10.00	25.00
Chess CH-50015	(S)	**Live And Cookin'**	1972	8.00	20.00
Chess CH-60008	(S)	**The London Howlin' Wolf Sessions**	1971	8.00	20.00
		(Features Ian Stewart, Charlie Watts and Bill Wyman.)			
Chess CH-50045	(M)	**The Back Door Wolf**	1974	8.00	20.00
Chess CH-60016	(E)	**Howlin' Wolf A.K.A. Chester Burnett** *(2 LPs)*	1972	10.00	25.00
		— Chess albums above have blue & white labels.—			
Chess CH-201	(S)	**Howlin' Wolf** *(2 LPs)*	1976	5.00	12.00
Chess CH-418	(S)	**Change My Way**	1977	5.00	12.00
HUDSON, ROCK					
Refer to Doris Day.					
Stanyan 10014	(S)	**Rock Gently**	1971	10.00	25.00
HUGHES, FREDDIE					
Wand WD-664	(M)	**Send My Baby Back**	1965	6.00	15.00
Wand WDS-664	(S)	**Send My Baby Back**	1965	8.00	20.00
Brunswick BL-754157	(S)	**Baby Boy**	1970	5.00	12.00
HUGHES, JIMMY					
Vee Jay VJ-1102	(M)	**Steal Away**	1965	6.00	15.00
Vee Jay SR-1102	(S)	**Steal Away**	1965	10.00	25.00
Atco 33-209	(M)	**Why Not Tonight**	1967	5.00	12.00
Atco SD-33-209	(S)	**Why Not Tonight**	1967	6.00	15.00
Volt VOS-6003	(S)	**Something Special**	1969	5.00	12.00
HULLABALOOS, THE					
Roulette R-25297	(M)	**England's Newest Singing Sensations**	1965	16.00	40.00
Roulette SR-25297	(E)	**England's Newest Singing Sensations**	1965	12.00	30.00
Roulette R-25310	(M)	**The Hullabaloos On Hullaballoo**	1965	12.00	30.00
Roulette SR-25310	(S)	**The Hullabaloos On Hullaballoo**	1965	16.00	40.00
HUMAN BEINZ, THE / THE MAMMALS					
Gateway GLP-3012	(S)	**Nobody But Me**	1968	12.00	30.00
HUMAN BEINZ, THE					
Capitol ST-2906	(S)	**Nobody But Me**	1968	10.00	25.00
Capitol ST-2926	(S)	**Evolutions**	1968	12.00	30.00

Label & Catalog #		Title	Year	VG+	NM
HUMAN ZOO, THE					
Accent ACS-5055	(S)	The Human Zoo	1971	35.00	70.00
HUMBLE PIE					
Immediate 101	(S)	As Safe As Yesterday Is	1968	6.00	15.00
Immediate 027	(S)	Town And Country	1972	5.00	12.00
HUMES, HELEN					
Contemporary M3571	(M)	T'ain't Nobody's Biz'ness If I Do	1960	8.00	20.00
Contemporary S7571	(S)	T'ain't Nobody's Biz'ness If I Do	1960	12.00	30.00
Contemporary M3582	(M)	Songs I Love To Sing	1961	8.00	20.00
Contemporary S7582	(S)	Songs I Love To Sing	1961	12.00	30.00
Contemporary M3598	(M)	Swingin' With Humes	1961	8.00	20.00
Contemporary S7598	(S)	Swingin' With Humes	1961	12.00	30.00
HUMPERDINCK, ENGELBERT					
Epic PAL-35020	(DJ)	Last Of The Romantics (Picture disc)	1978	20.00	50.00
HUNGER					
Public 1006	(S)	Strickly From Hunger	1969	180.00	300.00
HUNT, TOMMY					
Hunt was formerly a member of the Flamingos.					
Scepter 506	(M)	I Just Don't Know What To Do With Myself	1962	14.00	35.00
Scepter SS-506	(S)	I Just Don't Know What To Do With Myself	1962	20.00	50.00
Dynamo D-7001	(M)	Tommy Hunt's Greatest Hits	1967	8.00	20.00
Dynamo DS-8001	(S)	Tommy Hunt's Greatest Hits	1967	10.00	25.00
HUNTER, IVORY JOE					
MGM E-3488	(M)	I Get That Lonesome Feeling	1957	75.00	150.00
Sound 603	(M)	Ivory Joe Hunter	1957	75.00	150.00
King 605	(M)	16 Of His Greatest Hits	1958	75.00	150.00
Atlantic 8008	(M)	Ivory Joe Hunter (Black label)	1957	75.00	150.00
Atlantic 8008	(M)	Ivory Joe Hunter (Orange & purple label)	1960	50.00	100.00
Atlantic 8015	(M)	The Old & The New (Black label)	1958	75.00	150.00
Atlantic 8015	(M)	The Old & The New (Orange & purple label)	1960	50.00	100.00
Sage 603	(M)	Ivory Joe Hunter	1959	50.00	100.00
Lion L-70068	(M)	I Need You So	195?	50.00	100.00
Goldisc 403	(M)	The Fabulous Ivory Joe Hunter	1961	35.00	70.00
Smash MGS-27037	(M)	Ivory Joe Hunter's Golden Hits	1963	14.00	35.00
Smash SRS-67037	(S)	Ivory Joe Hunter's Golden Hits	1963	20.00	50.00
Dot DLP-3569	(M)	This Is Ivory Joe Hunter	1964	10.00	25.00
Dot DLP-25569	(S)	This Is Ivory Joe Hunter	1964	12.00	30.00
Epic SE-30348	(S)	The Return Of Ivory Joe Hunter	1971	8.00	20.00
Everest 289	(S)	Ivory Joe Hunter	1974	4.00	10.00
Paramount PAS-6080	(S)	I've Always Been Country	1974	5.00	12.00
HUNTER, LURLEAN					
RCA Victor LPM-1151	(M)	Lonesome Gal	1955	20.00	50.00
Vik 1061	(M)	Night Life	1956	16.00	40.00
Vik 1116	(M)	Stepping Out	1958	16.00	40.00
Atlantic 1344	(M)	Blue And Sentimental	1960	12.00	30.00
Atlantic SD-1344	(S)	Blue And Sentimental	1960	16.00	40.00
HUNTER, ROBERT					
Refer to The Grateful Dead.					
Round RX-101	(S)	Tales Of The Great Rum Runners	1974	8.00	20.00
Round RX-105	(S)	Tiger Rose	1975	8.00	20.00
HUNTER, TAB					
Warner Bros. W-1221	(M)	Tab Hunter	1958	12.00	30.00
Warner Bros. WS-1221	(S)	Tab Hunter	1958	16.00	40.00
Warner Bros. W-1292	(M)	When I Fall In Love	1959	12.00	30.00
Warner Bros. WS-1292	(S)	When I Fall In Love	1959	16.00	40.00
Warner Bros. W-1367	(M)	R.F.D. Tab Hunter	1960	12.00	30.00
Warner Bros. WS-1367	(S)	R.F.D. Tab Hunter	1960	16.00	40.00
Dot DLP-3370	(M)	Young Love	1961	8.00	20.00
Dot DLP-25370	(S)	Young Love	1961	12.00	30.00

Label & Catalog #		Title	Year	VG+	NM
HURT, MISSISSIPPI JOHN					
Vanguard VRS-9145	(M)	**Blues At Newport**	1965	10.00	25.00
Vanguard VSD-79145	(S)	**Blues At Newport**	1965	12.00	30.00
Vanguard VRS-9220	(M)	**Mississippi John Hurt Today**	1966	10.00	25.00
Vanguard VSD-79220	(S)	**Mississippi John Hurt Today**	1966	12.00	30.00
Vanguard VRS-9248	(M)	**The Immortal Mississippi John Hurt**	1967	10.00	25.00
Vanguard VSD-79248	(S)	**The Immortal Mississippi John Hurt**	1967	12.00	30.00
HURVITZ, SANDY					
Verve V6-5064	(S)	**Sandy's Album Is Here At Last**	1968	6.00	15.00
HUSKY, FERLIN					
Husky also recorded as Simon Crum.					
Capitol T-718	(M)	**Songs Of The Home And Heart**	1956	20.00	50.00
Capitol T-880	(M)	**Boulevard Of Broken Dreams**	1957	16.00	40.00
Capitol T-976	(M)	**Sittin' On A Rainbow**	1959	12.00	30.00
		— Original Capitol albums above have turquoise labels.—			
King 647	(M)	**Country Tunes Sung From The Heart**	1959	20.00	50.00
King 728	(M)	**Easy Livin'**	1960	20.00	50.00
Capitol T-1204	(M)	**Born To Lose**	1959	10.00	25.00
Capitol T-1280	(M)	**Ferlin's Favorites**	1960	10.00	25.00
Capitol T-1383	(M)	**Gone**	1960	8.00	20.00
Capitol T-1546	(M)	**Walkin' And Hummin'**	1961	6.00	15.00
Capitol ST-1546	(S)	**Walkin' And Hummin'**	1961	8.00	20.00
Capitol T-1633	(M)	**Memories Of Home**	1961	6.00	15.00
Capitol ST-1633	(S)	**Memories Of Home**	1961	8.00	20.00
		— Original Capitol albums above have black labels with the Capitol logo on the side.—			
Capitol T-1720	(M)	**Some Of My Favorites**	1962	5.00	12.00
Capitol ST-1720	(S)	**Some Of My Favorites**	1962	6.00	15.00
Capitol T-1885	(M)	**The Heart And Soul Of Ferlin Husky**	1963	5.00	12.00
Capitol ST-1885	(S)	**The Heart And Soul Of Ferlin Husky**	1963	6.00	15.00
Capitol T-1991	(M)	**The Hits Of Ferlin Husky**	1963	8.00	20.00
Capitol DT-1991	(E)	**The Hits Of Ferlin Husky**	1963	5.00	12.00
Capitol T-2101	(M)	**By Request**	1964	5.00	12.00
Capitol ST-2101	(S)	**By Request**	1964	6.00	15.00
Capitol T-2305	(M)	**True, True Lovin'**	1965	5.00	12.00
Capitol ST-2305	(S)	**True, True Lovin'**	1965	6.00	15.00
Capitol T-2439	(M)	**Songs Of Music City, U.S.A.**	1966	5.00	12.00
Capitol ST-2439	(S)	**Songs Of Music City, U.S.A.**	1966	6.00	15.00
Capitol T-2548	(M)	**I Could Sing All Night**	1966	5.00	12.00
Capitol ST-2548	(S)	**I Could Sing All Night**	1966	6.00	15.00
Capitol T-2705	(M)	**What Am I Gonna Do Now?**	1967	5.00	12.00
Capitol ST-2705	(S)	**What Am I Gonna Do Now?**	1967	6.00	15.00
Capitol T-2793	(M)	**Christmas All Year Long**	1967	5.00	12.00
Capitol ST-2793	(S)	**Christmas All Year Long**	1967	6.00	15.00
Capitol ST-2870	(S)	**Just For You**	1968	5.00	12.00
Capitol ST-2913	(S)	**Where No One Stands Alone**	1968	5.00	12.00
		— Original Capitol albums above have black labels with the Capitol logo on top.—			
HUTTON, BETTY					
Capitol H-256 (10")	(M)	**Square In The Social Circle**	1950	16.00	40.00
MGM E-509 (10")	(M)	**Annie Get Your Gun** *(Soundtrack)*	1950	40.00	80.00
RCA LPM-3097 (10")	(M)	**Somebody Loves Me** *(Soundtrack)*	1952	40.00	80.00
Capitol L-547 (10")	(M)	**Satins And Spurs** *(TV Soundtrack)*	1954	50.00	100.00
MGM E-3227	(M)	**Annie Get Your Gun** *(Soundtrack)*	1955	16.00	40.00
Warner Bros. W-1267	(M)	**At The Saints And Sinners Ball**	1959	5.00	12.00
Warner Bros. WS-1267	(S)	**At The Saints And Sinners Ball**	1959	6.00	15.00
HUTTON, DANNY					
Danny Hutton was a member of Three Dog Night.					
MGM SE-4664	(S)	**Pre-Dog Night**	1970	6.00	15.00
HUTTON, JUNE					
Capitol T-643	(M)	**Afterglow**	1955	12.00	30.00
Venise 10017	(M)	**Dream**	195?	12.00	30.00
HYLAND, BRIAN					
Kapp KL-1202	(M)	**The Bashful Blonde**	1960	12.00	30.00
Kapp KS-3202	(S)	**The Bashful Blonde**	1960	16.00	40.00

Label & Catalog #		Title	Year	VG+	NM
ABC-Paramount 400	(M)	Let Me Belong To You	1961	6.00	15.00
ABC-Paramount S-400	(S)	Let Me Belong To You	1961	8.00	20.00
ABC-Paramount 431	(M)	Sealed With A Kiss	1962	8.00	20.00
ABC-Paramount S-431	(P)	Sealed With A Kiss	1962	10.00	25.00
ABC-Paramount 463	(M)	Country Meets Folk	1964	6.00	15.00
ABC-Paramount S-463	(S)	Country Meets Folk	1964	8.00	20.00
Phillips PHM-200136	(M)	Here's To Our Love	1964	6.00	15.00
Phillips PHS-600136	(S)	Here's To Our Love	1964	8.00	20.00
Phillips PHM-200158	(M)	Rockin' Folk	1965	6.00	15.00
Phillips PHS-600158	(S)	Rockin, Folk	1965	8.00	20.00
Phillips PHM-200217	(M)	Joker Went Wild	1966	6.00	15.00
Phillips PHS-600217	(S)	Joker Went Wild	1966	8.00	20.00
Dot DLP-25926	(S)	Tragedy	1969	5.00	12.00
Dot DLP-25954	(S)	Stay And Love Me All Summer	1969	5.00	12.00
Uni 72097	(P)	Brian Hyland	1971	5.00	12.00
Private Stock PS-7003	(S)	In A State Of Bayou	1977	4.00	10.00

I

IAN, JANIS

Columbia PCQ-33394	(Q)	Between The Lines	1975	6.00	15.00
Columbia PCQ-33919	(Q)	Aftertones	1976	6.00	15.00
Columbia PCQ-34440	(Q)	Miracle Row	1977	6.00	15.00

IAN & THE ZODIACS

Phillips PHM-200176	(M)	Ian And The Zodiacs	1965	16.00	40.00
Phillips PHS-600176	(S)	Ian And The Zodiacs	1965	20.00	50.00

ID, THE

RCA Victor LPM-3805	(M)	The Inner Sounds Of The Id	1967	8.00	20.00
RCA Victor LSP-3805	(S)	The Inner Sounds Of The Id	1967	10.00	25.00
Aura 1000	(S)	Where Are We Going?	1976	12.00	30.00

IDLE, ERIC, & NEIL INNES
Refer to The Rutles.

Passport PPSD-98018	(S)	The Rutland Weekend Television Songbook	1976	10.00	25.00

IDLE RACE, THE
The Idle Race features Jeff Lynne. Refer to The Move.

Liberty LST-7603	(S)	Birthday Party	1969	12.00	30.00

IF

Capitol ST-539	(S)	If	1969	8.00	20.00
Capitol SW-676	(S)	If 2	1970	6.00	15.00
Capitol SMAS-820	(S)	If 3	1971	6.00	15.00
Metromedia BML1-057	(S)	Waterfall	1972	5.00	12.00
Metromedia BML1-074	(S)	Double Diamond	1973	5.00	12.00

IFIELD, FRANK
Refer to the Beatles.

Vee Jay LP-1054	(M)	I Re-mem-ber You	1963	10.00	25.00
Vee Jay SR-1054	(S)	I Re-mem-ber You	1963	16.00	40.00

Label & Catalog #	Title	Year	VG+	NM

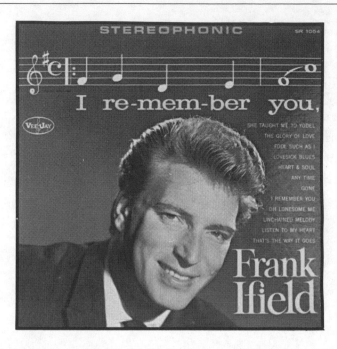

Known to collectors for his involvement with The Beatles on one of the world's most collectible LPs, the stereo version of crooner Frank Ifield's solo album for Vee Jay is, like many stereo albums on that label, very difficult to find in any condition

Capitol Int. T-10356	(M)	I'm Confessin'	196?	6.00	15.00
Capitol Int. ST-10356	(S)	I'm Confessin'	196?	8.00	20.00
Hickory LPM-132	(M)	The Best Of Frank Ifield	196?	6.00	15.00

IKETTES, THE
The Ikettes backed Ike & Tina Turner during the '60s.

Modern M-102	(M)	Soul Hits	1965	8.00	20.00
Modern MST-102	(S)	Soul Hits	1965	12.00	30.00

ILL WIND

ABC S-641	(S)	Flashes	1968	12.00	30.00

ILLUSION

Sinergia SR-7654	(S)	Illusion	1974	35.00	70.00

ILLUSTRATION

Janus 3010	(S)	Illustration	1969	10.00	25.00

ILMO SMOKEHOUSE

Beautiful Sound 3002	(S)	Ilmo Smokehouse	1971	14.00	35.00
Roulette SR-3002	(S)	Ilmo Smokehouse	1971	6.00	15.00

IMMIGRANTS, THE

Justice JLP	(M)	The Immigrants '66	1966	150.00	250.00

IMPACS, THE

King 886	(M)	Impact!	1964	35.00	70.00
King KS-886	(S)	Impact!	1964	50.00	100.00
King 916	(M)	Weekend With The Impacs	1964	35.00	70.00
King KS-916	(S)	Weekend With The Impacs	1964	50.00	100.00

Label & Catalog #		Title	Year	VG+	NM

IMPACTS, THE
The Impacts feature Merrel Fankhauser.

Label & Catalog #		Title	Year	VG+	NM
Del-Fi DFLP-1234	(M)	**Wipe Out**	*1963*	**10.00**	**25.00**
Del-Fi DFS-1234	(S)	**Wipe Out**	*1963*	**14.00**	**35.00**

IMPALA SYNDROME, THE

Parallax 4002	(S)	**The Impala Syndrome**	*1970*	**12.00**	**30.00**

IMPALAS, THE

Cub 8003	(M)	**Sorry (I Ran All The Way Home)**	*1959*	**180.00**	**300.00**
Cub S-8003	(S)	**Sorry (I Ran All The Way Home)**	*1959*	**360.00**	**600.00**

IMPRESSIONS, THE
The Impressions feature Curtis Mayfield. Refer to Jerry Butler.

ABC-Paramount 450	(M)	**The Impressions**	*1963*	**8.00**	**20.00**
ABC-Paramount S-450	(S)	**The Impressions**	*1963*	**12.00**	**30.00**
ABC-Paramount 468	(M)	**Never Ending Impressions**	*1964*	**8.00**	**20.00**
ABC-Paramount S-468	(S)	**Never Ending Impressions**	*1964*	**12.00**	**30.00**
ABC-Paramount 493	(M)	**Keep On Pushing**	*1964*	**6.00**	**15.00**
ABC-Paramount S-493	(S)	**Keep On Pushing**	*1964*	**8.00**	**20.00**
ABC-Paramount 505	(M)	**People Get Ready**	*1965*	**6.00**	**15.00**
ABC-Paramount S-505	(S)	**People Get Ready**	*1965*	**8.00**	**20.00**
ABC-Paramount 515	(M)	**The Impressions' Greatest Hits**	*1965*	**6.00**	**15.00**
ABC-Paramount S-515	(S)	**The Impressions' Greatest Hits**	*1965*	**8.00**	**20.00**
ABC-Paramount 523	(M)	**One By One**	*1965*	**5.00**	**12.00**
ABC-Paramount S-523	(S)	**One By One**	*1965*	**6.00**	**15.00**
ABC-Paramount 545	(M)	**Ridin' High**	*1966*	**5.00**	**12.00**
ABC-Paramount S-545	(S)	**Ridin' High**	*1966*	**6.00**	**15.00**
ABC-Paramount 606	(M)	**The Fabulous Impressions**	*1967*	**5.00**	**12.00**
ABC-Paramount S-606	(S)	**The Fabulous Impressions**	*1967*	**6.00**	**15.00**
ABC-Paramount S-635	(S)	**We're A Winner**	*1968*	**6.00**	**15.00**
ABC-Paramount S-654	(S)	**The Best Of The Impressions**	*1968*	**4.00**	**10.00**
Sire	(P)	**The Vintage Years** (2 LPs)	*1975*	**6.00**	**15.00**

IN-SECT, THE

Camden CAL-909	(M)	**Introducing The In-Sect**	*1965*	**12.00**	**30.00**
Camden CAS-909	(S)	**Introducing The In-Sect**	*1965*	**16.00**	**40.00**

INCREDIBLE STRING BAND, THE

Elektra EKL-322	(M)	**The Incredible String Band**	*1967*	**6.00**	**15.00**
Elektra EKS-7322	(S)	**The Incredible String Band**	*1967*	**8.00**	**20.00**
Elektra EKL-4010	(M)	**The 5,000 Spirits**	*1967*	**6.00**	**15.00**
Elektra EKS-74010	(S)	**The 5,000 Spirits**	*1967*	**8.00**	**20.00**
Elektra EKS-4021	(M)	**The Hangman's Beautiful Daughter**	*1968*	**6.00**	**15.00**
Elektra EKS-74021	(S)	**The Hangman's Beautiful Daughter**	*1968*	**8.00**	**20.00**
Elektra EKS-74036	(S)	**Wee Tam**	*1969*	**6.00**	**15.00**
Elektra EKS-74037	(S)	**The Big Huge**	*1969*	**6.00**	**15.00**
		— Original Elektra albums above have brown labels.—			
Elektra EKS-74057	(S)	**Changing Horses**	*1969*	**6.00**	**15.00**
Elektra EKS-74061	(S)	**I Looked Up**	*1970*	**4.00**	**10.00**
Decca DL7-9181	(S)	**Taking Off** (Soundtrack)	*1971*	**12.00**	**30.00**
Elektra EKS-2002	(S)	**"U"** (2 LPs)	*1971*	**6.00**	**15.00**
Elektra EKS-2004	(S)	**Relics Of The Incredible String Band** (2 LPs)	*1971*	**5.00**	**12.00**
Elektra EKS-74112	(S)	**Liquid Acrobat As Regards The Air**	*1972*	**4.00**	**10.00**
Reprise MS-2122	(S)	**Earthspan**	*1972*	**4.00**	**10.00**
Reprise MS-2198	(S)	**Hard Rope And Silver Twine**	*1974*	**4.00**	**10.00**
Reprise MS-2129	(S)	**No Ruinous Feud**	*1973*	**4.00**	**10.00**

INDEX, THE
Members of The Index later recorded as Just Us.

D. C. (No number)	(M)	**The Index**	*1965*	*See note below*	

(The first album features "New York Mining Disaster" as the first song on the second side. Only a few copies were issued with an original cover and there are no documented sales from which to derive a value! Copies with covers from the second album have an estimated near mint value of $1,000-2,000.)

D. C. (No number)	(M)	**The Index**	*1967*	*See note below*	

(The second album features "Fire Eyes" as the first song on the second side. Estimated near mint value $500-1,000.)

Label & Catalog #		Title	Year	VG+	NM
INDIAN SUMMER					
RCA Victor/Neon NE-3	(S)	**Indian Summer**	1971	8.00	20.00
INFLITE					
Anchor	(S)	**First In Flite**	1985	20.00	50.00
INFLUENCE					
ABC-Paramount S-630	(S)	**Influence**	1968	8.00	20.00
INGMANN, JORGEN					
Mercury MG-20200	(M)	**Swinging Guitar**	1956	20.00	50.00
Atco 33-130	(M)	**Apache**	1961	12.00	30.00
Atco 33-139	(M)	**The Many Guitars Of Jorgen Ingmann**	1962	12.00	30.00
United Arts. Int. 15549	(S)	**Movie Themes**	1968	5.00	12.00
INGRAM, LUTHER					
Koko KOS-2201	(S)	**I've Been Here All The Time**	1971	5.00	12.00
Koko KOS-2202	(S)	**If Loving You Is Wrong** (With bonus photo)	1972	6.00	15.00
INK SPOTS, THE					
Waldorf Music 144 (10")	(M)	**Spirituals And Jubilees**	195?	30.00	60.00
Waldorf Music 152 (10")	(M)	**Spirituals And Jubilees, Volume 2**	195?	30.00	60.00
Decca DL-5056 (10")	(M)	**The Ink Spots, Volume 1**	1950	20.00	50.00
Decca DL-5071 (10")	(M)	**The Ink Spots, Volume 2**	1950	20.00	50.00
Decca DL-5333 (10")	(M)	**Precious Memories**	1951	20.00	50.00
Decca DL-5541 (10")	(M)	**Street Of Dreams**	1954	20.00	50.00
Decca DL-8154	(M)	**The Ink Spots**	1955	16.00	40.00
Decca DL-8232	(M)	**Time Out For Tears**	1956	16.00	40.00
Decca DL-8768	(M)	**Torch Time**	1958	16.00	40.00
Decca DL-4297	(M)	**Our Golden Favorites**	1962	6.00	15.00
Decca DXB-182	(M)	**The Best Of The Ink Spots** (2 LPs)	1965	8.00	20.00
Decca DXSB-182	(P)	**The Best Of The Ink Spots** (2 LPs)	1965	6.00	15.00
Grand Award 328	(M)	**The Ink Spots' Greatest, Volume 1**	1956	10.00	25.00
Grand Award 354	(M)	**The Ink Spots' Greatest, Volume 2**	1956	10.00	25.00
King LP-535	(M)	**Something Old, Something New**	1958	50.00	100.00
King LP-642	(M)	**Songs That Will Live Forever**	1959	35.00	70.00
Colortone 4901	(M)	**The Ink Spots**	1958	35.00	70.00
Colortone 4947	(M)	**The Ink Spots (Volume 2)**	1959	35.00	70.00
Grand LP-328	(M)	**The Ink Spots' Greatest**	1959	10.00	25.00
Grand LP-354	(M)	**The Ink Spots' Greatest, Volume 2**	1959	10.00	25.00
Verve V-6096	(M)	**The Ink Spots' Favorites**	1960	10.00	25.00
Verve VS-606	(S)	**The Ink Spots' Favorites**	1960	16.00	40.00
Crown CST-144	(E)	**The Ink Spots' Greatest Hits** (Red vinyl)	196?	16.00	40.00
Crown CST-217	(S)	**The Sensational Ink Spots** (Red vinyl)	196?	16.00	40.00
Mayfair 9685S	(S)	**In The Spotlight** (Yellow vinyl)	196?	16.00	40.00
Vocalion VL-3606	(M)	**Sincerely Yours**	1964	6.00	15.00
Vocalion VL-3725	(M)	**Lost In A Dream**	1965	6.00	15.00
Vocalion VL-73725	(S)	**Lost In A Dream**	1965	6.00	15.00
INNOCENCE, THE					
The Innocence is Pete Anders and Vinnie Poncia.					
Kama Sutra KLP-8059	(M)	**The Innocence**	1967	5.00	12.00
Kama Sutra KLPS-8059	(S)	**The Innocence**	1967	8.00	20.00
INNOCENTS, THE					
The Innocents also recorded with Kathy Young.					
Indigo 503	(M)	**Innocently Yours**	1961	100.00	200.00
INSECT TRUST, THE					
Capitol SKAO-109	(S)	**The Insect Trust**	1968	14.00	35.00
Atco SD-33-313	(S)	**Hoboken Saturday Night**	1970	14.00	35.00
INSTINCTS, THE / THE METEORS					
TCA 3952	(M)	**The Loving Sandwich**	196?	180.00	300.00
INTERNATIONAL SUBMARINE BAND, THE					
The I.S.B. features Gram Parsons.					
L.H.I. 12001	(S)	**Safe At Home** (Multi-color label)	1968	40.00	80.00
		(Reproductions exist with white labels.)			

Label & Catalog #		Title	Year	VG+	NM
INTRIGUES, THE					
Yew YS-777	(S)	In A Moment	1970	16.00	40.00
INTRUDERS, THE					
Gamble 5001	(M)	The Intruders Are Together	1967	6.00	15.00
Gamble KZ-5001	(S)	The Intruders Are Together	1967	8.00	20.00
Gamble KZ-5004	(S)	Cowboys To Girls	1968	6.00	15.00
Gamble KZ-5005	(P)	The Intruders' Greatest Hits	1969	6.00	15.00
Gamble KZ-5008	(S)	When We Get Married	1970	6.00	15.00
INVADERS, THE					
Justice JLP-125	(M)	On The Right Track	196?	100.00	200.00
INVADERS, THE					
Duane 1006	(M)	Spacing Out	1968	60.00	120.00
INVICTAS, THE					
Sahara 101	(M)	The Invictas A-Go-Go	1965	50.00	100.00
IRON BUTTERFLY					
Atco 33-227	(M)	Heavy	1967	6.00	15.00
Atco SD-33-227	(S)	Heavy	1967	5.00	12.00
Atco 33-250	(M)	In-A-Gadda-Da-Vida	1968	8.00	20.00
Atco SD-33-250	(S)	In-A-Gadda-Da-Vida (Brown & purple label)	1968	6.00	15.00
ISLEY BROTHERS, THE					
RCA Victor LPM-2156	(M)	Shout!	1959	35.00	70.00
RCA Victor LSP-2156	(S)	Shout!	1959	50.00	100.00
Wand WD-653	(M)	Twist And Shout	1962	14.00	35.00
Wand WDS-653	(S)	Twist And Shout	1962	20.00	50.00
United Arts. UAL-6313	(M)	The Famous Isley Brothers	1963	12.00	30.00
United Arts. UAS-6313	(S)	The Famous Isley Brothers	1963	16.00	40.00
Scepter SC-552	(M)	Take Some Time Out For The Isley Brothers	1966	6.00	15.00
Scepter SCS-552	(S)	Take Some Time Out For The Isley Brothers	1966	8.00	20.00
Tamla T-269	(M)	This Old Heart Of Mine	1966	6.00	15.00
Tamla TS-269	(S)	This Old Heart Of Mine	1966	8.00	20.00
Tamla 275	(M)	Soul On The Rocks	1967	5.00	12.00
Tamla TS-275	(S)	Soul On The Rocks	1967	6.00	15.00
Tamla TS-287	(S)	Doin' Their Thing	1969	5.00	12.00
T-Neck ZQ-32453	(Q)	3 + 3	1974	5.00	12.00
T-Neck ZQ-33070	(Q)	The Isley Brothers Live It Up	1974	5.00	12.00
T-Neck PZQ-33536	(Q)	The Heat Is On	1975	5.00	12.00
T-Neck PZQ-33809	(Q)	Harvest For The World	1976	5.00	12.00
T-Neck A5Z-137	(DJ)	Everything You Always Wanted To Hear	1976	6.00	15.00
T-Neck PZQ-34432	(Q)	Go For Your Guns	1977	5.00	12.00
ISLEY BROTHERS, THE, & THE BROOKLYN BRIDGE					
T-Neck TNS-3004	(S)	Live At Yankee Stadium	1971	5.00	12.00
ISLEY BROTHERS, THE, & JIMI HENDRIX					
T-Neck TNS-3007	(S)	In The Beginning	1971	5.00	12.00
ISAACS, BUD					
Jabs 101	(M)	The Best Of Bud Isaacs	195?	20.00	50.00
IT'S A BEAUTIFUL DAY					
Columbia CS-9768	(S)	It's A Beautiful Day ("360 Sound" label)	1969	12.00	30.00
Columbia CS-9768	(S)	It's A Beautiful Day (Red & gold label)	1969	4.00	10.00
Columbia CS-1058	(S)	Marrying Maiden	1970	8.00	20.00
Columbia C-30734	(S)	Choice Quality Stuff/Anytime	1971	8.00	20.00
Columbia KC-31338	(S)	Live At Carnegie Hall	1972	8.00	20.00
Columbia KC-32181	(S)	It's A Beautiful Day Today	1973	8.00	20.00
San Fran. Sound 11790	(S)	It's A Beautiful Day (Half-speed master)	1985	12.00	30.00
IVES, BURL					
Columbia CL-6058 (10")	(M)	Return Of The Wayfaring Stranger	195?	12.00	30.00
Columbia CL-6109 (10")	(M)	Wayfaring Stranger	195?	12.00	30.00
Columbia CL-6144 (10")	(M)	More Folksongs	195?	12.00	30.00
Decca DL-5013 (10")	(M)	Ballads And Folk Songs, Volume 1	1950	12.00	30.00

Label & Catalog #		Title	Year	VG+	NM
Decca DL-5080 (10")	(M)	Ballads And Folk Songs, Volume 2	1950	12.00	30.00
Decca DL-5093 (10")	(M)	Ballads Folk And Country Songs	1950	12.00	30.00
Decca DL-5428 (10")	(M)	Christmas Day In The Morning	1952	12.00	30.00
Decca DL-5467 (10")	(M)	Folk Songs Dramatic And Dangerous	1953	12.00	30.00
Decca DL-5490 (10")	(M)	Women: Folk Songs About The Fair	1954	12.00	30.00
Columbia CL-628	(M)	Wayfaring Stranger	1955	8.00	20.00
Columbia CL-980	(M)	Burl Ives Sings Songs For All Ages	1957	8.00	20.00
Decca DL-8080	(M)	Coronation Concert	1956	8.00	20.00
Decca DL-8125	(M)	Men	1956	8.00	20.00
Decca DL-8245	(M)	Down To The Sea In Ships	1956	8.00	20.00
Decca DL-8246	(M)	Women	1956	8.00	20.00
Decca DL-8247	(M)	In The Quiet Of Night	1956	8.00	20.00
Decca DL-8248	(M)	Burl Ives Sings For Fun	1956	8.00	20.00
Decca DL-8391	(M)	Christmas Eve With Ives	1957	8.00	20.00
Decca DL-8444	(M)	Songs Of Ireland	1958	8.00	20.00
Decca DL-8587	(M)	Captain Burl Ives' Ark	1958	8.00	20.00
Decca DL-8749	(M)	Australian Folk Songs	1958	8.00	20.00
Decca DL-4815	(M)	Rudolph The Red-Nossed Reindeer	1966	12.00	30.00
Decca DL-74815	(S)	Rudolph The Red-Nossed Reindeer (TV Soundtrack)	1966	16.00	40.00

IVEYS, THE
The Iveys later recorded as Badfinger.

Apple SAPCOR-8S	(S)	Maybe Tomorrow	1968	300.00	500.00

(This Italian record is listed here due to the heavy sales in the U.S. of confusing counterfeits. The originals have green Apple labels while the counterfeits have black labels. This album was also issued in several other countries, including Japan and West Germany.)

IVORY

Tetragrammaton T-104	(S)	Ivory	1968	8.00	20.00
Playboy 115	(S)	Ivory	1973	5.00	12.00

IVORY, JACKIE

Atco 33-178	(M)	Soul Discovery	1965	8.00	20.00
Atco SD-33-178	(S)	Soul Discovery	1965	10.00	25.00

IVORY LIBRARY

Dairyland	(S)	Ivory Library	1985	5.00	12.00

IVY LEAGUE, THE

Cameo C-2000	(M)	Tossing And Turning	1965	8.00	20.00
Cameo CS-2000	(S)	Tossing And Turning	1965	12.00	30.00

IVY LEAGUE TRIO, THE

Coral CRL-57399	(M)	On And Off Campus	1962	6.00	15.00
Coral CRL-757399	(S)	On And Off Campus	1962	8.00	20.00
Coral CRL-57404	(M)	Folk Songs Bare And Well Done	1962	6.00	15.00
Coral CRL-757404	(S)	Folk Songs Bare And Well Done	1962	8.00	20.00
Reprise R-6087	(M)	Folk Ballads From The World Of Edgar Allan Poe	1963	6.00	15.00
Reprise R9-6087	(S)	Folk Ballads From The World Of Edgar Allan Poe	1963	8.00	20.00

Records With Estimated Values

Records with "See note below" in the price column have fluctuating values in the current market, illustrated by the estimated prices. A seller with a near mint copy should expect to get the minimum listed in the price spread in an open auction. While a buyer might win this record for the minimum, he should not be surprised to find the bidding escalate to the maximum listed value.

Label & Catalog #		Title	Year	VG+	NM

J.A. BLUEZY
| Apollo Music ERK-0782 | (S) | At The Delta Lady | 1980 | 30.00 | 60.00 |

J. TEAL BAND, THE
| Mother Cleo MCPLP-7721 | (S) | The J. Peal Band Cooks | 1977 | 75.00 | 150.00 |

JACKIE & ROY: *Refer to* JACKIE CAIN & ROY KRAL

JACKS, THE
The Jacks also recorded as The Cadets.
R.P.M. LRP-3006	(M)	Jumpin' With The Jacks	1956	180.00	300.00
Crown CLP-5021	(M)	Jumpin' With The Jacks	1960	50.00	100.00
Crown CLP-5372	(M)	Jumpin' With The Jacks	1962	20.00	50.00
Crown CST-372	(E)	Jumpin' With The Jacks	1962	14.00	35.00

JACKSON, BULL MOOSE
| Audio Lab LP-1524 | (M) | Bull Moose Jackson | 195? | 100.00 | 200.00 |

JACKSON, CHUBBY
| Laurie LLP-2011 | (M) | Twist Calling | 1962 | 10.00 | 25.00 |

JACKSON, CHUCK
Wand WD-650	(M)	I Don't Want To Cry	1961	12.00	30.00
Wand WDS-650	(S)	I Don't Want To Cry	1961	16.00	40.00
Wand WD-654	(M)	Any Day Now	1962	12.00	30.00
Wand WDS-654	(S)	Any Day Now	1962	16.00	40.00
Wand WD-655	(M)	Encore	1963	8.00	20.00
Wand WDS-655	(S)	Encore	1963	12.00	30.00
Wand WD-658	(M)	Chuck Jackson On Tour	1964	8.00	20.00
Wand WDS-658	(S)	Chuck Jackson On Tour	1964	12.00	30.00
Wand WD-667	(M)	Mr. Everything	1965	8.00	20.00
Wand WDS-667	(S)	Mr. Everything	1965	12.00	30.00
Wand WD-673	(M)	A Tribute To Rhythm & Blues	1966	8.00	20.00
Wand WDS-673	(S)	A Tribute To Rhythm & Blues	1966	12.00	30.00
Wand WD-676	(M)	A Tribute To Rhythm & Blues, Volume 2	1966	8.00	20.00
Wand WDS-676	(S)	A Tribute To Rhythm & Blues, Volume 2	1966	12.00	30.00
Wand WD-680	(M)	Dedicated To The King!!	1966	8.00	20.00
Wand WDS-680	(S)	Dedicated To The King!!	1966	12.00	30.00
Wand WD-683	(M)	Chuck Jackson's Greatest Hits	1967	6.00	15.00
Wand WDS-683	(S)	Chuck Jackson's Greatest Hits	1967	8.00	20.00
Motown MS-667	(S)	Chuck Jackson Arrives	1968	8.00	20.00
Motown MS-687	(S)	Goin' Back To Chuck Jackson	1969	8.00	20.00

JACKSON, CHUCK, & MAXINE BROWN
Wand WD-669	(M)	Saying Something	1965	6.00	15.00
Wand WDS-669	(S)	Saying Something	1965	8.00	20.00
Wand WD-678	(M)	Hold On, We're Coming	1966	6.00	15.00
Wand WDS-678	(S)	Hold On, We're Coming	1966	8.00	20.00

JACKSON, CHUCK, & TAMMI TERRELL
| Wand LP-682 | (M) | The Early Show | 1967 | 6.00 | 15.00 |
| Wand WDS-682 | (S) | The Early Show | 1967 | 8.00 | 20.00 |

JACKSON, DEON
| Atco 33-188 | (M) | Love Makes The World Go Round | 1966 | 10.00 | 25.00 |
| Atco SD-33-188 | (S) | Love Makes The World Go Round | 1966 | 14.00 | 35.00 |

JACKSON, J.J.
| Calla C-1101 | (M) | But It's Alright/I Dig Girls | 1967 | 6.00 | 15.00 |
| Calla CS-1101 | (S) | But It's Alright/I Dig Girls | 1967 | 8.00 | 20.00 |

Label & Catalog #		Title	Year	VG+	NM
Warner Bros. WS-1797	(S)	**The Great J.J. Jackson**	1969	6.00	15.00

JACKSON, JACKIE
Jackie is a member of The Jackson Five.

Perception 3	(S)	**J.J. Jackson's Dilemma**	1969	6.00	15.00
Perception	(S)	**Perception**	1970	5.00	12.00
Motown M-785	(S)	**Jackie Jackson**	1973	5.00	12.00

JACKSON, JERMAINE
Jermaine is a member of The Jackson Five.

Motown M-752	(S)	**Jermaine**	1972	5.00	12.00
Motown M-775	(S)	**Come Into My Life**	1973	5.00	12.00

JACKSON, JOE

Mobile Fidelity MFSL-080	(S)	**Night And Day**	1979	6.00	15.00

JACKSON, LIL' SON

Imperial 9142	(M)	**Rockin' And Rollin'**	1961	100.00	200.00

JACKSON, MICHAEL
Michael was a member of The Jackson Five.

Motown M-747	(S)	**Got To Be There**	1972	6.00	15.00
Motown M-755	(S)	**Ben** *(Soundtrack)*	1972	6.00	15.00
Motown M-767	(S)	**Music And Me**	1973	5.00	12.00
Motown M-825	(S)	**Forever Michael**	1975	5.00	12.00
Motown 6099ML	(S)	**14 Greatest Hits** *(Picture disc)*	1984	2.00	10.00
Epic HE-47545	(S)	**Off The Wall** *(Half-speed master)*	1982	16.00	40.00
Epic HE-48112	(S)	**Thriller** *(Half-speed master)*	1982	14.00	35.00
Epic 8E8-38867	(S)	**Thriller** *(Picture disc)*	1983	2.00	10.00
Epic 9E9-44043	(S)	**Bad** *(Picture disc)*	1987	2.00	10.00

JACKSON, STONEWALL

Columbia CL-1391	(M)	**The Dynamic Stonewall Jackson**	1959	10.00	25.00
Columbia CS-8186	(S)	**The Dynamic Stonewall Jackson**	1959	14.00	35.00
Columbia CL-1770	(M)	**Sadness In A Song**	1962	8.00	20.00
Columbia CS-8570	(S)	**Sadness In A Song**	1962	10.00	25.00

— *Original Columbia albums above have three white "eye" logos on each side of the spindle hole.*—

Columbia CL-2059	(M)	**I Love A Song**	1963	6.00	15.00
Columbia CS-8859	(S)	**I Love A Song**	1963	8.00	20.00
Columbia CL-2278	(M)	**Trouble And Me**	1965	6.00	15.00
Columbia CS-9078	(S)	**Trouble And Me**	1965	8.00	20.00
Columbia CL-2377	(M)	**Stonewall Jackson's Greatest Hits**	1965	5.00	12.00
Columbia CS-9177	(S)	**Stonewall Jackson's Greatest Hits**	1965	6.00	15.00
Columbia CL-2509	(M)	**All's Fair In Love 'N' War**	1966	5.00	12.00
Columbia CS-9309	(S)	**All's Fair In Love 'N' War**	1966	6.00	15.00
Columbia CL-2674	(M)	**Help Stamp Out Loneliness**	1967	5.00	12.00
Columbia CS-9474	(S)	**Help Stamp Out Loneliness**	1967	6.00	15.00
Columbia CL-2762	(M)	**Stonewall Jackson Country**	1967	5.00	12.00
Columbia CS-9562	(S)	**Stonewall Jackson Country**	1967	6.00	15.00
Columbia CL-2869	(M)	**Nothing Takes The Place Of Loving You**	1968	10.00	25.00
Columbia CS-9669	(S)	**Nothing Takes The Place Of Loving You**	1968	6.00	15.00

— *Columbia albums above have "360 Sound" on the bottom of the label.*—

JACKSON, WALTER

OKeh OKM-12107	(M)	**It's All Over**	1965	5.00	12.00
OKeh OKS-14107	(S)	**It's All Over**	1965	6.00	15.00
OKeh OKM-12108	(M)	**Welcome Home**	1965	5.00	12.00
OKeh OKS-14108	(S)	**Welcome Home**	1965	6.00	15.00
OKeh OKM-12120	(M)	**Speak Her Name**	1967	5.00	12.00
OKeh OKS-14120	(S)	**Speak Her Name**	1967	6.00	15.00
OKeh OKS-14128	(S)	**Walter Jackson's Greatest Hits**	1969	5.00	12.00

JACKSON, WANDA (& THE PARTY TIMERS)

Capitol T-1041	(M)	**Wanda Jackson**	1958	75.00	150.00
Capitol T-1384	(M)	**Rockin' With Wanda!**	1960	150.00	250.00

("Rockin'" is a collection of her earlier rockabilly singles.
Reissued on Capitol's Starline label, listed below.)

Capitol T-1384	(M)	**Rockin' With Wanda!** *(Gold Starline label)*	1962	75.00	150.00
Capitol T-1384	(M)	**Rockin' With Wanda!** *(Black Starline label)*	1963	20.00	50.00

Label & Catalog #		Title	Year	VG+	NM
Capitol T-1511	(M)	There's A Party Goin' On	1961	50.00	100.00
Capitol ST-1511	(S)	There's A Party Goin' On	1961	75.00	150.00
Capitol T-1596	(M)	Right Or Wrong	1961	16.00	40.00
Capitol ST-1596	(S)	Right Or Wrong	1961	20.00	50.00

— *Original Capitol albums above have black labels with the Capitol logo on the side.* —

Decca DL-4224	(M)	Lovin' Country Style	1962	20.00	50.00
Capitol T-1776	(M)	Wonderful Wanda	1962	8.00	20.00
Capitol ST-1776	(S)	Wonderful Wanda	1962	12.00	30.00
Capitol T-1911	(M)	Love Me Forever	1963	8.00	20.00
Capitol ST-1911	(S)	Love Me Forever	1963	12.00	30.00
Capitol T-2030	(M)	Two Sides Of Wanda Jackson	1964	12.00	30.00
Capitol ST-2030	(S)	Two Sides Of Wanda Jackson	1964	16.00	40.00
Capitol T-2306	(M)	Blues In My Heart	1964	12.00	30.00
Capitol ST-2306	(S)	Blues In My Heart	1964	16.00	40.00
Capitol T-2438	(M)	Wanda Jackson Sings Country Songs	1966	8.00	20.00
Capitol ST-2438	(S)	Wanda Jackson Sings Country Songs	1966	12.00	30.00
Capitol T-2606	(M)	Salutes The Country Music Hall Of Fame	1966	6.00	15.00
Capitol ST-2606	(S)	Salutes The Country Music Hall Of Fame	1966	8.00	20.00
Capitol T-2704	(M)	Reckless Love Affair	1967	5.00	12.00
Capitol ST-2704	(S)	Reckless Love Affair	1967	6.00	15.00
Capitol T-2812	(M)	You'll Always Have My Love	1967	5.00	12.00
Capitol ST-2812	(S)	You'll Always Have My Love	1967	6.00	15.00
Capitol T-2883	(M)	The Best Of Wanda Jackson	1967	5.00	12.00
Capitol ST-2883	(S)	The Best Of Wanda Jackson	1967	6.00	15.00
Capitol ST-2976	(S)	Cream Of The Crop	1968	6.00	15.00

— *Original Capitol albums above have black labels with the Capitol logo on top.* —

JACKSON FIVE, THE [THE JACKSONS]
The Jacksons feature Jackie, Jermaine and Michael Jackson.

Motown MS-700	(S)	Diana Ross Presents The Jackson Five	1969	8.00	20.00
Motown MS-709	(S)	ABC	1970	6.00	15.00
Motown MS-718	(S)	The Jackson Five's Third Album	1970	6.00	15.00
Motown MS-735	(S)	Maybe Tomorrow	1971	5.00	12.00
Motown M-741	(S)	The Jackson Five's Greatest Hits	1971	5.00	12.00
Motown M-742	(S)	Goin' Back To Indiana	1971	5.00	12.00
Epic PAL-34835	(DJ)	Goin' Places (Picture disc)	1978	6.00	15.00
Epic HE-46424	(S)	Triumph (Half-speed master)	1981	14.00	35.00
Epic 8E8-39576	(S)	Victory (Picture disc)	1984	4.00	10.00

JACKSON HEIGHTS

Mercury SR-61331	(S)	King Progress	1970	10.00	25.00
Verve V6-5089	(S)	Jackson Heights	1973	8.00	20.00

JACOBS, HANK

Sue 1023	(M)	So Far Away	1964	12.00	30.00

JADE

Gar 11311	(M)	The Faces Of Jade	196?	14.00	35.00

JADE STONE & LUV

Jade JS-4351	(S)	Mosaics-Pieces Of Stone	1977	50.00	100.00

JADES, THE

Jarrett 21517	(M)	Live At The Disc A-Go-Go	196?	50.00	100.00

JAGGER, MICK
Mick Jagger is a member of The Rolling Stones.

Warner Bros. BS-1846	(S)	Performance (Soundtrack)	1970	10.00	25.00
Warner Bros. BS-2554	(S)	Performance (Soundtrack)	1972	5.00	12.00
United Arts. UAS-5213	(S)	Ned Kelly (Soundtrack)	1970	6.00	15.00
Rolling Stones PRB-164	(DJ)	Interview With Mick Jagger (White label)	1971	100.00	200.00
Rolling Stones PRB-164	(DJ)	Interview With Mick Jagger (Yellow label)	1971	600	120.00

JAIM

Ethereal 1001	(S)	Prophesy Fulfilled	1970	20.00	50.00

JALOPY FIVE, THE

Compatible C-561	(M)	I Love That West Coast Sound	1965	5.00	12.00
Compatible CS-561	(S)	I Love That West Coast Sound	1965	6.00	15.00

Label & Catalog #		Title	Year	VG+	NM
JAMES, DIAN, & THE GREENBRIAR BOYS					
Elektra EKL-233	(M)	**Dian & The Greenbriar Boys**	1963	5.00	12.00
Elektra EKS-7233	(S)	**Dian & The Greenbriar Boys**	1963	6.00	15.00
JAMES, ELMORE					
Crown CLP-5168	(M)	**Blues After Hours**	1961	35.00	70.00
Sphere Sound SR-7002	(M)	**The Sky Is Crying**	1965	14.00	35.00
Sphere Sound SSR-7002	(S)	**The Sky Is Crying**	1965	20.00	50.00
Sphere Sound SR-7008	(M)	**I Need You**	1966	14.00	35.00
Sphere Sound SSR-7008	(S)	**I Need You**	1966	20.00	50.00
Kent KLP-5022	(M)	**Original Folk Blues**	1964	16.00	40.00
Kent KLP-9001	(M)	**Anthology Of The Blues Legend**	196?	10.00	25.00
Kent KLP-9010	(M)	**The Resurrection Of Elmore James**	196?	10.00	25.00
Chess 1537	(S)	**Whose Muddy Shoes**	1969	10.00	25.00
Bell 6037	(S)	**Elmore James**	1969	10.00	25.00
JAMES, ETTA					
Argo LP-4003	(M)	**At Last**	1961	8.00	20.00
Argo LPS-4003	(S)	**At Last**	1961	12.00	30.00
Argo LP-4011	(M)	**The Second Time Around**	1961	8.00	20.00
Argo LPS-4011	(S)	**The Second Time Around**	1961	12.00	30.00
Argo LP-4013	(M)	**Etta James**	1962	8.00	20.00
Argo LPS-4013	(S)	**Etta James**	1962	12.00	30.00
Argo LP-4018	(M)	**Etta James Sings For Lovers**	1962	8.00	20.00
Argo LPS-4018	(S)	**Etta James Sings For Lovers**	1962	12.00	30.00
Argo LP-4025	(M)	**Top Ten**	1963	8.00	20.00
Argo LPS-4025	(S)	**Top Ten**	1963	12.00	30.00
Argo LP-4032	(M)	**Etta James Rocks The House**	1964	8.00	20.00
Argo LPS-4032	(S)	**Etta James Rocks The House**	1964	12.00	30.00
Argo LP-4040	(M)	**The Queen Of Soul**	1965	8.00	20.00
Argo LPS-4040	(S)	**The Queen Of Soul**	1965	12.00	30.00
Cadet LPS-4003	(S)	**At Last**	1969	5.00	12.00
Cadet LPS-4011	(S)	**The Second Time Around**	1969	5.00	12.00
Cadet LPS-4013	(S)	**Etta James**	1969	5.00	12.00
Cadet LPS-4018	(S)	**Etta James Sings For Lovers**	1969	5.00	12.00
Cadet LPS-4025	(S)	**Top Ten**	1969	5.00	12.00
Cadet LPS-4032	(S)	**Etta James Rocks The House**	1969	5.00	12.00
Cadet LPS-4040	(S)	**The Queen Of Soul**	1969	5.00	12.00
Chess 2CH-60004	(S)	**Praches** (2 LPs)	1971	6.00	15.00
Chess CH-50042	(S)	**Etta James**	1973	4.00	10.00
Chess 2CH-60029	(S)	**Come A Little Bit Closer** (2 LPs)	1974	6.00	15.00
JAMES, JIMMY, & THE VAGABONDS					
Atco 33-222	(M)	**The New Religion**	1967	5.00	12.00
Atco SD-33-222	(S)	**The New Religion**	1967	6.00	15.00
JAMES, JONI					
MGM E-222 (10")	(M)	**Let There Be Love**	1955	20.00	50.00
MGM E-234 (10")	(M)	**Award Winning Album**	1955	20.00	50.00
MGM E-272 (10")	(M)	**Little Girl Blue**	1955	20.00	50.00
MGM E-3328	(M)	**In The Still Of The Night**	1956	16.00	40.00
MGM E-3240	(M)	**When I Fall In Love**	1955	16.00	40.00
MGM E-3346	(M)	**Award Winning Album**	1956	16.00	40.00
MGM E-3347	(M)	**Little Girl Blue**	1956	16.00	40.00
MGM E-3348	(M)	**Let There Be Love**	1956	16.00	40.00
MGM E-3349	(M)	**Songs By Victor Young And Frank Loesser**	1956	16.00	40.00
MGM E-3468	(M)	**Merry Christmas From Joni**	1957	16.00	40.00
MGM E-3528	(M)	**Give Us This Day**	1957	16.00	40.00
MGM E-3533	(M)	**Songs By Kern & Warren**	1957	16.00	40.00
		— Original MGM albums above have yellow labels.—			
MGM E-3739	(M)	**Songs Of Hank Williams**	1959	12.00	30.00
MGM SE-3739	(S)	**Songs Of Hank Williams**	1959	16.00	40.00
MGM E-3749	(M)	**Irish Favorites**	1959	8.00	20.00
MGM SE-3749	(S)	**Irish Favorites**	1959	12.00	30.00
MGM E-3755	(M)	**100 Strings And Joni**	1959	8.00	20.00
MGM SE-3755	(S)	**100 Strings And Joni**	1959	12.00	30.00
MGM E-3772	(M)	**Joni James Swings Sweet**	1959	8.00	20.00
MGM SE-3772	(S)	**Joni James Swings Sweet**	1959	12.00	30.00

Label & Catalog #		Title	Year	VG+	NM
MGM E-3800	(M)	Joni James At Carnegie Hall	1959	8.00	20.00
MGM SE-3800	(S)	Joni James At Carnegie Hall	1959	12.00	30.00
MGM E-3837	(M)	I'm In The Mood For Love	1960	8.00	20.00
MGM SE-3837	(S)	I'm In The Mood For Love	1960	10.00	25.00
MGM E-3839	(M)	100 Strings And Joni On Broadway	1960	8.00	20.00
MGM SE-3839	(S)	100 Strings And Joni On Broadway	1960	10.00	25.00
MGM E-3840	(M)	Joni James Sings Hollywood	1960	8.00	20.00
MGM SE-3840	(S)	Joni James Sings Hollywood	1960	10.00	25.00
MGM E-3885	(M)	More Joni Hits	1960	8.00	20.00
MGM SE-3885	(S)	More Joni Hits	1960	10.00	25.00
MGM E-3892	(M)	100 Voices, 100 Strings	1960	8.00	20.00
MGM SE-3892	(S)	100 Voices, 100 Strings	1960	10.00	25.00
MGM E-3958	(M)	Folk Songs By Joni James	1961	8.00	20.00
MGM SE-3958	(S)	Folk Songs By Joni James	1961	10.00	25.00
MGM E-3987	(M)	The Mood Is Swinging	1961	8.00	20.00
MGM SE-3987	(S)	The Mood Is Swinging	1961	10.00	25.00
MGM E-3990	(M)	The Mood Is Romance	1961	8.00	20.00
MGM SE-3990	(S)	The Mood Is Romance	1961	10.00	25.00
MGM E-3991	(M)	The Mood Is Blue	1961	8.00	20.00
MGM SE-3991	(S)	The Mood Is Blue	1961	10.00	25.00
MGM E-4053	(M)	I Feel A Song Comin' On	1962	8.00	20.00
MGM SE-4053	(S)	I Feel A Song Comin' On	1962	10.00	25.00
MGM E-4054	(M)	I'm Your Girl	1962	8.00	20.00
MGM SE-4054	(S)	I'm Your Girl	1962	10.00	25.00
MGM E-4088	(M)	After Hours	1962	8.00	20.00
MGM SE-4088	(S)	After Hours	1962	10.00	25.00
MGM E-4101	(M)	Country Girl Style	1962	8.00	20.00
MGM SE-4101	(S)	Country Girl Style	1962	10.00	25.00
MGM E-4151	(M)	The Very Best Of Joni James	1963	8.00	20.00
MGM SE-4151	(S)	The Very Best Of Joni James	1963	10.00	25.00
MGM E-4158	(M)	Something For The Boys	1963	8.00	20.00
MGM SE-4158	(S)	Something For The Boys	1963	10.00	25.00
MGM E-4182	(M)	Three O' Clock In The Morning	1963	8.00	20.00
MGM SE-4182	(S)	Three O' Clock In The Morning	1963	10.00	25.00
MGM E-4200	(M)	My Favorite Things	1963	8.00	20.00
MGM SE-4200	(S)	My Favorite Things	1963	10.00	25.00
MGM E-4208	(M)	Italianissime!	1963	8.00	20.00
MGM E-4208	(S)	Italianissime!	1963	10.00	25.00
MGM E-4248	(M)	Put On A Happy Face	1964	8.00	20.00
MGM SE-4248	(S)	Put On A Happy Face	1964	10.00	25.00
MGM E-4255	(M)	Joni James Sings The Gershwins	1964	8.00	20.00
MGM SE-4255	(S)	Joni James Sings The Gershwins	1964	10.00	25.00
MGM E-4263	(M)	Beyond The Reef	1964	8.00	20.00
MGM SE-4263	(S)	Beyond The Reef	1964	10.00	25.00
MGM E-4286	(M)	Bossa Nova Style	1965	8.00	20.00
MGM SE-4286	(S)	Bossa Nova Style	1965	10.00	25.00
		— Original MGM albums above have black labels.—			

JAMES, LEONARD

Label & Catalog #		Title	Year	VG+	NM
Decca DL-8772	(M)	Boppin' And A Strollin'	1958	20.00	50.00

JAMES, NICKY

Label & Catalog #		Title	Year	VG+	NM
Threshold 19	(DJ)	Thunderthroat	1976	8.00	20.00

JAMES, SKIP

Label & Catalog #		Title	Year	VG+	NM
Vanguard VSR-9219	(M)	Skip James Today!	1966	8.00	20.00
Vanguard VSD-79219	(S)	Skip James Today!	1966	10.00	25.00
Vanguard VSD-79273	(S)	Devil Got My Woman	1968	8.00	20.00

JAMES, SONNY

Label & Catalog #		Title	Year	VG+	NM
Capitol T-779	(M)	The Southern Gentleman	1957	16.00	40.00
Capitol T-867	(M)	Sonny	1957	16.00	40.00
Capitol T-988	(M)	Honey	1958	16.00	40.00
Capitol T-1178	(M)	This Is Sonny James	1959	16.00	40.00
		— Original Capitol albums above have turquoise labels.—			
Dot DLP-3462	(M)	Young Love	1962	8.00	20.00
Dot DLP-25462	(S)	Young Love	1962	12.00	30.00
Capitol T-2017	(M)	The Minute You're Gone	1964	5.00	12.00
Capitol ST-2017	(S)	The Minute You're Gone	1964	6.00	15.00

Label & Catalog #		Title	Year	VG+	NM
Capitol T-2209	(M)	You're The Only World I Know	1965	5.00	12.00
Capitol ST-2209	(S)	You're The Only World I Know	1965	6.00	15.00
Capitol T-2317	(M)	I'll Keep Holding On	1965	5.00	12.00
Capitol ST-2317	(S)	I'll Keep Holding On	1965	6.00	15.00
Capitol T-2415	(M)	Behind The Tear	1965	5.00	12.00
Capitol ST-2415	(S)	Behind The Tear	1965	6.00	15.00
Capitol T-2500	(M)	True Love's A Blessing	1966	5.00	12.00
Capitol ST-2500	(S)	True Love's A Blessing	1966	6.00	15.00
Capitol T-2561	(M)	Till The Last Leaf Shall Fall	1966	5.00	12.00
Capitol ST-2561	(S)	Till The Last Leaf Shall Fall	1966	6.00	15.00
Capitol T-2589	(M)	My Christmas Dream	1966	5.00	12.00
Capitol ST-2589	(S)	My Christmas Dream	1966	6.00	15.00
Capitol T-2615	(M)	The Best Of Sonny James	1966	5.00	12.00
Capitol ST-2615	(P)	The Best Of Sonny James	1966	6.00	15.00
Capitol T-2703	(M)	Need You	1967	5.00	12.00
Capitol ST-2703	(S)	Need You	1967	6.00	15.00
Capitol T-2788	(M)	I'll Never Find Another You	1967	5.00	12.00
Capitol ST-2788	(S)	I'll Never Find Another You	1967	6.00	15.00
Capitol ST-2884	(S)	A World Of Our Own	1968	5.00	12.00
Capitol ST-2937	(S)	Heaven Says Hello	1968	5.00	12.00

— Original Capitol albums above have black labels with the Capitol logo on top.—

JAMES, TOMMY, & THE SHONDELLS

Roulette R-25336	(M)	Hanky Panky	1966	8.00	20.00
Roulette SR-25336	(P)	Hanky Panky	1966	10.00	25.00
Roulette R-25344	(M)	It's Only Love	1967	6.00	15.00
Roulette SR-25344	(S)	It's Only Love	1967	8.00	20.00
Roulette R-25353	(M)	I Think We're Alone Now	1967	6.00	15.00
Roulette SR-25353	(P)	I Think We're Alone Now (Photo cover)	1967	8.00	20.00
Roulette SR-25353	(P)	I Think We're Alone Now (Footprint cover)	1968	6.00	15.00
Roulette SR-25355	(P)	Something Special!	1968	5.00	12.00
Roulette SR-25357	(S)	Gettin' Together	1968	5.00	12.00
Roulette SR-42012	(P)	Mony Mony	1968	6.00	15.00
Roulette SR-42023	(S)	Crimson And Clover	1968	6.00	15.00
Roulette SR-42030	(S)	Cellophane Symphony	1969	6.00	15.00
Roulette SR-42040	(P)	The Best Of Tommy James & The Shondells	1969	4.00	10.00
Roulette SR-42044	(S)	Travelin'	1970	4.00	10.00

JAN & DEAN
Jan Berry and Dean Torrence.

Dore 101	(M)	Jan & Dean (Light blue label)	1960	75.00	150.00
		(Issued with a bonus photo, priced separately below.)			
Dore 101		Jan & Dean Bonus Photo	1960	75.00	150.00
Liberty LRP-3248	(M)	Jan & Dean's Golden Hits	1962	14.00	35.00
Liberty LST-7248	(P)	Jan & Dean's Golden Hits	1962	16.00	40.00
Liberty LRP-3294	(M)	Jan & Dean Take Linda Surfing	1963	16.00	40.00
Liberty LST-7294	(S)	Jan & Dean Take Linda Surfing	1963	20.00	50.00
		(The Beach Boys provide backing on several tracks.)			
Liberty LRP-3314	(M)	Surf City	1963	12.00	30.00
Liberty LST-7314	(S)	Surf City	1963	16.00	40.00
Liberty LRP-3339	(M)	Drag City	1963	8.00	20.00
Liberty LST-7339	(S)	Drag City	1963	12.00	30.00
L-J 101	(M)	Jan & Dean With The Soul Surfers	1963	8.00	20.00
Inter. Award AKS-250	(M)	Jan & Dean & The Satellites	196?	6.00	15.00
Liberty LRP-3361	(M)	Dead Man's Curve/New Girl In School	1964	16.00	40.00
Liberty LST-7361	(S)	Dead Man's Curve/New Girl In School	1964	20.00	50.00
		(The cover photo is black & white with pink overtones.)			
Liberty LRP-3361	(M)	Dead Man's Curve/New Girl In School	1964	12.00	30.00
Liberty LST-7361	(S)	Dead Man's Curve/New Girl In School	1964	16.00	40.00
		(The cover photo is full color.)			
Liberty LRP-3361	(M)	New Girl In School/Dead Man's Curve	1964	8.00	20.00
Liberty LST-7361	(S)	New Girl In School/Dead Man's Curve	1964	12.00	30.00
Liberty LRP-3368	(M)	Ride The Wild Surf (Soundtrack)	1964	12.00	30.00
Liberty LST-7368	(S)	Ride The Wild Surf (Soundtrack)	1964	16.00	40.00
Liberty LRP-3377	(M)	Little Old Lady From Pasadena	1964	8.00	20.00
Liberty LST-7377	(S)	Little Old Lady From Pasadena	1964	10.00	25.00
Liberty LRP-3403	(M)	Command Performance	1965	8.00	20.00
Liberty LST-7403	(S)	Command Performance	1965	10.00	25.00

Label & Catalog #		Title	Year	VG+	NM
Liberty LRP-3414	(M)	Jan & Dean's Pop Symphony No.1	1965	20.00	50.00
Liberty LST-7414	(S)	Jan & Dean's Pop Symphony No.1	1965	50.00	100.00
Liberty LRP-3417	(M)	Jan & Dean's Golden Hits, Volume 2	1965	8.00	20.00
Liberty LRP-7417	(S)	Jan & Dean's Golden Hits, Volume 2	1965	10.00	25.00
Liberty LRP-3431	(M)	Folk 'N' Roll	1965	8.00	20.00
Liberty LST-7431	(S)	Folk 'N' Roll	1965	10.00	25.00
Liberty LRP-3441	(M)	Filet Of Soul	1966	8.00	20.00
Liberty LST-7441	(S)	Filet Of Soul	1966	10.00	25.00
Liberty LRP-3444	(M)	Jan & Dean Meet Batman	1966	20.00	50.00
Liberty LST-7444	(S)	Jan & Dean Meet Batman	1966	30.00	60.00
Liberty LRP-3458	(M)	Popsicle	1966	12.00	30.00
Liberty LST-7458	(S)	Popsicle	1966	12.00	30.00
Liberty LRP-3460	(M)	Jan & Dean's Golden Hits, Volume 3	1966	8.00	20.00
Liberty LST-7460	(S)	Jan & Dean's Golden Hits, Volume 3	1966	10.00	25.00
Columbia CL-2661	(M)	Save For A Rainy Day	1967	See note below	
Columbia CS-9461	(S)	Save For A Rainy Day	1967	See note below	
		(A U.S. pressing of this album is not known to exist.)			
J&D 101	(M)	Save For A Rainy Day	1967	100.00	200.00
United Arts. UAS-9961	(P)	The Jan And Dean Anthology Album (2 LPs)	1971	8.00	20.00
United Arts. UA-341	(P)	Gotta Take That One Last Ride (2 LPs)	1971	5.00	12.00
Deadman's Curve	(M)	Live At The Keystone Berkeley	1981	12.00	30.00
		(Issued in plain cardboard jackets with inserts.)			
Deadman's Curve	(M)	Live At The Keystone Berkeley	1981	8.00	20.00
		(Front and backs pasted on.)			
JANIS, JOHNNY					
ABC-Paramount 140	(M)	For The First Time	1956	20.00	50.00
Columbia CL-1674	(M)	The Start Of Something New	1961	6.00	15.00
Columbia CS-8474	(S)	The Start Of Something New	1961	8.00	20.00
Monument MLP-8036	(M)	Once In A Blue Moon	1965	6.00	15.00
Monument SLP-18036	(S)	Once In A Blue Moon	1965	8.00	20.00
JANSSEN, DAVID					
Epic LN-24150	(M)	Hidden Island	1965	6.00	15.00
Epic BN-26150	(S)	Hidden Island	1965	8.00	20.00
JASPER WRAITH					
Sunflower SNF-5003	(S)	Jasper Wraith (With insert)	1971	8.00	20.00
JAY & THE AMERICANS					
United Arts. UAL-3222	(M)	She Cried	1962	8.00	20.00
United Arts. UAS-6222	(S)	She Cried	1962	12.00	30.00
United Arts. UAL-3300	(M)	At The Cafe Wha?	1963	8.00	20.00
United Arts. UAS-6300	(S)	At The Cafe Wha?	1963	12.00	30.00
United Arts. UAL-3407	(M)	Come A Little Bit Closer	1964	6.00	15.00
United Arts. UAS-6407	(S)	Come A Little Bit Closer	1964	8.00	20.00
United Arts. UAL-3417	(M)	Blockbusters	1965	6.00	15.00
United Arts. UAS-6417	(S)	Blockbusters	1965	8.00	20.00
United Arts. UAL-3453	(M)	Jay & The Americans' Greatest Hits	1965	5.00	12.00
United Arts. UAS-6453	(P)	Jay & The Americans' Greatest Hits	1965	6.00	15.00
United Arts. UAL-3474	(M)	Sunday And Me	1966	5.00	12.00
United Arts. UAS-6474	(S)	Sunday And Me	1966	6.00	15.00
United Arts. UAL-3534	(M)	Livin' Above Your Head	1966	5.00	12.00
United Arts. UAS-6534	(S)	Livin' Above Your Head	1966	6.00	15.00
United Arts. UAL-3555	(M)	Jay & The Americans' Greatest Hits, Vol. 2	1966	5.00	12.00
United Arts. UAS-6555	(S)	Jay & The Americans' Greatest Hits, Vol. 2	1966	6.00	15.00
United Arts. UAL-3562	(M)	Try Some Of This	1967	5.00	12.00
United Arts. UAS-6562	(S)	Try Some Of This	1967	6.00	15.00
		— Original U.A. albums above have black labels.—			
United Arts. UAS-6671	(S)	Sands Of Time	1969	5.00	12.00
United Arts. UAS-6719	(S)	Wax Museum	1970	5.00	12.00
United Arts. UAS-6751	(S)	Wax Museum, Volume 2	1970	5.00	12.00
United Arts. UAS-6762	(S)	Capture The Moment	1970	5.00	12.00
JAY & THE TECHNIQUES					
Smash MGS-27095	(M)	Apples, Peaches, Pumpkin Pie	1967	6.00	15.00
Smash SRS-67095	(S)	Apples, Peaches, Pumpkin Pie	1967	8.00	20.00
Smash SRS-67102	(S)	Love Lost And Found	1968	8.00	20.00

Label & Catalog #		Title	Year	VG+	NM

JAYNETTES, THE

| Tuff LP-13 | (M) | Sally Go Round The Roses | 1963 | 90.00 | 180.00 |

JEFFERSON

| Janus JLS-3006 | (S) | Baby, Take Me In Your Arms | 1969 | 10.00 | 25.00 |

JEFFERSON, BLIND LEMON

Riverside 1014 (10")	(M)	The Folk Blues Of Blind Lemon Jefferson	1953	75.00	150.00
Riverside 1053 (10")	(M)	Penitentiary Blues	1955	75.00	150.00
Riverside RLP-12-125	(M)	Classic Folk Blues	1957	20.00	50.00
Riverside RLP-12-126	(M)	Blind Lemon Jefferson	1957	20.00	50.00

JEFFERSON, EDDIE

| Riverside 411 | (M) | Letter From Home | 1962 | 10.00 | 25.00 |
| Riverside 9411 | (S) | Letter From Home | 1962 | 12.00 | 30.00 |

JEFFERSON AIRPLANE, THE

The original Airplane (RCA 3584) was Signe Andersson, Marty Balin, Jack Casady, Paul Kantner, Jorma Kaukonen and Alexander Spence. Andersson and Spence were replaced by Grace Slick and Spencer Dryden. Refer to The Great Society; Hot Tuna.

| RCA Victor LPM-3584 | (M) | The Jefferson Airplane Takes Off! | 1966 | | See note below |

> (LPM-3584 was originally issued with several alternate takes and "Runnin' Round The World," which was deleted from all subsequent pressings. Stereo copies are not known to exist. Estimated near mint value $1,000-2,000.)

| RCA Victor LPM-3584 | (M) | The Jefferson Airplane Takes Off! | 1966 | 10.00 | 25.00 |
| RCA Victor LSP-3584 | (S) | The Jefferson Airplane Takes Off! | 1966 | 8.00 | 20.00 |

A quintessential example of San Francisco psychedelia, "Surrealistic Pillow" is sought after in its original mono mix, which is a cleaner, more forceful musical statement than the more common stereo mix.

RCA Victor LPM-3766	(M)	Surrealistic Pillow	1967	16.00	40.00
RCA Victor LSP-3766	(S)	Surrealistic Pillow	1967	10.00	25.00
RCA Victor LCO-1511	(M)	After Bathing At Baxter's	1967	10.00	25.00
RCA Victor LOS-1511	(S)	After Bathing At Baxter's	1967	8.00	20.00
RCA Victor LSP-4058	(S)	Crown Of Creation	1968	6.00	15.00

— Original RCA albums above have black labels. —

Label & Catalog #		Title	Year	VG+	NM
RCA Victor LSP-4133	(S)	**Bless Its Pointed Little Head** (Orange label)	1969	6.00	15.00
RCA Victor LSP-4238	(S)	**Volunteers** (Orange label)	1969	5.00	12.00
RCA Victor LSP-4448	(DJ)	**Blows Against The Empire** (Clear vinyl)	1970	75.00	150.00
RCA Victor LSP-4448	(S)	**Blows Against The Empire** (Orange label)	1970	5.00	12.00
Grunt FTR-1001	(S)	**Bark** (Issued in a brown paper bag)	1971	6.00	15.00
RCA Victor APD1-0320	(Q)	**Volunteers**	1973	8.00	20.00
JEFFERSON STARSHIP, THE					
Grunt BFD1-0717	(Q)	**Dragonfly**	1974	6.00	15.00
Grunt BFD1-0999	(Q)	**Red Octopus**	1975	6.00	15.00
Grunt BFD1-1557	(Q)	**Spitfire**	1976	6.00	15.00
Grunt CYL1-3363	(S)	**Gold** (Picture disc)	1976	4.00	10.00
JEFFREY, JOE					
Wand WDS-686	(S)	**My Pledge Of Love**	1969	8.00	20.00
JELLY BEAN BANDITS, THE					
Mainstream 56103	(M)	**Jelly Bean Bandits**	1967	14.00	35.00
Mainstream S-6103	(S)	**Jelly Bean Bandits**	1967	16.00	40.00
JELLYBREAD					
Blue Horizon BH-4801	(S)	**First Slice**	1970	8.00	20.00
JELLYROLL					
Kapp KS-3626	(S)	**Jellyroll**	1971	8.00	20.00
JENNINGS, WAYLON					
Bat 1001	(M)	**Waylon Jennings At JD's**	1964	240.00	400.00
Sounds 1001	(M)	**Waylon Jennings At JD's**	1964	50.00	100.00
RCA Victor LPM-3523	(M)	**Folk Country**	1966	8.00	20.00
RCA Victor LSP-3523	(S)	**Folk Country**	1966	10.00	25.00
RCA Victor LPM-3620	(M)	**Leavin' Town**	1966	8.00	20.00
RCA Victor LSP-3620	(S)	**Leavin' Town**	1966	10.00	25.00
RCA Victor LPM-3660	(M)	**Waylon Sings Ol' Harlan**	1967	12.00	30.00
RCA Victor LSP-3660	(S)	**Waylon Sings Ol' Harlan**	1967	16.00	40.00
RCA Victor LPM-3736	(M)	**Nashville Rebel** (Soundtrack)	1967	6.00	15.00
RCA Victor LSP-3736	(S)	**Nashville Rebel** (Soundtrack)	1967	8.00	20.00
RCA Victor LPM-3825	(M)	**Love Of The Common People**	1967	5.00	12.00
RCA Victor LSP-3825	(S)	**Love Of The Common People**	1967	6.00	15.00
RCA Victor LPM-3918	(M)	**Hangin' On**	1968	20.00	50.00
RCA Victor LSP-3918	(S)	**Hangin' On**	1968	6.00	15.00
RCA Victor LSP-4023	(S)	**Only The Greatest**	1968	6.00	15.00
		— Original RCA albums above have black labels.—			
A&M SP-4238	(S)	**Don't Think Twice**	1969	12.00	30.00
RCA Victor SPS-570	(DJ)	**Get Into Waylon Jennings**	1972	20.00	50.00
RCA Victor CPL1-3406	(S)	**Greatest Hits** (Picture disc)	1979	4.00	10.00
JENSEN, KRIS					
Hickory MH-110	(M)	**Torture**	1962	20.00	50.00
JESSE & THE BANDITS					
Re-Car 2001	(M)	**Top Teen Hits**	1965	50.00	100.00
JETHRO TULL					
Reprise RS-6336	(S)	**This Was**	1969	8.00	20.00
Reprise RS-6360	(S)	**Stand Up**	1969	8.00	20.00
		(Gatefold cover with a stand-up of the group on the inside.)			
Reprise RS-6400	(S)	**Benefit**	1970	6.00	15.00
Reprise MS-2035	(S)	**Aqualung**	1971	6.00	15.00
Reprise MS-2072	(DJ)	**Thick As A Brick** (Air-play sampler)	1972	12.00	30.00
Reprise MS-2072	(S)	**Thick As A Brick** (With booklet)	1972	6.00	15.00
Reprise MS-2106	(S)	**Living In The Past** (With booklet)	1972	6.00	15.00
Chrysalis CHR-1040	(DJ)	**A Passion Play** (Edited for airplay)	1973	10.00	25.00
Chrysalis CHR-1040	(S)	**A Passion Play** (With booklet)	1973	6.00	15.00
Chrysalis CH4-1044	(Q)	**Aqualung**	1973	10.00	25.00
Chrysalis CH4-1067	(Q)	**War Child**	1974	10.00	25.00
Mobile Fidelity MFSL-061	(S)	**Aqualung**	1980	30.00	60.00
Mobile Fidelity MFSL-092	(S)	**The Broadsword And The Beast**	1982	10.00	25.00
Mobile Fidelity MFSL-187	(S)	**Thick As A Brick**	1982	8.00	20.00

Label & Catalog #		Title	Year	VG+	NM
JETSONS, THE					
Colpix CP-213	(M)	**The Jetsons** (TV Soundtrack)	196?	50.00	100.00
HBR HLP-2037	(M)	**First Family On The Moon**	196?	30.00	60.00
JIM & JEAN					
Phillips PHM-600182	(M)	**Jim And Jean**	1965	5.00	12.00
Phillips PHS-600182	(S)	**Jim And Jean**	1965	6.00	15.00
Folkways FT-3001	(M)	**Changes**	1966	5.00	12.00
Folkways FTS-3001	(S)	**Changes**	1966	6.00	15.00
Forecast FT-3015	(M)	**People World**	1967	5.00	12.00
Forecast FTS-3015	(S)	**People World**	1967	6.00	15.00
JIVE FIVE, THE					
United Arts. UAL-3455	(M)	**The Jive Five**	1965	12.00	30.00
United Arts. UAS-6455	(S)	**The Jive Five**	1965	14.00	35.00
Ambient Sound 37717	(S)	**Here We Are**	1982	4.00	10.00
JOEL, BILLY					
Billy Joel originally recorded with The Hassles; Attila.					
Family Prod. 2700	(S)	**Cold Spring Harbor** (Color label)	1971	20.00	50.00
Columbia CQ-32544	(Q)	**Piano Man**	1974	6.00	15.00
Columbia PCQ-33146	(Q)	**Streetlife Serenade**	1974	6.00	15.00
Columbia PCQ-33848	(Q)	**Turnstiles**	1976	6.00	15.00
Columbia AS-326	(DJ)	**Souvenir**	1976	10.00	25.00
Columbia HC-34987	(S)	**The Stranger** (Half-speed master)	1981	16.00	40.00
Columbia HC-44987	(S)	**The Stranger** (Half-speed master)	1982	12.00	30.00
Columbia HC-45609	(S)	**52nd Street** (Half-speed master)	1982	12.00	30.00
Columbia HC-47461	(S)	**Songs In The Attic** (Half-speed master)	1982	10.00	25.00
Columbia HC-48837	(S)	**An Innocent Man** (Half-speed master)	1983	10.00	25.00
Columbia AS-1433	(DJ)	**Billy Joel Interview**	1982	6.00	15.00

The last vinyl release from Mobile Fidelity's Original Master Recording series, "Goodbye Yellow Brick Road" was pressed in a run of a mere 5,000 copies, guaranteeing its collectibility.

JOHN, ELTON					
Viking 105	(S)	**The Games** (Soundtrack)	1970	75.00	150.00
Uni 73090	(S)	**Elton John** (With booklet)	1970	8.00	20.00

Label & Catalog #		Title	Year	VG+	NM
Uni 73096	(S)	**Tumbleweed Connection** (With booklet)	1971	8.00	20.00
Uni 93090	(S)	**Elton John** (With booklet)	1971	6.00	15.00
Uni 93096	(S)	**Tumbleweed Connection** (With booklet)	1971	6.00	15.00
Uni 93105	(S)	**11-17-70**	1971	5.00	12.00
Uni 93120	(S)	**Madman Across The Water** (With booklet)	1971	6.00	15.00
Uni 93135	(S)	**Honky Chateau**	1972	5.00	12.00
Paramount DJ-1	(DJ)	**Friends** (Open-end interview)	1971	75.00	150.00
Paramount PAS-6004	(S)	**Friends** (Soundtrack)	1971	6.00	15.00
MCA 2100	(S)	**Don't Shoot Me, I'm Only The Piano Player**	1972	6.00	15.00
		(Solid black label with a lyric book.)			
MCA 2142	(DJ)	**Capt. Fantastic & The Brown Dirt Cowboy**	1979	150.00	250.00
		(Brown vinyl. All copies are autographed on the inside cover			
		by Elton and Bernie Taupin.)			
MCA L33-1995	(DJ)	**A Single Man** (Picture disc)	1979	16.00	40.00
MCA 14591	(S)	**A Single Man** (Picture disc)	1979	3.50	8.00
Nautilus NR-43	(S)	**Greatest Hits**	198?	14.00	35.00
Direct Disk 10003	(S)	**Goodbye Yellow Brick Road** (2 LPs)	1980	20.00	50.00
Geffen GHS-24031	(DJ)	**Breaking Hearts** (Quiex II vinyl)	1984	6.00	15.00
Mobile Fidelity MFSL-160	(S)	**Goodbye Yellow Brick Road** (2 LPs)	1990	20.00	50.00

JOHN, LITTLE WILLIE

King 395-564	(M)	**Fever** (Brown cover)	1956	180.00	300.00
King 564	(M)	**Fever** (Blue cover)	1957	75.00	150.00
King 395-596	(M)	**Talk To Me**	1958	75.00	150.00
King 603	(M)	**Mister Little Willie John**	1958	75.00	150.00
King 691	(M)	**Action**	1960	35.00	70.00
King 739	(M)	**Sure Things**	1961	20.00	50.00
King 767	(M)	**The Sweet, The Hot, The Teenage Beat**	1961	20.00	50.00
King 802	(M)	**Come On And Join Little Willie John**	1962	20.00	50.00
King 895	(M)	**These Are My Favorite Songs**	1964	20.00	50.00
King K-949	(M)	**Little Willie Sings All Originals**	1966	14.00	35.00
King KS-949	(S)	**Little Willie Sings All Originals**	1966	20.00	50.00
		—King albums above have crownless balck labels.—			
King KS-1081	(P)	**Free At Last**	1970	16.00	40.00
BluesWay 6069	(P)	**Free At Last**	1970	6.00	15.00

JOHN STREET ROCKETS, THE

Confidential SCR-5001	(S)	**Rot And Roll The Hard Way**	1979	20.00	50.00

JOHN'S CHILDREN

White Whale WWS-7128	(S)	**Orgasm**	1970	65.00	130.00

JOHNNIE & JOE

Ambient Sound 38345	(S)	**Kingdom Of Love**	1982	4.00	10.00

JOHNNY & JACK

RCA Victor LPM-1587	(M)	**The Tennessee Mountain Boys**	1957	14.00	35.00
RCA Victor LPM-2017	(M)	**Hits By Johnny And Jack**	1959	14.00	35.00
Decca DL-4308	(M)	**Smiles And Tears**	1962	6.00	15.00
Decca DL-74308	(S)	**Smiles And Tears**	1962	8.00	20.00

JOHNNY & THE BLUE BEATS

Winsor R-1001	(M)	**Smile**	196?	12.00	30.00
Winsor RL-1001	(S)	**Smile**	196?	12.00	30.00

JOHNNY & THE HURRICANES

Warwick W-2007	(M)	**Johnny & The Hurricanes**	1959	50.00	100.00
Warwick WST-2007	(P)	**Johnny & The Hurricanes**	1959	75.00	150.00
Warwick W-2010	(M)	**Stormsville**	1960	50.00	100.00
Warwick WST-2010	(S)	**Stormsville**	1960	75.00	150.00
Big Top 12-1302	(M)	**Big Sound Of Johnny & The Hurricanes**	1960	50.00	100.00
Big Top ST-1302	(S)	**Big Sound Of Johnny & The Hurricanes**	1960	75.00	150.00
Attila 1030	(M)	**Live At The Star Club**	1962	50.00	100.00

JOHNSON, BETTY

Atlantic 8017	(M)	**Betty Johnson**	1958	16.00	40.00
Atlantic 8027	(M)	**Songs You Heard When You Fell In Love**	1959	16.00	40.00

Label & Catalog #		Title	Year	VG+	NM
JOHNSON, BLIND WILLIE					
Folkways F-3585	(M)	**Blues**	1959	20.00	50.00
JOHNSON, BUBBER					
King 395-569	(M)	**Come Home**	1957	75.00	150.00
King 624	(M)	**Sings Sweet Love Songs**	1959	50.00	100.00
JOHNSON, BUDD					
Argo 736	(M)	**Ya Ya**	1964	10.00	25.00
JOHNSON, BUDDY					
Wing MGW-12005	(M)	**Rock 'N' Roll Stage Show**	1956	35.00	70.00
Mercury MG-20072	(M)	**Buddy Johnson Wails**	1958	30.00	60.00
Mercury MG-20209	(M)	**Rock 'N' Roll**	1958	30.00	60.00
Mercury MG-20322	(M)	**Walkin'**	1958	30.00	60.00
JOHNSON, BUDDY & ELLA					
Mercury MG-20347	(M)	**Swing Me**	1958	20.00	50.00
Roulette R-25085	(M)	**Go Ahead And Rock And Roll**	1959	16.00	40.00
Roulette SR-25085	(S)	**Go Ahead And Rock And Roll**	1959	20.00	50.00
JOHNSON, CANDY					
Canjo LP-1001	(M)	**The Candy Johnson Show**	1964	6.00	15.00
Canjo LP-1002	(M)	**Bikini Beach**	1964	6.00	15.00
JOHNSON, LONNIE					
King 395-520	(M)	**Lonesome Road**	1958	180.00	300.00
Bluesville BV-1007	(M)	**Blues By Lonnie Johnson**	1960	20.00	50.00
Bluesville BV-1011	(M)	**Blues And Ballads**	1960	20.00	50.00
Bluesville BV-1024	(M)	**Losing Game**	1961	20.00	50.00
Bluesville BV-1044	(M)	**Idle Hours**	1961	20.00	50.00
Bluesville BV-1054	(M)	**Woman Blues**	1963	14.00	35.00
Bluesville BV-1062	(M)	**Another Night To Cry**	1963	14.00	35.00
King K-958	(M)	**Sings 24 Twelve Bar Blues**	1966	30.00	60.00
King KS-958	(S)	**Sings 24 Twelve Bar Blues**	1966	40.00	80.00
King KS-1083	(S)	**Tomorrow Night**	1970	6.00	15.00
Prestige 7724	(S)	**Losing Game**	1969	6.00	15.00
JOHNSON, MARV					
United Arts. UAL-3081	(M)	**Marvelous Marv Johnson**	1960	20.00	50.00
United Arts. UAS-6081	(S)	**Marvelous Marv Johnson**	1960	35.00	70.00
United Arts. UAL-3118	(M)	**More Marv Johnson**	1960	20.00	50.00
United Arts. UAS-6118	(S)	**More Marv Johnson**	1960	35.00	70.00
United Arts. UAL-3187	(M)	**I Believe**	1962	18.00	45.00
United Arts. UAS-6187	(S)	**I Believe**	1962	30.00	60.00
JOHNSON, OLLIE					
RCA Victor LPM-1369	(M)	**A Bit Of The Blues**	1957	16.00	40.00
JOHNSON, PETE					
Savoy MG-14018	(M)	**Pete's Blues**	196?	14.00	35.00
JOHNSON, ROBERT					
Columbia CL-1654	(M)	**King Of The Delta Blues Singers**	1961	50.00	100.00
		(Label has three white "eye" logos on each side of the spindle hole.)			
Columbia CL-1654	(M)	**King Of The Delta Blues Singers**	1963	12.00	30.00
		(Label reads "Guaranteed High Fidelity" on the bottom.)			
Columbia CL-1654	(M)	**King Of The Delta Blues Singers**	1965	6.00	15.00
		(Label with "360 Sound Mono" in white print on the bottom.)			
Columbia CL-1654	(M)	**King Of The Delta Blues Singers**	1970	4.00	10.00
		(Label with "Columbia" in gold print around the perimeter.)			
Columbia C-30034	(M)	**King Of The Delta Blues Singers, Volume 2**	1970	4.00	10.00

JOHNSTON, BRUCE
Johnston is a member of The Beach Boys. Refer to The Catalinas; The De-Fenders; The Hot Doggers; The Rip Chords; The Vettes.

Del-Fi DFLP-1228	(M)	**Surfer's Pajama Party**	1963	20.00	50.00
Del-Fi DFST-1228	(S)	**Surfer's Pajama Party**	1963	35.00	70.00

Label & Catalog #		Title	Year	VG+	NM
Columbia CL-2057	(DJ)	**Surfin' 'Round The World** (White label)	1963	50.00	100.00
Columbia CL-2057	(M)	**Surfin' 'Round The World**	1963	75.00	150.00
Columbia CS-8857	(S)	**Surfin' 'Round The World**	1963	100.00	200.00
Columbia KC-34459	(S)	**Going Public** (Produced by Gary Usher)	1976	5.00	12.00

JOKER'S MEMORY
M.S. 11843	(S)	**Joker's Memory**	1975	50.00	100.00

JONES, ANN, & HER AMERICAN SWEETHEARTS
Audio Lab AL-1521	(M)	**Ann Joes & Her American Sweethearts**	195?	35.00	70.00
Audio Lab AL-1556	(M)	**Hit And Run**	195?	35.00	70.00

JONES, BRIAN
Brian Jones was formerly a member of The Rolling Stones.
Roll. Stones RSR-49100	(DJ)	**Pipes Of Pan At Joujouka** (With inserts)	1971	40.00	80.00
Roll. Stones RSR-49100	(S)	**Pipes Of Pan At Joujouka** (With inserts)	1971	16.00	40.00

JONES, CURTIS
Bluesville BV-102	(M)	**Trouble Blues**	1961	20.00	50.00
Delmar DL-605	(M)	**Lonesome Bedroom Blues**	1963	16.00	40.00

JONES, DAVY
Davy Jones is a member of The Monkees.
Colpix CP-493	(M)	**David Jones**	1965	8.00	20.00
Colpix SCP-493	(S)	**David Jones**	1965	12.00	30.00
Bell 6067	(S)	**Davy Jones**	1971	8.00	20.00

JONES, DEAN
Valiant LP-407	(M)	**Introducing Dean Jones**	1962	6.00	15.00
Valiant LPS-407	(S)	**Introducing Dean Jones**	1962	8.00	20.00
Dot DLP-25890	(S)	**The Names Of My Sorrow**	1968	5.00	12.00

JONES, ETTA
King 544	(M)	**Etta Jones Sings**	1958	35.00	70.00
King 707	(M)	**Etta Jones Sings**	1960	20.00	50.00
Prestige PRLP-7186	(M)	**Don't Go To Strangers**	1960	16.00	40.00
Prestige PRLP-7194	(M)	**Something Nice**	1961	16.00	40.00
Prestige PRLP-7204	(M)	**So Warm**	1961	16.00	40.00
Prestige PRLP-7214	(M)	**From The Heart**	1962	16.00	40.00
Prestige PRLP-7241	(M)	**Lonely And Blue**	1962	16.00	40.00
Prestige PRLP-7272	(M)	**Love Shout**	1963	16.00	40.00
Prestige PRLP-7284	(M)	**Holler**	1963	16.00	40.00
		— Original Prestige albums above have yellow labels.—			
Prestige PRLP-7186	(M)	**Don't Go To Strangers**	1965	8.00	20.00
Prestige PRLP-7194	(M)	**Something Nice**	1965	8.00	20.00
Prestige PRLP-7204	(M)	**So Warm**	1965	8.00	20.00
Prestige PRLP-7214	(M)	**From The Heart**	1965	8.00	20.00
Prestige PRLP-7241	(M)	**Lonely And Blue**	1965	8.00	20.00
Prestige PRLP-7272	(M)	**Love Shout**	1965	8.00	20.00
Prestige PRLP-7284	(M)	**Holler**	1965	8.00	20.00
Prestige PRLP-7443	(M)	**Etta Jones' Greatest Hits**	1965	8.00	20.00
Prestige PRST-7443	(E)	**Etta Jones' Greatest Hits**	1965	5.00	12.00
		— Original Prestige albums above have blue labels.—			

JONES, GEORGE
Refer to The Jones Boys; Dolly Parton.
Starday SLP-101	(M)	**The Grand Ole Opry's New Star**	1958	100.00	200.00
Starday SLP-125	(M)	**The Crown Prince Of Country Music**	1960	30.00	60.00
Starday SLP-150	(M)	**His Greatest Hits**	1962	20.00	50.00
Starday SLP-151	(M)	**The Fabulous Country Music Sound Of George Jones**	1962	20.00	50.00
Starday SLP-335	(M)	**George Jones**	1965	12.00	30.00
Starday SLP-344	(M)	**Long Live King George**	1965	12.00	30.00
Starday SLP-366	(M)	**The George Jones Story**	1966	12.00	30.00
		(Issued with a n 8 1/2 x 11 bonus photo, priced separately below.)			
Starday SLP-366		**The George Jones Story Bonus Photo**	1966	12.00	30.00
Starday SLP-401	(M)	**Song Book & Picture Album** (With book)	1967	20.00	50.00
Starday SLP-401	(M)	**Song Book & Picture Album** (Without book)	1967	12.00	30.00
Starday SLP-440	(M)	**The Golden Country Hits Of George Jones**	1969	6.00	15.00

Label & Catalog #		Title	Year	VG+	NM
Mercury MG-20306	(M)	14 Country Favorites	1957	30.00	60.00
Mercury MG-20462	(M)	Country Church Time	1959	35.00	70.00
Mercury MG-20477	(M)	White Lightning And Other Favorites	1959	35.00	70.00
Mercury MG-20596	(M)	George Jones Salutes Hank Williams	1960	14.00	35.00
Mercury SR-60596	(S)	George Jones Salutes Hank Williams	1960	20.00	50.00
Mercury MG-20621	(M)	George Jones' Greatest Hits	1961	10.00	25.00
Mercury SR-60621	(S)	George Jones' Greatest Hits	1961	14.00	35.00
Mercury MG-20624	(M)	Country And Western Hits	1961	10.00	25.00
Mercury SR-60624	(S)	Country And Western Hits	1961	14.00	35.00
Mercury MG-20694	(M)	From The Heart	1962	10.00	25.00
Mercury SR-60694	(S)	From The Heart	1962	14.00	35.00
Mercury MG-20793	(M)	The Novelty Side Of George Jones	1963	16.00	40.00
Mercury SR-60793	(S)	The Novelty Side Of George Jones	1963	20.00	50.00
Mercury MG-20836	(M)	The Ballad Side Of George Jones	1963	10.00	25.00
Mercury SR-60836	(S)	The Ballad Side Of George Jones	1963	14.00	35.00
— Original Mercury albums above have black labels.—					
Mercury MG-20906	(M)	Blue And Lonesome	1964	8.00	20.00
Mercury SR-60906	(S)	Blue And Lonesome	1964	12.00	30.00
Mercury MG-20937	(M)	Country & Western #1 Male Singer	1964	8.00	20.00
Mercury SR-60937	(S)	Country & Western #1 Male Singer	1964	12.00	30.00
Mercury MG-20990	(M)	Heartaches And Tears	1965	8.00	20.00
Mercury SR-60990	(S)	Heartaches And Tears	1965	12.00	30.00
Mercury MG-21029	(M)	Singing The Blues	1965	8.00	20.00
Mercury SR-61029	(S)	Singing The Blues	1965	12.00	30.00
Mercury MG-21048	(M)	George Jones' Greatest Hits, Volume 2	1965	8.00	20.00
Mercury SR-61048	(S)	George Jones' Greatest Hits, Volume 2	1965	12.00	30.00
— Original Mercury albums above have red labels.—					
United Arts. UAL-3193	(M)	The New Favorites Of George Jones	1962	8.00	20.00
United Arts. UAS-6193	(S)	The New Favorites Of George Jones	1962	12.00	30.00
United Arts. UAL-3218	(M)	The Hits Of His Country Cousins	1962	8.00	20.00
United Arts. UAS-6218	(S)	The Hits Of His Country Cousins	1962	12.00	30.00
United Arts. UAL-3219	(M)	Homecoming In Heaven	1962	8.00	20.00
United Arts. UAS-6219	(S)	Homecoming In Heaven	1962	12.00	30.00
United Arts. UAL-3220	(M)	My Favorites Of Hank Williams	1962	8.00	20.00
United Arts. UAS-6220	(S)	My Favorites Of Hank Williams	1962	12.00	30.00
United Arts. UAL-3221	(M)	George Jones Sings Bob Wills	1962	8.00	20.00
United Arts. UAS-6221	(S)	George Jones Sings Bob Wills	1962	12.00	30.00
United Arts. UAL-3270	(M)	I Wish Tonight Would Never End	1963	8.00	20.00
United Arts. UAS-6270	(S)	I Wish Tonight Would Never End	1963	12.00	30.00
United Arts. UAL-3291	(M)	The Best Of George Jones	1963	6.00	15.00
United Arts. UAS-6291	(S)	The Best Of George Jones	1963	8.00	20.00
United Arts. UAL-3338	(M)	More New Favorites	1964	12.00	30.00
United Arts. UAS-6338	(S)	More New Favorites	1964	16.00	40.00
United Arts. UAL-3364	(M)	George Jones Sings Like The Dickens	1964	16.00	40.00
United Arts. UAS-6364	(S)	George Jones Sings Like The Dickens	1964	20.00	50.00
United Arts. UAL-3388	(M)	I Get Lonely In A Hurry	1964	8.00	20.00
United Arts. UAS-6388	(S)	I Get Lonely In A Hurry	1964	12.00	30.00
United Arts. UAL-3408	(M)	Trouble In Mind	1965	8.00	20.00
United Arts. UAS-6408	(S)	Trouble In Mind	1965	12.00	30.00
United Arts. UAL-3422	(M)	The Race Is On	1965	8.00	20.00
United Arts. UAS-6422	(S)	The Race Is On	1965	12.00	30.00
United Arts. UAL-3442	(M)	King Of Broken Hearts	1965	8.00	20.00
United Arts. UAS-6442	(S)	King Of Broken Hearts	1965	12.00	30.00
United Arts. UAL-3457	(M)	The Great George Jones	1966	8.00	20.00
United Arts. UAS-6457	(S)	The Great George Jones	1966	12.00	30.00
United Arts. UAL-3532	(M)	George Jones' Golden Hits, Volume 1	1966	6.00	15.00
United Arts. UAS-6532	(S)	George Jones' Golden Hits, Volume 1	1966	8.00	20.00
United Arts. UAL-3558	(M)	The Young George Jones	1967	6.00	15.00
United Arts. UAS-6558	(S)	The Young George Jones	1967	8.00	20.00
United Arts. UAL-3566	(M)	George Jones' Golden Hits, Volume 1	1967	6.00	15.00
United Arts. UAS-6566	(S)	George Jones' Golden Hits, Volume 1	1967	8.00	20.00
— Original U.A. albums above have black labels.—					
Musicor M-2060	(M)	New Country Hits	1965	8.00	20.00
Musicor MS-3060	(S)	New Country Hits	1965	12.00	30.00
Musicor M-2061	(M)	Old Brush Arbors	1966	8.00	20.00
Musicor MS-3061	(S)	Old Brush Arbors	1966	12.00	30.00
Musicor M-2088	(M)	Love Bug	1966	8.00	20.00
Musicor MS-3088	(S)	Love Bug	1966	12.00	30.00

abel & Catalog #		Title	Year	VG+	NM
Iusicor P2-5094	(M)	Country Heart	1966	8.00	20.00
Iusicor P2S-5094	(S)	Country Heart	1966	12.00	30.00
Iusicor M-2099	(M)	I'm A People	1966	6.00	15.00
Iusicor MS-3099	(S)	I'm A People	1966	8.00	20.00
Iusicor M-2106	(M)	We Found Heaven Right Here On Earth	1966	6.00	15.00
Iusicor MS-3106	(S)	We Found Heaven Right Here On Earth	1966	8.00	20.00
Iusicor M-2116	(M)	George Jones' Greatest Hits	1967	6.00	15.00
Iusicor MS-3116	(S)	George Jones' Greatest Hits	1967	8.00	20.00
Iusicor M-2119	(M)	Walk Through This World With Me	1967	6.00	15.00
Iusicor MS-3119	(S)	Walk Through This World With Me	1967	8.00	20.00
Iusicor M-2124	(M)	Cup Of Loneliness	1967	6.00	15.00
Iusicor MS-3124	(S)	Cup Of Loneliness	1967	8.00	20.00
Iusicor M-2128	(M)	Hits By George	1967	6.00	15.00
Iusicor MS-3128	(S)	Hits By George	1967	8.00	20.00
Iusicor MS-3149	(S)	The Songs Of Dallas Frazier	1968	6.00	15.00
Iusicor MS-3158	(S)	If My Heart Had Windows	1968	6.00	15.00
Iusicor MS-3159	(S)	The Musical Loves, Life And Sorrows Of America's Great Country Star	1968	10.00	25.00
Iusicor MS-3169	(S)	My Country	1969	8.00	20.00
Iusicor MS-3177	(S)	I'll Share My World With You	1969	6.00	15.00
Iusicor MS-3181	(S)	Where Grass Won't Grow	1969	6.00	15.00
Iusicor MS-3188	(S)	Will You Visit Me On Sunday?	1970	6.00	15.00
Iusicor MS-3191	(S)	The Best Of George Jones	1970	6.00	15.00
Iusicor MS-3194	(S)	With Love	1971	6.00	15.00
Iusicor MS-3203	(S)	The Best Of Sacred Music	1971	6.00	15.00
Iusicor MS-3204	(S)	The Great Songs Of Leon Payne	1971	6.00	15.00

— Original Musicor albums above have black labels.—

JONES, GEORGE, & MELBA MONTGOMERY

Jnited Arts. UAL-3301	(M)	What's In Our Hearts	1963	8.00	20.00
Jnited Arts. UAS-6301	(S)	What's In Our Hearts	1963	12.00	30.00
Jnited Arts. UAL-3352	(M)	Bluegrass Hootenanny	1964	8.00	20.00
Jnited Arts. UAS-6352	(S)	Bluegrass Hootenanny	1964	12.00	30.00
Jnited Arts. UAL-3472	(M)	Blue Moon Of Kentucky	1966	8.00	20.00
Jnited Arts. UAS-6420	(S)	Blue Moon Of Kentucky	1966	8.00	20.00
Musicor M-3046	(M)	Mr. Country And Western	1965	8.00	20.00
Musicor MS-3046	(S)	Mr. Country And Western	1965	12.00	30.00
Musicor M-3079	(M)	Famous Country Duets	1965	6.00	15.00
Musicor MS-3079	(S)	Famous Country Duets	1965	8.00	20.00
Musicor M-3109	(M)	Close Together As You And Me	1966	6.00	15.00
Musicor MS-3109	(S)	Close Together As You And Me	1966	8.00	20.00
Musicor M-3127	(M)	Let's Get Together/Boy Meets Girl	1967	6.00	15.00
Musicor MS-3127	(S)	Let's Get Together/Boy Meets Girl	1967	8.00	20.00

JONES, GEORGE; MELBA MONTGOMERY & GENE PITNEY

Musicor M-3079	(M)	Famous Country Duets	1965	6.00	15.00
Musicor MS-3079	(S)	Famous Country Duets	1965	8.00	20.00

JONES, GEORGE, & GENE PITNEY

Musicor M-2044	(M)	For The First Time! Two Great Singers	1965	6.00	15.00
Musicor MS-3044	(S)	For The First Time! Two Great Singers	1965	8.00	20.00
Musicor M-2044	(M)	Recorded In Nashville	1965	6.00	15.00
Musicor MS-3044	(S)	Recorded In Nashville	1965	8.00	20.00
Musicor M-3065	(M)	It's Country Time Again!	1965	6.00	15.00
Musicor MS-3065	(S)	It's Country Time Again!	1965	8.00	20.00

JONES, GEORGE, & MARGE SINGLETON

Mercury MG-20747	(M)	Duets Country Style	1962	10.00	25.00
Mercury SR-60747	(S)	Duets Country Style	1962	12.00	30.00

JONES, GRANPA

Granpa also recorded as a member of The Brown's Ferry Four.

King 554	(M)	Granpa Jones Sings His Greatest Hits	1958	20.00	50.00
King 625	(M)	Strictly Country Tunes	1959	20.00	50.00
King 809	(M)	Rollin' Along With Granpa Jones	1963	16.00	40.00
King 822	(M)	16 Sacred Gospel Songs	1963	14.00	35.00
King 845	(M)	Do You Remember?	1963	14.00	35.00
King 888	(M)	The Other Side Of Granpa Jones	1964	10.00	25.00
King 1042	(M)	The Living Legend Of Country Music	1969	6.00	15.00

Label & Catalog #		Title	Year	VG+	NM
Decca DL-4364	(M)	An Evening With Granpa Jones	1963	8.00	20.00
Monument MLP-4006	(M)	Granpa Jones Makes The Rafters Ring	1962	8.00	20.00
Monument MLP-8001	(M)	Yodeling Hits	1963	8.00	20.00
Monument MLP-8021	(M)	Real Folk Songs	1964	6.00	15.00
Monument SLP-18021	(S)	Real Folk Songs	1964	8.00	20.00
Monument MLP-8041	(M)	Remembers The Brown's Ferry Four	1966	6.00	15.00
Monument SLP-18041	(S)	Remembers The Brown's Ferry Four	1966	8.00	20.00
Monument SLP-18083	(S)	Everybody's Grandpa	1968	6.00	15.00

JONES, JIMMY
| MGM E-3847 | (M) | Good Timin' | 1960 | 20.00 | 50.00 |
| MGM SE-3847 | (S) | Good Timin' | 1960 | 35.00 | 70.00 |

JONES, JOE
| Roulette R-25143 | (M) | You Talk Too Much | 1961 | 16.00 | 40.00 |
| Roulette SR-25143 | (S) | You Talk Too Much | 1961 | 20.00 | 50.00 |

JONES, LINDA
| Loma 5907 | (S) | Hypnotized | 1967 | 10.00 | 25.00 |
| Turbo 7007 | (S) | Your Precious Love | 196? | 10.00 | 25.00 |

JONES, PAUL
Paul Jones was formerly a member of Manfred Mann.
Universal 3005	(M)	Privilege (Soundtrack)	1967	6.00	15.00
Universal 73005	(S)	Privilege (Soundtrack)	1967	8.00	20.00
Capitol T-2795	(M)	Songs From The Film "Privilege"	1967	6.00	15.00
Capitol ST-2795	(S)	Songs From The Film "Privilege"	1967	8.00	20.00
London XPS-605	(S)	Crucifix In A Horseshoe	1971	4.00	10.00

JONES, RICKIE LEE
| Mobile Fidelity MFSL-089 | (S) | Rickie Lee Jones | 1980 | 20.00 | 50.00 |

JONES, RUFUS
| Cameo C-1076 | (M) | Five On Eight | 1964 | 6.00 | 15.00 |
| Cameo SC-1076 | (S) | Five On Eight | 1964 | 10.00 | 25.00 |

JONES, SPIKE
RCA Victor LPT-18 (10")	(M)	Spike Jones Plays The Charleston	1952	50.00	100.00
RCA Victor LPM-3054 (10")	(M)	Bottoms Up	1952	35.00	70.00
RCA Victor LPM-3128 (10")	(M)	Spike Jones Murders Carmen	1953	35.00	70.00
Verve V-2021	(M)	Let's Sing A Song For Christmas	1956	20.00	50.00
Verve V-4005	(M)	Dinner Music For People Who Aren't Very Hungry	1957	20.00	50.00
Verve V-8564	(M)	35 Reasons Why Christmas Can Be Fun	1958	14.00	35.00
Liberty LRP-3140	(M)	Omnibust	1959	16.00	40.00
Liberty LST-7140	(S)	Omnibust	1959	20.00	50.00
Liberty LST-7140	(S)	Omnibust (Red vinyl)	1959	50.00	100.00
Liberty LRP-3154	(M)	60 Years Of Music America Hates Best	1959	16.00	40.00
Liberty LST-7154	(S)	60 Years Of Music America Hates Best	1959	20.00	50.00
Warner Bros. B-1332	(M)	Spike Jones In Hi Fi	1960	14.00	35.00
Warner Bros. WS-1332	(S)	Spike Jones In Stereo	1960	20.00	50.00
Liberty LRP-3338	(M)	Washington Square	1963	12.00	30.00
Liberty LST-7338	(S)	Washington Square	1963	16.00	40.00
Liberty LRP-3349	(M)	Spike Jones' New Band	1963	12.00	30.00
Liberty LST-7349	(S)	Spike Jones' New Band	1963	16.00	40.00
Liberty LRP-3401	(M)	Hank Williams Hits	1965	12.00	30.00
Liberty LST-7401	(S)	Hank Williams Hits	1965	16.00	40.00
RCA Victor LPM-2224	(M)	Thank You, Music Lovers	1960	20.00	50.00
RCA Victor LOC-3235	(M)	Spike Jones Is Murdering The Classics	1965	12.00	30.00
RCA Victor LSC-3235	(E)	Spike Jones Is Murdering The Classics	1965	10.00	25.00
RCA Victor LPM-3849	(M)	The Best Of Spike Jones	1967	10.00	25.00
RCA Victor LSP-3849	(E)	The Best Of Spike Jones	1967	8.00	20.00
MGM SE-4731	(S)	Let's Sing A Song For Christmas	1970	8.00	20.00

JONES, TOM
Parrot PA-61004	(M)	It's Not Unusual	1965	6.00	15.00
Parrot PAS-71004	(S)	It's Not Unusual	1965	8.00	20.00
United Arts. UAL-4128	(M)	What's New, Pussycat? (Soundtrack)	1965	6.00	15.00
United Arts. UAS-5128	(S)	What's New, Pussycat? (Soundtrack)	1965	8.00	20.00

Label & Catalog #		Title	Year	VG+	NM
arrot PA-61006	(M)	**What's New Pussycat?**	1965	6.00	15.00
arrot PAS-71006	(S)	**What's New Pussycat?**	1965	8.00	20.00
nited Arts. UAL-4132	(M)	**Thunderball** (Soundtrack)	1965	4.00	10.00
nited Arts. UAS-5132	(S)	**Thunderball** (Soundtrack)	1965	5.00	12.00
arrot PA-61007	(M)	**A-Tomic Jones**	1966	6.00	15.00
arrot PAS-71007	(S)	**A-Tomic Jones**	1966	8.00	20.00
app KL-1476	(M)	**Promise Her Anything** (Soundtrack)	1966	8.00	20.00
app KS-3476	(S)	**Promise Her Anything** (Soundtrack)	1966	12.00	30.00

ONES BOYS, THE
George Jones' boys.

usicor M-2017	(M)	**Country & Western Songbook**	1964	12.00	30.00
usicor MS-3017	(S)	**Country & Western Songbook**	1964	16.00	40.00
usicor MS-3182	(S)	**My Boys, The Jones Boys**	1970	8.00	20.00

OPLIN, JANIS
anis was formerly a member of Big Brother & The Holding Company. Refer to Hot Tuna.

olumbia CS-9913	(S)	**I Got Dem Ol' Kozmic Blues Again!** ("360 Sound" label)	1969	6.00	15.00
olumbia CQ-30322	(Q)	**Pearl**	1974	8.00	20.00

ORDAN, KING

oral CRL-57372	(M)	**Phantom Guitar**	1962	6.00	15.00
oral CRL-757372	(S)	**Phantom Guitar**	1962	10.00	25.00

ORDAN, LOUIS

ercury MG-20242	(M)	**Somebody Up There Digs Me**	1957	100.00	200.00
ercury MG-20331	(M)	**Man, We're Wailin'**	1958	50.00	100.00
core 4007	(M)	**Go Blow Your Horn**	1958	50.00	100.00
ecca DL-8551	(M)	**Let The Good Times Roll**	1958	35.00	70.00

ORDAN, SHEILA

lue Note 9002	(M)	**Portrait Of Sheila Jordan**	1962	16.00	40.00
lue Note 89002	(S)	**Portrait Of Sheila Jordan**	1962	20.00	50.00

ORDANAIRES, THE
he Jordanaies backed Elvis on virtually everything he recorded from 1956-1966.

CA Victor LPM-3081 (10")	(M)	**Beautiful City**	1953	35.00	70.00
ecca DL-8681	(M)	**Peace In The Valley**	1957	12.00	30.00
esac 1401	(M)	**Of Rivers And Plains**	195?	20.00	50.00
apitol T-1011	(M)	**Heavenly Spirit**	1958	10.00	25.00
apitol T-1167	(M)	**Gloryland**	1959	10.00	25.00
apitol T-1311	(M)	**Land Of Jordan**	1960	8.00	20.00
apitol ST-1311	(S)	**Land Of Jordan**	1960	10.00	25.00
apitol T-1742	(M)	**Spotlight On The Jordanaires**	1962	10.00	25.00
apitol ST-1742	(S)	**Spotlight On The Jordanaires**	1962	12.00	30.00
apitol T-1559	(M)	**To God Be The Glory**	1961	8.00	20.00
apitol ST-1559	(S)	**To God Be The Glory**	1961	10.00	25.00
olumbia CL-2214	(M)	**This Land**	1964	6.00	15.00
olumbia CS-9014	(S)	**This Land**	1964	8.00	20.00
olumbia CL-2458	(M)	**Big Country Hits**	1966	6.00	15.00
olumbia CS-9258	(S)	**Big Country Hits**	1966	8.00	20.00

OSEFUS

ookah 330	(S)	**Dead Man**	1969	75.00	150.00
ainstream 6127	(S)	**Josefus**	1970	20.00	50.00

OSEPH

cepter 674	(S)	**Stoneage Man**	1970	8.00	20.00

OSHUA FOX

etragrammaton 125	(S)	**Joshua Fox**	1968	8.00	20.00

OSIE & THE PUSSYCATS
Cheryl Ladd is the voice of Josie.

apitol ST-665	(S)	**Josie And The Pussycats**	1970	65.00	130.00

OURNEY

olumbia AS-914	(DJ)	**Journey**	1975	6.00	15.00

Label & Catalog #		Title	Year	VG+	NM
Columbia PCQ-33904	(Q)	**Look Into The Future**	1976	5.00	12.00
Columbia AS-1606	(DJ)	**A Candid Conversation**	197?	6.00	15.00
Columbia HC-46339	(S)	**Departure** (Half-speed master)	1981	8.00	20.00
Columbia HC-47408	(S)	**Escape** (Half-speed master)	1981	8.00	20.00
Columbia HC-4912	(S)	**Infinity** (Half-speed master)	1981	8.00	20.00
Columbia HC-47998	(S)	**Dream After Dream** (Half-speed master)	1982	8.00	20.00
Mobile Fidelity MFSL-144	(S)	**Escape**	1981	75.00	150.00

JOURNEYMEN, THE
The Journeymen are John Phillips, Scott McKenzie and Dick Weissman.

Capitol T-1629	(M)	**The Journeymen**	1961	10.00	25.00
Capitol ST-1629	(S)	**The Journeymen**	1961	14.00	35.00
Capitol T-1951	(M)	**New Directions In Folk Music**	1963	10.00	25.00
Capitol ST-1951	(S)	**New Directions In Folk Music**	1963	12.00	30.00

JOY

Paula LPS-2217	(S)	**Thunderfoot**	1972	6.00	15.00

JOYFUL NOISE

RCA Victor LSP-3963	(S)	**Joyful Noise**	1968	6.00	15.00

JOYOUS NOISE

Capitol SMAS-844	(S)	**Joyous Noise**	1971	6.00	15.00

JUDAS PRIEST

Columbia 9C9-39926	(S)	**Great Vinyl And Concert Hits** (Picture disc)	1984	4.00	10.00

JUICY LUCY

Atco SD-33-325	(S)	**Juicy Lucy**	1970	6.00	15.00
Atco SD-33-345	(S)	**Lie Back And Enjoy It**	1970	6.00	15.00
Atco SD-33-367	(S)	**Get A Whiff Of This**	1971	6.00	15.00

JULIAN, DON

Amazon 1009	(M)	**Greatest Oldies**	1963	20.00	50.00

JULY

Epic BN-26416	(S)	**July**	1969	50.00	100.00

JUPITER

Jupiter 1005	(S)	**Multiple Choice**	1980	16.00	40.00

JUST IV

Liberty LRP-3340	(M)	**First Twelve Sides**	1964	5.00	12.00
Liberty LST-7340	(S)	**First Twelve Sides**	1964	6.00	15.00

JUST US
Just Us features former members of The Index.

Valord AR-2634	(S)	**The U.S.A. From The Air**	197?	50.00	100.00

JUSTIS, BILL

Phillips Int. 1950	(M)	**Cloud Nine**	1959	180.00	300.00
Smash MGS-27021	(M)	**Twelve Big Instrumental Hits**	1962	6.00	15.00
Smash SRS-67021	(S)	**Twelve Big Instrumental Hits**	1962	8.00	20.00
Smash MGS-67030	(M)	**Twelve More Big Instrumental Hits**	1962	6.00	15.00
Smash SRS-67030	(S)	**Twelve More Big Instrumental Hits**	1962	8.00	20.00
Smash MGS-27036	(M)	**Twelve Top Tunes**	1963	6.00	15.00
Smash SRS-67036	(S)	**Twelve Top Tunes**	1963	8.00	20.00
Smash MGS-27043	(M)	**Twelve Other Instrumental Hits**	1964	6.00	15.00
Smash SRS-67043	(S)	**Twelve Other Instrumental Hits**	1964	8.00	20.00
Smash MGS-27047	(M)	**Dixieland Folk Style**	1964	6.00	15.00
Smash SRS-67047	(S)	**Dixieland Folk Style**	1964	8.00	20.00
Smash MGS-27065	(M)	**More Instrumental Hits**	1965	5.00	12.00
Smash SRS-67065	(S)	**More Instrumental Hits**	1965	6.00	15.00
Smash MGS-27077	(M)	**A Taste Of Honey**	1966	5.00	12.00
Smash SRS-67077	(S)	**A Taste Of Honey**	1966	6.00	15.00

bel & Catalog #		Title	Year	VG+	NM

.O. BOSSY
| ga TSTLP-2003 | (M) | K.O. Bossy | 196? | 16.00 | 40.00 |

-DOE, ERNIE
rnie K-Doe is a pseudonym for Ernest Kador.
| init LP-0002 | (M) | Mother-In-Law | 1961 | 75.00 | 150.00 |
| anus JLS-3030 | (S) | Ernie K-Doe | 1971 | 6.00 | 15.00 |

AILUA, PRINCE, & THE TROPICAL ISLANDERS
rince Kailua is a pseudonym for Roy Smeck
| pic LN-24055 | (M) | Hawaii's Greatest Hits | 1963 | 5.00 | 12.00 |
| pic BN-26055 | (S) | Hawaii's Greatest Hits | 1963 | 6.00 | 15.00 |

AK
| pic BN-26429 | (S) | Kak | 1969 | 50.00 | 100.00 |

ALABASH CORP., THE
| ncle Bill KB-3114 | (S) | The Kalabash Corp. | 197? | 50.00 | 100.00 |

ALEIDOSCOPE
pic LN-24304	(M)	Side Trips	1967	10.00	25.00
pic BN-26304	(S)	Side Trips	1967	14.00	35.00
pic LN-24333	(M)	Beacon From Mars	1967	16.00	40.00
pic BN-26333	(S)	Beacon From Mars	1967	20.00	50.00
pic BN-26467	(S)	Incredible Kaleidoscope	1969	10.00	25.00
pic BN-26508	(S)	Bernice	1970	8.00	20.00
acific Arts 102	(S)	When Scopes Collide	1978	4.00	10.00

ALIN TWINS, THE
| ecca DL-8812 | (M) | The Kalin Twins | 1959 | 30.00 | 60.00 |

ALLEN, KITTY
efer to Ann-Margret / Kitty Kallen / Della Reese.
ercury MG-25206 (10")	(M)	Pretty Kitty Kallen Sings	1955	16.00	40.00
ecca DL-8397	(M)	It's A Lonesome Old Town	1958	12.00	30.00
ocalion VL-3679	(M)	Little Things Mean A Lot	1959	10.00	25.00
olumbia CL-1404	(M)	If I Give My Heart To You	1960	6.00	15.00
olumbia CS-8204	(S)	If I Give My Heart To You	1960	8.00	20.00
olumbia CL-1662	(M)	Honky Tonk Angel	1961	6.00	15.00
olumbia CS-8462	(S)	Honky Tonk Angel	1961	8.00	20.00
CA Victor LPM-2640	(M)	My Coloring Book	1963	6.00	15.00
CA Victor LSP-2640	(S)	My Coloring Book	1963	8.00	20.00

AMMERZELL
| rtco-Alpha 50-1209 | (S) | Hot For Your Love | 1979 | 20.00 | 50.00 |

ANGAROO
angaroo features Barbara Keith.
| GM SE-4586 | (S) | Kangaroo | 1968 | 6.00 | 15.00 |

ANNIBAL KOMIX
| olossus CS-1004 | (S) | Kannibal Komix | 1970 | 6.00 | 20.00 |

ANSAS
irshner AS-555	(DJ)	Two For The Show (Album sampler)	1978	6.00	15.00
irshner HZ-44224	(S)	Leftoverture (Half-speed master)	1981	12.00	30.00
irshner HZ-44929	(S)	Point Of Know Return (Half-speed master)	1981	12.00	30.00
irshner JZ-44929	(DJ)	Point Of Know Return (Picture disc)	1981	30.00	60.00
irshner HZ-46008	(S)	Monolith (Half-speed master)	1982	14.00	35.00
irshner HZ-48002	(S)	Vinyl Confessions (Half-speed master)	1982	12.00	30.00

Label & Catalog #		Title	Year	VG+	NM
KANSAS CITY JAMMERS, THE					
No label	(S)	**Got Good (If You Get It)**	197?	20.00	50.00
KANTNER, PAUL, & THE JEFFERSON STARSHIP					
RCA Victor LSP-4448	(S)	**Blows Against The Empire** (Orange label)	1970	6.00	15.00
KARLOFF, BORIS					
Cricket CR-32	(M)	**Tales Of Mystery And Imagination**	1959	12.00	30.00
Mercury MG-20815	(M)	**Tales Of The Frightened, Volume 1**	1963	14.00	35.00
Mercury SR-60815	(S)	**Tales Of The Frightened, Volume 1**	1963	16.00	40.00
Mercury MG-20816	(M)	**Tales Of The Frightened, Volume 2**	1963	14.00	35.00
Mercury SR-60816	(S)	**Tales Of The Frightened, Volume 2**	1963	16.00	40.00
MGM E-901	(M)	**How The Grinch Stole Christmas** (TV Sdtk)	1966	10.00	25.00
MGM SE-901	(S)	**How The Grinch Stole Christmas** (TV Sdtk)	1966	14.00	35.00
Decca DL-4833	(M)	**An Evening With Karloff And His Friends**	1967	8.00	20.00
Decca DL-74833	(S)	**An Evening With Karloff And His Friends**	1967	10.00	25.00
KAUFMANN, BOB					
L.H.I. 12002	(S)	**Trip Through A Blown Mind**	1967	16.00	40.00
KAY, JOHN, & SPARROW					
Kay was formerly a member of Steppenwolf.					
Columbia CS-9758	(S)	**John Kay & Sparrow** ("360 Sound" label)	1970	8.00	20.00
KAY, JOHN, & STEPPENWOLF					
Nautilus NR-53	(S)	**Wolftracks**	198?	6.00	15.00
KAYE, MARY					
Decca DL-8238	(M)	**The Mary Kaye Trio**	1956	12.00	30.00
Decca DL-8454	(M)	**Music On A Silver Platter**	1957	12.00	30.00
Decca DL-8650	(M)	**You Don't Know What Love Is**	1958	12.00	30.00
Warner Bros. W-1263	(M)	**Jackpot**	1959	8.00	20.00
Warner Bros. WS-1263	(S)	**Jackpot**	1959	10.00	25.00
KELLER, JERRY					
Kapp KL-1178	(M)	**Here Comes Jerry Keller**	1960	6.00	15.00
Kapp KS-3178	(S)	**Here Comes Jerry Keller**	1960	8.00	20.00
KELLY, BEVERLY					
Audio Fidelity 1874	(M)	**Beverly Kelly Sings**	1958	10.00	25.00
Audio Fidelity 5874	(S)	**Beverly Kelly Sings**	1958	14.00	35.00
Riverside RLP-12-328	(M)	**Love Locked Out**	1959	10.00	25.00
Riverside RLP-12-9328	(S)	**Love Locked Out**	1959	14.00	35.00
Riverside RLP-12-345	(M)	**Beverly Kelly In Person**	1960	10.00	25.00
Riverside RLP-12-9345	(S)	**Beverly Kelly In Person**	1960	14.00	35.00
KENNEDY, JERRY					
Refer to Tom & Jerry.					
Smash MGS-27004	(M)	**Dancing Guitars Rock Elvis' Hits**	1962	8.00	20.00
Smash SRS-67004	(S)	**Dancing Guitars Rock Elvis' Hits**	1962	12.00	30.00
Smash MGS-27024	(M)	**The Golden Standards**	1963	5.00	12.00
Smash SRS-67024	(S)	**The Golden Standards**	1963	6.00	15.00
Smash MGS-27066	(M)	**From Nashville To Soulville**	1965	5.00	12.00
Smash SRS-67066	(S)	**From Nashville To Soulville**	1965	6.00	15.00
KENNEDY, MIKE					
Mike Kennedy was formerly a member of Los Bravos.					
ABC X-754	(S)	**Louisiana**	1972	6.00	15.00
KENNEY, BEVERLY					
Roost 2206	(M)	**Beverly Kenney Sings For Jimmy Smith**	195?	12.00	30.00
Roost 2212	(M)	**Come Swing With Me**	195?	12.00	30.00
Roost 2218	(M)	**Beverly Kenney With Jimmy Jones And The Basic-Ites**	195?	12.00	30.00
Decca DL-8743	(M)	**Beverly Kenney Sings For Playboys**	1958	6.00	20.00
Decca DL-8850	(M)	**Born To Be Blue**	1959	6.00	20.00
Decca DL-8948	(M)	**Like Yesterday**	1959	6.00	20.00
Decca DL-78948	(S)	**Like Yesterday**	1959	12.00	30.00

abel & Catalog #		Title	Year	VG+	NM
ENNY & THE KASUALS					
Iark 5000	(M)	**Live At The Studio Club**	1966	300.00	500.00
Iark 5000	(M)	**Live At The Studio Club** (Reissue)	1977	12.00	30.00
Iark 6000	(M)	**Teen Dreams** (Red vinyl)	1978	100.00	200.00
		(Mark 6000 is a signed, numbered edition of 200 copies.)			
Iark 7000	(S)	**Garage Kings**	1979	12.00	30.00
ENTUCKY COLONELS, THE					
he Colonels feature Clarence White, later of The Byrds.					
Vorld Pacific T-1821	(M)	**Appalachian Swing**	1964	16.00	40.00
Vorld Pacific ST-1821	(S)	**Appalachian Swing**	1964	20.00	50.00
EROUAC, JACK					
Jot DLP-3154	(M)	**Poetry For The Beat Generation**	1959	See note below	
		(Pressed in minute quantities and then deleted, there are			
		no known documented sales from which to draw a value.)			
Ianover HML-5000	(M)	**Poetry For The Beat Generation**	1959	150.00	250.00
Ianover HML-5006	(M)	**Blues And Haikus**	1959	150.00	250.00
Ierve MGV-15005	(M)	**Readings On The Beat Generation**	1959	100.00	200.00
ESEY, KEN					
Jound City 27690	(M)	**The Acid Test** (With the Grateful Dead)	1967	100.00	200.00
ICKSTANDS, THE					
he Kickstands are a creation of Gary Usher & Co.					
Japitol T-2078	(M)	**Black Boots And Bikes**	1964	16.00	40.00
Japitol ST-2078	(S)	**Black Boots And Bikes**	1964	20.00	50.00
ILGORE, MERLE					
Jtarday SLP-251	(M)	**There's Gold In Them Thar Hills**	196?	12.00	30.00
Ving MGW-12316	(M)	**The Tall Man**	196?	8.00	20.00
ILLING FLOOR					
Killing Floor features Rory Gallagher.					
Jire SES-97019	(S)	**Killing Floor**	1970	20.00	50.00
ING, ALBERT					
Jing 852	(M)	**Big Blues**	1963	100.00	200.00
Jtax 723	(M)	**Born Under A Bad Sign**	1967	20.00	50.00
Jtax 723	(E)	**Born Under A Bad Sign**	1967	14.00	35.00
Jtax STS-2003	(S)	**Live Wire/Blues Power**	1968	8.00	20.00
Jing KS-1060	(S)	**Travelin' To California**	1969	8.00	20.00
Atlantic SD-8213	(S)	**King Of The Blues Guitar**	1969	8.00	20.00
Jtax STS-2010	(S)	**Years Gone By**	1969	6.00	15.00
Jtax STS-2015	(S)	**King Does The King's Thing**	1969	8.00	20.00
Jtax STS-2040	(S)	**Love Joy**	1971	6.00	15.00
Jtax STS-3009	(S)	**I'll Play The Blues For You**	1972	5.00	12.00
Jtax 5505	(S)	**I Wanna Get Funky**	1974	5.00	12.00
ING, ALBERT, & OTIS RUSH					
Jhess 1538	(S)	**Door To Door**	1969	6.00	15.00
ING, B.B.					
Jrown CLP-5020	(M)	**Singin' The Blues**	1960	12.00	30.00
Jrown CLP-5063	(M)	**The Blues**	1960	12.00	30.00
Jrown CLP-5115	(M)	**B.B. King Wails**	1960	12.00	30.00
Jrown CST-147	(E)	**B.B. King Wails** (Red vinyl)	1960	35.00	70.00
Jrown CLP-5119	(M)	**B.B. King Sings Spirituals**	1960	12.00	30.00
Jrown CST-152	(E)	**B.B. King Sings Spirituals** (Red vinyl)	1960	35.00	70.00
Jrown CLP-5143	(M)	**The Great B.B. King**	1961	12.00	30.00
Jrown CLP-5167	(M)	**King Of The Blues**	1961	12.00	30.00
Jrown CST-195	(E)	**King Of The Blues** (Red vinyl)	1961	35.00	70.00
Jrown CLP-5188	(M)	**My Kind Of Blues**	1961	12.00	30.00
Jrown CLP-5230	(M)	**More B.B. King**	1962	12.00	30.00
Jrown CLP-5248	(M)	**Twist With B.B. King**	1962	12.00	30.00
Jrown CLP-5286	(M)	**Easy Listening Blues**	1962	12.00	30.00
Jrown CLP-5309	(M)	**Blues In My Heart**	1962	12.00	30.00
Jrown CST-309	(E)	**Blues In My Heart**	1962	12.00	30.00
Jrown CLP-5359	(M)	**B.B. King**	1963	12.00	30.00

Label & Catalog #		Title	Year	VG+	NM
Galaxy 202	(M)	The Best Of B.B. King	1963	8.00	20.0
Galaxy 8202	(S)	The Best Of B.B. King	1963	12.00	30.0
ABC-Paramount 456	(M)	Mr. Blues	1963	8.00	20.0
ABC-Paramount S-456	(S)	Mr. Blues	1963	12.00	30.0
ABC-Paramount 509	(M)	Live At The Regal	1965	8.00	20.0
ABC-Paramount S-509	(S)	Live At The Regal	1965	12.00	30.0
ABC-Paramount 528	(M)	Confessin' The Blues	1965	8.00	20.0
ABC-Paramount S-528	(S)	Confessin' The Blues	1965	12.00	30.0
Kent KLP-5012	(M)	Rock Me Baby	1964	5.00	12.0
Kent KST-512	(S)	Rock Me Baby	1964	6.00	15.0
Kent KLP-5013	(M)	Let Me Love You	1965	5.00	12.0
Kent KST-513	(S)	Let Me Love You	1965	6.00	15.0
Kent KLP-5015	(M)	B.B. King Live On Stage	1965	5.00	12.0
Kent KST-515	(S)	B.B. King Live On Stage	1965	6.00	15.0
Kent KLP-5016	(M)	The Soul Of B.B. King	1966	5.00	12.0
Kent KST-516	(S)	The Soul Of B.B. King	1966	6.00	15.0
Kent KST-517	(S)	Pure Soul	1966	6.00	15.0
Kent KLP-5021	(M)	The Jungle	1967	5.00	12.0
Kent KST-521	(S)	The Jungle	1967	6.00	15.0
Kent KLP-5029	(M)	Boss Of The Blues	1968	5.00	12.0
Kent KST-529	(S)	Boss Of The Blues	1968	6.00	15.0
Kent KST-533	(S)	From The Beginning	1969	4.00	10.0
Kent KST-535	(S)	Underground Blues	1969	4.00	10.0
Kent KST-539	(S)	The Incredible Soul Of B.B. King	1970	4.00	10.0
Kent KST-548	(S)	Turn On With B.B. King	1971	4.00	10.0
Kent KST-552	(S)	Greatest Hits, Volume 1	1971	4.00	10.0
Kent KST-561	(S)	Better Than Ever	1971	4.00	10.0
Kent KST-563	(S)	Doing My Thing, Lord	1971	4.00	10.0
Kent KST-565	(S)	B.B. King Live	1972	4.00	10.0
Kent KST-568	(S)	The Original Sweet Sixteen	1972	4.00	10.0
Kent 9011	(S)	B.B. King Anthology	197?	4.00	10.0
BluesWay BL-6001	(S)	Blues Is King	1967	5.00	12.0
BluesWay BLS-6001	(S)	Blues Is King	1967	6.00	15.0
BluesWay BLS-6011	(S)	Blues On Top Of Blues	1968	5.00	12.0
BluesWay BLS-6016	(S)	Lucille	1968	5.00	12.0
BluesWay BLS-6022	(S)	His Best/The Electric B.B. King	1968	5.00	12.0
BluesWay BLS-6031	(S)	Live And Well	1969	4.00	10.0
BluesWay BLS-6037	(S)	Completely Well	1969	4.00	10.0
BluesWay BLS-6050	(S)	Back In The Alley	1970	4.00	10.0
Direct Disk SD-16616	(S)	Midnight Believer	1980	12.00	30.0

KING, BEN E.
Ben E. King was formerly a member of The Drifters.

Atco SD-33-133	(M)	Spanish Harlem	1961	14.00	35.0
Atco SD-33-133	(S)	Spanish Harlem	1961	20.00	50.0
Atco SD-33-137	(M)	Ben E. King Sings For Soulful Lovers	1962	12.00	30.0
Atco SD-33-137	(S)	Ben E. King Sings For Soulful Lovers	1962	16.00	40.0
Atco SD-33-142	(M)	Don't Play That Song	1962	12.00	30.0
Atco SD-33-142	(S)	Don't Play That Song	1962	16.00	40.0
Atco SD-33-165	(M)	Ben E. King's Greatest Hits	1964	10.00	25.0
Atco SD-33-165	(S)	Ben E. King's Greatest Hits	1964	12.00	30.0
Atco SD-33-174	(M)	Seven Letters	1965	10.00	25.0
Atco SD-33-174	(S)	Seven Letters	1965	12.00	30.0

KING, CAROLE

Ode SQ-88013	(Q)	Carole King Music	1971	5.00	12.0
Epic/Ode HE-44946	(S)	Tapestry (Half-speed master)	1980	16.00	40.0

KING, CLAUDE

Columbia CL-1810	(M)	Meet Claude King ("Eyes" logo label)	1962	8.00	20.0
Columbia CS-8610	(S)	Meet Claude King ("Eyes" logo label)	1962	12.00	30.0
Columbia CL-2415	(M)	Tiger Woman	1965	5.00	12.0
Columbia CS-9215	(S)	Tiger Woman	1965	6.00	15.0

KING, FREDDIE

King 762	(M)	Freddie King Sings The Blues	1961	45.00	90.0
King 773	(M)	Let's Hide Away And Dance Away	1961	45.00	90.0
King 777	(M)	Boy-Girl-Boy	1962	40.00	80.0
King 821	(M)	Bossa Nova And Blues	1962	40.00	80.0

Label & Catalog #		Title	Year	VG+	NM
King 856	(M)	Freddie King Goes Surfin'	1963	16.00	40.00
King 856	(S)	Freddie King Goes Surfin'	1963	20.00	50.00
King 928	(M)	A Bonanza Of Instrumentals	1965	10.00	25.00
King 928	(S)	A Bonanza Of Instrumentals	1965	12.00	30.00
King 964	(M)	24 Vocals And Instrumentals	1966	10.00	25.00
King KS-1059	(S)	Hide Away	1969	6.00	15.00
Cotillion SD-9004	(S)	Freddie King Is A Blues Master	1969	5.00	12.00
Cotillion SD-9016	(S)	My Feeling For The Blues	1970	5.00	12.00
Shelter SW-8905	(S)	Getting Ready	1971	5.00	12.00
Shelter SW-8913	(S)	Texas Cannonball	1972	5.00	12.00
Shelter SW-8919	(S)	Woman Across The River	1973	5.00	12.00
KING, JONATHON					
Parrot PA-61013	(M)	Or Then Again	1967	12.00	30.00
Parrot PAS-71013	(P)	Or Then Again	1967	16.00	40.00
UK S-53101	(S)	Bubble Rock Is Here To Stay	1972	6.00	15.00
UK S-53104	(S)	Pandora's Box	1973	6.00	15.00
KING, MORGANA					
EmArcy MG-36079	(M)	For You, For Me, Forever More	1956	16.00	40.00
Mercury MG-20231	(M)	Morgana King Sings The Blues	1958	16.00	40.00
Camden CAL-543	(M)	The Greatest Songs Ever Swung	1959	10.00	25.00
United Arts. UAL-3020	(M)	Let Me Love You	1960	10.00	25.00
United Arts. UAS-6020	(S)	Let Me Love You	1960	14.00	35.00
United Arts. UAL-3028	(M)	Folk Songs Ala King	1960	10.00	25.00
United Arts. UAS-6028	(S)	Folk Songs Ala King	1960	14.00	35.00
Ascot ALM-13014	(M)	The Winter Of My Discontent	1965	6.00	15.00
Ascot ALS-16014	(S)	The Winter Of My Discontent	1965	8.00	20.00
Ascot ALM-13019	(M)	The End Of A Love Affair	1965	6.00	15.00
Ascot ALS-16019	(S)	The End Of A Love Affair	1965	8.00	20.00
Ascot ALM-13020	(M)	Everybody Loves Saturday Night	1965	6.00	15.00
Ascot ALS-16020	(S)	Everybody Loves Saturday Night	1965	8.00	20.00
Reprise R-6205	(M)	Wild Is Love	1966	6.00	15.00
Reprise RS-6205	(S)	Wild Is Love	1966	8.00	20.00
Reprise R-6257	(M)	Gemini Changes	1967	6.00	15.00
Reprise RS-6257	(S)	Gemini Changes	1967	8.00	20.00
KING, PEE WEE					
RCA Victor LPM-3028 (10")	(M)	Pee Wee King	1954	30.00	60.00
RCA Victor LPM-3071 (10")	(M)	Western Hits	1954	30.00	60.00
RCA Victor LPM-3109 (10")	(M)	Waltzes	1955	30.00	60.00
RCA Victor LPM-3280 (10")	(M)	Swing West	1955	30.00	60.00
RCA Victor LPM-1237	(M)	Swing West	1955	20.00	50.00
Longhorn 1236	(M)	The Legendary Pee Wee King	1967	10.00	25.00
KING, PEGGY					
Columbia CL-2549 (10")	(M)	Wish Upon A Star	1055	14.00	35.00
Columbia CL-713	(M)	Girl Meets Boy	1055	10.00	25.00
Imperial LP-9026	(M)	Peggy King	1959	8.00	20.00
Imperial LP-12026	(S)	Peggy King	1959	12.00	30.00
KING, TEDDI					
Storyville STLP-302 (10")	(M)	'Round Midnight	1954	100.00	200.00
Storyville STLP-314 (10")	(M)	Storyville Presents Teddi King	1954	50.00	100.00
Storyville STLP-903	(M)	Now In Vogue	1955	35.00	70.00
RCA Victor LPM-1147	(M)	Bidin' My Time	1956	30.00	60.00
RCA Victor LPM-1313	(M)	To You From Teddi King	1956	20.00	50.00
RCA Victor LPM-1454	(M)	A Girl And Her Songs	1957	20.00	50.00
Coral CRL-57278	(M)	All The King's Songs	1959	14.00	35.00
Coral CRL-757278	(S)	All The King's Songs	1959	20.00	50.00
Inner City 1044	(S)	This Is New	1978	5.00	12.00
KING, TYLER, & THE TWISTEENS					
Startime TW-100	(M)	Twistin' Time	1961	8.00	20.00
KING CRIMSON					
Mobile Fidelity MFSL-075	(S)	In The Court Of The Crimson King	1980	16.00	40.00

Label & Catalog #		Title	Year	VG+	NM
KING CURTIS					
Refer to the Shirelles.					
Atco 33-113	(M)	Have Tenor Sax, Will Blow	1959	14.00	35.00
Atco SD-33-113	(S)	Have Tenor Sax, Will Blow	1959	20.00	50.00
New Jazz 8237	(M)	The New Scene Of King Curtis	1960	16.00	40.00
Everest DBR-1121	(M)	Azure	1961	16.00	40.00
Tru-Sound TS-15009	(M)	Doin' The Dixie Twist	1962	12.00	30.00
Tru-Sound STS-15009	(S)	Doin' The Dixie Twist	1962	16.00	40.00
Tru-Sound TS-15008	(M)	It's Party Time	1962	12.00	30.00
Tru-Sound STS-15008	(S)	It's Party Time	1962	16.00	40.00
Capitol T-2095	(M)	Soul Serenade	1964	8.00	20.00
Capitol ST-2095	(S)	Soul Serenade	1964	12.00	30.00
Capitol T-2341	(M)	Hits Made Famous By Sam Cooke	1965	8.00	20.00
Capitol ST-2341	(S)	Hits Made Famous By Sam Cooke	1965	12.00	30.00
Capitol ST-2858	(S)	The Best Of King Curtis	1968	8.00	20.00
Atco 33-189	(M)	That Lovin' Feeling	1966	6.00	15.00
Atco SD-33-189	(S)	That Lovin' Feeling	1966	8.00	20.00
Atco 33-198	(M)	Live At Small's Paradise	1966	6.00	15.00
Atco SD-33-198	(S)	Live At Small's Paradise	1966	8.00	20.00
Atco 33-211	(M)	The Great Memphis Hits	1967	6.00	15.00
Atco SD-33-211	(S)	The Great Memphis Hits	1967	8.00	20.00
Atco 33-231	(M)	King Size Soul	1967	6.00	15.00
Atco SD-33-231	(S)	King Size Soul	1967	8.00	20.00
Atco SD-33-247	(S)	Sweet Soul	1968	8.00	20.00
Atco SD-33-266	(S)	The Best Of King Curtis	1968	6.00	15.00
Atco SD-33-293	(S)	Instant Groove	1969	6.00	15.00
Atco SD-33-338	(S)	Get Ready	1970	6.00	15.00
Atco SD-33-359	(S)	Live At Fillmore West	1971	6.00	15.00
Atco SD-33-385	(S)	Everybody's Talkin'	1972	6.00	15.00
KING PINS, THE					
King 865	(M)	It Won't Be This Way Always	1963	16.00	40.00
KING'S HENCHMEN, THE					
Coral CRL-57216	(M)	Alan Freed Presents The King's Henchmen	1958	16.00	40.00
KINGDOM					
Specialty 2135	(S)	Kingdom	1970	45.00	90.00
KINGFISH					
Kingfish features Bob Weir of The Grateful Dead.					
Round RX-108	(S)	Kingfish	1976	6.00	15.00
Jet LA732-G	(S)	Live 'N' Kickin'	1977	4.00	10.00
KINGSMEN, THE					
Wand WD-657	(M)	The Kingsmen In Person	1964	8.00	20.00
Wand WDS-657	(S)	The Kingsmen In Person	1964	10.00	25.00
Wand WD-659	(M)	More Great Sounds	1964	8.00	20.00
Wand WDS-659	(S)	More Great Sounds	1964	10.00	25.00
		(Originally issued with "Death Of An Angel")			
Wand WDS-659	(S)	More Great Sounds	196?	6.00	15.00
Wand WD-662	(M)	The Kingsmen, Volume 3	1965	6.00	15.00
Wand WDS-662	(S)	The Kingsmen, Volume 3	1965	8.00	20.00
Wand WD-670	(M)	The Kingsmen On Campus	1965	5.00	12.00
Wand WDS-670	(S)	The Kingsmen On Campus	1965	6.00	15.00
Wand WD-674	(M)	15 Great Hits	1966	5.00	12.00
Wand WDS-674	(S)	15 Great Hits	1966	6.00	15.00
Wand WD-675	(M)	Up And Away	1966	5.00	12.00
Wand WDS-675	(S)	Up And Away	1966	6.00	15.00
Wand WD-681	(M)	The Kingsmen's Greatest Hits	1967	5.00	12.00
Wand WDS-681	(S)	The Kingsmen's Greatest Hits	1967	6.00	15.00
KINGSTON TRIO, THE					
Members include Bob Shane, Nick Reynolds and Dave Guard, later replaced by John Stewart..					
Capitol T-996	(M)	The Kingston Trio *(Turquoise label)*	1958	16.00	40.00
Capitol T-996	(M)	The Kingston Trio *(Black label)*	1958	10.00	25.00
Capitol T-1107	(M)	From The Hungry i	1959	10.00	25.00
Capitol ST-1183	(S)	Stereo Concert	1959	12.00	30.00

Label & Catalog #		Title	Year	VG+	NM
Capitol T-1199	(M)	The Kingston Trio At Large	1959	8.00	20.00
Capitol ST-1199	(S)	The Kingston Trio At Large	1959	12.00	30.00
Capitol T-1258	(M)	Here We Go Again	1959	8.00	20.00
Capitol ST-1258	(S)	Here We Go Again	1959	12.00	30.00
Capitol T-1352	(M)	Sold Out	1960	8.00	20.00
Capitol ST-1352	(S)	Sold Out	1960	12.00	30.00
Capitol T-1497	(M)	String Along	1960	8.00	20.00
Capitol ST-1497	(S)	String Along	1960	12.00	30.00
Capitol T-1446	(M)	The Last Month Of The Year	1960	8.00	20.00
Capitol ST-1446	(S)	The Last Month Of The Year	1960	12.00	30.00
Capitol T-1474	(M)	Make Way!	1961	8.00	20.00
Capitol ST-1474	(S)	Make Way!	1961	12.00	30.00
Capitol T-1564	(M)	Goin' Places	1961	8.00	20.00
Capitol ST-1564	(S)	Goin' Places	1961	12.00	30.00
Capitol DT-1612	(E)	Encores	1961	10.00	25.00
Capitol T-1642	(M)	Close Up	1961	8.00	20.00
Capitol ST-1642	(S)	Close Up	1961	12.00	30.00
— Original Capitol albums above have black labels with the logo on the left side.—					
Capitol T-1658	(M)	College Concert	1962	6.00	15.00
Capitol ST-1658	(S)	College Concert	1962	8.00	20.00
Capitol T-1705	(M)	Best Of The Kingston Trio	1962	5.00	12.00
Capitol ST-1705	(S)	Best Of The Kingston Trio	1962	6.00	15.00
Capitol T-1747	(M)	Something Special	1962	6.00	15.00
Capitol ST-1747	(S)	Something Special	1962	8.00	20.00
Capitol T-1809	(M)	New Frontier	1962	6.00	15.00
Capitol ST-1809	(S)	New Frontier	1962	8.00	20.00
Capitol T-1871	(M)	Kingston Trio #16	1963	6.00	15.00
Capitol ST-1871	(S)	Kingston Trio #16	1963	8.00	20.00
Capitol T-1935	(M)	Sunny Side!	1963	6.00	15.00
Capitol ST-1935	(S)	Sunny Side!	1963	8.00	20.00
Capitol T-2011	(M)	Time To Think	1963	8.00	20.00
Capitol ST-2011	(S)	Time To Think	1963	10.00	25.00
Capitol T-2081	(M)	Back In Town	1964	6.00	15.00
Capitol ST-2081	(S)	Back In Town	1964	8.00	20.00
Capitol TCL-2180	(M)	The Folk Era	1964	12.00	30.00
Capitol STCL-2180	(S)	The Folk Era	1964	16.00	40.00
Capitol T-2280	(M)	Best Of The Kingston Trio, Volume 2	1965	5.00	12.00
Capitol ST-2280	(S)	Best Of The Kingston Trio, Volume 2	1965	6.00	15.00
Capitol T-2614	(M)	Best Of The Kingston Trio, Volume 3	1966	5.00	12.00
Capitol ST-2614	(S)	Best Of The Kingston Trio, Volume 3	1966	6.00	15.00
— Original Capitol albums above have black labels with the logo on top.—					
Capitol DT-996	(E)	The Kingston Trio	1969	6.00	15.00
Decca DL-4613	(M)	The Kingston Trio: Nick-Bob-John	1965	8.00	20.00
Decca DL-74613	(S)	The Kingston Trio: Nick-Bob-John	1965	10.00	25.00
Decca DL-4656	(M)	Stay Awhile	1965	8.00	20.00
Decca DL-74656	(S)	Stay Awhile	1965	10.00	25.00
Decca DL-4694	(M)	Somethin' Else	1965	8.00	20.00
Decca DL-74694	(S)	Somethin' Else	1965	10.00	25.00
Decca DL-4758	(M)	Children In The Morning	1966	10.00	25.00
Decca DL-74758	(S)	Children In The Morning	1966	12.00	30.00
Tetragrammaton 5101	(S)	Once Upon A Time	1969	10.00	25.00
Longines SYS-5507	(P)	The World Needs A Melody	1973	8.00	20.00
Longines SYS-5569-5574	(P)	American Gold (6 LPs)	1973	20.00	50.00
Nautilus NR-2	(S)	Aspen Gold	1979	8.00	20.00

KINKS, THE

The original Kinks were Ray and Dave Davies, Pete Quaife and Mick Avory. Quaife was replaced by John Dalton in 1966.

Label & Catalog #		Title	Year	VG+	NM
Reprise R-6143	(M)	You Really Got Me	1965	20.00	50.00
Reprise RS-6143	(P)	You Really Got Me	1965	16.00	40.00
Reprise R-6158	(M)	Kinks Size	1965	16.00	40.00
Reprise RS-6158	(E)	Kinks Size	1965	12.00	30.00
Reprise R-6173	(M)	Kinda Kinks	1965	16.00	40.00
Reprise RS-6173	(E)	Kinda Kinks	1965	12.00	30.00
Reprise R-6184	(M)	Kinks' Kinkdom	1965	16.00	40.00
Reprise RS-6184	(E)	Kinks' Kinkdom	1965	12.00	30.00
Reprise R-6197	(M)	Kink Kontroversy	1966	16.00	40.00
Reprise RS-6197	(E)	Kink Kontroversy	1966	12.00	30.00

Label & Catalog #		Title	Year	VG+	NM
Reprise R-6217	(M)	The Kinks' Greatest Hits	1966	10.00	25.00
Reprise RS-6217	(E)	The Kinks' Greatest Hits	1966	8.00	20.00
Reprise R-6228	(M)	Face To Face	1967	12.00	30.00
Reprise RS-6228	(E)	Face To Face	1967	10.00	25.00
Reprise R-6260	(M)	Live Kinks	1967	12.00	30.00
Reprise RS-6260	(S)	Live Kinks	1967	10.00	25.00
Reprise R-6279	(M)	Something Else By The Kinks	1968	50.00	100.00
Reprise RS-6279	(S)	Something Else By The Kinks	1968	10.00	25.00
Reprise PRO-328	(P)	God Save The Kinks Box	1969	240.00	400.00
		(Boxed set includes a postcard, a decal, a bag of grass, a letter, a Union Jack pin, Kinks consumer guide, a "God Save The Kinks" button; and an album, "Then, Now And In Between.".)			
Reprise PRO-328	(P)	Then, Now And In Between	1969	75.00	150.00
Reprise RS-6327	(S)	The Village Green Preservation Society	1969	10.00	25.00
Reprise RS-6366	(S)	Arthur	1969	10.00	25.00
		— Original Reprise albums above have multi-color labels.—			
Reprise RS-6143	(P)	You Really Got Me	1969	5.00	12.00
Reprise RS-6217	(E)	The Kinks' Greatest Hits	1969	5.00	12.00
Reprise RS-6228	(E)	Face To Face	1969	5.00	12.00
Reprise RS-6260	(S)	Live Kinks	1969	5.00	12.00
Reprise RS-6279	(S)	Something Else By The Kinks	1969	5.00	12.00
Reprise RS-6327	(S)	The Village Green Preservation Society	1969	5.00	12.00
Reprise RS-6366	(S)	Arthur	1969	5.00	12.00
Reprise RS-6423	(S)	Lola Vs. The Powerman	1969	5.00	12.00
Reprise MS-2172	(P)	The Great Lost Kinks Album	1973	16.00	40.00
		— Reprise albums above have brown labels.—			
RCA Victor LSP-4644	(S)	Muswell Hillbillies	1971	6.00	15.00
RCA Victor VPS-6065	(S)	Everybody's In Show Biz (2 LPs)	1972	6.00	15.00
RCA Victor LPL1-5002	(S)	Preservation, Act 1	1973	5.00	12.00
RCA Victor CPL2-5040	(S)	Preservation, Act 2 (2 LPs)	1974	6.00	15.00
RCA Victor APL1-5081	(S)	Soap Opera	1975	5.00	12.00
		— Original RCA albums above orange labels.—			
Arista SP-69	(DJ)	Low Budget Radio Interview	1979	12.00	30.00
Mobile Fidelity MFSL-070	(S)	Misfits	1981	6.00	15.00
MCA 17281	(DJ)	A Look At "Think Visual"	1986	16.00	40.00

KIRBY STONE FOUR, THE
Columbia CL-1297	(S)	The Go Sound	1959	8.00	20.00

KISS
The original Kiss was Peter Criss, Ace Frehely, Gene Simmons and Paul Stanley.

Casablanca NBLP-9001	(DJ)	Kiss (White label)	1974	50.00	100.00
Casablanca NBLP-9001	(S)	Kiss	1974	16.00	40.00
Casablanca NBLP-7001	(S)	Kiss	1974	8.00	20.00
Casablanca NBLP-7006	(S)	Hotter Than Hell	1974	8.00	20.00
Casablanca NBLP-7016	(S)	Dressed To Kill (Embossed cover)	1975	8.00	20.00
Casablanca NBLP-7020	(S)	Alive!	1975	8.00	20.00
Casablanca NBLP-7025	(S)	Destroyer	1976	8.00	20.00
		— Original Casablanca albums above have blue/grey labels.—			
Casablanca NB Kiss-76	(DJ)	Special Kiss Album For Their Summer Tour	1976	14.00	35.00
Casablanca NBLP-7032	(S)	Kiss: The Originals (With inserts)	1976	40.00	80.00
Casablanca NBLP-7037	(DJ)	Rock And Roll Over-Special Edition	1976	14.00	35.00
Casablanca NBLP-7037	(S)	Rock And Roll Over	1976	6.00	15.00
		— Original Casablanca albums above have beige labels with Casablanca on top and the bottom.—			
Casablanca NBLP-7001	(S)	Kiss	1977	4.00	10.00
Casablanca NBLP-7006	(S)	Hotter Than Hell	1977	4.00	10.00
Casablanca NBLP-7016	(S)	Dressed To Kill	1977	4.00	10.00
Casablanca NBLP-7020	(S)	Alive!	1977	4.00	10.00
Casablanca NBLP-7025	(S)	Destroyer	1977	4.00	10.00
Casablanca NBLP-7032	(S)	Kiss: The Originals (With inserts)	1977	16.00	40.00
Casablanca NBLP-7037	(S)	Rock And Roll Over	1977	4.00	10.00
Casablanca NBLP-7057	(S)	Love Gun (With inserts)	1977	8.00	20.00
Casablanca NBLP-7076	(S)	Alive II (With inserts)	1977	4.00	10.00
Casablanca NBLP-7100	(S)	Double Platinum (2 LPs with insert)	1978	4.00	10.00
Casablanca NB 20128	(DJ)	A Taste Of Platinum	1978	12.00	30.00
Casablanca NBLP-7120	(S)	Gene Simmons (With poster)	1978	8.00	20.00
Casablanca NBLP-7120	(S)	Gene Simmons (Without poster)	1978	4.00	10.00
Casablanca NBLP-7120	(S)	Gene Simmons (Picture disc)	1978	10.00	25.00

Label & Catalog #		Title	Year	VG+	NM
Casablanca NBLP-7121	(S)	**Ace Frehley** (With poster)	1978	8.00	20.00
Casablanca NBLP-7121	(S)	**Ace Frehley** (Without poster)	1978	4.00	10.00
Casablanca NBLP-7121	(S)	**Ace Frehley** (Picture disc)	1978	10.00	25.00
Casablanca NBLP-7122	(S)	**Peter Criss** (With poster)	1978	8.00	20.00
Casablanca NBLP-7122	(S)	**Peter Criss** (Without poster)	1978	4.00	10.00
Casablanca NBLP-7122	(S)	**Peter Criss** (Picture disc)	1978	10.00	25.00
Casablanca NBLP-7123	(S)	**Paul Stanley** (With poster)	1978	8.00	20.00
Casablanca NBLP-7123	(S)	**Paul Stanley** (Without poster)	1978	4.00	10.00
Casablanca NBLP-7123	(S)	**Paul Stanley** (Picture disc)	1978	10.00	25.00
Casablanca NB 20137	(DJ)	**Solo Album Sampler**	1978	12.00	30.00
Casablanca NBLP-7152	(DJ)	**Dynasty** (With poster)	1979	8.00	20.00
Casablanca NBLP-7152	(S)	**Dynasty** (With poster)	1979	4.00	10.00
Casablanca NBLP-7225	(S)	**Unmasked** (With poster)	1980	4.00	10.00

— Casablanca albums above have Filmworks on top of the label with Casablanca on the bottom.—

Casablanca NBLP-7261	(S)	**Music From The Elder** (Soundtrack)	1981	14.00	35.00
Casablanca NBLP-7270	(S)	**Creatures Of The Night**	1982	8.00	20.00
Mercury 814 297-1	(S)	**Lick It Up**	1983	4.00	10.00
Mercury 822 495-1	(S)	**Animalize**	1984	4.00	10.00
Mercury 824 154-1	(S)	**Creatures Of The Night**	1984	4.00	10.00
Mercury 826 099-1	(S)	**Asylum**	1985	4.00	10.00
Mercury 832 626-1	(S)	**Crazy Nights**	1987	4.00	10.00
Mercury 832 903-1	(S)	**Crazy Nights** (Picture disc)	1987	6.00	15.00
Mercury 836 427-1	(S)	**Smashes, Thrashes And Hits**	1988	4.00	10.00
Mercury 836 8871-	(S)	**Smashes, Thrashes And Hits** (Picture disc)	1988	6.00	15.00
Mercury 838 913-1	(S)	**Hot In The Shade**	1989	4.00	10.00
Mercury 792	(DJ)	**First Kiss, Last Licks**	1990	16.00	40.00

KIT KATS, THE

Jamie LPM-3029	(M)	**It's Just A Matter Of Time**	1966	16.00	40.00
Jamie LPS-3029	(E)	**It's Just A Matter Of Time**	1966	12.00	30.00
Jamie LPM-3032	(M)	**Do Their Thing Live**	1967	12.00	30.00
Jamie LPS-3032	(S)	**Do Their Thing Live**	1967	16.00	40.00

KITCHEN CINQ, THE

L.II.I. 12000	(S)	**Everything But The Kitchen Cinq**	1967	8.00	20.00

KITT, EARTHA

RCA Victor LOC-1008	(M)	**New Faces Of 1952** (Original Cast)	1952	16.00	40.00
RCA Victor LPM-3062 (10")	(M)	**Songs**	1953	12.00	30.00
RCA Victor LPM-3187 (10")	(M)	**That Bad Eartha**	1953	12.00	30.00
RCA Victor LPM-1109	(M)	**Down To Eartha**	1955	12.00	30.00
RCA Victor LPM-1183	(M)	**That Bad Eartha**	1955	12.00	30.00
RCA Victor LPM-1300	(M)	**Thursday's Child**	1956	12.00	30.00
RCA Victor LPM-1661	(M)	**St. Louis Blues**	1958	8.00	20.00
RCA Victor LSP-1661	(S)	**St. Louis Blues**	1958	12.00	30.00
Kapp KL-1162	(M)	**The Fabulous Eartha Kitt**	1959	8.00	20.00
Kapp KS-3046	(S)	**The Fabulous Eartha Kitt**	1959	10.00	25.00
Kapp KL-1192	(M)	**Eartha Kitt Revisited**	1960	8.00	20.00
Kapp KS-3192	(S)	**Eartha Kitt Revisited**	1960	10.00	25.00
MGM E-4009	(M)	**Bad But Beautiful**	1962	6.00	15.00
MGM SE-4009	(S)	**Bad But Beautiful**	1962	8.00	20.00

KLUGMAN, JACK, & TONY RANDALL

London XPS-903	(S)	**The Odd Couple Sings**	1973	6.00	15.00

KNICKERBOCKERS, THE

Challenge LP-12664	(M)	**Sing And Sync Along With Lloyd Thaxton**	1965	35.00	70.00
Challenge LP-621	(M)	**Jerk And Twine Time**	1965	60.00	120.00
Challenge CH-622	(M)	**Lies**	1966	20.00	50.00
Challenge CHS-622	(S)	**Lies**	1966	35.00	70.00

KNIGHT, CHRIS, & MAUREEN McCORMICK

Paramount PAS-6062	(S)	**Chris Knight And Maureen McCormick**	1973	10.00	25.00

KNIGHT, CURTIS

Knight's group features a young Jimi Hendrix on guitar.

Capitol T-2856	(M)	**Get That Feeling**	1967	6.00	15.00
Capitol ST-2856	(S)	**Get That Feeling**	1967	8.00	20.00
Capitol ST-2894	(S)	**Flashing**	1968	8.00	20.00

Label & Catalog #		Title	Year	VG+	NM
KNIGHT, GLADYS, & THE PIPS					
Fury 1003	(M)	Letter Full Of Tears	1962	100.00	200.00
Maxx 3000	(M)	Gladys Knight And The Pips	1964	35.00	70.00
Sphere Sound SR-7006	(M)	Gladys Knight And The Pips	1965	20.00	50.00
Soul 706	(M)	Everybody Needs Love	1967	6.00	15.00
Soul SS-706	(S)	Everybody Needs Love	1967	8.00	20.00
Soul SS-707	(S)	Feelin' Bluesy	1968	6.00	15.00
Soul SS-711	(S)	Silk And Soul	1968	6.00	15.00
Bell 6013	(S)	Tastiest Hits	1968	6.00	15.00
Bell 1323	(S)	In The Beginning	1969	6.00	15.00
KNIGHT, ROBERT					
Monument 1-7000	(S)	Everlasting Love	1967	10.00	25.00
KNIGHT, SONNY					
Aura AR-3001	(M)	If You Want This Love	1964	8.00	20.00
Aura AS-3001	(S)	If You Want This Love	1964	10.00	25.00
KNIGHT, TERRY, & THE PACK					
The Pack features Mark Farner and Don Brewer, later of Grank Funk.					
Lucky Eleven LE-8000	(M)	Terry Knight & The Pack	1966	8.00	20.00
Lucky Eleven LES-8000	(S)	Terry Knight & The Pack	1966	12.00	30.00
Lucky Eleven LE-8001	(S)	Reflections	1966	8.00	20.00
Lucky Eleven LES-8001	(S)	Reflections	1966	12.00	30.00
Cameo C-2007	(M)	Reflections	1967	6.00	15.00
Cameo CS-2007	(S)	Reflections	1967	8.00	20.00
KNIGHTS, THE					
The Knights are a creation of Gary Usher & Co.					
Capitol T-2189	(M)	Hot Rod High	1964	75.00	150.00
Capitol DT-2189	(E)	Hot Rod High	1964	75.00	150.00
KNIGHTS, THE					
Ace MG-200854	(M)	Across The Road	1966	65.00	130.00
Ace MG-201303	(M)	The Knights 1967	1967	50.00	100.00
KNOCKOUTS, THE					
Tribute 1202	(M)	Go Ape With The Knockouts	1964	20.00	50.00
KNOWBODY ELSE					
Hip HIS-7003	(S)	Knowbody Else	1969	8.00	20.00
KNOTTS, DON					
United Arts. UAL-4090	(M)	Don Knotts	1961	6.00	15.00
United Arts. UAS-5090	(S)	Don Knotts	1961	8.00	20.00
KNOX, BUDDY					
Roulette R-25003	(M)	Buddy Knox	1957	65.00	130.00
Liberty LRP-3251	(M)	Buddy Knox's Golden Hits	1962	12.00	30.00
Liberty LSP-7251	(P)	Buddy Knox's Golden Hits	1962	16.00	40.00
United Arts. UAS-6689	(S)	Gypsy Man	1969	10.00	25.00
KNOX, BUDDY, & JIMMY BOWEN					
Roulette R-25048	(M)	Buddy Knox And Jimmy Bowen	1958	75.00	150.00
KOALA, THE					
Capitol SKAO-176	(S)	The Koala	1969	8.00	20.00
KODAKS, THE / THE STARLITES					
Sphere Sound SR-7005	(M)	The Kodaks Vs. The Starlites	1965	50.00	100.00
KEORNER, "SPIDER" JOHN					
Elektra EKL-290	(M)	Spider Blues	1965	6.00	15.00
Elektra EKS-7290	(S)	Spider Blues	1965	8.00	20.00
Elektra EKS-74041	(S)	Running, Jumping, Standing Still	1969	6.00	15.00
KOERNER, JOHN; DAVE RAY & TONY GLOVER					
Elektra EKL-240	(M)	Blue Rags And Hollers	1963	6.00	15.00
Elektra EKS-7240	(S)	Blue Rags And Hollers	1963	8.00	20.00

Label & Catalog #		Title	Year	VG+	NM
Elektra EKL-67	(M)	**Lots More Blues Rags And Hollers**	1964	6.00	15.00
Elektra EKS-7267	(S)	**Lots More Blues Rags And Hollers**	1964	8.00	20.00
Elektra EKL-305	(M)	**The Return Of Koerner, Ray & Glover**	1966	6.00	15.00
Elektra EKS-7305	(S)	**The Return Of Koerner, Ray & Glover**	1966	8.00	20.00

KOKI, SAM, & THE PARADISE ISLANDERS

Kapp KL-1321	(M)	**Surfin' At Waikiki**	1963	5.00	12.00
Kapp KS-3321	(S)	**Surfin' At Waikiki**	1963	6.00	15.00

KOLE, JERRY, & THE STROKERS
Jerry Kole is a pseudonym for Jerry Cole. Refer to Ritchie Valens / Jerry Kole.

Crown CLP-5385	(M)	**Hot Rod Alley**	1963	5.00	12.00
Crown CST-385	(S)	**Hot Rod Alley**	1963	6.00	15.00

KOOL & THE GANG

De-Lite DSR-2003	(S)	**Kool & The Gang**	1969	6.00	15.00
De-Lite MK-48	(DJ)	**History Of Kool & The Gang**	1979	6.00	15.00

KOPPERFIELD

Kopperdisc 5014N5	(S)	**Tales Untold**	1974	300.00	500.00

KORNER, ALEXIS

Warner Bros. 2XS-1966	(S)	**Bootleg Him** *(2 LPs with Charlie Watts)*	1972	10.00	25.00
Warner Bros. BS-2647	(S)	**Accidently Borne In New Orleans**	1972	5.00	12.00
Columbia PC-33427	(S)	**Get Off Of My Cloud** *(With Keith Richards)*	1975	6.00	15.00

KOTTKE, LEO

Oblivion 1	(S)	**Live At The Scholar Coffee House**	197?	10.00	25.00
Symposium 2001	(S)	**Circle 'Round The Sun**	1970	6.00	15.00

KRACKER

Primo PS-001	(S)	**Kracker**	1978	8.00	20.00

KRAL, IRENE

United Arts. UAL-4016	(M)	**The Band And I**	1959	20.00	50.00
United Arts. UAS-5016	(S)	**The Band And I**	1959	30.00	60.00
Ava 33	(M)	**Better Than Anything**	1963	6.00	20.00
Ava 33	(S)	**Better Than Anything**	1963	12.00	30.00
Mainstream 56058	(M)	**Wonderful Life**	1965	6.00	20.00
Mainstream 6058	(S)	**Wonderful Life**	1965	10.00	25.00

KRAL, IRENE, & STEVE ALLEN

United Arts. UAL-3052	(M)	**Steve-Irene-O!**	1959	12.00	30.00
United Arts. UAS-6052	(S)	**Steve-Irene-O!**	1959	16.00	40.00

KRAMER, BILLY J., & THE DAKOTAS

Imperial LP-9267	(M)	**Little Children** *(Black label with stars)*	1964	14.00	35.00
Imperial LP-12267	(P)	**Little Children** *(Black & silver label)*	1964	20.00	50.00
Imperial LP-9267	(M)	**Little Children** *(Black & pink label)*	1964	8.00	20.00
Imperial LP-12267	(P)	**Little Children** *(Black & pink label)*	1964	10.00	25.00
Imperial LP-9273	(M)	**I'll Keep You Satisfied**	1964	8.00	20.00
Imperial LP-12273	(S)	**I'll Keep You Satisfied**	1964	10.00	25.00
Imperial LP-9291	(M)	**Trains And Boats And Planes**	1965	8.00	20.00
Imperial LP-12291	(S)	**Trains And Boats And Planes**	1965	10.00	25.00

KRAZY KATS, THE

Damon 12478	(S)	**Movin' Out**	196?	35.00	70.00

KRISTOFFERSON, KRIS

Monument SLP-18139	(S)	**Kristofferson**	1970	8.00	20.00
Monument ZQ-30679	(Q)	**The Silver-Tongued Devil And I**	1972	5.00	12.00
Monument ZQ-31909	(Q)	**Jesus Was A Capricorn**	1972	5.00	12.00
Monument PZQ-32914	(Q)	**Spooky Lady's Sideshow**	1974	5.00	12.00

KRISTYL

No label	(M)	**Kristyl**	196?	150.00	250.00

Label & Catalog #		Title	Year	VG+	NM

KUBAN, BOB, & THE IN-MEN

| Musicland LP-3500 | (M) | Look Out For The Cheater | 1966 | 8.00 | 20.00 |
| Musicland SLP-3500 | (S) | Look Out For The Cheater | 1966 | 10.00 | 25.00 |

KUPFERBERG, TULI
Tuli was formerly a member of The Fugs.

| ESP 1035 | (S) | No Deposit No Return *(With insert)* | 1967 | 10.00 | 25.00 |
| ESP 1035 | (S) | No Deposit No Return *(Gold vinyl)* | 1967 | 16.00 | 40.00 |

KUSTOM KINGS, THE

| Smash MGS-27051 | (M) | Kustom City, U.S.A. | 1964 | 35.00 | 70.00 |
| Smash SRS-67051 | (S) | Kustom City, U.S.A. | 1964 | 50.00 | 100.00 |

KWESKIN, JIM, & THE JUG BAND

Vanguard VRS-9163	(M)	Jug Band Music	1966	5.00	12.00
Vanguard VSD-79163	(S)	Jug Band Music	1966	6.00	15.00
Vanguard VRS-9234	(M)	See Reverse Side For Title	1967	5.00	12.00
Vanguard VSD-79234	(S)	See Reverse Side For Title	1967	6.00	15.00
Vanguard VSD-13/14	(S)	Greatest Hits	1970	5.00	12.00
Reprise R-6266	(M)	Garden Of Joy	1967	6.00	15.00
Reprise RS-6266	(S)	Garden Of Joy	1967	8.00	20.00

L

LaBELLE (PATTI LaBELLE)

| Epic PEQ-33579 | (Q) | Phoenix | 1975 | 5.00 | 12.00 |

LaBELLE, PATTI, & THE BLUEBELLES

Newtown 631	(M)	Apollo Presents The Bluebelles	1963	65.00	130.00
Newtown 632	(M)	Sleigh Bells, Jingle Bells And Blue Bells	1963	65.00	130.00
Parkway 7043	(M)	The Bluebelles On Stage	1965	20.00	50.00
Atlantic 8101	(M)	Dreamer	1965	10.00	25.00
Atlantic SD-8101	(S)	Dreamer	1965	12.00	30.00
Atlantic 8119	(M)	Over The Rainbow	1966	10.00	25.00
Atlantic SD-8119	(S)	Over The Rainbow	1966	12.00	30.00

LADD, CHERYL
Refer to Josie & The Pussycats.

| Capitol SW-11808 | (S) | Cheryl Ladd | 1978 | 6.00 | 15.00 |

LaFARGE, PETER (PETER LaFORGE)

Folkways FV-9004	(M)	Women Blues	1965	5.00	12.00
Folkways FVS-9004	(S)	Women Blues	1965	6.00	15.00
Folkways 31014	(S)	As Long As The Grass Shall Grow	1968	4.00	10.00

LAINE, DENNY

| Capitol ST-11588 | (S) | Holly Days *(With Paul McCartney)* | 1977 | 6.00 | 15.00 |

LAINE, FRANKIE
Refer to Doris Day; The Four Lads; Jo Stafford.

Mercury MG-25007 (10")	(M)	Favorites	1949	14.00	35.00
Mercury MG-25024 (10")	(M)	Songs From The Heart	1950	14.00	35.00
Mercury MG-25025 (10")	(M)	Frankie Laine	1950	14.00	35.00

Label & Catalog #		Title	Year	VG+	NM
Mercury MG-25026 (10")	(M)	Frankie Laine	1950	14.00	35.00
Mercury MG-25027 (10")	(M)	Frankie Laine	1950	14.00	35.00
Mercury MG-25097 (10")	(M)	Mr. Rhythm Sings	1951	14.00	35.00
Mercury MG-25082 (10")	(M)	Christmas Favorites	1951	14.00	35.00
Mercury MG-25124 (10")	(M)	Listen To laine	1952	14.00	35.00
Mercury MG-20069	(M)	Songs By Frankie Laine	1956	14.00	35.00
Mercury MG-20080	(M)	That's My Desire	1957	14.00	35.00
Mercury MG-20083	(M)	Frankie Laine Sings For Us	1957	14.00	35.00
Mercury MG-20085	(M)	Concert Date	1957	14.00	35.00
Mercury MG-20105	(M)	With All My Heart	1957	14.00	35.00
Mercury MG-20587	(M)	Frankie Laine's Golden Hits	1960	10.00	25.00
Columbia CL-6200 (10")	(M)	One For My Baby	1952	14.00	35.00
Columbia CL-6278 (10")	(M)	Mr. Rhythm	1954	14.00	35.00
Columbia CL-2504 (10")	(M)	Lover's Laine	1955	14.00	35.00
Columbia CL-2548 (10")	(M)	One For My Baby	1955	14.00	35.00
Columbia CL-625	(M)	Command Performance	1956	14.00	35.00
Columbia CL-808	(M)	Jazz Spectacular	1956	12.00	30.00
Columbia CL-975	(M)	Rockin'	1957	12.00	30.00
Columbia CL-1116	(M)	Foreign Affair	1958	12.00	30.00
Columbia CL-1231	(M)	Frankie Laine's Greatest Hits	1959	10.00	25.00
Columbia CL-1224	(M)	Torchin'	1960	6.00	15.00
Columbia CS-8024	(S)	Torchin'	1960	8.00	20.00
Columbia CL-1287	(M)	Reunion In Rhythm	1961	6.00	15.00
Columbia CS-8087	(S)	Reunion In Rhythm	1961	8.00	20.00
Columbia CL-1319	(M)	You Are My Love	1961	6.00	15.00
Columbia CS-8119	(S)	You Are My Love	1961	8.00	20.00
Columbia CL-1388	(M)	Frankie Laine, Balladeer	1961	6.00	15.00
Columbia CS-8188	(S)	Frankie Laine, Balladeer	1961	8.00	20.00
Columbia CL-1615	(M)	Hell Bent For Leather!	1961	6.00	15.00
Columbia CS-8415	(S)	Hell Bent For Leather!	1961	8.00	20.00
Columbia CL-1696	(M)	Deuces Wild	1962	6.00	15.00
Columbia CS-8496	(S)	Deuces Wild	1962	8.00	20.00
— Original Columbia albums above have three white "eye" logos on each side of the spindle hole.—					
Columbia CL-1829	(M)	Call Of The Wild	1962	6.00	15.00
Columbia CS-8629	(S)	Call Of The Wild	1962	8..00	20.00
Columbia CL-1836	(M)	Frankie Laine's Greatest Hits	1962	6.00	15.00
Columbia CS-8636	(S)	Frankie Laine's Greatest Hits	1962	8..00	20.00
Columbia CL-1962	(M)	Wanderlust	1963	6.00	15.00
Columbia CS-8762	(S)	Wanderlust	1963	8..00	20.00
Capitol T-2277	(M)	I Believe	1965	5.00	12.00
Capitol ST-2277	(S)	I Believe	1965	6.00	15.00
Tower T-5092	(M)	Memory Laine	1967	5.00	12.00
Tower ST-5092	(S)	Memory Laine	1967	6.00	15.00

LAKE, GREG

Sweet Thunder 11	(S)	Greg Lake (Half-speed master)	198?	8.00	20.00

LAMB

Fillmore F-30003	(S)	Sign Of Change	1970	6.00	15.00

LAMBERT, DAVE

United Artists UAL-3084	(M)	Sings And Swings Alone	1959	14.00	35.00
United Artists UAS-6084	(S)	Sings And Swings Alone	1959	20.00	50.00

LAMBERT, HENDRICKS & BAVAN
Dave Lambert, Jon Hendricks and Yolanda Bavan.

RCA Victor LPM-2635	(M)	Live At Basin Street East	1963	8.00	20.00
RCA Victor LSP-2635	(S)	Live At Basin Street East	1963	12.00	30.00
RCA Victor LPM-2747	(M)	At Newport	1963	8.00	20.00
RCA Victor LSP-2747	(S)	At Newport	1963	12.00	30.00
RCA Victor LPM-2861	(M)	At The Village Gate	1965	8.00	20.00
RCA Victor LSP-2861	(S)	At The Village Gate	1965	12.00	30.00

LAMBERT, HENDRICKS & ROSS
Dave Lambert, Jon Hendricks and Annie Ross.

ABC-Paramount 223	(M)	Sing A Song Of Basie	1957	20.00	50.00
Roulette R-52018	(M)	Sing Along With Basie	1958	16.00	40.00
World Pacific WP-1264	(M)	The Swingers	1959	16.00	40.00

Label & Catalog #		Title	Year	VG+	NM
Columbia CL-1403	(M)	The Hottest New Group In Jazz	1959	8.00	20.00
Columbia CS-8198	(S)	The Hottest New Group In Jazz	1959	12.00	30.00
Columbia CL-1510	(M)	Lambert, Hendricks & Ross Sing Ellington	1960	8.00	20.00
Columbia CS-8310	(S)	Lambert, Hendricks & Ross Sing Ellington	1960	12.00	30.00
Columbia CL-1675	(M)	High Flying	1961	8.00	20.00
Columbia CS-8475	(S)	High Flying	1961	12.00	30.00

— Original Columbia albums above have three white "eye" logos on each side of the spindle hole.—

LAMEGO, DANNY, & HIS JUMPIN' JACKS

Forget-Me-Not 105A	(M)	The Big Weekend	1964	20.00	50.00

LAMOUR, DOROTHY

Decca DL-5115 (10")	(M)	Favorite Hawaiian Songs	1950	30.00	60.00
Design 45	(M)	The Road To Romance	195?	14.00	35.00

LANCE, MAJOR

OKeh OKM-12105	(M)	The Monkey Time	1963	8.00	20.00
OKeh OKS-14105	(S)	The Monkey Time	1963	10.00	25.00
OKeh OKM-12106	(M)	Um, Um, Um, Um, Um, Um	1964	8.00	20.00
OKeh OKS-14106	(S)	Um, Um, Um, Um, Um, Um	1964	10.00	25.00
OKeh OKM-12110	(M)	Major Lance's Greatest Hits	1965	6.00	15.00
OKeh OKS-14110	(P)	Major Lance's Greatest Hits	1965	8.00	20.00

LANCELOT LINK

ABC S-715	(S)	Lancelot Link & The Evolution Revolution	1970	10.00	25.00

LANCERS, THE

Trend TL-1009 (10")	(M)	The Lancers	1954	16.00	40.00
Coral CRL-57100	(M)	Dixieland Ball	1957	10.00	25.00

LANCHESTER, ELSA

HiFi R-405	(M)	Songs For A Smoke Filled Room	195?	10.00	25.00

LANE, VICKI

RCA Victor LPM-2056	(M)	I Swing For You	1959	12.00	30.00

LANGDON, DORY

Verve V-2101	(M)	Leprechauns Are Upon Me	195?	8.00	20.00

LARKS, THE
The Larks feature Don Julian.

Money LP-1102	(M)	The Jerk	1965	14.00	35.00
Money LP-1107	(M)	Soul Kaleidoscope	1966	8.00	20.00
Money MS-1107	(S)	Soul Kaleidoscope	1966	10.00	25.00
Money MY-1110	(M)	Superslick	1967	8.00	20.00
Money MS-1110	(S)	Superslick	1967	10.00	25.00

LaROSA, JULIUS

RCA Victor LPM-1299	(M)	Julius LaRosa	1956	16.00	40.00
Cadence CLP-1007	(M)	Julius LaRosa	1957	12.00	30.00
Roulette R-25054	(M)	Love Songs A LaRosa	1959	8.00	20.00
Roulette SR-25054	(S)	Love Songs A LaRosa	1959	12.00	30.00
Roulette R-25083	(M)	On The Sunny Side	1960	8.00	20.00
Roulette SR-25083	(S)	On The Sunny Side	1960	10.00	25.00
Forum S-16012	(M)	Just Say I Love Her	1960	6.00	15.00
Forum SF-16012	(S)	Just Say I Love Her	1960	8.00	20.00
Kapp KL-1245	(M)	The New Julie LaRosa	1961	6.00	15.00
Kapp KS-3245	(S)	The New Julie LaRosa	1961	8.00	20.00
MGM E-4398	(M)	You're Gonna Hear From Me	1966	5.00	12.00
MGM SE-4398	(S)	You're Gonna Hear From Me	1966	6.00	15.00

LAST DAYS, THE

No label	(S)	The Last Days	197?	20.00	50.00

LAST POETS, THE

Juggernaut 8802	(S)	Right On	1971	6.00	15.00
Douglas Z-30583	(S)	This Is Madness	1971	8.00	20.00
Douglas Z-30811	(S)	Last Poets	1971	10.00	25.00

Label & Catalog #		Title	Year	VG+	NM
LAST WORDS, THE					
Atco SD-33-235	(S)	The Last Words	1968	6.00	15.00
LAUGHTON, CHARLES					
Capitol TBO-1650	(M)	The Story Teller	1962	8.00	20.00
Capitol STBO-1650	(S)	The Story Teller	1962	10.00	25.00
LAUREN, ROD					
RCA Victor LPM-2176	(M)	I'm Rod Lauren	1961	8.00	20.00
RCA Victor LSP-2176	(S)	I'm Rod Lauren	1961	12.00	30.00
LAURIE SISTERS, THE					
Camden CAL-545	(M)	Hits Of The Great Girl Groups	1960	8.00	20.00
Camden CAS-545	(S)	Hits Of The Great Girl Groups	1960	12.00	30.00
LAWRENCE, CAROL					
Chancellor CHL-5015	(M)	Tonight At 8:30	1960	5.00	12.00
Chancellor CHLS-5015	(S)	Tonight At 8:30	1960	6.00	15.00
Choreo A-2	(M)	This Heart Of Mine	196?	6.00	15.00
Cameo S-1077	(M)	An Evening With Carol Lawrence	1964	5.00	12.00
Cameo SC-1077	(S)	An Evening With Carol Lawrence	1964	6.00	15.00
LAWRENCE, GERTRUDE					
Decca DL-5418 (10")	(M)	Souvenir Album	1952	16.00	40.00
RCA Victor LPM-1156	(M)	Noel And Gertie	1955	12.00	30.00
Decca DL-8673	(M)	A Remembrance	1958	12.00	30.00
Audio Fidelity AF-709	(M)	The Star	195?	12.00	30.00
LAWRENCE, STEVE					
Coral CRL-57050	(M)	About That Girl	1956	12.00	30.00
Coral CRL-57182	(M)	Songs	1957	12.00	30.00
Coral CRL-57204	(M)	Here's Steve Lawrence	1958	12.00	30.00
Coral CRL-57268	(M)	All About Love	1959	8.00	20.00
Coral CRL-757268	(S)	All About Love	1959	12.00	30.00
Coral CRL-57434	(M)	Songs Everybody Knows	1963	6.00	15.00
Coral CRL-757434	(S)	Songs Everybody Knows	1963	8.00	20.00
ABC-Paramount 290	(M)	Swing Softly With Me	1959	6.00	15.00
ABC-Paramount S-290	(S)	Swing Softly With Me	1959	8.00	20.00
ABC-Paramount 392	(M)	The Best Of Steve Lawrence	1960	6.00	15.00
ABC-Paramount S-392	(S)	The Best Of Steve Lawrence	1960	8.00	20.00
United Arts. UAL-3098	(M)	The Steve Lawrence Sound	1960	5.00	12.00
United Arts. UAS-6098	(S)	The Steve Lawrence Sound	1960	6.00	15.00
United Arts. UAL-3150	(M)	Portrait Of My Love	1961	5.00	12.00
United Arts. UAS-6150	(S)	Portrait Of My Love	1961	6.00	15.00
United Arts. UAL-3190	(M)	The Very Best Of Steve Lawrence	1962	5.00	12.00
United Arts. UAS-6190	(S)	The Very Best Of Steve Lawrence	1962	6.00	15.00
United Arts. UAL-3265	(M)	People Will Say We're In Love	1963	5.00	12.00
United Arts. UAS-6265	(S)	People Will Say We're In Love	1963	6.00	15.00
Columbia CL-1870	(M)	Come Waltz With Me	1962	5.00	12.00
Columbia CS-8670	(S)	Come Waltz With Me	1962	6.00	15.00
Columbia CL-1953	(M)	Winners	1963	4.00	10.00
Columbia CS-8753	(S)	Winners	1963	5.00	12.00
Columbia CL-2052	(M)	Swinging West	1964	5.00	12.00
Columbia CS-8852	(M)	Swinging West	1964	6.00	15.00
Columbia CL-2419	(M)	The Steve Lawrence Show	1965	4.00	10.00
Columbia CS-9219	(S)	The Steve Lawrence Show	1965	5.00	12.00
Columbia KOL-2440	(S)	What Makes Sammy Run? *(Soundtrack)*	1965	6.00	15.00
Columbia KOS-9240	(S)	What Makes Sammy Run? *(Soundtrack)*	1965	8.00	20.00
LAWRENCE, STEVE, & EYDIE GORME					
ABC-Paramount 300	(M)	We Got Us	1960	5.00	12.00
ABC-Paramount S-300	(S)	We Got Us	1960	6.00	15.00
ABC-Paramount 311	(M)	Steve & Eydie Sing The Golden Hits	1960	5.00	12.00
ABC-Paramount S-311	(S)	Steve & Eydie Sing The Golden Hits	1960	6.00	15.00
ABC-Paramount 469	(M)	Our Best To You	1964	5.00	12.00
ABC-Paramount S-469	(S)	Our Best To You	1964	6.00	15.00
United Arts. WWL-4509	(M)	Cozy	1961	5.00	12.00
United Arts. WWS-8509	(S)	Cozy	1961	6.00	15.00

Label & Catalog #		Title	Year	VG+	NM
United Arts. WWL-4518	(M)	Two On The Aisle	1963	5.00	12.00
United Arts. WWS-8518	(S)	Two On The Aisle	1963	6.00	15.00
United Arts. UAL-3191	(M)	The Very Best Of Eydie & Steve	1962	5.00	12.00
United Arts. UAS-6191	(S)	The Very Best Of Eydie & Steve	1962	6.00	15.00
Columbia CL-2021	(M)	At The Movies	1963	4.00	10.00
Columbia CS-8821	(S)	At The Movies	1963	5.00	12.00
Columbia CL-2262	(M)	That Holiday Feeling	1964	4.00	10.00
Columbia CS-9062	(S)	That Holiday Feeling	1964	5.00	12.00
Columbia CL-2636	(M)	Together On Broadway	1967	4.00	10.00
Columbia CS-9436	(S)	Together On Broadway	1967	5.00	12.00
Calendar KOM-1001	(M)	Golden Rainbow *(Soundtrack)*	1968	5.00	12.00
Calendar KOS-1001	(S)	Golden Rainbow *(Soundtrack)*	1968	6.00	15.00
RCA Victor LSP-4115	(S)	What It Was, Was Love *(Soundtrack)*	1969	5.00	12.00

LAWSON, DEE

Roulette R-52017	(M)	'Round Midnight	1958	16.00	40.00

LAY, SAM

Blue Thumb BTS-14	(S)	Sam Lay In Bluesland	1968	6.00	15.00

LAYTON, EDDIE

Mercury MG-20814	(M)	Folk Sounds	1963	5.00	12.00
Mercury SR-60814	(S)	Folk Sounds	1963	6.00	15.00

LAZAR, BILLY

Scarlett 100	(M)	Surfin' Around	1963	8.00	20.00

LAZY LESTER

Excello LP-8006	(M)	True Blues	1966	10.00	25.00

LAZY SMOKE

Onyx 6903	(M)	Corridor Of Faces	196?	500.00	750.00

LEA, BARBARA

Riverside 2518 (10")	(M)	A Woman In Love	1955	30.00	60.00
Prestige 7065	(M)	Barbara Lea	1956	16.00	40.00
Prestige 7100	(M)	Lea In Love	1957	16.00	40.00

LEACH, CURTIS

Longhorn 003	(M)	Indescribable	1965	20.00	50.00

LEADBELLY (HUDDIE LEDBETTER)

Folkways 4 (10")	(M)	Leadbelly	1950	16.00	40.00
Folkways 14 (10")	(M)	Leadbelly	1950	16.00	40.00
Folkways 24 (10")	(M)	Leadbelly	1950	16.00	40.00
Folkways 43 (10")	(M)	Leadbelly	1950	16.00	40.00
Folkways 2004 (10")	(M)	Take This Hammer	1951	16.00	40.00
Folkways 2013 (10")	(M)	Huddie Ledbetter	1951	16.00	40.00
Folkways 2014 (10")	(M)	Rock Island Line	1951	16.00	40.00
Folkways 2024 (10")	(M)	Leadbelly's Legacy	1951	16.00	40.00
Stinson SLP-17 (10")	(M)	Leadbelly Memorial *(Red vinyl)*	1951	20.00	50.00
Stinson SLP-19 (10")	(M)	Leadbelly Memorial *(Red vinyl)*	1951	20.00	50.00
Stinson SLP-39 (10")	(M)	Leadbelly Plays Party Songs	1951	12.00	30.00
Stinson SLP-41 (10")	(M)	Leadbelly Plays More Party Songs	1951	12.00	30.00
Stinson SLP-48 (10")	(M)	Leadbelly Memorial *(Red vinyl)*	1951	20.00	50.00
Stinson SLP-51 (10")	(M)	Leadbelly Memorial	1951	12.00	30.00
Stinson SLP-72 (10")	(M)	Leadbelly Memorial	1951	12.00	30.00
Allegro 4027 (10")	(M)	Sinful Songs	195?	100.00	200.00
Capitol H-369 (10")	(M)	Leadbelly	1952	100.00	200.00
Capitol T-1821	(M)	Leadbelly (Huddie Ledbetter's Best)	1962	20.00	50.00
Capitol DT-1891	(E)	Leadbelly (Huddie Ledbetter's Best)	1962	16.00	40.00
Folkways 2941	(M)	Leadbelly's Last Sessions, Part 1	1963	8.00	20.00
Folkways 2941	(E)	Leadbelly's Last Sessions, Part 1	1963	6.00	15.00
Folkways 2942	(M)	Leadbelly's Last Sessions, Part 2	1963	8.00	20.00
Folkways 2942	(E)	Leadbelly's Last Sessions, Part 2	1963	6.00	15.00
Folkways FV-9001	(M)	Take This Hammer	1965	8.00	20.00
Folkways FVS-9001	(E)	Take This Hammer	1965	10.00	25.00
Folkways FV-9021	(M)	Keep Your Hands Off Her	1965	8.00	20.00
Folkways FVS-9021	(E)	Keep Your Hands Off Her	1965	6.00	15.00

Label & Catalog #		Title	Year	VG+	NM
Folkways 3019	(M)	**From The Last Sessions**	1967	8.00	20.00
Folkways 3019	(E)	**From The Last Sessions**	1967	6.00	15.00
Folkways 3106	(E)	**Leadbelly Sings Folk Songs**	1968	6.00	15.00
RCA Victor LPV-505	(M)	**Midnight Special**	1964	20.00	50.00
Elektra EKL-301-2	(M)	**Library Of Congress Recordings** (2 LPs)	1966	10.00	25.00

LEADBELLY / JOSH WHITE / SONNY TERRY

Tradition 2093	(M)	**Legend Of Leadbelly, Josh White And Sonny Terry**	1969	6.00	15.00

LEARY, TIMOTHY

Pixie CA-1069	(M)	**L.S.D.**	1966	20.00	50.00
ESP 1027	(M)	**Turn On, Tune In, Drop Out**	1966	16.00	40.00
Mercury MG-21131	(M)	**Turn On, Tune In, Drop Out** (Soundtrack)	1967	20.00	50.00
Mercury SR-61131	(S)	**Turn On, Tune In, Drop Out** (Soundtrack)	1967	30.00	60.00
Douglas 1	(M)	**You Can Be Anyone This Time Around**	196?	50.00	100.00

LEASEBREAKERS, THE

United Arts. UAL-3423	(M)	**The Leasebreakers**	1965	5.00	12.00
United Arts. UAS-6423	(S)	**The Leasebreakers**	1965	6.00	15.00

LEATHERCOATED MINDS, THE
The Minds feature J.J. Cale.

Viva V-36003	(M)	**Trip Down Sunset Strip**	1967	12.00	30.00
Viva VS-36003	(S)	**Trip Down Sunset Strip**	1967	16.00	40.00

LEAVES, THE

Surrey 3005	(M)	**Hey Joe**	1966	50.00	100.00
Mira 3005	(M)	**Hey Joe**	1966	16.00	40.00
Mira LPS-3005	(S)	**Hey Joe**	1966	20.00	50.00
Capitol T-2638	(M)	**All The Good That's Happening**	1967	10.00	25.00
Capitol ST-2638	(S)	**All The Good That's Happening**	1967	12.00	30.00

LED ZEPPELIN

Atlantic SD-8216	(DJ)	**Led Zeppelin** (White label. Mono)	1968	100.00	200.00
Atlantic SD-8216	(DJ)	**Led Zeppelin** (White label. Stereo)	1968	75.00	150.00
Atlantic SD-8216	(S)	**Led Zeppelin** (Purple & brown label)	1968	75.00	150.00
Atlantic SD-8216	(S)	**Led Zeppelin**	1968	8.00	20.00
Atlantic SD-8236	(DJ)	**Led Zeppelin II** (White label. Mono)	1969	100.00	200.00
Atlantic SD-8236	(DJ)	**Led Zeppelin II** (White label. Stereo)	1969	75.00	150.00
Atlantic SD-8236	(S)	**Led Zeppelin II**	1969	8.00	20.00
Atlantic SD-7201	(DJ)	**Led Zeppelin III** (White label. Mono)	1970	100.00	200.00
Atlantic SD-7201	(DJ)	**Led Zeppelin III** (White label. Stereo)	1970	75.00	150.00
Atlantic SD-7201	(S)	**Led Zeppelin III**	1970	6.00	15.00
Atlantic SD-7208	(DJ)	**Led Zeppelin IV** (White label. Mono)	1971	100.00	200.00
Atlantic SD-7208	(DJ)	**Led Zeppelin IV** (White label. Stereo)	1971	75.00	150.00
Atlantic SD-7208	(S)	**Led Zeppelin IV**	1971	4.00	10.00
Atlantic SD-7255	(DJ)	**Houses Of The Holy** (White label. Mono)	1973	180.00	300.00
Atlantic SD-7255	(DJ)	**Houses Of The Holy** (White label. Stereo)	1973	100.00	200.00
Atlantic SD-7255	(S)	**Houses Of The Holy**	1973	4.00	10.00

— Original Atlantic albums above have green & orange labels with "1841 Broadway" on the bottom.—

Mobile Fidelity MFSL-065	(S)	**Led Zeppelin II**	1980	20.00	50.00

LED ZEPPELIN / DUSTY SPRINGFIELD

Atlantic SP-135	(DJ)	**Led Zeppelin / Dusty Springfield**	1969	75.00	150.00

(Album sampler with one side devoted to each artist; this is known among Zep collectors as "Climb Aboard Led Zeppelin.")

LEE, ADA

Atco 33-132	(M)	**Ada Lee Comes On**	1961	6.00	15.00
Atco SD-33-132	(S)	**Ada Lee Comes On**	1961	8.00	20.00

LEE, BRENDA

Decca DL-8873	(M)	**Grandma, What Great Songs You Sang**	1959	10.00	25.00
Decca DL-78873	(S)	**Grandma, What Great Songs You Sang**	1959	16.00	40.00
Decca DL-4039	(M)	**Brenda Lee**	1960	10.00	25.00
Decca DL-74039	(S)	**Brenda Lee**	1960	14.00	35.00
Decca DL-4082	(M)	**This Is Brenda**	1960	10.00	25.00
Decca DL-74082	(S)	**This Is Brenda**	1960	14.00	35.00

Label & Catalog #		Title	Year	VG+	NM
Decca DL-4104	(M)	**Emotions**	1961	8.00	20.00
Decca DL-74104	(S)	**Emotions**	1961	12.00	30.00
Decca DL-4176	(M)	**All The Way**	1961	8.00	20.00
Decca DL-74176	(S)	**All The Way**	1961	12.00	30.00
Decca DL-4216	(M)	**Sincerely, Brenda Lee**	1962	8.00	20.00
Decca DL-74216	(S)	**Sincerely, Brenda Lee**	1962	12.00	30.00
Decca DL-4326	(M)	**That's All**	1962	6.00	15.00
Decca DL-74326	(S)	**That's All**	1962	12.00	30.00
Decca DL-4370	(M)	**All Alone Am I**	1963	6.00	15.00
Decca DL-74370	(S)	**All Alone Am I**	1963	8.00	20.00
Decca DL-4439	(M)	**Let Me Sing**	1963	6.00	15.00
Decca DL-74439	(S)	**Let Me Sing**	1963	8.00	20.00
Decca DL-4509	(M)	**By Request**	1964	6.00	15.00
Decca DL-74509	(S)	**By Request**	1964	8.00	20.00
Decca DL-4583	(M)	**Merry Christmas From Brenda Lee**	1964	6.00	15.00
Decca DL-74583	(S)	**Merry Christmas From Brenda Lee**	1964	8.00	20.00
Decca DL-4626	(M)	**Top Teen Hits**	1965	6.00	15.00
Decca DL-74626	(S)	**Top Teen Hits**	1965	8.00	20.00
Decca DL-4661	(M)	**The Versatile Brenda Lee**	1965	6.00	15.00
Decca DL-74661	(S)	**The Versatile Brenda Lee**	1965	8.00	20.00
Decca DL-4684	(M)	**Too Many Rivers**	1965	6.00	15.00
Decca DL-74684	(S)	**Too Many Rivers**	1965	8.00	20.00
Decca DL-4755	(M)	**Bye, Bye Blues**	1966	6.00	15.00
Decca DL-74755	(S)	**Bye, Bye Blues**	1966	8.00	20.00
Decca DL-4757	(M)	**Ten Golden Years** (Fold-open cover)	1966	8.00	20.00
Decca DL-74757	(S)	**Ten Golden Years** (Fold-open cover)	1966	10.00	25.00
Decca DL-4825	(M)	**Coming On Strong**	1966	5.00	12.00
Decca DL-74825	(S)	**Coming On Strong**	1966	6.00	15.00
— Original Decca albums above have black labels with "Mfrd by Decca" beneath the rainbow.—					
Decca DL-4941	(M)	**Reflections In Blue**	1967	5.00	12.00
Decca DL-74941	(S)	**Reflections In Blue**	1967	6.00	15.00
Decca DL-74955	(S)	**For The First Time**	1968	6.00	15.00
Decca DL-75111	(S)	**Johnny One Time**	1969	6.00	15.00
Decca DL-75232	(S)	**Memphis Portrait**	1970	6.00	15.00

LEE, BRENDA / TENNESSEE ERNIE FORD

Decca MG-9226	(M)	**The Show For Christmas Seals**	1962	10.00	25.00
Decca MG-79226	(S)	**The Show For Christmas Seals**	1962	14.00	35.00

LEE, DICKEY

Smash MGS-27020	(M)	**Tales Of Patches**	1962	8.00	20.00
Smash SRS-67020	(S)	**Tales Of Patches**	1962	12.00	30.00
TCF Hall T-9001	(M)	**Laurie And The Girl From Peyton Place**	1965	6.00	15.00
TCF Hall ST-9001	(S)	**Laurie And The Girl From Peyton Place**	1965	8.00	20.00

LEE, JULIA

Capitol H-228 (10")	(M)	**Party Time**	1950	50.00	100.00
Capitol T-228	(M)	**Party Time**	1955	30.00	60.00

LEE, KATIE

Specialty 5000	(M)	**Spicy Songs For Cool Knights**	195?	10.00	25.00

LEE, KUI

Columbia CL-2603	(M)	**The Extraordinary Kui Lee**	1966	5.00	12.00
Columbia CS-9403	(S)	**The Extraordinary Kui Lee**	1966	6.00	15.00

LEE, MICHELE

Columbia OL-5800	(M)	**Bravo Giovanni!** (Soundtrack)	1962	6.00	15.00
Columbia OS-2200	(S)	**Bravo Giovanni!** (Soundtrack)	1962	8.00	20.00
Columbia CL-2486	(M)	**A Taste Of The Fantastic**	1967	5.00	12.00
Columbia CS-9286	(S)	**A Taste Of The Fantastic**	1967	6.00	15.00
Columbia CS-9682	(S)	**L. David Sloane**	1968	6.00	15.00

LEE, PEGGY
Ms. Lee also recorded with Doris Day.

Columbia CL-6033 (10")	(M)	**Benny Goodman And Peggy Lee**	1949	20.00	50.00
Decca DL-5482 (10")	(M)	**Black Coffee**	1953	35.00	70.00
Capitol H-151 (10")	(M)	**Rendezvous With Peggy Lee**	1952	20.00	50.00
Capitol H-204 (10")	(M)	**My Best To You**	1952	20.00	50.00

Label & Catalog #		Title	Year	VG+	NM
Decca DL-5539 (10")	(M)	Song In Intimate Style	1953	20.00	50.00
Decca DL-5557 (10")	(M)	The Lady And The Tramp (Soundtrack)	1955	50.00	100.00
Decca DL-8083	(M)	White Christmas (Soundtrack)	1954	20.00	50.00
Decca DL-8166	(M)	Songs From Pete Kelly's Blues (Soundtrack)	1955	30.00	60.00
Decca DL-8358	(M)	Black Coffee	1956	20.00	50.00
Decca DL-8411	(M)	Dream Street	1956	16.00	40.00
Decca DL-8462	(M)	The Lady And The Tramp (Soundtrack)	1957	50.00	100.00
Decca DL-8591	(M)	Sea Shells	1958	16.00	40.00
Decca DL-8816	(M)	Miss Wonderful	1959	16.00	40.00
— Original Decca albums above have black & silver labels.—					
Decca DL-4478	(M)	Lover	1964	6.00	15.00
Decca DL-74478	(S)	Lover	1964	8.00	20.00
Decca DL-4461	(M)	The Fabulous Peggy Lee	1964	6.00	15.00
Decca DL-74461	(S)	The Fabulous Peggy Lee	1964	8.00	20.00
Decca DXB-164	(M)	The Best Of Peggy Lee (2 LPs)	1964	8.00	20.00
Decca DXSB-164	(S)	The Best Of Peggy Lee (2 LPs)	1964	12.00	30.00
Capitol T-864	(M)	The Man I Love (Turquoise label)	1957	16.00	40.00
		(Capitol 864 conducted by Frank Sinatra.)			
Capitol T-975	(M)	Jump For Joy (Turquoise label)	1957	16.00	40.00
Capitol T-1049	(M)	Things Are Swingin'	1959	8.00	20.00
Capitol ST-1049	(S)	Things Are Swingin'	1959	12.00	30.00
Capitol T-1131	(M)	I Like Men	1959	8.00	20.00
Capitol ST-1131	(S)	I Like Men	1959	12.00	30.00
Capitol T-1219	(M)	Beauty And The Beat	1960	8.00	20.00
Capitol ST-1219	(S)	Beauty And The Beat	1960	12.00	30.00
— Original Capitol albums above have black labels with the logo on the left side.—					
Capitol T-1290	(M)	Latin Ala Lee!	1960	6.00	15.00
Capitol ST-1290	(S)	Latin Ala Lee!	1960	8.00	20.00
Capitol T-1366	(M)	All Aglow Again	1960	6.00	15.00
Capitol ST-1366	(S)	All Aglow Again	1960	8.00	20.00
Capitol T-1401	(M)	Pretty Eyes	1960	6.00	15.00
Capitol ST-1401	(S)	Pretty Eyes	1960	8.00	20.00
Capitol T-1423	(M)	Christmas Carousel	1960	6.00	15.00
Capitol ST-1423	(S)	Christmas Carousel	1960	8.00	20.00
Capitol T-1520	(M)	Basin Street East	1960	6.00	15.00
Capitol ST-1520	(S)	Basin Street East	1960	8.00	20.00
Capitol T-1671	(M)	Blue Cross Country	1961	6.00	15.00
Capitol ST-1671	(S)	Blue Cross Country	1961	8.00	20.00
Capitol T-1630	(M)	If You Go	1961	6.00	15.00
Capitol ST-1630	(S)	If You Go	1961	8.00	20.00
Capitol T-1743	(M)	Bewitching Lee	1962	6.00	15.00
Capitol ST-1743	(S)	Bewitching Lee	1962	8.00	20.00
Capitol T-1772	(M)	Sugar 'N' Spice	1962	6.00	15.00
Capitol ST-1772	(S)	Sugar 'N' Spice	1962	8.00	20.00
Capitol T-1850	(M)	Mink Jazz	1963	8.00	20.00
Capitol ST-1850	(S)	Mink Jazz	1963	12.00	30.00
Capitol T-1857	(M)	I'm A Woman	1963	5.00	12.00
Capitol ST-1857	(S)	I'm A Woman	1963	6.00	15.00
Capitol T-1969	(M)	In Love Again	1963	5.00	12.00
Capitol ST-1969	(S)	In Love Again	1963	6.00	15.00
Capitol T-2096	(M)	In The Name Of Love	1964	4.00	10.00
Capitol ST-2096	(S)	In The Name Of Love	1964	5.00	12.00
Capitol T-2320	(M)	Pass Me By	1965	4.00	10.00
Capitol ST-2320	(S)	Pass Me By	1965	5.00	12.00
Capitol T-2388	(M)	Then Was Then Now Is Now	1965	4.00	10.00
Capitol ST-2388	(S)	Then Was Then Now Is Now	1965	5.00	12.00
Capitol T-2475	(M)	Big Spender	1966	4.00	10.00
Capitol ST-2475	(S)	Big Spender	1966	5.00	12.00
Capitol T-2732	(M)	Extra Special	1967	4.00	10.00
Capitol ST-2732	(S)	Extra Special	1967	5.00	12.00
Capitol ST-2887	(S)	The Hits Of Peggy Lee	1968	5.00	12.00
— Original Capitol albums above have black labels with the logo on top.—					

LEE, PINKY

Decca DL-8421	(M)	The Surprise Party	1957	14.00	35.00

LEE, WILMA, & STONEY COOPER

Hickory 100	(M)	There's A Big Wheel	1960	16.00	40.00
Hickory 106	(M)	Family Favorites	1960	16.00	40.00

Label & Catalog #		Title	Year	VG+	NM
LEFT BANKE, THE					
Smash MGS-27088	(M)	**Walk Away Renee/Pretty Ballerina**	1967	20.00	50.00
Smash SRS-67088	(P)	**Walk Away Renee/Pretty Ballerina**	1967	16.00	40.00
Smash SRS-67113	(P)	**Left Banke, Too**	1968	16.00	40.00
		(Both stereo albums counterfieted with poor cover reproduction.)			
LEGEND					
Bell 6027	(S)	**Legend**	1969	16.00	40.00
LEGEND					
Megaphone 101	(S)	**Legend**	1970	30.00	60.00
LEGEND					
Empire 11186	(S)	**From The Fjords** *(With insert)*	1979	180.00	270.00
LEGENDS, THE					
Columbia CL-1707	(M)	**Hit Sounds Of Today's Smash Hit Combos**	1961	12.00	30.00
Columbia CS-8507	(S)	**Hit Sounds Of Today's Smash Hit Combos**	1961	16.00	40.00
LEGENDS, THE					
Ermine 101	(M)	**The Legends Let Loose**	1963	50.00	100.00
Capitol T-1925	(M)	**The Legends Let Loose**	1963	16.00	40.00
Capitol ST-1925	(S)	**The Legends Let Loose**	1963	20.00	50.00

Humorist Tom Lehrer's early albums were released on his own Lehrer label. He went on to both success and notoriety in the '60s with the topical TV show "That Was The Week That Was."

LEHRER, TOM					
Rivoli 4 (10")	(M)	**Song Satires**	1954	20.00	50.00
Lehrer 101 (10")	(M)	**Songs By Tom Lehrer**	1954	20.00	50.00
Lehrer TL-101	(M)	**Songs By Tom Lehrer**	1958	12.00	30.00
Lehrer TL-202	(M)	**An Evening Wasted With Tom Lehrer**	1958	8.00	20.00
Lehrer TL-202S	(S)	**An Evening Wasted With Tom Lehrer**	1958	12.00	30.00
Lehrer TL-102	(M)	**More Of Tom Lehrer**	1958	8.00	20.00
Lehrer TL-102S	(M)	**More Of Tom Lehrer**	1958	12.00	30.00
		(Lehrer 102 contains the same live tracks as Lehrer 202 with Tom's spoken commentary and the audience sounds edited out.)			

Label & Catalog #		Title	Year	VG+	NM
Reprise R-6179	(M)	That Was The Year That Was	1965	5.00	12.00
Reprise RS-6179	(S)	That Was The Year That Was	1965	6.00	15.00
Reprise R-6199	(M)	An Evening Wasted With Tom Lehrer	1966	5.00	12.00
Reprise RS-6199	(S)	An Evening Wasted With Tom Lehrer	1966	6.00	15.00

LEIBER, JERRY

Kapp KL-1127	(M)	Scooby-Doo	1959	20.00	50.00

LEIBER & STOLLER BIG BAND

Atlantic 8047	(M)	Yakety Yak	1960	12.00	30.00
Atlantic SD-8047	(S)	Yakety Yak	1960	16.00	40.00

LEMMON, JACK

Epic LN-3491	(M)	A Twist Of Lemmon	1959	8.00	20.00
Epic BN-3491	(S)	A Twist Of Lemmon	1959	10.00	25.00
Epic LN-3551	(M)	Music From "Some Like It Hot"	1959	8.00	20.00
Epic BN-3551	(S)	Music From "Some Like It Hot"	1959	10.00	25.00
Riverside RLP-12-849	(M)	E.B. White's "Here Is New York"	196?	8.00	20.00
Capitol T-1943	(M)	Piano Selections From "Irma La Douce"	1963	8.00	20.00
Capitol ST-1943	(S)	Piano Selections From "Irma La Douce"	1963	10.00	25.00

LEMON PIPERS, THE
Refer to 1910 Fruitgum Co. / The Lemon Pipers.

Buddah BD-5009	(M)	Green Tambourine	1968	6.00	15.00
Buddah BDS-5009	(S)	Green Tambourine	1968	8.00	20.00
Buddah BDS-5016	(S)	Jungle Marmalade	1968	6.00	15.00

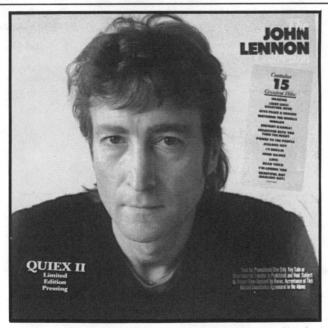

The term 'rock & roll genius' was invented for John Lennon. This collection of his final recordings before his assassination in 1980 is the most collectible album of those pressed on Quiex II virgin vinyl.

LENNON, JOHN (& THE PLASTIC ONO BAND)
John Lennon was formerly a member of The Beatles. Refer to Elephant's Memory; Nilsson; Yoko Ono.

Apple SW-3362	(S)	Live Peace In Toronto (With calendar)	1969	8.00	20.00
		(The label reads "Mfd. by Apple Records" on the bottom.)			
Apple SW-3362	(S)	Live Peace In Toronto (With calendar)	1969	12.00	30.00
		(The label reads "Mfd. by Capitol Industries" on the bottom.)			
Apple SW-3372	(S)	John Lennon/Plastic Ono Band	1970	8.00	20.00

Label & Catalog #		Title	Year	VG+	NM
Apple SW-3379	(S)	Imagine *(With poster and a postcard)*	1971	10.00	25.00
Apple SW-3379	(S)	Imagine *(Without the poster and postcard)*	1971	6.00	15.00
Apple SW-3414	(S)	Mind Games	1973	6.00	15.00
Apple SW-3416	(S)	Walls And Bridges *(With book)*	1974	6.00	15.00
Apple SK-3419	(S)	Rock 'N' Roll	1975	6.00	15.00
Adam VIII	(S)	Roots *(Counterfeits exist)*	1975	360.00	600.00
Apple SW-3421	(S)	Shaved Fish	1975	6.00	15.00
Capitol SW-3414	(S)	Mind Games *(Purple label)*	1978	12.00	30.00
Capitol SK-3419	(S)	Rock 'N' Roll *(Purple label)*	1978	10.00	25.00
Geffen GHSP-2023	(DJ)	The John Lennon Collection *(Quiex II vinyl)*	1982	16.00	40.00
Geffen GHSP-2023	(S)	The John Lennon Collection	1982	4.00	10.00
Silhouette SM-10012	(S)	Reflections And Poetry	1984	6.00	15.00
Mobile Fidelity MFSL-153	(S)	Imagine	1984	8.00	20.00

LENNON, JOHN, & YOKO ONO

Label & Catalog #		Title	Year	VG+	NM
Apple T-5001	(S)	Two Virgins: Unfinished Music No. 1	1968	35.00	70.00
		(Issued in a brown paper outer sleeve that opens on the right.)			
Apple/Tetragram. T-5001	(S)	Two Virgins: Unfinished Music No. 1	1968	6.00	15.00
Zapple ST-3357	(S)	Unfinished Music #2: Life With The Lions	1969	8.00	20.00
Apple 3361	(S)	Wedding Album	1969	65.00	130.00
		(Boxed set contains photos, postcard, poster of wedding photos, poster of lithographs, a booklet of press clippings, duplicate of marriage certificate, a "bagism" bag.)			
Apple SVBB-3392	(DJ)	Some Time In New York City *(2 LPs)*	1972	500.00	750.00
Apple SVBB-3392	(S)	Some Time In New York City *(2 LPs)*	1972	10.00	25.00
Capitol SVBB-3392	(S)	Some Time In New York City	1978	100.00	200.00
		(Single album reissue on purple label.)			
Nautilus NR-47	(DJ)	Double Fantasy *(With poster)*	1980	75.00	150.00
		(Issued in a plain white jacket with a nautilus seashell.)			
Nautilus NR-47	(S)	Double Fantasy *(With poster)*	1980	16.00	40.00
Polydor 817-160-1	(S)	Milk And Honey *(Green vinyl)*	1984	75.00	150.00
Polydor 817-160-1	(S)	Milk And Honey *(Gold vinyl)*	1984	50.00	100.00
		(These are unauthorized pressings done by a Polydor company employee "after hours." Issued without a cover.)			

LENOIR, J.B.

Label & Catalog #		Title	Year	VG+	NM
Chess 1410	(M)	Natural Man	1963	20.00	50.00
Polydor 24-4011	(S)	J.B. Lenoir	1970	6.00	15.00

LESTER, BOBBY, & THE MOONGLOWS: *Refer to* THE MOONGLOWS

LESTER, KETTY

Label & Catalog #		Title	Year	VG+	NM
Era EL-108	(M)	Love Letters	1963	12.00	30.00
Era ES-108	(S)	Love Letters	1963	16.00	40.00
RCA Victor LPM-2945	(M)	Soul Of Me	1964	6.00	15.00
RCA Victor LSP-2945	(S)	Soul Of Me	1964	8.00	20.00
RCA Victor LPM-3326	(M)	Where Is Love	1965	6.00	15.00
RCA Victor LSP-3326	(S)	Where Is Love	1965	8.00	20.00
Tower T-5029	(M)	When A Woman Loves A Man	1967	5.00	12.00
Tower ST-5029	(S)	When A Woman Loves A Man	1967	6.00	15.00

LETTERMEN, THE

Label & Catalog #		Title	Year	VG+	NM
Capitol T-1669	(M)	A Song For Young Love	1962	5.00	12.00
Capitol ST-1669	(S)	A Song For Young Love	1962	6.00	15.00
Capitol T-1711	(M)	Once Upon A Time	1962	5.00	12.00
Capitol ST-1711	(S)	Once Upon A Time	1962	6.00	15.00
Capitol T-1761	(M)	Jim, Tony, Bob	1962	5.00	12.00
Capitol ST-1761	(S)	Jim, Tony, Bob	1962	6.00	15.00
Capitol T-1829	(M)	College Standards	1963	5.00	12.00
Capitol ST-1829	(S)	College Standards	1963	6.00	15.00
Capitol T-1936	(M)	The Lettermen In Concert	1963	4.00	10.00
Capitol ST-1936	(S)	The Lettermen In Concert	1963	5.00	12.00
Capitol T-2013	(M)	A Lettermen Kind Of Love	1964	4.00	10.00
Capitol ST-2013	(S)	A Lettermen Kind Of Love	1964	5.00	12.00
Capitol T-2083	(M)	The Lettermen Look At Love	1964	4.00	10.00
Capitol ST-2083	(S)	The Lettermen Look At Love	1964	5.00	12.00
Capitol T-2142	(M)	She Cried	1964	4.00	10.00
Capitol ST-2142	(S)	She Cried	1964	5.00	12.00

Label & Catalog #		Title	Year	VG+	NM
Capitol T-2270	(M)	Portrait Of My Love	1965	4.00	10.00
Capitol ST-2270	(S)	Portrait Of My Love	1965	5.00	12.00
Capitol T-2213	(M)	You'll Never Walk Alone	1965	4.00	10.00
Capitol ST-2213	(S)	You'll Never Walk Alone	1965	5.00	12.00
Capitol T-2359	(M)	The Hit Sounds Of The Lettermen	1965	4.00	10.00
Capitol ST-2359	(S)	The Hit Sounds Of The Lettermen	1965	5.00	12.00
Capitol T-2428	(M)	More Hit Sounds Of The Lettermen	1966	4.00	10.00
Capitol ST-2428	(S)	More Hit Sounds Of The Lettermen	1966	5.00	12.00
Capitol T-2496	(M)	A New Song For Young Love	1966	4.00	10.00
Capitol ST-2496	(S)	A New Song For Young Love	1966	5.00	12.00
Capitol T-2554	(M)	The Best Of The Lettermen	1966	3.50	8.00
Capitol ST-2554	(S)	The Best Of The Lettermen	1966	4.00	10.00
Capitol T-2587	(M)	For Christmas This Year	1966	3.50	8.00
Capitol ST-2587	(S)	For Christmas This Year	1966	4.00	10.00
Capitol T-2633	(M)	Warm	1967	3.50	8.00
Capitol ST-2633	(S)	Warm	1967	4.00	10.00
Capitol T-2711	(M)	Spring!!	1967	3.50	8.00
Capitol ST-2711	(S)	Spring!!	1967	4.00	10.00
Capitol T-2758	(M)	The Lettermen!! And Live!	1967	3.50	8.00
Capitol ST-2758	(S)	The Lettermen!! And Live!	1967	4.00	10.00
Capitol ST-2865	(S)	Goin' Out Of My Head	1968	4.00	10.00

— Original Capitol albums above have black labels with the logo on top. —

LEVIATHAN

Mach XMA-12501	(S)	Leviathan	1974	6.00	15.00

LEWIS, BARBARA

Atlantic 8086	(M)	Hello Stranger	1963	14.00	35.00
Atlantic SD-8086	(S)	Hello Stranger	1963	20.00	50.00
Atlantic 8090	(M)	Snap Your Fingers	1964	14.00	35.00
Atlantic SD-8090	(S)	Snap Your Fingers	1964	20.00	50.00
Atlantic 8110	(M)	Baby, I'm Yours	1965	10.00	25.00
Atlantic SD-8110	(S)	Baby, I'm Yours	1965	14.00	35.00
Atlantic 8118	(M)	It's Magic	1966	8.00	20.00
Atlantic SD-8118	(S)	It's Magic	1966	10.00	25.00
Atlantic SD-8173	(S)	Workin' On A Groovy Thing	1968	8.00	20.00
Atlantic SD-8286	(S)	The Best Of Barbara Lewis	1971	8.00	20.00

LEWIS, BOBBY

Beltone 4000	(M)	Tossin' And Turnin'	1961	75.00	150.00

LEWIS, FURRY

Bluesville BV-1036	(M)	Back On My Feet Again	1961	14.00	35.00
Bluesville BVS-1036	(S)	Back On My Feet Again	1961	20.00	50.00
Prestige 7810	(S)	Back On My Feet Again	1970	5.00	12.00
Adelphi 1007	(S)	On The Road Again	1970	5.00	12.00
Ampex A-10140	(S)	Live At The Gaslight	1971	6.00	15.00
Fantasy F-24709	(S)	Shake 'Em On Down (2 LPs)	1972	5.00	12.00

LEWIS, GARY (& THE PLAYBOYS)

Liberty LRP-3408	(M)	This Diamond Ring	1965	6.00	15.00
Liberty LST-7408	(S)	This Diamond Ring	1965	8.00	20.00
Liberty LRP-3419	(M)	A Session With Gary Lewis	1965	4.00	10.00
Liberty LST-7419	(S)	A Session With Gary Lewis	1965	5.00	12.00
Liberty LRP-3428	(M)	Everybody Loves A Clown	1965	4.00	10.00
Liberty LST-7428	(S)	Everybody Loves A Clown	1965	5.00	12.00
Liberty LRP-3435	(M)	She's Just My Style	1966	4.00	10.00
Liberty LST-7435	(S)	She's Just My Style	1966	5.00	12.00
Liberty LRP-3452	(M)	Hits Again!	1966	4.00	10.00
Liberty LST-7452	(S)	Hits Again!	1966	5.00	12.00
Liberty LRP-3468	(M)	Gary Lewis' Golden Greats	1966	4.00	10.00
Liberty LST-7468	(S)	Gary Lewis' Golden Greats	1966	5.00	12.00
Liberty LRP-3487	(M)	You Don't Have To Paint Me A Picture	1967	3.50	8.00
Liberty LST-7487	(S)	You Don't Have To Paint Me A Picture	1967	4.00	10.00
Liberty LRP-3519	(M)	New Directions	1967	3.50	8.00
Liberty LST-7519	(S)	New Directions	1967	4.00	10.00
Liberty LRP-3524	(M)	Listen	1967	3.50	8.00
Liberty LST-7524	(S)	Listen	1967	4.00	10.00
Liberty LST-7568	(S)	Gary Lewis Now!	1968	4.00	10.00

Label & Catalog #		Title	Year	VG+	NM
Liberty LST-7589	(S)	More Golden Greats	1968	4.00	10.00
Liberty LST-7606	(S)	Close Cover Before Playing	1969	4.00	10.00
Liberty LST-7623	(S)	Rhythm Of The Rain	1969	4.00	10.00
Liberty LST-7633	(S)	I'm On The Right Road Now	1969	4.00	10.00

LEWIS, HUEY, & THE NEWS

Mobile Fidelity MFSL-181	(S)	Sports	198?	6.00	15.00

LEWIS, JERRY

Decca DL-8410	(M)	Jerry Lewis Just Sings	1956	12.00	30.00
Decca DL-8595	(M)	More Jerry Lewis	1956	12.00	30.00
Decca DL-8936	(M)	Big Songs For Little People	1959	12.00	30.00
Decca DL-78936	(S)	Big Songs For Little People	1969	16.00	40.00
Dot DLP-8001	(M)	Cinderfella (Soundtrack)	1960	14.00	35.00
Dot DLP-38001	(S)	Cinderfella (Soundtrack)	1960	20.00	50.00
Dot DLP-8001	(M)	Cinderfella (Soundtrack. Colored vinyl)	1960	35.00	70.00
Dot DLP-38001	(S)	Cinderfella (Soundtrack. Colored vinyl)	1960	50.00	100.00
Capitol J-3267	(M)	Nagger	1963	12.00	30.00
Vocalion VL-3781	(M)	Jerry Lewis Sings For Children	196?	6.00	15.00
Vocalion VL-73781	(S)	Jerry Lewis Sings For Children	196?	8.00	20.00

LEWIS, JERRY LEE

Sun LP-1230	(M)	Jerry Lee Lewis	1958	75.00	150.00
Sun LP-1265	(M)	Jerry Lee's Greatest	1961	100.00	200.00
Design DLP-165	(M)	Rockin' With Jerry Lee Lewis	1963	8.00	20.00
Smash MGS-27040	(M)	The Golden Hits Of Jerry Lee Lewis	1964	10.00	25.00
Smash SRS-67040	(S)	The Golden Hits Of Jerry Lee Lewis	1964	14.00	35.00
Smash MGS-27056	(M)	The Greatest Live Show On Earth	1964	35.00	70.00
Smash SRS-67056	(S)	The Greatest Live Show On Earth	1964	50.00	100.00
Smash MGS-27063	(M)	The Return Of Rock	1965	14.00	35.00
Smash SRS-67063	(S)	The Return Of Rock	1965	20.00	50.00
Smash MGS-27071	(M)	Country Songs For City Folks	1965	6.00	15.00
Smash SRS-67071	(S)	Country Songs For City Folks	1965	10.00	25.00
Smash MGS-27079	(M)	Memphis Beat	1966	8.00	20.00
Smash SRS-67079	(S)	Memphis Beat	1966	12.00	30.00
Smash MGS-27086	(M)	By Request	1966	8.00	20.00
Smash SRS-67086	(S)	By Request	1966	12.00	30.00
Smash MGS-27097	(M)	Soul My Way	1967	12.00	30.00
Smash SRS-67097	(S)	Soul My Way	1967	16.00	40.00
Smash SRS-67014	(S)	Another Place, Another Time	1968	6.00	15.00
Smash SRS-67040	(S)	Golden Rock Hits	1968	6.00	15.00
Smash SRS-67040	(S)	The Golden Rock Hits Of Jerry Lee Lewis	1969	6.00	15.00
Smash SRS-67071	(S)	All Country	1969	6.00	15.00
Smash SRS-67112	(S)	She Still Comes Around	1968	6.00	15.00
Smash SRS-67117	(S)	Country Music Hall Of Fame Hits, Volume 1	1969	6.00	15.00
Smash SRS-67118	(S)	Country Music Hall Of Fame Hits, Volume 2	1969	6.00	15.00
Smash SRS-67128	(S)	She Even Woke Me Up To Say Goodbye	1970	6.00	15.00
Smash SRS-67131	(S)	The Best Of Jerry Lee Lewis	1970	6.00	15.00
Wing MGW-12340	(M)	The Return Of Rock	1967	5.00	12.00
Wing SRW-16340	(S)	The Return Of Rock	1967	6.00	15.00
Wing SRW-16340	(S)	In Demand	1968	6.00	15.00
Wing SRW-16406	(S)	Unlimited	1968	6.00	15.00
Wing PKW2-125	(S)	The Legend Of Jerry Lee Lewis (2 LPs)	1969	10.00	25.00
Mercury SR-61278	(S)	Live At The International	1970	6.00	15.00
Mercury SR-61318	(S)	In Loving Memories	1971	10.00	25.00
Mercury SR-61323	(S)	There Must Be More To Love Than This	1971	6.00	15.00
Mercury SR-61343	(S)	Touching Home (Drawing cover)	1971	10.00	25.00
Mercury SR-61343	(S)	Touching Home (Photo cover)	1971	6.00	15.00
Mercury SR-61346	(S)	Would You Take Another Chance On Me	1971	6.00	15.00
Mercury SR-61366	(S)	Who's Gonna Play This Old Piano	1972	5.00	12.00
Mercury SRM-1-637	(S)	The Killer Rocks On	1972	8.00	20.00
Mercury MK-3	(DJ)	Southern Roots Radio Special	1973	20.00	50.00
Mercury SRM-2-803	(S)	The Session (2 LPs)	1973	10.00	25.00
Mercury SRM-1-710	(S)	I-40 Country	1974	8.00	20.00

LEWIS, JERRY LEE, & LINDA GAIL LEWIS

Smash SRS-67126	(S)	Together	1969	6.00	15.00

Label & Catalog #		Title	Year	VG+	NM
LEWIS, LINDA GAIL					
Smash SRS-67119	(S)	Two Sides Of Linda Gail Lewis	1969	6.00	15.00
LEWIS, KATHERINE HANDY					
Folkways FG-3540	(M)	W.C. Handy Blues	196?	10.00	25.00
LEWIS, MEADE LUX					
Stinson 25 (10")	(M)	Meade Lux Lewis	1950	50.00	100.00
Blue Note BLP-7018 (10")	(M)	Boogie Woogie Classics	1951	50.00	100.00
Atlantic 133 (10")	(M)	Boogie Woogie	1952	50.00	100.00
Clef C-632	(M)	Meade Lux Lewis With Louis Bellson	1955	20.00	50.00
Tops L-1533	(M)	Barrel House Piano	1956	20.00	50.00
ABC-Paramount 164	(M)	Out Of The Roaring '20s	1957	20.00	50.00
Riverside RLP-9402	(M)	Blues Piano Artistry Of Meade Lux Lewis	1961	20.00	50.00
LEWIS, SHARI					
RCA Victor LBY-1006	(M)	Fun In Shariland	195?	10.00	25.00
Golden GLP-39	(M)	Hi, Kids!	1962	8.00	20.00
LEWIS, SMILEY					
Imperial LP-9141	(M)	I Hear You Knocking	1961	180.00	300.00
LEWIS & CLARKE EXPEDITION					
Colgems COM-105	(M)	The Lewis And Clarke Expedition	1967	6.00	15.00
Colgems COS-105	(S)	The Lewis And Clarke Expedition	1967	8.00	20.00
LIBERMAN, JEFFREY					
Librah 1545	(S)	Jeffrey Liberman	1975	30.00	60.00
Librah 6969	(S)	Solitude Within	1975	40.00	80.00
Librah 12157	(S)	Synergy	1978	50.00	100.00
LICK					
Big Dog BD-1001	(S)	Just A Taste	1979	30.00	60.00
LT. GARCIA'S MAGIC MUSIC BOX					
Kama Sutra KLPS-8071	(S)	Cross The Border	1968	6.00	15.00
LIGHTCRUST DOUGHBOYS, THE					
Audio Lab LP-1525	(M)	The Lightcrust Doughboys	1959	40.00	80.00
LIGHTFOOT, GORDON					
United Arts. UAL-3487	(M)	Lightfoot	1965	5.00	12.00
United Arts. UAS-6487	(S)	Lightfoot	1965	6.00	15.00
United Arts. UAL-3587	(M)	The Way I Feel	1967	5.00	12.00
United Arts. UAS-6587	(S)	The Way I Feel	1967	6.00	15.00
Reprise MS4-2177	(Q)	Sundown	1974	6.00	15.00
Reprise MS4-2206	(Q)	Cold On The Shoulder	1975	6.00	15.00
Mobile Fidelity MFSL-018	(S)	Sundown	1979	10.00	25.00
LIGHTNIN' SLIM					
Excello 8000	(M)	Rooster Blues	1960	35.00	70.00
Excello 8004	(M)	Lightnin' Slim's Bell Ringer	1965	14.00	50.00
Excello S-8004	(S)	Lightnin' Slim's Bell Ringer	1965	16.00	40.00
Excello 8018	(S)	High And Low Down	1971	6.00	15.00
Excello 8023	(S)	London Gumbo	1972	6.00	15.00
LIGHTNING					
P.I.P. 6807	(S)	Lightning	1971	12.00	30.00
LIMELITERS, THE					
The Limeliters feature Glenn Yarbrough.					
Elektra EKL-180	(M)	The Limeliters	1960	6.00	15.00
Elektra EKS-7180	(S)	The Limeliters	1960	8.00	20.00
RCA Victor LPM-2272 —	(M)	Tonight: In Person	1961	5.00	12.00
RCA Victor LSP-2272	(S)	Tonight: In Person	1961	8.00	20.00
RCA Victor LPM-2393	(M)	The Slightly Fabulous Limeliters	1961	5.00	12.00
RCA Victor LSP-2393	(S)	The Slightly Fabulous Limeliters	1961	8.00	20.00
RCA Victor LPM-2445	(M)	The Limeliters Sing Out!	1962	5.00	12.00
RCA Victor LSP-2445	(S)	The Limeliters Sing Out!	1962	8.00	20.00

Label & Catalog #		Title	Year	VG+	NM
RCA Victor LPM-2512	(M)	Through Children's Eyes	1962	5.00	12.00
RCA Victor LSP-2512	(S)	Through Children's Eyes	1962	8.00	20.00
RCA Victor LPM-2547	(M)	Folk Matinee	1962	5.00	12.00
RCA Victor LSP-2547	(S)	Folk Matinee	1962	8.00	20.00
RCA Victor LPM-2588	(M)	Makin' A Joyful Noise	1963	5.00	12.00
RCA Victor LSP-2588	(S)	Makin' A Joyful Noise	1963	8.00	20.00
RCA Victor LPM-2609	(M)	Our Men In San Francisco	1963	5.00	12.00
RCA Victor LSP-2609	(S)	Our Men In San Francisco	1963	8.00	20.00
RCA Victor LPM-2671	(M)	Fourteen 14K Folk Songs	1963	5.00	12.00
RCA Victor LSP-2671	(S)	Fourteen 14K Folk Songs	1963	8.00	20.00

— Original RCA mono albums above have "Long Play" on the bottom of the label;
stereo albums have "Living Stereo" on the bottom.—

RCA Victor LPM-2844	(M)	More Of Everything	1964	4.00	10.00
RCA Victor LSP-2844	(S)	More Of Everything	1964	5.00	12.00
RCA Victor LPM-2889	(M)	The Best Of The Limeliters	1964	4.00	10.00
RCA Victor LSP-2889	(S)	The Best Of The Limeliters	1964	5.00	12.00
RCA Victor LPM-2906	(M)	Leave It To The Limeliters	1964	4.00	10.00
RCA Victor LSP-2906	(S)	Leave It To The Limeliters	1964	5.00	12.00
RCA Victor LPM-2907	(M)	London Concert	1965	4.00	10.00
RCA Victor LSP-2907	(S)	London Concert	1965	5.00	12.00
RCA Victor LPM-3385	(M)	The Limeliters Look At Love In Depth	1965	4.00	10.00
RCA Victor LSP-3385	(S)	The Limeliters Look At Love In Depth	1965	5.00	12.00

— Original RCA albums above have black labels.—

LILLIE, BEATRICE

Liberty Music 1002 (10")	(M)	Thirty Minutes With Beatrice	1952	20.00	50.00
Decca DL-5453 (10")	(M)	Souvenir Album	1953	16.00	40.00
London LL-1373	(M)	An Evening With Beatrice Lillie	1957	10.00	25.00

LIMOUSINE

G.S.F 1002	(S)	Limousine	1972	6.00	15.00

LINCOLN, ABBEY

Liberty LRP-3025	(M)	Affair	1957	20.00	50.00
Riverside RLP-12-251	(M)	That's Him	1957	16.00	40.00
Riverside RLP-12-277	(M)	It's Magic	1958	16.00	40.00
Riverside RLP-12-308	(M)	Abbey's Blue	1959	16.00	40.00
Candid 8015	(M)	Straight Ahead	1961	12.00	30.00
Candid 9015	(S)	Straight Ahead	1961	16.00	40.00

LINCOLN, PHILAMORE

Epic BN-26497	(S)	North Wind Blew South	1970	6.00	15.00

LINCOLN STREET EXIT

Mainstream S-6126	(S)	Drive It	1970	12.00	30.00

LIND, BOB

Folkways FT-3005	(M)	Elusive Bob Lind	1966	5.00	12.00
Folkways FTS-3005	(S)	Elusive Bob Lind	1966	6.00	15.00
World Pacific WP-1841	(M)	Don't Be Concerned	1966	5.00	12.00
World Pacific ST-21841	(S)	Don't Be Concerned	1966	6.00	15.00
World Pacific WP-1851	(M)	Photographs Of Feeling	1966	4.00	10.00
World Pacific ST-21851	(S)	Photographs Of Feeling	1966	5.00	12.00
Capitol ST-780	(S)	Since There Were Circles	1971	4.00	10.00

LINDE, DENNIS

Intrepid 74004	(M)	Linde Manor	1966	10.00	25.00

LINDEN, KATHY

Felsted 7501	(M)	That Certain Boy	195?	16.00	40.00

LINDSAY, MARK
Lindsay was formerly a member of Paul Revere's Raiders.

Columbia CS-9986	(S)	Arizona ("360 Sound" label)	1970	6.00	15.00

LINN COUNTRY

Mercury SR-61181	(S)	Proud Flesh Soothseer	1968	6.00	15.00
Mercury SR-61218	(S)	Fever Shot	1969	6.00	15.00
Philips PHS-600326	(S)	Till The Break Of Dawn	1970	5.00	12.00

Label & Catalog #		Title	Year	VG+	NM
LINTON, SHERWOOD, & THE COTTON KINGS					
Re-Car 2108	(S)	Sherwood Linton & The Cotton Kings	1968	35.00	70.00
LIPSCOMB, MANCE					
Reprise R-2012	(M)	Trouble In Mind	1961	10.00	25.00
Reprise R9-2012	(S)	Trouble In Mind	1961	14.00	35.00

A member of TV's "Mod Squad" (another of that medium's attempts to turn the unending stress of police work into cotton candy), Ms. Lipton's solo album is collected as an example of '60s pop culture.

LIPTON, PEGGY					
Ode Z12-44006	(S)	Peggy Lipton	1968	8.00	20.00
LIQUID SMOKE					
Avco Embassy AVE-33005	(S)	Liquid Smoke	196?	6.00	15.00
LISTENING					
Vanguard VSD-6504	(S)	Listening	1968	8.00	20.00
LITE STORM					
Beverly Hills 1135	(S)	Lite Storm Warning	1973	16.00	40.00
LITTER, THE					
Warick UR-5M-1940	(M)	Distortions	1968	180.00	300.00
Hexagon HX-681	(S)	$100 Fine	1969	150.00	250.00
Probe CPLP-4504	(S)	Emerge	1969	12.00	30.00
LITTLE, KEN					
Dharma 801	(S)	Solo	1973	8.00	20.00
LITTLE ANTHONY (& THE IMPERIALS)					
Little Anthony is Anthony Guardine.					
End 303	(M)	We Are Little Anthony & The Imperials	1959	100.00	200.00
End 311	(M)	Shades Of The 40's	1960	75.00	150.00
DCP DCL-3801	(M)	I'm On The Outside Looking In	1964	8.00	20.00
DCP DCS-6801	(S)	I'm On The Outside Looking In	1964	10.00	25.00

Label & Catalog #		Title	Year	VG+	NM
DCP DCL-3808	(M)	Goin' Out Of My Head	1965	8.00	20.00
DCP DCS-6808	(S)	Goin' Out Of My Head	1965	10.00	25.00
DCP DCL-3809	(M)	Best Of Little Anthony & The Imperials	1966	8.00	20.00
DCP DCS-6809	(S)	Best Of Little Anthony & The Imperials	1966	10.00	25.00
Roulette R-25294	(M)	Greatest Hits	1965	6.00	15.00
Roulette SR-25294	(S)	Greatest Hits	1965	8.00	20.00
Veep VP-13510	(M)	I'm On The Outside Looking In	1966	5.00	12.00
Veep VPS-16510	(S)	I'm On The Outside Looking In	1966	6.00	15.00
Veep VP-13513	(M)	Payin' Our Dues	1966	5.00	12.00
Veep VPS-16513	(S)	Payin' Our Dues	1966	6.00	15.00
Veep VP-13514	(M)	Reflections	1967	5.00	12.00
Veep VPS-16514	(S)	Reflections	1967	6.00	15.00
Veep VP-13516	(M)	Movie Grabbers	1967	5.00	12.00
Veep VPS-16516	(S)	Movie Grabbers	1967	6.00	15.00
Veep VPS-16519	(S)	The Best Of Little Anthony, Volume 2	1968	6.00	15.00
United Arts. UAS-6720	(S)	Out Of Sight, Out Of Mind	1969	6.00	15.00
United Arts. LA026	(S)	Legendary Masters (2 LPs)	1973	8.00	20.00

LITTLE BOY BLUES

Fontana MGF-27578	(M)	In The Woodland Of Weir	1967	10.00	25.00
Fontana SRF-67578	(S)	In The Woodland Of Weir	1967	12.00	30.00

LITTLE CAESAR & THE ROMANS

Del-Fi DFLP-1218	(M)	Memories Of Those Oldies But Goodies	1961	40.00	80.00

LITTLE ESTHER: Refer to PHILLIPS, ESTHER

LITTLE EVA (EVA BOYD)

Dimension DLP-6000	(M)	L-L-L-L-Loco-Motion	1962	40.00	80.00
Dimension DLPS-6000	(E)	L-L-L-L-Loco-Motion	1962	60.00	120.00

LITTLE FEAT
The Feat were formed and led by Lowell George.

Warner Bros. WS-1890	(S)	Little Feat	1970	6.00	15.00
		(Originals do not have a photo of the group on the back cover.)			
Mobile Fidelity MFSL-013	(S)	Waiting For Columbus (2 LPs)	1978	16.00	40.00
Nautilus NR-24	(S)	Time Loves A Hero	198?	14.00	35.00

LITTLE MILTON
Little Milton is a pseudonym for Milton Campbell.

Checker 2995	(M)	We're Gonna Make It (Black label)	1965	20.00	50.00
Checker 3002	(M)	Little Milton Sings Big Blues	1966	14.00	35.00
Checker 3011	(S)	Grits Ain't Groceries	1969	8.00	20.00
Checker 3012	(S)	If Walls Could Talk	1970	6.00	15.00
Chess CH-50013	(S)	Little Milton's Greatest Hits	1972	4.00	10.00

LITTLE RICHARD
Little Richard is a pseudonym for Richard Penniman. Refer to Canned Heat; Jimi Hendrix.

Camden CAL-420	(M)	Little Richard	1956	75.00	150.00
Specialty 100	(M)	Here's Little Richard	1957	180.00	300.00
Specialty 2100	(M)	Here's Little Richard	1957	75.00	150.00
Specialty SP-2103	(M)	Little Richard	1957	50.00	100.00
Specialty SP-2104	(M)	The Fabulous Little Richard	1958	50.00	100.00
Specialty SP-2113	(E)	Grooviest 17 Original Hits	1968	8.00	20.00
Specialty SP-2136	(E)	Well Alright	1970	8.00	20.00
		— Original Specialty albums above have black & gold labels.—			
20th Century FXG-5010	(M)	Little Richard Sings Gospel	1959	14.00	35.00
20th Century SGM-5010	(S)	Little Richard Sings Gospel	1959	20.00	50.00
Mercury MG-20656	(M)	It's Real	1961	14.00	35.00
Mercury SR-60656	(S)	It's Real	1961	20.00	50.00
Crown CLP-5362	(M)	Little Richard Sings Freedom Songs	1963	8.00	20.00
Coral CRL-57446	(M)	Coming Home	1963	12.00	30.00
Coral CRL-757446	(S)	Coming Home	1963	16.00	40.00
Specialty SP-2111	(M)	Little Richard's Biggest Hits	1963	16.00	40.00
Wing MGW-122288	(M)	King Of The Gospel Singers	1964	8.00	20.00
Wing SRW-162288	(S)	King Of The Gospel Singers	1964	12.00	30.00
Vee Jay LP-1107	(M)	Little Richard Is Back	1964	8.00	20.00
Vee Jay SR-1107	(S)	Little Richard Is Back	1964	16.00	40.00

abel & Catalog #		Title	Year	VG+	NM

After leaving his rambunctious career as one of rock & roll's founding fathers, Little Richard staged many comeback attempts via vinyl, including signing with Vee Jay in 1964, to no avail...

Label & Catalog #		Title	Year	VG+	NM
Vee Jay LP-1124	(M)	**Little Richard's Greatest Hits**	1965	10.00	25.00
Vee Jay VJS-2-100	(S)	**Little Richard's Gold** *(2 LPs)*	196?	10.00	25.00
Modern 100	(M)	**His Greatest Hits/Recorded Live**	196?	6.00	15.00
Modern 1000	(S)	**His Greatest Hits/Recorded Live**	196?	6.00	15.00
Modern 103	(M)	**The Wild And Frantic Little Richard**	196?	6.00	15.00
Modern 1003	(S)	**The Wild And Frantic Little Richard**	196?	6.00	15.00
Dynasty DYS-730	(S)	**Talkin' 'Bout Soul**	196?	6.00	15.00
Custom 2061	(M)	**Little Richard Sings Spirituals**	196?	6.00	15.00
Okeh OKM-12121	(M)	**Greatest Hits Recorded Live**	1967	6.00	15.00
Okeh OKS-14121	(S)	**Greatest Hits Recorded Live**	1967	8.00	20.00
Okeh OKM-12117	(M)	**The Explosive Little Richard**	1967	6.00	15.00
Okeh OKS-14117	(S)	**The Explosive Little Richard**	1967	8.00	20.00
Roulette RS-42007	(S)	**Forever Yours**	1968	6.00	15.00
Buddah BDS-7501	(S)	**Little Richard**	1969	8.00	20.00
Kama Sutra NSBS-2023	(S)	**Little Richard**	1970	8.00	20 00
Reprise RS-6406	(S)	**The Rill Thing**	1970	6.00	15.00
Reprise RS-6462	(S)	**The King Of Rock And Roll**	1971	6.00	15.00
Reprise MS-2107	(S)	**The Second Coming**	1972	6.00	15.00
Epic EG-3042	(S)	**Cast A Long Shadow**	1971	6.00	15.00
Scepter 18020	(S)	**The Best Of Little Richard**	1971	6.00	15.00
Audio Encores 1002	(S)	**Little Richard**	1980	10.00	25.00
LITTLE RIVER BAND, THE					
Mobile Fidelity MFSL-036	(S)	**First Under The Wire**	197?	6.00	15.00
LITTLE WALTER					
Refer to Bo Diddley.					
Chess LP-1428	(M)	**The Best Of Little Walter**	1963	45.00	90.00
Chess LPS-1535	(S)	**Hate To See You Go**	1969	6.00	15.00
Chess 2CH-60014	(S)	**Boss Blues Harmonica** *(2 LPs)*	1972	5.00	12.00
Chess 416	(S)	**Confessin' The Blues**	1974	4.00	10.00
LIVELY ONES, THE					
Del-Fi DFLP-1226	(M)	**Surf-Rider**	1963	10.00	25.00
Del-Fi DFST-1226	(S)	**Surf-Rider**	1963	16.00	40.00

Label & Catalog #		Title	Year	VG+	NM
Del-Fi DFLP-1231	(M)	**Surf Drums**	1963	10.00	25.00
Del-Fi DFST-1231	(S)	**Surf Drums**	1963	16.00	40.00
Del-Fi DFLP-1237	(M)	**This Is Surf City**	1963	10.00	25.00
Del-Fi DFST-1237	(S)	**This Is Surf City**	1963	16.00	40.00
Del-Fi DFLP-1238	(M)	**Great Surf Hits**	1963	10.00	25.00
Del-Fi DFST-1238	(S)	**Great Surf Hits**	1963	16.00	40.00
Del-Fi DFLP-1240	(M)	**Surfin' South Of The Border**	1964	10.00	25.00
Del-Fi DFST-1240	(S)	**Surfin' South Of The Border**	1964	16.00	40.00
MGM E-4449	(M)	**Bugalu Party**	1967	6.00	15.00
MGM SE-4449	(S)	**Bugalu Party**	1967	8.00	20.00

LIVERPOOL BEATS, THE: *Refer to* **THE BEATS**

LIVERPOOL FIVE, THE
Refer to The Astronauts / The Liverpool Five.

RCA Victor LPM-3583	(M)	**Arrive**	1966	8.00	20.00
RCA Victor LSP-3583	(S)	**Arrive**	1966	10.00	25.00
RCA Victor LPM-3682	(M)	**Out Of Sight**	1967	8.00	20.00
RCA Victor LSP-3682	(S)	**Out Of Sight**	1967	10.00	25.00

LIVERPOOL KIDS, THE

Palace 777	(M)	**Beatle Mash**	1964	16.00	40.00

LIVERPOOL SCENE, THE

Epic LN-24336	(M)	**The Incredible New Liverpool Scene**	1967	8.00	20.00
Epic BN-26336	(S)	**The Incredible New Liverpool Scene**	1967	10.00	25.00
RCA Victor LSP-4189	(S)	**Amazing Adventures**	1969	6.00	15.00
RCA Victor LSP-4267	(S)	**Bread On The Night**	1970	6.00	15.00

LIVERPOOLS, THE

Wyncote W-9001	(M)	**Beatle Mania! In The USA**	1964	6.00	15.00
Wyncote WS-9001	(S)	**Beatle Mania! In The USA**	1964	12.00	30.00

LIVIN' BLUES

Dwarf 2003	(S)	**Dutch Treat**	1971	12.00	30.00

LOADING ZONE, THE

RCA Victor LSP-3959	(S)	**The Loading Zone**	1968	10.00	25.00
Umbrella US-101	(S)	**One For All**	1970	35.00	70.00

LOCKLIN, HANK
Refer to Hank Snow / Hank Locklin / Porter Wagoner.

RCA Victor LPM-1673	(M)	**Foreign Love**	1958	16.00	40.00
RCA Victor LPM-2291	(M)	**Please Help Me, I'm Falling**	1960	12.00	30.00
RCA Victor LSP-2291	(S)	**Please Help Me, I'm Falling**	1960	16.00	40.00
King 672	(M)	**The Best Of Hank Locklin**	1961	16.00	40.00
King 738	(M)	**Encores**	1961	16.00	40.00
RCA Victor LPM-2464	(M)	**Happy Journey**	1962	8.00	20.00
RCA Victor LSP-2464	(S)	**Happy Journey**	1962	12.00	30.00
RCA Victor LPM-2597	(M)	**A Tribute To Roy Acuff**	1962	8.00	20.00
RCA Victor LSP-2597	(S)	**A Tribute To Roy Acuff**	1962	12.00	30.00
RCA Victor LPM-2680	(M)	**The Ways Of Love**	1963	8.00	20.00
RCA Victor LSP-2680	(S)	**The Ways Of Love**	1963	12.00	30.00

— Original RCA mono albums above have "Long Play" on the bottom of the label.
Stereo albums have "Living Stereo" on the bottom. —

RCA Victor LPM-2801	(M)	**Irish Songs, Country Style**	1964	5.00	12.00
RCA Victor LSP-2801	(S)	**Irish Songs, Country Style**	1964	6.00	15.00
RCA Victor LPM-2997	(M)	**Hank Locklin Sings Hank Williams**	1964	5.00	12.00
RCA Victor LSP-2997	(S)	**Hank Locklin Sings Hank Williams**	1964	6.00	15.00
RCA Victor LPM-3391	(M)	**Hank Locklin Sings Eddy Arnold**	1965	5.00	12.00
RCA Victor LSP-3391	(S)	**Hank Locklin Sings Eddy Arnold**	1965	6.00	15.00
RCA Victor LPM-3465	(M)	**Once Over Lightly**	1965	5.00	12.00
RCA Victor LSP-3465	(S)	**Once Over Lightly**	1965	6.00	15.00
RCA Victor LPM-3559	(M)	**The Best Of Hank Locklin**	1966	5.00	12.00
RCA Victor LSP-3559	(E)	**The Best Of Hank Locklin**	1966	5.00	12.00
RCA Victor LPM-3588	(M)	**The Girls Get Prettier**	1966	5.00	12.00
RCA Victor LSP-3588	(S)	**The Girls Get Prettier**	1966	6.00	15.00
RCA Victor LPM-3656	(M)	**The Gloryland Way**	1966	5.00	12.00
RCA Victor LSP-3656	(S)	**The Gloryland Way**	1966	6.00	15.00

abel & Catalog #		Title	Year	VG+	NM
CA Victor LPM-3770	(M)	**Send Me The Pillow You Dream On**	_1967_	5.00	12.00
CA Victor LSP-3770	(S)	**Send Me The Pillow You Dream On**	_1967_	6.00	15.00
CA Victor LPM-3841	(M)	**Nashville Women**	_1967_	5.00	12.00
CA Victor LSP-3841	(S)	**Nashville Women**	_1967_	6.00	15.00
CA Victor LPM-3946	(M)	**Country Hall Of Fame**	_1968_	12.00	30.00
CA Victor LSP-3946	(S)	**Country Hall Of Fame**	_1968_	5.00	12.00
		— Original RCA Victor albums above have black labels.—			

OFGREN, NILS
efer to Crazy Horse.

&M SP-8362	(DJ)	**Authorized Bootleg** _(Counterfeits exist)_	_1976_	16.00	40.00

OGGINS, KENNY

olumbia AS-946	(DJ)	**Kenny Loggins** _(Radio sampler)_	_1981_	6.00	15.00
olumbia HC-45387	(S)	**Nightwatch** _(Half-speed master)_	_1981_	6.00	15.00

OGGINS & MESSINA
enny Loggins and Jim Messina.

olumbia CQ-32540	(Q)	**Full Sail**	_1974_	5.00	12.00
olumbia PCQ-33578	(Q)	**Native Sons**	_1976_	5.00	12.00
olumbia HC-44388	(S)	**Best Of Friends** _(Half-speed master)_	_1982_	8.00	20.00
irect Disk SD-16606	(S)	**Full Sail**	_197?_	8.00	20.00

OGSDON, JIMMIE

ing 843	(M)	**Howdy, Neighbors**	_1963_	12.00	30.00

OLLIPOP SHOPPE, THE
he Lollipop Shoppe features Nik Pascal Raicevic.

ower ST-5128	(S)	**Angels From Hell** _(Soundtrack)_	_1968_	12.00	30.00
ni 73019	(S)	**The Lollipop Shoppe**	_1968_	16.00	40.00

OMAX, ALAN

app KL-1316	(M)	**Raise A Ruckus And Have A Hootenanny**	_1963_	6.00	15.00
app KS-3316	(S)	**Raise A Ruckus And Have A Hootenanny**	_1963_	8.00	20.00
radition TLP-1029	(M)	**Texas Folk Songs**	_196?_	8.00	20.00

OMAX, JACKIE

pple ST-3354	(S)	**Is This What You Want**	_1969_	6.00	15.00

ONDON, JULIE

iberty LRP-3006	(M)	**Julie Is Her Name**	_1955_	16.00	40.00
iberty LRP-3012	(M)	**Lonely Girl**	_1956_	16.00	40.00
iberty SL-9002	(M)	**Calendar Girl** _(Fold-open cover)_	_1956_	30.00	60.00
iberty LRP-3027	(M)	**Julie Is Her Name**	_1957_	12.00	30.00
iberty LST-7027	(S)	**Julie Is Her Name**	_1957_	16.00	40.00
iberty LST-7027	(S)	**Julie Is Her Name** _(Blue vinyl)_	_195?_	20.00	50.00
iberty LST-7027	(S)	**Julie Is Her Name** _(Red vinyl)_	_195?_	20.00	50.00
iberty LRP-3043	(M)	**About The Blues**	_1957_	12.00	30.00
iberty LRP-3060	(M)	**Make Love To Me**	_1957_	12.00	30.00
iberty LRP-3096	(M)	**Julie**	_1957_	12.00	30.00
iberty LRP-3100	(M)	**Julie Is Her Name, Volume 2**	_1958_	12.00	30.00
iberty LST-7100	(S)	**Julie Is Her Name, Volume 2**	_1958_	16.00	40.00
iberty LRP-3105	(M)	**London By Night**	_1958_	12.00	30.00
iberty LST-7105	(S)	**London By Night**	_1958_	16.00	40.00
iberty LRP-3119	(M)	**Swing Me An Old Song**	_1959_	12.00	30.00
iberty LST-7119	(S)	**Swing Me An Old Song**	_1959_	16.00	40.00
iberty LRP-3130	(M)	**Your Number Please**	_1959_	12.00	30.00
iberty LST-7130	(S)	**Your Number Please**	_1959_	16.00	40.00
		— Original Liberty mono albums above have turquoise labels; stereo albums have black & silver labels.—			
iberty LRP-3152	(M)	**Julie London At Home**	_1959_	8.00	20.00
iberty LST-7152	(S)	**Julie London At Home**	_1959_	12.00	30.00
iberty LRP-3164	(M)	**Around Midnight**	_1960_	8.00	20.00
iberty LST-7164	(S)	**Around Midnight**	_1960_	12.00	30.00
iberty LRP-3171	(M)	**Send For Me**	_1960_	8.00	20.00
iberty LST-7171	(S)	**Send For Me**	_1960_	12.00	30.00
iberty LRP-3192	(M)	**Whatever Julie Wants**	_1961_	6.00	15.00
iberty LST-7192	(S)	**Whatever Julie Wants**	_1961_	8.00	20.00
iberty LRP-3203	(M)	**Sophisticated Lady**	_1962_	6.00	15.00
iberty LST-7203	(S)	**Sophisticated Lady**	_1962_	8.00	20.00

Julie London was a popular chanteuse and accomplished actress, turning out remarkably well made records while enjoying a career on both movie and, later, television screens. Her covers invariably displayed her rather obvious physical attributes while the grooves inside contained some very sensual readings, often more than a match for the cover.

abel & Catalog #		Title	Year	VG+	NM
iberty LRP-3231	(M)	Love Letters	1962	6.00	15.00
iberty LST-7231	(S)	Love Letters	1962	8.00	20.00
iberty LRP-3278	(M)	Latin In A Satin Mood	1963	6.00	15.00
iberty LST-7278	(S)	Latin In A Satin Mood	1963	8.00	20.00
iberty LRP-3291	(M)	Golden Greats	1963	6.00	15.00
iberty LST-7291	(S)	Golden Greats	1963	8.00	20.00
iberty LRP-3300	(M)	The End Of The World	1963	6.00	15.00
iberty LST-7300	(S)	The End Of The World	1963	8.00	20.00
iberty LRP-3324	(M)	The Wonderful World Of Julie London	1963	6.00	15.00
iberty LST-7324	(S)	The Wonderful World Of Julie London	1963	8.00	20.00
iberty LRP-3342	(M)	Julie London	1964	6.00	15.00
iberty LST-7342	(S)	Julie London	1964	8.00	20.00
iberty LRP-3375	(M)	In Person At The Americana	1964	6.00	15.00
iberty LST-7375	(S)	In Person At The Americana	1964	8.00	20.00
iberty LRP-3392	(M)	Our Fair Lady	1965	6.00	15.00
iberty LST-7392	(S)	Our Fair Lady	1965	8.00	20.00
iberty LRP-3434	(M)	All Through The Night	1965	6.00	15.00
iberty LST-7434	(S)	All Through The Night	1965	8.00	20.00
iberty LRP-3478	(M)	For The Night People	1966	6.00	15.00
iberty LST-7478	(S)	For The Night People	1966	8.00	20.00

— Original Liberty albums above have black labels with a gold & white logo on the side.—

ONDON, LAURIE

Capitol T-1016	(M)	Laurie London	1958	12.00	30.00

ONE RANGER, THE

Decca DL-8578	(M)	The Adventures Of The Lone Ranger	1958	30.00	60.00

ONG, BARBARA

Savoy MG-12161	(M)	Soul	1961	10.00	25.00

ONGBRANCH PENNYWHISTLE

Members include J.D. Souther, Glen Frey, James Burton, Ry Cooder, Doug Kershaw; Buddy Emmons.

Amos AAS-7007	(S)	Longbranch Pennywhistle	1969	16.00	40.00

ONZO & OSCAR

Starday SLP-119	(M)	America's Greatest Country Comedians	1960	12.00	30.00
Starday SLP-244	(M)	Country Music Time	1963	10.00	25.00

OOSE

Necturne 906	(S)	Freaky Billie, The Wheelie King	1970	12.00	30.00

OPEZ, TRINI

King 863	(M)	Teenage Love Songs	1963	14.00	35.00
King 877	(M)	More Of Trini Lopez	1964	14.00	35.00

OPEZ, TRINI / SCOTT GREGORY

This album includes early, rare tracks by Bill Haley a.k.a. Scott Gregory.

Guest Star 1499	(M)	Trini Lopez And Scott Gregory	1964	20.00	50.00
Guest Star 1499	(E)	Trini Lopez And Scott Gregory	1964	14.00	35.00

ORD, BOBBY

Harmony HL-7322	(M)	Bobby Lord's Best	1964	12.00	30.00

ORD SITAR

Capitol ST-3916	(S)	Lord Sitar	1968	10.00	25.00

ORD SUTCH

Cotillion SD-9015	(S)	Lord Sutch And His Heavy Friends	1972	12.00	30.00
Cotillion SD-9049	(S)	Hands Of Jack The Ripper	1972	10.00	25.00

OREN, DONNA

Capitol T-2323	(M)	Beach Blanket Bingo	1965	10.00	25.00
Capitol ST-2323	(S)	Beach Blanket Bingo	1965	12.00	30.00

OREN, SOPHIA

Ms. Loren also recorded with Peter Sellers.

Columbia CL-1222	(M)	Houseboat *(Soundtrack)*	1958	75.00	150.00

Label & Catalog #		Title	Year	VG+	NM
RCA Victor Int. FOC-5	(M)	**Boccaccio '70** (Soundtrack)	1962	20.00	50.00
RCA Victor Int. FSO-5	(S)	**Boccaccio '70** (Soundtrack)	1962	35.00	70.00
Columbia OL-6310	(M)	**Sophia Loren In Rome** (TV Soundtrack)	1964	12.00	30.00
Columbia OS-2710	(S)	**Sophia Loren In Rome** (TV Soundtrack)	1964	20.00	50.00
Mace MXX-10020	(S)	**The Poems Of Salvatore Di Giacomo**	196?	6.00	15.00

Like many '60s albums, there are no stereo masters for Los Bravos' first album and the rechannelled stereo's echo and distortion makes a mess of the music.

LOS BRAVOS
Los Bravos features Mike Kennedy.

Press PR-73003	(M)	**Black Is Black**	1966	12.00	30.00
Press PAS-83003	(E)	**Black Is Black**	1966	10.00	25.00
Parrot PAS-71021	(S)	**Bring A Little Lovin**	1968	12.00	30.00

LOS LOBOS [LOS LOBOS DEL ESTE DE LOS ANGELES]

Pan American 101	(S)	**Si Se Puede!**	1976	75.00	150.00
New Vista 1001	(S)	**Just Another Band From East L.A.**	1978	180.00	300.00

LOST & FOUND

International Art. 3	(S)	**Everybody's Here**	1968	16.00	40.00
International Art. 3	(S)	**Everybody's Here**	1979	6.00	15.00
		(Reissues have "Masterfonics" stamped in the trail-off vinyl.)			
Tempo 7064	(S)	**Number Two**	1973	6.00	15.00

LOTHAR & THE HAND PEOPLE

Capitol ST-2997	(S)	**Presenting Lothar & The Hand People**	1968	16.00	40.00
Capitol ST-247	(S)	**Space Hymn**	1969	16.00	40.00

LOUDERMILK, JOHN D.

RCA Victor LPM-2434	(M)	**Language Of Love**	1961	5.00	12.00
RCA Victor LSP-2434	(S)	**Language Of Love**	1961	8.00	20.00
RCA Victor LPM-2539	(M)	**Twelve Sides Of Loudermilk**	1962	5.00	12.00
RCA Victor LSP-2539	(S)	**Twelve Sides Of Loudermilk**	1962	8.00	20.00

— Original RCA mono albums above have "Long Play" on the bottom of the label; stereo albums have "Living Stereo" on the bottom.—

Label & Catalog #		Title	Year	VG+	NM
RCA Victor LPM-3497	(M)	A Bizarre Collection Of... Unusual Songs	1965	8.00	20.00
RCA Victor LSP-3497	(S)	A Bizarre Collection Of... Unusual Songs	1965	10.00	25.00
RCA Victor LPM-3807	(M)	Suburban Attitudes In Country Verse	1967	5.00	12.00
RCA Victor LSP-3807	(S)	Suburban Attitudes In Country Verse	1967	6.00	15.00
RCA Victor LSP-4040	(S)	Country Love Songs	1968	5.00	12.00
RCA Victor LSP-4097	(S)	The Open Mind Of John D. Loudermilk	1968	5.00	12.00

LOUDON, DOROTHY

| Coral CRL-57265 | (M) | Live At The Blue Angel | 1959 | 6.00 | 15.00 |
| Coral CRL-757265 | (S) | Live At The Blue Angel | 1959 | 10.00 | 25.00 |

LOUIE & THE LOVERS

| Epic KE-30026 | (S) | Rise | 1970 | 6.00 | 15.00 |

LOUISIANA RED

| Roulette R-25200 | (M) | The Lowdown Back Porch Blues | 1963 | 14.00 | 35.00 |
| Atco SD-33-389 | (S) | Louisiana Red Sings The Blues | 1972 | 5.00 | 12.00 |

LOUVIN, CHARLIE

Capitol T-2208	(M)	Less And Less	1965	6.00	15.00
Capitol ST-2208	(S)	Less And Less	1965	8.00	20.00
Capitol T-2437	(M)	The Many Moods Of Charlie Louvin	1966	6.00	15.00
Capitol ST-2437	(S)	The Many Moods Of Charlie Louvin	1966	8.00	20.00
Capitol T-2482	(M)	Lonesome Is Me	1966	5.00	12.00
Capitol ST-2482	(S)	Lonesome Is Me	1966	6.00	15.00
Capitol T-2689	(M)	I'll Remember Always	1967	5.00	12.00
Capitol ST-2689	(S)	I'll Remember Always	1967	6.00	15.00
Capitol T-2787	(M)	I Forgot To Cry	1967	5.00	12.00
Capitol ST-2787	(S)	I Forgot To Cry	1967	6.00	15.00
Capitol ST-2958	(S)	Will You Visit Me On Sundays	1968	6.00	15.00

LOUVIN, IRA

| Capitol T-2413 | (M) | The Unforgettable Ira Louvin | 1965 | 8.00 | 20.00 |
| Capitol ST-2413 | (S) | The Unforgettable Ira Louvin | 1965 | 12.00 | 30.00 |

LOUVIN BROTHERS, THE
Charlie and Ira Louvin.

MGM E-3426	(M)	The Louvin Brothers	1956	100.00	200.00
Capitol T-769	(M)	Tragic Songs Of Life	1956	50.00	100.00
Capitol T-825	(M)	Nearer My God To Thee	1957	40.00	80.00
Capitol T-910	(M)	Ira And Charlie	1958	40.00	80.00
		— Original Capitol albums above have turquoise labels.—			
Capitol T-1061	(M)	The Family Who Prays	1958	20.00	50.00
Capitol T-1106	(M)	Country Love Ballads	1959	20.00	50.00
Capitol T-1277	(M)	Satan Is Real	1960	20.00	50.00
Capitol T-1385	(M)	My Baby's Gone	1960	20.00	50.00
Capitol T-1449	(M)	A Tribute To The Delmore Brothers	1960	35.00	70.00
Capitol T-1547	(M)	Encore	1961	20.00	50.00
Capitol T-1616	(M)	Country Christmas	1961	14.00	35.00
Capitol ST-1616	(S)	Country Christmas	1961	20.00	50.00
		— Original Capitol albums above have black labels with the logo on the left side.—			
Capitol T-1721	(M)	Weapon Of Prayer	1962	12.00	30.00
Capitol ST-1721	(S)	Weapon Of Prayer	1962	16.00	40.00
Capitol T-1834	(M)	Keep Your Eyes On Jesus	1963	12.00	30.00
Capitol ST-1834	(S)	Keep Your Eyes On Jesus	1963	16.00	40.00
Capitol T-2091	(M)	Sing And Play Their Current Hits	1964	12.00	30.00
Capitol ST-2091	(S)	Sing And Play Their Current Hits	1964	16.00	40.00
Capitol T-2331	(M)	Thank God For My Christian Home	1965	12.00	30.00
Capitol ST-2331	(S)	Thank God For My Christian Home	1965	16.00	40.00
Capitol T-2827	(M)	The Great Roy Acuff Songs	1967	12.00	30.00
Capitol ST-2827	(S)	The Great Roy Acuff Songs	1967	16.00	40.00
Tower T-5038	(M)	Two Different Worlds	1966	12.00	30.00
Tower DT-5038	(E)	Two Different Worlds	1966	8.00	20.00
Tower DT-5122	(E)	Country Heart And Soul	1968	10.00	25.00

LOVE
Love was the brainchild of Arthur Lee.

| Elektra EKL-4001 | (M) | Love | 1966 | 10.00 | 25.00 |
| Elektra EKS-74001 | (S) | Love | 1966 | 6.00 | 15.00 |

Label & Catalog #		Title	Year	VG+	NM
Elektra EKL-4005	(M)	**Da Capo**	1966	10.00	25.00
Elektra EKS-74005	(S)	**Da Capo**	1966	6.00	15.00
Elektra EKL-4013	(M)	**Forever Changes**	1967	14.00	35.00
Elektra EKS-74013	(S)	**Forever Changes**	1967	6.00	15.00
		— Original Elektra albums above have brown labels.—			
Elektra EKS-74049	(S)	**Four Sail**	1969	5.00	12.00
Elektra EKS-74058	(S)	**Revisited**	1970	4.00	10.00
Blue Thumb BTS-9000	(S)	**Out Here** (2 LPs)	1969	5.00	12.00
Blue Thumb BTS-8822	(S)	**False Start**	1970	6.00	15.00

LOVE EXCHANGE, THE
Tower ST-5115	(S)	**The Love Exchange**	1968	6.00	15.00

LOVE GENERATION, THE
Imperial LP-9351	(M)	**The Love Generation**	1967	5.00	12.00
Imperial LP-12351	(S)	**The Love Generation**	1967	6.00	15.00
Imperial LP-12364	(S)	**A Generation Of Love**	1968	5.00	12.00
Imperial LP-12408	(S)	**Montage**	1968	5.00	12.00

LOVE SCULPTURE
Love Sculpture features Dave Edmunds.
Rare Earth RS-505	(S)	**Blues Helping**	1969	14.00	35.00
Parrot PAS-71035	(S)	**Forms And Feeling**	1970	10.00	25.00

LOVECRAFT: *Refer to* H.P. LOVECRAFT

LOVESONG
Lovesong features Chuck Girard of The Hondells.
Good News 8100	(S)	**Lovesong**	197?	5.00	12.00
Good News 8101	(S)	**The Final Touch**	197?	5.00	12.00
Good News 8104	(S)	**Feel The Touch**	197?	5.00	12.00

LOVIN' SPOONFUL, THE
The original Spoonful (1965-67) were Steve Boone, Joe Butler, John Sebastian and Zal Yanovsky.
Kama Sutra KLP-8050	(M)	**Do You Believe In Magic?**	1965	6.00	15.00
Kama Sutra KLPS-8050	(S)	**Do You Believe In Magic?**	1965	8.00	20.00
Kama Sutra KLP-8051	(M)	**Daydream**	1966	6.00	15.00
Kama Sutra KLPS-8051	(S)	**Daydream**	1966	8.00	20.00
Kama Sutra KLP-8053	(M)	**What's Up, Tiger Lily?** (Soundtrack)	1966	6.00	15.00
Kama Sutra KLPS-8053	(S)	**What's Up, Tiger Lily?** (Soundtrack)	1966	8.00	20.00
Kama Sutra KLP-8054	(M)	**Hums Of The Lovin' Spoonful**	1966	6.00	15.00
Kama Sutra KLPS-8054	(S)	**Hums Of The Lovin' Spoonful**	1966	8.00	20.00
Kama Sutra KLP-8056	(M)	**The Best Of The Lovin' Spoonful**	1967	5.00	12.00
Kama Sutra KLPS-8056	(S)	**The Best Of The Lovin' Spoonful**	1967	6.00	15.00
Kama Sutra KLP-8058	(M)	**You're A Big Boy Now**	1967	5.00	12.00
Kama Sutra KLPS-8058	(S)	**You're A Big Boy Now**	1967	6.00	15.00
Kama Sutra KLPS-8061	(S)	**Everything's Playing**	1968	6.00	15.00
Kama Sutra KLPS-8064	(S)	**The Best Of The Lovin' Spoonful, Volume 2**	1968	5.00	12.00
Kama Sutra KOPS-750-2	(S)	**24 Karat Hits** (2 LPs)	1968	6.00	15.00
Kama Sutra KLPS-8073	(S)	**Revelations: Revolution '69**	1969	5.00	12.00
Kama Sutra KLPS-2011	(S)	**The John Sebastian Songbook**	1970	5.00	12.00
Kama Sutra KSBS-2013	(S)	**The Very Best Of The Lovin' Spoonful**	1970	5.00	12.00
Kama Sutra KLPS-2029	(S)	**Once Upon A Time**	1971	5.00	12.00

LOWE, JIM
Mercury MG-20246	(M)	**The Door Of Fame**	1957	30.00	60.00
Dot DLP-3051	(M)	**Songs They Sang Behind The Green Door**	1957	50.00	100.00
Dot DLP-3114	(M)	**Wicked Women**	1958	30.00	60.00

LOWE, NICK
Columbia AS-1408	(DJ)	**An Interrogation Of Nick Lowe**	1982	6.00	15.00

LUCAS, NICK
Cavalier 5003 (10")	(M)	**Tiptoe Thru The Tulips**	1955	12.00	30.00
Decca DL-8653	(M)	**Painting The Clouds With Sunshine**	1957	20.00	50.00

LULU
Fontana MGF-18030	(M)	**To Sir With Love** (Soundtrack)	1967	6.00	15.00
Fontana SRF-67569	(S)	**To Sir With Love** (Soundtrack)	1967	8.00	20.00

The term folk-rock has a somewhat constricted interpretation these days. When first applied during the mid '60s it embraced not only the Byrds and Dylan, but also the Jefferson Airplane's first album, the early Youngbloods and everything by the Lovin' Spoonful. Melding hip New York sounds with traditional jug band and country blues, the Spoonful produced several albums of intelligence, wit and eminent musicality; leader John Sebastian was often hailed as one of the leading writers in the then contemporary hip Rock-with-a-capital-R world. *Do You Believe In Magic* and *Hums* are arguably their two strongest efforts, with the first displaying their love for jug band music while the latter displays Sebastian's prodigious talents as a singer and songwriter.

Label & Catalog #		Title	Year	VG+	NM
Epic LN-24339	(M)	To Sir With Love	1967	6.00	15.00
Epic BN-26339	(S)	To Sir With Love	1967	8.00	20.00
Parrot PA-61016	(M)	From Lulu With Love	1967	6.00	15.00
Parrot PAS-71016	(S)	From Lulu With Love	1967	8.00	20.00
Chelsea 518	(S)	Heaven & Earth & Stars (With David Bowie)	1977	8.00	20.00

LULU BELLE & SCOTTY

Super 6201	(M)	Lulu Belle & Scotty	1963	20.00	50.00
Starday SLP-206	(M)	The Sweethearts Of Country Music	1963	12.00	30.00
Starday SLP-285	(M)	Down Memory Lane	1964	12.00	30.00
Starday SLP-351	(M)	Lulu Belle & Scotty	1965	12.00	30.00

LUMAN, BOB

Warner Bros. W-1396	(M)	Let's Think About Livin'	1960	20.00	50.00
Warner Bros. WS-1396	(S)	Let's Think About Livin'	1960	35.00	70.00
Hickory LPM-124	(M)	Livin' Lovin' Sounds	1965	6.00	15.00
Hickory LPS-124	(S)	Livin' Lovin' Sounds	1965	8.00	20.00

LUMBER

Radnor 2003	(S)	Overdose	197?	20.00	50.00
		(Issued with a bonus game, priced separately below.)			
Radnor 2003		Overdose Game	197?	10.00	25.00

LUND, GARRETT

No label	(S)	Almost Grown (With insert)	1975	300.00	500.00

LUTCHER, NELLIE

Capitol H-232 (10")	(M)	Real Gone	1950	20.00	50.00
Capitol T-232	(M)	Real Gone	1955	16.00	40.00
Epic 1108 (10")	(M)	Whee! Nellie	1955	20.00	50.00
Liberty LRP-3014	(M)	Our New Nellie	1956	10.00	25.00

LYMON, FRANKIE, & THE TEENAGERS: *Refer to* **THE TEENAGERS**

LYNN, BARBARA

Jamie JLP-3023	(M)	You'll Lose A Good Thing	1962	10.00	25.00
Jamie JLPS-70-3023	(S)	You'll Lose A Good Thing	1962	14.00	35.00
Jamie JLP-3026	(M)	Sister Of Soul	1964	6.00	15.00
Jamie JLPS-3026	(S)	Sister Of Soul	1964	8.00	20.00
Atlantic SD-8171	(S)	Here Is Barbara Lynn	1968	6.00	15.00

LYNN, DONNA

Capitol T-2085	(M)	Java Jones	1964	6.00	15.00
Capitol ST-2085	(S)	Java Jones	1964	8.00	20.00

LYNN, LORETTA

Decca DL-4457	(M)	Loretta Lynn Sings	1963	16.00	40.00
Decca DL-74457	(S)	Loretta Lynn Sings	1963	20.00	50.00
Decca DL-4541	(M)	Before I'm Over You	1964	12.00	30.00
Decca DL-74541	(S)	Before I'm Over You	1964	16.00	40.00
Decca DL-4620	(M)	Songs From My Heart	1965	12.00	30.00
Decca DL-74620	(S)	Songs From My Heart	1965	16.00	40.00
Decca DL-4665	(M)	Blue Kentucky Girl	1965	12.00	30.00
Decca DL-74665	(S)	Blue Kentucky Girl	1965	16.00	40.00
Decca DL-4695	(M)	Hymns	1965	8.00	20.00
Decca DL-74695	(S)	Hymns	1965	10.00	25.00
Decca DL-4744	(M)	I Like 'Em Country	1966	8.00	20.00
Decca DL-74744	(S)	I Like 'Em Country	1966	10.00	25.00
Decca DL-4783	(M)	You Ain't Woman Enough	1966	8.00	20.00
Decca DL-74783	(S)	You Ain't Woman Enough	1966	10.00	25.00
Decca DL-4817	(M)	A Country Christmas	1966	8.00	20.00
Decca DL-74817	(S)	A Country Christmas	1966	10.00	25.00
		— Original Decca albums above have black labels with "Mfrd. by Decca" beneath the rainbow.—			
Decca DL-4842	(M)	Don't Come Home Drinkin'	1967	6.00	15.00
Decca DL-74842	(S)	Don't Come Home Drinkin'	1967	8.00	20.00
Decca DL-4930	(M)	Singin' With Feelin'	1967	8.00	20.00
Decca DL-74930	(S)	Singin' With Feelin'	1967	8.00	20.00
Decca DL-74928	(S)	Who Says God Is Dead?	1968	8.00	20.00
Decca DL-74997	(S)	Fist City	1968	8.00	20.00

Label & Catalog #		Title	Year	VG+	NM
Decca DL-75000	(S)	Loretta Lynn's Greatest Hits	1968	8.00	20.00
Decca DL-75084	(S)	Your Squaw Is On The Warpath	1969	16.00	40.00
		(Originally issued with "Barney.")			
Decca DL-75084	(S)	Your Squaw Is On The Warpath	1969	6.00	15.00
Decca DL-75113	(S)	A Woman Of The World	1969	6.00	15.00
Decca DL-75163	(S)	Wings Upon Your Horns	1970	6.00	15.00
Decca DL-75198	(S)	Loretta Lynn Writes 'Em And Sings 'Em	1970	5.00	12.00
Decca DL-75253	(S)	Coal Miner's Daughter	1971	8.00	20.00
Decca DL-75282	(S)	I Wanna Be Free	1971	5.00	12.00
Decca DL-75310	(S)	You're Lookin' At Country	1971	5.00	12.00
Decca DL-75334	(S)	One's On The Way	1972	5.00	12.00
Decca DL-75351	(S)	God Bless America Again	1972	5.00	12.00
Decca DL-75381	(S)	Here I Am Again	1972	5.00	12.00
MCA PRO-1934	(DJ)	Loretta Lynn	1974	12.00	30.00
MCA 35013	(DJ)	Allis-Chambers Presents Loretta Lynn	1978	12.00	30.00
MCA 35018	(DJ)	Crisco Presents Loretta Lynn	1979	12.00	30.00

LYNN, LORETTA, & ERNEST TUBB

Decca DL-4639	(M)	Mr & Mrs Used To Be	1965	10.00	25.00
Decca DL-74639	(S)	Mr & Mrs Used To Be	1965	12.00	30.00
Decca DL-4872	(M)	Singin' Again	1967	6.00	15.00
Decca DL-74872	(S)	Singin' Again	1967	8.00	20.00
Decca DL-75115	(S)	If We Put Our Heads Together	1969	6.00	15.00

LYNYRD SKYNYRD

MCA 3029	(S)	Street Survivors	1977	8.00	20.00
		(Original covers pictures the group in flames.)			

MABON, WILLIE

Chess 1439	(M)	Willie Mabon	1959	40.00	80.00

MacARTHUR

R.P.C.	(S)	MacArthur	1978	100.00	200.00
Bay Music	(S)	MacArthur II	1982	35.00	70.00

MacCOLL, EWAN

Riverside RLP-12-632	(M)	Bad Lads And Hard Cases	195?	12.00	30.00
Riverside RLP-12-642	(M)	Bless 'Em All	195?	12.00	30.00
Riverside RLP-12-652	(M)	Champions And Sporting Blades	195?	12.00	30.00

MacDONALD, JEANETTE, & NELSON EDDY

RCA Victor LPM-1738	(M)	Favorites In Hi-Fi	1959	12.00	30.00

MACK, LONNIE

Fraternity SF-1014	(M)	The Wham Of That Memphis Man	1963	16.00	40.00
Fraternity SSF-1014	(S)	The Wham Of That Memphis Man	1963	35.00	70.00
Elektra EKS-74050	(S)	Whatever's Right	1969	8.00	20.00
Elektra EKS-74040	(S)	Glad I'm In The Band	1969	8.00	20.00
Elektra EKS-74077	(M)	For Collectors Only	1970	8.00	20.00
Elektra EKS-74012	(S)	The Hills Of Indiana	1971	8.00	20.00

Label & Catalog #		Title	Year	VG+	NM
MacKENZIE, GISELE					
Vik LX-1055	(M)	**Gisele MacKenzie**	1956	12.00	30.00
Vik LX-1075	(M)	**Mam' Selle Giselle**	1956	12.00	30.00
Vik LX-1099	(M)	**Christmas With Giselle**	1957	12.00	30.00
RCA Victor LPM-1790	(M)	**Gisele**	1958	12.00	30.00
RCA Victor LPM-2006	(M)	**Christmas With Gisele**	1959	12.00	30.00
Everest 5069	(M)	**In Person At The Empire Room**	196?	5.00	12.00
Everest 1069	(S)	**In Person At The Empire Room**	196?	8.00	20.00
MACON, UNCLE DAVE					
Decca DL-4760	(M)	**Uncle Dave Macon**	1966	8.00	20.00
Decca DL-74760	(S)	**Uncle Dave Macon**	1966	10.00	25.00
MacRAE, GORDON					
Refer to Jane Powell; Jo Stafford.					
Capitol H-231 (10")	(M)	**Songs**	1950	16.00	40.00
MGM E-104 (10")	(M)	**Prisoner Of Love** *(Soundtrack)*	1952	16.00	40.00
Capitol L-334 (10")	(M)	**Roberta** *(Studio Cast)*	1952	16.00	40.00
Capitol L-335 (10")	(M)	**Merry Widow** *(Studio Cast)*	1952	16.00	40.00
Capitol L-351 (10")	(M)	**Desert Song** *(Studio Cast)*	1953	20.00	50.00
Capitol L-407 (10")	(M)	**Student Prince** *(Studio Cast)*	1953	16.00	40.00
Capitol H-422 (10")	(M)	**By The Light Of The Silvery Moon** *(Sdtk)*	1953	20.00	50.00
Capitol L-530 (10")	(M)	**The Red Mill** *(Soundtrack)*	1954	16.00	40.00
Capitol T-219	(M)	**New Moon / Vagabond King** *(Soundtrack)*	1952	12.00	30.00
Capitol T-384	(M)	**The Desert Song / Roberta** *(Soundtrack)*	1953	16.00	40.00
Capitol T-437	(M)	**Merry Widow / The Student Prince** *(Sdtk)*	1954	16.00	40.00
Capitol T-537	(M)	**Romantic Ballads**	1955	14.00	35.00
Capitol P-551	(M)	**The Red Mill / Naughty Marietta** *(Sdtk)*	1954	16.00	40.00
Capitol SAO-595	(M)	**Oklahoma** *(Soundtrack)*	1955	8.00	20.00
Capitol T-681	(M)	**Operetta Favorites**	1956	12.00	30.00
Capitol W-694	(M)	**Carousel** *(Soundtrack)*	1956	12.00	30.00
Capitol T-765	(M)	**The Best Things In Life Are Free**	1956	12.00	30.00
Capitol T-834	(M)	**Cowboy's Lament**	1957	12.00	30.00
Capitol T-875	(M)	**Motion Picture Soundstage**	1957	12.00	30.00
Capitol T-980	(M)	**Gordon McRae In Concert**	1958	12.00	30.00
Capitol T-1050	(M)	**This Is Gordon McRae**	1958	12.00	30.00
MAD DOG					
Fish Head	(S)	**Mad Dog**	1975	16.00	40.00
MAD FABLE					
Magic MAD-101	(S)	**Get Off!**	1977	50.00	100.00
MAD LADS, THE					
Volt 414	(M)	**The Mad Lads In Action**	1966	6.00	15.00
Volt 414	(S)	**The Mad Lads In Action**	1966	8.00	20.00
Volt VOS-6005	(S)	**The Mad Mad Mad Mad Mad Lads**	1969	6.00	15.00
Volt VOS-6020	(S)	**A New Beginning**	1973	5.00	12.00
MAD RIVER					
Capitol ST-2985	(S)	**Mad River**	1968	20.00	50.00
Capitol ST-185	(S)	**Paradise Bar And Grill**	1969	16.00	40.00
		(Counterfeits of 185— perhaps 2985— exist.)			
MADDOX, ROSE					
Rose also recorded with her brothers.					
Columbia CL-1159	(M)	**Precious Memories**	1958	20.00	50.00
Capitol T-1312	(M)	**The One Rose**	1960	10.00	25.00
Capitol ST-1312	(S)	**The One Rose**	1960	14.00	35.00
Capitol T-1437	(M)	**Glorybound Train**	1960	10.00	25.00
Capitol ST-1437	(S)	**Glorybound Train**	1960	14.00	35.00
Capitol T-1548	(M)	**A Big Bouquet Of Roses**	1961	10.00	25.00
Capitol ST-1548	(S)	**A Big Bouquet Of Roses**	1961	14.00	35.00
Capitol T-1779	(M)	**Rose Maddox Sing Bluegrass**	1962	12.00	30.00
Capitol ST-1779	(S)	**Rose Maddox Sing Bluegrass**	1962	16.00	40.00
Capitol T-1993	(M)	**Alone With You**	1963	8.00	20.00
Capitol ST-1993	(S)	**Alone With You**	1963	12.00	30.00
Starday SLP-463	(M)	**Rosie**	196?	8.00	20.00

Label & Catalog #		Title	Year	VG+	NM
MADDOX BROTHERS, THE, & ROSE					
King 669	(M)	**A Collection Of Standard Sacred Songs**	1956	50.00	100.00
King 677	(M)	**The Maddox Brothers And Rose**	1961	30.00	60.00
King 752	(M)	**I'll Write Your Name In The Sand**	1961	30.00	60.00
MADIGAN, BETTY					
MGM E-3448	(M)	**Am I Blue?**	1957	10.00	25.00
Coral CRL-57192	(M)	**The Jerome Kern Songbook**	1958	10.00	25.00

Madonnamania maintains its juggernaut pace through print, CDs, film and personal performance. Anything remotely collectible associated with her promises to be a good long-term investment, including her original Sire albums, especially this promotional white vinyl "Virgin."

MADONNA					
Sire 25157	(DJ)	**Like A Virgin** *(White vinyl)*	1984	16.00	40.00
MAESTRO, JOHNNY					
Johnny Maestro was formerly the lead singer for The Crests; The Brooklyn Bridge.					
Buddah BDS-5091	(P)	**The Johnny Maestro Story** *(With inserts)*	1971	16.00	40.00
MAGI					
Uncle Dirty 6102-N13	(S)	**Win Or Lose**	1975	100.00	200.00
MAGIC					
Armadillo 8031	(S)	**Enclosed**	1970	150.00	250.00
MAGIC FERN, THE					
Piccadilly PIC-	(S)	**The Magic Fern**	1980	50.00	100.00
MAGIC LANTERNS, THE					
Atlantic SD-8217	(S)	**Shame Shame**	1969	5.00	12.00
MAHAL, TAJ					
Columbia CS-9579	(S)	**Taj Mahal**	1968	6.00	15.00
Columbia CS-9698	(S)	**Natch'l Blues**	1969	6.00	15.00
Columbia GP-18	(S)	**Giant Step** *(2 LPs)*	1969	6.00	15.00

— Original Columbia albums above have "360 Sound" on the bottom of the label.—

Label & Catalog #		Title	Year	VG+	NM
MAHOGANY RUSH					
Nine 936	(S)	Maxoom	1972	20.00	50.00
20th Century S-451	(S)	Child Of Novelty	1973	6.00	15.00
20th Century S-463	(S)	Maxoom	1975	6.00	15.00
20th Century S-482	(S)	Strange Universe	1975	6.00	15.00
MAIDA					
Audio Fidelity 6136	(M)	Maida Sings Folk	1965	5.00	12.00
Audio Fidelity SD-6136	(S)	Maida Sings Folk	1965	6.00	15.00
MAIN ATTRACTION, THE					
Tower ST-5177	(S)	And Now	1968	8.00	20.00
MAINER, J. E.					
King 765	(M)	Variety Album	1961	12.00	30.00
MAINER, WADE					
King 769	(M)	Soulful Sacred Songs	1961	12.00	30.00
MAINER'S MOUNTAINEERS					
King 666	(M)	Good Old Mountain Music	195?	12.00	30.00
MAIZE, JOE (& HIS CORDSMEN)					
Decca DL-8590	(M)	Presenting Joe Maize & His Cordsmen	1958	16.00	40.00
Decca DL-8817	(M)	Hawaiian Dreams	1959	12.00	30.00
Decca DL-4555	(M)	Isle Of Dreams	1965	8.00	20.00
Decca DL-74555	(S)	Isle Of Dreams	1965	10.00	25.00
MAJIC SHIP					
Bel Ami BA-711	(S)	Majic Ship	1968	150.00	250.00
MAJORS, THE					
Imperial LP-9222	(M)	Meet The Majors	1963	14.00	35.00
Imperial LP-12222	(P)	Meet The Majors	1963	20.00	50.00
MAKEBA, MIRIAM					
RCA Victor LPM-2267	(M)	Miriam Makeba	1960	8.00	20.00
RCA Victor LSP-2267	(S)	Miriam Makeba	1960	12.00	30.00
Kapp KL-1274	(M)	The Many Voices Of Miriam Makeba	1962	6.00	15.00
Kapp KS-3274	(S)	The Many Voices Of Miriam Makeba	1962	8.00	20.00
RCA Victor LPM-2750	(M)	The World Of Miriam Makeba	1963	6.00	15.00
RCA Victor LSP-2750	(S)	The World Of Miriam Makeba	1963	8.00	20.00
RCA Victor LPM-2845	(M)	The Voice Of Africa	1964	6.00	15.00
RCA Victor LSP-2845	(S)	The Voice Of Africa	1964	8.00	20.00
RCA Victor LPM-3321	(M)	Makeba Sings	1965	6.00	15.00
RCA Victor LSP-3321	(S)	Makeba Sings	1965	8.00	20.00
RCA Victor LPM-3512	(M)	The Magic Of Makeba	1966	6.00	15.00
RCA Victor LSP-3512	(S)	The Magic Of Makeba	1966	8.00	20.00
		— Original RCA albums above have black labels.—			
Mercury MG-21082	(M)	The Magnificent Miriam Makeba	1966	5.00	12.00
Mercury SR-61082	(S)	The Magnificent Miriam Makeba	1966	6.00	15.00
Mercury MG-261095	(M)	All About Miriam	1966	5.00	12.00
Mercury SR-61095	(S)	All About Miriam	1966	6.00	15.00
Reprise R-6253	(M)	Miriam Makeba In Concert!	1967	5.00	12.00
Reprise RS-6253	(S)	Miriam Makeba In Concert!	1967	6.00	15.00
Reprise R-6274	(M)	Pata Pata	1967	5.00	12.00
Reprise RS-6274	(S)	Pata Pata	1967	6.00	15.00
Reprise RS-6381	(S)	Keep Me In Mind	1970	5.00	12.00

MAMAS & THE PAPAS, THE
The Mamas were Michelle Phillips and Cass Elliott; the Papas were John Phillips and Denny Doherty.

Dunhill D-50006	(M)	If You Can Believe Your Eyes And Ears	1966	75.00	150.00
Dunhill DS-50006	(S)	If You Can Believe Your Eyes And Ears	1966	100.00	200.00
		(First pressing: The toilet in the lower right corner of the cover is clearly and wholly visible. On all subsequent pressings a scroll with the titles of the singles has been placed over the toilet.)			
Dunhill D-50006	(M)	If You Can Believe Your Eyes And Ears	1966	8.00	20.00
Dunhill DS-50006	(S)	If You Can Believe Your Eyes And Ears	1966	6.00	15.00
		(The toilet on the cover is concealed by the a scroll.)			

Label & Catalog #		Title	Year	VG+	NM
Dunhill DS-50006	(S)	**If You Can Believe Your Eyes And Ears**	196?	**20.00**	**50.00**
		(Record Club release has a black border along the bottom			
		of the cover, effectively obstructing the offending john.)			
Dunhill D-50010	(M)	**The Mamas & The Papas**	1966	**8.00**	**20.00**
Dunhill DS-50010	(S)	**The Mamas & The Papas**	1966	**6.00**	**15.00**

While albums by The Mamas & The Papas are used record shop staples, original pressings of their first three classic albums, when Dunhill was an independent label distributed by ABC-Paramount, are scarce in collectible condition.

Dunhill D-50014	(M)	**The Mamas & The Papas Deliver**	1967	**8.00**	**20.00**
Dunhill DS-50014	(S)	**The Mamas & The Papas Deliver**	1967	**6.00**	**15.00**
— *Original Dunhill albums above read "Dist. by ABC-Paramount" on the bottom of the label.*—					
Dunhill D-50025	(M)	**Farewell To The First Golden Era**	1967	**6.00**	**15.00**
Dunhill DS-50025	(S)	**Farewell To The First Golden Era**	1967	**5.00**	**12.00**
Dunhill DS-50031	(S)	**The Papas And The Mamas**	1968	**6.00**	**15.00**
— *Original Dunhill albums above read "A Subsidiary of ABC Records" on the bottom of the label.*—					
Dunhill DS-50032	(S)	**Book Of Songs**	1968	**5.00**	**12.00**
Dunhill DS-50038	(S)	**Golden Era, Volume 2**	1968	**5.00**	**12.00**
Dunhill DS-50073	(S)	**A Gathering Of Flowers** *(2 LP box)*	1970	**10.00**	**25.00**

MANCHESTER, MELISSA

Arista AQ-4031	(Q)	**Melissa**	1975	**5.00**	**12.00**
Arista AQ-4067	(Q)	**Better Days And Happy Endings**	1976	**5.00**	**12.00**
Mobile Fidelity MFSL-028	(S)	**Melissa**	1979	**6.00**	**15.00**
Nautilus NR-33	(S)	**Don't Cry Out Loud**	198?	**6.00**	**15.00**

MANDEL, HARVEY

Phillips PHS-600281	(S)	**Cristo Redentor**	1968	**6.00**	**15.00**
Phillips PHS-600306	(S)	**Righteous**	1969	**6.00**	**15.00**
Phillips PHS-600325	(S)	**Games Guitars Play**	1969	**6.00**	**15.00**

MANDRAKE MEMORIAL

Poppy PYS-40,002	(S)	**Mandrake Memorial**	1968	**8.00**	**20.00**
Poppy PYS-40,003	(S)	**Medium**	1969	**8.00**	**20.00**
Poppy PYS-40,006	(S)	**Puzzle**	1970	**8.00**	**20.00**

Label & Catalog #		Title	Year	VG+	NM

MANFRED MANN

Label & Catalog #		Title	Year	VG+	NM
Ascot ALM-13015	(M)	The Manfred Mann Album	1964	12.00	30.00
Ascot ALS-16015	(S)	The Manfred Mann Album	1964	16.00	40.00
Ascot ALM-13018	(M)	The Five Faces Of Manfred Mann	1965	12.00	30.00
Ascot ALS-16018	(S)	The Five Faces Of Manfred Mann	1965	16.00	40.00
Ascot ALM-13021	(M)	My Little Red Book Of Winners	1965	12.00	30.00
Ascot ALS-16021	(S)	My Little Red Book Of Winners	1965	16.00	40.00
Ascot ALM-13024	(M)	Mann Made	1966	12.00	30.00
Ascot ALS-16024	(S)	Mann Made	1966	16.00	40.00
United Arts. UAL-4128	(M)	What's New, Pussycat? (Soundtrack)	1965	6.00	15.00
United Arts. UAS-5128	(S)	What's New, Pussycat? (Soundtrack)	1965	8.00	20.00
United Arts. UAL-3549	(M)	Pretty Flamingo	1966	8.00	20.00
United Arts. UAS-6549	(S)	Pretty Flamingo	1966	12.00	30.00
United Arts. UAL-3551	(M)	Manfred Mann's Greatest Hits	1966	8.00	20.00
United Arts. UAS-6551	(P)	Manfred Mann's Greatest Hits	1966	12.00	30.00
United Arts. UAS-5177	(S)	Charge Of The Light Brigade (Soundtrack)	1968	16.00	40.00
Mercury SR-61168	(S)	The Mighty Quinn	1968	8.00	20.00

MANHATTANS, THE

Carnival CLPS-201	(S)	Dedicated To You	196?	6.00	15.00
Carnival CLPS-202	(S)	For You And Yours	196?	6.00	15.00
Deluxe DLP-12000	(S)	With These Hands	1970	6.00	15.00
Deluxe DLP-12004	(S)	A Million To One	1972	6.00	15.00
Columbia PCQ-34450	(Q)	It Feels So Good	1977	5.00	12.00

MANILOW, BARRY

Bell 1129	(S)	Barry Manilow (Original cover)	1972	8.00	20.00
Arista AQ-4016	(Q)	Barry Manilow II	1974	6.00	15.00
Arista AQ-6060	(Q)	Tryin' To Get That Feeling	1975	6.00	15.00
Mobile Fidelity MFSL-097	(S)	I	1979	5.00	12.00

MANN, BARRY

ABC-Paramount 399	(M)	Who Put The Bomp	1963	20.00	50.00
ABC-Paramount S-399	(S)	Who Put The Bomp	1963	35.00	70.00

MANN, CARL

Phillips Int. 1960	(M)	Like Mann	1960	300.00	500.00

MANN, SHADOW

Tomorrow's TPS-69001	(S)	Come Live With Me	1974	45.00	90.00

MANSFIELD, JAYNE

20th Century	(M)	Jayne Mansfield Busts Up Las Vegas	195?	30.00	60.00
MGM E-4204	(M)	Shakespeare, Tchaikovsky And Me	1964	10.00	25.00
MGM SE-4204	(S)	Shakespeare, Tchaikovsky And Me	1964	14.00	35.00

MANSON, CHARLES

ESP 2003	(M)	Lie: The Love And Terror Cult	1970	50.00	100.00

MAPHIS, JOE

Maphis also recorded with Merle Travis.

Columbia CL-1005	(M)	Fire On The Strings ("Eyes" logo label)	1957	35.00	70.00
MacGregor MGR-1205	(M)	King Of The Strings	196?	35.00	70.00
Starday SLP-316	(M)	King Of The Strings	1966	16.00	40.00
Starday SLP-322	(M)	Golden Gospel	1966	12.00	30.00
Starday SLP-373	(M)	Country Guitar Goes To The Jimmy Dean Show	1966	16.00	40.00
Mosrite MA-400	(M)	The New Sound Of Joe Maphis	196?	16.00	40.00

MAPHIS, JOE & ROSE LEE

Capitol T-1778	(M)	With The Blue Ridge Mountain Boys	1962	12.00	30.00
Capitol ST-1778	(S)	With The Blue Ridge Mountain Boys	1962	16.00	40.00
Starday SLP-286	(S)	Mr. And Mrs. Country Music	1964	10.00	25.00

MAPHIS, ROSE LEE

Columbia CL-1598	(M)	Rose Lee Maphis ("Eyes" logo label)	1961	10.00	25.00
Columbia CS-8398	(S)	Rose Lee Maphis ("Eyes" logo label)	1961	14.00	35.00

Label & Catalog #		Title	Year	VG+	NM
MAR-KEYS, THE					
Refer to Booker T. & The MG's.					
Atlantic 8055	(M)	**Last Night**	1961	12.00	30.00
Atlantic SD-8055	(E)	**Last Night**	1961	10.00	25.00
Atlantic 8062	(M)	**Do The Pop-Eye With The Mar-Kays**	1962	8.00	20.00
Atlantic SD-8062	(S)	**Do The Pop-Eye With The Mar-Keys**	1962	12.00	30.00
Stax ST-707	(M)	**Great Memphis Sound**	1966	6.00	15.00
Stax STS-707	(S)	**Great Memphis Sound**	1966	8.00	20.00
Stax STS-2025	(S)	**Damifiknew**	1969	6.00	15.00
Stax STS-2036	(S)	**Memphis Experience**	1971	4.00	10.00
MAR-KEYS, THE, & BOOKER T. & THE MG'S					
Stax ST-720	(M)	**Back To Back**	1967	5.00	12.00
Stax STS-720	(S)	**Back To Back**	1967	6.00	15.00
MARAIS & MIRANDA					
Decca DL-8711	(M)	**Sundown Songs**	1958	10.00	25.00
Decca DL-9087	(M)	**Songs Of Spirit And Humor**	1959	8.00	20.00
Decca DL-79087	(S)	**Songs Of Spirit And Humor**	1959	10.00	25.00
Decca DL-9026	(M)	**Marais & Miranda In Person, Volume 1**	1959	8.00	20.00
Decca DL-79026	(S)	**Marais & Miranda In Person, Volume 1**	1959	10.00	25.00
Decca DL-9027	(M)	**Marais & Miranda In Person, Volume 2**	1959	8.00	20.00
Decca DL-79027	(S)	**Marais & Miranda In Person, Volume 2**	1959	10.00	25.00
MARATHONS, THE					
Arvee A-428	(M)	**Peanut Butter**	1961	50.00	100.00
MARAUDERS, THE					
No label	(M)	**The Marauders Check In**	1964	20.00	50.00
No label	(M)	**Maraudin' '65**	1965	20.00	50.00
MARBLE PHROGG, THE					
Derrick 8868	(S)	**The Marble Phrogg**	1968	360.00	600.00
MARCELS, THE					
Colpix CP-416	(M)	**Blue Moon** *(Gold Label)*	1961	35.00	70.00
Colpix CSP-416	(S)	**Blue Moon** *(Gold Label)*	1961	75.00	150.00
MARCH, LITTLE PEGGY					
RCA Victor LPM-2732	(M)	**I Will Follow Him**	1963	10.00	25.00
RCA Victor LSP-2732	(S)	**I Will Follow Him**	1963	14.00	35.00
RCA Victor LPM-3408	(M)	**In Our Fashion**	1965	14.00	35.00
RCA Victor LSP-3408	(S)	**In Our Fashion**	1965	16.00	45.00
RCA Victor LSP-3883	(S)	**No Foolin'**	1968	10.00	25.00
MARCHAN, BOBBY					
Sphere Sound SR-7004	(M)	**There's Something On Your Mind**	1964	20.00	50.00
Sphere Sound SSR-7004	(S)	**There's Something On Your Mind**	1964	30.00	60.00
MARCUS					
NR 10788	(S)	**From The House Of Trax**	1979	660.00	1,000.00
MARESCA, ERNIE					
Seville SV-77001	(M)	**Shout! Shout! Knock Yourself Out**	1962	12.00	30.00
Seville SV-87001	(S)	**Shout! Shout! Knock Yourself Out**	1962	16.00	40.00
MARIANI					
Sonobeat 1001	(M)	**Perpetuum Mobile** *(No cover)*	196?	*See note below*	
		(Rare. Estimated near mint value $1,500-3,000.)			
MARIE, ROSE					
Kapp KRL-4500	(M)	**Songs For Single Girls**	195?	10.00	25.00
MARKETTS, THE [THE MAR-KETTS]					
Liberty LRP-3226	(M)	**Surfer's Stomp**	1962	8.00	20.00
Liberty LST-7226	(S)	**Surfer's Stomp**	1962	12.00	30.00
Liberty LRP-3226	(M)	**The Surfing Scene**	1963	8.00	20.00
Liberty LST-7226	(S)	**The Surfing Scene**	1963	12.00	30.00

Label & Catalog #		Title	Year	VG+	NM
Warner Bros. T-1509	(M)	The Marketts Take To Wheels	1963	6.00	15.00
Warner Bros. ST-1509	(S)	The Marketts Take To Wheels	1963	8.00	20.00
Warner Bros. T-1537	(M)	Out Of Limits	1964	6.00	15.00
Warner Bros. ST-1537	(S)	Out Of Limits	1964	8.00	20.00
Warner Bros. T-1642	(M)	Batman Theme	1966	8.00	20.00
Warner Bros. ST-1642	(S)	Batman Theme	1966	10.00	25.00
World Pacific WP-1870	(M)	Sun Power	1967	5.00	12.00
World Pacific ST-1870	(S)	Sun Power	1967	6.00	15.00
Mercury SRM-1-679	(S)	AM, FM, Etc.	1973	6.00	15.00

MARKLEY

Forward 1007	(S)	Markley: A Group	1969	8.00	20.00

MARKS, GUY

ABC-Paramount 549	(M)	Hollywood Sings	1966	4.00	10.00
ABC-Paramount S-549	(S)	Hollywood Sings	1966	5.00	12.00
ABC-Paramount 648	(M)	Loving You Has Made Me Bananas	1967	5.00	12.00
ABC-Paramount S-648	(S)	Loving You Has Made Me Bananas	1967	6.00	15.00

MARKS, J., & SHIPEN LEBZELTER

Columbia 7193	(S)	Rock And Other Four Letter Words (2 LPs)	1968	12.00	30.00

(This is a McLuhanesque collage of related sounds, events, etc. and includes a one line quote from Brian Wilson.)

MARLENE [MARLENE VERPLANCK]

Savoy MG-12058	(M)	I Think Of You With Every Breath I Take	1956	35.00	70.00
Mounted 108	(M)	A Breath Of Fresh Air	1963	12.00	30.00

MARLEY, BOB, & THE WAILERS

Island ILPS-9256	(S)	Burnin'	1975	4.00	10.00
Island ILPS-9281	(S)	Natty Dread	1975	4.00	10.00
Island ILPS-9329	(S)	Catch A Fire	1975	16.00	40.00

(The cover is shaped like a cigarette lighter with a hinge that allows the top to flip open.)

Island ILPS-9329	(S)	Catch A Fire (Standard cover)	1975	4.00	10.00
Island ILPS-9376	(S)	Bob Marley Live	1976	4.00	10.00
Island ILPS-9383	(S)	Rastaman Vibrations	1976	4.00	10.00

— Original Island albums above have black labels with an "i" on the bottom.—

MARMALADE

Epic BN-26553	(S)	The Best Of Marmalade	1970	6.00	15.00
London PS-575	(P)	Reflections Of My Life	1970	6.00	15.00

MARSHALL, JACK, & THE NEWPORT BEACH LITTLE THEATER SURFING GROUP

Capitol T-1939	(M)	My Son The Surf Nut	1963	6.00	15.00
Capitol ST-1939	(S)	My Son The Surf Nut	1963	8.00	20.00

MARSHMALLOW WAY

United Arts. UAS-6708	(S)	Marshmellow Way	1969	6.00	15.00

MARTHA & THE VANDELLAS
Martha is Ms. Martha Reeves.

Gordy 902	(M)	Come And Get These Memories	1963	35.00	70.00
Gordy GS-902	(S)	Come And Get These Memories	1963	50.00	100.00
Gordy 907	(M)	Heat Wave	1963	14.00	35.00
Gordy GS-907	(S)	Heat Wave	1963	16.00	40.00
Gordy 915	(M)	Dance Party	1965	10.00	25.00
Gordy GS-915	(S)	Dance Party	1965	12.00	30.00
Gordy 917	(M)	Martha & The Vandellas' Greatest Hits	1966	6.00	15.00
Gordy GS-917	(S)	Martha & The Vandellas' Greatest Hits	1966	8.00	20.00
Gordy 920	(M)	Watchout!	1967	6.00	15.00
Gordy GS-920	(S)	Watchout!	1967	8.00	20.00
Gordy 925	(M)	Martha & The Vandellas' Live!	1967	5.00	12.00
Gordy GS-925	(S)	Martha & The Vandellas' Live!	1967	6.00	15.00
Gordy GS-926	(S)	Ridin' High	1968	6.00	15.00
Gordy GS-944	(S)	Sugar 'N Spice	1969	6.00	15.00
Gordy GS-952	(S)	Natural Resources	1970	5.00	12.00
Gordy GS-958	(S)	Black Magic	1972	5.00	12.00

Label & Catalog #		Title	Year	VG+	NM

One of Motown's best female groups, Martha & The Vandellas' classics, "Dancing In The Street" and "Nowhere To Run," are included on their third album, which also features great cover graphics!

MARTIN, BENNY

Starday SLP-131	(M)	Country Music's Sensational Entertainer	1961	12.00	30.00

MARTIN, DEAN

Refer to The Reprise Repertory Theatre.

Label & Catalog #		Title	Year	VG+	NM
Capitol L-401 (10")	(M)	The Stooge (Soundtrack)	1953	50.00	100.00
Capitol T-401	(M)	The Stooge (Soundtrack)	1953	20.00	50.00
Capitol T-576	(M)	Swingin' Down Yonder	1955	12.00	30.00
Capitol T-849	(M)	Pretty Baby	1957	12.00	30.00
Capitol T-1047	(M)	This Is Martin	1958	12.00	30.00
		— Original Capitol albums above have turquoise labels—			
Capitol T-1150	(M)	Sleep Warm	1959	8.00	20.00
Capitol ST-1150	(S)	Sleep Warm	1959	12.00	30.00
		(Capitol 1150 conducted by Frank Sinatra.)			
Capitol T-1285	(M)	Winter Romance	1959	8.00	20.00
Capitol ST-1285	(S)	Winter Romance	1959	12.00	30.00
Capitol W-1435	(M)	Bells Are Ringing (Soundtrack)	1960	14.00	35.00
Capitol SW-1435	(S)	Bells Are Ringing (Soundtrack)	1960	20.00	50.00
Capitol T-1442	(M)	This Time I'm Swingin'	1961	6.00	15.00
Capitol ST-1442	(S)	This Time I'm Swingin'	1961	8.00	20.00
Capitol W-1580	(M)	Dean Martin	1961	6.00	15.00
Capitol SW-1580	(S)	Dean Martin	1961	8.00	20.00
Capitol T-1659	(M)	Dino	1962	6.00	15.00
Capitol ST-1659	(S)	Dino	1962	8.00	20.00
		— Original Capitol albums above have black labels with the logo on the left side.—			
Capitol T-2212	(M)	Hey Brother, Pour The Wine	1964	6.00	15.00
Capitol DT-2212	(E)	Hey Brother, Pour The Wine	1964	5.00	12.00
Capitol T-2297	(M)	Dean Martin Sings, Sinatra Conducts	1965	6.00	15.00
Capitol ST-2297	(S)	Dean Martin Sings, Sinatra Conducts	1965	8.00	20.00
Capitol T-2333	(M)	Southern Style	1965	6.00	15.00
Capitol DT-2333	(E)	Southern Style	1965	5.00	12.00
Capitol TT-2343	(M)	Holiday Cheer	1965	5.00	12.00
Capitol STT-2343	(S)	Holiday Cheer	1965	6.00	15.00
Capitol T-2601	(M)	The Best Of Dean Martin	1966	5.00	12.00
Capitol DT-2601	(E)	The Best Of Dean Martin	1966	4.00	10.00

Label & Catalog #		Title	Year	VG+	NM
Capitol TCL-2815	(M)	**Deluxe Set** *(3 LPs)*	1967	10.00	25.00
Capitol DTCL-2815	(P)	**Deluxe Set** *(3 LPs)*	1967	8.00	20.00
Capitol DT-2941	(E)	**Favorites**	1968	6.00	15.00
— *Original Capitol albums above have black labels with the logo on top.*—					
Tower T-5006	(M)	**Lush Years**	1965	5.00	12.00
Tower ST-5006	(S)	**Lush Years**	1965	6.00	15.00
Tower T-5018	(M)	**Relaxin'**	1966	5.00	12.00
Tower ST-5018	(S)	**Relaxin'**	1966	6.00	15.00
Tower T-5036	(M)	**Happy In Love**	1966	5.00	12.00
Tower ST-5036	(S)	**Happy In Love**	1966	6.00	15.00
Reprise R-6021	(M)	**French Style**	1962	4.00	10.00
Reprise RS-6021	(S)	**French Style**	1962	5.00	12.00
Reprise R-6054	(M)	**Dino Latino**	1963	4.00	10.00
Reprise RS-6054	(S)	**Dino Latino**	1963	5.00	12.00
Reprise R-6061	(M)	**Country Style**	1963	5.00	12.00
Reprise RS-6061	(S)	**Country Style**	1963	6.00	15.00
Reprise R-6085	(M)	**Dean "Tex" Martin Rides Again**	1963	5.00	12.00
Reprise RS-6085	(S)	**Dean "Tex" Martin Rides Again**	1963	6.00	15.00

MARTIN, DEWEY
Dewey Martin was formerly a member of The Buffalo Springfield.

Uni 73088	(S)	**Dewey Martin And Medicine Ball**	1970	6.00	15.00

MARTIN, GEORGE (& HIS ORCHESTRA)
Mr. Martin was the "fifth" Beatle, producer of all of their work, 1962-1969. Martin's scores for the "A Hard Day's Night," "Help!" and "Yellow Submarine" soundtracks are listed under The Beatles.

United Arts. UAL-3377	(M)	**Off The Beatle Track**	1964	16.00	40.00
United Arts. UAS-6377	(S)	**Off The Beatle Track**	1964	20.00	50.00
United Arts. UAL-3420	(M)	**George Martin**	1965	10.00	25.00
United Arts. UAS-6420	(S)	**George Martin**	1965	12.00	30.00
United Arts. UAL-3387	(M)	**Ferry Cross The Mersey** *(Soundtrack)*	1965	14.00	35.00
United Arts. UAS-6387	(S)	**Ferry Cross The Mersey** *(Soundtrack)*	1965	20.00	50.00
United Arts. UAL-3448	(M)	**George Martin Plays "Help"**	1965	12.00	30.00
United Arts. UAS-6448	(S)	**George Martin Plays "Help"**	1965	16.00	40.00
United Arts. UAL-3539	(M)	**George Martin Salutes The Beatle Girls**	1966	12.00	30.00
United Arts. UAS-6539	(S)	**George Martin Salutes The Beatle Girls**	1966	16.00	40.00
United Arts. UAL-3647	(M)	**London By George**	1967	8.00	20.00
United Arts. UAS-6647	(S)	**London By George**	1967	10.00	25.00
United Arts. LA100	(S)	**Live And Let Die** *(Soundtrack)*	1973	6.00	15.00

MARTIN, GRADY

Decca DL-5566 (10")	(M)	**Dance-O-Rama #6**	1955	90.00	180.00

MARTIN, JIMMY (& THE SUNNY MOUNTAIN BOYS)

Decca DL-4016	(M)	**Good 'N' Country**	1960	6.00	15.00
Decca DL-74016	(S)	**Good 'N' Country**	1960	8.00	20.00
Decca DL-4285	(M)	**Country Music Time**	1962	6.00	15.00
Decca DL-74285	(S)	**Country Music Time**	1962	8.00	20.00
Decca DL-4360	(M)	**This World Is Not My Home**	1963	6.00	15.00
Decca DL-74360	(S)	**This World Is Not My Home**	1963	8.00	20.00
Decca DL-4536	(M)	**Widow Maker**	1964	5.00	12.00
Decca DL-74536	(S)	**Widow Maker**	1964	6.00	15.00
Decca DL-4643	(M)	**Sunny Side Of The Mountain**	1965	5.00	12.00
Decca DL-74643	(S)	**Sunny Side Of The Mountain**	1965	6.00	15.00
Decca DL-4769	(M)	**Mr. Good 'N' Country Music**	1966	5.00	12.00
Decca DL-74769	(S)	**Mr. Good 'N' Country Music**	1966	6.00	15.00
Decca DL-4891	(M)	**Big Country Instrumentals**	1967	5.00	12.00
Decca DL-74891	(S)	**Big Country Instrumentals**	1967	6.00	15.00
Decca DL-74996	(S)	**Tennessee**	1968	5.00	12.00
Decca DL-75116	(S)	**Free Born Man**	1969	5.00	12.00

MARTIN, MARTY
Marty later recorded as Boxcar Willie.

A.H.M.C. 118	(S)	**Marty Martin Sings Country Music**	197?	20.00	50.00

MARTIN, MARY

Decca DL-7027 (10")	(M)	**The Ford 50th Anniversary Show**	195?	14.00	35.00
Disneyland 3031	(M)	**A Musical Love Story**	195?	10.00	25.00
Disneyland 3038	(M)	**Hi Ho**	195?	10.00	25.00

Label & Catalog #		Title	Year	VG+	NM

MARTINEZ, TONY

Label & Catalog #		Title	Year	VG+	NM
Del Fi DFLP-1205	(M)	The Many Sides Of Pepino	1959	10.00	25.00
Del Fi DFLP-1205S	(S)	The Many Sides Of Pepino	1959	14.00	35.00

MARTINO, AL

20th Century SF-3025	(M)	Al Martino	1959	12.00	30.00
20th Century SF-3032	(M)	Sing Along With Al Martino	1959	8.00	20.00
20th Century SFX-3032	(S)	Sing Along With Al Martino	1959	12.00	30.00
20th Century TF-4168	(M)	Al Martino Sings	1962	6.00	15.00
20th Century TFS-4168	(S)	Al Martino Sings	1962	8.00	20.00
20th Century TF-5009	(M)	Love Notes	1963	6.00	15.00
20th Century TFS-5009	(S)	Love Notes	1963	8.00	20.00
Capitol T-1774	(M)	The Exciting Voice Of Al Martino	1962	5.00	12.00
Capitol ST-1774	(S)	The Exciting Voice Of Al Martino	1962	6.00	15.00
Capitol T-1807	(M)	The Italian Voice Of Al Martino	1962	5.00	12.00
Capitol ST-1807	(S)	The Italian Voice Of Al Martino	1962	6.00	15.00
Capitol T-1914	(M)	I Love You Because	1963	5.00	12.00
Capitol ST-1914	(S)	I Love You Because	1963	6.00	15.00
Capitol T-1975	(M)	Painted, Tainted Rose	1963	5.00	12.00
Capitol ST-1975	(S)	Painted, Tainted Rose	1963	6.00	15.00
Capitol T-2040	(M)	Living A Lie	1964	5.00	12.00
Capitol ST-2040	(S)	Living A Lie	1964	6.00	15.00
Capitol T-2107	(M)	I Love You More And More Every Day	1964	5.00	12.00
Capitol ST-2107	(S)	I Love You More And More Every Day	1964	6.00	15.00
Capitol T-2165	(M)	Merry Christmas	1964	5.00	12.00
Capitol ST-2165	(S)	Merry Christmas	1964	6.00	15.00
Capitol T-2200	(M)	We Could	1965	5.00	12.00
Capitol ST-2200	(S)	We Could	1965	6.00	15.00
Capitol T-2312	(M)	Somebody Else Is Taking My Place	1965	5.00	12.00
Capitol ST-2312	(S)	Somebody Else Is Taking My Place	1965	6.00	15.00
Capitol T-2362	(M)	My Cherie	1965	5.00	12.00
Capitol ST-2362	(S)	My Cherie	1965	6.00	15.00
Capitol T-2435	(M)	Spanish Eyes	1966	5.00	12.00
Capitol ST-2435	(S)	Spanish Eyes	1966	6.00	15.00
Capitol T-2528	(M)	Think I'll Go Somewhere And Cry Myself To Sleep	1966	5.00	12.00
Capitol ST-2528	(S)	Think I'll Go Somewhere And Cry Myself To Sleep	1966	6.00	15.00
Capitol T-2592	(M)	This Is Love	1966	5.00	12.00
Capitol ST-2592	(S)	This Is Love	1966	6.00	15.00
Capitol T-2654	(M)	This Love For You	1967	5.00	12.00
Capitol ST-2654	(S)	This Love For You	1967	6.00	15.00
Capitol T-2733	(M)	Daddy's Little Girl	1967	5.00	12.00
Capitol ST-2733	(S)	Daddy's Little Girl	1967	6.00	15.00
Capitol T-2780	(M)	Mary In The Morning	1967	5.00	12.00
Capitol ST-2780	(S)	Mary In The Morning	1967	6.00	15.00
Capitol ST-2843	(S)	This Is Al Martino	1968	5.00	12.00
Capitol ST-2908	(S)	Love Is Blue	1968	5.00	12.00
Capitol ST-2946	(S)	The Best Of Al Martino	1968	5.00	12.00

— Original Capitol albums above have black labels with the logo on top.—

MARVELETTES, THE

Tamla 228	(M)	Please Mr. Postman	1961	100.00	200.00
Tamla 229	(M)	The Marvelettes Sing	1962	100.00	200.00
Tamla 231	(M)	Playboy	1962	100.00	200.00

— Original Tamla albums above have a disc over-lapping a globe at the top of the label.—

Tamla 228	(M)	Please Mr. Postman	1963	50.00	100.00
Tamla 229	(M)	The Marvelettes Sing	1963	50.00	100.00
Tamla 231	(M)	Playboy	1963	50.00	100.00
Tamla 237	(M)	The Marvelous Marvelettes	1963	50.00	100.00
Tamla 243	(M)	On Stage	1963	30.00	60.00
Tamla 253	(M)	The Marvelettes' Greatest Hits	1966	6.00	15.00
Tamla TS-253	(S)	The Marvelettes' Greatest Hits	1966	8.00	20.00
Tamla 274	(M)	The Marvelettes	1967	5.00	12.00
Tamla TS-274	(S)	The Marvelettes	1967	6.00	15.00
Tamla TS-286	(S)	Sophisticated Soul	1968	5.00	12.00
Tamla TS-288	(S)	The Marvelettes In Full Bloom	1969	5.00	12.00
Tamla TS-305	(S)	Return Of The Marvelettes	1970	5.00	12.00

— Tamla albums above have two side-by-side circles at the top of the label.—

Label & Catalog #		Title	Year	VG+	NM
MARX, GROUCHO					
Decca DL-5405 (10")	(M)	**Hooray For Captain Spaulding**	1952	100.00	200.00
A&M SP-3515	(M)	**An Evening With Groucho**	1972	6.00	15.00
A&M SP-3515	(M)	**An Evening With Groucho** (Picture disc)	1972	4.00	10.00
MARX, HARPO					
RCA Victor LPM-27 (10")	(M)	**Harp By Harpo**	1951	50.00	100.00
Mercury MG-20232	(M)	**Harpo In Hi-Fi**	1957	20.00	50.00
Mercury SR-60232	(S)	**Harpo In Hi-Fi**	1957	35.00	70.00
Mercury MG-20363	(M)	**Harpo At Work**	1959	20.00	50.00
Mercury SR-60016	(S)	**Harpo At Work**	1959	35.00	70.00
RCA Victor LPM-2720	(M)	**Harp By Harpo**	1963	20.00	50.00
RCA Victor LSP-2720	(E)	**Harp By Harpo**	1963	16.00	40.00
MARX BROTHERS, THE					
The Marx Brothers were Chico, Groucho, Harpo and Zeppo.					
Decca DL-79168	(E)	**The Marx Brothers**	1969	8.00	20.00
MARY BUTTERWORTH					
Custom Fidelity	(M)	**Mary Butterworth**	1968	180.00	300.00
MASKED MARAUDERS, THE					
Reprise/Deity RS-6378	(S)	**The Masked Marauders**	1969	8.00	20.00
MASON, BARBARA					
Arctic ALP-1000	(M)	**Yes, I'm Ready**	1965	8.00	20.00
Arctic ALPS-1000	(S)	**Yes, I'm Ready**	1965	10.00	25.00
Arctic ALPS-1004	(S)	**Oh, How It Hurts**	1968	6.00	15.00
MASON, DAVE					
Dave Mason was formerly a member of Traffic.					
Blue Thumb BTS-19	(S)	**All Together** (Multi-colored vinyl)	1970	4.00	10.00
		(Frst pressings on pseudo-psychedelic vinyl are common.)			
Blue Thumb BTS-19	(S)	**All Together** (Black vinyl)	1971	8.00	20.00
Columbia PCQ-31721	(Q)	**It's Like You Never Left**	1974	5.00	12.00
Columbia PCQ-33096	(Q)	**Dave Mason**	1974	5.00	12.00
Columbia PCQ-33698	(Q)	**Split Coconut**	1976	5.00	12.00
MASON, DAVE, & CASS ELLIOT					
Blue Thumb BTS-25	(S)	**Dave Mason & Cass Elliot**	1969	8.00	20.00
Blue Thumb BTS-8825	(S)	**Dave Mason & Cass Elliot**	1971	4.00	10.00
MATHIS, JOHNNY					
Columbia CL-887	(M)	**Johnny Mathis**	1957	14.00	35.00
Columbia CL-1028	(M)	**Wonderful, Wonderful**	1957	14.00	35.00
Columbia CL-1078	(M)	**Warm**	1957	14.00	35.00
Columbia CL-1090	(M)	**Wild Is The Wind** (Soundtrack)	1957	75.00	150.00
Columbia CL-1119	(M)	**Good Night, Dear Lord**	1958	14.00	35.00
Columbia CL-1133	(M)	**Johnny's Greatest Hits**	1958	14.00	35.00
Columbia CL-1165	(M)	**Swing Softly**	1958	14.00	35.00
Columbia CL-1194	(M)	**A Certain Smile** (Soundtrack)	1958	75.00	150.00
Columbia CL-1195	(M)	**Merry Christmas**	1958	14.00	35.00
Columbia CL-1270	(M)	**Open Fire, Two Guitars**	1959	14.00	35.00
Columbia CL-1344	(M)	**More Johnny's Greatest Hits**	1959	10.00	25.00
Columbia CL-1351	(M)	**Heavenly**	1959	6.00	15.00
Columbia CS-8151	(S)	**Heavenly**	1959	8.00	20.00
Columbia CL-1419	(M)	**Faithfully**	1960	6.00	15.00
Columbia CS-8219	(S)	**Faithfully**	1960	8.00	20.00
Columbia CL-1526	(M)	**Johnny's Moods**	1960	6.00	15.00
Columbia CS-8326	(S)	**Johnny's Moods**	1960	8.00	20.00
Columbia C2L-803	(M)	**The Rhythms And Ballads Of Broadway**	1960	8.00	20.00
Columbia C2S-803	(S)	**The Rhythms And Ballads Of Broadway**	1960	10.00	25.00
Columbia CL-1623	(M)	**I'll Buy You A Star**	1961	5.00	12.00
Columbia CS-8423	(S)	**I'll Buy You A Star**	1961	6.00	15.00
Columbia CL-1644	(M)	**Portrait Of Johnny** (With portrait)	1961	6.00	15.00
Columbia CS-8444	(S)	**Portrait Of Johnny** (With portrait)	1961	8.00	20.00
Columbia CL-1711	(M)	**Live It Up!**	1962	5.00	12.00
Columbia CS-8511	(S)	**Live It Up!**	1962	6.00	15.00

— Original Columbia albums above have three white "eye" logos on each side of the spindle hole.—

Label & Catalog #		Title	Year	VG+	NM
Columbia CL-1834	(M)	Johnny's Greatest Hits	1962	6.00	15.00
Columbia CS-8634	(E)	Johnny's Greatest Hits	1962	4.00	10.00
Columbia CL-1915	(M)	Rapture	1962	4.00	10.00
Columbia CS-8715	(S)	Rapture	1962	5.00	12.00

Because Johnny's records were often used in creating a "proper" ambience for romance, they were played often and, consequently, first pressings of his earlier albums are scarce in nearly mint condition.

Columbia CL-2016	(M)	Johnny's Newest Hits	1963	5.00	12.00
Columbia CS-8816	(S)	Johnny's Newest Hits	1963	6.00	15.00
Columbia CL-2044	(M)	Johnny	1963	4.00	10.00
Columbia CS-8844	(S)	Johnny	1963	5.00	12.00
Columbia CL-2098	(M)	Romantically	1963	4.00	10.00
Columbia CS-8898	(S)	Romantically	1963	5.00	12.00
Columbia CL-2143	(M)	I'll Search My Heart And Other Great Hits	1964	4.00	10.00
Columbia CS-8943	(S)	I'll Search My Heart And Other Great Hits	1964	5.00	12.00
Columbia C2L-834	(M)	The Great Years	1964	4.00	10.00
Columbia C2S-834	(S)	The Great Years	1964	5.00	12.00
Columbia CL-2223	(M)	The Ballads Of Broadway	1964	4.00	10.00
Columbia CS-9023	(S)	The Ballads Of Broadway	1964	5.00	12.00
Columbia CL-2224	(M)	The Rhythms Of Broadway	1964	4.00	10.00
Columbia CS-9024	(S)	The Rhythms Of Broadway	1964	5.00	12.00
Columbia CL-2246	(M)	Wonderful! Wonderful!	1964	5.00	12.00
Columbia CS-9046	(E)	Wonderful! Wonderful!	1964	3.20	8.00

— Original Columbia albums above have "360 Sound Mono/Stereo" on the bottom of the label.—

Mercury MG-20837	(M)	The Sound Of Christmas	1964	4.00	12.00
Mercury SR-60837	(S)	The Sound Of Christmas	1964	5.00	15.00
Mercury MG-20890	(M)	Tender Is The Night	1964	4.00	12.00
Mercury SR-60890	(S)	Tender Is The Night	1964	5.00	15.00
Mercury MG-20913	(M)	The Wonderful World Of Make Believe	1964	4.00	12.00
Mercury SR-60913	(S)	The Wonderful World Of Make Believe	1964	5.00	15.00
Mercury MG-20942	(M)	This Is Love	1964	4.00	12.00
Mercury SR-60942	(S)	This Is Love	1964	5.00	15.00
Mercury MG-20988	(M)	Johnny Mathis Ole	1964	4.00	12.00
Mercury SR-60988	(S)	Johnny Mathis Ole	1964	5.00	15.00
Mercury MG-20991	(M)	Love Is Everything	1965	4.00	12.00
Mercury SR-60991	(S)	Love Is Everything	1965	5.00	15.00

Label & Catalog #		Title	Year	VG+	NM
Mercury MG-21041	(M)	The Sweetheart Tree	1965	4.00	12.00
Mercury SR-61041	(S)	The Sweetheart Tree	1965	5.00	15.00
Mercury MG-21073	(M)	The Shadow Of Your Smile	1966	4.00	12.00
Mercury SR-61073	(S)	The Shadow Of Your Smile	1966	5.00	15.00
Mercury MG-21091	(M)	So Nice	1966	4.00	12.00
Mercury SR-61091	(S)	So Nice	1966	5.00	15.00
Mercury MG-21107	(M)	Johnny Mathis Sings	1967	4.00	12.00
Mercury SR-61107	(S)	Johnny Mathis Sings	1967	5.00	15.00
Columbia CQ-30740	(Q)	You've Got A Friend	1971	4.00	12.00
Columbia CQ-30979	(Q)	Johnny Mathis In Person	1972	6.00	15.00
Columbia CQ-31626	(Q)	Song Sung Blue	1972	4.00	12.00
Columbia CQ-32114	(Q)	Me And Mrs Jones	1973	4.00	12.00
Columbia CQ-32435	(Q)	I'm Coming Home	1973	4.00	12.00
Columbia CQ-33420	(Q)	When Will I See You Again	1975	4.00	12.00
Mobile Fidelity MFSL-171	(S)	Heavenly	198?	8.00	20.00

MAUDS, THE

Mercury MG-21135	(M)	The Mauds Hold On	1967	5.00	12.00
Mercury SR-61135	(S)	The Mauds Hold On	1967	6.00	15.00

MAXWELL, DIANE

Challenge CHL-607	(M)	Almost Seventeen	1959	10.00	25.00
Challenge CHS-2501	(S)	Almost Seventeen	1959	14.00	35.00

MAY BLITZ

Paramount PAS-5020	(S)	May Blitz	1970	8.00	20.00

MAYA, CANTA

Roulette R-25052	(M)	A Long, Long Kiss	1958	8.00	20.00

MAYALL, JOHN [JOHN MAYALL'S BLUESBREAKERS]
Refer to the Groundhogs.

London LL-3492	(M)	Blues Breakers With Eric Clapton	1967	6.00	15.00
London PS-492	(S)	Blues Breakers With Eric Clapton	1967	8.00	20.00
London LL-3502	(M)	A Hard Road	1967	5.00	12.00
London PS-502	(S)	A Hard Road	1967	6.00	15.00
London PS-529	(S)	Crusade	1968	6.00	15.00
London PS-534	(S)	The Blues Alone	1968	5.00	12.00
London PS-537	(S)	Bare Wires	1968	4.00	10.00
London PS-545	(S)	Blues From Laurel Canyon	1969	4.00	10.00
Mobile Fidelity MFSL-183	(S)	Blues Breakers With Eric Clapton	198?	8.00	20.00

MAYER, NATHANIEL

Fortune 8014	(M)	Going Back To The Village Of Love	1964	14.00	35.00

MAYFIELD, PERCY

Tangerine TRC-1505	(M)	My Jug And I	1966	6.00	15.00
Tangerine TRCS-1505	(S)	My Jug And I	1966	8.00	20.00
Tangerine TRC-1510	(M)	Bought Blues	1967	6.00	15.00
Tangerine TRCS-1510	(S)	Bought Blues	1967	8.00	20.00
Brunswick BL7-54145	(S)	Walking On A Tightrope	1969	6.00	15.00
Specialty SPS-2186	(E)	The Best Of Percy Mayfield	1970	6.00	15.00
RCA Victor LSP-4269	(S)	Percy Mayfield Sings Percy Mayfield	1970	6.00	15.00
RCA Victor LSP-4444	(S)	Weakness Is A Thing Called Man	1970	6.00	15.00
RCA Victor LSP-4558	(S)	Blues And Then Some	1971	6.00	15.00

MAZANTI

Mazanti Music	(S)	Philosopher	1979	35.00	70.00

MAZE

M.T.A. 5012	(S)	Armageddon	1971	40.00	80.00

MC-5, THE [THE MOTOR CITY FIVE]

Elektra EKS-74042	(S)	Kick Out The Jams *(Brown label)*	1969	30.00	60.00
		(Original pressings open side one with the anthem, "Kick out the jams, motherfuckers!" and feature liner notes on the back cover.)			
Elektra EKS-74042	(S)	Kick Out The Jams	1969	16.00	40.00
		(Later pressings replace the expletive with "Kick out the jams, brothers and sisters" and delete the liner notes.)			

Label & Catalog #		Title	Year	VG+	NM
Atlantic SD-8247	(S)	Back In The U.S.A.	1970	16.00	40.00
Atlantic SD-8285	(S)	High Time	1971	16.00	40.00

McAULIFFE, LEON (& HIS CIMMARON BOYS)

Sesac 1601	(M)	Points West	195?	50.00	100.00
Sesac 1602	(M)	Just A Minute	195?	35.00	70.00
Dot DLP-3139	(M)	Take Off	1958	20.00	50.00
Cimarron 202	(M)	Swingin' Western Strings	1960	30.00	60.00
ABC-Paramount 394	(M)	Cozy Inn	1961	14.00	35.00
ABC-Paramount S-394	(S)	Cozy Inn	1961	20.00	50.00
Starday SLP-171	(M)	Mr. Western Swing	1962	16.00	40.00
Starday SLP-280	(M)	Swinging West	1962	16.00	40.00
Starday SLP-309	(M)	Swingin' Western Strings	1962	16.00	40.00
Capitol T-2016	(M)	The Dancin'est Band Around	1964	12.00	30.00
Capitol ST-2016	(S)	The Dancin'est Band Around	1964	16.00	40.00
Capitol T-2148	(M)	Everybody Dance! Everybody Swing!	1964	12.00	30.00
Capitol ST-2148	(S)	Everybody Dance! Everybody Swing!	1964	16.00	40.00
Dot DLP-3689	(M)	Golden Country Hits	1966	12.00	30.00
Dot DLP-25689	(E)	Golden Country Hits	1966	8.00	20.00

McCALL, MARY ANN

Discovery DL-3011 (10")	(M)	Mary Ann McCall Sings	1950	35.00	70.00
Norgran 20 (10")	(M)	An Evening With Mary Ann McCall	1954	35.00	70.00
Norgran 1013	(M)	Another Evening With Mary Ann McCall	1954	30.00	60.00
Norgran 1053	(M)	An Evening With Mary Ann McCall	1955	20.00	50.00
Verve V-8143	(M)	An Evening With Mary Ann McCall	1957	16.00	40.00
Regent 6040	(M)	Easy Living	1956	14.00	35.00
Jubilee 1078	(M)	Detour To The Moon	1958	14.00	35.00
Coral CRL-57276	(M)	Melancholy Baby	1959	14.00	35.00

McCARTNEY, PAUL (& WINGS)

Some albums are credited to Wings. Refer to The Beatles; Denny Laine; Percy Thrillington.

Warner Bros. PRO (10")	(DJ)	The Family Way Radio Spots	1967	150.00	250.00
London M-76007	(M)	The Family Way (Soundtrack)	1967	20.00	50.00
London MS-82007	(S)	The Family Way (Soundtrack)	1967	35.00	70.00
Apple STAO-3363	(S)	McCartney ("Mfd. by Apple" label)	1970	6.00	15.00
Apple STAO-3363	(S)	McCartney (Capitol logo label)	1970	14.00	40.00
Apple STAO-3363	(S)	McCartney ("All rights reserved" label)	1970	12.00	30.00
Apple MAS-3375	(DJ)	Ram	1971	See note below	
		(Rare mono promo. Estimated near mint value $1,000-3,000.)			
Apple SMAS-3375	(S)	Ram ("Mfd. by Apple" label)	1971	6.00	15.00
Apple SMAS-3375	(S)	Ram (Capitol logo label)	1971	10.00	25.00
Apple SMAS-3375	(S)	Ram ("All rights reserved" label)	1971	12.00	30.00
Apple SPRO-6210	(DJ)	Brung To Ewe By	1971	180.00	300.00
Apple SW-3386	(S)	Wild Life	1971	6.00	15.00
Apple SMAL-3409	(S)	Red Rose Speedway	1973	4.00	10.00
Apple SO-3415	(S)	Band On The Run (With poster)	1973	4.00	10.00
Capitol SEAX-11901	(S)	Band On The Run (Picture disc)	1975	14.00	35.00
Capitol SMAS-11419	(S)	Venus And Mars (With inserts)	1975	4.00	10.00
Capitol SW-11525	(DJ)	Wings At The Speed Of Sound	1976	65.00	130.00
Capitol SWCO-11593	(S)	Wings Over America	1976	6.00	15.00
Columbia C3X-37990	(S)	Wings Over America	1976	14.00	35.00
Columbia JC-36482	(S)	Band On The Run	1981	10.00	25.00
		(MPL logo in lower left corner of cover.)			
Columbia HC-46482	(S)	Band On The Run (Half-speed master)	1981	14.00	35.00
Columbia FC-36057	(DJ)	Back To The Egg	1979	16.00	40.00
Columbia AS2-821	(DJ)	The McCartney Interview (2 LPs)	1980	10.00	25.00
Columbia FC-36511	(DJ)	McCartney II (White label)	1980?	8.00	20.00
Columbia FC-36511	(S)	McCartney II (With "Coming Up" single)	1980	4.00	10.00

McCOY, VAN

Columbia CL-2497	(M)	Night Time Is Lonely Time	1966	5.00	12.00
Columbia CS-9297	(S)	Night Time Is Lonely Time	1966	6.00	15.00

McCOYS, THE

Bang BLP-212	(M)	Hang On Sloopy	1965	12.00	30.00
Bang BLPS-212	(P)	Hang On Sloopy	1965	16.00	40.00
Bang BLP-213	(M)	You Make Me Feel So Good	1966	12.00	30.00
Bang BLPS-213	(S)	You Make Me Feel So Good	1966	16.00	40.00

Label & Catalog #		Title	Year	VG+	NM
Mercury SR-61163	(S)	Infinite McCoys	1968	6.00	15.00
Mercury SR-61207	(S)	Human Ball	1969	6.00	15.00

McCRACKLIN, JIMMY

Chess 1464	(M)	Jimmy McCracklin Sings	1961	35.00	70.00
Stax 8506	(M)	I Just Gotta Know	1963	20.00	50.00
Imperial LP-9285	(M)	Every Night, Every Day	1965	8.00	20.00
Imperial LP-12285	(S)	Every Night, Every Day	1965	10.00	25.00
Imperial LP-9297	(M)	Think	1965	8.00	20.00
Imperial LP-12297	(S)	Think	1965	10.00	25.00
Imperial LP-9306	(M)	My Answer	1966	8.00	20.00
Imperial LP-12306	(S)	My Answer	1966	10.00	25.00
Imperial LP-9316	(M)	New Soul Of Jimmy McCracklin	1966	8.00	20.00
Imperial LP-12316	(S)	New Soul Of Jimmy McCracklin	1966	10.00	25.00
Minit LP-4009	(M)	The Best Of Jimmy McCracklin	1967	5.00	12.00
Minit LP-24009	(S)	The Best Of Jimmy McCracklin	1967	6.00	15.00
Minit LP-24011	(S)	Let's Get Together	1968	6.00	15.00
Minit LP-24017	(S)	Stinger Man	1969	6.00	15.00
Stax STS-2047	(S)	Yesterday Is Gone	1972	4.00	10.00

McCULLOCH, DANNY
Danny was formerly a member of The Animals.

Capitol ST-174	(S)	Wings Of A Man	1969	6.00	15.00

McCURDY, ED

Riverside RLP-12-180	(M)	The Legend Of Robin Hood	195?	8.00	20.00
Riverside RLP-12-601	(M)	The Ballad Record	195?	8.00	20.00
Riverside RLP-12-807	(M)	Bar Room Ballads	195?	8.00	20.00
Elektra EKL-24	(M)	Sin Songs, Pro And Con	195?	8.00	20.00
Elektra EKL-108	(M)	Blood, Booze 'N Bones	195?	8.00	20.00
Elektra EKL-112	(M)	Songs Of The Old West	195?	8.00	20.00
Elektra EKL-170	(M)	When Dalliance Was In Flower	195?	8.00	20.00
Tradition TLP-1003	(M)	A Ballad Singer's Choice	195?	8.00	20.00
Tradition TLP-1027	(M)	Children's Songs	195?	8.00	20.00
Dawn DLP-1127	(M)	The Folk Singer	195?	8.00	20.00
By-Line 1	(M)	Frankie And Johnny	195?	8.00	20.00

McDANIELS, GENE

Liberty LRP-3146	(M)	In Times Like These	1960	8.00	20.00
Liberty LST-7146	(S)	In Times Like These	1960	10.00	25.00
Liberty LST-7146	(S)	In Times Like These (Blue vinyl)	1960	30.00	60.00
Liberty LRP-3175	(M)	Sometimes I'm Happy, Sometimes I'm Blue	1960	8.00	20.00
Liberty LST-7175	(S)	Sometimes I'm Happy, Sometimes I'm Blue	1960	10.00	25.00
Liberty LRP-3191	(M)	100 Lbs. Of Clay	1961	8.00	20.00
Liberty LST-7191	(S)	100 Lbs. Of Clay	1961	10.00	25.00
Liberty LRP-3204	(M)	Gene McDaniels Sings Movie Memories	1962	6.00	15.00
Liberty LST-7204	(S)	Gene McDaniels Sings Movie Memories	1962	8.00	20.00
Liberty LRP-3215	(M)	Tower Of Strength	1962	8.00	20.00
Liberty LST-7215	(S)	Tower Of Strength	1962	10.00	25.00
Liberty LRP-3258	(M)	Hit After Hit	1962	6.00	15.00
Liberty LST-7258	(S)	Hit After Hit	1962	8.00	20.00
Liberty LRP-3275	(M)	Spanish Lace	1963	8.00	20.00
Liberty LST-7275	(S)	Spanish Lace	1963	10.00	25.00
Liberty LRP-3311	(M)	The Wonderful Word Of Gene McDaniels	1963	6.00	15.00
Liberty LST-7311	(S)	The Wonderful Word Of Gene McDaniels	1963	8.00	20.00

McDONALD, "COUNTRY" JOE
Refer to Country Joe & The Fish.

Mobile Fidelity MFSL-056	(S)	Paradise With An Ocean View	1980	6.00	15.00

McDONALD, KATHY
Ms. McDonald was formerly a member of Big Brother & The Holding Company.

Capitol ST-11224	(S)	Insane Asylum	1974	10.00	25.00

McDONALD, MARIE

RCA Victor LPM-1585	(M)	The Body Sings!	1957	20.00	50.00

McDONALD, MICHAEL

Mobile Fidelity MFSL-149	(S)	If That's What It Takes	198?	5.00	12.00

Label & Catalog #		Title	Year	VG+	NM
McDONALD, SKEETS					
Capitol T-1040	(M)	Goin' Steady With The Blues	1958	30.00	60.00
Capitol T-1179	(M)	The Country's Best	1959	20.00	50.00
Columbia CL-2170	(M)	Call Me Skeets!	1964	8.00	20.00
Columbia CS-8970	(S)	Call Me Skeets!	1964	12.00	30.00
Fortune 3001	(S)	Tattooed Lady	1969	10.00	25.00
McDOWELL, "MISSISSIPPI" FRED					
Sire 97018	(S)	Mississippi Fred McDowell In London	1970	6.00	15.00
Everest 253	(S)	Mississippi Fred McDowell	1971	5.00	12.00
Capitol ST-403	(S)	I Do Not Play No Rock & Roll	1973	6.00	15.00
McDOWELL, "MISSISSIPPI" FRED / GUITAR JR.					
Capitol SAT-403	(DJ)	I Do Not Play No Rock & Roll (Picture disc)	1973	30.00	60.00
McDUFF, BROTHER JACK					
Prestige 7259	(M)	Screamin'	1963	10.00	25.00
Prestige 7274	(M)	Live!	1963	10.00	25.00
Blue Note 84322	(S)	Down Home Style	1969	6.00	15.00
McGHEE, BROWNIE					
Refer to Sonny Terry & Brownie McGhee.					
Sharp 2003	(M)	Brownie McGhee	195?	35.00	70.00
Smash MGS-27067	(M)	Brownie McGhee At The Bunkhouse	1965	12.00	30.00
Smash SRS-67067	(S)	Brownie McGhee At The Bunkhouse	1965	16.00	40.00
McGHEE, STICKS, & JOHN LEE HOOKER					
Audio Lab AL-1520	(M)	Highway Of Blues	1959	75.00	150.00
McGOVERN, PATTY					
Atlantic 1245	(M)	Patty McGovern With Thomas Talbert	1956	16.00	40.00
McGUINN, ROGER					
Roger was formerly a member of The Byrds.					
Columbia AS-353	(DJ)	The Roger McGuinn Airplay Anthology	1977	12.00	30.00
McGUIRE, BARRY					
Barry McGuire was formerly a member of The New Christy Minstrels.					
Horizon WP-1608	(M)	Barry Here And Now	1962	5.00	12.00
Horizon ST-1608	(S)	Barry Here And Now	1962	6.00	15.00
Horizon WP-1636	(M)	The Barry McGuire Album	1963	6.00	15.00
Dunhill D-50003	(M)	Eve Of Destruction	1966	8.00	20.00
Dunhill DS-50003	(S)	Eve Of Destruction	1966	12.00	30.00
Dunhill D-50005	(M)	This Precious Time	1966	5.00	12.00
Dunhill DS-50005	(S)	This Precious Time	1966	6.00	15.00
Dunhill DS-50033	(S)	The World's Last Private Citizen	1968	5.00	12.00
Ode SP-77004	(S)	McGuire And The Doctor	1970	5.00	12.00
McGUIRE SISTERS, THE					
Coral CRL-56123 (10")	(M)	By Request	1955	20.00	50.00
Coral CRL-57097	(M)	Children's Holiday	1956	14.00	35.00
Coral CRL-57026	(M)	Do You Remember When?	1956	14.00	35.00
Coral CRL-57028	(M)	S'Wonderful	1956	14.00	35.00
Coral CRL-57033	(M)	He	1956	14.00	35.00
Coral CRL-57052	(M)	Sincerely	1956	14.00	35.00
Coral CRL-57134	(M)	Teenage Party	1957	14.00	35.00
Coral CRL-57145	(M)	When The Lights Are Low	1957	14.00	35.00
Coral CRL-57180	(M)	Musical Magic	1957	12.00	30.00
Coral CRL-57217	(M)	Sugartime	1958	12.00	30.00
Coral CRL-57225	(M)	Greetings From The McGuire Sisters	1958	12.00	30.00
Coral CRL-57296	(M)	May You Always	1959	8.00	20.00
Coral CRL-757296	(S)	May You Always	1959	12.00	30.00
Coral CRL-57303	(M)	In Harmony With Him	1959	8.00	20.00
Coral CRL-757303	(S)	In Harmony With Him	1959	12.00	30.00
Coral CRL-57337	(M)	His And Her's	1960	8.00	20.00
Coral CRL-757337	(S)	His And Her's	1960	12.00	30.00
Coral CRL-57349	(M)	Our Golden Favorites	1961	8.00	20.00
Coral CRL-757349	(S)	Our Golden Favorites	1961	12.00	30.00

Label & Catalog #		Title	Year	VG+	NM
Coral CRL-57385	(M)	**Just For Old Times Sake**	1961	8.00	20.00
Coral CRL-757385	(S)	**Just For Old Times Sake**	1961	12.00	30.00
Coral CRL-57398	(M)	**Subways Are For Sleeping**	1961	6.00	15.00
Coral CRL-757398	(S)	**Subways Are For Sleeping**	1961	8.00	20.00
Coral CRL-57415	(M)	**Songs Everybody Knows**	1962	6.00	15.00
Coral CRL-757415	(S)	**Songs Everybody Knows**	1962	8.00	20.00

— Original Coral albums above have maroon & silver labels.—

The McGuire Sisters created an easy blend of related voices over the popular arrangements of their day. Their later work included participation in the loosely knit Reprise Repertory Theatre.

Coral CRL-57443	(M)	**Showcase**	1964	5.00	12.00
Coral CRL-757443	(S)	**Showcase**	1964	6.00	15.00
Coral CXB-6	(M)	**The Best Of The McGuire Sisters**	1966	5.00	12.00
Coral CXSB-6	(S)	**The Best Of The McGuire Sisters**	1966	6.00	15.00
ABC-Paramount 530	(S)	**The McGuire Sisters Today**	1966	5.00	12.00
ABC-Paramount S-530	(S)	**The McGuire Sisters Today**	1966	6.00	15.00

McKAY, SCOTTY

Ace LP-1017	(M)	**Tonight In Person**	1961	10.00	25.00

McKENZIE, SCOTT

Ode Z12-44001	(M)	**The Voice Of Scott McKenzie**	1967	5.00	12.00
Ode Z12-44002	(S)	**The Voice Of Scott McKenzie**	1967	6.00	15.00
Ode SP-77007	(S)	**Stained Glass Morning**	1970	5.00	12.00

McKUEN, ROD

Liberty LRP-3011	(M)	**Lazy Afternoon**	1956	16.00	40.00
Decca DL-8714	(M)	**Summer Love** *(Soundtrack)*	1958	50.00	100.00
Decca DL-8882	(M)	**Anywhere I Wander**	1958	8.00	20.00
Decca DL-78882	(S)	**Anywhere I Wander**	1958	12.00	30.00
Decca DL-8946	(M)	**Alone After Dark**	1958	8.00	20.00
Decca DL-78946	(S)	**Alone After Dark**	1958	12.00	30.00
Hi Fi R-419	(M)	**Beatsville**	1959	6.00	15.00
Hi Fi SR-419	(S)	**Beatsville**	1959	8.00	20.00
Jubilee J-5013	(M)	**Mr. Oliver Twist**	1962	5.00	12.00
Jubilee SJ-5013	(S)	**Mr. Oliver Twist**	1962	6.00	15.00

Label & Catalog #		Title	Year	VG+	NM
Horizon T-1612	(M)	New Sounds In Folk Music	1963	5.00	12.00
Horizon ST-1612	(S)	New Sounds In Folk Music	1963	6.00	15.00
In 1003	(M)	Seasons In The Sun	1964	5.00	12.00
In S-1003	(S)	Seasons In The Sun	1964	6.00	15.00
Capitol T-2079	(M)	Rod McKuen Sings Rod McKuen	1964	5.00	12.00
Capitol ST-2079	(S)	Rod McKuen Sings Rod McKuen	1964	6.00	15.00
Tradition 2063	(M)	A San Francisco Hippie Trip	1967	8.00	20.00

McLAIN, DENNY
Denny was formerly a member of the Detroit Tigers.

Capitol ST-204	(S)	Denny McLain In Las Vegas	1969	10.00	25.00

McLEAN, DON

Mediarts 41-4	(S)	Tapestry	1970	6.00	15.00
Millenium DJL1-3933	(DJ)	RCA Special Radio Series *(With insert)*	197?	4.00	10.00

McLUHAN, MARSHALL

Columbia CL-2701	(M)	The Medium Is The Message	1967	8.00	20.00
Columbia CS-9501	(S)	The Medium Is The Message	1967	10.00	25.00

McNAIR, BARBARA

Warner Bros. W-1541	(M)	I Enjoy Being A Girl	1964	6.00	15.00
Warner Bros. WS-1541	(S)	I Enjoy Being A Girl	1964	8.00	20.00
Warner Bros. W-1570	(M)	Livin' End	1964	6.00	15.00
Warner Bros. WS-1570	(S)	Livin' End	1964	8.00	20.00
Motown 644	(M)	Where I Am	1966	6.00	15.00
Motown S-644	(S)	Where I Am	1966	8.00	20.00
Motown S-680	(S)	The Real Barbara McNair	1969	6.00	15.00

McNEELY, BIG JAY

Federal 295-96 (10")	(M)	Big Jay McNeely	1954	660.00	1,000.00
Savoy MG-15045 (10")	(M)	A Rhythm And Blues Concert	1955	300.00	500.00
Federal 395-530	(M)	Big Jay McNeely In 3-D	1956	300.00	500.00
King 395-530	(M)	Big Jay McNeely In 3-D	1956	150.00	250.00
King 650	(M)	Big Jay McNeely In 3-D	1959	50.00	100.00
Warner Bros. W-1523	(M)	Big Jay McNeely	1963	16.00	40.00
Warner Bros. WS-1523	(S)	Big Jay McNeely	1963	20.00	50.00

McPHATTER, CLYDE
Clyde was formerly the lead singer for Billy Ward & The Dominoes; The Drifters.

Atlantic 8024	(M)	Love Ballads *(Black label)*	1958	100.00	200.00
Atlantic 8024	(M)	Love Ballads *(Orange & purple label)*	1960	50.00	100.00
Atlantic 8031	(M)	Clyde *(Black label)*	1959	100.00	200.00
Atlantic 8031	(M)	Clyde *(Orange & purple label)*	1960	50.00	100.00
Atlantic 8077	(M)	The Best Of Clyde McPhatter	1963	16.00	40.00
MGM E-3775	(M)	Let's Start Over Again	1959	16.00	40.00
MGM SE-3775	(S)	Let's Start Over Again	1959	20.00	50.00
MGM E-3866	(M)	Clyde McPhatter's Greatest Hits	1960	16.00	40.00
MGM SE-3866	(S)	Clyde McPhatter's Greatest Hits	1960	20.00	50.00
Mercury MG-20597	(M)	Ta Ta	1960	10.00	25.00
Mercury SR-60597	(S)	Ta Ta	1960	14.00	35.00
Mercury MG-20655	(M)	Golden Blues Hits	1962	10.00	25.00
Mercury SR-60655	(S)	Golden Blues Hits	1962	14.00	35.00
Mercury MG-20711	(M)	Lover Please	1962	10.00	25.00
Mercury SR-60711	(S)	Lover Please	1962	14.00	35.00
Mercury MG-20750	(M)	Rhythm And Soul	1962	10.00	25.00
Mercury SR-60750	(S)	Rhythm And Soul	1962	14.00	35.00
Mercury MG-20783	(M)	Clyde McPhatter's Greatest Hits	1963	10.00	25.00
Mercury SR-60783	(S)	Clyde McPhatter's Greatest Hits	1963	14.00	35.00
Mercury MG-20902	(M)	Songs Of The Big City	1964	10.00	25.00
Mercury SR-60902	(S)	Songs Of The Big City	1964	14.00	35.00
Mercury MG-20915	(M)	Live At The Apollo	1964	10.00	25.00
Mercury SR-60915	(S)	Live At The Apollo	1964	14.00	35.00
Decca DL-75231	(S)	Welcome Home	1970	8.00	20.00

McRAE, CARMEN
Ms. McRae also recorded with Sammy Davis, Jr.

Bethlehem 1023 (10")	(M)	Carmen McRae	1954	16.00	40.00
Decca DL-8173	(M)	By Special Request	1955	12.00	30.00

Label & Catalog #		Title	Year	VG+	NM
Decca DL-8267	(M)	Torchy	1955	12.00	30.00
Decca DL-8347	(M)	Blue Moon	1956	16.00	40.00
Decca DL-8583	(M)	After Glow	1957	12.00	30.00
Decca DL-8662	(M)	Mad About The Man	1957	16.00	40.00
Decca DL-8738	(M)	Carmen For Cool Ones	1958	12.00	30.00
Decca DL-8815	(M)	Birds Of A Feather	1958	16.00	40.00
Kapp KL-1117	(M)	Book Of Ballads	1958	8.00	20.00
Kapp KS-1117S	(S)	Book Of Ballads	1960	8.00	20.00
Kapp KL-1135	(M)	When You're Away	1959	8.00	20.00
Kapp KS-3018	(S)	When You're Away	1960	8.00	20.00
Kapp KL-1169	(M)	Something To Swing About	1959	8.00	20.00
Kapp KS-3053	(S)	Something To Swing About	1960	8.00	20.00
Columbia CL-1609	(M)	Tonight's The Night	1961	5.00	12.00
Columbia CS-8409	(S)	Tonight's The Night	1961	6.00	15.00
Columbia CL-1730	(M)	Lover Man	1962	5.00	12.00
Columbia CS-8530	(S)	Lover Man	1962	6.00	15.00
Columbia CL-1943	(M)	Something Wonderful	1962	5.00	12.00
Columbia CS-8743	(S)	Something Wonderful	1962	6.00	15.00
Time 52104	(M)	Live At Sugar Hill	1963	5.00	12.00
Time 2104	(S)	Live At Sugar Hill	1963	6.00	15.00
Focus 334	(M)	Bittersweet	1965	5.00	12.00
Focus 334	(S)	Bittersweet	1965	6.00	15.00
Mainstream 56028	(M)	Second To None	1965	5.00	12.00
Mainstream 6028	(S)	Second To None	1965	6.00	15.00
Mainstream 56044	(M)	Haven't We Met?	1965	5.00	12.00
Mainstream 6044	(S)	Haven't We Met?	1965	6.00	15.00

McTELL, "BLIND" WILLIE

Melodeon 7323	(M)	1940	1956	75.00	150.00
Bluesville BV-1040	(M)	Last Session	1962	16.00	40.00
Atlantic SD-7224	(S)	Blues Original, Volume 1	1972	6.00	15.00

McVIE, CHRISTINE
Refer to Chickenshack; Fleetwood Mac.

Sire 7522	(S)	The Legendary Christine Perfect Album	1976	5.00	12.00
Warner Bros. 25059	(DJ)	Christine McVie (Quiex II vinyl)	1984	6.00	15.00

MEAT LOAF
Refer to Stoney & Meatloaf

Epic E99-34974	(S)	Bat Out Of Hell (Picture disc)	1979	6.00	15.00
Epic HE-44974	(S)	Bat Out Of Hell (Half-speed master)	1981	10.00	25.00

MECKI MARK MEN, THE

Limelight LS-86054	(S)	The Mecki Mark Men	1968	8.00	20.00
Limelight LS-86068	(S)	Running In The Summer Night	1969	8.00	20.00

MEDIUM

Gamma GS-503	(S)	Medium	196?	10.00	25.00

MEL & TIM
Mel Hardin and Tim McPherson.

Bamboo BMS-8001	(S)	Good Guys Only Win In The Movies	1970	5.00	12.00
Stax STS-3007	(S)	Starting All Over Again	1972	6.00	15.00
Stax STS-5501	(S)	Mel And Tim	1974	5.00	12.00

MELACHRINO, GEORGE

RCA Victor LPM-1045	(M)	Christmas In High Fidelity	1955	10.00	25.00
RCA Victor LPM-1676	(M)	Under Western Skies	1957	10.00	25.00

MELLANCAMP COUGAR, JOHN [JOHN COUGAR]

MCA 2225	(S)	Chestnut Street Incident	1977	10.00	25.00
Riva	(DJ)	The Kid Inside (Picture disc)	198?	16.00	40.00

MELLO-LARKS, THE

Epic LN-1106 (10")	(M)	The Mello-Larks & Jamie	1955	20.00	50.00
Camden CAL-530	(M)	Just For A Lark	1959	16.00	40.00

MELLO-KINGS, THE

Herald H-1013	(M)	Tonight-Tonight	1960	180.00	300.00

Label & Catalog #		Title	Year	VG+	NM

MELLOMEN, THE

| Columbia CL-6338 | (M) | **White Christmas** (Soundtrack) | 1954 | 12.00 | 30.00 |

MELVIN, HAROLD, & THE BLUENOTES

| Phila. Inter. PZQ-32407 | (Q) | **Black And Blue** | 1974 | 5.00 | 12.00 |
| Phila. Inter. PZ-33808 | (Q) | **Wake Up Everybody** | 1975 | 5.00 | 12.00 |

MEMPHIS SLIM

Memphis Slim is a pseudonym for Peter Chapman. Refer to Willie Dixon.

Vee Jay VJLP-1012	(M)	**Memphis Slim At The Gate Of The Horn**	1959	50.00	100.00
Chess LP-1455	(M)	**Memphis Slim** (Black label)	1961	50.00	100.00
Chess LP-1510	(M)	**Real Folk Blues**	1966	16.00	40.00
United Arts. UAL-3137	(M)	**Broken Soul Blues**	1961	16.00	40.00
United Arts. UAS-6137	(S)	**Broken Soul Blues**	1961	20.00	50.00
Bluesville BV-1018	(M)	**Just Blues**	1961	12.00	30.00
Bluesville BVS-1018	(S)	**Just Blues**	1961	16.00	40.00
Bluesville BV-1031	(M)	**No Strain**	1962	8.00	20.00
Bluesville BVS-1031	(S)	**No Strain**	1962	12.00	30.00
Bluesville BV-1053	(M)	**All Kinds Of Blues**	1963	8.00	20.00
Bluesville BVS-1053	(S)	**All Kinds Of Blues**	1963	12.00	30.00
Bluesville BV-1075	(M)	**Steady Rollin' Blues**	1964	8.00	20.00
Bluesville BVS-1075	(S)	**Steady Rollin' Blues**	1964	12.00	30.00
Candid 9023	(M)	**Tribute To Big Bill Broonzy**	1961	16.00	40.00
Candid 9023	(S)	**Tribute To Big Bill Broonzy**	1961	20.00	50.00
Candid 9024	(M)	**Memphis Slim, U.S.A.**	1962	16.00	40.00
Candid 9024	(S)	**Memphis Slim, U.S.A.**	1962	20.00	50.00
Battle BM-6118	(M)	**Alone With My Friends**	1963	12.00	30.00
King LP-885	(M)	**Memphis Slim**	1964	20.00	50.00
Scepter SM-535	(M)	**Self Portrait**	1966	10.00	25.00
Strand SLS-1046	(S)	**The World's Foremost Blues Singer**	196?	8.00	20.00
Jubilee 8003	(S)	**Legend Of The Blues**	1967	6.00	15.00
Everest 215	(S)	**Memphis Slim**	1968	6.00	15.00
Buddah BDS-7505	(S)	**Mother Earth**	1969	6.00	15.00
King KS 1082	(S)	**Messin' Around With The Blues**	1970	6.00	15.00
Jewell 5004	(S)	**Born With The Blues**	1971	4.00	10.00
Warner Bros. WS-1899	(S)	**Blue Memphis**	1971	6.00	15.00
Warner Bros. BS-2646	(S)	**South Side Reunion**	1972	6.00	15.00
Fantasy 24705	(S)	**Raining The Blues** (2 LPs)	1972	5.00	12.00

MEMPHIS WILLIE B.

| Bluesville BV-1034 | (M) | **Introducing Memphis Willie B.** | 1961 | 6.00 | 15.00 |
| Bluesville BVS-1034 | (S) | **Introducing Memphis Willie B.** | 1961 | 10.00 | 25.00 |

MEN AT WORK

Epic PAL-37978	(DJ)	**Business As Usual** (Picture disc)	1983	16.00	40.00
Epic HE-47978	(S)	**Business As Usual** (Half-speed master)	1982	6.00	15.00
Epic HE-48660	(S)	**Cargo** (Half-speed master)	1982	6.00	15.00

MERCER, MABEL

Atlantic ALS-402 (10")	(M)	**Songs, Volume 1**	1952	20.00	50.00
Atlantic ALS-403 (10")	(M)	**Songs, Volume 2**	1953	20.00	50.00
Atlantic 1213	(M)	**Mabel Mercer Sings Cole Porter**	1955	16.00	40.00
Atlantic 1244	(M)	**Midnight At Mabel Mercer's**	1957	16.00	40.00
Atlantic 1301	(M)	**Once In A Blue Moon**	1959	12.00	30.00
Atlantic 1322	(M)	**Merely Marvelous**	1959	12.00	30.00

MERKIN

| Windi 1004 | (S) | **Music From Merkin Manor** | 1972 | 180.00 | 300.00 |

MERRILL, HELEN

EmArcy MG-36006	(M)	**Helen Merrill**	1955	20.00	50.00
EmArcy MG-36057	(M)	**Helen Merrill With Strings**	1956	20.00	50.00
EmArcy MG-36078	(M)	**Dream Of You**	1956	20.00	50.00
EmArcy MG-36107	(M)	**Merrill At Midnight**	1956	16.00	40.00
EmArcy MG-36134	(M)	**The Nearness Of You**	1958	16.00	40.00
Metrojazz 1010	(M)	**You've Got A Date With The Blues**	1959	14.00	35.00
Atco 33-112	(M)	**American Country Songs**	1959	12.00	30.00
Atco SD-33-112	(S)	**American Country Songs**	1959	16.00	40.00

Label & Catalog #		Title	Year	VG+	NM
Mainstream 56014	(M)	The Artistry Of Helen Merrill	1965	6.00	15.00
Mainstream 6014	(S)	The Artistry Of Helen Merrill	1965	8.00	20.00

MERRIWEATHER, BIG MACEO, & JOHN LEE HOOKER

Fortune 3002	(M)	Big Maceo Merriweather & John Lee Hooker	196?	50.00	100.00

Leader Emitt Rhodes' first album, "American Dream," was a continuation of The Merry-Go-Round sound and later pressings included a new version of "You're A Very Lovely Woman."

MERRY-GO-ROUND, THE

A&M LP-132	(M)	The Merry-Go-Round	1967	10.00	25.00
A&M SP-4132	(S)	The Merry-Go-Round	1967	14.00	35.00

MERRYWEATHER [NEIL MERRYWEATHER]

Capitol SKAO-220	(S)	Merryweather	1969	5.00	12.00
Capitol STBB-278	(S)	Word Of Mouth	1969	6.00	15.00
RCA Victor LSP-4442	(S)	Ivar Avenue Reunion	1970	6.00	15.00
RCA Victor LSP-4485	(S)	Vacuum Cleaner	1971	5.00	12.00
Kent KST-546	(S)	Neil Merryweather And The Boers	1972	8.00	20.00

MERSEYBEATS, THE

ARC International 834	(M)	Englands Best Sellers	1964	16.00	40.00

MERSEYBOYS, THE

Vee Jay VJ-1101	(DJ)	15 Greatest Songs Of The Beatles	1964	75.00	150.00
Vee Jay VJ-1101	(M)	15 Greatest Songs Of The Beatles	1964	20.00	50.00
Vee Jay VJS-1101	(S)	15 Greatest Songs Of The Beatles	1964	40.00	80.00

MESMERIZING EYE, THE

Smash MGS-27090	(M)	Psychedelia/A Musical Light Show	1967	8.00	20.00
Smash SRS-67090	(S)	Psychedelia/A Musical Light Show	1967	10.00	25.00

MESSINA, JIM, & HIS JESTERS

Messina was later a member of The Buffalo Springfield.

Audio Fidelity DFM-3037	(M)	The Dragsters	1964	16.00	40.00
Audio Fidelity DFS-7037	(S)	The Dragsters	1964	30.00	60.00

Label & Catalog #		Title	Year	VG+	NM
MESSINA, JIM					
Warner Bros. 3559	(DJ)	**Messina** (Quiex II vinyl)	1981	5.00	12.00
METERS, THE					
Josie JOS-4010	(S)	**The Meters**	1969	10.00	25.00
Josie JOS-4011	(S)	**Look-Ka Py Py**	1970	10.00	25.00
Josie JOS-4012	(S)	**Struttin'**	1970	8.00	20.00
Reprise MS-2076	(S)	**Cabbage Alley**	1972	8.00	20.00
Reprise MS-2200	(S)	**Rejuvenation**	1972	8.00	20.00
METRONOMES, THE					
Strand 3002	(M)	**The Standard Hits**	196?	12.00	30.00
Strand S-3002	(S)	**The Standard Hits**	196?	16.00	40.00
METROTONES, THE					
Columbia 6341 (10")	(M)	**Tops In Rock And Roll**	1955	100.00	200.00
MFSB					
Phila. Inter. PZQ-32707	(Q)	**Love Is The Message**	1974	5.00	12.00
Phila. Inter. PZQ-33845	(Q)	**Philadelphia Freedom**	1975	5.00	12.00
MICAH					
Sterling World ST-1001	(S)	**I'm Only One Man**	197?	150.00	250.00
MICHAELS, JORDAN					
Hold Tight 001	(S)	**Armageddon**	1982	100.00	200.00
MICHAELS, LEE					
Columbia CQ-32275	(Q)	**Nice Day For Something**	1973	5.00	12.00
MICKEY & SYLVIA					
Mickey Baker and Sylvia Vanderpool.					
Vik LX-1102	(M)	**New Sounds**	1957	180.00	300.00
Camden CAL-863	(M)	**Love Is Strange**	1965	20.00	50.00
RCA Victor APM1-0327	(M)	**Do It Again**	1973	6.00	15.00
MIDAS TOUCH, THE					
Decca DL-75151	(S)	**Midas Touch**	1969	6.00	15.00
Decca DL-75240	(S)	**Color My World With Love**	1970	5.00	12.00
MIDLER, BETTE					
Atlantic QD-7238	(Q)	**The Divine Miss M**	1973	5.00	12.00
MIGHTY BABY					
Head LPS-025	(S)	**Mighty Baby**	1969	30.00	60.00
MIGHTY MARVELOWS, THE					
ABC-Paramount S-643	(S)	**The Mighty Marvelows**	1968	6.00	15.00
MILBURN, AMOS					
Aladdin 704 (10")	(M)	**Rockin' The Boogie**	1954	500.00	750.00
Aladdin 704 (10")	(M)	**Rockin' The Boogie** (Red vinyl)	1954	1,000.00	1,500.00
Aladdin 810	(M)	**Rockin' The Boogie**	1958	300.00	500.00
Score LP-4012	(M)	**Let's Have A Party**	1957	180.00	300.00
Imperial LP-9176	(M)	**Million Sellers**	1962	50.00	100.00
Motown 608	(M)	**The Blues Boss**	1963	See note below	
		(Probably the rarest of all Motown albums. Estimated near mint value $1,000-3,000.)			
MILBURN, AMOS / WYNONIE HARRIS / CROWN PRINCE WATERFORD					
Aladdin 703 (10")	(M)	**Party After Hours**	1954	500.00	750.00
Aladdin 703 (10")	(M)	**Party After Hours** (Red vinyl)	1954	1,000.00	1,500.00
MILES, JACKIE					
Imperial LP-9154	(M)	**120 Pounds Dripping Wet**	1961	8.00	20.00
MILES, LIZZIE					
Cook 1182	(M)	**Moans And Blues**	1955	16.00	40.00
Cook 1183	(M)	**Hot Songs My Mother taught Me**	1955	16.00	40.00

Label & Catalog #		Title	Year	VG+	NM
Cook 1184	(M)	Torchy Lullabies	1955	14.00	35.00
Cook 1185	(M)	Clambake On Bourbon St.	1955	14.00	35.00

MILES, LONG GONE

World Pacific WP-1820	(M)	Country Born	1964	6.00	15.00
World Pacific ST-1820	(S)	Country Born	1964	8.00	20.00

MILKWOOD

A&M SP-4226	(S)	Under Milkwood	1969	6.00	15.00

MILKWOOD

Paramount PAS-6046	(S)	How's The Weather?	1973	12.00	30.00

MILLARD & DYCE

Kaymar KS-7-265	(S)	Open	1973	50.00	100.00

MILLENIUM
Millenium features Curt Boetcher. Executive producer: Gary Usher.

Columbia CS-9663	(S)	Begin	1968	8.00	20.00

MILLER, FRANKIE

Starday SLP-134	(M)	Country Music's New Star	1961	30.00	60.00
Starday SLP-199	(M)	The True Country Style Of Frankie Miller	1962	20.00	50.00
Audio Lab AL-1562	(M)	The Fine Country Singing Of Frankie Miller	1963	20.00	50.00
Starday SLP-338	(M)	Backland Farmer	1965	10.00	25.00

MILLER, JODY

Capitol T-1913	(M)	Wednesday's Child Is Full Of Woe	1963	5.00	12.00
Capitol ST-1913	(S)	Wednesday's Child Is Full Of Woe	1963	6.00	15.00
Capitol T-2349	(M)	Queen Of The House	1965	5.00	12.00
Capitol ST-2349	(S)	Queen Of The House	1965	6.00	15.00
Capitol T-2414	(M)	Home Of The Brave	1965	5.00	12.00
Capitol ST-2414	(S)	Home Of The Brave	1965	6.00	15.00
Capitol T-2446	(M)	The Great Hits Of Buck Owens	1966	4.00	10.00
Capitol ST-2446	(S)	The Great Hits Of Buck Owens	1966	5.00	12.00
Capitol ST-2996	(S)	The Nashville Sound Of Jody Miller	1969	4.00	10.00

MILLER, MICKEY

Folkways FA-2393	(M)	American Folk Songs	1959	8.00	20.00

MILLER, NED

Fabor FLP-1001	(M)	From A Jack To A King	1963	16.00	40.00
Fabor FLP-1001	(M)	From A Jack To A King (Colored vinyl)	1963	50.00	100.00

MILLER, ROGER

Camden CAL-851	(M)	Roger Miller	1964	5.00	12.00
Camden CAS-851	(S)	Roger Miller	1964	6.00	15.00
Camden CAL-903	(M)	The One And Only Roger Miller	1965	5.00	12.00
Camden CAS-903	(S)	The One And Only Roger Miller	1965	6.00	15.00
Starday SLP-318	(M)	Wild-Child Roger Miller	1965	10.00	25.00
Starday SLP-318	(M)	The Country Side Of Roger Miller	1965	10.00	25.00

MILLER, STEVE [THE STEVE MILLER BAND]
Refer to Chuck Berry.

Capitol SKAO-2920	(S)	Children Of The Future	1968	8.00	20.00
Capitol ST-2984	(S)	Sailor	1968	8.00	20.00
Capitol STBB-177	(S)	Children Of The Future / Sailor	1969	8.00	20.00
Capitol ST-184	(S)	Brave New World	1969	8.00	20.00
		— Original Capitol albums above have black rainbow labels.—			
Capitol SEAX-11903	(S)	Book Of Dreams (Picture disc)	1978	4.00	10.00
Capitol SOO-11872	(DJ)	Greatest Hits 1974-78 (Blue vinyl)	1978	12.00	30.00
Mobile Fidelity MFSL-021	(S)	Fly Like An Eagle	1976	12.00	30.00

MILLER, STEVE / QUICKSILVER MESSENGER SERVICE / THE BAND

Capitol STCR-288	(S)	Steve Miller Band / Quicksilver Messenger Service / The Band (3 LP box)	1969	12.00	30.00
		(This boxed set contains three lime green label albums: "Sailor," "Quicksilver Messenger Service" and "Music From Big Pink.")			

abel & Catalog #		Title	Year	VG+	NM

MILLS, ALAN

olkways FC-7021	(M)	Folk Songs For Young Folk	195?	8.00	20.00
olkways FA-2312	(M)	Songs Of The Sea	195?	8.00	20.00
olkways FA-3001	(M)	O Canada	196?	8.00	20.00

MILLS, HAYLEY

efer to Annette & Hayley Mills.

isneyland ST-1960	(M)	Pollyanna *(Soundtrack)*	1960	14.00	35.00
uena Vista BV-3311	(M)	Let's Get Together	1962	10.00	25.00
uena Vista STER-3311	(S)	Let's Get Together	1962	14.00	35.00
isneyland ST-3916	(M)	In Search Of The Castaways *(Soundtrack)*	1962	40.00	80.00
isneyland ST-3916	(S)	In Search Of The Castaways *(Soundtrack)*	1962	60.00	120.00
uena Vista BV-4025	(M)	Summer Magic *(Soundtrack)*	1963	30.00	60.00
uena Vista STER-4025	(S)	Summer Magic *(Soundtrack)*	1963	50.00	100.00
ainstream 56090	(M)	Gypsy Girl *(Soundtrack)*	1966	14.00	35.00
ainstream 6090	(S)	Gypsy Girl *(Soundtrack)*	1966	20.00	50.00

MILLS BROTHERS, THE

ecca DL-5050 (10")	(M)	Barber Shop Ballads	1950	20.00	50.00
ecca DL-5051 (10")	(M)	Barber Shop Ballads	1950	20.00	50.00
ecca DL-5102 (10")	(M)	Souvenir Album	1950	20.00	50.00
ecca DL-5337 (10")	(M)	Wonderful Words	1951	20.00	50.00
ecca DL-5506 (10")	(M)	Meet The Mills Brothers	1954	20.00	50.00
ecca DL-5509 (10")	(M)	Louis Armstrong And The Mills Brothers	1954	20.00	50.00
ecca DL-5516 (10")	(M)	Four Boys And A Guitar	1954	20.00	50.00
ecca DL-8148	(M)	Souvenir Album	1955	12.00	30.00
ecca DL-8209	(M)	Singin' And Swingin'	1956	12.00	30.00
ecca DL-8219	(M)	Memory Lane	1956	12.00	30.00
ecca DL-8491	(M)	One Dozen Roses	1957	12.00	30.00
ecca DL-8664	(M)	The Mills Brothers In Hi-Fi	1958	12.00	30.00
ecca DL-8827	(M)	Glow With The Mills Brothers	1959	12.00	30.00
ecca DL-8890	(M)	Barber Shop Harmony	1959	12.00	30.00
ecca DL-8892	(M)	Harmonizin' With The Mills Brothers	1959	12.00	30.00

— Original Decca albums above have black & silver labels.—

ecca DXB-193	(M)	The Best Of The Mills Brothers	1965	8.00	20.00
ecca DXSB-193	(P)	The Best Of The Mills Brothers	1965	8.00	20.00
ot DLP-3103	(M)	Mmmm, The Mills Brothers	1958	8.00	20.00
ot DLP-25103	(S)	Mmmm, The Mills Brothers	1958	12.00	30.00
ot DLP-3157	(M)	The Mills Brothers' Greatest Hits	1958	8.00	20.00
ot DLP-25157	(S)	The Mills Brothers' Greatest Hits	1958	12.00	30.00
ot DLP-3208	(M)	Great Barbershop Hits	1959	8.00	20.00
ot DLP-25208	(S)	Great Barbershop Hits	1959	12.00	30.00
ot DLP-3232	(M)	Merry Christmas	1959	8.00	20.00
ot DLP-25232	(S)	Merry Christmas	1959	12.00	30.00
ot DLP-3237	(M)	The Mills Brothers Sing	1960	8.00	20.00
ot DLP-25237	(S)	The Mills Brothers Sing	1960	12.00	30.00
ot DLP-3308	(M)	Great Hits, Volume 2	1961	6.00	15.00
ot DLP-25308	(S)	Great Hits, Volume 2	1961	8.00	20.00
ot DLP-3338	(M)	Yellow Bird	1961	6.00	15.00
ot DLP-25338	(S)	Yellow Bird	1961	8.00	20.00
ot DLP-3363	(M)	San Antonio Rose	1961	6.00	15.00
ot DLP-25363	(S)	San Antonio Rose	1961	8.00	20.00
ot DLP-3368	(M)	Great Hawaiian Hits	1961	6.00	15.00
ot DLP-25368	(S)	Great Hawaiian Hits	1961	8.00	20.00
ot DLP-3465	(M)	The Beer Barrel Polka And Other Hits	1962	5.00	12.00
ot DLP-25465	(S)	The Beer Barrel Polka And Other Hits	1962	6.00	15.00
ot DLP-3508	(M)	The End Of The World	1963	5.00	12.00
ot DLP-25508	(S)	The End Of The World	1963	6.00	15.00
ot DLP-3565	(M)	Gems By The Mills Brothers	1964	5.00	12.00
ot DLP-25565	(S)	Gems By The Mills Brothers	1964	6.00	15.00
ot DLP-3568	(M)	Hymns We Love	1964	5.00	12.00
ot DLP-25568	(S)	Hymns We Love	1964	6.00	15.00
ot DLP-3592	(M)	Say Si Si And Other Great Latin Hits	1964	5.00	12.00
ot DLP-25592	(S)	Say Si Si And Other Great Latin Hits	1964	6.00	15.00
amilton HL-12116	(M)	The Mills Brothers Sing For You	1964	5.00	12.00
amilton HS-12116	(S)	The Mills Brothers Sing For You	1964	5.00	12.00
ot DLP-3652	(M)	Ten Years Of Hits 1954-1964	1965	5.00	12.00
ot DLP-25652	(S)	Ten Years Of Hits 1954-1964	1965	6.00	15.00

Label & Catalog #		Title	Year	VG+	NM
Dot DLP-3699	(M)	These Are The Mills Brothers	1966	5.00	12.00
Dot DLP-25699	(S)	These Are The Mills Brothers	1966	6.00	15.00
Dot DLP-3744	(M)	That Country Feeling	1966	5.00	12.00
Dot DLP-25744	(S)	That Country Feeling	1966	6.00	15.00
Dot DLP-3783	(M)	The Mills Brothers Live	1967	5.00	12.00
Dot DLP-25783	(S)	The Mills Brothers Live	1967	6.00	15.00
Dot DLP-25809	(S)	Fortuosity	1968	6.00	15.00
Dot DLP-25838	(S)	The Board Of Directors	1968	6.00	15.00
Dot DLP-25872	(S)	My Shy Violet	1968	6.00	15.00
Dot DLP-25927	(S)	Dream	1969	6.00	15.00

MILTON, ROY
Refer to Chuck Higgins / Roy Milton.

Kent 554	(M)	The Great Roy Milton	1963	20.00	50.00

MIMMS, GARNET, & THE ENCHANTERS

United Arts. UAL-3305	(M)	Cry Baby And 11 Other Hits	1963	10.00	25.00
United Arts. UAS-6305	(S)	Cry Baby And 11 Other Hits	1963	14.00	35.00
United Arts. UAL-3396	(M)	As Long As I Have You	1964	8.00	20.00
United Arts. UAS-6396	(S)	As Long As I Have You	1964	10.00	25.00
United Arts. UAL-3498	(M)	I'll Take Good Care Of You	1966	8.00	20.00
United Arts. UAS-6498	(S)	I'll Take Good Care Of You	1966	10.00	25.00

MIND EXPANDERS, THE

Dot DLP-3773	(M)	What's Happening	1967	20.00	50.00
Dot DLP-25773	(S)	What's Happening	1967	30.00	60.00

MIND GARAGE

RCA Victor LSP-4218	(S)	Mind Garage	1969	6.00	15.00
RCA Victor LSP-4319	(S)	Mind Garage Again!	1970	6.00	15.00

MINDBENDERS, THE
The Mindbenders originally recorded with Wayne Fontana.

Fontana MGF-27554	(M)	A Groovy Kind Of Love	1966	10.00	25.00
Fontana SRF-67554	(E)	A Groovy Kind Of Love	1966	8.00	20.00
		(Originally issued with "Ashes To Ashes.")			
Fontana MGF-27554	(M)	A Groovy Kind Of Love	1966	8.00	20.00
Fontana SRF-67554	(E)	A Groovy Kind Of Love	1966	6.00	15.00
		(Later pressings replace "Ashes" with "Don't Cry No More.")			
Fontana MGF-18030	(M)	To Sir With Love *(Soundtrack)*	1967	6.00	15.00
Fontana SRF-67569	(S)	To Sir With Love *(Soundtrack)*	1967	8.00	20.00

MINEO, SAL

Epic LN-3405	(M)	Sal	1958	30.00	60.00

MINNELLI, LIZA
Refer to Judy Garland & Liza Minnelli.

Cadence CE-4012	(M)	Best Foot Forward *(Soundtrack)*	1963	20.00	50.00
Cadence CLP-24012	(S)	Best Foot Forward *(Soundtrack)*	1963	30.00	60.00
Capitol T-2174	(M)	Liza! Liza!	1964	6.00	15.00
Capitol ST-2174	(S)	Liza! Liza!	1964	8.00	20.00
Capitol T-2271	(M)	It Amazes Me	1965	6.00	15.00
Capitol ST-2271	(S)	It Amazes Me	1965	8.00	20.00
Capitol TAO-2295	(M)	Live At The London Palladium	1965	8.00	20.00
Capitol STAO-2295	(S)	Live At The London Palladium	1965	10.00	25.00
Capitol T-2448	(M)	There Is A Time	1966	6.00	15.00
Capitol ST-2448	(S)	There Is A Time	1966	8.00	20.00
RCA Victor LOC-1111	(M)	Flora The Red Menace *(Soundtrack)*	1965	20.00	50.00
RCA Victor LSO-1111	(S)	Flora The Red Menace *(Soundtrack)*	1965	35.00	70.00
A&M SP-4141	(S)	Liza Minelli	1969	6.00	15.00
A&M SP-4164	(S)	Come Saturday Morning	1969	6.00	15.00
Columbia CQ-32149	(Q)	The Singer	1973	6.00	15.00
Columbia CQ-32149	(Q)	The Singer	1973	6.00	15.00

MINT TATTOO

Dot DLP-25918	(S)	Mint Tattoo	1969	10.00	25.00

MIRACLES, THE: *Refer to* SMOKEY ROBINSON & THE MIRACLES

Label & Catalog #		Title	Year	VG+	NM
MIRACLES, THE					
Columbia PCQ-24460	(Q)	**Love Crazy**	*1977*	**5.00**	**12.00**
MIRTHRANDER					
Mirth Music	(S)	**For You, The Old Woman**	*1976*	**75.00**	**150.00**
MR. ED					
Colpix CP-209	(M)	**Mr. Ed, The Talking Horse**	*196?*	**60.00**	**120.00**
Golden LP-88	(M)	**Straight From The Horses' Mouth**	*1962*	**75.00**	**150.00**
MR. FLOOD'S PARTY					
Cotillion SD-9003	(S)	**Mr. Flood's Party**	*1969*	**5.00**	**12.00**
MR. GASSER & THE WEIRDOS					
Mr. Gasser is a pseudonym for Ed "Big Daddy" Roth. The Weirdos are a creation of Gary Usher & Co.					
Capitol T-2010	(M)	**Hot Rod Hootenanny**	*1963*	**20.00**	**50.00**
Capitol ST-2010	(S)	**Hot Rod Hootenanny**	*1963*	**35.00**	**70.00**
Capitol T-2057	(M)	**Rods N' Ratfinks** *(With ratfink decal)*	*1963*	**30.00**	**60.00**
Capitol ST-2057	(S)	**Rods N' Ratfinks** *(With ratfink decal)*	*1963*	**40.00**	**80.00**
Capitol T-2057	(M)	**Rods N' Ratfinks** *(Without decal)*	*1963*	**20.00**	**50.00**
Capitol ST-2057	(S)	**Rods N' Ratfinks** *(Without decal)*	*1963*	**35.00**	**70.00**
Capitol T-2114	(M)	**Surfink!**	*1964*	**40.00**	**80.00**
Capitol ST-2114	(S)	**Surfink!**	*1964*	**50.00**	**100.00**
		(Includes the bonus single, "Santa Barbara" / "Midnight Run," by the Super Stocks.)			
Capitol T-2114	(M)	**Surfink!** *(Without bonus single)*	*1964*	**20.00**	**50.00**
Capitol ST-2114	(S)	**Surfink!** *(Without bonus single)*	*1964*	**35.00**	**70.00**
MR. MAGOO					
Mr. Magoo's voice was supplied by Jim Backus.					
RCA Victor LPM-1362	(M)	**MaGoo In Hi Fi**	*1956*	**20.00**	**50.00**
MRS. MILLER					
Capitol T-2494	(M)	**Mrs. Miller's Greatest Hits**	*1966*	**5.00**	**12.00**
Capitol ST-2494	(S)	**Mrs. Miller's Greatest Hits**	*1966*	**6.00**	**15.00**
Capitol T-2579	(M)	**Will Success Spoil Mrs. Miller?**	*1966*	**6.00**	**15.00**
Capitol ST-2579	(S)	**Will Success Spoil Mrs. Miller?**	*1966*	**8.00**	**20.00**
Capitol T-2734	(M)	**The Country Soul Of Mrs. Miller**	*1967*	**6.00**	**15.00**
Capitol ST-2734	(S)	**The Country Soul Of Mrs. Miller**	*1967*	**8.00**	**20.00**
Sidewalk T-5911	(M)	**Mary Jane** *(Soundtrack)*	*1968*	**8.00**	**20.00**
Sidewalk DT-5911	(P)	**Mary Jane** *(Soundtrack)*	*1968*	**8.00**	**20.00**
Amaret 5000	(S)	**Mrs. Miller Does Her Thing**	*1969*	**10.00**	**25.00**
MITCHELL, CHAD [CHAD MITCHELL TRIO]					
Kapp KL-1262	(M)	**Mighty Day On Campus**	*1962*	**6.00**	**15.00**
Kapp KS-3262	(S)	**Mighty Day On Campus**	*1962*	**8.00**	**20.00**
Kapp KL-1281	(M)	**At The Bitter End**	*1962*	**6.00**	**15.00**
Kapp KS-3281	(S)	**At The Bitter End**	*1962*	**8.00**	**20.00**
Kapp KL-1313	(M)	**Blowin' In The Wind**	*1963*	**6.00**	**15.00**
Kapp KS-3313	(S)	**Blowin' In The Wind**	*1963*	**8.00**	**20.00**
Kapp KL-1334	(M)	**The Best Of The Chad Mitchell Trio**	*1963*	**5.00**	**12.00**
Kapp KS-3334	(S)	**The Best Of The Chad Mitchell Trio**	*1963*	**6.00**	**15.00**
Colpix CP-411	(M)	**The Chad Mitchell Trio Arrives**	*1963*	**6.00**	**15.00**
Colpix SCP-411	(S)	**The Chad Mitchell Trio Arrives**	*1963*	**10.00**	**25.00**
Colpix CP-463	(M)	**In Concert**	*1964*	**6.00**	**15.00**
Colpix SCP-463	(S)	**In Concert**	*1964*	**10.00**	**25.00**
Mercury MG-20838	(M)	**Singin' Our Mind**	*1963*	**5.00**	**12.00**
Mercury SR-60838	(S)	**Singin' Our Mind**	*1963*	**6.00**	**15.00**
Mercury MG-20891	(M)	**Reflecting**	*1964*	**5.00**	**12.00**
Mercury SR-60891	(S)	**Reflecting**	*1964*	**6.00**	**15.00**
Mercury MG-20944	(M)	**The Slightly Irreverent Mitchell Trio**	*1964*	**5.00**	**12.00**
Mercury SR-60944	(S)	**The Slightly Irreverent Mitchell Trio**	*1964*	**6.00**	**15.00**
Mercury MG-20992	(M)	**Typical American Boys**	*1965*	**5.00**	**12.00**
Mercury SR-60992	(S)	**Typical American Boys**	*1965*	**6.00**	**15.00**
Mercury MG-21049	(M)	**That's The Way It's Gonna Be**	*1965*	**5.00**	**12.00**
Mercury SR-61049	(S)	**That's The Way It's Gonna Be**	*1965*	**6.00**	**15.00**
Mercury MG-21067	(M)	**Violets Of Dawn**	*1966*	**5.00**	**12.00**
Mercury SR-61067	(S)	**Violets Of Dawn**	*1966*	**6.00**	**15.00**

Label & Catalog #		Title	Year	VG+	NM

MITCHELL, GUY

Columbia CL-6231 (10")	(M)	**Songs Of Open Spaces**	1953	20.00	50.00
Columbia CL-6282 (10")	(M)	**Red Garters** (Soundtrack)	1954	50.00	100.00
Columbia CL-1211	(M)	**A Guy In Love**	1959	12.00	30.00
Columbia CS-8011	(S)	**A Guy In Love**	1959	16.00	40.00
Columbia CL-1226	(M)	**Guy Mitchell's Greatest Hits**	1959	14.00	35.00
Columbia CL-1552	(M)	**Sunshine Guitar**	1960	10.00	25.00
Columbia CS-8352	(S)	**Sunshine Guitar**	1960	14.00	35.00

— Original Columbia albums above have three white "eye" logos on each side of the spindle hole.—

MITCHELL, JONI

Asylum EQ-1001	(Q)	**Court And Spark**	1974	8.00	20.00
Asylum EQ-1051	(Q)	**The Hissing Of Summer Lawns**	1975	8.00	20.00
Nautilus NR-11	(S)	**Court And Spark**	1980	14.00	35.00
Geffen 2019	(DJ)	**Wild Things Run Fast** (Quiex II vinyl)	198?	10.00	25.00

MITCHELL, WILLIE

Hi HL-32010	(M)	**Sunrise Serenade**	1963	6.00	15.00
Hi SHL-32010	(S)	**Sunrise Serenade**	1963	8.00	20.00
Hi HL-32021	(M)	**Hold It**	1964	5.00	12.00
Hi SHL-32021	(S)	**Hold It**	1964	6.00	15.00
Hi HL-32026	(M)	**It's Dance Time**	1965	5.00	12.00
Hi SHL-32026	(S)	**It's Dance Time**	1965	6.00	15.00
Hi HL-32029	(M)	**Driving Beat**	1966	5.00	12.00
Hi SHL-32029	(S)	**Driving Beat**	1966	6.00	15.00
Hi HL-32034	(M)	**Hit Sound Of Willie Mitchell**	1967	5.00	12.00
Hi SHL-32034	(S)	**Hit Sound Of Willie Mitchell**	1967	6.00	15.00
Hi HL-32039	(M)	**Ooh Baby, You Turn Me On**	1967	5.00	12.00
Hi HL-32039	(S)	**Ooh Baby, You Turn Me On**	1967	6.00	15.00

MITCHUM, ROBERT

Capitol T-853	(M)	**Calypso Is Like So**	1957	35.00	70.00
Monument MLP-8086	(M)	**That Man, Robert Mitchum, Sings**	1967	8.00	20.00
Monument SLP-18086	(S)	**That Man, Robert Mitchum, Sings**	1967	10.00	25.00

MIXTURES, THE

| Linda 3301 | (M) | **Stompin' At The Rainbow** | 1962 | 20.00 | 50.00 |

MOB, THE

| Colossus CS-1006 | (S) | **The Mob** | 1971 | 6.00 | 15.00 |

MOBY GRAPE

Alexander "Skip" Spence, Bob Mosley, Jerry Miller, Peter Lewis and Don Stephenson.

| Columbia CL-2698 | (M) | **Moby Grape** | 1967 | 14.00 | 35.00 |
| Columbia CS-9498 | (S) | **Moby Grape** | 1967 | 14.00 | 35.00 |

("360 Sound" label. The cover features Don Stephenson "giving the finger" while holding a washboard. Issued with a poster, priced separately below.)

| Columbia | | **Moby Grape Bonus Poster #1** | 1967 | 8.00 | 20.00 |

(The poster also features Stephenson "giving the finger.")

| Columbia CL-2698 | (M) | **Moby Grape** | 1967 | 8.00 | 20.00 |
| Columbia CS-9498 | (S) | **Moby Grape** | 1967 | 8.00 | 20.00 |

(Second pressings have "360 Sound" labels and Don's offending phalange removed. Issued with a poster, priced separately below.)

| Columbia CS-9498 | (S) | **Moby Grape** | 1970 | 6.00 | 15.00 |

(Third pressings have red labels with gold print. and Don's Issued in the altered cover with an altered poster.)

| Columbia CS-9613 | (S) | **Wow** | 1968 | 6.00 | 15.00 |
| Columbia MGS-1 | (S) | **Grape Jam** | 1968 | 3.50 | 8.00 |

("Grape Jam" was issued as bonus album with "Wow.")

| Columbia CS-9696 | (S) | **Moby Grape '69** | 1969 | 8.00 | 20.00 |
| Columbia CS-9912 | (S) | **Truly Fine Citizen** | 1969 | 6.00 | 15.00 |

— Original Columbia albums above have "360 Sound" on the bottom of the label.—

Columbia AS-341098	(S)	**Great Grape**	1972	4.00	10.00
Harmony KH-30392	(M)	**Omaha**	1971	4.00	10.00
Reprise RS-6460	(S)	**20 Granite Creek**	1971	5.00	12.00
Escape ESA1A	(S)	**Live Grape** (Marble vinyl)	1978	5.00	12.00
San Francisco 04805	(S)	**Moby Grape**	1983	6.00	15.00

Label & Catalog #		Title	Year	VG+	NM
San Francisco 04801	(S)	**Wow/Grape Jam** (2 LPs)	1983	8.00	20.00
San Francisco 04830	(S)	**Moby Grape '84** (Picture disc)	1984	8.00	20.00

MOD & THE ROCKERS

| Justice JLP-153 | (M) | **Mod & The Rockers Now!** | 196? | 180.00 | 300.00 |

MODERN FOLK QUARTET, THE

Warner Bros. W-1511	(M)	**Modern Folk Quartet**	1963	8.00	20.00
Warner Bros. WS-1511	(S)	**Modern Folk Quartet**	1963	12.00	30.00
Warner Bros. W-1546	(M)	**Changes**	1964	8.00	20.00
Warner Bros. WS-1546	(S)	**Changes**	1964	12.00	30.00

MODERN LOVERS, THE: *Refer to* **JONATHAN RICHMAN**

MODLIN, DAN, & DAVE SCOTT

| 700 West 760715 | (S) | **The Train Don't Stop Here Anymore** | 1976 | 150.00 | 250.00 |

MODUGNO, DOMENICO

| Decca DL-8808 | (M) | **Nel Blu Dipinti Blu** | 1958 | 20.00 | 50.00 |
| Decca DL-4133 | (M) | **Viva Italia** | 1961 | 12.00 | 30.00 |

MOLLY HATCHET

Epic PJE-35347	(DJ)	**Molly Hatchet** (Picture disc)	1979	10.00	25.00
Epic AS-99-694	(DJ)	**Flirtin' With Disaster** (Picture disc)	1979	8.00	20.00
Epic AS-99-884	(DJ)	**Beatin' The Odds** (Picture disc)	1980	6.00	15.00
Epic AS-99-1320	(DJ)	**Take No Prisoners** (Picture disc)	1981	5.00	12.00

MOM'S APPLIE PIE

Brown Bag 14200	(S)	**Mom's Apple Pie**	1972	3.50	8.00
		(Original covers feature a vagina in mom's apple pie.)			
Brown Bag 14200	(S)	**Mom's Apple Pie**	1972	4.00	10.00
		(Later covers replace the vagina with a barbed wire wall!)			

MONICA, CORBETT

| Dot DLP-3303 | (M) | **For Laughs** | 1960 | 10.00 | 25.00 |

MONITORS, THE

| Soul SS-714 | (S) | **Greetings, We're The Monitors** | 1969 | 6.00 | 15.00 |

MONKEES, THE

Michael Nesmith, Mickey Dolenz, Peter Tork and Davey Jones.

Colgems COM-101	(M)	**The Monkees** (With "Papa Jean's Blues")	1966	16.00	40.00
Colgems COS-101	(S)	**The Monkees** (With "Papa Jean's Blues")	1966	20.00	50.00
Colgems COM-101	(M)	**The Monkees** (With "Papa Gene's Blues")	1966	12.00	30.00
Colgems COS-101	(S)	**The Monkees** (With "Papa Gene's Blues")	1966	16.00	40.00
Colgems COM-102	(DJ)	**More Of The Monkees** (Clear vinyl)	1967	300.00	500.00
Colgems COM-102	(M)	**More Of The Monkees**	1967	12.00	30.00
Colgems COS-102	(S)	**More Of The Monkees**	1967	16.00	40.00
Colgems COM-103	(M)	**Headquarters**	1967	12.00	30.00
Colgems COS-103	(S)	**Headquarters**	1967	16.00	40.00
Colgems COM-104	(M)	**Pisces, Aquarius, Capricorn & Jones**	1967	12.00	30.00
Colgems COS-104	(S)	**Pisces, Aquarius, Capricorn & Jones**	1967	16.00	40.00
		— Original Colgems albums above read "TM of Colgems Records" at the top of the label.—			
Colgems COS-101	(S)	**The Monkees**	1968	12.00	30.00
Colgems COS-102	(S)	**More Of The Monkees**	1968	12.00	30.00
Colgems COS-103	(S)	**Headquarters**	1968	16.00	40.00
		(The back cover has a photo of Mike, Pete and Mickey with beards.)			
Colgems COS-104	(S)	**Pisces, Aquarius, Capricorn & Jones**	1968	12.00	30.00
		— Colgems albums above do not have "TM of Colgems Records" on the label and have an "RE-1" on the cover.—			
Colgems COM-109	(M)	**The Birds, The Bees And The Monkees**	1968	75.00	150.00
Colgems COS-109	(S)	**The Birds, The Bees And The Monkees**	1968	12.00	30.00
Colgems COSO-5008	(S)	**Head**	1968	20.00	50.00
Colgems COS-113	(S)	**Instant Replay**	1969	16.00	40.00
Colgems COS-115	(S)	**The Monkees' Greatest Hits**	1969	12.00	30.00
Colgems COS-117	(S)	**The Monkees Present**	1969	16.00	40.00
Colgems COS-119	(S)	**Changes**	1970	30.00	60.00
Colgems SCOS-1001	(S)	**A Barrel Full Of Monkees** (2 LPs)	1971	50.00	100.00
		— Colgems albums above delete "TM of Colgems Records" from the label.—			

Label & Catalog #		Title	Year	VG+	NM

An excellent if incomplete summation of their run on the charts, by the time this hits package was released in 1969, The Monkees' heyday had passed and it racked up sparse sales. Consequently, it has been a difficult record to locate for years.

Label & Catalog #		Title	Year	VG+	NM
RCA Victor PRS-329	(S)	**The Monkees' Golden Hits**	1972	50.00	100.00
Bell 6081	(S)	**Refocus**	1973	20.00	50.00
Arista AL-4089	(S)	**The Monkees' Greatest Hits**	1976	6.00	15.00
RCA/Pair DPL2-0188	(S)	**The Monkees** *(2 LPs)*	1976	14.00	35.00
Rhino RNLP-144	(S)	**The Birds, The Bees And The Monkees**	1984	12.00	30.00
		(First pressings issued with an alternate take of "Valleri." There is an "RE-1" etched in the trail-off vinyl.)			
MONRO, MATT					
London LL-1611	(M)	**Blue And Sentimental**	1957	12.00	30.00
Warwick 2045	(M)	**My Kind Of Girl**	1961	14.00	35.00
Liberty LRP-3240	(M)	**Matt Monro**	1962	6.00	15.00
Liberty LST-7240	(S)	**Matt Monro**	1962	8.00	20.00
United Arts. UAL-4114	(M)	**From Russia With Love** *(Soundtrack)*	1964	5.00	12.00
United Arts. UAS-5114	(S)	**From Russia With Love** *(Soundtrack)*	1964	6.00	15.00
Liberty LRP-3356	(M)	**From Russia With Love**	1964	6.00	15.00
Liberty LST-7356	(S)	**From Russia With Love**	1964	8.00	20.00
Liberty LRP-3402	(M)	**Walk Away**	1965	6.00	15.00
Liberty LST-7402	(S)	**Walk Away**	1965	8.00	20.00
Liberty LRP-3423	(M)	**All My Loving**	1965	6.00	15.00
Liberty LST-7423	(S)	**All My Loving**	1965	8.00	20.00
Liberty LRP-3437	(M)	**Yesterday**	1966	6.00	15.00
Liberty LST-7437	(S)	**Yesterday**	1966	8.00	20.00
Liberty LRP-3459	(M)	**Matt Monro's Best**	1966	6.00	15.00
Liberty LST-7459	(S)	**Matt Monro's Best**	1966	8.00	20.00
MGM E-4368	(M)	**Born Free** *(Soundtrack)*	1966	6.00	15.00
MGM SE-4368	(S)	**Born Free** *(Soundtrack)*	1966	6.00	15.00
Columbia OL-6660	(M)	**The Quiller Memorandum** *(Soundtrack)*	1966	40.00	80.00
Columbia OS-3060	(S)	**The Quiller Memorandum** *(Soundtrack)*	1966	50.00	100.00
Capitol T-2730	(M)	**Invitation To The Movies/Born Free**	1967	5.00	12.00
Capitol ST-2730	(S)	**Invitation To The Movies/Born Free**	1967	6.00	15.00
Decca DL-9160	(M)	**A Matter Of Innocence** *(Soundtrack)*	1968	16.00	40.00
Decca DL-79160	(S)	**A Matter Of Innocence** *(Soundtrack)*	1968	20.00	50.00

Label & Catalog #		Title	Year	VG+	NM
Colgems COSO-5009	(S)	The Southern Star (Soundtrack)	1969	50.00	100.00
Paramount PAS-5007	(S)	The Italian Job (Soundtrack)	1969	14.00	35.00

MONROE, BILL (& HIS BLUEGRASS BOYS)

Decca DL-8731	(M)	Knee Deep In Bluegrass	1958	16.00	40.00
Decca DL-78731	(S)	Knee Deep In Bluegrass	1958	30.00	60.00
Decca DL-8769	(M)	I Saw The Light	1959	16.00	40.00
Decca DL-78769	(S)	I Saw The Light	1959	20.00	50.00
— Original Decca albums above have black & silver labels.—					
Decca DL-4080	(M)	Mr. Bluegrass	1960	12.00	30.00
Decca DL-74080	(S)	Mr. Bluegrass	1960	14.00	35.00
Decca DL-4266	(M)	Bluegrass Ramble	1962	8.00	20.00
Decca DL-74266	(S)	Bluegrass Ramble	1962	10.00	25.00
Decca DL-4327	(M)	My All Time Country Favorites	1962	8.00	20.00
Decca DL-74327	(S)	My All Time Country Favorites	1962	10.00	25.00
Decca DL-4382	(M)	Bluegrass Special	1963	8.00	20.00
Decca DL-74382	(S)	Bluegrass Special	1963	10.00	25.00
Decca DL-4537	(M)	I'll Meet You In Church Sunday Morning	1964	6.00	15.00
Decca DL-74537	(S)	I'll Meet You In Church Sunday Morning	1964	8.00	20.00
Decca DL-4601	(M)	Bluegrass Instrumentals	1965	6.00	15.00
Decca DL-74601	(S)	Bluegrass Instrumentals	1965	8.00	20.00
Decca DL-4780	(M)	The High Lonesome Sound Of Bill Monroe	1966	6.00	15.00
Decca DL-74780	(S)	The High Lonesome Sound Of Bill Monroe	1966	8.00	20.00
— Original Decca albums above have black labels with "Mfd by Decca" beneath the rainbow.—					
Decca DL-4896	(M)	Bluegrass Time	1967	6.00	15.00
Decca DL-74896	(S)	Bluegrass Time	1967	8.00	20.00
Decca DL-75010	(E)	Bill Monroe's Greatest Hits	1968	4.00	10.00
Decca DL-75135	(S)	A Voice From On High	1969	6.00	15.00
Decca DL-75213	(S)	Kentucky Bluegrass	1970	6.00	15.00
Decca DL-75281	(S)	Country Music Hall Of Fame	1971	6.00	15.00
Decca DL-75348	(S)	Uncle Pen	1972	6.00	15.00
Harmony HL-7290	(M)	The Great Bill Monroe	1961	8.00	20.00
Harmony HL-7315	(M)	Bill Monroe's Best	1964	6.00	15.00
Harmony HL-7338	(M)	Original Blue Grass Sound	1965	6.00	15.00
Camden CAL-719	(M)	Father Of Bluegrass Music	1962	8.00	20.00
Camden CAL-774	(M)	Early Bluegrass	1963	8.00	20.00
Vocalion VL-3702	(M)	Bill Monroe Sings Country Songs	1964	6.00	15.00

MONROE, MARILYN

MGM E-208 (10")	(M)	Gentlemen Prefer Blondes (Soundtrack)	1953	75.00	150.00
MGM E-3231	(M)	Gentlemen Prefer Blondes (Soundtrack)	1955	35.00	70.00
		("Blondes" also features Ms. Jane Russell.)			
United Arts. UAL-4030	(M)	Some Like It Hot (Soundtrack)	1959	20.00	50.00
United Arts. UAS-5030	(S)	Some Like It Hot (Soundtrack)	1959	35.00	70.00
		(This soundtrack was released simultaneously on U.A.			
		credited to Sweet Sue & Her Society Syncopaters.)			
Columbia CL-1527	(M)	Let's Make Love (Soundtrack)	1960	20.00	50.00
Columbia CS-8327	(S)	Let's Make Love (Soundtrack)	1960	35.00	70.00
20th Century FXG-5000	(M)	Marilyn	1959	40.00	80.00
20th Century SXG-5000	(E)	Marilyn	1959	35.00	70.00
		(Issued with a full color poster, priced separately below.)			
20th Century 5000		Marilyn Poster	1959	35.00	70.00
20th Century T-901	(M)	Remember Marilyn	1959	35.00	70.00
Ascot ALM-13008	(M)	Marilyn Monroe	196?	16.00	40.00
Ascot ALS-16008	(S)	Marilyn Monroe	196?	20.00	50.00
Ascot US-13500	(M)	Some Like It Hot (Soundtrack)	1964	8.00	20.00
Ascot US-16500	(S)	Some Like It Hot (Soundtrack)	1964	12.00	30.00
Movietone 72016	(M)	The Unforgettable Marilyn Monroe	1967	10.00	25.00
Movietone S-72016	(S)	The Unforgettable Marilyn Monroe	1967	12.00	30.00

MONROE, VAUGHN

RCA Victor LPM-1799	(M)	There I Sing, Swing It Again	1958	8.00	20.00
RCA Victor LSP-1799	(S)	There I Sing, Swing It Again	1958	12.00	30.00
Dot DLP-3431	(M)	His Greatest Hits	1962	5.00	12.00
Dot DLP-25431	(S)	His Greatest Hits	1962	6.00	15.00
Dot DLP-3470	(M)	Great Themes Of Famous Bands And Great Singers	1962	5.00	12.00
Dot DLP-25470	(S)	Great Themes Of Famous Bands And Great Singers	1962	6.00	15.00

Label & Catalog #		Title	Year	VG+	NM
MONROE BROTHERS, THE					
Bill and Charlie Monroe.					
Camden CAL-774	(M)	**Early Bluegrass Music**	*1963*	**6.00**	**15.00**
Camden CAS-774	(S)	**Early Bluegrass Music**	*1963*	**6.00**	**15.00**
Decca DL-75066	(S)	**The Monroe Brothers**	*1969*	**5.00**	**12.00**
MONTAGE					
Montage features Steve Martin of The Left Banke.					
Laurie SLP-2049	(S)	**Montage**	*1969*	**6.00**	**15.00**
MONTANA, PATSY					
Sims LP-122	(M)	**The New Sound Of Patsy Montana**	*1964*	**12.00**	**30.00**
MONTANA, SLIM					
Montana Slim is a pseudonym for Wilf Carter.					
Camden CAL-527	(M)	**Wilf Carter/Montana Slim**	*1958*	**14.00**	**35.00**
Camden CAL-668	(M)	**Reminiscin'**	*1962*	**8.00**	**20.00**
Camden CAL-846	(M)	**32 Wonderful Years**	*1965*	**8.00**	**20.00**
Decca DL-8917	(M)	**I'm Ragged But I'm Right**	*1959*	**30.00**	**60.00**
Decca DL-4092	(S)	**The Dynamite Trail**	*1960*	**30.00**	**60.00**
Starday SLP-300	(M)	**Wilf Carter As Montana Slim**	*1964*	**14.00**	**35.00**
MONTENEGRO, HUGO, & HIS ORCHESTRA					
RCA Victor LPM-3475	(M)	**Music From "The Man From U.N.C.L.E."**	*1966*	**6.00**	**15.00**
RCA Victor LSP-3475	(S)	**Music From "The Man From U.N.C.L.E."**	*1966*	**8.00**	**20.00**
RCA Victor LPM-3574	(M)	**More Music From**			
		"The Man From U.N.C.L.E."	*1966*	**6.00**	**15.00**
RCA Victor LSP-3574	(S)	**More Music From**			
		"The Man From U.N.C.L.E."	*1966*	**8.00**	**20.00**
		(Both "U.N.C.L.E. albums are TV soundtracks.)			
MONTEZ, CHRIS					
Monogram M-100	(M)	**Let's Dance And Have Some Kinda' Fun!!!**	*1963*	**35.00**	**70.00**
A&M LP-115	(M)	**The More I See You/Call Me**	*1966*	**8.00**	**20.00**
A&M SP-4115	(P)	**The More I See You/Call Me**	*1966*	**10.00**	**25.00**
A&M LP-120	(M)	**Time After Time**	*1966*	**5.00**	**12.00**
A&M SP-4120	(S)	**Time After Time**	*1966*	**6.00**	**15.00**
A&M LP-128	(M)	**Foolin' Around**	*1967*	**5.00**	**12.00**
A&M SP-4128	(S)	**Foolin' Around**	*1967*	**6.00**	**15.00**
A&M LP-157	(M)	**Watch What Happens**	*1967*	**5.00**	**12.00**
A&M SP-4157	(S)	**Watch What Happens**	*1967*	**6.00**	**15.00**
MONTGOMERY, "LITTLE BROTHER"					
Riverside RLP-12-403	(M)	**Southside Blues**	*1961*	**20.00**	**50.00**
Bluesville BV-1012	(M)	**Tasty Blues**	*1965*	**10.00**	**25.00**
Adelphi AD-1003	(S)	**No Special Rider**	*196?*	**10.00**	**25.00**
MONTGOMERY, MARIAN					
Capitol T-1884	(M)	**Swings For Winners And Losers**	*1963*	**5.00**	**12.00**
Capitol ST-1884	(S)	**Swings For Winners And Losers**	*1963*	**6.00**	**15.00**
Capitol T-1982	(M)	**Let There Be Marian Montgomery**	*1963*	**5.00**	**12.00**
Capitol ST-1982	(S)	**Let There Be Marian Montgomery**	*1963*	**6.00**	**15.00**
MONTGOMERY, MELBA					
Ms. Montgomery also recorded with George Jones; Gene Pitney.					
United Arts. UAL-3341	(M)	**#1 Country & Western Girl Singer**	*1964*	**5.00**	**12.00**
United Arts. UAS-6341	(S)	**#1 Country & Western Girl Singer**	*1964*	**6.00**	**15.00**
United Arts. UAL-3369	(M)	**Down Home**	*1964*	**5.00**	**12.00**
United Arts. UAS-6369	(S)	**Down Home**	*1964*	**6.00**	**15.00**
United Arts. UAL-3391	(M)	**I Can't Get Used To Being Lonely**	*1964*	**5.00**	**12.00**
United Arts. UAS-6391	(S)	**I Can't Get Used To Being Lonely**	*1964*	**6.00**	**15.00**
Musicor M-2074	(M)	**Country Girl**	*1966*	**4.00**	**10.00**
Musicor MS-3074	(S)	**Country Girl**	*1966*	**5.00**	**12.00**
Musicor M-2097	(M)	**The Hallelujah Road**	*1966*	**4.00**	**10.00**
Musicor MS-3097	(S)	**The Hallelujah Road**	*1966*	**5.00**	**12.00**
Musicor M-2113	(M)	**Melba Toast**	*1966*	**4.00**	**10.00**
Musicor MS-3113	(S)	**Melba Toast**	*1966*	**5.00**	**12.00**
Musicor M-2114	(M)	**Don't Keep Me Lonely Too Long**	*1966*	**4.00**	**10.00**
Musicor MS-3114	(S)	**Don't Keep Me Lonely Too Long**	*1966*	**5.00**	**12.00**

Label & Catalog #		Title	Year	VG+	NM
Musicor M-2129	(M)	I'm Just Living	1967	4.00	10.00
Musicor MS-3129	(S)	I'm Just Living	1967	5.00	12.00

MOODY, CLYDE
| King 891 | (M) | The Best Of Clyde Moody | 1964 | 12.00 | 30.00 |

MOODY BLUES
The Moodies are Graeme Edge, Justin Haywood, John Lodge, Denny Laine and Ray Thomas.

London LL-3428	(M)	Go Now/Moody Blues #1	1965	20.00	50.00
London PS-428	(E)	Go Now/Moody Blues #1	1965	10.00	25.00
Deram DES-18012	(S)	Days Of Future Passed	1968	8.00	20.00
Deram DES-18017	(S)	In Search Of The Lost Chord	1968	8.00	20.00
Deram DES-18025	(S)	On The Threshold Of A Dream	1969	8.00	20.00

— Original Deram albums above have the "London" logo beneath Deram at the top of the label.—

| Threshold THS-1 | (S) | To Our Children's Children's Children | 1969 | 6.00 | 15.00 |

(White & blue label reads "Distributed by London.")

Threshold THS-3	(S)	A Question Of Balance	1970	5.00	12.00
Threshold THX-100	(DJ)	Special Moody Blues Interview Kit	1971	30.00	60.00
Threshold THS-5	(S)	Every Good Boy Deserves Favour	1971	5.00	12.00
Threshold THS-7	(S)	Seventh Sojourn	1972	5.00	12.00

— Original Threshold albums above have white labels with a purple logo on top.—

London PS-708	(DJ)	Octave (Blue vinyl)	1978	10.00	25.00
Mobile Fidelity MFSL-042	(S)	Days Of Future Passed	1980	16.00	40.00
Mobile Fidelity MFSL-151	(S)	Seventh Sojourn	1984	8.00	20.00
Nautilus NR-21	(S)	On The Threshold Of A Dream	198?	8.00	20.00

MOOLAH
| Annuit Septus M-1 | (S) | Whoa, Ye Demons Possessed | 1974 | 50.00 | 100.00 |

MOON, KEITH
Keith Moon was formerly a member of The Who.

| MCA 2136 | (S) | Two Sides Of The Moon | 1975 | 14.00 | 35.00 |

MOONDOG
Epic LN-1002 (10")	(M)	Moondog And His Friends	1954	35.00	70.00
Prestige 7042	(M)	Caribea	1956	16.00	40.00
Prestige 7069	(M)	More Moondog	1956	16.00	40.00
Prestige 7099	(M)	The Story Of Moondog	1957	16.00	40.00
Columbia MS-7335	(S)	Moondog	1970	6.00	15.00
Columbia KC-30897	(S)	Moondog II	1971	6.00	15.00

MOONEY, JOE
Decca DL-5555 (10")	(M)	You Go To My Head	1953	16.00	40.00
Atlantic 1255	(M)	Lush Life	1957	14.00	35.00
Decca DL-8468	(M)	On The Rocks	1957	10.00	25.00

MOONEY, RALPH, & JAMES BURTON
| Capitol T-2872 | (M) | Corn Pickin' And Slick Slidin' | 1967 | 16.00 | 40.00 |
| Capitol ST-2872 | (S) | Corn Pickin' And Slick Slidin' | 1967 | 20.00 | 50.00 |

MOONGLOWS, THE
Refer to The Flamingos / The Moonglows.

Chess LP-1430	(M)	Look, It's The Moonglows	1959	180.00	300.00
Chess LP-1471	(M)	The Best Of Bobby Lester & The Moonglows	1962	75.00	150.00
Constellation CS-2	(M)	The Moonglows: Collectors Showcase	1964	12.00	30.00
RCA Victor LSP-4722	(S)	The Return Of The Moonglows	1972	6.00	15.00

MOORE, ADA
Refer to Jimmy Rushing & Ada Moore.

| Debut DLP-15 (10") | (M) | Jazz Workshop (Volume 3) | 1956 | 20.00 | 50.00 |

MOORE, BOBBY, & THE RHYTHM ACES
| Checker LP-3000 | (M) | Searching For My Love | 1966 | 8.00 | 20.00 |
| Checker LPS-3000 | (E) | Searching For My Love | 1966 | 6.00 | 15.00 |

MOORE, DANNY
| Everest 1211 | (M) | Folk Songs From Here And There | 1963 | 6.00 | 15.00 |
| Everest SD-1211 | (S) | Folk Songs From Here And There | 1963 | 8.00 | 20.00 |

Label & Catalog #		Title	Year	VG+	NM
MOORE, DEBBY					
Top Rank TR-301	(M)	**Debby Moore**	1959	12.00	30.00
MOORE, DUDLEY					
Atlantic 1403	(M)	**"Beyond The Fringe" And All That Jazz**	1962	10.00	25.00
London MS-82009	(S)	**Bedazzled** (Soundtrack)	1968	12.00	30.00
London MS-82010	(S)	**30 Is A Dangerous Age, Cynthia** (Soundtk.)	1968	10.00	25.00
MOORE, GATEMOUTH					
King 684	(M)	**I'm A Fool To Care**	1960	300.00	500.00
MOORE, LATTIE					
Audio Lab AL-1555	(M)	**The Best Of Lattie Moore**	1960	20.00	50.00
Audio Lab AL-1573	(M)	**Country Side**	1962	20.00	50.00
Derbytown 102	(M)	**Lattie Moore**	196?	6.00	15.00
MOORE, MARILYN					
Bethlehem 73	(M)	**Moody**	1957	16.00	40.00
MOORE, SCOTTY					
Scotty was formerly a member of Elvis, Scotty & Bill.					
Epic LN-24103	(M)	**The Guitar That Changed The World**	1964	20.00	50.00
Epic BN-26103	(S)	**The Guitar That Changed The World**	1964	35.00	70.00
MOORE, SHELLY					
Argo 4106	(M)	**For The First Time**	1962	8.00	20.00
MORENO, RITA					
Strand 1039	(M)	**Rita Moreno Sings**	195?	14.00	35.00
Wynne 103	(M)	**Warm, Wonderful And Wild**	195?	14.00	35.00
MORGAN, GEORGE					
Columbia CL-1044	(M)	**Morgan, By George**	1957	16.00	40.00
Columbia CL-1831	(M)	**Golden Memories**	1961	6.00	15.00
Columbia CS-8431	(S)	**Golden Memories**	1961	8.00	20.00
Columbia CL-2111	(M)	**Tender Lovin' Care**	1964	5.00	12.00
Columbia CS-8911	(S)	**Tender Lovin' Care**	1964	6.00	15.00
Columbia CL-2197	(M)	**Slippin' Around**	1964	5.00	12.00
Columbia CS-8997	(S)	**Slippin' Around**	1964	6.00	15.00
Columbia CL-2333	(M)	**Red Roses For A Blue Lady**	1965	5.00	12.00
Columbia CS-9133	(S)	**Red Roses For A Blue Lady**	1965	6.00	15.00
MORGAN, JANE					
Kapp KL-1023	(M)	**Jane Morgan**	1956	12.00	30.00
Kapp KL-1066	(M)	**Fascination**	1957	12.00	30.00
Kapp KS-3017	(M)	**Fascination**	195?	12.00	30.00
Kapp KL-1098	(M)	**Jane Morgan**	1958	12.00	30.00
Kapp KL-1105	(M)	**The Day The Rain Came**	1958	12.00	30.00
Kapp KL-1105S	(S)	**The Day The Rain Came**	1958	12.00	30.00
Kapp KL-1129	(M)	**Jane In Spain**	1959	10.00	25.00
Kapp KS-3014	(S)	**Jane In Spain**	1959	10.00	25.00
Kapp KL-1191	(M)	**Ballads Of Lady Jane**	1960	6.00	15.00
Kapp KS-3191	(S)	**Ballads Of Lady Jane**	1960	8.00	20.00
Kapp KL-1239	(M)	**Second Time Around**	1961	6.00	15.00
Kapp KS-3239	(S)	**Second Time Around**	1961	8.00	20.00
Kapp KL-1246	(M)	**The Great Golden Hits**	1961	6.00	15.00
Kapp KS-3246	(S)	**The Great Golden Hits**	1961	8.00	20.00
Kapp KL-1247	(M)	**Big Hits From Broadway**	1961	6.00	15.00
Kapp KS-3247	(S)	**Big Hits From Broadway**	1961	8.00	20.00
Kapp KL-1250	(M)	**Love Makes The World Go 'Round**	1961	6.00	15.00
Kapp KS-3250	(S)	**Love Makes The World Go 'Round**	1961	8.00	20.00
Kapp KL-1268	(M)	**Jane Morgan At The Cocoanut Grove**	1962	6.00	15.00
Kapp KS-3268	(S)	**Jane Morgan At The Cocoanut Grove**	1962	8.00	20.00
Kapp KL-1296	(M)	**What Now My Love**	1962	6.00	15.00
Kapp KS-3296	(S)	**What Now My Love**	1962	8.00	20.00
Kapp KL-1329	(M)	**Jane Morgan's Greatest Hits**	1963	5.00	12.00
Kapp KS-3329	(S)	**Jane Morgan's Greatest Hits**	1963	6.00	15.00
Epic LN-24166	(M)	**In My Style**	1965	5.00	12.00
Epic BN-26166	(S)	**In My Style**	1965	6.00	15.00

Label & Catalog #		Title	Year	VG+	NM
Epic LN-24190	(M)	Today's Hits... Tomorrow's Golden Favorites	1966	5.00	12.00
Epic BN-26190	(S)	Today's Hits... Tomorrow's Golden Favorites	1966	6.00	15.00
Epic LN-24211	(M)	Fresh Flavor	1966	5.00	12.00
Epic BN-26211	(S)	Fresh Flavor	1966	6.00	15.00
Colpix CP-497	(M)	The Jane Morgan Album	1966	5.00	12.00
Colpix SCP-497	(S)	The Jane Morgan Album	1966	6.00	15.00

MORGAN, JAYE P.

Label & Catalog #		Title	Year	VG+	NM
RCA Victor LPM-1155	(M)	Jaye P. Morgan	1955	12.00	30.00
MGM E-3774	(M)	Slow And Easy	1959	8.00	20.00
MGM SE-3774	(S)	Slow And Easy	1959	12.00	30.00
MGM E-3830	(M)	Up North	1960	5.00	12.00
MGM SE-3830	(S)	Up North	1960	8.00	20.00
MGM E-3867	(M)	Down South	1960	5.00	12.00
MGM SE-3867	(S)	Down South	1960	8.00	20.00
MGM E-3940	(M)	That Country Sound	1961	5.00	12.00
MGM SE-3940	(S)	That Country Sound	1961	8.00	20.00

MORGEN

Label & Catalog #		Title	Year	VG+	NM
Probe CPLP-4507	(M)	Morgen (With insert)	1969	50.00	100.00

MOREL, TERRY

Label & Catalog #		Title	Year	VG+	NM
Bethlehem 47	(M)	Songs Of A Woman In Love	1955	16.00	40.00

MORLY GREY

Label & Catalog #		Title	Year	VG+	NM
Starshine 69000	(M)	The Only Truth	1968	150.00	250.00

MORNING

Label & Catalog #		Title	Year	VG+	NM
Vault 138	(S)	Morning	1970	8.00	20.00
Fantasy 9402	(S)	Struck Like Silver	1972	6.00	15.00

MORNING DEW

Label & Catalog #		Title	Year	VG+	NM
Roulette R-41045	(M)	Morning Dew	1970	35.00	70.00
Roulette RS-41045	(S)	Morning Dew	1970	60.00	120.00

MORNING GLORY

Label & Catalog #		Title	Year	VG+	NM
Fontana MGF-27573	(M)	Two Suns Worth	1967	5.00	12.00
Fontana SRF-67573	(S)	Two Suns Worth	1967	6.00	15.00

MORNINGLORY

Label & Catalog #		Title	Year	VG+	NM
Toya STLP-003	(S)	Growing	1972	14.00	35.00

MORRISEY, PAT

Label & Catalog #		Title	Year	VG+	NM
Mercury MG-20197	(M)	I'm Pat Morrisey, I Sing	1956	16.00	40.00

MORRISON, VAN

Van The Man was formerly lead singer for Them.

Label & Catalog #		Title	Year	VG+	NM
Bang BLP-218	(M)	Blowin' Your Mind (Red & white label)	1967	10.00	25.00
Bang BLPS-218	(S)	Blowin' Your Mind (Red & white label)	1967	12.00	30.00
		(Originally issued with the complete single version of "Brown-Eyed Girl" with the line "Making love in the green grass.")			
Bang BLPS-218	(S)	Blowin' Your Mind (Red & white label)	1967	12.00	30.00
		(Reissued with a censored version of "Brown-Eyed Girl" that deletes "Making love in the green grass.")			
Bang BLPS-218	(S)	Blowin' Your Mind (Yellow label)	1970	4.00	10.00
Bang BLPS-222	(S)	The Best Of Van Morrison	1970	8.00	20.00
Bang BLPS-400	(S)	T.B. Sheets	1973	6.00	15.00
Warner Bros. WS-1768	(S)	Astral Weeks	1968	6.00	15.00
Warner Bros. WS-1835	(S)	Moondance	1970	5.00	12.00
Warner Bros. WS-1885	(S)	Van Morrison, His Band And Street Choir	1970	5.00	12.00
Warner Bros. WS-1950	(S)	Tupelo Honey	1971	5.00	12.00
		— Original Warner albums above have green labels with a "W7" on top.—			
Warner Bros. WBMS-102	(DJ)	Live At The Roxy	1978	12.00	30.00
		(Part of the "Warner Brothers Music Sho.w")			
Direct Disk SD-16604	(S)	Moondance	1981	16.00	40.00

Label & Catalog #		Title	Year	VG+	NM

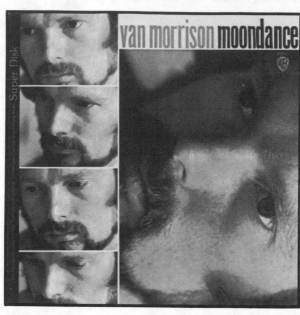

While Van's entire canon can be viewed as an ongoing work-in-progess, it is "Moondance" that remains the quintessential Morrison to many of his fans. This half-speed mastered Super Disk from Direct Disk Labs offers the music in its best available setting.

MORSE, ELLA MAE

Capitol H-513 (10")	(M)	**Barrelhouse Boogie And The Blues**	1954	150.00	250.00
Capitol T-513	(M)	**Barrelhouse Boogie And The Blues**	1955	50.00	100.00
Capitol T-898	(M)	**Morse Code**	1957	35.00	70.00
Capitol T-1802	(M)	**Hits Of Ella Mae Morse And Freddie Slack**	1962	20.00	50.00

MORY STORM BAND, THE

Sound Machine SMS-49007	(S)	**Cry For The Dreamer**	197?	40.00	80.00

MOSER, J., & THE HOTS

Moco FIT-003	(S)	**For Life**	1975	35.00	70.00

MOSS, GENE

RCA Victor LPM-2977	(M)	**Dracula's Greatest Hits**	1964	8.00	20.00
RCA Victor LSP-2977	(S)	**Dracula's Greatest Hits**	1964	10.00	25.00

MOTHER EARTH
Mother Earth features Tracy Nelson.

Mercury SR-61194	(S)	**Living With The Animals**	1968	8.00	20.00
Mercury SR-61226	(S)	**Make A Joyful Noise**	1969	6.00	15.00
Mercury SR-61230	(S)	**Tracy Nelson Country**	1969	6.00	15.00
Mercury SR-61270	(S)	**Satisfied**	1970	5.00	12.00
Reprise RS-6431	(S)	**Bring Me Home**	1971	5.00	12.00

MOTHERS OF INVENTION, THE: *Refer to* FRANK ZAPPA

MOTLEY CRUE

Leather	(S)	**Too Fast For Love** (Black letter cover)	198?	50.00	100.00
Leather	(S)	**Too Fast For Love** (White letter cover)	198?	35.00	70.00
Elektra 60395	(S)	**Helter Skelter** (Picture disc)	1984	10.00	25.00

MOTIONS, THE

Phillips PHS-600317	(S)	**Electric Baby**	1969	6.00	15.00

Label & Catalog #		Title	Year	VG+	NM
MOTT THE HOOPLE [MOTT]					
Atlantic SD-8272	(S)	**Mad Shadows**	1970	5.00	12.00
Atlantic SD-8258	(S)	**Mott The Hoople**	1970	5.00	12.00
Atlantic SD-8284	(S)	**Wildlife**	1971	5.00	12.00
Atlantic SD-8304	(S)	**Brain Capers**	1972	5.00	12.00
Columbia PCQ-32871	(Q)	**The Hoople**	1974	8.00	20.00
MOUNTAIN					
Mountain features Leslie West.					
Columbia CQ-32079	(Q)	**The Best Of Mountain**	1973	6.00	15.00
Columbia CQ-33088	(Q)	**Avalanche**	1974	6.00	15.00
MOUNTAIN BUS					
Good 101	(S)	**Sundance**	1971	40.00	80.00
MOUNTAIN RAMBLERS, THE					
Atlantic 1347	(M)	**Blue Ridge Mountain Music**	1962	14.00	35.00
MOUSEKETEERS, THE					
Disneyland T-3918	(M)	**How To Be A Mouseketeer**	1962	10.00	25.00
Disneyland ST-3918	(S)	**How To Be A Mouseketeer**	1962	14.00	35.00
MOUZOKIS					
British Main 90069	(S)	**Magic Tube**	1972	50.00	100.00

The brainchild of Roy Wood, it was the addition of The Idle Race's Jeff Lynne in 1970 that moved the group toward their metamorphosis into The Electric Light Orchestra,

MOVE, THE					
A&M SP-4259	(S)	**Shazam**	1969	10.00	25.00
A&M SP-3181	(S)	**Shazam**	1982	4.00	10.00
Capitol ST-658	(S)	**Looking On**	1971	6.00	15.00
Capitol ST-811	(S)	**Message From The Country**	1971	6.00	15.00
United Arts. UAS-5666	(S)	**Split Ends**	1973	4.00	10.00
A&M SP-3625	(S)	**Best Of The Move/First Move** *(2 LPs)*	1974	5.00	12.00

Label & Catalog #		Title	Year	VG+	NM

MOVING SIDEWALKS
The Sidewalks featured Billy Gibbons, later of ZZ Top.

Tantara 6919	(S)	**Flash**	1968	85.00	170.00

MU
Mu is a creation of Merrell Fenkhauser.

R.T.V. 300	(S)	**Mu** *(With insert)*	1972	60.00	120.00
C.A.S. 300	(S)	**Mu** *(With insert)*	1972	50.00	100.00

MUDDY WATERS
Muddy Waters is a pseudonym for McKinley Morganfield. Refer to Bo Diddley.

Chess LP-1427	(M)	**The Best Of Muddy Waters**	1957	50.00	100.00
Chess LP-1444	(M)	**Muddy Waters Sings Big Bill**	1960	40.00	80.00
Chess LP-1449	(M)	**Muddy Waters At Newport**	1963	35.00	70.00
Chess LP-1483	(M)	**Folk Singer**	1964	35.00	70.00
		— Original Chess albums above have black & silver labels.—			
Chess LP-1501	(M)	**The Real Folk Blues Of Muddy Waters**	1965	16.00	40.00
Chess LPS-1501	(S)	**The Real Folk Blues Of Muddy Waters**	1965	35.00	70.00
Chess LP-1507	(M)	**Muddy, Brass And Blues**	1966	14.00	35.00
Chess LPS-1507	(S)	**Muddy, Brass And Blues**	1966	20.00	50.00
Chess LP-1511	(M)	**More Real Folk Blues**	1966	14.00	35.00
Chess LPS-1511	(S)	**More Real Folk Blues**	1966	20.00	50.00
Chess LP-1533	(M)	**Blues From Big Bill's Copacabana**	1967	12.00	30.00
Chess LPS-1533	(S)	**Blues From Big Bill's Copacabana**	1967	14.00	35.00
Cadet Concept 314	(S)	**Electric Mud**	1968	8.00	20.00
Cadet Concept 320	(S)	**After The Rain**	1969	8.00	20.00
Chess LPS-1539	(S)	**Sail On**	1969	10.00	25.00
Chess LPS-1553	(S)	**They Call Me Muddy Waters**	1971	6.00	15.00
Chess 2CH-60006	(S)	**McKinley Morganfield A.K.A. Muddy Waters** *(2 LPs)*	1971	10.00	25.00
Chess CH-50012	(S)	**Muddy Waters Live**	1972	5.00	12.00
Chess CH-60013	(S)	**The London Muddy Waters Sessions**	1972	6.00	15.00
		— Original Chess albums above have blue labels.—			
Chess CH-50023	(S)	**Can't Get No Grindin'**	1973	8.00	20.00
Chess CH-60026	(S)	**London Revisited**	1974	5.00	12.00
Chess CH-60031	(S)	**Unk In Funk**	1974	5.00	12.00
Chess CH-50033	(S)	**Fathers And Sons** *(2 LPs)*	1975	10.00	20.00

MUELLER, BILL, & THE BRAT

Brat CT-3301	(S)	**No Place Like Home**	1979	35.00	70.00

MUGWUMPS
The Mugwumps were Cass Elliot, Denny Doherty, Jim Hendricks and Zal Yanovsky.

Warner Bros. W-1697	(M)	**The Mugwumps**	1967	10.00	25.00
Warner Bros. WS-1697	(S)	**The Mugwumps**	1967	12.00	30.00

MULDAUR, MARIA

Reprise MS4-2194	(Q)	**Waitress In A Donut Shop**	1974	5.00	12.00

MULLICAN, MOON

Coral CRL-57235	(M)	**Moon Over Mullican**	1958	210.00	350.00
Sterling ST-601	(M)	**I'll Sail My Ship Alone**	1958	50.00	100.00
King 555	(M)	**His All-Time Greatest Hits**	1958	50.00	100.00
King 628	(M)	**16 Of His Favorite Tunes**	1959	50.00	100.00
King 681	(M)	**The Many Moods Of Moon Mullican**	1960	50.00	100.00
King 937	(M)	**24 Of His Favorite Tunes**	1965	10.00	25.00
Audio Lab AL-1568	(M)	**Instrumentals**	1962	50.00	100.00
Starday SLP-267	(M)	**Mister Piano Man**	1964	14.00	35.00
Starday SLP-398	(M)	**The Unforgettable Moon Mullican**	1967	10.00	25.00

MUMY, BILL

BB 103	(S)	**Bill Mumy**	1980	10.00	25.00

MUNSTERS, THE

Decca DL-4588	(M)	**The Munsters**	1964	16.00	40.00
Decca DL-74588	(S)	**The Munsters**	1964	20.00	50.00
Golden LP-139	(M)	**At Home With The Minsters**	1964	30.00	60.00

Label & Catalog #		Title	Year	VG+	NM

MURE, BILLY

Label & Catalog #		Title	Year	VG+	NM
United Arts. UAL-3031	(M)	**Bandstand Record Hop**	1959	10.00	25.00
United Arts. UAS-6031	(S)	**Bandstand Record Hop**	1959	16.00	40.00
MGM E-4131	(M)	**Teen Bossa Nova**	1963	8.00	20.00
MGM SE-4131	(S)	**Teen Bossa Nova**	1963	10.00	25.00

MURPHEY, MICHAEL

Epic PEQ-33851	(Q)	**Swans Against The Sun**	1975	5.00	12.00

MURPHY, MARK

Decca DL-8390	(M)	**Meet Mark Murphy**	1956	16.00	40.00
Decca DL-8632	(M)	**Let Yourself Go**	1958	12.00	30.00
Capitol T-1177	(M)	**This Could Be The Start Of Something**	1959	8.00	20.00
Capitol ST-1177	(S)	**This Could Be The Start Of Something**	1959	10.00	25.00
Capitol T-1299	(M)	**Hip Parade**	1960	6.00	15.00
Capitol ST-1299	(S)	**Hip Parade**	1960	8.00	20.00
Capitol T-1458	(M)	**Playing The Field**	1960	6.00	15.00
Capitol ST-1458	(S)	**Playing The Field**	1960	8.00	20.00
Riverside RLP-395	(M)	**Rah!**	1961	6.00	15.00
Riverside RSP-9395	(S)	**Rah!**	1961	8.00	20.00
Riverside RLP-441	(M)	**That's How I Love The Blues**	1962	6.00	15.00
Riverside RSP-9441	(S)	**That's How I Love The Blues**	1962	8.00	20.00
Fontana MGF-27537	(M)	**A Swingin' Singin' Affair**	1965	5.00	12.00
Fontana SRF-67537	(S)	**A Swingin' Singin' Affair**	1965	6.00	15.00

MURPHY, ROSE

Royale 1835 (10")	(M)	**Rose Murphy And Quartette**	195?	12.00	30.00
Verve V-2070	(M)	**Not Cha-Cha, But Chi-Chi**	1957	10.00	25.00
United Arts. UAL-12025	(M)	**Jazz, Joy And Happiness**	195?	10.00	25.00
United Arts. UAS-15025	(S)	**Jazz, Joy And Happiness**	195?	12.00	30.00

MURRAY, ANNE

Capitol 11743	(DJ)	**Let's Keep It That Way** (Picture disc)	1978	20.00	50.00

MUSIC EMPORIUM, THE

Sentinal 69001	(S)	**The Music Emporium**	1969	See note below	
		(Rare. Estimated near mint value $1,000-2,000.)			

MUSIC EXPLOSION, THE

Laurie LLP-2040	(M)	**A Little Bit O' Soul**	1967	6.00	15.00
Laurie SLLP-2040	(S)	**A Little Bit O' Soul**	1967	8.00	20.00

MUSIC MACHINE, THE
Refer to Bonniwell's Music Machine.

Original Sound 5015	(M)	**Turn On The Music Machine**	1966	6.00	15.00
Original Sound 8875	(S)	**Turn On The Music Machine**	1966	16.00	40.00

MUSTANGS, THE

Providence PLP-001	(M)	**Dartell Stomp**	1963	16.00	40.00

MUTHA GOOSE

Alpha Omega 264-01	(S)	**Mutha Goose I**	197?	80.00	160.00

MYERS, DAVE

Del-Fi DFLP-1239	(M)	**Hangin' Twenty**	1963	8.00	20.00
Del-Fi DFST-1239	(S)	**Hangin' Twenty**	1963	12.00	30.00
		(Del-Fi 1239 is credited to Dave Myers & The Surftones.)			
Carole CAR-8002	(M)	**Greatest Racing Themes**	1966	12.00	30.00
		(Carole 8002 is credited to The Dave Myers Effect.)			

MYSTIC ASTROLOGIC CRYSTAL BAND, THE

Carole 8001	(M)	**Mystic Astrologic Crystal Band**	1967	5.00	12.00
Carole S-8001	(S)	**Mystic Astrologic Crystal Band**	1967	6.00	15.00
Carole S-8003	(S)	**Clip Out, Put On Book**	1968	6.00	15.00

MYSTIC MOODS ORCHESTRA, THE

Mobile Fidelity MFSL-001	(S)	**Emotions**	1979	16.00	40.00
Mobile Fidelity MFSL-002	(S)	**Cosmic Force**	1979	16.00	40.00
Mobile Fidelity MFSL-003	(S)	**Stormy Weekend**	1979	16.00	40.00

Label & Catalog #		Title	Year	VG+	NM

MYSTIC NUMBER NATIONAL BANK, THE
| Probe CPLPS-4501 | (S) | The Mystic Number National Bank | 1969 | 6.00 | 15.00 |

MYSTIC SIVA
| V.O. 19713 | (S) | Mystic Siva | 1970 | 300.00 | 500.00 |

NAGLE, RON
| Warner Bros. WS-1902 | (S) | Bad Rice | 1970 | 8.00 | 20.00 |

NAPOLEON XIV
| Warner Bros. W-1661 | (M) | They're Coming To Take Me Away Ha-Haaa! | 1966 | 30.00 | 60.00 |
| Warner Bros. WS-1661 | (S) | They're Coming To Take Me Away Ha-Haaa! | 1966 | 40.00 | 80.00 |

NASH, JOHNNY
ABC-Paramount 244	(M)	Johnny Nash	1958	8.00	20.00
ABC-Paramount S-244	(S)	Johnny Nash	1958	12.00	30.00
ABC-Paramount 276	(M)	Quiet Hour	1959	8.00	20.00
ABC-Paramount S-276	(S)	Quiet Hour	1959	12.00	30.00
ABC-Paramount 299	(M)	I Got Rhythm	1959	8.00	20.00
ABC-Paramount S-299	(S)	I Got Rhythm	1959	12.00	30.00
ABC-Paramount 344	(M)	Let's Get Lost	1960	8.00	20.00
ABC-Paramount S-344	(S)	Let's Get Lost	1960	12.00	30.00
ABC-Paramount 383	(M)	Studio Time	1961	6.00	15.00
ABC-Paramount S-383	(S)	Studio Time	1961	10.00	25.00
Jad JS-1207	(S)	Hold Me Tight	1968	6.00	15.00
Jad JS-1001	(S)	Prince Of Peace	1969	6.00	15.00
Jad JS-1006	(S)	Folk Soul	1969	6.00	15.00
Epic KE-31607	(S)	I Can See Clearly Now (Yellow label)	1972	4.00	10.00

NASHVILLE ALL-STARS, THE
The All-Stars feature Chet Atkins, Gary Burton and Hank Garland.
| RCA Victor LPM-2302 | (M) | After The Riot At Newport | 1960 | 12.00 | 30.00 |
| RCA Victor LSP-2302 | (S) | After The Riot At Newport | 1960 | 16.00 | 40.00 |

NASHVILLE TEENS, THE
| London LL-3407 | (M) | Tobacco Road | 1964 | 35.00 | 70.00 |
| London PS-407 | (E) | Tobacco Road | 1964 | 30.00 | 60.00 |

NAZZ, THE
The Nazz features Todd Rundgren.
SGC 5001	(S)	Nazz	1968	12.00	30.00
SGC 5002	(S)	Nazz Nazz (Black vinyl)	1969	30.00	60.00
SGC 5002	(S)	Nazz Nazz (Red vinyl)	1969	16.00	40.00
SGC 5004	(S)	Nazz III	1971	12.00	30.00

(Poorly reproduced counterfeits of each of the Nazz albums exist.)

NEGATIVE SPACE
| Evil 1001 | (M) | Hard, Heavy, Mean | 196? | 180.00 | 300.00 |

(Heavy cardboard cover with the title in blue print on the front.)
| Evil 1001 | (M) | Hard, Heavy, Mean | 196? | 100.00 | 200.00 |

(Plain cardboard jacket with a sticker.)

Label & Catalog #		Title	Year	VG+	NM
NEIGHB'RHOOD CHILDR'N, THE					
Acta 8005	(M)	The Neighb'rhood Childr'n	1968	12.00	30.00
Acta 38005	(S)	The Neighb'rhood Childr'n	1968	30.00	60.00
NEIL, FRED					
Capitol T-2665	(M)	Fred Neil	1966	6.00	15.00
Capitol ST-2665	(S)	Fred Neil	1966	8.00	20.00
Capitol T-2862	(M)	Sessions	1967	6.00	15.00
Capitol ST-2862	(S)	Sessions	1967	8.00	20.00
NELSON, PORTIA					
Columbia CL-4722 (10")	(M)	Love Songs For A Late Evening	195?	12.00	30.00
Dolphin 4	(M)	Autumn Leaves	195?	10.00	25.00
NELSON, RICK					
Verve V-2083	(M)	Teen Time	1957	100.00	200.00
		(Vrious artists album with the cover devoted to Ricky.)			
Imperial LP-9048	(M)	Ricky	1957	50.00	100.00
Imperial LP-9050	(M)	Ricky Nelson	1958	30.00	60.00
Imperial LP-9061	(M)	Ricky Sings Again	1959	30.00	60.00
Imperial LP-9082	(M)	Songs By Ricky	1959	20.00	50.00
Imperial LP-9122	(M)	More Songs By Ricky	1960	16.00	40.00
Imperial LP-12059	(S)	More Songs By Ricky	1960	30.00	60.00
Imperial LP-12059	(DJ)	More Songs By Ricky *(Blue vinyl)*	1960	210.00	350.00
		(Issued with a poster, priced separately below.)			
		More Songs By Ricky Bonus Poster		50.00	100.00
Imperial LP-9152	(M)	Rick Is 21	1961	16.00	40.00
Imperial LP-12071	(S)	Rick Is 21	1961	30.00	60.00
Imperial LP-9167	(M)	Album Seven By Rick	1962	16.00	40.00
Imperial LP-12082	(S)	Album Seven By Rick	1962	30.00	60.00
Imperial LP-9218	(M)	Best Sellers	1963	16.00	40.00
Imperial LP-9232	(M)	Million Sellers	1963	16.00	40.00
Imperial LP-9223	(M)	It's Up To You	1963	16.00	40.00
Imperial LP-9244	(M)	A Long Vacation	1963	12.00	30.00
Imperial LP-12244	(E)	A Long Vacation	1963	10.00	25.00
Imperial LP-9251	(M)	Rick Nelson Sings For You	1964	12.00	30.00
Imperial LP-12251	(E)	Rick Nelson Sings For You	1964	10.00	25.00
		— Original Imperial mono albums above have black labels with stars on top; stereo albums have black labels with silver print.—			
Imperial LP-9048	(M)	Ricky	1966	8.00	20.00
Imperial LP-9218	(M)	Best Sellers	1966	8.00	20.00
Imperial LP-12218	(E)	Best Sellers	1966	5.00	12.00
Imperial LP-9232	(M)	Million Sellers	1966	8.00	20.00
Imperial LP-12232	(E)	Million Sellers	1966	5.00	12.00
		— Imperial albums above have black & green labels.—			
Decca DL-4419	(M)	For Your Sweet Love	1963	10.00	25.00
Decca DL-74419	(S)	For Your Sweet Love	1963	16.00	40.00
Decca DL-4479	(M)	Rick Nelson Sings For You	1963	10.00	25.00
Decca DL-74479	(S)	Rick Nelson Sings For You	1963	16.00	40.00
Decca DL-4559	(M)	The Very Thought Of You	1964	10.00	25.00
Decca DL-74559	(S)	The Very Thought Of You	1964	16.00	40.00
Decca DL-4608	(M)	Spotlight On Rick	1964	10.00	25.00
Decca DL-74608	(S)	Spotlight On Rick	1964	14.00	35.00
Decca DL-4660	(M)	Best Always	1965	10.00	25.00
Decca DL-74660	(S)	Best Always	1965	14.00	35.00
Decca DL-4678	(M)	Love And Kisses	1965	10.00	25.00
Decca DL-74678	(S)	Love And Kisses	1965	14.00	35.00
Decca DL-4779	(M)	Bright Lights And Country Music	1966	10.00	25.00
Decca DL-74779	(S)	Bright Lights And Country Music	1966	14.00	35.00
Decca DL-4827	(M)	Country Fever	1967	10.00	25.00
Decca DL-74827	(S)	Country Fever	1967	14.00	35.00
Decca DL-4836	(M)	On The Flip Side *(TV Soundtrack)*	1967	12.00	30.00
Decca DL-74836	(S)	On The Flip Side *(TV Soundtrack)*	1967	16.00	40.00
		— Original Decca albums above have black labels with "Mfrd by Decca" beneath the rainbow.—			
Decca DL-4944	(M)	Another Side Of Rick	1967	12.00	30.00
Decca DL-74944	(S)	Another Side Of Rick	1967	16.00	40.00
Decca DL-75014	(S)	Perspective	1968	16.00	40.00
Decca DL-75162	(S)	Rick Nelson In Concert *(Gatefold cover)*	1970	8.00	20.00
Decca DL-75236	(S)	Rick Sings Nelson *(With poster)*	1970	10.00	25.00

Another overlooked figure in the development of '60s country rock, former teen idol-cum-crooner Rick Nelson began recording albums that expertly blended country, rock, pop and folk in 1966. *Rick Nelson Country* is a two-record compilation from his previous Decca country/rock albums. With the always excellent Stone Canyon Band, Nelson continued in this vein throughout the rest of his career, although he only enjoyed minimal chart success: "Garden Party" the single was a big hit in 1972 while *Garden Party* the album was a more modest seller.

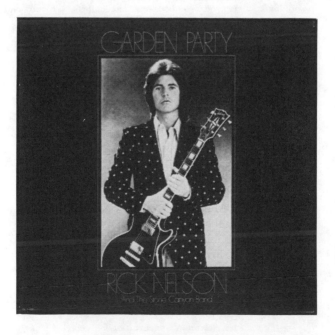

Label & Catalog #		Title	Year	VG+	NM
Decca DL-75297	(S)	**Rudy The Fifth**	1971	6.00	15.00
Decca DL-75391	(S)	**Garden Party**	1972	6.00	15.00
Sunset SUM-4118	(M)	**Ricky Nelson**	1966	6.00	15.00
Sunset SUS-5118	(P)	**Ricky Nelson**	1966	8.00	20.00
Sunset SUS-5205	(S)	**I Need You**	1968	6.00	15.00
United Arts. UAS-960	(M)	**Legendary Masters** (2 LPs. Brown label)	1971	10.00	25.00
MCA 2-4004	(S)	**Rick Nelson Country** (2 LPs)	1973	8.00	20.00
NELSON, SANDY					
Imperial LP-9105	(M)	**Sandy Nelson Plays Teen Beat**	1960	8.00	20.00
Imperial LP-9136	(M)	**He's A Drummer Boy**	1962	8.00	20.00
Imperial LP-9159	(M)	**Let There Be Drums**	1962	8.00	20.00
Imperial LP-9168	(M)	**Drums Are My Beat**	1962	8.00	20.00
Imperial LP-12083	(P)	**Drums Are My Beat**	196?	6.00	15.00
Imperial LP-9189	(M)	**Drummin' Up A Storm**	1962	8.00	20.00
Imperial LP-12189	(S)	**Drummin' Up A Storm**	1962	6.00	15.00
Imperial LP-9202	(M)	**Golden Hits**	1962	8.00	20.00
Imperial LP-12202	(P)	**Golden Hits**	1962	6.00	15.00
Imperial LP-9203	(M)	**On The Wild Side**	1962	8.00	20.00
Imperial LP-12203	(S)	**On The Wild Side**	1962	6.00	15.00
Imperial LP-9204	(M)	**Compelling Percussion**	1962	8.00	20.00
Imperial LP-12204	(S)	**Compelling Percussion**	1962	6.00	15.00
Imperial LP-9215	(M)	**Teenage House Party**	1962	8.00	20.00
Imperial LP-9224	(M)	**The Best Of The Beats**	1963	5.00	12.00
Imperial LP-12224	(S)	**The Best Of The Beats**	1963	6.00	15.00
Imperial LP-9249	(M)	**Sandy Nelson Plays**	1963	5.00	12.00
Imperial LP-12249	(S)	**Sandy Nelson Plays**	1963	6.00	15.00
Imperial LP-9258	(M)	**Be True To Your School**	1963	5.00	12.00
Imperial LP-12258	(S)	**Be True To Your School**	1963	6.00	15.00

— Original Imperial mono albums above have black labels with stars on top; stereo albums have black labels with silver print.—

NELSON, WILLIE					
Liberty LRP-3238	(M)	**And Then I Wrote**	1962	12.00	30.00
Liberty LST-7238	(S)	**And Then I Wrote**	1962	16.00	40.00
Liberty LRP-3308	(M)	**Here's Willie Nelson**	1963	12.00	30.00
Liberty LST-7308	(S)	**Here's Willie Nelson**	1963	16.00	40.00
RCA Victor LPM-3418	(M)	**Country Willie: His Own Songs**	1965	8.00	20.00
RCA Victor LSP-3418	(S)	**Country Willie: His Own Songs**	1965	10.00	25.00
RCA Victor LPM-3528	(M)	**Country Favorites, Willie Nelson Style**	1966	6.00	15.00
RCA Victor LSP-3528	(S)	**Country Favorites, Willie Nelson Style**	1966	8.00	20.00
RCA Victor LPM-3659	(M)	**Live Country Music Concert**	1966	6.00	15.00
RCA Victor LSP-3659	(S)	**Live Country Music Concert**	1966	8.00	20.00
RCA Victor LPM-3748	(M)	**Make Way For Willie Nelson**	1967	6.00	15.00
RCA Victor LSP-3748	(S)	**Make Way For Willie Nelson**	1967	8.00	20.00
RCA Victor LPM-3858	(M)	**The Party's Over**	1967	8.00	20.00
RCA Victor LSP-3858	(S)	**The Party's Over**	1967	8.00	20.00
RCA Victor LPM-3937	(M)	**Texas In My Soul**	1968	20.00	50.00
RCA Victor LSP-3937	(S)	**Texas In My Soul**	1968	8.00	20.00

— Original RCA Victor albums above have black labels.—

RCA Victor LSP-4057	(S)	**Good Times**	1968	6.00	15.00
RCA Victor LSP-4111	(S)	**My Own Peculiar Way**	1969	6.00	15.00
RCA Victor LSP-4294	(S)	**Both Sides Now**	1970	5.00	12.00
RCA Victor LSP-4404	(S)	**Laying My Burdens Down**	1970	5.00	12.00
RCA Victor LSP-4489	(S)	**Willie Nelson And Family**	1971	5.00	12.00
RCA Victor LSP-4568	(S)	**Yesterday's Wine**	1971	5.00	12.00
RCA Victor LSP-4653	(S)	**The Words Don't Fit The Picture**	1971	5.00	12.00
RCA Victor LSP-4760	(S)	**The Willie Way**	1972	5.00	12.00

— Original RCA Victor albums above have orange labels.—

Columbia PAL-35305	(DJ)	**Stardust** (Picture disc)	1978	12.00	30.00
Columbia HC-43482	(S)	**Red Headed Stranger** (Half-speed master)	1982	10.00	25.00
Columbia HC-45305	(S)	**Stardust** (Half-speed master)	1981	20.00	50.00
Columbia HC-47951	(S)	**Always On My Mind** (Half-speed master)	1982	10.00	25.00
Columbia HC-48248	(S)	**Tougher Than Leather** (Half-speed master)	1983	10.00	25.00
Columbia CX-38258	(DJ)	**Always On My Mind** (Picture disc)	1983	10.00	25.00
Columbia 9C-39943	(S)	**Always On My Mind** (Picture disc)	1983	4.00	10.00
Columbia XSM-171010	(DJ)	**Willie Nelson And Family** (Picture disc)	1983	6.00	15.00

Label & Catalog #		Title	Year	VG+	NM

NEP-TUNES, THE

Label & Catalog #		Title	Year	VG+	NM
Family FLP-152	(M)	**Surfer's Holiday**	1963	14.00	35.00
Family SFLP-552	(S)	**Surfer's Holiday**	1963	20.00	50.00

Michael Nesmith's first album went a long way to replace his somewhat awkward image as the "intellectual Monkee" with that of a careful craftsman and a talented singer and songwriter.

NESMITH, MICHAEL

Nesmith was formerly a member of The Monkees. Refer to Wichita Train Whistle.

Label & Catalog #		Title	Year	VG+	NM
RCA Victor LSP-4371	(S)	**Magnetic South**	1970	12.00	30.00
RCA Victor LSP-4415	(S)	**Loose Salute**	1970	10.00	25.00
RCA Victor LSP-4497	(S)	**Nevada Fighter**	1971	10.00	25.00
RCA Victor LSP-4563	(S)	**Tantamount To Treason**	1971	10.00	25.00
RCA Victor LSP-4696	(S)	**And The Hits Just Keep On Comin'**	1972	10.00	25.00
Pacific Arts 7-101	(S)	**The Prison** *(Box with booklet)*	1978	16.00	40.00
Pacific Arts 7-101	(S)	**The Prison** *(Standard cover)*	1978	6.00	15.00
Pacific Arts 7-106	(S)	**Michael Nesmith Compilation**	1978	6.00	15.00
Pacific Arts 7-107	(S)	**From A Radio Engine To The Photon Wing**	1978	6.00	15.00
Pacific Arts 7-116	(S)	**And The Hits Just Keep On Comin'**	1978	6.00	15.00
Pacific Arts 7-117	(S)	**Pretty Much Your Standard Ranch Stash**	1978	6.00	15.00
Pacific Arts 7-118	(S)	**Live At The Palais**	1978	6.00	15.00
Pacific Arts 7-130	(S)	**Infinite Rider On The Big Dogma**	1979	6.00	15.00
Pacific Arts	(DJ)	**The Michael Nesmith Radio Special**	1979	16.00	40.00

NETHERWORLD

Label & Catalog #		Title	Year	VG+	NM
R.E.M. 4441	(S)	**Netherworld**	1981	35.00	70.00

NEVILLE, ARON

Label & Catalog #		Title	Year	VG+	NM
Par-Lo LP-1	(M)	**Tell It Like It Is**	1967	14.00	35.00
Par-Lo LP-1	(S)	**Tell It Like It Is**	1967	20.00	50.00
Minit LP-40007	(M)	**Like It 'Tis**	1967	10.00	25.00
Minit LP-40007	(E)	**Like It 'Tis**	1967	8.00	20.00

NEW COLONY SIX, THE

Label & Catalog #		Title	Year	VG+	NM
Sentar LP-101	(M)	**Breakthrough**	1966	180.00	300.00
Sentar ST-3001	(M)	**Colonization**	1967	8.00	20.00
Sentar SST-3001	(S)	**Colonization**	1967	12.00	30.00

Aaron Neville took "Tell It Like It Is" to the top of many American charts in the early weeks of 1967. The original release on Par-Lo is true stereo; the Minit reissue is rechanneled stereo.

Arguably the most successful female vocalist of the '70s, Olivia's "Physical" album was one of the few to be issued on MCA's short lived half-speed mastered Audiophile series.

Label & Catalog #		Title	Year	VG+	NM
Mercury SR-61165	(S)	Revelations	1968	6.00	15.00
Mercury SR-61228	(S)	Attacking A Straw Man	1969	6.00	15.00

NEW DAWN

| Hoot GR70-4569 | (M) | There's A New Dawn | 1969 | 210.00 | 350.00 |

NEW DIMENSIONS, THE

Sutton SU-331	(M)	Dueces And Eights	1963	8.00	20.00
Sutton SSU-331	(S)	Dueces And Eights	1963	12.00	30.00
Sutton SU-332	(M)	Surf 'N' Bongos	1963	8.00	20.00
Sutton SSU-332	(S)	Surf 'N' Bongos	1963	12.00	30.00
Sutton SU-336	(M)	Soul Surf	1964	8.00	20.00
Sutton SSU-336	(S)	Soul Surf	1964	12.00	30.00

NEW HOPE

| Jamie LPS-3034 | (S) | To Understand Is To Love | 1970 | 8.00 | 20.00 |

NEW LEGION ROCK SPECTACULAR, THE

| Spectacular SPLP-7777 | (S) | Wild Ones! | 197? | 35.00 | 70.00 |

NEW RIDERS OF THE PURPLE SAGE, THE

| Columbia CQ-32450 | (Q) | Adventures Of Panama Red | 1974 | 6.00 | 15.00 |

NEW TWEEDY BROTHERS, THE

| Ridon 234 | (S) | The New Tweedy Brothers | 196? | | See note below |

(Issued in an oversized, hexagonal cover designed to look like an acid laced sugar cube, only a few of which exist today! Estimated near mint value $1,000-2,000.)

| Ridon 234 | (S) | The New Tweedy Brothers (Without cover) | 196? | 180.00 | 300.00 |

NEW VAUDEVILLE BAND, THE

Fontana MGF-27560	(M)	Winchester Cathedral	1966	5.00	12.00
Fontana SRF-67560	(S)	Winchester Cathedral	1966	6.00	15.00
Fontana MGF-27688	(M)	The New Vaudeville Band On Tour	1967	4.00	10.00
Fontana SRF-67588	(S)	The New Vaudeville Band On Tour	1967	5.00	12.00
RCA Victor LSP-4080	(S)	The Bliss Of Mrs. Blossom (Soundtrack)	1968	8.00	20.00

NEW LOST CITY RAMBLERS, THE

Folkways FA-2395	(M)	The New Lost City Ramblers, Volume 1	1960	10.00	25.00
Folkways FA-2396	(M)	The New Lost City Ramblers, Volume 2	1960	10.00	25.00
Folkways FA-2397	(M)	The New Lost City Ramblers, Volume 3	1960	10.00	25.00
Folkways FA-2398	(M)	The New Lost City Ramblers, Volume 4	1960	10.00	25.00
Folkways FA-2399	(M)	The New Lost City Ramblers, Volume 5	1960	10.00	25.00
Folkways FA-2491	(M)	The New Lost City Ramblers	1964	8.00	20.00
Folkways FA-2492	(M)	String Band Instrumentals	1964	8.00	20.00
Folkways FA-2494	(M)	Songs Of The New Lost City Ramblers	1965	8.00	20.00
Folkways FA-2496	(M)	Rural Delivery No. 1	1965	8.00	20.00
Folkways FA-5264	(M)	Songs Of The Depression	1965	8.00	20.00

NEW YORK DOLLS, THE

Both Dolls albums were originally issued with custom dolls labels and inner sleeves.

| Mercury SRM-1-675 | (S) | New York Dolls | 1973 | 10.00 | 25.00 |
| Mercury SRM-1-1001 | (S) | Too Much, Too Soon | 1974 | 10.00 | 25.00 |

NEW YORK ROCK & ROLL ENSEMBLE, THE [THE NEW YORK ROCK ENSEMBLE]

The Ensemble features Michael Kamen.

Atco SD-33-240	(S)	New York Rock & Roll Ensemble	1968	6.00	15.00
Atco SD-33-294	(S)	Faithful Friends	1969	6.00	15.00
Atco SD-33-312	(S)	Reflections	1970	6.00	15.00

NEWBEATS, THE

Larry Henley, Dean Mathis and Mark Mathis.

Hickory LP-120	(M)	Bread And Butter	1964	35.00	70.00
Hickory LPS-120	(S)	Bread And Butter	1964	75.00	150.00
Hickory LP-122	(M)	Big Beat Sounds By The Newbeats	1965	20.00	50.00
Hickory LPS-122	(S)	Big Beat Sounds By The Newbeats	1965	35.00	70.00
Hickory LP-128	(M)	Run Baby Run	1965	20.00	50.00
Hickory LPS-128	(S)	Run Baby Run	1965	35.00	70.00

Label & Catalog #		Title	Year	VG+	NM
NEWMAN, BOB					
Audio Lab AL-1536	(M)	The Kentucky Colonel	195?	20.00	50.00
NEWMAN, JIMMY C.					
MGM E-3777	(M)	This Is Jimmy Newman	1959	8.00	20.00
MGM SE-3777	(S)	This Is Jimmy Newman	1959	10.00	25.00
MGM E-4045	(M)	Songs By Jimmy Newman	1962	6.00	15.00
MGM SE-4045	(S)	Songs By Jimmy Newman	1962	8.00	20.00
Decca DL-4221	(M)	Jimmy Newman	1962	5.00	12.00
Decca DL-74221	(S)	Jimmy Newman	1962	6.00	15.00
Decca DL-4398	(M)	Folk Songs Of The Bayou Country	1963	5.00	12.00
Decca DL-74398	(S)	Folk Songs Of The Bayou Country	1963	6.00	15.00
Decca DL-4748	(M)	Artificial Rose	1966	4.00	10.00
Decca DL-74748	(S)	Artificial Rose	1966	5.00	12.00
Decca DL-4781	(M)	Jimmy Newman Sings Country Songs	1966	4.00	10.00
Decca DL-74781	(S)	Jimmy Newman Sings Country Songs	1966	5.00	12.00
Dot DLP-3390	(M)	A Fallen Star	1966	5.00	12.00
Dot DLP-25390	(E)	A Fallen Star	1966	4.00	10.00
Dot DLP-3736	(M)	Country Crossroads	1966	4.00	10.00
Dot DLP-25736	(S)	Country Crossroads	1966	5.00	12.00
NEWMAN, RANDY					
Epic LN-24147	(M)	Peyton Place (TV Soundtrack)	1965	16.00	40.00
Epic BN-26147	(S)	Peyton Place (TV Soundtrack)	1965	20.00	50.00
Reprise RS-6286	(S)	Randy Newman	1968	8.00	20.00
		(Full color cover of Newman in the clouds.)			
Reprise RS-6286	(S)	Randy Newman	1969	5.00	12.00
		(Black & white close-up cover.)			
Reprise RS-6373	(S)	12 Songs	1970	5.00	12.00
Reprise PRO-484	(DJ)	Randy Newman Live	1971	20.00	50.00
Reprise MS-2064	(S)	Sail Away (With poster)	1972	6.00	15.00
		(Original covers do not list the song titles on the back.)			
Reprise MS4-2193	(Q)	Good Old Boys	1974	6.00	15.00
NEWTON-JOHN, OLIVIA					
Uni 73117	(S)	If Not For You	1971	16.00	40.00
MCA 3067	(S)	Totally Hot (Picture disc)	1979	8.00	20.00
MCA 16011	(S)	Physical (Half-speed master)	1981	8.00	20.00
Mobile Fidelity MFSL-040	(S)	Totally Hot	1981	6.00	15.00
NEXT MORNING, THE					
Calla SC-2002	(S)	The Next Morning	1972	75.00	150.00
NICE, THE					
Immediate Z12-52004	(S)	Thoughts of Emerlist Davjack	1968	5.00	12.00
Immediate Z12-52020	(S)	Ars Longa Vita Brevis	1969	5.00	12.00
Immediate Z12-52022	(S)	The Nice	1969	5.00	12.00
Immediate Z12-52026	(S)	Nice	1971	5.00	12.00
Sire SASH-3710	(S)	The Immediate Story (2 LPs)	1975	5.00	12.00
NICHOLAS BROTHERS, THE					
Mercury MG-20355	(M)	We Do Sing, Too	195?	8.00	20.00
NICHOLS, MIKE, & ELAINE MAY					
Mercury MG-20376	(M)	Improvisations To Music	1959	16.00	40.00
Mercury OCM-2200	(M)	An Evening With Mike Nichols & Elaine May	1960	12.00	30.00
Mercury OCS-6200	(S)	An Evening With Mike Nichols & Elaine May	1960	16.00	40.00
Mercury MG-20680	(M)	Examine Doctors	1962	6.00	15.00
Mercury SR-60680	(S)	Examine Doctors	1962	8.00	20.00
Mercury MG-20997	(M)	The Best Of Mike Nichols & Elaine May	1965	5.00	12.00
Mercury SR-60997	(S)	The Best Of Mike Nichols & Elaine May	1965	6.00	15.00
NICHOLS, NICHELLE					
Epic LN-24351	(M)	Down To Earth	1968	16.00	40.00
Epic BN-26351	(S)	Down To Earth	1968	16.00	40.00
NICKEL BAG, THE					
Kama Sutra KLPS-8066	(S)	Doing Their Love Thing	1968	6.00	15.00

Berlin's contribution to the art of monotone, Nico first captured the eye of Brian Jones, who steered her to Stones manager Andrew Oldham, who recorded her on his Immediate label in 1965. She met Andy Warhol and, after accepting a role in his film "Chelsea Girls," performed as a member of the Velvet Underground (their first album is, appropriately, titled *The Velvet Underground & Nico*).

For this, her first solo album, she recorded songs by both Lou Reed and John Cale (and a teenaged Jackson Browne), making this album a peripheral Velvet collectible. She continued to work with Cale, who produced two of her later albums, *The Marble Index* and *Desert Shore*.

Label & Catalog #		Title	Year	VG+	NM
NICKS, STEVIE					
Refer to Buckingham/Nicks; Fleetwood Mac.					
Mobile Fidelity MFSL-121	(S)	Bella Donna	1982	10.00	25.00
NICO					
Verve V-5032	(M)	Chelsea Girl	1967	8.00	20.00
Verve V6-5032	(S)	Chelsea Girl	1967	10.00	25.00
Elektra EKS-74029	(S)	The Marble Index	1968	8.00	20.00
Reprise RS-6424	(S)	Desert Shore	1970	8.00	20.00
Island ILPS-9311	(S)	The End	1975	6.00	15.00
NIGHT OWLS, THE					
Valmor 79	(M)	Twisting The Oldies	1962	20.00	50.00
NIGHT SHADOWS, THE					
Spectrum	(S)	The Square Root Of Two	1968	660.00	1,000.00
Hottrax 1414	(S)	The Square Root Of Two	1968	75.00	150.00
Hottrax 1430	(S)	Live At The Spot	1981	10.00	25.00
NIGHTCAPS, THE					
Vandan VRLP-8124	(M)	Wine, Wine, Wine	196?	60.00	120.00
NIGHTCRAWLERS, THE					
Kapp KL-1520	(M)	The Little Black Egg	1967	30.00	60.00
Kapp KS-3520	(E)	The Little Black Egg	1967	20.00	50.00
NIGHTHAWKS, THE					
Aladdin 101	(M)	Rock And Roll	195?	100.00	200.00
NIELSEN, GERTRUDE					
Decca DL-5138 (10")	(M)	Gertrude Nielsen	1951	14.00	35.00
NILES, JOHN JACOB					
Camden CAL-219	(M)	American Folk And Gambling Songs	195?	8.00	20.00
Camden CAL-245	(M)	American Folk Songs	195?	8.00	20.00
Camden CAL-330	(M)	50th Anniversary Album	196?	6.00	15.00
Boone Tolliver BTR-22	(M)	American Folk Love Songs	196?	8.00	20.00
Boone Tolliver BTR-23	(M)	Ballads	196?	8.00	20.00
Tradition TRP-1023	(M)	I Wonder As I Wander	196?	6.00	15.00
NILSSON [HARRY NILSSON]					
Tower T-5095	(M)	Spotlight On Nilsson	1967	6.00	15.00
Tower DT-5095	(E)	Spotlight On Nilsson	1967	5.00	12.00
RCA Victor LPM-3874	(M)	Pandemonium Shadow Show	1967	5.00	12.00
RCA Victor LSP-3874	(S)	Pandemonium Shadow Show	1967	6.00	15.00
RCA Victor	(DJ)	The True One	1967	50.00	100.00
		(Boxed set includes a copy of LPM-3874, two black & white			
		glossy photos, a button, poster, stickers and bios.)			
RCA Victor LPM-3956	(M)	Aerial Ballet	1968	12.00	30.00
RCA Victor LSP-3956	(S)	Aerial Ballet	1968	6.00	15.00
RCA Victor LSO-1152	(S)	Skidoo (Soundtrack)	1968	8.00	20.00
		— Original RCA albums above have black labels.—			
RCA Victor LSP-4197	(S)	Harry	1969	4.00	10.00
RCA Victor LSP-4289	(S)	Nilsson Sings Newman	1969	6.00	15.00
RCA SPS-33-567	(DJ)	Scatalogue (With insert)	197?	20.00	50.00
Musicor MS-2505	(S)	Eary Times	1970	5.00	12.00
RCA Victor LSP-4417	(S)	The Point (TV Soundtrack with booklet)	1971	5.00	12.00
RCA Victor LSP-4543	(S)	Aerial Pandemonium Ballet	1971	4.00	10.00
RCA Victor LSP-4515	(S)	Nilsson Schmilsson	1971	4.00	10.00
RCA Victor LSP-4717	(S)	Son Of Schmilsson	1972	4.00	10.00
RCA Victor APL1-0097	(S)	A Little Touch Of Schmilsson In The Night	1973	4.00	10.00
Rapple ABL1-0220	(S)	Son Of Dracula (Soundtrack)	1974	4.00	10.00
RCA Victor CPL1-0570	(S)	Pussy Cats	1974	6.00	15.00
RCA Victor APD1-0570	(Q)	Pussy Cats	1974	8.00	20.00
		("Pussy Cats" features John Lennon as producer and performer.)			
RCA Victor APD1-0817	(Q)	Duit On Mon Dei	1975	5.00	12.00
RCA Victor APD1-1031	(Q)	Sandman	1976	5.00	12.00
		— Original RCA albums above have orange labels.—			

After his first two albums of charm, ingenuity and vocal acrobatics, *Pandemonium Shadow Show* and *Aerial Ballet*, failed to set the charts on fire (even though *Ballet* was mentioned by John Lennon as his favorite American album), RCA condensed the two into one, *Aerial Pandemonium Ballet*, remixing the tracks along the way, making the hybrid a unique listening experience and an essential for any fan of the man... Beginning in 1966, several artists took notice of an idiosyncratic songwriter from L.A., Randy Newman, recording several of his songs on their albums. But it took equally idiosyncratic Harry Nilsson to dedicate an entire album to the talented tunesmith. While *Nilsson Sings Newman* enjoyed immediate critical success, it dropped out of sight on the marketplace.

Label & Catalog #		Title	Year	VG+	NM

NIMOY, LEONARD
Mr. Nimoy was formerly a member of the U.S.S. Enterprise.

Label & Catalog #		Title	Year	VG+	NM
Dot DLP-3794	(M)	Mr. Spock's Music From Outer Space	1967	16.00	40.00
Dot DLP-25794	(S)	Mr. Spock's Music From Outer Space	1967	20.00	50.00
Dot DLP-3835	(M)	Two Sides Of Leonard Nimoy	1968	12.00	30.00
Dot DLP-25835	(S)	Two Sides Of Leonard Nimoy	1968	12.00	30.00
Dot DLP-25883	(S)	The Way I Feel	1968	10.00	25.00
Dot DLP-25910	(S)	The Touch Of Leonard Nimoy	1969	10.00	25.00
Dot DLP-25966	(S)	The New World Of Leonard Nimoy	1969	14.00	35.00
Paramount 1030	(S)	Outer Space/Inner Mind	1970	12.00	30.00
Pickwick SPC-3199	(S)	Space Odyssey	197?	10.00	25.00
Sears SPS-491	(S)	Leonard Nimoy	197?	10.00	25.00
Caedmon TC-1520	(S)	H.G. Wells' "War Of The Worlds"	1976	16.00	40.00

NINA & FREDERIK

Label & Catalog #		Title	Year	VG+	NM
Atco 33-119	(M)	Introducing The Fabulous Nina & Frederik	1960	5.00	12.00
Atco SD-33-119	(S)	Introducing The Fabulous Nina & Frederik	1960	6.00	15.00
Atco 33-154	(M)	Where Have All The Flowers Gone?	1963	5.00	12.00
Atco SD-33-154	(S)	Where Have All The Flowers Gone?	1963	6.00	15.00
Atco 33-217	(M)	Lovers Of The World Unite	1967	4.00	10.00
Atco SD-33-217	(S)	Lovers Of The World Unite	1967	5.00	12.00

NIRVANA

Label & Catalog #		Title	Year	VG+	NM
Bell 6015	(S)	The Story Of Simon Simopath	1968	10.00	25.00
Bell 6024	(S)	All Of Us	1969	10.00	25.00
Metromedia 1018	(S)	Nirvana	1970	10.00	25.00

NITTY GRITTY DIRT BAND, THE [THE DIRT BAND]

Label & Catalog #		Title	Year	VG+	NM
Liberty LRP-3501	(M)	The Nitty Gritty Dirt Band	1967	6.00	15.00
Liberty LST-7501	(S)	The Nitty Gritty Dirt Band	1967	8.00	20.00
Liberty LRP-3516	(M)	Ricochet	1967	6.00	15.00
Liberty LST-7516	(S)	Ricochet	1967	8.00	20.00
Liberty LST-7540	(S)	Rare Junk	1968	8.00	20.00
Liberty LST-7611	(S)	Alive	1969	8.00	20.00

This attractive promo pack is a book-like folder that includes: a copy of the album; a 7" interview,
SP-37, in a special sleeve; a 10" 78 rpm interview; four glossy black & white photos; and
a sixty page collection of articles, reviews, etc. from the group's past.

Label & Catalog #		Title	Year	VG+	NM
Liberty LST-7642	(S)	Uncle Charlie & His Dog Teddy	1970	6.00	15.00
Liberty LST-7642	(DJ)	Uncle Charlie & His Dog Teddy Promo Pack	1970	75.00	150.00
United Arts. SP-117	(DJ)	The Nitty Gritty Dirt Band Interview	1975	8.00	20.00
United Arts. LA469	(DJ)	A Programmers Guide To Dream	1975	12.00	30.00
NITZSCHE, JACK					
Reprise R-6101	(M)	The Lonely Surfer	1963	20.00	50.00
Reprise RS-6101	(S)	The Lonely Surfer	1963	35.00	70.00
Reprise R-6115	(M)	Dance To The Hits Of The Beatles	1964	12.00	30.00
Reprise RS-6115	(S)	Dance To The Hits Of The Beatles	1964	16.00	40.00
Reprise R-6200	(M)	Chopin '66	1966	6.00	15.00
Reprise RS-6200	(S)	Chopin '66	1966	8.00	20.00
Reprise MS-2092	(S)	St. Giles Cripplegate	1972	8.00	20.00
NOBLES, CLIFF, & COMPANY					
Phil L.A. Of Soul 4001	(S)	The Horse	1968	12.00	30.00
Moon Shot 601	(S)	Pony The Horse	1969	6.00	15.00
NOLAND, TERRY					
Brunswick BL-54041	(M)	Terry Noland	1958	100.00	200.00
NORDINE, KEN					
Decca DL-8550	(M)	Concert In The Sky	1957	20.00	50.00
Dot DLP-3075	(M)	Word Jazz	1957	20.00	50.00
Dot DLP-3096	(M)	Son Of Word Jazz	1958	14.00	35.00
Dot DLP-25096	(S)	Son Of Word Jazz	1958	20.00	50.00
Dot DLP-3115	(M)	Love Words	1958	14.00	35.00
Dot DLP-25115	(S)	Love Words	1958	20.00	50.00
Dot DLP-3142	(M)	My Baby	1958	14.00	35.00
Dot DLP-25142	(S)	My Baby	1958	20.00	50.00
Dot DLP-3196	(M)	Next!	1959	14.00	35.00
Dot DLP-25196	(S)	Next!	1959	20.00	50.00
Dot DLP-3301	(M)	Word Jazz, Volume 2	1960	14.00	35.00
Dot DLP-25301	(S)	Word Jazz, Volume 2	1960	20.00	50.00
Hamilton H-12102	(M)	The Voice Of Love	1959	10.00	25.00
Philips PHM-200224	(M)	Colors	196?	10.00	25.00
Philips PHS-600224	(S)	Colors	196?	14.00	35.00
Philips PHM-200258	(M)	Twink	196?	10.00	25.00
Philips PHS-600258	(S)	Twink	196?	14.00	35.00
Dot DLP-25880	(S)	Classic Collection/Best Of Word Jazz	1968	10.00	25.00
NORMA JEAN					
Norma Jean also recorded with Porter Wagoner.					
RCA Victor LPM-2961	(M)	Let's Go All The Way	1964	5.00	12.00
RCA Victor LSP-2961	(S)	Let's Go All The Way	1964	6.00	15.00
RCA Victor LPM-3449	(M)	Pretty Miss Norma Jean	1965	5.00	12.00
RCA Victor LSP-3449	(S)	Pretty Miss Norma Jean	1965	6.00	15.00
RCA Victor LPM-3541	(M)	Please Don't Hurt Me	1966	5.00	12.00
RCA Victor LSP-3541	(S)	Please Don't Hurt Me	1966	6.00	15.00
RCA Victor LPM-3664	(M)	A Tribute To Kitty Wells	1966	5.00	12.00
RCA Victor LSP-3664	(S)	A Tribute To Kitty Wells	1966	6.00	15.00
RCA Victor LPM-3700	(M)	Norma Jean Sings Porter Wagoner	1967	5.00	12.00
RCA Victor LSP-3700	(S)	Norma Jean Sings Porter Wagoner	1967	6.00	15.00
RCA Victor LPM-3836	(M)	Jackson Ain't A Very Big Town	1967	5.00	12.00
RCA Victor LSP-3836	(S)	Jackson Ain't A Very Big Town	1967	6.00	15.00
RCA Victor LPM-3910	(M)	Heaven's Just A Prayer Away	1968	10.00	25.00
RCA Victor LSP-3910	(S)	Heaven's Just A Prayer Away	1968	6.00	15.00
— Original RCA albums above have black labels.—					
NORMAN, LARRY					
Larry was formerly a member of People.					
Capitol ST-446	(S)	Upon This Rock	1970	16.00	40.00
One Way JC-7937	(S)	Street Level	1970	10.00	25.00
One Way JC-900	(S)	Bootleg	1971	10.00	25.00
MGM SE-4942	(S)	So Long Ago/The Garden	1973	12.00	30.00
Solid Rock SRA-2001	(S)	In Another Land	197?	6.00	15.00
Street Level 8885	(S)	Only Visiting This Planet	197?	6.00	15.00
Sunrise AB-777	(S)	Streams Of White Light	197?	6.00	15.00
Impac HWS-3121	(S)	Upon This Rock	197?	6.00	15.00

Label & Catalog #		Title	Year	VG+	NM
NORTH, JAY					
Kem LP-27	(M)	**Look Who's Singing!**	195?	35.00	70.00
Colpix CP-204	(M)	**The Mis-Adventures Of Dennis The Menace** (TV Soundtrack)	196?	50.00	100.00
NORTHERN FRONT, THE					
No label	(M)	**The Furniture Store**	196?	40.00	80.00
NOSY PARKER					
No label	(S)	**Nosy Parker**	1975	180.00	300.00
NOTES FROM THE UNDERGROUND					
Vanguard VSD-6502	(S)	**Notes From The Underground**	1970	8.00	20.00
NOVA LOCAL, THE					
Decca DL-74977	(S)	**Nova 1**	1968	10.00	25.00
NOVELLS, THE					
Mother's MLPS-73	(S)	**That Did It!**	197?	20.00	50.00
NOVY, LEN & JUDY					
Prestige PR-7355	(M)	**Folk Songs, Sweet And Bittersweet**	1965	5.00	12.00
Prestige PRS-7355	(S)	**Folk Songs, Sweet And Bittersweet**	1965	6.00	15.00
NRBQ [THE NEW RHYTHM & BLUES QUINTET]					
Refer to Carl Perkins; Wildweeds.					
Columbia CS-9858	(S)	**NRBQ** ("360 Sound" label)	1969	6.00	15.00
Kama Sutra KSBS-2045	(S)	**Scraps**	1972	8.00	20.00
Kama Sutra KSBS-2065	(S)	**Workshop**	1973	12.00	30.00
Annuit Coeptis 1001	(S)	**Scraps/Workshop** (2 LPs)	1976	6.00	15.00
Mercury SRM-1-3712	(S)	**NRBQ At Yankee Stadium**	1978	5.00	12.00
Red Rooster 101	(S)	**All Hopped Up**	1977	6.00	15.00
Red Rooster 3029	(S)	**All Hopped Up**	1979	4.00	10.00
Red Rooster 3030	(S)	**Kick Me Hard**	1979	4.00	10.00
Red Rooster 3048	(S)	**Tiddly Winks**	1980	4.00	10.00
Red Rooster 3055	(S)	**Scraps**	1982	4.00	10.00
Red Rooster 3066	(S)	**Tapdancin' Bats**	1983	4.00	10.00
Bearsville 23187	(S)	**Grooves In Orbit**	1983	4.00	10.00
NUGENT, TED					
Nugent was formerly a member of The Amboy Dukes.					
Epic PEQ-34121	(Q)	**Free For All**	1976	6.00	15.00
Epic AS-99-607	(DJ)	**State Of Shock** (Picture disc)	1979	6.00	15.00
NUTMEGS, THE					
Herald H-452	(M)	**The Nutmegs**	1958	180.00	300.00
NUTTY SQUIRRELS, THE					
Hanover HML-8014	(M)	**The Nutty Squirrels**	1960	10.00	25.00
Columbia CL-1589	(M)	**Bird Watching**	1961	6.00	15.00
Columbia CS-8389	(S)	**Bird Watching**	1961	10.00	25.00
MGM E-4272	(M)	**A Hard Day's Night**	1964	8.00	20.00
MGM SE-4272	(S)	**A Hard Day's Night**	1964	10.00	25.00
NYE, LOUIS					
Riverside 842	(M)	**Heigh-Ho, Madison Avenue**	196?	8.00	20.00
Signature SM-2004	(M)	**Man On The Street**	196?	8.00	20.00
United Arts. UAL-4089	(M)	**Here's Nye In You Eye**	196?	8.00	20.00
NYRO, LAURA					
Folkways FT-3020	(M)	**More Than A New Discovery**	1967	6.00	15.00
Folkways FTS-3020	(S)	**More Than A New Discovery**	1967	8.00	20.00
Columbia CL-2826	(M)	**Eli And The 13th Confession**	1968	8.00	20.00
Columbia CS-9626	(S)	**Eli And The 13th Confession**	1968	6.00	15.00
Columbia CS-9737	(S)	**New York Tendaberry**	1969	6.00	15.00
— Original Columbia albums above have "360 Sound" on the bottom of the label.—					
Columbia KC-30259	(S)	**Christmas And The Beads Of Sweat**	1970	4.00	10.00
Columbia KC-30987	(S)	**Gonna Take A Miracle**	1971	4.00	10.00
Columbia KC-31410	(S)	**The First Songs**	1971	4.00	10.00

Label & Catalog #		Title	Year	VG+	NM

O' BRIEN, HUGH

ABC-Paramount 203	(M)	Wyatt Earp Sings	1957	20.00	50.00

O' CONNELL, HELEN

Vik LX-1093	(M)	Green Eyes	1957	16.00	40.00
Cameo C-1045	(M)	An Era Reborn	1963	6.00	15.00
Cameo CS-1045	(S)	An Era Reborn	1963	8.00	20.00

O' DAY, ANITA

Advance 8 (10")	(M)	Anita O' Day Specials	1951	75.00	150.00
Clef 130 (10")	(M)	Anita O' Day Collates	1953	50.00	100.00
Coral CRL-56073 (10")	(M)	Singin' And Swingin'	1953	50.00	100.00
Norgran 30 (10")	(M)	Anita O' Day	1954	50.00	100.00
Norgran 1049	(M)	Anita O' Day Sings Jazz	1955	20.00	50.00
Norgran 1057	(M)	An Evening With Anita O' Day	1956	16.00	40.00
Verve V-2000	(M)	Anita	1956	16.00	40.00
Verve V-2043	(M)	Pick Yourself Up	1956	16.00	40.00
Verve V-2049	(M)	The Lady Is A Tramp	1956	16.00	40.00
Verve V-2050	(M)	An Evening With Anita O' Day	1956	16.00	40.00
Verve V-8259	(M)	Anita Sings The Most	1958	16.00	40.00
A.R.S. G-426	(M)	For Oscar	1957	20.00	50.00
		(Issued in a plastic sleeve with four page insert.)			
Verve V-8283	(M)	Anita O' Day Sings The Winners	1958	12.00	30.00
Verve V6-6002	(S)	Anita O' Day Sings The Winners	1958	16.00	40.00
Verve V-2113	(M)	Anita O' Day At Mr. Kelly's	1958	12.00	30.00
Verve V6-6043	(S)	Anita O' Day At Mr. Kelly's	1958	16.00	40.00
Verve V-2118	(M)	Anita O' Day Swings Cole Porter	1959	12.00	30.00
Verve V6-6059	(S)	Anita O' Day Swings Cole Porter	1959	16.00	40.00
Verve V-8312	(M)	Cool Heat	1959	12.00	30.00
Verve V6-6046	(S)	Cool Heat	1959	16.00	40.00
Verve V-2141	(M)	Anita O' Day Swings Rodgers And Hart	1959	12.00	30.00
Verve V-2145	(M)	Waiter, Make Mine Blues	1960	8.00	20.00
Verve V6-2145	(S)	Waiter, Make Mine Blues	1960	12.00	30.00
Verve V-2157	(M)	Trav'lin' Light	1961	8.00	20.00
Verve V6-2157	(S)	Trav'lin' Light	1961	12.00	30.00
Verve V-8442	(M)	All The Sad Young Men	1961	8.00	20.00
Verve V6-8442	(S)	All The Sad Young Men	1961	12.00	30.00

— Original Verve albums above have black labels with "Verve Records, Inc" on the bottom.—

Verve V-8472	(M)	Time For Two	1962	8.00	20.00
Verve V6-8472	(S)	Time For Two	1962	10.00	25.00
Verve V-8483	(M)	That Is Anita	1962	8.00	20.00
Verve V6-8483	(E)	That Is Anita	1962	5.00	12.00
Verve V-8514	(M)	Anita O' Day And The Three Sounds	1963	8.00	20.00
Verve V6-8514	(S)	Anita O' Day And The Three Sounds	1963	10.00	25.00
Verve V-8572	(M)	Incomparable Anita O' Day	1964	8.00	20.00
Verve V6-8572	(S)	Incomparable Anita O' Day	1964	10.00	25.00

O' DELL, MAC

Audio Lab AL-1544	(M)	Hymns For The Country Folk	1960	50.00	100.00

O' HARA, MAUREEN

Columbia CL-1750	(M)	Her Favorite Irish Songs	1961	16.00	40.00
Columbia CS-8550	(S)	Her Favorite Irish Songs	1961	20.00	50.00

O' JAYS, THE

Imperial LP-9290	(M)	Comin' Through	1965	10.00	25.00
Imperial LP-12290	(S)	Comin' Through	1965	12.00	30.00
Minit LP-4008	(M)	Soul Sounds	1967	8.00	20.00
Minit LP-24008	(S)	Soul Sounds	1967	10.00	25.00
Bell 6014	(S)	Back On Top	1968	6.00	15.00

Label & Catalog #		Title	Year	VG+	NM
Sunset SUS-5222	(S)	Full Of Soul	1968	4.00	10.00
United Arts. UAS-5655	(P)	The O' Jays' Greatest Hits	1972	4.00	10.00
Bell 6082	(S)	The O' Jays	1973	4.00	10.00
Phila. Inter. ASZ-140	(DJ)	Everything You Always Wanted To Hear	197?	5.00	12.00
Phila. Inter. ZQ-32408	(Q)	Ship Ahoy	1974	5.00	12.00
Phila. Inter. ZQ-32953	(Q)	The O' Jays Live In London	1974	5.00	12.00
Phila. Inter. PZQ-33807	(Q)	Family Reunion	1975	5.00	12.00

O' KAYSIONS, THE

ABC S-664	(P)	Girl Watcher	1968	10.00	25.00

OAK RIDGE BOYS, THE [THE OAK RIDGE QUARTET]

Cadence CLP-3019	(M)	The Oak Ridge Quartet	1959	20.00	50.00
Warner Bros. W-1497	(M)	The Oak Ridge Boys	1963	8.00	20.00
Warner Bros. WS-1497	(S)	The Oak Ridge Boys	1963	12.00	30.00
Warner Bros. W-1521	(M)	Folk Minded Spirituals	1963	8.00	20.00
Warner Bros. WS-1521	(S)	Folk Minded Spirituals	1963	12.00	30.00
Skylite M-6020	(M)	The Oak Ridge Boys Sing For You	1964	8.00	20.00
Skylite M-6030	(M)	I Wouldn't Take Nothing For My Journey Now	1965	6.00	15.00
Skylite S-6030	(S)	I Wouldn't Take Nothing For My Journey Now	1965	8.00	20.00
Starday SLP-356	(M)	The Sensational Oak Ridge Boys	1965	8.00	20.00
Skylite M-6040	(M)	The Solid Gospel Sound Of The Oak Ridge Boys	1966	5.00	12.00
Skylite S-6040	(S)	The Solid Gospel Sound Of The Oak Ridge Boys	1966	6.00	15.00
Skylite M-6045	(M)	River Of Love	1967	5.00	12.00
Skylite S-6045	(S)	River Of Love	1967	6.00	15.00
United Arts. UAL-3554	(M)	The Oak Ridge Boys At Their Best	1966	6.00	15.00
United Arts. UAS-6554	(S)	The Oak Ridge Boys At Their Best	1966	8.00	20.00
Columbia PC-33935	(S)	The Oak Ridge Boys	1976	6.00	15.00
MCA 51247	(DJ)	Sail Away (Picture disc)	1979	20.00	50.00

OBJECTS, THE

No label	(S)	Live At The Greatwood Cafe	1980	50.00	100.00

OBOLER, ARCH

Capitol T-1763	(M)	Drop Dead! An Exercise In Horror	1962	5.00	12.00
Capitol ST-1763	(S)	Drop Dead! An Exercise In Horror	1962	6.00	15.00

OCHS, PHIL

Elektra EKL-269	(M)	All The News That's Fit To Sing	1964	8.00	20.00
Elektra EKS-7269	(S)	All The News That's Fit To Sing	1964	12.00	30.00
Elektra EKL-287	(M)	I Ain't Marching Anymore	1965	8.00	20.00
Elektra EKS-7287	(S)	I Ain't Marching Anymore	1965	12.00	30.00
Elektra EKL-310	(M)	Phil Ochs In Concert	1965	8.00	20.00
Elektra EKS-7310	(S)	Phil Ochs In Concert	1965	12.00	30.00
A&M LP-133	(M)	Pleasures Of The Harbor	1967	6.00	15.00
A&M SP-4133	(S)	Pleasures Of The Harbor	1967	8.00	20.00
A&M SP-4148	(S)	Tape From California	1968	8.00	20.00
A&M SP-4181	(S)	Rehearsals For Retirement	1969	8.00	20.00
A&M SP-4253	(S)	Phil Ochs' Greatest Hits	1970	8.00	20.00

— Original A&M albums above have brown labels. —

ODA

Loud A0011	(S)	Oda	197?	180.00	300.00

ODETTA

Fantasy 3-15 (10")	(M)	Odetta And Lary	1955	16.00	40.00
Fantasy F-3252	(M)	Odetta	1957	12.00	30.00
Tradition TRP-1010	(M)	Ballads And Blues	1956	12.00	30.00
Tradition TRP-1025	(M)	Odetta At The Gate Of Horn	1957	12.00	30.00
Vanguard VRS-9059	(M)	My Eyes Have Seen	1960	6.00	15.00
Vanguard VSD-72046	(S)	My Eyes Have Seen	1960	8.00	20.00
Vanguard VRS-9066	(M)	Ballads For Americans	1960	6.00	15.00
Vanguard VSD-72057	(S)	Ballads For Americans	1960	8.00	20.00
Vanguard VRS-9076	(M)	Odetta At Carnegie Hall	1961	6.00	15.00
Vanguard VSD-72072	(S)	Odetta At Carnegie Hall	1961	8.00	20.00

Label & Catalog #		Title	Year	VG+	NM
Vanguard VRS-2079	(M)	**Christmas Spirituals**	1961	6.00	15.00
Vanguard VSD-72079	(S)	**Christmas Spirituals**	1961	8.00	20.00
Riverside RLP-417	(M)	**Odetta And The Blues**	1962	6.00	15.00
Riverside RS-9417	(S)	**Odetta And The Blues**	1962	8.00	20.00
Vanguard VRS-2109	(M)	**Odetta At Town Hall**	1962	6.00	15.00
Vanguard VSD-72109	(S)	**Odetta At Town Hall**	1962	8.00	20.00
Vanguard VRS-2153	(M)	**One Grain Of Sand**	1963	6.00	15.00
Vanguard VSD-72153	(S)	**One Grain Of Sand**	1963	8.00	20.00
Vanguard VRS-3003	(M)	**Odetta At Carnegie Hall**	1964	5.00	12.00
Vanguard VSD-73003	(S)	**Odetta At Carnegie Hall**	1964	6.00	15.00
RCA Victor LPM-2573	(M)	**Sometimes I Feel Like Crying**	1962	6.00	15.00
RCA Victor LSP-2573	(S)	**Sometimes I Feel Like Crying**	1962	8.00	20.00
RCA Victor LPM-2643	(M)	**Odetta Sings Folk Songs**	1963	6.00	15.00
RCA Victor LSP-2643	(S)	**Odetta Sings Folk Songs**	1963	8.00	20.00
RCA Victor LPM-2792	(M)	**It's A Mighty World**	1964	6.00	15.00
RCA Victor LSP-2792	(S)	**It's A Mighty World**	1964	8.00	20.00
RCA Victor LPM-2923	(M)	**Odetta Sings Of Many Things**	1964	6.00	15.00
RCA Victor LSP-2923	(S)	**Odetta Sings Of Many Things**	1964	8.00	20.00
RCA Victor LPM-3324	(M)	**Odetta Sings Dylan**	1965	8.00	20.00
RCA Victor LSP-3324	(S)	**Odetta Sings Dylan**	1965	10.00	25.00
RCA Victor LPM-3457	(M)	**Odetta In Japan**	1966	6.00	15.00
RCA Victor LSP-3457	(S)	**Odetta In Japan**	1966	8.00	20.00

— Original RCA albums above have black labels.—

ODYSSEY

Organic ORG-1	(M)	**Odyssey**	196?	660.00	1,000.00

OHIO EXPRESS, THE

Cameo CS-20,000	(S)	**Beg, Borrow And Steal**	1968	16.00	40.00

OHIO PLAYERS, THE

Capitol ST-192	(S)	**Observations In Time**	1969	8.00	20.00

OLAY, RUTH

EmArcy 36125	(M)	**Ole! Olay**	1958	14.00	35.00
Mercury MG-20390	(M)	**Easy Living**	1959	12.00	30.00
Mercury SR-60390	(S)	**Easy Living**	1959	16.00	40.00
United Arts. UAL-3115	(M)	**Ruth Olay In Person**	1960	8.00	20.00
United Arts. UAL-6115	(S)	**Ruth Olay In Person**	1960	12.00	30.00
Everest 5218	(M)	**Olay! OK!**	1963	6.00	15.00
Everest 1218	(S)	**Olay! OK!**	1963	8.00	20.00

OLD & IN THE WAY
Features Jerry Garcia of The Grateful Dead.

Round RX-103	(S)	**Old And In The Way**	1975	8.00	20.00

OLDFIELD, MIKE

Virgin HE-44116	(S)	**Tubular Bells** *(Half-speed master)*	198?	10.00	25.00

OLDHAM ORCHESTRA, ANDREW

London LL-3457	(M)	**The Rolling Stones Songbook**	1965	20.00	50.00
London PS-457	(S)	**The Rolling Stones Songbook**	1965	30.00	60.00
Parrot PA-61003	(M)	**East Meets West**	1965	16.00	40.00
Parrot PAS-71003	(S)	**East Meets West**	1965	20.00	50.00

OLENN, JOHNNY

Liberty LRP-3029	(M)	**Just Rollin' With Johnny Olenn**	1957	150.00	250.00

OLIVER & THE TWISTERS

Colpix CP-423	(M)	**Look Who's Twistin' Everybody**	1961	16.00	40.00

OLYMPICS, THE

Arvee A-423	(M)	**Doin' The Hully Gully**	1960	75.00	150.00
Arvee A-424	(M)	**Dance By The Light Of The Moon**	1961	50.00	100.00
Arvee A-429	(M)	**Party Time**	1961	50.00	100.00
Tri-Disc 1001	(M)	**Do The Bounce**	1963	16.00	40.00
Tri-Disc 1001	(S)	**Do The Bounce**	1963	20.00	50.00
Mirwood M-7003	(M)	**Something Old, Something New**	1966	12.00	30.00
Mirwood MS-7003	(S)	**Something Old, Something New**	1966	16.00	40.00

abel & Catalog #		Title	Year	VG+	NM
•NE					
illage	(S)	**Creation Earth**	1977	20.00	50.00
•NES, THE					
shwood House 1105	(S)	**The Ones**	196?	300.00	500.00
•NO, YOKO					
Is. Ono also recorded with her husband, John Lennon, who co-produced her first three albums.					
pple SW-3373	(S)	**Plastic Ono Band**	1971	6.00	15.00
pple SVBB-3380	(S)	**Fly** *(With insert)*	1971	8.00	20.00
pple SVBB-3399	(S)	**Approximately Infinite Universe**	1972	8.00	20.00
pple SW-3412	(S)	**Feeling The Space**	1973	6.00	15.00
•RANG-UTAH					
•ell 6054	(S)	**Orang-Utah**	1971	8.00	20.00
•RBISON, ROY					
•un 1260	(DJ)	**Roy Orbison At The Rockhouse**	1961	300.00	500.00
•un 1260	(M)	**Roy Orbison At The Rockhouse**	1961	100.00	200.00
•un 113	(E)	**The Original Sun Sound Of Roy Orbison**	1969	6.00	15.00
		(Sun 113 is a repackage of the "Rockhouse" album.)			
Ionument M-4002	(M)	**Lonely And Blue**	1961	35.00	70.00
Ionument SM-14002	(S)	**Lonely And Blue**	1961	50.00	100.00
Ionument M-4007	(M)	**Crying**	1962	35.00	70.00
Ionument SM-14007	(S)	**Crying**	1962	50.00	100.00
Ionument M-4009	(M)	**Roy Orbison's Greatest Hits**	1962	14.00	35.00
Ionument SM-14009	(S)	**Roy Orbison's Greatest Hits**	1962	20.00	50.00
Ionument MLP-8000	(M)	**Roy Orbison's Greatest Hits**	1963	8.00	20.00
Ionument SLP-18000	(S)	**Roy Orbison's Greatest Hits**	1963	12.00	30.00
Ionument MLP-8003	(M)	**In Dreams**	1963	30.00	60.00
Ionument SLP-18003	(S)	**In Dreams**	1963	35.00	70.00
Ionument MLP-8023	(M)	**Early Orbison**	1964	12.00	30.00
Ionument SLP-18023	(S)	**Early Orbison**	1964	18.00	45.00
Ionument MLP-8024	(M)	**More Of Roy Orbison's Greatest Hits**	1964	12.00	30.00
Ionument SLP-18024	(S)	**More Of Roy Orbison's Greatest Hits**	1964	16.00	40.00
Ionument MLP-8035	(M)	**Orbisongs**	1965	8.00	20.00
Ionument SLP-18035	(S)	**Orbisongs**	1965	12.00	30.00
Ionument MLP-8045	(M)	**The Very Best Of Roy Orbison**	1966	8.00	20.00
Ionument SLP-18045	(P)	**The Very Best Of Roy Orbison**	1966	12.00	30.00
pectrum DLP-164	(M)	**Orbiting With Roy Orbison**	196?	6.00	15.00
•pectrum DLPS-164	(E)	**Orbiting With Roy Orbison**	196?	5.00	12.00
IGM E-4308	(M)	**There Is Only One Roy Orbison**	1965	5.00	12.00
IGM SE-4308	(S)	**There Is Only One Roy Orbison**	1965	8.00	20.00
IGM E-4322	(M)	**The Orbison Way**	1965	5.00	12.00
IGM SE-4322	(S)	**The Orbison Way**	1965	8.00	20.00
IGM E-4379	(M)	**The Classic Roy Orbison**	1966	5.00	12.00
IGM SE-4379	(S)	**The Classic Roy Orbison**	1966	8.00	20.00
IGM E-4424	(M)	**Roy Orbison Sings Don Gibson**	1966	5.00	12.00
IGM SE-4424	(S)	**Roy Orbison Sings Don Gibson**	1966	8.00	20.00
IGM E-4514	(M)	**Cry Softly, Lonely One**	1967	5.00	12.00
IGM SE-4514	(S)	**Cry Softly, Lonely One**	1967	8.00	20.00
IGM SE-4475	(S)	**The Fastest Guitar Alive** *(Soundtrack)*	1968	10.00	25.00
IGM SE-4636	(S)	**The Many Moods Of Roy Orbison**	1969	6.00	15.00
IGM SE-4659	(S)	**The Great Songs Of Roy Orbison**	1970	6.00	15.00
IGM SE-4683	(S)	**Hank Williams The Roy Orbison Way**	1970	8.00	20.00
IGM SE-4835	(S)	**Roy Orbison Sings**	1972	5.00	12.00
IGM SE-4867	(S)	**Memphis**	1972	6.00	15.00
IGM SE-4934	(S)	**Milestones**	1973	5.00	12.00
Ionument KZG-31484	(P)	**All-Time Greatest Hits** *(2 LPs)*	1972	10.00	25.00
Iercury SRM-1-1045	(S)	**I'm Still In Love With You**	1975	5.00	12.00
Ionument MG-7600	(S)	**Regeneration**	1976	5.00	12.00
Ionument MP-8600	(P)	**All-Time Greatest Hits** *(2 LPs)*	1977	6.00	15.00
Ionument MC-6619	(S)	**Roy Orbison's Greatest Hits**	1977	5.00	12.00
Ionument MC-6620	(S)	**In Dreams**	1977	5.00	12.00
Ionument MC-6621	(S)	**More Of Roy Orbison's Greatest Hits**	1977	5.00	12.00
Ionument MC-6622	(P)	**The Very Best Of Roy Orbison**	1977	5.00	12.00
•RIENT EXPRESS, THE					
Iainstream 6117	(S)	**The Orient Express**	1969	8.00	20.00

Original copies of Roy's stereo Monument albums have risen dramatically in recent years.
Overlooked is the fact that four of the titles were reissued in the '70s and can be found
for under $10 at many shops or shows.

Label & Catalog #		Title	Year	VG+	NM
ORIGINAL SURFARIS, THE					
Diplomat D-2309	(M)	**Wheels-Shorts-Hot Rods**	196?	5.00	12.00
Diplomat DS-2309	(S)	**Wheels-Shorts-Hot Rods**	196?	6.00	15.00
ORIOLES, THE					
Refer to The Cadillacs; Sonny Til & The Orioles.					
Parker PLP-816	(M)	**Modern Sounds Of The Orioles**	196?	100.00	200.00
ORION					
Orion is a pseudonym for Jimmy Ellis.					
Sun 1012	(S)	**Orion Reborn** *(Coffin cover. Gold vinyl)*	1978	6.00	15.00
ORION, P.J., & THE MAGNATES					
Magnate 122459	(M)	**P.J. Orion And The Magnates**	196?	100.00	200.00
ORLANDO, TONY					
Epic LN-611	(M)	**Bless You And 11 Other Great Hits**	1961	12.00	30.00
Epic BN-611	(S)	**Bless You And 11 Other Great Hits**	1961	16.00	40.00
ORLONS, THE					
Cameo C-1020	(M)	**The Wah Watusi**	1962	16.00	40.00
Cameo C-1033	(M)	**All The Hits**	1962	14.00	35.00
Cameo C-1041	(M)	**South Street**	1963	16.00	40.00
Cameo C-1054	(M)	**Not Me**	1963	14.00	35.00
Cameo C-1061	(M)	**Biggest Hits**	1963	14.00	35.00
Cameo C-1073	(M)	**Down Memory Lane**	1963	14.00	35.00
ORLONS, THE / THE DOVELLS					
Cameo C-1067	(M)	**Golden Hits Of The Orlons & The Dovells**	1963	14.00	35.00
ORPHAN EGG					
Carole CARS-8004	(S)	**Orphan Egg**	1968	10.00	25.00
American Inter. ST-A-1033	(S)	**The Cycle Savages** *(Soundtrack)*	1970	10.00	25.00
ORPHANN					
O.M.I. M-70021	(S)	**Up For Adoption**	1977	35.00	70.00
ORPHEUS					
MGM SE-4524	(S)	**Orpheus**	1968	6.00	15.00
MGM SE-4569	(S)	**Ascending**	1968	6.00	15.00
MGM SE-4599	(S)	**Joyful**	1969	6.00	15.00
OSBORNE, JIMMY					
Audio Lab AL-1527	(M)	**Singing Songs He Wrote**	1959	30.00	60.00
King 730	(M)	**The Legendary Jimmy Osborne**	1961	16.00	40.00
King 782	(M)	**Golden Harvest, Volume 3**	1962	12.00	30.00
King 892	(M)	**The Very Best Of Jimmy Osborne**	1964	10.00	25.00
OSBORNE, MARY					
Warwick 2004	(M)	**A Girl And Her Guitar**	1961	12.00	30.00
OSBORNE BROTHERS, THE					
MGM E-3734	(M)	**Country Pickin' And Hillside Singin'**	1959	16.00	40.00
MGM E-4018	(M)	**Blue Grass Music**	1959	12.00	30.00
Decca DL-4602	(M)	**Voices In Bluegrass**	1965	6.00	15.00
Decca DL 74602	(S)	**Voices In Bluegrass**	1965	8.00	20.00
Decca DL-4767	(M)	**Up This Hill And Down**	1966	6.00	15.00
Decca DL-74767	(S)	**Up This Hill And Down**	1966	8.00	20.00
Decca DL-4903	(M)	**Modern Sounds Of Bluegrass Music**	1967	6.00	15.00
Decca DL-74903	(S)	**Modern Sounds Of Bluegrass Music**	1967	8.00	20.00
Decca DL-74993	(S)	**Yesterday, Today & The Osborne Brothers**	1968	6.00	15.00
OSMOND, MARIE					
MGM SE-4910	(S)	**Paper Roses**	1973	5.00	12.00
OSMOND BROTHERS, THE					
The Osmonds feature Donny Osmond.					
MGM E-4146	(M)	**Songs We Sang On The Andy Williams Show**	1963	8.00	20.00
MGM SE-4146	(S)	**Songs We Sang On The Andy Williams Show**	1963	10.00	25.00

Fronted by Sonny Til, the Orioles were one of the first black groups to make inroads on the r'n'b charts (on National in 1948), where their harmony sound was a direct precursor of the doo wop movement of the early '50s, and then on the pop charts, where their incredible version of "Crying In The Chapel" was a huge hit in 1953. Along with the Ravens, the Orioles were also responsible for the flock of groups with bird derived names; the Orioles chose their name after the baseball team from their native Baltimore. *The Cadillacs Meet The Orioles* features one of the more bizarre covers gracing an album of black vocal group music...

Label & Catalog #		Title	Year	VG+	NM
MGM E-4187	(M)	We Sing You A Merry Christmas	1963	8.00	20.00
MGM SE-4187	(S)	We Sing You A Merry Christmas	1963	10.00	25.00
MGM E-4235	(M)	All-Time Hymn Favorites	1964	8.00	20.00
MGM SE-4235	(S)	All-Time Hymn Favorites	1964	10.00	25.00
MGM E-4291	(M)	The New Sound Of The Osmond Brothers	1965	8.00	20.00
MGM SE-4291	(S)	The New Sound Of The Osmond Brothers	1965	10.00	25.00

OSMOSIS

RCA Victor LSP-4369	(S)	Osmosis	1970	8.00	20.00

OSWALD, LEE HARVEY

Truth 22-65	(M)	Lee Harvey Oswald Speaks	1967	20.00	50.00
Inca 1001	(M)	Self Portrait In Red	1967	20.00	50.00

OTHER HALF, THE

"7/2"	(M)	The Other Half	196?	180.00	300.00

*(Original covers open on the left; counterfeits open on the right.
Counterfeits vinyl shows blue when held up to a light.)*

OTHER HALF, THE

The Other Half features Randy Holden, later of Blue Cheer.

Acta A-38004	(S)	The Other Half	1968	16.00	40.00

OTIS, JOHNNY

Refer to Mel Williams.

Dig 104	(M)	Rock And Roll Hit Parade, Volume 1	1957	180.00	300.00
Capitol T-940	(M)	The Johnny Otis Show	1958	100.00	200.00
Kent KST-534	(S)	Cold Shot	196?	10.00	25.00
Epic BN-26524	(S)	Cuttin' Up	1970	8.00	20.00
Epic EG-30473	(S)	Live At Monterey	1971	8.00	20.00

OUTLAWS, THE

Direct Disk SD-16617	(S)	Outlaws	198?	8.00	20.00

OUTSIDERS, THE

Capitol T-2501	(M)	Time Won't Let Me	1966	8.00	20.00
Capitol ST-2501	(S)	Time Won't Let Me	1966	10.00	25.00
Capitol T-2568	(M)	Album #2	1966	6.00	15.00
Capitol ST-2568	(P)	Album #2	1966	8.00	20.00
Capitol T-2636	(M)	In	1967	6.00	15.00
Capitol ST-2636	(S)	In	1967	8.00	20.00
Capitol T-2745	(M)	Happening Live	1967	6.00	15.00
Capitol ST-2745	(S)	Happening Live	1967	8.00	20.00

OWEN, REG

RCA Victor LPM-1906	(M)	I'll Sing You 1,000 Love Songs	1958	8.00	20.00
RCA Victor LPM-1908	(M)	Girls Were Made To Take Care Of Boys	1958	8.00	20.00
RCA Victor LPM-1914	(M)	Cuddle Up A Little Closer	1959	6.00	15.00
RCA Victor LSP-1914	(S)	Cuddle Up A Little Closer	1959	8.00	20.00
Decca DL-8859	(M)	Under Paris Skies	1959	6.00	15.00
Decca DL7-8859	(S)	Under Paris Skies	1959	8.00	20.00

OWEN-B

No label	(S)	Mus-I-Col	197?	40.00	80.00

OWENS, BONNIE (& THE STRANGERS)

Refer to Merle Haggard.

Capitol T-2403	(M)	Don't Take Advantage Of Me	1965	6.00	15.00
Capitol ST-2403	(S)	Don't Take Advantage Of Me	1965	8.00	20.00
Capitol T-2660	(M)	All Of Me Belongs To You	1967	6.00	15.00
Capitol ST-2660	(S)	All Of Me Belongs To You	1967	8.00	20.00
Capitol ST-2861	(S)	Somewhere Between	1968	6.00	15.00
Capitol ST-195	(S)	Lead Me On	1969	6.00	15.00
Capitol ST-341	(S)	Hifi To Cry By	1969	6.00	15.00
Capitol ST-557	(S)	Mother's Favorite Hymns	1970	6.00	15.00

OWENS, BUCK (& THE BUCKAROOS)

Refer to The Buckaroos.

LaBrea 8017	(M)	Buck Owens	1961	50.00	100.00

Label & Catalog #		Title	Year	VG+	NM
Starday SLP-172	(M)	Fabulous Country Music Sound	1962	20.00	50.00
Starday SLP-324	(M)	Country Hit Maker #1	196?	16.00	40.00
Starday SLP-324	(M)	Fabulous Country Music Sound	196?	16.00	40.00
Capitol T-1482	(M)	Buck Owens Sings Harlan Howard	1961	16.00	40.00
Capitol ST-1482	(S)	Buck Owens Sings Harlan Howard	1961	20.00	50.00
Capitol T-1489	(M)	Under Your Spell Again	1961	16.00	40.00
Capitol DT-1489	(E)	Under Your Spell Again	1961	10.00	25.00
Capitol T-1777	(M)	You're For Me	1962	16.00	40.00
Capitol ST-1777	(S)	You're For Me	1962	20.00	50.00
Capitol T-1879	(M)	On The Bandstand	1963	16.00	40.00
Capitol ST-1879	(S)	On The Bandstand	1963	20.00	50.00
Capitol T-1989	(M)	Buck Owens Sings Tommy Collins	1963	16.00	40.00
Capitol ST-1989	(S)	Buck Owens Sings Tommy Collins	1963	20.00	50.00
Capitol T-2105	(M)	The Best Of Buck Owens	1964	6.00	15.00
Capitol ST-2105	(S)	The Best Of Buck Owens	1964	8.00	20.00
Capitol T-2135	(M)	Together Again	1964	6.00	15.00
Capitol ST-2135	(S)	Together Again	1964	8.00	20.00
Capitol T-2186	(M)	I Don't Care	1964	6.00	15.00
Capitol ST-2186	(S)	I Don't Care	1964	8.00	20.00
Capitol T-2283	(M)	I've Got A Tiger By The Tail	1965	6.00	15.00
Capitol ST-2283	(S)	I've Got A Tiger By The Tail	1965	8.00	20.00
Capitol T-2353	(M)	Before You Go	1965	6.00	15.00
Capitol ST-2353	(S)	Before You Go	1965	8.00	20.00
Capitol T-2367	(M)	The Instrumental Hits	1965	6.00	15.00
Capitol ST-2367	(S)	The Instrumental Hits	1965	8.00	20.00
Capitol T-2396	(M)	Christmas With Buck Owens	1965	6.00	15.00
Capitol ST-2396	(S)	Christmas With Buck Owens	1965	8.00	20.00
Capitol T-2443	(M)	Roll Out The Red Carpet	1966	6.00	15.00
Capitol ST-2443	(S)	Roll Out The Red Carpet	1966	8.00	20.00
Capitol T-2497	(M)	Dust On Mother's Bible	1966	6.00	15.00
Capitol ST-2497	(S)	Dust On Mother's Bible	1966	8.00	20.00
Capitol SPRO-2980	(DJ)	Minute Masters (Radio sampler)	1966	20.00	50.00
Capitol T-2556	(M)	Carnegie Hall Concert	1966	6.00	15.00
Capitol ST-2556	(S)	Carnegie Hall Concert	1966	8.00	20.00
Capitol T-2640	(M)	Open Up Your Heart	1967	6.00	15.00
Capitol ST-2640	(S)	Open Up Your Heart	1967	8.00	20.00
Capitol T-2715	(M)	Buck Owens & His Buckaroos In Japan	1967	6.00	15.00
Capitol ST-2715	(S)	Buck Owens & His Buckaroos In Japan	1967	8.00	20.00
Capitol T-2760	(M)	Your Tender Loving Care	1967	6.00	15.00
Capitol ST-2760	(S)	Your Tender Loving Care	1967	8.00	20.00
Capitol ST-2841	(S)	It Takes People Like You	1968	8.00	20.00
Capitol ST-2897	(S)	The Best Of Buck Owens, Volume 2	1968	8.00	20.00
Capitol ST-2902	(S)	A Night On The Town	1968	8.00	20.00
Capitol ST-2962	(S)	Sweet Rosie Jones	1968	8.00	20.00
Capitol ST-2977	(S)	Christmas Shopping	1968	8.00	20.00
Capitol ST-2994	(S)	The Guitar Player	1968	8.00	20.00
Capitol ST-131	(S)	I've Got You On My Mind Again	1969	6.00	15.00
Capitol SKAO-145	(S)	The Best Of Buck Owens, Volume 3	1969	6.00	15.00
Capitol ST-212	(S)	Tall Dark Stranger	1969	6.00	15.00
Capitol ST-232	(S)	Live At The London Palladium	1969	6.00	15.00

— Original Capitol albums above have black labels with the Capitol logo on top.—

Capitol SWBB-257	(S)	Close-Up (2 LPs)	1969	6.00	15.00
Capitol ST-413	(S)	Big In Vegas (The Buck Owens Show)	1969	6.00	15.00
Capitol ST-439	(S)	Your Mother's Prayer	1970	6.00	15.00
Capitol ST-476	(S)	Kansas City Song	1970	6.00	15.00
Capitol STBB-486	(S)	A Merry "Hee Haw" Christmas (2 LPs)	1970	8.00	20.00
Capitol STBB-532	(E)	My Heart Skips A Beat / Under Your Spell Again (2 LPs)	1970	6.00	15.00
Capitol ST-574	(S)	Buck Owens (3 LPs)	1970	10.00	25.00
Capitol ST-628	(S)	I Wouldn't Live In New York City	1970	6.00	15.00
Capitol ST-685	(S)	Bridge Over Troubled Water	1971	6.00	15.00
Capitol ST-795	(S)	Ruby	1971	6.00	15.00
Capitol ST-830	(S)	The Best Of Buck Owens, Volume 4	1971	6.00	15.00
Capitol ST-860	(S)	The Songs Of Merle Haggard	1972	6.00	15.00

OXFORD, VERNON

RCA Victor LPM-3704	(M)	Woman, Let Me Sing You A Song	1967	8.00	20.00
RCA Victor LSP-3704	(S)	Woman, Let Me Sing You A Song	1967	10.00	25.00

Label & Catalog #		Title	Year	VG+	NM
OZ KNOZZ					
Ozone 02-1000	(S)	**Russ Nix**	1975	90.00	180.00
OZZIE & HARRIET (NELSON)					
Imperial LP-9049	(M)	**The Ozzie And Harriet Show**	1957	35.00	70.00
Sunset SUM-1146	(M)	**Ozzie And Harriet Sing**	1967	8.00	20.00
Sunset SUS-5146	(S)	**Ozzie And Harriet Sing**	1967	10.00	25.00

Label & Catalog #		Title	Year	VG+	NM
P.H. PHACTOR					
Piccadilly PIC-3343	(S)	**Merryjuana**	1980	50.00	100.00
PABLO CRUISE					
Mobile Fidelity MFSL-029	(S)	**A Place In The Sun**	1979	6.00	15.00
Nautilus NR-6	(S)	**Lifeline**	198?	5.00	12.00
Nautilus NR-28	(S)	**Worlds Away**	198?	5.00	12.00
PACE, JOHNNY					
Riverside 12-292	(M)	**Chet Baker Introduces Johnny Pace**	1958	12.00	30.00
PACIFIC GAS & ELECTRIC					
Bright Orange 701	(S)	**Get It On**	1968	10.00	25.00
PAGE, JIMMY					
Refer to Cartoone; Led Zepplin; The Yardbirds.					
Springboard SPB-4038	(S)	**Special Early Works**	1972	10.00	25.00
PAGE, PATTI					
Mercury MG-25059 (10")	(M)	**Songs**	1950	16.00	40.00
Mercury MG-25101 (10")	(M)	**Folksong Favorites**	1951	16.00	40.00
Mercury MG-25109 (10")	(M)	**Christmas**	1951	16.00	40.00
Mercury MG-25154 (10")	(M)	**Tennessee Waltz**	1952	16.00	40.00
Mercury MG-25185 (10")	(M)	**Patti Sings For Romance**	1954	16.00	40.00
Mercury MG-25187 (10")	(M)	**Song Souvenirs**	1954	16.00	40.00
Mercury MG-25196 (10")	(M)	**Just Patti**	1954	16.00	40.00
Mercury MG-25197 (10")	(M)	**Patti's Songs**	1954	16.00	40.00
Mercury MG-25209 (10")	(M)	**And I Thought About You**	1954	16.00	40.00
Mercury MG-25210 (10")	(M)	**So Many Memories**	1954	16.00	40.00
EmArcy MG-36074	(M)	**In The Land Of Hi Fi**	1956	14.00	35.00
EmArcy MG-36116	(M)	**The East Side**	1957	12.00	30.00
EmArcy SR-60014	(S)	**The East Side**	1959	14.00	35.00
EmArcy MG-36136	(M)	**The West Side**	1957	12.00	30.00
EmArcy SR-60113	(S)	**The West Side**	1959	14.00	35.00
Mercury MG-20076	(M)	**Romance On The Range**	1955	12.00	30.00
Mercury MG-20093	(M)	**Christmas With Patti Page**	1956	12.00	30.00
Mercury MG-20095	(M)	**Page I**	1955	12.00	30.00
Mercury MG-20096	(M)	**Page II**	1955	12.00	30.00
Mercury MG-20097	(M)	**Page III**	1955	12.00	30.00
Mercury MG-20098	(M)	**You Go To My Head**	1955	12.00	30.00
Mercury MG-20099	(M)	**Music For Two In Love**	1955	12.00	30.00
Mercury MG-20100	(M)	**The Voices Of Patti Page**	1955	12.00	30.00
Mercury MG-20101	(M)	**Page IV**	1955	12.00	30.00

Label & Catalog #		Title	Year	VG+	NM
Mercury MG-20102	(M)	My Song	1955	12.00	30.00
Mercury MG-20318	(M)	The Waltz Queen	1957	12.00	30.00
Mercury SR-60049	(S)	The Waltz Queen	1959	14.00	35.00
Mercury MG-20387	(M)	Let's Get Away From It All	1957	12.00	30.00
Mercury SR-60010	(S)	Let's Get Away From It All	1959	14.00	35.00
Mercury MG-20388	(M)	I've Heard That Song Before	1958	12.00	30.00
Mercury SR-60011	(S)	I've Heard That Song Before	1959	14.00	35.00
Mercury MG-20398	(M)	Patti Page On Camera	1959	12.00	30.00
Mercury SR-60025	(S)	Patti Page On Camera	1959	14.00	35.00
Mercury MG-20417	(M)	Three Little Words	1960	12.00	30.00
Mercury SR-60037	(S)	Three Little Words	1960	14.00	35.00
Mercury MG-20405	(M)	Indiscretion	1959	12.00	30.00
Mercury SR-60059	(S)	Indiscretion	1959	14.00	35.00
Mercury MG-20406	(M)	I'll Remember April	1959	12.00	30.00
Mercury SR-60081	(S)	I'll Remember April	1959	14.00	35.00
Mercury MG-20226	(M)	Manhattan Tower	1956	12.00	30.00
Mercury MG-20573	(M)	Just A Closer Walk With Thee	1960	12.00	30.00
Mercury SR-60233	(S)	Just A Closer Walk With Thee	1960	14.00	35.00
Mercury MG-20599	(M)	Sings And Stars In "Elmer Gantry"	1960	8.00	20.00
Mercury SR-60260	(M)	Sings And Stars In "Elmer Gantry"	1960	12.00	30.00
Mercury MG-20495	(M)	Patti Page's Golden Hits	1961	6.00	15.00
Mercury SR-60495	(S)	Patti Page's Golden Hits	1961	8.00	20.00
Mercury MG-20615	(M)	Country & Western Golden Hits	1961	6.00	15.00
Mercury SR-60615	(S)	Country & Western Golden Hits	1961	8.00	20.00
Mercury MG-20689	(M)	Go On Home	1962	6.00	15.00
Mercury SR-60689	(S)	Go On Home	1962	8.00	20.00
Mercury MG-20712	(M)	Golden Hits Of The Boys	1962	6.00	15.00
Mercury SR-60712	(S)	Golden Hits Of The Boys	1962	8.00	20.00
Mercury MG-20758	(M)	Patti Page On Stage	1963	6.00	15.00
Mercury SR-60758	(S)	Patti Page On Stage	1963	8.00	20.00
Mercury MG-20794	(M)	Patti Page's Golden Hits, Volume 2	1963	5.00	12.00
Mercury SR-60794	(S)	Patti Page's Golden Hits, Volume 2	1963	6.00	15.00
Mercury MG-20819	(M)	The Singing Rage	1963	5.00	12.00
Mercury SR-60819	(S)	The Singing Rage	1963	5.00	12.00
Mercury MG-20909	(M)	Blue Dream Street	1964	5.00	12.00
Mercury SR-60909	(S)	Blue Dream Street	1964	6.00	15.00

— Original Mercury albums above have black labels with silver print.—

PAISLEYS, THE

Audio City 70	(M)	Cosmic Mind At Play	196?	75.00	150.00

PALANCE, JACK

Warner Bros. WS-1865	(S)	Palance	1970	6.00	15.00

PALEY, TOM

Elektra EKL-12	(M)	Folk Songs From The South Appalachian Mountains	1956	10.00	25.00

PALEY, TOM, & PEGGY SEEGER

Elektra EKL-295	(M)	Tom Paley And Peggy Seeger	1965	5.00	12.00
Elektra EKS-7295	(S)	Tom Paley And Peggy Seeger	1965	6.00	15.00

PALEY & ALEXANDER

Sounds Int. 005	(M)	Boston Incest Album	196?	20.00	50.00

PALMER, BRUCE

Palmer was formerly a member of The Buffalo Springfield.

Forecast FTS-3086	(S)	Bruce Palmer	1970	6.00	15.00

PALMER, ROBERT

Island PRO-819	(DJ)	Secrets (Picture disc)	1979	8.00	20.00

PANICS, THE

Chancellor CHL-5026	(M)	Panicsville	1962	8.00	20.00
Chancellor CHLS-5026	(S)	Panicsville	1962	10.00	25.00
Phillips PHM-200159	(M)	Discotheque Dance Party	1964	5.00	12.00
Phillips PHS-600159	(S)	Discotheque Dance Party	1964	6.00	15.00

Van Dyke Parks captured the ear of the rock world when he joined Brian Wilson's then work in progress, known as *Smile*. Working primarily as Brian's lyricist, Parks wove dense, swirling arabesques of pose around Brian's demanding music. When *Smile* collapsed, Parks accepted a contract from Warner Bros. and prepared the equally arresting *Song Cycle*, a stunning collection that summed up the "art rock" aspirations of the time (and remains, along with several of the released *Smile* pieces, "Surf's Up" and "Heroes And Villains," among the most intelligent and ambitious lyrics ever placed on a pop record). After that, Parks discovered the sublime joy of Trinidad's steel drum music, which makes up the entirety of *Discover America*.

Label & Catalog #		Title	Year	VG+	NM

PARAGONS, THE / THE JESTERS

| Jubilee JLP-1098 | (M) | Paragons Meet The Jesters | 1959 | 75.00 | 150.00 |
| Jubilee JLP-1098 | (M) | Paragons Meet The Jesters (Colored vinyl) | 1959 | 240.00 | 400.00 |

PARAGONS, THE / THE HARPTONES

| Musicnote M-8001 | (M) | The Paragons Vs. The Harptones | 1964 | 14.00 | 35.00 |

PARAMOR, NORRIE

| Capitol Int. 10025 | (M) | In London, In Love | 1956 | 12.00 | 30.00 |

PARIS, JACKIE

Coral CRL-56118 (10")	(M)	Jackie Paris	1955	20.00	50.00
EmArcy MC-36095	(M)	Songs By Jackie Paris	1955	14.00	35.00
Brunswick BL-54019	(M)	Skylark	1958	12.00	30.00
Time 70009	(M)	The Lyrics Of Ira Gershwin	195?	12.00	30.00
East/West 4002	(M)	The Jackie Paris Sound	195?	14.00	35.00
Impulse 17	(M)	The Song Is Paris	1959	8.00	20.00
Impulse 17	(S)	The Song Is Paris	1959	12.00	30.00

PARKER, FESS

Columbia CL-576	(M)	TV Sweethearts (With Marion Marlowe)	1955	20.00	50.00
Columbia CL-666	(M)	Davy Crockett	1955	20.00	50.00
Disneyland WDA-3007	(M)	Three Adventures Of Davy Crockett	195?	16.00	40.00
Disneyland WDA-3602	(M)	Yarns And Songs	195?	16.00	40.00
Disneyland 1336	(M)	Cowboy And Indian Songs	195?	14.00	35.00
RCA Victor LPM-2973	(M)	Fess Parker Sings	1964	8.00	20.00
RCA Victor LSP-2973	(S)	Fess Parker Sings	1964	12.00	30.00

PARKER, GRAHAM, & THE RUMOUR

| Arista SP-63 | (DJ) | Live Sparks | 1979 | 12.00 | 30.00 |

PARKER, LITTLE JUNIOR

Duke DLP-76	(M)	Driving Wheel	1962	30.00	60.00
Mercury MG-21101	(M)	Like It Is	1967	6.00	15.00
Mercury SR-61101	(S)	Like It Is	1967	8.00	20.00
Minit 24024	(S)	Blues Man	1969	6.00	15.00
Blue Rock SRB-64004	(S)	Honey-Drippin' Blues	1969	6.00	15.00
Capitol ST-64	(S)	The Outside Man	1970	6.00	15.00
United Arts. UAS-6823	(S)	I Tell Stories Sad And True	1971	5.00	12.00
BluesWay BLS-6066	(S)	Sometime Tomorrow	1973	5.00	12.00
Duke X-72	(S)	Barefoot Rock And You Got Me	1974	5.00	12.00
Duke DLP-83	(M)	The Best Of Junior Parker	1974	5.00	12.00

PARKER, LITTLE JUNIOR, & JIMMY McGRIFF

| Capitol ST-569 | (S) | Dudes Doin' Business | 1971 | 6.00 | 15.00 |
| United Arts. UAS-6814 | (S) | 100 Proof Black Magic | 1971 | 5.00 | 12.00 |

PARKER, ROBERT

| Nola LP-1001 | (M) | Barefootin' | 1966 | 12.00 | 30.00 |
| Nola LPS-1001 | (S) | Barefootin' | 1966 | 20.00 | 50.00 |

PARKS, VAN DYKE

Warner Bros. WS-2727	(S)	Song Cycle (Gold Label)	1968	10.00	25.00
Warner Bros. WS-2727	(S)	Song Cycle (Green Label)	1968	4.00	10.00
Warner Bros. BS-2589	(S)	Discover America	1972	6.00	15.00
Warner Bros. BS-2878	(S)	Clang Of The Yankee Reaper	1975	6.00	15.00

PARLIAMENT

Parliament, who also recorded as Funkadelic, features George Clinton.

Casablanca NBLP-9003	(S)	Up For The Down Stroke	1974	12.00	30.00
Casablanca NBLP-7014	(S)	Chocolate City	1975	8.00	20.00
Casablanca NBLP-7034	(S)	Clones Of Dr. Funkenstein	1976	8.00	20.00
Casablanca NBLP-7053	(S)	Parliament Live/Funk Earth Tour	1977	8.00	20.00
Casablanca NBLP-7084	(S)	Funkentelechy Vs. The Placebo Syndrome	1977	8.00	20.00
Casablanca NBLP-7125	(S)	Motor Booty Affair	1978	8.00	20.00
Casablanca NBLP-7125	(S)	Motor Booty Affair (Picture disc)	1979	12.00	30.00
Casablanca NBLP-7146	(S)	Invasion Of The Body Snatchers	1979	8.00	20.00
Casablanca NBLP-7195	(S)	Gloryhallastoopid	1979	8.00	20.00
Casablanca NBLP-7249	(S)	Trombipulation	1980	8.00	20.00

A top tenner in 1966, Robert Parker's infectious "Barefootin'" was the title for his sole album and bore a rather distinctive cover graphic.

The Partridge Family enjoyed a two year run on the charts before their star waned. Twenty years after the fact their records remain popular with an ever widening audience of collectors.

Label & Catalog #		Title	Year	VG+	NM
PARRISH, PAUL					
ABC 1013	(DJ)	**Song For A Young Girl** (Picture disc)	1979	4.00	10.00
PARSONS, ALAN [ALAN PARSONS PROJECT]					
Mobile Fidelity MFSL-084	(S)	**I, Robot**	1980	12.00	30.00
Mobile Fidelity MFQR-084	(S)	**I, Robot** (UHQR in a box)	1982	35.00	70.00
Arista PD-8263	(DJ)	**Vulture Culture**	1985	6.00	15.00
PARTON, DOLLY					
Dolly originally recorded with Porter Wagoner.					
Monument MLP-8085	(M)	**Hello, I'm Dolly**	1967	8.00	20.00
Monument SLP-18085	(S)	**Hello, I'm Dolly**	1967	10.00	25.00
Monument SLP-18136	(S)	**As Long As I Love**	1970	6.00	15.00
RCA Victor LPM-3949	(M)	**Just Because I'm A Woman**	1968	20.00	50.00
RCA Victor LSP-3949	(S)	**Just Because I'm A Woman** (Black label)	1968	6.00	15.00
RCA Victor LSP-4099	(S)	**In The Good Old Days**			
		(When Times Were Bad)	1969	8.00	20.00
RCA Victor LSP-4188	(S)	**My Blue Ridge Mountain Boy**	1969	8.00	20.00
RCA Victor LSP-4288	(S)	**The Fairest Of Them All**	1970	8.00	20.00
RCA Victor LSP-4387	(S)	**A Real Live Dolly**	1970	6.00	15.00
RCA Victor LSP-4396	(S)	**Golden Streets Of Glory**	1971	6.00	15.00
RCA Victor LSP-4449	(S)	**The Best Of Dolly Parton**	1970	6.00	15.00
RCA Victor LSP-4507	(S)	**Joshua**	1971	6.00	15.00
RCA Victor LSP-4603	(S)	**Coat Of Many Colors**	1971	6.00	15.00
RCA Victor LSP-4686	(S)	**Touch Your Woman**	1972	6.00	15.00
RCA Victor LSP-4752	(S)	**My Favorite Song Writer: Porter Wagoner**	1972	6.00	15.00
		— Original RCA albums above have orange labels.—			
RCA Victor APD1-0033	(Q)	**My Tennessee Mountain Home**	1973	5.00	12.00
RCA Victor CPL1-1343	(DJ)	**Great Balls Of Fire** (Picture disc)	1979	4.00	10.00
RCA Victor 812	(DJ)	**HBO Presents Dolly Parton** (Picture disc)	1983	5.00	12.00
PARTON, DOLLY, & GEORGE JONES					
Starday SLP-429	(E)	**Dolly Parton And George Jones**	1968	16.00	40.00
PARTON, DOLLY, & FAYE TUCKER					
Somerset SF-19700	(S)	**Hits Made Famous By Country Queens**	1963	12.00	30.00
PARTRIDGE FAMILY, THE					
Bell 6050	(S)	**Album**	1970	6.00	15.00
Bell 6059	(S)	**Up To Date**	1971	6.00	15.00
		(Issued with a 12" x 20" Partridge Family school book cover, priced separately below.)			
Bell 6059		**Up To Date Book Cover**	1971	4.00	10.00
Bell 6064	(S)	**Sound Magazine**	1971	6.00	15.00
Bell 6066	(S)	**A Christmas Card** (With card)	1971	10.00	25.00
Bell 6066	(S)	**A Christmas Card** (Without card)	1971	6.00	15.00
Bell 6072	(S)	**Shopping Bag** (With bag)	1972	10.00	25.00
Bell 6072	(S)	**Shopping Bag** (Without bag)	1972	6.00	15.00
Bell 1107	(S)	**At Home With Their Greatest Hits**	1972	6.00	15.00
Bell 1111	(S)	**The Partridge Family Notebook**	1972	6.00	15.00
Bell 1122	(S)	**Crossword Puzzle**	1973	6.00	15.00
Bell 1137	(S)	**Bulletin Board**	1973	6.00	15.00
Bell 1319	(S)	**The World Of The Partridge Family** (2 LPs)	1974	8.00	20.00
Laurie House H-8014	(S)	**The Partridge Family** (2 LPs)	197?	12.00	30.00
PASTEL SIX, THE					
Zen 1001	(M)	**Cinnamon Cinder**	1963	16.00	40.00
Mark-56 MLP-511	(M)	**Golden Oldies**	1963	14.00	35.00
PATRON SAINTS, THE					
No label	(M)	**Fohhoh Bohob**	1969	See note below	
		(Rare. Estimated near mint value $1,200-2,000.)			
PATTON, JIMMY					
Stereophonic LP-1002	(S)	**Take 30 Minutes With Jimmy Patton**	196?	50.00	100.00
Sourdough 127	(M)	**Blue Darlin'**	1965	20.00	50.00
Sims 127	(M)	**Blue Darlin'**	1965	16.00	40.00
Moon 101	(M)	**Make Room For The Blues**	1966	20.00	50.00

Label & Catalog #		Title	Year	VG+	NM
PAUL, BILLY					
Phila. Inter. ZQ-31793	(Q)	**360 Degrees Of Billy Paul**	1972	5.00	12.00
Phila. Inter. ZQ-32409	(Q)	**War Of The Gods**	1973	5.00	12.00
Phila. Inter. ZQ-32952	(Q)	**Billy Paul Live In Europe**	1974	5.00	12.00

The recordings of Les Paul and pop vocalist Mary Ford are often collected by guitar players:
Paul was the inventor of the solid body guitar and an originator of many recording techniques
that are part and parcel of today's studios.

Label & Catalog #		Title	Year	VG+	NM
PAUL, LES, & MARY FORD					
Decca DL-5018 (10")	(M)	**Hawaiian Paradise**	1949	40.00	80.00
Decca DL-5376 (10")	(M)	**Galloping Guitars**	1952	40.00	80.00
Capitol H-226 (10")	(M)	**New Sound, Volume 1**	1950	35.00	70.00
Capitol H-286 (10")	(M)	**New Sound, Volume 2**	1951	35.00	70.00
Capitol H-356 (10")	(M)	**Bye Bye Blues**	1952	35.00	70.00
Capitol H-416 (10")	(M)	**The Hit Makers**	1953	35.00	70.00
Capitol H-577 (10")	(M)	**Les A Mary**	1955	35.00	70.00
Capitol T-226	(M)	**New Sound, Volume 1**	1955	20.00	50.00
Capitol T-286	(M)	**New Sound, Volume 2**	1955	20.00	50.00
Capitol T-356	(M)	**Bye Bye Blues**	1955	20.00	50.00
Capitol T-416	(M)	**The Hitmakers**	1955	20.00	50.00
Capitol T-577	(M)	**Les And Mary**	1955	20.00	50.00
Capitol T-802	(M)	**Time To Dream**	1957	20.00	50.00
Capitol T-1476	(M)	**The Hits Of Les And Mary**	1960	10.00	25.00
Columbia CL-1276	(M)	**Lover's Luau**	1959	8.00	20.00
Columbia CL-1688	(M)	**Warm And Wonderful**	1962	6.00	15.00
Columbia CS-8488	(S)	**Warm And Wonderful**	1962	8.00	20.00
Columbia CL-1821	(M)	**Bouquet Of Roses**	1962	6.00	15.00
Columbia CS-8621	(S)	**Bouquet Of Roses**	1962	8.00	20.00
—Original Columbia albums above have three white "eye" logos on each side of the spindle hole.—					
Columbia CL-1928	(M)	**Swingin' South**	1963	6.00	15.00
Columbia CS-8728	(S)	**Swingin' South**	1963	8.00	20.00
PAUL & PAULA					
Phillips PHM-200078	(M)	**Paul And Paula Sing For Young Lovers**	1963	8.00	20.00
Phillips PHS-600078	(S)	**Paul And Paula Sing For Young Lovers**	1963	10.00	25.00

Label & Catalog #		Title	Year	VG+	NM
Phillips PHM-200089	(M)	We Go Together	1963	8.00	20.00
Phillips PHS-600089	(S)	We Go Together	1963	10.00	25.00
Phillips PHM-200101	(M)	Holiday For Teens	1963	6.00	15.00
Phillips PHS-600101	(S)	Holiday For Teens	1963	8.00	20.00

PAXTON, SANDY

Elektra EKL-148	(M)	The Many Sides Of Sandy Paxton	195?	8.00	20.00

PAYNE, FREDA

Impulse 53	(M)	After The Lights Go Down Low	1964	6.00	15.00
Impulse S-53	(S)	After The Lights Go Down Low	1964	8.00	20.00
MGM E-4370	(M)	How Do You Say I Don't Love You Anymore	1966	5.00	12.00
MGM SE-4370	(S)	How Do You Say I Don't Love You Anymore	1966	6.00	15.00
MGM GAS-128	(S)	Freda Payne	1970	4.00	10.00

PAYNE, LEON

Starday SLP-231	(M)	Leon Payne	1963	16.00	40.00
Starday SLP-236	(M)	Americana	1963	14.00	35.00

PEACE, JOE

No label	(S)	Finding Peace Of Mind	1972	75.00	150.00

PEACHES & HERB

Date TE-3004	(M)	Let's Fall In Love	1967	5.00	12.00
Date TES-4004	(S)	Let's Fall In Love	1967	6.00	15.00
Date TE-3005	(M)	For Your Love	1967	5.00	12.00
Date TES-4005	(S)	For Your Love	1967	6.00	15.00
Date TES-4007	(S)	Peaches And Herbs' Golden Duets	1968	5.00	12.00
Date TES-4012	(S)	Peaches And Herbs' Greatest Hits	1968	5.00	12.00

PEANUT BUTTER CONSPIRACY, THE
The Conspiracy Columbia albums were produced by Gary Usher.

Challenge 2000	(M)	For Children Of All Ages	1968	10.00	25.00
Columbia CL-2654	(M)	Peanut Butter Conspiracy Is Spreading	1967	6.00	15.00
Columbia CS-9495	(S)	Peanut Butter Conspiracy Is Spreading	1967	8.00	20.00
Columbia CL-2790	(M)	The Great Conspiracy	1968	12.00	30.00
Columbia CS-9590	(S)	The Great Conspiracy	1968	8.00	20.00

PEARL, MINNIE

Starday SLP-224	(M)	Howdee	1963	10.00	25.00
Starday SLP-380	(M)	America's Beloved Minnie Pearl	1965	10.00	25.00
Starday SLP-397	(M)	The Country Music Story	1966	10.00	25.00
Nashville NLP-2043	(M)	Lookin' For A Feller	196?	8.00	20.00
Nashville NLPS-2043	(S)	Lookin' For A Feller	196?	10.00	25.00

PEARLS BEFORE SWINE
Pearls features Tom Rapp.

ESP 1054	(M)	One Nation Under Ground (Brown cover)	1967	8.00	20.00
ESP 1054	(S)	One Nation Under Ground (Brown cover)	1967	10.00	25.00
ESP 1054	(S)	One Nation Under Ground (Color cover)	196?	6.00	15.00
ESP 1075	(S)	Balaklava	1968	8.00	20.00
Reprise MS-6364	(S)	These Things Too	1969	6.00	15.00
Reprise MS-6405	(S)	The Use Of Ashes	1970	6.00	15.00
Reprise MS-6442	(S)	City Of Gold	1971	6.00	15.00
Reprise MS-6467	(S)	Beautiful Lies You Could Live In	1971	6.00	15.00

PECK, GREGORY

Decca DL-8009	(M)	Lullabye Of Christmas	1966	5.00	12.00
Decca DL-78009	(S)	Lullabye Of Christmas	1966	6.00	15.00

PEDICIN, MIKE

Apollo LP-484	(M)	Musical Medicine	1957	50.00	100.00

PEEL, DAVID (& THE LOWER EAST SIDE)

Elektra EKS-74032	(S)	Have A Marijuana	1968	10.00	25.00
Elektra EKS-74069	(S)	The American Revolution	1970	8.00	20.00
Apple SW-3391	(S)	The Pope Smokes Dope	1972	35.00	70.00
		(Apple 3391 produced by John & Yoko.)			

Label & Catalog #		Title	Year	VG+	NM
PEELS, THE					
Karate 5402	(M)	**Juanita Banana**	1966	35.00	70.00
PENDERGRASS, TEDDY					
Phila. Inter. JZ-30595	(DJ)	**Life Is A Song Worth Singing** (Picture disc)	1978	6.00	15.00
Phila. Inter. JE-47491	(S)	**It's Time For Love** (Half-speed master)	1981	6.00	15.00
PENETRATION					
Higher Key 33071	(S)	**An Aquarian Symphony**	1974	50.00	100.00
PENGUINS, THE					
Dooto DTL-242	(M)	**The Cool Cool Penguins** (Yellow & red label)	1959	180.00	300.00
PENNY, HANK					
Audio Lab AL-1508	(M)	**Hank Penny Sings**	195?	45.00	90.00
PENTANGLE, THE					
Reprise RS-6315	(S)	**The Pentangle**	1968	6.00	15.00
Reprise 2RS-6334	(S)	**Sweet Child** (2 LPs)	1969	6.00	15.00
Reprise RS-6372	(S)	**Basket Of Light**	1969	4.00	10.00
Reprise RS-6430	(S)	**Cruel Sister**	1971	4.00	10.00
Reprise RS-6463	(S)	**Reflections**	1971	4.00	10.00
Reprise MS-2100	(S)	**Solomon's Seal**	1972	4.00	10.00
PEOPLE					
People features Larry Norman.					
Capitol ST-2924	(S)	**I Love You**	1968	12.00	30.00
Capitol ST-151	(S)	**Both Sides Of People**	1969	10.00	25.00
Paramount PAS-5013	(S)	**There Are People And There Are People**	1970	8.00	20.00
PEPPER, JIM					
Embryo SD-7312	(S)	**Pepper's Pow Wow**	196?	20.00	50.00
PEPPERMINT RAINBOW, THE					
Decca DL-75129	(S)	**Will You Be Staying After Sunday**	1969	5.00	12.00
PEPPERMINT TROLLEY COMPANY, THE					
Acta 8007	(M)	**The Peppermint Trolley Company**	1968	6.00	15.00
Acta 38007	(S)	**The Peppermint Trolley Company**	1968	8.00	20.00
PERKINS, CARL					
Sun LP-1225	(M)	**The Dance Album Of Carl Perkins**	1957	300.00	500.00
Columbia CL-1234	(DJ)	**Whole Lotta Shakin'** (White label)	1958	75.00	150.00
Columbia CL-1234	(M)	**Whole Lotta Shakin'**	1958	150.00	250.00
Sun LP-1225	(M)	**Teen Beat (The Best Of Carl Perkins)**	1961	240.00	400.00
		("Teen Beat" is a repackage of "Dance Album.")			
Sun 112	(E)	**Blue Suede Shoes**	1969	4.00	10.00
Columbia CS-9833	(S)	**Carl Perkins' Greatest Hits**	1969	8.00	20.00
Columbia CS-9931	(S)	**On Top**	1969	8.00	20.00
Columbia CS-9981	(S)	**Boppin' The Blues** (With NRBQ)	1970	6.00	15.00
		— Original Columbia albums above have "360 Sound" labels. —			
PERKINS, TONY					
Epic LN-3394	(M)	**Tony Perkins**	1957	12.00	30.00
RCA Victor LPM-1679	(M)	**From My Heart**	1958	12.00	30.00
RCA Victor LPM-1853	(M)	**On A Rainy Afternoon**	1958	12.00	30.00
RCA Victor LSP-1853	(S)	**On A Rainy Afternoon**	1958	16.00	40.00
PERRINE, PEP					
Hideout 1003	(M)	**Pep Perrine Live And In Person**	196?	75.00	150.00
PERSUADERS, THE					
Saturn SAT-5000	(M)	**Surfer's Nightmare**	1963	50.00	100.00
Saturn SATS-5000	(S)	**Surfer's Nightmare**	1963	75.00	150.00
PERSUASIONS, THE					
Straight STS-6394	(S)	**Acappella**	1970	12.00	30.00
Capitol ST-791	(S)	**We Came To Play**	1971	8.00	20.00
Capitol ST-872	(S)	**Street Corner Symphony**	1972	8.00	20.00

Before his now legendary role as Norman Bates in Alfred Hitchcock's "Psycho,"
Tony Perkins put in time as a teen heart-throb in several major films,
including "Desire Under The Elms" with Sophia Loren.

This, his second album for RCA in 1958, was one of that company's earlier stereo albums
and is, needless to say, rather rare in that format.

Label & Catalog #		Title	Year	VG+	NM
Capitol ST-11101	(S)	Spread The Word	1972	6.00	15.00
MCA 326	(S)	We Still Ain't Got No Band	1973	4.00	10.00
A&M SD-3656	(S)	I Just Want To Sing With My Friends	1974	4.00	10.00
A&M SD-3635	(S)	More Than Before	1974	4.00	10.00
Elektra 7E-1099	(S)	Chirpin'	1977	4.00	10.00

While oft compared to fellow Anglo duo Chad & Jeremy, the main difference between the two — or four— was the folkie basis of the former and the pure pop aspirations of the latter (Mr. Asher's sibling relationship to a Mr. McCartney's beau-of-the-moment certainly helped).

PETER & GORDON
Peter Asher and Gordon Waller.

Label & Catalog #		Title	Year	VG+	NM
Capitol T-2115	(M)	A World Without Love	1964	6.00	15.00
Capitol ST-2115	(S)	A World Without Love	1964	8.00	20.00
Capitol T-2220	(M)	I Don't Want To See You Again	1964	6.00	15.00
Capitol ST-2220	(S)	I Don't Want To See You Again	1964	8.00	20.00
Capitol T-2324	(M)	I Go To Pieces	1965	6.00	15.00
Capitol ST-2324	(S)	I Go To Pieces	1965	8.00	20.00
Capitol T-2368	(M)	True Love Ways	1965	6.00	15.00
Capitol ST-2368	(S)	True Love Ways	1965	8.00	20.00
Capitol T-2430	(M)	The Hits Of Nashville	1966	6.00	15.00
Capitol ST-2430	(S)	The Hits Of Nashville	1966	8.00	20.00
Capitol T-2477	(M)	Woman	1966	6.00	15.00
Capitol ST-2477	(S)	Woman	1966	8.00	20.00
Capitol T-2549	(M)	The Best Of Peter And Gordon	1966	4.00	10.00
Capitol ST-2549	(S)	The Best Of Peter And Gordon	1966	5.00	12.00
Capitol T-2664	(M)	Lady Godiva	1967	6.00	15.00
Capitol ST-2664	(S)	Lady Godiva	1967	8.00	20.00
Capitol T-2729	(M)	A Knight In Rusty Armour	1967	5.00	12.00
Capitol ST-2729	(S)	A Knight In Rusty Armour	1967	6.00	15.00
Capitol T-2747	(M)	In London For Tea	1967	6.00	15.00
Capitol ST-2747	(S)	In London For Tea	1967	8.00	20.00
Capitol T-2882	(M)	Hot, Cold And Custard	1968	10.00	25.00
Capitol ST-2882	(S)	Hot, Cold And Custard	1968	8.00	20.00

Label & Catalog #		Title	Year	VG+	NM

PETER, PAUL & MARY
Peter Yarrow, Paul Stookey & Mary Travers.

Warner Bros. W-1473	(M)	Peter, Paul And Mary Moving	1962	5.00	12.00
Warner Bros. WS-1473	(S)	Peter, Paul And Mary Moving	1962	6.00	15.00
Warner Bros. W-1449	(M)	Peter, Paul And Mary	1962	5.00	12.00
Warner Bros. WS-1449	(S)	Peter, Paul And Mary	1962	6.00	15.00
Warner Bros. W-1507	(M)	Peter, Paul And Mary In The Wind	1963	5.00	12.00
Warner Bros. WS-1507	(S)	Peter, Paul And Mary In The Wind	1963	6.00	15.00
Warner Bros. W2-1555	(M)	In Concert	1964	5.00	12.00
Warner Bros. W2S-1555	(S)	In Concert	1964	6.00	15.00
Warner Bros. W-1589	(M)	A Song Will Rise	1965	5.00	12.00
Warner Bros. WS-1589	(S)	A Song Will Rise	1965	6.00	15.00
Warner Bros. W-1615	(M)	See What Tomorrow Brings	1965	5.00	12.00
Warner Bros. WS-1615	(S)	See What Tomorrow Brings	1965	6.00	15.00
		— Original Warner albums above have grey labels. —			
Warner Bros. W-1648	(M)	The Peter, Paul And Mary Album	1966	4.00	10.00
Warner Bros. WS-1648	(S)	The Peter, Paul And Mary Album	1966	5.00	12.00
Warner Bros. W-1700	(M)	Album 1700	1967	4.00	10.00
Warner Bros. WS-1700	(S)	Album 1700	1967	5.00	12.00
		— Original Warner albums above have gold labels. —			

PETERS, BROCK

United Arts. UAL-3041	(M)	Sing'a Man	1959	10.00	25.00
United Arts. UAL-3062	(M)	At The Village Gate	1959	10.00	25.00

PETERSEN, PAUL

Colpix CP-429	(M)	Lollipops And Roses	1962	10.00	25.00
Colpix SCP-429	(S)	Lollipops And Roses	1962	16.00	40.00
Colpix CP-442	(M)	My Dad	1963	10.00	25.00
Colpix SCP-442	(S)	My Dad	1963	16.00	40.00

PETERSON, RAY

RCA Victor LPM-2297	(M)	Tell Laura I Love Her	1960	35.00	70.00
RCA Victor LSP-2297	(S)	Tell Laura I Love Her	1960	50.00	100.00
MGM E-4250	(M)	The Very Best Of Ray Peterson	1964	10.00	25.00
MGM SE-4250	(S)	The Very Best Of Ray Peterson	1964	12.00	30.00
MGM E-4277	(M)	The Other Side Of Ray Peterson	1965	10.00	25.00
MGM SE-4277	(S)	The Other Side Of Ray Peterson	1965	12.00	30.00
Uni 73078	(S)	The Best Of Ray Peterson	1969	8.00	20.00
Decca DL-75307	(S)	Ray Peterson Country	1971	8.00	20.00

PETTY TRIO, NORMAN

Vik LX-1073	(M)	Corsage	1957	20.00	50.00
Columbia CL-1092	(M)	Moondreams	1958	75.00	150.00
		(Features Buddy Holly on guitar on the title track.)			
Top Rank RS-639	(S)	Petty For Your Thoughts	1960	14.00	35.00

PETTY, TOM (& THE HEARTBREAKERS)

Shelter SRL-52006	(S)	Tom Petty & The Heartbreakers	1976	8.00	20.00
		(Yellow label. Issued with a sheet of black & white photos of TP.)			
Shelter/ABC TP-12677	(DJ)	Official Live 'Leg	1976	16.00	40.00
		(One-sided. Convincing counterfeits exist.)			
Shelter/ABC DA-52029	(DJ)	You're Gonna Get It! (Red vinyl)	1978	10.00	25.00
MCA 8021	(DJ)	Pack Up The Plantation (Sampler)	1985	6.00	15.00

PHANTOM'S DIVINE COMEDY, THE

Capitol ST-11313	(S)	Part One	1974	20.00	50.00

PHAPHNER

Dragon LP-101	(S)	Overdrive	197?	See note below	
		(Rare. Estimated near mint value $2,000-3,000.)			

PHARAOHS, THE

Scarab 001	(S)	Awakening	1972	6.00	15.00

PHILLIPS, BILL

Harmony HL-7309	(M)	Bill Phillips' Best	1964	8.00	20.00
Decca DL-4792	(M)	Put It Off Until Tomorrow	1966	8.00	20.00
Decca DL-74792	(S)	Put It Off Until Tomorrow	1966	10.00	25.00

Label & Catalog #		Title	Year	VG+	NM
PHILLIPS, ESTHER [LITTLE ESTHER]					
King LP-622	(M)	**Down Memory Lane With Little Esther**	1956	800.00	1,200.00
Lenox 227	(M)	**Release Me**	1962	35.00	70.00
Atlantic 8102	(M)	**And I Love Him**	1965	12.00	30.00
Atlantic SD-8102	(S)	**And I Love Him**	1965	16.00	40.00
Atlantic 8122	(M)	**Esther**	1966	10.00	25.00
Atlantic SD-8122	(S)	**Esther**	1966	12.00	30.00
Atlantic 8130	(M)	**The Country Side Of Esther Phillips**	1966	10.00	25.00
Atlantic SD-8130	(S)	**The Country Side Of Esther Phillips**	1966	12.00	30.00
		(Atlantic 8130 is a repackage of Lenox 227.)			
Atlantic SD-1565	(S)	**Burnin'**	1970	6.00	15.00
PHILLIPS, JOHN					
Mr. Phillips was formerly a member of The Journeymen; The Mamas & The Papas.					
Dunhill DS-50077	(S)	**John Phillips/Wolf King Of L.A.**	1970	6.00	15.00
20th Century 4210	(DJ)	**Myra Breckinridge** *(Soundtrack)*	1970	*See note below*	
		(Rare. Estimated near mint value $500-1,000.)			
MGM 1SE-28ST	(S)	**Brewster McCloud** *(Soundtrack)*	1970	6.00	15.00
PHILLIPS, WARREN, & THE ROCKETS					
Parrot PAS-71044	(S)	**Rocked Out**	1970	8.00	20.00
PHILOSOPHERS, THE					
Philo Spectrum LP-1001	(S)	**After Sundown**	1970	45.00	90.00
PHLUPH					
Verve V6-5054	(S)	**Phluph**	1968	6.00	15.00
PIANO RED					
Groove LG-1001	(M)	**Jump Man, Jump**	1956	180.00	300.00
Groove LG-1002	(M)	**Piano Red In Concert**	1956	180.00	300.00
PICKETT, BOBBY "BORIS" (& THE CRYPT KICKERS)					
Garpax GP-67001	(M)	**The Monster Mash**	1962	35.00	70.00
Garpax SGP-67001	(S)	**The Monster Mash**	1962	75.00	150.00
Parrott XPAS-71063	(E)	**The Original Monster Mash**	1973	10.00	25.00
PICKETT, WILSON					
Double-L DL-2300	(M)	**It's Too Late**	1963	16.00	40.00
Double-L SDL-8300	(S)	**It's Too Late**	1963	20.00	50.00
Atlantic 8114	(M)	**In The Midnight Hour**	1965	12.00	30.00
Atlantic SD-8114	(S)	**In The Midnight Hour**	1965	16.00	40.00
Atlantic 8129	(M)	**The Exciting Wilson Pickett**	1966	8.00	20.00
Atlantic SD-8129	(S)	**The Exciting Wilson Pickett**	1966	12.00	30.00
Atlantic 8138	(M)	**The Wicked Pickett**	1967	8.00	20.00
Atlantic SD-8138	(S)	**The Wicked Pickett**	1967	12.00	30.00
Atlantic 8145	(M)	**The Sound Of Wilson Pickett**	1967	8.00	20.00
Atlantic SD-8145	(S)	**The Sound Of Wilson Pickett**	1967	12.00	30.00
Atlantic 8151	(M)	**The Best Of Wilson Pickett**	1967	8.00	20.00
Atlantic SD-8151	(E)	**The Best Of Wilson Pickett**	1967	6.00	15.00
Atlantic SD-8175	(S)	**I'm In Love**	1968	6.00	15.00
Atlantic SD-8183	(S)	**Midnight Mover**	1968	6.00	15.00
Atlantic SD-8215	(S)	**Hey Jude**	1869	5.00	12.00
Atlantic SD-8250	(S)	**Right On**	1970	5.00	12.00
Atlantic SD-8270	(S)	**Wilson Pickett In Philadelphia**	1970	5.00	12.00
Atlantic SD-8290	(S)	**The Best Of Wilson Pickett, Volume 2**	1971	5.00	12.00
Atlantic SD-8300	(S)	**Don't Knock My Love**	1971	5.00	12.00
Atlantic SD-2501	(P)	**Wilson Pickett's Greatest Hits**	1973	5.00	12.00
PIERCE, WEBB					
Decca DL-5536 (10")	(M)	**That Wondering Boy**	1953	50.00	100.00
Decca DL-8129	(M)	**Webb Pierce**	1955	20.00	50.00
Decca DL-8295	(M)	**That Wondering Boy**	1956	20.00	50.00
Decca DL-8728	(M)	**Just Imagination**	1957	16.00	40.00
Decca DL-8889	(M)	**Bound For The Kingdom**	1959	10.00	25.00
Decca DL-78889	(S)	**Bound For The Kingdom**	1959	16.00	40.00
Decca DL-8899	(M)	**Webb!**	1959	10.00	25.00
Decca DL-78899	(S)	**Webb!**	1959	16.00	40.00

— Original Decca albums above have black & silver labels.—

Label & Catalog #		Title	Year	VG+	NM
King 648	(M)	The One And Only Webb Pierce	1959	20.00	50.00
Decca DL-4015	(M)	Webb With A Beat	1960	6.00	15.00
Decca DL-74015	(S)	Webb With A Beat	1960	8.00	20.00
Decca DL-4079	(M)	Walking The Streets	1960	6.00	15.00
Decca DL-74079	(S)	Walking The Streets	1960	8.00	20.00
Decca DL-4110	(M)	Golden Favorites	1961	6.00	15.00
Decca DL-74110	(E)	Golden Favorites	1961	4.00	10.00
Decca DL-4144	(M)	Fallen Angel	1961	5.00	12.00
Decca DL-74144	(S)	Fallen Angel	1961	6.00	15.00
Decca DL-4218	(M)	Hideaway Heart	1962	5.00	12.00
Decca DL-74218	(S)	Hideaway Heart	1962	6.00	15.00
Decca DL-4294	(M)	Cross Country	1962	5.00	12.00
Decca DL-74294	(S)	Cross Country	1962	6.00	15.00
Decca DL-4358	(M)	I've Got A New Heartache	1963	5.00	12.00
Decca DL-74358	(S)	I've Got A New Heartache	1963	6.00	15.00
Decca DL-4384	(M)	Bow Thy Head	1963	5.00	12.00
Decca DL-74384	(S)	Bow Thy Head	1963	6.00	15.00
Decca DXB-181	(M)	The Webb Pierce Story (2 LPs with booklet)	1964	8.00	20.00
Decca DXSB-181	(S)	The Webb Pierce Story (2 LPs with booklet)	1964	10.00	25.00
Decca DL-4486	(M)	Sands Of Gold	1964	5.00	12.00
Decca DL-74486	(S)	Sands Of Gold	1964	6.00	15.00
Decca DL-4604	(M)	Memory No. 1	1965	5.00	12.00
Decca DL-74604	(S)	Memory No. 1	1965	6.00	15.00
Decca DL-4659	(M)	Country Music Time	1965	5.00	12.00
Decca DL-74659	(S)	Country Music Time	1965	6.00	15.00
Decca DL-4739	(M)	Sweet Memories	1966	5.00	12.00
Decca DL-74739	(S)	Sweet Memories	1966	6.00	15.00
Decca DL-4782	(M)	Webb's Choice	1966	5.00	12.00
Decca DL-74782	(S)	Webb's Choice	1966	6.00	15.00

— Original Decca albums above have black labels with "Mfrd by Decca" beneath the rainbow. —

PIERCE, WEBB / MARVIN RAINWATER / STUART HAMBLEN

Audio Lab AL-1563	(M)	Sing For You	195?	30.00	60.00

PIKE, PETE

Audio Lab AL-1559	(M)	Pete Pike	1960	20.00	50.00

PILOT

RCA Victor LSP-4730	(S)	Pilot	1972	5.00	12.00
RCA Victor LSP-4825	(S)	Point Of View	1973	8.00	20.00

PINK FLOYD

Pink Floyd is Nick Mason, Roger Waters, Roger Wright and Syd Barrett, who was replaced by David Gilmour in 1968.

Tower T-5093	(DJ)	Piper At The Gates Of Dawn (White label)	1967	100.00	200.00
Tower T-5093	(M)	Piper At The Gates Of Dawn (Orange label)	1967	75.00	150.00
Tower ST-5093	(S)	Piper At The Gates Of Dawn (Orange label)	1967	16.00	40.00
Tower ST-5093	(S)	Piper At The Gates Of Dawn (Striped label)	1968	20.00	50.00
Tower ST-5131	(DJ)	A Saucerful Of Secrets (White label)	1968	50.00	100.00
Tower ST-5131	(S)	A Saucerful Of Secrets (Orange label)	1968	16.00	40.00
Tower ST-5169	(DJ)	More (Soundtrack. White label)	1968	50.00	100.00
Tower ST-5169	(S)	More (Soundtrack)	1968	16.00	40.00
Harvest 388	(S)	Ummagumma (2 LPs)	1969	16.00	40.00
		(First pressing covers have a copy of "Ummagumma" leaning against the wall in the left foreground.)			
Harvest SMAS-382	(S)	Atom Heart Mother	1970	8.00	20.00
Harvest SW-759	(S)	Relics	1971	5.00	12.00
Harvest SMAS-832	(S)	Meddle	1971	6.00	15.00
Harvest ST-11078	(S)	Obscured By Clouds (Soundtrack)	1972	6.00	15.00
Harvest SMAS-11163	(S)	The Dark Side Of The Moon	1973	5.00	12.00
Harvest SABB-11257	(S)	Nice Pair (2 LPs)	1973	6.00	15.00
Capitol SPRO-8116	(DJ)	Pink Floyd Tour '75	1975	35.00	70.00
Capitol SEAX-11902	(S)	The Dark Side Of The Moon (Picture disc)	1978	12.00	30.00
Columbia PC-33453	(S)	Wish You Were Here	1975	4.00	10.00
Columbia PCQ-33453	(Q)	Wish You Were Here	1975	16.00	40.00
Columbia AP-1	(DJ)	Animals (With insert)	1977	12.00	30.00
Columbia PCQ-34474	(Q)	Animals	1977	16.00	40.00
Columbia HC-33453	(S)	Wish You Were Here (Half-speed master)	1981	20.00	50.00
Columbia HC-43453	(S)	Wish You Were Here (Half-speed master)	1982	14.00	35.00

Label & Catalog #		Title	Year	VG+	NM
Columbia H2C-46183	(S)	**The Wall** *(2 LPs. Half-speed master)*	1983	60.00	120.00
Columbia HC-47680	(S)	**Collection Of Great Dance Songs** *(Half-speed master)*	1983	14.00	35.00
Columbia AS-	(DJ)	**Off The Wall**	1983	35.00	70.00
Columbia AS-1636	(DJ)	**Final Cut** *(Banded for airplay)*	1983	8.00	20.00
Mobile Fidelity MFSL-017	(S)	**The Dark Side Of The Moon**	1977	16.00	40.00
Mobile Fidelity MFHR-017	(S)	**The Dark Side Of The Moon** *(UHQR in a box)*	1982	180.00	300.00
Mobile Fidelity MFSL-197	(S)	**Meddle**	198?	12.00	30.00

PINK GRASS

No label	(S)	**Rhubarb's Revenge, or, Confessions Of A Big, Lanky Dope**	197?	300.00	500.00

PINK PUZZ: *Refer to* **PAUL REVERE & THE RAIDERS**

PIPKINS, THE

Capitol ST-483	(S)	**Gimme Dat Ding**	1970	6.00	15.00

PISANI, FRANK

Dellwood DLD-56010	(S)	**Sky**	1977	50.00	100.00

PITNEY, GENE
Gene also recorded with George Jones.

Musicor MM-2001	(M)	**The Many Sides Of Gene Pitney**	1962	8.00	20.00
Musicor MS-3001	(S)	**The Many Sides Of Gene Pitney** *(Musicor 3001 originally issued on a brown label.)*	1962	12.00	30.00
Musicor MM-2001	(M)	**The Many Sides Of Gene Pitney**	1962	6.00	15.00
Musicor MS-3001	(S)	**The Many Sides Of Gene Pitney**	1962	8.00	20.00
Musicor MM 2003	(M)	**Only Love Can Break A Heart**	1962	6.00	15.00
Musicor MS-3003	(S)	**Only Love Can Break A Heart**	1962	8.00	20.00
Musicor MM-2004	(M)	**Gene Pitney Sings Just For You**	1963	6.00	15.00
Musicor MS-3004	(S)	**Gene Pitney Sings Just For You**	1963	8.00	20.00
Musicor MM-2005	(M)	**World-Wide Winners**	1963	6.00	15.00
Musicor MS-3005	(S)	**World-Wide Winners**	1963	8.00	20.00
Musicor MM-2006	(M)	**Blue Gene**	1963	6.00	15.00
Musicor MS-3006	(S)	**Blue Gene**	1963	8.00	20.00
Musicor MM-2007	(M)	**The Fair Young Ladies Of Folkland**	1964	6.00	15.00
Musicor MS-3007	(S)	**The Fair Young Ladies Of Folkland**	1964	8.00	20.00
Musicor MM-2008	(M)	**Gene Pitney's Big Sixteen**	1964	5.00	12.00
Musicor MS-3008	(S)	**Gene Pitney's Big Sixteen**	1964	6.00	15.00

— Original Musicor albums above have black labels with "Distributed by United Artists."—

Musicor MM-2015	(M)	**Gene Italiano**	1964	5.00	12.00
Musicor MS-3015	(S)	**Gene Italiano**	1964	6.00	15.00
Musicor MM-2019	(M)	**It Hurts To Be In Love**	1964	5.00	12.00
Musicor MS-3019	(S)	**It Hurts To Be In Love**	1964	6.00	15.00
Musicor MM-2043	(M)	**Big Sixteen, Volume 2**	1965	5.00	12.00
Musicor MS-3043	(S)	**Big Sixteen, Volume 2**	1965	6.00	15.00
Musicor MM-2056	(M)	**I Must Be Seeing Things**	1965	5.00	12.00
Musicor MS-3056	(S)	**I Must Be Seeing Things**	1965	6.00	15.00
Musicor MM-2069	(M)	**Looking Through The Eyes Of Love**	1965	5.00	12.00
Musicor MS-3069	(S)	**Looking Through The Eyes Of Love**	1965	6.00	15.00
Musicor MM-2072	(M)	**Gene Pitney Espanol**	1965	5.00	12.00
Musicor MS-3072	(S)	**Gene Pitney Espanol**	1965	6.00	15.00
Musicor MM-2085	(M)	**Big Sixteen, Volume 3**	1966	5.00	12.00
Musicor MS-3085	(S)	**Big Sixteen, Volume 3**	1966	6.00	15.00
Musicor MM-2095	(M)	**Backstage I'm Lonely**	1966	5.00	12.00
Musicor MS-3095	(S)	**Backstage I'm Lonely**	1966	6.00	15.00
Musicor MM-2100	(M)	**Messumo Mi Puo Giudicare**	1966	5.00	12.00
Musicor MS-3100	(S)	**Messumo Mi Puo Giudicare**	1966	6.00	15.00
Musicor MM-2101	(M)	**The Gene Pitney Show**	1966	5.00	12.00
Musicor MS-3101	(S)	**The Gene Pitney Show**	1966	6.00	15.00
Musicor MM-2102	(M)	**Greatest Hits Of All Time**	1966	5.00	12.00
Musicor MS-3102	(S)	**Greatest Hits Of All Time**	1966	6.00	15.00
Musicor MM-2104	(M)	**The Country Side Of Gene Pitney**	1966	5.00	12.00
Musicor MS-3104	(S)	**The Country Side Of Gene Pitney**	1966	6.00	15.00
Musicor MM-2108	(M)	**Young And Warm And Wonderful**	1966	5.00	12.00
Musicor MS-3108	(S)	**Young And Warm And Wonderful**	1966	6.00	15.00
Musicor MM-2117	(M)	**Just One Smile**	1967	5.00	12.00
Musicor MS-3117	(S)	**Just One Smile**	1967	6.00	15.00

Label & Catalog #		Title	Year	VG+	NM
Musicor MM-2134	(M)	Golden Greats	1967	5.00	12.00
Musicor MS-3134	(S)	Golden Greats	1967	6.00	15.00
Musicor M2S-3148	(S)	The Gene Pitney Story	1968	6.00	15.00
Musicor MS-3161	(S)	Gene Pitney Sings Burt Bacharach	1968	5.00	12.00
Musicor MS-3164	(S)	She's A Heartbreaker	1968	6.00	15.00
Musicor P2S-5025	(S)	This Is Gene Pitney (2 LPs. Record Club)	1968	6.00	15.00
Musicor MS-3174	(S)	The Greatest Hits Of Gene Pitney	1969	5.00	12.00
Musicor MS-3183	(S)	This Is Gene Pitney	1970	5.00	12.00
Musicor MS-3206	(S)	Ten Years After	1971	5.00	12.00
Musicor MS-3250	(S)	The Golden Hits Of Gene Pitney	1971	5.00	12.00
		— Original Musicor albums above have black labels.—			
PIXIES THREE, THE					
Mercury MG-20912	(M)	Party With The Pixies Three	1964	50.00	100.00
Mercury SR-60912	(P)	Party With The Pixies Three	1964	75.00	150.00
PLAIN JANE					
Hobbit 5000	(S)	Plain Jane	1969	10.00	25.00
PLANT & SEE					
White Whale S-7120	(S)	Plant And See	1969	8.00	20.00
PLATTERS, THE					
The original Platters feature Tony Williams.					
Federal 395-549	(M)	The Platters	1955	660.00	1,000.00
King 395-549	(M)	The Platters	1955	300.00	500.00
King 651	(M)	Only You (Repackage of King 549)	1959	240.00	400.00
Mercury MG-20146	(M)	The Platters	1956	50.00	100.00
Mercury MG-20216	(M)	The Platters, Volume 2	1956	50.00	100.00
Mercury MG-20298	(M)	Flying Platters	1957	50.00	100.00
Mercury MG-20366	(M)	Flying Platters Around The World	1959	14.00	35.00
Mercury SR-60043	(S)	Flying Platters Around The World	1959	20.00	50.00
Mercury MG-20410	(M)	Remember When?	1959	14.00	35.00
Mercury SR-60087	(S)	Remember When?	1959	20.00	50.00
Mercury MG-20472	(M)	Encore Of Golden Hits	1960	10.00	25.00
Mercury SR-60243	(S)	Encore Of Golden Hits	1960	14.00	35.00
Mercury MG-20481	(M)	Reflections	1960	10.00	25.00
Mercury SR-60160	(S)	Reflections	1960	14.00	35.00
Mercury MG-20589	(M)	Life Is Just A Bowl Of Cherries	1960	10.00	25.00
Mercury SR-60254	(S)	Life Is Just A Bowl Of Cherries	1960	14.00	35.00
Mercury MG-20591	(M)	More Encore Of Golden Hits	1960	10.00	25.00
Mercury SR-60252	(S)	More Encore Of Golden Hits	1960	14.00	35.00
Mercury MG-20669	(M)	The Platters Sing For The Lonely	1962	10.00	25.00
Mercury SR-60669	(S)	The Platters Sing For The Lonely	1962	14.00	35.00
Mercury MG-20693	(M)	Encore Of Golden Hits Of The Groups	1962	10.00	25.00
Mercury SR-60693	(S)	Encore Of Golden Hits Of The Groups	1962	14.00	35.00
Mercury MG-20759	(M)	Moonlight Memories	1963	10.00	25.00
Mercury SR-60759	(S)	Moonlight Memories	1963	14.00	35.00
Mercury MG-20782	(M)	The Platters Sing All The Movie Hits	1963	10.00	25.00
Mercury SR-60782	(S)	The Platters Sing All The Movie Hits	1963	14.00	35.00
Mercury MG-20808	(M)	The Platters Sing Latino	1963	10.00	25.00
Mercury SR-60808	(S)	The Platters Sing Latino	1963	14.00	35.00
Mercury MG-20841	(M)	Christmas With The Platters	1963	10.00	25.00
Mercury SR-60841	(S)	Christmas With The Platters	1963	14.00	35.00
		— Original Mercury albums above have black & silver labels.—			
Mercury MG-20983	(M)	The New Soul Of The Platters	1965	8.00	20.00
Mercury SR-60983	(S)	The New Soul Of The Platters	1965	10.00	25.00
Wing MGW-12112	(M)	Encores	1962	5.00	12.00
Wing SRW-16112	(S)	Encores	1962	6.00	15.00
Wing MGW-12226	(M)	Flying Platters	1963	5.00	12.00
Wing SRW-16226	(S)	Flying Platters	1963	6.00	15.00
Wing MGW-12272	(M)	Reflections	1964	5.00	12.00
Wing SRW-16272	(S)	Reflections	1964	6.00	15.00
Wing MGW-12346	(M)	10th Anniversary Album	1965	5.00	12.00
Wing SRW-16346	(S)	10th Anniversary Album	1965	6.00	15.00
Musicor MM-2091	(M)	I Love You 1,000 Times	1966	5.00	12.00
Musicor MS-3091	(S)	I Love You 1,000 Times	1966	6.00	15.00
Musicor MM-2111	(M)	The Platters Have The Magic Touch	1966	5.00	12.00
Musicor MS-3111	(S)	The Platters Have The Magic Touch	1966	6.00	15.00

Label & Catalog #		Title	Year	VG+	NM
Musicor MM-2125	(M)	**Going Back To Detroit**	1967	5.00	12.00
Musicor MS-3125	(S)	**Going Back To Detroit**	1967	6.00	15.00
Musicor MM-2141	(M)	**New Golden Hits Of The Platters**	1967	5.00	12.00
Musicor MS-3141	(S)	**New Golden Hits Of The Platters**	1967	6.00	15.00
Musicor MS-3156	(S)	**Sweet, Sweet Lovin'**	1968	6.00	15.00
Musicor MS-3171	(S)	**I Get The Sweetest Feeling**	1968	6.00	15.00
Musicor MS-3185	(S)	**Singing The Great Hits Our Way**	1969	6.00	15.00
Music Disc MDS-1002	(S)	**Only You**	1969	6.00	15.00

PLAYBACKS, THE

Round LP-1111	(M)	**Greatest Of The Latest**	196?	20.00	50.00

PLAYERS, THE

Minit 4006	(M)	**He'll Be Back**	1966	5.00	12.00
Minit 24006	(S)	**He'll Be Back**	1966	6.00	15.00

PLAYMATES, THE

Roulette R-25001	(M)	**Calypso**	1958	8.00	20.00
Roulette SR-25001	(S)	**Calypso**	1958	10.00	25.00
Roulette R-25043	(M)	**At Play With The Playmates**	1958	8.00	20.00
Roulette SR-25043	(S)	**At Play With The Playmates**	1958	10.00	25.00
Roulette R-25059	(M)	**Rock And Roll Record Hop**	1959	8.00	20.00
Roulette SR-25059	(S)	**Rock And Roll Record Hop**	1959	10.00	25.00
Roulette R-25068	(M)	**Cuttin' Capers**	1959	8.00	20.00
Roulette SR-25068	(S)	**Cuttin' Capers**	1959	10.00	25.00
Roulette R-25084	(M)	**Broadway Show Stoppers**	1959	8.00	20.00
Roulette SR-25084	(S)	**Broadway Show Stoppers**	1959	10.00	25.00
Forum F-16001	(M)	**The Playmates Visit West Of The Indies**	1960	6.00	15.00
Forum SF-16001	(S)	**The Playmates Visit West Of The Indies**	1960	8.00	20.00
Roulette R-25139	(M)	**Wait For Me**	1961	6.00	15.00
Roulette SR-25139	(S)	**Wait For Me**	1961	8.00	20.00

PLEASURE FAIR, THE

Uni 3009	(M)	**The Pleasure Fair**	1967	5.00	12.00
Uni 73009	(S)	**The Pleasure Fair**	1967	6.00	15.00

PLIMSOULS, THE

Beat BE-1001	(S)	**Zero Hour** *(Five tracks)*	1980	10.00	25.00
Planet P-13	(S)	**The Plimsouls**	1981	8.00	20.00

POCO

Poco's original line-up included Richie Furay and Jim Messina of The Buffalo Springfield.

Epic EQ-30209	(Q)	**Deliverin'**	1971	5.00	12.00
Epic EQ-32354	(Q)	**Crazy Eyes**	1973	5.00	12.00
Epic PEQ-33192	(Q)	**Cantamos**	1974	5.00	12.00
Mobile Fidelity MFSL-020	(S)	**Legend**	1978	6.00	15.00

POINT, THE

No label	(S)	**The Point** *(10" on white vinyl)*	1981	75.00	150.00

POLICE

A&M SP-3735	(S)	**Synchronicity** *(Brown & grey cover)*	1983	12.00	30.00
A&M SP-3735	(S)	**Synchronicity** *(Black & white cover)*	1983	20.00	50.00
Nautilus NR-19	(S)	**Zenyatta Mondatta**	198?	8.00	20.00
Nautilus NR-40	(S)	**Ghost In The Machine**	198?	10.00	25.00

POLK, LUCY ANN

Trend TL-1008 (10")	(M)	**Lucy Ann Polk With Dave Pell**	1953	35.00	70.00
Mode MOD-115	(M)	**Lucky Lucy Ann**	1957	30.00	60.00
Interlude MO-504	(M)	**Easy Livin'**	1959	10.00	25.00
Interlude ST-1004	(S)	**Easy Livin'**	1959	14.00	35.00

PONCE, PONCIE

Warner Bros. W-1453	(M)	**Poncie Ponce Sings**	1962	8.00	20.00
Warner Bros. WS-1453	(S)	**Poncie Ponce Sings**	1962	10.00	25.00

PONTY, JEAN LUC

World Pacific WPS-20172	(S)	**King Kong/Ponty Plays Zappa**	1970	10.00	25.00

(Although uncredited, Zappa produces and plays guitar.)

Label & Catalog #		Title	Year	VG+	NM

In addition to the common colored graphics on the cover of "Synchronicity," A&M released the album in a muted brown and grey and a rare black and white variation.

POOBAH

Peppermint	(S)	**Let Me In**	1969	240.00	400.00
Peppermint	(S)	**U.S. Rock**	1969	60.00	120.00
Peppermint	(S)	**Steamroller**	1969	50.00	100.00

POOLE, BILLIE

Riverside RLP-425	(M)	**Sermonette/The Voice Of Billie Poole**	1962	10.00	25.00
Riverside RLP-9425	(S)	**Sermonette/The Voice Of Billie Poole**	1962	14.00	35.00
Riverside RLP-458	(M)	**Confessin' The Blues**	1962	10.00	25.00
Riverside RLP-9458	(S)	**Confessin' The Blues**	1962	14.00	35.00

POOLE, BRIAN, & THE TREMELOES

Audio Fidelity AF-2151	(M)	**Brian Poole Is Here**	1966	8.00	20.00
Audio Fidelity AFS-6151	(S)	**Brian Poole Is Here**	1966	12.00	30.00
Audio Fidelity AF-2177	(M)	**The Tremeloes Are Here**	1967	8.00	20.00
Audio Fidelity AFS-6177	(S)	**The Tremeloes Are Here**	1967	12.00	30.00
		(These are the same albums with different titles.)			

POPCORN BLIZZARD, THE

(No label)	(M)	**Explode!**	196?	50.00	100.00

PORTER, PEPPER

First American FA-7756	(S)	**Invasion**	197?	10.00	25.00

POWELL, DICK

Decca DL-8837	(S)	**Song Book**	1958	10.00	25.00
Dot DLP-3421	(M)	**Themes From Original TV Soundtracks**	1962	10.00	25.00
Dot DLP-25421	(S)	**Themes From Original TV Soundtracks**	1962	12.00	30.00
Columbia C2L-44	(M)	**Dick Powell In Hollywood** *(2 LPs)*	1966	8.00	20.00
Columbia C2S-44	(S)	**Dick Powell In Hollywood** *(2 LPs)*	1966	10.00	25.00

Label & Catalog #		Title	Year	VG+	NM

POWELL, JANE
Refer to Gordon MacRae; Marilyn Monroe.

Label & Catalog #		Title	Year	VG+	NM
Columbia CL-2034 (10")	(M)	**Romance**	1949	**30.00**	**60.00**
Columbia CL-2045 (10")	(M)	**A Date With Jane Powell**	1949	**30.00**	**60.00**
Columbia ML-4148	(M)	**Alice In Wonderland**	1950	**40.00**	**80.00**
MGM E-508 (10")	(M)	**Nancy Goes To Rio** *(Soundtrack)*	1950	**50.00**	**100.00**
MGM E-530 (10")	(M)	**Two Weeks With Love** *(Soundtrack)*	1950	**50.00**	**100.00**
MGM E-543 (10")	(M)	**Royal Wedding** *(Soundtrack)*	1951	**50.00**	**100.00**
MGM E-86 (10")	(M)	**Rich, Young And Pretty** *(Soundtrack)*	1951	**50.00**	**100.00**
Mercury MG-25202	(M)	**Athena** *(Soundtrack)*	1954	**100.00**	**200.00**
MGM E-224 (10")	(M)	**Seven Brides For Seven Brothers** *(Soundtk.)*	1954	**50.00**	**100.00**
MGM E-3233	(M)	**Two Weeks With Love** *(Soundtrack)*	1955	**20.00**	**50.00**
MGM E-3236	(M)	**Rich, Young And Pretty** *(Soundtrack)*	1955	**20.00**	**50.00**
MGM E-3451	(M)	**Something Wonderful**	1957	**16.00**	**40.00**
Verve V-2023	(M)	**Can't We Be Friends?**	1956	**14.00**	**35.00**

POWERS OF BLUE, THE

Label & Catalog #		Title	Year	VG+	NM
M.T.A. 1002	(M)	**Flipout**	1967	**5.00**	**12.00**
M.T.A. 5002	(S)	**Flipout**	1967	**6.00**	**15.00**

PREMIERS, THE

Label & Catalog #		Title	Year	VG+	NM
Warner Bros. W-1565	(M)	**Farmer John**	1964	**12.00**	**30.00**
Warner Bros. WS-1565	(S)	**Farmer John**	1964	**16.00**	**40.00**

PRESLEY, ELVIS
With few exceptions, each of Elvis' albums remained in print since release through the vinyl era. Since this covers many RCA label changes through the years—there are a staggering number of variations— reissues for these titles would, if listed, take up more room than this book can provide (and that does not count the hundreds of record club, mail order, off label and movie related albums). Thus, for albums released from 1956 through 1973, first pressings (with essential promos) are listed.

Elvis' albums were issued on RCA's classic black label with Nipper on top through 1968 (with various label changes, noted below). Beginning with LPM-4088 and continuing through 4445, original pressings have orange labels and were pressed on thick, non-flexible vinyl. These were reissued with identical labels but on flimsy, flexible vinyl in 1971-73. Similarly, Camden CAS-2304 through 2428 were pressed on the non-flexible vinyl and also reissued on the flexible vinyl. The flexible of the RCA and the Camden reissues are worth 50-60% of the non-flexible prices.

Most of the early albums (1956-1962) were reissued several times: mono albums were changed in 1963 to read "Mono" on the bottom of the label. These reissues are generally worth 40-50% of the originals. The monaural albums received a further label change in 1965 when the motto on the bottom of the label was changed to "Monaural;" these are worth approximately 60-80% of the "Mono" labels.

The "Living Stereo" albums were reissued in 1965 with "Stereo" on the bottom; these reissues are generally worth 40-50% of the originals. Most of the stereo albums were reissued with an orange label in 1969 on stiff, non-flexible vinyl; with the same orange label on flimsy flexible vinyl in 1971; on the brown label in 1975; and on the "new" black label, with Nipper in the upper right, in the late '70s. The values for these vary dramatically and are not listed here; for more information on where to acquire data for these records, refer to the main introduction of this book.

Label & Catalog #		Title	Year	VG+	NM
RCA Victor F70P-9681	(DJ)	**E-Z Pop Programming #5**	1955	**300.00**	**500.00**
RCA Victor G70L-0108	(DJ)	**E-Z Country Programming #2**	1955	**300.00**	**500.00**
RCA Victor G70L-0197	(DJ)	**E-Z Pop Programming #6**	1956	**240.00**	**400.00**
RCA Victor G70L-0108	(DJ)	**E-Z Country Programming #3**	1956	**240.00**	**400.00**
		(The above four albums contain Elvis' first appearance on LP. Elvis appeared on a variety of compilations; many are listed in the "Various Artists" section of the book.)			
RCA Victor LPM-1254	(M)	**Elvis Presley**	1956	**75.00**	**150.00**
		(The word "Elvis" on the cover is in pale pink letters.)			
RCA Victor LPM-1254	(M)	**Elvis Presley**	1956	**50.00**	**100.00**
		(The word "Elvis" on the cover is in dark pink letters.)			
RCA Victor LPM-1382	(M)	**Elvis** *(With ads on back cover)*	1956	**60.00**	**120.00**
RCA Victor LPM-1382	(M)	**Elvis** *(Without the ads)*	1956	**50.00**	**100.00**
RCA Victor LPM-1382	(M)	**Elvis**	1956	**180.00**	**300.00**
		(The label prefixes each track with "Band 1" through "Band 6.")			
RCA Victor LPM-1382	(M)	**Elvis**	1956	**660.00**	**1,000.00**
		(Contains an alternate take of "Old Shep." The matrix number in the trail-off vinyl ends with either "17S" or "19S.")			

Label & Catalog #		Title	Year	VG+	NM
RCA Victor LPM-1515	(M)	Loving You	1957	50.00	100.00
RCA Victor LOC-1035	(M)	Elvis' Christmas Album	1957	300.00	500.00
		(With special "gift certificate" sticker on the cover.)			
RCA Victor LOC-1035	(M)	Elvis' Christmas Album	1957	240.00	400.00
		(Without the "gift certificate" sticker.)			
RCA Victor LPM-1707	(M)	Elvis' Golden Records	1958	50.00	100.00
		(The title on the front cover is in blue print.)			
RCA Victor LPM-1707	(M)	Elvis' Golden Records	1959	30.00	60.00
		(The title on the front cover is in blue print with "RE" on the back.)			
RCA Victor LPM-1884	(M)	King Creole	1958	50.00	100.00
RCA Victor LPM-1884		King Creole Bonus Photo	1958	50.00	100.00
RCA Victor LPM-1951	(M)	Elvis' Christmas Album	1958	50.00	100.00
RCA Victor LPM-1990	(M)	For LP Fans Only	1959	60.00	120.00
RCA Victor LPM-2011	(M)	A Date With Elvis	1959	75.00	150.00
		(Issued in a gatefold jacket with a 1960 calendar on the back. The song titles were not printed on the cover.)			
RCA Victor LPM-2011	(M)	A Date With Elvis	1959	100.00	200.00
		(Issued in a gatefold jacket with a 1960 calendar on the back. The song titles were not printed on the cover but a red sticker on front reads "Never Before On LP" and lists the songs.)			
RCA Victor LPM-2075	(M)	Elvis' Gold Records, Volume 2	1960	50.00	100.00
RCA Victor LPM-2231	(M)	Elvis Is Back!	1960	40.00	80.00
RCA Victor LSP-2231	(S)	Elvis Is Back!	1960	50.00	100.00
		(Issued in a gatefold jacket; the song titles were not printed on the cover.)			
RCA Victor LPM-2231	(M)	Elvis Is Back!	1960	50.00	100.00
RCA Victor LSP-2231	(S)	Elvis Is Back!	1960	75.00	150.00
		(Issued in a gatefold jacket; the song titles were not printed on the cover but a yellow sticker on the cover lists the songs.)			
RCA Victor LPM-2256	(M)	G.I. Blues	1960	16.00	40.00
RCA Victor LSP-2256	(S)	G.I. Blues	1960	30.00	60.00
RCA Victor LPM-2328	(M)	His Hand In Mine	1961	20.00	50.00
RCA Victor LSP-2328	(S)	His Hand In Mine	1961	35.00	70.00
RCA Victor LPM-2370	(M)	Something For Everybody	1961	35.00	70.00
RCA Victor LSP-2370	(S)	Something For Everybody	1961	40.00	80.00
		(Back cover advertises Elvis' latest Compact-33 releases.)			
RCA Victor LPM-2426	(M)	Blue Hawaii	1961	20.00	50.00
RCA Victor LSP-2426	(S)	Blue Hawaii	1961	30.00	60.00
RCA Victor LPM-2426	(M)	Blue Hawaii	1961	40.00	80.00
RCA Victor LSP-2426	(S)	Blue Hawaii	1961	50.00	100.00
		(Some copies of 2426 were issued with a red sticker on the cover that reads "Contains the Twist Special Rock-A-Hula Baby.")			
RCA Victor LPM-2523	(M)	Pot Luck With Elvis	1962	30.00	60.00
RCA Victor LSP-2523	(S)	Pot Luck With Elvis	1962	40.00	80.00
RCA Victor LPM-2621	(M)	Girls! Girls! Girls!	1962	16.00	40.00
RCA Victor LSP-2621	(S)	Girls! Girls! Girls!	1962	30.00	60.00
RCA Victor 2621		Girls! Girls! Girls! Bonus Calendar #1	1962	40.00	80.00
		(1963 calendar with ads for Elvis' EPs and LPs on the back)			
RCA Victor 2621		Girls! Girls! Girls! Bonus Calendar #2	1962	50.00	100.00
		(1963 calendar with ads for Elvis' 45s on the back)			
RCA Victor 2621		Girls! Girls! Girls! Bonus Calendar #3	1962	150.00	250.00
		(1963 calendar with Col. Parker as Santa Claus on the back)			
RCA Victor LPM-2697	(M)	It Happened At The World's Fair	1963	20.00	50.00
RCA Victor LSP-2697	(S)	It Happened At The World's Fair	1963	30.00	60.00
RCA Victor 2697		It Happened At The World's Fair Bonus Photo	1963	75.00	150.00

— Original RCA mono albums above have "Long Play" on the bottom of the label;
stereo albums have "Living Stereo" on the bottom.—

RCA Victor LPM-2756	(M)	Fun In Acapulco	1963	16.00	40.00
RCA Victor LSP-2756	(S)	Fun In Acapulco	1963	20.00	50.00
RCA Victor LPM-2765	(M)	Elvis' Golden Records, Volume 3	1963	16.00	40.00
RCA Victor LSP-2765	(S)	Elvis' Golden Records, Volume 3	1963	20.00	50.00
RCA Victor LPM-2894	(M)	Kissin' Cousins	1964	16.00	40.00
RCA Victor LSP-2894	(S)	Kissin' Cousins	1964	20.00	50.00
RCA Victor LPM-2999	(M)	Roustabout	1964	20.00	50.00
RCA Victor LSP-2999	(S)	Roustabout	1964	240.00	400.00

— Original RCA mono albums above have "Mono" on the bottom of the label;
stereo albums have a silver "RCA Victor" on top.—

Label & Catalog #		Title	Year	VG+	NM
RCA Victor LSP-2999	(S)	**Roustabout**	1965	20.00	50.00
RCA Victor LPM-3338	(M)	**Girl Happy**	1965	20.00	50.00
RCA Victor LSP-3338	(S)	**Girl Happy**	1965	20.00	50.00
RCA Victor LPM-3450	(M)	**Elvis For Everyone**	1965	20.00	50.00
RCA Victor LSP-3450	(S)	**Elvis For Everyone**	1965	16.00	40.00
RCA Victor LPM-3468	(M)	**Harum Scarum**	1965	16.00	40.00
RCA Victor LSP-3468	(S)	**Harum Scarum**	1965	16.00	40.00
RCA Victor 3468		**Harum Scarum Bonus Photo**	1965	12.00	30.00
RCA Victor LPM-3553	(M)	**Frankie And Johnny**	1966	16.00	40.00
RCA Victor LSP-3553	(S)	**Frankie And Johnny**	1966	16.00	40.00
RCA Victor 3553		**Frankie And Johnny Bonus Photo**	1966	12.00	30.00
RCA Victor LPM-3643	(M)	**Paradise Hawaiian Style**	1966	16.00	40.00
RCA Victor LSP-3643	(S)	**Paradise Hawaiian Style**	1966	16.00	40.00
RCA Victor LPM-3702	(M)	**Spinout**	1966	16.00	40.00
RCA Victor LSP-3702	(S)	**Spinout**	1966	16.00	40.00
RCA Victor 3702		**Spinout Bonus Photo**	1966	12.00	30.00
RCA SP-33-461	(DJ)	**Special Palm Sunday Programming**	1967	300.00	500.00
RCA Victor LPM-3758	(M)	**How Great Thou Art**	1967	20.00	50.00
RCA Victor LSP-3758	(S)	**How Great Thou Art**	1967	16.00	40.00
		(RCA 3758 reads "Dynagroove" on the bottom of the label.)			
RCA Victor LSP-3758	(S)	**How Great Thou Art**	1967	12.00	30.00
		("Stereo Dynagroove" label with an RIAA Gold Record Award			
		notification printed on the front cover.)			
RCA Victor LPM-3787	(M)	**Double Trouble**	1967	16.00	40.00
RCA Victor LSP-3787	(S)	**Double Trouble**	1967	16.00	40.00
RCA Victor 3787		**Double Trouble Bonus Photo**	1967	12.00	30.00
RCA Victor LPM-3893	(M)	**Clambake**	1967	75.00	150.00
RCA Victor LSP-3893	(S)	**Clambake**	1967	20.00	50.00
RCA Victor 3893		**Clambake Bonus Photo**	1967	12.00	30.00
RCA UNMR-5697	(DJ)	**Special Christmas Programming**	1967	660.00	1,000.00
RCA Victor LPM-3921	(M)	**Elvis' Gold Records, Volume 4**	1968	500.00	750.00
RCA Victor LSP-3921	(S)	**Elvis' Gold Records, Volume 4**	1968	20.00	50.00
RCA Victor 3921		**Elvis' Gold Records, Volume 4 Bonus Photo**	1968	50.00	100.00
RCA Victor LPM-3989	(M)	**Speedway**	1968	500.00	750.00
RCA Victor LSP-3989	(S)	**Speedway**	1968	16.00	40.00
		("Speedway" contains one track by Nancy Sinatra.)			
RCA Victor 3989		**Speedway Bonus Photo**	1968	14.00	35.00
		— *Original RCA mono albums above have "Monaural" on the bottom of the label;*			
		stereo albums have a white "RCA Victor" on top.—			
RCA Victor PRS-279	(P)	**Singer Presents Elvis**	1968	10.00	25.00
RCA Victor PRS-279	(P)	**Singer Presents Elvis Bonus Photo**	1968	6.00	15.00
RCA Victor LPM-4088	(M)	**Elvis (NBC TV Special)**	1968	8.00	20.00
RCA Victor LSP-4155	(S)	**From Elvis In Memphis**	1969	8.00	20.00
RCA Victor LSP-4155		**From Elvis In Memphis Bonus Photo**	1969	6.00	15.00
RCA Victor LSP-6020	(S)	**From Memphis To Vegas** (2 LPs)	1969	10.00	25.00
RCA Victor LSP-6020		**From Memphis To Vegas Bonus Photo**	1969	6.00	15.00
		(Issued with two photos; the price is for either one.)			
RCA Victor (No number)	(DJ)	**International Hotel Presents Elvis, 1969**	1969	——	1,100.00
		(Box given to attenders of Elvis' opening show in Vegas, 1969,			
		includes a copy of LPM-4088; a copy of LSP-4155; three photos;			
		an Elvis Record Catalog; and a letter from Elvis and the Colonel.			
		Approximately $750 of the value is for the box alone.)			
RCA Victor (No number)	(DJ)	**International Hotel Presents Elvis, 1970**	1970	——	1,200.00
		(Box given to attenders of Elvis' opening show in Vegas, 1970,			
		includes a copy of LSP-6020; a copy of "Kentucky Rain;" one			
		photo; an Elvis Record Catalog; a wallet calendar; a hotel menu;			
		a photo album; and a letter from Elvis and the Colonel.			
		Approximately $750 of the value is for the box alone.)			
RCA Victor LSP-4362	(S)	**On Stage-February, 1970**	1970	8.00	20.00
RCA Victor LPM-6401	(M)	**Worldwide 50 Gold Award Hits** (4 LP box)	1970	30.00	60.00
RCA Victor LPM-6401		**Worldwide 50 Gold Award Hits Bonus Book**	1970	10.00	25.00
RCA Victor LSP-4428	(S)	**In Person At The International Hotel**	1970	8.00	20.00
RCA Victor LSP-4429	(S)	**Back In Memphis**	1970	8.00	20.00
RCA Victor LSP-4445	(S)	**That's The Way It Is**	1970	10.00	25.00
RCA Victor LSP-4460	(S)	**Elvis Country**	1971	8.00	20.00
RCA Victor LSP-4460		**Elvis Country Bonus Photo**	1971	6.00	15.00

— *Original RCA albums above have orange labels and were pressed on non-flexible vinyl.*
Identical orange label second pressings on flexible vinyl exist for each title.—

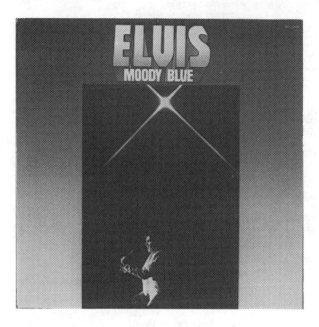

The initial pressing (250,000 copies) of Elvis' *Moody Blue* was pressed on translucent blue vinyl. When those copies were gone, RCA began pressing the album on black vinyl, only to learn of Elvis' unfortunate demise on August 16, 1977. In commemoration, they switched back to the blue. Thus, blue vinyl copies are common, with several millions sold in the U.S. The black vinyl version of AFL1-2428 is quite rare, although the album was reissued on black vinyl as AQL1-2428.

Copies of the the original album also exist on a variety of different colors including solid gold, green, red and white; white vinyl with either purple, red or yellow "splashed" into the pressing; and a very rare multi-color splash vinyl. Long believed to be experimental test pressings, there is reason to believe that they may have been run off by employees as private collectibles...

Label & Catalog #		Title	Year	VG+	NM
RCA Victor LSP-4530	(S)	**Love Letters From Elvis** *(Orange label)*	1971	**16.00**	**40.00**
		(The cover has the RCA logo at top center.)			
RCA Victor LSP-4530	(S)	**Love Letters From Elvis** *(Orange label)*	1971	**14.00**	**35.00**
		(The cover has the RCA logo in the lower right corner.)			
RCA Victor LPM-6402	(M)	**The Other Sides** *(4 LP box. Orange labels)*	1971	**16.00**	**40.00**
		(Subtitled "Worldwide Gold Award Hits, Volume 2." Printed on			
		the cover are ads for two bonuses, priced separately below.)			
RCA Victor LPM-6402		**The Other Sides Bonus Poster**	1971	**6.00**	**15.00**
RCA Victor LPM-6402		**The Other Sides Bonus Envelope**	1971	**6.00**	**15.00**
		(Small envelope holds a piece of cloth from Elvis' wardrobe.)			
RCA Victor LSP-4579	(S)	**The Wonderful World Of Christmas**	1971	**10.00**	**25.00**
		(Orange label)			
RCA Victor LSP-4579		**The Wonderful World Of Christmas Photo**	1971	**6.00**	**15.00**
RCA Victor LSP-4671	(S)	**Elvis Now** *(Orange label)*	1972	**8.00**	**20.00**
RCA Victor LSP-4690	(S)	**He Touched Me** *(Orange label)*	1972	**8.00**	**20.00**
RCA SPS-33-571-1	(DJ)	**Recorded At Madison Square Garden**	1972	**100.00**	**200.00**
		(2 LPs banded for air-play and issued in a plain white cover.)			
RCA Victor LSP-4776	(S)	**Recorded At Madison Square Garden**	1972	**6.00**	**15.00**
		(Orange label)			
RCA Victor VPSX-6089	(S)	**Aloha From Hawaii Via Satellite** *(2 LPs)*	1973	**1,000.00**	**1,500.00**
		(With "Chicken of the Sea" tuna sticker on cover.)			
RCA Victor VPSX-6089	(S)	**Aloha From Hawaii Via Satellite** *(2 LPs)*	1973	**10.00**	**25.00**
		(Dark orange label with a dark "Quadradisc" on top			
		and "RCA" on the bottom.)			
RCA Victor APL1-0283	(S)	**Elvis (Featuring "Fool")** *(Orange label)*	1973	**16.00**	**40.00**
RCA Victor APL1-0388	(S)	**Raised On Rock/For Ol' Times Sake**	1973	**8.00**	**20.00**
RCA Victor DPL2-0056	(E)	**Elvis** *(2 LPs. Brown label)*	1973	**12.00**	**30.00**
RCA Victor CPL1-0341	(P)	**A Legendary Performer, Volume 1**	1974	**8.00**	**20.00**
		(Custom black label. The cover has a die-cut circular window.			
		Issued with a booklet, included in the price.)			
RCA Victor CPL1-0475	(S)	**Good Times** *(Orange label)*	1974	**10.00**	**25.00**
RCA Victor DJL1-0606	(DJ)	**Live On Stage In Memphis** *(White label)*	1974	**100.00**	**200.00**
RCA Victor CPL1-0606	(S)	**Live On Stage In Memphis** *(Orange label)*	1974	**6.00**	**15.00**
RCA Victor APD1-0606	(Q)	**Live On Stage In Memphis** *(Orange label)*	1974	**75.00**	**150.00**
Boxcar	(M)	**Having Fun With Elvis On Stage**	1974	**75.00**	**150.00**
RCA Victor CPM1-0818	(M)	**Having Fun With Elvis On Stage** *(Orange)*	1974	**8.00**	**20.00**
RCA Victor APL1-0873	(S)	**Promised Land** *(Orange label)*	1975	**20.00**	**50.00**
RCA Victor APL1-0873	(S)	**Promised Land** *(Brown label)*	1975	**6.00**	**15.00**
RCA Victor APD1-0873	(Q)	**Promised Land** *(Orange label)*	1975	**75.00**	**150.00**
RCA Victor APD1-0873	(Q)	**Promised Land** *(Black label)*	1975	**30.00**	**60.00**
RCA Victor APL1-1039	(S)	**Elvis Today** *(Orange label)*	1975	**20.00**	**50.00**
RCA Victor APL1-1039	(S)	**Elvis Today** *(Brown label)*	1975	**6.00**	**15.00**
RCA Victor APD1-1039	(Q)	**Elvis Today** *(Orange label)*	1975	**75.00**	**150.00**
RCA Victor APD1-1039	(Q)	**Elvis Today** *(Black label)*	1975	**30.00**	**60.00**
RCA Victor ANL1-0971	(P)	**Pure Gold** *(Orange label)*	1975	**3.50**	**8.00** —
RCA Victor CPL1-1349	(P)	**A Legendary Performer, Volume 2**	1976	**8.00**	**20.00**
		(Custom black label. The cover has a die-cut circular window.			
		Issued with a booklet, included in the price.)			
RCA Victor APM1-1675	(M)	**The Sun Sessions** *(Brown label)*	1976	**6.00**	**15.00**
RCA Victor APL1-1506	(S)	**From Elvis Presley Boulevard** *(Brown label)*	1976	**6.00**	**15.00**
RCA Victor DPL2-0168	(P)	**Elvis In Hollywood** *(2 LPs. Blue label with book)*	1976	**12.00**	**30.00**
RCA Victor AFL1-2428	(S)	**Moody Blue** *(Blue vinyl)*	1977	**3.50**	**8.00** —
RCA Victor AFL1-2428	(S)	**Moody Blue** *(Colored vinyl)*	1977	**660.00**	**1,000.00**
		(Copies exist of gold, green, red or white vinyl.)			
RCA Victor AFL1-2428	(S)	**Moody Blue** *("Splash" colored vinyl)*	1977	**800.00**	**1,200.00**
		(Copies exist of purple, red or yellow on white vinyl.)			
RCA Victor AFL1-2428	(S)	**Moody Blue** *(Black vinyl)*	1977	**100.00**	**200.00**
RCA Victor CPL1-3078	(P)	**A Legendary Performer, Volume 3** *(Picture disc)*	1979	**8.00**	**20.00**
RCA Victor CPL1-3078	(P)	**A Legendary Performer, Volume 3**	1979	**8.00**	**20.00**
		(Custom black label. The cover has a die-cut circular window.			
		Issued with a booklet, included in the price.)			
RCA DJL1-3455	(DJ)	**Pure Elvis**	1979	**150.00**	**250.00**
RCA Victor CPL8-3699	(P)	**Elvis Aron Presley** *(8 LP box with book)*	1980	**15.00**	**60.00**
RCA Victor CPL1-4848	(P)	**A Legendary Performer, Volume 4**	1980	**5.00**	**12.00**
		(Custom black label. The cover has a die-cut circular window.			
		Issued with a booklet, included in the price.)			
RCA Victor FJ-1981	(DJ)	**Felton Jarvis Talks About Elvis** *(No cover)*	1981	**50.00**	**100.00**

Label & Catalog #		Title	Year	VG+	NM
RCA Victor CPM6-5172	(P)	A Golden Celebration (6 LP box with photo)	1984	12.00	30.00
RCA Victor DVM1-0704	(M)	Elvis (One Night With You) (With poster)	1985	12.00	30.00
RCA Victor DJM1-0835	(DJ)	An Audio Self Portrait	1985	20.00	50.00
Mobile Fidelity MFSL-059	(S)	From Elvis In Memphis	1980	10.00	25.00
Camden CAS-2304	(P)	Elvis Sings Flaming Star	1969	8.00	20.00
Camden CAS-2408	(P)	Let's Be Friends	1970	6.00	15.00
Camden CAS-2440	(P)	Almost In Love (With "Stay Away, Joe")	1970	6.00	15.00
Camden CAS-2440	(P)	Almost In Love (With "Stay Away")	1970	3.50	8.00
Camden CAL-2428	(P)	Elvis' Christmas Album	1970	6.00	15.00
— Original Camden albums above were pressed on non-flexible vinyl. —					
Camden CALX-2472	(P)	You'll Never Walk Alone	1971	8.00	10.00
Camden CAL-2518	(P)	C'mon Everybody	1971	8.00	10.00
Camden CAL-2533	(P)	I Got Lucky	1971	8.00	10.00
Camden CAS-2567	(S)	Elvis Sings Hits From His Movies, Volume 1	1972	8.00	10.00
Camden CAS-2595	(S)	Elvis Sings Burning Love	1972	10.00	25.00
		(Cover has a star on the front for the bonus photo, priced below.)			
Camden CAS-2595		Elvis Sings Burning Love Bonus Photo	1972	20.00	50.00
Camden CAS-2595	(S)	Elvis Sings Burning Love	1972	5.00	12.00
		(Cover does not mention a bonus photo.)			
Camden CAS-2611	(S)	Separate Ways	1973	8.00	10.00
		(Issued with a bonus photo, priced below.)			
Camden CAS-2611		Separate Ways Bonus Photo	1973	8.00	10.00

PRESTON, BILLY

Vee Jay LP-1123	(M)	The Most Exciting Organ Ever	1965	8.00	20.00
Vee Jay LPS-1123	(S)	The Most Exciting Organ Ever	1965	12.00	30.00
Exodus EX-304	(M)	Early Hits Of 1965	1965	6.00	15.00
Exodus EX-304	(S)	Early Hits Of 1965	1965	8.00	20.00
Capitol T-2532	(M)	Wildest Organ In Town	1966	6.00	15.00
Capitol ST-2532	(S)	Wildest Organ In Town	1966	8.00	20.00
Buddah BDS-7502	(S)	Billy Preston	1969	5.00	12.00
Apple ST-3359	(S)	That's The Way God Planned It	1969	20.00	50.00
		(The cover features a close-up of Preston's face.)			
Apple ST-3359	(S)	That's The Way God Planned It	1969	8.00	20.00
		(The cover features multiple images of Preston.)			
Apple ST-3370	(S)	Encouraging Words	1970	8.00	20.00

PRESTON, JOHNNY

Mercury MG-20592	(M)	Running Bear	1960	30.00	60.00
Mercury SR-60250	(P)	Running Bear	1960	35.00	70.00
Mercury MG-20609	(M)	Come Rock With Me	1961	20.00	50.00
Mercury SR-60609	(P)	Come Rock With Me	1961	30.00	60.00

PRETENDERS, THE

Nautilus NR-38	(S)	The Pretenders	198?	8.00	20.00
Sire 23980	(DJ)	Learning To Crawl (Quiex II vinyl)	198?	8.00	20.00

PRETTY THINGS, THE

Fontana MGF-27544	(M)	The Pretty Things	1966	30.00	60.00
Fontana SRF-67544	(P)	The Pretty Things	1966	35.00	70.00
Rare Earth RS-506	(S)	S.F. Sorrow	1969	16.00	40.00
Rare Earth RS-515	(S)	Parachute	1970	10.00	25.00
Sire SASH-3713	(S)	The Vintage Years (2 LPs)	1976	6.00	15.00
Rare Earth R-459	(S)	Real Pretty (2 LPs)	1976	6.00	15.00

PRICE, ALAN
Price was formerly a member of the original Animals.

Parrot PA-1018	(M)	The Price Is Right	1968	8.00	20.00
Parrot PAS-71018	(S)	The Price Is Right	1968	10.00	25.00
Warner Bros. DS-2710	(S)	O Lucky Man (Soundtrack)	1973	6.00	15.00

PRICE, LLOYD

Specialty SP-2105	(M)	Lloyd Price	1959	35.00	70.00
ABC-Paramount 277	(M)	The Exciting Lloyd Price	1959	14.00	35.00
ABC-Paramount S-277	(S)	The Exciting Lloyd Price	1959	20.00	50.00
ABC-Paramount 297	(M)	Mr. Personality	1959	14.00	35.00
ABC-Paramount S-297	(S)	Mr. Personality	1959	20.00	50.00

One of the most prominent proponents of early New Orleans r'n'b based rock & roll (vividly presented on his eponymous Specialty album above), Lloyd Price began as just that, an r'n'b singer/songwriter who scored big with the great "Lawdy Miss Clawdy." He continued to have success with the black market when he signed with ABC-Paramount in 1957, who had picked up his own KRC recording of "Just Because" and had a national hit on both the r'n'b and pop charts. From there he streamlined his sound and approach, taking on more of the accoutrements of the rock and pop sound, and enjoyed a string of hits, culminating in "Stagger Lee" and "Personality."

Label & Catalog #		Title	Year	VG+	NM
ABC-Paramount 315	(M)	Mr. Personality Sings The Blues	1960	14.00	35.00
ABC-Paramount S-315	(S)	Mr. Personality Sings The Blues	1960	20.00	50.00
ABC-Paramount 324	(M)	Mr. Personality's 15 Hits	1960	12.00	30.00
ABC-Paramount S-324	(E)	Mr. Personality's 15 Hits	1960	10.00	25.00
ABC-Paramount 346	(M)	The Fantastic Lloyd Price	1960	12.00	30.00
ABC-Paramount S-346	(E)	The Fantastic Lloyd Price	1960	10.00	25.00
ABC-Paramount 366	(M)	Lloyd Price Sings The Million Sellers	1961	10.00	25.00
ABC-Paramount S-366	(S)	Lloyd Price Sings The Million Sellers	1961	14.00	35.00
ABC-Paramount 382	(M)	Cookin' With Lloyd Price	1961	10.00	25.00
ABC-Paramount S-382	(S)	Cookin' With Lloyd Price	1961	14.00	35.00
Double-L D-2301	(M)	The Lloyd Price Orchestra	1963	8.00	20.00
Double-L SDL-8301	(S)	The Lloyd Price Orchestra	1963	10.00	25.00
Double-L D-2303	(M)	Misty	1963	8.00	20.00
Double-L SDL-8303	(S)	Misty	1963	10.00	25.00
Monument MLP-8032	(M)	Lloyd Swings For Sammy	1965	8.00	20.00
Monument SMP-18032	(S)	Lloyd Swings For Sammy	1965	10.00	25.00
Jad 1002	(S)	Lloyd Price Now	1969	6.00	15.00

PRICE, RAY

Label & Catalog #		Title	Year	VG+	NM
Columbia CL-1015	(M)	Ray Price Sings Heart Songs	1957	20.00	50.00
Columbia CL-1148	(M)	Talk To Your Heart	1958	16.00	40.00
Columbia CL-1494	(M)	Faith	1960	12.00	30.00
Columbia CS-8285	(S)	Faith	1960	16.00	40.00
Columbia CL-1566	(M)	Ray Price's Greatest Hits	1961	12.00	30.00
Columbia CL-1758	(M)	San Antonio Rose	1962	8.00	20.00
Columbia CS-8556	(S)	San Antonio Rose	1962	12.00	30.00

— *Original Columbia albums above have three white "eye" logos on each side of the spindle hole.*—

Columbia CL-1971	(M)	Night Life	1963	5.00	12.00
Columbia CS-8771	(S)	Night Life	1963	6.00	15.00
Columbia CL-1976	(M)	Greatest Western Hits, Volume 1	1963	5.00	12.00
Columbia CS-8776	(S)	Greatest Western Hits, Volume 1	1963	6.00	15.00
Columbia CL-2189	(M)	Love Life	1964	5.00	12.00
Columbia CS-8989	(S)	Love Life	1964	6.00	15.00
Columbia CL-2289	(M)	Burning Memories	1965	5.00	12.00
Columbia CS-9089	(S)	Burning Memories	1965	6.00	15.00
Columbia CL-2339	(M)	Western Strings	1965	8.00	20.00
Columbia CS-9139	(S)	Western Strings	1965	10.00	25.00
Columbia CL-2382	(M)	The Other Woman	1965	5.00	12.00
Columbia CS-9182	(S)	The Other Woman	1965	6.00	15.00
Columbia CL-2528	(M)	Another Bridge To Burn	1966	4.00	10.00
Columbia CS-9328	(S)	Another Bridge To Burn	1966	5.00	12.00
Columbia CL-2606	(M)	Touch My Heart	1967	4.00	10.00
Columbia CS-9406	(S)	Touch My Heart	1967	5.00	12.00
Columbia CL-2670	(M)	Ray Price's Greatest Hits, Volume 2	1967	4.00	10.00
Columbia CS-9470	(S)	Ray Price's Greatest Hits, Volume 2	1967	5.00	12.00
Columbia CL-2677	(M)	Danny Boy	1967	4.00	10.00
Columbia CS-9477	(S)	Danny Boy	1967	5.00	12.00
Columbia CL-2806	(M)	Take Me As I Am	1968	12.00	30.00
Columbia CS-9606	(S)	Take Me As I Am	1968	5.00	12.00
Columbia CS-9733	(S)	She Wears My Ring	1968	5.00	12.00
Columbia CS-9822	(S)	Sweetheart Of The Year	1969	5.00	12.00
Columbia CS-9861	(S)	Ray Price's Christmas Album	1969	5.00	12.00
Columbia CS-9918	(S)	You Wouldn't Know Love	1970	5.00	12.00

— *Original Columbia albums above have "360 Sound" on the bottom of the label.*—

Columbia CQ-30106	(Q)	For The Good Times	1970	5.00	12.00

PRICE, RUTH

Label & Catalog #		Title	Year	VG+	NM
Kapp KL-1006	(M)	My Name Is Ruth Price, I Sing	1955	16.00	40.00
Kapp KL-1054	(M)	The Party's Over	1957	16.00	40.00
Roost 2217	(M)	Ruth Price Sings	1956	14.00	35.00
Contemporary M3590	(M)	Ruth Price At The Manne-Hole	1961	12.00	30.00
Contemporary S7590	(S)	Ruth Price At The Manne-Hole	1961	16.00	40.00
Ava A-54	(M)	Live And Beautiful	1963	8.00	20.00
Ava AS-54	(S)	Live And Beautiful	1963	12.00	30.00
Mainstream 56078	(M)	Harper (Soundtrack)	1966	14.00	35.00
Mainstream S-6078	(S)	Harper (Soundtrack)	1966	18.00	45.00

Label & Catalog #		Title	Year	VG+	NM
PRICE, VINCENT					
Columbia ML-5668	(M)	**America The Beautiful**	1961	8.00	20.00
Dot DLP-3195	(M)	**Gallery**	1962	8.00	20.00
Dot DLP-25195	(S)	**Gallery**	1962	10.00	25.00
Capitol SWBB-342	(S)	**Witchcraft/Magic** (2 LPs)	1969	8.00	20.00
Pro-Star CS-110	(S)	**Vincent Price**	1977	5.00	12.00
PRIMA, LOUIS					
Mercury MG-25142 (10")	(M)	**Louis Prima Plays**	1953	20.00	50.00
Capitol T-755	(M)	**The Wildest**	1956	14.00	35.00
Capitol T-836	(M)	**Call Of The Wildest**	1957	14.00	35.00
Capitol T-908	(M)	**The Wildest Show Art Tahoe**	1957	14.00	35.00
Capitol T-1010	(M)	**Las Vegas Prima Style**	1958	14.00	35.00
Capitol T-1132	(M)	**Strictly Prima**	1959	14.00	35.00
Capitol T-1723	(M)	**The Wildest Comes Home**	1962	10.00	25.00
Capitol ST-1723	(S)	**The Wildest Comes Home**	1962	12.00	30.00
Columba CL-1206	(M)	**Breakin' It Up**	1958	14.00	35.00
Rondo 842	(M)	**Louis Prima**	1959	14.00	35.00
Dot DLP-3262	(M)	**His Greatest Hits**	1960	6.00	15.00
Dot DLP-25262	(S)	**His Greatest Hits**	1960	8.00	20.00
Dot DLP-3352	(M)	**Wonderland By Night**	1961	6.00	15.00
Dot DLP-25352	(S)	**Wonderland By Night**	1961	8.00	20.00
Dot DLP-3410	(M)	**Doin' The Twist**	1961	6.00	15.00
Dot DLP-25410	(S)	**Doin' The Twist**	1961	8.00	20.00
PRIMA, LOUIS, & KEELY SMITH					
Capitol T-1160	(M)	**Hey Boy, Hey Girl** (Soundtrack)	1959	16.00	40.00
Dot DLP-3210	(M)	**Louis And Keely**	1959	10.00	25.00
Dot DLP-25210	(S)	**Louis And Keely**	1959	14.00	35.00
Dot DLP-3263	(M)	**Together**	1960	10.00	25.00
Dot DLP-25263	(S)	**Together**	1960	14.00	35.00
Capitol T-1531	(M)	**The Hits Of Louis And Keely**	1961	12.00	30.00
PRIMEVAL					
700 West 740105	(S)	**Smokin' Bats At Campton's**	1974	35.00	70.00
PRINCE					
Warner Bros. 25110	(DJ)	**Purple Rain** (Purple vinyl)	1984	12.00	30.00
Warner Bros. 25677DJ	(S)	**The Black Album** (2 LPs)	1987	See note below	
		(45 rpm promo contains the complete album. Estimated near mint value $3,000-5,000.)			
Warner Bros. 25677	(S)	**The Black Album**	1987	See note below	
		(Withdrawn. Estimated near mint value $2,000-4,000.)			
PRINCE BUSTER					
RCA Victor LPM-3792	(M)	**Ten Commandments**	1967	10.00	25.00
RCA Victor LSP-3792	(S)	**Ten Commandments**	1967	14.00	35.00
PROBE					
Eborp SS-21396-01	(S)	**Direction**	197?	240.00	400.00
PROBY, P.J.					
Liberty LRP-3406	(M)	**Go Go P.J. Proby**	1965	8.00	20.00
Liberty LST-7406	(S)	**Go Go P.J. Proby**	1965	10.00	25.00
Liberty LRP-3421	(M)	**P.J. Proby**	1965	8.00	20.00
Liberty LST-7421	(S)	**P.J. Proby**	1965	10.00	25.00
Liberty LRP-3497	(M)	**Enigma**	1967	8.00	20.00
Liberty LST-7497	(S)	**Enigma**	1967	10.00	25.00
Liberty LRP-3515	(M)	**Phenomenon**	1967	8.00	20.00
Liberty LST-7515	(S)	**Phenomenon**	1967	10.00	25.00
Liberty LRP-3561	(M)	**What's Wrong With My World?**	1968	10.00	25.00
Liberty LST-7561	(S)	**What's Wrong With My World?**	1968	10.00	25.00
PROCOL HARUM					
Deram DE-16008	(M)	**Procol Harum** (Black & white cover)	1967	20.00	50.00
Deram DES-18008	(E)	**Procol Harum** (Black & white cover)	1967	8.00	20.00
		(Issued with a poster of the cover, priced separately below.)			
Deram		**Procol Harum Poster**	1967	10.00	25.00

Label & Catalog #		Title	Year	VG+	NM
A&M SP-4151	(S)	**Shrine On Brightly**	1968	6.00	15.00
A&M SP-4179	(S)	**A Salty Dog**	1969	6.00	15.00
A&M SP-4261	(S)	**Home**	1970	4.00	10.00
A&M SP-4294	(S)	**Broken Barricades**	1971	4.00	10.00
		— Original A&M albums above have brown labels.—			
A&M SP-8503	(DJ)	**Procol Harum Lives**	197?	16.00	40.00

PROCTOR, PHIL, & PETER BERGMAN
Proctor and Bergman are members of The Firesign Theatre.

Columbia KC-32199	(S)	**TV Or Not TV**	1973	4.00	10.00

PROFESSOR LONGHAIR (HENRY ROLAND BYRD)

Atlantic SD-7225	(S)	**New Orleans Piano**	1972	10.00	25.00
Harvest SW-11790	(S)	**Live On The Queen Mary**	1978	6.00	15.00
Atlantic SD-2-4001	(S)	**The Last Mardi Gras** *(2 LPs)*	1982	6.00	15.00
Nighthawk 108	(S)	**Mardi Gras In New Orleans**	1982	4.00	10.00

PROOF

Proof Prod.	(S)	**Proof**	197?	240.00	400.00

PROVINE, DOROTHY

Warner Bros. W-1394	(M)	**The Roaring '20's**	1961	6.00	15.00
Warner Bros. WS-1394	(S)	**The Roaring '20's**	1961	8.00	20.00
Warner Bros. W-1419	(M)	**The Vamp Of The Roaring '20's**	1961	6.00	15.00
Warner Bros. WS-1419	(S)	**The Vamp Of The Roaring '20's**	1961	8.00	20.00

PRYSOCK, ARTHUR

Old Town LP-102	(M)	**I Worry About You**	1962	14.00	35.00
Old Town LP-2004	(M)	**Arthur Prysock Sings Only For You**	1962	10.00	25.00
Old Town LP-2005	(M)	**Coast To Coast**	1963	10.00	25.00
Old Town LP-2006	(M)	**Portrait**	1963	10.00	25.00
Old Town LP-2007	(M)	**Everlasting Songs For Everlasting Lovers**	1964	10.00	25.00
Old Town LP-2008	(M)	**Intimately Yours**	1964	10.00	25.00
Old Town LP-2009	(M)	**Double Header**	1965	10.00	25.00
Old Town LP-2010	(M)	**In A Mood**	1965	10.00	25.00
Decca DL-4581	(M)	**Strictly Sentimental**	1965	6.00	15.00
Decca DL-74581	(S)	**Strictly Sentimental**	1965	8.00	20.00
Decca DL-4628	(M)	**Showcase**	1965	6.00	15.00
Decca DL-74628	(S)	**Showcase**	1965	8.00	20.00
Verve V-8646	(M)	**Arthur Prysock/Count Basie**	1965	6.00	15.00
Verve V6-8646	(S)	**Arthur Prysock/Count Basie**	1965	8.00	20.00
Verve V6-5009	(M)	**Art And Soul**	1966	6.00	15.00
Verve V-5009	(S)	**Art And Soul**	1966	8.00	20.00
Verve V6-5011	(M)	**The Best Of Arthur Prysock**	1967	5.00	12.00
Verve V-5011	(S)	**The Best Of Arthur Prysock**	1967	6.00	15.00
Verve V6-5038	(M)	**The Best Of Arthur Prysock, Volume 2**	1967	5.00	12.00
Verve V-5038	(S)	**The Best Of Arthur Prysock, Volume 2**	1967	6.00	15.00
Verve V6-650	(S)	**24 Karat Hits** *(2 LPs)*	1968	6.00	15.00
Verve V6-5073	(S)	**Funny Thing**	1969	4.00	10.00

PRYSOCK, RED

Mercury MG-20086	(M)	**Rock 'N' Roll**	1955	75.00	150.00
Mercury MG-20106	(M)	**Battle Royal**	1956	50.00	100.00
Mercury MG-20188	(M)	**Swing Softly Red**	1956	50.00	100.00
Mercury MG-20211	(M)	**Fruit Boots**	1957	50.00	100.00
Mercury MG-20307	(M)	**The Beat**	1959	20.00	50.00
Mercury SR-60307	(S)	**The Beat**	1959	35.00	70.00

PUGSLEY MUNION

J&S SLP-0001	(S)	**Just Like You**	196?	30.00	60.00

PURE PRAIRIE LEAGUE

RCA Victor APD1-0933	(Q)	**Two Lane Highway**	1975	5.00	12.00

PURIFY, JAMES & BOBBY

Bell 6003	(M)	**James And Bobby Purify**	1967	6.00	15.00
Bell 6003	(S)	**James And Bobby Purify**	1967	8.00	20.00

Label & Catalog #		Title	Year	VG+	NM
...ell 6010	(M)	The Pure Sound Of The Purifys	1967	6.00	15.00
...ell 6010	(S)	The Pure Sound Of The Purifys	1967	8.00	20.00
PURPLE GANG, THE					
...ire/London SES-97006	(S)	The Purple Gang Strikes	1969	6.00	15.00
PURSELL, BILL					
Columbia CL-1972	(M)	Our Winter Love	1963	6.00	15.00
Columbia CS-8972	(S)	Our Winter Love	1963	8.00	20.00
PYRAMIDS, THE					
...est BR-16501	(M)	Penetration	1964	75.00	150.00
...est BRS-36501	(E)	Penetration	1964	50.00	100.00

QUARTERMASS					
Harvest SKAO-314	(S)	Quartermass	1970	8.00	20.00
QUATTLEBAUM, DOUG					
Bluesville BV-1065	(M)	Softee Man Blues	1962	10.00	25.00
QUATRO, SUZI					
Bell 1302	(S)	Suzi Quatro	1974	8.00	20.00
Bell 1313	(S)	Quatro	1974	8.00	20.00
QUEEN					
Elektra EQ-5064	(Q)	Queen	1973	12.00	30.00
Mobile Fidelity MFSL-067	(S)	Night At The Opera	1980	16.00	40.00
QUEENSRYCHE					
EMI SPRO-1436	(DJ)	Operation Mind Control (Picture disc)	1988	8.00	20.00
QUESTION MARK & THE MYSTERIANS					
Cameo C-2004	(M)	96 Tears	1966	16.00	40.00
Cameo CS-2004	(E)	96 Tears	1966	12.00	30.00
Cameo C-2006	(M)	Action	1967	16.00	40.00
Cameo SC-2006	(E)	Action	1967	12.00	30.00

QUICKSILVER MESSENGER SERVICE [QUICKSILVER]
Original members were John Cippolina, Gary Duncan, Greg Elmore and David Freiberg. Later members include Nicky Hopkins and Dino Valenti. Refer to The Steve Miller Band ; Rocky Sullivan.

Capitol ST-2904	(S)	Quicksilver Messenger Service	1968	12.00	30.00
Capitol ST-120	(S)	Happy Trails	1969	8.00	20.00
		— Original Capitol albums above have black rainbow labels.—			
Capitol ST-2904	(S)	Quicksilver Messenger Service	1969	4.00	10.00
Capitol ST-120	(S)	Happy Trails	1969	4.00	10.00
Capitol ST-391	(S)	Shady Grove	1969	4.00	10.00
Capitol ST-498	(S)	Just For Love	1970	4.00	10.00
Capitol ST-630	(S)	What About Me?	1970	4.00	10.00
Capitol ST-819	(S)	Quicksilver	1971	4.00	10.00
		— Capitol albums above have green rainbow labels.—			

Label & Catalog #		Title	Year	VG+	NM
QUIET RIOT					
Pasha 8Z8-39203	(S)	**Metal Health** (Picture disc)	1983	4.00	10.00
QUINTESSENCE					
Island ST-9306	(S)	**Dive Deep**	1971	8.00	20.00
Island SMAS-9301	(S)	**Quintessence**	1971	8.00	20.00

R

Label & Catalog #		Title	Year	VG+	NM
R.E.O. SPEEDWAGON					
Epic AS-410	(DJ)	**Live Again**	1978	8.00	20.00
Epic AS-643	(DJ)	**Nine Lives**	1979	8.00	20.00
Epic HE-45082	(S)	**You Can Tune A Piano But You Can't Tuna Fish** (Half-speed master)	1982	8.00	20.00
Epic HE-46844	(S)	**Hi Infidelity** (Half-speed master)	1982	8.00	20.00
Epic HE-48100	(DJ)	**Good Trouble** (Half-speed master)	1982	8.00	20.00
R.P.S.					
Mars/Mid-America	(S)	**R.P.S.**	197?	35.00	70.00
RADHA KRSNA TEMPLE, THE					
Produced by George Harrison.					
Apple SKAO-3376	(S)	**Radha Krsna Temple**	1971	8.00	20.00
RAEBURN, BOYD					
Columbia CL-889	(M)	**Dance Spectacular** ("Eyes" logo label)	1956	16.00	40.00
Columbia CL-957	(M)	**Fraternity Rush** ("Eyes" logo label)	1957	16.00	40.00
Columbia CL-1073	(M)	**Teen Rock** ("Eyes" logo label)	1957	16.00	40.00
RAFFERTY, GERRY					
Mobile Fidelity MFSL-058	(S)	**City To City**	1978	10.00	25.00
RAICEVIC, NIK PASCAL					
Nik was formerly a member of The Lollipop Shoppe.					
Narco 102	(S)	**Beyond The End Eternity**	1971	8.00	20.00
Narco 666	(S)	**Sixth Ear**	1972	8.00	20.00
Narco 321	(S)	**Magnetic Web**	1973	8.00	20.00
Narco 123	(S)	**Zero Gravity**	1975	8.00	20.00
RAIDERS, THE					
Liberty LRP-3225	(M)	**Twistin' The Country Classics**	1962	8.00	20.00
Liberty LST-7225	(S)	**Twistin' The Country Classics**	1962	12.00	30.00
RAIDERS, THE: Refer to PAUL REVERE & THE RAIDERS					
RAIN					
Project-3 5072	(S)	**Rain**	1970	6.00	15.00
RAIN					
Whazoo USR-3049	(S)	**Live, Christmas Night** (No cover)	1969	40.00	80.00

Label & Catalog #		Title	Year	VG+	NM
RAINBOW PROMISE, THE					
New Wine LPS-251-01	(S)	The Rainbow Promise	196?	150.00	250.00
RAINDROPS, THE					
The Raindrops feature Jeff Barry and Ellie Greenwich.					
Jubilee J-5023	(M)	The Raindrops	1963	18.00	45.00
Jubilee SJ-5023	(S)	The Raindrops	1963	35.00	70.00
RAINWATER, MARVIN					
Refer to Webb Pierce / Marvin Rainwater / Stuart Hamblen.					
MGM E-3534	(M)	Songs By Marvin Rainwater *(Yellow label)*	1957	75.00	150.00
MGM E-3721	(M)	With A Heart, With A Beat *(Yellow label)*	1958	50.00	100.00
MGM E-4046	(M)	Gonna Find Me A Bluebird *(Black label)*	1962	35.00	70.00
RAINY DAZE					
Uni 3002	(M)	That Acapulco Gold	1967	6.00	15.00
Uni 73002	(S)	That Acapulco Gold	1967	8.00	20.00
RAITT, JOHN					
Capitol T-583	(M)	Highlights Of Broadway	1955	12.00	30.00
Capitol T-714	(M)	Mediterranean Magic	1956	12.00	30.00
Capitol T-1058	(M)	Under Open Skies	1958	12.00	30.00
Capitol ST-1058	(S)	Under Open Skies	1958	16.00	40.00
RAM, BUCK					
Mercury MG-20392	(M)	The Magic Touch	1960	8.00	20.00
Mercury SR-60067	(S)	The Magic Touch	1960	12.00	30.00
RAMBEAU, EDDIE					
DynoVoice 9001	(M)	Concrete And Clay	1965	6.00	15.00
DynoVoice DS-9001	(S)	Concrete And Clay	1965	8.00	20.00
RAMBLERS THREE, THE					
MGM E-4072	(M)	Make Way For The Ramblers Three	1962	6.00	15.00
MGM SE-4072	(S)	Make Way For The Ramblers Three	1962	8.00	20.00
RAMJET, RODGER					
Camden CAL-1075	(M)	Rodger Ramjet & The American Eagles	1966	10.00	25.00
Camden CAS-1075	(S)	Rodger Ramjet & The American Eagles	1966	14.00	35.00
RAMONES, THE					
Sire SASD-7520	(S)	The Ramones	1976	6.00	15.00
Sire SA-7528	(S)	The Ramones Leave Home	1976	8.00	20.00
		(First pressing with "Carbona Not Glue".)			
Sire SR-6042	(S)	Rocket To Russia	1977	5.00	12.00
RANDALL, TONY					
Imperial LP-9090	(M)	Tony Randall	196?	8.00	20.00
Mercury MG-21108	(M)	Vo, Vo, De, Oh, Doe	1967	5.00	12.00
Mercury SR-61108	(M)	Vo, Vo, De, Oh, Doe	1967	6.00	15.00
Mercury MG-21178	(M)	Warm And Wavery	1967	5.00	12.00
Mercury SR-61178	(S)	Warm And Wavery	1967	6.00	15.00
RANDALL, TONY, & JACK KLUGMAN					
London XPS-903	(S)	The Odd Couple Sings	1973	8.00	20.00
RANDAZZO, TEDDY					
Randazzo was formerly a member of The Three Chuckles.					
Vik LX-1121	(M)	I'm Confessin'	195?	20.00	50.00
ABC-Paramount 352	(M)	Journey To Love	1961	12.00	30.00
ABC-Paramount S-352	(S)	Journey To Love	1961	16.00	40.00
ABC-Paramount 421	(M)	Teddy Randazzo Twists	1962	12.00	30.00
ABC-Paramount S-421	(S)	Teddy Randazzo Twists	1962	16.00	40.00
Roulette R-25168	(M)	Hey, Let's Twist *(Soundtrack)*	1962	12.00	30.00
Roulette SR-25168	(S)	Hey, Let's Twist *(Soundtrack)*	1962	16.00	40.00
Colpix CP-445	(M)	Big Wide World	1963	10.00	25.00
Colpix SCP-445	(S)	Big Wide World	1963	16.00	40.00

The original figureheads of the punk movement who inspired countless British bands, the Ramones were a sort of supergroup, especially within the confines of New York City, where their appearances were guaranteed sell-outs. The Ramones themselves functioned almost as a cartoon version of a rock 'n roll band, even adopting stage names such as Joey Ramone, Dee Dee Ramone, etc.

Ramones Leave Home was originally issued with "Carbona Not Glue," a track which was deleted and replaced on subsequent pressings by "Sheena Is A Punk Rocker," a minor national hit that was played endlessly on university and alternative radio stations around the country.

Label & Catalog #		Title	Year	VG+	NM
RANEY, WAYNE					
King 588	(M)	**Songs From The Hills**	1958	20.00	50.00
Starday SLP-124	(M)	**Wayne Raney And The Raney Family**	1960	12.00	30.00
Starday SLP-279	(M)	**Don't Try To Be What You Ain't**	1962	12.00	30.00
RANGER, ANDY					
Dot DLP-3028	(M)	**Singing From "The Song That Never Ends"**	1956	30.00	60.00
RANDY & THE RAINBOWS					
Ambient Sound 37715	(S)	**C'mon Let's Go**	1982	4.00	10.00
RARE BIRD					
Probe 24-4514	(S)	**Rare Bird**	1970	8.00	20.00
RARE EARTH					
Verve V6-5066	(S)	**Dreams/Answers**	1968	8.00	20.00
Rare Earth 6-507	(S)	**Get Ready** (Shape cover)	1969	8.00	20.00
Rare Earth 6-507	(S)	**Get Ready** (Square cover)	1969	5.00	12.00
Rare Earth 6-514	(S)	**Ecology**	1970	5.00	12.00
RASCALS, THE [THE YOUNG RASCALS]					
The [Young] Rascals were Eddie Brigati, Felix Cavaliere, Gene Cornish and Dino Danelli.					
Atlantic 8123	(M)	**The Young Rascals**	1966	14.00	35.00
Atlantic SD-8123	(S)	**The Young Rascals**	1966	10.00	25.00
Atlantic 8134	(M)	**Collections**	1967	12.00	30.00
Atlantic SD-8134	(S)	**Collections**	1967	8.00	20.00
Atlantic 8148	(M)	**Groovin'**	1967	12.00	30.00
Atlantic SD-8148	(S)	**Groovin'**	1967	8.00	20.00
Atlantic SD-8169	(S)	**Once Upon A Dream**	1968	6.00	15.00
Atlantic SD-8190	(S)	**Time Peace/The Rascals' Greatest Hits**	1968	5.00	12.00
Atlantic SD-2-091	(S)	**Freedom Suite** (2 LPs)	1969	8.00	20.00
Atlantic ST-137	(DJ)	**Freedom Suite**	1969	14.00	35.00
Atlantic SD-8246	(S)	**See**	1970	4.00	10.00
Atlantic SD-8276	(S)	**Search And Nearness**	1971	4.00	10.00
Columbia 30462	(S)	**Peaceful World**	1971	6.00	15.00
Columbia 31103	(S)	**The Island Of Real**	1972	6.00	15.00
RASPBERRIES, THE					
The Raspberries feature Eric Carmen.					
Capitol ST-11036	(S)	**Raspberries**	1972	8.00	20.00
Capitol ST-11123	(S)	**Fresh Raspberries** (Shape cover)	1972	12.00	30.00
Capitol SMAS-11220	(S)	**Side Three**	1973	10.00	25.00
Capitol ST-11329	(S)	**Starting Over**	1974	8.00	20.00
Capitol ST-11524	(S)	**Raspberries' Best**	1976	4.00	10.00
RATHBONE, BASIL					
Refer to Errol Flynn.					
Columbia ML-4038 (10")	(M)	**Peter And The Wolf / Treasure Island**	195?	14.00	35.00
Columbia ML-4072 (10")	(M)	**Sinbad The Sailor / Oliver Twist**	195?	14.00	35.00
Columbia CL-673	(M)	**Treasure Island / Robin Hood**	1955	14.00	35.00
RATIONALS, THE					
Crewe CR-1334	(S)	**The Rationals**	1968	8.00	20.00
RATTLES, THE					
Refer to The Searchers / The Rattles.					
Mercury MG-21127	(M)	**The Rattles' Greatest Hits**	1967	20.00	50.00
Mercury SR-61127	(S)	**The Rattles' Greatest Hits**	1967	35.00	70.00
RAVEN					
Owl	(M)	**Back To Ohio Blues**	196?	240.00	400.00
RAVEN					
Discovery 36133	(M)	**Live At The Inferno**	1967	30.00	60.00
Columbia CS-9903	(S)	**Raven**	1969	6.00	15.00
RAVENS, THE					
Regent MG-6062	(M)	**Write Me A Letter** (Green label)	195?	100.00	200.00
Regent MG-6062	(M)	**Write Me A Letter** (Red label)	196?	20.00	50.00

Label & Catalog #		Title	Year	VG+	NM
RAW					
Coral CRL7-57515	(S)	**Raw Holly**	1971	12.00	30.00
RAY, DIANE					
Mercury MG-20903	(M)	**The Exciting Years**	1964	6.00	15.00
Mercury SR-60903	(S)	**The Exciting Years**	1964	8.00	20.00
RAY, JAMES					
Caprice LP-1002	(M)	**If You Gotta Make A Fool Of Somebody**	1962	12.00	30.00
Caprice SLP-1002	(S)	**If You Gotta Make A Fool Of Somebody**	1962	16.00	40.00
RAY, JOHNNY					
Columbia CL-6199 (10")	(M)	**Johnnie Ray**	1951	20.00	50.00
Columbia CL-2510 (10")	(M)	**I Cry For You**	1955	20.00	50.00
Epic LN-1120 (10")	(M)	**Johnnie Ray**	1955	20.00	50.00
Columbia CL-961	(M)	**Johnnie Ray Sings The Big Beat**	1957	16.00	40.00
Columbia CL-1093	(M)	**At The Desert Inn In Las Vegas**	1959	16.00	40.00
Columbia CL-1225	(M)	**'Til Morning**	1959	12.00	30.00
Columbia CL-1227	(M)	**Johnnie Ray's Greatest Hits**	1959	12.00	30.00
Columbia CL-1385	(M)	**On The Trail**	1959	12.00	30.00
— *Original Columbia albums above have three white "eye" logos on each side of the spindle hole.*—					
Liberty LRP-3221	(M)	**Johnnie Ray**	1962	8.00	20.00
Liberty LST-7221	(S)	**Johnnie Ray**	1962	12.00	30.00
RAY, WADE					
ABC-Paramount 539	(M)	**A Ray Of Country**	1966	6.00	15.00
ABC-Paramount S-539	(S)	**A Ray Of Country**	1966	8.00	20.00
RAYBURN, MARGE					
Liberty LRP-3126	(M)	**Margie**	1959	6.00	15.00
Liberty LST-7126	(S)	**Margie**	1959	10.00	25.00
RAYE, JERRY, & FENWICK					
DeVille LP-101	(M)	**The Many Sides Of Jerry Raye & Fenwick**	1969	40.00	80.00
RAYE, MARTHA					
Discovery 3010 (10")	(M)	**Martha Raye Sings**	1951	14.00	35.00
Epic LG-3061	(M)	**Here's Martha Raye**	1954	12.00	30.00
RAYNE					
No label	(S)	**Rayne**	1979	180.00	300.00
REBS, THE					
Fredlo 6830	(M)	**1968 A.D. Breakthrough**	1968	100.00	200.00
RED CRAYOLA					
International Art.	(S)	**Parable Of Arable**	1968	20.00	50.00
International Art.	(S)	**Parable Of Arable**	1979	8.00	20.00
International Art.	(S)	**God Bless The Crayon**	1968	20.00	50.00
International Art.	(S)	**God Bless The Crayon**	1979	8.00	20.00
(Reissues have "Masterfonics" stamped in the trail-off vinyl.)					
REDBONE					
Epic EQ-33053	(Q)	**Beaded Dreams Through Turquoise Eyes**	1974	6.00	15.00
REDD, VI					
United Arts. UAL-14106	(M)	**Bird Call**	1962	8.00	20.00
United Arts. UAS-15106	(S)	**Bird Call**	1962	10.00	25.00
Atco 33-157	(M)	**Lady Soul**	1963	8.00	20.00
Atco SD-33-157	(S)	**Lady Soul**	1963	10.00	25.00
REDDING, OTIS					
Refer to Jimi Hendrix / Otis Redding.					
Atco 33-161	(M)	**Pain In My Heart**	1964	20.00	50.00
Atco SD-33-161	(S)	**Pain In My Heart**	1964	35.00	70.00
Volt 411	(M)	**Soul Ballads**	1965	20.00	50.00
Volt S-411	(S)	**Soul Ballads**	1965	30.00	60.00
Volt 412	(M)	**Otis Blue/Otis Redding Sings Soul**	1965	10.00	25.00
Volt S-412	(S)	**Otis Blue/Otis Redding Sings Soul**	1965	14.00	35.00

From his humble origins as a Little Richard imitator, through his adaptation of the smoother approach of Sam Cooke, Otis Redding's impassioned vocals were, for many, the quintessential Memphis soul sound. His distinctive, raspy voice could belt a rocker or croon a ballad to melt a heart. Otis was on his way to conquering the white market following his enormous (and unexpected) success at the Monterey Pop Festival in 1967 when he was killed in an airplane crash, which also took the talents of four members of the Bar-Kays. The posthumous success of "(Sittin' On The) Dock Of The Bay," an instant classic, cemented his reputation as one of the '60's top black soul singers. On *The Best Of Otis Redding*, the original session musicians returned to the studio and recut their parts so the tracks could be released in stereo; this actually worked better than it probably sounds...

Label & Catalog #		Title	Year	VG+	NM
Volt 413	(M)	The Soul Album	1966	10.00	25.00
Volt S-413	(S)	The Soul Album	1966	14.00	35.00
Volt 415	(M)	Dictionary Of Soul	1966	10.00	25.00
Volt S-415	(S)	Dictionary Of Soul	1966	14.00	35.00
Volt 416	(M)	Live In Europe	1967	10.00	25.00
Volt S-416	(S)	Live In Europe	1967	14.00	35.00
Volt 418	(M)	The History Of Otis Redding	1967	10.00	25.00
Volt S-418	(P)	The History Of Otis Redding	1967	14.00	35.00
Volt S-419	(S)	The Dock Of The Bay	1968	12.00	30.00
Atco SD-33-252	(S)	The Immortal Otis Redding	1968	8.00	20.00
Atco SD-33-261	(P)	The History Of Otis Redding	1968	12.00	30.00
Atco SD-33-265	(S)	In Person At The Whiskey A Go Go	1968	8.00	20.00
Atco SD-33-288	(S)	The Dock Of The Bay	1969	8.00	20.00
Atco SD-33-289	(S)	Love Man	1969	8.00	20.00
Atco SD-33-333	(S)	Tell The Truth	1970	8.00	20.00
Atco SD-2-801	(S)	The Best Of Otis Redding (2 LPs)	1972	8.00	20.00

REDDING, OTIS, & CARLA THOMAS

Stax 716	(M)	King And Queen	1967	10.00	25.00
Stax S-716	(S)	King And Queen	1967	14.00	35.00

REED, JIMMY

Vee Jay LP-1004	(M)	I'm Jimmy Reed (Maroon label)	1958	75.00	150.00
Vee Jay LP-1004	(M)	I'm Jimmy Reed (Black label)	196?	30.00	60.00
Vee Jay LP-1008	(M)	Rockin' With Reed (Maroon label)	1959	75.00	150.00
Vee Jay LP-1008	(M)	Rockin' With Reed (Black label)	196?	30.00	60.00
Vee Jay LP-1022	(M)	Found Love	1960	16.00	40.00
Vee Jay LP-1025	(M)	Now Appearing	1960	16.00	40.00
Vee Jay 2LP-1035	(M)	Jimmy Reed At Carnegie Hall (2 LPS)	1961	12.00	30.00
Vee Jay 2SR-1035	(P)	Jimmy Reed At Carnegie Hall (2 LPS)	1961	16.00	40.00
Vee Jay LP-1039	(M)	The Best Of Jimmy Reed	1962	8.00	20.00
Vee Jay SR-1039	(P)	The Best Of Jimmy Reed	1962	12.00	30.00
Vee Jay LP-1050	(M)	Just Jimmy Reed	1962	12.00	30.00
Vee Jay LP-1067	(M)	T'Ain't No Big Thing	1963	12.00	30.00
Vee Jay LP-1072	(M)	The Best Of The Blues	1963	12.00	30.00
Vee Jay LP-1073	(M)	The 12 String Guitar Blues	1963	10.00	25.00
Vee Jay SR-1073	(S)	The 12 String Guitar Blues	1963	12.00	30.00
Vee Jay LP-1080	(M)	More Of The Best Of Jimmy Reed	1964	10.00	25.00
Vee Jay LP-1080	(P)	More Of The Best Of Jimmy Reed	1964	12.00	30.00
Vee Jay LP-1095	(M)	Jimmy Reed At Soul City	1964	10.00	25.00
Vee Jay VJ-8501	(M)	The Legend, The Man	1965	10.00	25.00
Vee Jay VJS-8501	(S)	The Legend, The Man	1965	12.00	30.00

— Original Vee Jay albums above have black labels with a rainbow border.—

BluesWay BL-6004	(M)	The New Jimmy Reed Album	1967	6.00	15.00
BluesWay BLS-6004	(S)	The New Jimmy Reed Album	1967	8.00	20.00
BluesWay BL-6009	(M)	Soulin'	1967	6.00	15.00
BluesWay BLS-6009	(S)	Soulin'	1967	8.00	20.00
BluesWay BLS-6013	(S)	Big Boss Man	1968	6.00	15.00
BluesWay BLS-6024	(S)	Down In Virginia	1969	6.00	15.00
BluesWay BLS-6054	(S)	I Ain't From Chicago	1973	5.00	12.00
BluesWay BLS-6067	(S)	The Ultimate Jimmy Reed	1973	5.00	12.00
BluesWay BLX-6073	(P)	Jimmy Reed At Carnegie Hall (2 LPs)	1973	6.00	15.00

REED, LUCY

Fantasy 3-212	(M)	The Singing Reed	1956	20.00	50.00
Fantasy 3243	(M)	This Is Lucy Reed	1957	20.00	50.00

REED, LOU

RCA Victor LSP-4701	(S)	Lou Reed (Orange label)	1972	6.00	15.00
RCA Victor LSP-4807	(S)	Transformer (Orange label)	1972	5.00	12.00
RCA Victor APL1-0207	(S)	Berlin (Orange label with booklet)	1973	5.00	12.00
RCA Victor CPL22-1101	(S)	Metal Machine Music	1973	16.00	40.00
RCA Victor APD2-1101	(Q)	Metal Machine Music	1973	40.00	80.00
RCA Victor DJL1-4266	(DJ)	Special Radio Series, Vol. XVII (Interview)	1980	8.00	20.00
RCA Victor DJL1-4267	(DJ)	Blue Mask Interview Album	1980	8.00	20.00

REED, LULU

King 604	(M)	Blue And Moody	1959	300.00	500.00

Label & Catalog #		Title	Year	VG+	NM
REED, SUSAN					
Columbia ML-54368	(M)	**Folk Songs**	195?	10.00	25.00
RCA Victor LXA-3019	(M)	**I Know My Love**	195?	10.00	25.00
Elektra EKL-116	(M)	**Folk Songs**	195?	8.00	20.00
Elektra EKL-126	(M)	**Susan Reed Sings Old Airs**	195?	8.00	20.00
REESE, DELLA					
Refer to Ann-Margret / Kitty Kallen / Della Reese.					
Jubilee JLP-1026	(M)	**Melancholy Baby**	1957	10.00	25.00
Jubilee JLP-1071	(M)	**A Date With Della Reese**	1958	6.00	15.00
Jubilee SDJLP-1071	(S)	**A Date With Della Reese**	1958	10.00	25.00
Jubilee JLP-1083	(M)	**Amen**	1958	6.00	15.00
Jubilee SDJLP-1083	(S)	**Amen**	1958	10.00	25.00
Jubilee JLP-1095	(M)	**The Story Of The Blues**	1958	6.00	15.00
Jubilee SDJLP-1095	(S)	**The Story Of The Blues**	1958	10.00	25.00
Jubilee JLP-1109	(M)	**What Do You Know About Love?**	1959	6.00	15.00
Jubilee SDJLP-1109	(S)	**What Do You Know About Love?**	1959	10.00	25.00
Jubilee JLP-1116	(M)	**And That Reminds Me**	1959	6.00	15.00
Jubilee SDJLP-1116	(S)	**And That Reminds Me**	1959	10.00	25.00
RCA Victor LPM-2157	(M)	**Della**	1960	6.00	15.00
RCA Victor LSP-2157	(S)	**Della**	1960	10.00	25.00
RCA Victor LPM-2204	(M)	**Della By Starlight**	1960	6.00	15.00
RCA Victor LSP-2204	(S)	**Della By Starlight**	1960	10.00	25.00
RCA Victor LPM-2280	(M)	**Della Della Cha-Cha-Cha**	1961	6.00	15.00
RCA Victor LSP-2280	(S)	**Della Della Cha-Cha-Cha**	1961	10.00	25.00
RCA Victor LPM-2391	(M)	**Special Delivery**	1961	6.00	15.00
RCA Victor LSP-2391	(S)	**Special Delivery**	1961	10.00	25.00
RCA Victor LPM-2419	(M)	**Classic Della**	1961	6.00	15.00
RCA Victor LSP-2419	(S)	**Classic Della**	1961	10.00	25.00
RCA Victor LPM-2568	(M)	**Della Reese On Stage**	1962	6.00	15.00
RCA Victor LSP-2568	(S)	**Della Reese On Stage**	1962	10.00	25.00

— Original RCA mono albums above have "Long Play" on the bottom of the label;
stereo albums have "Living Stereo" on the bottom.—

Label & Catalog #		Title	Year	VG+	NM
RCA Victor LPM-2711	(M)	**Waltz With Me**	1963	5.00	12.00
RCA Victor LSP-2711	(S)	**Waltz With Mc**	1963	6.00	15.00
RCA Victor LPM-2872	(M)	**Della Reese At Basin Street East**	1964	5.00	12.00
RCA Victor LSP-2872	(S)	**Della Reese At Basin Street East**	1964	6.00	15.00
ABC-Paramount 569	(M)	**Della Reese Live**	1965	5.00	12.00
ABC-Paramount S-569	(S)	**Della Reese Live**	1965	6.00	15.00
REEVES, JIM					
Abbott LP-5001	(M)	**Jim Reeves Sings**	1956	*See note below*	
		(Rare. Estimated near mint value $1,000-1,500.)			
RCA Victor LPM-1256	(M)	**Singing Down The Lane**	1956	75.00	150.00
RCA Victor LPM-1410	(M)	**Bimbo**	1957	35.00	70.00
RCA Victor LPM-1576	(M)	**Jim Reeves**	1957	20.00	50.00
RCA Victor LPM-1685	(M)	**Girls I Have Known**	1958	16.00	40.00
RCA Victor LPM-1950	(M)	**God Be With You**	1958	12.00	30.00
RCA Victor LSP-1950	(S)	**God Be With You**	1958	16.00	40.00
RCA Victor LPM-2001	(M)	**Songs To Warm Your Heart**	1959	12.00	30.00
RCA Victor LSP-2001	(S)	**Songs To Warm Your Heart**	1959	14.00	35.00
RCA Victor LPM-2216	(M)	**The Intimate Jim Reeves**	1960	8.00	20.00
RCA Victor LSP-2216	(S)	**The Intimate Jim Reeves**	1960	12.00	30.00
RCA Victor LPM-2223	(M)	**He'll Have To Go**	1960	12.00	30.00
RCA Victor LSP-2223	(E)	**He'll Have To Go**	1962	6.00	15.00
RCA Victor LPM-2284	(M)	**Tall Tales And Short Tempers**	1961	8.00	20.00
RCA Victor LSP-2284	(S)	**Tall Tales And Short Tempers**	1961	12.00	30.00
RCA Victor LPM-2339	(M)	**Talkin' To Your Heart**	1961	8.00	20.00
RCA Victor LSP-2339	(S)	**Talkin' To Your Heart**	1961	12.00	30.00
RCA Victor LPM-2487	(M)	**A Touch Of Velvet**	1962	8.00	20.00
RCA Victor LSP-2487	(S)	**A Touch Of Velvet**	1962	12.00	30.00
RCA Victor LPM-2552	(M)	**We Thank Thee**	1962	8.00	20.00
RCA Victor LSP-2552	(S)	**We Thank Thee**	1962	12.00	30.00
RCA Victor LPM-2605	(M)	**Gentleman Jim**	1963	8.00	20.00
RCA Victor LSP-2605	(S)	**Gentleman Jim**	1963	12.00	30.00
RCA Victor LPM-2704	(M)	**The International Jim Reeves**	1963	8.00	20.00
RCA Victor LSP-2704	(S)	**The International Jim Reeves**	1963	12.00	30.00

— Original RCA mono albums above have "Long Play" on the bottom of the label;
stereo albums have "Living Stereo" on the bottom.—

Label & Catalog #		Title	Year	VG+	NM
RCA Victor LPM-2758	(M)	Twelve Songs Of Christmas	1963	6.00	15.00
RCA Victor LSP-2758	(S)	Twelve Songs Of Christmas	1963	8.00	20.00
RCA Victor LPM-2780	(M)	Kimberley Jim (Soundtrack)	1964	6.00	15.00
RCA Victor LSP-2780	(S)	Kimberley Jim (Soundtrack)	1964	8.00	20.00
RCA Victor LPM-2854	(M)	Moonlight And Roses	1964	6.00	15.00
RCA Victor LSP-2854	(S)	Moonlight And Roses	1964	8.00	20.00
RCA Victor LPM-2890	(M)	The Best Of Jim Reeves	1964	5.00	12.00
RCA Victor LSP-2890	(P)	The Best Of Jim Reeves	1964	6.00	15.00
RCA Victor LPM-2968	(M)	The Jim Reeves Way	1965	5.00	12.00
RCA Victor LSP-2968	(S)	The Jim Reeves Way	1965	6.00	15.00
RCA Victor LPM-3427	(M)	Up Through The Years	1965	5.00	12.00
RCA Victor LSP-3427	(S)	Up Through The Years	1965	6.00	15.00
RCA Victor SP-33-479	(DJ)	Something Special For Disc Jockeys	1966	50.00	100.00
RCA Victor LPM-3482	(M)	The Best Of Jim Reeves, Volume 2	1966	5.00	12.00
RCA Victor LSP-3482	(P)	The Best Of Jim Reeves, Volume 2	1966	6.00	15.00
RCA Victor LPM-3542	(M)	Distant Drums	1966	5.00	12.00
RCA Victor LSP-3542	(S)	Distant Drums	1966	6.00	15.00
RCA Victor LPM-3709	(M)	Yours Sincerely, Jim Reeves	1966	5.00	12.00
RCA Victor LSP-3709	(S)	Yours Sincerely, Jim Reeves	1966	6.00	15.00
RCA Victor LPM-3793	(M)	The Blue Side Of Lonesome	1967	5.00	12.00
RCA Victor LSP-3793	(S)	The Blue Side Of Lonesome	1967	6.00	15.00
RCA Victor LPM-3903	(M)	My Cathedral	1967	5.00	12.00
RCA Victor LSP-3903	(S)	My Cathedral	1967	6.00	15.00
RCA Victor LPM-3987	(M)	A Touch Of Sadness	1968	20.00	50.00
RCA Victor LSP-3987	(S)	A Touch Of Sadness	1968	6.00	15.00
RCA Victor LSP-4062	(S)	Jim Reeves On Stage	1968	5.00	12.00

— Original RCA albums above have black labels.—

REFLECTIONS, THE

Golden World 300	(M)	(Just Like) Romeo And Juliet	1964	35.00	70.00

REGENTS, THE

Gee GLP-708	(M)	Barbara Ann	1961	40.00	80.00
Gee SGLP-708	(S)	Barbara Ann	1961	50.00	100.00
Capitol KAO-2153	(M)	Live At The AM/PM Discotheque	1964	20.00	50.00
Capitol SKAO-2153	(S)	Live At The AM/PM Discotheque	1964	35.00	70.00

REID, IRENE

MGM E-4159	(M)	It's Only The Beginning	1964	6.00	15.00
MGM SE-4159	(S)	It's Only The Beginning	1964	8.00	20.00
Verve V-8621	(M)	Room For One More	1965	6.00	15.00

RELAYER

H.S.R. LSR-1006	(S)	Relayer	1979	35.00	70.00

REMAINS, THE

Epic LN-24214	(M)	The Remains	1966	50.00	100.00
Epic BN-26214	(S)	The Remains	1966	100.00	200.00

REMINGTON, HERBIE

"D" 7002	(M)	Herbie Remington Plays The Steel	195?	20.00	50.00
"D" 7005	(M)	Aloha Hawaii	195?	20.00	50.00
United Arts. UAL-3167	(M)	Steel Guitar Holiday	1961	6.00	15.00
United Arts. UAS-6167	(E)	Steel Guitar Holiday	1961	6.00	15.00
		(Repackage of "D" 7002.)			

RENAISSANCE

Elektra 74068 features Keith Relf and Jim McCarty of The Yardbirds.

Elektra EKS-74068	(S)	Renaissance	1969	8.00	20.00
Mobile Fidelity MFSL-099	(S)	Scheherezade	1980	16.00	40.00

RENAISSANCE SOCIETY, THE

HBR HLP-8504	(S)	Baroque 'N Stones	1969	8.00	20.00

RENAY, DIANE

20th Century TF-3133	(M)	Navy Blue	1964	20.00	50.00
20th Century TFS-3133	(P)	Navy Blue	1964	40.00	80.00

Label & Catalog #		Title	Year	VG+	NM

Containing both her hit singles, "Navy Blue" and "Kiss Me, Sailor," Diane Renay's album is tough to find in mono... and is one of the rarer stereo albums by a pop singer from the '60s.

RENO & SMILEY

Label & Catalog #		Title	Year	VG+	NM
King 550	(M)	Sacred Songs	1958	20.00	50.00
King 579	(M)	Folk Ballads And Instrumentals	1958	20.00	50.00
King 621	(M)	Good Old Country Ballads	1959	20.00	50.00
King 646	(M)	A Variety Of Country Songs	1959	20.00	50.00
King 693	(M)	Hymns Sacred And Gospel	1959	20.00	50.00
King 701	(M)	Country Songs	1959	20.00	50.00
King 756	(M)	Folk Songs Of The Civil War	1961	20.00	50.00

REPARATA & THE DELRONS

Label & Catalog #		Title	Year	VG+	NM
World Artists WAM-2006	(M)	Whenever A Teenager Cries	1965	12.00	30.00
World Artists WAS-3006	(S)	Whenever A Teenager Cries	1965	16.00	40.00

REPRISE REPERTORY THEATRE, THE

Rosemary Clooney, Bing Crosby, Sammy Davis, Jr., the Hi-Lo's, Dean Martin, the McGuire Sisters, Debbie Reynolds, Allan Sherman, Dinah Shore, Frank Sinatra, Keely Smith and Jo Stafford.

Label & Catalog #		Title	Year	VG+	NM
Reprise F-2015	(M)	Finian's Rainbow	1964	12.00	30.00
Reprise FS-2015	(S)	Finian's Rainbow	1964	16.00	40.00
Reprise F-2016	(M)	Guys And Dolls	1964	12.00	30.00
Reprise FS-2016	(S)	Guys And Dolls	1964	16.00	40.00
Reprise F-2017	(M)	Kiss Me, Kate	1964	12.00	30.00
Reprise FS-2017	(S)	Kiss Me, Kate	1964	16.00	40.00
Reprise F-2018	(M)	South Pacific	1964	12.00	30.00
Reprise FS-2018	(S)	South Pacific	1964	16.00	40.00
Reprise F-2019	(M)	The Reprise Repertory Theatre *(4 LP box)*	1964	75.00	150.00
Reprise FS-2019	(S)	The Reprise Repertory Theatre *(4 LP box)*	1964	100.00	200.00
Reprise F-2020	(M)	America, I Hear You Singing	1964	8.00	20.00
Reprise FS-2020	(S)	America, I Hear You Singing	1964	12.00	30.00
Reprise F-2021	(M)	Robin And The Seven Hoods	1964	20.00	50.00
Reprise FS-2021	(S)	Robin And The Seven Hoods	1964	30.00	60.00
Reprise F-2022	(M)	Twelve Songs Of Christmas	1964	8.00	20.00
Reprise FS-2022	(S)	Twelve Songs Of Christmas	1964	12.00	30.00

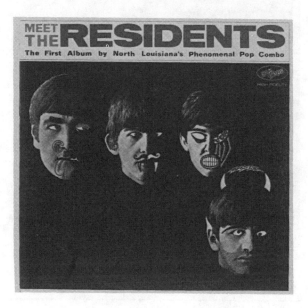

Long renowned as America's #1 Underground group, the Residents received their name when
a demo tape of their material sent to one label was returned addressed to "Residents."
After giving up on the majors, the group formed their own label, the redoubtable Ralph,
and pressed up 1,000 copies of this, their first album, a gently wicked lampoon of much of rock
that was held sacred by the pundits.

The most obvious joke was the cover itself, a grotesque parody of the Beatles first Capitol album
with alterations added by the band. After the threat of a lawsuit from the ever serious heads
of Capitol, the album was reissued with a completely different cover, but not before several
hundred copies were circulated.

Label & Catalog #		Title	Year	VG+	NM

RESIDENTS, THE

Label & Catalog #		Title	Year	VG+	NM
Ralph RR-0274	(M)	**Meet The Residents**	1974	100.00	200.00
		(Back cover reads "First Pressing-1,000 Discs-February, 1974.")			
Ralph RR-0677	(S)	**Meet The Residents**	1977	10.00	25.00
		(Remixed reissue with non-ligitative cover art, this pressing			
		has a split "a" in the Ralph logo on the back cover.)			
Ralph RR-0677	(S)	**Meet The Residents** *(Picture disc)*	1985	10.00	25.00
Ralph RR-1075	(S)	**Third Reich 'N' Roll**	1976	20.00	50.00
		(Back cover reads "First Pressing-1,000 Copies.")			
Ralph RR-1276	(S)	**Fingerprince**	1976	20.00	50.00
		(Textured chocolate-brown cover states "First Pressing			
		December 1976" on the back)			
Ralph RR-1276	(S)	**Fingerprince**	1977	6.00	15.00
		(Second pressing has a slick, light brown cover.)			
Ralph RR-1174	(S)	**Not Available** *(Maroon & purple label)*	1978	10.00	25.00
Ralph DJ-7901	(DJ)	**Please Do Not Steal It!**	1979	10.00	25.00
Ralph ESK-7906	(S)	**Eskimo** *(White vinyl)*	1980	10.00	25.00
Ralph RZ-8006	(S)	**Diskomo**	1980	6.00	15.00
Ralph RZ-8052	(S)	**Commercial Album**	1980	6.00	15.00
		(Back cover has incorrect song listings.)			
Ralph RZ-8152	(S)	**Mark Of The Mole** *(Brown vinyl)*	1981	20.00	50.00
Ralph ESK-7906	(S)	**Eskimo** *(Picture disc)*	1983	6.00	15.00
Ralph RZ-0001	(S)	**The Mole Show**	1983	12.00	30.00
Ralph RZ-0001	(S)	**The Mole Show** *(Picture disc)*	1983	10.00	25.00
Ralph RZ-8402	(S)	**George And James**	1984	10.00	25.00
		(The matrix number in the trail-off vinyl is #"RZ-8402-ARe-1.")			
Ralph RZ-8402	(S)	**George And James** *(Clear vinyl)*	1984	10.00	25.00
Ralph RZ-8452	(S)	**Vileness Fats** *(Red vinyl)*	1984	10.00	25.00
Ralph RR-0677	(S)	**Meet The Residents** *(Picture disc)*	1985	10.00	25.00
Episode ED-21	(S)	**Census Taker** *(Soundtrack)*	1985	20.00	50.00

RESTIVO, JOHNNY

Label & Catalog #		Title	Year	VG+	NM
RCA Victor LPM-2149	(M)	**Oh, Johnny**	1959	16.00	40.00
RCA Victor LSP-2149	(S)	**Oh, Johnny**	1959	20.00	50.00

REVELLS, THE

The Revells are a creation of Gary Usher & Co.

Label & Catalog #		Title	Year	VG+	NM
Reprise R-6160	(M)	**The Go Sound Of The Slots**	1965	50.00	100.00
Reprise RS-6160	(S)	**The Go Sound Of The Slots**	1965	75.00	150.00

REVELS, THE

Label & Catalog #		Title	Year	VG+	NM
Impact LPM-1	(M)	**Revels On A Rampage**	1964	50.00	100.00

REVENGERS, THE

Label & Catalog #		Title	Year	VG+	NM
Metro M-565	(M)	**Batman And Other Supermen**	1966	6.00	15.00
Metro MS-565	(S)	**Batman And Other Supermen**	1966	8.00	20.00

REVERE, PAUL, & THE RAIDERS [THE RAIDERS]

Revolving around Revere and Mark Lindsay were various Raiders, including Phil Volk, Michael Smith , Drake Levin (through 1967), Jim Valley, Freddy Weller and Keith Allison. Refer to Brotherhood; The Falconaires; Friendsound.

Label & Catalog #		Title	Year	VG+	NM
Gardena LP-G1000	(M)	**Like, Long Hair**	1961	150.00	250.00
Sande S-1001	(M)	**Paul Revere & The Raiders**	1963	180.00	300.00
Jerden JRL-7004	(M)	**In The Beginning**	1966	12.00	30.00
Jerden JRS-7004	(E)	**In The Beginning**	1966	8.00	20.00
Sears SPS-493	(E)	**Paul Revere & The Raiders**	1966	20.00	50.00
		(The Jerden and Sears albums repackage the Sande material.)			
Columbia CL-2307	(M)	**Here They Come!**	1965	12.00	30.00
		(Label reads "Guaranteed High Fidelity" on the bottom.)			
Columbia CS-9107	(S)	**Here They Come!**	1965	14.00	35.00
		(Label reads "360 Sound Stereo" in black on the bottom.)			
Columbia Cl-2307	(M)	**Here They Come!**	1965	8.00	20.00
		(Label reads "360 Sound Mono" on the bottom.)			
Columbia CS-9107	(S)	**Here They Come!**	1965	10.00	25.00
		(Label reads "360 Sound Stereo" in white on the bottom.)			
Columbia CL-2451	(M)	**Just Like Us!**	1966	6.00	15.00
Columbia CS-9251	(S)	**Just Like Us!**	1966	8.00	20.00
Columbia CS-9308	(M)	**Midnight Ride**	1966	6.00	15.00
Columbia CS-9308	(S)	**Midnight Ride**	1966	8.00	20.00

One of the most popular American bands during a period where few groups lacking a British accent had their records played, Paul Revere & The Raiders produced a body of work that, while not always great rock, was usually exceptional pop! Both of these albums were recorded after the crest of their popularity had passed, and, while *Revolution* is a typically solid set of pop and rock, *Goin' To Memphis* was an ignominious failure, one of the few to come out of Chips Moman's red hot American Sound Studios. Mark Lindsay's attempts at blue-eyed soul were one dimensional and the record quickly became a cut-out bin staple. (Note: *Memphis* is the last Raiders' album issued in mono and is rather rare in that format; unfortunately, the lack of real collector attention in the group's later work has left it as a modestly valued late '60's mono rarity.)

Label & Catalog #		Title	Year	VG+	NM
Columbia CL-2595	(M)	The Spirit Of '67	1966	5.00	12.00
Columbia CS-9395	(P)	The Spirit Of '67	1966	6.00	15.00
Columbia KCL-2662	(M)	Greatest Hits (With booklet)	1967	6.00	15.00
Columbia KCS-9462	(P)	Greatest Hits (With booklet)	1967	8.00	20.00
Columbia CL-2721	(M)	Revolution!	1967	5.00	12.00
Columbia CS-9521	(S)	Revolution!	1967	6.00	15.00
Columbia CL-755	(M)	Christmas Past... And Present	1967	8.00	20.00
Columbia CS-9555	(S)	Christmas Past... And Present	1967	8.00	20.00
Columbia CL-2805	(M)	Goin' To Memphis	1968	5.00	12.00
Columbia CS-9605	(S)	Goin' To Memphis	1968	4.00	10.00
Columbia CS-9665	(S)	Something Happening	1968	6.00	15.00
Columbia CS-9753	(S)	Hard 'N' Heavy (With Marshmallow)	1969	6.00	15.00
		(The cover photo is in black and white.)			
Columbia CS-9753	(S)	Hard 'N' Heavy (With Marshmallow)	1969	4.00	10.00
		(The cover photo is colored.)			
Columbia CS-9905	(S)	Alias Pink Puzz	1969	6.00	15.00
Columbia GP-12	(P)	Paul Revere & The Raiders (2 LPs)	1969	6.00	15.00
		(Columbia GP-12 repackages "Spirit Of '67" and "Revolution.")			
— Original Columbia albums above have "360 Sound" on the bottom of the label. —					
Raider/America	(S)	Special Edition Featuring Michael Bradley	1982	6.00	15.00
Hitbound	(S)	Paul Revere Rides Again	1983	5.00	12.00
No label	(S)	Still Live	1984	6.00	15.00
No label	(S)	Generic Rock Album	1984	6.00	15.00

REVOLUTIONARY BLUES BAND, THE

Label & Catalog #		Title	Year	VG+	NM
Coral CRL-757506	(S)	The Revolutionary Blues Band	1969	6.00	15.00

REXROTH, KENNETH

Label & Catalog #		Title	Year	VG+	NM
Fantasy 700-8	(M)	Poetry & Jazz At The Blackhawk (Red vinyl)	195?	16.00	40.00

REY, ALVINO

Label & Catalog #		Title	Year	VG+	NM
Capitol T-808	(M)	Aloha	1957	12.00	30.00
Capitol T-1085	(M)	Swinging Fling	1958	8.00	20.00
Capitol ST-1085	(S)	Swinging Fling	1958	12.00	30.00
Capitol T-1262	(M)	Ping Pong	1960	8.00	20.00
Capitol ST-1262	(S)	Ping Pong	1960	12.00	30.00
Capitol T-1395	(M)	That Lonely Feeling	1960	8.00	20.00
Capitol ST-1395	(S)	That Lonely Feeling	1960	12.00	30.00
Decca DL-8403	(M)	My Reverie	1958	8.00	20.00
Dot DLP-3391	(M)	His Greatest Hits	1961	6.00	15.00
Dot DLP-25391	(S)	His Greatest Hits	1961	8.00	20.00
Dot DLP-3448	(M)	As I Remember Hawaii	1962	6.00	15.00
Dot DLP-25448	(S)	As I Remember Hawai	1962	8.00	20.00

REYNOLDS, DEBBIE
Refer to The Reprise Repertory Theatre.

Label & Catalog #		Title	Year	VG+	NM
MGM E-530 (10")	(M)	Two Weeks With Love (Soundtrack)	1950	50.00	100.00
MGM E-113 (10")	(M)	Singing In The Rain (Soundtrack)	1952	50.00	100.00
MGM E-190 (10")	(M)	I Love Melvin (Soundtrack)	1953	50.00	100.00
Mercury MG-25202	(M)	Athena (Soundtrack)	1954	100.00	200.00
MGM E-3233	(M)	Two Weeks With Love (Soundtrack)	1955	20.00	50.00
MGM E-3236	(M)	Singing In The Rain / Rich Young And Pretty	1955	16.00	40.00
RCA Victor LPM-1339	(M)	A Bundle Of Joy (Soundtrack)	1956	35.00	70.00
Coral CRL-57159	(M)	Tammy And The Bachelor (Soundtrack)	1957	100.00	200.00
Columbia CL-1337	(M)	Say One For Me (Soundtrack)	1959	35.00	70.00
Columbia CS-8137	(S)	Say One For Me (Soundtrack)	1959	50.00	100.00
Dot DLP-3191	(M)	Debbie	1959	12.00	30.00
Dot DLP-25191	(S)	Debbie	1959	16.00	40.00
Dot DLP-3295	(M)	Am I That Easy To Forget	1960	8.00	20.00
Dot DLP-25295	(S)	Am I That Easy To Forget	1960	12.00	30.00
Dot DLP-25295	(S)	Am I That Easy To Forget (Blue vinyl)	1960	20.00	50.00
Dot DLP-3298	(M)	Fine And Dandy	1960	8.00	20.00
Dot DLP-25298	(S)	Fine And Dandy	1960	12.00	30.00
Dot DLP-3492	(M)	Tammy	1963	8.00	20.00
Dot DLP-25492	(S)	Tammy	1963	12.00	30.00
MGM 1E-5	(M)	How The West Was Won (Soundtrack)	1963	14.00	35.00
MGM S1E-5	(S)	How The West Was Won (Soundtrack)	1963	18.00	45.00
MGM E-4232	(M)	The Unsinkable Molly Brown (Soundtrack)	1964	6.00	15.00
MGM SE-4232	(S)	The Unsinkable Molly Brown (Soundtrack)	1964	8.00	20.00

Label & Catalog #		Title	Year	VG+	NM
MGM 1E-7	(M)	The Singing Nun (Soundtrack)	1966	8.00	20.00
MGM S1E-7	(S)	The Singing Nun (Soundtrack)	1966	12.00	30.00
United Arts. UAL-4163	(M)	Divorce American Style (Soundtrack)	1967	8.00	20.00
United Arts. UAS-5163	(S)	Divorce American Style (Soundtrack)	1967	12.00	30.00
Paramount 1008	(S)	Charlotte's Web (Soundtrack)	1973	6.00	15.00
Columbia KC-32266	(S)	Irene (Soundtrack)	1973	12.00	30.00
MGM SE-3806	(S)	From Debbie With Love	197?	6.00	15.00
A.V.I. AVL-1033	(S)	And Then I Sing	197?	6.00	15.00

REYS, RITA

Columbia CL-903	(M)	The Cool Sound Of Rita Reys	1956	12.00	30.00
Epic LN-3522	(M)	Her Name Is Rita Reys	1957	12.00	30.00
Dawn 1125	(M)	New Voices	195?	12.00	30.00

RHINOCEROUS

Elektra EKS-74030	(S)	Rhinocerous	1968	8.00	20.00
Elektra EKS-74056	(S)	Satin Chickens	1969	5.00	12.00
Elektra EKS-74075	(S)	Better Times Are Coming	1970	5.00	12.00

RHODES, EMITT
Emitt Rhodes was the leader of The Merry-Go-Round.

A&M SP-4254	(S)	American Dream	1970	8.00	20.00
		(Originally issued with "Saturday Night.")			
A&M SP-4254	(S)	American Dream	1970	5.00	12.00
		(Second pressings feature "You're A Very Lovely Woman.")			

RHODES, TODD

King 295-88	(M)	Todd Rhodes Playing His Greatest Hits	1954	50.00	100.00
King 658	(M)	Dance Music	1960	30.00	60.00

RHYTHM DEVILS, THE
The Rhythm Devils are Mickey Hart and Bill Kreutzmann of The Grateful Dead.

Passport PB-9844	(S)	The Rhythm Devils Play River Music	1980	8.00	20.00

RHYTHM ROCKERS, THE

Challenge CHL-617	(M)	Soul Surfin'	1963	20.00	50.00

RICH, CHARLIE

Philips Int. 1970	(M)	Lonely Weekends	1960	300.00	500.00
Groove G-1000	(M)	Charlie Rich	1964	20.00	50.00
Groove GS-1000	(S)	Charlie Rich	1964	35.00	70.00
RCA Victor LPM-3352	(M)	That's Rich	1965	10.00	25.00
RCA Victor LSP-3352	(S)	That's Rich	1965	12.00	30.00
RCA Victor LPM-3537	(M)	Big Boss Man	1966	10.00	25.00
RCA Victor LSP-3537	(S)	Big Boss Man	1966	12.00	30.00
Smash MGS-27070	(M)	The Many Sides Of Charlie Rich	1965	8.00	20.00
Smash SRS-67070	(S)	The Many Sides Of Charlie Rich	1965	10.00	25.00
Smash MGS-27078	(M)	The Best Years	1966	8.00	20.00
Smash SRS-67078	(S)	The Best Years	1966	10.00	25.00
Hi HL-32037	(M)	Charlie Rich Sings Country And Western	1967	5.00	12.00
Hi SHL-32037	(S)	Charlie Rich Sings Country And Western	1967	6.00	15.00
Epic EQ-31933	(Q)	The Best Of Charlie Rich	1972	5.00	12.00
Epic EQ-32247	(Q)	Behind Closed Doors	1973	5.00	12.00
Epic EQ-32531	(Q)	Very Special Love Songs	1974	5.00	12.00
Epic PEQ-33250	(Q)	The Silver Fox	1974	5.00	12.00
Epic PEQ-33455	(Q)	Every Time You Touch Me	1975	5.00	12.00

RICHARD, CLIFF (& THE SHADOWS)
Refer to The Shadows.

ABC-Paramount 321	(M)	Cliff Sings	1960	16.00	40.00
ABC-Paramount S-321	(S)	Cliff Sings	1960	20.00	50.00
ABC-Paramount 391	(M)	Listen To Cliff	1961	16.00	40.00
ABC-Paramount S-391	(S)	Listen To Cliff	1961	20.00	50.00
Dot DLP-3474	(M)	Wonderful To Be Young (Soundtrack)	1962	16.00	40.00
Dot DLP-25474	(S)	Wonderful To Be Young (Soundtrack)	1962	20.00	50.00
Epic LN-24063	(M)	Summer Holiday (Soundtrack)	1963	20.00	50.00
Epic BN-26063	(S)	Summer Holiday (Soundtrack)	1963	35.00	70.00
Epic LN-24089	(M)	It's All In The Game	1964	10.00	25.00
Epic BN-26089	(S)	It's All In The Game	1964	12.00	30.00

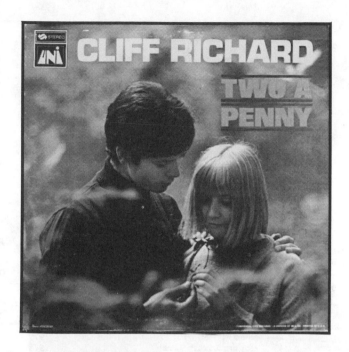

Cliff Richard's soundtrack for *Two A Penny* was issued on both Uni without a catalog number, raising the possibility that it was intended for promotional use only, and on the Christian oriented Light label, which did see commercial distribution.

Label & Catalog #		Title	Year	VG+	NM
Epic LN-24115	(M)	Cliff Richard In Spain	1964	10.00	25.00
Epic BN-26115	(S)	Cliff Richard In Spain	1964	12.00	30.00
Epic LN-24145	(M)	Swinger's Paradise (Soundtrack)	1965	12.00	30.00
Epic BN-26145	(S)	Swinger's Paradise (Soundtrack)	1965	16.00	40.00
Uni (No number)	(S)	Two A Penny (Soundtrack)	1971	20.00	50.00
Light LS-5530	(S)	Two A Penny (Soundtrack)	1971	6.00	15.00

RICHARD, CYRIL

Riverside RLP-406	(M)	Alice In Wonderland	1961	12.00	30.00

RICHARDS, ANN

Capitol T-1087	(M)	I'm Shooting High	1958	16.00	40.00
Capitol T-1406	(M)	The Many Moods Of Ann Richards	1960	10.00	25.00
Capitol ST-1406	(S)	The Many Moods Of Ann Richards	1960	14.00	35.00
Capitol T-1495	(M)	Two Much	1961	10.00	25.00
Capitol ST-1495	(S)	Two Much	1961	14.00	35.00
Atco 33-136	(M)	Ann, Man!	1961	6.00	15.00
Atco SD-33-136	(S)	Ann, Man!	1961	10.00	25.00
Vee Jay LP-1070	(M)	Live... At The Losers	1963	6.00	15.00
Vee Jay SR-1070	(M)	Live... At The Losers	1963	10.00	25.00

RICHARDS, TRUDY

Capitol T-838	(M)	Crazy In Love	1957	12.00	30.00

RICHMAN, JONATHAN, & THE MODERN LOVERS

Home Of The Hits HH-1910	(S)	The Modern Lovers	1975	20.00	50.00
Beserkley JBX-0048	(S)	Jonathan Richman & The Modern Lovers	1976	14.00	35.00
Beserkley BZ-0050	(S)	The Modern Lovers	1976	14.00	35.00
Beserkley PZ-34800	(S)	Rock 'N' Roll With The Modern Lovers	1977	8.00	20.00
Beserkley JBZ-0055	(S)	Modern Lovers 'Live'	1978	8.00	20.00
Beserkley BZ-0060	(S)	Back In Your Life	1979	8.00	20.00
Mohawk SCALP-0002	(S)	The Original Modern Lovers	1981	8.00	20.00
Sire 23939	(S)	Jonathan Sings!	1983	6.00	15.00

RICKS, JIMMY

Mr. Ricks was formerly a member of The Ravens.

Signature 1032	(M)	Jimmy Ricks	1961	50.00	100.00
Mainstream 56050	(M)	Vibrations	1965	8.00	20.00
Mainstream 6050	(S)	Vibrations	1965	12.00	30.00
Jubilee 8021	(M)	Tell Her You Love Her	1969	8.00	20.00

RIDDLE, NELSON

20th Century TF-4180	(M)	Batman (TV Soundtrack)	1966	20.00	50.00
20th Century TFS-4180	(S)	Batman (TV Soundtrack)	1966	35.00	70.00

RIGHTEOUS BROTHERS, THE

The brothers righteous are Bobby Hatfield and Bill Medley.

Moonglow MLP-1001	(M)	Right Now!	1963	8.00	20.00
Moonglow MSP-1001	(S)	Right Now!	1963	12.00	30.00
Moonglow MLP-1002	(M)	Some Blue-Eyed Soul	1964	8.00	20.00
Moonglow MSP-1002	(S)	Some Blue-Eyed Soul	1964	12.00	30.00
Moonglow MLP-1003	(M)	This Is New!	1965	8.00	20.00
Moonglow MSP-1003	(S)	This Is New!	1965	12.00	30.00
Moonglow MLP-1004	(M)	The Best Of The Righteous Brothers	1966	8.00	20.00
Moonglow MSP-1004	(S)	The Best Of The Righteous Brothers	1966	12.00	30.00
Philles PHLP-4007	(M)	You've Lost That Loving Feelin'	1965	8.00	20.00
Philles PHLP-ST-4007	(P)	You've Lost That Loving Feelin'	1965	12.00	30.00
Philles PHLP-4008	(M)	Just Once In My Life	1965	8.00	20.00
Philles PHLP-ST-4008	(P)	Just Once In My Life	1965	12.00	30.00
Philles PHLP-4009	(M)	Back To Back	1966	5.00	12.00
Philles PHLP-ST-4009	(P)	Back To Back	1966	8.00	20.00
		(Portions of Philles 4007 and 4009 were produced by Phil Spector.)			
Verve V-5001	(M)	Soul And Inspiration	1966	5.00	12.00
Verve V6-5001	(S)	Soul And Inspiration	1966	6.00	15.00
Verve V-5004	(S)	Go Ahead And Cry	1966	5.00	12.00
Verve V6-5004	(S)	Go Ahead And Cry	1966	6.00	15.00
Verve V-5010	(M)	Sayin' Somethin'	1967	5.00	12.00
Verve V6-5010	(S)	Sayin' Somethin'	1967	6.00	15.00

Along with Don Van Vliet, a.k.a. Captain Beefheart, Jonathan Richman may be rock & roll's "most difficulty acquired taste," although for disparate reasons. Originally the leader of the Modern Lovers, one of endless bands inspired by the Velvet Underground, Richman eventually opted for an acoustic based sound to sing songs that have more in common with nursery rhymes than rhythm 'n' blues. He sings such self-penned tunes as "I'm A Little Dinosaur" with a complete lack of pretension, charming even the most effete rock fan. (Note: *The Modern Lovers* collects tracks originally recorded years earlier for Warner Brothers.)

Label & Catalog #		Title	Year	VG+	NM
Verve V-5020	(M)	**The Righteous Brothers' Greatest Hits**	1967	5.00	12.00
Verve V6-5020	(P)	**The Righteous Brothers' Greatest Hits**	1967	6.00	15.00
Verve V-5031	(M)	**Souled Out**	1967	5.00	12.00
Verve V6-5031	(S)	**Souled Out**	1967	6.00	15.00

RINCON SURFSIDE BAND, THE
The Rincons are a creation of Steve Barri and Phil Sloan. Refer to The Grass Roots; The Fantastic Baggys.

Dunhill D-50001	(M)	**Surfing Songbook**	1965	35.00	70.00
Dunhill DS-50001	(S)	**Surfing Songbook**	1965	50.00	100.00

RIP CHORDS, THE
The Rip Chords are a creation of Bruce Johnston and Terry Melcher & Co.

Columbia CL-2151	(M)	**Hey, Little Cobra (& Other Hot Rod Hits)**	1964	8.00	20.00
Columbia CS-8951	(S)	**Hey, Little Cobra (& Other Hot Rod Hits)**	1964	12.00	30.00
Columbia CL-2216	(M)	**Three Window Coupe**	1964	16.00	40.00
Columbia CS-9016	(S)	**Three Window Coupe**	1964	20.00	50.00
		(Originally issued with a borderless, full view cover.)			
Columbia CS-9016	(S)	**Three Window Coupe**	196?	6.00	15.00
		(Special Products reissue with a black border on the cover.)			

RIPPERTON, MINNIE

Epic PEQ-3345	(Q)	**Adventures In Paradise**	1975	5.00	12.00

RISERS, THE

Imperial LP-9269	(M)	**She's A Bad Motorcycle**	1964	10.00	25.00
Imperial LP-12269	(S)	**She's A Bad Motorcycle**	1964	14.00	35.00

RISING STORM, THE

Remnant BBA-3571	(M)	**Calm Before The Rising Storm**	1968	500.00	750.00

RITCHIE, JEAN

Elektra EKL-2	(M)	**Traditional Songs Of Her Kentucky Mountain Home**	195?	8.00	20.00
Elektra EKL-125	(M)	**Kentucky Mountain Songs**	195?	8.00	20.00
Riverside RLP-12-620	(M)	**Saturday Night And Sunday, Too**	195?	8.00	20.00
Riverside RLP-12-646	(M)	**Songs From Kentucky**	195?	8.00	20.00
Westminster WP-6037	(M)	**Songs From Kentucky**	195?	8.00	20.00
Folkways FC-7054	(M)	**Southern Mountain Children's Songs And Games**	195?	8.00	20.00
Folkways FC-2316	(M)	**The Ritchie Family Of Kentucky**	195?	8.00	20.00

RITCHIE, JEAN, & OSCAR BRAND

Riverside RLP-12-646	(M)	**Riddle Me This**	195?	8.00	20.00

RITTER, TEX

Capitol H-4004 (10")	(M)	**Cowboy Favorites**	1949	40.00	80.00
Capitol T-971	(M)	**Songs From The Western Screen**	1958	20.00	50.00
		(Turquoise label.)			
Capitol T-1100	(M)	**Psalms**	1959	12.00	30.00
Capitol T-1292	(M)	**Blood On The Saddle**	1960	8.00	20.00
Capitol ST-1292	(S)	**Blood On The Saddle**	1960	10.00	25.00
Capitol W-1562	(M)	**The Lincoln Hymns**	1961	8.00	20.00
Capitol SW-1562	(S)	**The Lincoln Hymns**	1961	10.00	25.00
Capitol T-1623	(M)	**Hillbilly Heaven**	1961	8.00	20.00
Capitol ST-1623	(S)	**Hillbilly Heaven**	1961	10.00	25.00
		— Original Capitol albums above have black labels with the logo on the left side.—			
Capitol T-1757	(M)	**Stan Kenton / Tex Ritter**	1962	10.00	25.00
Capitol ST-1757	(S)	**Stan Kenton / Tex Ritter**	1962	14.00	35.00
Capitol T-1910	(M)	**Border Affair**	1963	6.00	15.00
Capitol ST-1910	(S)	**Border Affair**	1963	8.00	20.00
Capitol T-2402	(M)	**The Friendly Voice Of Tex Ritter**	1965	6.00	15.00
Capitol ST-2402	(S)	**The Friendly Voice Of Tex Ritter**	1965	8.00	20.00
Capitol T-2595	(M)	**The Best Of Tex Ritter**	1966	5.00	12.00
Capitol ST-2595	(S)	**The Best Of Tex Ritter**	1966	6.00	15.00
Capitol T-2743	(M)	**Sweet Land Of Liberty**	1967	5.00	12.00
Capitol ST-2743	(S)	**Sweet Land Of Liberty**	1967	6.00	15.00
Capitol T-2786	(M)	**Just Beyond The Moon**	1967	5.00	12.00
Capitol ST-2786	(S)	**Just Beyond The Moon**	1967	6.00	15.00
Capitol ST-2890	(S)	**Bump Tiddil Dee Bum Bum!**	1968	6.00	15.00

Label & Catalog #		Title	Year	VG+	NM
Capitol ST-2974	(S)	**Tex Ritter's Wild West**	*1968*	**6.00**	**15.00**
Capitol ST-213	(S)	**Chuck Wagon Days**	*1969*	**5.00**	**12.00**
		— Original Capitol albums above have black labels with the logo on top.—			

RIVERA, LUIS, & DOC BAGBY

King 631	(M)	**Battle Of The Organs**	*196?*	**20.00**	**50.00**

RIVERS, JOHNNY

Capitol T-2161	(M)	**The Sensational Johnny Rivers**	*1964*	**6.00**	**15.00**
Capitol ST-2161	(S)	**The Sensational Johnny Rivers**	*1964*	**8.00**	**20.00**
United Arts. UAL-3386	(M)	**Go Johnny, Go**	*1964*	**6.00**	**15.00**
United Arts. UAS-6386	(S)	**Go Johnny, Go**	*1964*	**8.00**	**20.00**

Johnny's first album for Imperial was a collection of r&b, folk and rock chestnuts in a loose, funky "live, very live!" setting. Success followed, as did a string of similar albums, leading Rivers to a career as one of the finest— and most underrated— white interpreters of the '60s and '70s.

Imperial LP-9264	(M)	**Johnny Rivers At The Whiskey A-Go-Go**	*1964*	**6.00**	**15.00**
Imperial LP-12264	(S)	**Johnny Rivers At The Whiskey A-Go-Go**	*1964*	**8.00**	**20.00**
Imperial LP-9274	(M)	**Here We A-Go-Go Again**	*1964*	**6.00**	**15.00**
Imperial LP-12274	(S)	**Here We A-Go-Go Again**	*1964*	**8.00**	**20.00**
Imperial LP-9280	(M)	**Johnny Rivers In Action**	*1965*	**6.00**	**15.00**
Imperial LP-12280	(S)	**Johnny Rivers In Action**	*1965*	**8.00**	**20.00**
Imperial LP-9284	(M)	**Meanwhile Back At The Whiskey A-Go-Go**	*1965*	**6.00**	**15.00**
Imperial LP-12284	(S)	**Meanwhile Back At The Whiskey A-Go-Go**	*1965*	**8.00**	**20.00**
Imperial LP-9293	(M)	**Johnny Rivers Rocks The Folk**	*1965*	**6.00**	**15.00**
Imperial LP-12293	(S)	**Johnny Rivers Rocks The Folk**	*1965*	**8.00**	**20.00**
Imperial LP-9307	(M)	**And I Know You Wanna Dance**	*1966*	**6.00**	**15.00**
Imperial LP-12307	(S)	**And I Know You Wanna Dance**	*1966*	**8.00**	**20.00**
Imperial LP-9324	(M)	**Johnny Rivers' Golden Hits**	*1966*	**5.00**	**12.00**
Imperial LP-12324	(S)	**Johnny Rivers' Golden Hits**	*1966*	**6.00**	**15.00**
Imperial LP-9334	(M)	**Changes**	*1966*	**5.00**	**12.00**
Imperial LP-12334	(S)	**Changes**	*1966*	**6.00**	**15.00**

Label & Catalog #		Title	Year	VG+	NM
Imperial LP-9341	(M)	Rewind	1967	5.00	12.00
Imperial LP-12341	(S)	Rewind	1967	6.00	15.00
Imperial LP-9372	(M)	Realization	1968	6.00	15.00
Imperial LP-12372	(S)	Realization	1968	6.00	15.00
Imperial LP-12427	(S)	A Touch Of Gold	1969	4.00	10.00
Imperial LP-16001	(S)	Slim Slo Rider	1969	4.00	10.00

RIVERS, MAVIS

Capitol T-1408	(M)	The Simple Life	1960	5.00	12.00
Capitol ST-1408	(S)	The Simple Life	1960	6.00	15.00
Reprise R-2002	(M)	Mavis	1961	5.00	12.00
Reprise R9-2002	(S)	Mavis	1961	6.00	15.00
Reprise R-2009	(M)	Swing Along	1961	5.00	12.00
Reprise R9-2009	(S)	Swing Along	1961	6.00	15.00
Reprise R-6074	(M)	Mavis Rivers Meets Shorty Rogers	1962	5.00	12.00
Reprise RS-6074	(S)	Mavis Rivers Meets Shorty Rogers	1962	6.00	15.00
Vee Jay LP-1132	(M)	We Remember Mildred Bailey	1964	5.00	12.00
Vee Jay LPS-1132	(S)	We Remember Mildred Bailey	1964	6.00	15.00

RIVIERAS, THE

Riviera 701	(M)	Campus Party	1964	50.00	100.00
U.S.A. 102	(M)	Let's Have A Party	1964	30.00	60.00

RIVINGTONS, THE

Liberty LRP-3282	(M)	Doin' The Bird	1963	35.00	70.00
Liberty LST-7282	(S)	Doin' The Bird	1963	50.00	100.00

ROAD, THE

Kama Sutra KSBS-8075	(S)	The Road	1969	6.00	15.00
Kama Sutra KSBS-2012	(S)	The Road	1970	5.00	12.00
Kama Sutra KSBS-2032	(S)	Cognition	1970	5.00	12.00

ROAD RUNNERS, THE
The Road Runners are a creation of Gary Usher & Co.

London LL-3381	(M)	The New Mustang (& Other Hot Rod Hits)	1964	35.00	70.00
London PS-381	(S)	The New Mustang (& Other Hot Rod Hits)	1964	50.00	100.00

ROBBINS, MARTY
Refer to Carl Smith.

Columbia CL-2601 (10")	(M)	Rock 'N Roll 'N Robbins	1956	500.00	750.00
Columbia CL-976	(M)	The Song Of Robbins	1957	35.00	70.00
Columbia CL-1087	(M)	Song Of The Islands	1957	35.00	70.00
Columbia CL-1189	(M)	Marty Robbins	1958	20.00	50.00
Columbia CL-1325	(M)	Marty's Greatest Hits	1959	12.00	30.00
Columbia CL-1349	(M)	Gunfighter Ballads And Trail Songs	1959	12.00	30.00
Columbia CS-8158	(S)	Gunfighter Ballads And Trail Songs	1959	16.00	40.00
Columbia CL-1481	(M)	More Gunfighter Ballads And Trail Songs	1960	8.00	20.00
Columbia CS-8272	(S)	More Gunfighter Ballads And Trail Songs	1960	12.00	30.00
Columbia CL-1558	(M)	The Alamo *(Soundtrack)*	1960	8.00	20.00
Columbia CS-8358	(S)	The Alamo *(Soundtrack)*	1960	12.00	30.00
Columbia CS-1635	(M)	More Greatest Hits	1961	8.00	20.00
Columbia CS-8435	(S)	More Greatest Hits	1961	12.00	30.00
Columbia CL-1666	(M)	Just A Little Sentimental	1961	8.00	20.00
Columbia CS-8466	(S)	Just A Little Sentimental	1961	12.00	30.00
— Original Columbia albums above have three white "eye" logos on each side of the spindle hole.—					
Columbia CL-1801	(M)	Marty After Midnight	1962	20.00	50.00
Columbia CS-8601	(S)	Marty After Midnight	1962	30.00	60.00
Columbia CL-1855	(M)	Portrait Of Marty	1962	10.00	25.00
Columbia CS-8655	(S)	Portrait Of Marty	1962	14.00	35.00
		(Issued with a bonus photo, priced separately below.)			
Columbia		Portrait Of Marty Bonus Photo	1962	12.00	30.00
Columbia CL-1918	(M)	Devil Woman	1962	8.00	20.00
Columbia CS-8718	(S)	Devil Woman	1962	12.00	30.00
Columbia CL-2040	(M)	Hawaii's Calling Me	1963	12.00	30.00
Columbia CS-8840	(S)	Hawaii's Calling Me	1963	16.00	40.00
Columbia CL-2072	(M)	Return Of The Gunfighter	1963	8.00	20.00
Columbia CS-8872	(S)	Return Of The Gunfighter	1963	12.00	30.00
Columbia CL-2176	(M)	Island Woman	1964	12.00	30.00
Columbia CS-8976	(S)	Island Woman	1964	16.00	40.00

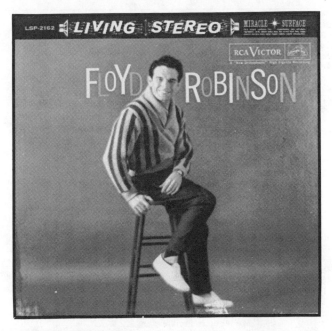

Floyd's sole entry on the major pop charts was 1959's "Makin' Love," a top 40 hit everywhere.
His first album is a stereo collectible.

Jimmie Rodgers placed two dozen sides on the charts from 1957-67. Only four albums during
this period sold enough to dent the charts, including this, his sole entry for Dot.

Label & Catalog #		Title	Year	VG+	NM
Columbia CL-2220	(M)	R.F.D. Marty Robbins	1964	12.00	30.00
Columbia CS-9020	(S)	R.F.D. Marty Robbins	1964	16.00	40.00
Columbia CL-2304	(M)	Turn The Lights Down Low	1965	8.00	20.00
Columbia CS-9104	(S)	Turn The Lights Down Low	1965	12.00	30.00
Columbia CL-2448	(M)	What God Has Done	1965	6.00	15.00
Columbia CS-9248	(S)	What God Has Done	1965	8.00	20.00
Columbia CL-2527	(M)	The Drifter	1966	6.00	15.00
Columbia CS-9327	(S)	The Drifter	1966	8.00	20.00
Columbia CLP-445	(P)	Bend In The River	1966	16.00	40.00
Columbia DL-237	(M)	Saddle Tramp (Record Club)	1966	6.00	15.00
Columbia DS-237	(S)	Saddle Tramp (Record Club)	1966	8.00	20.00
Columbia CL-2621	(M)	The Song Of Robbins	1967	10.00	25.00
Columbia CS-9421	(E)	The Song Of Robbins	1967	8.00	20.00
Columbia CL-2625	(M)	Song Of The Islands	1967	10.00	25.00
Columbia CS-9425	(E)	Song Of The Islands	1967	8.00	20.00
Columbia CL-2645	(M)	My Kind Of Country	1967	8.00	20.00
Columbia CS-9445	(S)	My Kind Of Country	1967	12.00	30.00
Columbia CL-2725	(M)	Tonight Carmen	1967	6.00	15.00
Columbia CS-9525	(S)	Tonight Carmen	1967	8.00	20.00
Columbia CL-2735	(M)	Christmas With Marty Robbins	1967	12.00	30.00
Columbia CS-9535	(S)	Christmas With Marty Robbins	1967	12.00	30.00
Columbia CL-2817	(M)	By The Time I Get To Phoenix	1968	20.00	50.00
Columbia CS-9617	(S)	By The Time I Get To Phoenix	1968	8.00	20.00
Columbia CS-9725	(S)	I Walk Alone	1968	6.00	15.00
Columbia CSP-445	(S)	Bend In The River (Record Ckub)	1968	20.00	50.00
Columbia STS-2016	(E)	The Heart Of Marty Robbins (2 LPs)	1969	20.00	50.00
Columbia CS-9811	(S)	It's A Sin	1969	10.00	25.00
Columbia GP-15	(S)	Marty's Country	1969	6.00	15.00
Columbia CS-9978	(S)	My Woman, My Woman, My Wife	1970	6.00	15.00

— Original Columbia albums above have "360 Sound" on the bottom of the label.—

ROBBS, THE

Mercury MG-21130	(M)	The Robbs	1967	10.00	25.00
Mercury SR-61130	(S)	The Robbs	1967	12.00	30.00

ROBERTS, JOAN

Quality 719-26 (10")	(M)	Joan Roberts Sings	195?	14.00	35.00

ROBERTS, PERNELL

RCA Victor LPM-2662	(M)	Come All Ye Fair And Tender Ladies	1963	10.00	25.00
RCA Victor LSP-2662	(S)	Come All Ye Fair And Tender Ladies	1963	14.00	35.00

ROBERTSON, DALE

RCA Victor LPM-2158	(M)	His Album Of Western Classics	1960	35.00	70.00
RCA Victor LSP-2158	(S)	His Album Of Western Classics	1960	50.00	100.00

ROBINS, THE

Whippet WLP-703	(M)	Rock 'N' Roll With The Robins	1958	300.00	500.00

ROBINSON, CARSON

MGM E-3594	(M)	Life Get's Tee-jus, Don't It	1958	16.00	40.00

ROBINSON, FLOYD

RCA Victor LPM-2162	(M)	Floyd Robinson	1960	10.00	25.00
RCA Victor LSP-2162	(S)	Floyd Robinson	1960	13.00	35.00

ROBINSON, SMOKEY, & THE MIRACLES [THE MIRACLES]

Tamla 220-254 simply credit The Miracles. The Miracles who recorded for Tamla from 1974 on are a different group.

Tamla 220	(M)	Hi! We're The Miracles	1961	150.00	250.00
Tamla 223	(M)	Cookin' With The Miracles	1962	150.00	250.00
Tamla 224	(M)	Shop Around	1962	100.00	200.00
Tamla 230	(M)	I'll Try Something New	1962	100.00	200.00

— Original Tamla albums above have a disc over-lapping a globe at the top of the label.—

Tamla 236	(M)	Christmas With The Miracles	1963	100.00	200.00
Tamla 238	(M)	The Fabulous Miracles	1963	75.00	150.00
Tamla 238	(M)	You've Really Got A Hold On Me	1963	75.00	150.00
		(Repackage of "The Fabulous Miracles.")			
Tamla 241	(M)	The Miracles On Stage	1963	75.00	150.00

While fans focused on the artists of the Motown roster, it was actually those behind the scenes responsible for the string of incredible singles churned out from 1964 through the early '70s. Along with the Holland-Dozier-Holland team, William "Smokey" Robinson was most responsible for the great songs that the Motown acts were fortunate to record. *Greatest Hits From The Beginning* is a two-record set that reprises the Miracles' first two albums and is a showcase for Robinson's singing as well as his writing. The sound on these early recordings (way back in 1961-62) are positively primitive compared to the glossy, polished production of *Away We A Go-Go*, one of the quintessential Motown albums from their golden period.

Label & Catalog #		Title	Year	VG+	NM
Tamla 245	(M)	Doin' Mickey's Monkey	1963	75.00	150.00
Tamla T-245	(S)	Doin' Mickey's Monkey	1963	100.00	200.00
Tamla 254	(M)	Greatest Hits From The Beginning (2 LPs)	1965	14.00	35.00
Tamla T-2-254	(E)	Greatest Hits From The Beginning (2 LPs)	1965	8.00	20.00
Tamla 267	(M)	Going To A Go-Go	1965	8.00	20.00
Tamla T-267	(S)	Going To A Go-Go	1965	10.00	25.00
Tamla 271	(M)	Away We A Go-Go	1966	6.00	15.00
Tamla T-271	(S)	Away We A Go-Go	1966	8.00	20.00
Tamla 276	(M)	Make It Happen	1967	6.00	15.00
Tamla T-276	(S)	Make It Happen	1967	8.00	20.00
Tamla T-276	(S)	Tears Of A Clown	1970	6.00	15.00
		(Repackage of "Make It Happen.")			
Tamla T-280	(S)	Greatest Hits, Volume 2	1968	6.00	15.00

— Tamla albums above have two side-by-side circles at the top of the label. —

Tamla T-289	(S)	Live!	1969	6.00	15.00
Tamla T-290	(S)	Special Occasion	1968	6.00	15.00
Tamla T-295	(S)	Time Out	1969	6.00	15.00
Tamla T-297	(S)	Four In Blue	1969	6.00	15.00
Tamla T-301	(S)	What Love Has Joined Together	1970	6.00	15.00
Tamla T-306	(S)	A Pocketful Of Miracles	1970	6.00	15.00
Tamla T-307	(S)	The Season For Miracles	1970	6.00	15.00
Tamla T-312	(S)	One Dozen Roses	1971	6.00	15.00
Tamla T-318	(S)	Flying High Together	1972	6.00	15.00
Tamla T-320	(S)	The Miracles 1957-1972 (2 LPs)	1973	6.00	15.00

ROBINSON, SUGAR CHILE

Capitol T-589	(M)	Boogie Woogie	1955	50.00	100.00

ROBINSON, SUGAR RAY

Continental 16009	(S)	I'm Still Swinging	195?	10.00	25.00

ROCHE, BETTY

Bethlehem 64	(M)	Take The 'A' Train	1956	35.00	70.00
Prestige PR-7187	(M)	Singin' And Swingin'	1961	16.00	40.00
Prestige PRS-7187	(S)	Singin' And Swingin'	1961	20.00	50.00
Prestige PR-7198	(M)	Lightly And Politely	1961	16.00	40.00
Prestige PRS-7198	(S)	Lightly And Politely	1961	20.00	50.00

ROCK-A-TEENS, THE

Roulette R-25109	(M)	Woo-Hoo	1960	50.00	100.00
Roulette SR-25109	(P)	Woo-Hoo	1960	75.00	150.00

ROCK SHOP, THE

LeeMo	(M)	The Rock Shop	1969	100.00	200.00

ROCKET 88

Rocket 88 is a creation of Charlie Watts of The Rolling Stones.

Atlantic 19293	(S)	Rocket 88	1981	4.00	10.00

ROCKETS, THE

The Rockets feature Ralph Molina and Danny Talbot, later of Crazy Horse.

White Whale S-7116	(S)	The Rockets	1968	10.00	25.00

ROCKIN' FOO

Hobbit HB-5001	(S)	Rockin' Foo	1969	8.00	20.00
Uni 73115	(S)	Rockin' Foo	1971	5.00	12.00

ROCKIN' REBELS, THE

Swan SLP-509	(M)	Wild Weekend	1963	75.00	150.00

ROCKY FELLERS, THE

Scepter SP-512	(M)	Killer Joe	1963	10.00	25.00
Scepter SPS-512	(S)	Killer Joe	1963	14.00	35.00

ROD & THE COBRAS

Somerset SF-20500	(M)	At A Drag Race At Surf City	1964	5.00	12.00
Somerset SF-20500	(S)	At A Drag Race At Surf City	1964	6.00	15.00

Label & Catalog #		Title	Year	VG+	NM
RODERICK, JUDY					
Columbia CL-2153	(M)	Ain't Nothin' But The Blues	1964	5.00	12.00
Columbia CS-8953	(S)	Ain't Nothin' But The Blues	1964	6.00	15.00
Vanguard VRS-9197	(M)	Woman Blue	1964	5.00	12.00
Vanguard VSD-79197	(S)	Woman Blue	1964	6.00	15.00
RODGERS, JIMMIE					
RCA Victor LPT-3037 (10")	(M)	Memorial Album, Volume 1	1952	75.00	150.00
RCA Victor LPT-3038 (10")	(M)	Memorial Album, Volume 2	1952	75.00	150.00
RCA Victor LPT-3039 (10")	(M)	Memorial Album, Volume 3	1952	75.00	150.00
RCA Victor LPT-3073 (10")	(M)	Travelin' Blues	1952	75.00	150.00
RCA Victor LPM-1232	(M)	Never No Mo' Blues/Memorial Album	1955	50.00	100.00
RCA Victor LPM-1640	(M)	Train Whistle Blues	1957	50.00	100.00
RCA Victor LPM-2112	(M)	My Rough And Rowdy Ways	1960	20.00	50.00
RCA Victor LPM-2213	(M)	Jimmie The Kid	1961	20.00	50.00
RCA Victor LPM-2531	(M)	Country Music Hall Of Fame	1962	20.00	50.00
RCA Victor LPM-2634	(M)	The Short But Brilliant Life Of Jimmie Rodgers	1963	20.00	50.00

— Original RCA albums above have "Long Play" on the bottom of the label.—

Label & Catalog #		Title	Year	VG+	NM
RCA Victor LPM-2865	(M)	My Time Ain't Long	1964	10.00	25.00
RCA Victor LPM-3315	(M)	Best Of The Legendary Jimmie Rodgers	1965	10.00	25.00
RCA Victor LSP-3315	(E)	Best Of The Legendary Jimmie Rodgers	1965	6.00	15.00

— Original RCA albums above have black labels.—

Label & Catalog #		Title	Year	VG+	NM
RODGERS, JIMMIE					
Roulette R-25020	(M)	Folk Songs And Readings	1958	12.00	30.00
Roulette R-25026	(M)	The Long Hot Summer (Soundtrack)	1958	16.00	40.00
Roulette R-25033	(M)	Number One Ballads	1958	8.00	25.00
Roulette R-25042	(M)	Jimmie Rodgers Sings Folk Songs	1958	8.00	25.00

— Original Roulette albums above have black labels.—

Label & Catalog #		Title	Year	VG+	NM
Roulette R-25057	(M)	His Golden Year	1959	8.00	25.00
Roulette R-25071	(M)	TV Favorites	1959	6.00	15.00
Roulette SR-25071	(S)	TV Favorites	1959	8.00	20.00
Roulette R-25081	(M)	Twilight On The Trail	1959	6.00	15.00
Roulette SR-25081	(S)	Twilight On The Trail	1959	8.00	20.00
Roulette R-25095	(M)	It's Christmas Once Again	1959	6.00	15.00
Roulette SR-25095	(S)	It's Christmas Once Again	1959	8.00	20.00
Roulette R-25103	(M)	When The Spirit Moves You	1960	6.00	15.00
Roulctte SR-25103	(S)	When The Spirit Moves You	1960	8.00	20.00
Roulette R-25128	(M)	At Home With Jimmie Rodgers	1960	6.00	15.00
Roulette SR-25128	(S)	At Home With Jimmie Rodgers	1960	8.00	20.00
Roulette R-25150	(M)	The Folk Song World Of Jimmie Rodgers	1961	6.00	15.00
Roulette SR-25150	(S)	The Folk Song World Of Jimmie Rodgers	1961	8.00	20.00
Roulette R-25160	(M)	The Best Of Jimmie Rodgers Folk Songs	1961	6.00	15.00
Roulette SR-25160	(S)	The Best Of Jimmie Rodgers Folk Songs	1961	8.00	20.00
Roulette R-25179	(M)	15 Million Sellers	1962	5.00	12.00
Roulette SR-25179	(S)	15 Million Sellers	1962	6.00	15.00

— Original Roulette albums above have white labels.—

Label & Catalog #		Title	Year	VG+	NM
Roulette R-25199	(M)	Folk Songs	1963	5.00	12.00
Roulette SR-25199	(S)	Folk Songs	1963	6.00	15.00
Dot DLP-3453	(M)	No One Will Ever Know	1962	5.00	12.00
Dot DLP-25453	(S)	No One Will Ever Know	1962	6.00	15.00
Dot DLP-3496	(M)	Folk Concert	1963	5.00	12.00
Dot DLP-25496	(S)	Folk Concert	1963	6.00	15.00
Dot DLP-3502	(M)	My Favorite Hymns	1963	5.00	12.00
Dot DLP-25502	(S)	My Favorite Hymns	1963	6.00	15.00
Dot DLP-3525	(M)	Honeycomb And Kisses Sweeter Than Wine	1963	5.00	12.00
Dot DLP-25525	(S)	Honeycomb And Kisses Sweeter Than Wine	1963	6.00	15.00
Dot DLP-3???	(M)	Town And Country	1963	4.00	10.00
Dot DLP-25???	(S)	Town And Country	1963	5.00	12.00
Dot DLP-3???	(M)	The World I Used To Know	1964	4.00	10.00
Dot DLP-25???	(S)	The World I Used To Know	1964	5.00	12.00
Dot DLP-3579	(M)	Twelve Great Hits	1964	4.00	10.00
Dot DLP-25579	(S)	Twelve Great Hits	1964	5.00	12.00
Dot DLP-3614	(M)	Deep Purple	1965	4.00	10.00
Dot DLP-25614	(S)	Deep Purple	1965	5.00	12.00
Dot DLP-3657	(M)	Christmas With Jimmie Rodgers	1965	4.00	10.00
Dot DLP-25657	(S)	Christmas With Jimmie Rodgers	1965	5.00	12.00

Label & Catalog #		Title	Year	VG+	NM
Dot DLP-3687	(M)	Nashville Sound	1966	4.00	10.00
Dot DLP-25687	(S)	Nashville Sound	1966	5.00	12.00
Dot DLP-3710	(M)	Country Music 1966	1966	4.00	10.00
Dot DLP-25710	(S)	Country Music 1966	1966	5.00	12.00
Dot DLP-3717	(M)	It's Over	1966	4.00	10.00
Dot DLP-25717	(S)	It's Over	1966	5.00	12.00
Dot DLP-3780	(M)	Love Me, Please Love Me	1967	4.00	10.00
Dot DLP-25780	(S)	Love Me, Please Love Me	1967	5.00	12.00
Dot DLP-3815	(M)	Golden Hits/15 Hits Of Jimmie Rodgers	1967	4.00	10.00
Dot DLP-25815	(S)	Golden Hits/15 Hits Of Jimmie Rodgers	1967	5.00	12.00

ROE, TOMMY

Label & Catalog #		Title	Year	VG+	NM
ABC-Paramount 432	(M)	Sheila	1962	10.00	25.00
ABC-Paramount S-432	(S)	Sheila	1962	14.00	35.00
ABC-Paramount 467	(M)	Something For Everybody	1964	8.00	20.00
ABC-Paramount S-467	(S)	Something For Everybody	1964	10.00	25.00
ABC-Paramount 575	(M)	Sweet Pea	1966	6.00	15.00
ABC-Paramount S-575	(S)	Sweet Pea	1966	8.00	20.00
ABC-Paramount 594	(M)	It's Now Winter's Day	1967	5.00	12.00
ABC-Paramount S-594	(S)	It's Now Winter's Day	1967	6.00	15.00
ABC 610	(M)	Phantasy	1967	5.00	12.00
ABC S-610	(S)	Phantasy	1967	6.00	15.00
ABC S-683	(S)	Dizzy	1969	6.00	15.00
ABC S-700	(S)	Twelve In A Roe (Greatest Hits)	1969	5.00	12.00
ABC S-714	(S)	We Can Make Music	1970	4.00	10.00
ABC S-732	(S)	Beginnings	1971	4.00	10.00
ABC X-762	(S)	16 Greatest Hits	1972	4.00	10.00

ROGERS, EILEEN

Label & Catalog #		Title	Year	VG+	NM
Columbia CL-1229	(M)	Blue Swing	1959	6.00	15.00
Columbia CS-8029	(S)	Blue Swing	1959	10.00	25.00

ROGERS, GINGER

Label & Catalog #		Title	Year	VG+	NM
Decca DL-5040 (10")	(M)	Alice In Wonderland	195?	20.00	50.00
Citel CLP-201	(M)	Hello, Ginger!	195?	12.00	30.00

ROGERS, KENNY
Kenny also recorded with The First Edition.

Label & Catalog #		Title	Year	VG+	NM
Jolly Rogers 5001	(S)	Backroads (Picture disc)	1975	50.00	100.00
United Artists LA934	(DJ)	The Gambler (Picture disc)	1978	20.00	50.00
Mobile Fidelity MFSL-044	(S)	The Gambler	1979	5.00	12.00
Mobile Fidelity MFSL-049	(S)	Greatest Hits	1979	6.00	15.00
Liberty SLL-8344	(DJ)	HBO Presents Kenny Rogers (Picture disc)	1983	4.00	10.00

ROGERS, ROY (& DALE EVANS)

Label & Catalog #		Title	Year	VG+	NM
RCA Victor LPT-3041 (10")	(M)	Roy Rogers Souvenir Album	1952	50.00	100.00
RCA Victor LPT-3168 (10")	(M)	Hymns Of Faith	1954	40.00	80.00
RCA Victor LPM-1439	(M)	Sweet Hour Of Prayer	1957	20.00	50.00
Golden A-1978	(M)	16 Great Songs Of The Old West	195?	14.00	35.00
Bluebird LBY-1022	(M)	Jesus Loves Me	1959	10.00	25.00
Capitol T-1745	(M)	The Bible Tells Me So	1962	10.00	25.00
Capitol ST-1745	(S)	The Bible Tells Me So	1962	12.00	30.00
Camden CAL-1054	(M)	Pecos Bill	1964	10.00	25.00
Camden CAL-1074	(M)	Lore Of The West	1966	10.00	25.00
Capitol T-2818	(M)	Christmas Is Always	1967	12.00	30.00
Capitol ST-2818	(S)	Christmas Is Always	1967	12.00	30.00
Camden CAL-1097	(M)	Peter Cottontail And His Friends	1968	6.00	15.00
Capitol ST-594	(S)	The Country Side Of Roy Rogers	1970	6.00	15.00
Capitol ST-785	(S)	A Man From Duck Run	1971	6.00	15.00
Capitol ST-11020	(S)	Take A Little Love And Pass It On	1972	5.00	12.00
20th Century 467	(S)	Happy Trails To You	1975	5.00	12.00

ROKES, THE

Label & Catalog #		Title	Year	VG+	NM
RCA Victor Int. FPM-185	(M)	Che Mondo Strano	1968	35.00	70.00

.abel & Catalog #		Title	Year	VG+	NM

ROLLING STONES, THE

Mick Jagger, Brian Jones, Keith Richards, Charlie Watts and Bill Wyman with Ian Stewart. Jones was replaced by Mick Taylor, 1969-72; Ron Wood joined for good in 1976. Refer to Howlin' Wolf; Alexis Korner; Rocket 88.

.abel & Catalog #		Title	Year	VG+	NM
London LL-3375	(DJ)	The Rolling Stones (White label)	1964	800.00	1,200.00
London LL-3375	(M)	The Rolling Stones	1964	50.00	100.00
		(Issued with a bonus photo, which is advertised in the lower left corner of the front cover. The photo is priced separately below.)			
London LL-3375		The Rolling Stones Bonus Photo	1964	75.00	150.00
London LL-3402	(M)	12 X 5	1964	50.00	100.00
London LL-3420	(M)	The Rolling Stones, Now!	1965	50.00	100.00
London LL-3429	(M)	Out Of Our Heads	1965	50.00	100.00
		— London albums above have maroon labels with the London/ffrr" logo and "Made in England by the Decca Group" at the top.—			
London LL-3375	(M)	The Rolling Stones	1964	16.00	40.00
London LL-3402	(M)	12 X 5 (Blue vinyl)	1964	See note below	
		(Rare. Estimated near mint value $3,000-5,000.)			
London LL-3402	(M)	12 X 5	1964	16.00	40.00
London LL-3420	(M)	The Rolling Stones, Now!	1965	16.00	40.00
London LL-3429	(M)	Out Of Our Heads	1965	16.00	40.00
London LL-3451	(M)	December's Children	1965	16.00	40.00
		— London mono albums above have maroon labels with a silver "London" on top against a plain maroon background.—			
London LL-3375	(M)	The Rolling Stones	1966	10.00	25.00
London LL-3402	(M)	12 X 5	1966	10.00	25.00
London LL-3420	(M)	The Rolling Stones, Now!	1966	10.00	25.00
London LL-3429	(M)	Out Of Our Heads	1966	10.00	25.00
London LL-3451	(M)	December's Children	1966	10.00	25.00
London NP-1	(M)	High Tide And Green Grass	1966	10.00	25.00
London LL-3476	(M)	Aftermath	1966	10.00	25.00
London LL-4493	(M)	Got Live If You Want It	1966	10.00	25.00
London LL-499	(M)	Between The Buttons	1967	10.00	25.00
London LL-509	(M)	Flowers	1967	10.00	25.00
London NP-2	(M)	Their Satanic Majesties Request (3-D cover)	1967	75.00	150.00
		— London mono albums above have maroon labels with a maroon "London" on top in a silver box.—			
London PS-375	(E)	The Rolling Stones	1964	10.00	25.00
London PS-402	(E)	12 X 5	1964	10.00	25.00
London PS-420	(E)	The Rolling Stones, Now!	1965	10.00	25.00
London PS-429	(E)	Out Of Our Heads	1965	10.00	25.00
London PS-451	(E)	December's Children	1965	10.00	25.00
		— London stereo albums above have blue labels with a silver "London" on top against a plain blue background.—			
I.N.S. Radio 1003	(M)	It's Here Luv!! (Counterfeits are common)	1965	100.00	200.00
London PS-375	(E)	The Rolling Stones	1966	4.00	10.00
London PS-402	(E)	12 X 5	1966	4.00	10.00
London PS-420	(E)	The Rolling Stones, Now!	1966	4.00	10.00
London PS-429	(E)	Out Of Our Heads	1966	4.00	10.00
London PS-451	(E)	December's Children	1966	4.00	1C.00
London NPS-1	(E)	High Tide And Green Grass	1966	4.00	10.00
London PS-476	(S)	Aftermath	1966	4.00	10.00
London PS-493	(P)	Got Live If You Want It	1966	4.00	10.00
London PS-499	(S)	Between The Buttons	1967	4.00	10.00
London PS-509	(P)	Flowers	1967	4.00	10.00
London NPS-2	(P)	Their Satanic Majesties Request (3-D cover)	1967	14.00	35.00
London NPS-2	(P)	Their Satanic Majesties Request (2-D cover)	1967	6.00	15.00
London PS-539	(S)	Beggar's Banquet	1968	6.00	15.00
		(First pressings of 539 credit all songs to Jagger-Richard.)			
London NPS-3	(P)	Through The Past, Darkly	1969	4.00	10.00
London NPS-4	(S)	Let It Bleed (With poster)	1969	8.00	20.00
London NPS-4	(S)	Let It Bleed (Without poster)	1969	4.00	10.00
London NPS-5	(S)	Get Your Ya-Ya's Out!	1970	4.00	10.00
London RSD-1	(DJ)	The Rolling Stones/The Promotional Album	1969	600.00	900.00
		(Counterfeits are common.)			
London 2PS-606/7	(P)	Hot Rocks 1964-1971 (2 LPs)	1971	5.00	12.00
London 2PS-626/7	(P)	More Hot Rocks (2 LPs)	1972	5.00	12.00
		— London stereo albums above have deep blue labels with a blue "London" on top in a silver box.—			

Label & Catalog #		Title	Year	VG+	NM

Long a source of frustration and a hindrance to both collectors and dealers has been the confusing data on London label variations, especially with the under-valued Stones. An accurate breakdown of those changes, both mono and stereo, is included in this edition.

Abkco DVL2-0268	(P)	**The Rolling Stones' Greatest Hits** *(2 LPs.)*	1975	8.00	20.00
Abkco MPD-1	(S)	**Songs Of The Rolling Stones**	1975	100.00	200.00
		(Cover photo is a shot of the group in a field.)			
Abkco MPD-1	(S)	**Songs Of The Rolling Stones**	1975	660.00	1,000.00
		(Cover shot taken from the "Rock & Roll Circus.")			
Roll. Stones COC 59100	(DJ)	**Sticky Fingers** *(White label. Mono)*	1971	180.00	300.00
Roll. Stones COC 59100	(DJ)	**Sticky Fingers** *(White label. Stereo)*	1971	100.00	200.00
Roll. Stones COC 59100	(S)	**Sticky Fingers** *(Zipper cover)*	1971	4.00	10.00
Roll. Stones COC-39100	(DJ)	**Jamming With Edward** *(White label)*	1972	16.00	40.00
Roll. Stones COC-39100	(S)	**Jamming With Edward**	1972	6.00	15.00
Roll. Stones COC-2-2900	(S)	**Exile On Main Street** *(2 LPs)*	1972	6.00	15.00
		(Fold-out jacket with pockets that open on the inside. Includes a tear-sheet of postcards.)			
Roll. Stones COC 39113	(S)	**Still Life** *(Picture disc)*	1982	8.00	20.00
Mobile Fidelity MFSL-060	(S)	**Sticky Fingers**	1980	10.00	25.00
Mobile Fidelity MFSL-087	(S)	**Some Girls**	1982	8.00	20.00
Mobile Fidelity (No #)	(P)	**The Rolling Stones** *(11 LP box)*	1984	150.00	250.00

ROMEOS, THE
| Mark-II 1001 | (M) | **Precious Memories** | 1967 | 10.00 | 25.00 |

ROMNEY, HUGH
Mr. Romney later claimed fame in the counter-culture as Digger deluxe "Wavy Gravy."
| World Pacific WP-1805 | (M) | **Third Stream Humor** | 1962 | 10.00 | 25.00 |

RONETTES, THE
The Ronettes feature Veronica Bennett, a.k.a. Ronnie Spector. Philles 4006 was produced by Phil Spector.
Colpix CLP-486	(DJ)	**The Ronettes Featuring Veronica**	1965	150.00	250.00
Colpix CLP-486	(M)	**The Ronettes Featuring Veronica**	1965	75.00	150.00
Colpix CST-486	(S)	**The Ronettes Featuring Veronica**	1965	100.00	200.00
		(First pressings are on a gold label.)			
Colpix CLP-486	(M)	**The Ronettes Featuring Veronica**	196?	50.00	100.00
Colpix CST-486	(S)	**The Ronettes Featuring Veronica**	196?	75.00	150.00
		(Second pressings are on a blue label.)			

Label & Catalog #		Title	Year	VG+	NM
Philles PHLP-4006	(DJ)	**Presenting The Fabulous Ronettes**	1965	300.00	500.00
Philles PHLP-4006	(M)	**Presenting The Fabulous Ronettes**	1965	100.00	200.00
		(First pressings are on a blue label.)			
Philles PHLP-4006	(M)	**Presenting The Fabulous Ronettes**	1965	75.00	150.00
		(Second pressings are on a yellow label.)			
Philles PHLP-ST-4006	(S)	**Presenting The Fabulous Ronettes**	1965	210.00	350.00
		(Yellow label with red print.)			
Philles ST-	(S)	**Presenting The Fabulous Ronettes**	1965	150.00	250.00
		(Capitol Record Club. Yellow label with black print.)			
RONNIE & THE DEADBEATS					
Check 103	(M)	**Groovin' With Ronnie & The Deadbeats**	197?	8.00	20.00
RONNY & THE DAYTONAS					
Mala 4001	(M)	**G.T.O.**	1964	35.00	70.00
Mala 4002	(M)	**Sandy**	1966	12.00	30.00
Mala 4002-S	(S)	**Sandy**	1966	35.00	70.00
RONNIE & THE POMONA CASUALS					
Donna 2112	(M)	**Everybody Jerk**	1965	12.00	30.00
RONSTADT, LINDA, & THE STONE PONEYS					
Capitol T-2666	(M)	**The Stone Poneys**	1967	8.00	20.00
Capitol ST-2666	(S)	**The Stone Poneys**	1967	12.00	30.00
Capitol T-2763	(M)	**Evergreen, Volume II**	1967	8.00	20.00
Capitol ST-2763	(S)	**Evergreen, Volume II**	1967	12.00	30.00
Capitol ST-2863	(S)	**Linda Ronstadt, Stone Poneys & Friends**	1968	16.00	40.00

By 1968 Capitol could grace the third album by The Stone Poneys with a this stunning photo of Linda and give the album the ungainly title "Linda Ronstadt, Stone Poneys And Friends, Vol. III."

RONSTADT, LINDA					
Capitol ST-208	(S)	**Hand Sown** *(Green label)*	1969	6.00	15.00
Capitol ST-407	(S)	**Silk Purse** *(Green label)*	1970	6.00	15.00
Capitol SMAS-635	(S)	**Linda Ronstadt** *(Green label)*	1972	6.00	15.00
Asylum DP-401	(S)	**Living In The U.S.A.** *(Picture disc)*	1978	3.50	8.00
Mobile Fidelity MFSL-158	(S)	**What's New?**	198?	8.00	20.00
Nautilus NR-26	(S)	**Simple Dreams**	198?	12.00	30.00

Label & Catalog #		Title	Year	VG+	NM
ROOFTOP SINGERS, THE					
Vanguard VRS-2136	(M)	**Walk Right In**	1963	5.00	12.00
Vanguard VSD-72136	(S)	**Walk Right In**	1963	6.00	15.00
Vanguard VRS-9134	(M)	**Goodtime**	1964	4.00	10.00
Vanguard VSD-79134	(S)	**Goodtime**	1964	5.00	12.00
Vanguard VRS-9190	(M)	**Rainy River**	1965	4.00	10.00
Vanguard VSD-79190	(S)	**Rainy River**	1965	5.00	12.00
ROONEY, MICKEY					
RCA Victor LPM-1520	(M)	**Mickey Rooney Sings George M. Cohan**	1957	14.00	35.00
ROSE GARDEN, THE					
Atco SD-33-225	(S)	**The Rose Garden**	1968	5.00	12.00
ROSE MARIE					
Kapp KRL-2500	(M)	**Songs For Single Girls**	1964	5.00	12.00
Kapp KRS-4500	(S)	**Songs For Single Girls**	1964	6.00	15.00

Ms. Rosie Hamlin, formerly of Rosie & The Originals ("Angel Baby"), recorded her sole solo album for Brunswick in 1961. Highly collectible, the stereo version is much rarer than the mono.

Label & Catalog #		Title	Year	VG+	NM
ROSIE					
Rosalie Hamlin of Rosie & The Originals.					
Brunswick BL-54102	(M)	**Lonely Blue Nights**	1961	50.00	100.00
Brunswick BL7-54102	(S)	**Lonely Blue Nights**	1961	75.00	150.00
ROSS, ANNIE					
Refer to Lambert, Hendricks & Ross.					
World Pacific WP-1253	(M)	**Annie Ross Sings A Song With Mulligan**	1959	16.00	40.00
World Pacific WP-1020	(S)	**Annie Ross Sings A Song With Mulligan**	1959	20.00	50.00
World Pacific WP-1276	(M)	**Gypsy**	1959	16.00	40.00
World Pacific WP-1028	(S)	**Gypsy**	1959	20.00	50.00
World Pacific WP-1285	(M)	**A Gasser**	1959	20.00	50.00
Decca DL-4922	(M)	**Fill My Heart With Song**	1967	8.00	20.00
Decca DL-74922	(S)	**Fill My Heart With Song**	1967	10.00	25.00

Label & Catalog #		Title	Year	VG+	NM
ROSS, DIANA					
Motown M7-923	(DJ)	**The Boss** (Gold vinyl)	1979	8.00	20.00
Nautilus NR-37	(S)	**Diana**	1981	6.00	15.00
ROSS, DIANA / NEIL DIAMOND					
MCA SM-734727	(S)	**It's Happening! Diana Ross-Neil Diamond**	1972	20.00	50.00
ROSS, JOE E.					
Mr. Ross also recorded as Officer Gunther Toody.					
Roulette R-25281	(M)	**Love Songs From A Cop**	1964	6.00	15.00
Roulette SR-25281	(S)	**Love Songs From A Cop**	1964	8.00	20.00
ROTH, LILLIAN					
Tops 1567	(M)	**Lillian Roth Sings**	195?	14.00	35.00
Epic LN-3206	(M)	**I'll Cry Tomorrow**	195?	14.00	35.00
ROUND ROBIN					
Domain 101	(M)	**Greatest Hits, Slauson Style**	1964	10.00	25.00
Challenge LP-620	(M)	**Lloyd Thaxton Presents The Land Of 1,000 Dances Featuring Round Robin**	1965	8.00	20.00
ROUTERS, THE					
Warner Bros. W-1490	(M)	**Let's Go With The Routers**	1963	6.00	15.00
Warner Bros. WS-1490	(S)	**Let's Go With The Routers**	1963	8.00	20.00
Warner Bros. W-1524	(M)	**1963's Great Instrumental Hits**	1964	5.00	12.00
Warner Bros. WS-1524	(S)	**1963's Great Instrumental Hits**	1964	6.00	15.00
Warner Bros. W-1559	(M)	**Charge!**	1964	5.00	12.00
Warner Bros. WS-1559	(S)	**Charge!**	1964	6.00	15.00
Warner Bros. W-1595	(M)	**Go Go Go With The Chuck Berry Songbook**	1965	5.00	12.00
Warner Bros. WS-1595	(S)	**Go Go Go With The Chuck Berry Songbook**	1965	6.00	15.00
Mercury SRM-1-682	(S)	**Superbird**	197?	4.00	10.00
ROXX					
Sit On It & Spin	(S)	**Get Your Roxx Off**	1976	20.00	50.00

Initially issued with a cover featuring these lovely but barely clad ladies, "Country Life" was pulled and a new cover, the background sans the ladies, was issued in its stead.

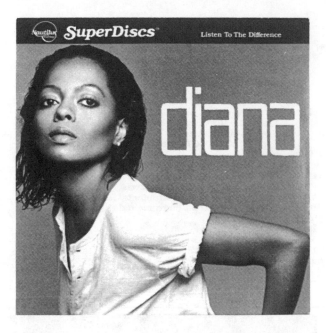

Originally gaining worldwide fame as one of the lead singers for the most popular female vocal group of the '60s, the Supremes, Diana Ross saw her star rise to top billing (many of their records were released as Diana Ross & The Supremes) to a solo career that can best be described as extraordinarily successful...

Sticking with Motown and mentor Berry Gordy through 1981, she scored a number of massive hits, including the disco drivel "Upside Down," the centerpiece for the above album. This half-speed master is fairly difficult to find but has yet to attract a sizeable following...

Label & Catalog #		Title	Year	VG+	NM

ROXY MUSIC
The original Roxy Music featured Brian Eno and Brian Ferry.

Reprise MS-2114	(S)	**Roxy Music**	1972	10.00	25.00
Reprise BS-2969	(S)	**For Your Pleasure**	1973	10.00	25.00
Atlantic SD-7045	(S)	**Stranded**	1974	6.00	15.00
Atco SD-33-106	(S)	**Country Life** (Nearly naked ladies cover)	1975	10.00	25.00
Atco SD-38114	(DJ)	**Manifesto** (Picture disc)	1979	8.00	20.00

The perennially underrated Billy Joe Royal was, for all practical purposes, the first lead singer for Joe South's band, The Believers. For Billy Joe, South wrote most of the material, played guitar and arranged and produced his albums!

ROYAL, BILLY JOE

Columbia CL-2403	(M)	**Down In The Boondocks**	1965	6.00	15.00
Columbia CS-9203	(S)	**Down In The Boondocks**	1965	8.00	20.00
Columbia CL-2781	(M)	**Billy Joe Royal**	1967	6.00	15.00
Columbia CS-9581	(S)	**Billy Joe Royal**	1967	8.00	20.00
Columbia CS-9974	(S)	**Cherry Hill Park**	1969	6.00	15.00

ROYAL GUARDSMEN, THE

Laurie LLP-2038	(M)	**Snoopy Vs. The Red Baron**	1967	8.00	20.00
Laurie SLLP-2038	(S)	**Snoopy Vs. The Red Baron**	1967	10.00	25.00
Laurie LLP-2039	(M)	**The Return Of The Red Baron**	1967	6.00	15.00
Laurie SLLP-2039	(S)	**The Return Of The Red Baron**	1967	8.00	20.00
Laurie LLP-2042	(M)	**Snoopy And His Friends**	1967	10.00	25.00
Laurie SLLP-2042	(S)	**Snoopy And His Friends**	1967	12.00	30.00
		(Issued with a "Merry Snoopy's Christmas" tear-off sheet attached to the back cover.)			
Laurie LLP-2042	(M)	**Snoopy And His Friends** (Without sheet)	1967	6.00	15.00
Laurie SLLP-2042	(S)	**Snoopy And His Friends** (Without sheet)	1967	8.00	20.00
Laurie SLLP-2046	(S)	**Snoopy For President**	1968	8.00	20.00

ROYAL JOKERS, THE

Dawn 1119	(M)	**Rock And Roll Spectacular**	195?	50.00	100.00

In 1966 the Royal Guardsmen captured the nation's fancy with their set of singles chronicling the valiant efforts of dogfighting Snoopy and the equally cunning Red Baron. Their third album, *Snoopy & His Friends,* issued for Christmas of '67, originally had a tear-off "poster" of Snoopy attached to the back cover. Needless to say, few copies have survived with the poster intact...

Label & Catalog #		Title	Year	VG+	NM
ROYAL PLAYBOYS, THE					
Waldorf 33-136 (10")	(M)	**Spirituals And Jubilees**	195?	50.00	100.00
ROYALETTES, THE					
MGM E-4332	(M)	**It's Gonna Take A Miracle**	1965	6.00	15.00
MGM SE-4332	(S)	**It's Gonna Take A Miracle**	1965	8.00	20.00
MGM E-4366	(M)	**The Elegant Sound Of The Royalettes**	1966	6.00	15.00
MGM SE-4366	(S)	**The Elegant Sound Of The Royalettes**	1966	8.00	20.00
RUBBER BAND, THE					
GRT 10007	(S)	**The Jimi Hendrix Songbook**	1969	6.00	15.00
GRT 10010	(S)	**The Cream Songbook**	1969	6.00	15.00
GRT 10015	(S)	**The Beatles Songbook**	1969	6.00	15.00
RUBBER MEMORY					
R.P.C. 69401	(M)	**Welcome**	1966	240.00	400.00
RUBEN & THE JETS					
Mercury SRM-1-659	(S)	**For Real** (Produced by Frank Zappa)	1973	6.00	15.00
RUBY & THE ROMANTICS					
Kapp KL-1323	(M)	**Our Day Will Come**	1963	8.00	20.00
Kapp KS-3323	(S)	**Our Day Will Come**	1963	10.00	25.00
Kapp KL-1341	(M)	**Till Then**	1963	6.00	15.00
Kapp KS-3341	(S)	**Till Then**	1963	8.00	20.00
Kapp KL-1458	(M)	**Greatest Hits Album**	1966	5.00	12.00
Kapp KS-3458	(S)	**Greatest Hits Album**	1966	6.00	15.00
Kapp KL-1526	(M)	**Ruby And The Romantics**	1967	5.00	12.00
Kapp KS-3526	(S)	**Ruby And The Romantics**	1967	6.00	15.00
ABC S-638	(S)	**More Than Yesterday**	1968	6.00	15.00
RUFFIN, DAVID					

David Ruffin was formerly a member of The Temptations.

Motown MS-685	(S)	**My Whole World Ended**	1969	8.00	20.00
Motown MS-696	(S)	**Feelin' Good**	1969	6.00	15.00
RUFFIN, JIMMY					
Soul 704	(M)	**Jimmy Ruffin Sings Top 10**	1967	6.00	15.00
Soul S-704	(S)	**Jimmy Ruffin Sings Top 10**	1967	8.00	20.00
Soul S-708	(S)	**Ruff 'N Ready**	1969	5.00	12.00
RUFFIN, JIMMY & DAVID					
Soul S-728	(S)	**I Am My Brother's Keeper**	1970	5.00	12.00
RUFUS					
Command QD-40023	(Q)	**Rufusized**	1975	6.00	15.00
Command QD-40024	(Q)	**Rags To Rufus**	1975	6.00	15.00
ABC AA-1049	(DJ)	**Street Player** (Picture disc)	1979	5.00	12.00
ABC AA-1049	(DJ)	**Numbers** (Picture disc)	1979	5.00	12.00
RUMBLERS, THE					
Downey DLP-1001	(M)	**Boss!**	1963	30.00	60.00
Downey DLPS-1001	(S)	**Boss!**	1963	35.00	70.00
Dot DLP-3509	(M)	**Boss!**	1963	12.00	30.00
Dot DLP-25509	(S)	**Boss!**	1963	16.00	40.00
Bell 6047	(S)	**Rumplestiltskin**	1970	5.00	12.00
RUNAWAYS, THE					

The Runaways feature Joan Jett.

Mercury SRM-1-1090	(S)	**The Runaways**	1976	6.00	15.00
Mercury SRM-1-1126	(S)	**Queens Of Noise**	1977	6.00	15.00
Mercury SRM-1-3705	(S)	**Waitin' For The Night**	1977	6.00	15.00
RUNDGREN, TODD					

Mr. Rundgren was formerly a member of The Nazz.

Ampex 10105	(S)	**Runt** (With "Say No More")	1970	50.00	100.00
Ampex 10105	(S)	**Runt**	1970	16.00	40.00
Ampex 10116	(S)	**Ballad Of Todd Rundgren**	1971	16.00	40.00

(Counterfeits of both Ampex albums are plentiful.)

Label & Catalog #	Title	Year	VG+	NM

Formerly the leader of The Nazz, Todd Rundgren's first two albums for Ampex, "Runt" and "The Ballad Of Todd Rundgren," have been heavily counterfeited. The most tell-tale sign: the cover artwork is rather obviously photocopied from the original.

Label & Catalog #		Title	Year	VG+	NM
Bearsville 10105	(S)	**Runt**	1972	8.00	20.00
Bearsville 21066	(DJ)	**Something/Anything** *(2 LPs)*	1972	150.00	250.00
		(One album is on blue vinyl, the other, red.)			
Bearsville 524	(DJ)	**The Todd Rundgren Radio Show**	1977	75.00	150.00
Bearsville 597	(DJ)	**Banded Radio Interview**	1977	50.00	100.00
Bearsville 788	(DJ)	**Todd Rundgren Radio Sampler**	1979	20.00	50.00
RUSH					
Mercury MK-32	(DJ)	**Everything Your Listener Ever Wanted...**	1975	20.00	50.00
Mercury SRP-1300	(S)	**Hemisheres** *(Picture disc)*	1979	10.00	25.00
RUSH, MERILEE					
Bell 6020	(P)	**Angel Of The Morning**	1968	5.00	12.00
RUSH, OTIS					
Blue Horizion BM-4602	(S)	**Blues Masters, Volume 2**	1968	6.00	15.00
Blue Horizion BM-4805	(S)	**Chicago Blues**	1970	6.00	15.00
Cotillion SD-9006	(S)	**Mourning In The Morning**	1969	6.00	15.00
RUSH, TOM					
Folklore PR-7374	(M)	**Blues, Songs And Ballads**	1965	5.00	12.00
Folklore PRS-7374	(S)	**Blues, Songs And Ballads**	1965	6.00	15.00
Elektra EKL-288	(M)	**Tom Rush**	1965	5.00	12.00
Elektra EKS-7288	(S)	**Tom Rush**	1965	6.00	15.00
Elektra EKL-308	(M)	**Take A Little Walk With Me**	1966	5.00	12.00
Elektra EKS-7308	(S)	**Take A Little Walk With Me**	1966	6.00	15.00
Elektra EKS-74018	(S)	**The Circle Game**	1968	4.00	10.00
Elektra EKS-74062	(S)	**Classic Rush**	1970	4.00	10.00
Ly Cornu SA-70-2	(S)	**Tom Rush At The Unicorn**	1970	8.00	20.00
RUSHING, JIMMY					
Vanguard 8011 (10")	(M)	**Going To Chicago**	1954	50.00	100.00
Vanguard 8505	(M)	**Listen To The Blues**	1955	20.00	50.00

Label & Catalog #		Title	Year	VG+	NM
Vanguard 8513	(M)	If This Ain't The Blues	1957	20.00	50.00
Vanguard 8518	(M)	Going To Chicago	1957	20.00	50.00
Vanguard VDS-2008	(M)	If This Ain't The Blues	1958	20.00	50.00
Jazztone 1244	(M)	Listen To The Blues	1957	20.00	50.00
Columbia CL-963	(M)	The Jazz Odyssey Of James Rushing, Esq.	1957	20.00	50.00
Columbia CL-1152	(M)	Little Jimmy Rushing And The Big Brass	1958	14.00	35.00
Columbia CS-8060	(S)	Little Jimmy Rushing And The Big Brass	1958	20.00	50.00
Columbia CL-1401	(M)	Rushing Lullabies	1959	14.00	35.00
Columbia CS-8196	(S)	Rushing Lullabies	1959	20.00	50.00
Columbia CL-1553	(M)	Brubeck And Rushing	1960	12.00	30.00
Columbia CS-8353	(S)	Brubeck And Rushing	1960	16.00	40.00
Columbia CL-1605	(M)	Jimmy Rushing And The Smith Girls	1961	12.00	30.00
Columbia CS-8405	(S)	Jimmy Rushing And The Smith Girls	1961	16.00	40.00
— Original Columbia albums above have three white "eye" logos on each side of the spindle hole.—					
Audio Lab 1512	(M)	Two Shades Of Blue	1959	20.00	50.00
Colpix CLP-446	(M)	Five Feet Of Soul	1963	10.00	25.00
Colpix SCP-446	(S)	Five Feet Of Soul	1963	16.00	40.00
BluesWay BL-3005	(M)	Everyday I Have The Blues	1967	6.00	15.00
BluesWay BLS-6005	(S)	Everyday I Have The Blues	1967	8.00	20.00
BluesWay BLS-6107	(S)	Livin' The Blues	1968	6.00	15.00

RUSHING, JIMMY, & ADA MOORE

Columbia CL-778	(M)	Cat Meets Chick	1956	20.00	50.00

RUSKIN-SPEAR, ROGER
Ruskin-Spear was formerly a member of The Bonzo Dog Band.

United Arts. LA097	(S)	Electric Shocks	1973	10.00	25.00

RUSSELL, JANE
Refer to Marilyn Monroe.

Mercury MG-25182 (10")	(M)	The French Line (Soundtrack)	1954	50.00	100.00
Coral CRL-57158	(M)	Make A Joyful Noise Unto The Lord	1957	14.00	35.00
MGM E-3715	(M)	Jane Russell	1959	35.00	70.00

RUSSELL, KURT

Capitol SKAO-492	(S)	Kurt Russell	1970	8.00	20.00

RUTLES, THE
The Rutles feature Neil Innes of The Bonzo Dog Band and Eric Idle.

Warner Bros. H-3151	(S)	Meet The Rutles (With booklet)	1978	8.00	20.00
Warner Bros. PRO-723	(DJ)	Meet The Rutles (Gold vinyl)	1978	10.00	25.00

RYAN, CHARLIE

King 751	(M)	Hot Rod	1961	45.00	90.00
Hilltop JM-6006	(M)	Hot Rod Lincoln Drags Again	1964	8.00	20.00
Hilltop JS-6006	(E)	Hot Rod Lincoln Drags Again	1964	6.00	15.00

RYDELL, BOBBY

Cameo C-1006	(M)	We Got Love	1959	16.00	40.00
Cameo C-1007	(M)	Bobby Sings	1960	16.00	40.00
Cameo C-1009	(M)	Biggest Hits (Fold-open cover with insert)	1961	16.00	40.00
Cameo C-1010	(M)	Bobby Rydell Salutes The Great Ones	1961	12.00	30.00
Cameo C-1011	(M)	Rydell At The Copa	1961	12.00	30.00
Cameo C-1019	(M)	All The Hits	1962	12.00	30.00
Cameo C-1028	(M)	Biggest Hits, Volume 2	1962	12.00	30.00
Cameo C-1040	(M)	All The Hits, Volume 2	1963	12.00	30.00
Cameo C-1043	(M)	Bye Bye Birdie	1963	12.00	30.00
Cameo C-1055	(M)	Wild (Wood) Days	1963	10.00	25.00
Cameo CS-1055	(S)	Wild (Wood) Days	1963	16.00	40.00
Cameo C-1070	(M)	The Top Hits Of '63	1964	10.00	25.00
Cameo CS-1070	(S)	The Top Hits Of '63	1964	16.00	40.00
Cameo C-1080	(M)	Forget Him	1964	10.00	25.00
Cameo CS-1080	(S)	Forget Him	1964	16.00	40.00
Cameo C-2001	(M)	16 Golden Hits	1965	8.00	20.00
Cameo CS-2001	(E)	16 Golden Hits	1965	8.00	20.00
Cameo C-4017	(M)	An Era Reborn	196?	6.00	15.00
Cameo CS-4017	(S)	An Era Reborn	196?	8.00	20.00
Capitol T-2281	(M)	Somebody Loves You	1965	6.00	15.00
Capitol ST-2281	(S)	Somebody Loves You	1965	8.00	20.00

Label & Catalog #		Title	Year	VG+	NM
RYDELL, BOBBY, & CHUBBY CHECKER					
Cameo C-1013	(M)	**Bobby Rydell / Chubby Checker**	1961	12.00	30.00
Cameo C-1063	(M)	**Chubby Checker And Bobby Rydell**	1963	12.00	30.00
RYDER, MITCH (& THE DETROIT WHEELS)					
New Voice 2000	(M)	**Take A Ride**	1966	8.00	20.00
New Voice S-2000	(S)	**Take A Ride**	1966	12.00	30.00
New Voice 2002	(M)	**Breakout!!!**	1966	8.00	20.00
New Voice S-2002	(S)	**Breakout!!!**	1966	12.00	30.00
New Voice 2003	(M)	**Sock It To Me!**	1967	8.00	20.00
New Voice S-2003	(S)	**Sock It To Me!**	1967	12.00	30.00
New Voice 2004	(M)	**All Mitch Ryder Hits!**	1967	6.00	15.00
New Voice S-2004	(S)	**All Mitch Ryder Hits!**	1967	8.00	20.00
DynoVoice 1901	(M)	**What Now My Love**	1967	4.00	10.00
DynoVoice 31901	(S)	**What Now My Love**	1967	5.00	12.00
New Voice S-2005	(S)	**Mitch Ryder Sings The Hits**	1968	8.00	20.00
Dot DLP-25963	(S)	**The Detroit-Memphis Experiment**	1969	8.00	20.00

SABRAS, THE [BEZALEL & THE SABRAS]					
Tikva 122	(M)	**The Sabras**	196?	180.00	300.00
SACRED MUSHROOM, THE					
Parallax P-4001	(S)	**The Sacred Mushroom**	1969	50.00	100.00
SAGITTARIUS					
Sagittarius features Curt Boetcher.					
Columbia CS-9644	(S)	**Present Tense** (*Produced by Gary Usher*)	1968	10.00	25.00
Together STT-1002	(S)	**The Blue Marble**	1969	14.00	35.00
SAHM, DOUG					
Doug Sahm is Sir Doug of The Sir Douglas Quintet.					
Mercury SRM-1-655	(S)	**Rough Edges**	1972	12.00	30.00
Atlantic SD-7254	(S)	**Doug Sahm & Band** (*With Bob Dylan*)	1973	5.00	12.00
Warner Bros. BS-2810	(S)	**Groover's Paradise**	1974	8.00	20.00
Takoma TAK-7075	(S)	**Hell Of A Spell**	1980	4.00	10.00
ST. ANTHONY'S FIRE					
Zonk	(M)	**St. Anthony's Fire**	1968	240.00	400.00
ST. CLAIRE, BETTY					
Jubilee 15 (10")	(M)	**Mal McHusick Plays/Betty St. Claire Sings**	1955	20.00	50.00
Jubilee 23 (10")	(M)	**Cool And Clearer**	1955	20.00	50.00
Jubilee 1011	(M)	**What Is There To Say?**	1956	16.00	40.00
Seeco 456	(M)	**Betty St. Claire At Basin Street East**	1960	12.00	30.00
ST. JOHN GREEN					
Flick Disc FLS-45001	(S)	**St. John Green**	1968	8.00	20.00
ST. LOUIS, JIMMY					
Bluesville BV-1028	(M)	**Goin' Down Slow**	1961	8.00	20.00

"Sir" Doug Sahm has made an admirable career out of introducing his rock oriented fans to a whole body of a different aspect of American culture (most of it from the Lone Star state). Primarily mixing folk blues with Texas' Mexican rhythms, Sahm has produced a delightful ouvre that continues to grow. *Rough Edges* is a collection of outtakes from his two previous albums that holds together as a strong complement to either. *Groover's Paradise* features former CCR rhythm section Stu Cook and Doug Clifford. Both albums were hard to find within months of release.

Label & Catalog #		Title	Year	VG+	NM
ST. LOUIS HOUNDS, THE					
No label	(S)	The St. Louis Hounds	197?	100.00	200.00
ST. PETERS, CRISPIAN					
Jamie JLPM-3027	(M)	The Pied Piper	1966	12.00	30.00
Jamie JLPS-3027	(E)	The Pied Piper	1966	8.00	20.00
SAKAMOTO, KYU					
Capitol Int. T-10349	(M)	Sukiyaki	1963	10.00	25.00
Capitol Int. DT-10349	(E)	Sukiyaki	1963	8.00	20.00
SALES, SOUPY					
Reprise R-6010	(M)	The Soupy Sales Show	1961	10.00	25.00
Reprise R9-6010	(S)	The Soupy Sales Show	1961	14.00	35.00
Reprise R96052	(M)	Up In The Air	1962	8.00	20.00
Reprise R9-6052	(S)	Up In The Air	1962	10.00	25.00
ABC-Paramount 503	(M)	Spy With A Pie	1965	8.00	20.00
ABC-Paramount S-503	(S)	Spy With A Pie	1965	10.00	25.00
ABC-Paramount 517	(M)	Soupy Sez Do The Mouse	1965	8.00	20.00
ABC-Paramount S-517	(S)	Soupy Sez Do The Mouse	1965	10.00	25.00
Motown MS-686	(S)	A Bag Of Soup	1969	6.00	15.00
MCA 5274	(S)	Still Soupy After All These Years	1981	4.00	10.00
SALEM MASS					
Salem Mass SM-101	(S)	Witch Burning	1972	150.00	250.00
SALLYANGIE					
Sallyangie is Sally and Mike Oldfield.					
Warner Bros. WS-1783	(S)	Children Of The Sun	1969	6.00	15.00
SALVATION					
ABC S-623	(S)	Salvation	1968	6.00	15.00
ABC S-653	(S)	Gypsy Carnival Caravan	1968	6.00	15.00
SAM & DAVE					
Sam Moore and Dave Prater.					
Roulette R-25323	(M)	Sam And Dave	1966	12.00	30.00
Roulette SR-25323	(S)	Sam And Dave	1966	16.00	40.00
Stax 708	(M)	Hold On I'm Comin'	1966	12.00	30.00
Stax 708	(S)	Hold On I'm Comin'	1966	16.00	40.00
Stax 712	(M)	Double Dynamite	1966	12.00	30.00
Stax 712	(S)	Double Dynamite	1966	16.00	40.00
Stax 725	(M)	Soul Men	1967	8.00	20.00
Stax 725	(S)	Soul Men	1967	12.00	30.00
Atlantic SD-8205	(S)	I Thank You	1968	8.00	20.00
Atlantic SD-8218	(S)	The Best Of Sam And Dave	1969	6.00	15.00
United Arts. LA262	(S)	Back At 'Cha!	1974	5.00	12.00
United Arts. LA524	(S)	Back At 'Cha!	1975	4.00	10.00
SAM THE SHAM & THE PHARAOHS					
MGM E-4297	(M)	Wooly Bully	1965	12.00	30.00
MGM SE-4297	(S)	Wooly Bully	1965	16.00	40.00
MGM E-4314	(M)	Their Second Album	1965	8.00	20.00
MGM SE-4314	(S)	Their Second Album	1965	10.00	25.00
MGM E-4347	(M)	On Tour	1966	8.00	20.00
MGM SE-4347	(S)	On Tour	1966	10.00	25.00
MGM E-4407	(M)	Lil' Red Riding Hood	1966	10.00	25.00
MGM SE-4407	(S)	Lil' Red Riding Hood	1966	12.00	30.00
MGM E-4422	(M)	The Best Of Sam The Sham	1967	6.00	15.00
MGM SE-4422	(S)	The Best Of Sam The Sham	1967	8.00	20.00
MGM E-4479	(M)	Nefertiti	1967	6.00	15.00
MGM SE-4479	(S)	Nefertiti	1967	8.00	20.00
MGM SE-4479	(S)	Sam The Sham Revue	1968	6.00	15.00
MGM SE-4526	(S)	Ten Of Pentacles	1968	6.00	15.00
SAMUDIO, SAM					
Atlantic SD-8271	(S)	Hard And Heavy	1971	5.00	12.00

Label & Catalog #		Title	Year	VG+	NM

SANDALS, THE [THE SANDELLS]

World Pacific WP-1818	(M)	**Scramblers**	*1964*	**16.00**	**40.00**
World Pacific ST-1818	(S)	**Scramblers**	*1964*	**20.00**	**50.00**
World Pacific ST-1818	(S)	**Scramblers** *(Red vinyl)*	*1964*	**50.00**	**100.00**
		(World Pacific 1818 is credited to The Sandells.)			
World Pacific WP-1832	(M)	**The Endless Summer** *(Soundtrack)*	*1966*	**8.00**	**20.00**
World Pacific ST-1832	(S)	**The Endless Summer** *(Soundtrack)*	*1966*	**10.00**	**25.00**
		(World Pacific 1832 is a repackage of W.P. 1818.)			
World Pacific WPS-21884	(S)	**The Last Of The Ski Bums** *(Soundtrack)*	*1969*	**8.00**	**20.00**
		(Orange cover with three skiers' silhouettes.)			
World Pacific WPS-21884	(S)	**The Last Of The Ski Bums** *(Soundtrack)*	*1969*	**8.00**	**20.00**
		(Blue cover with cartoon skiers in a VW bus.)			

While record collectors know him as a member of the delightfully obscene Fugs, Ed Sanders is known to the rest of the world as the author of "The Family," in which Sanders set out from New York to California to prove that Charles Manson was a poor hippie framed by The Establishment... and came back horrified by what he learned!

SANDERS, ED

Mr. Sanders was formerly a member of The Fugs.

Reprise RS-6374	(S)	**Sanders' Truckstop**	*1969*	**8.00**	**20.00**
Reprise MS-2105	(S)	**Beer Cans On The Moon**	*1973*	**8.00**	**20.00**

SANDERS, FELICIA

Columbia CL-654	(M)	**Felicia Sanders At The Blue Angel**	*1955*	**14.00**	**35.00**
Columbia CL-713	(M)	**Girl Meets Boy**	*1955*	**14.00**	**35.00**
Decca DL-8762	(M)	**That Certain Feeling**	*1958*	**10.00**	**25.00**
Decca DL-78762	(S)	**That Certain Feeling**	*1958*	**14.00**	**35.00**
Time 2007	(M)	**The Songs Of Kurt Weill**	*1963*	**6.00**	**15.00**
Time 52007	(S)	**The Songs Of Kurt Weill**	*1963*	**8.00**	**20.00**
Time 2110	(M)	**Felicia Sanders**	*1964*	**5.00**	**12.00**
Time 52110	(S)	**Felicia Sanders**	*1964*	**6.00**	**15.00**

SANDERS, GEORGE

ABC-Paramount 231	(M)	**The George Sanders Touch**	*1958*	**12.00**	**30.00**

Label & Catalog #		Title	Year	VG+	NM

SANDS, TOMMY
Tommy also recorded soundtrack songs with Annette.

Label & Catalog #		Title	Year	VG+	NM
Capitol T-848	(M)	Steady Date With Tommy Sands	1957	20.00	50.00
Capitol T-929	(M)	Sing Boy Sing *(Soundtrack)*	1958	20.00	50.00
Capitol T-1081	(M)	Sands Storm	1959	16.00	40.00
Capitol T-1109	(M)	Teenage Rock	1959	16.00	40.00
Capitol T-1123	(M)	This Thing Called Love	1959	10.00	25.00
Capitol ST-1123	(S)	This Thing Called Love	1959	14.00	35.00
Capitol T-1239	(M)	When I'm Thinking Of You	1960	10.00	25.00
Capitol ST-1239	(S)	When I'm Thinking Of You	1960	14.00	35.00
Capitol T-1364	(M)	Sands At The Sands	1960	10.00	25.00
Capitol ST-1364	(S)	Sands At The Sands	1960	14.00	35.00
Capitol T-1426	(M)	Dream With Me	1961	10.00	25.00
Capitol ST-1426	(S)	Dream With Me	1961	14.00	35.00

SANDY COAST: *Refer to* VANITY FARE

SANTANA

Label & Catalog #		Title	Year	VG+	NM
Columbia CS-9781	(S)	Santana *("360 Sound" label)*	1969	6.00	15.00
Columbia KC-30130	(S)	Abraxas *(With poster)*	1970	6.00	15.00
Columbia CQ-30130	(Q)	Abraxas	1974	6.00	15.00
Columbia CQ-31610	(Q)	Caravanserai	1974	6.00	15.00
Columbia PCQ-32445	(Q)	Welcome	1974	6.00	15.00
Columbia PCQ-32900	(Q)	Illuminations	1974	6.00	15.00
Columbia PCQ-32964	(Q)	Santana	1974	6.00	15.00
Columbia PCQ-33050	(Q)	Greatest Hits	1974	6.00	15.00
Columbia PCQ-33135	(Q)	Borboletta	1974	6.00	15.00
Columbia PCQ-33576	(Q)	Amigos	1976	6.00	15.00
Columbia PCQ-34423	(Q)	Festival	1977	6.00	15.00
Columbia HC-40130	(S)	Abraxas *(Half-speed master)*	1981	12.00	30.00
Columbia HC-47158	(S)	Zebop! *(Half-speed master)*	1981	8.00	20.00

SANTO & JOHNNY
Santo and Johnny Farina.

Label & Catalog #		Title	Year	VG+	NM
Canad. Am. CALP-1001	(M)	Santo & Johnny	1959	20.00	50.00
Canad. Am. SCALP-1001	(S)	Santo & Johnny	1959	35.00	70.00
Canad. Am. CALP-1002	(M)	Encore	1960	12.00	30.00
Canad. Am. SCALP-1002	(S)	Encore	1960	16.00	40.00
Canad. Am. CALP-1004	(M)	Hawaii	1961	12.00	30.00
Canad. Am. SCALP-1004	(S)	Hawaii	1961	16.00	40.00
Canad. Am. CALP-1006	(M)	Come On In	1962	12.00	30.00
Canad. Am. SCALP-1006	(S)	Come On In	1962	16.00	40.00
Canad. Am. CALP-1011	(M)	Off Shore	1963	12.00	30.00
Canad. Am. SCALP-1011	(S)	Off Shore	1963	16.00	40.00
Canad. Am. CALP-1014	(M)	In The Still Of The Night	1963	12.00	30.00
Canad. Am. SCALP-1014	(S)	In The Still Of The Night	1963	16.00	40.00
Canad. Am. CALP-1016	(M)	Wish You Were Here	1964	12.00	30.00
Canad. Am. SCALP-1016	(S)	Wish You Were Here	1964	16.00	40.00
Canad. Am. CALP-1017	(M)	The Beatles' Greatest Hits	1964	16.00	40.00
Canad. Am. SCALP-1017	(S)	The Beatles' Greatest Hits	1964	20.00	50.00
Canad. Am. CALP-1018	(M)	Mucho	1965	10.00	25.00
Canad. Am. SCALP-1018	(S)	Mucho	1965	14.00	35.00
Imperial LP-9363	(M)	Brilliant Guitar Sounds	1967	6.00	15.00
Imperial LP-12363	(S)	Brilliant Guitar Sounds	1967	8.00	20.00
Imperial LP-12366	(S)	Golden Guitars	1968	8.00	20.00
Imperial LP-12418	(S)	On The Road Again	1968	8.00	20.00

SAPPHIRES, THE

Label & Catalog #		Title	Year	VG+	NM
Swan LP-513	(M)	Who Do You Love	1964	50.00	100.00

SAPPHIRE THINKERS, THE

Label & Catalog #		Title	Year	VG+	NM
Hobbit HB-5003	(S)	From Within	1969	8.00	20.00

SATAN & THE DE-CIPLES

Label & Catalog #		Title	Year	VG+	NM
Goldband 7750	(S)	Underground	1969	20.00	50.00

SATANS, THE

Label & Catalog #		Title	Year	VG+	NM
No label	(M)	Raisin' Hell	1962	100.00	200.00

Label & Catalog #		Title	Year	VG+	NM
SATINS FOUR, THE, & THE CINNAMON ANGELS					
B.T. Puppy BTS-1010	(S)	Mixed Soul	1970	50.00	100.00
SAUNDERS, MERL, & JERRY GARCIA					
Fantasy F-79002	(S)	Live At The Keystone	1973	6.00	15.00
SAUVAGE, KATHERINE					
Epic LN-3489	(M)	The Songs Of Kurt Weill	195?	14.00	35.00
SAVAGE ROSE					
Polydor 24-6001	(S)	In The Plain	1969	6.00	15.00
SAVAGE SONS OF YO HO WA, THE					
Higher Key 3306	(S)	The Savage Sons Of Yo Ho Wa	1974	75.00	150.00
Higher Key 3309	(S)	I'm Gonna Take You Home	1975	75.00	150.00
SAVAGES, THE					
Duane 1047	(M)	Live And Wild	1966	150.00	250.00
SAVOY BROWN					
Parrot PAS-71024	(S)	Getting To The Point	1968	6.00	15.00
Parrot PAS-71027	(S)	Blue Matter	1969	6.00	15.00
Parrot PAS-71029	(S)	A Step Further	1969	6.00	15.00
Parrot PAS-71036	(S)	Raw Sienna	1970	6.00	15.00
Parrot PAS-71042	(S)	Looking In	1970	6.00	15.00
Parrot PAS-71047	(S)	Street Corner Talking	1971	6.00	15.00

— Parrot albums above read "Distributed by London" on the label.—

SAXONS, THE					
Mirrosonic AS-1017	(M)	Love Minus Zero	1966	30.00	60.00
SCAFFOLD					
Bell 6018	(S)	Thank U Very Much	1968	10.00	25.00
SCAGGS, BOZ					

Boz was formerly a member of the Steve Miller Band.

Columbia AS-203	(DJ)	The Boz Scaggs Sampler	1976	6.00	15.00
Columbia HC-43920	(S)	Silk Degrees (Half-speed master)	1981	10.00	25.00
SCAMPS, THE					
Project 8002	(M)	Teen Dance And Sing Along Party	1962	16.00	40.00
SCHILLER, LAWRENCE					
Capitol TAO-2574	(M)	LSD	1966	6.00	15.00
Capitol STAO-2574	(S)	LSD	1966	8.00	20.00
Capitol KAO-2630	(M)	Why Did Lenny Bruce Die?	1967	8.00	20.00
Capitol SKAO-2630	(S)	Why Did Lenny Bruce Die?	1967	10.00	25.00
Capitol KAO-2652	(M)	Homosexuality In The American Male	1967	6.00	15.00
Capitol SKAO-2652	(S)	Homosexuality In The American Male	1967	8.00	20.00
SCHLAMME, MARTHA					
Vanguard VRS-9011	(M)	Folk Songs	195?	8.00	20.00
SCHOOLBOYS, THE					
Palace 778	(M)	Beatle Mania	1964	16.00	40.00
SCHORY, DICK [DICK SCHORY'S NEW PERCUSSION ENSEMBLE]					
RCA Victor LPM-1866	(M)	Music For Bang, Barroom And Harp	1958	8.00	20.00
RCA Victor LSP-1866	(S)	Music For Bang, Barroom And Harp	1958	40.00	80.00
RCA Victor LPM-2125	(M)	Music To Break Any Mood	1960	6.00	15.00
RCA Victor LSP-2125	(S)	Music To Break Any Mood	1960	30.00	60.00
SCORPION					
Tower ST-5171	(S)	Scorpion	1969	12.00	30.00
SCOTT, BOBBY					
Bethlehem 1004 (10")	(M)	Great Scott	1954	20.00	50.00
Bethlehem 1009 (10")	(M)	The Compositions, Volume 1	1954	20.00	50.00
Bethlehem 1029 (10")	(M)	The Compositions, Volume 2	1954	20.00	50.00

One of several albums issued to exploit the massive explosion of publicity that the formerly legal chemical lysergic acid diethylamide was amassing during the mid '60s. Lawrence Schiller's simply titled *LSD* is a hilarious attempt to paint a picture of acid's more bizarre effects and at the same time make everyone involved read like a public savior. "At Capitol Records we live in a world of the young... We are, therefore, perhaps more aware of, and more sensitive to, the widespread use of LSD among the school age population."

The liner notes include a glossary that defines the following terms as:
"Flip: Go psychotic." "The Grateful Dead: A West Coast rock-and-roll group under the entrepreneurial aegis of Owsley Stanley." "Guide: A person who baby-sits for the psychedelic user during a session." "Travel agent: The person who provides the trip."

The entire album's reactionary babble, and the tortured rantings of the supposed head having a bummer, function as low comedy for anyone who has been experienced...

Label & Catalog #		Title	Year	VG+	NM
Bethlehem 8	(M)	The Compositions	1955	16.00	40.00
ABC-Paramount 102	(M)	Scott Free	1956	16.00	40.00
ABC-Paramount 148	(M)	Bobby Scott And Two Horns	1957	16.00	40.00
Atlantic 1341	(M)	The Complete Musician	1960	10.00	25.00
Atlantic SD-1341	(S)	The Complete Musician	1960	16.00	40.00
Atlantic 1355	(M)	A Taste Of Honey	1960	10.00	25.00
Atlantic SD-1355	(S)	A Taste Of Honey	1960	16.00	40.00
Mercury MG-20701	(M)	Joyful Noises	1962	8.00	20.00
Mercury SR-60701	(S)	Joyful Noises	1962	12.00	30.00
Mercury MG-20767	(M)	When The Feeling Hits You	1963	8.00	20.00
Mercury SR-60767	(S)	When The Feeling Hits You	1963	12.00	30.00
Mercury MG-20854	(M)	108 Pounds Of Heartache	1963	8.00	20.00
Mercury SR-60854	(S)	108 Pounds Of Heartache	1963	12.00	30.00

SCOTT, CLIFORD

Label & Catalog #		Title	Year	VG+	NM
World Pacific WP-1811	(M)	The Big Ones	1964	6.00	15.00
World Pacific ST-1811	(S)	The Big Ones	1964	8.00	20.00
World Pacific ST-1811	(S)	The Big Ones (Green vinyl)	1964	20.00	50.00

SCOTT, FREDDIE

Label & Catalog #		Title	Year	VG+	NM
Colpix CP-461	(M)	Freddie Scott Sings (Gold label)	1964	14.00	35.00
Colpix SCP-461	(S)	Freddie Scott Sings (Gold label)	1964	20.00	50.00
Colpix CP-461	(M)	Freddie Scott Sings (Blue label)	1965	10.00	25.00
Colpix SCP-461	(E)	Freddie Scott Sings (Blue label)	1965	10.00	25.00
Columbia CL-2258	(M)	Everything I Have Is Yours	1964	6.00	15.00
Columbia CS-9058	(S)	Everything I Have Is Yours	1964	8.00	20.00
Columbia CL-2660	(M)	Lonely Man	1967	5.00	12.00
Columbia CS-9460	(S)	Lonely Man	1967	6.00	15.00
Shout SLP-501	(M)	Are You Lonely For Me	1967	5.00	12.00
Shout SLPS-501	(S)	Are You Lonely For Me	1967	6.00	15.00
Probe CPLP-4517	(S)	I Shall Be Released	1970	4.00	10.00

SCOTT, HAZEL

Label & Catalog #		Title	Year	VG+	NM
Capitol H-364 (10")	(M)	Late Show	1952	16.00	40.00
Debut 12 (10")	(M)	Relaxed Piano Moods	1955	16.00	40.00

SCOTT, JACK

Label & Catalog #		Title	Year	VG+	NM
Carlton LP-12-107	(M)	Jack Scott	1958	50.00	100.00
Carlton STLP-12-107	(S)	Jack Scott	1958	100.00	200.00
Carlton LP-12-122	(M)	What Am I Living For	1958	50.00	100.00
Carlton STLP-12-122	(S)	What Am I Living For	1958	100.00	200.00
Top Rank RM-319	(M)	I Remember Hank Williams	1960	50.00	100.00
Top Rank RS-619	(S)	I Remember Hank Williams	1960	75.00	150.00
Top Rank RM-326	(M)	What In The World's Come Over You?	1960	50.00	100.00
Top Rank RS-626	(S)	What In The World's Come Over You?	1960	75.00	150.00
Top Rank RM-348	(M)	The Spirit Moves Me	1961	50.00	100.00
Top Rank RS-648	(S)	The Spirit Moves Me	1961	75.00	150.00
Capitol T-2035	(M)	Burning Bridges (Black label)	1964	35.00	70.00
Capitol ST-2035	(S)	Burning Bridges (Black label)	1964	50.00	100.00
Capitol ST-2035	(S)	Burning Bridges (Green label)	1964	20.00	50.00
Jade 33-202	(M)	Great Scott	196?	50.00	100.00
Sesac 4201	(DJ)	Soul Stirring	196?	75.00	150.00

SCOTT, JIMMY

Label & Catalog #		Title	Year	VG+	NM
Savoy MG-12027	(M)	Very Truly Yours	1955	20.00	50.00
Savoy MG-14003	(M)	If You Only Knew	1958	16.00	40.00
Savoy MG-12150	(M)	The Fabulous Songs Of Jimmy Scott	1959	12.00	30.00
Savoy MGS-12150	(S)	The Fabulous Songs Of Jimmy Scott	1959	16.00	40.00
		— Original Savoy albums above have maroon labels.—			
Tangerine T-1501	(M)	Little Jimmy Scott	196?	6.00	15.00
Tangerine TS-1501	(S)	Little Jimmy Scott	196?	8.00	20.00

SCOTT, LINDA

Label & Catalog #		Title	Year	VG+	NM
Canad. Am. CALP-1005	(M)	Starlight, Starbright	1961	16.00	40.00
Canad. Am. SCALP-1005	(S)	Starlight, Starbright	1961	20.00	50.00
Canad. Am. CALP-1007	(M)	Great Scott!! Her Greatest Hits	1962	16.00	40.00
Canad. Am. SCALP-1007	(S)	Great Scott!! Her Greatest Hits	1962	20.00	50.00
Congress 3001	(M)	Linda	1962	12.00	30.00
Congress S-3001	(S)	Linda	1962	16.00	40.00

Label & Catalog #		Title	Year	VG+	NM
Kapp KL-1424	(M)	Hey, Look At Me Now	1965	10.00	25.00
Kapp KS-3424	(S)	Hey, Look At Me Now	1965	12.00	30.00
SCOTT, LIZABETH					
Vik 1130	(M)	Lizabeth	195?	16.00	40.00
SCOTT, PATRICIA					
ABC-Paramount 301	(M)	Once Around The Clock	1959	8.00	20.00
ABC-Paramount S-301	(S)	Once Around The Clock	1959	12.00	30.00
SCOTTSVILLE SQUIRREL BARKERS, THE					
The Barkers feature Chris Hillman. Refer to The Hillmen; The Byrds.					
Crown CLP-5346	(M)	Blue-Grass Favorites	1963	12.00	30.00
Crown CST-346	(S)	Blue-Grass Favorites	1963	16.00	40.00
SCRUGGS, EARL					
Refer to Flatt & Scruggs.					
Folkways FA-2314	(M)	American Banjo Scruggs Style	195?	8.00	20.00
SEALS & CROFTS					
T.A. 5001	(S)	Seals And Crofts	1969	8.00	20.00
T.A. 5004	(S)	Down Home	1970	8.00	20.00
Warner Bros. BS4-2629	(Q)	Summer Breeze	1974	5.00	12.00
Warner Bros. BS4-2699	(Q)	Diamond Girl	1973	5.00	12.00
Warner Bros. WS4-2761	(Q)	Unborn Child	1974	5.00	12.00
Warner Bros. BS4-2848	(Q)	I'll Play For You	1975	5.00	12.00
Nautilus NR-10	(S)	Summer Breeze	197?	8.00	20.00
SEARCHERS, THE					
Mercury MG-20914	(M)	Hear! Hear!	1964	12.00	30.00
Mercury SR-60914	(S)	Hear! Hear!	1964	16.00	40.00
Kapp KL-1363	(M)	Meet The Searchers	1964	10.00	25.00
Kapp KS-3363	(S)	Meet The Searchers	1964	14.00	35.00
Kapp KL-1409	(M)	This Is Us	1964	10.00	25.00
Kapp KS-3409	(S)	This Is Us	1964	14.00	35.00
Kapp KL-1412	(M)	The New Searchers LP	1965	10.00	25.00
Kapp KS-3412	(S)	The New Searchers LP	1965	14.00	35.00
Kapp KL-1449	(M)	The Searchers No. 4	1965	8.00	20.00
Kapp KS-3449	(S)	The Searchers No. 4	1965	12.00	30.00
Kapp KL-1477	(M)	Take Me For What I'm Worth	1966	10.00	25.00
Kapp KS-3477	(S)	Take Me For What I'm Worth	1966	14.00	35.00
SEARCHERS, THE / THE RATTLES					
Mercury MG-20994	(M)	The Searchers Meet The Rattles	1965	16.00	40.00
Mercury SR-60994	(S)	The Searchers Meet The Rattles	1965	20.00	50.00
SEASTONES					
Seastones features Jerry Garcia, Micky Hart and Phil Lesh of The Grateful Dead.					
Round RX-106	(S)	Seastones	1975	10.00	25.00
SEATRAIN					
Seatrain was formed by Ray Blumefeld and Andy Kulberg of The Blues Project.					
A&M SP-4171	(S)	Seatrain	1969	6.00	15.00
Capitol SMAS-650	(S)	Seatrain	1971	5.00	12.00
Capitol SMAS-829	(S)	Marblehead Messenger	1972	5.00	12.00
SEDAKA, NEIL					
RCA Victor LPM-2035	(M)	Rock With Sedaka	1959	20.00	50.00
RCA Victor LSP-2035	(S)	Rock With Sedaka	1959	30.00	60.00
RCA Victor LPM-2317	(M)	Circulate	1960	12.00	30.00
RCA Victor LSP-2317	(S)	Circulate	1960	16.00	40.00
RCA Victor LPM-2421	(M)	Little Devil And His Other Hits	1961	12.00	30.00
RCA Victor LSP-2421	(S)	Little Devil And His Other Hits	1961	16.00	40.00
RCA Victor LPM-2627	(M)	Neil Sedaka Sings His Greatest Hits	1962	10.00	25.00
RCA Victor LSP-2627	(S)	Neil Sedaka Sings His Greatest Hits	1962	14.00	35.00

— Original RCA mono albums above have "black labels with Long Play" on the bottom;
stereo albums have have black labels with "Living Stereo" on the bottom. —

Label & Catalog #		Title	Year	VG+	NM
SEEDS, THE					
Crescendo GNP-2023	(M)	**The Seeds**	1966	8.00	20.00
Crescendo GNPS-2023	(S)	**The Seeds**	1966	6.00	15.00
Crescendo GNP-2033	(M)	**A Web Of Sound**	1966	6.00	15.00
Crescendo GNPS-2033	(S)	**A Web Of Sound**	1966	5.00	12.00
Crescendo GNP-2038	(M)	**Future**	1967	6.00	15.00
Crescendo GNPS-2038	(S)	**Future**	1967	5.00	12.00
Crescendo GNP-2040	(M)	**Full Spoon of Seedy Blues**	1967	6.00	15.00
Crescendo GNPS-2040	(S)	**Full Spoon of Seedy Blues**	1967	5.00	12.00
Crescendo GNP-2043	(M)	**Raw And Alive**	1967	6.00	15.00
Crescendo GNPS-2043	(S)	**Raw And Alive**	1967	5.00	12.00
		— Original GNP albums above have red labels.—			
SEEGER, PEGGY					
Ms. Seeger also recorded with Tom Paley.					
Riverside RLP-12-655	(M)	**Peggy Seeger**	195?	8.00	20.00
Tradition 2059	(M)	**Manchester Angel**	196?	5.00	12.00
Folkways FA-	(M)	**Songs Of Courting And Complaint**	195?	8.00	20.00
SEEGER, PETE					
Pete was formerly a member of The Weavers. Refer to Big Bill Broonzy.					
Folkways FP-3 (10")	(M)	**Darling Corey**	1950	16.00	40.00
Stinson 52 (10")	(M)	**Lincoln Brigade**	1953	14.00	35.00
Stinson 57 (10")	(M)	**Pete Seeger In Concert**	1953	14.00	35.00
Stinson 90	(M)	**Pete**	195?	12.00	30.00
Folkways 43 (10")	(M)	**Pete Seeger Sampler**	1955	10.00	25.00
Folkways 85-1	(M)	**Talking Union**	1955	12.00	30.00
Folkways 85-2	(M)	**Peter Seeger Sings**	1956	10.00	25.00
Folkways 85-3	(M)	**Love Songs**	1956	10.00	25.00
Folkways FPH-	(M)	**Champlain Valley Song Bag**	195?	10.00	25.00
Folkways FH-	(M)	**American Industrial Ballads**	195?	10.00	25.00
Folkways FH-5285	(M)	**Talking Union**	195?	10.00	25.00
Folkways FH-5412	(M)	**Pete Seeger At Carnegie Hall**	195?	10.00	25.00
Folkways FA-2003 (10")	(M)	**Darling Corey**	1957	10.00	25.00
Folkways FA-2005 (10")	(M)	**Seegers**	1957	10.00	25.00
Folkways 7053 (10")	(M)	**American Christmas Songs**	1957	10.00	25.00
Folkways FA-2043	(M)	**Pete Seeger Sampler**	1958	10.00	25.00
Folkways FA-2045	(M)	**Goofing Off Suite**	1958	10.00	25.00
Folkways FA-	(M)	**Ballads**	1958	10.00	25.00
Folkways FA-2175/6	(M)	**Frontier Ballads** *(2 LPs)*	1958	10.00	25.00
Folkways FA-2319	(M)	**American Favorite Ballads, Volume 1**	1958	10.00	25.00
Folkways FA-2320	(M)	**American Favorite Ballads, Volume 2**	1959	10.00	25.00
Folkways FA-2321	(M)	**American Favorite Ballads, Volume 3**	1959	10.00	25.00
Folkways FA-2351	(M)	**Pete Seeger At Carnegie Hall**	1963	10.00	25.00
Folkways FA-2452	(M)	**With Voices Together We Sing**	1963	10.00	25.00
Folkways FA-2453	(M)	**Love Songs For Friends And Foes**	1963	10.00	25.00
Folkways FA-2454	(M)	**Rainbow Design**	1963	10.00	25.00
Folkways FA-2456	(M)	**Broadsides**	1964	8.00	20.00
Folkways FN-2501	(M)	**Gazette**	1964	8.00	20.00
Folkways FN-2512	(M)	**Hootenanny At Carnegie Hall**	1964	8.00	20.00
Folkways FI-8303	(M)	**How To Play The Five String Banjo**	196?	8.00	20.00
Folkways FV-9009	(M)	**Pete Seeger On Campus**	1965	6.00	15.00
Folkways FVS-9009	(S)	**Pete Seeger On Campus**	1965	8.00	20.00
Folkways FV-9013	(M)	**Folk Music Live At The Village Gate**	1965	6.00	15.00
Folkways FVS-9013	(S)	**Folk Music Live At The Village Gate**	1965	8.00	20.00
Folkways FV-9020	(M)	**Little Boxes And Other Broadsides**	1965	6.00	15.00
Folkways FVS-9020	(S)	**Little Boxes And Other Broadsides**	1965	8.00	20.00
Columbia CL-1101	(M)	**We Shall Overcome**	1958	16.00	40.00
Columbia CL-1648	(M)	**Story Songs**	1961	8.00	20.00
Columbia CS-8448	(S)	**Story Songs**	1961	12.00	30.00
Columbia CL-1916	(M)	**In Person At The Bitter End**	1962	8.00	20.00
Columbia CS-8716	(S)	**In Person At The Bitter End**	1962	12.00	30.00
		— Original Columbia albums above have three white "eye" logos on each side of the spindle hole.—			
Columbia CL-1947	(M)	**Children's Concert At Town Hall**	1963	5.00	12.00
Columbia CS-8747	(S)	**Children's Concert At Town Hall**	1963	6.00	15.00
Columbia CL-2257	(M)	**I Can See A New Day**	1964	5.00	12.00
Columbia CS-9057	(S)	**I Can See A New Day**	1964	6.00	15.00
Columbia CL-2334	(M)	**Strangers And Cousins**	1965	5.00	12.00
Columbia CS-9134	(S)	**Strangers And Cousins**	1965	6.00	15.00

Label & Catalog #		Title	Year	VG+	NM
Columbia CL-2432	(M)	God Bless The Grass	1965	5.00	12.00
Columbia CS-9232	(S)	God Bless The Grass	1965	6.00	15.00
Columbia CL-2503	(M)	Dangerous Songs	1966	5.00	12.00
Columbia CS-9303	(S)	Dangerous Songs	1966	6.00	15.00
Columbia CL-2616	(M)	Pete Seeger's Greatest Hits	1967	4.00	10.00
Columbia CS-9416	(S)	Pete Seeger's Greatest Hits	1967	5.00	12.00
Columbia CL-2705	(M)	Waist Deep In The Big Muddy	1967	4.00	10.00
Columbia CS-9505	(S)	Waist Deep In The Big Muddy	1967	5.00	12.00
Columbia CS-9717	(S)	Pete Seeger Now	1968	5.00	12.00
Columbia CS-9873	(S)	Young Vs. Old	1969	5.00	12.00
— Original Columbia albums above have "360 Sound" on the bottom of the label.—					
Philips PHM-2-300	(M)	The Story Of The Nativity (2 LPs)	1963	6.00	15.00
Broadside BR-302	(M)	Broadside Ballads	1963	6.00	15.00
Capitol W-2172	(M)	Folk Songs By Pete Seeger	1964	8.00	20.00
Capitol DW-2172	(E)	Folk Songs By Pete Seeger	1964	5.00	12.00
Capitol T-2718	(M)	Freight Train	1967	8.00	20.00
Capitol DT-2718	(E)	Freight Train	1967	5.00	12.00
Prestige PR-7375	(M)	Folk Songs With Pete Seeger (2 LPs)	1965	6.00	15.00

SEEGER, PETE, & FRANK HAMILTON

Folkways FA-2439	(M)	Nonesuch And Other Folk Tunes	1959	8.00	20.00

SEGAL, GEORGE

Philips PHM-200242	(M)	The Yama Yama Man	1967	6.00	15.00
Philips PHS-600242	(S)	The Yama Yama Man	1967	8.00	20.00

SEGER, BOB

Capitol ST-172	(S)	Ramblin' Gamblin' Man	1969	12.00	30.00
Capitol ST-236	(S)	Noah	1969	30.00	60.00
Capitol SKAO-499	(S)	Mongrel (Fold-open cover)	1970	10.00	25.00
Capitol ST-731	(S)	Brand New Morning	1971	30.00	60.00
Palladium P-1006	(S)	Smokin' O.P.'s	1972	12.00	30.00
Reprise MS-2109	(S)	Smokin' O.P.'s	1972	8.00	20.00
Reprise MS-2126	(S)	Back In '72	1973	8.00	20.00
Reprise MS-2184	(S)	Seven	1974	8.00	20.00
Capitol SPRO-8433	(DJ)	"Live" Bullet	1976	16.00	40.00
Capitol ST-11557	(DJ)	Night Moves (Picture disc)	1978	14.00	35.00
Capitol SEAX-11904	(S)	Stranger In Town (Picture disc)	1979	14.00	35.00
Mobile Fidelity MFSL-034	(S)	Night Moves	1980	12.00	30.00
Mobile Fidelity MFSL-127	(S)	Against The Wind	1983	8.00	20.00

SELAH JUBILEE QUARTET, THE

Remington 1023 (10")	(M)	Spirituals	195?	50.00	100.00

SELLERS, BROTHER JOHN

Vanguard VRS-8005 (10")	(M)	Brother John Sellers	1954	14.00	35.00
Vanguard VRS-9036	(M)	Blues And Folksongs	195?	12.00	30.00

SELLERS, BROTHER JOHN, & MICKEY BAKER

Monitor 505	(M)	Big Beat Up The River	1959	12.00	30.00

SELLERS, PETER

Angel 35884	(M)	The Best Of Peter Sellers	1960	8.00	20.00
Angel 35884	(S)	The Best Of Peter Sellers	1960	12.00	30.00
United Arts. UAL-4148	(M)	After The Fox (Soundtrack)	1966	8.00	20.00
United Arts. UAS-5148	(P)	After The Fox (Soundtrack)	1966	12.00	30.00
		(The Hollies back Sellers on the title tune.)			
Warner Bros. W-1711	(M)	The Bobo (Soundtrack)	1967	12.00	30.00
Warner Bros. WS-1711	(S)	The Bobo (Soundtrack)	1967	16.00	40.00

SELLERS, PETER, & SOPHIA LOREN

Angel 35910	(M)	Peter Sellers And Sophia Loren	1961	10.00	25.00
Angel 35910	(S)	Peter Sellers And Sophia Loren	1961	14.00	35.00

SENSATIONS, THE

The Sensations feature Yvonne Baker.

Argo LP-4022	(M)	Let Me In	1963	60.00	120.00

Label & Catalog #		Title	Year	VG+	NM

SENTINALS, THE

Del-Fi DFLP-1232	(M)	Big Surf	1963	12.00	30.00
Del-Fi DFST-1232	(S)	Big Surf	1963	16.00	40.00
Del-Fi DFLP-1241	(M)	Surfer Girl	1963	12.00	30.00
Del-Fi DFST-1241	(S)	Surfer Girl	1963	16.00	40.00
Sutton SU-338	(M)	Vegas Go-Go	1964	10.00	25.00
Sutton SSU-338	(S)	Vegas Go-Go	1964	14.00	35.00

SERPENT POWER, THE

Vanguard VSD-79252	(S)	The Serpent Power	1967	8.00	20.00

SEVENTH SONS, THE

ESP 1078	(S)	The Seventh Sons	1967	8.00	20.00

SEVILLE, DAVID
David Seville is a pseudonym for Ross Bagdasarian, the creator of The Chipmunks.

Liberty LRP-3073	(M)	The Music Of David Seville	1957	50.00	100.00
Liberty LRP-3092	(M)	The Witch Doctor	1958	50.00	100.00

SEX PISTOLS, THE

Warner Bros. BSK-3147	(S)	Never Mind The Bollocks	1977	6.00	15.00
		(With custom label and inner sleeve.)			

SHACKLEFORDS, THE

Mercury MG-20806	(M)	You Ain't Heard Nothing Yet	1963	6.00	15.00
Mercury SR-60806	(S)	You Ain't Heard Nothing Yet	1963	8.00	20.00
Capitol T-2450	(M)	The Shacklefords	1966	5.00	12.00
Capitol ST-2450	(S)	The Shacklefords	1966	6.00	15.00

SHADES OF BLUE, THE

Impact IM-101	(M)	Happiness Is The Shades Of Blue	1966	10.00	25.00
Impact IM-1001	(S)	Happiness Is The Shades Of Blue	1966	16.00	40.00

SHADOWFAX

Passport 98013	(S)	Watercourse Way	1976	6.00	15.00

SHADOWS, THE
The Shadows also recorded with Cliff Richard.

Atlantic 8089	(M)	Surfing With The Shadows	1963	20.00	50.00
Atlantic SD-8089	(S)	Surfing With The Shadows	1963	35.00	70.00
Atlantic 8097	(M)	The Shadows Know	1964	14.00	35.00
Atlantic SD-8097	(S)	The Shadows Know	1964	20.00	50.00

SHADOWS OF KNIGHT, THE

Dunwich 666	(M)	Gloria	1966	16.00	40.00
Dunwich S-666	(S)	Gloria	1966	20.00	50.00
Dunwich 667	(M)	Back Door Men	1966	16.00	40.00
Dunwich S-667	(S)	Back Door Men	1966	20.00	50.00
Super-K SKS-6002	(S)	The Shadows Of Knight	1969	8.00	20.00

SHADRACK CHAMELEON

No label	(S)	Shadrack Chameleon	1972	100.00	200.00

SHAGGS, THE

Third World 3001	(S)	Philosophy Of The World	196?	*See note below*	
		(Rare. Estimated near mint value $250-750.)			

SHAKERS, THE

Audio Fidelity 2155	(M)	The Break It All	1966	14.00	35.00
Audio Fidelity S-2155	(S)	The Break It All	1966	16.00	40.00

SHAKEY JAKE

Bluesville BV-1008	(M)	Shakey Jake	1960	16.00	40.00
Bluesville BV-1027	(M)	Mouth Harp Blues	1961	16.00	40.00
World Pacific WPS-21886	(S)	Blues Makers	196?	6.00	15.00

SHANGRI-LAS, THE

Red Bird 20-101	(M)	Leader Of The Pack	1965	50.00	100.00
Red Bird 20-104	(M)	I Can Never Go Home Anymore	1965	50.00	100.00

Label & Catalog #		Title	Year	VG+	NM
Red Bird 20-104	(M)	The Shangri-Las '65	1965	40.00	80.00
		(Repackage of "I Can Never Go Home Anymore.")			
Mercury MG-21099	(M)	The Shangri-Las' Golden Hits	1966	16.00	40.00
Mercury SR-61099	(P)	The Shangri-Las' Golden Hits	1966	20.00	50.00
Post 4000	(S)	The Shangri-Las Sing	196?	10.00	25.00

SHANKAR, L.

| Zappa SRZ-1-1602 | (S) | Touch Me There (Produced by Frank Zappa) | 1979 | 10.00 | 25.00 |

SHANNON, DEL

Big Top 12-3003	(M)	Runaway	1961	50.00	100.00
Big Top S-12-3003	(S)	Runaway	1961	300.00	500.00
Big Top 12-1308	(M)	Little Town Flirt	1963	20.00	50.00
Big Top S-12-1308	(S)	Little Town Flirt	1963	50.00	100.00
Amy 8003	(M)	Handy Man	1964	16.00	40.00
Amy S-8003	(S)	Handy Man	1964	20.00	50.00
Amy 8004	(M)	Del Shannon Sings Hank Williams	1965	16.00	40.00
Amy S-8004	(S)	Del Shannon Sings Hank Williams	1965	20.00	50.00
Amy 8006	(M)	1,661 Seconds	1965	20.00	50.00
Amy S-8006	(S)	1,661 Seconds	1965	35.00	70.00
Liberty LRP-3453	(M)	This Is My Bag	1966	8.00	20.00
Liberty LST-7453	(S)	This Is My Bag	1966	12.00	30.00
Liberty LRP-3479	(M)	Total Commitment	1966	8.00	20.00
Liberty LST-7479	(S)	Total Commitment	1966	12.00	30.00
Liberty LRP-3539	(M)	Further Adventures Of Charles Westover	1968	12.00	30.00
Liberty LST-7539	(S)	Further Adventures Of Charles Westover	1968	16.00	40.00
Dot DLP-3834	(M)	The Best Of Del Shannon	1967	8.00	20.00
Dot DLP-25834	(E)	The Best Of Del Shannon	1967	6.00	15.00
Post 9000	(E)	Del Shannon Sings	196?	6.00	15.00
United Arts. LA151	(S)	Live In England	1973	8.00	20.00
Sire SHAH-3708-2	(P)	The Vintage Years (2 LPs)	1975	10.00	25.00

SHANNON, HUGH

| Atlantic 406 (10") | (M) | Hugh Shannon Sings | 195? | 20.00 | 50.00 |

SHAPIRO, HELEN

| Epic LN-24075 | (M) | A Teenager In Love | 1963 | 8.00 | 20.00 |
| Epic BN-26075 | (S) | A Teenager In Love | 1963 | 10.00 | 25.00 |

SHARKEY

| Fireworks 1234 | (S) | Signposts | 1975 | 6.00 | 15.00 |

SHARP, DEE DEE

Cameo C-1018	(M)	It's Mashed Potato Time	1962	20.00	50.00
Cameo C-1022	(M)	Songs Of Faith	1962	16.00	40.00
Cameo C-1032	(M)	All The Hits	1962	14.00	35.00
Cameo SC-1032	(S)	All The Hits	1962	20.00	50.00
Cameo C-1050	(M)	Do The Bird	1963	14.00	35.00
Cameo SC-1050	(S)	Do The Bird	1963	20.00	50.00
Cameo C-1062	(M)	Biggest Hits	1963	14.00	35.00
Cameo C-1074	(M)	Down Memory Lane	1963	14.00	35.00
Cameo C-2002	(M)	18 Golden Hits	1964	14.00	35.00
Cameo SC-2002	(S)	18 Golden Hits	1964	20.00	50.00

SHARP, DEE DEE, & CHUBBY CHECKER

| Cameo C-1029 | (M) | Down To Earth | 1962 | 14.00 | 35.00 |
| Cameo SC-1029 | (S) | Down To Earth | 1962 | 20.00 | 50.00 |

SHARPE, MIKE

Liberty LRP-3507	(M)	Spooky Sound Of Mike Sharpe	1967	5.00	12.00
Liberty LST-7507	(S)	Spooky Sound Of Mike Sharpe	1967	6.00	15.00
Liberty LST-7615	(S)	Mystic Light	1969	5.00	12.00

SHARPE, RAY

| Award LMP-711 | (M) | Welcome Back, Linda Lou | 1964 | 60.00 | 120.00 |

SHATNER, WILLIAM

| Decca DL-5043 | (M) | Transformed Man | 1968 | 14.00 | 35.00 |
| Decca DL-75043 | (S) | Transformed Man | 1968 | 16.00 | 40.00 |

Del Shannon's early '70s comeback included the stunning *Live In England* recorded in a small club in England (the vocals were later re-recorded in the more favorable setting of a studio). *The Vintage Years*, part of a series of double album compilations from Sire, collects the essential hit singles with some great non-hits and some of the recordings Del did in England in the '60s, previously unavailable on the American market.

Label & Catalog #		Title	Year	VG+	NM
Caedmon TC-1508	(S)	Isaac Asimov's "Foundation"	1976	12.00	30.00
Lemli 00001	(S)	William Shatner "Live"	1977	16.00	40.00
Century-21 2476/7	(DJ)	Interview With The Star Of "Big Bad Mama"	197?	35.00	70.00
		(Issued without a cover.)			

SHAW, SANDIE

Reprise R-6166	(M)	Sandi Shaw	1965	10.00	25.00
Reprise RS-6166	(E)	Sandi Shaw	1965	8.00	20.00
Reprise R-6191	(M)	Me	1966	10.00	25.00
Reprise RS-6191	(E)	Me	1966	8.00	20.00

SHELDON, ERNIE, & THE VILLAGERS

Columbia CL-1515	(M)	Big Men, Bold And Bad	1960	6.00	15.00
Columbia CS-8315	(S)	Big Men, Bold And Bad	1960	8.00	20.00

SHELTON, ROSCOE

Excello 8002	(M)	Roscoe Shelton	1961	35.00	70.00
Sound Stage-7 500	(S)	Music In His Soul, Soul In His Music	196?	14.00	35.00

SHEP & THE LIMELITES

Hull 1001	(M)	Our Anniversary	1962	300.00	500.00
Roulette R-25350	(M)	Our Anniversary	1967	20.00	50.00
Roulette RS-25350	(E)	Our Anniversary	1967	16.00	40.00

SHEPARD, JEAN (& THE SECOND FIDDLES)

Capitol T-728	(M)	Songs Of A Love Affair *(Turquoise label)*	1956	20.00	50.00
Capitol T-1126	(M)	Lonesome Love	1959	14.00	35.00
Capitol T-1253	(M)	This Is Jean Shepard	1959	14.00	35.00
Capitol T-1525	(M)	Got You On My Mind	1961	10.00	25.00
Capitol ST-1525	(S)	Got You On My Mind	1961	12.00	30.00
Capitol T-1663	(M)	Heartaches And Tears	1962	10.00	25.00
Capitol ST-1663	(S)	Heartaches And Tears	1962	12.00	30.00

— Original Capitol albums above have black labels with the logo on the left side.—

Capitol T-1922	(M)	The Best Of Jean Shepard	1963	5.00	12.00
Capitol T-1922	(P)	The Best Of Jean Shepard	1963	6.00	15.00
Capitol T-2187	(M)	Lighthearted And Blue	1964	5.00	12.00
Capitol ST-2187	(S)	Lighthearted And Blue	1964	6.00	15.00
Capitol T-2416	(M)	It's A Man Everytime	1965	5.00	12.00
Capitol ST-2416	(S)	It's A Man Everytime	1965	6.00	15.00
Capitol T-2537	(M)	I'll Take The Dog	1966	5.00	12.00
Capitol ST-2537	(S)	I'll Take The Dog	1966	6.00	15.00
Capitol T-2547	(M)	Many Happy Hangovers	1966	5.00	12.00
Capitol ST-2547	(S)	Many Happy Hangovers	1966	6.00	15.00
Capitol T-2690	(M)	Heart, We Did All That We Could	1967	5.00	12.00
Capitol ST-2690	(S)	Heart, We Did All That We Could	1967	6.00	15.00
Capitol T-2765	(M)	Your Forevers Don't Last Very Long	1967	5.00	12.00
Capitol ST-2765	(S)	Your Forevers Don't Last Very Long	1967	6.00	15.00
Capitol ST-2871	(S)	Heart To Heart	1968	5.00	12.00
Capitol ST-2966	(S)	A Real Good Woman	1968	5.00	12.00

— Original Capitol albums above have black labels with the logo on top.—

SHEPHARD, JEAN

Abbott 5003	(M)	Into The Unknown With Jazz	1956	35.00	70.00
Elektra EKL-172	(M)	Jean Shephard And Other Foibles	195?	16.00	40.00

SHEPHERD, CYBIL

Paramount PAS-1018	(S)	Cybil Does It To Cole Porter *(Gatefold cover)*	1972	8.00	20.00

SHEPPARDS, THE

Constellation CS-4	(M)	The Sheppards	1964	20.00	50.00

SHERRYS, THE

Guyden GLP-503	(M)	At The Hop With The Sherry's	1962	150.00	250.00

SHIGETA, JAMES

Choreo A-7	(M)	We Speak The Same Language	196?	10.00	25.00
Choreo AS-7	(S)	We Speak The Same Language	196?	12.00	30.00

Label & Catalog #		Title	Year	VG+	NM

SHILOH
Shiloh features Don Henley, later of The Eagles.

| Amos AAS-7015 | (S) | Shiloh | 196? | 16.00 | 40.00 |

SHIP, THE

| Elektra EKS-75036 | (S) | The Ship (Produced by Gary Usher) | 1972 | 10.00 | 25.00 |

SHIRELLES, THE

Scepter SRM-501	(M)	Tonight's The Night	1961	35.00	70.00
Scepter SPS-501	(S)	Tonight's The Night	1961	50.00	100.00
Scepter SRM-502	(M)	The Shirelles Sing To Trumpets & Strings	1961	14.00	35.00
Scepter SPS-502	(S)	The Shirelles Sing To Trumpets & Strings	1961	20.00	50.00
Scepter SRM-504	(M)	Baby It's You	1962	16.00	40.00
Scepter SPS-504	(S)	Baby It's You	1962	20.00	50.00
Scepter SRM-505	(M)	A Twist Party (With King Curtis)	1962	16.00	40.00
Scepter SPS-505	(S)	A Twist Party (With King Curtis)	1962	20.00	50.00
Scepter SRM-507	(M)	The Shirelles' Greatest Hits	1963	12.00	30.00
Scepter SPS-507	(S)	The Shirelles' Greatest Hits	1963	16.00	40.00
Scepter SRM-511	(M)	Foolish Little Girl	1963	12.00	30.00
Scepter SPS-511	(S)	Foolish Little Girl	1963	16.00	40.00
Scepter SRM-514	(M)	It's A Mad, Mad, Mad, Mad, World	1963	10.00	25.00
Scepter SPS-514	(S)	It's A Mad, Mad, Mad, Mad, World	1963	14.00	35.00
Scepter SRM-516	(M)	The Shirelles Sing The Golden Oldies	1964	10.00	25.00
Scepter SPS-516	(S)	The Shirelles Sing The Golden Oldies	1964	14.00	35.00
Scepter SRM-560	(M)	The Shirelles' Greatest Hits, Volume 2	1967	8.00	20.00
Scepter SPS-560	(S)	The Shirelles' Greatest Hits, Volume 2	1967	10.00	25.00
Scepter SRM-562	(M)	Spontaneous Combustion	1967	8.00	20.00
Scepter SPS-562	(S)	Spontaneous Combustion	1967	10.00	25.00
Scepter SPS-2-599	(S)	Remember When	1972	6.00	15.00
Pricewise P-4001	(M)	Swing The Most	196?	10.00	25.00
Pricewise P-4002	(M)	Here And Now	196?	10.00	25.00

SHIRLEY & LEE
Shirley Goodman and Leonard Lee.

Aladdin 807	(M)	Let The Good Times Roll	1956	300.00	500.00
Score SLP-4023	(M)	Let The Good Times Roll	1957	150.00	250.00
Warwick 2028	(M)	Let The Good Times Roll	1961	50.00	100.00
Warwick WST-2028	(S)	Let The Good Times Roll	1961	75.00	150.00
		(New recordings with a rerecorded title tune.)			
Imperial LP-9179	(M)	Let The Good Times Roll	1962	50.00	100.00
United Arts. LA-026-G	(P)	Legendary Masters (2 LPs)	1974	12.00	30.00

SHIVA'S HEADBAND

Armadillo	(S)	Coming To A Head	1969	50.00	100.00
Capitol ST-538	(S)	Take Me To The Mountains	1970	20.00	50.00
Ape 1001	(S)	Psychedlic Yesterday	1981	10.00	25.00

SHOCKING BLUE, THE

| Colossus CS-1000 | (P) | The Shocking Blue | 1970 | 8.00 | 20.00 |

SHONDELLS, THE

| La Louisianne 109 | (M) | The Shondells At The Saturday Hop | 1964 | 50.00 | 100.00 |

SHORE, DINAH
Refer to The Reprise Repertory Theatre.

Columbia CL-6004 (10")	(M)	Dinah Shore Sings	1949	16.00	40.00
Columbia CL-6069 (10")	(M)	Reminiscing	1949	16.00	40.00
Columbia JL-8503	(M)	Bongo / Land Of The Lost	1950	16.00	40.00
RCA Victor LOC-1000 (10")	(M)	Call Me Madam	1950	50.00	100.00
RCA Victor LPM-39 (10")	(M)	Two Tickets To Broadway	1951	20.00	50.00
RCA Victor LPM-3006 (10")	(M)	Aaron Slick From Punkin Crick (Sdtk)	1952	50.00	100.00
RCA Victor LPM-3103 (10")	(M)	Dinah Shore Sings The Blues	1953	14.00	35.00
RCA Victor LPM-3214 (10")	(M)	The Dinah Shore TV Show	1954	14.00	35.00
RCA Victor LPM-1154	(M)	Holding Hands At Midnight	1955	14.00	35.00
RCA Victor LPM-1214	(M)	Bouquet Of Blues	1956	10.00	25.00
RCA Victor LPM-1719	(M)	Moments Like These	1958	10.00	25.00

— Original RCA mono albums above have "black labels with Long Play" on the bottom; stereo albums have have black labels with "Living Stereo" on the bottom.—

Label & Catalog #		Title	Year	VG+	NM
Capitol T-1247	(M)	Dinah, Yes Indeed	1959	6.00	15.00
Capitol ST-1247	(S)	Dinah, Yes Indeed	1959	8.00	20.00
Capitol T-1296	(M)	Somebody Loves Me	1959	6.00	15.00
Capitol ST-1296	(S)	Somebody Loves Me	1959	8.00	20.00
Capitol T-1354	(M)	Dinah Sings Some Blues With Red	1960	6.00	15.00
Capitol ST-1354	(S)	Dinah Sings Some Blues With Red	1960	8.00	20.00
Capitol T-1422	(M)	Dinah Sings/Previn Plays	1960	6.00	15.00
Capitol ST-1422	(S)	Dinah Sings/Previn Plays	1960	8.00	20.00
Capitol T-1655	(M)	Dinah Down Home	1962	5.00	12.00
Capitol ST-1655	(S)	Dinah Down Home	1962	6.00	15.00
Capitol T-1704	(M)	Fabulous Hits Newly Recorded	1962	5.00	12.00
Capitol ST-1704	(S)	Fabulous Hits Newly Recorded	1962	6.00	15.00

— Original Capitol albums above have black labels with the logo on the left side.—

SHORT, BOBBY

Atlantic 606 (10")	(M)	Bobby Short Loves Cole Porter	1952	35.00	70.00
Atlantic 1214	(M)	Songs By Bobby Short	1955	20.00	50.00
Atlantic 1230	(M)	Bobby Short, Volume 2	1956	20.00	50.00
Atlantic 1262	(M)	Speaking Of Love	1957	16.00	40.00
Atlantic 1285	(M)	Sing Me A Swing Song	1958	16.00	40.00
Atlantic 1302	(M)	The Mad Twenties	1959	16.00	40.00
Atlantic 1321	(M)	On The East Side	1959	16.00	40.00

SHORT CROSS

Grizly S16-013	(S)	Arising	197?	50.00	100.00

SICKNICKS, THE

Amy 2	(M)	Sick # 2	196?	12.00	30.00

SIDEKICKS, THE

RCA Victor LPM-3712	(M)	Fifi The Flea	1966	6.00	15.00
RCA Victor LSP-3712	(S)	Fifi The Flea	1966	8.00	20.00

SIEGEL-SCHWALL BAND, THE

Vanguard VRS-9235	(M)	The Siegel-Schwall Band	1966	5.00	12.00
Vanguard VSD-79235	(S)	The Siegel-Schwall Band	1966	6.00	15.00
Vanguard VSD-79249	(M)	The Siegel-Schwall Band Say	1967	5.00	12.00
Vanguard VSD-79249	(S)	The Siegel-Schwall Band Say	1967	6.00	15.00
Vanguard VSD-79289	(S)	Shake!	1968	6.00	15.00
Vanguard VSD-6562	(S)	Siegal-Schwall '70	1970	5.00	12.00

SIGLER, BUNNY

Parkway P-50000	(M)	Let The Good Times Roll	1967	10.00	25.00
Parkway PS-50000	(S)	Let The Good Times Roll	1967	12.00	30.00

SIGNATURES, THE

Whippet W-702	(M)	Their Voices And Instruments	1957	30.00	60.00
Warner Bros. W-1250	(M)	The Signatures Sing In	1959	8.00	20.00
Warner Bros. WS-1250	(S)	The Signatures Sing In	1959	12.00	30.00
Warner Bros. W-1353	(M)	Prepare To Flip!	1959	8.00	20.00
Warner Bros. WS-1353	(S)	Prepare To Flip!	1959	12.00	30.00

SILHOUETTES, THE

Goodway GLP-100	(M)	Get A Job	1958	180.00	300.00

SILKIE, THE

Fontana MGF-27548	(M)	You've Got To Hide Your Love Away	1965	16.00	40.00
Fontana SRF-67548	(E)	You've Got To Hide Your Love Away	1965	12.00	30.00
		(Full color cover.)			
Fontana MGF-27548	(M)	You've Got To Hide Your Love Away	1965	12.00	30.00
Fontana SRF-67548	(E)	You've Got To Hide Your Love Away	1965	8.00	20.00
		(Black & white cover with a violet tone.)			

SILLY SURFERS, THE / THE WEIRD-OHS

Issued by the Hawk Model Co., The Surfers and The Weird-Ohs are Gary Usher & Co. projects. The tracks on this album were later used by Gary to create individual albums by The Surfers and The Weird-Ohs.

Hairy 101	(DJ)	Music To Make Models By	1964	50.00	100.00

Label & Catalog #		Title	Year	VG+	NM

SILLY SURFERS, THE
The Surfers are a creation of Gary Usher & Co.

Label & Catalog #		Title	Year	VG+	NM
Mercury MG-20977	(M)	Sounds Of The Silly Surfers	1965	10.00	25.00
Mercury SR-60977	(S)	Sounds Of The Silly Surfers	1965	14.00	35.00

SILVER

Grammie Fonics 8322	(S)	Children Of The Lord	1975	50.00	100.00

SILVERMAN, JERRY

Audio Video 101	(M)	Folk Blues	195?	10.00	25.00

SILVERSTEIN, SHEL

Elektra EKL-176	(M)	Hairy Jazz	1959	30.00	60.00
Elektra EKS-7176	(S)	Hairy Jazz	1959	40.00	80.00
Atlantic 8072	(M)	Inside Folk Songs	1963	12.00	30.00
Atlantic SD-8072	(S)	Inside Folk Songs	1963	16.00	40.00
Cadet LP-4052	(M)	I'm So Good I Don't Have To Brag!	1965	6.00	15.00
Cadet LPS-4052	(S)	I'm So Good I Don't Have To Brag!	1965	8.00	20.00
Cadet LP-4054	(M)	Drain My Brain	1966	6.00	15.00
Cadet LPS-4054	(S)	Drain My Brain	1966	8.00	20.00
RCA Victor LSP-4192	(S)	A Boy Named Sue	1969	8.00	20.00

SIMMONS, "JUMPIN'" GENE

Hi HL-2018	(M)	Jumpin' Gene Simmons	1964	6.00	15.00
Hi SHL-32018	(S)	Jumpin' Gene Simmons	1964	8.00	20.00

SIMMONS, GENE: *Refer to* KISS

SIMMONS, JEFF
Mr. Simmons was formerly a member of The Easy Chair.

Straight STS-1057	(S)	Lucille Has Messed Up My Mind	1969	20.00	50.00
Reprise STS-1057	(S)	Lucille Has Messed Up My Mind	1970	10.00	25.00

Ms. Simon's popularity with the pre-yuppie crowd ensured the release of her catalogue in the quadraphonic format. This, her most popular LP, was issued in quad in a gatefold cover, making it far more attractive than the standard stereo release.

Label & Catalog #		Title	Year	VG+	NM
SIMON, CARLY					
Ms. Simon was formerly of The Simon Sisters.					
Decca DL-79181	(S)	**Taking Off** *(Soundtrack)*	1971	6.00	15.00
Elektra EQ-4082	(Q)	**Carly Simon**	1973	6.00	15.00
Elektra EQ-5049	(Q)	**No Secrets**	1973	6.00	15.00
Elektra EQ-1002	(Q)	**Hotcakes**	1974	6.00	15.00
Elektra EQ-1033	(Q)	**Playing Possum**	1975	6.00	15.00
Elektra EQ-1064	(Q)	**Another Passenger**	1975	6.00	15.00
Elektra EQ-1048	(Q)	**The Best Of Carly Simon**	1977	6.00	15.00
Direct Disk SD-16608	(S)	**Boys In The Trees**	198?	8.00	20.00
SIMON, PAUL					
Columbia CQ-30750	(Q)	**Paul Simon**	1973	6.00	15.00
Columbia PCQ-33540	(Q)	**Still Crazy After All These Years**	1975	6.00	15.00
Columbia HC-43540	(S)	**Still Crazy After All These Years** *(Half-speed)*	1981	10.00	25.00
Columbia HC-45032	(S)	**Greatest Hits, Etc.** *(Half-speed master)*	1981	12.00	30.00
Warner Bros. 23942	(DJ)	**Hearts And Bones** *(Quiex II vinyl)*	198?	6.00	15.00
SIMON & GARFUNKEL					
Paul Simon and Art Garfunkel.					
Columbia CL-2249	(M)	**Wednesday Morning 3 A.M.**	1964	8.00	20.00
Columbia CS-9049	(S)	**Wednesday Morning 3 A.M.**	1964	6.00	15.00
Columbia CL-2469	(M)	**Sounds Of Silence**	1966	8.00	20.00
Columbia CS-9269	(S)	**Sounds Of Silence**	1966	6.00	15.00
Columbia CL-2563	(M)	**Parsley, Sage, Rosemary & Thyme**	1966	8.00	20.00
Columbia CS-9363	(S)	**Parsley, Sage, Rosemary & Thyme**	1966	6.00	15.00
Columbia KCL-2729	(M)	**Bookends**	1968	12.00	30.00
Columbia KCS-9529	(S)	**Bookends**	1968	6.00	15.00
Columbia OS-3180	(S)	**The Graduate** *(Soundtrack)*	1968	4.00	10.00
— Original Columbia albums above have "360 Sound" on the bottom of the label.—					
Columbia CQ-30995	(Q)	**Bridge Over Troubled Water**	1971	6.00	15.00
Columbia HC-41350	(S)	**Greatest Hits** *(Half-speed master)*	1982	10.00	25.00
Columbia HC-49914	(S)	**Bridge Over Troubled Water** *(Half-speed)*	1982	8.00	20.00
Pickwick SPC-3059	(S)	**The Hit Sounds Of Simon & Garfunkel**	1966	12.00	30.00
Sears 435	(S)	**Simon & Garfunkel**	1969	10.00	25.00
Mobile Fidelity MFSL-173	(S)	**Bridge Over Troubled Water**	198?	6.00	15.00
SIMON & ILANA					
Coral CRL-57409	(M)	**The Wonderful World Of Folk Music**	1962	6.00	15.00
Coral CRL-757409	(S)	**The Wonderful World Of Folk Music**	1962	8.00	20.00
SIMON SISTERS, THE					
Carly and Lucy Simon.					
Kapp KL-1359	(M)	**Winkin,' Blinkin' And Nod**	1964	12.00	30.00
Kapp KS-3359	(S)	**Winkin,' Blinkin' And Nod**	1964	16.00	40.00
Kapp KL-1397	(M)	**Cuddlebug**	1964	12.00	30.00
Kapp KS-3397	(S)	**Cuddlebug**	1964	16.00	40.00
Columbia CC-24506	(S)	**The Lobster Quadrille** *(With booklet)*	1969	6.00	15.00
Columbia CR-21539	(S)	**The Simon Sisters Sing For Children**	1973	4.00	10.00
(Columbia 21539 is a remixed repackage of 24506.)					
SIMONE, NINA					
Bethlehem BCP-6028	(M)	**Little Girl Blue**	1959	16.00	40.00
Bethlehem BCP-6041	(M)	**Nina Simone And Her Friends**	1959	16.00	40.00
Bethlehem BCP-6028	(M)	**The Original Nina Simone**	1961	10.00	25.00
Bethlehem BCPS-6028	(E)	**The Original Nina Simone**	1961	6.00	15.00
(Reissue of Nina's first album with the same catalogue number.)					
Colpix CP-407	(M)	**The Amazing Nina Simone**	1959	8.00	20.00
Colpix SCP-407	(S)	**The Amazing Nina Simone**	1959	12.00	30.00
Colpix CP-409	(M)	**Nina At Town Hall**	1959	8.00	20.00
Colpix SCP-409	(S)	**Nina At Town Hall**	1959	12.00	30.00
Colpix CP-412	(M)	**Nina Simone At Newport**	1960	6.00	15.00
Colpix SCP-412	(S)	**Nina Simone At Newport**	1960	10.00	25.00
Colpix CP-419	(M)	**Forbidden Fruit**	1961	6.00	15.00
Colpix SCP-419	(S)	**Forbidden Fruit**	1961	10.00	25.00
Colpix CP-421	(M)	**Nina Simone At The Village Gate**	1961	6.00	15.00
Colpix SCP-421	(S)	**Nina Simone At The Village Gate**	1961	10.00	25.00
Colpix CP-425	(M)	**Nina Simone Sings Ellington**	1962	6.00	15.00
Colpix SCP-425	(S)	**Nina Simone Sings Ellington**	1962	10.00	25.00

Label & Catalog #		Title	Year	VG+	NM
Colpix CP-443	(M)	Nina's Choice	1963	5.00	12.00
Colpix SCP-443	(S)	Nina's Choice	1963	8.00	20.00
Colpix CP-455	(M)	Nina Simone At Carnegie Hall	1963	5.00	12.00
Colpix SCP-455	(S)	Nina Simone At Carnegie Hall	1963	8.00	20.00
Colpix CP-465	(M)	Folksy Nina	1964	5.00	12.00
Colpix SCP-465	(S)	Folksy Nina	1964	8.00	20.00
Colpix CP-496	(M)	Nina With Strings	1966	5.00	12.00
Colpix SCP-496	(S)	Nina With Strings	1966	8.00	20.00
Philips PHM-200135	(M)	Nina Simone In Concert	1964	5.00	12.00
Philips PHS-600135	(S)	Nina Simone In Concert	1964	6.00	15.00
Philips PHM-200148	(M)	Blues: Ballads	1964	5.00	12.00
Philips PHS-600148	(S)	Blues: Ballads	1964	6.00	15.00
Philips PHM-200172	(M)	I Put A Spell On You	1965	5.00	12.00
Philips PHS-600172	(S)	I Put A Spell On You	1965	6.00	15.00
Philips PHM-200187	(M)	Pastel Blues	1965	5.00	12.00
Philips PHS-600187	(S)	Pastel Blues	1965	6.00	15.00
Philips PHM-200202	(M)	Let It All Out	1966	5.00	12.00
Philips PHS-600202	(S)	Let It All Out	1966	6.00	15.00
Philips PHM-200207	(M)	Wild Is The Wind	1966	5.00	12.00
Philips PHS-600207	(S)	Wild Is The Wind	1966	6.00	15.00
Philips PHM-200219	(M)	The High Priestess Of Soul	1967	5.00	12.00
Philips PHS-600219	(S)	The High Priestess Of Soul	1967	6.00	15.00
RCA Victor LPM-3789	(M)	Nina Simone Sings The Blues	1966	5.00	12.00
RCA Victor LSP-3789	(S)	Nina Simone Sings The Blues	1966	6.00	15.00
RCA Victor LPM-3837	(M)	Silk And Soul	1967	4.00	10.00
RCA Victor LSP-3837	(S)	Silk And Soul	1967	5.00	12.00
RCA Victor LSP-4065	(S)	Nuff Said	1968	4.00	10.00
RCA Victor LSP-4248	(S)	Black Gold	1970	4.00	10.00
RCA Victor LSP-4347	(S)	The Best Of Nina Simone	1970	4.00	10.00
RCA Victor LSP-4536	(S)	Here Comes The Sun	1972	4.00	10.00

SIMPSON, CAROLE

Capitol T-878	(M)	All About Carole	1957	12.00	30.00
Tops 1732	(M)	Singin' And Swingin'	1960	10.00	25.00

SIMPSON, FRANK

Audio Lab AL-1552	(M)	Four Star Hits	1960	20.00	50.00

SIMPSON, MIKE, & THE RAUNCH HANDS

Mercury MG-20697	(M)	Dixie Twist	1962	6.00	15.00
Mercury SR-60697	(S)	Dixie Twist	1962	8.00	20.00

SIMPSON, RED

Portland 1003	(M)	Hello, I'm A Truck	1965	20.00	50.00
Capitol T-2468	(M)	Roll Truck, Roll	1966	6.00	15.00
Capitol ST-2468	(S)	Roll Truck, Roll	1966	8.00	20.00
Capitol T-2569	(M)	The Man Behind The Badge	1966	5.00	12.00
Capitol ST-2569	(S)	The Man Behind The Badge	1966	6.00	15.00
Capitol T-2691	(M)	Truck Drivin' Fool	1967	5.00	12.00
Capitol ST-2691	(S)	Truck Drivin' Fool	1967	6.00	15.00
Capitol T-2829	(M)	A Bakersfield Dozen	1967	5.00	12.00
Capitol ST-2829	(S)	A Bakersfield Dozen	1967	6.00	15.00
Capitol ST-881	(S)	I'm A Truck	1971	5.00	12.00

SIMS, FRANKIE LEE

Specialty SPS-2124	(S)	Lucy Mae Blues	1969	14.00	35.00

SIN SAY SHUNS, THE

Venett V-940	(M)	I'll Be There	196?	8.00	20.00
Venett VS-940	(S)	I'll Be There	196?	10.00	25.00

SINATRA, FRANK

Refer to Peggy Lee; Dean Martin; The Reprise Repertory Theater.

Columbia C-124 (10")	(M)	Songs By Sinatra	1947	50.00	100.00
Columbia CL-6001 (10")	(M)	The Voice Of Frank Sinatra	1949	16.00	40.00
Columbia CL-6019 (10")	(M)	Christmas Songs By Sinatra	1949	16.00	40.00
Columbia CL-6059 (10")	(M)	Frankly Sentimental Sinatra	1949	16.00	40.00
Columbia CL-6087 (10")	(M)	Songs By Sinatra, Volume 1	1950	16.00	40.00
Columbia CL-6??? (10")	(M)	Songs By Sinatra, Volume 2	1950	16.00	40.00

Label & Catalog #		Title	Year	VG+	NM
Columbia CL-6096 (10")	(M)	Dedicated To You	1950	16.00	40.00
Columbia CL-6143 (10")	(M)	Sing And Dance With Frank Sinatra	1950	16.00	40.00
Columbia CL-6212 (10")	(M)	This Is My Best	1953	16.00	40.00
Columbia CL-6254 (10")	(M)	Requested By You	1953	16.00	40.00
Columbia CL-6290 (10")	(M)	I've Got A Crush On You	1954	16.00	40.00
Columbia CL-6339 (10")	(M)	Young At Heart (Sdtk with Doris Day)	1954	30.00	60.00
Columbia CL-2521 (10")	(M)	Get Happy	1955	12.00	30.00
Columbia CL-2530 (10")	(M)	Boys And Gils Together	1955	12.00	30.00
Columbia CL-2539 (10")	(M)	I've Got A Crush On You	1955	12.00	30.00
Columbia CL-2542 (10")	(M)	Christmas With Sinatra	1955	12.00	30.00
RCA Victor LPT-3063 (10")	(M)	Fabulous Frankie	1955	16.00	40.00
Columbia ML-4271	(M)	Conducts The Music Of Alec Wilder	195?	14.00	35.00
Columbia CL-112	(M)	The Voice Of Frank Sinatra	1950	14.00	35.00
Columbia CL-167	(M)	Christmas Songs By Sinatra	1950	14.00	35.00
Columbia CL-606	(M)	Frankie	1955	10.00	25.00
— Original Columbia albums above have labels with "Long LP Playing" on the bottom.—					
Columbia CL-743	(M)	The Voice	1955	8.00	20.00
Columbia CL-884	(M)	Conducts The Music Of Alec Wilder	1956	10.00	25.00
Columbia CL-902	(M)	That Old Feeling	1956	8.00	20.00

The 1960s saw three different labels— Columbia, Capitol and Reprise— promoting Sinatra's extensive catalog. While Capitol kept many of his LPs in print (often as truncated budget albums), the Columbia material was often only partially available on anthologies.

Columbia CL-953	(M)	Adventures Of The Heart	1957	8.00	20.00
Columbia CL-1032	(M)	Christmas Dreaming	1957	8.00	20.00
Columbia CL-1130	(M)	The Frank Sinatra Story In Music, Volume 1	1957	8.00	20.00
Columbia CL-1131	(M)	The Frank Sinatra Story In Music, Volume 2	1957	8.00	20.00
Columbia C2L-6	(M)	The Frank Sinatra Story In Music (2 LPs)	1958	10.00	25.00
Columbia CL-1136	(M)	Put Your Dreams Away	1958	8.00	20.00
Columbia CL-1241	(M)	Love Is A Kick	1958	8.00	20.00
Columbia CL-1297	(M)	The Broadway Kick	1959	8.00	20.00
Columbia CL-1359	(M)	Come Back To Sorrento	1959	8.00	20.00
Columbia CL-1448	(M)	Reflections	1960	8.00	20.00
— Original Columbia albums above have three white "eye" logos on each side of the spindle hole.—					
Columbia CL-2474	(M)	Greatest Hits: The Early Years	1965	6.00	15.00
Columbia CS-9274	(E)	Greatest Hits: The Early Years	1965	5.00	12.00

Label & Catalog #		Title	Year	VG+	NM
Columbia C3L-42	(M)	The Essential Frank Sinatra (3 LPs)	1966	12.00	30.00
Columbia C3S-42	(E)	The Essential Frank Sinatra (3 LPs)	1966	8.00	20.00
Columbia CL-2739	(M)	The Essential Frank Sinatra, Volume 1	1967	6.00	15.00
Columbia CS-9539	(M)	The Essential Frank Sinatra, Volume 1	1967	4.00	10.00
Columbia CL-2740	(M)	The Essential Frank Sinatra, Volume 2	1967	6.00	15.00
Columbia CS-9540	(E)	The Essential Frank Sinatra, Volume 2	1967	4.00	10.00
Columbia CL-2741	(M)	The Essential Frank Sinatra, Volume 3	1967	6.00	15.00
Columbia CS-9541	(E)	The Essential Frank Sinatra, Volume 3	1967	4.00	10.00
— Original Columbia albums above have "360 Sound" on the bottom of the label.—					
Capitol H-488 (10")	(M)	Songs For Young Lovers	1954	14.00	35.00
Capitol H-528 (10")	(M)	Swing Easy	1954	14.00	35.00
Capitol H-581 (10")	(M)	In The Wee Small Hours	1955	14.00	35.00
Capitol T-528	(M)	Swing Easy	1954	10.00	25.00
Capitol W-581	(M)	In The Wee Small Hours	1955	10.00	25.00
Capitol W-587	(M)	Swing Easy / Songs For Young Lovers	1955	10.00	25.00
Capitol W-653	(M)	Songs For Swingin' Lovers	1956	10.00	25.00
Capitol W-735	(M)	Conducts Tone Poems Of Color	1956	12.00	30.00
Capitol W-750	(M)	High Society (Soundtrack)	1956	12.00	30.00
Capitol T-768	(M)	This Is Sinatra!	1956	10.00	25.00
Capitol W-789	(M)	Close To You	1957	10.00	25.00
Capitol W-803	(M)	A Swingin' Affair	1957	10.00	25.00
Capitol SW-803	(S)	A Swingin' Affair	1957	14.00	35.00
— Original Capitol albums above have turquoise or grey labels with "Long Playing" on the bottom.—					
Capitol W-855	(M)	Where Are You?	1957	8.00	20.00
Capitol SW-855	(S)	Where Are You?	1957	14.00	35.00
Capitol W-894	(M)	A Jolly Christmas From Frank Sinatra	1957	10.00	25.00
Capitol W-912	(M)	Pal Joey (Soundtrack)	1957	10.00	25.00
Capitol W-920	(M)	Come Fly With Me	1958	8.00	20.00
Capitol SW-920	(S)	Come Fly With Me	1958	14.00	35.00
Capitol W-982	(M)	This Is Sinatra, Volume 2	1958	8.00	20.00
— Original Capitol albums above have turquoise or grey labels with "Long Playing High Fidelity" on the bottom.—					
Capitol W-1053	(M)	Frank Sinatra Sings For Only The Lonely	1958	6.00	15.00
Capitol SW-1053	(S)	Frank Sinatra Sings For Only The Lonely	1958	10.00	25.00
Capitol W-1069	(M)	Come Dance With Me!	1959	6.00	15.00
Capitol SW-1069	(S)	Come Dance With Me!	1959	10.00	25.00
Capitol W-1164	(M)	Look To Your Heart	1959	6.00	15.00
Capitol W-1221	(M)	No One Cares	1959	6.00	15.00
Capitol SW-1221	(S)	No One Cares	1959	10.00	25.00
Capitol W-1301	(M)	Can-Can (Soundtrack)	1960	8.00	20.00
Capitol SW-1301	(S)	Can-Can (Soundtrack)	1960	12.00	30.00
Capitol W-1417	(M)	Nice 'N' Easy	1960	5.00	12.00
Capitol SW-1417	(S)	Nice 'N' Easy	1960	6.00	15.00
Capitol W-1429	(M)	Swing Easy	1960	6.00	15.00
Capitol W-1432	(M)	Songs For Young Lovers	1960	6.00	15.00
Capitol W-1491	(M)	Sinatra's Swingin' Session!!!	1961	5.00	12.00
Capitol SW-1491	(S)	Sinatra's Swingin' Session!!!	1961	6.00	15.00
Capitol W-1538	(M)	All The Way	1961	5.00	12.00
Capitol SW-1538	(S)	All The Way	1961	6.00	15.00
Capitol W-1594	(M)	Come Swing With Me!	1961	5.00	12.00
Capitol SW-1594	(S)	Come Swing With Me!	1961	6.00	15.00
Capitol W-1676	(M)	Point Of No Return	1962	5.00	12.00
Capitol SW-1676	(S)	Point Of No Return	1962	6.00	15.00
— Original Capitol albums above have black labels with the logo on the left side.—					
Capitol W-1729	(M)	Sinatra Sings... Of Love And Things	1962	5.00	12.00
Capitol SW-1729	(S)	Sinatra Sings.., Of Love And Things	1962	6.00	15.00
Capitol TCO-1762	(M)	The Great Years (3 LPs)	1962	12.00	30.00
Capitol STCO-1762	(P)	The Great Years (3 LPs)	1962	16.00	40.00
Capitol W-1825	(M)	Frank Sinatra Sings Rodgers And Hart	1963	6.00	15.00
Capitol DW-1825	(E)	Frank Sinatra Sings Rodgers And Hart	1963	5.00	12.00
Capitol T-1919	(M)	Tell Her You Love Her	1963	6.00	15.00
Capitol DT-1919	(E)	Tell Her You Love Her	1963	5.00	12.00
Capitol W-1984	(M)	The Select Johnny Mercer	1963	6.00	15.00
Capitol DW-1984	(E)	The Select Johnny Mercer	1963	5.00	12.00
Capitol T-2036	(M)	The Great Hits Of Frank Sinatra	1964	6.00	15.00
Capitol DT-2036	(E)	The Great Hits Of Frank Sinatra	1964	5.00	12.00
Capitol T-2123	(M)	The Select Harold Arlen	1964	6.00	15.00
Capitol W-2301	(M)	The Select Cole Porter	1965	6.00	15.00
Capitol DW-2301	(E)	The Select Cole Porter	1965	5.00	12.00

Label & Catalog #		Title	Year	VG+	NM
Capitol PRO-2974/5	(DJ)	**Minute Masters**	1965	16.00	40.00
Capitol T-2602	(M)	**Forever Frank**	1966	6.00	15.00
Capitol DT-2602	(E)	**Forever Frank**	1966	5.00	12.00
Capitol T-2700	(M)	**The Movie Songs**	1967	6.00	15.00
Capitol DT-2700	(E)	**The Movie Songs**	1967	5.00	12.00
Capitol STFL-2814	(M)	**Deluxe Set** (3 LP box)	1968	16.00	40.00
Capitol DKAO-2950	(E)	**The Best Of Frank Sinatra**	1969	4.00	10.00
— Original Capitol albums above have black labels with the logo on top. —					
Capitol DWBB-254	(E)	**Close-Up** (2 LPs)	1969	5.00	12.00
Capitol DKAO-374	(E)	**Frank Sinatra's Greatest**	1969	4.00	10.00
Capitol STBB-50074	(E)	**My One And Only Love** (2 LPs)	197?	5.00	12.00
Capitol SMAS-94408	(E)	**The Cole Porter Song Book** (Record Club)	197?	6.00	15.00
Reprise F-1001	(M)	**Ring-A-Ding-Ding!**	1961	5.00	12.00
Reprise FS-1001	(S)	**Ring-A-Ding-Ding!**	1961	6.00	15.00
Reprise F-1002	(M)	**Sinatra Swings**	1961	5.00	12.00
Reprise FS-1002	(S)	**Sinatra Swings**	1961	6.00	15.00
Reprise F-1003	(M)	**I Remember Tommy**	1961	5.00	12.00
Reprise FS-1003	(S)	**I Remember Tommy**	1961	6.00	15.00
Reprise F-1004	(M)	**Sinatra And Strings**	1962	5.00	12.00
Reprise FS-1004	(S)	**Sinatra And Strings**	1962	6.00	15.00
Reprise F-1005	(M)	**Sinatra And Swingin' Brass**	1962	5.00	12.00
Reprise FS-1005	(S)	**Sinatra And Swingin' Brass**	1962	6.00	15.00
Reprise F-1007	(M)	**All Alone**	1962	5.00	12.00
Reprise FS-1007	(S)	**All Alone**	1962	6.00	15.00
Reprise R-6045	(M)	**Conducts Music From Pictures**	1962	6.00	15.00
Reprise R9-6045	(S)	**Conducts Music From Pictures**	1962	8.00	20.00
Colpix CP-516	(M)	**The Victors** (Soundtrack)	1963	16.00	40.00
Colpix SCP-516	(S)	**The Victors** (Soundtrack)	1963	30.00	60.00
Reprise F-1008	(M)	**Sinatra-Basie**	1963	4.00	10.00
Reprise FS-1008	(S)	**Sinatra-Basie**	1963	5.00	12.00
Reprise F-1009	(M)	**The Concert Sinatra**	1963	4.00	10.00
Reprise FS-1009	(S)	**The Concert Sinatra**	1963	5.00	12.00
Reprise F-1010	(M)	**Sinatra's Sinatra**	1963	4.00	10.00
Reprise FS-1010	(S)	**Sinatra's Sinatra**	1963	5.00	12.00
Reprise R-6071	(M)	**Come Blow Your Horn** (Soundtrack)	1963	35.00	70.00
Reprise R9-6071	(S)	**Come Blow Your Horn** (Soundtrack)	1963	45.00	90.00
Reprise R-6116	(M)	**Greatest Hits From The Greatest Films**	1964	5.00	12.00
Reprise RS-6116	(S)	**Greatest Hits From The Greatest Films**	1964	6.00	15.00
Reprise F-1011	(M)	**Days Of Wine And Roses**	1964	4.00	10.00
Reprise FS-1011	(S)	**Days Of Wine And Roses**	1964	5.00	12.00
Reprise F-1012	(M)	**It Might As Well Be Swing**	1964	4.00	10.00
Reprise FS-1012	(S)	**It Might As Well Be Swing**	1964	5.00	12.00
Reprise F-1013	(M)	**Softly, As I Leave You**	1964	4.00	10.00
Reprise FS-1013	(S)	**Softly, As I Leave You**	1964	5.00	12.00
Reprise R-6167	(M)	**Sinatra '65**	1965	4.00	10.00
Reprise RS-6167	(S)	**Sinatra '65**	1965	5.00	12.00
Reprise F-1014	(M)	**September Of My Years**	1965	4.00	10.00
Reprise FS-1014	(S)	**September Of My Years**	1965	5.00	12.00
Reprise F-1015	(M)	**My Kind Of Broadway**	1965	4.00	10.00
Reprise FS-1015	(S)	**My Kind Of Broadway**	1965	5.00	12.00
Reprise 2F-1016	(M)	**A Man And His Music** (2 LPs)	1965	6.00	15.00
Reprise 2FS-1016	(S)	**A Man And His Music** (2 LPs)	1965	8.00	20.00
Reprise F-1017	(M)	**Strangers In The Night**	1966	4.00	10.00
Reprise FS-1017	(S)	**Strangers In The Night**	1966	6.00	15.00
Reprise F-1018	(M)	**Moonlight Sinatra**	1966	5.00	12.00
Reprise FS-1018	(S)	**Moonlight Sinatra**	1966	6.00	15.00
Reprise 2F-1019	(M)	**Sinatra At The Sands** (2 LPs)	1966	5.00	12.00
Reprise 2FS-1019	(S)	**Sinatra At The Sands** (2 LPs)	1966	6.00	15.00
Reprise F-1020	(M)	**That's Life**	1966	4.00	10.00
Reprise FS-1020	(S)	**That's Life**	1966	5.00	12.00
Reprise F-1021	(M)	**Francis Albert Sinatra And Antonio Carlos Jobim**	1967	5.00	12.00
Reprise FS-1021	(S)	**Francis Albert Sinatra And Antonio Carlos Jobim**	1967	6.00	15.00
Reprise F-1022	(M)	**The World We Knew**	1967	4.00	10.00
Reprise FS-1022	(S)	**The World We Knew**	1967	5.00	12.00
Reprise F-1023	(M)	**Frank Sinatra And Frank, Jr., And Nancy**	1967	5.00	12.00
Reprise FS-1023	(S)	**Frank Sinatra And Frank, Jr., And Nancy**	1967	6.00	15.00

Label & Catalog #		Title	Year	VG+	NM
Reprise F-1024	(M)	Francis A. And Edward K.	1968	6.00	15.00
Reprise FS-1024	(S)	Francis A. And Edward K.	1968	6.00	15.00
		— Original Reprise albums have pink, gold & green labels.—			

"After all these years, Francis Albert Sinatra conjoins with Edward Kennedy Ellington."

Reprise FS-1026	(S)	The Sinatra Family Wish You A Merry Christmas *(With Nancy Sinatra)*	1968	5.00	12.00
Reprise FS-1031	(S)	Watertown	1970	6.00	15.00
Reprise FS-2155	(S)	Ol' Blue Eyes Is Back	1973	6.00	15.00
Reprise FS4-2155	(Q)	Ol' Blue Eyes Is Back	1973	6.00	15.00
Reprise FS4-2195	(Q)	Some Nice Things I've Missed	1974	6.00	15.00
Mobile Fidelity MFSL-086	(S)	Nice 'N' Easy	1980	8.00	20.00
Mobile Fidelity MFSL-135	(S)	A Jolly Christmas	1980	8.00	20.00
Mobile Fidelity	(P)	Sinatra *(16 LP box)*	1984	180.00	300.00

SINATRA, FRANK, & TOMMY DORSEY

RCA Victor LPT-10 (10")	(M)	Getting Sentimental	195?	16.00	40.00
RCA Victor LPT-15 (10")	(M)	Tommy Dorsey All-Time Hits	195?	16.00	40.00
RCA Victor LPV-583	(M)	This Love of Mine	195?	12.00	30.00
RCA Victor LPM-1229	(M)	Yes Indeed	1956	12.00	30.00
RCA Victor LPM-1432	(M)	Tribute To Dorsey, Volume 1	1956	12.00	30.00
RCA Victor LPM-1433	(M)	Tribute To Dorsey, Volume 2	1956	12.00	30.00
RCA Victor LPM-1569	(M)	Frankie And Tommy	1957	12.00	30.00
RCA Victor LPM-1632	(M)	We Three	1957	12.00	30.00
RCA Victor LPM-1643	(M)	Having A Wonderful Time	1957	12.00	30.00
RCA Victor VPM-6038	(M)	This Is Tommy Dorsey *(2 LPs)*	195?	14.00	35.00
RCA Victor VPM-6038	(M)	This Is Tommy Dorsey, Volume 2 *(2 LPs)*	195?	14.00	35.00
		— Original RCA Victor albums have "Long Play" on the bottom of the label.—			

SINATRA, NANCY
Ms. Sinatra also recorded with Elvis Presley.

Reprise R-6202	(M)	Boots	1966	8.00	20.00
Reprise RS-6202	(S)	Boots	1966	12.00	30.00
Dot DLP-3714	(M)	Last Of The Secret Agents *(Soundtrack)*	1966	6.00	15.00
Dot DLP-25714	(S)	Last Of The Secret Agents *(Soundtrack)*	1966	8.00	20.00

After struggling for several years with Reprise, Nancy scored big in early 1966 with "These Boots Are Made For Walkin,'" a record that has enjoyed a large following since. After several more years of solo hits team-ups with Lee Hazlewood— creating some of the most downright odd and unfashionable records of that or any other time— and soundtrack work (including the dubious distinction of being the only person to have a track on an Elvis album by anyone but the King— the hilarious "Your Groovy Self" on *Speedway*), her recording career with Daddy's label came to an end. She was picked up by RCA, who released a two-disc set of her biggest hits, *This Is Nancy Sinatra*, and graced it with this knockout cover. (Note: This is also Ms. Sinatra's rarest album.)

abel & Catalog #		Title	Year	VG+	NM
eprise R-6207	(M)	**How Does That Grab You?**	1966	5.00	12.00
eprise RS-6207	(S)	**How Does That Grab You?**	1966	8.00	20.00
eprise R-6221	(M)	**Nancy In London**	1966	4.00	10.00
eprise RS-6221	(S)	**Nancy In London**	1966	5.00	12.00
eprise R-6239	(M)	**Sugar**	1966	5.00	12.00
eprise RS-6239	(S)	**Sugar**	1966	6.00	15.00
nited Arts. UAL-4155	(M)	**You Only Live Twice** (Soundtrack)	1967	5.00	12.00
nited Arts. UAS-5155	(S)	**You Only Live Twice** (Soundtrack)	1967	6.00	15.00
eprise R-6251	(M)	**Country, My Way**	1967	4.00	10.00
eprise RS-6251	(S)	**Country, My Way**	1967	5.00	12.00
eprise R-6277	(M)	**Movin' With Nancy**	1968	5.00	12.00
eprise RS-6277	(S)	**Movin' With Nancy**	1968	4.00	10.00
eprise RS-6333	(S)	**Nancy**	1969	5.00	12.00
eprise RS-6409	(S)	**Nancy's Greatest Hits**	1970	8.00	20.00
RCA Victor VPS-6078	(S)	**This Is Nancy Sinatra** (2 LPs)	1972	12.00	30.00
RCA Victor LSP-4774	(S)	**Woman**	1972	6.00	15.00

SINATRA, NANCY, & LEE HAZLEWOOD

eprise R-6273	(M)	**Nancy And Lee**	1968	8.00	20.00
eprise RS-6273	(S)	**Nancy And Lee**	1968	6.00	15.00
RCA Victor LSP-4645	(S)	**Nancy And Lee Again**	1972	6.00	15.00

SINATRA, NANCY, & MEL TILLIS

Elektra 5E-549	(S)	**Mel And Nancy**	1981	6.00	15.00

SIR DOUGLAS QUINTET, THE [DOUG SAHM]
Refer to Doug Sahm.

ribe TR-37001	(M)	**The Best Of The Sir Douglas Quintet**	1966	12.00	30.00
ribe TRS-47001	(P)	**The Best Of The Sir Douglas Quintet**	1966	16.00	30.00
mash SRS-67108	(S)	**Honkey Blues**	1968	12.00	30.00
mash SRS-67115	(S)	**Mendocino**	1969	10.00	25.00
mash SRS-67130	(S)	**Together After Five**	1970	10.00	25.00
hilips PHS-600344	(S)	**1+1+1=4**	1970	10.00	25.00
hilips PHS-600353	(S)	**The Return Of Doug Saldana**	1971	10.00	25.00
tlantic SD-7267	(S)	**Texas Tornado**	1973	5.00	12.00
ot 2057	(S)	**Texas Rock For Country Rollers**	1976	6.00	15.00

SIR LANCELOT

ercury MG-25159 (10")	(M)	**Calypso**	1952	16.00	40.00

SIR LORD BALTIMORE

ercury SR-61328	(S)	**Kingdom Come**	1970	6.00	15.00
ercury SRM-1-613	(S)	**Sir Lord Baltimore**	1971	6.00	15.00

SKIFFLERS, THE

erfect S-14015	(M)	**Folk Songs**	1960	6.00	15.00
erfect PS-14015	(S)	**Folk Songs**	1960	8.00	20.00
Harmony HL-7307	(M)	**Hootenanny**	1964	5.00	12.00

SKINNER, CORNELIA & OTIS

amden CAL-190	(M)	**Cornelia Skinner With Otis Skinner**	195?	10.00	25.00

SKINNER, JIMMIE

ercury MG-20352	(M)	**Songs That Make The Juke Box Play**	1957	30.00	60.00
ecca DL-4132	(M)	**Country Singer**	1961	12.00	30.00
ecca DL-74132	(S)	**Country Singer**	1961	16.00	40.00
ercury MG-20700	(M)	**Jimmie Skinner Sings Jimmie Rodgers**	1962	12.00	30.00
ercury SR-60700	(S)	**Jimmie Skinner Sings Jimmie Rodgers**	1962	16.00	40.00
tarday SLP-240	(M)	**The Kentucky Colonel**	1963	12.00	30.00
Wing MGW-12277	(M)	**Country Blues**	1964	6.00	15.00
Wing SRW-16277	(S)	**Country Blues**	1964	8.00	20.00

SKIP & THE CREATIONS

Justice JLP-	(S)	**Mobam** (With cover)	196?	240.00	400.00
Justice JLP-	(S)	**Mobam** (No cover)	196?	100.00	200.00

SKULL SNAPS, THE

G.S.F. 1011	(S)	**The Skull Snaps**	1973	6.00	15.00

Label & Catalog #		Title	Year	VG+	NM

SKUNKS, THE

Teen Town TTLP-101	(S)	Gettin' Started	196?	16.00	40.00

SKYLINERS, THE

Calico LP-3000	(M)	The Skyliners	1959	150.00	250.00
Original Sound 8873	(M)	Since I Don't Have You	1963	14.00	35.00
Original Sound S-8873	(P)	Since I Don't Have You	1963	20.00	50.00
Kama Sutra KSBS-2026	(S)	Once Upon A Time	1971	8.00	20.00

SLACK, FREDDIE

Capitol H-83 (10")	(M)	Boogie Woogie	1950	30.00	60.00
EmArcy 36094	(M)	Boogie Woogie On The 88	1956	20.00	50.00
Wing MGW-60003	(M)	Boogie Woogie On The 88	1957	14.00	35.00

SLEDGE, PERCY

Atlantic 8125	(M)	When A Man Loves A Woman	1966	10.00	25.00
Atlantic SD-8125	(S)	When A Man Loves A Woman	1966	12.00	30.00
Atlantic 8132	(M)	Warm And Tender Soul	1966	10.00	25.00
Atlantic SD-8132	(S)	Warm And Tender Soul	1966	12.00	30.00
Atlantic 8146	(M)	The Percy Sledge Way	1967	8.00	20.00
Atlantic SD-8146	(S)	The Percy Sledge Way	1967	10.00	25.00
Atlantic SD-8180	(S)	Take Time To Know Her	1968	10.00	25.00
Atlantic SD-8210	(S)	The Best Of Percy Sledge	1969	6.00	15.00
Capricorn 0147	(S)	I'll Be Your Everything	1974	4.00	10.00

SLEEPY HOLLOW

Family Prod. 2708	(S)	Sleepy Hollow	1973	6.00	15.00

SLICK, GRACE
Refer to The Great Society; The Jefferson Airplane; The Jefferson Starship; Paul Kantner.

RCA Victor DJL1-3922	(DJ)	The Grace Slick Interview	1981	4.00	10.00
RCA Victor DJL1-3923	(DJ)	RCA Special Radio Series (Interview)	1981	4.00	10.00

SLIM JIM

Soma 1225	(M)	Slim Jim Sings (Black label)	1958	20.00	50.00

SLOAN, P.F.
Refer to The Fantastic Baggys; The Grass Roots.

Dunhill D-50004	(M)	Songs Of Our Times	1965	6.00	15.00
Dunhill DS-50004	(S)	Songs Of Our Times	1965	8.00	20.00
Dunhill D-50007	(S)	Twelve More Times	1966	6.00	15.00
Dunhill DS-50007	(S)	Twelve More Times	1966	8.00	20.00
Atco SD-33-268	(S)	Measure Of Pleasure	1968	6.00	15.00
Mums KZ-31260	(S)	Raised On Records	1972	4.00	10.00

SLOANE, CAROL

Columbia CL-1766	(M)	Out Of The Blue	1962	8.00	20.00
Columbia CS-8566	(S)	Out Of The Blue	1962	12.00	30.00
Columbia CL-1923	(M)	Live At 30th St.	1963	8.00	20.00
Columbia CS-8723	(S)	Live At 30th St.	1963	12.00	30.00

SLY & THE FAMILY STONE (SLY)

Epic LN-24324	(M)	A Whole New Thing	1967	8.00	20.00
Epic BN-26324	(S)	A Whole New Thing	1967	10.00	25.00
Epic BN-26371	(S)	Dance To The Music	1968	6.00	15.00
Epic BN-26397	(S)	Life	1968	6.00	15.00
Epic BN-26456	(S)	Stand!	1969	6.00	15.00
Epic KE-30325	(P)	Sly & The Family Stone's Greatest Hits	1970	5.00	12.00
Epic KE-30986	(S)	There's A Riot Goin' On	1971	5.00	12.00
		— Original Epic albums above have yellow labels.—			
Epic EQ-30325	(Q)	Sly & The Family Stone's Greatest Hits	1973	20.00	50.00
Epic PEQ-32930	(Q)	Small Talk	1974	8.00	20.00
Epic PEQ-33835	(Q)	High On You	1975	8.00	20.00

SMALL, MILLIE

Smash MGS-27055	(M)	My Boy Lollipop	1964	16.00	40.00
Smash SRS-67055	(E)	My Boy Lollipop	1964	12.00	30.00

Label & Catalog #		Title	Year	VG+	NM

Perhaps the most desirable of the early '70s quadraphonic albums, this title,
remixed to four channels from the original multi-tracks, contains hits in true stereo that are
available only in rechanneled stereo elsewhere.

SMALL FACES, THE [THE FACES]
Features Steve Marriott, Ronnie Lane, Kenny Jones and Ian McLagen. The Warners and Mercury albums
include Rod Stewart and Ron Wood.

Label & Catalog #		Title	Year	VG+	NM
Immediate Z12-52-002	(S)	**There Are But Four Small Faces**	1968	12.00	30.00
Immediate Z12-52-008	(S)	**Ogden's Nut Gone Flake** *(Round cover)*	1968	12.00	30.00
Immediate 4225	(S)	**Ogden's Nut Gone Flake** *(Square cover)*	1973	6.00	15.00
Warner Bros. WS-1851	(S)	**First Step**	1970	6.00	15.00
Warner Bros. WS-1892	(S)	**Long Player**	1971	4.00	10.00
Warner Bros. BS-2574	(S)	**A Nod Is As Good As A Wink**	1971	4.00	10.00
Warner Bros. BS-2665	(S)	**Ooh La La**	1973	4.00	10.00
Pride 0001	(P)	**Early Faces**	1972	4.00	10.00
Pride 0014	(P)	**The History Of The Small Faces**	1973	4.00	10.00

SMART SET, THE

Warner Bros. W-1203	(M)	**A New Experience In Vocal Styles**	1958	8.00	20.00

SMECK, ROY
Smeck also recorded as Prince Kailua.

"X" LPX-3012 (10")	(M)	**South Of The Border**	195?	40.00	80.00
"X" LPA-3016 (10")	(M)	**Christmas In Hawaii**	195?	40.00	80.00
Coral CRL-56013 (10")	(M)	**Drifting And Dreaming**	195?	20.00	50.00
Decca DL-5458 (10")	(M)	**Memory Lane**	1953	20.00	50.00
Decca DL-5473 (10")	(M)	**Songs Of The Range**	1953	20.00	50.00
Decca DL-8674	(M)	**Memories Of You**	1958	12.00	30.00
ABC-Paramount 119	(M)	**South Seas Serenade**	1956	8.00	20.00
ABC-Paramount 174	(M)	**Melodies With Memories**	1957	8.00	20.00
ABC-Paramount 234	(M)	**Hi Fi Paradise**	1958	8.00	20.00
ABC-Paramount 330	(M)	**The Haunting Hawaiian Guitar**	1960	6.00	15.00
ABC-Paramount S-330	(S)	**The Haunting Hawaiian Guitar**	1960	8.00	20.00
ABC-Paramount 379	(M)	**His Singing Guitar**	1961	6.00	15.00
ABC-Paramount S-379	(S)	**His Singing Guitar**	1961	8.00	20.00
ABC-Paramount 412	(M)	**Stringing Along**	1962	6.00	15.00
ABC-Paramount S-412	(S)	**Stringing Along**	1962	8.00	20.00

Label & Catalog #		Title	Year	VG+	NM
ABC-Paramount 452	(M)	The Many Guitar Moods Of Roy Smeck	1963	6.00	15.00
ABC-Paramount S-452	(S)	The Many Guitar Moods Of Roy Smeck	1963	8.00	20.00
Kapp KL-1491	(M)	Hawaiian Guitar Hits	1966	5.00	12.00
Kapp KS-3491	(M)	Hawaiian Guitar Hits	1966	6.00	15.00

SMILE

Pickwick SPC-3288	(S)	Smile	1973	12.00	30.00

SMITH, "FIDDLIN'" ARTHUR

Starday SLP-202	(M)	Rare Old Time Fiddle Tunes	1962	12.00	30.00

SMITH, ARTHUR "GUITAR BOOGIE" (& HIS CRACKERJACKS)

MGM E-236 (10")	(M)	Foolish Questions	1954	30.00	60.00
MGM E-533 (10")	(M)	Fingers On Fire	1955	30.00	60.00
MGM E-3301	(M)	Specials	1955	20.00	50.00
MGM E-3525	(M)	Fingers On Fire	1957	16.00	40.00
— Original MGM albums above have yellow labels.—					
Starday SLP-173	(M)	Mister Guitar	1962	12.00	30.00
Starday SLP-186	(M)	Arthur Smith And The Crossroads Quartet	1962	12.00	30.00
Starday SLP-216	(M)	Arthur Guitar Boogie Smith Goes To Town	1963	12.00	30.00
Starday SLP-241	(M)	In Person	1963	12.00	30.00
Starday SLP-266	(M)	Down Home	1964	12.00	30.00
Starday SLP-415	(M)	The Guitars Of Arthur Smith	1968	6.00	15.00
ABC Paramount 441	(M)	Arthur Guitar Smith And Voices	1963	6.00	15.00
ABC Paramount S-441	(S)	Arthur Guitar Smith And Voices	1963	8.00	20.00
Folkways FA-2379	(M)	Old Timers Of The Grand Ole Opry	1964	6.00	15.00
Hamilton HLP-12134	(M)	The Arthur Smith Show	1964	5.00	12.00
Hamilton HLPS-12134	(S)	The Arthur Smith Show	1964	6.00	15.00
Dot DLP-3600	(M)	Original Guitar Boogie	1964	8.00	20.00
Dot DLP-25600	(S)	Original Guitar Boogie	1964	10.00	25.00
Dot DLP-3636	(M)	Great Country And Western Hits	1965	5.00	12.00
Dot DLP-25636	(S)	Great Country And Western Hits	1965	6.00	15.00
Dot DLP-3642	(M)	Singing On The Mountain	1965	5.00	12.00
Dot DLP-25642	(S)	Singing On The Mountain	1965	6.00	15.00
Dot DLP-3769	(M)	A Tribute To Jim Reeves	1966	5.00	12.00
Dot DLP-25769	(S)	A Tribute To Jim Reeves	1966	6.00	15.00

SMITH, BOB

Kent KST-551	(S)	The Visit (2 LPs with poster)	1969	40.00	80.00
Kent KST-551	(S)	The Visit (2 LPs without poster)	1969	30.00	60.00

SMITH, BUSTER

Atlantic 1323	(M)	The Legendary Buster Smith	1960	20.00	50.00

SMITH, CARL

Columbia HL-9023 (10")	(M)	Sentimental Songs	195?	20.00	50.00
Columbia HL-9026 (10")	(M)	Softly And Tenderly	195?	20.00	50.00
Columbia HL-2579 (10")	(M)	Carl Smith	1956	20.00	50.00
Columbia CL-959	(M)	Sunday Down South	1957	14.00	30.00
Columbia CL-1022	(M)	Smith's The Name	1957	14.00	30.00
Columbia CL-1172	(M)	Let's Live A Little	1958	14.00	30.00
Columbia CL-1532	(M)	The Carl Smith Touch	1960	6.00	15.00
Columbia CS-8332	(S)	The Carl Smith Touch	1960	10.00	25.00
Columbia CL-1740	(M)	Easy To Please	1962	6.00	15.00
Columbia CS-8540	(S)	Easy To Please	1962	10.00	25.00
— Original Columbia albums above have three white "eye" logos on each side of the spindle hole.—					
Columbia CL-1937	(M)	Carl Smith's Greatest Hits	1962	6.00	15.00
Columbia CS-8737	(P)	Carl Smith's Greatest Hits	1962	6.00	15.00
Columbia CL-2091	(M)	Tall, Tall Gentleman	1963	5.00	12.00
Columbia CS-8891	(S)	Tall, Tall Gentleman	1963	6.00	15.00
Columbia CL-2173	(M)	There Stands The Glass	1964	4.00	10.00
Columbia CS-8973	(S)	There Stands The Glass	1964	5.00	12.00
Columbia CL-2293	(M)	I Want To Live And Love	1965	4.00	10.00
Columbia CS-9093	(S)	I Want To Live And Love	1965	5.00	12.00
Columbia CL-2358	(M)	Kisses Don't Lie	1965	4.00	10.00
Columbia CS-9158	(S)	Kisses Don't Lie	1965	5.00	12.00
Columbia CL-2501	(M)	Man With A Plan	1966	4.00	10.00
Columbia CS-9301	(S)	Man With A Plan	1966	5.00	12.00

Label & Catalog #		Title	Year	VG+	NM
Columbia CL-2610	(M)	The Country Gentleman	1967	4.00	10.00
Columbia CS-9410	(S)	The Country Gentleman	1967	5.00	12.00
Columbia CL-2687	(M)	The Country Gentleman Sings	1967	4.00	10.00
Columbia CS-9487	(S)	The Country Gentleman Sings	1967	5.00	12.00
		— Original Columbia albums above have "360 Sound" on the bottom of the label.—			

SMITH, CARL / LEFTY FRIZZELL / MARTY ROBBINS

Columbia CL-2544 (10")	(M)	Carl, Lefty And Marty	1956	100.00	200.00

SMITH, HUEY "PIANO"

Ace LP-1004	(M)	Having A Good Time	1959	100.00	200.00
Ace LP-1015	(M)	For Dancing	1961	75.00	150.00
Ace LP-1027	(M)	Twas The Night Before Christmas	1962	75.00	150.00
Ace LP-2021	(S)	Rock 'N' Roll Revival	1971	8.00	20.00

SMITH, JENNIE

RCA Victor LPM-1523	(M)	Jennie	1957	14.00	35.00

SMITH, KEELY

Keely Smith also recorded with Louis Prima. Refer to The Reprise Repertory Theatre.

Capitol W-914	(M)	I Wish You Love (Turquoise label)	1957	16.00	40.00
Capitol T-1073	(M)	Politely	1958	12.00	30.00
Capitol ST-1073	(S)	Politely	1958	16.00	40.00
Capitol T-1145	(M)	Swingin' Pretty	1959	12.00	30.00
Capitol ST-1145	(S)	Swingin' Pretty	1959	16.00	40.00
		— Original Capitol albums above have black labels with the logo on the left side.—			
Dot DLP-3241	(M)	Be My Love	1961	6.00	15.00
Dot DLP-25241	(S)	Be My Love	1961	8.00	20.00
Dot DLP-3387	(M)	Dearly Beloved	1961	6.00	15.00
Dot DLP-25387	(S)	Dearly Beloved	1961	8.00	20.00
Dot DLP-3345	(M)	A Keely Christmas	1961	6.00	15.00
Dot DLP-25345	(S)	A Keely Christmas	1961	8.00	20.00
Dot DLP-3415	(M)	Because You're Mine	1962	6.00	15.00
Dot DLP-25415	(S)	Because You're Mine	1962	8.00	20.00
Dot DLP-3423	(M)	Twist With Keely Smith	1962	6.00	15.00
Dot DLP-25423	(S)	Twist With Keely Smith	1962	8.00	20.00
Reprise R-6086	(M)	Little Girl Blue, Little Girl New	1963	6.00	15.00
Reprise R9-6086	(S)	Little Girl Blue, Little Girl New	1963	8.00	20.00
Reprise R-6142	(M)	The Lennon-McCartney Songbook	1964	6.00	15.00
Reprise R9-6142	(S)	The Lennon-McCartney Songbook	1964	8.00	20.00

SMITH, LaVERGNE

Cook 1081 (10")	(M)	Angel In The Absinthe House	1955	50.00	100.00
Savoy MG-12031	(M)	New Orleans Nightingale	1955	20.00	50.00
Vik LX-1056	(M)	LaVergne Smith	1956	16.00	40.00

SMITH, OSBORNE

Argo 4000	(M)	Eyes Of Love	1960	8.00	20.00

SMITH, RAY

Judd JLPA-701	(M)	Travelin' With Ray	1960	240.00	400.00
"T" 56062	(M)	The Best Of Ray Smith	196?	20.00	50.00
Columbia CL-1937	(M)	Greatest Hits ("360 Sound" label)	1963	8.00	20.00
Columbia CS-8737	(S)	Greatest Hits ("360 Sound" label)	1963	10.00	25.00

SMITH, RAY / PAT CUPP

Crown CLP-5364	(M)	Ray Smith And Patt Cupp	1963	8.00	20.00

SMITH, ROGER

Warners W-1305	(M)	Beach Romance	1959	10.00	25.00
Warners WS-1305	(S)	Beach Romance	1959	14.00	35.00

SMITH, TAB

United LP-001 (10")	(M)	Music Styled By Tab Smith	1955	50.00	100.00
United LP-003 (10")	(M)	Red, Hot And Cool Blues	1955	50.00	100.00

SMITH, WARREN

Liberty LRP-3199	(M)	The First Country Collection	1961	20.00	50.00
Liberty LST-7199	(S)	The First Country Collection	1961	30.00	60.00

Label & Catalog #		Title	Year	VG+	NM

SMOKE, THE

Sidewalk ST-5912	(S)	The Smoke	1968	16.00	40.00
Tower ST-5912	(S)	The Smoke	1968	16.00	40.00

SMOKE, THE

Uni 73052	(S)	The Smoke	1969	8.00	20.00
Uni 73065	(S)	At Georges Coffee Shop	1970	8.00	20.00

SMOTHERS, SMOKEY

King 779	(M)	The Backporch Blues	1962	100.00	200.00

SMOTHERS BROTHERS, THE

Mercury MG-20611	(M)	Songs And Comedy	1961	5.00	12.00
Mercury SR-60611	(S)	Songs And Comedy	1961	6.00	15.00
Mercury MG-20675	(M)	The Two Sides Of The Smothers Brothers	1962	5.00	12.00
Mercury SR-60675	(S)	The Two Sides Of The Smothers Brothers	1962	6.00	15.00
Mercury MG-20777	(M)	Think Ethnic!	1963	5.00	12.00
Mercury SR-60777	(S)	Think Ethnic!	1963	6.00	15.00

— Original Mercury albums above have black & silver labels.—

Mercury MG-20862	(M)	Curb Your Tongue, Knave!	1963	4.00	10.00
Mercury SR-60862	(S)	Curb Your Tongue, Knave!	1963	5.00	12.00
Mercury MG-20904	(M)	It Must Have Been Something I Said	1964	4.00	10.00
Mercury SR-60904	(S)	It Must Have Been Something I Said	1964	5.00	12.00
Mercury MG-20948	(M)	Tour De Farce: American History	1964	4.00	10.00
Mercury SR-60948	(S)	Tour De Farce: American History	1964	5.00	12.00
Mercury MG-20989	(M)	Aesop's Fables	1965	4.00	10.00
Mercury SR-60989	(S)	Aesop's Fables	1965	5.00	12.00
Mercury MG-21051	(M)	Mom Always Liked You Best!	1965	4.00	10.00
Mercury SR-61051	(S)	Mom Always Liked You Best!	1965	5.00	12.00
Mercury MG-21064	(M)	The Smothers Brothers Play It Straight	1965	4.00	10.00
Mercury SR-61064	(S)	The Smothers Brothers Play It Straight	1965	5.00	12.00
Mercury MG-21089	(M)	Golden Hits, Volume 2	1966	4.00	10.00
Mercury SR-61089	(S)	Golden Hits, Volume 2	1966	5.00	12.00

SNAKEFINGER

Ralph SN-7909	(S)	Chewing Hides The Sound	1980	5.00	12.00
Ralph SN-8053	(S)	Green Pastures	1981	5.00	12.00
Ralph SN-8203	(S)	Manual Of Errors	1982	5.00	12.00

SNAKEGRINDER

Alligator Shoes 40004	(S)	Snakegrinder & The Shredded Field Mice	1977	60.00	120.00

SNOW, HANK

RCA Victor LPT-3026 (10")	(M)	Country Classics	1952	50.00	100.00
RCA Victor LPT-3070 (10")	(M)	Hank Snow Sings	1952	50.00	100.00
RCA Victor LPT-3131 (10")	(M)	Hank Snow Salutes Jimmie Rodgers	1953	50.00	100.00
RCA Victor LPT-3267 (10")	(M)	Hank Snow's Country Guitar	1954	50.00	100.00
RCA Victor LPM-1113	(M)	Just Keep A-Movin'	1955	20.00	50.00
RCA Victor LPM-1156	(M)	Old Doc Brown & Other Narrations (2 LPs)	1955	75.00	150.00
RCA Victor LPM-1233	(M)	Country Classics	1955	20.00	50.00
RCA Victor LPM-1419	(M)	Country And Western Jamboree	1957	20.00	50.00
RCA Victor LPM-1435	(M)	Hank Snow's Country Guitar	1957	20.00	50.00
RCA Victor LPM-1638	(M)	Hank Snow Sings Sacred Songs	1958	20.00	50.00
RCA Victor LPM-1861	(M)	When Tragedy Struck	1958	30.00	60.00
School Of Music 1149	(M)	The Guitar (With booklet)	1958	100.00	200.00
RCA Victor LPM-2043	(M)	Hank Snow Sings Jimmie Rodgers Songs	1959	14.00	35.00
RCA Victor LSP-2043	(S)	Hank Snow Sings Jimmie Rodgers Songs	1959	20.00	50.00
RCA Victor LPM-2285	(M)	Souvenirs	1961	12.00	30.00
RCA Victor LSP-2285	(S)	Souvenirs	1961	16.00	40.00
RCA Victor LPM-2458	(M)	Big Country Hits	1961	12.00	30.00
RCA Victor LSP-2458	(S)	Big Country Hits	1961	16.00	40.00
RCA Victor LPM-2675	(M)	I've Been Everywhere	1963	10.00	25.00
RCA Victor LSP-2675	(S)	I've Been Everywhere	1963	14.00	35.00
RCA Victor LPM-2705	(M)	Railroad Man	1963	10.00	25.00
RCA Victor LSP-2705	(S)	Railroad Man	1963	14.00	35.00

— Original RCA mono albums above have "black labels with Long Play" on the bottom; stereo albums have have black labels with "Living Stereo" on the bottom.—

RCA Victor LPM-2812	(M)	More Hank Snow Souvenirs	1964	8.00	20.00
RCA Victor LSP-2812	(S)	More Hank Snow Souvenirs	1964	12.00	30.00

Label & Catalog #		Title	Year	VG+	NM
RCA Victor LPM-2901	(M)	Songs Of Tragedy	1964	8.00	20.00
RCA Victor LSP-2901	(S)	Songs Of Tragedy	1964	12.00	30.00
RCA Victor LPM-3317	(M)	Your Favorite Country Hits	1965	8.00	20.00
RCA Victor LSP-3317	(S)	Your Favorite Country Hits	1965	12.00	30.00
RCA Victor LPM-3378	(M)	Gloryland March	1965	12.00	30.00
RCA Victor LSP-3378	(S)	Gloryland March	1965	16.00	40.00
RCA Victor LPM-3471	(M)	Heartbreak Trail	1965	8.00	20.00
RCA Victor LSP-3471	(S)	Heartbreak Trail	1965	12.00	30.00
RCA Victor LPM-3478	(M)	The Best Of Hank Snow	1966	6.00	15.00
RCA Victor LSP-3478	(S)	The Best Of Hank Snow	1966	10.00	25.00
RCA Victor LPM-3548	(M)	The Guitar Stylings Of Hank Snow	1966	12.00	30.00
RCA Victor LSP-3548	(S)	The Guitar Stylings Of Hank Snow	1966	16.00	40.00
RCA Victor LPM-3595	(M)	Gospel Train	1966	12.00	30.00
RCA Victor LSP-3595	(S)	Gospel Train	1966	16.00	40.00
RCA Victor LPM-6014	(M)	This Is My Story	1966	10.00	25.00
RCA Victor LSP-6014	(S)	This Is My Story (2 LPs)	1966	12.00	30.00
RCA Victor LPM-3737	(M)	Snow In Hawaii	1967	10.00	25.00
RCA Victor LSP-3737	(S)	Snow In Hawaii	1967	12.00	30.00
RCA Victor LPM-3826	(M)	Christmas With Hank Snow	1967	10.00	25.00
RCA Victor LSP-3826	(S)	Christmas With Hank Snow	1967	12.00	30.00
RCA Victor LPM-3857	(M)	Spanish Fireball	1967	10.00	25.00
RCA Victor LSP-3857	(S)	Spanish Fireball	1967	12.00	30.00
RCA Victor LPM-3965	(M)	Hits, Hits And More Hits	1968	12.00	30.00
RCA Victor LSP-3965	(S)	Hits, Hits And More Hits	1968	8.00	20.00
RCA Victor LSP-4032	(S)	Tales Of The Yukon	1968	12.00	30.00
		— Original RCA albums above have black labels.—			
RCA Victor LSP-4122	(S)	Snow In All Seasons	1969	10.00	25.00
RCA Victor LSP-4166	(S)	Hits Covered By Snow	1969	8.00	20.00
RCA Victor LSP-4306	(S)	In Memory Of Jimmie Rodgers	1970	8.00	20.00
RCA Victor LSP-4379	(S)	Cure For The Blues	1970	6.00	15.00
RCA Victor LSP-4501	(S)	Tracks And Trains	1971	6.00	15.00
RCA Victor LSP-4601	(S)	Award Winners	1971	6.00	15.00
RCA Victor LSP-4708	(S)	The Jimmie Rodgers Story	1972	6.00	15.00
		— Original RCA albums above have orange labels.—			
RCA/Reader's Digest 216	(P)	I'm Movin' On (6 LP box)	197?	50.00	100.00
RCA Victor DPL2-0134	(P)	The Living Legend (2 LPs)	1978	50.00	100.00

SNOW, HANK, & CHET ATKINS
RCA Victor LPM-2952	(M)	Reminiscing	1964	8.00	20.00
RCA Victor LSP-2952	(S)	Reminiscing	1964	10.00	25.00
RCA Victor LSP-4254	(S)	By Special Request	1970	8.00	20.00

SNOW, HANK, & ANITA CARTER
RCA Victor LPM-2580	(M)	Together Again	1962	10.00	25.00
RCA Victor LSP-2580	(S)	Together Again	1962	14.00	35.00

SNOW, HANK / HANK LOCKLIN / PORTER WAGONER
RCA Victor LPM-2723	(M)	Three Country Gentlemen	1963	6.00	15.00
RCA Victor LSP-2723	(S)	Three Country Gentlemen	1963	8.00	20.00

SOFT MACHINE, THE
Probe 4500	(S)	The Soft Machine	1968	10.00	25.00
		(The cover is a "machine" with movable parts.)			
Probe 4500	(S)	The Soft Machine (Standard cover)	1969	6.00	15.00
Probe 4505	(S)	Soft Machine, Volume 2	1969	6.00	15.00

SOMMER, ELKE
MGM E-4321	(M)	Love In Any Language	1966	6.00	15.00
MGM SE-4321	(S)	Love In Any Language	1966	8.00	20.00

SOMMERS, JOANIE
Warner Bros. W-1346	(M)	Positively The Most	1960	8.00	20.00
Warner Bros. WS-1346	(S)	Positively The Most	1960	12.00	30.00
Warner Bros. B-1348	(M)	Behind Closed Doors At A Recording Session	1960	20.00	50.00
		(Boxed set includes one album and a booklet.)			
Warner Bros. W-1412	(M)	The Voice Of The 60's	1961	8.00	20.00
Warner Bros. WS-1412	(S)	The Voice Of The 60's	1961	12.00	30.00

Label & Catalog #		Title	Year	VG+	NM
Warner Bros. W-1436	(M)	**For Those Who Think Young**	1962	8.00	20.00
Warner Bros. WS-1436	(S)	**For Those Who Think Young**	1962	12.00	30.00
Warner Bros. W-1470	(M)	**Johnny Get Angry**	1962	12.00	30.00
Warner Bros. WS-1470	(S)	**Johnny Get Angry**	1962	16.00	40.00
Warner Bros. W-1474	(M)	**Let's Talk About Love**	1962	8.00	20.00
Warner Bros. WS-1474	(S)	**Let's Talk About Love**	1962	12.00	30.00
Warner Bros. W-1504	(M)	**Sommer's Seasons**	1964	8.00	20.00
Warner Bros. WS-1504	(S)	**Sommer's Seasons**	1964	12.00	30.00
Warner Bros. W-1575	(M)	**Softly, The Brazilian Sound**	1965	8.00	20.00
Warner Bros. WS-1575	(S)	**Softly, The Brazilian Sound**	1965	12.00	30.00
		—Original Warner albums above have grey labels.—			
Columbia CL-2495	(M)	**Come Alive**	1966	6.00	15.00
Columbia CS-9295	(S)	**Come Alive**	1966	8.00	20.00
Decca DL-4836	(M)	**On The Flip Side** *(TV Soundtrack)*	1967	12.00	30.00
Decca DL-74836	(S)	**On The Flip Side** *(TV Soundtrack)*	1967	16.00	40.00

This 1967 television drama that paired two performers whose stars as pop singers had waned.

SONICS, THE

Etiquette LP-024	(M)	**Here Are The Sonics!!!**	1965	60.00	120.00
Etiquette LP-027	(M)	**The Sonics Boom**	1966	60.00	120.00
Etiquette LPS-027	(E)	**The Sonics Boom**	1966	50.00	100.00
Jerden JRL-7007	(M)	**Introducing The Sonics**	1967	75.00	150.00
Buckshot BSR-001	(S)	**Explosives**	1974	16.00	40.00
First American FA-7715	(S)	**Original Northwest Punk**	1977	6.00	15.00
First American FA-7719	(S)	**Unreleased**	1980	6.00	15.00
First American FA-7779	(S)	**Fire And Ice**	1981	4.00	10.00

SONICS, THE / THE WAILERS / THE GALAXIES

Etiquette ALB-02	(M)	**Merry Christmas**	1965	100.00	200.00

Label & Catalog #		Title	Year	VG+	NM

SONNY [SONNY BONO]

Atco 33-229	(M)	Inner Views	1967	5.00	12.00
Atco SD-33-229	(S)	Inner Views	1967	6.00	15.00

SONNY & CHER
Sonny Bono and Cher.

Reprise R-6177	(M)	Baby Don't Go	1965	8.00	20.00
Reprise RS-6177	(S)	Baby Don't Go	1965	12.00	30.00
Atco 33-177	(M)	Look At Us	1965	6.00	15.00
Atco SD-33-177	(S)	Look At Us	1965	8.00	20.00
Atco 33-183	(M)	The Wondrous World Of Sonny & Cher	1966	5.00	12.00
Atco SD-33-183	(S)	The Wondrous World Of Sonny & Cher	1966	6.00	15.00
Atco 33-203	(M)	In Case You're In Love	1967	5.00	12.00
Atco SD-33-203	(S)	In Case You're In Love	1967	6.00	15.00
Atco 33-214	(M)	Good Times (Soundtrack)	1967	5.00	12.00
Atco SD-33-214	(S)	Good Times (Soundtrack)	1967	6.00	15.00
Atco 33-219	(M)	The Best Of Sonny & Cher	1967	5.00	12.00
Atco SD-33-219	(S)	The Best Of Sonny & Cher	1967	6.00	15.00
Atco A2-5178	(M)	Sonny & Cher's Greatest Hits (2 LPs)	1967	8.00	20.00
Atco A2S-5178	(S)	Sonny & Cher's Greatest Hits (2 LPs)	1967	6.00	15.00
Atco SD-2-804	(S)	The Two Of Us (2 LPs)	1972	6.00	15.00

SONNY & THE CASCADES

Columbia CL-2172	(M)	Exciting New Liverpool Sound	1964	12.00	30.00
Columbia CS-8972	(S)	Exciting New Liverpool Sound	1964	16.00	40.00

SONNY & THE DEMONS

United Arts. UAL-3316	(M)	Drag Kings	1964	8.00	20.00
United Arts. UAS-6316	(S)	Drag Kings	1964	10.00	25.00

SONNY TERRY
Refer to Leadbelly; Pete Seeger.

Stinson 55 (10")	(M)	Blues	1950	30.00	60.00
Folkways 2006 (10")	(M)	Washboard Band	1950	20.00	50.00
Folkways 2035 (10")	(M)	Harmonica	1952	20.00	50.00
Elektra EKL-14 (10")	(M)	Folk Blues	195?	20.00	50.00
Riverside RLP-644	(M)	Sonny Terry and His Mouth Harp	195?	12.00	30.00
Washington W-702	(M)	Talkin' 'Bout The Blues	1961	16.00	40.00
Bluesville BV-1025	(M)	Sonny's Story	1961	14.00	35.00
Bluesville BV-1059	(M)	Sonny Is King	1963	12.00	30.00
Everest 206	(S)	Sonny Terry	1968	6.00	15.00
Brut 6002	(S)	The Book Of Numbers (Soundtrack)	1973	6.00	15.00

SONNY TERRY & BROWNIE McGHEE
Sonny & Brownie are Saunders Terrell and Walter Brown McGhee. Refer to Big Bill Broonzy.

Savoy MG-14019	(M)	Back Country Blues	195?	30.00	60.00
Folkways 2028 (10")	(M)	Get On Board	1951	30.00	60.00
Folkways 2030 (10")	(M)	Blues	1951	30.00	60.00
Columbia OL-5240	(M)	Simply Heavenly (Soundtrack)	1957	50.00	100.00
Folkways F6-3557	(M)	Blues	1959	16.00	40.00
Folkways F-2327	(M)	Blues And Folksongs	1961	12.00	30.00
Folkways FS-2327	(S)	Blues And Folksongs	1961	16.00	40.00
Folkways F-2421	(M)	Traditional Blues, Volume 1	1961	12.00	30.00
Folkways FS-2422	(S)	Traditional Blues, Volume 2	1961	16.00	40.00
Folkways FV-9019	(M)	Guitar Highway	1965	8.00	20.00
Folkways FVS-9019	(S)	Guitar Highway	1965	10.00	25.00
Roulette R-25074	(M)	The Folk Songs Of Sonny & Brownie	1959	16.00	40.00
World Pacific WP-1294	(M)	Blues Is A Story	1960	12.00	30.00
World Pacific ST-1294	(S)	Blues Is A Story	1960	16.00	40.00
World Pacific WP-1296	(M)	Way Down South Summit Meetin'	1960	12.00	30.00
World Pacific ST-1296	(S)	Way Down South Summit Meetin'	1960	16.00	40.00
Bluesville BV-1002	(M)	Down Home Blues	1960	12.00	30.00
Bluesville BVS-1002	(S)	Down Home Blues	1960	16.00	40.00
Bluesville BV-1005	(M)	Blues & Folk	1960	12.00	30.00
Bluesville BVS-1005	(S)	Blues & Folk	1960	16.00	40.00
Bluesville BV-1020	(M)	Blues All Around My Head	1961	12.00	30.00
Bluesville BVS-1020	(S)	Blues All Around My Head	1961	16.00	40.00
Bluesville BV-1033	(M)	Blues In My Soul	1961	12.00	30.00
Bluesville BVS-1033	(S)	Blues In My Soul	1961	16.00	40.00

Label & Catalog #		Title	Year	VG+	NM
Bluesville BV-1042	(M)	Brownie's Blues	1962	10.00	25.00
Bluesville BVS-1042	(S)	Brownie's Blues	1962	12.00	30.00
Bluesville BV-1058	(M)	At The 2nd Fret	1962	12.00	30.00
Verve V6-3008	(M)	Blues Is My Companion	1961	12.00	30.00
Verve V6-3008	(S)	Blues Is My Companion	1961	14.00	35.00
Fantasy F-3254	(M)	Sonny Terry & Brownie McGhee	1961	12.00	30.00
Fantasy F-3254	(M)	Sonny Terry & Brownie McGhee (Red vinyl)	1961	35.00	70.00
Fantasy F-3296	(M)	Just A Closer Walk With Thee	1962	12.00	30.00
Fantasy F-3296	(M)	Just A Closer Walk With Thee (Red vinyl)	1962	35.00	70.00
Fantasy F-8091	(M)	Sonny & Brownie At Sugar Hill	1962	12.00	30.00
Fantasy F-8091	(M)	Sonny & Brownie At Sugar Hill (Red vinyl)	1962	35.00	70.00
Fantasy F-3317	(M)	Blues & Shouts	1962	12.00	30.00
Fantasy F-3317	(M)	Blues & Shouts (Red vinyl)	1962	35.00	70.00
Mainstream MS-6049	(M)	Hometown Blues	1965	8.00	20.00
Mainstream MS-6049	(S)	Hometown Blues	1965	10.00	25.00
Everest 242	(S)	Brownie McGhee & Sonny Terry	1969	6.00	15.00
Prestige 7715	(S)	Best Of Sonny Terry & Brownie McGhee	1969	6.00	15.00
Fontana SGF-67599	(S)	Where The Blues Begin	1969	8.00	20.00
BluesWay 6028	(S)	Long Way From Home	1969	6.00	15.00
BluesWay 6059	(S)	I Couldn't Believe My Eyes	1973	6.00	15.00
Olympic 7108	(S)	Hootin' & Hollerin'	1973	4.00	10.00
Savoy 12218	(S)	Down Home Blues	1973	4.00	10.00
A&M SP-34379	(S)	Sonny & Brownie	1973	5.00	12.00
Fantasy 24708	(S)	Back To New Orleans	1972	6.00	15.00

SONS OF CHAMPLIN

Capitol SWBB-200	(S)	Loosen Up Naturally (2 LPs)	1969	6.00	15.00
Capitol SKAO-322	(S)	The Sons	1969	5.00	12.00
Capitol ST-675	(S)	Follow Your Heart	1971	5.00	12.00

— Original Capitol albums above have green labels.—

SONS OF HEROES

MCA 39010	(S)	Sons Of Heroes (With Bill Wyman)	1983	8.00	20.00

SONS OF THE PIONEERS, THE

RCA Victor LPM-3032 (10")	(M)	Cowboy Classics	1952	30.00	60.00
RCA Victor LPM-3095 (10")	(M)	Cowboy Hymns And Spirituals	1952	30.00	60.00
RCA Victor LPM-3162 (10")	(M)	Western Classics	1953	30.00	60.00
RCA Victor LPM-1130	(M)	Favorite Cowboy Songs	1955	14.00	35.00
RCA Victor LPM-1431	(M)	How Great Thou Art	1957	14.00	35.00
RCA Victor LPM-1483	(M)	One Man's Songs	1957	14.00	35.00
RCA Victor LPM-2118	(M)	Cool Water	1960	6.00	15.00
RCA Victor LSP-2118	(S)	Cool Water	1960	10.00	25.00
RCA Victor LPM-2356	(M)	Lure Of The West	1961	6.00	15.00
RCA Victor LSP-2356	(S)	Lure Of The West	1961	10.00	25.00
RCA Victor LPM-2456	(M)	Tumbleweed Trails	1962	6.00	15.00
RCA Victor LSP-2456	(S)	Tumbleweed Trails	1962	10.00	25.00
RCA Victor LPM-2603	(M)	Our Men Out West	1963	6.00	15.00
RCA Victor LSP-2603	(S)	Our Men Out West	1963	10.00	25.00
RCA Victor LPM-2652	(M)	Hymns Of The Cowboy	1963	6.00	15.00
RCA Victor LSP-2652	(S)	Hymns Of The Cowboy	1963	10.00	25.00

— Original RCA mono albums above have "black labels with Long Play" on the bottom; stereo albums have have black labels with "Living Stereo" on the bottom.—

RCA Victor LPM-2737	(M)	Trail Dust	1963	5.00	12.00
RCA Victor LSP-2737	(S)	Trail Dust	1963	8.00	20.00
RCA Victor LPM-2855	(M)	Country Fare	1964	5.00	12.00
RCA Victor LSP-2855	(S)	Country Fare	1964	8.00	20.00
RCA Victor LPM-2957	(M)	Down Memory Trail	1964	5.00	12.00
RCA Victor LSP-2957	(S)	Down Memory Trail	1964	8.00	20.00
RCA Victor LPM-3351	(M)	Legends Of The West	1965	5.00	12.00
RCA Victor LSP-3351	(S)	Legends Of The West	1965	8.00	20.00
RCA Victor LPM-3476	(M)	The Best Of The Sons Of The Pioneers	1966	4.00	10.00
RCA Victor LSP-3476	(S)	The Best Of The Sons Of The Pioneers	1966	6.00	15.00
RCA Victor LPM-3554	(M)	The Songs Of Bob Nolan	1966	4.00	10.00
RCA Victor LSP-3554	(S)	The Songs Of Bob Nolan	1966	6.00	15.00
RCA Victor LPM-3714	(M)	Campfire Favorites	1967	4.00	10.00
RCA Victor LSP-3714	(S)	Campfire Favorites	1967	6.00	15.00
RCA Victor LSP-3964	(S)	South Of The Border	1968	6.00	15.00

— Original RCA albums above have black labels.—

Label & Catalog #		Title	Year	VG+	NM
SONS OF THE PURPLE SAGE					
Waldorf 143 (10")	(M)	Songs Of the Golden West	1955	16.00	40.00
SOPHOMORES, THE					
Seeco CELP-451	(M)	The Sophomores	195?	20.00	50.00
SOPWITH CAMEL, THE					
Kama Sutra KLP-8060	(M)	The Sopwith Camel	1967	12.00	30.00
Kama Sutra KLPS-8060	(S)	The Sopwith Camel	1967	14.00	35.00
Kama Sutra KSBS-2063	(S)	The Sopwith Camel In Hello, Hello	1973	10.00	25.00
Reprise MS-2108	(S)	The Miraculous Hump Returns	1973	8.00	20.00
SORKIN, DAN					
Mercury MG-20681	(M)	Folk Singing One	1963	5.00	12.00
Mercury SR-60681	(S)	Folk Singing One	1963	6.00	15.00
SORRELL, FRANK					
Coral CRL-57234	(M)	Frank Sorrell And His Four Guitars	1958	12.00	30.00
SOTHERN, ANN					
Craftsmen C-8061	(M)	It's Ann Sothern Time!	195?	12.00	30.00
SOUL, JIMMY					
S.P.Q.R. E-16001	(M)	If You Wanna Be Happy	1963	20.00	50.00
Spinorama 123	(M)	Jimmy Soul And The Belmonts	1963	8.00	20.00
SOUL SISTERS, THE					
Sue LP-1022	(M)	I Can't Stand It	1964	12.00	30.00
SOUL STIRRERS, THE					
The Stirrers lead singers included Sam Cooke and Johnny Taylor.					
Specialty SPS-2106	(M)	The Soul Stirrers Featuring Sam Cooke	1969	6.00	15.00
Specialty SPS-2116	(M)	The Gospel Soul Of Sam Cooke, Volume 1	1969	6.00	15.00
Specialty SPS-2128	(M)	The Gospel Soul Of Sam Cooke, Volume 2	1970	6.00	15.00
Specialty SPS-2137	(M)	The Original Soul Stirrers	1970	6.00	15.00
SOUL SURVIVORS, THE					
Crimson LP-502	(M)	When The Whistle Blows Anything Goes	1967	8.00	20.00
Crimson LP-502	(P)	When The Whistle Blows Anything Goes	1967	10.00	25.00
Atco SD-33-277	(S)	Take Another Look	1969	6.00	15.00
SOUP					
Arf Arm 1	(S)	Soup *(Insert cover)*	1970	60.00	120.00
Big Tree BTS-2007	(S)	The Soup Album	1971	8.00	20.00
SOUTH, JOE (& THE BELIEVERS)					
Refer to Billy Joe Royal.					
Capitol ST-108	(S)	Introspect *(Black label)*	1968	8.00	20.00
Capitol ST-108	(S)	Introspect	1969	4.00	10.00
Capitol ST-235	(S)	Games People Play	1969	4.00	10.00
Capitol ST-392	(S)	Don't It Make You Want To Go Home	1969	4.00	10.00
Capitol ST-450	(S)	Joe South's Greatest Hits	1970	4.00	10.00
Capitol ST-637	(S)	So The Seeds Are Growing	1971	4.00	10.00
Capitol ST-845	(S)	Joe South	1972	4.00	10.00
— Original Capitol albums above have green labels.—					
Capitol ST-1074	(S)	Look Inside	1972	4.00	10.00
Island ILPS-9328	(S)	Midnight Rainbows	1975	4.00	10.00
SOUTH 40					
Metrobeat MBS-1000	(S)	Live At The Someplace Else	1968	14.00	35.00
SOUTH PAW					
Bad Man RHBP-318	(S)	South Paw	1980	20.00	50.00
SOUTHERN, JERI					
Decca DL-5531 (10")	(M)	Intimate Songs	1954	20.00	50.00
Decca DL-8055	(M)	Southern Style	1955	16.00	40.00
Decca DL-8214	(M)	You Better Go Now	1956	16.00	40.00
Decca DL-8394	(M)	When Your Heart's On Fire	1957	16.00	40.00

Label & Catalog #		Title	Year	VG+	NM
Decca DL-8472	(M)	Jeri Gently Jumps	1957	16.00	40.00
Decca DL-8745	(M)	Prelude To A Kiss	1958	16.00	40.00
Decca DL-8761	(M)	Southern Hospitality	1958	16.00	40.00
Roulette R-52010	(M)	Southern Breeze	1958	12.00	30.00
Roulette SR-52010	(S)	Southern Breeze	1958	16.00	40.00
Roulette R-52016	(M)	Jeri Southern Meets Johnny Smith	1958	12.00	30.00
Roulette SR-52016	(S)	Jeri Southern Meets Johnny Smith	1958	16.00	40.00
Roulette R-52039	(M)	Coffee, Cigarettes And Memories	1958	12.00	30.00
Roulette SR-52039	(S)	Coffee, Cigarettes And Memories	1958	16.00	40.00
Capitol T-1173	(M)	Jeri Southern Meets Cole Porter	1959	8.00	20.00
Capitol ST-1173	(S)	Jeri Southern Meets Cole Porter	1959	12.00	30.00
Capitol T-1278	(M)	Jeri Southern At The Crescendo	1960	8.00	20.00
Capitol ST-1278	(S)	Jeri Southern At The Crescendo	1960	12.00	30.00

SOUTHWEST F.O.B.

Hip HIS-7001	(S)	Smell Of Incense	1969	12.00	30.00

SOVINE, RED

MGM E-3465	(M)	Red Sovine	1957	35.00	70.00
Starday SLP-132	(M)	The One And Only Red Sovine	1961	10.00	25.00
Starday SLP-197	(M)	The Golden Country Ballads Of The 1960s	1962	10.00	25.00
Decca DL-4445	(M)	Red Sovine	1964	8.00	20.00
Decca DL-74445	(S)	Red Sovine	1964	10.00	25.00
Decca DL-4736	(M)	Country Music Time	1966	6.00	15.00
Decca DL-74736	(S)	Country Music Time	1966	8.00	20.00
Starday SLP-341	(M)	Little Rosa	1966	6.00	15.00
Starday SLP-341	(S)	Little Rosa	1966	8.00	20.00
Starday SLP-363	(M)	Giddy-Up Go	1966	6.00	15.00
Starday SLP-363	(S)	Giddy-Up Go	1966	8.00	20.00
Starday SLP-383	(M)	Town And Country Action	1966	6.00	15.00
Starday SLP-383	(S)	Town And Country Action	1966	8.00	20.00
Starday SLP-396	(M)	The Nashville Sound Of Red Sovine	1967	6.00	15.00
Starday SLP-396	(S)	The Nashville Sound Of Red Sovine	1967	8.00	20.00
Starday SLP-405	(M)	I Didn't Jump The Fence	1967	6.00	15.00
Starday SLP-405	(S)	I Didn't Jump The Fence	1967	8.00	20.00
Starday SLP-414	(M)	Phantom 309	1967	6.00	15.00
Starday SLP-414	(S)	Phantom 309	1967	8.00	20.00

SOXX, BOBB B., & THE BLUE JEANS

Philles PHLP-4002	(DJ)	Zip A Dee Doo Dah (White label)	1963	300.00	500.00
Philles PHLP-4002	(M)	Zip A Dee Doo Dah	1963	150.00	250.00

SPACE

Hand 5167	(S)	Space	1969	10.00	25.00

SPACE ARK

Color World CW-1001	(S)	Space Ark	197?	6.00	15.00

SPACEMEN, THE

Roulette MG-25275	(M)	Rockin' In The 25th Century	1964	6.00	15.00
Roulette SR-25275	(S)	Rockin' In The 25th Century	1964	8.00	20.00
Roulette MG-25322	(M)	Music For Batman And Robin	1966	10.00	25.00
Roulette SR-25322	(S)	Music For Batman And Robin	1966	12.00	30.00

SPANDAU BALLET

Mobile Fidelity MFSL-152	(S)	True	198?	6.00	15.00

SPANIELS, THE

Vee Jay LP-1002	(M)	Goodnite, It's Time To Go (Maroon label)	1958	240.00	400.00
Vee Jay LP-1002	(M)	Goodnite, It's Time To Go (Black label)	1961	100.00	200.00
		(Reproductions of Vee Jay 1002 exist.)			
Vee Jay LP-1024	(M)	The Spaniels	1960	100.00	200.00
Upfront UPF-131	(M)	The Hits Of The Spaniels	196?	4.00	10.00
Lost-Nite LP-137	(M)	The Spaniels	196?	10.00	25.00
Solid Smoke 8028	(M)	Greatest Hits	1984	4.00	10.00

SPANKY & OUR GANG

Mercury MG-21124	(M)	Spanky And Our Gang	1967	4.00	10.00
Mercury SR-61124	(S)	Spanky And Our Gang	1967	5.00	12.00

Label & Catalog #		Title	Year	VG+	NM
Mercury SR-61161	(S)	**Like To Get To Know You**	1968	5.00	12.00
Mercury SR-61183	(S)	**Without Rhyme Or Reason**	1969	4.00	10.00
Mercury SR-61227	(S)	**Greatest Hits**	1969	4.00	10.00
Mercury SR-61326	(S)	**Live**	1971	4.00	10.00

SPANN, OTIS

Label & Catalog #		Title	Year	VG+	NM
Candid CJ-9001	(M)	**Otis Spann Is The Blues**	1960	50.00	100.00
BluesWay BL-6003	(M)	**The Blues Is Where It's At**	1967	10.00	25.00
BluesWay BLS-6003	(S)	**The Blues Is Where It's At**	1967	12.00	30.00
BluesWay BLS-6013	(S)	**The Bottom Of The Blues**	1968	10.00	25.00
Archive Of Folk Music 217	(S)	**Otis Spann**	1968	6.00	15.00
London PS-543	(S)	**Raw Blues**	1968	10.00	25.00
London PS-551	(S)	**Cracked Spanner Head**	1969	10.00	25.00
Prestige 7719	(S)	**The Blues Never Die**	1969	8.00	20.00
Vanguard VDS-6514	(S)	**Cryin' Time**	1970	8.00	20.00
Blues Time 9006	(S)	**Sweet Giant Of The Blues**	1970	5.00	12.00
Barnaby KZ-30246	(S)	**Otis Spann Is The Blues**	1970	5.00	12.00
Barnaby KZ-31290	(S)	**Walking The Blues**	1972	5.00	12.00
BluesWay BLS-6063	(S)	**Heart Loaded With Trouble**	1973	5.00	12.00

SPANN, OTIS, & FLEETWOOD MAC

Label & Catalog #		Title	Year	VG+	NM
Blue Horizon BH-66227	(S)	**Blues Jam At Chess**	1969	12.00	30.00
Blue Horizon BH-4802	(S)	**The Biggest Thing Since Colossus**	1970	14.00	35.00
Blue Horizon BH-4803	(S)	**Blues Jam In Chicago**	1970	10.00	25.00
Blue Horizon BH-4803	(S)	**Blues Jam In Chicago, Volume 2**	1970	6.00	15.00
Blue Horizon BH-3801	(S)	**Blues Jam In Chicago** (2 LPs)	1970	8.00	20.00
Sire SASH-3715	(S)	**Fleetwood Mac In Chicago** (2 LPs)	1975	6.00	15.00
Sire 2XS-6009	(S)	**Fleetwood Mac In Chicago** (2 LPs)	1977	5.00	12.00

SPARKS, RANDY

Randy originally recorded with The Back Porch Majority.

Label & Catalog #		Title	Year	VG+	NM
Verve V-2103	(M)	**Randy Sparks**	1959	10.00	25.00
Verve V-2126	(M)	**Walkin' The Low Road**	1960	10.00	25.00
Verve V-2143	(M)	**Randy Sparks Three**	1960	8.00	20.00
Verve VS-2143	(S)	**Randy Sparks Three**	1960	10.00	25.00
MGM SE-4769	(S)	**Hazy Sunshine**	1971	4.00	10.00

SPARROWS, THE

Label & Catalog #		Title	Year	VG+	NM
Elkay 3009	(M)	**The Mersey Sound**	1964	12.00	30.00

SPAT

Label & Catalog #		Title	Year	VG+	NM
ABC-Paramount 502	(M)	**Cookin' With The Spats**	1965	6.00	15.00
ABC-Paramount S-502	(S)	**Cookin' With The Spats**	1965	8.00	20.00

SPECTOR, PHIL

These albums are compilations; refer to "There Are Producers..." in the main introduction.

Label & Catalog #		Title	Year	VG+	NM
Philles PHLP-4004	(DJ)	**Today's Hits** (White label)	1963	300.00	500.00
Philles PHLP-4004	(M)	**Today's Hits**	1963	150.00	250.00
Philles PHLP-4005	(DJ)	**A Christmas Gift For You** (White label)	1963	300.00	500.00
Philles PHLP-4005	(M)	**A Christmas Gift For You** (Blue label)	1963	50.00	100.00
Philles PHLP-4005	(M)	**A Christmas Gift For You** (Yellow label)	1964	20.00	50.00
Apple SW-3400	(M)	**Phil Spector's Christmas Album**	1972	12.00	30.00
		(The Apple album bears a stereo prefix but plays mono.)			
Warner Bros. 9103	(S)	**Phil Spector's Christmas Album**	1975	8.00	20.00
		(The Warner album claims to be mono but plays stereo.)			
Warner Bros. 9104	(M)	**Phil Spector's 20 Greatest Hits** (2 LPs)	1977	10.00	25.00
Pavillion PZ-37686	(S)	**Phil Spector's Christmas Album**	1981	8.00	20.00
Passport PB-3604	(S)	**Phil Spector's Christmas Album**	1984	6.00	15.00

SPELLBINDERS, THE

Label & Catalog #		Title	Year	VG+	NM
Columbia CL-2514	(M)	**The Magic Of The Spellbinders**	1966	6.00	15.00
Columbia CS-9314	(S)	**The Magic Of The Spellbinders**	1966	8.00	20.00

SPENCE, ALEXANDER "SKIP"

Mr. Spence was formerly a member of The Jefferson Airplane; Moby Grape.

Label & Catalog #		Title	Year	VG+	NM
Columbia CS-9831	(S)	**Oar**	1969	20.00	50.00

SPIDERS, THE

Label & Catalog #		Title	Year	VG+	NM
Imperial LP-9140	(M)	**I Didn't Wanna Do It**	1961	180.00	300.00

Released in 1963 as *A Christmas Gift For You* on Philles, this album is considered along with *Elvis' Christmas Album* as the best rock 'n roll seasonal sets. Unlike Elvis' album, the Philles album was out of print between 1965 and 1972, when it reappeared as *Phil Spector's Christmas Album* on Apple. It has since been reissued on Warner Brothers, Pavillion and Passport.

Now, along with the title change, another, more interesting transformation took place: originally issued only in mono, the entire album turned up in true stereo on Warners despite the fact that Uncle Phil's photo on the cover has him sporting a "back to mono" button on his Santa suit (and the fact that Spector always denied the existence of stereo masters).

Collectors should note that while the Apple album bears a stereo prefix, the album plays mono and that both the Pavillion and Passport versions are in stereo.

Label & Catalog #					NM

SPIDERS FROM MARS, THE
The Spiders were formerly David
Pye 12125 (S) — 0 15.00

SPIFFYS, THE
R.I. 2597 (M) — 00 160.00

SPINNERS, THE
Time 52092 (M) — 00 20.00
Time S-2092 (S) — 00 25.00

SPINNERS, THE
Motown 639 (M) — .00 15.00
Motown 639 (S) — .00 20.00
V.I.P. 405 (S) — .00 15.00
Atlantic QD-7256 (Q) — .00 15.00
Atlantic QD-18118 (Q) — .00 15.00

SPIRAL STARECASE, THE
The Starecase was produced by
Columbia CS-9852 (S) — 5.00 12.00

SPIRIT

Label & Catalog #			Year		NM
Ode Z12-44004	(S)	Spirit		8.00	20.00
Ode Z12-44014	(S)	The Family That Plays Together	1968	8.00	20.00
Ode Z12-44016	(S)	Clear Spirit	1969	8.00	20.00
Epic KE-30267	(S)	Twelve Dreams Of Dr. Sardonicus	1970	6.00	15.00
Epic KE-31175	(S)	Feedback	1972	5.00	12.00
Epic KEG-31457	(S)	Spirit	1972	5.00	12.00
Epic KE-31461	(S)	The Family That Plays Together	1972	5.00	12.00

— Original Epic albums above have yellow labels with a oval logo on top.—

SPIRIT & WORM

A&M SP-4229	(S)	Spirit And Worm	1969	100.00	200.00

SPOKESMEN, THE

Decca DL-4712	(M)	Dawn Of Correction	1965	8.00	20.00
Decca DL-74712	(S)	Dawn Of Correction	1965	10.00	25.00

SPOOKY TOOTH

Bell 6019	(S)	Spooky Tooth	1968	6.00	15.00

SPOONER

Mountain Rail. 8005	(S)	Every Corner Dance	1982	5.00	12.00
Boat 1004	(S)	Wildest Dreams	1984	4.00	10.00

SPRING
Spring is Marilyn and Diane Rovell of The Honeys. Production by Brian Wilson.

United Arts. 5571	(S)	Spring (With insert)	1972	10.00	25.00

SPRINGFIELD, DUSTY
Ms. Springfield was originally a member of The Springfields. Refer to Led Zeppelin / Dusty Springfield.

Philips PHM-200133	(M)	Stay Awhile	1964	8.00	20.00
Philips PHS-600133	(S)	Stay Awhile	1964	12.00	30.00
Philips PHM-200156	(M)	Dusty	1964	8.00	20.00
Philips PHS-600156	(S)	Dusty	1964	12.00	30.00
Philips PHM-200174	(M)	Ooooooo Weeee!!!	1965	8.00	20.00
Philips PHS-600174	(S)	Ooooooo Weeee!!!	1965	12.00	30.00
Philips PHM-200210	(M)	You Don't Have To Say You Love Me	1966	8.00	20.00
Philips PHS-600210	(S)	You Don't Have To Say You Love Me	1966	12.00	30.00
Philips PHM-200220	(M)	Dusty Springfield's Golden Hits	1966	8.00	20.00
Philips PHS-600220	(P)	Golden Hits (With "Goin' Back")	1966	12.00	30.00
Philips PHS-600220	(P)	Golden Hits (Without "Goin' Back")	1967	6.00	15.00
Philips PHM-200256	(M)	The Look Of Love	1967	5.00	12.00
Philips PHS-600256	(S)	The Look Of Love	1967	8.00	20.00
Phillips PHM-200303	(M)	Everything's Coming Up Dusty	1967	6.00	15.00
Phillips PHS-600303	(S)	Everything's Coming Up Dusty	1967	8.00	20.00
Colgems COMO-5005	(M)	Casino Royale (Soundtrack)	1967	12.00	30.00
Colgems COSO-5005	(S)	Casino Royale (Soundtrack)	1967	75.00	150.00

Label & Catalog #		Title	Year	VG+	NM
United Arts. UAL-4158	(M)	**The Corrupt Ones** (Soundtrack)	1967	20.00	50.00
United Arts. UAS-5158	(S)	**The Corrupt Ones** (Soundtrack)	1967	30.00	60.00
20th Century TFS-4198	(S)	**The Sweet Ride** (Soundtrack)	1968	8.00	20.00

After being written off, Dusty Springfield journeyed to the confines of Chip Moman's American Sound Studios in Memphis, TN, and cut what many believe to be one of the finest albums of the decade.

Atlantic SD-8214	(S)	**Dusty In Memphis**	1969	6.00	15.00
Atlantic SD-8249	(S)	**A Brand New Me**	1970	6.00	15.00
Dunhill DSX-50128	(S)	**Cameo**	1973	5.00	12.00
United Arts. LA791	(S)	**It Begins Again**	1978	4.00	10.00
United Arts. LA936	(S)	**Living Without Your Love**	1979	4.00	10.00

SPRINGFIELDS, THE
Tom and Dusty Springfield.

Philips PHM-200052	(M)	**Silver Threads And Golden Needles**	1962	8.00	20.00
Philips PHS-600052	(S)	**Silver Threads And Golden Needles**	1962	12.00	30.00
Philips PHM-200076	(M)	**Folksongs From The Hills**	1963	8.00	20.00
Philips PHS-600076	(S)	**Folksongs From The Hills**	1963	12.00	30.00

SPRINGSTEEN, BRUCE (& THE E STREET BAND)

Columbia KC-31903	(DJ)	**Greetings From Asbury Park** (White label)	1973	20.00	50.00
Columbia KC-31903	(S)	**Greetings From Asbury Park**	1973	6.00	15.00
Columbia KC-32432	(DJ)	**Wild, The Innocent & The E Street Shuffle** (White label)	1973	20.00	50.00
Columbia KC-32432	(S)	**Wild, The Innocent & The E Street Shuffle** *(The title on the cover is in yellow print.)*	1973	6.00	15.00
Columbia PC-33795	(DJ)	**Born To Run** (White label) *(Promotional copy with the title in script on the cover.)*	1975	500.00	750.00
Columbia PC-33795	(DJ)	**Born To Run** (White label)	1975	20.00	50.00
Columbia PC-33795	(S)	**Born To Run** *(Jon Landau's name is misspelled as "John" on the back cover.)*	1975	6.00	15.00
Columbia PC-33795	(S)	**Born To Run** *(A strip with Landau's name is added to the back cover.)*	1975	6.00	15.00
Columbia PAL-35318	(DJ)	**Darkness On The Edge Of Town** *(Picture disc)*	1978	50.00	100.00
Columbia JC-35318	(DJ)	**Darkness On The Edge Of Town** *(White label)*	1978	20.00	50.00

Label & Catalog #		Title	Year	VG+	NM
Columbia HC-33795	(S)	**Born To Run** (Half-speed master)	1980	16.00	40.00
Columbia HC-43795	(S)	**Born To Run** (Half-speed master)	1981	12.00	30.00
Columbia HC-45318	(S)	**Darkness On The Edge Of Town** (Half-speed master)	1981	14.00	35.00
Columbia AS-978	(DJ)	**As Requested Around The World**	1981	14.00	35.00
Columbia FC-36854	(DJ)	**The River** (2 LPs. White label)	1984	20.00	50.00
		(Issued with a letter to radio programmers, priced separately below.)			
Columbia FC-36854		**The River CBS Letter**	1984	16.00	40.00

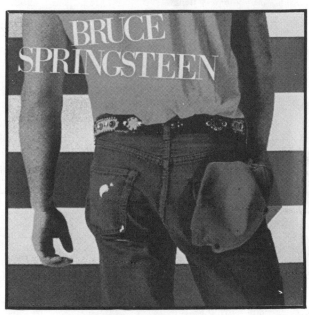

This contains five tracks, mainly previously uncollected b-sides. Check the label before purchase: second pressings, bearing the same catalog number and cover, are noted there.

Columbia AS-1957	(DJ)	**Born In The U.S.A.**	1985	14.00	35.00
Columbia AS-1957	(DJ)	**Born In The U.S.A.**	1987	8.00	20.00
		(Second pressings note so on the label.)			
Columbia QC-38358	(DJ)	**Nebraska** (White label)	1982	12.00	30.00
SPUR					
Cinema CSLP-1500	(M)	**Spur Of The Moment**	1969	35.00	70.00
SPYRO GYRA					
Nautilus NR-9	(S)	**Morning Dance**	197?	10.00	25.00
SQUIDDLY DIDDLY					
HBR HLP-2043	(M)	**Squiddly Diddly's Surfin' Surfari**	1965	16.00	40.00
HBR HST-2043	(S)	**Squiddly Diddly's Surfin' Surfari**	1965	20.00	50.00
SRC					
Capitol ST-2991	(S)	**SRC**	1968	16.00	40.00
Capitol ST-134	(S)	**Milestones**	1969	12.00	30.00
Capitol SKAO-273	(S)	**Travellers Tale**	1970	12.00	30.00
STACK					
Charisma CRS-303	(M)	**Above All**	1966	See note below	
		(Rare. Estimated near mint value $1,000-2,000.)			

Label & Catalog #		Title	Year	VG+	NM

STAFFORD, JO
Refer to Doris Day; Frank Sinatra; The Reprise Repertory Theatre.

Label & Catalog #		Title	Year	VG+	NM
Capitol H-75 (10")	(M)	American Folk Songs	1950	20.00	50.00
Capitol H-157 (10")	(M)	Kiss Me Kate (Studio Cast)	1950	35.00	70.00
Capitol H-9014 (10")	(M)	Songs Of Faith	1950	20.00	50.00
Capitol H-197 (10")	(M)	Autumn In New York	1950	20.00	50.00
Capitol H-247 (10")	(M)	Songs For Sunday Evening	1950	20.00	50.00
Capitol H-435 (10")	(M)	Starring Jo Stafford	1953	20.00	50.00
Capitol T-197	(M)	Autumn In New York	1955	14.00	35.00
Capitol T-428	(M)	Memory Songs	1955	14.00	35.00
Capitol T-435	(M)	Starring Jo Stafford	1955	14.00	35.00
Columbia CL-6210 (10")	(M)	As You Desire Me	1952	20.00	50.00
Columbia CL-6238 (10")	(M)	Broadway's Best	1953	20.00	50.00
Columbia CL-6274 (10")	(M)	My Heart's In The Highland	1954	20.00	50.00
Columbia CL-6286 (10")	(M)	Garden Of Prayers	1954	20.00	50.00
Columbia CL-2501 (10")	(M)	Soft And Sentimental	1955	16.00	40.00
Columbia CL-2591 (10")	(M)	A Gal Named Jo	1956	16.00	40.00
Columbia CL-2597 (10")	(M)	My Fair Lady (Studio Cast)	1956	35.00	70.00
Columbia CL-584	(M)	Broadway's Best	1954	12.00	30.00
Columbia CL-691	(M)	Happy Holiday	1955	12.00	30.00
Columbia CL-910	(M)	Ski Trails	1956	12.00	30.00
Columbia CL-968	(M)	Once Over Lightly	1957	12.00	30.00
Columbia CL-1043	(M)	Songs Of Scotland	1957	14.00	35.00
Columbia CL-1124	(M)	Swingin' Down Broadway	1958	14.00	35.00
Columbia CL-1228	(M)	Jo Stafford's Greatest Hits	1959	12.00	30.00
Columbia CL-1280	(M)	I'll Be Seeing You	1959	8.00	20.00
Columbia CS-8080	(S)	I'll Be Seeing You	1959	12.00	30.00
Columbia CL-1339	(M)	Ballad Of The Blues	1959	8.00	20.00
Columbia CS-8139	(S)	Ballad Of The Blues	1959	12.00	30.00
Columbia CL-1561	(M)	Jo + Jazz	1960	12.00	30.00
Columbia CS-8361	(S)	Jo + Jazz	1960	16.00	40.00

— Original Columbia albums above have three white "eye" logos on each side of the spindle hole.—

Label & Catalog #		Title	Year	VG+	NM
Capitol T-1653	(M)	American Folk Songs	1962	8.00	20.00
Capitol ST-1653	(S)	American Folk Songs	1962	10.00	25.00
Capitol T-1921	(M)	The Hits Of Jo Stafford	1963	8.00	20.00
Capitol ST-1921	(S)	The Hits Of Jo Stafford	1963	10.00	25.00
Capitol T-2069	(M)	Sweet Hour Of Prayer	1964	8.00	20.00
Capitol ST-2069	(S)	Sweet Hour Of Prayer	1964	10.00	25.00
Capitol T-2166	(M)	Joyful Season	1964	8.00	20.00
Capitol ST-2166	(S)	Joyful Season	1964	10.00	25.00
Reprise R-6090	(M)	Getting Sentimental Over Tommy Dorsey	1963	8.00	20.00
Reprise R9-6090	(S)	Getting Sentimental Over Tommy Dorsey	1963	10.00	25.00
Dot DLP-3673	(M)	Do I Hear A Waltz?	1966	6.00	15.00
Dot DLP-25673	(S)	Do I Hear A Waltz?	1966	8.00	20.00
Dot DLP-3745	(M)	This Is Jo Stafford	1966	6.00	15.00
Dot DLP-25745	(S)	This Is Jo Stafford	1966	8.00	20.00

STAFFORD, JO, & FRANKIE LAINE

Label & Catalog #		Title	Year	VG+	NM
Columbia CL-6268 (10")	(M)	New Orleans	1954	20.00	50.00
Columbia CL-2567 (10")	(M)	Guys And Dolls (Soundtrack)	1955	50.00	100.00
Columbia CL-2598 (10")	(M)	Mosy Happy Fella	1956	16.00	40.00
Columbia CL-578	(M)	New Orleans	1954	12.00	30.00

STAFFORD, JO, & GORDON McRAE

Label & Catalog #		Title	Year	VG+	NM
Capitol T-423	(M)	Memory Songs	1954	14.00	35.00
Capitol T-1696	(M)	Whispering Hope	1962	5.00	12.00
Capitol ST-1696	(S)	Whispering Hope	1962	6.00	15.00
Capitol T-1916	(M)	Peace In The Valley	1963	5.00	12.00
Capitol ST-1916	(S)	Peace In The Valley	1963	6.00	15.00

STAFFORD, TERRY

Label & Catalog #		Title	Year	VG+	NM
Crusader CLP-1001	(M)	Suspicion!	1964	14.00	35.00
Crusader CLP-1001S	(P)	Suspicion!	1964	16.00	40.00

STAINED GLASS

Label & Catalog #		Title	Year	VG+	NM
Capitol ST-154	(S)	Crazy Horse Roads	1969	8.00	20.00
Capitol ST-242	(S)	Aurora	1969	8.00	20.00

STAIRSTEPS, THE: *Refer to* **THE FIVE STAIRSTEPS & CUBIE**

Label & Catalog #		Title	Year	VG+	NM

Until recently a rather rare stereo album, a warehouse find turned up cases of Crusader CLP-1001S.

STALLINGS, MARY

Fantasy 3325	(M)	Cal Tjader Plays, Mary Stallings Sings	1961	8.00	20.00
Fantasy 8068	(S)	Cal Tjader Plays, Mary Stallings Sings	1961	12.00	30.00

STANDELLS, THE

Liberty LRP-3384	(M)	The Standells In Person At P.J.'s	1964	20.00	50.00
Liberty LST-7384	(S)	The Standells In Person At P.J.'s	1964	30.00	60.00
Sunset SUM-1186	(M)	Live And Out Of Sight	1966	10.00	25.00
Sunset SUS-5186	(S)	Live And Out Of Sight	1966	12.00	30.00
		(The Sunset album is a reissue of the Liberty album.)			
Tower T-5027	(M)	Dirty Water	1966	16.00	40.00
Tower ST-5027	(S)	Dirty Water	1966	20.00	50.00
Tower T-5044	(M)	Why Pick On Me	1966	16.00	40.00
Tower ST-5044	(S)	Why Pick On Me	1966	20.00	50.00
Tower T-5049	(M)	Hot Ones	1966	16.00	40.00
Tower ST-5049	(S)	Hot Ones	1966	20.00	50.00
Tower T-5098	(M)	Try It	1967	16.00	40.00
Tower ST-5098	(S)	Try It	1967	20.00	50.00

STANDLEY, JOHNNY

Capitol T-732	(M)	Comedy Caravan	1956	10.00	25.00

STANLEY, PAUL: Refer to KISS

STANLEY BROTHERS, THE

Mercury MG-20349	(M)	Country Pickin' And Singin'	1958	30.00	60.00
Starday SLP-106	(M)	Mountain Song Favorites	1959	16.00	40.00
Starday SLP-122	(M)	Sacred Songs Of The Hills	1960	16.00	40.00
King 615	(M)	The Stanley Brothers	1959	20.00	50.00
King 645	(M)	Hymns And Sacred Songs	1960	16.00	40.00
King 690	(M)	Everybody's Country Favorites	1961	16.00	40.00
King 698	(M)	For The Good People	1961	16.00	40.00
King 719	(M)	The Stanleys In Person	1961	16.00	40.00
King 750	(M)	Old Time Camp Meeting	1961	16.00	40.00
King 772	(M)	The Songs They Like Best	1961	16.00	40.00

Label & Catalog #		Title	Year	VG+	NM
King 791	(M)	**Award Winners**	1962	14.00	35.00
King 805	(M)	**Good Old Camp Meeting Songs**	1962	14.00	35.00
Vintage 002	(M)	**Live At Antioch College**	1961	20.00	50.00
Mercury MG-20884	(M)	**Hard Times**	1963	8.00	20.00
Mercury SR-60884	(S)	**Hard Times**	1963	10.00	25.00
Cabin Creek 203	(M)	**Bluegrass Gospel Favorites**	1966	16.00	40.00
STARCASTLE					
Epic PE-34935	(DJ)	**Citadel** (Picture disc)	1979	8.00	20.00
STRAFIRE					
Crimson S-4476/7	(S)	**Starfire**	1974	50.00	100.00
STARFIRES, THE					
Ohio Recording Serv. 34	(M)	**The Starfires Play**	1964	20.00	50.00
La Brea LS-8018	(M)	**Teenbeat A-Go-Go**	1965	20.00	50.00
STARK NAKED					
RCA Victor LSP-4592	(S)	**Stark Naked**	1971	10.00	25.00
STARR, EDWIN					
Gordy GS-931	(S)	**Soul Master**	1969	6.00	15.00
Gordy GS-940	(S)	**25 Miles**	1969	6.00	15.00
Gordy GS-948	(S)	**War And Peace**	1970	5.00	12.00
Gordy GS-956	(S)	**Involved**	1971	5.00	12.00
STARR, KAY					
Capitol H-211 (10")	(M)	**Songs By Starr**	1950	20.00	50.00
Capitol H-363 (10")	(M)	**Kay Starr Style**	1953	20.00	50.00
Capitol H-415 (10")	(M)	**The Hits Of Kay Starr**	1953	20.00	50.00
Capitol T-211	(M)	**Songs By Starr**	1955	14.00	35.00
Capitol T-363	(M)	**Kay Starr Style**	1955	14.00	35.00
Capitol T-415	(M)	**The Hits Of Kay Starr**	1955	14.00	35.00
Capitol T-580	(M)	**In A Blue Mood**	1955	14.00	35.00
		— Original Capitol albums above have turquoise labels.—			
Liberty LRP-9001	(M)	**Swingin' With The Starr**	1956	12.00	30.00
Modern 1203	(M)	**Singin' Kay Starr, Swingin' Erroll Garner**	1956	12.00	30.00
Rondo-Lette 3	(M)	**Them There Eyes**	1958	12.00	30.00
RCA Victor LPM-1149	(M)	**The One And Only Kay Starr**	1955	12.00	30.00
RCA Victor LPM-1549	(M)	**Blue Starr**	1957	12.00	30.00
RCA Victor LPM-1720	(M)	**Rockin' With Kay**	1958	20.00	50.00
RCA Victor LPM-2055	(M)	**I Hear The Word**	1959	8.00	20.00
RCA Victor LSP-2055	(S)	**I Hear The Word**	1959	12.00	30.00
		— Original RCA mono albums above have "black labels with Long Play" on the bottom;			
		stereo albums have have black labels with "Living Stereo" on the bottom.—			
Capitol T-1254	(M)	**Movin'**	1959	8.00	20.00
Capitol ST-1254	(S)	**Movin'**	1959	12.00	30.00
Capitol T-1303	(M)	**Losers, Weepers**	1960	8.00	20.00
Capitol ST-1303	(S)	**Losers, Weepers**	1960	12.00	30.00
Capitol T-1358	(M)	**One More Time**	1960	8.00	20.00
Capitol ST-1358	(S)	**One More Time**	1960	12.00	30.00
Capitol T-1374	(M)	**Movin' On Broadway**	1960	8.00	20.00
Capitol ST-1374	(S)	**Movin' On Broadway**	1960	12.00	30.00
Capitol T-1438	(M)	**Jazz Singer**	1960	8.00	20.00
Capitol ST-1438	(S)	**Jazz Singer**	1960	12.00	30.00
Capitol T-1468	(M)	**All Starr Hits**	1961	8.00	20.00
Capitol ST-1468	(S)	**All Starr Hits**	1961	10.00	25.00
Capitol T-1681	(M)	**I Cry By Night**	1962	8.00	20.00
Capitol ST-1681	(S)	**I Cry By Night**	1962	10.00	25.00
		— Original Capitol albums above have black labels with the logo on the left side.—			
Capitol T-1795	(M)	**Just Plain Country**	1962	6.00	15.00
Capitol ST-1795	(S)	**Just Plain Country**	1962	8.00	20.00
Capitol T-2106	(M)	**Fabulous Favorites**	1964	4.00	10.00
Capitol ST-2106	(S)	**Fabulous Favorites**	1964	5.00	12.00
Capitol T-2550	(M)	**Tears And Heartaches**	1966	4.00	10.00
Capitol ST-2550	(S)	**Tears And Heartaches**	1966	5.00	12.00
		— Original Capitol albums above have black labels with the logo on top.—			
ABC S-631	(S)	**When The Lights Go On Again**	1968	4.00	10.00
Paramount 5001	(S)	**How About This** (With Count Basie)	1969	4.00	10.00

Label & Catalog #		Title	Year	VG+	NM
STARR, RINGO					
Apple SMAS-3365	(S)	**Sentimental Journey**	1970	6.00	15.00
Apple SMAS-3368	(S)	**Beaucoups Of Blues**	1970	6.00	15.00
Apple SWAL-3413	(S)	**Ringo**	1973	6.00	15.00
Apple SWAL-3413	(S)	**Ringo**	1973	75.00	150.00
		(Contains 5:26 version of "Six O' Clock.")			
Apple SW-3417	(S)	**Goodnight Vienna**	1974	4.00	10.00
Apple SW-3422	(S)	**Blast From Your Past**	1975	4.00	10.00
Portrait JR-35378	(DJ)	**Bad Boy** *(White label)*	1978	6.00	15.00
Capitol SMAS-3365	(S)	**Sentimental Journey**	197?	10.00	25.00
Boardwalk NB1-33246	(S)	**Stop And Smell The Roses**	1981	4.00	10.00
STATLER BROTHERS, THE					
Columbia CL-2449	(M)	**Flowers On The Wall**	1966	6.00	15.00
Columbia CS-9249	(S)	**Flowers On The Wall**	1966	8.00	20.00
Columbia CL-2719	(M)	**The Big Hits**	1967	5.00	12.00
Columbia CS-9519	(S)	**The Big Hits**	1967	6.00	15.00
Columbia CS-9878	(S)	**Oh Happy Day**	1969	5.00	12.00
STATON, DAKOTA					
Capitol T-876	(M)	**The Late, Late Show**	1957	14.00	35.00
Capitol T-1003	(M)	**In The Night**	1958	14.00	35.00
		— Original Capitol albums above have turquoise labels.—			
Capitol T-1054	(M)	**Dynamic!**	1958	12.00	30.00
Capitol T-1170	(M)	**Crazy He Calls Me**	1958	12.00	30.00
Capitol T-1241	(M)	**Time To Swing**	1959	8.00	20.00
Capitol ST-1241	(S)	**Time To Swing**	1959	12.00	30.00
Capitol T-1325	(M)	**More Than The Most**	1959	8.00	20.00
Capitol ST-1325	(S)	**More Than The Most**	1959	12.00	30.00
Capitol T-1387	(M)	**Ballads And The Blues**	1959	8.00	20.00
Capitol ST-1387	(S)	**Ballads And The Blues**	1959	12.00	30.00
Capitol T-1427	(M)	**Softly**	1960	8.00	20.00
Capitol ST-1427	(S)	**Softly**	1960	12.00	30.00
Capitol T-1490	(M)	**Dakota**	1960	8.00	20.00
Capitol ST-1490	(S)	**Dakota**	1960	12.00	30.00
Capitol T-1597	(M)	**Round Midnight**	1960	8.00	20.00
Capitol ST-1597	(S)	**Round Midnight**	1960	12.00	30.00
Capitol T-1649	(M)	**Dakota At Storyville**	1961	8.00	20.00
Capitol ST-1649	(S)	**Dakota At Storyville**	1961	12.00	30.00
		— Original Capitol albums above have black labels with the logo on the left side.—			
United Arts. UAL-3292	(M)	**From Dakota With Love**	1963	6.00	15.00
United Arts. UAS-6292	(S)	**From Dakota With Love**	1963	8.00	20.00
United Arts. UAL-3312	(M)	**Live And Swinging**	1963	6.00	15.00
United Arts. UAS-6312	(S)	**Live And Swinging**	1963	8.00	20.00
United Arts. UAL-3355	(M)	**Dakota Staton With Strings**	1964	6.00	15.00
United Arts. UAS-6355	(S)	**Dakota Staton With Strings**	1964	8.00	20.00
STATUS QUO, THE					
Cadet Concept LPS-315	(E)	**Messages From The Status Quo**	1968	16.00	40.00
STEAM					
Mercury SR-61254	(S)	**Steam**	1969	6.00	15.00
STEAMHAMMER					
Steamhammer features Rod Stewart.					
Epic BN-26490	(S)	**Reflection**	1969	8.00	20.00
Epic BN-26552	(S)	**Steamhammer**	1970	8.00	20.00
STEELEYE SPAN					
Big Tree BTS-2004	(S)	**Please To See The King**	1971	8.00	20.00
Chrysalis CHR-1008	(S)	**Below The Salt**	1972	5.00	12.00
Chrysalis CHR-1046	(S)	**Parcel Of Rogues**	1973	5.00	12.00
Chrysalis CHR-1053	(S)	**Now We Are Six**	1974	5.00	12.00
Chrysalis CHR-1071	(S)	**Commoners Crown**	1975	5.00	12.00
Chrysalis CHR-1091	(S)	**All Around My Hat**	1975	5.00	12.00
Chrysalis CHR-1120	(S)	**Hark The Village Wait**	1976	5.00	12.00
Chrysalis CHR-1119	(S)	**Please To See The King**	1976	5.00	12.00
Chrysalis CHR-1121	(S)	**Ten Man Mop**	1976	5.00	12.00
Chrysalis CHR-1123	(S)	**Rocket Cottage**	1976	5.00	12.00

Label & Catalog #		Title	Year	VG+	NM
Chrysalis CHR-2-1136	(S)	The Steeleye Span Story (2 LPs)	1977	6.00	15.00
Chrysalis CHR-1151	(S)	Storm Force Ten	1978	4.00	10.00
Chrysalis CHR-1199	(S)	Live At Last	1978	4.00	10.00
Mobile Fidelity MFSL-027	(S)	All Around My Hat	1978	8.00	20.00

STEELY DAN

Command QD-40009	(Q)	Can't Buy A Thrill	1974	6.00	15.00
Command QD-40010	(Q)	Countdown To Ecstasy	1974	6.00	15.00
Command QD-40015	(Q)	Pretzel Logic	1974	6.00	15.00
Mobile Fidelity MFSL-007	(S)	Katy Lied	1978	35.00	70.00
Mobile Fidelity MFSL-033	(S)	Aja	1979	12.00	30.00

STEPHENS, LEIGH
Stevens was formerly a member of Blue Cheer.

Phillips PHS-600294	(S)	Red Weather	1969	12.00	30.00

STEPPENWOLF
Steepenwolf features John Kay.

Dunhill D-50029	(M)	Steppenwolf	1968	20.00	50.00
Dunhill DS-50029	(S)	Steppenwolf	1968	10.00	25.00
		(Label reads "A Subsidiary of ABC Records" on the bottom.)			
Dunhill D-50037	(M)	The Second	1968	See note below	
		(If it exists, estimated near mint value $100-200.)			
Dunhill DS-50037	(S)	The Second (Chrome border cover)	1968	8.00	20.00
Dunhill DS-50037	(S)	The Second (White border cover)	197?	12.00	30.00
ABC S-OC-9	(S)	Candy (Soundtrack)	1968	6.00	15.00

STEVENS, APRIL
Refer to Nino Tempo & April Stevens.

Audio Lab AL-1534	(M)	Torrid Tunes	1959	45.00	90.00
Imperial LP-9118	(M)	Teach Me Tiger	1960	16.00	40.00
Imperial LP-12055	(S)	Teach Me Tiger	1960	20.00	50.00

STEVENS, CAROL

Atlantic 1256	(M)	That Satin Doll	1957	14.00	35.00

STEVENS, CAT

Deram DE-18005	(M)	Matthew And Son	1967	6.00	15.00
Deram DES-18005	(E)	Matthew And Son	1967	5.00	12.00
Deram DES-18010	(S)	New Masters	1968	6.00	15.00
Deram DES-18005/10	(P)	Matthew And Son/New Masters (2 LPs)	1971	5.00	12.00
A&M QU-54280	(Q)	Tea For The Tillerman	1972	5.00	12.00
A&M QU-54313	(Q)	Teaser And The Firecat	1972	5.00	12.00
A&M QU-54365	(Q)	Catch Bull At Four	1972	5.00	12.00
A&M QU-54391	(Q)	Foreigner	1974	5.00	12.00
A&M QU-53623	(Q)	Buddha And The Chocolate Box	1974	5.00	12.00
A&M QU-54519	(Q)	Greatest Hits	1975	5.00	12.00
Mobile Fidelity MFSL-035	(S)	Tea For The Tillerman	1979	12.00	30.00
Mobile Fidelity MFQR-035	(S)	Tea For The Tillerman (UHQR in a box)	1984	20.00	50.00

STEVENS, CONNIE

Warner Bros. W-1208	(M)	Conchetta	1958	20.00	50.00
Warner Bros. W-1335	(M)	Hawaiian Eye (TV Soundtrack)	1959	20.00	50.00
Warner Bros. WS-1335	(S)	Hawaiian Eye (TV Soundtrack)	1959	35.00	70.00
Warner Bros. W-1382	(M)	Connie Stevens From "Hawaiian Eye"	1960	10.00	25.00
Warner Bros. WS-1382	(S)	Connie Stevens From "Hawaiian Eye"	1960	12.00	30.00
Warner Bros. W-1431	(M)	From Me To You	1962	10.00	25.00
Warner Bros. WS-1431	(S)	From Me To You	1962	12.00	30.00
Warner Bros. W-1432	(M)	Connie	1962	10.00	25.00
Warner Bros. WS-1432	(S)	Connie	1962	12.00	30.00
Warner Bros. W-1460	(M)	The Hank Williams Songbook	1962	10.00	25.00
Warner Bros. WS-1460	(S)	The Hank Williams Songbook	1962	12.00	30.00
Warner Bros. W-1519	(M)	Palm Springs Weekend (Soundtrack)	1963	20.00	50.00
Warner Bros. WS-1519	(S)	Palm Springs Weekend (Soundtrack)	1963	35.00	70.00
		—Original Warner albums above have grey labels.—			

STEVENS, DODIE

Dot DLP-3212	(M)	Dodie Stevens	1960	8.00	20.00
Dot DLP-25212	(S)	Dodie Stevens	1960	12.00	30.00

The quintessential studio group, Steely Dan consists primarily of writers/vocalists Donald Fagen and Walter Becker plus a plethora of studio musicians. While the quadraphonic pressings of their early albums have yet to set the market afire, the "Original Master Recording" of *Katy Lied* is among the most desirable of all audiophile pressings.

Label & Catalog #		Title	Year	VG+	NM
Dot DLP-3323	(M)	Over The Rainbow	1960	8.00	20.00
Dot DLP-25323	(S)	Over The Rainbow	1960	12.00	30.00
Dot DLP-3371	(M)	Pink Shoelaces	1961	8.00	20.00
Dot DLP-25371	(S)	Pink Shoelaces	1961	12.00	30.00

STEVENS, RAY
Ray also recorded as Baby Ray.

Mercury MG-20732	(M)	1,837 Seconds Of Humor	1962	16.00	40.00
Mercury SR-60732	(S)	1,837 Seconds Of Humor	1962	20.00	50.00
Mercury MG-20732	(M)	Ahab The Arab	1963	8.00	20.00
Mercury SR-60732	(S)	Ahab The Arab	1963	12.00	30.00
		(Repackage of "1,837 Seconds Of Humor.")			
Mercury MG-20028	(M)	This Is Ray Stevens	1963	6.00	15.00
Mercury SR-60028	(S)	This Is Ray Stevens	1963	8.00	20.00

STEWART, AL

Epic BN-26564	(S)	Love Chronicles	1970	6.00	15.00
Arista SP-40	(DJ)	The Live Radio Concert	1980	16.00	40.00
Mobile Fidelity MFSL-009	(S)	Year Of The Cat	1979	12.00	30.00
Mobile Fidelity MFSL-082	(S)	Time Passages	1981	8.00	20.00
Nautilus NR-34	(S)	24 Carrots	198?	6.00	15.00

STEWART, BILLY

Chess LP-1496	(M)	I Do Love You	1965	12.00	30.00
Chess LPS-1496	(S)	I Do Love You	1965	16.00	40.00
Chess LP-1499	(M)	Unbelievable	1965	12.00	30.00
Chess LPS-1499	(S)	Unbelievable	1965	16.00	40.00
Chess LP-1513	(M)	Teaches Old Standards New Tricks	1967	10.00	25.00
Chess LPS-1513	(S)	Teaches Old Standards New Tricks	1967	12.00	30.00
Chess LPS-1547	(S)	Billy Stewart Remembered	1968	12.00	30.00

STEWART, HELEYNE

Contemporary W3601	(M)	Love Moods	1961	12.00	30.00
Contemporary S7601	(S)	Love Moods	1961	16.00	40.00

STEWART, JOHN
Stewart was formerly a member of The Cumberland Three; The Kingston Trio.

Capitol T-2975	(M)	Signals Through The Glass	1968	8.00	20.00
Capitol ST-2975	(S)	Signals Through The Glass	1968	6.00	15.00
Capitol ST-203	(S)	California Bloodlines	1969	6.00	15.00
Capitol ST-540	(S)	Willard	1970	4.00	10.00

STEWART, RED

Audio Lab AL-1528	(M)	Favorite Old Songs	1959	35.00	70.00

STEWART, ROD
Refer to Steampacket; The Jeff Beck Group; The Small Faces.

Warner Bros. BSP-3276	(S)	Blondes Have More Fun *(Picture disc)*	1979	4.00	10.00
Warner Bros. 1-23473	(DJ)	Absolutely Live *(2 LPs. Quiex II vinyl)*	1982	8.00	20.00
Mobile Fidelity MFSL-054	(S)	Blondes Have More Fun	1981	8.00	20.00

STEWART, WYNN (& THE TOURISTS)

Wrangler W-1006	(M)	Wynn Stewart	1962	8.00	20.00
Wrangler WS-1006	(S)	Wynn Stewart	1962	12.00	30.00
Capitol T-2332	(M)	The Songs Of Wynn Stewart	1965	6.00	15.00
Capitol ST-2332	(S)	The Songs Of Wynn Stewart	1965	8.00	20.00
Capitol T-2737	(M)	It's Such A Pretty World Today	1967	6.00	15.00
Capitol ST-2737	(S)	It's Such A Pretty World Today	1967	8.00	20.00
Capitol ST-2849	(S)	Love's Gonna Happen To Me	1968	6.00	15.00
Capitol ST-2921	(S)	Something Pretty	1968	6.00	15.00

STEWART, WYNN, & JAN HOWARD

Challenge CHL-611	(M)	Sweethearts Of Country Music	1961	16.00	40.00

STIDHAM, ARBEE

Bluesville BV-1021	(M)	Tired Of Wandering	1961	20.00	50.00

STING

Mobile Fidelity MFSL-185	(S)	Dream Of The Blue Turtles	198?	8.00	20.00

Label & Catalog #		Title	Year	VG+	NM
STITES, GARY					
Carlton LP-120	(M)	**Lonely For You**	1960	20.00	50.00
Carlton STLP-120	(S)	**Lonely For You**	1960	35.00	70.00
STONE, CLIFFIE [CLIFFIE STONE'S HOMBRES]					
Capitol H-4009 (10")	(M)	**Square Dances**	1958	20.00	50.00
Capitol T-1080	(M)	**The Party's On Me**	1958	20.00	50.00
Capitol T-1230	(M)	**Cool Cowboy**	1959	12.00	30.00
Capitol ST-1230	(S)	**Cool Cowboy**	1959	16.00	40.00
Capitol T-1286	(M)	**Square Dance Promenade**	1960	8.00	20.00
Capitol ST-1286	(S)	**Square Dance Promenade**	1960	12.00	30.00
Capitol KAO-1555	(M)	**Original Cowboy Sing-A-Long**	1961	8.00	20.00
Capitol SKAO-1555	(S)	**Original Cowboy Sing-A-Long**	1961	12.00	30.00
— Original Capitol albums above have black labels with the logo on the left side.—					
Tower T-5073	(M)	**Together Again**	1967	5.00	12.00
Tower ST-5073	(S)	**Together Again**	1967	6.00	15.00
STONE, ROLAND					
Ace LP-1018	(M)	**Just A Moment**	1961	16.00	40.00
STONE COUNTRY					
RCA Victor LSP-3958	(S)	**Stone Country**	1968	20.00	50.00
STONE HARBOUR					
Stone Harbour 398	(S)	**Stone Harbour Emerges**	1974	360.00	600.00
STONE PONEYS: *Refer to* **LINDA RONSTADT & THE STONE PONEYS**					
STONEGROUND					
Stoneground features Sal Valentino of The Beau Brummels.					
Warner Bros. WS-1895	(S)	**Stoneground**	1971	6.00	15.00
Warner Bros. 2ZS-1956	(S)	**Family Album** *(2 LPs)*	1971	8.00	20.00
Warner Bros. BS-2645	(S)	**Stoneground 3**	1972	5.00	12.00
Flat Out 101	(S)	**Flat Out**	1976	8.00	20.00
Crystal Clear	(S)	**Play It Loud**	198?	6.00	15.00
STONEMANS, THE [THE STONEMAN FAMILY]					
World Pacific WP-1828	(M)	**Big Ball In Monterey**	1964	6.00	15.00
World Pacific ST-1828	(S)	**Big Ball In Monterey**	1964	8.00	20.00
Starday SLP-393	(M)	**White Lightning**	1965	8.00	20.00
MGM E-4363	(M)	**Those Singin,' Swingin,' Stompin,' Sensational Stonemans**	1966	5.00	12.00
MGM SE-4363	(S)	**Those Singin,' Swingin,' Stompin,' Sensational Stonemans**	1966	6.00	15.00
MGM E-4453	(M)	**Stoneman's Country**	1967	5.00	12.00
MGM SE-4453	(S)	**Stoneman's Country**	1967	6.00	15.00
MGM E-4511	(M)	**All In The Family**	1967	5.00	12.00
MGM SE-4511	(S)	**All In The Family**	1967	6.00	15.00
MGM SE-4578	(S)	**The Great Stonemans**	1968	5.00	12.00
MGM SE-4588	(S)	**Pop Stoneman Memorial Album**	1969	5.00	12.00
MGM SE-4613	(S)	**A Stoneman Christmas**	1968	5.00	12.00
MGM GAS-125	(S)	**The Stonemans**	1970	4.00	10.00
STOOGES, THE					
The Stooges feature Iggy Pop.					
Elektra EKS-74051	(S)	**The Stooges** *(Red label)*	1969	14.00	35.00
Elektra EKS-74051	(S)	**The Stooges** *(Butterfly label)*	197?	6.00	15.00
Elektra EKS-74701	(S)	**Fun House** *(Red label)*	1970	14.00	35.00
Elektra EKS-74701	(S)	**Fun House** *(Butterfly label)*	197?	6.00	15.00
Columbia KC-32111	(S)	**Raw Power** *(With inner sleeve)*	1973	12.00	30.00
STORM, BILLY (& THE VALIANTS)					
Buena Vista BV-3315	(M)	**Billy Storm**	1963	50.00	100.00
Famous F-504	(M)	**This Is The Night**	1969	12.00	30.00
STORM, GALE					
Dot DLP-3011	(M)	**Gale Storm**	1956	12.00	30.00
Dot DLP-3017	(M)	**Sentimental Me**	1956	12.00	30.00
Dot DLP-3098	(M)	**Gale Storm Hits**	1958	12.00	30.00

Label & Catalog #		Title	Year	VG+	NM
Dot DLP-3197	(M)	Softly And Tenderly	1959	8.00	20.00
Dot DLP-25197	(S)	Softly And Tenderly	1959	12.00	30.00
Dot DLP-3209	(M)	Gale Storm Sings	1959	8.00	20.00
Dot DLP-25209	(S)	Gale Storm Sings	1959	12.00	30.00

STOWAWAYS, THE

Justice SLP-	(S)	The Stowaways	196?	300.00	500.00

STRACKE, WIN

Bally 12013	(M)	Americana	195?	10.00	25.00
Golden GLP-31	(M)	Golden Treasury Of Songs	195?	10.00	25.00

STRANGE

Outer Galaxie 1000	(S)	Translucent World	1973	16.00	40.00
Outer Galaxie 1001	(S)	Raw Power	1976	12.00	30.00
Star People 0013	(S)	High Flyer (Colored vinyl)	1981	8.00	20.00

STRANGELOVES, THE

Bang BLP-211	(M)	I Want Candy	1965	20.00	50.00
Bang BLPS-211	(S)	I Want Candy	1965	40.00	80.00

STRAWBERRY ALARM CLOCK, THE
Refer to The Who / The Strawberry Alarm Clock.

Uni 3014	(M)	Incense And Peppermints	1967	12.00	30.00
Uni 73014	(S)	Incense And Peppermints	1967	16.00	40.00
Uni 3025	(M)	Wake Up It's Tomorrow	1967	8.00	20.00
Uni 73025	(S)	Wake Up It's Tomorrow	1967	10.00	25.00
Uni 73035	(S)	The World In A Sea Shell	1968	8.00	20.00
Uni 73054	(S)	Good Morning Starshine	1969	8.00	20.00
Uni 73074	(S)	The Best Of The Strawberry Alarm Clock	1970	8.00	20.00
20th Century TFS-4211	(S)	Beyond The Valley Of The Dolls (Sdtk)	1970	20.00	50.00
Vocalion 73915	(S)	Changes	1971	6.00	15.00

STRAY

Transatlantic TRA-216	(S)	Stray	197?	12.00	30.00
Mercury SRM-1-611	(S)	Suicide	1971	6.00	15.00
Mercury SRM-1-624	(S)	Saturday Morning Pictures	1971	6.00	15.00

STRAYWINDS

Shamyn-Alexus 413504	(S)	Straywinds	1973	45.00	90.00

STREISAND, BARBRA

Columbia OS-2210	(M)	Pins And Needles (Soundtrack)	1962	10.00	25.00
Columbia KOL-5780	(M)	I Can Get It For You Wholesale (Soundtrack)	1962	8.00	20.00
Columbia KOS-2180	(S)	I Can Get It For You Wholesale (Soundtrack)	1962	10.00	25.00
Columbia CL-2007	(M)	The Barbra Streisand Album	1963	5.00	12.00
Columbia CS-8807	(S)	The Barbra Streisand Album	1963	6.00	15.00
Columbia CL-2054	(DJ)	Second Album (Mono. Blue vinyl)	1963	35.00	70.00
Columbia CS-8854	(DJ)	Second Album (Stereo. Blue vinyl)	1963	50.00	100.00
Columbia CL-2054	(M)	Second Barbra Streisand Album	1963	5.00	12.00
Columbia CS-8854	(S)	Second Barbra Streisand Album	1963	6.00	15.00
Columbia CL-2154	(M)	The Third Barbra Streisand Album	1964	5.00	12.00
Columbia CS-8954	(S)	The Third Barbra Streisand Album	1964	6.00	15.00
Capitol VAS-2059	(M)	Funny Girl (Soundtrack)	1964	8.00	20.00
Capitol SVAS-2059	(S)	Funny Girl (Soundtrack)	1964	10.00	25.00
Columbia CL-2215	(M)	People	1964	5.00	12.00
Columbia CS-9015	(S)	People	1964	6.00	15.00
Columbia CL-2336	(M)	My Name Is Barbra	1965	5.00	12.00
Columbia CS-9136	(S)	My Name Is Barbra	1965	6.00	15.00
Columbia CL-2409	(M)	My Name Is Barbra, Two	1965	5.00	12.00
Columbia CS-9209	(S)	My Name Is Barbra, Two	1965	6.00	15.00
Columbia CL-2478	(DJ)	Color Me Barbra (Mono. Red vinyl)	1966	35.00	70.00
Columbia CS-9278	(DJ)	Color Me Barbra (Stereo. Red vinyl)	1966	50.00	100.00
Columbia CL-2478	(M)	Color Me Barbra	1966	5.00	12.00
Columbia CS-9278	(S)	Color Me Barbra	1966	6.00	15.00
Columbia CL-2547	(M)	Je M'appelle Barbra	1966	5.00	12.00
Columbia CS-9347	(S)	Je M'appelle Barbra	1966	6.00	15.00
Columbia CL-2682	(M)	Simply Streisand	1967	5.00	12.00
Columbia CS-9482	(S)	Simply Streisand	1967	6.00	15.00

For many, "Incense And Peppermints" remains a classic psychedelic single, a bravura display of the hippie accoutrements associated with consciousness expansion by the uninitiated. The group's albums are all collectible, although the first appears on everyone's want list. Their soundtrack work included several tracks for *Beyond The Valley Of The Dolls* (screenplay by Roger Ebert), a unique cinematic achievement that needs to be seen by every film fan with a penchant for the well turned cliche...

Label & Catalog #		Title	Year	VG+	NM
Columbia CL-2757	(M)	**Barbra's Christmas Album**	1967	5.00	12.00
Columbia CS-9557	(S)	**Barbra's Christmas Album**	1967	6.00	15.00
Columbia BOS-3220	(S)	**Funny Girl** (Soundtrack)	1968	6.00	15.00
Columbia CS-9710	(S)	**A Happening In Central Park**	1968	4.00	10.00
Columbia CS-9816	(S)	**What About Today?**	1969	4.00	10.00
Columbia CS-9968	(S)	**Barbra Streisand's Greatest Hits**	1970	4.00	10.00
— Original Columbia albums above have "360 Sound" on the bottom of the label.—					
Columbia PCQ-30378	(Q)	**Stoney End**	1971	6.00	15.00
Columbia PCQ-30792	(Q)	**Barbra Joan Streisand**	1971	6.00	15.00
Columbia SQ-30992	(Q)	**Funny Girl** (Soundtrack)	1972	6.00	15.00
Columbia PCQ-31760	(Q)	**Live In Concert At The Forum**	1972	6.00	15.00
Columbia PCQ-32801	(Q)	**The Way We Were**	1974	6.00	15.00
Columbia PCQ-33005	(Q)	**Butterfly**	1974	6.00	15.00
Columbia PCQ-33815	(Q)	**Lazy Afternoon**	1975	6.00	15.00
Arista AQ-9004	(Q)	**Funny Lady** (Soundtrack)	1975	8.00	20.00
Columbia HC-42801	(S)	**The Way We Were** (Half-speed master)	1982	12.00	30.00
Columbia HC-45679	(S)	**Greatest Hits, Vol. 2** (Half-speed master)	1982	10.00	25.00
Columbia HC-46750	(S)	**Guilty** (Half-speed master)	1982	8.00	20.00
Columbia HC-47678	(S)	**Memories** (Half-speed master)	1982	12.00	30.00

Ms. Streisand saw four of her albums receive the half-speed mastering process from Columbia, of which "Memories" is both the rarest and the most sought-after.

Columbia S-30410	(S)	**The Owl And The Pussycat** (Soundtrack)	1970	6.00	15.00
Columbia AS-1779	(DJ)	**The Legend Of Barbra Streisand** (2 LPs)	1983	12.00	30.00
Columbia AS-99-1891	(DJ)	**Yentl** (Picture disc)	1983	6.00	15.00
Columbia 9C9-39909	(S)	**Emotion** (Picture disc)	1985	4.00	10.00

STRIDER

Warner Bros. BS-2722	(S)	**Exposed**	1973	6.00	15.00

STRIDERS, THE

Apollo 480	(M)	**Hesitating Fool**	1955	100.00	200.00

STRINGBEAN

Starday SLP-142	(M)	**Old Time Pickin' And Singin'**	1961	20.00	50.00
Starday SLP-179	(M)	**Stringbean**	1962	16.00	40.00

Label & Catalog #		Title	Year	VG+	NM
Starday SLP-215	(M)	A Salute To Uncle Dave Macon	1963	16.00	40.00
Starday SLP-260	(M)	Way Back In The Hills Of Old Kentucky	1964	14.00	35.00
STROKE BAND, THE					
Abacus 78-095	(S)	Green And Yellow	1978	75.00	150.00
STRONG, NOLAN, & THE DIABLOS					
Fortune LP-8010	(M)	Fortune Of Hits	1961	50.00	100.00
Fortune LP-8012	(M)	Fortune Of Hits, Volume 2	1962	50.00	100.00
Fortune LP-8015	(M)	Mind Over Matter	1963	50.00	100.00
STYX					
A&M SP-8431	(DJ)	The Styx Radio Special (2 LPs)	1977	10.00	25.00
A&M SP-17053	(DJ)	The Styx Radio Special (3 LP box)	1978	16.00	40.00
A&M SP-17222	(DJ)	The Styx Radio Sampler (2 LPs)	1978	10.00	25.00
Mobile Fidelity MFSL-026	(S)	The Grand Illusion	1978	10.00	25.00
Nautilus NR-15	(S)	Pieces Of Eight	198?	6.00	15.00
Nautilus NR-45	(S)	Paradise Theatre	198?	6.00	15.00
Nautilus NR-27	(S)	Cornerstone	198?	6.00	15.00
SUB-ZERO BAND, THE					
Sub-Zero 1172	(S)	The Sub-Zero Band	197?	75.00	150.00
SUGAR BEARS, THE					
The Bears feature Kim Carnes.					
Big Tree BTS-2009	(S)	Introducing The Sugar Bears	1971	8.00	20.00
SUGARLOAF					
Sugarloaf features Jerry Corbetta, later of The Four Seasons.					
Liberty LST-7640	(S)	Sugarloaf	1970	6.00	15.00
Liberty LST-11010	(S)	Spaceship Earth	1971	5.00	12.00
SULLIVAN, MAXINE					
Period 1909	(M)	Maxine Sullivan	1955	20.00	50.00
Period 1207	(M)	Maxine Sullivan, Volume 2	1956	20.00	50.00
Jazztone 1229	(M)	Flow Gently, Sweet Rhythm	1956	20.00	50.00
Bethlehem 67	(M)	The Complete Charlie Shavers With Maxine Sullivan	1957	20.00	50.00
SULLIVAN, ROCKY (WITH JOHN CIPPOLINA)					
Jupiter 2006	(S)	Illegal Entry	1980	10.00	25.00
Rag Baby 1021	(S)	Caught In The Crossfire	1984	6.00	15.00
SUMMER, DONNA					
Casablanca 7119	(S)	Best Of "Live & More" (Picture disc)	1979	4.00	10.00
Geffen GHS-24040	(DJ)	Cats Without Claws (Quiex II vinyl)	1984	5.00	12.00
SUMMER SOUNDS					
No label	(S)	Summer Sounds	197?	300.00	500.00
SUNDOG SUMMIT					
No label	(S)	On Summit Hill	1976	50.00	100.00
SUNDOWNERS, THE					
Liberty LRP-3269	(M)	Folk Songs For The Rich	1962	5.00	12.00
Liberty LST-7269	(S)	Folk Songs For The Rich	1962	6.00	15.00
Decca DL-75036	(S)	Captain Nemo	1968	6.00	15.00
SUNGLOWS, THE					
Sunglow SLP-103	(M)	The Original Peanuts	1965	20.00	50.00
SUNNY & THE SUNLINERS					
Tear Drop 2000	(M)	Talk To Me/Rags To Riches	1963	30.00	60.00
Tear Drop 2019	(M)	All Night Worker	1964	20.00	50.00
SUNNYLAND SLIM					
Bluesville BV-1016	(M)	Slim's Shout	1961	20.00	50.00
Prestige 7723	(S)	Slim's Shout	1969	6.00	15.00
World Pacific WPS-21890	(S)	Slim's Got His Thing Goin' On	1969	8.00	20.00

Label & Catalog #		Title	Year	VG+	NM
Blue Horizon BM-4608	(M)	**Blues Masters, Volume 8**	*197?*	**5.00**	**12.00**
BluesWay BLS-6068	(S)	**Ragtime Blues**	*1973*	**5.00**	**12.00**

Believe-It-Or-Not Dept: The Sunrays were Murry Wilson's (father of Brian, Dennis and Carl)
attempt to get even with his offspring. Believing that he was the genius behind the success
of The Beach Boys, Murry blew a gasket when his sons fired him as manager and immediately
brought The Sunrays to Capitol as "the new Beach Boys." They were signed to Capitol's
Tower subsidiary and Murry produced two decent hits for them...

SUNRAYS, THE
Tower T-5017	(M)	**Andrea**	*1966*	**10.00**	**25.00**
Tower ST-5017	(S)	**Andrea**	*1966*	**16.00**	**40.00**

SUNSET SURF, THE
Capitol T-1915	(M)	**The Sunset Surf**	*1963*	**6.00**	**15.00**
Capitol ST-1915	(S)	**The Sunset Surf**	*1963*	**8.00**	**20.00**

SUNSETS, THE
Palace 752	(M)	**Surfing With The Sunsets**	*1963*	**12.00**	**30.00**

SUNSHINE COMPANY, THE
Imperial LP-9359	(M)	**Happy Is The Sunshine Company**	*1967*	**5.00**	**12.00**
Imperial LP-12359	(S)	**Happy Is The Sunshine Company**	*1967*	**6.00**	**15.00**
Imperial LP-12368	(S)	**The Sunshine Company**	*1968*	**4.00**	**10.00**
Imperial LP-12399	(S)	**Sunshine And Shadows**	*1968*	**4.00**	**10.00**

SUPERFINE DANDELION
Mainstream 56102	(M)	**Superfine Dandelion**	*1967*	**5.00**	**12.00**
Mainstream S-6102	(S)	**Superfine Dandelion**	*1967*	**6.00**	**15.00**

SUPERSTOCKS, THE
The Superstocks are a creation of Gary Usher & Co.
Capitol T-1997	(M)	**Hot Rod Rally**	*1964*	**12.00**	**30.00**
Capitol ST-1997	(S)	**Hot Rod Rally**	*1964*	**16.00**	**40.00**
		(A various artists album with half the tracks by The Superstocks.)			
Capitol T-2060	(M)	**Thunder Road**	*1964*	**50.00**	**100.00**
Capitol ST-2060	(S)	**Thunder Road**	*1964*	**75.00**	**150.00**

Label & Catalog #		Title	Year	VG+	NM
Capitol T-2113	(M)	**Surf Route 101**	1964	60.00	120.00
Capitol ST-2113	(S)	**Surf Route 101**	1964	85.00	170.00
		(Issued with a Mr. Gasser bonus single by in a pocket on the cover.)			
Capitol T-2113	(M)	**Surf Route 101** *(Without the single)*	1964	50.00	100.00
Capitol ST-2113	(S)	**Surf Route 101** *(Without the single)*	1964	75.00	150.00
Capitol T-2190	(M)	**School Is A Drag**	1964	50.00	100.00
Capitol ST-2190	(S)	**School Is A Drag**	1964	75.00	150.00
SUPERSISTER					
Dwarf PDLP-2001	(S)	**Supersister**	197?	8.00	20.00
SUPERTRAMP					
A&M SP-3730	(S)	**Breakfast In America** *(Picture disc)*	1979	180.00	300.00
Mobile Fidelity MFSL-005	(S)	**Crime Of The Century**	1979	14.00	35.00
Mobile Fidelity MFSL-045	(S)	**Breakfast In America**	1980	10.00	25.00
Mobile Fidelity MFQR--005	(S)	**Crime Of The Century** *(UHQR in a box)*	1983	50.00	100.00
Sweet Thunder 5	(S)	**Even In The Quietest Moments** *(Half-speed)*	198?	8.00	20.00
SUPREMES, THE [DIANA ROSS & THE SUPREMES]					
Original members include Florence Ballard, Diana Ross and Mary Wilson.					
Motown M-606	(M)	**Meet The Supremes**	1964	300.00	500.00
		(The cover features the group seated on stools.)			
Motown M-606	(M)	**Meet The Supremes**	1964	8.00	20.00
Motown S-606	(S)	**Meet The Supremes**	1964	12.00	30.00
		(The cover features a close-up of the group.)			
Motown M-621	(M)	**Where Did Our Love Go**	1964	8.00	20.00
Motown S-621	(S)	**Where Did Our Love Go**	1964	12.00	30.00
Motown M-623	(M)	**A Bit Of Liverpool**	1964	14.00	35.00
Motown S-623	(S)	**A Bit Of Liverpool**	1964	20.00	50.00
Motown M-625	(M)	**Country, Western And Pop**	1965	8.00	20.00
Motown S-625	(S)	**Country, Western And Pop**	1965	12.00	30.00
Motown M-627	(M)	**More Hits By The Supremes**	1965	6.00	15.00
Motown S-627	(S)	**More Hits By The Supremes**	1965	8.00	20.00
Motown M-629	(M)	**We Remember Sam Cooke**	1965	8.00	20.00
Motown S-629	(S)	**We Remember Sam Cooke**	1965	12.00	30.00
Motown M-636	(M)	**The Supremes At The Copa**	1965	6.00	15.00
Motown S-636	(S)	**The Supremes At The Copa**	1965	8.00	20.00
Motown M-638	(M)	**Merry Christmas**	1965	8.00	20.00
Motown S-638	(S)	**Merry Christmas**	1965	10.00	25.00
Motown M-643	(M)	**I Hear A Symphony**	1966	6.00	15.00
Motown S-643	(S)	**I Hear A Symphony**	1966	8.00	20.00
Motown M-649	(M)	**Supremes A' Go-Go**	1966	6.00	15.00
Motown S-649	(S)	**Supremes A' Go-Go**	1966	8.00	20.00
Motown M-650	(M)	**Holland-Dozier-Holland**	1967	8.00	20.00
Motown S-650	(S)	**Holland-Dozier-Holland**	1967	12.00	30.00
Motown M-659	(M)	**The Supremes Sing Rodgers And Hart**	1967	8.00	20.00
Motown S-659	(S)	**The Supremes Sing Rodgers And Hart**	1967	12.00	30.00
Motown M-663	(M)	**Greatest Hits** *(With poster)*	1967	6.00	15.00
Motown S-663	(S)	**Greatest Hits** *(With poster)*	1967	8.00	20.00
Motown M-663	(M)	**Greatest Hits** *(Without poster)*	1967	10.00	25.00
Motown S-663	(S)	**Greatest Hits** *(Without poster)*	1967	12.00	30.00
Motown M-665	(M)	**Reflections**	1968	12.00	30.00
Motown S-665	(S)	**Reflections**	1968	6.00	15.00
Motown S-676	(S)	**Live At London's Talk Of The Town**	1968	6.00	15.00
Motown S-672	(S)	**Funny Girl**	1968	5.00	12.00
Motown S-670	(S)	**Love Child**	1968	5.00	12.00
Motown S-682	(S)	**TCB**	1968	5.00	12.00
Motown S-689	(S)	**Let The Sunshine In**	1969	6.00	15.00
Motown S-694	(S)	**Cream Of The Crop**	1969	5.00	12.00
Motown S-699	(S)	**On Broadway**	1969	5.00	12.00
— *Original Motown albums above have the company's Detroit, MI, address on the bottom of the label* —					
Motown PR-102	(DJ)	**Touch Interview**	1971	10.00	25.00
Motown S-794	(DJ)	**Anthology 1962-1969** *(3 LPs)*	1974	16.00	40.00
Motown S-794	(S)	**Anthology 1962-1969** *(3 LPs)*	1974	5.00	12.00
SURF SIDE FIVE, THE					
Intermountain 153	(M)	**Recorded Live**	196?	75.00	150.00

Label & Catalog #		Title	Year	VG+	NM
SURF STOMPERS, THE					
Del-Fi DFLP-1236	(M)	**The Original Surfer Stomp**	1963	37.50	75.00
Del-Fi DFST-1236	(S)	**The Original Surfer Stomp**	1963	50.00	100.00
		(This is a reissue of The Bruce Johnston Surfing Band album.)			
SURF TEENS, THE					
Sutton SU-339	(M)	**Surf Mania**	196?	8.00	20.00
Sutton SSU-339	(S)	**Surf Mania**	196?	10.00	25.00
SURFARIS, THE					
The final two Decca albums, 4614 and 4683, are essentially Gary Usher & Co. with vocalist Ron Wilson.					
Dot DLP-3535	(M)	**Wipe Out**	1963	16.00	40.00
Dot DLP-25535	(S)	**Wipe Out**	1963	20.00	50.00
		(The back cover of first pressings has a photo with five members.)			
Dot DLP-3535	(M)	**Wipe Out**	1963	14.00	35.00
Dot DLP-25535	(S)	**Wipe Out**	1963	16.00	40.00
		(The back cover has a photo with four members.)			
Dot DLP-3535	(M)	**Wipe Out**	1964	10.00	25.00
Dot DLP-25535	(S)	**Wipe Out**	1964	12.00	30.00
		(The back cover does not have a photo of the group at all.)			
Decca DL-4470	(M)	**The Surfaris Play Wipe Out**	1963	14.00	35.00
Decca DL-74470	(S)	**The Surfaris Play Wipe Out**	1963	20.00	50.00
Decca DL-4487	(M)	**Hit City '64**	1964	14.00	35.00
Decca DL-74487	(S)	**Hit City '64**	1964	20.00	50.00
Decca DL-4560	(M)	**Fun City, U.S.A.**	1964	20.00	50.00
Decca DL-74560	(S)	**Fun City, U.S.A.**	1964	30.00	60.00
Decca DL-4614	(M)	**Hit City '65**	1965	20.00	50.00
Decca DL-74614	(S)	**Hit City '65**	1965	30.00	60.00
Decca DL-4683	(M)	**It Ain't Me, Babe**	1965	16.00	40.00
Decca DL-74683	(S)	**It Ain't Me, Babe**	1965	20.00	50.00

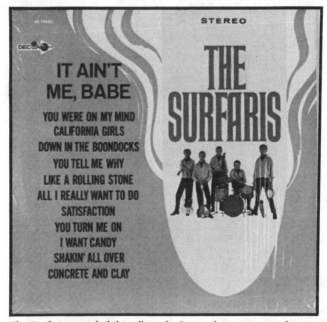

By the time The Surfaris recorded this album for Decca, they were a studio group headed by Gary Usher and featuring one lone original member, lead singer Ron Wilson.

SURFRIDERS, THE					
Vault V-105	(M)	**Surfbeat, Volume 2**	1963	10.00	25.00
Vault VS-105	(S)	**Surfbeat, Volume 2**	1963	12.00	30.00

Label & Catalog #		Title	Year	VG+	NM
SURFSIDERS, THE					
Design DLP-208	(M)	The Beach Boy's Songbook	1965	5.00	12.00
Design DLPS-208	(S)	The Beach Boy's Songbook	1965	6.00	15.00
SURPRISE					
No label	(S)	Assault On Merryland (With booklet)	197?	45.00	90.00
SURPRISE PACKAGE					
L.H.I. S-12005	(S)	Free Up	1968	10.00	25.00
SWAMP DOGG					
Canyon LP-7706	(S)	Total Destruction To Your Mind	1970	10.00	25.00
Elektra EKS-74089	(S)	Rat On	1971	6.00	15.00
Cream 9009	(S)	Cuffed, Collared And Tagged	1972	5.00	12.00
Musicor MUS-2504	(S)	Finally Caught Up With Myself	197?	5.00	12.00
SWAMPWATER					
King 1122	(S)	Swampwater	1970	6.00	15.00
RCA Victor LSP-4572	(S)	Swampwater	1971	5.00	12.00
SWANN, BETTYE					
Money 1103	(M)	Make Me Yours	1967	6.00	15.00
Money S-1103	(S)	Make Me Yours	1967	8.00	20.00
SWEET, THE					
Bell ST-1124	(S)	Sweet	1973	10.00	25.00
Capitol ST-11395	(S)	Desolation Boulevard	1975	6.00	15.00
Capitol ST-11496	(S)	Give Us A Wink	1976	6.00	15.00
Capitol SPRO-8849	(DJ)	Short And Sweet	1978	12.00	30.00
Capitol PRO-11929	(DJ)	Cut Above The Rest	1979	30.00	60.00
		(Box contains LP, cassette, 8-track, photo and biography.)			
SWEET INSPIRATIONS, THE					
Atlantic SD-8155	(S)	The Sweet Inspirations	1968	6.00	15.00
Atlantic SD-8201	(S)	What The World Needs Now Is Love	1969	6.00	15.00
Atlantic SD-8225	(S)	Sweets For My Sweet	1969	6.00	15.00
Atlantic SD-8253	(S)	Sweet, Sweet Soul	1970	6.00	15.00
SWEET PANTS					
Barkley LP-1141	(S)	Fat Peter Presents Sweet Pants	1972	150.00	250.00
SWEET SUE & HER SOCIETY SYNCOPATERS					
The Society Syncopaters were the group featuring Marilyn Monroe from the film "Some Like It Hot."					
United Arts. UAL-3029	(M)	Some Like It Hot (Soundtrack)	1959	40.00	80.00
United Arts. UAS-6029	(S)	Some Like It Hot (Soundtrack)	1959	50.00	100.00
SWEET TOOTHE					
Dominion NR-7360	(S)	Testing	1974	150.00	250.00
SWINGIN' MEDALLIONS, THE					
Smash MGS-27083	(M)	Double Shot	1966	14.00	35.00
Smash SRS-67083	(S)	Double Shot	1966	16.00	40.00
		(Includes the single version of "Double Shot.")			
Smash MGS-27083	(M)	Double Shot	1966	10.00	25.00
Smash SRS-67083	(S)	Double Shot	1966	12.00	30.00
		(Includes an edited version of "Double Shot.")			
SWINGING BLUE JEANS, THE					
Imperial LP-9261	(M)	Hippy Hippy Shake	1964	50.00	100.00
Imperial LP-12261	(E)	Hippy Hippy Shake	1964	40.00	80.00
SYKES, ROOSEVELT					
Bluesville BV-1006	(M)	The Return Of Roosevelt Sykes	1960	20.00	50.00
Bluesville BV-1014	(M)	The Honeydripper	1961	20.00	50.00
Crown CLP-5287	(M)	Roosevelt Sykes Sings The Blues	1962	6.00	15.00
Crown CST-287	(E)	Roosevelt Sykes Sings The Blues	1962	5.00	12.00
United 7792	(M)	Roosevelt Sykes Sings The Blues	1969	4.00	10.00
Prestige 7722	(S)	The Honeydripper	1969	6.00	15.00
Delmark 616	(S)	In Europe	1969	6.00	15.00

Label & Catalog #		Title	Year	VG+	NM
Delmark 632	(S)	Feel Like Blowing My Horn	1973	4.00	10.00
BluesWay BLS-6077	(S)	Double Dirty Mother	1973	4.00	10.00

SYNDICATE OF SOUND, THE

Label & Catalog #		Title	Year	VG+	NM
Bell LP-6001	(M)	Little Girl	1966	14.00	35.00
Bell SLP-6001	(S)	Little Girl	1966	20.00	50.00

SYMS, SYLVIA

Label & Catalog #		Title	Year	VG+	NM
Atlantic ALS-137 (10")	(M)	Songs By Sylvia Sims	1952	35.00	70.00
Version 103 (10")	(M)	There's A Man In My Life	1955	35.00	70.00
Decca DL-8188	(M)	Sylvia Sims Sings	1955	20.00	50.00
Decca DL-8639	(M)	Songs Of Love	1958	20.00	50.00
Atlantic 1243	(M)	Songs By Sylvia Sims (Black label)	1956	20.00	50.00
Columbia CL-1447	(M)	Torch Song	1960	6.00	15.00
Columbia CS-8243	(S)	Torch Song	1960	10.00	25.00

— Original Columbia albums above have three white "eye" logos on each side of the spindle hole.—

Label & Catalog #		Title	Year	VG+	NM
Kapp KL-1236	(M)	That Man/Love Songs To Frank Sinatra	1961	5.00	12.00
Kapp KS-3236	(S)	That Man/Love Songs To Frank Sinatra	1961	6.00	15.00
20th Century 4123	(M)	The Fabulous Sylvia Sims	1964	5.00	12.00
20th Century S-4123	(S)	The Fabulous Sylvia Sims	1964	6.00	15.00
Prestige 7439	(M)	Sylvia Is!	1965	5.00	12.00
Prestige S-7439	(S)	Sylvia Is!	1965	6.00	15.00
Prestige 7489	(M)	For Once In My Life	1965	5.00	12.00
Prestige S-7489	(S)	For Once In My Life	1965	6.00	15.00

T

T-BONES, THE

Label & Catalog #		Title	Year	VG+	NM
Liberty LRP-3346	(M)	Boss Drag	1964	6.00	15.00
Liberty LST-7346	(S)	Boss Drag	1964	8.00	20.00
Liberty LRP-3363	(M)	Boss Drag At The Beach	1964	6.00	15.00
Liberty LST-7363	(S)	Boss Drag At The Beach	1964	8.00	20.00
Liberty LRP-3404	(M)	Doin' The Jerk	1965	4.00	10.00
Liberty LST-7404	(S)	Doin' The Jerk	1965	5.00	12.00
Liberty LRP-3439	(M)	No Matter What Shape	1966	5.00	12.00
Liberty LST-7439	(S)	No Matter What Shape	1966	6.00	15.00
Liberty LRP-3446	(M)	Sippin' And Chippin'	1966	4.00	10.00
Liberty LST-7446	(S)	Sippin' And Chippin'	1966	5.00	12.00
Liberty LRP-3471	(M)	Everyone's Gone To The Moon	1966	4.00	10.00
Liberty LST-7471	(S)	Everyone's Gone To The Moon	1966	5.00	12.00

T.C. ATLANTIC

Label & Catalog #		Title	Year	VG+	NM
Dove LP-4459	(M)	T.C. Atlantic	196?	50.00	100.00

T.I.M.E. [TRUST IN MEN EVERYWHERE]

Label & Catalog #		Title	Year	VG+	NM
Liberty LST-7558	(S)	T.I.M.E.	1968	6.00	15.00
Liberty LST-7605	(S)	Smooth Ball	1969	6.00	15.00

T-REX [TYRANNOSAURUS REX]
T-Rex features Marc Bolan.

Label & Catalog #		Title	Year	VG+	NM
Blue Thumb BTS-7	(S)	Unicorn	1969	8.00	20.00
Blue Thumb BTS-18	(S)	A Beard Of Stars	1970	8.00	20.00
Reprise PRO-511	(DJ)	Interview With Marc Bolan	1971	75.00	150.00

Label & Catalog #		Title	Year	VG+	NM
Reprise RS-6440	(S)	T-Rex	1971	6.00	15.00
Reprise RS-6466	(S)	Electric Warrior	1971	6.00	15.00
Reprise MS-2095	(S)	The Slider	1972	6.00	15.00
Reprise MS-2132	(S)	Tanx	1973	6.00	15.00
A&M SP-3514	(S)	Tyrannosaurus Rex / A Beginning (2 LPs)	1972	5.00	12.00
Casablanca NBLP-9006	(S)	Light Of Love	1974	5.00	12.00

T.V. & THE TRIBESMEN

HBR HLP-9507	(M)	Barefootin'	1966	5.00	12.00
HBR HST-9507	(S)	Barefootin'	1966	6.00	15.00

TALISMEN, THE

Blue Star M-6323	(M)	Treasury Of American Railroad Songs And Ballads	1964	5.00	12.00
Blue Star MS-6323	(S)	Treasury Of American Railroad Songs And Ballads	1964	6.00	15.00
Prestige PR-7406	(M)	Folk Swingers Extraordinaire	1965	5.00	12.00
Prestige PRS-7406	(S)	Folk Swingers Extraordinaire	1965	6.00	15.00

TALKING HEADS, THE

Warner Bros. PRO-	(DJ)	Live At The Roxy (Coounterfeits exist)	1979	20.00	50.00
Sire 23771	(S)	Speaking In Togues (Clear vinyl)	1983	12.00	30.00

(Issued in a clear plastic box with artwork by Robert Rauschenberg.)

TAMPA RED

Bluesville BV-1030	(M)	Don't Tampa With The Blues	1961	20.00	50.00
Bluesville BV-1043	(M)	Don't Jive With Me	1962	20.00	50.00

TAMS, THE

ABC-Paramount 481	(M)	Presenting The Tams	1964	12.00	30.00
ABC-Paramount S-481	(E)	Presenting The Tams	1964	8.00	20.00
ABC-Paramount 499	(M)	Hey Girl, Don't Bother Me	1964	8.00	20.00
ABC-Paramount S-499	(S)	Hey Girl, Don't Bother Me	1964	12.00	30.00
ABC-Paramount 596	(M)	Time For The Tams	1967	5.00	12.00
ABC-Paramount S-596	(S)	Time For The Tams	1967	6.00	15.00
ABC-Paramount S-673	(S)	A Portrait Of The Tams	1969	6.00	15.00

TANEGA, NORMA

New Voice NV-2001	(M)	Walkin' My Cat Named Dog	1966	10.00	25.00
New Voice NVS-2002	(S)	Walkin' My Cat Named Dog	1966	16.00	40.00

TANGERINE

Stephen Prod. SPST-001	(S)	The Peeling Of Tangerine	197?	100.00	200.00

TANGERINE ZOO

Mainstream S-6107	(S)	Tangerine Zoo	1968	8.00	20.00
Mainstream S-6116	(S)	Outside Looking In	1968	8.00	20.00

TAR BABY

New South NR-4500	(S)	February (No cover)	197?	85.00	170.00

TARGAL, JEM

Sheavy	(M)	Lucky Guy	196?	150.00	250.00

TARRIERS, THE
Members include Alan Arkin, Erik Darling and Bob Carey.

Glory 1200	(M)	The Tarriers	1959	20.00	50.00
United Arts. UAL-4033	(M)	Hard Travelin'	1959	14.00	35.00
United Arts. UAS-5033	(S)	Hard Travelin'	1959	20.00	50.00
Atlantic 8042	(M)	Tell The World About This	1960	10.00	25.00
Atlantic SD-8042	(S)	Tell The World About This	1960	14.00	35.00
Decca DL-4342	(M)	The Tarriers	1962	6.00	15.00
Decca DL-74342	(S)	The Tarriers	1962	8.00	20.00
Kapp KL-1349	(M)	The Original Tarriers	1963	6.00	15.00
Kapp KS-3349	(S)	The Original Tarriers	1963	8.00	20.00

TASTE

Atco SD-33-296	(S)	Taste	1969	8.00	20.00
Atco SD-33-322	(S)	On The Boards	1970	8.00	20.00

Label & Catalog #		Title	Year	VG+	NM
TAVENER, JOHN					
Apple SMAS-3369	(S)	**The Whale**	1972	6.00	15.00
TAYLOR, BOBBY, & THE VANCOUVERS					
Gordy GS-930	(S)	**Bobby Taylor And The Vancouvers**	1968	8.00	20.00
Gordy GS-942	(S)	**Taylor Made Soul**	1968	6.00	15.00
TAYLOR, EARL (& THE STONEY MOUNTAIN BOYS)					
United Arts. UAL-3049	(M)	**Folk Songs From The Bluegrass**	1960	14.00	35.00
United Arts. UAS-6049	(S)	**Folk Songs From The Bluegrass**	1960	20.00	50.00
Capitol T-2090	(M)	**Bluegrass Taylor Made**	1963	14.00	35.00
Capitol ST-2090	(S)	**Bluegrass Taylor Made**	1963	20.00	50.00
TAYLOR, JAMES					
Refer to the Original Flying Machine.					
Apple SKAO-3352	(S)	**James Taylor**	1969	12.00	30.00
Warner Bros. BS4-2866	(Q)	**Gorilla**	1975	5.00	12.00
Columbia HC-47009	(S)	**Dad Loves His Work** *(Half-speed master)*	1983	10.00	25.00
Nautilus NR-29	(S)	**Gorilla**	1981	8.00	20.00
TAYLOR, JOHNNIE					
Johnnie Taylor originally recorded with The Soul Stirrers.					
Stax ST-715	(M)	**Wanted: One Soul Singer**	1967	6.00	15.00
Stax STS-715	(S)	**Wanted: One Soul Singer**	1967	8.00	20.00
Stax STS-2005	(S)	**Who's Making Love?**	1968	6.00	15.00
Stax STS-2008	(S)	**Raw Blues**	1969	6.00	15.00
Stax STS-2012	(S)	**Rare Stamps**	1969	6.00	15.00
Stax STS-2023	(S)	**The Philosophy Continues**	1969	6.00	15.00
Stax STS-2030	(S)	**One Step Beyond**	1971	4.00	10.00
Columbia PCQ-33951	(Q)	**Eargasm**	1976	5.00	12.00
Columbia PCQ-34401	(Q)	**Rated Extraordinaire**	1977	5.00	12.00
TAYLOR, LITTLE JOHNNY					
Galaxy 203	(M)	**Little Johnny Taylor**	1963	10.00	25.00
Galaxy 8203	(S)	**Little Johnny Taylor**	1963	12.00	30.00
TAYLOR, KINGSIZE, & THE DOMINOS					
Midnight HLP-2101	(M)	**Real Gonk Man**	196?	12.00	30.00
Midnight HST-2101	(S)	**Real Gonk Man**	196?	14.00	35.00
TAYLOR, MICK					
Mick Taylor was formerly a member of The Roling Stones.					
Columbia JC-35076	(S)	**Mick Taylor**	1979	5.00	12.00
TAYLOR, SAM "THE MAN"					
MGM E-293 (10")	(M)	**The Big Beat**	1956	50.00	100.00
TAYLOR, TED					
OKeh OKM-12104	(M)	**Be Ever Wonderful**	1963	6.00	15.00
OKeh OKS-14104	(S)	**Be Ever Wonderful**	1963	8.00	20.00
OKeh OKM-12109	(M)	**Blues And Soul**	1965	6.00	15.00
OKeh OKS-14109	(S)	**Blues And Soul**	1965	8.00	20.00
OKeh OKM-12113	(M)	**Greatest Hits**	1966	5.00	12.00
OKeh OKS-14113	(S)	**Greatest Hits**	1966	6.00	15.00
Ronn LPS-7528	(S)	**Shades Of Blue**	1969	4.00	10.00
Ronn KPS-7529	(S)	**You Can Dig It**	1970	4.00	10.00
Ronn LPS-7531	(S)	**Taylor Made**	1972	4.00	10.00
TEA COMPANY, THE					
Smash SRS-67105	(S)	**Come And Have Some Tea**	1968	10.00	25.00
TEDDY & THE PANDAS					
Tower ST-5125	(S)	**Basic Magnetism**	1968	3.00	8.00
		(A warehouse find drastically lowered its value.)			
TEDDY BEARS, THE					
Imperial LP-9067	(M)	**The Teddy Bears Sing!**	1959	180.00	300.00
Imperial SLP-12067	(S)	**The Teddy Bears Sing!**	1959	360.00	600.00

From the sunny funny spreads of Los Angeles, this softish rock trio featured Annette Bard, Marshall Lieb and future boy-genius Phil Spector and scored with "To Know Him Is To Love Him" in 1958. Following the single with an album was a natural, although what came out of the sessions is what is arguably the first true stereo rock 'n roll album!

While hardly classic material, the album is nonetheless highly sought-after, if only for its stature amongst stereophiles (and, of course, the fact that it is a Spector artifact).

Label & Catalog #		Title	Year	VG+	NM
TEDESCO, TOM					
Imperial LP-9263	(M)	**The Electric 12 String Guitar**	1964	5.00	12.00
Imperial LP-12263	(S)	**The Electric 12 String Guitar**	1964	6.00	15.00
TEEN QUEENS, THE					
Crown CLP-5022	(M)	**Eddie, My Love**	1956	100.00	200.00
Crown CLP-5373	(M)	**The Teen Queens**	1963	16.00	40.00
TEENAGERS, THE (FEATURING FRANKIE LYMON)					
Gee GLP-701	(M)	**The Teenagers Featuring Frankie Lymon** *(First pressings have a red label.)*	1957	180.00	300.00
Gee GLP-701	(M)	**The Teenagers Featuring Frankie Lymon** *(Second pressings have a grey label.)*	1961	75.00	150.00
Gee GLPS-701	(E)	**The Teenagers Featuring Frankie Lymon**	1961	50.00	100.00
Roulette R-25013	(M)	**The Teenagers At The London Palladium**	1958	100.00	200.00
Roulette R-25036	(M)	**Rock And Roll**	1958	100.00	200.00
Roulette R-25250	(M)	**Jerry Blavatt Presents The Teenagers**	1964	50.00	100.00

Fronted by the guitars of Tom Verlaine (a name he adopted from French Symbolist poet, Paul Verlaine) and Richard Lloyd, Television's two albums, marked by intelligent lyrics and passionate playing, sold poorly but gathered a critical and cultish following.

TELEVISION					
Elektra 7E-1098	(S)	**Marquee Moon**	1977	6.00	15.00
Elektra 6E-133	(S)	**Adventure**	1978	6.00	15.00
TEMPEST					
Earth 0378	(S)	**Tempest**	1976	45.00	90.00
TEMPESTS, THE					
Smash MGS-27098	(M)	**Would You Believe?**	1966	5.00	12.00
Smash SRS-67098	(S)	**Would You Believe?**	1966	6.00	15.00
TEMPLE, SHIRLY					
20th Century TCF-103	(M)	**Complete Shirley Temple Songbook** *(2 LPs)*	1961	14.00	35.00
20th Century TFM-3045	(M)	**More Little Miss Wonderful**	1961	10.00	25.00
20th Century TFM-3102	(M)	**The Best Of Shirley Temple**	1963	10.00	25.00

Label & Catalog #		Title	Year	VG+	NM
TEMPO, NICK					
Liberty LRP-3023	(M)	**Rock 'N Roll Beach Party**	1958	20.00	50.00
TEMPO, NINO, & APRIL STEVENS					
Atco 33-156	(M)	**Deep Purple**	1963	8.00	20.00
Atco SD-33-156	(S)	**Deep Purple**	1963	12.00	30.00
Atco 33-162	(M)	**Sing The Great Songs**	1964	6.00	15.00
Atco SD-33-162	(S)	**Sing The Great Songs**	1964	8.00	20.00
Atco 33-180	(M)	**Hey Baby**	1966	6.00	15.00
Atco SD-33-180	(S)	**Hey Baby**	1966	8.00	20.00
White Whale WW-113	(M)	**All Strung Out**	1967	5.00	12.00
White Whale WWS-7113	(S)	**All Strung Out**	1967	6.00	15.00
TEMPOS, THE					
Justice JLP-104	(M)	**Speaking Of The Tempos**	1966	240.00	400.00
TEMPTATIONS, THE					
Gordy G-911	(M)	**Meet The Temptations**	1964	8.00	20.00
Gordy GS-911	(S)	**Meet The Temptations**	1964	12.00	30.00
Gordy G-912	(M)	**The Temptations Sing Smokey**	1965	8.00	20.00
Gordy GS-912	(S)	**The Temptations Sing Smokey**	1965	12.00	30.00
Gordy G-914	(M)	**Temptin' Temptations**	1965	6.00	15.00
Gordy G-914	(S)	**Temptin' Temptations**	1965	8.00	20.00
Gordy G-918	(M)	**Gettin' Ready**	1966	6.00	15.00
Gordy GS-918	(S)	**Gettin' Ready**	1966	8.00	20.00
Gordy G-919	(M)	**The Temptations' Greatest Hits**	1966	6.00	15.00
Gordy GS-919	(S)	**The Temptations' Greatest Hits**	1966	8.00	20.00
Gordy G-921	(M)	**The Temptations Live**	1967	6.00	15.00
Gordy GS-921	(S)	**The Temptations Live**	1967	8.00	20.00
— Original Gordy albums above have "Gordy" in yellow script at the top of the label.—					
Gordy G-922	(M)	**With A Lot O' Soul**	1967	6.00	15.00
Gordy GS-922	(S)	**With A Lot O' Soul**	1967	8.00	20.00
Gordy G-924	(M)	**In A Mellow Mood**	1967	6.00	15.00
Gordy GS-924	(S)	**In A Mellow Mood**	1967	8.00	20.00
Gordy GS-927	(S)	**The Temptations Wish It Would Rain**	1968	6.00	15.00
Gordy GS-933	(S)	**The Temptations Show**	1969	6.00	15.00
Gordy GS-938	(S)	**Live At The Copa**	1969	6.00	15.00
Gordy GS-939	(S)	**Cloud Nine**	1969	5.00	12.00
Gordy GS-947	(S)	**Psychedelic Shack**	1970	5.00	12.00
Gordy GS-949	(S)	**Puzzle People**	1969	5.00	12.00
Gordy GS-951	(S)	**The Temptations' Christmas Album**	1970	6.00	15.00
Gordy GS-953	(S)	**Live At London's Talk Of The Town**	1970	5.00	12.00
Gordy GS-954	(S)	**The Temptations' Greatest Hits, Volume 2**	1970	5.00	12.00
Gordy GS-957	(S)	**The Sky's The Limit**	1971	5.00	12.00
TEMPTATIONS, THE / STEVIE WONDER					
Gordy PR-101	(DJ)	**The Sky's The Limit /**			
		Where I'm Coming From	1971	8.00	20.00
		(One side by The Tempts, one by Stevie Wonder.)			
TEN YEARS AFTER					
Deram DES-18009	(S)	**Ten Years After**	1968	6.00	15.00
Deram DES-18016	(S)	**Undead**	1968	6.00	15.00
Deram DES-18021	(S)	**Stonedhenge**	1969	5.00	12.00
Deram DES-18029	(S)	**Ssssh**	1969	5.00	12.00
Deram DES-18038	(S)	**Cricklewood Green**	1970	5.00	12.00
Deram DES-18050	(S)	**Watt**	1970	5.00	12.00
Columbia CQ-30801	(Q)	**A Space In Time**	1972	6.00	15.00
TERRELL, TAMMI					
Ms. Terrell also recorded with Marvin Gaye; Chuck Jackson.					
Motown 652	(M)	**Irresistible Tammi**	1967	8.00	20.00
Motown MS-652	(S)	**Irresistible Tammi**	1967	10.00	25.00
TERRY, DON					
Columbia CL-6288 (10")	(M)	**Teen-Age Dance Session**	1955	20.00	50.00
TEX, JOE					
Checker 2993	(M)	**Hold On**	1964	16.00	40.00

Label & Catalog #		Title	Year	VG+	NM
King 935	(M)	The Best Of Joe Tex	1965	16.00	40.00
King KS-935	(S)	The Best Of Joe Tex	1965	20.00	50.00
Parrot PA-61002	(M)	The Best Of Joe Tex	1965	6.00	15.00
Parrot PAS-71002	(S)	The Best Of Joe Tex	1965	8.00	20.00
Atlantic 8106	(S)	Hold What You've Got	1965	6.00	15.00
Atlantic SD-8106	(S)	Hold What You've Got	1965	8.00	20.00
Atlantic 8115	(M)	The New Boss	1965	6.00	15.00
Atlantic SD-8115	(S)	The New Boss	1965	8.00	20.00
Atlantic 8124	(M)	The Love You Save	1966	6.00	15.00
Atlantic SD-8124	(S)	The Love You Save	1966	8.00	20.00
Atlantic 8133	(M)	I've Got To Do A Little Better	1966	6.00	15.00
Atlantic SD-8133	(S)	I've Got To Do A Little Better	1966	8.00	20.00
Atlantic 8144	(S)	The Best Of Joe Tex	1967	6.00	15.00
Atlantic SD-8144	(S)	The Best Of Joe Tex	1967	8.00	20.00
Atlantic SD-8156	(S)	Live And Lively	1968	6.00	15.00
Atlantic SD-8187	(S)	Soul Country	1968	6.00	15.00
Atlantic SD-8211	(S)	Happy Soul	1969	5.00	12.00
Atlantic SD-8231	(S)	Buying A Book	1969	5.00	12.00
Atlantic SD-8254	(S)	With Strings And Things	1970	5.00	12.00
Atlantic SD-8292	(S)	From The Roots Came The Rapper	1972	5.00	12.00

TEXAS RUBY
Ms. Ruby also recorded with Curly Fox.

King 840	(M)	Favorite Songs Of Texas Ruby	195?	20.00	50.00

THAXTON, LLOYD

Decca DL-4594	(M)	Lloyd Thaxton Presents	1964	6.00	15.00
Decca DL-74594	(S)	Lloyd Thaxton Presents	1964	8.00	20.00

THEE IMAGE

Manticore MA6-50451	(S)	Thee Image	1975	5.00	12.00
Manticore MA6-50651	(S)	Inside The Triangle	1975	5.00	12.00

THEE MIDNIGHTERS

Chattahoochee CS-1001	(S)	Thee Midniters	1965	16.00	40.00
Whittier W-5000	(M)	Bring You Love Special Delivery	1966	10.00	25.00
Whittier W-5001	(M)	Unlimited	1966	10.00	25.00
Whittier WS-5002	(S)	The Giants	1967	10.00	25.00

THEE MUFFINS

Fan club issue	(M)	Thee Muffins Pop Up!	1967	100.00	200.00

THEE PROPHETS

Kapp KS-3596	(S)	Playgirl	1969	8.00	20.00

THEM
The Parrot and London albums feature Van Morrison.

Parrot PA-61005	(M)	Them	1965	16.00	40.00
Parrot PAS-71005	(E)	Them	1965	14.00	35.00
Parrot PA-61008	(M)	Them Again	1966	12.00	30.00
Parrot PAS-71008	(S)	Them Again	1966	14.00	35.00
Tower T-5104	(M)	Now And Them	1968	16.00	40.00
Tower ST-5104	(S)	Now And Them	1968	20.00	50.00
Tower T-5116	(M)	Time Out! Time In For Them	1968	20.00	50.00
Tower ST-5116	(S)	Time Out! Time In For Them	1968	30.00	60.00
Happy Tiger 1004	(S)	Them	1969	16.00	40.00
Happy Tiger 1012	(S)	Them In Reality	1971	30.00	60.00

THIN LIZZY

London PS-594	(S)	Thin Lizzy	1971	16.00	40.00
London PS-636	(S)	Vagabonds Of The Western World	1974	12.00	30.00
Vertigo 2002	(S)	Night Life	1974	6.00	15.00
Vertigo 2005	(S)	Fighting	1975	6.00	15.00

THIRD EAR BAND, THE

Harvest ST-376	(S)	Alchemy	1969	6.00	15.00

THIRD ESTATE, THE

3rd Estate PPE-LP1000	(S)	Years Before The Wine	197?	300.00	500.00

Label & Catalog #		Title	Year	VG+	NM

THIRD POWER, THE
| Vanguard VSD-6554 | (S) | The Third Power Believe | 1970 | 10.00 | 25.00 |

THIRD QUADRANT, THE
| No label | (S) | Seeing Yourself As You Really Are | 1982 | 75.00 | 150.00 |
| | | (Issued in a cardboad jacket with an insert cover.) | | | |

THIRD RAIL, THE
| Epic LN-24327 | (M) | Id Music | 1967 | 12.00 | 30.00 |
| Epic BN-26327 | (S) | Id Music | 1967 | 14.00 | 35.00 |

THIRTEENTH FLOOR ELEVATORS, THE
The Elevators feature Roky Erikson.
International Art. 1	(M)	Psychedelic Sounds	1967	30.00	60.00
International Art. 1	(S)	Psychedelic Sounds	1967	20.00	50.00
International Art. 5	(M)	Easter Everywhere	1967	30.00	60.00
International Art. 5	(S)	Easter Everywhere	1967	20.00	50.00
International Art. 8	(S)	Thirteenth Floor Elevators Live	1968	20.00	50.00
International Art. 9	(S)	Bull Of The Woods	1968	20.00	50.00
		— Original Int. Art. albums above copies were pressed on thick vinyl.—			
International Art. 1	(S)	Psychedelic Sounds	1979	8.00	20.00
International Art. 5	(S)	Easter Everywhere	1979	8.00	20.00
International Art. 8	(S)	Thirteenth Floor Elevators Live	1979	8.00	20.00
International Art. 9	(S)	Bull Of The Woods	1979	8.00	20.00
		— Int. Art. reissues above are on thinner vinyl with "Masterfonics" stamped in the trail-off vinyl.—			

31ST OF FEBRUARY, THE
| Vanguard VSD-6503 | (S) | The 31st Of February | 1969 | 8.00 | 20.00 |

THOMAS, B.J.
Pacemaker PLP-3001	(M)	B.J. Thomas & The Triumphs	1965	20.00	50.00
Hickory LP-133	(M)	The Very Best Of B.J. Thomas	1966	8.00	20.00
Hickory LPS-133	(S)	The Very Best Of B.J. Thomas	1966	10.00	25.00
Scepter SP-535	(M)	I'm So Lonesome I Could Cry	1966	6.00	15.00
Scepter SPS-535	(S)	I'm So Lonesome I Could Cry	1966	8.00	20.00
Scepter SP-556	(M)	Tomorrow Never Comes	1966	5.00	12.00
Scepter SPS-556	(S)	Tomorrow Never Comes	1966	6.00	15.00
Scepter SP-561	(M)	For Lovers And Losers	1967	5.00	12.00
Scepter SPS-561	(S)	For Lovers And Losers	1967	6.00	15.00

THOMAS, CARLA
Ms. Thomas also recorded with Otis Redding; Rufus Thomas.
Atlantic 8057	(M)	Gee Whiz	1961	20.00	50.00
Stax ST-706	(M)	Comfort Me	1966	10.00	25.00
Stax STS-706	(S)	Comfort Me	1966	14.00	35.00
Stax ST-709	(M)	Carla	1966	10.00	25.00
Stax STS-709	(S)	Carla	1966	14.00	35.00
Stax ST-718	(M)	The Queen Alone	1967	10.00	25.00
Stax STS-718	(S)	The Queen Alone	1967	12.00	30.00
Atlantic SD-8232	(P)	The Best Of Carla Thomas	1969	8.00	20.00
Stax STS-2019	(S)	Memphis Queen	1969	6.00	15.00
Stax STS-2044	(S)	Love Means Carla Thomas	1971	6.00	15.00

THOMAS, IRMA
Imperial LP-9266	(M)	Wish Someone Would Care	1964	12.00	30.00
Imperial LP-12266	(S)	Wish Someone Would Care	1964	16.00	40.00
Imperial 9302	(M)	Take A Look	1966	10.00	25.00
Imperial LP-12302	(S)	Take A Look	1966	14.00	35.00
Fungus FB-25150	(S)	In Between Tears	1973	6.00	15.00

THOMAS, JEANNIE
| Strand 1030 | (M) | Jeannie Thomas Sings For The Boys | 1961 | 6.00 | 15.00 |

THOMAS, JOE, & BILL ELLIOTT
| Sue 1025 | (S) | Speak Your Piece | 1964 | 10.00 | 25.00 |

THOMAS, JON
| ABC-Paramount 351 | (M) | Heartbreak | 1960 | 6.00 | 15.00 |
| ABC-Paramount S-351 | (S) | Heartbreak | 1960 | 8.00 | 20.00 |

Label & Catalog #		Title	Year	VG+	NM

THOMAS, RAY
Thomas is a member of The Moody Blues.

Threshold THS-017	(S)	Hopes, Wishes And Dreams	1976	8.00	20.00
Threshold THSX-102	(DJ)	Ray Thomas Discusses The Recording Of His First Solo Album	1975	16.00	40.00

THOMAS, RUFUS

Stax ST-704	(M)	Walking The Dog	1963	20.00	50.00
Stax STS-2022	(S)	May I Have Your Ticket Please	1969	6.00	15.00
Stax STS-2028	(S)	Do The Funky Chicken	1970	6.00	15.00
Stax STS-2039	(S)	Doing The Push And Pull Live At P.J.'s	1971	5.00	12.00
Stax STS-3004	(S)	Did You Heard Me	1972	5.00	12.00
Stax STS-3008	(S)	Crown Prince Of Dance	1973	5.00	12.00

THOMAS, TERRY

London 5764	(M)	Strictly It	1963	8.00	20.00
Warner Bros. W-1558	(M)	Terry Thomas Discovers America	1964	6.00	15.00
Warner Bros. WS-1558	(S)	Terry Thomas Discovers America	1964	8.00	20.00

THOMPSON, MAYO

Texas Revolution	(S)	Corky's Debt To His Father	1969	50.00	100.00

THOMPSON, HANK (& THE BRAZOS VALLEY BOYS)

Capitol H-418 (10")	(M)	Songs Of The Brazos Valley	1953	40.00	80.00
Capitol H-618 (10")	(M)	North Of The Rio Grande	1953	40.00	80.00
Capitol H-729 (10")	(M)	New Recordings Of Hank's All-Time Hits	1953	40.00	80.00
Capitol H-911 (10")	(M)	Hank Thompson Favorites	1953	40.00	80.00
Capitol T-418	(M)	Songs Of The Brazos Valley	1956	30.00	60.00
Capitol T-618	(M)	North Of The Rio Grande	1956	30.00	60.00
Capitol T-729	(M)	New Recordings Of Hank's All-Time Hits	1956	30.00	60.00
Capitol T-826	(M)	Hank!	1957	30.00	60.00
Capitol T-911	(M)	Hank Thompson Favorites	1957	20.00	50.00
Capitol T-975	(M)	Hank Thompson's Dance Ranch	1958	20.00	50.00
— Original Capitol albums above have turquoise or grey labels.—					
Capitol T-1111	(M)	Favorite Waltzes	1959	30.00	60.00
Capitol T-1246	(M)	Songs For Rounders	1959	12.00	30.00
Capitol ST-1246	(S)	Songs For Rounders	1959	16.00	40.00
Capitol T-1360	(M)	Most Of All	1960	8.00	20.00
Capitol ST-1360	(S)	Most Of All	1960	12.00	30.00
Capitol T-1469	(M)	This Broken Heart Of Mine	1960	8.00	20.00
Capitol ST-1469	(S)	This Broken Heart Of Mine	1960	12.00	30.00
Capitol T-1544	(M)	An Old Love Affair	1961	6.00	15.00
Capitol ST-1544	(S)	An Old Love Affair	1961	8.00	20.00
Capitol T-1632	(M)	At The Golden Nugget	1961	6.00	15.00
Capitol ST-1632	(S)	At The Golden Nugget	1961	10.00	25.00
Capitol T-1741	(M)	The #1 Country & Western Band	1962	12.00	30.00
Capitol DT-1741	(E)	The #1 Country & Western Band	1962	8.00	20.00
— Original Capitol albums above have black labels with the logo on the left side.—					
Capitol T-1775	(M)	Cheyenne Frontier Days	1962	8.00	20.00
Capitol ST-1775	(S)	Cheyenne Frontier Days	1962	10.00	25.00
Capitol T-1878	(M)	The Best Of Hank Thompson	1963	8.00	20.00
Capitol ST-1878	(P)	The Best Of Hank Thompson	1963	10.00	25.00
Capitol T-1955	(M)	At The State Fair Of Texas	1963	10.00	25.00
Capitol DT-1955	(E)	At The State Fair Of Texas	1963	6.00	15.00
Capitol T-2089	(M)	Golden Country Hits	1964	6.00	15.00
Capitol ST-2089	(S)	Golden Country Hits	1964	8.00	20.00
Capitol T-2154	(M)	It's Christmas Time	1964	6.00	15.00
Capitol ST-2154	(S)	It's Christmas Time	1964	8.00	20.00
Capitol T-2274	(M)	Breakin' In Another Heart	1965	6.00	15.00
Capitol ST-2274	(S)	Breakin' In Another Heart	1965	8.00	20.00
Capitol T-2342	(M)	The Luckiest Heartache In Town	1965	6.00	15.00
Capitol ST-2342	(S)	The Luckiest Heartache In Town	1965	8.00	20.00
Capitol T-2460	(M)	A Six Pack To Go	1966	8.00	20.00
Capitol DT-2460	(E)	A Six Pack To Go	1966	6.00	15.00
Capitol T-2575	(M)	Breakin' The Rules	1966	6.00	15.00
Capitol ST-2575	(S)	Breakin' The Rules	1966	8.00	20.00
Capitol T-2661	(M)	The Best Of Hank Thompson, Volume 2	1967	6.00	15.00
Capitol ST-2661	(S)	The Best Of Hank Thompson, Volume 2	1967	8.00	20.00

Label & Catalog #		Title	Year	VG+	NM
Capitol T-2826	(M)	Just An Old Flame	1967	6.00	15.00
Capitol ST-2826	(S)	Just An Old Flame	1967	8.00	20.00
— Original Capitol albums above have black labels with the logo on top.—					
Tower T-5120	(M)	Country Blues	1968	8.00	20.00
Tower DT-5120	(E)	Country Blues	1968	6.00	15.00

THOMPSON, HAYDEN

Kapp KL-1507	(M)	Here's Hayden Thompson	1966	10.00	25.00
Kapp KS-3507	(S)	Here's Hayden Thompson	1966	12.00	30.00

THOMPSON, KAY

MGM E-3146	(M)	Kay Thompson	1954	10.00	25.00

THOMPSON, RICHARD

Reprise MS-2112	(S)	Henry The Human Fly	1972	6.00	15.00

THOMPSON, SONNY

King 568	(M)	Moody Blues	1956	100.00	200.00
King 655	(M)	Mellow Blues For The Late Hours	1959	50.00	100.00

THOMPSON, SUE

Hickory LPM-104	(M)	Meet Sue Thompson	1962	12.00	30.00
Hickory LPS-104	(S)	Meet Sue Thompson	1962	16.00	40.00
Hickory LPM-107	(M)	Two Of A Kind	1962	12.00	30.00
Hickory LPS-107	(S)	Two Of A Kind	1962	16.00	40.00
Hickory LPM-111	(M)	Sue Thompson's Golden Hits	1963	12.00	30.00
Hickory LPS-111	(S)	Sue Thompson's Golden Hits	1963	16.00	40.00
Wing MGW-12317	(M)	The Country Side Of Sue Thompson	1964	8.00	20.00
Wing SRW-16317	(S)	The Country Side Of Sue Thompson	1964	12.00	30.00
Hickory LPM-121	(M)	Paper Tiger	1965	8.00	20.00
Hickory LPS-121	(S)	Paper Tiger	1965	12.00	30.00
Hickory LPM-130	(M)	Sue Thompson With Strings Attached	1966	8.00	20.00
Hickory LPS-130	(S)	Sue Thompson With Strings Attached	1966	12.00	30.00
Hickory LPS-148	(S)	This Is Sue Thompson	1969	8.00	20.00
Hickory H3F-4511	(S)	Sweet Memories	1974	5.00	12.00

THOMPSON'S BRAZOS VALLEY BOYS, HANK

Warner Bros. W-1664	(M)	Where Is The Circus	1966	5.00	12.00
Warner Bros. WS-1664	(S)	Where Is The Circus	1966	6.00	15.00
Warner Bros. W-1679	(M)	The Countrypolitan Sound	1967	5.00	12.00
Warner Bros. WS-1679	(S)	The Countrypolitan Sound	1967	6.00	15.00
Warner Bros. W-1686	(M)	The Gold Standard Collection	1967	5.00	12.00
Warner Bros. WS-1686	(S)	The Gold Standard Collection	1967	6.00	15.00
Dot DLP-25978	(S)	The Instrumental Sound	1970	5.00	12.00

THORINSHIELD

Phillips PHS-600251	(S)	Thorinshield	1968	6.00	15.00

THORNTON, BIG MAMA

Arhoolie F-1028	(M)	Big Mama Thornton In Europe	1966	8.00	20.00
Arhoolie F-1032	(M)	The Queen At Monterey	1967	8.00	20.00
Arhoolie F-1039	(M)	Ball And Chain	1967	8.00	20.00
Mercury SRM-1-61225	(S)	Stronger Than Dirt	1969	8.00	20.00
Mercury SRM-1-61249	(S)	The Way It Is	1970	8.00	20.00
Roulette SR-42050	(S)	Maybe	1970	6.00	15.00
Back Beat BLP-68	(S)	She's Back	1970	6.00	15.00
Pentagram PE-10,005	(S)	Saved	1971	5.00	12.00
Vanguard VSD-79351	(S)	Jail	1974	5.00	12.00
Vanguard VSD-79354	(S)	Sassy Mama	1975	5.00	12.00

THORNTON, TERI

Riverside RLP-12-352	(M)	Devil May Care	1960	6.00	15.00
Riverside RLP-12-9352	(S)	Devil May Care	1960	10.00	25.00
Dauntless 4306	(M)	Somewhere In The Night	1963	6.00	15.00
Dauntless 6306	(S)	Somewhere In The Night	1963	8.00	20.00
Columbia CL-2094	(M)	Open Highway	1963	6.00	15.00
Columbia CS-8894	(S)	Open Highway	1963	8.00	20.00

Label & Catalog #		Title	Year	VG+	NM

THREE CHUCKLES, THE
The Three Chuckles feature Teddy Randazzo.

Label & Catalog #		Title	Year	VG+	NM
Vik LX-1067	(M)	The Three Chuckles	1956	75.00	150.00

THREE D'S, THE

Capitol T-2171	(M)	New Dimensions In Folk Songs	1964	6.00	15.00
Capitol ST-2171	(S)	New Dimensions In Folk Songs	1964	8.00	20.00

THREE DOG NIGHT
Three Dog Night features Danny Hutton, Cory Wells and Chuck Negron.

Dunhill DS-50078	(S)	It Ain't Easy (Nude group cover)	1970	20.00	50.00
Dunhill DSD-50168	(S)	Hard Labor	1974	12.00	30.00
		(The cover depicts a hospital delivery with a woman giving birth to a record album.)			
Dunhill DSD-50168	(S)	Hard Labor	1974	6.00	15.00
		(The delivery has a band-aid pasted over it.)			
Dunhill DSD-50168	(S)	Hard Labor	1974	1.50	6.00
		(The delivery has a band-aid printed over it.)			
Command QD-40014	(Q)	Hard Labor	1974	6.00	15.00
Command QD-40018	(Q)	Coming Down Your Way	1975	6.00	15.00

THREE FLAMES, THE

Mercury MG-20239	(M)	At The Bon Soir	1957	12.00	30.00

THREE MAN ARMY
The Army features Adrian Gurvitz.

Kama Sutra SKBS-2044	(S)	A Third Of A Lifetime	1971	12.00	30.00
		(Pink label. Fold-open cover with die-cut holes.)			
Kama Sutra SKBS-2044	(S)	A Third Of A Lifetime (Single cover)	1971	6.00	15.00
Reprise MS-2150	(S)	Three Man Army	1973	6.00	15.00
Reprise MS-2182	(S)	Three Man Army Two	1974	6.00	15.00

THREE STOOGES, THE
The Stooges are Moe, Larry, Curly, Shemp and Curly Joe. The Stooges also recorded with Yogi Bear.

Coral CRL-57289	(M)	The Nonsense Songbook	1959	20.00	50.00
Coral CRL-757289	(S)	The Nonsense Songbook	1959	35.00	70.00
Vocalion VL-73823	(S)	The Three Stooges Sing For Kids	1968	10.00	25.00
		(Vocalion 73823 is a repackage of Coral 757289.)			
Golden GLP-43	(M)	Madcap Musical Nonsense	1959	35.00	70.00
Columbia CL-1650	(M)	Snow White & The Three Stooges (Sdtk)	1961	20.00	50.00
Columbia CS-8450	(S)	Snow White & The Three Stooges (Sdtk)	1961	30.00	60.00

THREE SUNS, THE

Varsity VLP-6001 (10")	(M)	Twilight Time	1950	12.00	30.00
Varsity VLP-6048 (10")	(M)	Midnight Time	1950	12.00	30.00
Royale 1 (10")	(M)	Twilight Time	1951	10.00	25.00
Royale 29 (10")	(M)	Midnight Time	1950	10.00	25.00
RCA Victor LPM-3 (10")	(M)	Three-Quarter Time	1951	10.00	25.00
RCA Victor LPM-20 (10")	(M)	Hands Across The Table	1951	10.00	25.00
RCA Victor LPM-52 (10")	(M)	Christmas Favorites	1951	10.00	25.00
RCA Victor LPM-3012 (10")	(M)	Twilight Moods	1952	10.00	25.00
RCA Victor LPM-3034 (10")	(M)	The Three Suns Present	1952	10.00	25.00
RCA Victor LPM-3040 (10")	(M)	Busy Fingers	1952	10.00	25.00
RCA Victor LPM-3056 (10")	(M)	Christmas Party	1952	10.00	25.00
RCA Victor LPM-3075 (10")	(M)	Slumbertime	1952	10.00	25.00
RCA Victor LPM-3113 (10")	(M)	Pop Concert Favorites	1953	10.00	25.00
RCA Victor LPM-3125 (10")	(M)	Mods	1953	10.00	25.00
RCA Victor LPM-3130 (10")	(M)	Top Pops	1953	10.00	25.00
RCA Victor LPM-3146 (10")	(M)	Polka Time	1953	10.00	25.00
RCA Victor LPM-3174 (10")	(M)	Sacred Hymns	1953	10.00	25.00
RCA Victor LPM-1041	(M)	Soft And Sweet	1955	8.00	20.00
RCA Victor LPM-1132	(M)	Sounds Of Christmas	1955	8.00	20.00
RCA Victor LPM-1171	(M)	Twilight Time	1956	8.00	20.00
RCA Victor LPM-1173	(M)	My Reverie	1956	8.00	20.00
RCA Victor LPM-1220	(M)	Malaguena	1956	8.00	20.00
RCA Victor LPM-1249	(M)	High Fi And Wide	1956	8.00	20.00
RCA Victor LPM-1316	(M)	Easy Listening	1956	8.00	20.00
RCA Victor LPM-1333	(M)	Midnight For Two	1957	8.00	20.00

Label & Catalog #		Title	Year	VG+	NM

THRILLINGTON, PERCY "THRILLS"
Thrills Thrillington is a pseudonym for Paul McCartney.

Capitol ST-11642	(S)	Thrillington	1977	50.00	100.00

THUNDER, JOHNNY

Diamond D-5001	(M)	Loop De Loop	1963	20.00	50.00
Diamond SD-5001	(S)	Loop De Loop	1963	35.00	70.00
Real Records RR1	(S)	So Alone	196?	4.00	10.00

THUNDERBIRDS, THE

Red Feather TH-1	(M)	Meet The Fabulous Thunderbirds	196?	100.00	200.00

THUNDERCLAP NEWMAN

Track SD-8264	(S)	Hollywood Dream	1970	8.00	20.00

TUNDERPUSSY

M.R.T. RL-31748	(S)	Document Of Captivity	1973	100.00	200.00

TIDE, THE

Mouth 7237	(S)	Almost Live	196?	20.00	50.00

TIDES, THE

Mercury MG-20714	(M)	Limbo Rock	1962	4.00	10.00
Mercury SR-60714	(S)	Limbo Rock	1962	5.00	12.00
Wing MGW-12248	(M)	The Best Of Bossa Nova	1963	4.00	10.00
Wing SRW-16248	(S)	The Best Of Bossa Nova	1963	5.00	12.00
Wing MGW-12265	(M)	Surf City And Other Surfin' Favorites	1963	5.00	12.00
Wing SRW-16265	(S)	Surf City And Other Surfin' Favorites	1963	6.00	15.00

TIEKIN, FREDDIE, & THE ROCKERS

I.T. 2301	(M)	By Popular Demand	1957	20.00	50.00
I.T. 2304	(M)	Freddie Tieken & The Rockers	1958	20.00	50.00

TIFFANY SHADE

Mainstream 56105	(S)	Tiffany Shade	1969	10.00	25.00

TIJUANA BEATLES, THE

Alshire 5165	(S)	The Tijuana Beatles	1969	6.00	15.00

TIKIS, THE

Minaret TLP-7001	(M)	The Tikis	196?	16.00	40.00
Philips PHM-200043	(M)	The Tikis	1962	8.00	20.00
Philips PHS-600043	(S)	The Tikis	1962	12.00	30.00

TIL, SONNY, & THE ORIOLES

RCA Victor LSP-4451	(S)	Sonny Til Returns	1970	6.00	15.00
RCA Victor LSP-4538	(S)	Old Gold / New Gold	1970	6.00	15.00

TILLIS, MEL (& THE STATESIDERS)
Mel also recorded with Nancy Sinatra.

Columbia CL-1724	(M)	Heart Over Mind ("Eyes" logo label)	1962	12.00	30.00
Columbia CS-8524	(S)	Heart Over Mind ("Eyes" logo label)	1962	16.00	40.00

TILLMAN, FLOYD

RCA Victor LPM-1686	(M)	Floyd Tillman's Best	1958	20.00	50.00
Sims 110	(M)	Slippin' Around	196?	20.00	50.00
Harmony HL-7316	(M)	Floyd Tillman's Best	196?	10.00	25.00
Starday SLP-310	(M)	Let's Make Memories	196?	8.00	20.00
Mus. MM-2136	(M)	Floyd Tillman's Country	196?	12.00	30.00

TILLOTSON, JOHNNY

Cadence CLP-3052	(M)	Johnny Tillotson's Best	1961	10.00	25.00
Cadence CLP-25052	(P)	Johnny Tillotson's Best	1961	16.00	40.00
Cadence CLP-3058	(M)	It Keeps Right On A-Hurtin'	1962	10.00	25.00
Cadence CLP-25058	(S)	It Keeps Right On A-Hurtin'	1962	16.00	40.00
Cadence CLP-3067	(M)	You Can Never Stop Me Loving You	1963	8.00	20.00
Cadence CLP-25067	(S)	You Can Never Stop Me Loving You	1963	12.00	30.00

Label & Catalog #		Title	Year	VG+	NM

By the end of the '60s, Johnny Tillotson was no longer a viable commercial concern and was looking at a bleak future. When Elvis cut "It Keeps Right On A-Hurtin'" for his "From Elvis In Memphis" album, the songwriter's royalty check was enough to pay for Johnny's wedding!

Label & Catalog #		Title	Year	VG+	NM
MGM E-4188	(M)	**Talk Back Trembling Lips**	1964	6.00	15.00
MGM SE-4188	(S)	**Talk Back Trembling Lips**	1964	8.00	20.00
MGM E-4224	(M)	**The Tillotson Touch**	1964	6.00	15.00
MGM SE-4224	(S)	**The Tillotson Touch**	1964	8.00	20.00
MGM E-4270	(M)	**She Understands Me**	1964	6.00	15.00
MGM SE-4270	(S)	**She Understands Me**	1964	8.00	20.00
MGM E-4302	(M)	**That's My Style**	1965	6.00	15.00
MGM SE-4302	(S)	**That's My Style**	1965	8.00	20.00
MGM E-4328	(M)	**Our World**	1965	6.00	15.00
MGM SE-4328	(S)	**Our World**	1965	8.00	20.00
MGM E-4395	(M)	**No Love At All**	1966	6.00	15.00
MGM SE-4395	(S)	**No Love At All**	1966	8.00	20.00
MGM E-4402	(M)	**The Christmas Touch**	1966	6.00	15.00
MGM SE-4402	(S)	**The Christmas Touch**	1966	8.00	20.00
MGM E-4452	(M)	**Here I Am**	1967	5.00	12.00
MGM SE-4452	(S)	**Here I Am**	1967	6.00	15.00
		— Original MGM albums above have black labels.—			
MGM SE-4532	(S)	**The Best Of Johnny Tillotson**	1968	5.00	12.00
MGM SE-4814	(S)	**The Very Best Of Johnny Tillotson**	1971	4.00	10.00
TIMBER CREEK					
Renegade JAH-95014	(S)	**Hellbound Highway**	1975	75.00	150.00
TINO & THE REVLONS					
Dearborn 1004	(M)	**By Request At The Sway-Zee**	1966	150.00	250.00
TIR NA NOG					
Chrysalis CHR-1006	(S)	**A Tear And A Smile**	1972	5.00	12.00
Chrysalis CHR-1047	(S)	**Strong In The Sun**	1973	5.00	12.00
TITANS, THE					
MGM E-3992	(M)	**Today's Teen Beat**	1961	10.00	25.00
MGM SE-3992	(S)	**Today's Teen Beat**	1961	12.00	30.00

Label & Catalog #		Title	Year	VG+	NM
TITUS OATES					
No label	(S)	**Jungle Lady**	197?	50.00	100.00
TOAD HALL					
Liberty LST-7580	(S)	**Toad Hall**	1968	6.00	15.00
TOADS, THE					
Wiggins 64021	(M)	**The Toads**	1964	50.00	100.00
TOKENS, THE					
RCA Victor LPM-2514	(M)	**The Lion Sleeps Tonight**	1961	20.00	50.00
RCA Victor LSP-2514	(S)	**The Lion Sleeps Tonight**	1961	35.00	70.00
RCA Victor LPM-2631	(M)	**We, The Tokens, Sing Folk**	1962	12.00	30.00
RCA Victor LSP-2631	(S)	**We, The Tokens, Sing Folk**	1962	16.00	40.00
		— Original RCA mono albums above have "Long Play" on the bottom of the label;			
		stereo albums have "Living Stereo" on the bottom.—			
RCA Victor LPM-2886	(M)	**Wheels**	1964	20.00	50.00
RCA Victor LST-2886	(S)	**Wheels**	1964	30.00	60.00
RCA Victor LPM-3685	(M)	**The Tokens Again**	1966	10.00	25.00
RCA Victor LSP-3685	(S)	**The Tokens Again**	1966	12.00	30.00
B.T. Puppy BTP-1000	(M)	**I Hear Trumpets Blow**	1966	8.00	20.00
B.T. Puppy BTPS-1000	(P)	**I Hear Trumpets Blow**	1966	10.00	25.00
B.T. Puppy BTPS-1006	(S)	**Tokens Of Gold**	1969	10.00	25.00
B.T. Puppy BTPS-1012	(S)	**Greatest Moments**	1970	10.00	25.00
B.T. Puppy BTPS-1014	(S)	**December 5th**	1971	10.00	25.00
Buddah BDS-5059	(S)	**Both Sides Now**	1971	6.00	15.00
TOKENS, THE / THE HAPPENINGS					
B.T. Puppy BTP-1002	(M)	**Back To Back**	1967	5.00	12.00
B.T. Puppy BTPS-1002	(S)	**Back To Back**	1967	6.00	15.00
TOM & JERRY					
Charlie Tomlinson and Jerry Kennedy.					
Mercury MG-20626	(M)	**Guitar's Greatest Hits**	1961	5.00	12.00
Mercury SR-60626	(S)	**Guitar's Greatest Hits**	1961	6.00	15.00
Mercury MG-20671	(M)	**Guitars Play The Sound Of Ray Charles**	1962	5.00	12.00
Mercury SR-60671	(S)	**Guitars Play The Sound Of Ray Charles**	1962	6.00	15.00
Mercury MG-20756	(M)	**Guitar's Greatest Hits, Volume 2**	1962	5.00	12.00
Mercury SR-60756	(S)	**Guitar's Greatest Hits, Volume 2**	1962	6.00	15.00
Mercury MG-20842	(M)	**Surfin' Hootenanny**	1963	6.00	15.00
Mercury SR-60842	(S)	**Surfin' Hootenanny**	1963	8.00	20.00
TOMORROW					
Tomorrow features Steve Howe; Twink.					
Sire SES-97912	(S)	**Tomorrow**	1968	12.00	30.00
TONEY, OSCAR, JR.					
Bell 6006	(M)	**For Your Precious Love**	1967	6.00	15.00
Bell S-6006	(S)	**For Your Precious Love**	1967	8.00	20.00
TONGUE					
Hemisphere HIS-101	(S)	**Tongue**	197?	35.00	70.00
TONGUE & GROOVE (FEATURING LYNN HUGHES)					
Fontana SRF-67593	(S)	**Tongue & Groove**	1968	5.00	12.00
TONTO'S EXPANDING HEAD BAND					
Embryo SD-732	(S)	**Zero Time**	1971	10.00	25.00
TOODY, OFFICER GUNTHER					
Gunther Toody is a pseudonym for Joe. E. Ross.					
Golden LP-91	(M)	**Tells Toody Tales**	1963	14.00	35.00
TOP DRAWER					
Wish Bone 721207	(S)	**Solid Oak**	197?	300.00	500.00
TOPSIDERS, THE					
Josie J-4000	(M)	**Rock Goes Folk**	1963	6.00	15.00
Josie JS-4000	(S)	**Rock Goes Folk**	1963	8.00	20.00

Label & Catalog #		Title	Year	VG+	NM
TORME, MEL					
Capitol P-200 (10")	(M)	**California Suite**	1950	30.00	60.00
MGM 552 (10")	(M)	**Songs**	1952	30.00	60.00
Coral CRL-57012	(M)	**Mel Torme At The Crescendo**	1954	20.00	50.00
Coral CRL-57044	(M)	**Musical Soundings**	1954	20.00	50.00
Bethlehem BCP-34	(M)	**It's A Blue World**	1955	20.00	50.00
Bethlehem BCP-52	(M)	**Mel Torme**	1956	20.00	50.00
Bethlehem BCP-6013	(M)	**Mel Torme Sings Fred Astaire**	1958	20.00	50.00
Bethlehem BCP-6016	(M)	**California Suite**	1958	20.00	50.00
Bethlehem BCP-6020	(M)	**Mel Torme At The Crescendo**	1958	20.00	50.00
Bethlehem BCP-6031	(M)	**Song For Any Taste**	1959	20.00	50.00
Tops L1615	(M)	**Prelude To A Kiss**	1958	12.00	30.00
Verve V-2105	(M)	**Torme**	1958	14.00	35.00
Verve VS-6015	(S)	**Torme**	1958	20.00	50.00
Verve V-2120	(M)	**Back In Town**	1959	14.00	35.00
Verve VS-6083	(S)	**Back In Town**	1959	20.00	50.00
Verve V-2132	(M)	**Mel Torme Swings Schubert Alley**	1960	14.00	35.00
Verve VS-6146	(S)	**Mel Torme Swings Schubert Alley**	1960	20.00	50.00
Strand 1076	(M)	**Mel Torme Sings**	1960	6.00	15.00
Strand S-1076	(S)	**Mel Torme Sings**	1960	8.00	20.00
Verve V-2144	(M)	**Swingin' On The Moon**	1960	14.00	35.00
Verve V6-2144	(S)	**Swingin' On The Moon**	1960	20.00	50.00
Verve V-8440	(M)	**My Kind Of Music**	1961	14.00	35.00
Verve V6-8440	(S)	**My Kind Of Music**	1961	20.00	50.00
Verve V-8491	(M)	**I Dig The Duke, I Dig The Count**	1961	14.00	35.00
Verve V6-8491	(S)	**I Dig The Duke, I Dig The Count**	1961	20.00	50.00
Atlantic 8066	(M)	**Mel Torme At The Red Hill**	1962	14.00	35.00
Atlantic SD-8066	(S)	**Mel Torme At The Red Hill**	1962	20.00	50.00
Atlantic 8069	(M)	**Comin' Home, Baby**	1962	14.00	35.00
Atlantic SD-8069	(S)	**Comin' Home, Baby**	1962	20.00	50.00
Atlantic 8091	(M)	**Sunday In New York**	1963	12.00	30.00
Atlantic SD-8091	(S)	**Sunday In New York**	1963	16.00	40.00
Columbia CL-2318	(M)	**That's All**	1964	6.00	15.00
Columbia CS-9118	(S)	**That's All**	1964	8.00	20.00
Metro 523	(M)	**I Wished On The Moon**	1965	5.00	12.00
Metro S-523	(S)	**I Wished On The Moon**	1965	6.00	15.00
TORME, MEL, & MARGARET WHITING					
Verve V-2146	(M)	**Broadway, Right Now**	1961	12.00	30.00
Verve V6-2146	(S)	**Broadway, Right Now**	1961	16.00	40.00
TORNADOES, THE [THE HOLLYWOOD TORNADOES]					
Josie JJ-4005	(M)	**Bustin' Surfboards**	1963	50.00	100.00
Josie S-4005	(S)	**Bustin' Surfboards**	1963	75.00	150.00
TORNADOS, THE					
London LL-3279	(M)	**Telstar**	1962	14.00	35.00
London LL-3293	(M)	**The Sounds Of The Tornados**	1963	12.00	30.00
TORQUES, THE					
Wiggins 64010	(M)	**Zoom!**	1967	50.00	100.00
Lemco 604	(M)	**Live**	1968	50.00	100.00
TOSSI, AARON					
Prestige INT-13027	(M)	**Folk Songs And Ballads**	1962	8.00	20.00
TOTO					
Columbia PJC-35317	(S)	**Toto** (Picture disc)	1979	6.00	15.00
Columbia PD-36813	(DJ)	**Turn Back** (Picture disc)	1979	6.00	15.00
Columbia PJC-37928	(DJ)	**Toto IV** (Picture disc)	1979	6.00	15.00
Columbia HC-47928	(DJ)	**Toto IV** (Half-speed master)	1981	6.00	15.00
Columbia 9C9-39911	(S)	**Isolation** (Picture disc)	1984	4.00	10.00
TOTTY					
Our First BT-205	(S)	**Totty**	197?	60.00	120.00
Our First OFRO-2	(S)	**Totty Too**	1981	12.00	30.00
TOUCH					
Mainline PS-70-116-7	(S)	**Street Suite**	197?	660.00	1,000.00

Label & Catalog #		Title	Year	VG+	NM
TOUCH, THE					
Coliseum DS-51004	(S)	**The Touch**	1968	8.00	20.00
TOUCHSTONE					
Touchstone features Tom Constanten of The Grateful Dead.					
United Arts. UAS-5563	(S)	**Tarot**	1972	12.00	30.00
TOUSSAINT, ALLEN					
RCA Victor LPM-1767	(M)	**The Wild Sound Of New Orleans**	1958	50.00	100.00
Scepter 24003	(S)	**Toussaint**	1971	6.00	15.00
Reprise MS-2062	(S)	**Life, Love And Faith**	1972	5.00	12.00
TOURISTS, THE					
The Tourists feature Annie Lennox and Dave Stewart, later The Eurythmics.					
Epic NJE-36386	(S)	**Reality Effect**	1979	6.00	15.00
Epic NJE-36757	(S)	**Luminous Basement**	1980	4.00	10.00
TOWER, THE					
Other World OUR-1001	(S)	**The Tower**	1975	30.00	60.00
TOWER OF POWER					
San Francisco 204	(S)	**East Bay Grease**	1971	8.00	20.00
Direst Disk SD-16601	(S)	**Back To Oakland**	198?	8.00	20.00
Sheffield Lab	(S)	**Direct!**	198?	6.00	15.00
TOWNSEND, ED					
Capitol T-1140	(M)	**New In Town**	1959	6.00	15.00
Capitol ST-1140	(S)	**New In Town**	1959	8.00	20.00
Capitol T-1214	(M)	**Glad To Be Here**	1959	6.00	15.00
Capitol ST-1214	(S)	**Glad To Be Here**	1959	8.00	20.00
TOWNSEND, HENRY					
Bluesville BV-1041	(M)	**Tired Of Bein' Mistreated**	1962	14.00	35.00
TOWNSHEND, PETE					
Townshend is a member of The Who.					
Track 79189	(S)	**Who Came First**	1972	10.00	25.00
TOYS, THE					
DynoVoice 9002	(M)	**A Lovers Concerto/Attack**	1966	10.00	25.00
DynoVoice 9002-S	(S)	**A Lovers Concerto/Attack**	1966	16.00	40.00
DynoVoice 9002-S	(P)	**A Lovers Concerto/Attack**	1967	12.00	30.00
		("Attack" is rechanneled.)			
TRADEWINDS, THE					
The Tradewinds are Pete Anders and Vinnie Poncia.					
Kama Sutra KLP-8057	(M)	**Excursions**	1967	8.00	20.00
Kama Sutra KLPS-8057	(S)	**Excursions**	1967	10.00	25.00
TRAFFIC					
Traffic features Steve Winwood and Dave Mason.					
United Arts. UAS-6651	(S)	**Heaven Is In Your Mind**	1968	20.00	50.00
United Arts. UAS-6651	(S)	**Mr. Fantasy** *(Black label)*	1968	8.00	20.00
United Arts. UAS-6651	(S)	**Mr. Fantasy**	1969	5.00	12.00
		("Mr. Fantasy" is a retitled "Heaven Is In Your Mind.")			
United Arts. UAS-6676	(S)	**Traffic**	1968	5.00	12.00
United Arts. UAS-6702	(S)	**Last Exit**	1969	5.00	12.00
		— U.A. albums above have orange & purple labels.—			
TRAMMELL, BOBBY LEE					
Atlantic 1503	(M)	**Arkansas Twist**	1962	35.00	70.00
TRASHMEN, THE					
Garrett GA-200	(M)	**Surfin' Bird**	1964	50.00	100.00
Garrett GAS-200	(S)	**Surfin' Bird**	1964	180.00	300.00
TRASK, DIANA					
Columbia CL-1601	(M)	**Diana Trask**	1961	6.00	15.00
Columbia CS-8401	(S)	**Diana Trask**	1961	8.00	20.00

Label & Catalog #		Title	Year	VG+	NM
Columbia CL-1705	(M)	Diana Trask On TV	1961	6.00	15.00
Columbia CS-8505	(S)	Diana Trask On TV	1961	8.00	20.00

TRAVEL AGENCY, THE

Viva V-36017	(S)	Viva	1969	5.00	12.00

TRAVELLERS, THE

Kapp KL-1051	(M)	Journey With The Travellers	1960	6.00	15.00
Kapp KS-3051	(S)	Journey With The Travellers	1960	8.00	20.00
Epic LN-124013	(M)	Introducing The Travellers	1962	5.00	12.00
Epic BN-26013	(S)	Introducing The Travellers	1962	8.00	20.00

TRAVELERS THREE, THE

Elektra EKL-216	(M)	The Travelers Three	1962	5.00	12.00
Elektra EKS-7216	(S)	The Travelers Three	1962	6.00	15.00
Elektra EKL-226	(M)	Open House	1962	5.00	12.00
Elektra EKS-7226	(S)	Open House	1962	6.00	15.00
Elektra EKL-236	(M)	Live, Live, Live	1963	5.00	12.00
Elektra EKS-7236	(S)	Live, Live, Live	1963	6.00	15.00

TRAVIS, MERLE

Capitol T-650	(M)	The Merle Travis Guitar (Turquoise label)	1956	50.00	100.00
Capitol T-891	(M)	Back Home (Grey label)	1957	35.00	70.00
Capitol T-1391	(M)	Walkin' The Strings	1960	20.00	50.00
Capitol T-1664	(M)	Travis	1962	12.00	30.00
Capitol ST-1664	(S)	Travis	1962	16.00	40.00

— Original Capitol albums above have black labels with the logo on the left side.—

Capitol T-1956	(M)	Songs Of The Coal Mines	1963	12.00	30.00
Capitol ST-1956	(S)	Songs Of The Coal Mines	1963	16.00	40.00
Capitol T-2662	(M)	The Best Of Merle Travis	1967	6.00	15.00
Capitol ST-2662	(P)	The Best Of Merle Travis	1967	8.00	20.00
Capitol ST-2938	(S)	Strictly Guitar	1969	6.00	15.00

— Original Capitol albums above have black labels with the logo on top.—

TRAVIS, MERLE, & JOE MAPHIS

Capitol T-2102	(M)	Merle Travis And Joe Maphis	1964	12.00	30.00
Capitol ST-2102	(S)	Merle Travis And Joe Maphis	1964	16.00	40.00

TRAVIS, MERLE, & JOHNNY BOND

Capitol ST-249	(S)	Great Songs Of The Delmore Brothers	1969	6.00	15.00

TREMELOES, THE

Refer to Brian Poole & the Tremeloes.

Epic LN-24310	(M)	Here Comes My Baby	1967	10.00	25.00
Epic BN-26310	(E)	Here Comes My Baby	1967	8.00	20.00
Epic LN-24326	(M)	Even The Bad Times Are Good	1967	8.00	20.00
Epic BN-26326	(P)	Even The Bad Times Are Good	1967	10.00	25.00
Epic LN-24363	(M)	Suddenly You Love Me	1968	8.00	20.00
Epic BN-26363	(E)	Suddenly You Love Me	1968	6.00	15.00
Epic BN-26388	(S)	World Explosion '58/'68	1968	8.00	20.00

TRENIERS, THE

Epic LG-3125	(M)	The Treniers On TV	1955	75.00	150.00
Dot DLP-3257	(M)	Souvenir Album	1960	50.00	100.00

TRIGGER, VICK

Sanctuary 12103	(S)	Electronic Wizzard	1977	35.00	70.00

TRIPSICHORD MUSIC BOX, THE

Janus JLS-3016	(S)	The Tripsichord Music Box	1971	6.00	15.00

TRIZO-50

Cavern Custom 740142	(S)	Cavern-50	197?	180.00	300.00

TROGGS, THE

Atco 33-193	(M)	Wild Thing	1966	20.00	50.00
Atco SD-33-193	(E)	Wild Thing	1966	14.00	35.00
Fontana SR-27556	(M)	The Troggs	1966	14.00	35.00
Fontana SRF-67556	(E)	The Troggs	1966	10.00	25.00

Label & Catalog #		Title	Year	VG+	NM
Fontana SRF-67576	(E)	**Love Ia All Around**	1968	10.00	25.00
Pye 12112	(S)	**The Troggs**	1975	4.00	10.00
Private Stock PS-2008	(S)	**The Trogg Tapes**	1976	4.00	10.00
Sire SASH-3714-2	(M)	**Vintage Years** (2 LPs)	1976	6.00	15.00
TROLL					
Smash SRS-67114	(S)	**Animated Music**	1969	8.00	20.00
TROMBONES, THE					
Chartmaker 1105	(S)	**The Trombones**	1969	8.00	20.00
TROUP, BOBBY					
Capitol H-484 (10")	(M)	**Bobby**	1953	40.00	80.00
Capitol T-484	(M)	**Bobby**	1955	20.00	50.00
Bethlehem BCP-19	(M)	**Bobby Troup Sings Johnny Mercer**	1955	20.00	50.00
Bethlehem BCP-35	(M)	**The Distinctive Style Of Bobby Troup**	1955	20.00	50.00
Liberty LRP-9005	(M)	**Escapade Reviews The Jazz Scene**	1957	16.00	40.00
Liberty LRP-3002	(M)	**Bobby Troup And His Trio**	1956	16.00	40.00
Liberty LRP-3026	(M)	**Do Re Mi**	1957	16.00	40.00
Liberty LRP-3078	(M)	**Here's To My Lady**	1958	16.00	40.00
		— Original Liberty albums above have turquoise labels.—			
Mode 111	(M)	**Bobby Swings Tenderly**	1957	16.00	40.00
Interlude 501	(M)	**Cool**	1959	14.00	35.00
Interlude 1001	(S)	**Cool**	1959	20.00	50.00
RCA Victor LPM-1959	(M)	**Bobby Troup And His Jazz All-Stars**	1959	14.00	35.00
RCA Victor LSP-1959	(S)	**Bobby Troup And His Jazz All-Stars**	1959	20.00	50.00
TROY, DORIS					
Atlantic 8088	(M)	**Just One Look**	1964	10.00	25.00
Atlantic SD-8088	(S)	**Just One Look**	1964	16.00	40.00
Apple ST-3371	(S)	**Doris Troy**	1970	6.00	15.00
TRUMAN, MARGARET					
RCA Victor LPM-57 (10")	(M)	**American Songs**	1951	16.00	40.00
TRUMPETEERS, THE					
Score 4021	(M)	**Milky White Way**	1956	100.00	200.00
Grand 7701	(M)	**The Last Supper**	195?	50.00	100.00
TRUTH & JANEY					
Montrose	(S)	**No Rest For The Wicked**	197?	35.00	70.00
Bee Bee 711X98	(S)	**Just A Little Bit Of Magic**	197?	16.00	40.00
T2					
London PS-583	(S)	**It'll All Work Out In Boomland**	1971	20.00	50.00
TUBB, ERNEST (& THE TEXAS TROUBADORS)					
Refer to Red Foley.					
Decca DL-5301 (10")	(M)	**Ernest Tubb Favorites**	1951	50.00	100.00
Decca DL-5334 (10")	(M)	**Old Rugged Cross**	1951	50.00	100.00
Decca DL-5336 (10")	(M)	**Jimmie Rodgers Songs**	1951	50.00	100.00
Decca DL-5497 (10")	(M)	**Sing A Song Of Christmas**	1954	50.00	100.00
Decca DL-8291	(M)	**Ernest Tubb Favorites**	1956	20.00	50.00
Decca DL-8553	(M)	**The Daddy Of 'Em All**	1956	20.00	50.00
Decca DXA-159	(M)	**The Ernest Tubb Story** (With booklet)	1958	20.00	50.00
Decca DXSA-159	(E)	**The Ernest Tubb Story** (With booklet)	1958	20.00	50.00
Decca DL-8834	(M)	**The Importance Of Being Ernest**	1959	16.00	40.00
Decca DL-78834	(S)	**The Importance Of Being Ernest**	1959	20.00	50.00
		— Original Decca albums above have black & silver labels.—			
Decca DL-4042	(M)	**Record Shop**	1960	10.00	25.00
Decca DL-74042	(S)	**Record Shop**	1960	16.00	40.00
Decca DL-4046	(M)	**All Time Hits**	1961	8.00	20.00
Decca DL-74046	(S)	**All Time Hits**	1961	12.00	30.00
Decca D-74118	(M)	**Ernest Tubb's Golden Favorites**	1961	8.00	20.00
Decca DL-74118	(S)	**Ernest Tubb's Golden Favorites**	1961	12.00	30.00
Decca DL-4321	(M)	**On Tour**	1962	12.00	30.00
Decca DL-74321	(S)	**On Tour**	1962	16.00	40.00
Decca DL-4385	(M)	**Just Call Me Lonesome**	1963	8.00	20.00
Decca DL-74385	(S)	**Just Call Me Lonesome**	1963	12.00	30.00

Label & Catalog #		Title	Year	VG+	NM
Decca DL-4397	(M)	The Family Bible	1964	6.00	15.00
Decca DL-74397	(S)	The Family Bible	1964	8.00	20.00
Decca DL-4514	(M)	Thanks A Lot	1964	6.00	15.00
Decca DL-74514	(S)	Thanks A Lot	1964	8.00	20.00
Decca DL-4518	(M)	Blue Christmas	1964	6.00	15.00
Decca DL-74518	(S)	Blue Christmas	1964	8.00	20.00
Decca DL-4640	(M)	My Pick Of The Hits	1965	6.00	15.00
Decca DL-74640	(S)	My Pick Of The Hits	1965	8.00	20.00
Decca DL-4644	(M)	Country Dance Time	1965	6.00	15.00
Decca DL-74644	(S)	Country Dance Time	1965	8.00	20.00
Decca DL-4681	(M)	Hittin' The Road	1965	6.00	15.00
Decca DL-74681	(S)	Hittin' The Road	1965	8.00	20.00
Decca DL-4746	(M)	By Request	1966	6.00	15.00
Decca DL-74746	(S)	By Request	1966	8.00	20.00
Decca DL-4772	(M)	Country Hits, Old And New	1966	6.00	15.00
Decca DL-74772	(S)	Country Hits, Old And New	1966	8.00	20.00
—Original Decca albums above have black labels with "Mfrd by Decca" beneath the rainbow.—					
Decca DL-4867	(M)	Another Story	1967	6.00	15.00
Decca DL-74867	(S)	Another Story	1967	8.00	20.00
Decca DL-74957	(S)	Ernest Tubb Sings Hank Williams	1968	8.00	20.00
Decca DL-75006	(S)	Ernest Tubb's Greatest Hits	1968	8.00	20.00
Decca DL-75072	(S)	Country Hit Time	1968	8.00	20.00
Decca DL-75114	(S)	Let's Turn Back The Years	1969	6.00	15.00
Decca DL-75122	(S)	Saturday Satan, Sunday Saint	1969	6.00	15.00
Decca DL-75222	(S)	A Good Year For The Wine	1970	5.00	12.00
Decca DL-75252	(S)	Ernest Tubb's Greatest Hits, Volume 2	1970	5.00	12.00
Decca DL-75301	(S)	One Sweet Hello	1971	5.00	12.00
Decca DL-75345	(S)	Say Something Nice To Sarah	1972	5.00	12.00
Decca DL-75388	(S)	Baby, It's So Hard To Be Good	1972	5.00	12.00

TUBB, ERNEST, & LORETTA LYNN

Decca DL-4639	(M)	Mr. And Mrs. Used To Be	1965	6.00	15.00
Decca DL-74639	(S)	Mr. And Mrs. Used To Be	1965	8.00	20.00
Decca DL-4872	(M)	Singin' Again	1967	6.00	15.00
Decca DL-74872	(S)	Singin' Again	1967	8.00	20.00
Decca DL-75115	(S)	If We Put Our Heads Together	1969	5.00	12.00

TUBB, JUSTIN

Decca DL-8644	(M)	Country Boy In Love	1957	20.00	50.00
Starday SLP-160	(M)	Star Of The Grand Ole Opry	1962	12.00	30.00
Starday SLP-198	(M)	The Modern Country Music Sound	1962	12.00	30.00
Starday SLP-334	(M)	The Best Of Justin Tubb	1965	10.00	25.00

TUBB, JUSTIN, & LORENE MANN

RCA Victor LPM-3339	(M)	Together And Alone	1966	8.00	20.00
RCA Victor LSP-3339	(S)	Together And Alone	1966	10.00	25.00

TUBB'S TEXAS TROUBADORS, ERNEST

Decca DL-4459	(M)	The Texas Troubadors	1964	12.00	30.00
Decca DL-74459	(S)	The Texas Troubadors	1964	16.00	40.00
Decca DL-4644	(M)	Country Dance Time	1965	12.00	30.00
Decca DL-74644	(S)	Country Dance Time	1965	16.00	40.00
Decca DL-4745	(M)	Ernest Tubb's Fabulous Texas Troubadors	1966	6.00	15.00
Decca DL-74745	(S)	Ernest Tubb's Fabulous Texas Troubadors	1966	8.00	20.00
Decca DL-75017	(S)	The Terrific Texas Troubadors	1968	6.00	15.00

TUCKER, TOMMY

Checker 2990	(M)	Hi Heel Sneakers	1964	20.00	50.00

TUNETOPPERS, THE

Amy A-1	(M)	At The Madison Dance Party	1960	14.00	35.00
Amy AS-1	(P)	At The Madison Dance Party	1960	20.00	50.00

TURNER, IKE

Crown CLP-5367	(M)	Rocks The Blues	1963	8.00	20.00
Crown CST-367	(E)	Rocks The Blues	1963	6.00	15.00
Pompeii SD-6003	(S)	A Black Man's Soul	1969	6.00	15.00
United Artists UAS-5576	(S)	Blues Roots	1972	4.00	10.00
United Artists LA087	(S)	Bad Dreams	1973	4.00	10.00

The stories surrounding the Turners' recording sessions with Phil Spector are the stuff of a book. Spector, who produced half of the album, scheduled it for release in 1966 as Philles PHLP-4011. Apparently disgusted with his dealings with Ike, he destroyed the Philles pressing saving a handful as momentos for friends and associates. As there were only a few hundred pressed, covers were never manufactured, so that the price listed is for the record only!

The album was eventually released in 1969 on A&M, where it was largely ignored by the buying public. While the album itself is uneven, reeling from Spector's bombastic productions to Ike Turner's R&B-ish numbers, the inclusion of the title track, the outrageous "River Deep-Mountain High," makes the album a favorite with fans and collectors.

Label & Catalog #		Title	Year	VG+	NM

TURNER, IKE & TINA

Label & Catalog #		Title	Year	VG+	NM
Sue LP-2001	(M)	The Sound Of Ike And Tina Turner	1961	50.00	100.00
Sue LP-2003	(M)	Dance With Ike And Tina Turner	1962	40.00	80.00
Sue LP-2004	(M)	Dynamite	1963	35.00	70.00
Sue LP-2005	(M)	Don't Play Me Cheap	1963	35.00	70.00
Sue LP-2007	(M)	It's Gonna Work Out Fine	1963	35.00	70.00
Sue LP-1038	(M)	Ike And Tina Turner's Greatest Hits	1965	20.00	50.00
Kent K-519	(M)	The Soul Of Ike And Tina	1961	8.00	20.00
Kent KST-519	(S)	The Soul Of Ike And Tina	1961	12.00	30.00
Kent K-538	(M)	Festival Of Live Performances	1962	8.00	20.00
Kent KST-538	(S)	Festival Of Live Performances	1962	12.00	30.00
Kent K-550	(M)	Please Please Please	1962	8.00	20.00
Kent KST-550	(S)	Please Please Please	1962	12.00	30.00
Kent K-5014	(M)	The Ike And Tina Turner Revue Live	1964	8.00	20.00
Kent KST-5014	(S)	The Ike And Tina Turner Revue Live	1964	12.00	30.00
Warner Bros. W-1579	(M)	The Ike And Tina Turner Show Live	1965	8.00	20.00
Warner Bros. WS-1579	(S)	The Ike And Tina Turner Show Live	1965	12.00	30.00
Warner Bros. WS-1810	(S)	Ike And Tina Turner's Greatest Hits	1969	6.00	15.00
Loma 5904	(M)	Live/The Ike And Tina Show	1966	12.00	30.00
Philles PHLP-4011	(M)	River Deep-Mountain High	1966	See note below	

(Manufactured and pressed in minute quantities, most of which were destroyed shortly afterward. No covers are to known to have been completed for Philles 4011. Estimated near mint value for the record without the cover $4,000-5,000.)

Label & Catalog #		Title	Year	VG+	NM
Pompeii SD-6000	(S)	So Fine	1968	8.00	20.00
Pompeii SD-6004	(S)	Cussin,' Cryin' And Carryin' On	1969	8.00	20.00
Pompeii SD-6006	(S)	Get It Together	1969	8.00	20.00
A&M SP-4178	(S)	River Deep-Mountain High (Brown label)	1969	8.00	20.00

(Repackage of the unreleased Philles 4011.)

Label & Catalog #		Title	Year	VG+	NM
Sunset SUS-5265	(S)	The Fantastic Ike And Tina Turner	1969	5.00	12.00
Sunset SUS-5286	(S)	Ike And Tina Turner's Greatest Hits	1969	5.00	12.00
Harmony HS-11360	(S)	Ooh Poo Pah Doo	1969	5.00	12.00
Capitol ST-571	(S)	Her Man, His Woman	1969	6.00	15.00
Blue Thumb BTS-5	(S)	Outta Season	1969	6.00	15.00
Blue Thumb BTS-11	(S)	The Hunter	1969	6.00	15.00
Blue Thumb BTS-49	(S)	The Best Of Ike And Tina Turner	1973	4.00	10.00
Liberty LST-7637	(S)	Come Together	1970	6.00	15.00
Liberty LST-7650	(S)	Workin' Together	1970	6.00	15.00
ABC 4014	(S)	16 Great Performances	1971	4.00	10.00
United Arts. UAS-9953	(S)	What You Hear Is What You Get (2 LPs)	1971	6.00	15.00
United Arts. UAS-5530	(S)	Nuff Said	1971	5.00	12.00
United Arts. UAS-5598	(S)	Feel Good	1972	5.00	12.00
United Arts. UAS-5660	(S)	Let Me Touch Your Mind	1973	5.00	12.00
United Arts. UAS-5667	(S)	Ike And Tina Turner's Greatest Hits	1972	5.00	12.00
United Arts. LA064	(S)	The World Of Ike And Tina Live	1973	5.00	12.00
United Arts. LA180	(S)	Nutbush City Limits	1973	6.00	15.00

TURNER, JOE ["BIG" JOE TURNER]

Label & Catalog #		Title	Year	VG+	NM
Decca DL-8044	(M)	Kansas City Jazz	1953	100.00	200.00
Atlantic 1234	(M)	Boss Of The Blues	1956	50.00	100.00
Atlantic SD-1234	(S)	Boss Of The Blues	195?	75.00	150.00
Atlantic 1235	(M)	Kansas City Jaz	1956	50.00	100.00
Atlantic SD-1235	(S)	Kansas City Jazz	195?	75.00	150.00
Atlantic 8005	(M)	Joe Turner	1957	50.00	100.00
Atlantic 8023	(M)	Rockin' The Blues	1958	75.00	150.00
Atlantic 8033	(M)	Big Joe Is Here	1959	75.00	150.00

— Original Atlantic mono albums above have black labels; stereo albums have green labels.—

Label & Catalog #		Title	Year	VG+	NM
Atlantic 8005	(M)	Joe Turner	1960	35.00	70.00
Atlantic 8023	(M)	Rockin' The Blues	1960	35.00	70.00
Atlantic 8033	(M)	Big Joe Is Here	1960	35.00	70.00
Atlantic 1332	(M)	Big Joe Rides Again	1960	35.00	70.00
Atlantic 8081	(M)	The Best Of Joe Turner	1963	20.00	50.00

—Atlantic albums above have orange & purple labels.—

Label & Catalog #		Title	Year	VG+	NM
Savoy MG-14012	(M)	Joe Turner And The Blues	1958	50.00	100.00
Savoy MG-14106	(M)	Careless Love	1963	35.00	70.00
BluesWay BL-6006	(M)	Singing The Blues	1967	8.00	20.00
BluesWay BLS-6006	(S)	Singing The Blues	1967	10.00	25.00
BluesWay BLS-6060	(S)	Roll 'Em	1973	6.00	15.00

Label & Catalog #		Title	Year	VG+	NM
TURNER, JOE, & PETE JOHNSON					
EmArcy 36014	(M)	Joe Turner And Pete Johnson	1955	50.00	100.00
TURNER, MICKEY					
Edmar E-1040	(M)	The Mickey Turner Show	1966	10.00	25.00
TURNER, SAMMY					
Big Top 12-1301	(M)	Lavender Blue Mods	1962	10.00	25.00
Big Top S-12-1301	(S)	Lavender Blue Mods	1962	12.00	30.00
TURNER, SPYDER					
MGM E-4450	(M)	Stand By Me	1967	6.00	15.00
MGM SE-4450	(S)	Stand By Me	1967	8.00	20.00
TURNER, TITUS					
Jamie JLP-70-3018	(M)	Sound Off	1961	8.00	20.00
Jamie JLP-3018	(S)	Sound Off	1961	10.00	25.00
TURNER, ZEB					
Audio Lab AL-1537	(M)	Country Music In The Turner Style	195?	30.00	60.00
TURTLES, THE					
White Whale WW-111	(M)	It Ain't Me Babe	1965	12.00	30.00
White Whale WWS-7111	(S)	It Ain't Me Babe	1965	16.00	40.00
White Whale WW-112	(M)	You Baby	1966	10.00	25.00
White Whale WWS-7112	(S)	You Baby	1966	12.00	30.00
White Whale WW-114	(M)	Happy Together	1967	6.00	15.00
White Whale WWS-7114	(S)	Happy Together	1967	8.00	20.00
White Whale WW-115	(M)	The Turtles' Golden Hits	1967	6.00	15.00
White Whale WWS-7115	(S)	The Turtles' Golden Hits	1967	8.00	20.00
White Whale WWS-7118	(S)	The Battle Of The Bands	1968	6.00	15.00
White Whale WWS-7124	(S)	Turtle Soup	1969	6.00	15.00
White Whale WWS-7127	(S)	More Golden Hits	1970	6.00	15.00
White Whale WWS-7133	(S)	Wooden Head	1971	6.00	15.00
Sire SASH-3703	(S)	Happy Together Again (2 LPs)	1974	10.00	25.00
TWEETY PIE: *Refer to* MEL BLANC					
TWENTIETH CENTURY ZOO					
Vault 122	(S)	Thunder On A Clear Day	1968	8.00	20.00
TWIGGY					
MGM 1SE-32	(S)	The Boy Friend (Soundtrack)	1971	6.00	15.00
Mercury SRM-1-1038	(S)	Please Get My Name Right	1975	6.00	15.00
Mercury SRM-1-1093	(S)	Twiggy	1976	6.00	15.00
TWINK					
Refer to The Pretty Things; Tomorrow.					
Sire SES-97022	(S)	Think Pink	1970	20.00	50.00
TWINS, THE					
RCA Victor LPM-1708	(M)	Teenagers Love The Twins	1958	20.00	50.00
TWISTERS, THE					
Treasure TLP-890	(M)	Doin' The Twist	1962	12.00	30.00
TWISTIN' KINGS, THE					
Motown MLP-601	(M)	Twistin' The World Around	1960	50.00	100.00
TWITTY, CONWAY					
MGM E-3744	(M)	Conway Twitty Sings	1959	40.00	80.00
MGM SE-3744	(S)	Conway Twitty Sings	1959	60.00	120.00
MGM E-3786	(M)	Saturday Night With Conway Twitty	1959	35.00	70.00
MGM SE-3786	(S)	Saturday Night With Conway Twitty	1959	50.00	100.00
MGM E-3818	(M)	Lonely Blue Boy	1960	35.00	70.00
MGM SE-3818	(S)	Lonely Blue Boy	1960	50.00	100.00
		— Original MGM albums above have yellow labels—			
MGM E-3744	(M)	Conway Twitty Sings	196?	16.00	40.00
MGM SE-3744	(S)	Conway Twitty Sings	196?	20.00	50.00

Label & Catalog #		Title	Year	VG+	NM
MGM E-3786	(M)	Saturday Night With Conway Twitty	1959	16.00	40.00
MGM SE-3786	(S)	Saturday Night With Conway Twitty	1959	20.00	50.00
MGM E-3818	(M)	Lonely Blue Boy	1960	16.00	40.00
MGM SE-3818	(S)	Lonely Blue Boy	1960	20.00	50.00
MGM E-3849	(M)	Conway Twitty's Greatest Hits	1960	16.00	40.00
MGM SE-3849	(P)	Conway Twitty's Greatest Hits	1960	20.00	50.00
		(Issued with a fold-open poster, priced separately below.)			
		Conway Twitty's Greatest Hits Poster	1960	10.00	25.00
MGM E-3907	(M)	The Rock And Roll Story	1961	20.00	50.00
MGM SE-3907	(S)	The Rock And Roll Story	1961	35.00	70.00
MGM E-3943	(M)	The Conway Twitty Touch	1961	20.00	50.00
MGM SE-3943	(S)	The Conway Twitty Touch	1961	35.00	70.00
MGM E-4019	(M)	Portrait Of A Fool And Others	1962	16.00	40.00
MGM SE-4019	(S)	Portrait Of A Fool And Others	1962	20.00	50.00
MGM E-4089	(M)	R&B '63	1963	16.00	40.00
MGM SE-4089	(S)	R&B '63	1963	20.00	50.00
MGM E-4217	(M)	Hit The Road	1964	10.00	25.00
MGM SE-4217	(S)	Hit The Road	1964	12.00	30.00
		— Original MGM albums above have black labels—			
Metro M-512	(M)	It's Only Make Believe	1965	5.00	12.00
Metro MS-512	(S)	It's Only Make Believe	1965	6.00	15.00
Decca DL-4724	(M)	Conway Twitty Sings	1966	5.00	12.00
Decca DL-74724	(S)	Conway Twitty Sings	1966	6.00	15.00
Decca DL-4828	(M)	Look Into My Teardrops	1966	5.00	12.00
Decca DL-74828	(S)	Look Into My Teardrops	1966	6.00	15.00
		— Original Decca albums above have black labels with "Mfrd. by Decca" beneath the rainbow.—			

TYLER, RED, & THE GYROS

Ace LP-1006	(M)	Rockin' And Rollin'	1960	35.00	70.00

TYLER, T. TEXAS

Sound 607	(M)	Deck Of Cards	1958	20.00	50.00
King 664	(M)	T. Texas Tyler	1959	35.00	70.00
King 689	(M)	The Great Texan	1960	35.00	70.00
King 721	(M)	T. Texas Tyler	1961	20.00	50.00
King 734	(M)	Songs Along The Way	1961	20.00	50.00
Wrangler 1002	(M)	T. Tyler Texas	1962	14.00	35.00
Capitol T-1662	(M)	Salvation	1962	10.00	25.00
Capitol ST-1662	(S)	Salvation	1962	14.00	35.00
Capitol T-2344	(M)	The Hits Of T. Texas Tyler	1965	8.00	20.00
Capitol ST-2344	(S)	The Hits Of T. Texas Tyler	1965	10.00	25.00
Starday SLP-379	(M)	The Man With A Million Friends	1966	10.00	25.00

TYMES, THE

Parkway P-7032	(M)	So Much In Love	1963	16.00	40.00
Parkway P-7038	(M)	The Sound Of Wonderful Tymes	1963	12.00	30.00
Parkway P-7039	(M)	Somewhere	1964	12.00	30.00
Columbia CS-9778	(S)	People	1969	6.00	15.00

U.F.O.

Rare Earth RS-524	(S)	U.F.O.	1971	10.00	25.00

Label & Catalog #		Title	Year	VG+	NM
ULTIMATE SPINACH, THE					
MGM SE-4518	(S)	The Ultimate Spinach	1968	6.00	15.00
MGM SE-4570	(S)	Behold And See	1968	6.00	15.00
MGM SE-4600	(S)	The Ultimate Spinach	1969	6.00	15.00
UNBEATABLES, THE					
Dawn LP-5050	(M)	Live At Palisades Park	1964	40.00	80.00
UNCLE JOSH & COUSIN JAKE					
Cotton Town 101	(M)	Just Joshing	196?	35.00	70.00
UNDERGROUND SUNSHINE					
Intrepid IT-4003	(S)	Let There Be Light	1969	12.00	30.00
UNDERGROUNDS, THE					
Mercury MG-16337	(M)	Psychedelic Visions	1967	8.00	20.00
Mercury SR-16337	(S)	Psychedelic Visions	1967	10.00	25.00
Gordy GS-970	(S)	Cosmic Truth	1975	4.00	10.00
UNFOLDING, THE					
Audio Fidelity 6184	(S)	How To Blow Your Mind And Have A Freakout Party	196?	35.00	70.00
UNIFICS, THE					
Kapp KS-3582	(S)	Sittin' In At The Court Of Love	1968	6.00	15.00
UNIQUES (FEATURING JOE STAMPLEY), THE					
Paula LP-2190	(M)	Uniquely Yours	1966	8.00	20.00
Paula LPS-2190	(S)	Uniquely Yours	1966	10.00	25.00
Paula LP-2194	(M)	Happening Now	1967	8.00	20.00
Paula LPS-2194	(S)	Happening Now	1967	10.00	25.00
Paula LP-2199	(M)	Playtime	1968	8.00	20.00
Paula LPS-2199	(S)	Playtime	1968	10.00	25.00
Paula LPS-2204	(S)	The Uniques	1969	8.00	20.00
Paula LPS-2208	(S)	Golden Hits	1970	8.00	20.00
UNITED STATES DOUBLE QUARTET, THE					
B.T. Puppy BTS-1005	(S)	Life Is Groovy	1969	12.00	30.00
UNITED STATES OF AMERICA, THE					
Columbia CS-9616	(S)	The United States Of America (With bag)	1968	12.00	30.00
Columbia CS-9616	(S)	The United States Of America (Without bag)	1968	8.00	20.00
UNIT 4 + 2					
London LL-3427	(M)	Unit 4 + 2 #1	1965	16.00	40.00
London PS-427	(P)	Unit 4 + 2 #1	1965	20.00	50.00
UNSPOKEN WORD, THE					
Ascot AS-16028	(S)	Tuesday, April 19th	1968	6.00	15.00
Atco SD-33-335	(S)	The Unspoken Work	1970	5.00	12.00
UNUSUAL WE					
Pulsar 10608	(S)	Unusual We	1969	10.00	25.00
UPCHURCH, PHIL					
Boyd B-398	(M)	You Can't Sit Down	1961	6.00	15.00
Boyd BS-398	(S)	You Can't Sit Down	1961	10.00	25.00
United Arts. UAL-3162	(M)	You Can't Sit Down, Part 2	1961	6.00	15.00
United Arts. UAS-6162	(S)	You Can't Sit Down, Part 2	1961	8.00	20.00
United Arts. UAL-3175	(M)	Big Hits Dances	1962	6.00	15.00
United Arts. UAS-6175	(S)	Big Hits Dances	1962	8.00	20.00
URSA MAJOR					
RCA Victor LSP-4777	(S)	Ursa Major	1972	6.00	15.00

USHER, GARY: *Refer to "There Are Producers..." in the main introduction.*

U2					
Warner Bros. WBMS-117	(DJ)	2 Sides Live	1981	30.00	60.00

Label & Catalog #		Title	Year	VG+	NM

VALE, RICKY, & HIS SURFERS

Strand SL-1104	(M)	Everybody's Surfin'	1963	6.00	15.00
Strand SLS-1104	(S)	Everybody's Surfin'	1963	8.00	20.00

VALENS, RITCHIE

Del Fi DFLP-1201	(M)	Ritchie Valens	1959	50.00	100.00
Del Fi DFLP-1206	(M)	Ritchie	1959	50.00	100.00
Del Fi DFLP-1214	(M)	In Concert At Pacoima Jr. High	1960	75.00	150.00
Del Fi DFLP-1225	(M)	His Greatest Hits	1963	35.00	70.00
Del Fi DFLP-1247	(M)	Ritchie Valens: His Greatest Hits, Volume 2	1965	35.00	70.00
— Original Del Fi albums above have black labels with a blue logo on top.—					
Guest Star 1469	(M)	The Original Ritchie Valens	1963	8.00	20.00
Guest Star S-1469	(E)	The Original Ritchie Valens	1963	5.00	12.00
Guest Star 1484	(M)	The Original La Bamba	1963	8.00	20.00
Guest Star S-1484	(E)	The Original La Bamba	1963	5.00	12.00
MGM GAS-117	(E)	Ritchie Valens	1970	8.00	20.00

VALENS. RITCHIE, & JERRY KOLE

Crown CLP-5336	(M)	Ritchie Valens And Jerry Kole	1963	8.00	20.00
Crown CST-336	(E)	Ritchie Valens And Jerry Kole	1963	5.00	12.00

VALENTE, DINO

Epic LN-24335	(M)	Dino Valente	1967	5.00	12.00
Epic BN-26335	(S)	Dino Valente	1967	6.00	15.00

VALENTE, CATERINA

Decca DL-8203	(M)	The HiFi Nightingale	1956	10.00	25.00
Decca DL-8436	(M)	Ole Caterina	1957	10.00	25.00
Decca DL-8440	(M)	Plenty Valante!	1957	10.00	25.00
RCA Victor LPM-2119	(M)	Classics With A Chaser	1960	8.00	20.00

VALENTINE, HILTON
Valentine was formerly a member of The Animals.

Capitol ST-330	(S)	All In Your Head	1969	10.00	25.00

VALENTINO, MARK

Swan LP-508	(M)	Mark Valentino	1963	20.00	50.00

VALLEE, RUDY

RCA Victor LPM-2507	(M)	Young Rudy Vallee	1961	6.00	15.00
RCA Victor LSP-2507	(S)	Young Rudy Vallee	1961	10.00	25.00
Decca DL-4242	(M)	Stein Songs	1962	6.00	15.00
Decca DL7-4242	(S)	Stein Songs	1962	8.00	20.00
Jubilee J-2051	(M)	The Funny Side Of Rudy Vallee	1964	6.00	15.00
Viva 6005	(M)	Ho Ho, Everybody	1966	5.00	12.00
Viva 16005	(S)	Ho Ho, Everybody	1966	6.00	15.00
RCA Victor LPM-3816	(M)	The Best Of Rudy Vallee	1967	5.00	12.00
RCA Victor LSP-3816	(S)	The Best Of Rudy Vallee	1967	6.00	15.00

VALLEY, JIM
Valley was formerly a member of Paul Revere's Raiders.

Panorama 104	(S)	Harpo (With Don & The Goodtimes)	1969	16.00	40.00
Light LS-5564	(S)	Family	197?	6.00	15.00

VALLI, FRANKI
Refer to The Four Lovers; The Four Seasons.

Phillips PHM-200247	(M)	Solo	1967	8.00	20.00
Phillips PHS-600247	(S)	Solo	1967	10.00	25.00
Phillips PHS-600274	(S)	Timeless	1968	6.00	15.00
Motown M6-852	(S)	Inside You	1975	5.00	12.00

Label & Catalog #		Title	Year	VG+	NM
VAMPIRES, THE					
United Arts. UAL-3378	(M)	At The Monster Ball	1964	6.00	15.00
United Arts. UAS-6378	(S)	At The Monster Ball	1964	8.00	20.00
VAN DER GRAAF GENERATOR					
Mercury SR-61238	(S)	The Aerosol Grey Machine	1969	8.00	20.00
Probe 4515	(S)	The Least We Can Do Is Wave	1970	8.00	20.00
Dunhill DS-50097	(S)	H To He Who Am The Only One	1970	6.00	15.00
Charisma CH-1051	(S)	Prawn Hearts	1971	5.00	12.00
VAN DYKE, LEROY					
Mercury MG-20682	(M)	Walk On By	1962	6.00	15.00
Mercury SR-60682	(S)	Walk On By	1962	8.00	20.00
Mercury MG-20716	(M)	Movin' Van Dyke	1963	5.00	12.00
Mercury SR-60716	(S)	Movin' Van Dyke	1963	6.00	15.00
Mercury MG-20802	(M)	LeRoy Van Dyke's Greatest Hits	1963	5.00	12.00
Mercury SR-60802	(S)	LeRoy Van Dyke's Greatest Hits	1963	6.00	15.00
Mercury MG-20922	(M)	Songs For Mon And Dad	1964	5.00	12.00
Mercury SR-60922	(S)	Songs For Mon And Dad	1964	6.00	15.00
VAN DYKES, THE					
Bell 6004	(M)	Tellin' It Like It Is	1967	6.00	15.00
Bell 6004	(S)	Tellin' It Like It Is	1967	8.00	20.00
VAN DYKES, THE					
Sutton LP-307	(M)	A Hootin' Hootenanny	196?	6.00	15.00
VAN EATON, LON & FERREK					
Apple SMAS-3390	(S)	Brother (With insert)	1972	6.00	15.00
VAN HALEN					
Warner Bros.	(DJ)	1984 (Quiex II vinyl)	1984	6.00	15.00
VAN RONK, DAVE					
Folkways F-3818	(M)	Ballads & Blues And Spirituals	1959	8.00	20.00
Prestige INT-13056	(M)	Dave Van Ronk, Folksinger	1962	6.00	15.00
Prestige F-14025	(M)	The Genius Of Dave Van Ronk	1964	6.00	15.00
Prestige PR-7527	(M)	Dave Van Ronk, Folksinger	1967	5.00	12.00
Prestige PRS-7527	(S)	Dave Van Ronk, Folksinger	1967	6.00	15.00
Forecast FVS-3041	(S)	Dave Van Ronk & The Hudson Dusters	1968	6.00	15.00
Prestige PRS-7716	(S)	Inside Dave Van Ronk	1969	5.00	12.00
Mercury MG-20908	(M)	Just Dave Van Ronk	1964	5.00	12.00
Mercury SR-60908	(S)	Just Dave Van Ronk	1964	6.00	15.00
Folkways FV-9006	(M)	Dave Van Ronk Sings The Blues	1965	5.00	12.00
Folkways FVS-9006	(S)	Dave Van Ronk Sings The Blues	1965	6.00	15.00
Folkways FV-9017	(M)	Gambler's Blues	1965	5.00	12.00
Folkways FVS-9017	(S)	Gambler's Blues	1965	6.00	15.00
Folkways FV-3009	(M)	No Dirty Names	1966	5.00	12.00
Folkways FVS-3009	(S)	No Dirty Names	1966	6.00	15.00
Polydor 24-4052	(S)	Van Ronk	1971	4.00	10.00
Fantasy 24170	(S)	Van Ronk	1972	5.00	12.00
VAN ZANDT, TOWNES					
Poppy PYS-40001	(S)	For The Sake Of A Song	1968	10.00	25.00
Poppy PYS-40004	(S)	Our Mother The Mountain	1969	6.00	15.00
Poppy PYS-40007	(S)	Townes Van Zandt	1969	6.00	15.00
Poppy PYS-40012	(S)	Delta Momma Blues	1970	6.00	15.00
Poppy PYS-5700	(S)	High, Low And In Between	1971	6.00	15.00
Poppy LAOO-F4	(S)	The Late Great Townes Van Zandt	1972	6.00	15.00
VANDROSS, LUTHER					
Epic HE-47451	(S)	Never Too Much (Half-speed master)	1981	8.00	20.00
VANGELIS					
RCA Victor DJL1-1849	(DJ)	The Vangelis Radio Special	1976	100.00	200.00
		(Issued in a jacket for RCA LPL1-5110, "Heaven And Hell" with a sticker that reads "Radio Special Self-Portrait.)			

Label & Catalog #		Title	Year	VG+	NM

VANILLA FUDGE
Refer to Cream / Vanilla Fudge.

Label & Catalog #		Title	Year	VG+	NM
Atco 33-224	(M)	Vanilla Fudge	1967	8.00	20.00
Atco SD-33-224	(S)	Vanilla Fudge	1967	6.00	15.00
Atco SD-33-237	(S)	The Beat Goes On	1968	6.00	15.00
Atco SD-33-244	(S)	Renaissance	1968	6.00	15.00

— Original Atco stereo albums above have purple & brwon labels.—

Atco SD-33-278	(S)	Near The Beginning	1969	5.00	12.00
Atco SD-33-303	(S)	Rock 'N' Roll	1969	5.00	12.00

VANITY FARE

Page One 2502	(S)	Early In The Morning	1970	50.00	100.00

(Mispressing plays one side from the unreleased Sandy Coast album. Mispressed albums have less tracks than the label credits.)

Page One 2502	(S)	Early In The Morning	1970	6.00	15.00

VANNELLI, GINO

Mobile Fidelity MFSL-041	(S)	Powerful People	198?	8.00	20.00
Nautilus NR-35	(S)	Brother To Brother	198?	6.00	15.00

VAUGHAN, SARAH

Remington 1024 (10")	(M)	Hot Jazz	1950	35.00	70.00
Columbia CL-6133 (10")	(M)	Sarah Vaughan	1950	35.00	70.00
MGM E-544 (10")	(M)	Sarah Vaughan Sings	1951	30.00	60.00
MGM E-165 (10")	(M)	Tenderly	1952	30.00	60.00
Mercury MG-25188 (10")	(M)	Divine Sarah	1954	16.00	50.00
EmArcy 26005 (10")	(M)	Images	1954	16.00	50.00
Riveride RLP-2511 (10")	(M)	Sarah Vaughan Sings With John Kirby	1955	16.00	50.00
EmArcy MG-36004	(M)	Sarah Vaughan	1954	16.00	40.00
EmArcy MG-36058	(M)	Sarah Vaughan In The Land Of Hi Fi	1955	16.00	40.00
EmArcy MG-36089	(M)	Sassy	1956	16.00	40.00
EmArcy MG-36109	(M)	Swingin' Easy	1957	16.00	40.00
MGM E-3274	(M)	My Kinda Love *(Yellow label)*	1955	16.00	40.00
Columbia CL-660	(M)	After Hours With Sarah Vaughan	1955	16.00	40.00
Columbia CL-745	(M)	Sarah Vaughan In Hi Fi	1955	16.00	40.00
Columbia CL-914	(M)	Linger Awhile	1956	16.00	40.00
Concord 3018	(M)	Sarah Vaughan Concert	1957	12.00	30.00
Rondo-Lette 35	(M)	Songs Of Broadway	1959	12.00	30.00
Lion 70052	(M)	Sarah Vaughan	1959	12.00	30.00
Mercury MG-20094	(M)	Sarah Vaughan At The Blue Note	1957	12.00	30.00
Mercury MGP-2-100	(M)	Great Songs From Hit Shows *(2 LPs)*	1957	16.00	40.00
Mercury MGP-2-101	(M)	George Gershwin *(2 LPs)*	1957	16.00	40.00
Mercury MG-20219	(M)	Wonderful Sarah	1957	12.00	30.00
Mercury MG-20223	(M)	In A Romantic Mood	1957	12.00	30.00
Mercury MG-20244	(M)	Great Songs From Hit Shows, Vol. 1	1958	10.00	25.00
Mercury MSR-60041	(S)	Great Songs From Hit Shows, Vol. 1	1958	12.00	30.00
Mercury MG-20245	(M)	Great Songs From Hit Shows, Volume 2	1958	10.00	25.00
Mercury SR-60078	(S)	Great Songs From Hit Shows, Volume 2	1958	12.00	30.00
Mercury MG-20310	(M)	George Gershwin, Vol. 1	1958	10.00	25.00
Mercury SR-60045	(S)	George Gershwin, Vol. 1	1958	12.00	30.00
Mercury MG-20311	(M)	George Gershwin, Vol. 2	1958	10.00	25.00
Mercury SR-60046	(S)	George Gershwin, Vol. 2	1958	12.00	30.00
Mercury MG-20326	(M)	Sarah Vaughan At Mr. Kelly's	1958	12.00	30.00
Mercury MG-20370	(M)	Vaughan And Violins	1958	10.00	25.00
Mercury SR-60038	(S)	Vaughan And Violins	1958	12.00	30.00
Mercury MG-20383	(M)	After Hours At The London House	1958	12.00	30.00
Mercury MG-20438	(M)	The Magic Of Sarah Vaughan	1959	10.00	25.00
Mercury SR-60110	(S)	The Magic Of Sarah Vaughan	1959	12.00	30.00
Mercury MG-20441	(M)	No Count Sarah	1959	10.00	25.00
Mercury SR-60116	(S)	No Count Sarah	1959	12.00	30.00
Mercury MG-20540	(M)	The Divine Sarah Vaughan	1959	8.00	20.00
Mercury SR-60255	(S)	The Divine Sarah Vaughan	1959	10.00	25.00
Mercury MG-20580	(M)	Close To You	1960	8.00	20.00
Mercury SR-	(S)	Close To You	1960	10.00	25.00
Mercury MG-20617	(M)	My Heart Sings	1961	8.00	20.00
Mercury SR-60617	(S)	My Heart Sings	1961	10.00	25.00
Mercury MG-20645	(M)	Sarah Vaughan's Golden Hits	1962	8.00	20.00
Mercury SR-60645	(S)	Sarah Vaughan's Golden Hits	1962	10.00	25.00

— Original Mercury albums above have black labels with "Long Playing Microgroove" on the bottom.—

Label & Catalog #		Title	Year	VG+	NM
Mercury MG-20831	(M)	Sassy Swings The Tivoli	1963	6.00	15.00
Mercury SR-60831	(S)	Sassy Swings The Tivoli	1963	8.00	20.00
Mercury MG-20882	(M)	Vaughan With Voices	1964	5.00	12.00
Mercury SR-60882	(S)	Vaughan With Voices	1964	6.00	15.00
— Original Mercury albums above have black labels with "Long Playing High Fidelity" on the bottom.—					
Mercury MG-20941	(M)	Viva Vaughan	1964	5.00	12.00
Mercury SR-60941	(S)	Viva Vaughan	1964	6.00	15.00
Mercury MG-21009	(M)	Mancini Songbook	1965	5.00	12.00
Mercury SR-61009	(S)	Mancini Songbook	1965	6.00	15.00
Mercury MG-21069	(M)	The Pop Artistry Of Sarah Vaughan	1966	5.00	12.00
Mercury SR-61069	(S)	The Pop Artistry Of Sarah Vaughan	1966	6.00	15.00
Mercury MG-21079	(M)	New Scene	1966	5.00	12.00
Mercury SR-61079	(S)	New Scene	1966	6.00	15.00
Mercury MG-21116	(M)	Sassy Swings Again	1967	5.00	12.00
Mercury SR-61116	(S)	Sassy Swings Again	1967	6.00	15.00
— Original Mercury albums above have red labels.—					
Roulette R-52046	(M)	Dreamy (Black label)	1960	12.00	30.00
Roulette SR-52046	(S)	Dreamy (Black label)	1960	16.00	40.00
Roulette R-52046	(M)	Dreamy	1960	8.00	20.00
Roulette SR-52046	(S)	Dreamy	1960	12.00	30.00
Roulette R-52060	(M)	Divine One	1960	8.00	20.00
Roulette SR-52060	(S)	Divine One	1960	12.00	30.00
Roulette R-52061	(M)	Count Basie/Sarah Vaughan	1960	8.00	20.00
Roulette SR-52061	(S)	Count Basie/Sarah Vaughan	1960	12.00	30.00
Roulette R-52070	(M)	After Hours	1961	8.00	20.00
Roulette SR-52070	(S)	After Hours	1961	12.00	30.00
Roulette R-52082	(M)	You're Mine, You	1962	8.00	20.00
Roulette SR-52082	(S)	You're Mine, You	1962	12.00	30.00
Roulette SR-52082	(S)	You're Mine, You (Red vinyl)	1962	35.00	70.00
Roulette R-52091	(M)	Snowbound	1962	6.00	15.00
Roulette SR-52091	(S)	Snowbound	1962	8.00	20.00
Roulette R-52092	(M)	The Explosive Side Of Sarah	1962	6.00	15.00
Roulette SR-52092	(S)	The Explosive Side Of Sarah	1962	8.00	20.00
Roulette R-52100	(M)	Star Eyes	1963	6.00	15.00
Roulette SR-52100	(S)	Star Eyes	1963	8.00	20.00
Roulette R-52104	(M)	Lonely Hours	1963	6.00	15.00
Roulette SR-52104	(S)	Lonely Hours	1963	8.00	20.00
Roulette R-52109	(M)	The World Of Sarah Vaughan	1964	5.00	12.00
Roulette SR-52109	(S)	The World Of Sarah Vaughan	1964	6.00	15.00
Roulette R-52112	(M)	Sweet 'N Sassy	1964	5.00	12.00
Roulette SR-52112	(S)	Sweet 'N Sassy	1964	6.00	15.00
Roulette R-52116	(M)	Sarah Sings Soulfully	1965	5.00	12.00
Roulette SR-52116	(S)	Sarah Sings Soulfully	1965	6.00	15.00
Roulette R-52118	(M)	Sarah Plus Two	1965	5.00	12.00
Roulette SR-52118	(S)	Sarah Plus Two	1965	6.00	15.00
— Original Roulette albums above have white labels.—					

VAUGHAN, SARAH, & BILLY ECKSTINE

Mercury MG-20316	(M)	The Best Of Irving Berlin	1958	10.00	25.00
Mercury SR-60002	(S)	The Best Of Irving Berlin	1958	12.00	30.00
Lion 70088	(M)	Billy And Sarah	1959	16.00	40.00

VAUGHAN, SARAH; DINAH WASHINGTON, & JOE WILLIAMS

Roulette R-52108	(M)	We Three	1964	6.00	15.00
Roulette SR-52108	(S)	We Three	1964	8.00	20.00

VAUGHAN, STEVIE RAY

Epic 8E8-39609	(S)	Couldn't Stand The Weather (Picture disc)	1984	8.00	20.00

VAUGHN, ROBERT

MGM E-4488	(M)	Readings From Hamlet	1962	8.00	20.00
MGM SE-4488	(S)	Readings From Hamlet	1962	10.00	25.00

VAUGHT, BOB, & THE RENEGAIDS

Crescendo GNP-83	(M)	Surf Crazy	1963	8.00	20.00
Crescendo GNPS-83	(S)	Surf Crazy	1963	10.00	25.00

Label & Catalog #		Title	Year	VG+	NM
VEE, BOBBY					
Liberty LRP-3165	(M)	**Bobby Vee Sings Your Favorites**	1960	12.00	30.00
Liberty LST-7165	(S)	**Bobby Vee Sings Your Favorites**	1960	16.00	40.00
Liberty LRP-3181	(M)	**Bobby Vee**	1961	10.00	25.00
Liberty LST-7181	(S)	**Bobby Vee**	1961	14.00	35.00
Liberty LRP-3186	(M)	**Bobby Vee With Strings And Things**	1961	10.00	25.00
Liberty LST-7186	(S)	**Bobby Vee With Strings And Things**	1961	14.00	35.00
Liberty LRP-3205	(M)	**Bobby Vee Sings Hits Of The Rockin' 50's**	1961	10.00	25.00
Liberty LST-7205	(S)	**Bobby Vee Sings Hits Of The Rockin' 50's**	1961	14.00	35.00
Liberty LRP-3211	(M)	**Take Good Care Of My Baby**	1961	10.00	25.00
Liberty LST-7211	(S)	**Take Good Care Of My Baby**	1961	14.00	35.00
Liberty LRP-3228	(M)	**Bobby Vee Meets The Crickets**	1962	12.00	30.00
Liberty LST-7228	(S)	**Bobby Vee Meets The Crickets**	1962	16.00	40.00
Liberty LRP-3232	(M)	**A Bobby Vee Recording Session**	1962	8.00	20.00
Liberty LST-7232	(S)	**A Bobby Vee Recording Session**	1962	12.00	30.00
Liberty LRP-3245	(M)	**Bobby Vee's Golden Greats**	1962	6.00	15.00
Liberty LST-7245	(S)	**Bobby Vee's Golden Greats**	1962	8.00	20.00
Liberty LRP-3267	(M)	**Merry Christmas From Bobby Vee**	1962	8.00	20.00
Liberty LST-7267	(S)	**Merry Christmas From Bobby Vee**	1962	12.00	30.00
Liberty LRP-3285	(M)	**The Night Has A Thousand Eyes**	1963	8.00	20.00
Liberty LST-7285	(S)	**The Night Has A Thousand Eyes**	1963	12.00	30.00
Liberty LRP-3289	(M)	**Bobby Vee Meets The Ventures**	1963	8.00	20.00
Liberty LST-7289	(S)	**Bobby Vee Meets The Ventures**	1963	12.00	30.00
Liberty LRP-3336	(M)	**I Remember Buddy Holly**	1963	12.00	30.00
Liberty LST-7336	(S)	**I Remember Buddy Holly**	1963	16.00	40.00
Liberty LRP-3352	(M)	**The New Sound From England!**	1964	8.00	20.00
Liberty LST-7352	(S)	**The New Sound From England!**	1964	10.00	25.00
Liberty LRP-3385	(M)	**30 Big Hits From The 60's**	1964	8.00	20.00
Liberty LST-7385	(S)	**30 Big Hits From The 60's**	1964	10.00	25.00
Liberty LRP-3393	(M)	**Bobby Vee Live On Tour**	1965	8.00	20.00
Liberty LST-7393	(S)	**Bobby Vee Live On Tour**	1965	10.00	25.00
		— Original Liberty albums above have black labels with a gold logo on the left side.—			
Liberty LRP-3464	(M)	**Bobby Vee's Golden Greats, Volume 2**	1966	6.00	15.00
Liberty LST-7464	(S)	**Bobby Vee's Golden Greats, Volume 2**	1966	8.00	20.00
Liberty LRP-3480	(M)	**Look At Me Girl**	1966	6.00	15.00
Liberty LST-7480	(S)	**Look At Me Girl**	1966	8.00	20.00
Liberty LRP-3534	(M)	**Come Back When You Grow Up**	1967	5.00	12.00
Liberty LST-7534	(S)	**Come Back When You Grow Up**	1967	6.00	15.00
Liberty LST-7554	(S)	**Just Today**	1968	5.00	12.00
Liberty LST-7592	(S)	**Do What You Gotta Do**	1968	5.00	12.00
Liberty LST-7612	(S)	**Gates, Grills And Railings**	1969	5.00	12.00
United Arts. LA025	(S)	**Legendary Masters** (2 LPs)	1973	12.00	30.00
United Arts. LA085	(S)	**Robert Thomas Velline**	1973	8.00	20.00
VEGAS, PAT & LOLLY					
Mercury MG-21059	(M)	**At The Haunted House**	1966	12.00	30.00
Mercury SR-61059	(S)	**At The Haunted House**	1966	14.00	35.00
VELASCO, VI					
Colpix CP-438	(M)	**Cantando Bossa Nova**	1963	8.00	20.00
VELEZ, MARTHA					
Sire SES-97008	(S)	**Fiends And Angels**	1969	12.00	30.00
VELVET, JIMMY					
Velvetone 101	(S)	**A Touch Of Velvet**	1968	8.00	20.00
United Arts. UAS-6653	(S)	**A Touch Of Velvet**	1968	4.00	10.00
VELVET UNDERGROUND, THE					
Verve V-5008	(DJ)	**The Velvet Underground & Nico** (White label)	1967	180.00	300.00
Verve V-5008	(M)	**The Velvet Underground & Nico**	1967	100.00	200.00
Verve V6-5008	(S)	**The Velvet Underground & Nico**	1967	80.00	160.00
		(First pressing: the cover has a yellow, peel-off banana over the pink banana printed on the cover. The photo of the group on the back cover is framed by a male torso. The price here is for copies with the banana sticker completely intact on the cover!)			
Verve V-5008	(M)	**The Velvet Underground & Nico**	1967	50.00	100.00
Verve V6-5008	(S)	**The Velvet Underground & Nico**	1967	40.00	80.00
		(The price here is for a first pressing with the banana peeled off!)			

For all intents and purposes, the Velvet Underground were virtually unknown in their day, selling records to a handful of insiders and critics. Today, their four albums are considered standards of a certain type of minimalist rock and predecessors of the punk and new wave of the late '70s and early '80s.

While their first three albums can be considered largely experimental (especially for the time), this, their fourth album, was an attempt to bridge the gap between the group's New York-streets-are-the-toughest attitude and a more acceptable pop sensibility. For the most part, they succeeded.

Loaded combines the familiar stuttering strut of Lou Reed's vocals and his heavily strummed electric lead, both dominating the songs Reed penned. While many hardcore fans panned the album at the time ("My God, they sound like the Beatles!"), it has become a favorite of bands looking to plunder the Velvet's trove of treasure with updated covers...

Label & Catalog #		Title	Year	VG+	NM
Verve V-5008	(M)	The Velvet Underground & Nico	1967	80.00	160.00
Verve V6-5008	(S)	The Velvet Underground & Nico	1967	60.00	120.00
		(Second pressing: the cover has a yellow, peel-off banana over the pink banana printed on the cover. The photo of the group on the back is covered with a sticker, hiding the torso. The price here is for copies with the banana sticker completely intact on the cover!)			
Verve V-5008	(M)	The Velvet Underground & Nico	1967	40.00	80.00
Verve V6-5008	(S)	The Velvet Underground & Nico	1967	30.00	60.00
		(The price here is for a second pressing with the banana peeled off!)			
Verve V-5008	(M)	The Velvet Underground & Nico	1967	70.00	140.00
Verve V6-5008	(S)	The Velvet Underground & Nico	1967	50.00	100.00
		(Third pressing: the cover has a yellow, peel-off banana over the pink banana printed on the cover. The torso on the back has been air-brushed out. The price here is for copies with the banana sticker completely intact on the cover!)			
Verve V-5008	(M)	The Velvet Underground & Nico	1967	35.00	70.00
Verve V6-5008	(S)	The Velvet Underground & Nico	1967	20.00	50.00
		(The price here is for a third pressing with the banana peeled off!)			
Verve V-5046	(M)	White Light/White Heat	1967	20.00	50.00
Verve V6-5046	(S)	White Light/White Heat	1967	16.00	40.00
		(Blue label. A black-on-black skull is visible in lower left corner of the front cover when viewed at an angle.)			
MGM SE-4617	(S)	The Velvet Underground	1969	16.00	40.00
MGM GAS-131	(S)	The Velvet Underground	1970	10.00	25.00
Cotillion SD-9034	(S)	Loaded (Light blue label)	1970	8.00	20.00
Mercury SRM-2-7504	(M)	Live 1969 (Gatefold cover)	1972	6.00	15.00

VENTURAS, THE

Drum Boy DBM-1003	(M)	Here They Are	1964	35.00	70.00
Drum Boy DBS-1003	(S)	Here They Are	1964	50.00	100.00

VENTURES, THE
The Ventures also recorded with Bobby Vee.

Dolton BLP-2003	(M)	Walk-Don't Run	1960	8.00	20.00
Dolton BST-8003	(S)	Walk-Don't Run	1960	12.00	30.00
Dolton BLP-2004	(M)	The Ventures	1961	8.00	20.00
Dolton BST-8004	(S)	The Ventures	1961	12.00	30.00
Dolton BLP-2006	(M)	Another Smash!!!	1961	8.00	20.00
Dolton BST-8006	(S)	Another Smash!!!	1961	12.00	30.00
Dolton BLP-2008	(M)	The Colorful Ventures	1961	8.00	20.00
Dolton BST-8008	(S)	The Colorful Ventures	1961	12.00	30.00
Dolton BLP-2010	(M)	Twist With The Ventures	1962	8.00	20.00
Dolton BST-8010	(S)	Twist With The Ventures	1962	12.00	30.00
Dolton BLP-2014	(M)	The Ventures' Twist Party	1962	8.00	20.00
Dolton BST-8014	(S)	The Ventures' Twist Party	1962	12.00	30.00

— Original Dolton albums above have light blue labels with the fish logo above the spindle hole.—

Dolton BLP-2003	(M)	Walk-Don't Run	1963	6.00	15.00
Dolton BST-8003	(S)	Walk-Don't Run	1963	8.00	20.00
Dolton BLP-2004	(M)	The Ventures	1963	6.00	15.00
Dolton BST-8004	(S)	The Ventures	1963	8.00	20.00
Dolton BLP-2006	(M)	Another Smash!!!	1963	6.00	15.00
Dolton BST-8006	(S)	Another Smash!!!	1963	8.00	20.00
Dolton BLP-2008	(M)	The Colorful Ventures	1963	6.00	15.00
Dolton BST-8008	(S)	The Colorful Ventures	1963	8.00	20.00
Dolton BLP-2010	(M)	Dance! (Repackage of "Twist")	1963	6.00	15.00
Dolton BST-8010	(S)	Dance! (Repackage of "Twist")	1963	8.00	20.00
Dolton BLP-2014	(M)	Dance With The Ventures	1963	6.00	15.00
Dolton BST-8014	(S)	Dance With The Ventures	1963	8.00	20.00
		(Repackage of "Twist Party.")			
Dolton BLP-2016	(M)	Mashed Potatoes And Gravy	1962	8.00	20.00
Dolton BST-8016	(S)	Mashed Potatoes And Gravy	1962	10.00	25.00
Dolton BLP-2016	(M)	Beach Party	196?	6.00	15.00
Dolton BST-8016	(S)	Beach Party	196?	8.00	20.00
		(Repackage of "Mashed Potatoes.")			
Dolton BLP-2017	(M)	Going To The Ventures' Dance Party!	1962	6.00	15.00
Dolton BST-8017	(S)	Going To The Ventures' Dance Party!	1962	8.00	20.00
Dolton BLP-2019	(M)	Telstar, The Lonely Bull	1963	6.00	15.00
Dolton BST-8019	(S)	Telstar, The Lonely Bull	1963	8.00	20.00

Label & Catalog #		Title	Year	VG+	NM
Dolton BLP-2022	(M)	**Surfing**	1963	6.00	15.00
Dolton BST-8022	(S)	**Surfing**	1963	8.00	20.00
Dolton BLP-2023	(M)	**The Ventures Play The Country Classics**	1963	5.00	12.00
Dolton BST-8023	(S)	**The Ventures Play The Country Classics**	1963	6.00	15.00
Dolton BLP-2024	(M)	**Let's Go!**	1963	5.00	12.00
Dolton BST-8024	(S)	**Let's Go!**	1963	6.00	15.00
Dolton BLP-2027	(M)	**The Ventures In Space**	1964	5.00	12.00
Dolton BST-8027	(S)	**The Ventures In Space**	1964	6.00	15.00
Dolton BLP-2029	(M)	**The Fabulous Ventures**	1964	5.00	12.00
Dolton BST-8029	(S)	**The Fabulous Ventures**	1964	6.00	15.00
Dolton BLP-2031	(M)	**Walk, Don't Run, Volume 2**	1964	5.00	12.00
Dolton BST-8031	(S)	**Walk, Don't Run, Volume 2**	1964	6.00	15.00
Dolton BLP-2033	(M)	**The Ventures Knock Me Out!**	1965	5.00	12.00
Dolton BST-8033	(S)	**The Ventures Knock Me Out!**	1965	6.00	15.00
Dolton BLP-2035	(M)	**The Ventures On Stage**	1965	5.00	12.00
Dolton BST-8035	(S)	**The Ventures On Stage**	1965	6.00	15.00

—Dolton albums above have dark blue labels with a color logo on the left side.—

Label & Catalog #		Title	Year	VG+	NM
Dolton BLP-16501	(M)	**Play Guitar With The Ventures**	1965	6.00	15.00
Dolton BST-17501	(S)	**Play Guitar With The Ventures**	1965	8.00	20.00
Dolton BLP-16502	(M)	**Play Guitar With The Ventures, Volume 2**	1965	6.00	15.00
Dolton BST-17502	(S)	**Play Guitar With The Ventures, Volume 2**	1965	8.00	20.00
Dolton BLP-16503	(M)	**Play Guitar With The Ventures, Volume 3**	1965	6.00	15.00
Dolton BST-17503	(S)	**Play Guitar With The Ventures, Volume 3**	1965	8.00	20.00
Dolton BLP-16504	(M)	**Play Guitar With The Ventures, Volume 4**	1965	6.00	15.00
Dolton BST-17504	(S)	**Play Guitar With The Ventures, Volume 4**	1965	8.00	20.00
Dolton BLP-2037	(M)	**The Ventures A Go-Go**	1965	5.00	12.00
Dolton BST-8037	(S)	**The Ventures A Go-Go**	1965	6.00	15.00
Dolton BLP-2038	(M)	**The Ventures' Christmas Album**	1965	6.00	15.00
Dolton BST-8038	(S)	**The Ventures' Christmas Album**	1965	8.00	20.00
Dolton BLP-2040	(M)	**Where The Action Is!**	1966	5.00	12.00
Dolton BST-8040	(S)	**Where The Action Is!**	1966	6.00	15.00
Dolton BLP-2042	(M)	**Batman Theme**	1966	8.00	20.00
Dolton BST-8042	(S)	**Batman Theme**	1966	10.00	25.00
Dolton BLP-2045	(M)	**Go With The Ventures!**	1966	5.00	12.00
Dolton BST-8045	(S)	**Go With The Ventures!**	1966	6.00	15.00
Dolton BLP-2047	(M)	**Wild Things!**	1966	5.00	12.00
Dolton BST-8047	(S)	**Wild Things!**	1966	6.00	15.00
Dolton BLP-2050	(M)	**Guitar Freakout**	1967	5.00	12.00
Dolton BST-8050	(S)	**Guitar Freakout**	1967	6.00	15.00
Liberty LRP-4052	(M)	**Super Psychedelics**	1967	5.00	12.00
Liberty LST-8052	(S)	**Super Psychedelics**	1967	6.00	15.00
Liberty LRP-4053	(M)	**Golden Greats By The Ventures**	1967	5.00	12.00
Liberty LST-8053	(S)	**Golden Greats By The Ventures**	1967	6.00	15.00
Liberty LRP-4054	(M)	**$1,000,000.00 Weekend**	1967	5.00	12.00
Liberty LST-8054	(S)	**$1,000,000.00 Weekend**	1967	6.00	15.00
Liberty LST-8055	(S)	**Flights Of Fantasy**	1968	6.00	15.00
Liberty LST-8057	(S)	**The Horse**	1968	6.00	15.00
Liberty LST-8059	(S)	**Underground Fire**	1969	6.00	15.00
Liberty LST-8060	(S)	**More Golden Greats**	1970	6.00	15.00
Liberty LST-8061	(S)	**Hawaii Five-O**	1969	6.00	15.00
Liberty LST-8062	(S)	**Swamp Rock**	1969	6.00	15.00
Liberty LST-35000	(S)	**The Ventures' 10th Anniversary Album**	1970	8.00	20.00
Liberty SCR-5	(S)	**The Versatile Ventures** *(Record club)*	196?	6.00	15.00

VERA, BILLY
Refer to Judy Clay & Billy Vera.

Atlantic SD-8197	(S)	**With Pen In Hand**	1968	6.00	15.00

VERDON, GWEN

RCA Victor LPM-1152	(M)	**The Girl I Left Home For**	1956	10.00	25.00

VERITY BAND, JOHN

Dunhill DSX-500170	(S)	**The John Verity Band**	1974	8.00	20.00

VERNE, LARRY

Era 104	(M)	**Mister Larry Verne**	196?	14.00	35.00

VERNON, MILLI

Storyville 910	(M)	**Introducing Milli Verdon**	1956	12.00	30.00

Label & Catalog #		Title	Year	VG+	NM
VERSATONES, THE					
RCA Victor LPM-1538	(M)	**The Versatones**	1957	16.00	40.00
VESTICH BROTHERS, THE					
Eclipse W11779VB	(S)	**Live At Woofendale's**	1979	35.00	70.00
VETTES, THE					
The Vettes feature Bruce Johnston.					
MGM E-4193	(M)	**Rev-Up**	1963	20.00	50.00
MGM SE-4193	(S)	**Rev-Up**	1963	30.00	60.00
VIBRATIONS, THE					
Checker 2978	(M)	**Watusi**	1961	35.00	70.00
OKeh OKM-4111	(M)	**Shout**	1965	12.00	30.00
OKeh OKS-14111	(S)	**Shout**	1965	14.00	35.00
OKeh OKM-4112	(M)	**Misty**	1966	10.00	25.00
OKeh OKS-14112	(S)	**Misty**	1966	12.00	30.00
OKeh OKS-14129	(S)	**Greatest Hits**	1969	16.00	40.00
Mandate 3006	(S)	**Taking A New Step**	1972	6.00	15.00
VICEROYS, THE					
Bolo BLP-8000	(M)	**The Viceroys At Granny's Pad**	1963	16.00	40.00
VICK TRIGGER BAND, THE					
Sanctuary 12103	(S)	**Electronic Wizard**	197?	40.00	80.00
VICTIMS OF CHANCE, THE					
Crestview CRS-3052	(S)	**The Victims Of Chance**	197?	12.00	30.00
VIGRASS & OSBORNE					
Uni 73129	(S)	**Queues**	1971	8.00	20.00
VILLAGE PEOPLE, THE					
Casablanca 7064	(S)	**Village People** *(Picture disc)*	1978	4.00	10.00
Casablanca 7096	(S)	**Macho Man** *(Picture disc)*	1978	4.00	10.00
VINCENT, GENE					
Capitol T-764	(DJ)	**Bluejean Bop!**	1957	300.00	500.00
Capitol T-764	(M)	**Bluejean Bop!**	1957	180.00	300.00
Capitol T-811	(DJ)	**Gene Vincent & The Blue Caps**	1957	300.00	500.00
Capitol T-811	(M)	**Gene Vincent & The Blue Caps**	1957	180.00	300.00
Capitol T-970	(DJ)	**Gene Vincent Rocks! & The Blue Caps Roll**	1958	300.00	500.00
Capitol T-970	(M)	**Gene Vincent Rocks! & The Blue Caps Roll**	1958	180.00	300.00
Capitol T-985	(DJ)	**Hot Rod Gang** *(Soundtrack)*	1958	300.00	500.00
Capitol T-985	(M)	**Hot Rod Gang** *(Soundtrack)*	1958	180.00	300.00
Capitol T-1059	(DJ)	**A Gene Vincent Record Date**	1958	300.00	500.00
Capitol T-1059	(M)	**A Gene Vincent Record Date**	1958	180.00	300.00
Capitol T-1207	(DJ)	**Sounds Like Gene Vincent**	1959	300.00	500.00
Capitol T-1207	(M)	**Sounds Like Gene Vincent**	1959	180.00	300.00
Capitol T-1342	(DJ)	**Crazy Times**	1960	300.00	500.00
Capitol T-1342	(M)	**Crazy Times**	1960	180.00	300.00
Capitol DKAO-380	(E)	**Gene Vincent's Greatest** *(Green label)*	1969	12.00	30.00
Dandelion 9-102	(S)	**I'm Back And I'm Proud**	1970	10.00	25.00
Kama Sutra 2019	(S)	**If Only You Could See Me Today**	1970	10.00	25.00
Kama Sutra 2027	(S)	**The Day The World Turned Blue**	1971	10.00	25.00
VINSON, EDDIE "CLEANHEAD"					
Refer to Roy Brown; Jimmy Witherspoon.					
Riverside 3502	(M)	**Backdoor Blues**	195?	20.00	50.00
Bethlehem BCP-5005	(M)	**Eddie Cleanhead Vinson Sings**	195?	20.00	50.00
Aamco 312	(M)	**Eddie Cleanhead Vinson Sings**	195?	8.00	20.00
BluesWay BL-6007	(M)	**Cherry Red**	1967	6.00	15.00
BluesWay BLS-6007	(S)	**Cherry Red**	1967	8.00	20.00
VINTON, BOBBY					
Epic BN-3727	(M)	**Dancing At The Hop**	1961	8.00	20.00
Epic LN-579	(S)	**Dancing At The Hop**	1961	10.00	25.00
Epic BN-3780	(M)	**Young Man With A Big Band**	1961	6.00	15.00
Epic LN-597	(S)	**Young Man With A Big Band**	1961	10.00	25.00

Label & Catalog #		Title	Year	VG+	NM
Epic LN-24020	(M)	Roses Are Red	1962	6.00	15.00
Epic BN-26020	(S)	Roses Are Red	1962	8.00	20.00
Epic LN-24035	(M)	Bobby Vinton Sings The Big Ones	1963	6.00	15.00
Epic BN-26035	(S)	Bobby Vinton Sings The Big Ones	1963	8.00	20.00
Epic LN-24049	(M)	The Greatest Hits Of The Greatest Groups	1963	8.00	20.00
Epic BN-26049	(S)	The Greatest Hits Of The Greatest Groups	1963	10.00	25.00
Epic LN-24068	(M)	Blue Velvet	1963	6.00	15.00
Epic BN-26068	(S)	Blue Velvet	1963	8.00	20.00
Epic LN-24081	(M)	There! I've Said It Again	1964	5.00	12.00
Epic BN-26081	(S)	There! I've Said It Again	1964	6.00	15.00
Epic LN-24098	(M)	Bobby Vinton's Greatest Hits	1964	5.00	12.00
Epic BN-26098	(S)	Bobby Vinton's Greatest Hits	1964	6.00	15.00
Epic LN-24113	(M)	Tell Me Why	1964	5.00	12.00
Epic BN-26113	(S)	Tell Me Why	1964	6.00	15.00
Epic LN-24122	(M)	A Very Merry Christmas	1964	5.00	12.00
Epic BN-26122	(S)	A Very Merry Christmas	1964	6.00	15.00
Epic LN-24136	(M)	Mr. Lonely	1965	5.00	12.00
Epic BN-26136	(S)	Mr. Lonely	1965	6.00	15.00
Epic LN-24154	(M)	Bobby Vinton Sings For Lonely Nights	1965	5.00	12.00
Epic BN-26154	(S)	Bobby Vinton Sings For Lonely Nights	1965	6.00	15.00
Epic LN-24170	(M)	Drive-In Movie Time	1965	5.00	12.00
Epic BN-26170	(S)	Drive-In Movie Time	1965	6.00	15.00
Epic LN-24182	(M)	Satin Pillows	1966	5.00	12.00
Epic BN-26182	(S)	Satin Pillows	1966	6.00	15.00
Epic LN-24187	(M)	More Of Bobby Vinton's Greatest Hits	1966	5.00	12.00
Epic BN-26187	(S)	More Of Bobby Vinton's Greatest Hits	1966	6.00	15.00
Epic LN-24188	(M)	Country Boy	1966	5.00	12.00
Epic BN-26188	(S)	Country Boy	1966	6.00	15.00
Epic LN-24203	(M)	Live At The Copa	1966	5.00	12.00
Epic BN-26203	(S)	Live At The Copa	1966	6.00	15.00
Epic LN-24245	(M)	Bobby Vinton Sings The Newest Hits	1967	5.00	12.00
Epic BN-26245	(S)	Bobby Vinton Sings The Newest Hits	1967	6.00	15.00
Epic LN-24341	(M)	Please Love Me Forever	1967	5.00	12.00
Epic BN-26341	(S)	Please Love Me Forever	1967	6.00	15.00
Epic BN-26382	(S)	Take Good Care Of Her	1968	5.00	12.00
Epic BN-26437	(S)	I Love How You Love Me	1969	5.00	12.00

— Original Epic albums above have yellow labels. —

VIRGIN INSANITY

Funky 71411	(S)	Illusions Of The Maintenance Man	1970	100.00	200.00

VIRTUE, FRANK, & THE VIRTUES,

Fayette 1816	(M)	Frank Virtue & The Virtues	196?	16.00	40.00

VIRTUES, THE

Wynne WLP-111	(M)	Guitar Boogie Shuffle	1960	20.00	50.00
Strand L-1061	(M)	Guitar Boogie Shuffle	1960	12.00	30.00
Strand SL-1061	(S)	Guitar Boogie Shuffle	1960	16.00	40.00

VISCOUNTS, THE

Madison 1001	(M)	The Viscounts	1960	50.00	100.00
Amy 8008	(M)	Harlem Nocturne	1965	12.00	30.00
Amy S-8008	(P)	Harlem Nocturne	1965	16.00	40.00

VOGUES, THE

Co&Ce 1229	(M)	Meet The Vogues	1965	10.00	25.00
Co&Ce 1229	(S)	Meet The Vogues	1965	14.00	35.00
Co&Ce 1230	(M)	Five O' Clock World	1966	10.00	25.00
Co&Ce 1230	(S)	Five O' Clock World	1966	14.00	35.00

VON SCHMIDT, ERIC

Prestige 7384	(M)	Eric Sings Von Schmidt	1964	6.00	15.00
Prestige 7384	(S)	Eric Sings Von Schmidt	1964	8.00	20.00
Prestige 7717	(S)	The Folk Blues Of Eric Von Schmidt	1969	6.00	15.00
Smash SRS-67124	(S)	Who Knocked The Brains Out Of The Sky	1969	6.00	15.00

VOYAGER

Camwood	(S)	Sound Barriers	1981	20.00	50.00

Label & Catalog #		Title	Year	VG+	NM

VULCAN
| 13th Records | (S) | **Vulcan** | 1985 | 80.00 | 160.00 |

WABASH RESURRECTION, THE
| Pepperland 76294 | (S) | **Get It Off!** | 197? | 50.00 | 100.00 |

WADE, ADAM
Coed LPC-902	(M)	**And Then Came Adam**	1960	16.00	40.00
Coed LPC-903	(M)	**Adam And Evening**	1961	12.00	30.00
Coed LPCS-903	(S)	**Adam And Evening**	1961	16.00	40.00
Epic LN-24019	(M)	**Adam Wade's Greatest Hits**	1962	6.00	15.00
Epic BN-26019	(S)	**Adam Wade's Greatest Hits**	1962	8.00	20.00
Epic LN-24026	(M)	**One Is A Lonely Number**	1962	6.00	15.00
Epic BN-26026	(S)	**One Is A Lonely Number**	1962	8.00	20.00
Epic LN-24044	(M)	**What Kind Of Fool Am I?**	1963	6.00	15.00
Epic BN-26044	(S)	**What Kind Of Fool Am I?**	1963	8.00	20.00
Epic LN-24056	(M)	**A Very Good Year For Girls**	1963	6.00	15.00
Epic BN-26056	(S)	**A Very Good Year For Girls**	1963	8.00	20.00

— Original Epic albums above have yellow labels.—

WAGONER, PORTER (& THE WAGONMASTERS)
Refer to Hank Snow / Hank Lochlin / Porter Wagoner.
RCA Victor LPM-1358	(M)	**A Satisfied Mind**	1956	20.00	50.00
RCA Victor LPM-2447	(M)	**A Slice Of Life-Songs Happy 'N' Sad**	1962	8.00	20.00
RCA Victor LSP-2447	(S)	**A Slice Of Life-Songs Happy 'N' Sad**	1962	12.00	30.00
RCA Victor LPM-2650	(M)	**The Porter Wagoner Show**	1963	8.00	20.00
RCA Victor LSP-2650	(S)	**The Porter Wagoner Show**	1963	12.00	30.00
RCA Victor LPM-2706	(M)	**Y'All Come**	1963	8.00	20.00
RCA Victor LSP-2706	(S)	**Y'All Come**	1963	12.00	30.00

— Original RCA mono albums above have "Long Play" on the bottom of the label;
stereo albums have "Living Stereo" on the bottom.—

RCA Victor LPM-2960	(M)	**The Bluegrass Story**	1964	8.00	20.00
RCA Victor LSP-2960	(S)	**The Bluegrass Story**	1964	10.00	25.00
RCA Victor LPM-3389	(M)	**The Thin Man From West Plains**	1965	8.00	20.00
RCA Victor LSP-3389	(S)	**The Thin Man From West Plains**	1965	10.00	25.00
RCA Victor LPM-3488	(M)	**Grand Old Gospel**	1966	8.00	20.00
RCA Victor LSP-3488	(S)	**Grand Old Gospel**	1966	10.00	25.00
RCA Victor LPM-3560	(M)	**The Best Of Porter Wagoner**	1966	5.00	12.00
RCA Victor LSP-3560	(S)	**The Best Of Porter Wagoner**	1966	6.00	15.00
RCA Victor LPM-3593	(M)	**Confessions Of A Broken Man**	1966	5.00	12.00
RCA Victor LSP-3593	(S)	**Confessions Of A Broken Man**	1966	6.00	15.00
RCA Victor LPM-3683	(M)	**Soul Of A Convict**	1967	5.00	12.00
RCA Victor LSP-3683	(S)	**Soul Of A Convict**	1967	6.00	15.00
RCA Victor LPM-3797	(M)	**The Cold Hard Facts Of Life**	1967	6.00	15.00
RCA Victor LSP-3797	(S)	**The Cold Hard Facts Of Life**	1967	8.00	20.00
RCA Victor LPM-3855	(M)	**More Grand Old Gospel**	1967	5.00	12.00
RCA Victor LSP-3855	(S)	**More Grand Old Gospel**	1967	6.00	15.00
RCA Victor LPM-3968	(M)	**The Bottom Of The Bottle**	1968	20.00	50.00
RCA Victor LSP-3968	(S)	**The Bottom Of The Bottle**	1968	5.00	12.00
RCA Victor LSP-4034	(S)	**Gospel Country**	1968	5.00	12.00

— Original RCA albums above have black labels.—

Label & Catalog #		Title	Year	VG+	NM
WAGONER, PORTER, & SKEETER DAVIS					
RCA Victor LPM-2529	(M)	**Duets**	1962	8.00	20.00
RCA Victor LSP-2529	(S)	**Duets**	1962	12.00	30.00
WAGONER, PORTER, & NORMA JEAN					
RCA Victor LPM-2840	(M)	**In Person**	1964	8.00	20.00
RCA Victor LSP-2840	(S)	**In Person**	1964	10.00	25.00
RCA Victor LPM-3509	(M)	**Live On The Road**	1966	6.00	15.00
RCA Victor LSP-3509	(S)	**Live On The Road**	1966	8.00	20.00
WAGONER, PORTER, & DOLLY PARTON					
RCA Victor LPM-3926	(M)	**Just Between You And Me** *(Black label)*	1968	20.00	50.00
RCA Victor LSP-3926	(S)	**Just Between You And Me** *(Black label)*	1968	8.00	20.00
RCA Victor LSP-4039	(S)	**Just The Two Of Us**	1968	6.00	15.00
RCA Victor LSP-4186	(S)	**Always, Always**	1969	6.00	15.00
RCA Victor LSP-4305	(S)	**Porter Wayne And Dolly Rebecca**	1970	6.00	15.00
RCA Victor LSP-4388	(S)	**Once More**	1970	6.00	15.00
RCA Victor LSP-4490	(S)	**Two Of A Kind**	1971	6.00	15.00
RCA Victor LSP-4556	(S)	**The Best Of Porter Wagoner & Dolly Parton**	1971	6.00	15.00
RCA Victor LSP-4628	(S)	**The Right Combination**	1972	6.00	15.00
RCA Victor LSP-4761	(S)	**Together Always**	1972	6.00	15.00
RCA Victor LSP-4841	(S)	**We Found It**	1973	6.00	15.00

— Original RCA albums above have orange labels.—

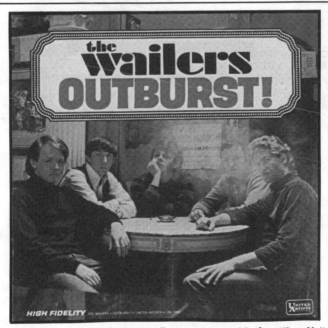

While their early albums garner the most collector attention, "Outburst!" on United Artists has become an increasingly difficult album to find, especially the stereo version.

WAILERS, THE					
Refer to The Sonics.					
Golden Crest CR-3075	(M)	**Fabulous Wailers** *(Color cover)*	1959	50.00	100.00
Golden Crest CR-3075	(M)	**Fabulous Wailers** *(Black & white cover)*	1959	35.00	70.00
Golden Crest CR-3075	(M)	**Fabulous Wailers** *(Titles cover)*	1959	20.00	50.00
Etiquette ALB-01	(M)	**Wailers At The Castle**	1962	20.00	50.00
Etiquette ALB-022	(M)	**Wailers & Company**	1963	20.00	50.00
Imperial LP-9262	(M)	**Tall Cool One**	1964	14.00	35.00
Imperial LP-12262	(S)	**Tall Cool One**	1964	20.00	50.00
Etiquette ALB-023	(M)	**Wailers, Wailers, Everywhere**	1965	20.00	50.00

Label & Catalog #		Title	Year	VG+	NM
Etiquette ALB-026	(M)	Out Of Our Tree	1966	20.00	50.00
United Arts. UAL-3557	(M)	Outburst!	1966	12.00	30.00
United Arts. UAS-6557	(P)	Outburst!	1966	16.00	40.00
Bell 6016	(M)	Walk Thru The People	1968	8.00	20.00

WAKELY, JIMMY
Wakely was formerly a member of Gene Autry's traveling band.

Capitol H-9004 (10")	(M)	Christmas On The Range	1950	20.00	50.00
Capitol H-4008 (10")	(M)	Songs Of The West	1950	30.00	60.00
Decca DL-8409	(M)	Santa Fe Trail	1956	16.00	40.00
Decca DL-8680	(M)	Enter And Rest And Pray	1957	16.00	40.00
Decca DL-78680	(E)	Enter And Rest And Pray	196?	5.00	12.00
Shasta SHLP-501	(M)	Country Million Sellers	1959	10.00	25.00
Shasta SHLP-502	(M)	Merry Christmas	1959	10.00	25.00
Shasta SHLP-505	(M)	Jimmy Wakely Sings	1960	10.00	25.00
Dot DLP-3711	(M)	Slippin' Around	1966	5.00	12.00
Dot DLP-25711	(S)	Slippin' Around	1966	6.00	15.00
Dot DLP-3754	(M)	Christmas With Jimmy Wakely	1966	5.00	12.00
Dot DLP-25754	(S)	Christmas With Jimmy Wakely	1966	6.00	15.00
Decca DL7-5077	(S)	Heartaches	1969	5.00	12.00
Decca DL7-5192	(S)	Now And Then	1970	5.00	12.00

WAKEMAN, RICK
Wakeman was formerly a member of Yes.

A&M QU-54361	(Q)	The Six Wives Of Henry The VIII	1973	6.00	15.00
A&M QU-53621	(Q)	Journey To The Center Of The Earth	1975	6.00	15.00
A&M QU-54515	(Q)	The Myths And Legends Of King Arthur	1975	6.00	15.00

WALES, HOWARD, & JERRY GARCIA

Douglas-5 KZ-30589	(S)	Hooteroll	1971	8.00	20.00

WALKER, BILLY

Columbia CL-1624	(M)	Everybody's Hits But Mine	1961	8.00	20.00
Columbia CS-8424	(S)	Everybody's Hits But Mine	1961	12.00	30.00

— Original Columbia album above has three white "eye" logos on each side of the spindle hole.—

Columbia CL-1935	(M)	Billy Walker's Greatest Hits	1963	5.00	12.00
Columbia CS-8735	(S)	Billy Walker's Greatest Hits	1963	6.00	15.00
Columbia CL-2206	(M)	Thank You For Calling	1964	5.00	12.00
Columbia CS-9006	(S)	Thank You For Calling	1964	6.00	15.00
Columbia CL-2331	(M)	The Gun, The Gold And The Girl	1965	5.00	12.00
Columbia CS-9131	(S)	The Gun, The Gold And The Girl	1965	6.00	15.00

WALKER, CHARLIE

Columbia CL-1691	(M)	Greatest Hits ("Eyes" logo label)	1961	8.00	20.00
Columbia CS-8491	(S)	Greatest Hits ("Eyes" logo label)	1961	12.00	30.00

WALKER, CINDY

Monument MLP-8020	(M)	Words And Music By Cindy Walker	1964	8.00	20.00
Monument SLP-18020	(S)	Words And Music By Cindy Walker	1964	10.00	25.00

WALKER, CLINT

Warner Bros. W-1343	(M)	Inspiration	1959	8.00	20.00

WALKER, JERRY JEFF

Atco SD-33-259	(S)	Mr. Bojangles	1968	8.00	20.00
Atco SD-33-297	(S)	Five Years Gone	1969	12.00	30.00
Atco SD-33-336	(S)	Bein' Free	1970	8.00	20.00
Vanguard VSD-6521	(S)	Driftin' Way Of Life	1969	8.00	20.00
Elektra 6E-163	(S)	Jerry Jeff	1971	5.00	12.00
Elektra 6E-239	(S)	Too Old To Change	1971	5.00	12.00
Decca DL-75384	(S)	Jerry Jeff Walker	1972	6.00	15.00

WALKER, JUNIOR (& THE ALL STARS)

Soul 701	(M)	Shotgun	1965	8.00	20.00
Soul SS-701	(S)	Shotgun	1965	12.00	30.00
Soul 702	(M)	Soul Session	1966	6.00	15.00
Soul SS-702	(S)	Soul Session	1966	8.00	20.00
Soul 703	(M)	Road Runner	1966	6.00	15.00
Soul SS-703	(S)	Road Runner	1966	8.00	20.00

Label & Catalog #		Title	Year	VG+	NM
Soul 705	(M)	Junior Walker & The All Stars Live	1967	6.00	15.00
Soul SS-705	(S)	Junior Walker & The All Stars Live	1967	8.00	20.00
Soul 710	(S)	Home Cookin'	1969	6.00	15.00
Soul SS-718	(S)	Greatest Hits	1969	6.00	15.00
Soul SS-721	(S)	Gotta Hold On To This Feeling	1969	6.00	15.00
Soul SS-721	(S)	What Does It Take To Win Your Love	1969	5.00	12.00
		(Repackage of "Gotta Hold On To This Feeling.")			
Soul SS-725	(S)	Junior Walker & The All Stars Live	1970	4.00	10.00
Soul SS-726	(S)	A Gasssss	1970	4.00	10.00
Soul SS-732	(S)	Rainbow Funk	1971	4.00	10.00
Soul SS-733	(S)	Moody Jr.	1971	4.00	10.00
Motown MS-786	(S)	Anthology (2 LPs)	1979	6.00	15.00

WALKER, LUCILLE

Label & Catalog #		Title	Year	VG+	NM
Checker 1428	(M)	The Best Of Lucille Walker	1957	50.00	100.00

WALKER, OLIVE

Label & Catalog #		Title	Year	VG+	NM
RCA Victor LPB-3001	(M)	Folk Songs Of Trinidad And Tobago	1962	6.00	15.00

WALKER, SCOTT

Scott Walker is a pseudonym for Scott Engel. Refer to Scott Engel; The Walker Brothers.

Label & Catalog #		Title	Year	VG+	NM
Smash SRS-67099	(S)	Aloner	1968	6.00	15.00
Smash SRS-67106	(S)	Scott, Volume 2	1968	6.00	15.00
Smash SRS-67121	(S)	Scott Walker 3	1969	6.00	15.00

WALKER, T-BONE

T-Bone is a pseudonym for Aaron Walker.

Label & Catalog #		Title	Year	VG+	NM
Capitol H-370 (10")	(M)	Classics In Jazz	1953	300.00	500.00
Capitol T-370	(M)	Classics In Jazz	1953	100.00	200.00
Atlantic 8020	(M)	T-Bone Blues (Black label)	1959	50.00	100.00
Atlantic 8020	(M)	T-Bone Blues (Red label)	196?	20.00	50.00
Atlantic SD-8256	(S)	T-Bone Blues	1970	8.00	20.00
Imperial LP-9098	(M)	Sings The Blues	1959	35.00	70.00
Imperial LP-9116	(M)	Singing The Blues	1960	35.00	70.00
Imperial LP-9146	(M)	I Get So Weary	1961	35.00	70.00
Capitol T-1958	(M)	Great Blues Vocals And Guitar	1963	20.00	50.00
Capitol ST-1958	(S)	Great Blues Vocals And Guitar	1963	35.00	70.00
Delmark D-633	(M)	I Want A Little Girl	1967	8.00	20.00
Delmark DS-633	(S)	I Want A Little Girl	1967	10.00	25.00
Wet Soul 1002	(M)	Stormy Monday Blues	1967	8.00	20.00
Wet Soul 1002	(S)	Stormy Monday Blues	1967	10.00	25.00
Brunswick BL-754126	(S)	The Truth	1968	8.00	20.00
Bluestime 29010	(S)	Blue Rocks	1968	8.00	20.00
BluesWay BLS-6014	(S)	Funky Town	1968	8.00	20.00
BluesWay BLS-6061	(S)	Blues Classics	1973	6.00	15.00
BluesWay BLS-6058	(S)	Dirty Mistreater	1973	6.00	15.00
Polydor PD-5521	(S)	Fly Walker Airlines	1973	6.00	15.00
Reprise 2XS-6483	(S)	Very Rare (2 LPs)	1973	8.00	20.00
Blue Note BNLA-533	(S)	T-Bone Walker	197?	6.00	15.00

WALKER BROTHERS, THE

Features Scott Engel, Gary Leeds and John Maus as Scott, Gary and John Walker.

Label & Catalog #		Title	Year	VG+	NM
Smash MGS-27076	(M)	Introducing The Walker Brothers	1966	10.00	25.00
Smash SRS-67076	(E)	Introducing The Walker Brothers	1966	8.00	20.00
Smash MGS-27082	(M)	The Sun Ain't Gonna Shine Anymore	1967	10.00	25.00
Smash SRS-67082	(E)	The Sun Ain't Gonna Shine Anymore	1967	8.00	20.00

WALLACE, JERRY

Label & Catalog #		Title	Year	VG+	NM
Challenge CHL-606	(M)	Just Jerry	1959	30.00	60.00
Challenge CHL-612	(M)	There She Goes	1961	10.00	25.00
Challenge CHS-612	(S)	There She Goes	1961	14.00	35.00
Challenge CHL-616	(M)	Shutters And Boards	1962	8.00	20.00
Challenge CHS-616	(S)	Shutters And Boards	1962	10.00	25.00
Challenge CHL-619	(M)	In The Misty Moonlight	1964	6.00	15.00
Challenge CHS-619	(S)	In The Misty Moonlight	1964	8.00	20.00
Mercury MG-21072	(M)	The Best Of Jerry Wallace	1966	5.00	12.00
Mercury SR-61072	(S)	The Best Of Jerry Wallace	1966	6.00	15.00

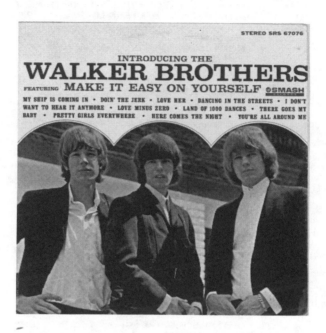

The British trio, the Walker Brothers, were not Walkers nor were they brothers nor were they British! Expatriate Americans John Maus a.k.a. John Stewart, Scott Engel and Gary Leeds had a lengthy history in rock 'n roll, having recorded surf, instrumentals and pop.

While they achieved enormous success in Great Britain with their good looks and Spectorized ballad style, they fared only modestly in the U.S., with both "Make It Easy On Yourself" and "The Sun Ain't Gonna Shine (Anymore)" racking up huge sales in late '65 and early '66.

Both of their Smash albums are extremely difficult to find in collectible condition...

Label & Catalog #		Title	Year	VG+	NM
WALLACE BROTHERS, THE					
Sims 128	(M)	Soul, Soul And More Soul	1965	6.00	15.00
Sims 128	(S)	Soul, Soul And More Soul	1965	8.00	20.00
WALLER, GORDON					
Gordon was formerly a member of Peter & Gordon.					
ABC X-749	(S)	And Gordon	1972	6.00	15.00
WALLER, JIM, & THE DELTAS					
Arvee A-432	(M)	Surfin' Wild	1963	10.00	25.00
Arvee AS-432	(S)	Surfin' Wild	1963	14.00	35.00
WALNUT BAND, THE					
Appaloosa CSL452	(S)	The Walnut Band Goes Nuts!	197?	90.00	180.00
WALSH, JOE					
Walsh was formerly a member of The James Gang; The Eagles.					
Command QD-40016	(Q)	The Smoker You Drink, The Player You Get	1974	6.00	15.00
Command QD-40017	(Q)	So What	1975	6.00	15.00
WALTONS, THE					
Columbia KC-33193	(S)	The Waltons' Christmas Album	1975	6.00	15.00
WANDERIN' FIVE, THE					
Somerset SF-8600	(M)	Pickin' And Singin' Folk Songs	1963	5.00	12.00
Somerset SF-18600	(S)	Pickin' And Singin' Folk Songs	1963	6.00	15.00
Somerset SF-9900	(M)	Hootenanny At The Limelight	1963	5.00	12.00
Somerset SF-19900	(S)	Hootenanny At The Limelight	1963	6.00	15.00
WAR					
War also recorded with Eric Burdon.					
United Arts. SP-103	(DJ)	Radio Free War *(Blue vinyl)*	1974	8.00	20.00
WARD, BILLY, & THE DOMINOES					
Federal 295-94 (10")	(M)	Billy Ward & His Dominoes	1954	3,500.00	5,000.00
Federal 395-548	(M)	Billy Ward & His Dominoes	1956	660.00	1,000.00
Federal 395-559	(M)	Clyde McPhatter With Billy Ward & His Dominoes	1957	660.00	1,000.00
King LP-548	(M)	Billy Ward & His Dominoes	1958	300.00	500.00
King LP-559	(M)	Clyde McPhatter With Billy Ward & His Dominoes	1958	300.00	500.00
King LP-733	(M)	Billy Ward & His Dominoes Featuring Clyde McPhatter And Jackie Wilson	1960	300.00	500.00
Decca DL-8621	(M)	Billy Ward & His Dominoes	1958	75.00	150.00
Liberty LRP-3056	(M)	Sea Of Glass	1957	30.00	60.00
Liberty LST-7056	(S)	Sea Of Glass	1957	40.00	80.00
Liberty LRP-3083	(M)	Yours Forever	1958	30.00	60.00
Liberty LST-7083	(S)	Yours Forever	1958	40.00	80.00
Liberty LRP-3113	(M)	Pagan Love Song	1959	30.00	60.00
Liberty LST-7113	(S)	Pagan Love Song	1959	40.00	80.00
King LP-952	(M)	Twenty Four Songs	1966	20.00	50.00
— Original King albums above have crownless black labels.—					
WARD, HELEN					
Columbia CL-6271 (10")	(M)	It's Been So Long	1954	16.00	40.00
RCA Victor LPM-1464	(M)	With A Little Bit Of Swing	1958	10.00	25.00
WARD, ROBIN					
Dot DLP-3555	(M)	Wonderful Summer	1963	16.00	40.00
Dot DLP-25555	(S)	Wonderful Summer	1963	20.00	50.00
WARREN, FRAN					
RCA Victor LM-61 (10")	(M)	Mr. Imperium *(Soundtrack)*	1951	50.00	100.00
MGM E-3394	(M)	Mood Indigo	1956	14.00	35.00
Venise 7019	(M)	Come Rain Or Come Shine	195?	8.00	20.00
Venise 10019	(S)	Come Rain Or Come Shine	195?	12.00	30.00
Warwick T-2012	(M)	Something's Coming	1960	6.00	15.00
Warwick ST-2012	(S)	Something's Coming	1960	8.00	20.00

Label & Catalog #		Title	Year	VG+	NM
WARWICK, DEE DEE					
Mercury MG-21100	(M)	I Want To Be With You	1967	6.00	15.00
Mercury SR-61100	(S)	I Want To Be With You	1967	8.00	20.00
Mercury SR-61221	(S)	Dee Dee Warwick	1969	6.00	15.00
Atco SD-33-337	(S)	Turnin' Around	1970	5.00	12.00
WARWICK, DIONNE					
Scepter S-508	(M)	Presenting Dionne Warwick	1963	6.00	15.00
Scepter S-508	(S)	Presenting Dionne Warwick	1963	8.00	20.00
Scepter S-517	(M)	Anyone Who Had A Heart	1964	6.00	15.00
Scepter SS-517	(S)	Anyone Who Had A Heart	1964	8.00	20.00
Scepter S-523	(M)	Make Way For Dionne Warwick	1964	4.00	10.00
Scepter SS-523	(S)	Make Way For Dionne Warwick	1964	5.00	12.00
Scepter S-528	(M)	The Sensitive Sound Of Dionne Warwick	1965	4.00	10.00
Scepter SS-528	(S)	The Sensitive Sound Of Dionne Warwick	1965	5.00	12.00
United Arts. UAL-4128	(M)	What's New, Pussycat? (Soundtrack)	1965	6.00	15.00
United Arts. UAS-5128	(S)	What's New, Pussycat? (Soundtrack)	1965	8.00	20.00
Scepter S-531	(M)	Here I Am	1966	4.00	10.00
Scepter SS-531	(S)	Here I Am	1966	5.00	12.00
Scepter S-534	(M)	Dionne Warwick In Paris	1966	4.00	10.00
Scepter SS-534	(S)	Dionne Warwick In Paris	1966	5.00	12.00
Scepter S-555	(M)	Here Where There Is Love	1966	4.00	10.00
Scepter SS-555	(S)	Here Where There Is Love	1966	5.00	12.00
Scepter S-559	(M)	On Stage And In The Movies	1967	4.00	10.00
Scepter SS-559	(S)	On Stage And In The Movies	1967	5.00	12.00
Scepter S-563	(M)	The Windows Of The World	1967	4.00	10.00
Scepter SS-563	(S)	The Windows Of The World	1967	5.00	12.00
Scepter S-565	(M)	Dionne Warwick's Golden Hits, Part One	1967	4.00	10.00
Scepter SS-565	(S)	Dionne Warwick's Golden Hits, Part One	1967	5.00	12.00
Scepter SS-573	(S)	Soulful	1969	6.00	15.00
		— Original Scepter albums above have orange labels. —			
Mobile Fidelity MFSL-098	(S)	Hot! Live And Otherwise (2 LPs)	1980	8.00	20.00
WASHINGTON, BABY					
Baby is a pseudonym for Jeanette Washington.					
Sue LP-1014	(M)	That's How Heartaches Are Made	1963	20.00	50.00
Veep 16528	(S)	With You In Mind	1968	8.00	20.00
WASHINGTON, DINAH					
Refer to Brook Benton; Sarah Vaughan.					
Mercury MG-25060 (10")	(M)	Dinah Washington Songs	1950	35.00	70.00
Mercury MG-25138 (10")	(M)	Dynamic Dinah	1951	35.00	70.00
Mercury MG-25140 (10")	(M)	Blazing Ballads	1951	35.00	70.00
EmArcy 26032 (10")	(M)	After Hours With Miss D	1954	20.00	50.00
EmArcy MG-36000	(M)	Dinah Jams	1954	20.00	50.00
EmArcy MG-36011	(M)	For Those In Love	1955	20.00	50.00
EmArcy MG-36028	(M)	After Hours With Miss D	1955	20.00	50.00
EmArcy MG-36065	(M)	Dinah	1956	16.00	40.00
EmArcy MG-36073	(M)	In The Land Of Hi Fi	1956	16.00	40.00
EmArcy MG-36104	(M)	The Swingin' Miss D	1956	16.00	40.00
EmArcy MG-36119	(M)	Dinah Washington Sings Fats Waller	1957	16.00	40.00
EmArcy MG-36130	(M)	Dinah Washington Sings Bessie Smith	1958	16.00	40.00
EmArcy MG-36141	(M)	Newport '58	1958	16.00	40.00
Mercury MG-20119	(M)	Music For A First Love	1957	12.00	30.00
Mercury MG-20120	(M)	Music For Late Hours	1957	12.00	30.00
Mercury MG-20247	(M)	The Best In Blues	1957	12.00	30.00
Mercury MG-20439	(M)	The Queen	1959	8.00	20.00
Mercury SR-60111	(S)	The Queen	1959	12.00	30.00
Mercury MG-20479	(M)	What A Diff'rence A Day Makes	1959	8.00	20.00
Mercury SR-60158	(S)	What A Diff'rence A Day Makes	1959	12.00	30.00
Mercury MG-20523	(M)	Newport '58	1959	10.00	20.00
Mercury SR-60200	(M)	Newport '58	1959	10.00	20.00
Mercury MG-20525	(M)	Dinah Washington Sings Fats Waller	1959	8.00	20.00
Mercury SR-60202	(S)	Dinah Washington Sings Fats Waller	1959	12.00	30.00
Mercury MG-20572	(M)	Unforgettable	1960	8.00	20.00
Mercury SR-60232	(S)	Unforgettable	1960	12.00	30.00
Mercury MG-20604	(M)	I Concentrate On You	1961	8.00	20.00
Mercury SR-60604	(S)	I Concentrate On You	1961	12.00	30.00

Label & Catalog #		Title	Year	VG+	NM
Mercury MG-20614	(M)	For Lonely Lovers	1961	8.00	20.00
Mercury SR-60614	(S)	For Lonely Lovers	1961	12.00	30.00
Mercury MG-20638	(M)	September In The Rain	1961	8.00	20.00
Mercury SR-60638	(S)	September In The Rain	1961	12.00	30.00
Mercury MG-20661	(M)	Tears And Laughter	1962	8.00	20.00
Mercury SR-60661	(S)	Tears And Laughter	1962	12.00	30.00
Mercury MG-20729	(M)	I Wanna Be Loved	1962	8.00	20.00
Mercury SR-60729	(S)	I Wanna Be Loved	1962	12.00	30.00
Mercury MG-20788	(M)	This Is My Story, Volume 1	1963	8.00	20.00
Mercury SR-60788	(S)	This Is My Story, Volume 1	1963	12.00	30.00
Mercury MG-20789	(M)	This Is My Story, Volume 2	1963	8.00	20.00
Mercury SR-60789	(S)	This Is My Story, Volume 2	1963	12.00	30.00
Mercury MG-20829	(M)	The Good Old Days	1963	10.00	25.00
Mercury SR-60829	(E)	The Good Old Days	1963	6.00	15.00
— Original Mercury albums above have black labels with silver print. —					
Roulette R-25170	(M)	Dinah '62 (White label)	1962	8.00	20.00
Roulette SR-25170	(S)	Dinah '62 (White label)	1962	10.00	25.00
Roulette R-25180	(M)	In Love	1962	6.00	15.00
Roulette SR-25180	(S)	In Love	1962	8.00	20.00
Roulette R-25183	(M)	Drinking Again	1962	6.00	15.00
Roulette SR-25183	(S)	Drinking Again	1962	8.00	20.00
Roulette R-25189	(M)	Back To The Blues	1962	6.00	15.00
Roulette SR-25189	(S)	Back To The Blues	1962	8.00	20.00
Roulette R-25220	(M)	Dinah '63	1963	6.00	15.00
Roulette SR-25220	(S)	Dinah '63	1963	8.00	20.00
— Original Roulette albums above have orange & pink labels. —					
Roulette R-25244	(M)	In Tribute	1963	5.00	12.00
Roulette SR-25244	(S)	In Tribute	1963	6.00	15.00
Roulette R-25253	(M)	Stranger On Earth	1964	5.00	12.00
Roulette SR-25253	(S)	Stranger On Earth	1964	6.00	15.00
Roulette R 25269	(M)	Dinah Washington	1964	5.00	12.00
Roulette SR-25269	(S)	Dinah Washington	1964	6.00	15.00
Roulette R-25289	(M)	The Best Of Dinah Washington	1965	5.00	12.00
Roulette SR-25289	(S)	The Best Of Dinah Washington	1965	6.00	15.00
Mercury R-60928	(M)	The Queen And Quincy	1965	5.00	12.00
Mercury SR-60928	(S)	The Queen And Quincy	1965	6.00	15.00
Mercury MG-21119	(M)	Dinah Discovered	1967	5.00	12.00
Mercury SR-61119	(S)	Dinah Discovered	1967	6.00	15.00
Mercury PKW-2-121	(S)	The Original Queen Of Soul	1969	5.00	12.00
Mercury SRM-2-603	(S)	This Is My Story (2 LPs)	197?	5.00	12.00

WASHINGTON, GINO
Kapp K-3415	(M)	Ram Jam Band	1967	6.00	15.00

WASHINGTON, JUSTINE
Sue 1042	(M)	Only Those In Love	1965	8.00	20.00
Sue S-1042	(S)	Only Those In Love	1965	10.00	25.00

WATERFORD, CROWN PRINCE: Refer to AMOS MILBURN

WATERS, ETHEL
Jay 3010 (10")	(M)	Ethel Waters Singing Her Best	195?	20.00	50.00
"X" 1009	(M)	Ethel Waters	195?	14.00	35.00
Continental 16008	(M)	Ethel Waters Sings	195?	14.00	35.00

WATSON, DOC (& MERLE WATSON)
Folkways FA-2366	(M)	Doc Watson And Family	1963	10.00	25.00
Vanguard VSD-9152	(M)	Doc Watson	1964	8.00	20.00
Vanguard VSD7-9152	(S)	Doc Watson	1964	10.00	25.00
Vanguard VSD-9170	(M)	Doc Watson And Son	1965	8.00	20.00
Vanguard VSD7-9170	(S)	Doc Watson And Son	1965	10.00	25.00
Vanguard VSD-9213	(M)	Southbound	1966	6.00	15.00
Vanguard VSD7-9213	(S)	Southbound	1966	8.00	20.00
Vanguard VSD-9239	(M)	Home Again	1967	6.00	15.00
Vanguard VSD7-9239	(S)	Home Again	1967	8.00	20.00
Vanguard VSD7-9276	(S)	Good Deal	1968	6.00	15.00
Poppy PYS-5703	(S)	The Elementary Doc Watson	1972	6.00	15.00
Poppy LA022	(S)	Then And Now	1973	6.00	15.00
Poppy LA210	(S)	Two Days In November	1974	6.00	15.00

Label & Catalog #		Title	Year	VG+	NM
WATSON, JOHNNY "GUITAR"					
King LP-857	(M)	**Johnny Guitar Watson**	1963	75.00	150.00
Chess 1490	(M)	**Blues Soul**	1965	35.00	70.00
OKeh OKM-4118	(M)	**Bad**	1967	10.00	25.00
OKeh OKS-14118	(S)	**Bad**	1967	14.00	35.00
OKeh OKM-4124	(M)	**In The Fats Bag**	1967	8.00	20.00
OKeh OKS-14124	(S)	**In The Fats Bag**	1967	10.00	25.00
Cadet 4056	(S)	**I Cried For You**	1967	8.00	20.00
WATSON, JOHNNY "GUITAR", & LARRY WILLIAMS					
OKeh OKM-4122	(M)	**Two For The Price Of One**	1967	10.00	25.00
OKeh OKS-14122	(S)	**Two For The Price Of One**	1967	14.00	35.00
WATTS, ALAN					
Together	(S)	**Dhyana: Of The Art Of Meditation**	1970	10.00	25.00
Ascension	(S)	**Dhyana: Of The Art Of Meditation, Volume 2**	1970	10.00	25.00
		(Both "Dhyana" albums produced by Gary Usher.)			
WAVECRESTS, THE					
Viking VKS-6606	(M)	**Surftime U.S.A.**	1963	12.00	30.00
WAYFARERS, THE					
RCA Victor LPM-1213	(M)	**The Wayfarers**	1956	12.00	30.00
RCA Victor LPM-2666	(M)	**Come Along With The Wayfarers**	1963	5.00	12.00
RCA Victor LSP-2666	(S)	**Come Along With The Wayfarers**	1963	6.00	15.00
RCA Victor LPM-2735	(M)	**The Wayfarers At The Hungry i**	1963	5.00	12.00
RCA Victor LSP-2735	(S)	**The Wayfarers At The Hungry i**	1963	6.00	15.00
— Original RCA mono albums above have "Long Play" on the bottom of the label; stereo albums have "Living Stereo" on the bottom.—					
RCA Victor LPM-2946	(M)	**The Wayfarers At The World's Fair**	1964	5.00	12.00
RCA Victor LSP-2946	(S)	**The Wayfarers At The World's Fair**	1964	6.00	15.00
WAYFARERS TRIO, THE					
Mercury MG-20634	(M)	**Songs Of The Blue And Grey**	1961	5.00	12.00
Mercury SR-60634	(S)	**Songs Of The Blue And Grey**	1961	6.00	15.00
WAYNE, FRANCES					
Coral CRL-56091 (10")	(M)	**Frances Wayne**	1954	20.00	50.00
Epic LN-3222	(M)	**Songs For My Man**	1956	14.00	35.00
Atlantic 1263	(M)	**The Warm Sound Of Frances Wayne**	1957	14.00	35.00
Brunswick BL-54022	(M)	**Frances Wayne**	1957	14.00	35.00
WAYNE, JOHN					
RCA Victor LSP-4828	(S)	**America, Why I Love Her**	1972	6.00	15.00
WAYNE, "WEE" WILLIE					
Imperial LP-9144	(M)	**Travelin' Mood**	1961	35.00	70.00
WEASELS, THE					
Wing MGW-12282	(M)	**The Liverpool Beat**	1964	8.00	20.00
Wing SRW-16282	(S)	**The Liverpool Beat**	1964	10.00	25.00
WEAVERS, THE					
The Weavers feature Pete Seeger.					
Decca DL-5285 (10")	(M)	**The Weavers**	1951	20.00	50.00
Decca DL-5373 (10")	(M)	**We Wish You A Merry Christmas**	1952	20.00	50.00
Decca DL-8893	(M)	**Best Of The Weavers**	1959	12.00	30.00
Decca DL-8909	(M)	**Folk Songs Around The World**	1959	12.00	30.00
Decca DXB-173	(M)	**Best Of The Weavers** (2 LPs)	1965	8.00	20.00
Decca DXSB-173	(P)	**Best Of The Weavers** (2 LPs)	1965	8.00	20.00
Vanguard VRS-9010	(M)	**The Weavers At Carnegie Hall**	1957	8.00	20.00
Vanguard VRS-9013	(M)	**The Weavers On Tour**	1957	8.00	20.00
Vanguard VRS-9022	(M)	**Travelling On With The Weavers**	1961	6.00	15.00
Vanguard VSD-2022	(S)	**Travelling On With The Weavers**	1961	8.00	20.00
Vanguard VRS-9024	(M)	**The Weavers At Home**	1962	6.00	15.00
Vanguard VSD-2024	(S)	**The Weavers At Home**	1962	8.00	20.00
Vanguard VRS-2043	(M)	**Travelling On**	1962	6.00	15.00
Vanguard VSD-2043	(S)	**Travelling On**	1962	8.00	20.00
Vanguard VRS-9075	(M)	**The Weavers At Carnegie Hall, Volume 2**	1962	8.00	20.00

Label & Catalog #		Title	Year	VG+	NM
Vanguard VRS-9101	(M)	Almanac	1963	6.00	15.00
Vanguard VSD-2101	(S)	Almanac	1963	8.00	20.00
Vanguard VRS-9150	(M)	Reunion At Carnegie Hall	1964	6.00	15.00
Vanguard VSD-2150	(S)	Reunion At Carnegie Hall	1964	8.00	20.00
Vanguard VRS-9161	(M)	Reunion At Carnegie Hall	1965	6.00	15.00
Vanguard VSD-79161	(S)	Reunion At Carnegie Hall	1965	8.00	20.00
Vanguard VRS-3001	(M)	Songbook	1967	5.00	12.00
Vanguard VSD-73001	(S)	Songbook	1967	6.00	15.00
Vanguard VSD-76533	(S)	The Weavers At Carnegie Hall	1970	4.00	10.00
Vanguard VSD-6537	(S)	The Weavers On Tour	1970	4.00	10.00
Vanguard VSD-15	(S)	The Weavers' Greatest Hits (2 LPs)	1971	5.00	12.00
Decca DL-74277	(S)	Weaver's Gold	1971	6.00	15.00

WEB, THE

Deram DES-18018	(S)	Fully Interlocking	1968	10.00	25.00

WEBB, JACK

RCA Victor LPM-1126	(M)	Pete Kelly's Blues (Soundtrack)	1955	10.00	25.00
Warner Bros. W-1207	(M)	You're My Girl	1958	8.00	20.00
Warner Bros. WS-1207	(S)	You're My Girl	1958	12.00	30.00

WEDGE

(No label)	(S)	Wedge	1972	150.00	250.00
(No label)	(S)	No One But Me	1975	100.00	200.00

WEDGES, THE

Time T-2090	(M)	Hang Ten (For Surfers Only)	1963	6.00	15.00
Time ST-2090	(S)	Hang Ten (For Surfers Only)	1963	8.00	20.00

WEIGHT

International 104	(S)	Music Is The Message	1970	8.00	20.00

WEIR, BOB
Refer to Bobby & The Midnites; The Grateful Dead.

Warner Bros. BS-2627	(S)	Ace	1972	12.00	30.00

WEIRD-OHS, THE
The Wierd-Ohs are a creation of Gary Usher & Co. Refer to The Silly Surfers / The Weird-Ohs.

Mercury MG-20976	(M)	New! The New Sounds Of Weird-Ohs	1964	20.00	50.00
Mercury SR-60976	(S)	New! The New Sounds Of Weird-Ohs	1964	35.00	70.00

WEISBERG, TIM
Weisberg aslo recorded with Dan Fogelberg.

Nautilus NR-7	(S)	The Tip Of The Weisberg	198?	6.00	15.00

WELCH, BOB
Welch was formerly a member of Fleetwood Mac.

Capitol ST-11663	(DJ)	French Kiss (Picture disc)	1979	6.00	15.00

WELCH, LENNY

Cadence CLP-5068	(M)	Since I Fell For You	1963	12.00	30.00
Cadence CLP-25068	(S)	Since I Fell For You	1963	16.00	40.00
Columbia CL-2430	(M)	Since I Fell For You ("360 Sound" label)	1965	8.00	20.00
Columbia CS-9230	(S)	Since I Fell For You ("360 Sound" label)	1965	12.00	30.00
Kapp KL-1457	(M)	Two Different Worlds	1965	5.00	12.00
Kapp KS-3457	(S)	Two Different Worlds	1965	6.00	15.00
Kapp KL-1481	(M)	Rags To Riches	1966	5.00	12.00
Kapp KS-3481	(S)	Rags To Riches	1966	6.00	15.00
Kapp KL-1517	(M)	Lenny	1967	5.00	12.00
Kapp KS-3517	(S)	Lenny	1967	6.00	15.00

WELLER, FREDDY
Weller was formerly a member of Paul Revere's Raiders.

Columbia CS-9904	(S)	Games People Play ("360 Sound" label)	1969	6.00	15.00

WELLS, JUNIOR

Delmark 612	(M)	Hoodoo Man Blues	1966	10.00	25.00
Vanguard VRS-9231	(M)	It's My Life Baby	1966	6.00	15.00
Vanguard VSD-79231	(S)	It's My Life Baby	1966	8.00	20.00

Label & Catalog #		Title	Year	VG+	NM
Delmark 628	(S)	Southside Blues Jam	1967	6.00	15.00
Vanguard 79262	(S)	Comin' At You	1968	6.00	15.00
Blue Rock 64002	(S)	You're Tuff Enough	1968	6.00	15.00
Delmark 640	(S)	Blues Hit Big Town	1969	6.00	15.00
WELLS, KITTY					
Decca DL-8293	(M)	Country Hit Parade	1956	20.00	50.00
Decca DL-8552	(M)	Winner Of Your Heart	1956	20.00	50.00
Decca DL-8858	(M)	Dust On The Bible	1959	20.00	50.00
Decca DL-8888	(M)	After Dark	1959	16.00	40.00
Decca DL-8979	(M)	Kitty's Choice	1960	12.00	30.00
Decca DL-78979	(S)	Kitty's Choice	1960	16.00	40.00
— Original Decca albums above have black & silver labels.—					
Decca DL-78293	(E)	Country Hit Parade	196?	6.00	15.00
Decca DL-78552	(E)	Winner Of Your Heart	196?	6.00	15.00
Decca DL-78858	(E)	Dust On The Bible	196?	6.00	15.00
Decca DL-78888	(E)	After Dark	196?	6.00	15.00
Decca DL-4075	(M)	Seasons Of My Heart	1960	8.00	20.00
Decca DL-74075	(S)	Seasons Of My Heart	1960	12.00	30.00
Decca DL-4108	(M)	Kitty Wells' Golden Favorites	1961	12.00	30.00
Decca DL-74108	(E)	Kitty Wells' Golden Favorites	196?	6.00	15.00
Decca DL-4141	(M)	Heartbreak U.S.A.	1961	8.00	20.00
Decca DL-74141	(S)	Heartbreak U.S.A.	1961	12.00	30.00
Decca DL-4197	(M)	Queen Of Country Music	1962	8.00	20.00
Decca DL-74197	(S)	Queen Of Country Music	1962	12.00	30.00
Decca DL-4270	(M)	Singing On Sunday	1962	8.00	20.00
Decca DL-74270	(S)	Singing On Sunday	1962	12.00	30.00
Decca DL-4349	(M)	Christmas With Kitty Wells	1962	8.00	20.00
Decca DL-74349	(S)	Christmas With Kitty Wells	1962	12.00	30.00
Decca DXB-174	(M)	The Kitty Wells Story (With booklet)	1963	8.00	20.00
Decca DXSB-174	(S)	The Kitty Wells Story (With booklet)	1963	12.00	30.00
Decca DL-4493	(M)	Especially For You	1964	6.00	15.00
Decca DL-74493	(S)	Especially For You	1964	8.00	20.00
Decca DL-4554	(M)	Country Music Time	1964	6.00	15.00
Decca DL-74554	(S)	Country Music Time	1964	8.00	20.00
Decca DL-4612	(M)	Burning Memories	1965	6.00	15.00
Decca DL-74612	(S)	Burning Memories	1965	8.00	20.00
Decca DL-4658	(M)	Lonesome, Sad And Blue	1965	6.00	15.00
Decca DL-74658	(S)	Lonesome, Sad And Blue	1965	8.00	20.00
Decca DL-4679	(M)	Family Gospel Sing	1965	6.00	15.00
Decca DL-74679	(S)	Family Gospel Sing	1965	8.00	20.00
Decca DL-4741	(M)	Songs Made Famous By Jim Reeves	1966	6.00	15.00
Decca DL-74741	(S)	Songs Made Famous By Jim Reeves	1966	8.00	20.00
Decca DL-4776	(M)	Country All The Way	1966	6.00	15.00
Decca DL-74776	(S)	Country All The Way	1966	8.00	20.00
Decca DL-4831	(M)	The Kitty Wells Show	1966	6.00	15.00
Decca DL-74831	(S)	The Kitty Wells Show	1966	8.00	20.00
— Original Decca albums above have black labels with "Mfrd by Decca" beneath the rainbow.—					
WELLS, KITTY, & RED FOLEY					
Decca DL-4906	(M)	Together Again	1967	5.00	12.00
Decca DL-74906	(S)	Together Again	1967	6.00	15.00
WELLS, MARY					
Motown 600	(M)	Bye, Bye Baby, I Don't Want To Take A Chance (White label)	1961	100.00	200.00
Motown 600	(M)	Bye, Bye Baby, I Don't Want To Take A Chance	1961	50.00	100.00
Motown 605	(M)	The One Who Really Loves You	1962	40.00	80.00
Motown 607	(M)	Two Lovers	1963	30.00	60.00
Motown 611	(M)	Live On Stage	1963	16.00	40.00
Motown 611	(S)	Live On Stage	1963	20.00	50.00
— Original Motown albums above have the company address above the spindle hole on the label.—					
Motown 616	(M)	Mary Wells' Greatest Hits	1964	10.00	25.00
Motown 617	(M)	My Guy	1964	14.00	35.00
Motown 653	(M)	Vintage Stock	1966	10.00	25.00
Motown 653	(S)	Vintage Stock	1966	12.00	30.00
20th Century TFM-3171	(M)	Mary Wells	1965	8.00	20.00
20th Century TFS-4171	(S)	Mary Wells	1965	12.00	30.00

Label & Catalog #		Title	Year	VG+	NM
20th Century TFM-3178	(M)	Love Songs To The Beatles	1965	14.00	35.00
20th Century TFS-4178	(S)	Love Songs To The Beatles	1965	20.00	50.00
Movietone 71010	(M)	Ooh	1966	8.00	20.00
Movietone 72010	(S)	Ooh	1966	12.00	30.00
Atco 33-199	(M)	Two Sides Of Mary Wells	1966	8.00	20.00
Atco SD-33-199	(S)	Two Sides Of Mary Wells	1966	12.00	30.00
Jubilee JGS-8018	(S)	Servin' Up Some Soul	1968	6.00	15.00

WEST

Epic BN-26380	(S)	West	1968	5.00	12.00
Epic BN-26433	(S)	Bridges	1969	5.00	12.00

WEST, ADAM, & BURT WARD: *Refer to* NELSON RIDDLE

WEST, MAE

Decca DL-9016	(M)	The Fabulous Mae West	1955	16.00	40.00
Decca DL-79016	(E)	The Fabulous Mae West	196?	10.00	25.00
Tower T-5028	(M)	Way Out West	1966	8.00	20.00
Tower ST-5028	(S)	Way Out West	1966	10.00	25.00
Dragonet D-64	(M)	Wild Christmas	196?	6.00	15.00
Decca DL-79176	(P)	Original Voice Tracks From Her Greatest Movies *(With poster)*	1970	8.00	20.00
MGM SE-4869	(S)	Great Balls Of Fire	1972	6.00	15.00

WEST, SPEEDY, & JIMMY BRYANT

Capitol H-520 (10")	(M)	Two Guitars Country Style	1954	100.00	200.00
Capitol T-520	(M)	Two Guitars Country Style	1956	50.00	100.00

WEST, SPEEDY

Capitol T-956	(M)	West Of Hawaii	1958	35.00	70.00
Capitol T-1341	(M)	Steel Guitar	1960	16.00	40.00
Capitol ST-1341	(S)	Steel Guitar	1960	20.00	50.00
Capitol T-1835	(M)	Guitar Spectacular	1962	14.00	35.00
Capitol ST-1835	(S)	Guitar Spectacular	1962	16.00	40.00

WEST, BRUCE & LAING

Columbia CQ-31929	(Q)	Why Dontcha'	1973	6.00	15.00
Columbia CQ-32216	(Q)	Whatever Turns You On	1973	6.00	15.00

WEST COAST POP ART EXPERIMENTAL BAND, THE
The WCPAEB features Dan Harris, Shaun Harris and Bob Markley.

Fifo M101	(M)	West Coast Pop Art Experimental Band	1966	*See note below*	
		(Rare. Estimated near mint value $1,000-1,500.)			
Reprise R-6247	(M)	Part One	1967	10.00	25.00
Reprise RS-6247	(S)	Part One	1967	12.00	30.00
Reprise R-6270	(M)	Volume 2	1967	10.00	25.00
Reprise RS-6270	(S)	Volume 2	1967	12.00	30.00
Reprise RS-6298	(S)	A Child's Guide To Good And Evil	1968	12.00	30.00
Amos AAS-7004	(S)	Where's My Daddy	1969	20.00	50.00

WESTFAUSTER

Nasco 9008	(S)	In A King's Dream	1971	35.00	70.00

WESTON, KIM
Ms. Weston also recorded with Marvin Gaye.

MGM E-4477	(M)	For The First Time	1967	6.00	15.00
MGM SE-4477	(S)	For The First Time	1967	8.00	20.00
Volt VOS-6014	(S)	Kim Kim Kim	1971	5.00	12.00

WET WILLIE

Epic PRO-428	(DJ)	Manorisms/Live Concert Series	1978	8.00	20.00

WHALEFEATHERS

Nasco 9003	(S)	Whalefeathers Declare	1969	20.00	50.00
Nasco 9005	(S)	Whalefeathers	1970	20.00	50.00

WHITCOMB, IAN

Tower T-5004	(M)	You Turn Me On	1965	8.00	20.00
Tower DT-5004	(E)	You Turn Me On	1965	6.00	15.00

Label & Catalog #		Title	Year	VG+	NM
Tower T-5042	(M)	Mod, Mod, Music Hall	1966	5.00	12.00
Tower ST-5042	(S)	Mod, Mod, Music Hall	1966	6.00	15.00
Tower T-5071	(M)	Yellow Underground	1967	5.00	12.00
Tower ST-5071	(S)	Yellow Underground	1967	6.00	15.00
Tower ST-5100	(S)	Sock Me Some Rock	1968	6.00	15.00

WHITE, BUKKA

Blue Horizon 4604	(M)	Blues Master, Volume 4	196?	6.00	15.00
Herwin 201	(M)	Sic'em Dogs	1969	6.00	15.00
Takoma 1001	(M)	Mississippi Blues	1969	5.00	12.00
Arhoolie 1019	(M)	Sky Songs, Volume 1	1975	5.00	12.00
Arhoolie 1020	(M)	Sky Songs, Volume 2	1975	5.00	12.00

WHITE, JOSH
Refer to Leadbelly.

Mercury MG-25015 (10")	(M)	Josh White Sings	1949	50.00	100.00
Decca DL-5082 (10")	(M)	Ballads	1950	35.00	70.00
Stinson 14 (10")	(M)	Blues	1950	20.00	50.00
Stinson 15 (10")	(M)	Folk Songs	1950	20.00	50.00
London LL-338 (10")	(M)	Josh White	1951	20.00	50.00
London LL-341 (10")	(M)	Josh White Program	1951	20.00	50.00
Decca DL-5247 (10")	(M)	Ballads, Volume 2	1952	20.00	50.00
EmArcy MG-26010 (10")	(M)	Strange Fruit	1954	20.00	50.00
Elektra 701 (10")	(M)	The Story Of John Henry	1955	16.00	40.00
Period 1115 (10")	(M)	Josh White Comes A-Visiting	1956	20.00	50.00
London LL-1341	(M)	A Josh White Program	1956	16.00	40.00
ABC-Paramount 124	(M)	Stories	1956	16.00	40.00
ABC-Paramount 166	(M)	Stories, Volume 2	1957	16.00	40.00
Mercury MG-20203	(M)	Josh White's Blues	1957	20.00	50.00
Elektra EKL-102	(M)	Josh At Midnight	1956	12.00	30.00
Elektra EKL-114	(M)	Josh	1957	12.00	30.00
Elektra EKL-123	(M)	25th Anniversary Album	1957	12.00	30.00
Elektra EKL-158	(M)	Chain Gang Songs	1958	12.00	30.00
Decca DL-8665	(M)	Josh White	1958	12.00	30.00
Mercury MG-20821	(M)	The Beginning	1963	8.00	20.00
Mercury SR-60821	(S)	The Beginning	1963	12.00	30.00

WHITE, JOSH, & BIG BILL BROONZY

Period 1209	(M)	Josh White & Big Bill Broonzy	1956	30.00	60.00

WHITE, KITTY

EmArcy MG-36020	(M)	A New Voice In Jazz	1955	20.00	50.00
EmArcy MG-36068	(M)	Kitty White	1955	20.00	50.00
Pacifica PL-802 (10")	(M)	Kitty White	1955	20.00	50.00
Pacifica 2002	(M)	A Moment Of Love	1956	16.00	40.00
Mercury MG-20183	(M)	Folk Songs	1957	16.00	40.00
World Pacific WP-1406	(M)	Intimate	195?	10.00	25.00
Roulette R-25020	(M)	Sweet Talk	1960	8.00	20.00
Roulette RS-25020	(S)	Sweet Talk	1960	12.00	30.00

WHITE BOY & THE AVERAGE RAT BAND

Tradewind MM-11761	(S)	White Boy & The Average Rat Band	1975	60.00	120.00

WHITE LIGHT

Century 39955	(S)	White Light (With "Heartbreak Hotel")	197?	75.00	150.00
Century 39955	(S)	White Light (Without "Heartbreak Hotel")	197?	100.00	200.00

WHITE LIGHTNIN'

ABC 690	(S)	File Under Rock	1969	6.00	15.00

WHITE PLAINS

Deram DES-18045	(S)	My Baby Loves Loving	1970	5.00	12.00

WHITE SUMMER

No label 6034N7	(S)	White Summer	197?	150.00	250.00

WHITE WITCH

Capricorn CPN-0107	(S)	White Witch	1973	6.00	15.00
Capricorn CPN-0129	(S)	A Spiritual Greeting	1974	5.00	12.00

Label & Catalog #		Title	Year	VG+	NM

WHITEHEAD, CHARLIE, & THE SWAMP DOGG BAND

| Fungus FB-25145 | (S) | Charlie Whitehead | 197? | 6.00 | 15.00 |

WHITING, MARGARET

Ms. Whiting also recorded with Mel Torme.

Capitol H-163 (10")	(M)	South Pacific	1950	20.00	50.00
Capitol H-209 (10")	(M)	Margaret Whiting Sings Rodgers & Hart	1950	20.00	50.00
Capitol H-234 (10")	(M)	Songs	1950	20.00	50.00
Capitol T-410	(M)	Love Songs	1955	14.00	35.00
Capitol T-685	(M)	For The Starry-Eyed	1955	14.00	35.00
Dot DLP-3072	(M)	Goin' Places	1957	10.00	25.00
Dot DLP-3113	(M)	Margaret	1958	6.00	15.00
Dot DLP-25113	(S)	Margaret	1958	8.00	20.00
Dot DLP-3176	(M)	Margaret Whiting Great Hits	1959	6.00	15.00
Dot DLP-25176	(S)	Margaret Whiting Great Hits	1959	8.00	20.00
Dot DLP-3235	(M)	Ten Top Hits	1960	6.00	15.00
Dot DLP-25235	(S)	Ten Top Hits	1960	8.00	20.00
Dot DLP-3337	(M)	Just A Dream	1960	6.00	15.00
Dot DLP-25337	(S)	Just A Dream	1960	8.00	20.00
Verve V-4038	(M)	The Jerome Kern Song Book	1960	6.00	15.00
Verve V6-4038	(S)	The Jerome Kern Song Book	1960	8.00	20.00
MGM E-4006	(M)	Past Midnight	1961	6.00	15.00
MGM SE-4006	(S)	Past Midnight	1961	8.00	20.00

Patterning himself after his idol, Slim Montana, "Yodelin' Slim" Whitman gave up a potential career in baseball to become— arguably— the most popular and successful country entertainer of the '50s.

WHITMAN, SLIM

RCA Victor LPM-3217 (10")	(M)	Slim Whitman Sings And Yodels	1954	100.00	200.00
Imperial LP-3004 (10")	(M)	America's Favorite Folk Artist	1954	180.00	300.00
Imperial LP-9003	(M)	Favorites	1956	20.00	50.00
Imperial LP-9026	(M)	Slim Whitman Sings	1957	20.00	50.00
Imperial LP-9056	(M)	Slim Whitman Sings	1958	20.00	50.00
Imperial LP-9064	(M)	Slim Whitman Sings	1959	20.00	50.00
		— Original Imperial albums above have maroon labels.—			
Imperial LP-9003	(M)	Favorites	1958	12.00	30.00
Imperial LP-9026	(M)	Slim Whitman Sings	195?	12.00	30.00

Label & Catalog #		Title	Year	VG+	NM
Imperial LP-9056	(M)	Slim Whitman Sings	195?	12.00	30.00
Imperial LP-9064	(M)	Slim Whitman Sings	195?	12.00	30.00
Imperial LP-9077	(M)	Annie Laurie	1959	12.00	30.00
Imperial LP-9088	(M)	I'll Walk With God	1960	12.00	30.00
Imperial LP-12032	(E)	I'll Walk With God	196?	5.00	12.00
Imperial LP-9100	(M)	Country Hits, Volume 1	1966	6.00	15.00
Imperial LP-9102	(M)	Million Record Hits	1960	12.00	30.00
Imperial LP-9102	(M)	Song Of The Old Waterwheel	1966	6.00	15.00
Imperial LP-9104	(M)	Country Hits, Volume 2	1966	6.00	15.00
Imperial LP-9105	(M)	My Best To You	1966	6.00	15.00
Imperial LP-9106	(M)	Country Favorites	1966	6.00	15.00
Imperial LP-9135	(M)	First Visit To Britain	1960	10.00	25.00
Imperial LP-9137	(M)	Just Call Me Lonesome	1961	10.00	25.00
Imperial LP-9156	(M)	Once In A Lifetime	1961	10.00	25.00
Imperial LP-9171	(M)	Forever	1966	6.00	15.00
Imperial LP-9194	(M)	Slim Whitman Sings	1962	10.00	25.00
Imperial LP-12194	(S)	Slim Whitman Sings	1962	12.00	30.00
Imperial LP-9209	(M)	Heart Songs And Love Songs	1962	10.00	25.00
Imperial LP-9226	(M)	I'm A Lonely Wanderer	1963	10.00	25.00
Imperial LP-9235	(M)	Yodeling	1963	10.00	25.00
Imperial LP-9245	(M)	Irish Songs, The Whitman Way	1963	10.00	25.00
Imperial LP-9252	(M)	All Time Favorites	1964	10.00	25.00
— Original Imperial albums above have black labels with stars on top.—					
Imperial LP-9268	(M)	Country Songs/City Hits	1964	6.00	15.00
Imperial LP-12268	(S)	Country Songs/City Hits	1964	8.00	20.00
Imperial LP-9277	(M)	Love Song Of The Waterfall	1964	6.00	15.00
Imperial LP-12277	(S)	Love Song Of The Waterfall	1964	8.00	20.00
Imperial LP-9288	(M)	Reminiscing	1965	6.00	15.00
Imperial LP-12288	(S)	Reminiscing	1965	8.00	20.00
Imperial LP-9303	(M)	More Than Yesterday	1965	6.00	15.00
Imperial LP-12303	(S)	More Than Yesterday	1965	8.00	20.00
Camden CAL-954	(M)	Birmingham Jail	1966	8.00	20.00
Camden CAS-954	(E)	Birmingham Jail	1966	5.00	12.00
(Camden 954 is a repackage of RCA 3217.)					
Imperial LP-9308	(M)	God's Hand In Mine	1966	5.00	12.00
Imperial LP-9313	(M)	A Travelin' Man	1966	5.00	12.00
Imperial LP-12313	(S)	A Travelin' Man	1966	6.00	15.00
Imperial LP-9333	(M)	A Time For Love	1966	5.00	12.00
Imperial LP-12333	(S)	A Time For Love	1966	6.00	15.00
Imperial LP-9342	(M)	15th Anniversary	1967	5.00	12.00
Imperial LP-12342	(S)	15th Anniversary	1967	6.00	15.00
Imperial LP-9356	(M)	Country Memories	1967	5.00	12.00
Imperial LP-12356	(S)	Country Memories	1967	6.00	15.00
Imperial LP-12375	(S)	In Love, The Whitman Way	1968	6.00	15.00
Imperial LP-12411	(S)	Happy Street	1969	6.00	15.00
Imperial LP-12436	(S)	Slim	1969	6.00	15.00
Imperial LP-12448	(S)	The Slim Whitman Christmas Album	1969	6.00	15.00

WHO, THE

The Who are Roger Daltrey, John Entwhistle, Keith Moon and Pete Townshend. Moon died in 1978 and was replaced by Kenny Jones of The Faces.

Decca DL-4664	(DJ)	The Who Sing My Generation (White label)	1966	75.00	150.00
Decca DL-4664	(M)	The Who Sing My Generation	1966	35.00	70.00
Decca DL-74664	(E)	The Who Sing My Generation	1966	30.00	60.00
Decca DL-4892	(DJ)	Happy Jack (White label)	1967	50.00	100.00
Decca DL-4892	(M)	Happy Jack	1967	35.00	70.00
Decca DL-74892	(S)	Happy Jack	1967	20.00	50.00
Decca DL-4950	(DJ)	The Who Sell Out (White label)	1967	100.00	200.00
(Promo with all of the commercials lumped together on one side.)					
Decca DL-4950	(DJ)	The Who Sell Out (White label)	1967	50.00	100.00
Decca DL-4950	(M)	The Who Sell Out	1967	35.00	70.00
Decca DL-74950	(S)	The Who Sell Out	1967	20.00	50.00
Decca DL-5064	(DJ)	Magic Bus (White label. Mono)	1968	75.00	150.00
Decca DL-75064	(S)	Magic Bus	1968	20.00	50.00
Decca DXW-7205	(DJ)	Tommy (White label. Mono)	1969	100.00	200.00
Decca DXSW-7205	(S)	Tommy (2 LPs with booklet)	1969	16.00	40.00
Decca DL-79175	(DJ)	Live At Leeds (White label)	1970	50.00	100.00
Decca DL-79175	(S)	Live At Leeds	1970	16.00	40.00
(Fold-open jacket includes twelve different inserts and photos.)					

Label & Catalog #		Title	Year	VG+	NM
Decca DL-79182	(S)	Who's Next	1971	8.00	20.00
Decca DL-79184	(P)	Meaty, Beaty, Big And Bouncy	1971	6.00	15.00
MCA 10004	(S)	Quadrophenia (2 LPs)	1973	5.00	12.00
Track 2126	(S)	Odds And Sods	1974	6.00	15.00
Track 2-4067	(S)	A Quick One / The Who Sell Out (2 LPs)	1974	5.00	12.00
Track 2-4068	(P)	Magic Bus / My Generation (2 LPs)	1974	5.00	12.00
MCA 2044	(E)	The Who Sing My Generation	1974	16.00	40.00
MCA 2045	(S)	Happy Jack	1974	16.00	40.00
MCA 3050	(DJ)	Who Are You (White label)	1978	10.00	25.00
MCAP-14950	(S)	Who Are You (Picture Disc)	1979	6.00	15.00
Direct Disc SD-16610	(S)	Who Are You	1979	10.00	25.00
Warner Bros. WBMS-116	(DJ)	Filling In The Gaps (2 LPs)	1981	30.00	60.00
Warner Bros. 23731	(DJ)	It's Hard (Quiex II vinyl)	1982	8.00	20.00
Mobile Fidelity MFSL-115	(S)	Face Dances	1984	6.00	15.00

WHO, THE / THE STRAWBERRY ALARM CLOCK

Decca DL-734568	(S)	The Who / The Strawberry Alarm Clock	1969	35.00	70.00

WICHITA TRAIN WHISTLE, THE
The Whistle features Michael Nesmith.

Dot DLP-25861	(S)	The Wichita Train Whistle Sings	1968	16.00	40.00

WIGGINS, LITTLE ROY

Starday SLP-188	(M)	Mister Steel Guitar	195?	12.00	30.00
Starday SLP-259	(M)	The Fabulous Steel Guitar Artistry	196?	10.00	25.00
Starday SLP-392	(M)	Nashville Steel Guitar	196?	10.00	25.00

WIGWAM

Forecast FTS-3089	(S)	Tombstone Valentine (2 LPs)	1971	8.00	20.00

WILBURN BROTHERS, THE

Decca DL-8576	(M)	The Wilburn Brothers	1957	20.00	50.00
Decca DL-8774	(M)	Side By Side	1958	14.00	35.00
Decca DL-78774	(S)	Side By Side	1958	20.00	50.00
Decca DL-8959	(M)	Livin' In God's Country	1959	14.00	35.00
Decca DL-78959	(S)	Livin' In God's Country	1959	20.00	50.00
		— Original Decca albums above have black & silver labels.—			
Decca DL-4058	(M)	The Big Heartbreak	1960	8.00	20.00
Decca DL-74058	(S)	The Big Heartbreak	1960	12.00	30.00
Decca DL-4122	(M)	City Limits	1961	8.00	20.00
Decca DL-74122	(S)	City Limits	1961	12.00	30.00
Decca DL-4142	(M)	The Wilburn Brothers Sing	1961	8.00	20.00
Decca DL-74142	(S)	The Wilburn Brothers Sing	1961	12.00	30.00
King 746	(M)	The Wonderful Wilburn Brothers	1961	30.00	60.00
Decca DL-4225	(M)	Folk Songs	1962	6.00	15.00
Decca DL-74225	(S)	Folk Songs	1962	8.00	20.00
Decca DL-4391	(M)	Trouble's Back In Town	1963	6.00	15.00
Decca DL-74391	(S)	Trouble's Back In Town	1963	8.00	20.00
Decca DL-4464	(M)	Take Up Thy Cross	1964	6.00	15.00
Decca DL-74464	(S)	Take Up Thy Cross	1964	8.00	20.00
Decca DL-4544	(M)	Never Alone	1964	6.00	15.00
Decca DL-74544	(S)	Never Alone	1964	8.00	20.00
Decca DL-4615	(M)	Country Gold	1965	6.00	15.00
Decca DL-74615	(S)	Country Gold	1965	8.00	20.00
Decca DL-4645	(M)	I'm Gonna Tie One On Tonight	1965	6.00	15.00
Decca DL-74645	(S)	I'm Gonna Tie One On Tonight	1965	8.00	20.00
Decca DL-4721	(M)	The Wilburn Brothers Show	1966	14.00	35.00
Decca DL-74721	(S)	The Wilburn Brothers Show	1966	16.00	40.00
Decca DL-4764	(M)	Let's Go Country	1966	5.00	12.00
Decca DL-74764	(S)	Let's Go Country	1966	6.00	15.00
Decca DL-4824	(M)	Two For The Show	1967	5.00	12.00
Decca DL-74824	(S)	Two For The Show	1967	6.00	15.00

WILDCATS, THE

United Arts. UAL-3031	(M)	Bandstand Record Hop	1958	20.00	50.00

WILDE, MARTY

Epic LN-3686	(M)	Bad Boy	1960	20.00	50.00
Epic LN-3711	(M)	Wilde About Marty	1960	14.00	35.00

Label & Catalog #		Title	Year	VG+	NM

WILDWEEDS, THE
Wildweeds features Al Anderson of NRBQ.

Vanguard VSD-6552	(S)	Wildweeds	1970	8.00	20.00

WILEY, LEE

Columbia CL-6169 (10")	(M)	Night In Manhattan	1952	20.00	50.00
Columbia CL-6215 (10")	(M)	Lee Wiley Sings Vincent Youmans	1952	20.00	50.00
Columbia CL-6216 (10")	(M)	Lee Wiley Sings Irving Berlin	1952	20.00	50.00
Columbia CL-656	(M)	Night In Manhattan	1955	10.00	25.00
Storyville STLP-312 (10")	(M)	Lee Wiley Sings Rodgers And Hart	1954	30.00	60.00
Storyville STLP-911	(M)	Duologue	1956	16.00	40.00
RCA Victor LPM-1408	(M)	West Of The Moon	1957	14.00	35.00
RCA Victor LPM-1566	(M)	A Touch Of The Blues	1957	14.00	35.00
Ric M-2002	(M)	One And Only Lee Wiley	1964	10.00	25.00
Ric MS-2002	(E)	One And Only Lee Wiley	1964	6.00	15.00

WILLETT, SLIM

Audio Lab 1542	(M)	Slim Willett	195?	35.00	70.00

WILLIAMS, ANDY

Cadence CLP-3030	(M)	Lonely Street	1960	6.00	15.00
Cadence CLP-25030	(S)	Lonely Street	1960	8.00	20.00
Cadence CLP-3054	(M)	Andy Williams' Best	1962	6.00	15.00
Cadence CLP-25054	(S)	Andy Williams' Best	1962	8.00	20.00
Cadence CLP-3061	(M)	Million Seller Songs	1962	6.00	15.00
Cadence CLP-25061	(S)	Million Seller Songs	1962	8.00	20.00

WILLIAMS, BILLY
Mr. Williams was formerly a member of The Charioteers.

Coral CRL-57184	(M)	Billy Williams	1957	20.00	50.00
MGM E-3400	(M)	The Billy Williams Quartet	1957	20.00	50.00
Mercury MG-20317	(M)	Billy Williams Singing Oh Yeah	1958	20.00	50.00
Wing MGW-12131	(M)	Vote For Billy Williams	1959	16.00	40.00
Coral CRL-57251	(M)	Half Sweet, Half Beat	1959	20.00	50.00
Coral CRL-57343	(M)	The Billy Williams Revue	1960	20.00	50.00

WILLIAMS, DON

ABC SPPD-44	(DJ)	Expression (Picture disc)	1978	6.00	15.00

WILLIAMS, HANK [LUKE THE DRIFTER]
On several albums, MGM addded strings and choruses to the original recordings; in some cases the mono albums do not have the sweetening but the stereos do. On the "Hank With Strings" albums, the sweetening is on both the mono and stereo versions; the stereo albums have Hank's original mono tracks with the sweetening in stereo. Most albums with the strings are avoided by all but the completist.

MGM E-107 (10")	(M)	Hank Williams Sings	1952	75.00	150.00
MGM E-168 (10")	(M)	Moanin' The Blues	1952	75.00	150.00
MGM E-202 (10")	(M)	Hank Williams Memorial Album	1953	75.00	150.00
MGM E-203 (10")	(M)	Hank Williams As Luke The Drifter	1953	75.00	150.00
MGM E-242 (10")	(M)	Honky Tonkin'	1954	75.00	150.00
MGM E-243 (10")	(M)	I Saw The Light	1954	75.00	150.00
MGM E-291 (10")	(M)	Ramblin' Man	1954	75.00	150.00
MGM E-3219	(M)	Ramblin' Man	1955	40.00	80.00
MGM E-3267	(M)	Hank Williams As Luke The Drifter	1955	40.00	80.00
MGM E-3272	(M)	Hank Williams Memorial Album	1955	40.00	80.00
MGM E-3330	(M)	Moanin' The Blues	1956	40.00	80.00
MGM E-3331	(M)	I Saw The Light (Yellow label. Green cover)	1956	40.00	80.00
MGM E-3331	(M)	I Saw The Light (Yellow label. Church cover)	1959	30.00	60.00
MGM E-3412	(M)	Honky Tonkin'	1957	40.00	80.00
MGM E-3560	(M)	Sing Me A Blue Song	1957	40.00	80.00
MGM E-3605	(M)	The Immortal Hank Williams	1958	40.00	80.00
MGM 3E-2	(M)	36 Of Hank Williams' Greatest Hits (3 LPs)	195?	100.00	200.00
MGM 3E-4	(M)	36 More Greatest Hits (3 LPs)	195?	100.00	200.00
MGM E-3733	(M)	The Unforgettable Hank Williams	1959	40.00	80.00
		—Original MGM albums above have yellow labels.—			
MGM E-3219	(M)	Ramblin' Man	1960	12.00	30.00
MGM E-3267	(M)	Hank Williams As Luke The Drifter	1960	12.00	30.00
MGM E-3272	(M)	Hank Williams Memorial Album	1960	12.00	30.00
MGM E-3330	(M)	Moanin' The Blues	1960	12.00	30.00
MGM E-3331	(M)	I Saw The Light	1960	12.00	30.00

Label & Catalog #		Title	Year	VG+	NM

This promotioanl boxed set contains spoken testimonials by a host of country legends, all of whom pay tribute to the king of country. Rare in any condition and a must on most Hank want-lists.

Label & Catalog #		Title	Year	VG+	NM
MGM E-3412	(M)	**Honky Tonkin'**	*1960*	**12.00**	**30.00**
MGM E-3560	(M)	**Sing Me A Blue Song**	*1960*	**12.00**	**30.00**
MGM E-3605	(M)	**The Immortal Hank Williams**	*1960*	**12.00**	**30.00**
MGM E-3733	(M)	**The Unforgettable Hank Williams**	*1960*	**12.00**	**30.00**
MGM 3E-2	(M)	**36 Of Hank Williams' Greatest Hits** (*3 LPs*)	*1960*	**50.00**	**100.00**
MGM 3E-4	(M)	**36 More Greatest Hits** (*3 LPs*)	*1960*	**50.00**	**100.00**
MGM E-3803	(M)	**The Lonesome Sound Of Hank Williams**	*1960*	**12.00**	**30.00**
MGM E-3850	(M)	**Wait For The Light To Shine**	*1960*	**16.00**	**40.00**
MGM E-3918	(M)	**Hank Williams' Greatest Hits**	*1961*	**12.00**	**30.00**
MGM E-3923	(M)	**Hank Williams Lives Again**	*1961*	**12.00**	**30.00**
MGM E-3924	(M)	**Sing Me A Blue Song**	*1961*	**12.00**	**30.00**
MGM E-3925	(M)	**Wanderin' Around**	*1961*	**12.00**	**30.00**
MGM E-3926	(M)	**I'm Blue Inside**	*1961*	**12.00**	**30.00**
MGM E-3928	(M)	**First, Last And Always, Hank Williams**	*1961*	**12.00**	**30.00**
		(*MGM 3928 is a repackage of MGM 3605.*)			
MGM E-3955	(M)	**The Spirit Of Hank Williams**	*1961*	**12.00**	**30.00**
MGM E-3999	(M)	**On Stage! Hank Williams Recorded Live**	*1962*	**12.00**	**30.00**
MGM SE-3999	(E)	**Hank Williams On Stage Recorded Live**	*1962*	**6.00**	**15.00**
MGM E-4040	(M)	**14 More Greatest Hits, Volume 2**	*1962*	**10.00**	**25.00**
MGM E-4109	(M)	**Hank Williams On Stage, Volume 2**	*1963*	**10.00**	**25.00**
MGM SE-4109	(E)	**Hank Williams On Stage, Volume 2**	*1963*	**6.00**	**15.00**
MGM E-4138	(M)	**Beyond The Sunset**	*1963*	**12.00**	**30.00**
MGM SE-4138	(E)	**Beyond The Sunset**	*196?*	**6.00**	**15.00**
MGM E-4140	(M)	**14 More Greatest Hits, Volume 3**	*1963*	**10.00**	**25.00**
MGM E-4168	(M)	**The Very Best Of Hank Williams**	*1963*	**8.00**	**20.00**
MGM SE-4168	(E)	**The Very Best Of Hank Williams**	*1963*	**6.00**	**15.00**
MGM E-4227	(M)	**The Very Best Of Hank Williams, Volume 2**	*1964*	**8.00**	**20.00**
MGM SE-4227	(E)	**The Very Best Of Hank Williams, Volume 2**	*1964*	**6.00**	**15.00**
MGM E-4254	(M)	**Lost Highway (And Other Folk Ballads)**	*1964*	**12.00**	**30.00**
MGM E-4267	(M)	**The Hank Williams Story** (*4 LP box.*)	*1965*	**20.00**	**50.00**
MGM E-4300	(M)	**Kaw-Liga And Other Humorous Songs**	*1965*	**10.00**	**25.00**
MGM SE-4300	(E)	**Kaw-Liga And Other Humorous Songs**	*1965*	**6.00**	**15.00**
MGM E-4377	(M)	**The Legend Lives Anew**			
		(Hank Williams With Strings)	*1966*	**8.00**	**20.00**

Label & Catalog #		Title	Year	VG+	NM
MGM SE-4377	(S)	The Legend Lives Ane			
		(Hank Williams With Strings)	1966	8.00	20.00
MGM E-4380	(M)	Luke The Drifter	1966	8.00	20.00
MGM SE-4380	(E)	Luke The Drifter	1966	6.00	15.00
MGM E-4429	(M)	More Hank Williams And Strings	1966	8.00	20.00
MGM SE-4429	(S)	More Hank Williams And Strings	1966	8.00	20.00
MGM E-4481	(M)	I Won't Be Home No More	1967	8.00	20.00
MGM SE-4481	(E)	I Won't Be Home No More	1967	6.00	15.00
		— MGM albums above have black labels.—			
MGM SE-4529	(S)	Hank Williams And Strings, Volume 3	1968	8.00	20.00
MGM E-4576	(M)	Hank Williams In The Beginning	1968	12.00	30.00
MGM SE-4576	(E)	Hank Williams In The Beginning	1968	6.00	15.00
MGM SE-4651	(E)	The Essential Hank Williams	1969	6.00	15.00
MGM SE-4680	(E)	Life To Legend	1970	6.00	15.00
MGM SE-4755	(E)	24 Of Hank Williams' Greatest Hits (2 LPs)	1970	8.00	20.00
MGM SE-240	(E)	24 Karat Hits (2 LPs)	1970	10.00	25.00
MGM 1SE-33ST	(E)	The Last Picture Show (Soundtrack)	1971	12.00	30.00
		— MGM albums above have blue & gold labels.—			
MGM PRO-912	(DJ)	Reflections Of Those Who Loved Him	1975	75.00	150.00
		(Promotional 3 LP boxed set of various artists eulogizing Hank.)			
Metro M-509	(M)	Hank Williams	1965	8.00	20.00
Metro MS-509	(E)	Hank Williams	1965	5.00	12.00
Metro M-547	(M)	Mr. And Mrs. Hank Williams	1965	8.00	20.00
Metro MS-547	(E)	Mr. And Mrs. Hank Williams	1965	5.00	12.00
Metro M-602	(M)	The Immortal Hank Williams	1966	8.00	20.00
Metro MS-602	(E)	The Immortal Hank Williams	1966	5.00	12.00
Columbia P4S-5616	(E)	The Hank Williams Treasury (4 LP box)	197?	12.00	30.00

WILLIAMS, HANK, & HANK WILLIAMS, JR.

Label & Catalog #		Title	Year	VG+	NM
MGM E-4276	(M)	Hank Williams, Sr., & Hank Williams. Jr.	1965	6.00	15.00
MGM SE-4276	(S)	Hank Williams, Sr., & Hank Williams. Jr.	1965	8.00	20.00
MGM E-4378	(M)	Again	1966	6.00	15.00
MGM SE-4378	(S)	Again	1966	8.00	20.00
		— Original MGM albums above have black labels.—			

WILLIAMS, HANK, JR. (& THE CHEATIN' HEARTS)
Hank Jr. also recorded with Connie Francis.

Label & Catalog #		Title	Year	VG+	NM
MGM E-4213	(M)	Songs Of Hank Williams	1963	6.00	15.00
MGM SE-4213	(S)	Songs Of Hank Williams	1963	8.00	20.00
MGM E-4260	(M)	Your Cheatin' Heart (Soundtrack)	1964	6.00	15.00
MGM SE-4260	(S)	Your Cheatin' Heart (Soundtrack)	1964	8.00	20.00
MGM E-4316	(M)	Ballads Of The Hills And Plains	1965	5.00	12.00
MGM SE-4316	(S)	Ballads Of The Hills And Plains	1965	6.00	15.00
MGM E-4344	(M)	Blue's My Name	1966	5.00	12.00
MGM SE-4344	(S)	Blue's My Name	1966	6.00	15.00
MGM E-4391	(M)	Country Shadows	1966	5.00	12.00
MGM SE-4391	(S)	Country Shadows	1966	6.00	15.00
MGM E-4428	(M)	In My Own Way	1967	5.00	12.00
MGM SE-4428	(S)	In My Own Way	1967	6.00	15.00
MGM E-4513	(M)	The Best Of Hank Williams, Jr.	1967	5.00	12.00
MGM SE-4513	(S)	The Best Of Hank Williams, Jr.	1967	6.00	15.00
		— Original MGM albums above have black labels.—			

WILLIAMS, JOE
* *Refer to Sarah Vaughan.*

Label & Catalog #		Title	Year	VG+	NM
Regent 6002	(M)	Joe Williams Sings Everyday	1956	20.00	50.00
Vanguard 8508	(M)	A Night At Count Basie's	1957	12.00	30.00
Roulette R-52005	(M)	Man Ain't Supposed To Cry	1958	10.00	25.00
Roulette RS-52005	(S)	Man Ain't Supposed To Cry	1958	14.00	35.00
Roulette R-52021	(M)	Memories Ad Lib	1959	10.00	25.00
Roulette RS-52021	(S)	Memories Ad Lib	1959	14.00	35.00
Roulette R-52030	(M)	Joe Williams Sings About You!	1959	10.00	25.00
Roulette RS-52030	(S)	Joe Williams Sings About You!	1959	14.00	35.00
Roulette R-52033	(M)	Everyday I Have The Blues	1959	10.00	25.00
Roulette RS-52033	(S)	Everyday I Have The Blues	1959	14.00	35.00
Roulette R-52039	(M)	That Kind Of Woman	1959	10.00	25.00
Roulette RS-52039	(S)	That Kind Of Woman	1959	14.00	35.00
		— Original Roulette albums above have white labels.—			

Label & Catalog #		Title	Year	VG+	NM
Roulette R-52054	(M)	Just The Blues	1960	8.00	20.00
Roulette RS-52054	(S)	Just The Blues	1960	12.00	30.00
Roulette R-52066	(M)	Sentimental And Melancholy	1960	8.00	20.00
Roulette RS-52066	(S)	Sentimental And Melancholy	1960	12.00	30.00
Roulette R-52069	(M)	Together	1961	8.00	20.00
Roulette RS-52069	(S)	Together	1961	10.00	25.00
Roulette R-52071	(M)	Have A Good Time	1961	6.00	15.00
Roulette RS-52071	(S)	Have A Good Time	1961	8.00	20.00
Roulette R-52085	(M)	Swingin' Night At Birdland	1962	6.00	15.00
Roulette RS-52085	(S)	Swingin' Night At Birdland	1962	8.00	20.00
Roulette R-52102	(M)	One Is A Lonesome Number	1962	6.00	15.00
Roulette RS-52102	(S)	One Is A Lonesome Number	1962	8.00	20.00
Roulette R-52105	(M)	New Kind Of Love	1964	6.00	15.00
Roulette RS-52105	(S)	New Kind Of Love	1964	8.00	20.00
— Original Roulette albums above have orange & pink labels.—					
Verve V-8488	(M)	Count Basie Swings / Joe Williams Sings	1962	8.00	20.00
Verve V6-8488	(S)	Count Basie Swings / Joe Williams Sings	1962	10.00	25.00
RCA Victor LPM-2713	(M)	Jump For Joy	1963	6.00	15.00
RCA Victor LSP-2713	(S)	Jump For Joy	1963	8.00	20.00
RCA Victor LPM-2762	(M)	Joe Williams At Newport '63	1963	6.00	15.00
RCA Victor LSP-2762	(S)	Joe Williams At Newport '63	1963	8.00	20.00
— Original RCA mono albums above have "Long Play" on the bottom of the label; stereo albums have "Living Stereo" on the bottom.—					
RCA Victor LPM-2879	(M)	Me And The Blues	1963	5.00	12.00
RCA Victor LSP-2879	(S)	Me And The Blues	1963	6.00	15.00
RCA Victor LPM-3433	(M)	Song Is You	1965	5.00	12.00
RCA Victor LSP-3433	(S)	Song Is You	1965	6.00	15.00
RCA Victor LPM-3461	(M)	The Exciting Joe Williams	1965	5.00	12.00
RCA Victor LSP-3461	(S)	The Exciting Joe Williams	1965	6.00	15.00
— Original RCA albums above have black labels.—					
WILLIAMS, "BIG" JOE					
Folkways F-3820	(M)	Mississippi's Big Joe Williams	1962	8.00	20.00
Folkways FS-3820	(S)	Mississippi's Big Joe Williams	1962	12.00	30.00
Delmark D-604	(M)	Blues On Highway 49	1962	10.00	25.00
Bluesville BV-1056	(M)	Blues For Nine Strings	1963	10.00	25.00
Bluesville BV-1067	(M)	Big Joe Williams At Folk City	1963	10.00	25.00
Bluesville BV-1083	(M)	Studio Blues	1964	10.00	25.00
Delmark D-609	(M)	Starvin' Chain Blues	1966	8.00	20.00
Delmark SD-609	(S)	Starvin' Chain Blues	1966	10.00	25.00
Milestone 3001	(M)	Classic Delta Blues	1966	6.00	15.00
Folkways 31004	(M)	Hell Bound And Heaven Sent	1967	6.00	15.00
World Pacific WPS-21897	(S)	Big Joe Williams	1969	6.00	15.00
WILLIAMS, LARRY					
Larry also recorded with Johnny Watson.					
Specialty SP-2109	(M)	Here's Larry Williams *(Black & gold label)*	1959	50.00	100.00
OKeh OKM-2123	(M)	Larry Williams' Greatest Hits	1967	10.00	25.00
OKeh OKS-12123	(S)	Larry Williams' Greatest Hits	1967	12.00	30.00
WILLIAMS, MAURICE, & THE ZODIACS					
Herald HLP-1014	(M)	Stay	1961	100.00	200.00
Sphere Sound SR-7007	(M)	Stay	196?	30.00	60.00
Sphere Sound SSR-7007	(E)	Stay	196?	20.00	50.00
Snyder 5586	(M)	At The Beach	196?	16.00	40.00
Relic 5017	(M)	Greatest Hits	197?	8.00	20.00
WILLIAMS, MEL, & JOHNNY OTIS					
Dig 103	(M)	All Through The Night	1955	180.00	300.00
WILLIAMS, OTIS, & THE CHARMS					
Deluxe 750	(M)	Their All Time Hits	1957	300.00	500.00
King 570	(M)	Their All Time Hits	1957	150.00	250.00
King 614	(M)	This Is Otis Williams And The Charms	1959	100.00	200.00
WILLIAMS, OTIS, & THE MIDNIGHT COWBOYS					
Stop STLP-1022	(S)	Otis Williams & The Midnight Cowboys	1971	6.00	15.00

Label & Catalog #		Title	Year	VG+	NM
WILLIAMS, TEX					
Decca DL-5565 (10")	(M)	**Dance-O-Rama #5**	1955	90.00	180.00
Camden CAL-363	(M)	**Tex Williams' Best**	1958	10.00	25.00
Capitol T-1463	(M)	**Smoke! Smoke! Smoke!**	1960	12.00	30.00
Capitol ST-1463	(S)	**Smoke! Smoke! Smoke!**	1960	16.00	40.00
Decca DL-4295	(M)	**Country Music Time**	1962	8.00	20.00
Liberty LRP-3304	(M)	**Tex Williams In Las Vegas**	1963	5.00	12.00
Liberty LST-7304	(S)	**Tex Williams In Las Vegas**	1963	6.00	15.00
Imperial LP-9309	(M)	**The Voice Of Authority**	1966	5.00	12.00
Imperial LP-12309	(S)	**The Voice Of Authority**	1966	6.00	15.00
WILLIAMS, TONY					
Tony Williams was formerly the lead singer for The Platters.					
Mercury MG-20454	(M)	**A Girl Is A Girl Is A Girl**	1959	12.00	30.00
Mercury SR-60138	(S)	**A Girl Is A Girl Is A Girl**	1959	16.00	40.00
Reprise R-6006	(M)	**His Greatest Hits**	1961	8.00	20.00
Reprise R9-6006	(S)	**His Greatest Hits**	1961	12.00	30.00
Phillips PHM-200051	(M)	**Magic Touch Of Tony**	1962	8.00	20.00
Phillips PHS-600051	(S)	**Magic Touch Of Tony**	1962	12.00	30.00
WILLIAMSON, CHRIS					
Ms. Williamson is a pioneer of contemporary women's music.					
Ampex 10134	(S)	**Chris Williamson**	1971	6.00	15.00
WILLIAMSON, SONNY BOY					
Sonny Boy (#1) was a pseudonym for John Lee Williamson.					
Blues Classics BC-3	(M)	**Sonny Boy Williamson, Volume 1**	1964	6.00	15.00
Blues Classics BC-20	(M)	**Sonny Boy Williamson, Volume 2**	1964	6.00	15.00
Blues Classics BC-24	(M)	**Sonny Boy Williamson, Volume 3**	1964	6.00	15.00
WILLIAMSON, SONNY BOY					
Sonny Boy (#2) was a pseudonym for Alec "Rice" Williamson.					
Chess LP-1437	(M)	**Sonny Boy Williamson** (Black label)	1958	75.00	150.00
Chess 1503	(M)	**The Real Folk Blues** (Blue label)	1966	20.00	50.00
Chess 1509	(M)	**More Real Folk Blues** (Blue label)	1966	20.00	50.00
Chess 1536	(S)	**Bummer Road** (Blue label)	1969	8.00	20.00
Chess 2CH-50027	(S)	**This Is My Story** (2 LPs)	1972	6.00	15.00
Chess 2CH-206	(S)	**Sonny Boy Williamson** (2 LPs)	1976	6.00	15.00
WILLIAMSON, SONNY BOY, & THE YARDBIRDS					
Mercury MG-21071	(M)	**Sonny Boy Williamson & The Yardbirds**	1966	16.00	40.00
Mercury SR-61071	(S)	**Sonny Boy Williamson & The Yardbirds**	1966	20.00	50.00
WILLING, FOY, & THE RIDERS OF THE PURPLE SAGE					
Varsity VLP-6032 (10")	(M)	**Riders Of The Purple Sage**	1950	20.00	50.00
Royale 6032 (10")	(M)	**Riders Of The Purple Sage**	1952	16.00	40.00
Roulette R-25035	(M)	**Cowboy**	1958	14.00	35.00
Jubilee 5028	(M)	**The New Sound Of American Folk**	1962	10.00	25.00
WILLIS, CHUCK					
Epic LN-3425	(M)	**Chuck Willis Wails The Blues**	1958	180.00	300.00
Epic LN-3728	(M)	**A Tribute To Chuck Willis**	1960	150.00	250.00
Atlantic 8018	(M)	**The King Of The Stroll** (Black label)	1958	150.00	250.00
Atlantic 8018	(M)	**The King Of The Stroll** (Red label)	1960	50.00	100.00
Atlantic 8079	(M)	**I Remember Chuck Willis**	1963	40.00	80.00
Atlantic SD-8079	(P)	**I Remember Chuck Willis**	1963	50.00	100.00
Atco SD-33-373	(P)	**His Greatest Recordings**	1971	6.00	15.00
WILLS, BOB (& HIS TEXAS PLAYBOYS)					
Columbia HL-9003 (10")	(M)	**Bob Wills Round-Up**	1949	100.00	200.00
Antones LP-6000 (10")	(M)	**Texas Playboys**	195?	180.00	300.00
Antones LP-6010 (10")	(M)	**Old Time Favorites**	195?	180.00	300.00
MGM E-91 (10")	(M)	**Ranch House Favorites**	1951	100.00	200.00
Decca DL-5562 (10")	(M)	**Dance-O-Rama #2**	1955	150.00	250.00
MGM E-3352	(M)	**Ranch House Favorites**	1956	40.00	80.00
Decca DL-8727	(M)	**Bob Wills And His Texas Playboys**	1957	30.00	60.00
Harmony HL-7036	(M)	**Bob Wills Special** (Maroon label)	1957	14.00	35.00
Harmony HL-7304	(M)	**The Best Of Bob Wills** (Blue label)	1963	10.00	25.00
Harmony HL-7345	(M)	**The Great Bob Wills** (Blue label)	1965	8.00	20.00

Label & Catalog #		Title	Year	VG+	NM
Liberty LRP-3182	(M)	**Living Legend**	1961	10.00	25.00
Liberty LST-7182	(S)	**Living Legend**	1961	14.00	35.00
Liberty LRP-3194	(M)	**Mr. Words And Music**	1961	10.00	25.00
Liberty LST-7194	(S)	**Mr. Words And Music**	1961	14.00	35.00
Liberty LRP-3303	(M)	**Bob Wills Sings And Plays**	1963	10.00	25.00
Liberty LST-7303	(S)	**Bob Wills Sings And Plays**	1963	14.00	35.00
Starday SLP-375	(M)	**San Antonio Rose**	1965	10.00	25.00
Longhorn LP-001	(M)	**Keepsake Album #1**	1965	20.00	50.00
Vocalion VL-3735	(M)	**Western Swing Band**	1965	8.00	20.00
Vocalion VL-73735	(E)	**Western Swing Band**	1965	5.00	12.00
Vocalion VL-3922	(M)	**San Antonio Rose**	1971	6.00	15.00
Metro M-594	(M)	**Bob Wills**	1967	6.00	15.00
Metro MS-594	(S)	**Bob Wills**	1967	4.00	10.00
Kapp KL-1506	(M)	**From The Heart Of Texas**	1967	6.00	15.00
Kapp KS-3506	(S)	**From The Heart Of Texas**	1967	6.00	15.00
Kapp KL-1523	(M)	**King Of Western Swing**	1967	6.00	15.00
Kapp KS-3523	(S)	**King Of Western Swing**	1967	6.00	15.00
Kapp KS-3542	(S)	**Here's That Man Again**	1968	6.00	15.00
Kapp KS-3587	(S)	**The Living Legend**	1969	6.00	15.00
Kapp KS-3601	(S)	**The Greatest String Band Hits**	1969	6.00	15.00
Kapp KS-3569	(S)	**Time Changes Everything**	1969	6.00	15.00
Kapp KS-3639	(S)	**Bob Wills In Person**	1970	6.00	15.00
Kapp KS-3641	(S)	**The Best Of Bob Wills**	1971	5.00	12.00
United Arts. UAS-9962	(P)	**Legendary Masters** (2 LPs)	1971	10.00	25.00

WILLS, BOB, & TOMMY DUNCAN

Liberty LRX-1912	(M)	**Bob Wills And Tommy Duncan**	195?	8.00	20.00
Liberty LSX-1912	(S)	**Bob Wills And Tommy Duncan**	195?	10.00	25.00
Liberty LRP-3173	(M)	**Together Again**	1960	8.00	20.00
Liberty LST-7173	(S)	**Together Again**	1960	10.00	25.00
Sunset SUM-1108	(M)	**Together Again**	1966	5.00	12.00
Sunset SUS-5108	(S)	**Together Again**	1966	6.00	15.00
United Arts. UAS-9962	(P)	**Legendary Masters** (2 LPs)	1971	8.00	20.00

WILLS, JOHNNY LEE

Sims 101	(M)	**Where There's A Wills, There's A Way**	1962	16.00	40.00
Sims 108	(M)	**At The Tulsa Stampede**	1963	16.00	40.00

WILMER & THE DUKES

Aphrodisiac 6001	(S)	**Wilmer And The Dukes**	1969	10.00	25.00

WILSON, AL

Soul City SCS-92006	(S)	**Searching For The Dolphins**	1969	6.00	15.00
Rocky Road RR-3601	(S)	**Show And Tell**	1973	5.00	12.00

WILSON, BRIAN
Brian Wilson was The Beach Boys. Refer to J. Marks & Shipen Lebzelter; Spring.

Crawdaddy (No number)	(DJ)	**The Brian Wilson Interview**	1977	75.00	150.00
Sire PRO-3248	(DJ)	**Words And Music** (Interview)	1988	8.00	20.00

WILSON, DENNIS
Dennis Wilson was a member of The Beach Boys.

Caribou PZ-35354	(S)	**Pacific Ocean Blue**	1977	6.00	15.00

WILSON, J. FRANK, & THE CAVALIERS

Josie JM-4006	(M)	**Last Kiss**	1964	12.00	30.00
Josie JS-4006	(S)	**Last Kiss**	1964	16.00	40.00
Dill Pickle 3470	(S)	**Doin' My Thing**	1971	6.00	15.00

WILSON, JACKIE
Mr. Wilson was formerly the lead singer for Billy Ward & The Dominoes.

Sesac	(M)	**Jackie Wilson**	1958	*See note below*	
		(Rare. Estimated near mint value $500-1,000.)			
Brunswick BL-54042	(M)	**He's So Fine**	1959	50.00	100.00
Brunswick BL-54045	(M)	**Lonely Teardrops**	1959	50.00	100.00
Brunswick BL-54050	(M)	**So Much**	1960	30.00	60.00
Brunswick BL-754050	(S)	**So Much**	1960	40.00	80.00
Brunswick BL-54055	(M)	**Jackie Sings The Blues**	1960	30.00	60.00
Brunswick BL-754055	(S)	**Jackie Sings The Blues**	1960	40.00	80.00

Label & Catalog #		Title	Year	VG+	NM
Brunswick BL-54058	(M)	My Golden Favorites	1960	16.00	40.00
Brunswick BL-754058	(S)	My Golden Favorites	1960	30.00	60.00
Brunswick BL-54059	(M)	A Woman, A Lover, A Friend	1961	12.00	30.00
Brunswick BL-754059	(S)	A Woman, A Lover, A Friend	1961	16.00	40.00
Brunswick BL-54100	(M)	You Ain't Heard Nothin' Yet	1961	10.00	25.00
Brunswick BL-754100	(S)	You Ain't Heard Nothin' Yet	1961	12.00	30.00
Brunswick BL-54101	(M)	By Special Request	1961	10.00	25.00
Brunswick BL-754101	(S)	By Special Request	1961	12.00	30.00
Brunswick BL-54105	(M)	Body And Soul	1962	10.00	25.00
Brunswick BL-754105	(S)	Body And Soul	1962	12.00	30.00
Brunswick BL-54106	(M)	The World's Greatest Melodies	1962	10.00	25.00
Brunswick BL-754106	(S)	The World's Greatest Melodies	1962	12.00	30.00
Brunswick BL-54108	(M)	Jackie Wilson At The Copa	1962	8.00	20.00
Brunswick BL-754108	(S)	Jackie Wilson At The Copa	1962	10.00	25.00
		— Original Brunswick albums above have black & silver labels.—			
Brunswick BL-54110	(M)	Baby Workout	1963	8.00	20.00
Brunswick BL-754110	(S)	Baby Workout	1963	10.00	25.00
Brunswick BL-54112	(M)	Merry Christmas From Jackie Wilson	1963	8.00	20.00
Brunswick BL-754112	(S)	Merry Christmas From Jackie Wilson	1963	10.00	25.00
Brunswick BL-54113	(M)	Shake A Hand	1963	6.00	15.00
Brunswick BL-754113	(S)	Shake A Hand	1963	8.00	20.00
Brunswick BL-54115	(M)	My Golden Favorites, Volume 2	1964	6.00	15.00
Brunswick BL-754115	(S)	My Golden Favorites, Volume 2	1964	8.00	20.00
Brunswick BL-54117	(M)	Somethin' Else	1964	6.00	15.00
Brunswick BL-754117	(S)	Somethin' Else	1964	8.00	20.00
Brunswick BL-54118	(M)	Soul Time	1965	6.00	15.00
Brunswick BL-754118	(S)	Soul Time	1965	8.00	20.00
Brunswick BL-54119	(M)	Spotlight On Jackie Wilson	1965	6.00	15.00
Brunswick BL-754119	(S)	Spotlight On Jackie Wilson	1965	8.00	20.00
Brunswick BL-54120	(M)	Soul Galore	1966	6.00	15.00
Brunswick BL-754120	(S)	Soul Galore	1966	8.00	20.00
Brunswick BL-54112	(M)	Whispers	1967	6.00	15.00
Brunswick BL-754112	(S)	Whispers	1967	6.00	15.00
Brunswick BL-54130	(M)	Higher And Higher	1967	6.00	15.00
Brunswick BL-754130	(S)	Higher And Higher	1967	6.00	15.00
Brunswick BL-754138	(S)	I Get The Sweetest Feeling	1968	6.00	15.00
Brunswick BL-754134	(S)	Manufacturers Of Soul	1968	6.00	15.00
		— Original Brunswick albums above have black labels with a "Division of Decca Records" on the left side.—			

WILSON, JULIE

Label & Catalog #		Title	Year	VG+	NM
Dolphin 6	(M)	Love	1956	14.00	35.00
Vik LX-1095	(M)	My Old Flame	1957	12.00	30.00
Vik LX-1118	(M)	Julie Wilson At The St. Regis	1958	12.00	30.00
Cameo C-1021	(M)	Meet Julie Wilson	1962	10.00	25.00

WILSON McKINLEY

Label & Catalog #		Title	Year	VG+	NM
Voice of Elijah 29005/6	(S)	Heaven's Gonna Be A Blast!	197?	70.00	140.00
Voice of Elijah 29077/8	(S)	Spirit Of Elijah	197?	165.00	275.00
No label	(S)	Wilson McKinley On Stage	197?	80.00	160.00

WILSON, MURRY

The father of Brian, Dennis and Carl Wilson of The Beach Boys. Refer to The Sunrays.

Label & Catalog #		Title	Year	VG+	NM
Capitol T-2819	(M)	The Many Moods Of Murry Wilson	1967	5.00	12.00
Capitol ST-2819	(S)	The Many Moods Of Murry Wilson	1967	6.00	15.00

WINCHESTER, JESSE

Label & Catalog #		Title	Year	VG+	NM
Ampex A-10104	(S)	Jesse Winchester	1970	8.00	20.00
Bearsville PRO-692	(DJ)	Live At The Bijuo Cafe	1975	12.00	30.00
Bearsville PRO-693	(DJ)	Live Interview From Montreal (2 LPs)	1975	20.00	50.00

WIND

Label & Catalog #		Title	Year	VG+	NM
Life LLPS-2000	(S)	Make Believe	1969	6.00	15.00

WIND IN THE WILLOWS, THE

Wind features Debbie Harry, later of Blondie.

Label & Catalog #		Title	Year	VG+	NM
Capitol SKAO-2956	(S)	The Wind In The Willows	1968	12.00	30.00

Label & Catalog #		Title	Year	VG+	NM

WINGS

| Dunhill DS-50046 | (S) | Wings | 1968 | 6.00 | 15.00 |

WINTER, EDGAR (& WHITE TRASH)

Epic EQ-31584	(Q)	They Only Come Out At Night	1973	6.00	15.00
Epic PEQ-32461	(Q)	Shock Treatment	1974	6.00	15.00
Blue Sky PZQ-33483	(Q)	Jasmine Nightdreams	1975	6.00	15.00
Blue Sky PZQ-33798	(Q)	The Edger Winter Group With Rick Derringer	1975	6.00	15.00
Blue Sky ASZ-242	(DJ)	Johnny And Edger Discuss "Together"	1976	8.00	20.00

WINTER, JOHNNY

Sonobeat RS-1002	(DJ)	Progressive Blues Experiment (No cover)	1968	100.00	200.00
Imperial 12431	(S)	Progressive Blues Experiment	1969	10.00	25.00
GRT 10010	(S)	The Johnny Winter Story	1969	6.00	15.00
Buddah BDS-7513	(S)	First Winter	1969	6.00	15.00
Janus 3008	(S)	About Blues	1969	6.00	15.00
Janus 3056	(S)	Before The Storm	1970	6.00	15.00
Columbia CS-9826	(S)	Johnny Winter	1969	6.00	15.00
Columbia CS-9947	(S)	Second Winter (2 LPs)	1969	8.00	20.00
Columbia KC-30221	(S)	Johnny Winter And	1970	6.00	15.00
— Original Columbia albums above have "360 Sound Stereo" on the bottom of the label.—					
Columbia CQ-32188	(Q)	Still Alive And Well	1973	6.00	15.00
Columbia CQ-32715	(Q)	Saints And Sinners	1974	6.00	15.00
Blue Sky PZQ-33292	(Q)	John Dawson Winter III	1974	6.00	15.00

WINWOOD, STEVE

Steve was formerly a member of the Spencer Davis Group; Traffic; Blind Faith.

| United Arts. UAS-9950 | (S) | Winwood (2 LPs with a booklet) | 1971 | 10.00 | 25.00 |
| United Arts. UAS-9950 | (S) | Winwood (2 LPs without booklet) | 1971 | 6.00 | 15.00 |

WISE, CHUBBY

| Starday SLP-154 | (M) | The Tennessee Fiddler | 1961 | 12.00 | 30.00 |

WISEMAN, MAC

Refer to Lester Flatt.

Dot DLP-3084	(M)	Tis Sweet To Be Remembered	1958	16.00	40.00
Dot DLP-25084	(E)	Tis Sweet To Be Remembered	196?	6.00	15.00
Dot DLP-3135	(M)	Beside The Still Waters	1959	12.00	30.00
Dot DLP-25135	(S)	Beside The Still Waters	1959	16.00	40.00
Dot DLP-3213	(M)	Great Folk Ballads	1959	12.00	30.00
Dot DLP-25213	(S)	Great Folk Ballads	1959	16.00	40.00
Dot DLP-3313	(M)	12 Great Hits	1960	12.00	30.00
Dot DLP-25313	(S)	12 Great Hits	1960	16.00	40.00
Dot DLP-3336	(M)	Keep On The Sunnyside	1960	16.00	40.00
Dot DLP-25336	(E)	Keep On The Sunnyside	196?	6.00	15.00
Dot DLP-3373	(M)	Best Loved Gospel Hymns	1961	8.00	20.00
Dot DLP-25373	(S)	Best Loved Gospel Hymns	1961	12.00	30.00
Dot DLP-3408	(M)	Fireball Mail	1961	12.00	30.00
Dot DLP-25408	(E)	Fireball Mail	196?	6.00	15.00
Capitol T-1800	(M)	Bluegrass Favorites	1962	12.00	30.00
Capitol ST-1800	(S)	Bluegrass Favorites	1962	16.00	40.00
Hamilton HLP-12130	(M)	Sincerely	1964	8.00	20.00
Hamilton HLP-12167	(M)	Songs Of The Dear Old Days	1966	8.00	20.00
Dot DLP-3697	(M)	This Is Mac Wiseman	1966	8.00	20.00
Dot DLP-25697	(S)	This Is Mac Wiseman	1966	10.00	25.00
Dot DLP-3730	(M)	A Master At Work	1966	8.00	20.00
Dot DLP-25730	(S)	A Master At Work	1966	10.00	25.00
Dot DLP-3731	(M)	Bluegrass	1966	8.00	20.00
Dot DLP-25731	(S)	Bluegrass	1966	10.00	25.00
Dot DLP-25896	(S)	Golden Hits Of Mac Wiseman	1968	8.00	20.00

WISHBONE ASH

| Decca DL-71919 | (DJ) | An Evening Program With Wishbone Ash | 1972 | 8.00 | 20.00 |
| Decca DL-71922 | (DJ) | Live From Memphis | 1972 | 8.00 | 20.00 |

WITHERSPOON, JIMMY

Jimmy Witherspoon also recorded with Eric Burdon.

| Atlantic 1266 | (M) | New Orleans Blues (Black label) | 1956 | 100.00 | 200.00 |
| RCA Victor LPM-1639 | (M) | Goin' To Kansas City Blues | 1958 | 50.00 | 100.00 |

Label & Catalog #		Title	Year	VG+	NM
Hi Fi 421	(M)	At The Monterey Jazz Festival	1959	20.00	50.00
Hi Fi 422	(M)	Feelin' The Spirit	1959	20.00	50.00
Hi Fi 426	(M)	Jimmy Witherspoon At The Renaissance	1959	20.00	50.00
World Pacific WP-1267	(M)	Singin' The Blues	1959	20.00	50.00
World Pacific WP-1402	(M)	There's Good Rockin' Tonight	1961	20.00	50.00
Reprise R-2008	(M)	Spoon	1961	12.00	30.00
Reprise R9-2008	(S)	Spoon	1961	16.00	40.00
Reprise R-6012	(M)	Hey, Mrs. Jones	1962	12.00	30.00
Reprise R9-6012	(S)	Hey, Mrs. Jones	1962	16.00	40.00
Reprise R-6059	(M)	Roots	1962	12.00	30.00
Reprise R9-6059	(S)	Roots	1962	16.00	40.00
Prestige PR-7290	(M)	Baby, Baby, Baby	1963	8.00	20.00
Prestige PRS-7290	(S)	Baby, Baby, Baby	1963	12.00	30.00
Prestige PR-7300	(M)	Evenin' Blues	1964	8.00	20.00
Prestige PRS-7300	(S)	Evenin' Blues	1964	12.00	30.00
Prestige PR-7314	(M)	Goin' To Chicago Blues	1964	8.00	20.00
Prestige PRS-7314	(S)	Goin' To Chicago Blues	1964	12.00	30.00
Prestige PR-7327	(M)	Blue Spoon	1964	8.00	20.00
Prestige PRS-7327	(S)	Blue Spoon	1964	12.00	30.00
Prestige PR-7356	(M)	Some Of My Best Friends Are The Blues	1964	8.00	20.00
Prestige PRS-7356	(S)	Some Of My Best Friends Are The Blues	1964	12.00	30.00
Constellation M-1422	(M)	Take This Hammer	1964	12.00	30.00
Surrey S-1106	(M)	Blues For Spoon And Groove	1965	6.00	15.00
Surrey SS-1106	(S)	Blues For Spoon And Groove	1965	8.00	20.00
Prestige PR-7418	(M)	Spoon In London	1965	6.00	15.00
Prestige PRS-7418	(S)	Spoon In London	1965	8.00	20.00
Verve V-5007	(M)	Blue Point Of View	1966	8.00	20.00
Verve V6-5007	(S)	Blue Point Of View	1966	12.00	30.00
Prestige PR-7475	(M)	Blues For Easy Livers	1967	5.00	12.00
Prestige PRS-7475	(S)	Blues For Easy Livers	1967	6.00	15.00
Prestige PRS-7713	(S)	The Best Of Jimmy Witherspoon	1969	6.00	15.00
Verve V6-5050	(S)	A Spoonful Of Soul	1968	6.00	15.00
ABC S-717	(S)	Handbags And Gladrags	1970	6.00	15.00
BluesWay BLS-6026	(S)	Blues Singer	1970	6.00	15.00

WITHERSPOON, JIMMY / EDDIE VINSON

King 634	(M)	Battle Of The Blues, Volume 3	1959	360.00	600.00

WIZARD

Peon 1069	(S)	Original Wizard	1971	150.00	250.00

WIZARDS FROM KANSAS, THE

Mercury SR-61309	(S)	The Wizards From Kansas	1970	30.00	60.00

WOMACK, BOBBY

Minit LP-24014	(S)	Fly Me To The Moon	1968	6.00	15.00
Minit LP-24027	(S)	My Prescription	1969	6.00	15.00

WOMB

Dot DLP-25933	(S)	Womb	1969	6.00	15.00
Dot DLP-25959	(S)	Overdub	1969	6.00	15.00

WOMENFOLK, THE

RCA Victor LPM-2821	(M)	We Give A Hoot	1963	6.00	15.00
RCA Victor LSP-2821	(S)	We Give A Hoot	1963	8.00	20.00
RCA Victor LPM-2832	(M)	The Womenfolk	1964	5.00	12.00
RCA Victor LSP-2832	(S)	The Womenfolk	1964	6.00	15.00
RCA Victor LPM-2919	(M)	Never Underestimate The Power	1964	5.00	12.00
RCA Victor LSP-2919	(S)	Never Underestimate The Power	1964	6.00	15.00
RCA Victor LPM-2991	(M)	The Womenfolk At The Hungry i	1965	5.00	12.00
RCA Victor LSP-2991	(S)	The Womenfolk At The Hungry i	1965	6.00	15.00
RCA Victor LPM-3527	(M)	Man, Oh Man	1966	5.00	12.00
RCA Victor LSP-3527	(S)	Man, Oh Man	1966	6.00	15.00

WONDER, STEVIE
Refer to The Temptations / Stevie Wonder.

Tamla TS-232	(M)	A Tribute To Uncle Ray	1963	50.00	100.00
Tamla TS-233	(M)	The Jazz Soul Of Stevie Wonder	1963	50.00	100.00

— Original Tamla albums above have a disc over-lapping a globe at the top of the label. —

Label & Catalog #		Title	Year	VG+	NM
Tamla TS-240	(M)	Recorded Live-The 12 Year Old Genius	1963	30.00	60.00
Tamla TS-248	(M)	Workout Stevie, Workout	1963	30.00	60.00
Tamla T-250	(M)	With A Song In My Heart	1964	20.00	50.00
Tamla T-255	(M)	Stevie At The Beach	1964	16.00	40.00
Tamla TS-255	(S)	Stevie At The Beach	1964	20.00	50.00
Tamla T-268	(M)	Up-Tight (Everything's Alright)	1966	10.00	25.00
Tamla TS-268	(S)	Up-Tight (Everything's Alright)	1966	12.00	30.00
Tamla 272	(M)	Down To Earth	1966	8.00	20.00
Tamla TS-272	(S)	Down To Earth	1966	10.00	25.00
Tamla 279	(M)	I Was Made To Love Her	1967	8.00	20.00
Tamla TS-279	(S)	I Was Made To Love Her	1967	10.00	25.00
Tamla T-281	(M)	Someday At Christmas	1967	12.00	30.00
Tamla TS-281	(S)	Someday At Christmas	1967	14.00	35.00
Gordy GS-932	(S)	Eivets Rednow	1968	8.00	20.00
Tamla TS-282	(P)	Stevie Wonder's Greatest Hits	1968	6.00	15.00
Tamla TS-291	(S)	For Once In My Life	1968	6.00	15.00
Tamla TS-296	(S)	My Cherie Amour	1969	6.00	15.00
Tamla TS-298	(S)	Stevie Wonder 'Live!'	1970	6.00	15.00
Tamla PR-61	(DJ)	Journey Through The Secret Life Of Plants	1979	6.00	15.00

WOOD, BRENTON

Double Shot 1002	(M)	Oogum Boogum	1967	8.00	20.00
Double Shot 5002	(S)	Oogum Boogum	1967	6.00	15.00
Double Shot 1003	(M)	Baby You Got It	1967	8.00	20.00
Double Shot 5003	(S)	Baby You Got It	1967	6.00	15.00

WOOD, RON
Currently a Rolling Stone, Ron was formerly a member of The Jeff Beck Group and The Small Faces.

Warner Bros. BS-2819	(S)	I've Got My Own Album To Do	1974	5.00	12.00
Warner Bros. BS-2872	(S)	New Look (With Keith Richards)	1975	5.00	12.00
Atco SD-36126	(S)	Mahoney's Last Stand	1976	5.00	12.00
Columbia JC-35702	(S)	Gimme Some Neck	1979	4.00	10.00

WOODPECKER, WOODY: *Refer to* MEL BLANC

WOODS, BILL

Country Town CTR-24803	(M)	Bill Woods From Bakersfield	196?	35.00	70.00

WOODY'S TRUCK STOP

Smash SRS-67111	(S)	Woody's Truck Stop	1969	8.00	20.00

WOOL

ABC S-676	(S)	Wool	1969	8.00	20.00

WOOLEY, SHEB
Sheb Wooley is a pseudonym for Ben Colder.

MGM E-3299	(M)	Sheb Wooley	1956	20.00	50.00
MGM E-4026	(M)	That's My Ma And That's My Pa	1962	6.00	15.00
MGM SE-4026	(S)	That's My Ma And That's My Pa	1962	8.00	20.00
MGM E-4136	(M)	Tales Of How The West Was Won	1963	6.00	15.00
MGM SE-4136	(S)	Tales Of How The West Was Won	1963	8.00	20.00
MGM E-4275	(M)	The Very Best Of Sheb Wooley	1965	5.00	12.00
MGM SE-4275	(S)	The Very Best Of Sheb Wooley	1965	6.00	15.00
MGM E-4325	(M)	It's A Big Land	1965	5.00	12.00
MGM SE-4325	(S)	It's A Big Land	1965	6.00	15.00

WOOLIES, THE

Spirit 9645-2001	(S)	Basic Rock	1972	8.00	20.00
Spirit 9645-2005	(S)	Live At Lizards	1973	8.00	20.00

WOOLY BEAR

Stereo Lab Sound NR-5057	(S)	Wouldya?	1974	50.00	100.00

WORLD OF OZ, THE

Deram DES-18022	(S)	The World Of Oz	1969	12.00	30.00

WRAY, LINK (& HIS WRAYMEN)
Wray also recorded with Robert Gordon.

Epic LN-3661	(M)	Link Wray And The Wraymen	1960	75.00	150.00

Label & Catalog #		Title	Year	VG+	NM
Swan SLP-510	(M)	Jack The Ripper	1963	75.00	150.00
Vermillion 1924	(M)	Great Guitar Hits	196?	50.00	100.00
Vermillion 1925	(M)	Link Wray Sings And Plays Guitar	196?	50.00	100.00
Record Factory 1929	(S)	Yesterday And Today	197?	12.00	30.00

WRAY, VERNON

Vermillion 1972	(S)	Wasted (With Link Wray)	196?	12.00	30.00

WRIGHT, NAT

Warwick 2040	(M)	The Biggest Voice In Jazz	1960	16.00	40.00

WRIGHT, O.V.

Back Beat 61	(M)	If It's Only For Tonight	1965	6.00	15.00
Back Beat 61	(S)	If It's Only For Tonight	1965	8.00	20.00
Back Beat 67	(S)	Nucleus Of Soul	1969	6.00	15.00
Back Beat 70	(S)	A Nickle And A Nail And Ace Of Spades	1972	5.00	12.00

WYMAN, BILL
Mr. Wyman is a member of The Rolling Stones. Refer to The End; John Hammond; Sons Of Heroes.

Roll. Stones COC-79100	(S)	Monkey Grip	1974	5.00	12.00
Roll. Stones QD-79100	(Q)	Monkey Grip	1974	8.00	20.00
Roll. Stones COC-79103	(S)	Stone Alone	1976	5.00	12.00
Roll. Stones QD-79103	(Q)	Stone Alone	1976	8.00	20.00
Ripple (No number)	(S)	Digital Dreams (Soundtrack)	1983	65.00	130.00

WYNETTE, TAMMY

Epic LN-24305	(M)	Your Good Girl's Gonna Go Bad	1967	5.00	12.00
Epic BN-26305	(S)	Your Good Girl's Gonna Go Bad	1967	6.00	15.00
Epic BN-26353	(S)	Take Me To Your World	1968	5.00	12.00
Epic BN-26392	(S)	D-I-V-O-R-C-E	1968	5.00	12.00
Epic BN-26423	(S)	Inspiration	1969	4.00	10.00
Epic BN-26451	(S)	Stand By Your Man	1969	4.00	10.00
Epic BN-26474	(S)	Run, Angel, Run (Soundtrack)	1969	6.00	15.00
Epic BN-26486	(S)	Tammy's Greatest Hits	1969	4.00	10.00
Epic BN-26519	(S)	The Ways To Love A Man	1970	4.00	10.00
Epic BN-26549	(S)	Tammy's Touch	1970	4.00	10.00
		— Original Epic albums above have yellow labels.—			
Epic KE-30456	(P)	Five Easy Pieces (Soundtrack)	1971	6.00	15.00
Epic EQ-30658	(Q)	We Sure Can Love Each Other	1971	5.00	12.00
Columbia P6S-5856	(S)	The Very Best Of Tammy Wynette (5 LPs)	1973	14.00	35.00

X

Slash 104	(S)	Los Angeles	1980	6.00	15.00
Slash 107	(S)	Wild Gift	1981	6.00	15.00

XTC

Virgin 13134	(S)	Drums And Wires	1979	6.00	15.00
Virgin 13147	(S)	Black Sea	1980	6.00	15.00

XXX

No label	(S)	Live First Legal Bootleg Album	1973	30.00	60.00

Label & Catalog #		Title	Year	VG+	NM

YANCEY, JIMMY & MAMA
Atlantic 103 (10")	(M)	Yancey Special	1952	75.00	150.00
Atlantic 130 (10")	(M)	Jimmy And Mama Yancey	1952	75.00	150.00
Atlantic 134 (10")	(M)	Jimmy And Mama Yancey	1952	75.00	150.00
Paramount CJS-101 (10")	(M)	Yancey Special	1951	50.00	100.00
RCA Victor LX-3000 (10")	(M)	Blues And Boogie	1954	50.00	100.00
Riverside RLP-1028 (10")	(M)	Lost Recording Date	1954	50.00	100.00
Pax LP-6011 (10")	(M)	Mixture	1954	50.00	100.00
Pax LP-6011 (10")	(M)	Evening With The Yancey's	1954	50.00	100.00
Riverside RLP-1211	(M)	Yancey's Getaway	1957	50.00	100.00
Atlantic 1283	(M)	Pure Blues	1958	50.00	100.00
Atlantic SD-7229	(M)	Blues Originals	1972	6.00	15.00

YANCEY, MAMA
Folkways FV-9015	(M)	Mama Yancey Sings	1965	6.00	15.00
Folkways FVS-9015	(S)	Mama Yancey Sings	1965	8.00	20.00

YANCY DERRINGER
Hemisphere H-15104	(S)	Openers	1975	30.00	60.00

YANKEE DOLLAR, THE
Dot DLP-3874	(M)	The Yankee Dollar	1968	12.00	30.00
Dot DLP-25874	(S)	The Yankee Dollar	1968	16.00	40.00

YANOVSKY, ZALMAN
Zallie was formerly a member of The Mugwumps; The Lovin' Spoonful.
Buddah BDS-5019	(S)	Alive And Well In Argentina	1968	10.00	25.00
Kama Sutra KSBS-2030	(S)	Alive And Well In Argentina	1971	6.00	15.00

YARBROUGH, GLENN
Glenn was formerly a member of The Limeliters.
Tradition 1019	(M)	Come Sit By My Side	1957	10.00	25.00
Elektra EKL-135	(M)	Here We Go, Baby	1957	10.00	25.00
RCA Victor LPM-2905	(M)	One More Sound	1964	4.00	10.00
RCA Victor LSP-2905	(S)	One More Sound	1964	5.00	12.00
RCA Victor LPM-3301	(M)	Come Share My Life	1965	4.00	10.00
RCA Victor LSP-3301	(S)	Come Share My Life	1965	5.00	12.00
RCA Victor LPM-3422	(M)	Baby, The Rain Must Fall	1965	5.00	12.00
RCA Victor LSP-3422	(S)	Baby, The Rain Must Fall	1965	6.00	15.00
RCA Victor LPM-3472	(M)	It's Gonna Be Fine	1965	4.00	10.00
RCA Victor LSP-3472	(S)	It's Gonna Be Fine	1965	5.00	12.00
RCA Victor LPM-3539	(M)	The Lonely Things	1966	4.00	10.00
RCA Victor LSP-3539	(S)	The Lonely Things	1966	5.00	12.00
RCA Victor LPM-3661	(M)	Live At The Hungry i	1966	4.00	10.00
RCA Victor LSP-3661	(S)	Live At The Hungry i	1966	5.00	12.00
RCA Victor LPM-3801	(M)	For Emily, Whenever I May Find Her	1967	4.00	10.00
RCA Victor LSP-3801	(S)	For Emily, Whenever I May Find Her	1967	5.00	12.00
RCA Victor LPM-3860	(M)	Honey And Wine	1967	4.00	10.00
RCA Victor LSP-3860	(S)	Honey And Wine	1967	5.00	12.00

— Original RCA albums above have black labels.—

YARBROUGH, GELNN, & MARILYN CHILD
Elektra EKL-143	(M)	English And American Folk Songs	195?	8.00	20.00

YARDBIRDS, THE
Members were Chris Dreja, Jim McCarty, Keith Relf, Paul Samwell-Smith and Eric Clapton. Later members were Jeff Beck and Jimmy Page. Refer to Armageddon; Renaissance; Sonny Boy Williamson.
Epic LN-24167	(DJ)	For Your Love (White label)	1965	100.00	200.00
Epic LN-24167	(M)	For Your Love	1965	30.00	60.00
Epic BN-26167	(P)	For Your Love	1965	35.00	70.00

Label & Catalog #		Title	Year	VG+	NM
Epic LN-24177	(DJ)	**Having A Rave Up** (White label)	1965	100.00	200.00
Epic LN-24177	(M)	**Having A Rave Up**	1965	30.00	60.00
Epic BN-26177	(E)	**Having A Rave Up**	1965	18.00	45.00
Epic LN-24210	(DJ)	**Over Under Sideways Down** (White label)	1966	100.00	200.00
Epic LN-24210	(M)	**Over Under Sideways Down**	1966	30.00	60.00
Epic BN-26210	(P)	**Over Under Sideways Down**	1966	30.00	60.00
Epic LN-24246	(DJ)	**The Yardbirds' Greatest Hits**	1966	100.00	200.00
Epic LN-24246	(M)	**The Yardbirds' Greatest Hits**	1966	14.00	35.00
Epic BN-26246	(E)	**The Yardbirds' Greatest Hits**	1966	10.00	25.00
MGM E-4447	(M)	**Blow-Up** (Soundtrack)	1967	10.00	25.00
MGM SE-4447	(S)	**Blow-Up** (Soundtrack)	1967	14.00	35.00
Epic LN-24313	(DJ)	**Little Games** (White label)	1967	100.00	200.00
Epic LN-24313	(M)	**Little Games**	1967	35.00	70.00
Epic BN-26313	(S)	**Little Games**	1967	30.00	60.00
Epic EG-30135	(P)	**The Yardbirds** (2 LPs)	1970	20.00	50.00
Epic KE-30615	(S)	**Live Yardbirds Featuring Jimmy Page**	1972	35.00	70.00
		(Originals have a color cover; counterfeit covers are black & white.)			
Columbia P-13311	(S)	**Live Yardbirds Featuring Jimmy Page**	1972	20.00	50.00
Epic HE-38455	(P)	**The Yardbirds** (Half-speed master)	1983	35.00	70.00

YEAGER, ATLEE
Refer to Atlee; Damon.

Chelsea BCL1-0366	(S)	**Plant Me Now And Dig Me Later**	197?	5.00	12.00

YEAR ONE
No label

	(S)	**Year One** (2 LPs)	197?	35.00	70.00

YELLOW BALLOON, THE

Canterbury CLPM-1502	(M)	**The Yellow Balloon**	1967	12.00	30.00
Canterbury CLPS-1502	(S)	**The Yellow Balloon**	1967	16.00	40.00

YELLOW PAYGES, THE

Uni 73045	(S)	**The Yellow Payges, Volume 1**	1969	10.00	25.00

YES

Mobile Fidelity MFSL-077	(S)	**Close To The Edge**	1982	14.00	35.00

YESTERDAY'S CHILDREN

Map 3012	(S)	**Yesterday's Children**	196?	8.00	20.00

YESTERDAY'S FOLK

Buddah BDS-5035	(S)	**U.S. 69**	1969	5.00	12.00

YETTI-MEN, THE / THE UPPA-TRIO

Kal KB-4348	(S)	**The Yetti-Men / The Uppa-Trio**	1967	See note below	
		(Rare. Estimated near mint value $500-1,000.)			

YMA & THE KARMA DUSTERS

Manhole 1	(S)	**Up From The Sewers** (With insert)	197?	75.00	150.00

YORK BROTHERS, THE

King 586	(M)	**The York Brothers**	1958	20.00	50.00
King 581	(M)	**The York Brothers, Volume 2**	1958	20.00	50.00
King 820	(M)	**16 Great Country & Western Hits**	1963	12.00	30.00

YOU KNOW WHO GROUP, THE

Inter.Allied 420	(M)	**The You Know Who Group**	1965	30.00	60.00

YOUNG, FARON

Capitol T-778	(M)	**Sweethearts Or Strangers**	1957	20.00	50.00
Capitol T-1004	(M)	**The Object Of My Affection**	1958	16.00	40.00
Capitol T-1096	(M)	**This Is Faron Young**	1959	12.00	30.00
		— Original Capitol albums above have turquoise labels.—			
Capitol T-1185	(M)	**My Garden Of Prayer**	1959	20.00	25.00
Capitol T-1245	(M)	**Talk About Hits**	1959	20.00	25.00
Capitol ST-1245	(S)	**Talk About Hits**	1959	14.00	35.00
Capitol T-1450	(M)	**The Best Of Faron Young**	1960	8.00	20.00
Capitol ST-1450	(P)	**The Best Of Faron Young**	1960	12.00	30.00

Label & Catalog #		Title	Year	VG+	NM
Capitol T-1528	(M)	Hello, Walls	1961	8.00	20.00
Capitol ST-1528	(S)	Hello, Walls	1961	12.00	30.00
Capitol T-1634	(M)	The Young Approach	1961	8.00	20.00
Capitol ST-1634	(S)	The Young Approach	1961	12.00	30.00

— *Original Capitol albums above have black labels with the logo on the left side.*—

Label & Catalog #		Title	Year	VG+	NM
Capitol T-1876	(M)	The All-Time Great Hits of Faron Young	1963	8.00	20.00
Capitol T-2037	(M)	Memory Lane	1965	6.00	15.00
Capitol DT-2037	(E)	Memory Lane	1965	5.00	12.00
Capitol T-2307	(M)	Falling In Love	1965	6.00	15.00
Capitol DT-2307	(E)	Falling In Love	1965	5.00	12.00
Capitol T-2536	(M)	If You Ain't Lovin,' You Ain't Livin'	1966	6.00	15.00
Capitol DT-2536	(E)	If You Ain't Lovin,' You Ain't Livin'	1966	5.00	12.00
SeSac	(DJ)	Church Songs	195?	16.00	40.00
Mary Carter 1000	(DJ)	On Stage For Mary Carter Paints	196?	16.00	40.00
Mercury MG-20785	(M)	This Is Faron	1963	6.00	15.00
Mercury SR-60785	(S)	This Is Faron	1963	6.00	15.00
Mercury MG-20840	(M)	Faron Young Aims At The West	1963	5.00	12.00
Mercury SR-60840	(S)	Faron Young Aims At The West	1963	6.00	15.00
Mercury MG-20896	(M)	Story Songs For Country Fans	1964	5.00	12.00
Mercury SR-60896	(S)	Story Songs For Country Fans	1964	6.00	15.00
Mercury MG-20931	(M)	Country Dance Favorites	1964	5.00	12.00
Mercury SR-60931	(S)	Country Dance Favorites	1964	6.00	15.00
Mercury MG-20971	(M)	Story Songs Of Mountains And Valleys	1964	5.00	12.00
Mercury SR-60971	(S)	Story Songs Of Mountains And Valleys	1964	6.00	15.00
Mercury MG-21007	(M)	Pen And Paper	1965	5.00	12.00
Mercury SR-61007	(S)	Pen And Paper	1965	6.00	15.00
Mercury MG-21047	(M)	Faron Young's Greatest Hits	1965	4.00	10.00
Mercury SR-61047	(S)	Faron Young's Greatest Hits	1965	5.00	12.00
Mercury MG-21058	(M)	Faron Young Sings The Best Of Jim Reeves	1966	5.00	12.00
Mercury SR-61058	(S)	Faron Young Sings The Best Of Jim Reeves	1966	6.00	15.00
Mercury MG-21110	(M)	Unmitigated Gall	1967	4.00	10.00
Mercury SR-61110	(S)	Unmitigated Gall	1967	5.00	12.00
Tower DT-5121	(E)	The World Of Faron Young	1968	4.00	12.00

YOUNG, JESSE COLIN
Jesse was a founding member of The Youngbloods.

Label & Catalog #		Title	Year	VG+	NM
Capitol T-2070	(M)	Soul Of A City Boy	1964	8.00	20.00
Capitol ST-2070	(S)	Soul Of A City Boy	1964	10.00	25.00
Mercury MG-21005	(M)	Young Blood	1965	10.00	25.00
Mercury SR-61005	(S)	Young Blood	1965	12.00	30.00

YOUNG, KATHY

Label & Catalog #		Title	Year	VG+	NM
Mainstream S-6121	(S)	A Spoonful Of Cathy Young	196?	12.00	30.00

YOUNG, KATHY, & THE INNOCENTS
The Innocents recorded independently of Ms. Young.

Label & Catalog #		Title	Year	VG+	NM
Indigo 504	(M)	The Sound Of Cathy Young	1961	75.00	150.00

YOUNG, NEIL (& CRAZY HORSE)
Crazy Horse backs Young up on 6349, 2221, 2242. Refer to The Buffalo Springfield; Crosby, Stills, Nash & Young; The Stills-Young Band.

Label & Catalog #		Title	Year	VG+	NM
Reprise RS-6317	(DJ)	Neil Young *(White label)*	1968	50.00	100.00
Reprise RS-6317	(S)	Neil Young	1968	35.00	70.00
		(First pressings: Brown & orange label with "W7" logo. Young's name does not appear on the front cover.)			
Reprise RS-6317	(S)	Neil Young	1969	20.00	50.00
		(Second pressings with four remixed tracks. Brown & orange label with "W7" logo. "RE 1" is etched in the trail-off vinyl.)			
Reprise RS-6317	(S)	Neil Young	197?	4.00	10.00
		(Third pressings: Brown label with "Neil Young" across the top of the cover.)			
Reprise RS-6349	(DJ)	Everybody Knows This Is Nowhere	1969	20.00	50.00
		(White label promo.)			
Reprise RS-6349	(S)	Everybody Knows This Is Nowhere	1969	6.00	15.00
		(Brown & orange label with "W7" logo.)			
Reprise RS-6383	(DJ)	After The Gold Rush *(White label)*	1970	14.00	35.00
Reprise RS-6383	(S)	After The Gold Rush	1970	12.00	30.00
		(Brown & orange label with "W7" logo. A photo of Marc Bolan of T-Rex erroneously printed on the inside cover.)			

Label & Catalog #		Title	Year	VG+	NM
Reprise RS-6383	(S)	**After The Gold Rush**	1970	8.00	20.00
		(Brown & orange label with "W7" logo. A photo of Neil erroneously printed upside down on the inside cover.)			
Reprise RS-6383	(S)	**After The Gold Rush**	1970	5.00	12.00
		(Brown & orange label with "W7" logo. The photos are correct.)			
Reprise RS-6383	(S)	**After The Gold Rush**	1970	16.00	40.00
		(Brown & orange label with "W7" logo includes a remixed, extended version of "When You Dance I Can Really Love." "RE 2" is etched in the trail-off vinyl and the title on the cover is in red print instead of the more common yellow/gold.)			
Reprise MS-2032	(DJ)	**Harvest**	1972	6.00	15.00
		(The jacket and the lyric sheet are printed on textured paper.)			
Reprise 2XS-6480	(DJ)	**Journey Through The Past** (2 LPs. White label)	1972	16.00	40.00
		(Cover bears a sticker that reads "Album must be played prior to airing; this album may contain words offensive to the public.")			
Reprise 2XS-6480	(S)	**Journey Through The Past** (2 LPs)	1972	6.00	15.00
		(First pressing covers are die-cut with special inner sleeves.)			
Reprise M-2151	(DJ)	**Time Fades Away** (White label. Mono)	1973	20.00	50.00
Reprise MS-2151	(DJ)	**Time Fades Away** (White label. Stereo)	1973	8.00	20.00
Reprise 3RS-2257	(DJ)	**Decade** (3 LPs. Test pressing)	1976	100.00	200.00
		("Campaigner" contains a verse deleted from the official version.)			
Reprise MSK-2266	(DJ)	**Ode To The Wind**	1978	See note below	
		(MSK-2266 was originally titled "Ode To The Wind" and eventually released as "Comes A Time." Issued in a plain jacket with inserts. Estimated near mint value $200-500.)			
Reprise MSK-2266	(S)	**Comes A Time** (With "Lotta Love")	1978	20.00	50.00
Warner Bros. WBMS-107	(DJ)	**The Warner Bros. Music Show** (Interview)	1979	16.00	40.00
Geffen GHS-2018	(DJ)	**Trans** (Quiex II vinyl)	1982	6.00	15.00
Geffen GHS-4013	(DJ)	**Everybody's Rockin'** (Quiex II vinyl)	1983	6.00	15.00
Nautilus NR-44	(S)	**Harvest**	1982	16.00	40.00

An idiosyncratic superstar, Neil's star has risen and fallen with each turn of his career.
"Harvest," Young's most successful album on the charts, was chosen by Nautilus for its SuperDisc
series, eventually amassing miniscule sales and achieving modest collectible status.

YOUNG RASCALS, THE: *Refer to* THE RASCALS

Label & Catalog #		Title	Year	VG+	NM
YOUNGBLOODS, THE					
Original members were Banana, Joe Bauer, Jerry Corbitt and Jesse Colin Young.					
RCA Victor LPM-3724	(M)	The Youngbloods	1967	8.00	20.00
RCA Victor LSP-3724	(S)	The Youngbloods *(Black label)*	1967	6.00	15.00
RCA Victor LPM-3865	(M)	Earth Music	1968	12.00	30.00
RCA Victor LSP-3865	(S)	Earth Music *(Black label)*	1968	6.00	15.00
RCA Victor LSP-4150	(S)	Elephant Mountain	1969	6.00	15.00
RCA Victor LSP-3724	(S)	Get Together	1970	4.00	10.00
		(Repackage of "The Youngbloods.")			
Mercury SR-61273	(S)	Two Trips	1970	8.00	20.00
YOUR GANG					
Mercury MG-21094	(M)	If You Want To Buy 'Em	1966	5.00	12.00
Mercury SR-61094	(S)	If You Want To Buy 'Em	1966	6.00	15.00
YUM YUM KIDS, THE					
MGM E-4396	(M)	Yummy In Your Tummy	1966	6.00	15.00
MGM SE-4396	(S)	Yummy In Your Tummy	1966	8.00	20.00
YURO, TIMI					
Liberty LRP-3208	(M)	Hurt	1961	12.00	30.00
Liberty LST-7208	(S)	Hurt	1961	16.00	40.00
Liberty LRP-3212	(M)	Soul	1962	6.00	15.00
Liberty LST-7212	(S)	Soul	1962	8.00	20.00
Liberty LRP-3234	(M)	Let Me Call You Sweetheart	1962	5.00	12.00
Liberty LST-7234	(S)	Let Me Call You Sweetheart	1962	6.00	15.00
Liberty LRP-3263	(M)	What's A Matter, Baby?	1962	6.00	15.00
Liberty LST-7263	(S)	What's A Matter, Baby?	1962	8.00	20.00
Liberty LRP 3286	(M)	The Best Of Timi Yuro	1963	5.00	12.00
Liberty LST-7286	(S)	The Best Of Timi Yuro	1963	6.00	15.00
Liberty LRP-3319	(M)	Make The World Go Away	1963	5.00	12.00
Liberty LST-7319	(S)	Make The World Go Away	1963	6.00	15.00
Mercury MG-20963	(M)	The Amazing Timi Yuro	1964	4.00	10.00
Mercury SR-60963	(S)	The Amazing Timi Yuro	1964	5.00	12.00

Key to Abbreviations

(DJ) The price is for a disc jockey, or promotional, copy. Traditionally these have white labels with black print although some companies have used other colors or variations on their standard label with "For Promotional Use" or "Audition Copy" added to the label *at the record's manufacturing!*

(M) The price is for a monaural (one signal emanating from both speakers) record, manufactured almost exclusively from inception through the late '50s and in tandem with stereo through the demise of mono in 1968.

(S) The price is for a stereo (two separate, individual signals, one emanating from each speaker) album, issued in tandem with monaural from the late '50s through the demise of vinyl in the late '80s.

(E) The price is for a record which has its stereo effects electronically created by engineers after the fact from the original monophonic signal. Known as "rechanneled stereo," these are generally frowned upon and normally only collected by completists.

(P) The price is for a record that is stereo overall but may contain one or more tracks (usually singles recorded in mono) in either rechanneled stereo or in mono.

(Q) The price is for a quadraphonic album (four separate signals intended for special equipment: a quadraphonic pre-amp and four speakers), in vogue in the early '70s.

Referred to by Paul Williams' as "perhaps the tightest group in the country" (*Crawdaddy*, January 1967),
the Youngbloods' stock with both critics and fans has waned since. One can still purchase copies of their
first two marvelous albums for a song (actually, clean copies can be had for under $10 in most markets).
A joyful meld of folk, rock, r'n'b and pop, either of these records can bring smiles to even the droopiest
of faces. (Note: Their self-titled first album was reissued as *Get Together* in 1969 following
the success of that single.)

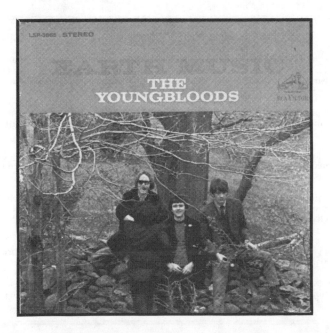

Label & Catalog #		Title	Year	VG+	NM

ZABACH, FLORIAN
| Decca DL-5367 (10") | (M) | The Hot Canary | 1951 | 16.00 | 40.00 |

ZACHERLY, JOHN
Elektra EKL-7190	(M)	Spook Along With Zacherley	1960	14.00	35.00
Elektra EKS-7190	(S)	Spook Along With Zacherley	1960	18.00	45.00
Parkway P-7018	(M)	Monster Mash	1962	16.00	40.00
Parkway P-7023	(M)	Scary Tales	1963	16.00	40.00
Crestview CR-803	(M)	Zacherley's Monster Gallery	1963	14.00	35.00
Crestview CRS7-803	(S)	Zacherley's Monster Gallery	1963	16.00	40.00

ZAPPA, FRANK [THE MOTHERS OF INVENTION]
While Zappa is always firmly in charge, the Verve albums and an occasional later album credits The Mothers Of Invention, or simply The Mothers. Refer to Captain Beefheart; Wild Man Fischer; The G.T.O.'s; Jean Luc Ponty; Ruben & The Jets; L. Shankar.
Verve V-5005	(DJ)	Freak Out! (2 LPs. White label)	1966	100.00	200.00
Verve V-5005	(M)	Freak Out! (2 LPs)	1966	40.00	80.00
Verve V6-5005	(DJ)	Freak Out! (2 LPs. Yellow label)	1966	75.00	150.00
Verve V6-5005	(S)	Freak Out! (2 LPs)	1966	20.00	50.00
		(Issued with a map, priced separately below.)			
Verve 5005		Freak Out! Map	1966	50.00	100.00
		(A map of "freak out hot spots" in L.A.)			
Verve V-5013	(DJ)	Absolutely Free (Yellow label)	1967	65.00	130.00
Verve V-5013	(M)	Absolutely Free	1967	40.00	80.00
Verve V6-5013	(S)	Absolutely Free	1967	20.00	50.00
Verve V-5045	(M)	We're Only In It For The Money	1968	65.00	130.00
		(Yellow label)			
Verve V-5045	(M)	We're Only In It For The Money	1968	40.00	80.00
Verve V6-5045	(S)	We're Only In It For The Money	1968	20.00	50.00
		(Issued with a "Sgt Pepper" parody insert.)			
Verve V6-5045	(S)	We're Only In It For The Money	1968	100.00	200.00
		(Edited version: in the song "Who Needs The Peace Corps?" the line "I will love the police as they kick the shit out of me" has been deleted. "REV" is etched in the trail-offf vinyl.)			
Verve V6-5055	(DJ)	Cruising With Ruben & The Jets	1968	65.00	130.00
		(Yellow label)			
Verve V6-5055	(S)	Cruising With Ruben & The Jets	1968	20.00	50.00
		(Issued with a set of bonuses, priced separately below.)			
Verve V6-5055		Cruising With Ruben & The Jets Insert #1	1968	20.00	50.00
		(Paper insert titled "The Story Of Ruben & The Jets.")			
Verve V6-5055		Cruising With Ruben & The Jets Insert #2	1968	20.00	50.00
		(Paper insert titled "How To Comb & Set A Jellyroll.")			
Verve V6-5055		Cruising With Ruben & The Jets Insert #3	1968	20.00	50.00
		(Paper insert guide on how to do the "bop.")			
Verve V6-8741	(DJ)	Lumpy Gravy (Yellow label)	1968	65.00	130.00
Verve V6-8741	(S)	Lumpy Gravy	1968	20.00	50.00
Verve V6-5068	(DJ)	Mothermania (Yellow label)	1969	50.00	100.00
Verve V6-5068	(S)	Mothermania	1969	30.00	60.00
Verve V6-5074	(DJ)	The XXXX Of The Mothers Of Invention	1969	50.00	100.00
		(Yellow label)			
Verve V6-5074	(S)	The XXXX Of The Mothers Of Invention	1969	20.00	50.00
MGM GAS-112	(DJ)	The Mothers Of Invention (Yellow label)	1970	30.00	60.00
MGM GAS-112	(S)	The Mothers Of Invention	1970	16.00	40.00
MGM SE-4754	(DJ)	The Worst Of The Mothers (Yellow label)	1971	35.00	70.00
MGM SE-4754	(S)	The Worst Of The Mothers	1971	20.00	50.00
Warner Bros. PRO-368	(DJ)	Zapped (Collage cover)	1969	16.00	40.00
Warner Bros. PRO-368	(DJ)	Zapped (Zappa cover)	1969	8.00	20.00
		(Various artists sampler for Zappa's Bizarre/Straight labels. First pressing covers have a black & white photo collage; second pressings have a black & white close-up of Frank.)			

As a rip-off artist— and I mean that in the '60's sense of the word— Frank Zappa was a genius. His early
albums for Verve are an awesome mosaic of influences: doo wop, surf, r'n'b, Varese, Webern and
Stravinsky are prominent. And while he was not above taking pot shots at pop— there is an hilarious
spoof of the Supremes on *Absolutely Free*— most of his better work at this time flailed away at the
pretensions of the culture and the supposedly hip counter-culture. Zappa's method of reaching
a market was also unorthodox: this cover graced the insides of many a comic book in 1967,
certainly proving that Zappa was anything but out of touch with his market...

Label & Catalog #		Title	Year	VG+	NM
Bizarre MS-2024	(DJ)	Uncle Meat (2 LPs)	1969	35.00	70.00
Bizarre MS-2024	(S)	Uncle Meat (2 LPs wth booklet)	1969	16.00	40.00
Bizarre RS-6356	(DJ)	Hot Rats	1969	20.00	50.00
Bizarre RS-6356	(S)	Hot Rats	1969	10.00	25.00
Bizarre RS-6370	(DJ)	Burnt Weenie Sandwich	1969	20.00	50.00
Bizarre RS-6370	(S)	Burnt Weenie Sandwich (With booklet)	1969	12.00	30.00
Bizarre MS-2028	(DJ)	Weasels Ripped My Flesh	1970	20.00	50.00
Bizarre MS-2028	(S)	Weasels Ripped My Flesh	1970	10.00	25.00
Bizarre MS-2030	(DJ)	Chunga's Revenge	1970	20.00	50.00
Bizarre MS-2030	(S)	Chunga's Revenge	1970	10.00	25.00
Bizarre MS-2042	(DJ)	Fillmore East, June 1971	1971	20.00	50.00
Bizarre MS-2042	(S)	Fillmore East, June 1971	1971	10.00	25.00
Bizarre MS-2075	(DJ)	Just Another Band From L.A.	1972	20.00	50.00
Bizarre MS-2075	(S)	Just Another Band From L.A.	1972	10.00	25.00
Bizarre MS-2093	(DJ)	The Grand Wazoo	1972	20.00	50.00
Bizarre MS-2093	(S)	The Grand Wazoo	1972	10.00	25.00
Bizarre MS-2094	(DJ)	Waka/Jawaka	1972	20.00	50.00
Bizarre MS-2094	(S)	Waka/Jawaka	1972	10.00	25.00

— Original copies of the Bizarre albums above have blue labels.—

Label & Catalog #		Title	Year	VG+	NM
Bizarre MS-2024	(S)	Uncle Meat (2 LPs)	197?	6.00	15.00
Bizarre RS-6356	(S)	Hot Rats	197?	4.00	10.00
Bizarre RS-6370	(S)	Burnt Weenie Sandwich	197?	4.00	10.00
Bizarre MS-2028	(S)	Weasels Ripped My Flesh	197?	4.00	10.00
Bizarre MS-2030	(S)	Chunga's Revenge	197?	4.00	10.00
Bizarre MS-2042	(S)	Fillmore East, June 1971	197?	4.00	10.00
Bizarre MS-2075	(S)	Just Another Band From L.A.	197?	4.00	10.00
Bizarre MS-2093	(S)	The Grand Wazoo	197?	4.00	10.00
Bizarre MS-2094	(S)	Waka/Jawaka	197?	4.00	10.00

— Second pressings of the Bizarre albums above have brown labels.—

Label & Catalog #		Title	Year	VG+	NM
DiscReet MS-2149	(S)	Over-Nite Sensation	1973	8.00	20.00
DiscReet MS4-2149	(Q)	Over-Nite Sensation	1973	16.00	40.00
DiscReet DS-2175	(S)	Apostrophe	1974	6.00	15.00
DiscReet DS4-2175	(Q)	Apostrophe	1974	14.00	35.00
DiscReet DSS-2202	(S)	Roxy & Elsewhere	1974	8.00	20.00
DiscReet DS-2216	(S)	One Size Fits All	1975	6.00	15.00
DiscReet DS-2234	(S)	Bongo Fury (With Captain Beefheart)	1975	6.00	15.00
Warner Bros. BS-2970	(S)	Zoot Allures	1976	6.00	15.00
DiscReet DSK-2288	(S)	Over-Nite Sensation	1977	8.00	20.00
DiscReet 2D-2290	(DJ)	Zappa In New York Cover (2 LPs)	1978	180.00	300.00
		(Test pressing with "Punky's Whips.")			
DiscReet 2D-2290	(S)	Zappa In New York Cover (2 LPs)	1978	75.00	150.00
		(Original covers erroneously list the deleted "Punky's Whips.")			
DiscReet 2D-2290	(S)	Zappa In New York (2 LPs)	1978	8.00	20.00
DiscReet DSK-2291	(S)	Studio Tan	1978	6.00	15.00
DiscReet DSK-2292	(S)	Sleep Dirt	1979	6.00	15.00
DiscReet DSK-2294	(S)	Orchestral Favorites	1979	6.00	15.00
Zappa	(DJ)	Lather (4 LP test pressing)	197?	See note below	
		(Rare. Estimated near mint value $500-1,000.)			
Zappa SRZ-2-1501	(S)	Sheik Yerbouti	1979	6.00	15.00
Zappa SRZ-1-1603	(S)	Joe's Garage, Act I	1979	5.00	12.00
Zappa SRZ-2-1502	(S)	Joe's Garage, Acts II & III (2 LPs)	1979	6.00	15.00
Barking Pumpkin 1115	(S)	Baby Snakes (Picture disc)	1982	6.00	15.00

ZEPHYR

Label & Catalog #		Title	Year	VG+	NM
Probe CPLP-4510	(S)	Zephyr	1969	10.00	25.00
Warner Bros. BS-1897	(S)	Going Back To Colorado	1971	6.00	15.00
Warner Bros. BS-2603	(S)	Sunset Ride	1972	6.00	15.00

ZERFAS

Label & Catalog #		Title	Year	VG+	NM
700 West 730710	(S)	Zerfas	197?	660.00	1,000.00

ZEVON, WARREN

Label & Catalog #		Title	Year	VG+	NM
Imperial LP-12456	(S)	Wanted Dead Or Alive	1970	6.00	15.00

ZIG ZAG PEOPLE

Label & Catalog #		Title	Year	VG+	NM
Decca DL-75110	(S)	Take Bubble Gum Music Underground	1969	8.00	20.00

Label & Catalog #		Title	Year	VG+	NM
ZIP CODES					
Liberty LRP-3367	(M)	**Mustang**	1964	20.00	50.00
Liberty LST-7367	(S)	**Mustang**	1964	35.00	70.00
ZOMBIES					
Features Rod Argent and Colin Blunstone.					
Parrot PAR-1001	(M)	**The Zombies**	1965	16.00	40.00
Parrot PAS-71001	(E)	**The Zombies**	1965	12.00	30.00
RCA Victor LOC-1115	(M)	**Bunny Lake Is Missing** *(Soundtrack)*	1965	30.00	60.00
RCA Victor LSO-1115	(S)	**Bunny Lake Is Missing** *(Soundtrack)*	1965	35.00	70.00
Date TES-4013	(S)	**Odessey And Oracle**	1968	12.00	30.00
		(First pressing covers make no mention of "Time Of The Season.")			
Date TES-4013	(S)	**Odessey And Oracle**	1969	8.00	20.00
		(Second pressing covers note the single "Time Of The Season.")			
London PS-557	(P)	**Early Days**	1969	5.00	12.00
Epic KEG-32861	(S)	**Time Of The Zombies** *(2 LPs)*	1974	5.00	12.00
ZOO					
Sunburst 7500	(S)	**The Zoo Presents The Chocolate Mousse**	1968	16.00	40.00
ZOO					
Mercury SR-61300	(S)	**The Zoo**	1970	6.00	15.00
ZZ TOP					
London PS-X-1001	(DJ)	**Takin' Texas to The People**	1976	20.00	50.00

Label & Catalog #		Title	Year	VG+	NM

Various Artists
Compilations & Soundtracks

A complete list of various artists compilations released over the past four decades would, quite literally, take up another whole volume. I have attempted to list those titles that are rare and need listings and those titles that require attention simply because they are sought by collectors. The listing here is a first and thus, even for its stated goals, far from complete. Titles are listed alphabetically by label and chronologically by catalogue number.

Rock'n Roll Soundtracks of The '50s

There are four various artists albums that deserve special attention: each was used as a soundtrack and each is among the most most collectible of all rock 'n roll albums (although they rank merely as mid-liners in the field of collectible soundtracks). Each of the big four are promotional, with three of them unissued except as publisher's demos (listed below as "No label"). The fourth was issued by Warner Brothers to radio stations. Each of these is a four figure record, with few, if any, recent sales; thus the values assigned are speculative: truly mint copies offered in a public auction could bring considerably more...

Carnival Rock remains a bit of a puzzler as it is on unattractive opaque red vinyl and came in a plain cardboard jacket. As there is only one copy in the hands of collectors, there is no documented value. Finally, the publishers demo for Rock, Rock, Rock should not be confused with the commercial copy issued on Chess.

	Label & Catalog #		Title	Year	VG+	NM
#1	No label	(DJ)	Carnival Rock	1956	——	
#2	No label	(DJ)	Rock, Rock, Rock	1956	1,500.00	
#3	No label	(DJ)	Go, Johnny, Go	1956	1,200.00	
#4	Warner Bros.	(DJ)	Jamboree (Soundtrack)	1957	1,000.00	

Label & Catalog #		Title	Year	VG+	NM
A&M SP-8022	(DJ)	The A&M Bootleg Album (2 LPs)	1973	10.00	25.00
A&M PR-4876	(DJ)	Propaganda (Picture disc)	1980	16.00	40.00
ABC-Paramount 216	(M)	A Million Or More	1958	16.00	40.00
ABC-Paramount 504	(M)	Shindig!	1964	10.00	25.00
ABC-Paramount S-504	(M)	Shindig!	1964	12.00	30.00
ABC OC-13	(S)	Zachariah (Soundtrack)	1970	6.00	15.00
Ace 1012	(M)	Greatest 15 Hits	1960	20.00	50.00
Ace 1019	(M)	Let's Have A Dance Party	1961	20.00	50.00
Ace 1020	(M)	For Twisters Only	1962	20.00	50.00
Aladdin 710	(M)	Rock & Roll With Rhythm & Blues	195?	180.00	300.00
Aladdin 812	(M)	Singing The Blues	195?	180.00	300.00
Aladdin 813	(M)	Party After Hours	195?	180.00	300.00
Almor A-108	(M)	The World Of Surfin'	1963	14.00	35.00
Almor AS-108	(S)	The World Of Surfin'	1963	20.00	50.00
Almor A-109	(M)	Hot Rod Drag Races	1963	10.00	25.00
Almor AS-109	(S)	Hot Rod Drag Races	1963	14.00	35.00
Amazon 1007	(M)	Greatest Rhythm & Blues Hits	195?	20.00	50.00
Amazon 1008	(M)	Greatest Rhythm & Blues Hits, Volume 2	195?	20.00	50.00
Apollo 490	(M)	Jackpot Of Hits	195?	75.00	150.00
Apple SW-3377	(S)	Come Together (Soundtrack)	1971	8.00	20.00
Argo 649	(DJ)	Remember The Oldies (Multi-color vinyl)	1963	75.00	150.00
Argo 649	(M)	Remember The Oldies	1963	20.00	50.00
Argo 656	(M)	Fanfare Of Hits	1963	10.00	25.00

The Bolo album, while quite desirable and often highly priced in some parts of the country, is a fairly common collectible in the Northwest.

Hardly known as a label for group vocal recordings, this early '70s Chess set contains twenty wonderful examples of the most collectible of all genres.

Label & Catalog #		Title	Year	VG+	NM
Argo 4026	(M)	The Blues, Volume 1	1963	10.00	25.00
Argo 4027	(M)	The Blues, Volume 2	1963	10.00	25.00
Argo 4031	(M)	Folk Festival Of The Blues	1964	20.00	50.00
Argo 4041	(M)	The Blues, Volume 3	1965	10.00	25.00
Argo 4042	(M)	The Blues, Volume 4	1965	10.00	25.00
Arrawak 100	(M)	A Night Train Of Oldies	195?	16.00	40.00
Arvee 433	(M)	Golden Echoes	1962	10.00	25.00
Ascot ALM-13007	(M)	All Girl Million Sellers	1964	14.00	35.00
Ascot ALS-16007	(P)	All Girl Million Sellers	1964	14.00	35.00
Astra 1001	(M)	Terry Lee Presents For Lovers Only	1964	20.00	50.00
Atco 33-103	(M)	Rockin' Together	1958	35.00	70.00
Atco 33-118	(M)	The Good Old '50's	1960	20.00	50.00
Atco 33-143	(M)	Great Group Goodies	1962	20.00	50.00
Atco 33-159	(M)	Apollo Saturday Night	1964	16.00	40.00
Atlantic 1239	(M)	Rock & Roll Forever	1956	75.00	150.00
Atlantic 1347	(M)	Blue Ridge Mountain Music	1960	16.00	40.00
Atlantic SD-1347	(S)	Blue Ridge Mountain Music	1960	20.00	50.00
Atlantic 8001	(M)	The Greatest Rock & Roll	1956	75.00	150.00
Atlantic 8010	(M)	Rock & Roll Forever, Volume 1	1956	50.00	100.00
Atlantic 8013	(M)	Dance The Rock & Roll	1957	50.00	100.00
Atlantic 8021	(M)	Rock & Roll Forever, Volume 1	1957	50.00	100.00
Atlantic 8037	(M)	The Rockin' '50's	1959	50.00	100.00
— Original Atlantic albums above have black labels.—					
Atlantic 8058	(M)	Greatest Twist Hits	1962	20.00	50.00
Atlantic 8098	(M)	Jamaica Ska	1963	8.00	20.00
Atlantic 8101	(M)	Saturday Night At The Uptown	1964	10.00	25.00
Atlantic SD-8101	(S)	Saturday Night At The Uptown	1964	14.00	35.00
Atlantic 8108	(M)	Killer Joe's International Disco	1965	8.00	20.00
Atlantic SD-8108	(S)	Killer Joe's International Disco	1965	12.00	30.00
Audio Fidelity AFLP-2168	(M)	Where It's At, Cheetah	1966	16.00	40.00
Audio Lab AL-1546	(M)	Swing Billies	195?	30.00	60.00
Audio Lab AL-1563	(M)	Pierce, Rainwater & Stuart Hamblen Sing For You	195?	30.00	60.00
Audio Lab AL-1566	(M)	Swing Billies, Volume 2	195?	30.00	60.00
August 100	(M)	Money Music	1967	180.00	300.00
Autumn 101	(M)	KYA's Memories Of The Cow Palace	1963	10.00	25.00
Bethlehem BLP-6071	(M)	Blues 'N' Folk	195?	50.00	100.00
Beta 1414S	(M)	Gathering At The Depot	196?	12.00	30.00
Blast 6803	(M)	Blasts From The Past With Clay Cole	196?	18.00	45.00
Blast 6805	(M)	16 Goodies: Blasts From The Past	196?	18.00	45.00
Bolo 8002	(M)	Bolo Bash	1964	12.00	30.00
Bonded 777	(M)	20 Original R&B Goodies	196?	20.00	50.00
Brunswick 5900 (10")	(M)	Mountain Frolic	195?	30.00	60.00
Brunswick 54001 (10")	(M)	Listen To Our Story	1958	30.00	60.00
Bud Jet 301	(M)	Country Western Hits (Volume 1)	1968	12.00	30.00
Bud Jet 302	(M)	Country Western Hits (Volume 2)	1968	12.00	30.00
Bud Jet 303	(M)	Country Western Hits (Volume 3)	1968	12.00	30.00
Bud Jet 311	(M)	Top Teen Bands (Volume 1)	1968	20.00	50.00
Bud Jet 312	(M)	Top Teen Bands (Volume 2)	1968	20.00	50.00
Bud Jet 313	(M)	Top Teen Bands (Volume 3)	1968	30.00	60.00

Label & Catalog #		Title	Year	VG+	NM
Cadence CLP-3041	(M)	Rock-A-Ballads	1960	20.00	50.00
Cadence CLP-3042	(M)	Rock-A-Hits	1960	20.00	50.00
Cadence CLP-3043	(M)	Golden Encores	1960	20.00	50.00
California Recording 101	(M)	Battle Of The Beat (Yellow label)	1964	180.00	300.00
Camay C-3001	(M)	Country & Western Bonanza	1962	8.00	20.00
Camay CS-3001	(S)	Country & Western Bonanza	1962	10.00	25.00
Capitol T-308	(M)	Top Banana	1951	20.00	50.00
Capitol T-830	(M)	Gold Record	1957	20.00	50.00
Capitol T-1009	(M)	Teenage Rock	1958	20.00	50.00
Capitol T-1025	(M)	Everybody Rocks	1958	20.00	50.00
Capitol T-1179	(S)	The Country's Best	1959	12.00	30.00
Capitol T-1414	(M)	Those Good Old Memories	195?	20.00	50.00
Capitol T-1561	(M)	Golden Gassers	1961	12.00	30.00
Capitol TBO-1572	(M)	Shake It And Break It (2 LPs)	1961	14.00	35.00
Capitol T-1837	(M)	Chartbusters	1963	8.00	20.00
Capitol DT-1837	(E)	Chartbusters	1963	6.00	15.00
Capitol T-1912	(M)	Country Hits By Country Stars	1963	6.00	15.00
Capitol ST-1912	(S)	Country Hits By Country Stars	1963	8.00	20.00
Capitol T-1939	(M)	My Son, The Surf Nut	1963	8.00	20.00
Capitol ST-1939	(S)	My Son, The Surf Nut	1963	12.00	30.00
Capitol T-1945	(M)	Chartbusters, Volume 2	1963	8.00	20.00
Capitol DT-1945	(E)	Chartbusters, Volume 2	1963	6.00	15.00
Capitol T-1995	(M)	Surfing's Greatest Hits	1963	6.00	15.00
Capitol ST-1995	(P)	Surfing's Greatest Hits	1963	8.00	20.00
Capitol T-2006	(M)	Chartbusters, Volume 3	1963	8.00	20.00
Capitol DT-2006	(E)	Chartbusters, Volume 3	1963	6.00	15.00
Capitol T-2009	(M)	Country Music Hootenanny	1963	12.00	30.00
Capitol ST-2009	(S)	Country Music Hootenanny	1963	16.00	40.00
Capitol T-2024	(M)	Big Hit Rod Hits	1963	8.00	20.00
Capitol ST-2024	(P)	Big Hit Rod Hits	1963	12.00	30.00
Capitol T-2094	(M)	Chartbusters, Volume 4	1964	16.00	40.00
Capitol ST-2094	(P)	Chartbusters, Volume 4	1964	30.00	60.00
Capitol T-2125	(M)	The Big Hits From England And The U.S.A.	1964	16.00	40.00
Capitol ST-2125	(S)	The Big Hits From England And The U.S.A.	1964	20.00	50.00
Capitol T-2538	(M)	Who's Who Of Country Music	1966	6.00	15.00
Capitol ST-2538	(S)	Who's Who Of Country Music	1966	8.00	20.00
Capitol T-2544	(M)	Liverpool Today	1966	8.00	20.00
Capitol ST-2544	(S)	Liverpool Today	1966	12.00	30.00

— Capitol Promotional Albums—

Label & Catalog #		Title	Year	VG+	NM
Capitol PRO-325	(DJ)	New Album Preview (2 LPs)	1957	100.00	200.00
Capitol PRO-326	(DJ)	New Album Preview (2 LPs)	1957	100.00	200.00
Capitol PRO-329	(DJ)	Merchandising Campaign (2 LPs)	1957	50.00	100.00
Capitol PRO-696	(DJ)	Preview Of New Sept. Albums (2 LPs)	1958	50.00	100.00
Capitol PRO-2376	(DJ)	Balanced For Broadcast	1963	12.00	30.00
Capitol PRO-2378	(DJ)	Salesmen's Demonstration Record	1963	16.00	40.00
Capitol PRO-2396	(DJ)	Big Surfin' Sounds	1963	35.00	70.00
Capitol PRO-2464	(DJ)	Salesmen's Demonstration Record	1963	16.00	40.00
Capitol PRO-2480	(DJ)	Hot Rod Music On Capitol	1963	50.00	100.00
Capitol PRO-2494	(DJ)	Salesmen's Demonstration Record	1963	16.00	40.00
Capitol PRO-2538	(DJ)	Great New Releases From The Sound Capitol Of The World	1964	50.00	100.00
Capitol PRO-2556	(DJ)	Balanced For Broadcast	1963	12.00	30.00
Capitol PRO-2658	(DJ)	Big Surfin' Sounds	1964	35.00	70.00
Capitol PRO-2685	(DJ)	Balanced For Broadcast	1964	12.00	30.00
Capitol PRO-2744	(DJ)	Programming Aids From Capitol	1964	75.00	150.00
Capitol PRO-3123	(DJ)	Silver Platter Service From Hollywood	1964	50.00	100.00
Capitol PRO-3133	(DJ)	Silver Platter Service From Hollywood	1964	150.00	250.00
Capitol PRO-3265	(DJ)	Silver Platter Service	1967	75.00	150.00
Capitol PRO-4411	(DJ)	Capitol's 25th Anniversary Celebration	1967	12.00	30.00
Capitol SPRO-4673	(DJ)	Capitol Disc Jockey Album	1969	12.00	30.00
Capitol SPRO-4724	(DJ)	Capitol Hits Through The Years	1969	16.00	40.00
Capitol SPRO-5003	(DJ)	Listen In Good Health	1970	12.00	30.00
Capitol SPRO-8511	(DJ)	The Greatest Music Ever Sold	1976	12.00	30.00
Capitol SPRO-9867	(DJ)	Capitol In-Store Sampler	198?	35.00	70.00

Label & Catalog #		Title	Year	VG+	NM
Carlton 121	(M)	One Dozen Goldies	1958	20.00	50.00
Chancellor CHL-5017	(M)	Wild Wildwood	1961	10.00	25.00
Chancellor CHS-5017	(S)	Wild Wildwood	1961	16.00	40.00
Checker LP-2973	(DJ)	Love Those Goodies (Multi-colored vinyl)	1959	75.00	150.00
Checker LP-2973	(M)	Love Those Goodies	1959	20.00	50.00
Checker LP-2975	(M)	Hits That Jumped	1959	20.00	50.00
Chess LP-1425	(M)	Rock, Rock, Rock (Soundtrack)	1958	85.00	170.00
Chess LP-1439	(DJ)	Oldies In Hi Fi (Multi-colored vinyl)	1959	300.00	500.00
Chess LP-1439	(M)	Oldies In Hi Fi	1959	35.00	70.00
Chess LP-1441	(DJ)	Bunch Of Goodies (Multi-colored vinyl)	1960	300.00	500.00
Chess LP-1441	(M)	Bunch Of Goodies	1960	35.00	70.00
Chess LP-1458	(M)	Murray The K's Golden Gassers	1961	16.00	40.00
Chess LP-1461	(M)	Murray The K's Blasts From The Past	1961	16.00	40.00
Chess LP-1470	(M)	Murray The K's Gassers For Submarine Race Watchers	1963	16.00	40.00
Chess LP-1474	(M)	Treasure Tunes From The Vault	1963	12.00	30.00
Chess LP-1476	(M)	Dance Tunes From The Vault	1964	12.00	30.00
— Original Chess albums above have black labels with silver print.—					
Chess LPS-1520	(S)	Petal Pushers	1968	10.00	25.00
Chess LPS-1544	(P)	Pop Origins	1969	10.00	25.00
Chess 2CH-50030	(M)	Golden Age Of Rhythm & Blues (2 LPs)	1972	12.00	30.00
Clarion 609	(M)	Discoteque In Astrosound	1966	60.00	120.00
Clarion 609	(S)	Discoteque In Astrosound	1966	85.00	170.00
Class 5004	(M)	Gone But Not Forgotten	1959	35.00	70.00
Colpix CP-444	(M)	Teenage Triangle	1964	16.00	40.00
Colpix SCP-444	(S)	Teenage Triangle	1964	35.00	70.00
Colpix CP-466	(M)	Groovy Goodies	1964	16.00	40.00
Colpix SCP-466	(M)	Groovy Goodies	1964	35.00	70.00
Colpix CP-468	(M)	More Teenage Triangle	1964	16.00	40.00
Colpix SCP-468	(S)	More Teenage Triangle	1964	35.00	70.00
Columbia HL-9008 (10")	(M)	Current Country Hits #1	195?	20.00	50.00
Columbia HL-9011 (10")	(M)	Current Country Hits #2	195?	20.00	50.00
Columbia HL-9016 (10")	(M)	Current Country Hits #3	195?	20.00	50.00
Columbia CL-894	(M)	Country Spectacular	1957	12.00	30.00
Columbia CL-1048	(M)	Phillip Morris Country Music Show	1958	10.00	25.00
Columbia CL-1072	(M)	Town Hall Party	1958	20.00	50.00
Columbia XLP-42371	(DJ)	Going Places On Columbia	1958	50.00	100.00
Columbia CL-1257	(M)	Greatest Western Hits	1959	10.00	25.00
Columbia CL-1408	(M)	The Greatest Western Hits	195?	10.00	25.00
Columbia CL-1583	(M)	Evolution Of The Blues Song	1960	8.00	20.00
Columbia CS-8383	(S)	Evolution Of The Blues Song	1960	12.00	30.00
— Original Columbia albums above have three white "eye" logos on each side of the spindle hole.—					
Columbia CL-1976	(M)	Greatest Western Hits, Volume 1	1963	5.00	12.00
Columbia CS-8776	(S)	Greatest Western Hits, Volume 1	1963	6.00	15.00
Columbia CL-2172	(M)	The Exciting New Liverpool Sound	1964	6.00	15.00
Columbia CS-8972	(M)	The Exciting New Liverpool Sound	1964	8.00	20.00
Columbia CL-2667	(M)	18 King Size R&B Hits	1967	6.00	15.00
Columbia CS-9467	(M)	18 King Size R&B Hits	1967	8.00	20.00
— Original Columbia albums above have "360 Sound" on the bottom of the label.—					
— Columbia Special Products/Promotional Albums—					
Columbia (No number)	(S)	Great Folk Ballads, Country & Western (4 LP box prepared for Zenith.)	1962	10.00	25.00
Columbia CLP-128	(M)	Hootenanny '64	1964	4.00	10.00
Columbia CSP-128	(S)	Hootenanny '64	1964	5.00	12.00
Columbia CLP-149	(M)	All-Star Hootenanny	1964	4.00	10.00
Columbia CSP-149	(S)	All-Star Hootenanny	1964	5.00	12.00
Columbia CLP-156	(M)	Songs Of The "Combat" Years	1964	6.00	15.00
Columbia CSP-156	(S)	Songs Of The "Combat" Years	1964	8.00	20.00
Columbia CLP-176	(M)	The Swingers	1964	4.00	10.00
Columbia CSP-176	(P)	The Swingers	1964	5.00	12.00

Label & Catalog #		Title	Year	VG+	NM
Columbia CLP-205	(M)	Folk Jamboree	1964	4.00	10.00
Columbia CSP-205	(S)	Folk Jamboree	1964	5.00	12.00
Columbia CLP-216	(M)	Zenith Presents A Hootenanny Special	1964	4.00	10.00
Columbia CSP-216	(S)	Zenith Presents A Hootenanny Special	1964	5.00	12.00
Columbia CLP-251	(M)	Power Train '66	1966	4.00	10.00
Columbia CSP-251	(S)	Power Train '66	1966	5.00	12.00
Columbia CLP-270	(M)	The Great Entertainers: The Folk Sound	1966	4.00	10.00
Columbia CSP-270	(S)	The Great Entertainers: The Folk Sound	1966	5.00	12.00
Columbia CLP-293	(M)	When We're Together With The Folk Sound	1966	4.00	10.00
Columbia CSP-293	(S)	When We're Together With The Folk Sound	1966	5.00	12.00
Columbia CLP-299	(M)	The Folk Sound	1966	4.00	10.00
Columbia CSP-299	(S)	The Folk Sound	1966	5.00	12.00
Columbia CLP-301	(M)	London Really Swings	1966	5.00	12.00
Columbia CSP-301	(S)	London Really Swings	1966	5.00	12.00
Columbia CLP-314	(M)	Sounds Of Mod Contact	1966	4.00	10.00
Columbia CSP-314	(P)	Sounds Of Mod Contact	1966	5.00	12.00
Columbia CLP-333	(M)	It's Happenin' Here	1966	4.00	10.00
Columbia CSP-333	(S)	It's Happenin' Here	1966	5.00	12.00
Columbia CLP-344	(M)	Just Plain Folk	1966	4.00	10.00
Columbia CSP-344	(S)	Just Plain Folk	1966	5.00	12.00
Columbia CSM-387	(M)	The Exciting Years	1966	4.00	10.00
Columbia CSS-387	(P)	The Exciting Years	1966	5.00	12.00
Columbia CLP-389	(M)	A Slice Of Lemon	1966	4.00	10.00
Columbia CSP-389	(S)	A Slice Of Lemon	1966	5.00	12.00
Columbia CSP-523	(M)	Zenith Salutes The Teen Sound	1966	4.00	10.00
Columbia CSS-523	(P)	Zenith Salutes The Teen Sound	1966	5.00	12.00
Columbia CLP-526	(M)	Zenith Salutes The Folk Singers	1966	4.00	10.00
Columbia CSP-526	(S)	Zenith Salutes The Folk Singers	1966	5.00	12.00
Columbia CSP-731	(M)	Groovy Sounds	1966	4.00	10.00
Columbia CSS-731	(P)	Groovy Sounds	1966	5.00	12.00
Columbia D-81	(M)	Disco Teen '65	1965	4.00	10.00
Columbia DS-81	(S)	Disco Teen '65	1965	5.00	12.00
Columbia D-155	(M)	Disco Teen '66	1966	4.00	10.00
Columbia DS-155	(S)	Disco Teen '66	1966	16.00	40.00
Columbia CL-2122	(M)	All-Star Hootenanny	1964	4.00	10.00
Columbia CS-8922	(S)	All-Star Hootenanny	1964	5.00	12.00
Columbia A2S-174	(DJ)	The Heavyweights (2 LPs)	1975	16.00	40.00
Columbia A2S-890	(DJ)	Hitline '80 (2 LPs)	1980	12.00	30.00
Columbia AS-902	(S)	Highlights From CBS Mastersound	1981	20.00	50.00
		(Issued with a booklet.)			
Constellation CS-5	(M)	Groups Three	1964	12.00	30.00
Constellation CS-7	(M)	Aces Three	1964	12.00	30.00
Coral CRL-57269	(M)	Hitsville	1959	35.00	70.00
Coral CRL-757269	(S)	Hitsville	1959	50.00	100.00
Coral CRL-57310	(M)	Million Airs	1959	12.00	30.00
Coral CRL-757310	(S)	Million Airs	1959	20.00	50.00
Coral CRL-57431	(M)	Teenage Goodies	1963	12.00	30.00
Coral CRL-757431	(S)	Teenage Goodies	1963	20.00	50.00
Cotillion SD-9037	(S)	Homer (Soundtrack)	1970	6.00	15.00
Cotillion CT3-500	(S)	Woodstock (3 LPs. Soundtrack)	1970	8.00	20.00
Cotillion CT2-400	(S)	Woodstock, Volume 2 (2 LPs)	1971	6.00	15.00
		— Original Cotillion albums above have grey labels with an 1841 Broadway address.—			
Dawn 119	(M)	Rock And Roll Spectacular	195?	20.00	50.00
Decca DL-38008	(DJ)	Fill The Air With Music	195?	50.00	100.00
Decca DL-738241	(DJ)	Admiral Stereophonic Demo	195?	50.00	100.00
Decca DL-8655	(M)	Let's Have A Party	1958	50.00	100.00
Decca DL-8860	(M)	Top Pops	1959	16.00	40.00
		— Original Decca albums above have black labels with silver print.—			
Decca DL-4004	(M)	The Early '50's	1960	20.00	50.00
Decca DL-4005	(M)	The Late '50's	1960	20.00	50.00
Decca DL-4011	(M)	Rhythm, Blues & Boogie Woogie	1960	20.00	50.00
Decca DL-4036	(M)	Golden Oldies	1960	20.00	50.00
Decca DL-4045	(M)	Midnight Jamboree	1960	12.00	30.00
Decca DL-74045	(S)	Midnight Jamboree	1960	16.00	40.00

Label & Catalog #		Title	Year	VG+	NM
Decca DL-4057	(M)	**Country Music Time**	*1960*	**12.00**	**30.00**
Decca DL-74057	(S)	**Country Music Time**	*1960*	**16.00**	**40.00**
Decca DL-4172	(M)	**Country Jubilee**	*1962*	**10.00**	**25.00**
Decca DL-74172	(S)	**Country Jubilee**	*1962*	**12.00**	**30.00**
Decca DL-4434	(M)	**Out Came The Blues**	*1964*	**16.00**	**40.00**
Decca DL-9119	(M)	**The Lively Set** *(Soundtrack)*	*1964*	**20.00**	**50.00**
Decca DL-79119	(S)	**The Lively Set** *(Soundtrack)*	*1964*	**35.00**	**70.00**
Decca DL-4671	(M)	**Saturday Night At The Grand Ole Opry**	*1966*	**6.00**	**15.00**
Decca DL-74671	(S)	**Saturday Night At The Grand Ole Opry**	*1966*	**8.00**	**20.00**
Decca DL-4699	(M)	**Wild, Wild Winter** *(Soundtrack)*	*1966*	**8.00**	**20.00**
Decca DL-74699	(S)	**Wild, Wild Winter** *(Soundtrack)*	*1966*	**12.00**	**30.00**
Decca DL-4751	(M)	**Out Of Sight** *(Soundtrack)*	*1966*	**12.00**	**30.00**
Decca DL-74751	(S)	**Out Of Sight** *(Soundtrack)*	*1966*	**16.00**	**40.00**
Del-Fi *(No number)*	(DJ)	**Del-Fi Album Sampler** *(Green vinyl)*	*1959*	**180.00**	**300.00**
Del-Fi DFLP-1210	(M)	**Del-Fi Record Hop**	*1960*	**35.00**	**70.00**
Del-Fi DFLP-1219	(M)	**Barrel Of Oldies**	*1961*	**20.00**	**50.00**
Del-Fi DFLP-1227	(M)	**Very Best Of The Oldies**	*1963*	**20.00**	**50.00**
Del-Fi DFLP-1235	(M)	**Battle Of The Surfing Bands**	*1964*	**20.00**	**50.00**
Del-Fi DFST-1235	(S)	**Battle Of The Surfing Bands**	*1964*	**35.00**	**70.00**
Del-Fi DFLP-1249	(M)	**Big Surf Hits**	*1964*	**20.00**	**50.00**
Del-Fi DFST-1249	(S)	**Big Surf Hits**	*1964*	**35.00**	**70.00**
Dimension DLP-6001	(M)	**The Dimension Dolls**	*1964*	**75.00**	**150.00**
Domain 102	(M)	**Rosko's Evergreens**	*1963*	**20.00**	**50.00**
Dooto LP-203	(M)	**Rock & Roll Vs. Rhythm & Blues**	*195?*	**20.00**	**50.00**
Dooto DTL-204	(M)	**Best In Rhythm 'N Blues** *(Colored vinyl)*	*1957*	**180.00**	**300.00**
		(First pressings have flat maroon labels.)			
Dooto DTL-204	(M)	**Best In Rhythm 'N Blues** *(Colored vinyl)*	*1959*	**50.00**	**100.00**
		(Second pressings have glossy maroon labels.)			
Dooto DTL-204	(M)	**Best In Rhythm 'N Blues** *(Colored vinyl)*	*1960*	**20.00**	**50.00**
		(Later pressings have multi-color labels.)			
Dooto LP-224	(M)	**Best Vocal Groups In Rhythm & Blues**	*1958*	**20.00**	**50.00**
Dooto LP-855	(M)	**Oldies**	*196?*	**6.00**	**15.00**
Dot DLP-3049	(M)	**Great Hits On Dot**	*1957*	**14.00**	**35.00**
Dot DLP-3183	(M)	**Young Love**	*1959*	**12.00**	**30.00**
Dot DLP-3425	(M)	**Million Dollar Music**	*1962*	**8.00**	**20.00**
Double-L DL-2302	(M)	**Washington Committee**	*1963*	**20.00**	**50.00**
Duke DLP-73	(M)	**Like 'Em Red Hot**	*1965*	**12.00**	**30.00**
Duke DLP-82	(M)	**Blues That Gave America Soul**	*1966*	**6.00**	**15.00**
Duke DLPS-82	(M)	**Blues That Gave America Soul**	*1966*	**8.00**	**20.00**
Elektra EKL-264	(M)	**The Blues Project**	*1964*	**8.00**	**20.00**
Elektra EKLS-7264	(S)	**The Blues Project**	*1964*	**12.00**	**30.00**
Elektra EKL-299	(M)	**Singer Songwriter Project**	*1965*	**8.00**	**20.00**
Elektra EKS-7299	(S)	**Singer Songwriter Project**	*1965*	**12.00**	**30.00**
Elektra EKL-4002	(M)	**What's Shakin'**	*1966*	**8.00**	**20.00**
Elektra EKS-74002	(S)	**What's Shakin'**	*1966*	**12.00**	**30.00**
Elektra 7E-2006	(P)	**Nuggets** *(2 LPs)*	*1972*	**12.00**	**30.00**
End LP-302	(M)	**Rock & Roll Jamboree**	*1959*	**30.00**	**60.00**
End LP-305	(M)	**Battle Of The Groups, Volume 1**	*1960*	**30.00**	**60.00**
End LP-309	(M)	**Battle Of The Groups, Volume 2**	*1960*	**30.00**	**60.00**
End LP-310	(M)	**12 + 3 + 15 Hits**	*1960*	**30.00**	**60.00**
End LP-313	(M)	**Alan Freed's Golden Picks**	*1961*	**16.00**	**40.00**
End LP-314	(M)	**Alan Freed's Memory Lane**	*1962*	**16.00**	**40.00**
End LP-315	(M)	**Alan Freed's Memory Lane**	*1962*	**16.00**	**40.00**
		—Original End albums above have grey labels with dogs on top.—			
Epic LN-3701	(M)	**Cream Of The Crop**	*1959*	**20.00**	**50.00**
Epic LN-3702	(M)	**Please Say You Want Me**	*1959*	**20.00**	**50.00**
Epic LN-24040	(M)	**Great Golden Grooves**	*1963*	**12.00**	**30.00**

Recorded live during the final shows from Bill Graham's legendary Fillmores West and East, this deluxe boxed set holds up well as both an artifact of a long gone period and as an example of how diverse that period really was.

Released in conjunction with International Artist's boxed set of their complete LP output in 1978, this sampler features an appropriate black and white line drawing on the cover.

Label & Catalog #		Title	Year	VG+	NM
Everlast 201	(M)	Our Best To You	196?	30.00	60.00
Famous 501	(M)	Rockin' Slumber Party	196?	12.00	30.00
Felsted 7503	(M)	Night At The Boulevard	196?	20.00	50.00
Fifth Pipe Dream 11680	(S)	San Francisco Sound (Black & white cover)	1969	75.00	150.00
Fifth Pipe Dream 11680	(S)	San Francisco Sound (Color cover)	1969	65.00	130.00
Fillmore 31390	(S)	The Last Days Of The Fillmore (2 LP box)	1972	14.00	35.00
Fire FLP-101	(M)	Memory Lane Hits By The Original Groups	1960	100.00	200.00
Flip 1001	(M)	Twelve Flip Hits	196?	30.00	60.00
Flip 1002	(M)	Original Recordings By The Artists Who Made Them Hits	196?	30.00	60.00
Fortune 8011	(M)	Treasure Chest Of Musty Dusties, Vol. 1	196?	30.00	60.00
Fortune 8017	(M)	Treasure Chest Of Musty Dusties, Vol. 2	196?	16.00	40.00
G.S.P. 6901	(M)	Beach Party	196?	50.00	100.00
Garrett 1243	(M)	Top Teen Bands	1968	35.00	70.00
Gateway 9004	(M)	1964 In Review	1965	16.00	40.00
Gee GLP-702	(M)	Teenage Party	1958	35.00	70.00
Golden Era 123	(M)	Golden Era (3 LPs)	196?	20.00	50.00
Groovemaster BR-140	(M)	Beat Battle Of The World	1964	10.00	25.00
Groovemaster GR-140	(E)	Beat Battle Of The World	1964	8.00	20.00
Happy Tiger 1017	(P)	Early Chicago	1969	20.00	50.00
HBR HLP-8500	(M)	A Swingin' Summer (Soundtrack)	1966	12.00	30.00
HBR HST-8500	(S)	A Swingin' Summer (Soundtrack)	1966	16.00	40.00
Herald 1010	(M)	Herald Of The Beat	1960	50.00	100.00
Herald 1015	(M)	Pot Of Golden Goodies	1960	50.00	100.00
Hideout	(M)	Best Of The Hideouts	1969	150.00	250.00
Hollywood 30	(M)	Rhythm & Blues In The Night	196?	30.00	60.00
Hollywood 501	(M)	Merry Christmas, Baby	196?	12.00	30.00
Hollywood 503	(M)	R&B Hits	196?	50.00	100.00
Hull 1002	(M)	Your Favorite Singing Groups	195?	100.00	200.00
I.G.L. 103	(M)	Roof Garden Jamboree	1967	100.00	200.00
Impact LP-2	(M)	Shake, Shout And Soul	196?	100.00	200.00
Imperial DJLP-1 (10")	(DJ)	Imperial Sampler	195?	50.00	100.00
Imperial LM-94000	(M)	Goin' Up The Country	196?	10.00	25.00
Imperial LM-94001	(M)	Saturday Night Function	196?	10.00	25.00
Imperial LM-94002	(M)	Blues Uptown	196?	10.00	25.00
Imperial LM-94003	(M)	The End Of An Era	196?	10.00	25.00
Imperial LM-94004	(M)	New Orleans Bounce	196?	10.00	25.00
Imperial LM-94005	(M)	Sweet And Greasy	196?	10.00	25.00
Imperial LP-9021	(M)	A Tribute To James Dean (Maroon label)	1957	20.00	50.00
Imperial LP-9084	(M)	Hitsville U.S.A., Volume 1	1960	16.00	40.00
Imperial LP-9099	(M)	Hitsville U.S.A., Volume 2	1960	16.00	40.00
Imperial LP-9210	(M)	A World Of Blues	1963	16.00	40.00
Imperial LP-9214	(M)	Hillbilly House Party	1963	8.00	20.00
Imperial LP-9257	(M)	Best Of The Blues, Volume 1	1964	8.00	20.00
Imperial LP-12257	(S)	Best Of The Blues, Volume 1	1964	10.00	25.00
Imperial LP-9259	(M)	Best Of The Blues, Volume 2	1964	8.00	20.00
Imperial LP-12259	(S)	Best Of The Blues, Volume 2	1964	10.00	25.00

Subtitled "Original Artyfacts From The First Psychedelic Era," this album is really a hodgepodge
of punk, garage, psych and pop. Which is not to denigrate the listening experience
or the import of the record on collectors' tastes...

While it might appear a bit presumptuous for a record to call itself "England's Greatest Hits"
and not include the Beatles, Stones, Kinks, Who, Yardbirds, etc. this collection from Fontana aptly
sums up the label's contributions to the Invasion period.

Label & Catalog #		Title	Year	VG+	NM
Imperial LP-9260	(M)	New Orleans, Our Home Town	1964	10.00	25.00
Imperial LP-12260	(S)	New Orleans, Our Home Town	1964	12.00	30.00
Imperial LP-9271	(M)	Giant Instrumental R&B Hits	1964	10.00	25.00
Imperial LP-12271	(S)	Giant Instrumental R&B Hits	1964	12.00	30.00

— Original Imperial mono albums above have black labels with stars on top;
stereo albums have black labels with silver print.—

Label & Catalog #		Title	Year	VG+	NM
Instant 7100	(M)	All These Things	196?	16.00	40.00
International Art. 13	(S)	Epitaph For A Legend (2 LPs)	1979	20.00	50.00
Jamie LPS-3031	(E)	Old 'N Golden	196?	8.00	20.00
JAS JAS-5001	(S)	San Francisco Roots (Photo cover)	1976	20.00	50.00
JAS JAS-5001	(S)	San Francisco Roots (Titles cover)	1976	6.00	15.00
Jerden JRL-7001	(M)	Original Great Northwest Hits, Volume 1	1965	20.00	50.00
Jerden JRL-7002	(M)	Original Great Northwest Hits, Volume 2	1965	20.00	50.00
Jerden JRL-7005	(M)	Hitmakers	1966	20.00	50.00
Jin 4002	(M)	Rockin' Date With The South Louisiana Stars	196?	16.00	40.00
Jobete PRO-1	(DJ)	The Top 10 Story In Sound	196?	20.00	50.00
Jobete PRO-4	(DJ)	The Songs Of Holland-Dozier-Holland	196?	20.00	50.00
Josie 4002	(M)	Original Goldies From The Fabulous '50's	1962	20.00	50.00
Jubilee J-1014	(M)	The Best of Rhythm And Blues	195?	50.00	100.00
Jubilee J-1014	(M)	The Best of Rhythm And Blues (Red vinyl)	195?	10.00	200.00
Jubilee J-1107	(M)	Surprise Party	196?	50.00	100.00
Jubilee J-1114	(M)	Rumble	195?	50.00	100.00
Jubilee J-1118	(M)	Boppin'	195?	50.00	100.00
Jubilee J-1119	(M)	Whoppers	195?	50.00	100.00
King 395 513	(M)	All Star Rock And Roll Revue	1958	100.00	200.00
King 395-528	(M)	After Hours	1958	180.00	300.00
King 395-536	(M)	Rock & Roll Dance Party	1958	100.00	200.00
King 395-537	(M)	All Time Country & Western Hits	1958	20.00	50.00
King 395-540	(M)	Piano Variations	1958	20.00	50.00
King 395-556	(M)	Sacred Songs	1958	20.00	50.00
King 395-562	(M)	Square Dance Music	1958	20.00	50.00
King 395-576	(M)	Spirituals, Volume 5	1958	20.00	50.00
King 395-607	(M)	Battle Of The Blues, Volume 1	1959	300.00	500.00
King 395-627	(M)	Battle Of The Blues, Volume 2	1959	300.00	500.00
King 395-634	(M)	Battle Of The Blues, Volume 3	1959	360.00	600.00
King 395-638	(M)	Rock & Roll Revue	1959	50.00	100.00
King 654	(M)	Rock & Roll Revue, Volume 2	1959	50.00	100.00
King 668	(M)	Battle Of The Blues, Volume 4	1959	660.00	1,000.00
King 680	(M)	Merry Christmas	1959	50.00	100.00
King 697	(M)	Country & Western Jamboree	1960	20.00	50.00
King 710	(M)	All Time Country & Western Hits	1960	20.00	50.00
King 725	(M)	25 Years Of Rhythm And Blues Hits	1960	35.00	70.00
King 726	(M)	Homespun Humor	1960	20.00	50.00
King 737	(M)	Hit Makers And Record Breakers	1960	20.00	50.00
King 745	(M)	Solo Spotlights	1961	20.00	50.00
King 749	(M)	25 Years Of R&B Hits	1961	20.00	50.00
King 753	(M)	Bumper Crop Of All Stars	1961	20.00	50.00
King 792	(M)	Forgotten Million Sellers	1962	20.00	50.00
King 807	(M)	All Star Country & Western	1962	20.00	50.00
King 811	(M)	Country Christmas	1962	20.00	50.00
King 813	(M)	Nashville Bandstand	1962	20.00	50.00
King 819	(M)	Carnival Of Songs	1963	16.00	40.00
King 837	(M)	Organ Jazz Giants	1963	14.00	35.00
King 847	(M)	Nashville Bandstand, Volume 2	1963	16.00	40.00
King 855	(M)	Surfin' On Wave Nine	1963	16.00	40.00
King 859	(M)	Turning Back The Clock Blue	1963	16.00	40.00
King 862	(M)	Hootenanny	1963	16.00	40.00
King 866	(M)	Truck Driver Songs	1963	16.00	40.00

Label & Catalog #		Title	Year	VG+	NM
King 869	(M)	Railroad Songs	1963	16.00	40.00
King 871	(M)	Songs Of Rivers, Oceans And Seas	1963	16.00	40.00
King 875	(M)	Everybody's Favorite Blues	1964	16.00	40.00
King 876	(M)	Western Swing	1964	16.00	40.00
King 882	(M)	Look Who's Surfin' Now	1964	20.00	50.00
King 884	(M)	Top R&B Artists Sing Country	1964	16.00	40.00
King 890	(M)	14 Great All Time C&W Waltzes	1964	16.00	40.00
King 893	(M)	14 Hit Flashbacks From The Group Era	1964	16.00	40.00
King K-951	(M)	Spirituals (Re-issue of #576)	1966	10.00	25.00
King K-965	(M)	24 Scared Songs	1966	10.00	25.00
King K-994	(M)	5 String Banjo Pickin' And Singin'	1966	10.00	25.00
King K-1004	(M)	25 Years Of R&B Hits	1966	10.00	25.00
King K-1006	(M)	25 Years Of C&W	1966	10.00	25.00
King K-1008	(M)	25 Years Of Popular Music	1966	10.00	25.00

— Original King albums above have crownless black labels.—

Label & Catalog #		Title	Year	VG+	NM
Liberty LST-101	(DJ)	This Is Stereo (Red vinyl)	1960	50.00	100.00
Liberty LRP-5503	(M)	Teensville	1962	16.00	40.00
Liberty LRP-5505	(M)	Golden Teen Hits	1962	16.00	40.00
Liberty MM-412	(DJ)	Explosive!	1962	20.00	50.00
Liberty MM-417	(DJ)	Spin Time With Liberty	1962	20.00	50.00
Liberty LRP-3178	(M)	Original Hits, Volume 1	1961	8.00	20.00
Liberty LST-7178	(P)	Original Hits, Volume 1	1961	10.00	25.00
Liberty LRP-3180	(M)	Original Hits, Volume 2	1961	8.00	20.00
Liberty LST-7180	(P)	Original Hits, Volume 2	1961	10.00	25.00
Liberty LRP-3187	(M)	Original Hits, Volume 3	1961	8.00	20.00
Liberty LST-7187	(P)	Original Hits, Volume 3	1961	10.00	25.00
Liberty LRP-3200	(M)	Original Hits, Volume 4	1962	8.00	20.00
Liberty LST-7200	(P)	Original Hits, Volume 4	1962	10.00	25.00
Liberty LRP-3235	(M)	15 Hits, Volume 5	1962	8.00	20.00
Liberty LST-7235	(P)	15 Hits, Volume 5	1962	10.00	25.00
Liberty LRP-3260	(M)	Original Hits, Volume 6	1962	6.00	15.00
Liberty LST-7260	(P)	Original Hits, Volume 6	1962	8.00	20.00
Liberty LRP-3274	(M)	Original Hits, Volume 7	1962	6.00	15.00
Liberty LST-7274	(P)	Original Hits, Volume 7	1962	8.00	20.00
Liberty LRP-3288	(M)	Original Hits, Volume 8	1963	6.00	15.00
Liberty LST-7288	(P)	Original Hits, Volume 8	1963	8.00	20.00
Liberty LRP-3325	(M)	Original Hits, Volume 9	1963	6.00	15.00
Liberty LST-7325	(P)	Original Hits, Volume 9	1963	8.00	20.00
Liberty LRP-3344	(M)	15 #1, Volume 10	1964	6.00	15.00
Liberty LST-7344	(P)	15 #1, Volume 10	1964	8.00	20.00
Liberty LRP-3366	(M)	Shut Downs And Hill Climbs	1963	8.00	20.00
Liberty LST-7366	(P)	Shut Downs And Hill Climbs	1963	10.00	25.00
Liberty LRP-3418	(M)	#1 Hits, Volume 11	1964	6.00	15.00
Liberty LST-7418	(P)	#1 Hits, Volume 11	1964	8.00	20.00
Liberty LRP-3430	(M)	C'mon Let's Live A Little (Soundtrack)	1966	6.00	15.00
Liberty LST-7430	(S)	C'mon Let's Live A Little (Soundtrack)	1966	8.00	20.00
Lion 70108	(M)	Celebrities	1960	10.00	25.00
Mainstream 56100	(M)	A Pot Of Flowers	1967	10.00	25.00
Mainstream S-6100	(S)	A Pot Of Flowers	1967	12.00	30.00
Mark-56	(M)	Mr. Faruki's Suzuki	196?	20.00	50.00
Mercury MG-20230	(M)	On The Shore Of Waikiki	1957	16.00	40.00
Mercury MG-20282	(M)	Hillbilly Hit Parade, Volume 1	1958	20.00	50.00
Mercury MG-20328	(M)	Hillbilly Hit Parade, Volume 2	1958	20.00	50.00
Mercury MG-20350	(M)	Opry Stars Jamboree	1958	16.00	40.00
Mercury MG-20360	(M)	A Night At The Louisiana Hayride	1958	16.00	40.00
Mercury MG	(M)	Rock All Night (Soundtrack)	195?	100.00	200.00
Mercury MG-20493	(M)	14 Newies But Goodies	195?	20.00	50.00
Mercury MG-20581	(M)	14 More Newies But Goodies	195?	20.00	50.00
Mercury MG-20687	(M)	Twist With The Stars	1962	20.00	50.00
Mercury MG-20809	(M)	Original Golden Hits Of The Great Groups	1963	20.00	50.00
Mercury MG-20826	(M)	The Great Blues Singers	1964	12.00	30.00
Mercury MG-20857	(M)	Hootenanny Bluegrass Style	1964	8.00	20.00
Mercury SRD-2-29	(S)	Zig Zag Festival [DB]	1970	16.00	40.00

Label & Catalog #		Title	Year	VG+	NM
MGM DJ-5	(DJ)	MGM Sounds Of 1959	1959	20.00	50.00
MGM E-3814	(M)	MGM Top Hits	1963	10.00	25.00
MGM E-3912	(M)	We Wrote 'Em And We Sing 'Em	1964	8.00	20.00
MGM SE-3912	(S)	We Wrote 'Em And We Sing 'Em	1964	12.00	30.00
MGM E-4273	(M)	Get Yourself A College Girl (Soundtrack)	1964	6.00	15.00
MGM SE-4273	(S)	Get Yourself A College Girl (Soundtrack)	1964	8.00	20.00
MGM E-4306	(M)	Mickie Most Presents British Go-Go	1964	4.00	10.00
MGM SE-4306	(S)	Mickie Most Presents British Go-Go	1964	6.00	15.00
MGM E-4312	(M)	Solid Gold	1965	8.00	20.00
MGM SE-4312	(P)	Solid Gold	1965	8.00	20.00
MGM E-4334	(M)	When The Boys Meet The Girls (Sdtk)	1965	8.00	20.00
MGM SE-4334	(S)	When The Boys Meet The Girls (Sdtk)	1965	10.00	25.00
MGM SE-4468	(S)	Zabriskie Point (Soundtrack)	1970	6.00	15.00
MGM SE-4506	(S)	What Am I Bid? (Soundtrack)	1971	8.00	20.00
MGM 2SE-14	(S)	The Strawberry Statement (2 LPs. Sdtk)	1971	8.00	20.00
MGM 1SE-21	(S)	Zigzag (Soundtrack)	1971	6.00	15.00
Minit 0001	(M)	New Orleans: Home Of The Blues	1961	12.00	30.00
Minit 0003	(M)	We Sing The Blues	1962	10.00	25.00
Minit 0004	(M)	New Orleans: Home Of The Blues, Volume 2	1962	10.00	25.00
Mobile Fidelity MFSL-200	(S)	Woodstock (5 LP box)	198?	50.00	100.00
Modern LMP-1210	(M)	Rock & Roll Dance Party	195?	40.00	80.00
Modern LMP-1211	(M)	Rock & Roll Record Hop	195?	40.00	80.00
Motown MLP-603	(M)	Motown Hits, Volume 1	1962	12.00	30.00
Motown MLP-609	(M)	The Motor-Town Revue, Volume 1	1963	12.00	30.00
Motown MLP-614	(M)	16 Original Big Hits, Volume 1	1963	6.00	15.00
Motown MLP-615	(M)	The Motor-Town Revue, Volume 2	1964	12.00	30.00
Motown MLP-624	(M)	16 Original Big Hits, Volume 3	1964	6.00	15.00
Motown MS-624	(S)	16 Original Big Hits, Volume 3	1964	6.00	15.00
Motown MLP-630	(M)	Nothing But A Man (Soundtrack)	1965	20.00	50.00
Motown MS-630	(S)	Nothing But A Man (Soundtrack)	1965	35.00	70.00
Motown MLP-633	(M)	16 Original Big Hits, Volume 4	1965	6.00	15.00
Motown MS-633	(S)	16 Original Big Hits, Volume 4	1965	6.00	15.00
Motown MS-642	(S)	In Loving Memory	1968	50.00	100.00
Motown MS-651	(S)	16 Original Big Hits, Volume 5	1968	6.00	15.00
Motown MS-655	(S)	16 Original Big Hits, Volume 6	1968	5.00	12.00
Motown MS-661	(S)	16 Original Big Hits, Volume 7	1968	5.00	12.00
Motown MS-666	(S)	16 Original Big Hits, Volume 8	1968	5.00	12.00
Motown MS-668	(S)	16 Original Big Hits, Volume 9	1968	5.00	12.00
Motown MS-681	(M)	Merry Christmas From Motown	1968	8.00	20.00
Motown MS-684	(S)	16 Original Big Hits, Volume 10	1969	4.00	10.00
Motown MS-688	(S)	The Motortown Revue Recorded Live!	1969	6.00	15.00
		— Original Motown albums above have a Detroit, MI, address on the label.—			
Muse 500	(M)	Carload Of Hits	196?	90.00	180.00
Northridge 101	(M)	Surf's Up At Banzai Pipeline	1963	16.00	40.00
Ode SP-99001	(S)	Tommy (Soundtrack)	1970	6.00	15.00
Ode SQ-99001	(Q)	Tommy (Soundtrack)	1970	16.00	40.00
Old Town 101	(M)	Rock & Roll On The Old Town	196?	30.00	60.00
Oldies-33 OL-8001	(M)	Oldies Dance Party, Volume 1	1964	8.00	20.00
Oldies-33 OL-8002	(M)	Oldies Dance Party, Volume 2	1964	8.00	20.00
Oldies-33 OL-8004	(M)	We Like Boys	1964	10.00	25.00
Panorama 103	(M)	Battle Of The Bands	1966	12.00	30.00
Parkway 7011	(M)	Don't Knock The Twist (Soundtrack)	1962	12.00	30.00
Parkway 7028	(M)	Million Seller Dance Hits	1963	10.00	25.00
Parkway 7031	(M)	12 Greatest Golden Oldies In The Whole World Ever	1963	10.00	25.00
Parkway 7035	(M)	Everybody's Goin' Surfin'	1963	12.00	30.00
Parrot PA-61010	(M)	Greatest Hits From England	1964	8.00	20.00
Parrot PAS-71010	(E)	Greatest Hits From England	1964	5.00	12.00

These two sets, visually unexciting grab-bag collections from RCA, stand as an example of the old maxim, "Don't believe everything you read." Both volumes of *Old 'N' Golden Goodies* are clearly marked as "electronically reprocessed," yet both contain several singles in... true stereo. While most ignore various artists albums, stereo collectors know how exciting it can be to discover a long sought after hit in glorious stereo on an obscure compilation.

Label & Catalog #		Title	Year	VG+	NM
Parrot PA-61017	(M)	Greatest Hits From England, Volume 2	1964	8.00	20.00
Parrot PAS-71017	(E)	Greatest Hits From England, Volume 2	1964	5.00	12.00
Parrot PA-61023	(M)	All American Hits	1964	8.00	20.00
Parrot PAS-71023	(E)	All American Hits	1964	5.00	12.00
Paul Winley Prod. 1001	(M)	New York City's Greatest Oldies	196?	50.00	100.00
Prestige PR-7539	(S)	Take A Trip With Psychedelic Hits	196?	10.00	25.00
Pricewise 4004	(M)	Best Of The Girl Groups	196?	10.00	25.00
Ralph	(DJ)	10th Anniversary Radio Special (2 LPs)	1981	12.00	30.00
Rampart LP-3303	(M)	East Side Revue (Multi-colored vinyl)	196?	50.00	100.00
Rampart LP-3305	(M)	East Side Revue, Volume 2	196?	12.00	30.00
RCA Victor LPM-3192 (10")	(M)	Tennessee Jamboree	1954	20.00	50.00
RCA Victor LPM-3220 (10")	(M)	Country And Western Caravan	1954	20.00	50.00
RCA Victor LPM-3282 (10")	(M)	Top Pops	1954	20.00	50.00
RCA Victor LPM-1540	(M)	Teenagers Dance	1957	14.00	35.00
RCA Victor LPM-1802	(M)	TV Record Hop	1958	10.00	25.00
RCA Victor LPM-2314	(M)	High Time (Soundtrack)	1960	8.00	20.00
RCA Victor LSP-2314	(S)	High Time (Soundtrack)	1960	12.00	30.00
RCA Victor LPM-2332	(M)	Twelve Big Ones	1960	6.00	15.00
RCA Victor LSP-2332	(P)	Twelve Big Ones	1960	8.00	20.00
— Original RCA albums above have "Long Play" on the bottom of the label.—					
RCA Victor LPM-2740	(M)	Old 'n' Golden Goodies	1963	8.00	20.00
RCA Victor LSP-2740	(P)	Old 'n' Golden Goodies	1963	12.00	30.00
RCA Victor LPM-3441	(M)	Wild On The Beach (Soundtrack)	1965	8.00	20.00
RCA Victor LSP-3441	(S)	Wild On The Beach (Soundtrack)	1965	12.00	30.00
RCA Victor LPM-3632	(M)	The Best Of The Best Of	1966	8.00	20.00
RCA Victor LSP-3632	(P)	The Best Of The Best Of	1966	10.00	25.00
RCA Victor LPM-3641	(M)	Old 'n' Golden Goodies, Volume 2	1966	8.00	20.00
RCA Victor LSP-3641	(P)	Old 'n' Golden Goodies, Volume 2	1966	12.00	30.00
RCA Victor LPM-6015	(M)	Stars Of The Grand Ole Opry (2 LP box)	1967	16.00	40.00
RCA Victor LPM-6015	(M)	Stars Of The Grand Ole Opry (2 LPs)	1967	6.00	15.00
— Original RCA albums above have black labels.—					
Red Bird 20102	(M)	Red Bird Goldies	196?	12.00	30.00
Regent MG-6015	(M)	Rock & Roll	195?	16.00	40.00
Regent MG-6042	(M)	Rock & Roll Party	195?	16.00	40.00
Reprise R-6094	(M)	Surf's Up At Banzai Pipeline	1963	14.00	35.00
Reprise RS-6094	(P)	Surf's Up At Banzai Pipeline	1963	20.00	50.00
Reprise 2MS-2031	(S)	The Strawberry Statement (2 LPs. Sdtk)	1970	35.00	70.00
(Issued in a plain jacket with a "Rush release" sticker.)					
Roadside RBF-20	(M)	Roots: Rhythm & Blues	196?	12.00	30.00
Ronco LP-1001	(P)	Do It Now! ("Speed Kills" cover)	1970	12.00	30.00
Roulette R-25021	(M)	Pajama Party (Black label)	195?	16.00	40.00
RPM 3001	(M)	Rock & Roll Dance Party	195?	20.00	50.00
Savoy MG-15008 (10")	(M)	Rhythm & Blues	195?	100.00	200.00
Savoy MG-15008	(M)	Rhythm & Blues	195?	16.00	40.00
Score LP-4002	(M)	I Dig Rock & Roll	195?	100.00	200.00
Score LP-4018	(M)	Rock & Roll Sock Hop	195?	100.00	200.00
Screen Gems/Colgems	(DJ)	212 Hits (2 LPs)	196?	10.00	25.00
Screen Gems/Colgems	(DJ)	More Solid Gold Programming (2 LPs)	196?	12.00	30.00
Screen Gems/Columbia	(DJ)	Solid Gold-Gerry Goffin And Carole King	196?	10.00	25.00
Shepherd 1300	(M)	Surf War	1963	14.00	35.00

Label & Catalog #		Title	Year	VG+	NM
Sidewalk T-5901	(M)	Freakout U.S.A.	1967	12.00	30.00
Sidewalk ST-5901	(E)	Freakout U.S.A.	1967	8.00	20.00
Sidewalk ST-5913	(S)	Psych-Out (Soundtrack)	1968	16.00	40.00
Sire	(P)	Nuggets (2 LPs)	197?	6.00	15.00
Soma MG-1243	(M)	Big Hits Of Mid America	1968	35.00	70.00
Soma MG-1246	(M)	Big Hits Of Mid America, Volume 2	1968	35.00	70.00
Somerset P-1300	(M)	Rock 'N' Roll Dance Party	1954	35.00	70.00
Sounds Of Hawaii 5014	(M)	Waikiki Surf Battle, Volume 1	1964	100.00	200.00
Sounds Of Hawaii 5014	(M)	Waikiki Surf Battle, Volume 2	1964	100.00	200.00
Specialty 2112	(M)	Our Significant Hits (Black & gold label)	1963	20.00	50.00
Star SRM-101	(M)	Battle Of The Bands	1964	60.00	120.00
Starday SLP-101	(M)	Hillbilly Jamboree	195?	20.00	50.00
Starday SLP-115	(M)	The Bluegrass Special	196?	12.00	30.00
Starday SLP-138	(M)	Nashville Steel Guitar	1961	16.00	40.00
Starday SLP-164	(M)	Country Music Hall Of fame	1962	12.00	30.00
Starday SLP-176	(M)	Tennessee Guitar	1962	10.00	25.00
Starday SLP-233	(M)	Steel Guitar Hall Of Fame	1963	12.00	30.00
Starday SLP-277	(M)	Unforgettable Country Instrumentals	1963	8.00	20.00
Starday SLP-293	(M)	Steel Guitar And Dobro Spectacular	1964	10.00	25.00
Starday SLP-306	(M)	Let's Hit The Road	1964	6.00	15.00
Starday SLP-324	(M)	Country Hitmaker #1	1964	12.00	30.00
Starday SLP-345	(M)	Spectacular C&W Instrumentals	1965	8.00	20.00
Starday SLP-346	(S)	Gone But Not Forgotten	1965	12.00	30.00
Starday SLP-350	(M)	Stars Of The Steel Guitar	1965	10.00	25.00
Starday SLP-352	(M)	Queens Of Country Music	1965	12.00	30.00
Starday SLP-7001	(M)	All-Star Country & Western Jamboree	197?	8.00	20.00
Starla LPM-1960	(M)	Art Laboe's Memories Of El Monte	1960	35.00	70.00
Stax 710	(M)	Memphis Gold (Blue label)	1966	6.00	15.00
Stax S-710	(S)	Memphis Gold (Blue label)	1966	8.00	20.00
Stax/Volt 11	(DJ)	Stay In School, Don't Be A Dropout	1967	300.00	500.00
Stax 721	(M)	The Stax/Volt Revue: Vol. 1, Live In London	1967	8.00	20.00
Stax S-721	(S)	The Stax/Volt Revue: Vol. 1, Live In London	1967	12.00	30.00
Stax 722	(M)	The Stax/Volt Revue: Vol. 2, Live In Paris	1967	8.00	20.00
Stax S-722	(S)	The Stax/Volt Revue: Vol. 2, Live In Paris	1967	12.00	30.00
Stax 726	(M)	Memphis Gold, Volume 2	1967	6.00	15.00
Stax SS-726	(S)	Memphis Gold, Volume 2	1967	8.00	20.00
Sue LP-1021	(M)	The Sue Story	196?	16.00	40.00
Sun LP-1250	(M)	Sun's Gold Hits	1961	30.00	60.00
Sutton SU-321	(M)	Jumpin'	1961	16.00	40.00
Sutton SSU-321	(S)	Jumpin'	1961	20.00	50.00
Sutton SU-323	(M)	Current Craze	1961	16.00	40.00
Sutton SSU-323	(S)	Current Craze	1961	20.00	50.00
Sutton SU-325	(M)	Great Popular Oldies, Volume 2	1961	16.00	40.00
Sutton SSU-325	(S)	Great Popular Oldies, Volume 2	1961	20.00	50.00
Swan 501	(M)	Treasure Chest Of Hits	1960	35.00	70.00
Swan 512	(M)	Hits I Forgot To Buy	1963	14.00	35.00
Tamla TM-222	(M)	The Great Gospel Stars	1961	16.00	40.00
Tamla TM-224	(M)	Tamla Special #1	1962	35.00	70.00
Tamla TM-256	(M)	A Collection Of 16 Original Big Hits, Vol. 2	1964	8.00	20.00
Tamla TS-256	(S)	A Collection Of 16 Original Big Hits, Vol. 2	1964	8.00	20.00
Teem 5002	(M)	Guaranteed To Please	196?	12.00	30.00
Teem 5003	(M)	Greatest Teenage Hits Of All Time	196?	14.00	35.00
Teem 5004	(M)	Approved By 10,000,000	196?	14.00	35.00

Label & Catalog #		Title	Year	VG+	NM
Teem 5005	(M)	Kings Sing The Blues	196?	12.00	30.00
Tempo Two T-2	(M)	A New High (With poster)	196?	50.00	100.00
Together ST-1014	(S)	Early L.A.	1971	10.00	25.00
Tops LP-941 (10")	(M)	Western Favorites	195?	20.00	50.00
Tower T-5007	(M)	Three At The Top (Soundtrack)	1965	8.00	20.00
Tower DT-5007	(E)	Three At The Top (Soundtrack)	1965	6.00	15.00
Tower T-5065	(M)	Riot On Sunset Strip (Soundtrack)	1967	16.00	40.00
Tower DT-5065	(E)	Riot On Sunset Strip (Soundtrack)	1967	12.00	30.00
Tower DT-5148	(E)	Best Of The Soundtracks	1969	10.00	25.00
Tower DT-5157	(E)	Instant Replay	1969	12.00	30.00
20th Century TFM-3131	(M)	Surf Party (Soundtrack)	1964	12.00	30.00
20th Century TFS-4131	(S)	Surf Party (Soundtrack)	1964	16.00	40.00
United Arts. UAS-5175	(S)	Here We Go 'Round The Mulberry Bush (Soundtrack)	1968	6.00	15.00
United Arts. UAS-5185	(S)	Revolution (Soundtrack)	1968	8.00	20.00
Vault LP-103	(M)	Oldies, Goodies And Woodies	1964	16.00	40.00
Vault VS-103	(S)	Oldies, Goodies And Woodies	1964	20.00	50.00
Vault LP-104	(M)	Hot Rod City	1964	16.00	40.00
Vault VS-104	(S)	Hot Rod City	1964	20.00	50.00
Vault VS-119	(S)	San Francisco Roots	1968	6.00	15.00
Vee Jay LP-1020	(M)	The Blues	1962	14.00	35.00
Vee Jay LP-1042	(M)	Tomorrow's Hits	1962	10.00	25.00
Vee Jay LP-1051	(M)	Unavailable	1962	12.00	30.00
— Original Vee Jay albums above have black rainbow labels.—					
Vee Jay LP-1112	(M)	Great Hits Of 1964	1964	8.00	20.00
Vee Jay SR-1112	(P)	Great Hits Of 1964	1964	12.00	30.00
Vee Jay LP-1136	(M)	More Great Hits Of 1964	1965	8.00	20.00
Vee Jay SR-1136	(P)	More Great Hits Of 1964	1965	12.00	30.00
Vernon 521	(M)	Chart Busters	196?	16.00	40.00
Wand WDM-652	(M)	Show Stoppers	1961	12.00	30.00
Wand WDM-660	(M)	The Greatest Sing Their Soul Favorites	1964	10.00	25.00
Wand WDM-677	(M)	Greatest Hits From The Soul Of Texas	1966	6.00	15.00
Wand WDS-677	(S)	Greatest Hits From The Soul Of Texas	1966	8.00	20.00
Warner Bros. W-1448	(M)	Hits Of The Hops	1962	6.00	15.00
Warner Bros. WS-1448	(M)	Hits Of The Hops	1962	8.00	20.00
Warner Bros. W-1511	(M)	Hoot Tonight	1963	8.00	20.00
Warner Bros. WS-1511	(S)	Hoot Tonight	1963	10.00	25.00
Warner Bros. W-1519	(M)	Palm Springs Weekend (Soundtrack)	1963	10.00	25.00
Warner Bros. WS-1519	(S)	Palm Springs Weekend (Soundtrack)	1963	14.00	35.00
Warner Bros. W-1725	(M)	Original Golden Instrumental Hits	1965	6.00	15.00
Warner Bros. WS-1725	(S)	Original Golden Instrumental Hits	1965	8.00	20.00
Warner Bros. BS-1846	(S)	Performance (Soundtrack)	1970	10.00	25.00
Warner Bros. (10")	(DJ)	Woodstock (Radio spots)	1970	240.00	400.00
Westchester 1005	(M)	Friday At The Cage A Go Go	196?	50.00	100.00
White Whale WWS-7125	(S)	Footprints In Time	1970	10.00	25.00
White Whale WWS-7129	(S)	Super Groups From Holland	1970	10.00	25.00
White Whale WWS-7130	(S)	Dutch Explosion	1970	12.00	30.00
Winley 6001	(M)	Everybody Digs The Boss Record Hop	195?	20.00	50.00
World Pacific WPS-21898	(S)	Bluegrass Special	196?	12.00	30.00
Zephyr ZP-12010H	(M)	Premiere	195?	12.00	30.00

Bibliography

Aside from the most obvious and basic sources — Phonolog, Schwann and Whitburn — the following books provided specific resource material for the discographies in this book:

Aeppli, Felix. *Heart Of Stone: The Definitive Rolling Stones Discography*. Pierian Press, 1985.

Beecher, John & Malcolm Jones. *The Buddy Holly Story: A Pictorial Account Of His Life & Music*. MCA/Coral, GT. Britain, 1980.

Blair, John. *The Illustrated Discography Of Surf Music*. Pierian Press, 1985.

Blair, John & Steve McParland. *The Illustrated Discography Of Hot Rod Music*. Popular Culture, Ink., 1990.

Brown, James, & Bruce Tucker. *James Brown: The Godfather Of Soul*. MacMillan, 1986.

Burt, Rob. *Surf City/Drag City*. Blandford Press, UK 1986.

Cox, Perry & Joe Lindsay. *Beatles Price Guide For American Records*. Cox Ent./BIOdisc. 1990.

Dalley, Robert. *Surfin' Guitars: Instrumental Surf Bands Of The Sixties*. Surf Publications, 1988.

DeWitt, Howard. *Chuck Berry: Rock 'N' Roll Music*. Pierian Press, 1985.

Elliott, Brad. *Surf's Up! The Beach Boys On Record*. Pierian Press, 1982.

Ferguson, Charles, & H. Johnson. *Mainstream Jazz Reference & Price Guide*. O'Sullivan Woodside, 1984.

Francis, Connie. *Who's Sorry Now?*. St. Martin's, 1984.

Goldmark, Joe. *International Steel Guitar Directory*. Privately printed, 1988.

Grafman, Howard & B. T. Manning. *Folk Music USA*. Citadel Press, 1962.

Haley, John & John van Hoelle. *Sound & Glory: The Incredible Story Of Bill Haley*. Dyne-American, 1990.

Heggeness, Fred. *The Rarest Of The Rare, Volumes 1-4*. FH Publishing.

Heggeness, Fred. *Country & Western Price Guide*. FH Publishing, 1991.

Hounsome, Terry, *Rock Record, 1st-3rd Editions*. Blandford, 1987.

Hudgeons, Thomas. *The Official Price Guide To Records, Volumes 1-7*. House Of Collectibles.

Joynson, Vernon. *Acid Trip: A Complete Guide To Psychedelic Music*. Babylon Books, 1984.

Lindsay, Joe. *Picture Discs Of The World Price Guide*. BIOdisc. 1990.

Malone, Bill. *Country Music USA*. Un. of Texas Press., 1968.

Malone, Bill & Judith McCulloh. *Stars Of Country Music*. Un. Of Illinois, 1975.

Morthland, John. *The Best Of Country Music*. Dolphin, 1984.

Peace, Warren. *Peace Record Price Guide,* Privately printed, 1979.

Docks, L.R. *American Premium Record Guide*. Books Americana, 1986.

Raymond, Jack. *Show Music On Record From The 1890s To The 1980s*. Ungar, 1982.

Rogers, Don. *Dance Halls, Armories & Teen Fairs: A History & Discography Of Pacific Northwest Rock*. Music Archives, 1988.

Savage, Jon. *The Kinks*. Faber & Faber, 1984.

Sawyer, Charles. *The Arrival Of B.B. King*. Doubleday, 1980.

Shaw, Arnold. *Sinatra: The Entertainer*. Delilah, 1982.

Shelton, Robert & Burt Goldblatt. *The Country Music Story*. Castle Books, 1966.

Shestack, Melvin. *Country Music Encyclopedia*. Thomas Crowell Co., 1974.

Tosches, Nick. *Unsung Heroes Of Rock 'n' Roll*. Charles Scribner's Sons, 1984.

Waller, Don. *The Motown Story*. Chares Scribner's Sons, 1985.

Williams, Roger. *Sing A Sad Song: The Life Of Hank Williams*. Ballantine, 1973.

Neal Umphred: A Brief Bio

My earliest memories of rock 'n roll really date to the first few years of the '60s. My grandmother had a nice old apartment in the same building the housed the Back Date Book Store on South Main Street, Wilkes-Barre, Pa., (pre-flood), which specialized in used magazines with their covers ripped off. I would hike over in the morning and load up on comic books (a nickel each, six for a quarter). With my reading I would spend the day at Gramma's, listening to Aunt Judy's record collection: Ricky, Fats, Little Richard, and lots of Elvis. Thus from 1960 through 1964 the bulk of my listening was oldies, 50% of which was Elvis.

While my contemporaries were wearing the grooves out of The Beatles and Herman's Hermits, I stuck to the "old" stuff: The first album that I remember buying were the first two volumes of *Elvis' Golden Records*. These were followed by more old rock 'n roll (Chuck Berry's *Golden Hits* on Mercury was definitely one of them and the wrong one to start with Mr. Berry.) When the British Invasion hit, I somehow managed to avoid the charm of The Beatles and The Stones and religiously purchased each new (cheesy) Elvis soundtrack.

In the summer of '65 everything changed: I realized that there was a potential for rock music to be something else, something other than the first generation of rockers had imagined. Call it what you like, but most of us, diehard collectos or merely casual listeners, remain inextricably bound to the sounds that first opened our ears and hearts to the possibilities of music. For one generation it was big bands, Harry James' horn and Frank Sinatra; for the next it was rockabilly, Scotty Moore's guitar and Elvis. For me it was The Byrds, jangling 12-strings and "Mr. Tambourine Man."

I was an avid reader of Paul Williams' *Crawdaddy,* which more than anything else helped shape my opinions on Rock-with-a capital-R. I had discovered *Pet Sounds*, the album that has remained #1 in my heart and soul for more than two decades (although not without its share of heady competition: *Blonde On Blonde, Rubber Soul, Beggar's Banquet, Music From Big Pink, Younger Than Yesterday, Clear Spot.*)

Through an odd series of events, in 1985 I was interviewed for the position of editor of O'Sullivan Woodside's line of record collectors price guides and was responsible for the sixth edition of their *Rock & Roll Record Albums Price Guide* (1985) and the third edition of the *Elvis Presley Record Price Guide* (1986). This led to my association with *Goldmine*, for which I compiled *Goldmine's Price Guide To Collectible Record Albums* in 1989 and *Goldmine's Rock 'n' Roll 45RPM Record Price Guide* in 1990. I am also associated with White Dragon Press, having produced *A Touch Of Gold: The Elvis Presley Record & Memorabilia Price Guide* in 1990 and their forthcoming (winter 1991) *Good Rockin' Tonight*, a price guide covering blues, rhythm 'n blues and black rock 'n roll of the '50s.

Neal Umphred
June 30, 1991